Human Sexuality
in a World of Diversity

fourth edition

Spencer A. Rathus
Montclair State University

Jeffrey S. Nevid
St. John's University

Lois Fichner-Rathus
The College of New Jersey

Allyn and Bacon
Boston ■ London ■ Toronto ■ Sydney ■ Tokyo ■ Singapore

Senior Editor: *Rebecca Pascal*
Editor-in Chief, Social Sciences: *Karen Hanson*
Editorial Assistant: *Jill Jeffrey*
Developmental Editor: *Mary Kriener*
Production Administrator: *Deborah Brown*
Editorial/Production Services: *Barbara Gracia*
Text Designer: *Carol Somberg, Omegatype Typography, Inc.*
Formatting/Page Layout: *Omegatype Typography, Inc.*
Cover Administrator: *Linda Knowles*
Composition Buyer: *Linda Cox*
Manufacturing Buyer: *Megan Cochran*
Photo Researcher: *Laurie Frankenthaler*

Copyright © 2000, 1997, 1995, 1993 by Allyn & Bacon
A Pearson Education Company
160 Gould Street
Needham Heights, MA 02494-2310
Internet: www.abacon.com

Library of Congress Cataloging-in-Publication Data

Rathus, Spencer A.
    Human sexuality in a world of diversity/Spencer A. Rathus,
Jeffrey S. Nevid, Lois Fichner-Rathus.   4th ed.
      p. cm.
    Includes bibliographical references and index.
    ISBN 0-205-27949-X
    1. Sex.   I. Nevid, Jeffrey S.   II. Fichner-Rathus, Lois, 1953-
HQ21.R23 2000
306.7--dc21   99-16469
                                              CIP

Printed in the United States of America
10 9 8 7 6 5 4 3 2 1 RRD 04 03 02 01 00 99

Photo Credits: **Chapter 1:** p. 7, Lou Jones; p. 8, Peter Vandermark/Stock, Boston; p. 13, Ali Meyer/The Bridgeman Art Library Ltd.; p. 15, Reuters/Jonathan Drake/Archive Photos; p. 16, Bettmann/Corbis; p. 17, Laurence Agron/Archive Photos; p. 24, Wolfgang Kaehler; p. 28, Elizabeth Crews/The Image Works; p. 31, A. Ramey/PhotoEdit. **Chapter 2:** p. 39, Courtesy of Farrall Instruments; p. 48, John Eastcott/Yva Momatiuk/Photo Researchers; p. 49, L. Ka Tai/Woodfin Camp & Associates. **Chapter 3:** p. 63 (all) L, Susan Lerner/Joel Gordon Photography; p. 67, Catherine Leroy/SIPA Press; p. 75, John Giannicchi/Science Source/Photo Researchers; p. 78 (left), Susan Lerner/Joel Gordon Photography; p. 78 (middle), Custom Medical Stock Photo; p. 78 (right), Joel Gordon; p. 81, Charles Gupton/ Stock, Boston; p. 91, David Young-Wolff/PhotoEdit; p. 95, Tony Neste. **Chapter 4:** p. 103 (left), Joel Gordon; p. 103 (middle), Custom Medical Stock Photo; p. 103 (right), Joel Gordon; p. 107, Cleo/PhotoEdit; p. 108 (top), Professor P. Motta/Dept. of Anatomy/Rome University/ SPL/Science Source/Photo Researchers; p. 108 (bottom), CNRI/SPL/Science Source/Photo Researchers; p. 112, AP/Wide World Photos; p. 114, Charles Gupton/Stock, Boston.

Photo credits continue on page iv, which constitutes a continuation of the copyright page.

Dedicated with love to our children
Taylor Lane Rathus and Michael Zev Nevid,
who were born at the time the first edition
of this book was being written.

Taylor Lane Rathus
November 3, 1990

Michael Zev Nevid
January 17, 1991

Photo Credits: *(continued from page ii)*   **Chapter 5:** p. 127, Bruce Ayres/Tony Stone Images; p. 131, David Madison/Tony Stone Images; p. 132, Bruce Lee Smith/Gamma Liaison; p. 137, Joel Gordon. **Chapter 6:** p. 158 and 159, from John Money, *Sex Errors of the Body and Related Syndromes: A Guide for Counseling Children, Adolescents and Their Families,* 1994, pp. 37 and 46. Published by Paul H. Brookes Publishing Co., P. O. Box 10624, Baltimore, MD 21285–0624; p. 164, Courtesy of Jayne Thomas; p. 166, Brian Smith; p. 170, Gary A. Conner/PhotoEdit; p. 173 (both), AP/Wide World Photos; p. 178 (left), Larry Kolvoord/The Image Works; p. 178 (right), Robert Harbison. **Chapter 7:** p. 191 (top left), Adam Wolfitt/Woodfin Camp & Associates; p. 191 (top middle), Lee/Archive Photos; p. 191 (top right), Claus Meyer/Black Star; p. 191 (bottom left), Mitch Kezar/Black Star; p. 191 (bottom right), Nicholas DeVore III/Photographers Aspen; p. 193, Stan Godlewski/Gamma Liaison; p. 194 (both), D. Perrett, K. May, and S. Yoshikawa, University of St. Andrews/SPL/Science Source/Photo Researchers; p. 197, Frank Siteman/Stock, Boston; p. 207, Roy Morsch/The Stock Market. **Chapter 8:** p. 215, Brian Smith; p. 218, Douglas Mason/Woodfin Camp & Associates; p. 220, M. Granitsas/The Image Works; p. 223, Joel Gordon; p. 225, Will Hart; p. 228, Robert Harbison. **Chapter 9:** p. 249, Peter Menzel/Tony Stone Images; p. 250, Catherine Smith/Impact Visuals; p. 253, Costa Manos/Magnum Photos. **Chapter 10:** p. 267, Zigy Kaluzny/Tony Stone Images; p. 277, Jonathan Nourok/PhotoEdit; p. 279, Rommel Pecson/Impact Visuals; p. 286, Stephen Marks; p. 289, Bill Aron/PhotoEdit; p. 294, Joel Gordon; p. 295, Chuck Nacke/Woodfin Camp & Associates. **Chapter 11:** p. 301, Francis LeRoy/Bio Cosmos/SPL/Science Source/Photo Researchers; p. 302, David Weintraub/Stock, Boston; p. 303, Todd Powell/Tony Stone Images; p. 305, Anna Zuckerman/PhotoEdit; p. 309, Mehau Kulyk/SPL/Science Source/Photo Researchers; p. 316 (all), Petit Format/Nestle/Science Source/Photo Researchers; p. 324, Will Hart; p. 330, SIU/Science Source/Photo Researchers; p. 332, James Stevenson/SPL/Science Source/Photo Researchers; p. 334, Willie J. Hill, Jr./The Image Works. **Chapter 12:** p. 343, Courtesy of Planned Parenthood of New York City; p. 348 and 352, Joel Gordon; p. 354 (left), Courtesy of Alza; p. 354 (right), Phototake; p. 369, Julie Houck/Stock, Boston; p. 381, David H. Hessell/Stock, Boston. **Chapter 13:** p. 387, Robert Harbison; p. 390, Rick Smolan/Stock, Boston; p. 399, Will Faller; p. 401, Bob Torrez/Tony Stone Images; p. 409, Yvonne Hemsey/Gamma Liaison. **Chapter 14:** p. 416, Frederick Charles/Liaison International; p. 417, Stephanie Maze/Woodfin Camp & Associates; p. 420, Frank Siteman/Tony Stone Images; p. 422, Leslye Borden/PhotoEdit; p. 425, Photo B. D. V./Corbis; p. 431 (left), B. Petry/Gamma Liaison; p. 431 (right) and 434, AP/Wide World Photos; p. 441, Paul Fusco/Magnum Photos; p. 444, Christopher Springman/The Stock Market. **Chapter 15:** p. 454, Mark Antman/The Image Works; p. 458, Nicholas DeVore III/Photographers Aspen; p. 463, Suzanne Arms/The Image Works; p. 469, G. Thomas Bishop/Custom Medical Stock Photo; p. 473, Bill Bachmann/PhotoEdit. **Chapter 16:** p. 484, Jim Corwin/Tony Stone Images (This photograph is used for illustrative purposes only.); p. 492, Courtesy of Dr. Nicholas J. Fiumara; p. 493, Dr. David Chase/Phototake; p. 495, Custom Medical Stock Photo; p. 496, Brian Palmer/Impact Visuals; p. 499, National Medical Slide/Custom Medical Stock Photo; p. 501, Bill Longcone/Science Source/Photo Researchers; p. 504, Douglas Mason/Woodfin Camp & Associates; p. 507, Jana Birchum/Impact Visuals; p. 509, Contact/Alon Reininger/Woodfin Camp & Associates; p. 511, Dr. John Wilson/Science Source/Photo Researchers; p. 515, BioPhoto Assoc./Science Source/Photo Researchers; p. 517, E. Gray/SPL/Science Source/Photo Researchers; p. 519, Tony Neste. **Chapter 17:** p. 528, Herb Snitzer/Stock, Boston; p. 529, Donna Binder/Impact Visuals; p. 534, Tom McCarthy/PhotoEdit; p. 541, North Wind Picture Archives; p. 548, Bob Daemmrich/The Image Works. **Chapter 18:** p. 555, AP/Wide World Photos; p. 556, Michael Nichols/Magnum Photos; p. 558, Steve McCurry/Magnum Photos; p. 565, PhotoDisc, Inc.; p. 570, Carolina Kroon/Impact Visuals; p. 571, Clark Jones/Impact Visuals; p. 575, Courtesy of the LaPorte County Child Abuse Prevention Council; p. 577, AP/Wide World Photos; p. 580, Charles Gupton/Tony Stone Images; p. 585, John Coletti; p. 588, Stewart Cohen/Tony Stone Images. **Chapter 19:** p. 595, Douglas Mason/Woodfin Camp & Associates; p. 599, Reuters/Sam Mircovich/Archive Photos; p. 604, Barnabus Bosshart/Corbis; p. 607 (left), AP/Wide World Photos; p. 607 (right), Patrice, 1977 Copyright © 1977 The Estate of Robert Mapplethorpe; p. 616, J. Kirk Condyles/Impact Visuals.

1   *What Is Human Sexuality?*   2

2   *Research Methods*   34

3   *Female Sexual Anatomy and Physiology*   60

4   *Male Sexual Anatomy and Physiology*   98

5   *Sexual Arousal and Response*   124

6   *Gender Identity and Gender Roles*   152

7   *Attraction and Love*   186

8   *Relationships and Communication*   210

9   *Sexual Techniques and Behavior Patterns*   236

10   *Sexual Orientation*   264

11   *Conception, Pregnancy, and Childbirth*   298

12   *Contraception and Abortion*   340

13   *Sexuality in Childhood and Adolescence*   384

14   *Sexuality in Adulthood*   414

15   *Sexual Dysfunctions*   448

16   *Sexually Transmitted Infections*   482

17   *Atypical Sexual Variations*   524

18   *Sexual Coercion*   552

19   *Commercial Sex*   592

20   *Making Responsible Sexual Decisions—An Epilogue*   618

contents

Preface   xvii

CHAPTER 1

What Is Human Sexuality?   2

OUTLINE   3

TRUTH OR FICTION?   3

What Is Human Sexuality?   4

The Study of Human Sexuality   5

Sexuality and Values   6

A World of Diversity   Around the World in Eighty
Ways—A Preview   6

Thinking Critically About Human Sexuality   9

Some Features of Critical Thinking   9

Perspectives on Human Sexuality   10

The Historical Perspective   11

The Biological Perspective   21

The Cross-Species Perspective   21

The Cross-Cultural Perspective   23

Psychological Perspectives   25

Sociocultural Perspectives   28

In the New Millennium   Human Sexuality—Where Are
We Headed?   31

Multiple Perspectives on Human Sexuality   31

SUMMING UP   32

CHAPTER 2

Research Methods   34

OUTLINE   35

TRUTH OR FICTION?   35

A Scientific Approach to Human Sexuality   36

The Scientific Method   36

Goals and Methods of the Science of Human
Sexuality   37

Operational Definitions   38

A Closer Look   Physiological Measures of Sexual
Arousal   39

**Populations and Samples: Representing the World
of Diversity**   40

Sampling Methods   41

Methods of Observation   42

The Case Study Method   42

Survey Method   43

A World of Diversity   Surveys of the Sexual Behavior
of Diverse Populations   48

The Naturalistic-Observation Method   50

The Ethnographic-Observation Method   51

The Participant-Observation Method   51

The Laboratory-Observation Method   51

The Correlational Method   53

Limitations of the Correlational Method   54

The Experimental Method   54

Aspects of the Experimental Method   55

Ethics in Sex Research   56

Pain and Stress   57

Confidentiality   57

Informed Consent   57

The Use of Deception   57

SUMMING UP   58

CHAPTER 3

*Female Sexual Anatomy and
Physiology   60*

OUTLINE   61

TRUTH OR FICTION?   61

External Sex Organs   62

The Mons Veneris   63

The Labia Majora   63

The Labia Minora   64

The Clitoris   64

The Vestibule   65

The Urethral Opening   65

A World of Diversity Clitoridectomy—Ritual Genital Mutilation   66

The Vaginal Opening   67

In the New Millennium Restoration of Virginity?   69

The Perineum   69

Structures That Underlie the External Sex Organs   69

A Closer Look Kegels   70

Internal Sex Organs   71

The Vagina   71

The Cervix   72

The Uterus   73

The Fallopian Tubes   74

The Ovaries   74

The Pelvic Examination   75

The Breasts   77

Breast Cancer   78

In the New Millennium Good News About Breast Cancer   81

A Closer Look Breast Self-Examination   82

The Menstrual Cycle   83

Menstruation Versus Estrus   84

Regulation of the Menstrual Cycle   84

Phases of the Menstrual Cycle   85

A World of Diversity Historical and Cross-Cultural Perspectives on Menstruation   89

Coitus During Menstruation   89

A Closer Look Myths About Menopause   90

Menopause   90

Menstrual Problems   92

Dysmenorrhea   92

Amenorrhea   94

Premenstrual Syndrome (PMS)   94

How to Handle Menstrual Discomfort   95

SUMMING UP   96

CHAPTER 4
Male Sexual Anatomy and Physiology   98

OUTLINE   99

TRUTH OR FICTION?   99

External Sex Organs   100

The Penis   100

The Scrotum   104

A Closer Look On Penis Size and Sexual Performance   105

Internal Sex Organs   105

The Testes   106

A Closer Look Is There a *Manopause*?   107

A Closer Look Big   109

The Vas Deferens   109

The Seminal Vesicles   109

The Prostate Gland   110

The Cowper's Glands   110

The Semen   111

Diseases of the Urogenital System   111

Urethritis   111

Cancer of the Testes   111

Disorders of the Prostate   112

A Closer Look Self-Examination of the Testes   113

In the New Millennium Good News About Prostate Cancer   114

Male Sexual Functions   115

Erection   115

Spinal Reflexes and Sexual Response   116

Ejaculation   120

SUMMING UP   122

CHAPTER 5
Sexual Arousal and Response   124

OUTLINE   125

TRUTH OR FICTION?   125

Making Sense of Sex: The Role of the Senses in Sexual Arousal   126

Vision: The Better to See You With   126

Smell: Does the Nose Know Best?   126

In the New Millennium Will We Finally Have Love Potions in the New Millennium?   127

The Skin Senses: Sex as a Touching Experience   127

Taste: On Savory Sex   128

Hearing: The Better to Hear You With   128

Aphrodisiacs: Of Spanish Flies and Rhino Horns   129

Anaphrodisiacs   130

Psychoactive Drugs   131

Sexual Response and the Brain: Cerebral Sex?   133

The Geography of the Brain   133

Brain Mechanisms in Sexual Functioning   134

On Pushing the Right Buttons: Are There Pleasure Centers in the Brain?   135

Sex Hormones: Do They "Goad" Us into Sex?   136

Sex Hormones and Sexual Behavior: Organizing and Activating Influences   137

Sex Hormones and Male Sexual Behavior   138

Sex Hormones and Female Sexual Behavior   138

The Sexual Response Cycle   140

Excitement Phase   140

Plateau Phase   141

Orgasmic Phase   142

Resolution Phase   144

Kaplan's Three Stages of Sexual Response: An Alternate Model   144

Controversies About Orgasm   145

Multiple Orgasms: When You're Having More Than One   145

How Many Kinds of Orgasms Do Women Have? One, Two, or Three?   146

The G-Spot   148

SUMMING UP   150

CHAPTER 6

Gender Identity and Gender Roles   152

OUTLINE   153

TRUTH OR FICTION?   153

Prenatal Sexual Differentiation   154

The Role of Sex Hormones in Sexual Differentiation   155

Descent of the Testes and the Ovaries   156

Sex Chromosomal Abnormalities   157

Prenatal Sexual Differentiation of the Brain   157

Gender Identity   157

Nature and Nurture in Gender Identity   158

Hermaphroditism   158

Transsexualism   161

A Closer Look Jayne Thomas, Ph.D.—In Her Own Words   164

Gender Roles and Stereotypes   166

A World of Diversity Machismo/Marianismo: Stereotypes and Hispanic Culture   168

Sexism   168

A World of Diversity Mom the Breadwinner   169

Gender Differences: Vive la Différence or Vive la Similarité?   169

Differences in Cognitive Abilities   170

Differences in Personality   171

In the New Millennium Will We See Differences in Fitness Evaporate in the New Millennium?   172

On Becoming a Man or a Woman: Gender Typing   173

Biological Perspectives   173

Sociobiology: It's Only Natural   173

Cross-Cultural Perspectives   174

Psychological Perspectives   175

Gender Roles and Sexual Behavior   180

Men as Sexually Aggressive, Women as Sexually Passive   180

Men as Overaroused, Women as Underaroused   181

Psychological Androgyny: The More Traits, the Merrier   181

Psychological Androgyny, Psychological Well-Being, and Personal Development   182

Psychological Androgyny and Sexual Behavior   183

SUMMING UP   183

CHAPTER 7

Attraction and Love   186

OUTLINE   187

TRUTH OR FICTION?   187

Attraction   189

Physical Attractiveness: How Important Is Looking Good?   189

In the New Millennium How Do We Compete with "Cyberbabes" and Cyberhunks"?   192

A World of Diversity Wide-Eyed with . . . Beauty?   194

A World of Diversity Gender Differences in Preferences in Mates Across 37 Cultures   196

The Matching Hypothesis: Who Is "Right" for You?   197

Similarity in Attitudes: Do Opposites Attract?   197

Reciprocity: If You Like Me, You Must Have Excellent Judgment 198

Love 198

The Greek Heritage 199

Romantic Love in Contemporary Western Culture 199

Questionnaire Are You a Romantic or a Realist? The Love Attitudes Scale 200

Contemporary Models of Love: Dare Science Intrude? 202

Questionnaire Sternberg's Triangular Love Scale 206

SUMMING UP 209

CHAPTER 8
Relationships and Communication   210

OUTLINE 211

TRUTH OR FICTION? 211

The ABC(DE)s of Romantic Relationships 212

The A's—Attraction 213

The B's—Building 213

In the New Millennium Modem Matchmaking 214

What Do You Say Now? How to Improve Date-Seeking Skills 216

The C's—Continuation 217

A World of Diversity Self-Disclosure: East May Be East and West May Be West, but Here, Perhaps, the 'Twain Do (Almost) Meet 218

The D's—Deterioration 219

The E's—Ending 220

Loneliness: "All the Lonely People, Where Do They All Come From?" 221

Causes of Loneliness 221

Coping with Loneliness 221

Intimacy 223

Knowing and Liking Yourself 223

Trusting and Caring 223

Being Honest 224

Making a Commitment 224

Maintaining Individuality When the *I* Becomes *We* 224

Communicating 224

Communication Skills for Enhancing Relationships and Sexual Relations 226

Common Difficulties in Sexual Communication 227

Getting Started 227

Listening to the Other Side 228

Learning About Your Partner's Needs 229

Providing Information 229

Making Requests 230

Delivering Criticism 231

Receiving Criticism 232

When Communication Is Not Enough: Handling Impasses 233

SUMMING UP 235

CHAPTER 9
Sexual Techniques and Behavior Patterns   236

OUTLINE 237

TRUTH OR FICTION? 237

Solitary Sexual Behavior 238

Masturbation 238

Sexual Fantasy 245

Sex with Others 247

Foreplay 247

Kissing 248

Touching 248

In the New Millennium Sex Becomes "Interactive" 249

Breast Stimulation 251

Oral-Genital Stimulation 251

A World of Diversity Sociocultural Factors and Oral Sex 253

Sexual Intercourse: Positions and Techniques 255

A World of Diversity Are African Americans Sexually Permissive? Cultural Mythology Versus Some Facts 260

SUMMING UP 263

CHAPTER 10
Sexual Orientation   264

OUTLINE 265

TRUTH OR FICTION? 265

Sexual Orientation   266

   Coming to Terms with Terms   267

   Sexual Orientation and Gender Identity   268

   Classification of Sexual Orientation   268

   Bisexuality   273

Perspectives on Gay Male and Lesbian Sexual Orientations   274

   Historical Perspectives   274

   Cross-Cultural Perspectives   275

   A World of Diversity Ethnicity and Sexual Orientation: A Matter of Belonging   276

   Cross-Species Perspectives   276

   Attitudes Toward Sexual Orientation in Contemporary Society   278

   Biological Perspectives   282

   Psychological Perspectives   284

   Gender Nonconformity   287

Adjustment of Gay Males and Lesbians   288

   Treatment of Gay Male and Lesbian Sexual Orientation   289

Coming Out: Coming to Terms with Being Gay   291

   Coming Out to Oneself   291

   Coming Out to Others   292

   In the New Millennium Out into the "Gay Global Village" of Cyberspace   293

Patterns of Sexual Activity Among Gay Males and Lesbians   293

   Sexual Techniques   293

Gay Lifestyles   294

   Lifestyle Differences Between Gay Males and Lesbians   295

   Variations in Gay Lifestyles   296

   SUMMING UP   297

CHAPTER 11

Conception, Pregnancy, and Childbirth   **298**

   OUTLINE   299

   TRUTH OR FICTION?   299

Conception: Against All Odds   300

   Optimizing the Chances of Conception   301

   In the New Millennium Two Views of Parenting: Childfree by Choice and Pushing the Biological Clock   302

   In the New Millennium Selecting the Gender of Your Child   304

   A Closer Look Sex and the Single Lizard   306

Infertility and Alternative Ways of Becoming Parents   306

   Male Fertility Problems   306

   Female Fertility Problems   308

   In the New Millennium Sperm and Egg Donations for Overnight Delivery?   310

Pregnancy   311

   Early Signs of Pregnancy   311

   Questionnaire Should *You* Have a Child?   312

   Pregnancy Tests   313

   Early Effects of Pregnancy   313

   Miscarriage (Spontaneous Abortion)   313

   Sex During Pregnancy   314

   Psychological Changes During Pregnancy   314

Prenatal Development   315

   The Germinal Stage   316

   The Embryonic Stage   317

   The Fetal Stage   319

   Environmental Influences on Prenatal Development   320

   Chromosomal and Genetic Abnormalities   325

Childbirth   327

   The Stages of Childbirth   328

   Methods of Childbirth   330

   Alternatives to the Hospital: Where Should a Child Be Born?   333

Birth Problems   333

   Anoxia   333

   A World of Diversity Ethnicity and Infant Mortality   334

   Preterm and Low-Birthweight Children   334

The Postpartum Period   335

   Maternal Depression   335

   Breast-Feeding Versus Bottle-Feeding   336

   Resumption of Ovulation and Menstruation   337

   Resumption of Sexual Activity   337

   SUMMING UP   338

CHAPTER 12
Contraception and Abortion   340

OUTLINE   341

TRUTH OR FICTION?   341

Contraception   342

Contraception in the United States: The Legal Battle   343

What Do You Say Now? Talking with Your Partner About Contraception   344

Selecting a Method of Contraception   345

Methods of Contraception   348

Oral Contraceptives ("the Pill")   348

Norplant   352

A Closer Look Congratulations, Wheat Ridge, It's a . . . !   353

Intrauterine Devices (IUDs)   353

The Diaphragm   355

Spermicides   357

The Cervical Cap   359

Condoms   359

Douching   363

Withdrawal (Coitus Interruptus)   363

Fertility Awareness Methods (Rhythm Methods)   363

Sterilization   366

In the New Millennium The Search Goes On   368

Abortion   371

When Does Human Life Begin?   371

Questionnaire Pro-Choice or Pro-Life? Where Do You Stand?   373

Historical and Legal Perspectives on Abortion   374

Methods of Abortion   377

A Closer Look Partial-Birth Abortion   379

Psychological Consequences of Abortion   380

A World of Diversity Japan's Abortion Agony: In a Country That Prohibited the Pill, Reality Collided with Religion   381

SUMMING UP   382

CHAPTER 13
Sexuality in Childhood and Adolescence   384

OUTLINE   385

TRUTH OR FICTION?   385

Infancy (0 to 2 Years): The Search for the Origins of Human Sexuality   386

The Infant's Capacity for Sexual Response   386

Masturbation   387

A World of Diversity Cross-Cultural Perspectives on Childhood Sexuality   388

Genital Play   388

Early Childhood (3 to 8 Years)   389

Masturbation   389

What Do You Say Now? How Should a Parent React to Childhood Masturbation?   390

Male-Female Sexual Behavior   390

Male-Male and Female-Female Sexual Behavior   391

Preadolescence (9 to 13 Years)   392

Masturbation   392

Male-Female Sexual Behavior   392

Male-Male and Female-Female Sexual Behavior   392

Sex Education and Miseducation   393

What Do You Say Now? Talking with Your Children about Sex   394

Adolescence   395

Puberty   395

A World of Diversity Menarche in Cross-Cultural Perspective   400

Masturbation   400

Male-Female Sexual Behavior   400

In the New Millennium Teenagers and Sex: Where Do We Stand?   402

A World of Diversity Ethnic Differences in Premarital Intercourse, Adolescent Use of Contraception, and Resolution of Unwanted Pregnancies   404

A Closer Look The First Time   406

Male-Male and Female-Female Sexual Behavior   408

Teenage Pregnancy   408

Contraceptive Use Among Sexually Active Teens   410

A Closer Look Should Public Schools Provide Students with Contraceptives?   412

SUMMING UP   413

CHAPTER 14
Sexuality in Adulthood   414

OUTLINE   415

TRUTH OR FICTION?   415

Singlehood   416

A World of Diversity Snug in Their Beds for Christmas Eve: In Japan, December 24 Has Become The Hottest Night of the Year   417

Cohabitation: Darling, Would You Be My POSSLQ?   418

Who Are the Cohabitors?   419

Reasons for Cohabitation   419

Cohabitation and Later Marriage: Benefit or Risk?   420

Marriage   421

Historical Perspectives   421

Why Do People Marry?   423

Types of Marriage   424

Whom Do We Marry: Are Marriages Made in Heaven or in the Neighborhood?   424

Marital Sexuality   426

The Sexual Revolution Hits Home   426

Sexual Satisfaction   429

Extramarital Sex   430

Patterns of Extramarital Sex   431

Attitudes Toward Extramarital Sex   432

Effects of Extramarital Sex   433

Swinging   433

Domestic Violence   434

Divorce   435

The Cost of Divorce   436

Alternative Forms of Marriage   437

Open Marriage   438

Group Marriage   438

Sex in the Later Years   439

Physical Changes   439

In the New Millennium Trends in Adult Sexuality   440

Patterns of Sexual Activity   441

Sex and Disability   443

Physical Disabilities   443

Psychological Disabilities   445

SUMMING UP   446

CHAPTER 15
Sexual Dysfunctions   448

OUTLINE   449

TRUTH OR FICTION?   449

Types of Sexual Dysfunctions   451

Sexual Desire Disorders   452

Sexual Arousal Disorders   453

Orgasmic Disorders   455

Sexual Pain Disorders   456

A World of Diversity Inis Beag and Mangaia—Worlds Apart   458

Origins of Sexual Dysfunctions   459

Organic Causes   459

Psychosocial Causes   460

A World of Diversity An Odd Couple: Koro and Dhat Syndromes   461

Treatment of Sexual Dysfunctions   465

The Masters-and-Johnson Approach   466

The Helen Singer Kaplan Approach   466

Sexual Desire Disorders   467

Sexual Arousal Disorders   468

In the New Millennium The Brave New World of Viagra   472

Orgasmic Disorders   473

In the New Millennium The "Orgasm Pill" for Women   476

Sexual Pain Disorders   477

Evaluation of Sex Therapy   478

How Do You Find a Qualified Sex Therapist?   480

SUMMING UP   481

CHAPTER 16
Sexually Transmitted Infections   482

OUTLINE   483

TRUTH OR FICTION?   483

An Epidemic   485

What Do You Say Now? Talking with Your Partner About STIs   486

Questionnaire STI Attitude Scale   487

Bacterial Infections   488

Gonorrhea   488

Syphilis   493

Chlamydia   495

Other Bacterial Infections   497

Vaginal Infections   498

Bacterial Vaginosis   499
Candidiasis   499
Trichomoniasis   500
Viral Infections   501
HIV Infection and AIDS   501
A World of Diversity Ethnicity and AIDS in the United States   502
In the New Millennium HIV Infection and AIDS—A Mixed Picture   508
Herpes   510
Viral Hepatitis   514
Genital Warts   515
Molluscum Contagiosum   516
Ectoparasitic Infestations   516
Pediculosis   516
Scabies   517
Prevention of STIs: It's More Than Safer Sex   517
A Closer Look Sources of Help   522
SUMMING UP   522

CHAPTER 17
Atypical Sexual Variations   524
OUTLINE   525
TRUTH OR FICTION?   525
Normal Versus Deviant Sexual Behavior   526
The Paraphilias   527
Fetishism   528
Transvestism   529
A Closer Look A Case of Transvestism   530
Exhibitionism   531
What Do You Say Now? How to Respond to an Exhibitionist   533
Obscene Telephone Calling   533
Voyeurism   534
In the New Millennium Exhibitionism, Voyeurism, and Videophones: Videoconferencing's Killer App May Be Sex   535
Sexual Masochism   535
Sexual Sadism   537
Frotteurism   538
Other Paraphilias   539

A Closer Look Paraphilias as Sexual Addictions   540
A World of Diversity Nymphomania, Satyriasis, and the Sexual Double Standard   541
Theoretical Perspectives   542
Biological Perspectives   542
Psychoanalytic Perspectives   542
Learning Perspectives   543
Sociological Perspectives   545
An Integrated Perspective: The "Lovemap"   545
Treatment of Paraphilias   546
Psychotherapy   547
Behavior Therapy   547
Biochemical Approaches   549
SUMMING UP   550

CHAPTER 18
Sexual Coercion   552
OUTLINE   553
TRUTH OR FICTION?   553
Rape   554
A World of Diversity Not All Sex Offenders Are Men   555
Incidence of Rape   556
Types of Rapes   557
A Closer Look Anatomy of a Date Rape: Ann and Jim   559
Social Attitudes and Myths That Encourage Rape   562
Sociocultural Factors in Rape   562
Psychological Characteristics of Rapists   563
A World of Diversity Rape-Prone and Rape-Free Societies: Whither the United States?   565
Adjustment of Rape Survivors   566
Treatment of Rape Survivors   568
A Closer Look Rape Prevention   569
Rape Prevention   569
Verbal Sexual Coercion   571
What Do You Say Now? Handling Sexual Pressure Lines   572
Sexual Abuse of Children   574
What Is Sexual Abuse of Children?   574
Patterns of Abuse   574

Pedophilia   576

Incest   577

Effects of Sexual Abuse of Children   579

In the New Millennium New Methods for Getting to the Truth in Cases of Child Abuse   580

Prevention of Sexual Abuse of Children   581

Treatment of Survivors of Sexual Abuse   581

Treatment of Rapists and Child Molesters   582

Sexual Harassment   583

Sexual Harassment in the Workplace   585

Sexual Harassment on Campus   586

Sexual Harassment in the Schools   587

How to Resist Sexual Harassment   587

SUMMING UP   589

CHAPTER 19

Commercial Sex   592

OUTLINE   593

TRUTH OR FICTION?   593

The Word of Commercial Sex: A Disneyland for Adults   594

Prostitution   594

Incidence of Prostitution in the United States Today   595

A World of Diversity From Russia, with . . . Sex?   596

Types of Female Prostitutes   596

Characteristics of Female Prostitutes   600

Customers of Female Prostitutes   601

A World of Diversity Schoolgirls as Sex Toys   603

Male Prostitution   603

HIV, AIDS, and Prostitution   605

Pornography and Obscenity   606

What Is Pornographic?   606

Pornography and the Law   608

Prevalence and Use of Erotica and Pornography   609

In the New Millennium Surfing for Sex   610

Pornography and Sexual Coercion   611

Sex in Advertising   615

Advertising and Gender-Role Stereotypes   615

SUMMING UP   617

CHAPTER 20

Making Responsible Sexual Decisions—An Epilogue   618

OUTLINE   619

Choices, Information, and Decision Making   620

Conflict   620

Decision, Decisions, Decisions . . .   620

Value Systems   621

Legalism   621

Situation Ethics   622

Ethical Relativism   622

Hedonism   623

Asceticism   623

Utilitarianism   623

Rationalism   624

The Balance Sheet for Decision Making   624

APPENDIX A: Scoring Keys for Self-Scoring Questionnaires   627

APPENDIX B: Additional Readings: Books on Human Sexuality and Related Topics   629

GLOSSARY   633

REFERENCES   649

NAME INDEX   689

SUBJECT INDEX   697

There are more things in heaven and earth, Horatio,
Than are dreamt of in your philosophy.

Shakespeare, *Hamlet*

There are, indeed, more kinds of people in this world, and more ways in which people experience their sexuality, than most of us might imagine. Human sexuality may be intimately related to human biology, but it is embedded in the sociocultural fabric of human society. For this reason, a core theme of the fourth edition of *Human Sexuality in a World of Diversity* is its multicultural perspective.

The fourth edition of *Human Sexuality in a World of Diversity* by Spencer Rathus, Jeffrey Nevid, and Lois Fichner-Rathus builds on the strong themes it has come to be known for:

- The rich diversity found in gender roles, sexual attitudes, and sexual behaviors and customs
- Critical thinking
- Making responsible sexual decisions
- Sexual health

Diversity

Colleges and universities are undertaking the mission of broadening students' perspectives so that they will appreciate and tolerate human diversity.

The United States is a nation of hundreds of different ethnic and religious groups, many of which endorse culturally distinctive beliefs about appropriate gender roles for men and women and sexual practices and customs. Diversity is even broader in the global village of the world's nearly 200 nations and those nations' own distinctive subcultures. *Human Sexuality in a World of Diversity, Fourth Edition*, incorporates a multicultural, multiethnic perspective that reflects the diversity of sexual experience in our society and around the world. Our book thereby broadens the student's understanding of the range of cultural differences in sexual attitudes and behavior of all people. Discussion of diversity encourages respect for people who hold diverse beliefs and attitudes. We also encourage students to question what is appropriate for women and men in terms of social roles and sexual conduct in light of cultural traditions and standards.

Critical Thinking

As we approach the new millennium, colleges and universities are encouraging students to become critical thinkers. Today's students are so inundated with information about gender and sexuality that it can be difficult to sort out truth from fiction. Not only do politicians, theologians, and community leaders influence our gender- and sex-related attitudes and behaviors, but newspapers, TV programs, and other media also brim with features about gender roles and issues concerning human sexuality.

Critical thinking means being skeptical of information that is presented in print or uttered by authority figures or celebrities. Critical thinking requires thoughtful analysis and probing of the claims and arguments of others in light of evidence. Moreover, it requires a willingness to challenge conventional wisdom and common knowledge that many of us take for granted. It means scrutinizing definitions of terms, evaluating the premises or assumptions that underlie arguments, and examining the logic of arguments.

Throughout the book, we raise issues that demand critical thinking. These issues are intended to stimulate students' interest in analyzing and evaluating their beliefs and attitudes toward gender roles and sexuality in light of the accumulated scientific evidence. Moreover, the fourth edition fosters critical thinking through the Reflections sections, which are found at the end of every major section within the text, and through self-scoring questionnaires. Closer Look boxes provide a close-up examination of topics of special interest. In the New Millennium boxes challenge students to consider recent changes in human sexuality, such as the advent of cybersex, and explore how these changes will affect them.

Responsible Sexual Decision Making

We encourage students to make responsible sexual decisions and to be aware of the psychological and physical dangers in "going with the flow" or being passive about their sexuality. We do not encourage students to be sexually active—such a decision is personal. Rather, we *do* encourage students to actively make their own sexual decisions on the basis of accurate information.

Decision making is deeply intertwined with our sexual experiences. For example, we need to decide

- Whom to date and whether, how, and when to become sexually intimate
- Whether to practice contraception and which methods to use
- How we will protect ourselves against AIDS and other sexually transmitted infections (STIs)

Responsible sexual decision making is based not only on accurate information, but also on carefully evaluating this information in the light of one's own moral values. We encourage students to actively consider their own values, needs, and interests, rather than going along with the crowd or acceding to the demands of their partners.

Throughout the text, we provide students with the information they need to make responsible decisions about their physical health, the gender roles they will enact, sexual practices, birth control, and prevention of sexually transmitted infections.

The Reflections sections help in the quest for values clarification. Moreover, the epilogue, "Making Responsible Sexual Decisions," explains the major ethical systems that are used in moral reasoning and provides a decision-making model that will help students to weigh the pluses and minuses of the options that are available to them.

Sexual Health

Human Sexuality in a World of Diversity places a strong emphasis on issues relating to sexual health, including extensive coverage of such topics as HIV/AIDS and other STIs, innovations in contraception and reproductive technologies, breast cancer, menstrual distress, sex and disabilities, and diseases that affect the reproductive tract. The text encourages students to take an active—in fact, a proactive—role in health promotion. For example, it includes exercises and features that will help students to examine their breasts and testes for abnormalities, reduce the risk of HIV infection, and cope with menstrual discomfort.

WHAT'S NEW IN THE FOURTH EDITION?

Although the themes of *Human Sexuality in a World of Diversity* remain constant, there are many exciting changes—changes that reflect our entrance into the unknown universe of the new millennium. The fourth edition of *A World of Diversity* includes general updates of information in each chapter as well as global changes that affect the pedagogy and message of the book. These changes help the book to retain the unique nature that sets it apart from other textbooks in the field.

New Feature

The single most exciting change in the fourth edition is the inclusion of a new boxed feature entitled "In the New Millennium." This feature highlights the ways in which human sexual experience is being transformed as we cross the threshold of the new millennium. One of the ways involves developments in electronics, as found in applications ranging from virtual reality to web sites for special interest groups to online interactivity with pornographic sites. Another way concerns changes in the trends that have characterized the last century of the old millennium, as shown in the apparent shifting of patterns of teenage sexuality, sex among older people, and transmission and treatment of STIs, particularly HIV/AIDS. Biological and medical transformations are also taking place, as in changes in the risks of cancer of the sex organs and new treatments for these cancers, contraceptive technology, and the possible use of human pheromones as aphrodisiacs. Throughout the fourth edition, these new developments and trends are incorporated into our understanding of human sexuality.

Reflection of Current Research

The text also includes recent survey results concerning sexual attitudes and behavior in our society and others. For example, recent findings of the ongoing NHSLS study are incorporated where appropriate throughout the book. We also incorporate findings of the Council on Aging study on sexuality and sexual activity among older adults.

STIs

We now use the name sexually transmitted infections (STIs) instead of sexually transmitted diseases (STDs) for health problems that can be transmitted via sexual contact. This change acknowledges the change in the discipline and refers to infections (such as HIV infection) and syndromes (such as the AIDS syndrome) as well as to diseases.

We have condensed the material on HIV/AIDS into the chapter on STIs in keeping with the transformation of HIV/AIDS into an increasingly more manageable health problem in the United States. At the same time, we retain our sensitivity to the worldwide devastation that continues to be unleashed by the epidemic.

FEATURES OF THE TEXT

The fourth edition of *Human Sexuality in a World of Diversity* contains various features that stimulate student interest and enhance understanding.

Pedagogical Boxes

The **In the New Millennium** boxes highlight the relationships between human sexuality and the technological and societal transformations that people are experiencing as they enter the new millennium. These include developments in electronics, as more and more people find relationships as they surf the Internet or seek sexual stimulation and gratification by visiting web sites. They include biomedical developments, as innovations aid in the detection and treatment of diseases of the sex organs and STIs and expand the methods of contraception that are available. They also report changes in the various so-cial and behavioral trends involving human sexual behavior, such as changes in patterns of teenage sexuality, sex among older people, and transmission and treatment of STIs.

World of Diversity boxes highlight the rich variety of human sexual customs and practices in our own society and around the world. Viewing human sexuality in a multi-cultural context helps students to better understand how cultural beliefs, values, and atti-tudes can influence the expression of sexuality. Students may come to understand that their partners, who might not share the same ethnic or religious heritages as themselves, can feel differently than they do about sexual intimacy. Students will learn about cultural differences that relate to gender roles, sexual orientation, sexual jealousy, and premarital and extramarital sexual patterns.

A Closer Look features provide in-depth discussions of scientific techniques, self-scoring questionnaires, skill-building exercises, explorations of controversial issues, and even humor.

What Do You Say Now? features are hands-on applications that place students in realistic, challenging situations and allow them to compare their own responses with re-sponses suggested by the authors. They encourage students to examine their attitudes and new ways of handling demanding situations..

The Writing Style

Human Sexuality in a World of Diversity, Fourth Edition, conveys the excitement of the sci-ence of human sexuality in all its dimensions. The text is written in a style that is intended to capture student interest in the material and at a level that students will find compelling and accessible but not oversimplified or patronizing. The selective use of humor and per-sonal asides builds interest and enlivens descriptions.

LEARNING AIDS

A textbook is more than a good read. It is also a teaching tool—a device for presenting material in a way that stimulates learning and critical thinking. *Human Sexuality in a World of Diversity, Fourth Edition,* was designed to maximize this goal by means of several peda-gogical aids.

- Chapter outlines at the beginning of each chapter organize the subject matter and better prepare students for understanding the concepts in human sexuality.
- Glossary terms, boldfaced in the text and defined in the margin, enable students to readily find the meanings of key terms and also maintain their concentration on the flow of the material.
- An upgraded and enriched art and photo program provides a better representation of the students taking the human sexuality course and the face of the population in the new millennium.
- **Truth or Fiction?** sections allow students to test their understanding of chapter subjects before reading. These unique chapter opening devices motivate students by challenging common sense, stereotypes, and folklore. **Truth or Fiction Revisited** sections interspersed throughout each chapter follow up by providing feedback to students on the accuracy of their assumptions in light of the evidence presented in the chapter.
- **Reflections** sections foster effective learning, critical thinking, values clarification, and applications of the subject matter to students' own lives.
- The **Summing Up** sections at the end of each chapter prompt students' memories and help them to organize and review the subject matter according to the heads within the chapter.

THE ANCILLARY PACKAGE

Human Sexuality in a World of Diversity, Fourth Edition, comes with a wide range of ancillaries and teaching aids. Students and instructors alike can stay current with the latest information by logging in on the *Human Sexuality in a World of Diversity* web site located on the Allyn and Bacon homepage at http://www.abacon.com. Students will find the *Student Resource Guide*, written by Lisa Davidson of Boston College, to be just the study tool they need for reviewing key concepts in human sexuality and for preparing for periodic tests. In addition, instructors will find the following as part of the package:

- *Instructor's Resource Manual*, Dr. Louis Montesinos, Montclair State University. Each chapter contains a chapter outline with suggested materials for enhancing instruction; learning objectives; chapter-by-chapter activities that reinforce concepts being taught and discussed in class; and listings of various resources, including videos, which can assist both new and experienced teachers.
- *Test-Item File*, Dr. Susan Troy, Northeast Iowa Community College. A separate test-item file containing over 2000 test items provides teachers with an array of items to use for assessing students' knowledge and retention of basic concepts in *Human Sexuality*. The test items are available as both a print supplement and in computerized format.
- *Computerized Testing*. In its computerized version, the *Allyn and Bacon Test Manager* is an integrated suite of testing and assessment tools for Windows and Macintosh. You can use *Test Manager* to create professional-looking exams in just minutes by building tests from the existing database of questions, by editing questions, or by writing your own. Course management features include a class roster, gradebook, and item analysis. *Test Manager* also has everything you need to create and administer online tests. For first-time users, there is a guided tour of the entire Test Manager system, and screen wizards to walk you through each area.
- *Transparencies*. Two sets of color acetates provide instructors with the tools for enhancing key points and include images from the text and other sources.
- *Videos*. Two custom videos are available with the adoption of *Human Sexuality in a World of Diversity, Fourth Edition*. These videos help bring a wide range of concepts to life and are designed for use as brief "lecture launchers" for the classroom, as well as highlighting related current events.
- *Web Site*. This extensive resource supports and enhances the main concepts of the human sexuality course through practice tests, links to related internet sites, learning objectives and much more for each chapter of the textbook. Visit www.abacon.com/ Rathus to explore this resource.
- *Contraception Kit*. This kit contains a range of sample contraceptives for a classroom demonstration.

ACKNOWLEDGMENTS

The authors owe a great debt of gratitude to the many researchers and scholars whose contributions to the body of knowledge in the field of human sexuality is represented in these pages. Underscoring the interdisciplinary nature of the field, we have drawn upon the work of scholars in such fields as psychology, sociology, medicine, anthropology, theology, and philosophy, to name a few. We are also indebted to the many researchers who have generously allowed us to quote from their work and reprint tabular material representing their findings. We also wish to thank our professional colleagues who reviewed this text at various stages in its development:

Reviewers for the fourth edition are G. David Johnson, University of South Alabama; Elizabeth A. Guillette, University of Florida; Robert Pollack, University of Georgia; Michael Cleary, Slippery Rock University; Laurie Desiderato, Bemidji State University;

Herbert H. Laube, University of Minnesota; Heinz Fischer, Long Beach City College; and Jerome Cerny, Indiana State University.

Reviewers of previous editions of *Human Sexuality in a World of Diversity* are Richard Archer, Southwest Texas State University; Elaine Baker, Marshall University; Judith Baker, Texas Women's University; Kenneth Beausang, Black Hawk College; Larry Bell, Northeastern University; Thomas Billimek, San Antonio College; Barry R. Burkhart, Auburn University; Jean Byrne, Kent State University; Willie A. Campbell, South Suburban College; Mona Coates, Orange Coast College; Clive Davis, Syracuse University; Linda DeVillers, Chaffey College; Beverly Drinnin, Des Moines Area Community College; Vera Dunwoody, Chaffey College; Katherine Ellison, Montclair College; Basil Fiorito, California Polytechnic State University; Julio R. Garcia, Southwestern College; Michael Gonzalez, University Psychological Associates; Ralph Hammond, University of Arkansas at Little Rock; Richard J. Hardy, Central Michigan University; Robert Holdsambeck, Allan Hancock College; Karen Huffman, Palomar College; David Johnson, University of Southern Alabama; Vicki Krenz, California State University, Fresno; R. Martin Lobdell, Pierce College; John T. Long, San Antonio College; Deborah McDonald, New Mexico State College; Gilbert Meyer, Illinois Valley Community College; Gregory D. Murrow, Edinboro University of Pennsylvania; Daphne Long Rankin, Virgina Commonwealth University; Jane Ellen Smith, University of New Mexico; Tom Springer, Louisiana Tech University; Marlene Tufts, Clackamus Community College; Mary Ann Watson, Metro State College of Denver; Charles Weichert, San Antonio College; and Paul Zelhart, East Texas State University.

We are also thankful to the many professionals at Allyn and Bacon who encouraged and supported us and helped to steer our course through the four editions of this text. Bill Barke, president of Allyn and Bacon, has been a friend to this text since its inception. We have profited from the vision and energy of a number of acquisitions editors, foremost among them Becky Pascal and Carolyn Merrill. Deborah Brown has overseen the production of the book for all four editions. We are also grateful to Mary Kriener for her developmental work. Thanks to all.

Spencer A. Rathus
Montclair State University
PsychLinks.com

Jeffrey S. Nevid
St. Johns University
nevidj@stjohns.edu

Lois Fichner-Rathus
The College of New Jersey
LoisFR@tcnj.edu

Human Sexuality

in a World of Diversity

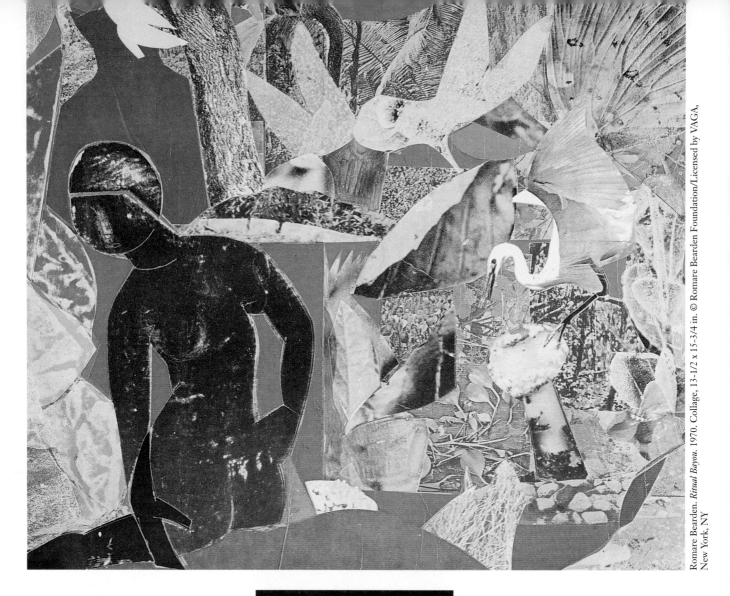

chapter

1

What Is Human Sexuality?

outline

TRUTH OR FICTION?

WHAT IS HUMAN SEXUALITY?

The Study of Human Sexuality

Sexuality and Values

A WORLD OF DIVERSITY:
Around the World in Eighty Ways—
A Preview

**THINKING CRITICALLY ABOUT
HUMAN SEXUALITY**

Some Features of Critical Thinking

**PERSPECTIVES ON HUMAN
SEXUALITY**

The Historical Perspective

The Biological Perspective

The Cross-Species Perspective

The Cross-Cultural Perspective

Psychological Perspectives

Sociocultural Perspectives

IN THE NEW MILLENNIUM:
Human Sexuality—Where Are We Headed?

Multiple Perspectives on
Human Sexuality

SUMMING UP

Truth or Fiction?

_____ Ancient civilizations worshiped women's ability to bear children and perpetuate the species.

_____ In ancient Greece, a mature man would take a sexual interest in an adolescent boy, often with the blessing of the boy's parents.

_____ The production of illustrated sex manuals originated in modern times.

_____ The graham cracker came into being as a means for helping young men to control their sexual appetites.

_____ Some African kings were literally the "fathers of their countries." That is, they had hundreds of wives and thousands of children.

_____ Trobrianders consider their children old enough to engage in sexual intercourse when they are . . . old enough.

_____ In our dreams, airplanes, bullets, snakes, sticks, and similar objects symbolize the male genitals.

We are about to embark on the study of human sexuality. But why, you might wonder, do we need to *study* human sexuality? Isn't sex something to *do* rather than to *talk about*? Isn't sex a natural function? Don't we learn what we need to know from personal experience or from our parents or our friends?

Yes, we can learn how our bodies respond to sexual stimulation—what turns us on and what turns us off—through personal experience. Personal experience teaches us little, however, about the biological processes that bring about sexual response and orgasm. Nor does experience inform us about the variations in sexual behavior that exist around the world or in the neighborhood. Experience does not prepare us to recognize the signs of sexually transmitted diseases or to evaluate the risks of pregnancy. Nor does experience help us to deal with most sexual problems or dysfunctions. What of our parents? What many of us learned about sex from our parents can probably be summarized in a single word: "Don't." The information we received from our friends was probably riddled with fabrication, exaggeration, and folklore. Yes, many young people today do receive accurate information through sex education courses in the schools, which is all the more important now that the specter of AIDS hangs over every sexual decision.

There is also something of a myth in our culture that love conquers all—that love is all we need to achieve and sustain satisfying and healthy relationships. But how likely are we to establish healthy and mutually satisfying relationships without some formal knowledge of our own and our partner's sexuality? Without some knowledge of the biology of how our bodies function? Without some awareness of the psychological aspects of our sexuality? In a scientific vacuum?

Concerns about AIDS and unwanted teenage pregnancies have focused greater attention today on the importance of sex education. Many children receive some form of sex education as early as elementary school. Courses on human sexuality, rarely offered as recently as the 1950s, are now routine on college campuses across the United States and Canada. You may know more about human sexuality than your parents or grandparents did at your age—or do today. But how much do you really know? What, for example, happens inside your body when you are sexually stimulated? What causes erection or vaginal lubrication? Can people who are paralyzed from the neck down become erect or lubricated? What do we know of the factors that determine a person's sexual orientation? What are the causes of sexual dysfunctions? How do our sexual responsiveness and interests change as we age? Why does the United States have the highest incidence of rape in the industrialized world? Can you contract a sexually transmitted disease and not know that you have it until you wind up sterile? Can you infect others without having any symptoms yourself?

These are just a few of the issues we will explore in this book. Much of the information that we present was discovered in recent years. It is almost as new to us as it may be to you. We also expect to debunk some common but erroneous ideas about sex that you may have picked up before you began this course. Before we proceed further, let us define our subject.

WHAT IS HUMAN SEXUALITY?

What *is* human sexuality? This is not a trick question. Consider the meaning, or rather meanings, of the word *sex*. The word derives from Latin roots meaning "to cut or divide," signifying the division of organisms into male and female genders. One use of the term *sex*, then, refers to our **gender,** or state of being male or female. The word *sex* (or *sexual*) is also used to refer to anatomic structures, called sex (or sexual) organs, that play a role in reproduction or sexual pleasure. We may also speak of sex when referring to physical activities involving our sex organs for purposes of reproduction or pleasure: masturbation, hugging, kissing, **coitus,** and so on. Sex also relates to **erotic** feelings, experiences, or desires, such as sexual fantasies and thoughts, sexual urges, or feelings of sexual attraction to another person.

We usually make our usage of the term "sex" clear enough in our everyday speech. When we ask about the sex of a newborn, we are referring to anatomic sex. When we talk of "having sex" (a rather ugly phrase, since it implies that we engage in sexual activity as we "have" a ham sandwich), we generally mean the physical expression of erotic feelings.

The terms *sex organs* and *sexual organs* may be used in different ways. Sometimes the terms are used to refer to those organs required for, and involved directly in, reproduction. These include the penis and testes in men and the vagina, uterus, and ovaries in women. The terms *sex organs* and *sexual organs* are also sometimes used to refer to organs or structures that are eroticized, even though they may play no direct role in reproduction (such as the clitoris or the breasts). Let us define sex (or sexual) organs as bodily structures that can be eroticized (such as the clitoris or the breasts) or that play a role in reproduction (such as the testes in the man and the uterus in the woman). They can also perform both functions, of course, as do the penis in the man and the vagina in the woman. We will use the term *gender* in this text to refer to the state of being male or female, as in **gender identity** and **gender roles.**

The term *sexual behavior* refers to physical activities that involve the body in the expression of erotic or affectionate feelings. This description of sexual behavior includes, but is not limited to, behavior involving reproduction. *Masturbation*, for example, is performed for pleasure, not reproduction. Kissing, hugging, manual manipulation of the genitals, and oral-genital contact are all sexual behaviors that can provide sensual stimulation, even though they do not directly lead to reproduction. They may also be used as forms of **foreplay,** which leads to coitus, which can lead to reproduction.

We can now define **human sexuality** as the ways in which we experience and express ourselves as sexual beings. Our awareness of ourselves as females or males is part of our sexuality, as is the capacity we have for erotic experiences and responses. Our sexuality is an essential part of ourselves, whether or not we ever engage in sexual intercourse or sexual fantasy, or even if we lose sensation in our genitals because of injury.

The Study of Human Sexuality

The study of human sexuality is an interdisciplinary enterprise that draws upon the scientific expertise of anthropologists, biologists, medical researchers, sociologists, and psychologists, to name but a few of the professional groups involved in the field. No other area of study draws on so many disciplines. These disciplines all have contributions to make, since sexual behavior reflects our biological capabilities, our psychological characteristics, and social and cultural influences. Biologists inform us about the physiological mechanisms of sexual arousal and response. Medical science teaches us about sexually transmitted diseases and the biological bases of sexual dysfunctions. Psychologists examine how our sexual behavior and attitudes are shaped by perception, learning, thought, motivation and emotion, and personality. Sociocultural theorists consider the sociocultural contexts of sexual behavior. For example, they examine relationships between sexual behavior and religion, race, and social class. Anthropologists focus on cross-cultural similarities and differences in sexual behavior. Scientists from many disciplines explore parallels between the sexual behavior of humans and other animals.

Science provides us with information, but it cannot make sexual decisions for us. Our **values** come into play in determining our sexual choices and behavior. The Declaration of Independence endorsed the fundamental values of "life, liberty, and the pursuit of happiness"—not a bad beginning. Our religious traditions also play a prominent role in

Gender One's personal, social, and legal status as male or female.

Coitus (co-it-us or co-EET-us) Sexual intercourse.

Erotic Arousing sexual feelings or desires. (From the Greek word for love, *eros*.)

Gender identity One's personal experience of being male or female.

Gender roles Complex clusters of ways in which males and females are expected to behave within a given culture.

Foreplay Mutual sexual stimulation that precedes sexual intercourse.

Human sexuality The ways in which we experience and express ourselves as sexual beings.

Values The qualities in life that are deemed important or unimportant, right or wrong, desirable or undesirable.

shaping our values. Our study of human sexuality will therefore consider how religious teachings shape sexual values.

Sexuality and Values

Our society is pluralistic. It embraces a wide range of sexual attitudes and values. Some readers may be liberal in their sexual views and behavior. Others may be conservative or traditional. Some will be staunchly pro-choice on abortion, others adamantly pro-life. Some will approve of premarital sex for couples who are dating casually. Others will hold the line at emotional commitment. Still others will believe that people should wait until marriage.

Since we encourage you through the course of this text to explore your own values about the issues we discuss, let us reveal two values that guided *our* writing:

1. *Sexual knowledge and critical thinking skills are of value because they allow us to make informed sexual decisions.* We hope that readers will confirm our belief. Having agreed on this much, your authors admit that they hold different values about a number of

A World of Diversity

AROUND THE WORLD IN EIGHTY WAYS— A PREVIEW

Like other aspects of human behavior, sexual beliefs and behaviors vary widely around the world. The United States alone is a nation of hundreds of different ethnic and religious groups, which vary in their sexual customs, attitudes, and beliefs. This diversity extends to the entire "global village" of the world's nearly 200 nations and to each nation's own distinctive subcultures.

The World of Diversity features that appear throughout this text explore the rich variety of sexual expression found worldwide. Seeing sexuality in contexts other than our own can help us to understand the role of a culture's beliefs, values, and attitudes in our own and others' expressions of sexuality. It can help us to understand why our partners, who might not share the same ethnic or religious heritage, may have different beliefs about sexual intimacy. Exploring diversity can also help us to understand cultural differences related to gender, sexual orientation, sexual attraction, sexual jealousy, premarital sex, teenage pregnancy, and risks of sexually transmitted diseases.

People in some societies believe, for instance, that a brother and sister who eat at the same table are engaging in a mildly erotic type of act. The practice is therefore

forbidden (Davenport, 1977). In contemporary Islamic societies, female sexuality is often viewed as dangerous. If women's behavior and attire are not kept under strict control, they can be "fatal attractions" for men (Kammeyer et al., 1990). What is sexually arousing varies from culture to culture, too. Among the Abkhazians in the southern part of what used to be the Soviet Union, men regard the female armpit as highly arousing. A woman's armpits are therefore a sight for her husband alone (Kammeyer et al., 1990).

Of course, one glaring reason for today's heightened interest in understanding sexuality in a broader perspective is the worldwide AIDS epidemic. Any effort to end this scourge requires that we open our eyes to cultural attitudes and traditions that may increase the risk of transmission of the disease.

If we take a quick tour of the world of diversity within our own borders and beyond, we find that:

- Kissing is practiced nearly universally as a form of petting in the United States, but it is unpopular in Japan and unknown among some cultures in Africa and South America (see Chapter 9).
- Some societies encourage sexual experimentation and even sexual intercourse

among children and adolescents, while others punish any form of childhood sexual play (see Chapter 13).
- Marital fidelity is a prominent value in Western culture, but among some people of the Arctic, it is considered hospitable for a man to offer his wife to a visiting fellow tribesman (see Chapter 14).
- In the United States, there remains a tendency to blame the victims of crimes—especially rape victims—rather than the perpetrators (see Chapter 18). In the strongly patriarchal society of Islamic Pakistan, however, the so-called Hudood Ordinance has actually resulted in prison sentences for some women who have brought rape charges against men. Hudood, you see, grants more credibility to the testimony of men than to that of women. An accused man may claim that any sexual contact between himself and the woman making the accusations was consensual, and the court will be inclined to believe him. Women are also frequently prevented from testifying in court. The result has been that some women who bring charges of rape are sometimes prosecuted for adultery and jailed if found guilty, while their assailants go free (Schork, 1990).

the issues we discuss. Therefore, we—your authors—do not try to persuade readers to adopt a particular stance concerning specific issues raised in the textbook. We present opposing points of view on controversial matters such as abortion and the distribution of condoms in schools. We hope that readers will critically consider their preconceptions and that the views that they form will be their own.

2. *Students should take an active role in enhancing their health.* In the course of this text, we will urge you, for example, to examine your bodies for possible abnormalities, to see your physician when you have questions about painful menstruation or other physical complaints, to become sensitive to the signs of sexually transmitted diseases, to get good prenatal care, and so forth.

People's sexual attitudes, experiences, and behaviors are shaped to a large extent by their cultural traditions and beliefs. Because our world consists of diverse peoples and cultures, the study of human sexuality is really the study of human sexuali*ties*. In this book, we highlight the many ways in which people experience their sexuality. We preview some of the findings of our review of sexuality in this chapter's A World of Diversity feature.

Kissing. Kissing is a nearly universal form of light petting in the United States, but it is unpopular in Japan and unknown in many African and South American cultures.

- Sex was typically considered "indecent and unmentionable" in Russia, according to Kon (1995), "a subject only for the degenerate underground." However, since the collapse of the Soviet Union, sex has apparently been escaping into the mainstream of Russian life. In today's Russia, newspapers and television regularly cover prostitution and pornography as well as the traditional bus accidents (Schillinger, 1995). As sex has grabbed the Russian imagination, the incidences of premarital sex and rape are also apparently on the rise (Kon, 1995).

- Perhaps in response to feelings of guilt or remorse, many Japanese women who have abortions place miniature stone statues known as *mizuko-jizo* in Buddhist temples in memory of their aborted fetuses (see Chapter 12). They sometimes decorate the statues with bibs or little hats and surround them with little stuffed animals, baby food, and pacifiers—all in the belief that it keeps the souls of their aborted fetuses warm and entertained (Bumiller, 1990).

- The United States has its romantic Valentine's Day, but Japan has a blatantly erotic day: Christmas Eve. (Yes, Christmas Eve.) Whereas Christmas Eve is a time of religious devotion in many Western nations, it has become a time of sexual devotion in Japan. On Christmas Eve, every single person must have a date—one that includes an overnight visit (Reid, 1990). The cost of a typical Christmas Eve date exceeds $1000. Where do Tokyo singles like to go before their overnight visits? Tokyo Disneyland (see Chapter 14).

We elaborate on such topics and issues concerning sexual diversity in subsequent chapters.

Students and Sexual Health. One theme of this text is that students should take an active role in enhancing their sexual health. Your attitudes, beliefs, and behaviors are shaped by those around you. The college years are filled with many new opportunities and experiences. The choices you make during this time can help set the foundation for your future, in all aspects of your life.

Reflections

A reflection is literally the image or likeness of a thing. In psychological terms, reflecting on things means *relating* them to things you already know (Willoughby et al., 1994). Things you know about already include your own experiences and the subject matter from other courses. Reflecting on the images and ideas raised in this textbook will help you to accomplish four goals:

- *Effective learning.* Reflecting on the material in this textbook will make it more meaningful and easy to remember (DeAngelis, 1994; Woloshyn et al., 1994). As noted by psychologist Wilbert McKeachie, "The research shows that if students are going to remember something, they have to think about it. They need to put it in their own heads in their own words, not just sit back passively and absorb it" (1994, p. 39).
- *Critical thinking.* Reflecting on the material will encourage you to analyze the definitions of terms, evaluate the adequacy of research methods, and examine the logic of arguments.
- *Values clarification.* Reflecting will enable you to identify and evaluate your values on matters relating to human sexuality.
- *Application of the material in the textbook to your own life.* Reflecting on the subject matter also enhances the likelihood that you will be able to *apply* it to your own life (Kintsch, 1994).

The Reflections questions in each major section will help you to accomplish these goals. For example, now that you have read the section "What Is Human Sexuality?," reflect on the following questions:

- Why do we need to study human sexuality?
- What are the meanings of the word *sex*? What is the meaning of *gender*? Why is it important to differentiate between the two?

■ How does the study of human sexuality help you to clarify your own values?

■ How is the study of human sexuality enriched by exploring the variety of sexual expression found worldwide?

THINKING CRITICALLY ABOUT HUMAN SEXUALITY

We are inundated with so much information about sex that it is difficult to separate truth from fiction. Newspapers, TV shows, and popular books and magazines contain one feature after another about sex. Many of them contradict one another, contain half-truths, or draw misleading or unsubstantiated conclusions. A scientific approach to human sexuality encourages people to think critically about the false claims and findings that are presented as truths.

Sad to say, most of us take certain "truths" for granted. We tend to assume that authority figures such as doctors and government officials provide us with factual information and are qualified to make decisions that affect our lives. When two doctors disagree on the need for a hysterectomy, however, or two officials disagree as to whether condoms should be distributed in public schools, we wonder how both can be correct. Critical thinkers never say, "This is true because so-and-so says that it is true."

To help students evaluate claims, arguments, and widely held beliefs, most colleges encourage *critical thinking*. Critical thinking has several features. One aspect of critical thinking is skepticism—not taking things for granted. It means being skeptical of things that are presented in print, uttered by authority figures or celebrities, or passed along by friends. Another aspect of critical thinking is thoughtful analysis and probing of claims and arguments. Critical thinking requires willingness to challenge the conventional wisdom and common knowledge that many of us take for granted. It means scrutinizing definitions of terms and evaluating the premises of arguments and their logic. It also means finding *reasons* to support your beliefs, rather than relying on feelings. When people think critically, they maintain open minds. They suspend their beliefs until they have obtained and evaluated the evidence.

Throughout the book, we raise issues that demand critical thinking. These issues may stimulate you to analyze and evaluate your beliefs and attitudes about sex in the light of scientific evidence. For example, upon reading Chapter 10, you may wish to reconsider your beliefs on whether or not gay males and lesbians *choose* their sexual orientation. Upon reading Chapter 4, you may reexamine folklore that suggests that sexual activity impairs a man's athletic performance on the following day. The discussion of abortion in Chapter 12 will encourage you to consider exactly when we begin to be *human*. When you read Chapters 13 and 17, you will face the question of whether or not schools should provide students with contraceptives.

Some Features of Critical Thinking

Critical thinkers maintain a healthy skepticism. They examine definitions of terms, weigh premises, consider evidence, and decide whether arguments are valid and logical. Here are suggestions for critical thinking:

1. *Be skeptical.* Politicians, religious leaders, and other authority figures attempt to convince you of their points of view. Even researchers and authors may hold certain biases. Have the attitude that you will accept nothing as true—including the comments of the authors of this text—until you have personally weighed the evidence.

2. *Examine definitions of terms.* Some statements are true when a term is defined in one way but not true when it is defined in another. Consider the statement "Love is

blind." If love is defined as head-over-heels infatuation, there may be substance to the statement. Infatuated people tend to idealize loved ones and overlook their faults. If love is defined as deep caring and commitment involving a more realistic (if still somewhat slanted) appraisal of the loved one, however, then love is not so much blind as a bit nearsighted.

3. *Examine the assumptions or premises of arguments.* Consider the statement "Abortion is murder." *Webster's New World Dictionary* defines murder as "the unlawful and malicious or premeditated killing of one human being by another." The statement can be true, according to this dictionary, only if the victim is held to be a human being (and if the act is unlawful and either malicious or premeditated). Pro-life advocates argue that embryos and fetuses are human beings. Pro-choice advocates claim that they are not, at least not until they are capable of surviving on their own. So the argument that abortion is murder would rest in part on the assumption that the embryo or fetus is a human being.

4. *Be cautious in drawing conclusions from evidence.* In Chapter 14, we shall discuss research findings that show that married people who cohabited before marriage are more likely to eventually get divorced than are those who didn't cohabit first. It might seem at first glance that cohabitation is a *cause* of divorce. However, married couples who cohabit before marriage may differ from those who do not in ways other than choosing cohabitation—which brings us to our next suggestion for critical thinking.

5. *Consider alternative interpretations of research evidence.* For example, cohabitors who later get married might be more likely to eventually get divorced because they are more liberal and less traditional than married couples who did not cohabit before marriage. Eventual divorce would then be *connected* with cohabitation but would not be *caused* by cohabitation.

6. *Consider the kinds of evidence upon which conclusions are based.* Some conclusions, even seemingly scientific conclusions, are based on anecdotes and personal endorsements. They are not founded on sound research.

7. *Do not oversimplify.* Consider the statement "Homosexuality is inborn." There is some evidence that sexual orientation may involve inborn biological predispositions, such as genetic influences. However, biology is not destiny in human sexuality. Gay male, lesbian, and heterosexual sexual orientations appear to develop as the result of a complex interaction of biological and environmental factors.

8. *Do not overgeneralize.* Consider the belief that gay males are effeminate and lesbians are masculine. Yes, some gay males and lesbians fit these stereotypes. However, many do not. Overgeneralizing makes us vulnerable to accepting stereotypes.

Reflections

- Why is critical thinking an important aspect of your education? Why is critical thinking essential to the study of human sexuality?
- Why is skepticism at the heart of critical thinking?
- What are some principles of critical thinking?
- A friend of yours insists that something is true because a noted sex researcher, his minister, or this textbook claims that it is true. Would a critical thinker accept your friend's argument as proof? Why or why not?

PERSPECTIVES ON HUMAN SEXUALITY

Human sexuality is a complex topic. No single theory or perspective can capture all its nuances. In this book, we explore human sexuality from many perspectives. In this section, we introduce a number of perspectives: historical, biological, cross-species, cross-cultural, psychological, and sociocultural. We draw on them in subsequent chapters.

The Historical Perspective

History places our sexual behavior in context. It informs us as to whether our sexual behavior reflects trends that have been with us through the millennia or the customs of a particular culture and era.

Our reading of history shows little evidence of universal sexual trends. Attitudes and behaviors vary extensively from one time and place to another. Contemporary U.S. society may be permissive when compared to the Victorian and postwar eras. Yet it looks staid when compared to the sexual excesses of some ancient societies, most notably the ruling class of ancient Rome.

History also involves the study of religious traditions. Religions provide explanations for natural events based on the existence of a supreme being or beings or on supernatural forces. Beliefs about the supernatural provide foundations for moral and ethical behavior. Religions have thus been major influences on sexual values and behavior. Yet the traditions and religions of diverse cultures have cast sexual behavior in different lights.

The rise of science since the Age of Enlightenment in the eighteenth century has also profoundly affected contemporary views of human sexuality. Let us trace some historical changes in attitudes toward sexuality. We begin by turning the clock back 20,000 or 30,000 years, to the days before written records were kept—that is, to *pre*history.

PREHISTORIC SEXUALITY: FROM FEMALE IDOLS TO PHALLIC WORSHIP   Information about life among our Stone Age ancestors is drawn largely from cave drawings, stone artifacts, and the customs of modern-day preliterate peoples whose existence may have changed little over the millennia. From such sources, historians and anthropologists infer a prehistoric division of labor. By and large, men hunted for game. Women tended to remain close to home. They nurtured children and gathered edible plants and nuts and crabs and other marine life that wandered along the shore or swam in shallow waters.

Art produced in the Stone Age, some 20,000 years ago, suggests the worship of women's ability to bear children and perpetuate the species (Fichner-Rathus, 1998). Primitive statues and cave drawings portray women with large, pendulous breasts, rounded hips, and prominent sex organs. Most theorists regard the figurines as fertility symbols.

It is true that ancient civilizations worshiped women's ability to bear children and perpetuate the species. Stone Age art suggests that people did worship women's ability to bear children and perpetuate the species. Primitive statues and cave drawings portraying women are regarded as fertility symbols. ■

Truth or Fiction?
REVISITED

Emphasis on the female reproductive role may also have signified ignorance of the male's contribution to reproduction.

As the ice sheets of the last ice age retreated (about 11,000 B.C.) and the climate warmed, human societies turned agrarian. Hunters and gatherers became farmers and herders. Villages sprang up around fields. Men tended the livestock. Women became farmers, supplementing their plant-gathering skills with expertise in cultivation. As people grew aware of the male role in reproduction, **phallic worship** sprang into being. Knowledge of paternity is believed to have developed around 9000 B.C., which is about the time that people shifted from being hunters and gatherers to being farmers and shepherds. The male's role in reproduction may seem obvious enough to us. However, uninformed people might not have connected childbirth to a sexual act that predated the most visible signs of pregnancy by months. Knowledge of paternity may have been a side benefit of the herding of livestock:

> For the first time, [people were] watching the same individual animals every day, all the year around, and [they] could scarcely fail to note the relatively constant length of the interval that elapsed between a ram servicing a ewe and the ewe dropping her lambs. (Tannahill, 1980, p. 46)

Phallic worship Worship of the penis as a symbol of generative power.

Of course, prehistoric people did not keep records that might help us to confirm this explanation. Had they done so, they would not have been *pre*historic.

In any event, the penis was glorified in art as a plough, an ax, or a sword. **Phallic symbols** played roles in religious ceremonies in ancient Egypt. Ancient Greek art revered phalluses, rendering them sometimes as rings and sometimes as necklaces. Some phalluses were given wings, suggesting the power ascribed to them. In ancient Rome, a large phallus was carried like a float in a parade honoring Venus, the goddess of love.

The **incest taboo** may have been the first human taboo (Tannahill, 1980). All human societies apparently have some form of incest taboo (Ember & Ember, 1990). Societies have varied in terms of the strictness of the taboo, however. Brother-sister marriages were permitted among the presumably divine rulers of ancient Egypt and among the royal families of the Incas and of Hawaii, even though they were generally prohibited among commoners. Father-daughter marriages were permitted among the aristocracy and royalty of ancient Egypt. Incestuous relationships in these royal blood lines may have ensured that wealth and power, as well as "divinity," would be kept in the family. Many societies, even today, permit marriages between some blood relatives, such as first cousins.

THE ANCIENT HEBREWS   The ancient Hebrews viewed sex, at least sex in marriage, as a fulfilling experience that was intended to fulfill the divine injunction to "be fruitful and multiply." The emphasis on the procreative function of sex led to some interesting social customs. For example, childlessness and the development of a repulsive abnormality, such as a boil, were grounds for divorce. After all, repulsiveness would dampen the mate's enthusiasm for reproducing. Male-male and female-female sexual behavior was strongly condemned, as it was believed to represent a threat to the perpetuation of the family. Adultery, too, was condemned—at least for a woman. Although the Hebrew Bible (called the Old Testament in the Christian faith) permitted **polygamy,** the vast majority of the Hebrews were **monogamous**.

The ancient Hebrews approved of sex within marriage not simply for procreation but also for mutual pleasure and fulfillment. They believed that the expression of sexual needs and desires helped to strengthen marital bonds and solidify the family. Jewish law even legislated the minimum frequency of marital relations, which varied according to the man's profession and the amount of time he spent at home:

> Every day for those who have no occupation, twice a week for laborers, once a week for ass-drivers; once every thirty days for camel drivers; and once every six months for sailors. (Mishna Ketubot 5:6; Ketubot 62b-62b; quoted in Telushkin, 1991, p. 616)

What of the feminine gender role among the ancient Hebrews? Women were to be good wives and mothers. What *is* a "good wife"? According to the Book of Proverbs, a good wife rises before dawn to tend to her family's needs, brings home the food, instructs the servants, tends the vineyards, makes the clothes, keeps the ledger, helps the needy, and works well into the night. For all this, among the ancient Hebrews, a wife was considered the property of her husband. If she offended him, she could be divorced on a whim (although wives almost never were). A wife could also be stoned to death for adultery. She might also have had to share her husband with his secondary wives and concubines. Men who committed adultery by consorting with the wives of other men were considered to have violated the property rights of the other men. Although they were subject to harsh penalties for violation of property rights, they would not be put to death.

THE ANCIENT GREEKS   The classical or golden age of ancient Greece lasted about 200 years, from about 500 B.C. to 300 B.C. Within this relatively short span lived the philosophers Socrates, Plato, and Aristotle; the playwrights Aristophanes, Aeschylus, and Sophocles; the natural scientist Archimedes; and the lawgiver Solon. Like the Hebrews, the Greeks valued family life. But the Greeks did not cement family ties by limiting sexual interests to marriage—at least not male sexual interests. The Greeks expressed sex-

Phallic symbols Images of the penis.

Incest taboo The prohibition against intercourse and reproduction among close blood relatives.

Polygamy The practice of having two or more spouses at the same time. (From the Greek roots meaning "many" [*poly-*] and "marriage" [*gamos*].)

Monogamy The practice of having a single spouse. (From the Greek *mono-,* meaning "single" or "alone.")

ual interests openly. They admired the well-developed male body and enjoyed nude wrestling among men in the arena. Erotic encounters and off-color jokes characterized the plays of Aristophanes and other playwrights. The Greeks held that the healthy mind must dwell in a healthy body. They cultivated muscle and movement along with mind.

The Greeks viewed their gods—Zeus, god of gods; Apollo, who inspired art and music; Aphrodite, the goddess of carnal love, whose name is the basis of the word *aphrodisiac;* and others—as voracious seekers of sexual variety. Not only were they believed to have sexual adventures among themselves, but they were also thought to have seduced mortals.

Three aspects of Greek sexuality are of particular interest to our study of sexual practices in the ancient world: male-male sexual behavior, pederasty, and prostitution. The Greeks viewed men and women as **bisexual.** One of their heroes was Heracles (Hercules). Heracles is said to have ravished 50 virgins in a night. Nevertheless, he also had affairs with men, including "sweet Hylas, he of the curling locks" (Tannahill, 1980, p. 85). Male-male *sex* was deemed normal. However, only a few male-male *relationships,* such as relationships between soldiers and between adolescents and older men, received the stamp of social approval. Male-male sexual behavior was tolerated as long as it did not threaten the institution of the family. Exclusive male-male sexual behavior was therefore discouraged. Some Greeks idealized romantic love between men, of the sort that bound Achilles to Patroclus in Homer's *Iliad.* The warrior Achilles could not be moved to fight the Trojans by love of country or the pleas of his king. He sprang into action, however, when the enemy slew his lover Patroclus.

Pederasty means love of boys. Greek men might take on an adolescent male as a lover and pupil. Sex between men and prepubescent boys was illegal, however. Families were generally pleased if their adolescent sons attracted socially prominent mentors. Pederasty did not impede the boy's future male-female functioning, since the pederast himself was usually married and Greeks believed people equally capable of male-female and male-male sexual activity.

The Venus of Willendorf.
Anthropologists believe that the Venus is an ancient fertility symbol.

It is true that in ancient Greece, a mature man would take a sexual interest in an adolescent boy, often with the blessing of the boy's parents. The Greeks viewed people as naturally bisexual. ■

Truth or Fiction?
REVISITED

Not all Greeks approved of pederasty, however. Aristotle, for one, considered it depraved. Prostitution flourished at every level of society. Prostitutes ranged from refined **courtesans** to **concubines,** who were usually slaves. Courtesans were similar to the geisha girls of Japan. They could play musical instruments, dance, engage in witty repartee, or discuss the latest political crisis. They were also skilled in the arts of love. No social stigma was attached to visiting a courtesan. Their clients included philosophers, playwrights, politicians, generals, and the very affluent. At the lower rungs of society were streetwalkers and prostitutes who lived in tawdry brothels. They were not hard to find. A wooden or painted penis invariably stood by the door.

Women in general held a low social status in society. The women of Athens had no more legal or political rights than slaves. They were subject to the authority of their male next-of-kin before marriage and to their husbands afterward. They received no formal education and were consigned most of the time to women's quarters in their homes. They were chaperoned when they ventured out of doors. A husband could divorce his wife without cause and was obligated to do so if she committed adultery. A wife, however, could divorce her husband only under extreme circumstances, which did not include adultery or pederasty. The legal and social rights of women in ancient Athens were similar to those of their contemporaries in Babylonia and Egypt and among the ancient Hebrews. All in all, the women of the ancient world were treated as *chattels*—property.

THE WORLD OF ANCIENT ROME   Much is made of the sexual excesses of the Roman emperors and ruling families. Julius Caesar is reputed to have been bisexual—"a man to

Bisexual Sexually responsive to either gender. (From the Latin *bi-,* meaning "two.")

Pederasty Sexual love of boys. (From the Greek *paidos,* meaning "boy.")

Courtesan A prostitute, especially the mistress of a noble or wealthy man. (From Italian roots meaning "court lady.")

Concubine A secondary wife, usually of inferior legal and social status. (From Latin roots meaning "lying with.")

every woman and a woman to every man." Other emperors, such as Caligula, sponsored orgies at which guests engaged in a wide variety of sexual practices, including **bestiality** and **sadism** in some cases. These sexual excesses were found more often among the upper classes of palace society than among average Romans, however. Unlike their counterparts in ancient Greece, Romans viewed male-male sexual behavior as a threat to the integrity of the Roman family and to the position of the Roman woman. Therefore, it was not held in favor.

Western society traces the roots of many of its sexual terms to Roman culture, as indicated by their Latin roots. **Fellatio,** for example, derives from the Latin *fellare*, meaning "to suck." **Cunnilingus** derives from *cunnus*, meaning "vulva," and *lingere*, "to lick." **Fornication** derives from *fornix*, an arch or vault. The term stems from Roman streetwalkers' practice of serving their customers in the shadows of archways near public buildings such as stadiums and theaters.

The family was viewed as the source of strength of the Roman empire. Although Roman women were more likely than their Greek counterparts to share their husbands' social lives, they too were considered to be the property of their husbands.

THE EARLY CHRISTIANS   Christianity emerged within the Roman Empire during the centuries following the death of Christ. According to the Christian Bible's New Testament, Jesus taught that love and tolerance are paramount in human relations and that God is forgiving. Little is known about Jesus's views on sex, however. Early Christian views on sexuality were largely shaped by Saint Paul and the church fathers in the first century and by Saint Augustine in the latter part of the fourth century. Adultery and fornication were rampant among the upper classes of Rome during this era. It was against this backdrop of sexual decadence that the early Christian leaders began to associate sexuality with sin.

In replacing the pagan values of Rome, the early Christians, like the Hebrews, sought to restrict sex to the marriage bed. They saw temptations of the flesh as distractions from spiritual devotion to God. Paul preached that celibacy was closer to the Christian ideal than marriage. He recognized that not everyone could achieve celibacy, however, so he said that it was "better to marry than to burn" (with passion, that is). Marriage was no sin, but it was spiritually inferior to celibacy.

Christians, like Jews before them, demanded virginity of brides. Masturbation and prostitution were condemned as sinful. Early Christians taught that men should love their wives with restraint, not passion. The goal of procreation should govern sexual behavior—the intellect should rule the flesh. Divorce was outlawed. Unhappiness with one's spouse might reflect sexual, thus sinful, restlessness. Dissolving a marriage might also jeopardize the tight social structure that supported the church.

Over subsequent centuries, Christian leaders took an even more negative view of sexuality. Particularly influential were the ideas of Saint Augustine (A.D. 353–430), who associated sexual lust with the original sin of Adam and Eve in the Garden of Eden. According to Augustine, lust had transformed the innocent procreative instinct, instilled in humanity by God, into sin. After their fall from grace, Adam and Eve cloaked their nakedness with fig leaves. Shame had entered the picture. To Augustine, lust and shame were passed down from Adam and Eve through the generations. Lust made any sexual expression, even intercourse in marriage, inherently evil and wicked. Only through celibacy, according to Augustine, could men and women attain a state of grace.

Nonprocreative sexual activity was deemed most sinful. Masturbation, male-male sexual behavior, female-female sexual behavior, oral-genital contact, anal intercourse—all were viewed as abominations in the eyes of God. To the Jews, sex was a natural and pleasurable function, as long as it was practiced within marriage. There was no sin attached to sexual pleasure. To the early Christians, however, sexual pleasure, even within marriage, was stained by the original sin of Adam and Eve. Marital sex was deemed somewhat less sinful when practiced for procreation and without passion.

Bestiality Sexual relations between a person and an animal.

Sadism The practice of achieving sexual gratification through hurting or humiliating others.

Fellatio A sexual activity involving oral contact with the penis.

Cunnilingus A sexual activity involving oral contact with the female genitals.

Fornication Sexual intercourse between people who are not married to one another. (If one of the partners is married, the act may be labeled *adultery*.)

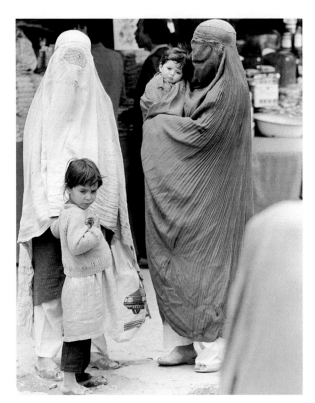

Traditional Islamic Women.
Women in traditional Islamic societies are expected to keep their heads and faces veiled in public and to avoid any touching of men other than their husbands. Yet the Islamic tradition values sexual fulfillment in marriage and frowns upon celibacy.

SEXUALITY AND THE EASTERN RELIGIONS An appreciation of the religious traditions of the Middle East and Far East can broaden our perspective of the history of sexual customs and practices. Islam, the dominant religion in the Middle East, was founded by the Prophet Muhammad. Muhammad was born in Mecca, in what is now Saudi Arabia, in about A.D. 570. The Islamic tradition treasures marriage and sexual fulfillment in marriage. Premarital intercourse invites shame and social condemnation—and, in some fundamentalist Islamic states, it incurs the death penalty.

The family is the backbone of Islamic society. Celibacy is frowned upon (Ahmed, 1991). Muhammad decreed that marriage represents the only road to virtue (Minai, 1981). Islamic tradition permits a sexual double standard, however. Men may take up to four wives, but women are permitted only one husband. Public social interactions between men and women are severely restricted in Islamic societies. In traditional Islamic cultures, social dancing between the genders is shunned. Women in most traditional Islamic societies are expected to keep their heads and faces veiled in public and to avoid all contact, even a handshake, with men other than their husbands.

In the cultures of the Far East, sexuality was akin to spirituality. To the Taoist masters of China, who influenced Chinese culture for millennia, sex was anything but sinful. Rather, they taught that sex was a sacred duty. It was a form of worship that was believed to lead toward immortality. Sex was to be performed well and often if one was to achieve harmony with nature.

The Chinese culture was the first to produce a detailed sex manual, which came into use about 200 years before the birth of Jesus. The manual helped to educate men and women in the art of lovemaking. The man was expected to extend intercourse as long as possible, thereby absorbing more of his wife's natural essence, or *yin*. Yin would enhance his own masculine essence, or *yang*. Moreover, he was expected to help bring his partner to orgasm so as to increase the flow of energy that he might absorb. (Her pleasure was incidental or secondary.)

Taoists believed that it was wasteful for a man to "spill his seed." Masturbation, acceptable for women, was ruled out for men. Sexual practices such as anal intercourse and

An Illustration from the *Kama Sutra*. The *Kama Sutra,* an Indian sex manual believed to have been written sometime between the third and fifth centuries A.D., contained graphic illustrations of sexual techniques and practices.

oral-genital contact (fellatio and cunnilingus) were permissible, as long as the man did not squander *yang* through wasteful ejaculation. Another parallel to Western cultures was the role accorded women in traditional Chinese society. The "good wife," like her Western counterparts, was limited largely to the domestic roles of child rearing and homemaking.

Perhaps no culture has cultivated sexual pleasure as a spiritual ideal to the extent of the ancient Hindus of India. From the fifth century onward, temples show sculptures of gods, heavenly nymphs, and ordinary people in erotic poses (Gupta, 1994). Hindu sexual practices were codified in a sex manual, the *Kama Sutra*. The *Kama Sutra* illustrates sexual positions, some of which would challenge a contortionist. It holds recipes for alleged aphrodisiacs, ways of making love, and so on. This manual remains the most influential sex manual ever produced. It is believed to have been written by the Hindu sage Vatsyayana sometime between the third and fifth centuries A.D., at about the time that Christianity was taking shape in the West as an organized religion.

Truth or Fiction?
REVISITED

It is not true that the production of illustrated sex manuals originated in modern times. Actually, the most influential sex manual ever produced was written and illustrated—profusely!—in ancient India. ■

In its graphic representations of sexual positions and practices, the *Kama Sutra* reflected the Hindu belief that sex was a religious duty, not a source of shame or guilt. In the Hindu doctrine of *karma* (the passage or transmigration of souls from one place to another), sexual fulfillment was regarded as one way to become reincarnated at a higher level of existence.

All in all, early Indian culture viewed sex as virtuous and natural. Indian society grew more restrictive toward sexuality after about A.D. 1000, however (Tannahill, 1980).

THE MIDDLE AGES   The Middle Ages, sometimes called medieval times, span the millennium of Western history from about A.D. 476 to A.D. 1450. These years are sometimes termed the Dark Ages because some historians have depicted them as an era of cultural and intellectual decay and stagnation. The Roman Catholic Church continued to grow in influence. Its attitudes toward sexuality, largely unchanged since the time of Augustine, dominated medieval thought. Some cross-currents of change crept across medieval Europe, however, especially in the social standing of women. The Roman Catholic Church had long regarded all women as being tainted by the sin of Eve, whom it blamed for humankind's downfall in the Garden of Eden. In the Eastern church of Constantinople, the cult of the Virgin Mary flourished. The ideal of womanhood was in the image of Mary: good, gracious, loving, and saintly.

Imported by the Crusaders and others who returned from the East, the cult of the Virgin Mary swept European Christendom and helped to elevate the status of women. Hundreds of new abbeys were founded across Europe. Their monks were devoted to the Virgin. They erected chapels in their churches in her honor and wore white in tribute to her purity.

Two conflicting concepts of women thus dominated medieval thought: one, *woman as Eve*, the temptress; the other, *woman as Mary*, virtuous and pure. Contemporary Western images of women still show the schism between the good girl and the bad girl—the Madonna and the whore. Part of the fascination of the rock star Madonna is that she combines the name of the Virgin Mary and crucifixes with an open display of undergarments and simulated lovemaking on the stage and in her videos. Note the Western dou-

What's the Message? Conflicting concepts of women have dominated much of Western thought. One concept has protrayed women as pure, Madonna-like. The other has depicted women as temptresses, as suggested in this photo. Many people thus think that women are either Madonnas or "whores"—not complex beings with a variety of attributes and tendencies.

ble standard: An unmarried, sexually active woman runs the risk of being branded a "slut." An unmarried, sexually active man is likely to receive more complimentary labels such as "stud," "playboy," or "ladies' man." Society has generally been more accepting of men's sexuality than women's.

Among the upper classes of medieval times, a concept of courtly love also emerged. It was part chivalry and part romance novel. Troubadours of the twelfth and thirteenth centuries sang of pure and ennobling love that burned brightly but remained unconsummated. Their verses often depicted the chaste love between a married lady of the court and a handsome suitor of lower rank who sought her favor through heroic deeds.

THE PROTESTANT REFORMATION   During the Reformation, Martin Luther (1483–1546) and other Christian reformers such as John Calvin (1509–1564) split off from the Roman Catholic Church and formed their own sects, which led to the development of the modern Protestant denominations of Western Europe (and later, the New World). Luther disputed many Roman Catholic doctrines on sexuality. He believed that priests should be allowed to marry and rear children. To Luther, marriage was as much a part of human nature as eating or drinking (Tannahill, 1980). Calvin rejected the Roman church's position that sex in marriage was permissible only for the purpose of procreation. To Calvin, sexual expression in marriage fulfilled other legitimate roles, such as strengthening the marriage bond and helping to relieve the stresses of everyday life. The Protestant Reformation encouraged a more accepting view of sexuality, although it maintained strict adherence to the belief that sex was permissible only in the context of marriage. Stern penalties were meted out for premarital and extramarital sex. The Puritans, one of the earliest Protestant sects to settle in America, subjected fornicators to flogging and sent parents to the pillory or the stocks if their children were born too soon after the wedding date. Adulterers, too, were flogged and sometimes branded. Remember the scarlet *A* that the adulteress Hester Prynne was compelled to wear in Nathaniel Hawthorne's novel *The Scarlet Letter.*

SHAPING THE PRESENT: FROM REPRESSION TO REVOLUTION TO REACTION Early settlers brought to the New World the religious teachings that had dominated Western thought and culture for centuries. Whatever their differences, each religion stressed the ideal of family life and viewed sex outside of marriage as immoral or sinful. A woman's place, by and large, was in the home and in the fields. Not until 1833, when Oberlin College opened its doors to women, were women permitted to attend college in the United States. Not until the twentieth century did women gain the right to vote.

In this century, social change has swept through Western culture at a sometimes dizzying pace. Sexual behaviors and attitudes that would have been unthinkable a couple of generations ago—such as cohabitation ("living together")—have become commonplace. The social barriers that had restricted women's roles have largely broken down.

The middle and later parts of the nineteenth century are generally called the Victorian period, named after Queen Victoria of England. Victoria assumed the throne in 1837 and ruled until her death in 1901. Her name has become virtually synonymous with sexual repression. Victorian society in Europe and the United States, on the surface at least, was prim and proper. Sex was not discussed in polite society. Even the legs of pianos were draped with cloth for the sake of modesty. Many women viewed sex as a marital duty to be performed for procreation or to satisfy their husbands' cravings. Consider the following quotation:

> I am happy now that Charles calls on my bed chamber less frequently than of old. As it is, I now endure but two calls a week and when I hear his steps outside my door I lie down on my bed, close my eyes, open my legs and think of England.
>
> —Attributed to Alice, Lady Hillingdon, wife of the Second Baron Hillingdon

Women were assumed not to experience sexual desires or pleasures. "I would say," observed Dr. William Acton (1814–1875), an influential English physician, in 1857, "that the majority of women (happily for society) are not much troubled with sexual feeling of any kind." Women, thought Acton, were born with a sort of *sexual anesthesia*.

It was widely believed among medical authorities in England and the United States that sex drains the man of his natural vitality. Physicians therefore recommended that intercourse be practiced infrequently, perhaps once a month or so. The Reverend Sylvester Graham (1794–1851) preached that ejaculation deprived men of the "vital fluids" they need to maintain health and vitality. Graham believed that the loss of an ounce of semen was equal to the loss of several ounces of blood. Each time a man ejaculated, in Graham's view, he risked his physical health. Graham preached against "wasting the seed" by masturbation or frequent marital intercourse. (How frequent was frequent? In Graham's view, intercourse more than once a month could dangerously deplete the man's vital energies.) Graham recommended that young men control their sexual appetites by a diet of simple foods based on whole-grain flours. To this day, his name is identified with a type of cracker he developed for this purpose in the 1830s: the graham cracker, derived from unbolted wheat (graham flour).

Truth or Fiction? **REVISITED**

It is true that the graham cracker came into being as a means for helping young men to control their sexual appetites. Graham believed that a diet based on whole-grain flours was a key to self-control. ■

It appears, though, that the actual behavior of Victorians was not as repressed as advertised. Despite the belief in female sexual anesthesia, Victorian women, as women before and after them, certainly did experience sexual pleasure and orgasm. One piece of evidence was provided by an early sex survey conducted in 1892 by a female physician, Celia Duel Mosher. Though her sample was small and nonrandom, 35 of the 44 women who responded admitted to desiring sexual intercourse. And 34 of them reported experiencing orgasm. Women's diaries of the time also contained accounts of passionate and sexually fulfilling love affairs (Gay, 1984).

Prostitution also flourished during the Victorian era. Men apparently thought that they were doing their wives a favor by looking elsewhere. Accurate statistics are hard to come by, but there may have been as many as 1 prostitute for every 12 London men during the nineteenth century; in Vienna, there were perhaps 1 for every 7 men.

THE FOUNDATIONS OF THE SCIENTIFIC STUDY OF SEXUALITY   Against this backdrop of sexual repression, scientists and scholars first began to approach sexuality as an area of legitimate scientific study. An early important contributor to the science of human sexuality was the English physician Havelock Ellis (1859–1939). Ellis compiled a veritable encyclopedia of sexuality: a series of volumes published between 1897 and 1910 entitled *Studies in the Psychology of Sex*. Ellis drew information from various sources, including case histories, anthropological findings, and medical knowledge. He challenged the prevailing view by arguing that sexual desires in women were natural and healthy. He promoted the view that many sexual problems had psychological rather than physical causes. He also promoted acceptance of the view that a gay male or lesbian sexual orientation was a naturally occurring variation within the spectrum of normal sexuality, not an aberration. Presaging some contemporary views, Ellis treated gay male and lesbian sexual orientations as inborn dispositions, not as vices or character flaws.

Another influential **sexologist,** the German psychiatrist Richard von Krafft-Ebing (1840–1902) described more than 200 case histories of individuals with various sexual deviations in his book *Psychopathia Sexualis*. His writings contain vivid descriptions of deviations ranging from sadomasochism (sexual gratification through inflicting or receiving pain) and bestiality (sex with animals) to yet more bizarre and frightening forms, such as necrophilia (intercourse with dead people). Krafft-Ebing viewed sexual deviations as mental diseases that could be studied and perhaps treated by medical science.

At about the same time, a Viennese physician, Sigmund Freud (1856–1939), was developing a theory of personality that has had an enormous influence on modern culture and science. Freud believed that the sex drive is our principal motivating force.

Alfred Kinsey (1894–1956), an Indiana University zoologist, conducted the first large-scale studies of sexual behavior in the 1930s and 1940s. It was then that sex research became recognized as a field of scientific study in its own right. In 1938, Kinsey had been asked to teach a course on marriage. When researching the course, Kinsey discovered that little was known about sexual practices in American society. He soon embarked upon an ambitious research project. Detailed personal interviews with nearly 12,000 people across the United States were conducted. The results of his surveys were published in two volumes, *Sexual Behavior in the Human Male* (1948) and *Sexual Behavior in the Human Female* (1953). They comprised the first scientific attempts to provide a comprehensive picture of sexual behavior in the United States.

These books made for rather dry reading and were filled with statistical tables rather than racy pictures or vignettes. Nevertheless, they became best-sellers. They exploded on a public that had not yet learned to discuss sex openly. Their publication—especially the book on female sexuality—unleashed the dogs of criticism. Kinsey's work had some methodological flaws, but much of the criticism branded it immoral and obscene. *The New York Times* refused to run advertisements for the 1948 volume on male sexuality. Many newspapers refused to report the results of his survey on female sexuality. A congressional committee in the 1950s went so far as to claim that Kinsey's work undermined the moral fiber of the nation, rendering it more vulnerable to a Communist takeover (Gebhard, 1976).

Kinsey died in 1956. His death may have been hastened by the emotional toll he suffered because of the public's reaction to his work (Gagnon, 1990). Even so, Kinsey and his colleagues made sex research a scientifically respectable field of study. They helped to lay the groundwork for greater openness in discussing sexual behavior.

THE PATH TO THE PRESENT: SEXUALITY IN THE TWENTIETH CENTURY   Victorian attitudes toward sexuality dominated society's view of sexuality well into the middle of the twentieth century. The belief that women did not desire sex was something of a self-fulfilling prophecy. That is, couples who held this belief might not have sought ways of enhancing the woman's sexual pleasure. Women were expected to remain virgins until marriage, although society gave tacit permission to men to sow their wild oats. Men

Sexologist A person who engages in the scientific study of sexual behavior.

were permitted to seek sex with prostitutes or "loose" women, or at least people looked the other way when they did.

Although steamy passages were found in early twentieth-century writings such as D. H. Lawrence's *Lady Chatterley's Lover*, the most explicit sexual contact permitted in the films of the 1930s and 1940s was a discreet kiss. Open-mouth kissing was not allowed. In TV shows of the 1950s, married couples were shown as having twin beds. No public forums featured sexual exotica or discussed sex openly. Nor was human sexuality widely taught in public schools, colleges, or even medical schools. By and large, sex remained shrouded in ignorance and secrecy.

THE SEXUAL REVOLUTION   The period of the mid-1960s to the mid-1970s is often referred to as the *sexual revolution*. Dramatic changes occurred in U.S. sexual attitudes and practices during the "Swinging Sixties." When folksinger Bob Dylan sang "The Times They Are A-Changin'," our society was on the threshold of major social upheaval, not only in sexual behavior, but also in science, politics, fashion, music, art, and cinema. The so-called Woodstock generation, disheartened by commercialism and the Vietnam War, tuned in (to rock music on the radio), turned on (to drugs), and dropped out (of mainstream society). The heat was on between the hippies and the hardhats. Long hair became the mane of men. Bell-bottomed jeans flared out. Films became sexually explicit. Critics seriously contemplated whether the pornography classic *Deep Throat* had deep social implications. Hard rock music bellowed the message of rebellion and revolution.

No single event marked the onset of the sexual revolution. There was no charge up a sexual Bunker Hill. Social movements often gain momentum from a timely interplay of scientific, social, political, and economic forces. The war (in Vietnam), the bomb (fear of the nuclear bomb), the pill (the introduction of the birth-control pill), and the tube (TV, that is) were four such forces. The pill drastically reduced the risk of unwanted pregnancy for young people. It permitted them to engage in recreational or casual sex, rather than procreative sex (Asbell, 1995). Pop psychology movements, such as the Human Potential Movement of the 1960s and 1970s (the "Me Decade"), spread the message that people should get in touch with and express their genuine feelings, including their sexual feelings. "Doing your own thing" became one catchphrase. "If it feels right, go with it" became another. The lamp was rubbed. Out popped the sexual genie.

The sexual revolution was tied to social permissiveness and political liberalism. In part reflecting the times, in part acting the catalyst, the media dealt openly with sex. Popular books encouraged people to explore their sexuality. Film scenes of lovemaking became so commonplace that the movie rating system was introduced to alert parents. Protests against the Vietnam War and racial discrimination spilled over into broader protests against conventional morality and hypocrisy. Traditional prohibitions against drugs, casual sex, and even group sex crumbled suddenly.

Some of the alternative lifestyles that preoccupied the media in the 1960s and 1970s have fallen by the wayside. We no longer hear much about mate-swapping (also called *swinging*) or open marriages. Casual sex may also be on the wane—in part because of fear of AIDS, in part as a pendulum swing back toward commitment and romance.

Yet if the pendulum has swung partway back, the incidence of premarital sex among teenagers, especially younger teens, appears to be headed in the opposite direction. More teenagers are sexually active today and at younger ages (Alan Guttmacher Institute, 1998). In addition to premarital sex, two other features of the sexual revolution have become permanent parts of our social fabric: the liberation of female sexuality and a greater willingness to discuss sex openly. In 1998, TV networks broadcast President Bill Clinton's grand jury testimony, with explicit references to oral sex with White House intern Monica Lewinsky, during daytime hours.

What, then, does history tell us about sex? Is there a universal standard for defining sexual values, or are there many standards? All societies have some form of an incest taboo. Most societies have placed a value on procreative sex within the context of an enduring relationship. The societal value of an enduring social, economic, and intimate relationship—usually in the form of marriage—lies in the roles its serves in providing security for children, maintaining or increasing the population, and ensuring the orderly transfer of property from generation to generation.

Other sexual practices—masturbation, promiscuous sex, male-male sexual behavior, female-female sexual behavior, prostitution, polygamy, and so on—have been condemned in some societies, tolerated by others, and encouraged by still others. Some societies have looked with favor upon nonprocreative sex, at least within the context of marriage. Others have condemned it. Some historians argue that the pagan "degradations" of Rome led to the empire's demise—that otherwise a "purer" Rome might still bestride the earth. They warn that the "excesses" of our own sexual revolution may also bring us down. Rome, however, also suffered from the administrative difficulties of tending to a far-flung empire. Rome was also besieged by "barbarians" in the outposts and, eventually, at the city gates. In fact, the civilizations of ancient Greece and Rome maintained their prominence for hundreds of years. When we consider their contributions to Western art, philosophical thought, and the languages we speak, we may question whether they fell at all.

The Biological Perspective

The biological perspective focuses on the roles of genes, hormones, the nervous system, and other biological factors in human sexuality. Sex, after all, serves the biological function of reproduction. We are biologically endowed with anatomic structures and physiological capabilities that make sexual behavior possible—and, for most people, pleasurable.

Study of the biology of sex informs us about the mechanisms of reproduction. It informs us of the physiological mechanisms of sexual arousal and response. By studying the biology of sex, we learn that erection occurs when the penis becomes engorged with blood. We learn that vaginal lubrication is the result of a "sweating" action of the vaginal walls. We learn that orgasm is a spinal reflex as well as a psychological event.

Researchers in biology have made major strides in assisting infertile couples to conceive through laboratory-based methods of fertilization. "Test-tube babies" have been conceived in laboratory dishes and inserted into their mothers' uteruses, where they have developed to term. In some cases in which women cannot provide egg cells of their own, other women have donated egg cells that are fertilized by the father's sperm and then inserted into the mother's uterus.

Knowledge of biology has furthered our understanding of sexuality and our ability to overcome sexual problems. To what extent does biology govern sexual behavior? Is sex controlled by biological instincts? Or are psychosocial factors, such as culture, experience, and decision-making ability more important? Although the sexuality of other species is largely governed by biological processes, culture and experience play vital roles—and in many cases, the key roles—in human sexuality. *Human* sexuality involves a complex interaction of biological and psychosocial factors. Biology indicates what is possible and, often, what is pleasurable or painful. Biology is not destiny, however. It does not imply what is proper and improper or determine the sexual decisions that we make. Religious tradition, cultural and personal values, and learning and experience guide these decisions.

The Cross-Species Perspective

The study of other animal species places human behavior in broader context. A surprising variety of sexual behaviors exists among nonhumans. There are animal examples, or **analogues,** of human male-male sexual behavior, female-female sexual behavior, oral-genital contact, and oral-oral behavior (i.e., kissing). Foreplay is also well known in the animal world. Turtles massage their mates' heads with their claws. Male mice nibble at their partner's necks. Most mammals use only a rear-entry position for **copulation,** but some animals, such as apes, use a variety of coital positions.

We even find analogues of deviant forms of sexual behavior, such as rape, in the animal world. We should be careful about drawing a connection between human rape and animal analogues, however. Human (perhaps we should say *in*human) rape is often motivated

Analogue Something that is similar or comparable to something else.

Copulation Sexual intercourse. (From the Latin *copulare,* meaning "to unite" or "to couple.")

by the desire to punish and humiliate the victim, a motive that may be entirely absent in the forced copulations among other animals that resemble rape among humans.

Cross-species research reveals an interesting pattern. Sexual behavior among "higher" mammals, such as primates, is less directly controlled by instinct than it is among the "lower" species, such as birds, fish, or lower mammals. Experience and learning play more important roles in sexuality as we travel up the evolutionary ladder.

Species vary not only in their physical characteristics but also in their social behavior, including their mating behavior. Scientists look to the process of **evolution** to help explain such variability. What is evolution? How might the sexual behavior of various species, including our own, be influenced by evolutionary forces?

The English naturalist Charles Darwin (1809–1882), the founder of the modern theory of evolution, believed that animal and plant species were not created independently, but evolved from other life-forms. The mechanism by which species evolved was **natural selection,** or, in the vernacular, "survival of the fittest." In each species, some individuals are better adapted to their environments than others. Better-adapted members are more likely to survive to reproduce. Therefore, they are also more likely to transmit their traits to succeeding generations. As the generations pass, a greater proportion of the species population carries the traits of the fittest members. Fitness, in the evolutionary sense, means reproductive success—the ability to produce surviving offspring. The fittest members of a species produce the greatest number of surviving offspring. They are not necessarily the strongest or fleetest of foot, although these traits may be adaptive in some environments and so enhance reproductive success.

Over time, natural selection favors traits that contribute to survival and reproduction. When environmental conditions change, natural selection favors those members of a species who possess traits that help them to adapt. These forms of the species proliferate, eventually replacing forms that fail to survive and reproduce. Species that lack forms that possess adaptive traits will eventually become extinct and be replaced by species that are better suited to their environmental conditions.

Darwin was too early. The technology of his day did not allow him to find the mechanisms that transmit traits from generation to generation. Nor could he explain how a species evolved from one form to another. Not until the discovery of the principles of genetic inheritance by the Austrian monk Gregor Mendel (1822–1884) did the pieces of the puzzle of evolution began to fall into place. Mendel discovered that traits are transmitted by units of heredity that we now call **genes.** Traits are determined by the combinations of genes that offspring inherit from their parents.

We now understand that genes are segments of **chromosomes,** which are composed of **DNA.** The chemical structure of genes provides genetic instructions. Each human cell normally contains a complement of 46 chromosomes, which are arranged in 23 pairs. Each human chromosome consists of more than 1,000 genes. A child normally inherits one member of each pair of chromosomes from each parent. So each offspring inherits 50% of his or her genes from each parent. The particular combinations of genes that one inherits from one's parents account for whether one has blue eyes or brown eyes, light or dark hair, and a wide range of other characteristics.

New variations in species are introduced through random genetic changes called **mutations.** Mutations occur randomly but are subject to natural selection. That is, some mutations are adaptive in that they enhance reproductive success. As a result, these adaptive mutations are more likely to be retained and to proliferate in a species. As more members of the species possess a variety of these adaptive traits, the species as a whole changes in form. Most mutations are not adaptive, however, and quickly disappear from the genetic pool.

In recent years, some theorists have suggested that there is a genetic basis to social behavior, including sexual behavior, among humans and other animals. This theory, called **sociobiology,** proposes that dispositions toward *behavior patterns* that enhance reproductive success—as well as physical traits that do so—may be genetically transmitted. If so, we may carry traits that helped our prehistoric ancestors to survive and reproduce successfully, even if these traits are no longer adaptive in modern culture. "Modern culture"—dating, say, from classical Greece—is but a moment in the lifetime of our species.

Evolution The development of a species to its present state, which is believed to involve adaptations to its environment.

Natural selection The evolutionary process by which adaptive traits enable members of a species to survive to reproductive age and transmit these traits to future generations.

Genes The basic units of heredity, which consist of chromosomal segments of DNA.

Chromosomes The rodlike structures that reside in the nuclei of every living cell and carry the genetic code in the form of genes.

DNA Deoxyribonucleic acid, the chemical substance whose molecules make up genes and chromosomes.

Mutations Random changes in the molecular structure of DNA.

Sociobiology The theory that dispositions toward behavior patterns that enhance reproductive success may be genetically transmitted.

There is a tendency to think of adaptive traits as somehow more "worthy," "good," or "admirable" than less adaptive traits. Evolution is not a moralistic enterprise, however. A trait either does or does not enhance reproductive success. It is not in itself good or bad. It may be adaptive for the female of a species to eat the male after mating. "Dad" then literally nourishes his offspring during the period of gestation. In evolutionary terms, his personal sacrifice is adaptive if it increases the chances that the offspring will survive and carry his genes. In other species, it may be adaptive for fathers to "love them and leave them"—that is, to mate with as many females as possible and abruptly abandon them to "plant their seed" elsewhere.

Sociobiologists are interested in sexual behavior because it is so interwoven with reproductive success. They seek common sexual themes across cultures in the belief that common themes may represent traits that helped our ancestors to survive and became part of the human genetic endowment. For example, there is considerable cross-cultural evidence that men are more promiscuous than women and have "spread their seed" widely.

Some sociobiologists argue that men are naturally more promiscuous because they are the genetic heirs of ancestors whose reproductive success was related to the number of women they could impregnate (Bjorklund & Kipp, 1996; Buss, 1994). Women, by contrast, can produce only a few offspring in their lifetimes. Therefore, the theory goes, they have to be more selective with respect to their mating partners. Women's reproductive success is enhanced by mating with the fittest males—not with any Tom, Dick, or Harry who happens by. From this perspective, the male's "roving eye" and the female's selectivity are embedded in their genes (Townsend, 1995). Sociobiological theory is also sometimes drawn upon to explain why the incidences of infanticide and sexual abuse of children are higher in stepfamilies than in families in which everyone is genetically related (Daly & Wilson, 1998).

To some sociobiologists, human beings are like marionettes on strings being tugged by invisible puppet masters: their genes. Genes govern the biological processes of sexual maturation and the production of sex hormones. Hormones, in turn, are largely responsible for regulating the sexual behavior of other animal species. Extending the sociobiological model to human behavior sparks considerable controversy, however. Critics contend that human behavior largely reflects learning and personal choice, not heredity.

Critics also claim that sociobiology is largely conjectural. No one, for example, has yet discovered genes for promiscuity. There is no direct evidence that either male promiscuity or female selectivity is genetically determined. Critics also point to examples of cultural diversity as evidence that culture and experience, not genetics, play the pivotal role in human behavior. Nor is cross-cultural similarity in sexual practices necessarily proof of a common genetic factor. Different cultures may adopt similar customs because such customs serve a similar function. For example, marriage exists in some form in every human society. Perhaps marriage serves similar functions in various cultures, such as in regulating the availability of sexual partners and providing an economic and social arrangement that will provide for the care of offspring. All in all, the evidence is far from clear (or compelling) for regarding human social and sexual behavior as direct products of our genes.

It is true that some African kings were literally the "fathers of their countries." They did have hundreds of wives and thousands of children. Some sociobiologists assert that male promiscuity is genetically determined. ■

Truth or Fiction?
REVISITED

The Cross-Cultural Perspective

The cross-cultural perspective, like the historical perspective, provides insight into the ways in which cultural beliefs affect sexual behavior and people's sense of morality. Unlike historians, who are limited in their sources to the eyewitness accounts of others and the shards of information that can be gleaned from fading relics, anthropologists can observe other cultures firsthand. Interest in the cross-cultural perspective on sexuality was spurred by the early-twentieth-century work of the anthropologists Margaret Mead (1901–1978) and Bronislaw Malinowski (1884–1942).

In *Sex and Temperament in Three Primitive Societies* (1935), Mead laid the groundwork for recent psychological and sociological research challenging gender-role stereotypes. In most cultures that are characterized by a gender division of labor, men typically go to business or to the hunt, and—when necessary—to war. In such cultures, men are perceived as strong, active, independent, and logical. Women are viewed as passive, dependent, nurturant, and emotional. Mead concluded that these stereotypes are not inherent in our genetic heritage. Rather, they are acquired through cultural expectations and socialization. That is, men and women learn to behave in ways that are expected of them in their particular culture.

Malinowski lived on the Trobriand island of Boyawa in the South Pacific during World War I. There he gathered data on two societies of the South Pacific, the Trobrianders and the Amphett islanders. The Amphett islanders maintained strict sexual prohibitions, whereas the Trobrianders enjoyed greater freedom. Trobrianders, for example, encouraged their children to masturbate. Boys and girls were expected to begin to engage in intercourse when they were biologically old enough. According to custom, they would pair off, exchange a coconut, a bit of betel nut, a few beads, or some fruit from the bush. Then they would go off together and engage in intercourse (Malinowski, 1929, p. 488). Adolescents were expected to have multiple sex partners until they married.

Truth or Fiction?
REVISITED

It is true that Trobrianders consider their children old enough to engage in sexual intercourse when they are . . . old enough. In traditional Trobriand society, children were encouraged by their elders to engage in sexual intercourse when they were biologically mature enough to do so. ■

Malinowski found the Trobrianders less anxiety-ridden than the Amphett islanders. He attributed the difference to their sexual freedom, thus making an early plea to relax prohibitions in Western societies. Even sexually permissive cultures like that of the Trobrianders, however, placed limits on sexual freedom. They frowned on extramarital relationships, for example. Other cultures, however, like that of the Toda of southern India, consider it immoral for a husband to restrict his wife's extramarital relations (Howard, 1989). Chukchee men of Arctic Siberia often exchange their wives with their friends.

CROSS-CULTURAL COMMONALITIES AND DIFFERENCES IN SEXUAL BEHAVIOR In 1951, Clellan Ford, an anthropologist, and Frank Beach, a psychologist, reviewed sexual behavior in preliterate societies around the world, as well as in other animals. They found great variety in sexual customs and beliefs among the almost 200 societies they studied. They also found some common threads, although there were exceptions to each. Although Ford and Beach's work is almost half a century old, it remains a valuable source of information about cross-cultural and cross-species patterns in sexuality (Frayser, 1985). Throughout the text, our discussion of cross-cultural patterns in sexuality is guided by their work and by more recent cross-cultural studies conducted by Gwen Broude and Sarah Greene (1976) and by Suzanne Frayser (1985), among others.

Ford and Beach reported that kissing was quite common across the cultures they studied, although not universal. The Thonga of Africa were one society that did not practice kissing. Upon witnessing two European visitors kissing each other, members of the tribe commented that they could not understand why Europeans "ate" each other's saliva and dirt. The frequency of sexual intercourse also varies from culture to culture, but intercourse is relatively more frequent among young people everywhere.

Societies differ in their attitudes toward childhood masturbation. Some societies, such as the Hopi Native Americans of the southwest United States, ignore it. Trobrianders encourage children to stimulate themselves. Other societies condemn it. The people of the Pacific island of East

Village Life. Anthropologists study sexual customs among preliterate societies to learn about the similarities and differences across cultures.

Bay discourage children from touching their genitals and may subject them to ridicule or scolding (Davenport, 1965).

Although all cultures place some prohibitions on incestuous relationships, intercourse between brother and sister has been viewed as natural and desirable in some cultures, such as that of the Dahomey of West Africa (Stephens, 1982). The acceptability of incestuous relations has also varied in some cultures according to social class. In some societies, incestuous marriages were permitted among the ruling classes. Virtually all cultures have strict incest taboos, however. Ford and Beach reported that marriage was even taboo between people speaking the same dialect in one Australian tribe—a prohibition that did not enhance marital communication.

Eighty-four percent of Ford and Beach's (1951) preliterate cultures practiced polygamy. The researchers concluded that monogamy was relatively uncommon. More common is the form of polygamy called **polygyny,** in which men are permitted to have more than one wife. Similarly, Frayser (1985) found that polygyny was practiced by the great majority (82%) of societies in her cross-cultural sample. In many cultures, the number of wives a man has is an emblem of his wealth and status. The cultures that were studied in Ford and Beach's and Frayser's cross-cultural samples typically had few members, however. Monogamy, which is the custom in the more populous, technologically advanced cultures, is therefore more prevalent worldwide. Even in polygynous cultures, the numbers of people who are monogamously married are greater than those who are married polygamously. Few societies have the oversupply of women that universal polygyny would entail (Ember & Ember, 1990). Rarer still is **polyandry,** a practice that permits women to have more than one husband. Frayser (1985) found polyandry in only 2% of the societies she studied. In fraternal polyandry, the most common form of polyandry, two or more brothers share a wife, and all live together in the same household. The wife "visits" each brother according to a schedule arranged by the men (Ember & Ember, 1990).

Polygyny has a long tradition in Western culture. King Solomon was reputed to have 700 wives. Polygyny was practiced in the nineteenth-century United States by an early leader of the Mormon church, Brigham Young, and by some of his followers. It has since been banned by the Mormon church as well by state laws, although it is still practiced in some disenfranchised Mormon communities.

The cross-cultural perspective illustrates the importance of learning in human sexual behavior. Societies differ widely in their sexual attitudes, customs, and practices. The members of all human societies share the same anatomic structures and physiological capacities for sexual pleasure, however. The same hormones flow through their arteries. Yet their sexual practices, and the pleasure they reap or fail to attain, may set them apart. Were human sexuality completely or predominantly determined by biology, we would not find such diversity.

Although sexual practices vary widely across cultures, there are some universal patterns. For one, all societies regulate sexual behavior in some fashion. No society allows unbounded sexual freedom. There is usually some societal control over the acceptability of sexual and marital partners, and extramarital relations. Nearly all societies have some form of an incest taboo. Nevertheless, cross-cultural comparisons show evidence of great variety. What is considered natural, normal, or moral in one culture may be deemed unnatural, abnormal, or immoral in another.

Yet people often apply an **ethnocentric** standard when judging other cultures. That is, they tend to treat the standards of their own cultures as the norm by which to judge other people's. Cross-cultural information helps us to appreciate the relativity of the concept of normalcy and to recognize the cultural contexts of sexual behavior. When we consider the historical and cross-cultural perspectives, we come to appreciate that our behavior exists in the context of both our own culture and our own time.

Psychological Perspectives

Psychological perspectives focus on the many psychological influences—perception, learning, motivation, emotion, personality, and so on—that affect our sexual behavior and

Polygyny A form of marriage in which a man has two or more wives. (From the Greek *gyne,* meaning "woman.")

Polyandry A form of marriage in which a woman has two or more husbands. (From the Greek *andros,* meaning "man" or "male.")

Ethnocentric Adjectival form of the noun *ethnocentrism,* meaning the tendency to view other groups or cultures according to the standards of one's own. (From the Greek *ethnos,* meaning "race," "culture," or "people," and *kentric,* meaning "center.")

our experience of ourselves as female or male. Some psychological theorists, such as Sigmund Freud, focus on the motivational role of sex in human personality. Others focus on how our experiences and mental representations of the world affect our sexual behavior.

SIGMUND FREUD AND PSYCHOANALYTIC THEORY Sigmund Freud, a Viennese physician, formulated a grand theory of personality termed **psychoanalysis.** Freud believed that we are all born with biologically based sex drives. These drives must be channeled through socially approved outlets if family and social life are to carry on without undue conflict. He hypothesized that conflicts between sexuality and society become internalized in the form of an inner conflict between two opposing parts of the personality: the **id,** which is the repository of biologically based drives or "instincts" (such as hunger, thirst, elimination, sex, and aggression) and the **ego,** which represents reason and good sense. The ego seeks socially appropriate outlets for satisfying the basic drives that arise from the id. Your id, for example, prompts you to feel sexual urges. Your ego attempts to find ways of satisfying those urges without incurring condemnation from others or from your own moral conscience, which Freud called the **superego.** How these internal conflicts are resolved, in Freud's view, largely determines our ability to love, work, and lead well-adjusted lives.

Freud proposed that the mind operates on conscious and unconscious levels. The conscious level corresponds to our state of present awareness. The **unconscious mind** refers to the darker reaches of the mind that lie outside our direct awareness. The ego shields the conscious mind from awareness of our baser sexual and aggressive urges by means of **defense mechanisms** such as **repression,** or motivated forgetting of traumatic experiences.

Although many sexual ideas and impulses are banished to the unconscious, they continue to seek expression. One avenue of expression is the dream, through which sexual impulses may be perceived in disguised, or symbolic, form. The therapists and scholars who follow in the Freudian tradition are quite interested in analyzing dreams, and the dream objects listed in Table 1.1 are often considered sexual symbols. Freud himself maintained a bit of skepticism about the import of dream symbols, however. He once remarked, "Sometimes a cigar is just a cigar."

Truth or Fiction?
REVISITED

To a psychoanalyst, dreams of airplanes, bullets, snakes, sticks, and similar objects may indeed symbolize the male genitals. Even Freud had to admit, however, that "sometimes a cigar is just a cigar"! ■

Freud introduced us to new and controversial ideas about ourselves as sexual beings. For example, he originated the concept of **erogenous zones**—the idea that many parts of the body, not just the genitals, are responsive to sexual stimulation.

One of Freud's most controversial beliefs was that children normally harbor erotic interests. He believed that the suckling of the infant in the oral stage was an erotic act. So too was anal bodily experimentation, through which children learn to experience pleasure in the control of their sphincter muscles and the processes of elimination. He theorized that it was normal for children to progress through stages of development in which the erotic interest shifts from one erogenous zone to another, as, for example, from the mouth or oral cavity to the anal cavity. According to Freud's theory of **psychosexual development,** children undergo five stages of development: oral, anal, phallic, latency, and genital, which are named according to the predominant erogenous zones of each stage. Each stage gives rise to certain kinds of conflicts. Moreover, inadequate or excessive gratification in any stage can lead to **fixation** in that stage and the development of traits and sexual preferences characteristic of that stage. (Parents who seek to rear their children according to psychoanalytic theory have been frustrated in that Freud never specified the proper amount of gratification in any stage or how to provide it.)

Freud believed that it was normal for children to develop erotic feelings toward the parent of the other gender during the phallic stage. These incestuous urges lead to conflict with the parent of the same gender. In later chapters, we shall see that these developments, which Freud termed the **Oedipus complex,** have profound implications for the assumption of gender roles and sexual orientation.

Psychoanalysis The theory of personality originated by Sigmund Freud, which proposes that human behavior represents the outcome of clashing inner forces.

Id In Freud's theory, the mental structure that is present at birth, embodies physiological drives, and is fully unconscious.

Ego In Freud's theory, the second mental structure to develop, which is characterized by self-awareness, planning, and delay of gratification.

Superego In Freud's theory, the third mental structure, which functions as a moral guardian and sets forth high standards for behavior.

Unconscious mind Those parts or contents of the mind that lie outside of conscious awareness.

table 1.1

Dream symbols in psychoanalytic theory*

Symbols for the Male Genital Organs

airplanes	fish	neckties	tools	weapons
bullets	hands	poles	trains	
feet	hoses	snakes	trees	
fire	knives	sticks	umbrellas	

Symbols for the Female Genital Organs

bottles	caves	doors	ovens	ships
boxes	chests	hats	pockets	tunnels
cases	closets	jars	pots	

Symbols for Sexual Intercourse

climbing a ladder	flying in an airplane
climbing a staircase	riding a horse
crossing a bridge	riding an elevator
driving an automobile	riding a roller coaster
entering a room	walking into a tunnel or down a hall

Symbols for the Breasts

apples	peaches

*Freud theorized that the content of dreams symbolized urges, wishes, and objects of fantasy that we would censor in the waking state.

Source: Adapted from Rathus, S. A. (1999). *Psychology in the new millennium,* 7th ed. Ft. Worth: Harcourt Brace College Publishers.

LEARNING THEORIES   To what extent does sexual behavior reflect experience? Would you hold the same sexual attitudes and do the same things if you had been reared in another culture? We think not. Even within the same society, family and personal experiences can shape unique sexual attitudes and behaviors. Whereas psychoanalytic theory plumbs the depths of the unconscious, learning theorists focus on environmental factors that shape behavior.

Behaviorists such as John B. Watson (1878–1958) and B. F. Skinner (1904–1990) emphasized the importance of rewards and punishments in the learning process. In psychology, events (such as rewards) that increase the frequency or likelihood of behavior are termed reinforcements. Children who are left to explore their bodies without parental condemnation will learn what feels good and tend to repeat it. The Trobriand child who is rewarded for masturbation and premarital coitus through parental praise and encouragement will be more likely to repeat these behaviors (at least openly!) than the child in a more sexually restrictive culture who is punished for the same behavior. When sexual behavior (such as masturbation) feels good but parents connect it with feelings of guilt and shame, the child is placed in conflict and may vacillate between masturbating and swearing off it.

Of course, parental punishment does not necessarily eliminate childhood masturbation. Nor has it stemmed the rising rate of teenage pregnancy in our society. Punishment tends to suppress behavior in circumstances in which it is expected to occur. People can learn to engage in prohibited behavior secretly, however. Still, if we as young children are severely punished for sexual exploration, we may come to associate sexual stimulation *in general* with feelings of guilt or anxiety. Such early learning experiences can set the stage for sexual dysfunctions in adulthood.

Defense mechanisms In psychoanalytic theory, automatic processes that protect the ego from anxiety by disguising or ejecting unacceptable ideas and urges.

Repression The automatic ejection of anxiety-evoking ideas from consciousness.

Erogenous zones Parts of the body, including but not limited to the sex organs, that are responsive to sexual stimulation.

Psychosexual development In psychoanalytic theory, the process by which sexual feelings shift from one erogenous zone to another.

Fixation In psychoanalytic theory, arrested development, which includes attachment to objects of an earlier stage of psychosexual development.

Oedipus complex In psychoanalytic theory, a conflict of the phallic stage in which the boy wishes to possess his mother sexually and perceives his father as a rival in love. (The analogous conflict for girls is the *Electra complex.*)

Behaviorists Learning theorists who argue that a scientific approach to understanding behavior must refer only to observable and measurable behaviors.

Acquisition of Gender Roles. According to social-learning theory, children learn gender roles that are considered appropriate in their society by means of reinforcement of certain behavior patterns and by observing the gender-role behaviors of their parents, peers, and other role models on TV, in films, and in books.

Social-learning theorists also use the concepts of reward and punishment, but they emphasize the importance of cognitive activity (anticipations, thoughts, plans, and so on) and learning by observation. Observational learning, or **modeling,** refers to acquiring knowledge and skills through observing others. Observational learning involves more than direct observation of other people. It includes seeing models in films or on television, hearing about them, and reading about them. According to social-learning theory, children acquire the gender roles that are deemed appropriate in a society through reinforcement of gender-appropriate behavior and through observing the gender-role behavior of their parents, their peers, and other models on television, in films, in books, and so on.

Psychological theories shed light on the ways in which sexuality is influenced by rewards, punishments, and mental processes such as fantasy, thoughts, attitudes, and expectations. Sigmund Freud helped to bring sexuality within the province of scientific investigation. He also helped to make it possible for people to recognize and talk about the importance of sexuality in their lives. Critics contend, however, that he may have placed too much emphasis on sexual motivation in determining behavior and on the role of unconscious processes.

The psychological perspective has much to offer to our understanding of human sexuality. Psychological factors affect every dimension of our sexuality. Those who harbor excessive guilt or anxiety over sexual activity may have difficulty enjoying sex or responding adequately to sexual stimulation. Even our basic gender identity is largely shaped by psychological factors, such as the experience in a given society of being reared as a girl or as a boy.

Sociocultural Perspectives

Sexual behavior is determined not only by biological and psychological factors, but also by social factors. Social factors contribute to the shaping of our sexual attitudes, beliefs, and behavior. Whereas anthropologists contribute to our understanding of cross-cultural variance in sexuality, sociocultural theorists focus on differences in sexuality among the subgroups of a society, as defined, for example, by differences in religion, race/ethnicity, country of origin, socioeconomic status, marital status, age, educational level, and gender. Such a society is the United States.

Consider the issue of the numbers of sex partners people have. Table 1.2 reports the results of a national survey concerning the number of sex partners people report having since the age of 18. It considers the factors of gender, age, marital status, level of education, religion, and race/ethnicity (Laumann et al., 1994).

Social-learning theory A cognitively oriented learning theory in which observational learning, values, and expectations play key roles in determining behavior.

Modeling Acquiring knowledge and skills by observing and imitating others.

t a b l e   1 . 2

Number of sex partners since age 18 as found in the NHSLS* study						
	NUMBER OF SEX PARTNERS (%)					
Social Characteristics	**0**	**1**	**2–4**	**5–10**	**11–20**	**21+**
Gender						
Male	3.4	19.5	20.9	23.3	16.3	16.6
Female	2.5	31.5	36.4	20.4	6.0	3.2
Age						
18–24	7.8	32.1	34.1	15.4	7.8	2.8
25–29	2.2	25.3	31.3	22.2	9.9	9.0
30–34	3.1	21.3	29.3	25.2	10.8	10.3
35–39	1.7	18.9	29.7	24.9	14.0	10.8
40–44	0.7	21.9	27.6	24.2	13.7	12.0
45–49	2.0	25.7	23.8	25.1	9.6	13.9
50–54	2.4	33.9	27.8	18.0	9.0	9.0
55–59	1.3	40.0	28.3	15.2	8.3	7.0
Marital Status						
Never married (not cohabiting)	12.3	14.8	28.6	20.6	12.1	11.6
Never married (cohabiting)	0.0	24.6	37.3	15.7	9.7	12.7
Married	0.0	37.1	28.0	19.4	8.7	6.8
Education						
Less than high school	4.2	26.7	36.0	18.6	8.8	5.8
High school graduate	3.4	30.2	29.1	20.0	9.8	7.4
Some college	2.1	23.9	29.4	23.3	11.9	9.3
College graduate	2.1	24.1	25.8	23.9	11.1	13.0
Advanced degree	3.5	24.6	26.3	22.8	9.6	13.2
Religion						
None	2.6	16.2	29.0	20.3	15.9	15.9
Liberal, moderate Protestant	2.3	22.8	31.2	23.0	12.4	8.3
Conservative Protestant	2.9	29.8	30.4	20.4	9.5	7.0
Catholic	3.8	27.2	29.2	22.7	8.1	9.1
Jewish†	0.0	24.1	13.0	29.6	16.7	16.7
Race/Ethnicity						
White (non-Hispanic)	3.0	26.2	28.9	22.0	10.9	9.1
African American	2.2	18.0	34.2	24.1	11.0	10.5
Hispanic American	3.2	35.6	27.1	17.4	8.2	8.5
Asian American†	6.2	46.2	24.6	13.8	6.2	3.1
Native American†	5.0	27.5	35.0	22.5	5.0	5.0

*National Health and Social Life Survey, conducted by a research team centered at the University of Chicago.
†These sample sizes are quite small.
Source: Adapted from Laumann, E. O., Gagnon, J. H., Michael, R. T., & Michaels, S. (1994). *The Social Organization of Sexuality: Sexual Practices in the United States.* Chicago: University of Chicago Press, Table 5.1C, p. 179.

Consider gender. Males, according to the survey, report having greater numbers of sex partners than females do. For example, 1 male in 3 (33%) reports having 11 or more sex partners since the age of 18, compared with fewer than 1 woman in 10 (9.2%). Throughout the text, we shall be focusing on gender differences and why men seem generally more likely than women to seek a wide range of sexual experience.

Concerning age, the numbers of sex partners appears to rise with age into the 40s. As people gain in years, they have had more opportunity to accumulate life experiences, including sexual experiences. But then the numbers of partners fall off among respondents in their 50s. Older respondents entered adulthood before the sexual revolution and were thus generally exposed to more conservative sexual attitudes. We shall find this sort of age difference, or age gradient, throughout the text as well.

Level of education is also connected with sexual behavior. Generally speaking, it would appear that education is something of a liberalizing influence. Therefore, it is not surprising that people with some college education, or who have completed college, are likely to have had more sex partners than those who attended only grade school or high school. We shall see that the effect of education is quite pronounced in the practices of oral and anal sex, as described in Chapter 9.

If education is a liberating influence on sexuality, conservative religious experience would appear to be a restraining factor. In Table 1.2, those who report no religion and liberal Protestants (e.g., Methodists, Lutherans, Presbyterians, Episcopalians, and United Church of Christ) report higher numbers of sex partners than do Catholics and conservative Protestants (e.g., members of Baptist Churches, Pentecostal Churches, Churches of Christ, and Assemblies of God). Results for Jews are obscured by a small sample size. Research in general would suggests that Orthodox Judaism is a restraining factor on sexual behavior, as compared to more liberal branches of Judaism.

The factor of ethnicity is also connected with sexual behavior. Throughout the text, our coverage of diversity will address differences between non-Hispanic White Americans, African Americans, Hispanic Americans, Asian Americans, and Native Americans. The research findings listed in Table 1.2 suggest that White (non-Hispanic) Americans and African Americans have the highest numbers of sex partners. Hispanic Americans are mostly Catholic, and Catholicism, as noted, provides something of a restraint on sexual behavior. Asian Americans would appear to be the most sexually restrained ethnic group. However, as noted in the footnote to the table, the sample sizes of Asian Americans and Native Americans are relatively small.

The sociocultural perspective informs us of the relationship between sexuality and one's social group within a society. Sociocultural theorists view sexual behavior as occurring within a particular sociocultural system. They study the ways in which the values, beliefs, and norms of a group influence the sexual behavior of its members. To a certain extent, we share attitudes and behavior patterns with people from similar backgrounds—for example, people with the same ethnic identity. Even so, not all Protestants or all members of a given ethnic group act or think alike.

GENDER ROLES   Sociocultural theorists also study gender roles. In Western cultures, men have traditionally been expected to be the breadwinners, whereas women have been expected to remain in the home and rear the children. Traditional gender roles also define sexual relations. Men, by this standard, are expected to be assertive; women, compliant. Men are to initiate romantic overtures. Women are to perform a gatekeeping role and determine which advances they will accept. Today, many of these traditions are falling by the wayside. Most women today are members of the workforce. Many are pursuing careers in traditionally male domains, such as law, medicine, and engineering. Some women command naval vessels. Others pilot military helicopters. Yet even women who become presidents and vice presidents of corporations are still burdened with the bulk of household chores (Rogan, 1984). Sexual practices are also changing to some degree. More women today initiate dates and sexual interactions than was the case in past generations.

Human Sexuality— Where Are We Headed?

How many people's lives have straddled two millennia? You are among the few.

Suddenly we are crossing the threshold into the new millennium. New years bring new hope, and we make resolutions to improve our lives. The thought of a new millennium brings yet greater hope and encourages us to examine and enhance our lives.

With the rapid pace of changing mores and the development of new technologies, we seem to be ever on the edge of important innovations and changes in lifestyle. The In the New Millennium features in the text explore the connections between such advances, human sexuality, and our styles of life.

The first of these features contains a wish list of changes that we would like to see sweep in on the winds of the new millennium. Some seem right around the corner. Others may be actualized within a few years:

- Further refinement of hormone replacement therapy for postmenopausal women such that it enhances postmenopausal women's cognitive, physical, and sexual functioning without heightening the risk of cancer.
- Increase in the number of men who become proactive about their sexual health—for example, seeking regular medical checkups for prostate cancer and other health problems that affect men's sex organs and general health.
- Further decline in gender polarization around the world. While women in the United States are entering professions in record numbers, women in some other cultures, such as that of the fundamentalist Islamic Taliban in Afghanistan, must cover themselves from head to toe when they leave home and cannot attend school or participate in the workforce.
- Further decline in prejudice against gay males and lesbians. Although the majority of Americans now believe that gay people should have equal access to job opportunities, many still would deny gay people access to jobs and housing.
- Development of safer, effective, less obtrusive contraceptives.
- More effective ways of preventing teenage pregnancies.
- Improvement of methods for treating sexual dysfunctions— for example, development of clearer standards for determining when to use psychological or biochemical methods, and development of Viagra-type drugs that have fewer side effects.

- Wider distribution of medicines that effectively combat HIV infection/AIDS. While people in the United States and other Western nations are living longer and better with HIV infection/AIDS because of the availability of combination drug therapies, the drugs are too expensive to be used in places such as sub-Saharan Africa, where nearly 90% of the world's deaths from AIDS occur.
- Development of effective programs for prevention and early detection of childhood sexual abuse.
- Effective means for controlling access to the pornography that is breaking out all over the Internet. Parents who don't exercise strict parental controls now find their children observing pornographic writings, pictures, videos, even live feeds from sex clubs in Amsterdam, Holland.

Trends in Human Sexuality in the New Millennium. What trends will we find or *create*? We can work to create further declines in prejudice against gay males and lesbians. Although most people in the United States now believe that gay people should have equal access to job opportunities, many still would deny them access to jobs and housing— particularly jobs and housing that might bring gay people into proximity with children.

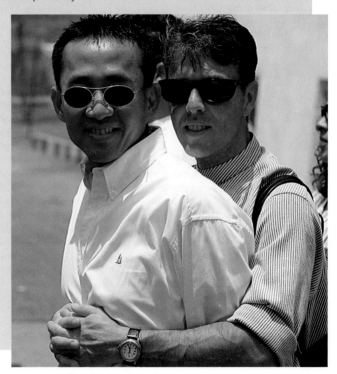

Multiple Perspectives on Human Sexuality

Given the complexity and range of human sexual behavior, we need to consider multiple perspectives to understand sexuality. Each perspective—historical, biological, cross-species, cross-cultural, psychological, and sociocultural—has something to offer to this enterprise. Let us venture a few conclusions based on our overview of these perspectives. First, human sexuality appears to reflect a combination of biological, social, cultural, sociocultural, and psychological factors that interact in complex ways, perhaps in combinations that are unique for each individual. Second, there are few universal patterns of sexual behavior, and views on what is right and wrong show great diversity. Third, although our own cultural values and beliefs may be deeply meaningful to us, they may not indicate what is normal, natural, or moral in terms of sexual behavior. The complexity of human sexuality—complexity that causes it to remain somewhat baffling to scientists—adds to the wonder and richness of our sexual experience.

Reflections

■ What is the relationship between our religious backgrounds and our judgments as to what kinds of sexual behavior are right and wrong? How have people from different cultures and different historical periods viewed human sexuality?

■ Why do we try to determine whether any sexual practices or prohibitions are universal? Are any universal?

■ Describe the development of the scientific study of sexuality.

■ Why is it important to understand the biological aspects of human sexuality? After all, isn't sex a natural function?

■ What do various psychological theories suggest about human sexuality?

■ How does the sociocultural perspective enhance our understanding of human sexuality?

s u m m i n g   u p

WHAT IS HUMAN SEXUALITY?

The term *human sexuality* refers to matters of gender, sexual behavior, sexual feelings, and the biology of sex. Human sexuality concerns the ways in which we experience and express ourselves as sexual beings.

The Study of Human Sexuality
The study of human sexuality draws upon the expertise of anthropologists, biologists, medical researchers, sociologists, psychologists, and other scientists.

Sexuality and Values
Our pluralistic society embraces a wide range of sexual attitudes and values.

THINKING CRITICALLY ABOUT HUMAN SEXUALITY

The text encourages critical thinking to help students evaluate claims, arguments, and widely held beliefs. Critical thinking encourages thoughtful analysis and probing of arguments, willingness to challenge conventional wisdom and common knowledge, and maintaining open minds.

Some Features of Critical Thinking
The text enumerates several features of critical thinking. These include being skeptical, examining definitions of terms, examining the assumptions or premises of arguments, being cautious in drawing conclusions from evidence, considering alternative interpretations of evidence, and avoiding oversimplification and overgeneralization.

PERSPECTIVES ON HUMAN SEXUALITY

Human sexuality is a complex field, and no single theory or perspective can capture all its nuances. The text offers diverse perspectives on sexuality.

The Historical Perspective
History places our sexual behavior in the context of time. History shows little evidence of universal sexual trends. There is evidence of prehistoric worship of generative power in women and men. Jews and Christians have emphasized the role of sex as a means of propagation and have generally restricted sex to the context of family life. The ancient Greeks and Romans dwelled in male-oriented societies that viewed women as chattel. Some Eastern civilizations have equated sexual pleasure with religious experience and have developed sex manuals. Repressive Victorian sexual attitudes gave way to the sexual revolution of the 1960s and 1970s in the West.

The Biological Perspective
The biological perspective focuses on the role of biological processes, such as genetic, hormonal, vascular, and neural factors, in explaining human sexual behavior. Knowledge of biology helps us to understand how our bodies respond to sexual stimulation and enhances aspects of our sexual health.

The Cross-Species Perspective
The study of other animal species reveals a surprising variety of sexual behaviors among nonhumans. There are, for example, animal analogues of male-male sexual behavior, female-female sexual behavior, oral sex, foreplay, and rape. Still, we must be cautious in generalizing from lower animals to hu-

mans. We find that experience and learning play more important roles in sexuality as we travel up the evolutionary ladder. Sociobiological theory proposes that dispositions toward behavior patterns that enhance reproductive success—as well as physical traits that do so—may be genetically transmitted.

The Cross-Cultural Perspective

This perspective, like the historical perspective, provides insight into the ways in which cultural beliefs affect sexual behavior and people's sense of morality. Anthropologists observe other cultures firsthand when possible. Cross-cultural evidence challenges the notion of the universality of gender-role stereotypes. All cultures apparently place some limits on sexual freedom (and almost all cultures place some prohibitions on incestuous relationships), but some cultures are more sexually permissive than others.

Psychological Perspectives

Psychological perspectives focus on the psychological factors of perception, learning, motivation, emotion, personality, and so on that affect gender and sexual behavior in the individual. Sigmund Freud formulated the theory of psychoanalysis, which proposes that biologically based sex drives come into conflict with social codes. Erogenous zones shift through the process of psychosexual development, and defense mechanisms keep threatening ideas and impulses out of conscious awareness. Learning theorists focus on the roles of rewards, punishments, and modeling on sexual behavior.

Sociocultural Perspectives

Sociocultural theorists focus on differences in sexuality among the groups within a society, as defined, for example, by differences in religion, race, country of origin, socioeconomic status, age, educational level, and gender.

Multiple Perspectives on Human Sexuality

Given the complexity and range of human sexual behavior, we need to consider multiple perspectives to understand human sexuality.

Jackson Pollock. *Male and Female*. 1942. Oil on canvas, 73-1/4 x 48-15/16 in. Philadelphia Museum of Art: Gift of Mr. and Mrs H. Gates Lloyd

chapter

2

Research Methods

outline

TRUTH OR FICTION?

A SCIENTIFIC APPROACH TO HUMAN SEXUALITY

The Scientific Method

Goals and Methods of the Science of Human Sexuality

Operational Definitions

A CLOSER LOOK:
Physiological Measures of Sexual Arousal

POPULATIONS AND SAMPLES: REPRESENTING THE WORLD OF DIVERSITY

Sampling Methods

METHODS OF OBSERVATION

The Case-Study Method

The Survey Method

A WORLD OF DIVERSITY:
Surveys of the Sexual Behavior of Diverse Populations

The Naturalistic-Observation Method

The Ethnographic-Observation Method

The Participant-Observation Method

The Laboratory-Observation Method

THE CORRELATIONAL METHOD

Limitations of the Correlational Method

THE EXPERIMENTAL METHOD

Aspects of the Experimental Method

ETHICS IN SEX RESEARCH

Pain and Stress

Confidentiality

Informed Consent

The Use of Deception

SUMMING UP

Truth or Fiction ?

_____ You could study the sexual behavior of millions of Americans and still not obtain an accurate picture of the sexual behavior of the general U.S. population.

_____ Researchers can overcome refusal of some people to participate in a study of sexual behavior by recruiting larger numbers of volunteers.

_____ Case studies have been carried out on people who are dead.

_____ Residents of China are more likely than people in the United States to approve of extramarital affairs.

_____ Some sex researchers have engaged in "swinging" with the people they have studied.

_____ Masters and Johnson created a transparent artificial penis containing photographic equipment to study female sexual response.

_____ Regular churchgoers report higher levels of sexual satisfaction.

ave you ever wondered about questions such as these: Are my sexual interests and behavior patterns unique or shared by many others? Does alcohol stimulate or dampen sexual response? Why do people engage in male-male or female-female sexual behavior? How do people contract AIDS? Does pornography cause rape?

You may have thought of such questions. You may even have expressed opinions on them. But scientists insist that opinions about behavior, including sexual behavior, be supported by evidence. Evidence, in turn, must be based upon careful observations in the laboratory or in the field.

In this chapter, we explore the methods that scientists use to study human sexuality. We then focus on ethical issues in research on sex. Researchers in all behavioral sciences confront ethical problems, but the problems are heightened in sex research. After all, the field of human sexuality touches on some of the most personal and intimate experiences of our lives.

A SCIENTIFIC APPROACH TO HUMAN SEXUALITY

Scientists and researchers who study human sexuality take an **empirical** approach. They base their knowledge on research evidence, rather than on intuition, faith, or superstition. Scientists' and other people's intuitions or religious beliefs may suggest topics to be studied scientifically. Yet once the topics are selected, answers are sought on the basis of the scientific method.

The Scientific Method

Critical thinking and the scientific approach share the hallmark of skepticism. As skeptics, scientists question prevailing assumptions and theories about sexual behavior. They are willing to dispute the assertions of authority figures such as political and religious leaders—even other scientists. Scientists also recognize that they cannot gain perfect knowledge. One era's "truths" may become another era's ancient myths and fallacies. Scientists are involved in the continuous quest for truth, but they do not see themselves as experiencing revelations or defining final truths.

The *scientific method* is a systematic way of gathering scientific evidence and testing assumptions through research. It has a number of elements:

1. *Formulating a research question.* For example, does alcohol inspire or impair sexual response? Scientists formulate research questions on the basis of their observations of, or theories about, events or behavior. They then seek answers to such questions by conducting empirical research.

2. *Framing the research question in the form of a hypothesis.* Experiments are usually undertaken with a **hypothesis** in mind—a precise prediction about behavior that is often derived from theory. A hypothesis is tested through research. For instance, a scientist might theorize that alcohol enhances sexual responsiveness either by directly stimulating sexual response or by reducing feelings of guilt associated with sex. He or she might then hypothesize that an intervention (called, in experimental terms, a "treatment"), such as drinking alcohol in a laboratory setting, will lead to heightened sexual arousal in the presence of erotic stimuli (such as sexually explicit films). Hypotheses, then, can be considered educated guesses that anticipate the results of an experiment in advance.

3. *Testing the hypothesis.* Scientists then test hypotheses through carefully controlled observation and experimentation. A specific hypothesis about alcohol and sexual arousal—that alcohol either increases or decreases sexual responsiveness—might be

Empirical Derived from or based on observation and experimentation.

Hypothesis A precise prediction about behavior that is tested through research.

36

tested by administering a certain amount of alcohol to one group of people and then comparing their level of sexual arousal following specific types of sexual stimulation (such as exposure to sexually explicit films) to the level of sexual arousal of another group of people who were shown the films but not given any alcohol.

4. *Drawing conclusions.* Scientists then draw conclusions or inferences about the correctness of their hypotheses, based on their analyses of the results of their studies. If the results of well-designed research studies fail to bear out certain hypotheses, scientists can revise the theories that served as the frameworks for the hypotheses. Research findings often lead scientists to modify their theories and, in turn, generate new hypotheses that can be tested in further research.

Some investigators include the publication of results in professional journals as part and parcel of the scientific method. Publication shares scientific knowledge with the public at large and also exposes research methods to evaluation by the scientific community. In this way, results can be interpreted in terms of potential flaws in methodology.

Goals and Methods of the Science of Human Sexuality

The goals of the science of human sexuality are congruent with those of other sciences: to describe, explain, predict, and control the events (in this case, the sexual behaviors) that are of interest. Let us discuss some of the general goals of science and how they relate to the study of human sexuality as a science.

Description is a basic objective of science. To understand sexual behavior, for example, we must first be able to describe it. So description of behavior precedes understanding. Scientists attempt to be clear, unbiased, and precise in their descriptions of events and behavior. The scientific approach to human sexuality describes sexual behavior through techniques as varied as the field study, the survey, the individual case study, and the laboratory experiment.

To underscore the importance of the need for unbiased description, consider the name of a tropical fish that will be familiar to many readers: the kissing gourami. These small, flat fish—particularly the males—approach each other frontally and press their open mouths against one another. Yet the term *kissing gourami* may well be something of a misnomer if the word "kissing" is meant to imply affection. Prolonged observations of the fish suggest that it is more likely that kissing in gouramis is a test of strength. More powerful "kissers" apparently achieve positions of social dominance that are connected with privileges in feeding and mating.

The error in describing the behavior of gouramis as "kissing" involves confusing **inference** with description. It is, in fact, an **anthropomorphic** inference, in that it involves applying human standards to explain animal behavior. One of the great challenges to scientists is the separation of description from inference.

Inference, like description, is crucial to science. Inference allows us to move from observations or descriptions of particular events or behavior to general principles that can be woven into models and theories that help to explain them, such as the psychoanalytic and learning theories or models. Without a means for organizing our descriptions of events and behavior in terms of models and theories, we would be left with nothing more than a buzzing confusion of disconnected observations. Scientists need to distinguish between *description* and *inference*, however—to recognize when they jump from a description of events to an inference based on an interpretation of those events. For example, one does not *describe* a person's sexual behavior as "deviant." Rather, one *labels* or *classifies* it as deviant when one believes it to deviate from a certain norm. But what is deviant in one culture may be normal in another. Incestuous relationships between brothers and sisters are permitted among the Dahomey of West Africa (Stephens, 1982). The same behavior is considered deviant in our own culture and virtually all others. Even within the same larger culture, behavior may be deviant by the standards of some subcultures and not by others.

Inference Conclusion or opinion.

Anthropomorphism The attributing of human characteristics to an animal.

Researchers attempt to relate their observations to other factors, or **variables,** that can help to explain them. For example, researchers may attempt to explain variations in the frequency of coitus by relating—or *correlating*—coitus with **demographic** variables such as age, religious or social background, or cultural expectations. The variables that are commonly used to explain sexual behavior include biological (age, health), psychological (anxieties, skills), and sociological (educational level, socioeconomic status, ethnicity) ones. Explanations of behavior can involve reference to many variables, even those that cannot be measured directly, such as unconscious motivation. Relationships among variables may be tied together into theories of behavior. For example, psychoanalytic theory emphasizes the role of unconscious forces in determining behavior. Learning theories focus on how variables such as rewards, punishments, and expectations shape behavior.

Theories provide frameworks within which scientists can explain what they observe and make predictions. It is not sufficient for theories to help us make sense of events that have already occurred. Theories must also allow us to make predictions. One test of the soundness of psychoanalytic and learning theories is whether or not they allow us to predict behavior. Prediction requires discovering variables that anticipate events. Geologists seek clues in the forces that affect the earth to forecast events such as earthquakes and volcanic eruptions. Sex researchers study factors that may predict various types of sexual behavior. Some researchers, for example, have examined childhood interests and behavior patterns that may predict the development of a gay male or lesbian sexual orientation. Others have explored factors, such as the age at which dating begins and the quality of the relationships between teens and their parents, that may predict the likelihood of premarital intercourse during adolescence.

The concept of "controlling" human behavior does not mean coercing people to do the bidding of others. Rather, it means drawing upon scientific knowledge to help people create their own goals and marshal their resources to meet them. Reputable scientists are held to ethical and professional standards that ban the use of harmful techniques in research or practice and that safeguard the rights of participants in research.

The science of human sexuality does not tell people how they *ought* to behave. It does not attempt to limit or expand their variety of sexual activities. Rather, it furnishes information that people may use to help themselves or others make decisions about their own behavior. For instance, the science of human sexuality provides information that increases the chances that a couple who are having difficulty becoming pregnant will be able to conceive. At the same time, it develops and evaluates means of birth control that can be used to help couples regulate their reproductive choices. The science of human sexuality also seeks to develop techniques that can help people overcome sexual dysfunctions and enhance the gratification they find in sexual relations. "Control" also takes the form of enabling couples to give and receive more sexual pleasure, of enhancing fetal health, and of preventing and curing sexually transmitted diseases.

Operational Definitions

How do we study concepts such as sexual satisfaction or an even broader concept, marital satisfaction? One of the requirements in sex research, as in other types of research, is specification of the definitions of the concepts, or *constructs*, of interest. Different investigators may define marital satisfaction or sexual satisfaction in different ways. They may be studying different events, although they may use the same terms.

What, for example, is sexual arousal? Many studies seek to assess the effects of various stimuli (such as sexually explicit material) on sexual arousal, but sexual arousal can mean several things. It can mean the *subjective* "feeling" that one is sexually aroused. It can mean one's self-report of genital sensations. It may refer to direct physiological measures of blood congestion (**vasocongestion**) in the genitals. We further explore the measurement of sexual arousal in the nearby A Closer Look feature.

The **operational definition** of a construct links its meaning to the methods that are used to measure it. In some studies reported in this book, sexual arousal is operationally

Variables Quantities or qualities that vary or may vary.

Demographic Concerning the vital statistics (density, race, age, etc.) of human populations.

Vasocongestion Congestion from the flow of blood. (From the Latin *vas,* meaning "vessel.")

Operational definition A definition of a construct or variable in terms of the methods used to measure it.

Penile strain gauge A device for measuring sexual arousal in men in terms of changes in the circumference of the penis.

a CLOSER look

Physiological Measures of Sexual Arousal

Scientific studies depend on the ability to measure the phenomena of interest. The phenomena of sexual arousal may be measured by different means, such as self-report and physiological measures. Self-report measures of sexual arousal are considered *subjective*. They ask people to give their impressions of the level of their sexual arousal at a given time, such as by circling their response on a ten-point scale that ranges from 0, "not at all aroused," to 10, "extremely aroused." Physiological devices measure the degree of vasocongestion that builds up in the genitals during sexual arousal. (Vasocongestion—that is, congestion with blood—leads to erection in men and vaginal lubrication in women.) In men, vasocongestion is frequently measured by a **penile strain gauge.** This device is worn under the man's clothing. It is fitted around the penis and measures his erectile response by recording changes in the circumference of the penis. The device is sensitive to small changes in circumference that may not be noticed (and therefore not reported) by the man.

Physiological measurement of sexual arousal in women is most often accomplished by means of a **vaginal photoplethysmograph.** The vaginal photoplethysmograph is a tampon-shaped probe with a light and a photocell in its tip. It is inserted in the vagina and indicates the level of blood congestion by means of measuring the amount of light reflected from the vaginal walls. The more light that is absorbed by the vaginal walls, the less that is reflected. Less reflected light indicates greater vasocongestion.

Sex researchers sometimes measure sexual arousal in response to stimuli such as erotic films or audiotaped dramatizations of erotic scenes. What happens when physiological devices give a different impression of sexual arousal than those offered by self-report? Objectively (physiologically) measured sexual arousal does not always agree with subjective feelings of sexual arousal, as measured by self-report. For example, a person may say that he or she is relatively unaroused while the physiological measures suggest otherwise. Which is the *truer* measure of arousal: the person's subjective reports or the levels shown on the objective instruments?

Discrepancies across measures suggest that people may be sexually aroused (as measured by physiological indicators) but psychologically unprepared to recognize it or unwilling to admit it. In the real world of human relationships, sexual arousal has psychological as well as physiological aspects. The reflexes of erection and vaginal lubrication do not necessarily translate into "Yes."

The Penile Strain Gauge and the Vaginal Photoplethysmograph. These devices measure vasocongestion in the genitals of men and women, providing an objective measure of their level of sexual arousal. Can you think of other aspects of sexual arousal?

defined as vasocongestion. In others, it is operationally defined as self-report of sexual interest or genital sensations. In still others, a combination of measures is used. It is important to recognize that our ability to generalize the results of research is limited by the operational definitions of the variables. That is, we may be able to generalize only to instances that define terms in the same way.

Vaginal plethysmograph A tampon-shaped probe that is inserted in the vagina and suggests the level of vasocongestion by measuring the light reflected from the vaginal walls.

Reflections

- What is the scientific method? Why do scholars of human sexuality use it?
- Does the science of human sexuality aim to tell people how they *ought* to behave? Why or why not?
- Which strikes you as the *truer* measure of sexual arousal: the person's subjective reports of arousal or the levels shown on objective instruments such as the penile strain gauge or vaginal photoplethysmograph? Support your answer.
- Do you believe that scientists should be permitted to use instruments such as the penile strain gauge or vaginal photoplethysmograph in their research? Why or why not?

Let us now examine the ways in which scientists study human sexuality. The first thing scientists do is to identify *whom* or *what* they will study, which brings us to the topic of sampling.

POPULATIONS AND SAMPLES: REPRESENTING THE WORLD OF DIVERSITY

Researchers undertake to learn about populations. **Populations** are complete groups of people or animals. Many researchers have attempted to learn about people in the United States, for example. (At the turn of the millennium, there are about 280 million of them—a sizable population.) Other researchers may identify American adults or American adolescents as their population. Still other researchers attempt to compare the sexual behavior of African Americans to that of Hispanic Americans and other Americans. These are termed the *populations of interest,* or *target populations.* These target populations are all sizable. It would be expensive, difficult, and, in fact, all but impossible to study every individual in them.

Because of the impossibility of studying all members of a population, scientists select individuals from the population and study them. The individuals who participate in research are said to compose a **sample.** However, we cannot truly learn about the population of interest unless the sample *represents* that population. A *representative sample* is a research sample of participants who accurately represent the population of interest.

If you wished to learn about dating practices at your college or university, the population of interest would be the total student population. If you were to select your research sample from one dormitory or class, it would probably not be a representative sample (unless the dormitory or class contained a true cross-section of the entire student body). If our samples do not represent the target populations, we cannot extend or **generalize** the results of our research to the populations of interest. If we wished to study the sexual behavior of Asian Americans, our population would consist of *all* Asian Americans. If we used only Asian American college students as our sample, we could not generalize our findings to all Asian Americans. Our sample would not *represent* all Asian Americans.

In a perfect world, research into populations would include every member of the target populations. Then we would know that our findings applied to these populations. Including all people in the United States in a study of sexual behavior would be impossible. We cannot even find all people in the United States when we conduct the census each decade. Sex research would undoubtedly cause many more people to refuse to participate than would a simple counting of noses. Sampling a part of a target population makes research practical and possible—if imperfect.

Population A complete group of organisms or events.

Sample Part of a population.

Generalize To go from the particular to the general.

Sampling Methods

Since we cannot sample every member of a population, we need to select samples that represent that population. One way of acquiring a representative sample is through random sampling. A **random sample** is one in which every member of the target population has an equal chance of participating. A random sample is a type of **probability sample.** Statisticians use the term *probability sample* to describe samples in which we know the probability of any particular member's being included in the sample.

Now and then, magazine editors boast that they have surveyed samples of 20,000 or 30,000 readers, but size alone does not mean that a sample is representative. As an example, the *Literary Digest* magazine polled thousands of voters by telephone to predict the outcome of the 1936 presidential election. On the basis of the survey, the magazine predicted that Alfred Landon would defeat Franklin D. Roosevelt, but Roosevelt won by a landslide of nearly 11 million votes. The problem was that the election was held during the Great Depression, when only relatively affluent people could afford telephones. Those who could afford phones were also more likely to be Republicans and to vote for the Republican candidate, Landon. Thus, the *Digest* poll, although large, was biased. A sample of 30 million voters will not provide an accurate picture if it is biased.

It is true that you could study the sexual behavior of millions of people in the United States and still not obtain an accurate picture of the sexual behavior of the general U.S. population. A sample of many millions might not represent the U.S. population. Sample size alone does not guarantee that the sample's members have been selected in an unbiased manner. ■

Truth or Fiction? REVISITED

Researchers overcome biased sampling by drawing *random* or *stratified random* samples of populations. In a random sample, every member of a population has an equal chance of participating. In a **stratified random sample,** known subgroups of a population are represented in proportion to their numbers in the population. For instance, about 12% of the U.S. population is African American. Researchers could therefore decide that 12% of their sample must be African American if they are to represent all people in the United States. The randomness of the sample would be preserved, since the members of the subgroups would be selected randomly from their particular subgroups. In practical terms, however, a reasonably large *random* sample with no prior stratification will turn out to be reasonably well stratified in the end. Put it another way: If you blindfold yourself, shake up a jar of jelly beans, and take out a scoopful, the proportions of the different colors of beans in the scoop are likely to approximate the proportions of those colors in the entire jar.

Random samples can be hard to come by, especially when it comes to asking people about their sexual attitudes or behavior. For instance, the Playboy Foundation (Hunt, 1974) sampled people listed in telephone directories in various cities in the United States in the early 1970s. Most people at the time had phones, yet the sample could not have included the very poor who may not have been able to afford to keep a phone, those who had unlisted numbers, and college students without private phones.

Another problem is that sexual research is almost invariably conducted with people who volunteer to participate. Volunteers may differ from people who refuse to participate. For example, volunteers tend to be more open about their sexuality than the general population. They may even tend to exaggerate behaviors that others might consider deviant or abnormal.

The problem of a **volunteer bias** is a thorny one for sex researchers, since the refusal of people who have been randomly selected to participate in the survey can ruin the representativeness of the sample. Since it would be unethical to coerce people to participate in a study on sexual behavior (or any other type of study), researchers must use samples of volunteers, rather than true random samples. A low response rate to a voluntary survey is an indication that the responses obtained may not be representative of the original sample (Biggar & Melbye, 1992). They may reflect only the type of people who chose to participate.

Random sample A sample in which every member of a population has an equal chance of participating.

Probability sample A sample in which the probability of inclusion in the sample of any particular member is known.

Stratified random sample A random sample in which known subgroups in a population are represented in proportion to their numbers in the population.

Volunteer bias A slanting of research data that is caused by the characteristics of individuals who volunteer to participate, such as willingness to discuss intimate behavior.

Truth or Fiction?
REVISITED

It is not true that researchers can overcome refusal of some people to participate by recruiting larger numbers of volunteers. Volunteers differ from people who refuse to participate. Therefore, volunteers do not *represent* the entire population. ■

In some cases, as in the Janus and Janus (1993) survey, samples are samples of convenience. They consist of individuals who happen to be available to the researcher and who share some characteristics with the target population, perhaps religious background or sexual orientation. Still, they might not truly represent the target group. Convenience samples often consist of White, middle-class college students who volunteer for studies conducted at their schools. They may not be (and probably are not) representative of students in general. They do not even represent the general student population at their own school. Random samples of gay males or lesbians are perhaps the most difficult to come by. The social stigma attached to their sexual orientations may discourage gay males and lesbians from disclosing them.

Reflections

■ To what "target populations" do you belong? How could researchers obtain representative samples of these populations?

■ Would you participate in a survey on sexual behavior? Why or why not? Why do you think many people are reluctant to participate in such surveys? What kinds of assurances might you seek from a researcher?

METHODS OF OBSERVATION

Once scientists have chosen those they will study, they observe them. In this section, we consider several methods of observation: the case-study method, the survey method, naturalistic observation, ethnographic observation, participant observation, and laboratory observation.

The Case-Study Method

A **case study** is a carefully drawn, in-depth biography of an individual or a small group. The focus is on understanding one or several individuals as fully as possible by unraveling the interplay of various factors in their backgrounds. In most case studies, the researcher comes to know the individual or group through interviews or other contacts conducted over a prolonged period of time. The interviewing pattern tends to build upon itself with a good deal of freedom, as opposed to the one-shot, standardized set of questions used in survey questionnaires.

Researchers may also conduct case studies by interviewing people who have known the individuals or by examining public records. Sigmund Freud, for example, drew upon historical records in his case study of the Renaissance inventor and painter Leonardo da Vinci. Freud concluded that Leonardo's artistic productions represented the sublimating, or channeling, of male-male sexual impulses.

Truth or Fiction?
REVISITED

It is true that case studies have been carried out on people who are dead. Such case studies rely on historic records rather than interviews with the individuals themselves or their contemporaries. ■

Case study A carefully drawn, in-depth biography of an individual or a small group of individuals that may be obtained through interviews, questionnaires, and historical records.

Reports of innovative treatments for sexual dysfunctions usually appear as well-described case studies. A clinician typically reports the background of the client in depth, describes the treatment, reports the apparent outcomes, and suggests factors that might have contributed to the treatment's success or failure. In writing a treatment case study, the therapist attempts to provide information that may be of help to therapists who treat clients with similar problems. Case studies or "multiple case studies" (reports concerning a few individuals) that hold promise may be subjected to controlled investigation—ideally, to experimental studies involving treatment and control groups.

LIMITATIONS OF THE CASE STUDY METHOD   Despite the richness of material that may be derived from the case study approach, it is not as rigorous a research design as an experiment. People often have gaps in memory, especially concerning childhood events. The potential for observer bias is also a prominent concern. Clinicians and interviewers may unintentionally guide people into saying what they expect to hear. Then, too, researchers may inadvertently color people's reports when they jot them down—shaping them subtly in ways that reflect their own views.

Remember that clinicians who test a treatment method with a single client (or with a few clients) through a course of therapy are manipulating an independent variable (the treatment) with one or more people who are unlikely to represent the general population. For one thing, the clients have sought (or been placed in) professional treatment. In a case study, we cannot be certain whether treatment outcomes are due to the treatment methods, giving clients hope that they will get better, having clients talk about their problems, or even improvement that comes about naturally as a result of time. We will see that the experiment allows us to eliminate such rival explanations.

The Survey Method

Surveys typically gather information about behavior through questionnaires or interviews. Researchers may interview or administer questionnaires to thousands of people from particular population groups to learn about their sexual behavior and attitudes. Interviews such as those used by Kinsey and his colleagues (1948, 1953) have the advantages of face-to-face contact and of giving the interviewer the opportunity to *probe*—that is, to follow up on answers that seem to lead toward useful information. A skilled interviewer may be able to set a respondent at ease and establish a sense of trust, or *rapport*, that encourages self-disclosure. On the other hand, unskilled interviewing may cause respondents to conceal information.

Questionnaires are inexpensive when compared to interviews. The major expenses in using questionnaires involve printing and distribution. Questionnaires can be administered to groups of people at once, and respondents can return them unsigned so that they are anonymous. Anonymity may encourage respondents to disclose intimate information. Questionnaires, of course, can be used only by people who can read and record their responses. Interviews can be used even with people who cannot read or write. But interviewers must be trained, sometimes extensively, and then paid for their time.

Some of the major surveys described in this book were conducted by Kinsey and his colleagues (1948, 1953), the Playboy Foundation (Hunt, 1974), Bell and his colleagues (1978, 1981), Coles and Stokes (1985), and the University of Chicago group (Laumann et al., 1994). The book also discusses surveys conducted by popular magazines such as *Redbook*. By and large, these surveys have reported the incidence and frequency of sexual activities among men and women, both married and single; male-female, male-male, and female-female sexual activity; and sexual behaviors of adolescents, adults, and older people.

Many of these surveys have *something* to offer to our understanding of human sexuality, but some are more methodologically sound than others. None represents the U.S. population at large, however. Most people consider their sexuality to be among the most intimate, *private* aspects of their lives. People who willingly agree to be polled as to their political preferences may resist participation in surveys concerning their sexual behavior. As a result, it is difficult, if not impossible, for researchers to recruit a truly representative sample of the population. Bear in mind, then, that survey results provide, at best, an approximation of the sexual attitudes, beliefs, and behaviors of the U.S. population.

Survey A detailed study of a sample obtained by means such as interviews and questionnaires.

Let us review the sampling techniques of some of the major studies of human sexuality. Throughout the book we shall reconsider the findings of these surveys, especially those that shed light on the changes that have occurred between Kinsey's surveys and the present. But for now let us focus on the methods used by Kinsey and others to survey sexual behavior patterns in the United States.

THE KINSEY REPORTS   Kinsey and his colleagues (1948, 1953) interviewed 5,300 males and 5,940 females in the United States between 1938 and 1949. They asked a wide array of questions on various types of sexual experiences, including masturbation, oral sex, and coitus that occurred before, during, and outside of marriage. The survey was a reasonable method for obtaining these data, since Kinsey was interested in studying the frequencies of various sexual behaviors, rather than their underlying causes. For obvious reasons, Kinsey could not use more direct observational methods, such as sending his researchers to peer through bedroom windows. Kinsey chose not to try to obtain a random sample. He believed that a high refusal rate would wreck the chances of accurately representing the general population. Instead, he adopted a *group sampling* approach. He recruited study participants from the organizations and community groups to which they belonged, such as college fraternities and sororities. He contacted representatives of groups in diverse communities and tried to persuade them to secure the cooperation of fellow group members. If he showed these individuals that they would not be subjected to embarrassment or discomfort, Kinsey hoped that they would persuade other members to participate. Kinsey understood that the groups he solicited were not necessarily representative of the general population. He believed, however, that his sampling approach was dictated by practical constraints. Even so, he made an attempt to sample as broadly as possible from the groups he solicited. In some cases, he obtained full participation. In other cases, he obtained a large enough proportion of the group membership to help ensure representativeness, at least of the group.

Still, Kinsey's samples did not represent the general population. People of color, people in rural areas, older people, the poor, and Catholics and Jews were all underrepresented in his samples. Statisticians who have reviewed Kinsey's methods have concluded that there were systematic biases in his sampling methods but that it would have been impossible to obtain a true probability sample from the general population (see, e.g., Cochran et al., 1953). There is therefore no way of knowing whether or not Kinsey's results accurately mirrored the U.S. population at the time. In Chapter 10, we shall see that his estimate that 37% of the male population had reached orgasm at least once through male-male sexual activity was probably too high. The *relationships* that Kinsey uncovered, however, such as the positive link between level of education and participation in oral sex, may be more generalizable (see Chapter 9).

To his credit, Kinsey took measures to encourage candor in the people he interviewed. For one, study participants were assured of the confidentiality of their records. For another, Kinsey's interviewers were trained to conduct the interviews in an objective and matter-of-fact style. To reduce the tendency to slant responses in a socially desirable direction, participants were reassured that the interviewers were not passing judgment on them. Interviewers were trained not to show emotional reactions that the people they interviewed could interpret as signs of disapproval (they maintained a "calm and steady eye" and a constant tone of voice).

Kinsey also checked the **reliability** of his data by evaluating the consistency of the responses given by several hundred interviewees who were reexamined after at least 18 months. Their reports of the **incidence** of sexual activities (for example, whether or not they had ever engaged in premarital or extramarital coitus) were highly reliable. That is, participants tended to give the same answers on both occasions. But reports of the **frequency** of sexual activities (such as the number of times the person had masturbated to orgasm or the frequency of coitus in marriage) were less consistent. People do tend to find it more difficult to compute the frequencies of their activities than to answer whether or not they have ever engaged in them.

Reliability The consistency or accuracy of a measure.

Incidence A measure of the occurrence or the degree of occurrence of an event.

Frequency The number of times an action is repeated within a given period.

Kinsey recognized that consistency of responses across time—or *retakes*, as he called them—did not guarantee their **validity.** That is, the retakes did not show whether the reported behaviors had some basis in fact. He could not validate self-reports directly, as one might validate reports that one is drug-free by means of urine analysis. He could not send his investigators to peer through bedroom windows, so he had to use indirect means to validate the data. One indirect measure was comparison of the reports of husbands and wives, for example, with respect to the *incidence* of oral-genital sex or the *frequency* of intercourse. There was a remarkable consistency in the reports of 706 pairs of spouses; this lends support to the view that their self-reports were accurate. (It is possible, but highly unlikely, that spouses colluded to misrepresent their behavior.)

THE NHSLS STUDY   The National Health and Social Life Survey was intended to provide general information about sexual behavior in the United States and also specific information that might be used to predict and prevent the spread of AIDS. It was conducted by Edward O. Laumann of the University of Chicago and three colleagues—John H. Gagnon, Robert T. Michael, and Stuart Michaels—in the 1990s and published as *The Social Organization of Sexuality: Sexual Practices in the United States* in 1994. A companion volume by Michael, Gagnon, Laumann, and Gina Kolata—a *New York Times* science reporter—was also published: *Sex in America: A Definitive Survey. Sex in America* is a bit less technical in presentation but offers some interesting data that are not found in the other version. The NHSLS study was to be originally supported by government funds, but Republican Senator Jesse Helms of North Carolina blocked federal financing on the grounds that it was inappropriate for the government to be supporting sex research (Bronner, 1998). The research team therefore obtained private funding but had to cut back the scope of the project.

The sample included 3,432 people. Of this number, 3,159 were drawn from English-speaking adults living in households (not dormitories, prisons, and so forth), ages 18 to 59. The other 273 were purposely obtained by oversampling African American and Hispanic American households so that more information could be obtained about these ethnic groups. Although the sample probably represents the overall U.S. population quite well (or at least those of ages 18 to 59), there may be too few Asian Americans, Native Americans, and Jews to offer much information about these groups.

The researchers identified samples of households in geographic areas—by addresses, not names. They sent a letter to each household, describing the purpose and methods of the study, and an interviewer visited each household one week later. The people who were targeted were assured that the purposes of the study were important and that the identities of participants would be kept confidential. Incentives of up to $100 were offered for cooperating. A high completion rate of close to 80% was obtained in this way. All in all, the NHSLS study could be the only one since Kinsey's day that offers a reasonably accurate picture of the sexual practices of the general population of the United States.

THE PLAYBOY FOUNDATION SURVEY   A survey of sexual practices in the 1970s was commissioned by the Playboy Foundation. The results were reported by Morton Hunt in his 1974 book, *Sexual Behavior in the 1970's.* The Playboy survey, or Hunt survey, as it is sometimes called, sought to examine the changes in sexual behavior in the United States between Kinsey's time and the early 1970s.

The Playboy sample was drawn randomly from phone book listings in 24 U.S. cities. People were asked to participate in small group discussions focusing on trends in sexual practices in the United States. They were not told that they would also be completing a questionnaire, an approach that has raised ethical concerns. That is, the participants were not fully informed about their role in the study when they agreed to participate. (Interestingly, though, none of 2,026 people who participated in the group meetings refused to complete the questionnaires.) The phone sampling method was supplemented by an additional sample of young people, who were likely to have been underrepresented in

Validity With respect to tests, the degree to which a particular test measures the constructs or traits it purports to measure.

telephone directories. But even with these additional people, rural people and inmates of prisons and mental hospitals remained underrepresented.

Because the Playboy Foundation did not sample rural people and selected only 24 urban centers, the study's participants do not represent the general U.S. population at the time. Hunt argues, perhaps with some justification, that the final sample of 2,026 is stratified properly as to the ages and races of urban residents across a diverse sample of U.S. cities. The major flaw in the method, however, is that 80% of the people contacted refused to participate. The final 2,026 were clearly willing to volunteer to participate in discussion groups and to then complete a sex questionnaire. We suspect that they were more open and frank about sexual issues than the population at large.

THE JANUS REPORT   Another nationwide survey of sexual behavior in the United States was conducted from 1988 to 1992 by a husband-and-wife team, Samuel and Cynthia Janus (1993). *The Janus Report on Sexual Behavior* was based on a survey of 2,765 people of age 18 years or older (1,347 men and 1,418 women) who anonymously completed written questionnaires assessing a wide range of sexual behaviors and attitudes. In-depth interviews were also conducted with a subset of the larger sample.

The Janus sample, like the Kinsey sample before it, was not randomly selected from the general population. Rather, the Januses assembled a team of researchers from every region of the contiguous 48 states, who then made contact with groups of potential respondents. In all, the survey team distributed 4,550 questionnaires in various sites across the country. Satisfactorily completed questionnaires (those with few missing responses) were returned from 2,765 respondents, representing a return rate of only 61%. The researchers attempted to construct a sample that represented a fairly typical cross-section of the U.S. population with respect to characteristics such as age, gender, income, and educational background. Although the findings may offer some insights into contemporary sexuality in American society, we have no assurance that the sample truly represented the general population. People who respond to sex surveys may not only be more open about discussing their sexuality than the general population. They may also hold more permissive views about sex.

THE MAGAZINE SURVEYS   Major readership surveys have also been conducted by popular magazines, such as *Psychology Today, Redbook, Ladies' Home Journal, McCall's, Cosmopolitan,* and even *Consumer Reports.* Although these surveys all offer some useful information and may be commended for attaining large samples (ranging from 20,000 to 106,000!), their sampling techniques are inherently unscientific and biased. Each sample represents, at best, the readers of the magazine in which the questionnaire appeared. Moreover, we learn only about readers who volunteered to respond to these questionnaires. They likely differed in important ways from the majority of readers who failed to respond. Finally, readers of these magazines are more affluent than the public at large, and readers of *Cosmopolitan, Psychology Today,* and even *Redbook* tend to be more liberal. So the samples may represent only those readers who were willing to complete and mail in the surveys.

A nonacademic researcher, Shere Hite, published several popular—perhaps we should say "notorious"—books on sexual behavior in men and women. Her samples for her 1976 book on female sexuality, *The Hite Report,* and her 1981 book on male sexuality, *The Hite Report on Male Sexuality,* were gleaned from people who completed questionnaires received in direct mailings, printed in sexually explicit magazines like *Penthouse,* and made available through other outlets, including some churches. Her final samples of some 3,000 women in the 1976 report and 7,000 men in the 1981 book might seem large. However, they actually represent small return rates of 3% and 6%, respectively. For these reasons, among others, the Hite reports cannot be considered scientific studies.

Laumann and his colleagues (1994) are particularly harsh in their judgment of such surveys. They write that "such studies, in sum, produce junk statistics of no value whatsoever in making valid and reliable population projections" (p. 45).

SURVEYS OF SPECIFIC POPULATIONS   The Kinsey and NHSLS studies were broad based. They queried men and women from different localities, socioeconomic strata, and age groups. Magazine surveys tend to recruit people more narrowly, as defined by reader characteristics. In some cases, however, researchers have focused their efforts on particular populations, such as adolescents, older people, people from particular racial/ethnic groups, and gay men and lesbians.

In recent years, large-scale studies in the United States and other countries have been conducted to acquire information concerning sexual practices that might prove useful in the fight against AIDS (Adler, 1993). In the United States, for example, researchers from the Battelle Memorial Institute of Seattle interviewed a nationally representative sample of 3,321 men between the ages of 20 and 39 to determine the prevalence of unsafe sexual practices among young adult men (Billy et al., 1993; Tanfer et al., 1993).

In later chapters, we shall discuss some of the findings from these various surveys. In this chapter's A World of Diversity feature, we consider some survey findings concerning Native Americans, African Americans, and people in China.

THE KINSEY INSTITUTE REPORTS ON GAY PEOPLE: 1978 AND 1981   These reports by the Indiana University Institute for Sex Research, also called the Kinsey Institute, were based on a sample of 979 gay people from the San Francisco area and a reference group of 477 people who were matched for age, race, and educational and occupational achievements (Bell & Weinberg, 1978; Bell et al., 1981). In their 1978 book, *Homosexualities*, researchers Alan Bell and Martin Weinberg recognized that their findings could not necessarily be extended to gay people who lived in other cities or sections of the country. Indeed, they acknowledged that their sample might not even represent gay people in San Francisco. It consisted of people who had "come out of the closet" to join gay rights organizations, who attended gay bars and baths, and so forth. Nevertheless, these reports have provided wide-ranging information on parent-child relationships and sexual orientation and on the diversity of lifestyles among gay people (see Chapter 10).

LIMITATIONS OF THE SURVEY METHOD   The Kinsey studies may be criticized because the interviewers were all men. Women respondents might have felt more free to open up to female interviewers. The interviewer's gender can have an impact on a respondent's willingness to disclose sensitive material. A recent investigation in the Asian country of Nepal, for example, showed that male interviewers generally elicited an underreporting of some sensitive aspects of sexual activity (Axinn, 1991). Problems in obtaining reliable estimates may also occur when interviewers and respondents are of different racial or socioeconomic backgrounds.

Yet another limitation of all surveys is that they require self-reports of respondents' behaviors. But self-reports are subject to inaccuracies or biases because of factors such as faulty memories of sexual behavior; tendencies to distort or conceal information because of embarrassment, shame, or guilt; or attempts to present a socially favorable image of oneself. Survey data may also be drawn from haphazard or nonrepresentative samples and thus not represent the target population. Let us consider several weaknesses of the survey method.

VOLUNTEER BIAS   Many people refuse to participate in surveys. Samples are thus biased by large numbers of volunteers. Volunteers are in general willing to take the time to participate. In the case of sex surveys, they also tend to be more sexually permissive and liberal-minded than nonvolunteers. The results of a survey based on a volunteer sample therefore may not accurately reflect the population at large.

FAULTY ESTIMATION   Respondents may recall their behavior inaccurately or purposely misrepresent it. People may not recall the age at which they first engaged in petting or masturbated to orgasm. People may have difficulty recalling or calculating the frequencies of certain behaviors, such as the weekly frequency of marital intercourse ("Well, let's see, this week I think it was four times, but last week only two times, and I can't remember the week before that"). Kinsey and Hunt speculated that people who desire more frequent sex tend to underestimate the frequency of marital coitus, whereas people who want less frequent sex tend to overestimate it.

SURVEYS OF THE SEXUAL BEHAVIOR OF DIVERSE POPULATIONS

Questions abound about the sexual behavior of Native Americans and African Americans. Kinsey did not survey Native Americans. Nor did Hunt, Wyatt, or other leading researchers. The 1982 government survey known as the National Survey of Family Growth (NSFG), which surveyed the reproductive behavior of more than 7,500 women nationwide, included only 83 Native American women in the sample, far too few to be a meaningful indicator of general patterns (Warren et al., 1990). The number of Native Americans in the NHSLS study was in the 40s (Laumann et al., 1994).

Kinsey obtained some data on the sexual behavior of African Americans but did not report it in his surveys because African Americans were clearly underrepresented in his samples. However, more recent studies by Gail Wyatt and the NHSLS group have reported some useful information.

It is interesting to compare results of these surveys with similar surveys in different countries and cultures, such as China. China was never a particularly prudish country. China's tradition of concubines and prostitution predates the birth of Jesus. Nevertheless, after the Communists came into power in 1949, China became transformed into one of the world's more puritanical societies. Yet according to a survey by Shanghai-based sociologist Liu Dalin, since China's opening to the outside world in the 1970s, the times have been a-changin'—a little.

Let us now have a glance at surveys of the sexual behavior of Native Americans, African Americans, and Chinese people.

The Billings Indian Health Service Survey

In one of the first efforts to survey the reproductive and health behavior of Native Americans, the Billings (Montana) Indian Health Service office surveyed 232 Native American women in the Billings area, ages 15 to 49. Half of the women lived on the Blackfeet Reservation. The other half lived off the reservation in nearby Great Falls

Native American Women. Research shows that the reproductive behavior of Native American women in urban areas is more similar to that of other U.S. minorities than to that of Native Americans living on reservations.

(Warren et al., 1990). Surveys were conducted in 1987. The results were compared to data on White and African American women obtained from the 1982 NSFG survey. Nearly 40% of the Native American households did not have telephones. Therefore, a face-to-face interview format was adopted. Virtually all of the women interviewed on the Blackfeet reservation were Blackfeet, but a variety of tribes were represented among interviewees living in Great Falls, including Chippewa-Cree, Little Shell, Assiniboine, and Chippewa, as well as Blackfeet.

Slightly more than half of the Native American women and African American women reported having engaged in sexual intercourse by the age of 17, compared to 28% of the White women. Native American women bore an average of 3.4 to 4.0 children. This figure exceeded the average among White women (2.7 children) but was similar to the average among African Americans (3.4). The percentage of last pregnancies that were unplanned was sim-

ilar for off-reservation Native American women (64%) and African American women (61%) but higher than that for White women (44.6%). Native American women living on the reservation showed an intermediate level (51.2%) of unplanned last pregnancies. Reservation women were more likely than White women to use contraception (79% versus 69%). The percentage of off-reservation Native American women who used contraception was lower, 58%—a figure that was similar to the level of contraceptive use among African American women (60%). Although female sterilization was the most commonly used contraceptive method among all three groups, its incidence was higher among Native Americans (more than 30%) than among White Americans (16%) or African Americans (21%).

Overall, the survey underscores the similarities in reproductive patterns between Native American women living off the reservation and African American women in the larger community. Both groups tended to initiate intercourse at an early age, have a high number of unplanned pregnancies, and make only moderate use of contraception. The reproductive patterns that they shared may reflect the plight of economically disadvantaged groups in the United States. Native American women living on the reservation showed reproductive patterns that were different from those of African Americans and White Americans and even from those of the urbanized, off-reservation Native American sample. Perhaps their reproductive behavior adheres more closely to traditional cultural norms than does that of Native American women living off the reservation, who may be attempting to assimilate into the larger community.

The Wyatt Survey on African American and White Women in Los Angeles

In the 1980s, UCLA researcher Gail Wyatt and her colleagues (Wyatt, 1985, 1989; Wyatt et al., 1988a, 1988b) examined the sexual behavior of a sample of 122 White and 126 African American women in Los Angeles County. The women ranged in age from 18 to 36 years. Women in the study were sampled randomly from telephone listings. People who agreed to participate were selected to balance the sample with respect to demographic characteristics such as age, education, number of children, and marital status. One in three prospective participants refused to cooperate. The participants were interviewed in Kinsey-style, face-to-face interviews that lasted 3 to 8 hours.

Because Wyatt and Kinsey used similar means to obtain data, direct comparisons can be made between their studies. Wyatt used statistical adjustments to control for differences in the sociodemographic characteristics (age, education, social class) between her samples and Kinsey's to enable comparisons between the two.

Wyatt's work is important for several reasons. It addresses changes in sexual behavior that have taken place in U.S. society since Kinsey's day. It focuses on social issues that have become prominent, such as sexual abuse in childhood. It also is one of the few detailed studies of sexual behavior among African American women.

One of the striking differences between Kinsey's data and Wyatt's was that women in her 1980s sample—African American and White—engaged in intercourse for the first time at earlier ages than was the case in Kinsey's sample. Kinsey reported that by the age of 20, about one in five women had engaged in premarital coitus. By contrast, Wyatt reported that 98% of the people in her study (African American and White) had experienced premarital intercourse by that age (Wyatt, 1989). When social class differences were taken into consideration, the ages of first intercourse for African American and White women in Wyatt's sample were quite similar.

Wyatt's research, of course, was limited to Los Angeles and might not represent the general U.S. population. Kinsey's sample was also geographically skewed. Kinsey overrepresented the northeastern United States, although he included respondents from other regions.

Let us also note the refusal rate in Wyatt's study. Wyatt was more successful in obtaining cooperation than the Playboy survey takers (67% of the people contacted agreed to participate, versus 20% for Playboy). Nonetheless, Wyatt's 33% refusal rate may have compromised representativeness. Also, to control for demographic differences between White and African American women, Wyatt limited the pool of cooperating individuals to demographically comparable women. Her sample of African American women did match the demographic characteristics of the larger population of African American women in Los Angeles County. However, her White sample did not match the population characteristics for White women in the county. It contained a greater proportion of White women from lower-income families. These kinds of trade-offs can occur when researchers attempt to control for demographic differences.

The Liu Report: Sexual Behavior in China

Liu interviewed 23,000 Chinese over a period of 18 months (Southerland, 1990). China's "Kinsey Report" was the first nationwide sex survey ever conducted in China. It polled twice as many people as Kinsey and his colleagues did. Participants included students, professionals, peasants, even convicted sex offenders drawn from 3 major cities and 12 provinces. The researchers encountered problems in lack of funds, illiteracy, and reluctance to reveal intimate sexual information.

Here are some of Liu's findings:

- Chinese youths today are reaching sexual maturity about a year earlier than their grandparents did, partly because of improved nutrition.

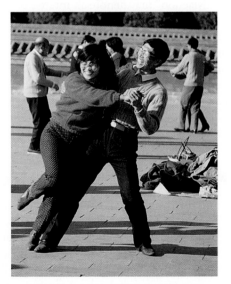

- About 50% of the young people in cities and on farms reported that they engaged in premarital intercourse.
- About 14% of the women living in large cities said that they engaged in extramarital sex. Overall, 69% of the respondents approved of such affairs. This is a larger approval rate than is found in the United States, where the majority of respondents to surveys disapprove of affairs (e.g., Blumstein & Schwartz, 1990; Hunt, 1974).

Truth or Fiction?
REVISITED

It does appear from the results of the Liu survey that the Chinese are more likely to approve of extramarital affairs than are people in the United States. ■

- Many Chinese couples use very little foreplay; 44% of urban wives and 37% of rural wives reported at least some pain during intercourse due to insufficient vaginal lubrication.
- Women are more likely than men to initiate divorces. Three out of five divorces are sought by women.

So go some survey findings of sexual attitudes and practices around the world.

Sex in China. Historically speaking, China was not a prudish country. China had a tradition of concubines and prostitution that predated the birth of Jesus. But after the Communist Revolution in 1949, China was transformed into a puritanical society. However, a survey by sociologist Liu Dalin finds that China is not as controlled as had been thought. For example, about half of China's young people engage in premarital intercourse and it would appear that more than half approve of extramarital affairs (though not nearly that many play around themselves).

SOCIAL-DESIRABILITY RESPONSE BIAS   Even people who consent to participate in surveys of sexual behavior may feel pressured to answer questions in the direction of **social desirability.** Some respondents, that is, try to ingratiate themselves with their interviewers by offering what they believe to be socially desirable answers. Although some respondents may readily divulge information concerning the frequency of marital coitus, they may deny experiences involving prohibited activities such as child molestation, voyeurism, or coerced sexual activity. (People who engage in these proscribed activities may also be more likely to decline to participate in sex surveys.)

Some people may not divulge sensitive information for fear of disapproval by the interviewer. Others may fear criminal prosecution. Even though interviewers may insist that they are nonjudgmental and that study participants will remain anonymous, respondents might fear that their identities may be uncovered someday.

EXAGGERATION   For some respondents, the "socially desirable" response is exaggeration. In our culture, men may tend to exaggerate their sexual exploits. Women may tend to play them down (Havemann & Lehtinen, 1990). Males and "liberated" females may fear that the interviewer will think less of them for reporting only infrequent sexual contacts or for sounding too "straight." Some respondents falsify their attitudes and exaggerate the bizarreness of their behavior, perhaps to draw attention to themselves, perhaps to foul up the results.

DENIAL   Another source of bias in sex survey research is denial. People may deny, even to themselves, sexual feelings or experiences that might elicit anxiety if they were acknowledged, such as male-male or female-female fantasies or feelings.

DIFFERENCES IN MEANINGS OF TERMS   In 1998, when the sex scandal broke loose in the White House, Bill Clinton asserted that he had never had "sexual relations" with a young intern there. The tabloids feasted on the fact that President Clinton did not consider "sexual relations" to include fellatio.

Survey respondents can respond only to the questions posed by interviewers or questionnaires. A word or phrase may mean different things to different people, however. One person who is asked whether he or she has engaged in French kissing might think of deep, open-mouthed tongue kissing (the generally accepted meaning of the term). To another, the term might denote a prolonged but gentle kiss on the lips. To some people, the term "sexual satisfaction" may denote an intense orgasm. To others, it signifies the pleasure of sharing physical intimacy with a loved one. To the extent that people interpret the same terms on sex surveys differently, they may differ in their responses because of differences in semantics, not because of differences in behavior.

You might think that these problems would render the survey method useless as a means of learning about human sexuality. Actually, carefully conceived and executed surveys offer many insights into sexual attitudes and practices. In many cases, they are the only available means. Before Kinsey, we had little information about the sexual practices of people in our society.

The Naturalistic-Observation Method

In **naturalistic observation,** also called the *field study,* scientists directly observe the behavior of animals and humans where it happens. Anthropologists, for example, have lived among preliterate societies and reported on their social and sexual customs. Other disciplines, too, have adopted methods of naturalistic observation in their research on human sexuality. Sociologists have observed the street life of prostitutes. Psychologists have observed patterns of nonverbal communication and body language between couples in dating situations.

Scientists take precautions to keep their naturalistic observations *unobtrusive.* They try not to influence the behavior of the individuals they study. Over the years, naturalis-

Social desirability A response bias to a questionnaire or interview in which the person provides a socially acceptable response.

Naturalistic observation A method in which organisms are observed in their natural environments.

tic observers have been placed in ethical dilemmas. They have allowed sick or injured animals to die, rather than intervene, when medical assistance could have saved them. They have allowed substance abuse and illicit sexual behavior to go unreported to authorities. The ethical trade-off is that unobtrusive observation may yield data that will benefit large numbers of people—the greatest good for the greatest number.

The Ethnographic-Observation Method

Anthropologists have lived among societies of people in the four corners of the earth to observe and study human diversity. Margaret Mead (1935) reported on the social and sexual customs of various peoples of New Guinea. Bronislaw Malinowski (1929) studied the Trobriand islanders, among other peoples. Ford and Beach's (1951) account of sexual practices around the world and in nonhuman species remains to this date a classic study of cross-cultural and cross-species comparisons. **Ethnographic** research has provided us with data about sexual behaviors and customs that occur widely across cultures and those that are limited to one or few cultures. Ethnographers are trained to be keen observers, but direct observation has its limits in the study of sexual behavior. Sexual activities are most commonly performed away from the watchful eyes of others, especially from those of visitors from other cultures. Ethnographers may therefore have to rely on methods such as personal interviewing to learn more about sexual customs.

The Participant-Observation Method

In **participant observation,** the investigators learn about people's behavior by directly interacting with them. Participant observation has been used in studies of male-male sexual behavior and mate-swapping. In effect, participation has been the "price of admission" for observation.

Investigators of mate-swapping, or **swinging,** have contacted swinging couples through newsletter ads and other sources and presented themselves as "baby swingers" (novices) seeking sexual relations (Bartell, 1970; Palson & Palson, 1972). Thus, some investigators may have deceived the people they studied. In some cases, however, as in Bartell's study, individuals were informed that the investigator was conducting research after he was admitted to the party. In some cases, researchers have engaged in coitus with study participants during "swinging parties," which raises questions about how far one should go "for the sake of science."

It is true that some sex researchers have engaged in "swinging" with the people they studied. But this is a rare occurrence, and the ethics of this research method have been questioned. ■

Truth or Fiction?
REVISITED

Sampling biases are another concern. There is no way of knowing whether the swingers who were contacted by newspaper ads were typical of swingers in general. The sampling methods also limited the investigations to active swingers and excluded people who had once "swung" but no longer did so.

The Laboratory-Observation Method

In *Human Sexual Response* (1966), William Masters and Virginia Johnson were among the first to report direct laboratory observations of individuals and couples engaged in sexual acts. In all, 694 people (312 men and 382 women) participated in the research. The women ranged from 18 to 78 in age; the men, from 21 to 80. There were 276 married couples, 106 single women, and 36 single men. The married couples engaged in intercourse and other forms of mutual stimulation, such as manual and oral stimulation of the genitals. The unmarried people participated in studies that did not require intercourse, such as measurement of female sexual arousal in response to insertion of a penis-shaped probe

Ethnography The branch of anthropology that deals descriptively with specific cultures, especially preliterate societies.

Participant observation A method in which observers interact with the people they study as they collect data.

Swinging Partner or mate swapping.

and male ejaculation during masturbation. Masters and Johnson performed similar laboratory observations of sexual response among gay people for their 1979 book *Homosexuality in Perspective.*

Direct laboratory observation of biological processes was not invented by Masters and Johnson. However, they were confronting a society that was still unprepared to speak openly of sex, let alone to observe people engaged in sexual activity in the laboratory. Masters and Johnson were accused of immorality, voyeurism, and an assortment of other evils. Nevertheless, their methods offered the first reliable set of data on what happens to the body during sexual response. Their instruments permitted them to directly measure vasocongestion (blood flow to the genitals), myotonia (muscle tension), and other physiological responses. Perhaps their most controversial device was a "coition machine." This was a transparent artificial penis outfitted with photographic equipment. It enabled them to study changes in women's internal sexual organs as they became sexually aroused. From these studies, Masters and Johnson observed that it is useful to divide sexual response into four stages (their "sexual response cycle").

Truth or Fiction? **REVISITED**

It is true that Masters and Johnson created a transparent artificial penis ("coition machine") containing photographic equipment to study female sexual response. ▪

Researchers have since developed more sophisticated physiological methods of measuring sexual arousal and response. Masters and Johnson's laboratory method is now used, with some variations but with less controversy, in research centers across the country (Rosen & Beck, 1988).

LIMITATIONS OF OBSERVATIONAL RESEARCH   One of the basic problems with naturalistic observation is the possibility that the behavior under study may be *reactive* to the measurement itself. This source of bias is referred to as the **observer effect.**

The ethnographer who studies a particular culture or subgroup within a culture may unwittingly alter the behavior of the members of the group by focusing attention on some facets of their behavior. Falling prey to social desirability, some people may "straighten out their act" while the ethnographer is present. Other people may try to impress the ethnographer by acting in ways that are more aggressive or sexually provocative than usual. In either case, people supply distorted or biased information. Ethnographers must corroborate self-reported information by using multiple sources. They must also consider whether their own behavior is more obtrusive than they think.

Observer bias can distort researchers' perceptions of the behaviors they observe. Observers who hold rigid sexual attitudes may be relatively unwilling to examine sexual activities that they consider to be offensive or objectionable. They may unwittingly (or intentionally) slant interviews in a way that presents a "sanitized" view of the behavior of those they study, or exaggerate or "sensationalize" certain sexual practices to conform to their preconceptions of the sexual behavior of the people they study.

The method of laboratory observation used by Masters and Johnson may be even more subject to distortion. Unlike animals, which naturalists may observe unobtrusively from afar, people who participate in laboratory observation know that they are being observed and that their responses are being measured. The problem of volunteer bias, troublesome for sex surveys, is even thornier in laboratory observation. How many of us would assent to performing sexual activities in the laboratory while we were connected to physiological monitoring equipment in full view of researchers? Some of the women that Masters and Johnson observed were patients of Dr. Masters who felt indebted to him and agreed to participate. Many were able to persuade their husbands to participate as well. Some were medical students and graduate students who may have been motivated to earn extra money (participants were paid for their time) as well as by scientific curiosity.

Observer effect A distortion of individuals' behavior caused by the act of observation.

Another methodological concern of the Masters and Johnson approach is that observing people engaged in sexual activities may in itself alter their responses. People might not respond publicly in the same way that they would in private. Perhaps sexual response in the laboratory bears little relationship to sexual response in the bedroom. The physiological monitoring equipment may also alter their natural responses. With these constraints in mind, it is perhaps remarkable that the people studied by Masters and Johnson were able to become sexually aroused and reach orgasm.

Reflections

- Consider your own knowledge of other people. Could you say that you have ever conducted a case study on anyone? What were the limitations of your "research"?
- How do the volunteer bias and social desirability response sets invalidate the results of many surveys? How did the Kinsey group, Morton Hunt, Shere Hite, and the University of Chicago group sample their target populations? Are the results of each survey believable? Why or why not?
- What are your own feelings about the methods of laboratory observation that Masters and Johnson used? Why?

THE CORRELATIONAL METHOD

What are the relationships between age and frequency of coitus among married couples? What is the connection between socioeconomic status and teenage pregnancy? In each case, two variables are being related to one another: age and frequency of coitus and socioeconomic status and rates of teenage pregnancy. Correlational research describes the relationship between variables such as these.

A **correlation** is a statistical measure of the relationship between two variables. In correlational studies, two or more variables are related, or linked to, one another by statistical means. The strength and direction (positive or negative) of the relationship between any two variables are expressed with a statistic called a **correlation coefficient.**

Research has shown relationships (correlations) between marital satisfaction and a host of variables: communication skills, shared values, flexibility, frequency of social interactions with friends, and churchgoing, to name a few. Although such research may give us an idea of the factors associated with marital satisfaction, the experimenters have not manipulated the variables of interest. For this reason we cannot say which, if any, of the factors is causally related to marital happiness. Consider the relationship between churchgoing and marital happiness. Couples who attend church more frequently report higher rates of marital satisfaction (Wilson & Filsinger, 1986). It is possible that churchgoing stabilizes marriages. It is also possible that people who attend church regularly are more stable and committed to marriage in the first place.

It is true that regular churchgoers report higher levels of sexual satisfaction. We cannot say, however, that churchgoing is causally related to marital satisfaction. ■

Truth or Fiction?
REVISITED

Correlations may be *positive* or *negative*. Two variables are positively correlated if one increases as the other increases. Frequency of intercourse, for example, has been found to be positively correlated with sexual satisfaction (Blumstein & Schwartz, 1983). That is, married couples who engage in coitus more frequently report higher levels of sexual satisfaction. However, the experimenters did not manipulate the variables. Therefore, we cannot conclude that sexual satisfaction *causes* high coital frequency. It could also be that frequent coitus contributes to greater sexual satisfaction. It is also possible that there is no causal relationship between the variables. Perhaps both coital frequency and sexual satisfaction are affected by other factors, such as communication ability, general marital

Correlation A statistical measure of the relationship between two variables.

Correlation coefficient A statistic that expresses the strength and direction (positive or negative) of the relationship between two variables.

figure 2.1

What Is the Relationship Between Frequency of Intercourse and Sexual Satisfaction? Married couples who engage in coitus more frequently report higher levels of sexual satisfaction, but why? Since researchers have not manipulated the variables, we cannot conclude that sexual satisfaction causes high coital frequency. Nor can we say that frequent coitus causes greater sexual satisfaction. Perhaps both variables are affected by other factors, such as communication ability, general marital satisfaction, and general health.

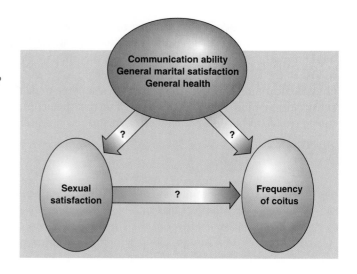

satisfaction, general health, and so on (see Figure 2.1). Similarly, height and weight are positively correlated but do not cause each another. Other factors that we label the growth process contribute to both.

Limitations of the Correlational Method

Correlation is not causation. Many variables are correlated but not causally related to one another.

Although correlations do not show cause and effect, they can be used to make predictions. For example, we can predict that people who were sexually traumatized as children are more likely to encounter psychological problems later on. They find it more difficult to establish intimate relationships in adulthood. However, we cannot demonstrate that sexual trauma directly causes these problems. Although correlation does not provide causal knowledge, it permits us to anticipate the needs of victims of sexual assault for treatment services. Knowledge of correlational relationships may also lead to controlled experiments that more directly address questions of cause and effect.

Reflections

■ Couples who attend church more frequently report higher rates of marital satisfaction. Can you suggest three possible cause-and-effect connections between church-going and marital satisfaction?

■ Here is another relationship between two variables: Men who are married live longer. (True.) It is possible that marriage "causes" longevity, but can you think of other possible reasons for the relationship?

THE EXPERIMENTAL METHOD

Experiment A scientific method that seeks to confirm cause-and-effect relationships by manipulating independent variables and observing their effects on dependent variables.

Treatment In experiments, an intervention that is administered to participants (e.g., a test, a drug, or sex-education program) so that its effects may be observed.

The best (if not always feasible) method for studying *cause-and-effect* relationships is the **experiment.** Experiments permit scientists to draw conclusions about cause-and-effect relationships because the experimenter is able to control or manipulate the factors or variables of interest directly and to observe their effects.

In an experiment on the effects of alcohol on sexual arousal, for example, a group of participants would receive an intervention, called a **treatment,** such as a dose of alcohol. (In other experiments, the intervention or treatment might involve the administration of a drug, exposure to violent pornography, a program of sex education, etc.). They would then be carefully observed to learn whether this treatment made a difference in their behavior—in this case, their sexual arousal.

Aspects of the Experimental Method

INDEPENDENT AND DEPENDENT VARIABLES   In an experiment, the variables (treatments) that are hypothesized to have a causal effect are manipulated or controlled by the researcher. Consider an experiment designed to determine whether or not alcohol stimulates sexual arousal. The design might involve giving one group of participants a certain dosage of alcohol, and then measuring its effects. In such an experimental arrangement, the dosage of alcohol is considered an **independent variable,** whose presence and quantity is manipulated by the researchers. The measured results are called **dependent variables,** since changes in their values are believed to depend on the independent variable or variables. In this experiment, measures of sexual arousal would be the dependent variables. Dependent variables are outcomes; they are observed and measured by the researchers but not manipulated. Sexual arousal might be measured by means such as physiological measurement (gauging the degree of penile erection in the male, for example) or self-report (asking participants to rate their sexual arousal on a rating scale).

In a study of the effects of sex education on teenage pregnancy, sex education would be the independent variable. The incidence of teenage pregnancy would be the dependent variable. Researchers would administer the experimental treatment (sex education) and track the participants for a period of time to determine their pregnancy rates. But how would experimenters know whether or not the treatment had made a difference in the pregnancy rate? One way would be to compare the pregnancy rate among people in experiments to rates found in public records. It could be argued, however, that the individuals in the experiment differed in other ways (besides having received sex education) from the people whose records were kept in the public documents, that the records were made at a different time, and so forth. So experimenters would prefer to compare the pregnancy rates of people in experimental groups with those of people in control groups.

EXPERIMENTAL AND CONTROL GROUPS   Well-designed experiments randomly assign people or animal study participants to experimental and control groups. Participants in **experimental groups** receive the treatment. Participants in **control groups** do not. Every effort is made to hold all other conditions constant for both groups. By using random assignment and holding other conditions constant, researchers can be reasonably confident that the independent variable (treatment), and not extraneous factors (such as the temperature of the room in which the treatment was administered or differences between the participants in the experimental and control groups), brought about the results.

WHY IS RANDOM ASSIGNMENT IMPORTANT?   Why do experimenters assign individuals at random to experimental and control groups whenever possible? Consider a study conducted to determine the effects of alcohol on sexual arousal in response to sexually explicit material, such as "XXX-rated" films. If we permitted study participants to choose whether or not they would drink alcohol, we might not know whether it was the alcohol itself that accounted for the results. Some other factor, called a **selection factor,** might discriminate between people who would or would not choose to drink alcohol. One difference might be that people who chose to drink might also have more permissive attitudes toward sexually explicit material than the others. Their permissiveness rather than the alcohol could affect their sexual responsiveness to these stimuli. If this were the case, experimental outcomes might reflect the effects of the selection factor rather than the alcohol.

EXPERIMENTATION WITH ANIMALS   Researchers frequently undertake studies with other animal species that would be impractical or unethical with people. For example, it may be hypothesized that prenatal sexual hormones "feminize" or "masculinize" the brain to give rise to gender-typed behaviors or predispose the individual to a heterosexual, gay male, or lesbian sexual orientation (see Chapters 6 and 10). The ideal method for examining these hypotheses would be to alter the balance of sex hormones systematically at various stages of fetal development and then monitor individuals' behavior in subsequent years. However, neither parents nor researchers would be willing to risk the

Independent variable   A condition in a scientific study that is manipulated so that its effects may be observed.

Dependent variables   The measured results of an experiment, which are believed to be a function of the independent variables.

Experimental group   A group of study participants who receive a treatment.

Control group   A group of study participants who do not receive the experimental treatment. However, other conditions are held comparable to those of individuals in the experimental group.

Selection factor   A bias that may operate in research when people are allowed to determine whether or not they will receive a treatment.

well-being of children through such an experiment. Therefore, studies of this kind have been conducted on animals to try to shed some light on similar processes in people.

To the extent that we share physiological processes with animals, experiments with other species may inform us about ourselves. Because of their physiological similarities to people, rats and monkeys are commonly used in laboratory experiments. Unfortunately—or fortunately?—these animals are more similar to humans biologically than psychologically. Therefore, we may make some generalizations from them to people concerning the effects of drugs and other biochemical treatments. We cannot, however, assume that their responses provide much of a clue to higher cognitive processes, such as thinking and reasoning. Nor can we claim that *pair bonding* between animals is equivalent to human marriage or that (apparently) affectionate displays between animals are the equivalent of romantic love between people.

LIMITATIONS OF THE EXPERIMENTAL METHOD   Although scientists agree that the experimental method provides the strongest evidence of cause-and-effect relationships, experimenters cannot manipulate many variables of interest directly. We might suspect that sexual trauma in the form of rape or sexual assault is a causal factor in the development of psychological or emotional problems (see Chapter 18). However, we would not expose people to sexual trauma to observe its effects. In the absence of a direct manipulation of the presumed causal factor (rape), we cannot be sure that adjustment problems in rape victims are directly attributable to rape itself, especially when they occur years later. Other factors may be involved, such as insensitive treatment of rape victims by their families or by representatives of the criminal justice system.

Nor can we conduct experiments to determine the effects of cohabitation on college students. We cannot assign an experimental group to cohabitation and a control group to separate living quarters. We can compare only groups of students who have chosen to cohabit to groups who have not. Our research may thus inform us that cohabitors have certain problems (for example, jealousy), but it cannot show that these problems are caused by cohabiting (see Chapter 14). Cohabitors and noncohabitors may differ on other factors that give rise to these differences in adjustment.

Similarly, we cannot conduct experiments to determine the effects of pornography on children and adolescents. Societal prohibitions and ethical standards preclude experimenters from exposing children or adolescents to erotic materials. Researchers must use other approaches, such as the correlational method, to study variables that cannot be manipulated.

Reflections

■ What would researchers have to do to run true experiments on the effects of cohabitation on college students or on the effects of pornography on children? Could such experiments be run? Why or why not?

■ To run a true experiment on the effect of a new drug on people with AIDS, some people with AIDS would have to be assigned to a control group. To control for the effects of expectations, they might be told they are being given the real drug when they are really receiving "sugar pills" that look like the real thing. Can researchers justify withholding the real drug from people in the control group? What do you think?

ETHICS IN SEX RESEARCH

Sex researchers are required to protect the people being studied. This means that people will not be subjected to physical or psychological harm and will participate of their own free will.

In colleges, universities, hospitals, and research institutions, ethics review committees help researchers weigh the potential harm of administering the independent variables and review proposed studies in light of ethical guidelines. If the committee finds fault with a proposal, it may advise the researcher how to modify the research design to comply with ethical standards and will withhold approval until the proposal has been so modified.

Pain and Stress

Individuals may be harmed if they are exposed to pain or placed in stressful situations. For this reason, many potentially informative or useful studies have not been done. Researchers have not exposed children to erotic materials to determine the effects. Researchers have not exposed human fetuses to male or female sex hormones to learn whether they create fundamental predispositions toward tomboyishness, gay male and lesbian sexual orientations, choices, and other variables of interest.

Sex researchers *have* studied children born to mothers who were given certain sex hormones to help maintain their pregnancies (see Chapter 6). But these treatments were standard medical procedures that were undertaken to help the women and their fetuses. The availability of these cases has made it possible for scientists to examine the effects on later gender-role behavior and sexual behavior of prenatal exposure to these hormones. But the investigators did not administer these treatments to the pregnant women for purposes of research.

When considering a study that poses a risk of harm, ethics review committees weigh the potential harm in light of the potential benefits to the participants, to science, and to society in general. Ethical standards require that research be conducted only when the expected benefits of the research outweigh the anticipated risks, when the experimenter attempts to minimize risks, and when the experimenter ensures that the pain and stress experienced by participants is neither excessive nor lasting. Moreover, participants are given general information about the stress or pain they may encounter before the study begins. Thus, they can decide whether or not they wish to participate and can prepare themselves.

Confidentiality

Sex researchers must keep the identities and responses of participants confidential to protect them from possible harm or embarrassment. Some participants may confide legally incriminating information to researchers, such as reports of illegal sexual activities. Some people might suffer harm or embarrassment if it were even known that they had participated in sex research.

Researchers can do many things to ensure the confidentiality of participants. They can make questionnaires anonymous. Interviewers may not be given the identities of interviewees. In reports of research, enough information about participants' backgrounds can be given to make the studies useful (size of city of origin, region of country, religion, age group, race, educational level, and so on) without divulging their identities. Once the need for follow-up has passed and the results have been fully analyzed, the names and addresses of participants and their records can be destroyed. If names and addresses are maintained, researchers can code them, keep them under lock and key, and spread the keys among several people so that no one person has enough information to divulge an individual's sexual behavior.

Informed Consent

The principle of **informed consent** requires that people freely agree to participate after being given enough information about the procedures and purposes of the research, and its risks and benefits, to make an informed decision. Information must be presented in a manner that potential participants can understand. People may not be coerced to participate. Once the study has begun, they must be free to withdraw at any time without penalty. In some cases, people may be told that some information about the study must be withheld until it is completed. This is especially so when deception is involved.

The Use of Deception

Ethical conflicts may emerge when experiments require that participants not know all about their purposes and methods. For example, in experiments on the effects of violent

Informed consent The term used by researchers to indicate that people have agreed to participate in research after receiving information about the purposes and nature of the study and its potential risks and benefits.

pornography on aggression against women, participants may be misled into believing that they are administering electric shocks to women (who are actually confederates of the experimenter), even though no shocks are actually delivered. The experimenter seeks to determine participants' willingness to hurt women following exposure to aggressive erotic films. Such studies could not be carried out if participants knew that no shocks would actually be delivered. In studies that involve deception, researchers must demonstrate that the effects of the treatment are not seriously harmful or prolonged and that the benefits of the information obtained outweigh the risks.

Research is the backbone of human sexuality as a science. This textbook focuses on scientific findings that can illuminate our understanding of sexuality, help to enhance sexual experience, prevent and treat sexually transmitted diseases, and build more rewarding relationships.

Reflections

■ What standards do ethics review committees use to determine whether or not proposed research is ethical? Do you agree with these standards? Why or why not?
■ Does any of the research discussed in the first two chapters of this book strike you as being unethical? Why? Would the researchers have been able to change their methods to agree with your standards of ethics? If so, how?

s u m m i n g   u p

A SCIENTIFIC APPROACH TO HUMAN SEXUALITY

Scientists insist that assumptions about sexual behavior be supported by evidence. Evidence is based on careful observations in the laboratory or in the field.

The Scientific Method
The scientific method is a systematic way of gathering scientific evidence and testing assumptions through empirical research. It entails formulating a research question, framing a hypothesis, testing the hypothesis, and drawing conclusions about the hypothesis.

Goals and Methods of the Science of Human Sexuality
The goals of the science of human sexuality are to describe, explain, predict, and control sexual behaviors. People often confuse description with inference. Inferences are woven into theories when possible.

Operational Definitions
The operational definition of a construct is linked to the methods used to measure it, enabling diverse researchers to understand what is being measured.

POPULATIONS AND SAMPLES: REPRESENTING THE WORLD OF DIVERSITY

Research samples should accurately represent the population of interest. Representative samples are usually obtained through random sampling.

METHODS OF OBSERVATION

The Case-Study Method
Case studies are carefully drawn biographies of individuals or small groups that focus on unraveling the interplay of various factors in individuals' backgrounds.

The Survey Method
Surveys typically gather information about behavior through interviews or questionnaires administered to large samples of people. Use of volunteers and the tendency of respondents to offer socially desirable responses are sources of bias in surveys.

The Naturalistic-Observation Method
In naturalistic observation, scientists directly observe the behavior of animals and humans where it happens—in the "field." The scientists remain unobtrusive.

The Ethnographic-Observation Method
Ethnographic research has provided us with data concerning sexual behaviors and customs that occur widely across cultures and those that are limited to one or few cultures.

The Participant-Observation Method
In participant observation, investigators learn about people's behavior by interacting with them.

The Laboratory-Observation Method
In the laboratory-observation method, people engage in the behavior under study in the laboratory setting. When methods of observation influence the behavior under study, that behavior may be distorted.

THE CORRELATIONAL METHOD

Correlational studies reveal the strength and direction of the relationships between variables. However, they do not show cause and effect.

THE EXPERIMENTAL METHOD

Experiments allow scientists to draw conclusions about cause-and-effect relationships because they directly control or manipulate the variables of interest and observe their effects. Well-designed experiments randomly assign individuals to experimental and control groups.

ETHICS IN SEX RESEARCH

Ethics concerns the ways in which researchers protect participants from harm.

Pain and Stress

Ethical standards require that research may be conducted only when the expected benefits of the research outweigh the anticipated risks to participants and when the experimenter attempts to minimize expected risks.

Confidentiality

Sex researchers keep the identities and responses of participants confidential to protect them from embarrassment and other potential sources of harm.

Informed Consent

The principle of informed consent requires that people agree to participate in research only after being given enough information about the purposes, procedures, risks, and benefits to make informed decisions.

The Use of Deception

Some research cannot be conducted without deceiving people as to its purposes and procedures. In such cases, the potential harm and benefits of the proposed research are weighed carefully.

Ruby Pearl. *Solitude*. Acrylic on rag paper, 22 x 30 in. Courtesy of Rae Temkin Edelson

chapter

3

Female Sexual Anatomy

and Physiology

o u t l i n e

TRUTH OR FICTION?

EXTERNAL SEX ORGANS
The Mons Veneris
The Labia Majora
The Labia Minora
The Clitoris
The Vestibule
The Urethral Opening

A WORLD OF DIVERSITY:
Clitoridectomy—Ritual Genital Mutilation

The Vaginal Opening

IN THE NEW MILLENNIUM:
Restoration of Virginity?

The Perineum
Structures That Underlie the External
Sex Organs

A CLOSER LOOK:
Kegels

INTERNAL SEX ORGANS
The Vagina
The Cervix
The Uterus
The Fallopian Tubes
The Ovaries
The Pelvic Examination

THE BREASTS
Breast Cancer

IN THE NEW MILLENNIUM:
Good News About Breast Cancer

A CLOSER LOOK:
Breast Self-Examination

THE MENSTRUAL CYCLE
Menstruation Versus Estrus
Regulation of the Menstrual Cycle
Phases of the Menstrual Cycle

A WORLD OF DIVERSITY:
*Historical and Cross-Cultural Perspectives
on Menstruation*

Coitus During Menstruation

A CLOSER LOOK:
Myths About Menopause

Menopause

MENSTRUAL PROBLEMS
Dysmenorrhea
Amenorrhea
Premenstrual Syndrome (PMS)
How to Handle Menstrual Discomfort

SUMMING UP

Truth or Fiction?

_____ A name for the external female genitals is derived from Latin roots that mean "something to be ashamed of."

_____ Women, but not men, have a sex organ whose only known function is the experiencing of sexual pleasure.

_____ One may determine whether or not a woman is a virgin by examining the hymen.

_____ Women with larger breasts produce more milk while nursing.

_____ The incidence of breast cancer is on the rise in the United States.

_____ Women who have had abortions are at greater risk of breast cancer.

_____ The ancient Romans believed that menstrual blood soured wine and killed crops.

_____ At menopause, women experience debilitating hot flashes.

_____ Menopause signals an end to a woman's sexual appetite.

t he French have a saying: *Vive la différence!* ("Long live the difference!"). It celebrates the differences between men and women. The differences between the genders, at least their anatomic differences, have often been met with prejudice and misunderstanding, however. Men have historically exalted their own genitals. Too often, the less visible genitals of women have been deemed inferior. The derivation of the word **pudendum,** which refers to the external female genitals, speaks volumes about sexism in the ancient Mediterranean world. *Pudendum* derives from the Latin *pudendus.* It literally means "something to be ashamed of."

Truth or Fiction?
REVISITED

It is true that a name for the external female genitals is derived from the Latin word *pudere,* meaning "to be ashamed." ▥

Even today, this cultural heritage may lead women to develop negative attitudes toward their genitals. Girls and boys are both sometimes reared to regard their genitals with shame or disgust. Both may be reprimanded for expressing normal curiosity about them. They may be reared with a "hands-off" attitude, to keep their "private parts" private, even to themselves. Touching them except for hygienic purposes may be discouraged. One woman recalls:

> When I was six years old I climbed up on the bathroom sink and looked at myself naked in the mirror. All of a sudden I realized I had three different holes. I was very excited about my discovery and ran down to the dinner table and announced it to everyone. "I have three holes!" Silence. "What are they for?" I asked. Silence even heavier than before. I sensed how uncomfortable everyone was and answered for myself. "I guess one is for pee-pee, the other for doo-doo and the third for ca-ca." A sigh of relief; no one had to answer my question. But I got the message—I wasn't supposed to ask "such" questions, though I didn't fully realize what "such" was about at that time.
> —Boston Women's Health Book Collective, *The New Our Bodies, Ourselves* (1992)

In this chapter, we tour the female sex organs. Even generally sophisticated students may fill in some gaps in their knowledge. Most of us know what a vagina is, but how many of us realize that only the female gender has an organ that is exclusively dedicated to pleasure? Or that a woman's passing of urine does not involve the vagina? How many of us know that a newborn girl already has all the **ova** she will ever produce?

As women readers encounter the features of their sexual anatomy in their reading, they might wish to examine their own genitals with a mirror. By following the text and the illustrations, students may discover some new anatomic features. They will see that their genitals can resemble those in the illustrations yet also be unique.

EXTERNAL SEX ORGANS

Pudendum The external female genitals.

Ova Egg cells. (Singular: ovum.)

Vulva The external sexual structures of the female.

Taken collectively, the external sexual structures of the female are termed the pudendum or the **vulva.** Pudendum, because of its derivation, may be a less desirable term than *vulva.* Vulva is a Latin word that means "wrapper" or "covering." The vulva consists of the *mons veneris,* the *labia majora* and *labia minora* (major and minor lips), the *clitoris,* and the vaginal opening (see Figure 3.1). Figure 3.2 shows variations in the appearance of women's genitals.

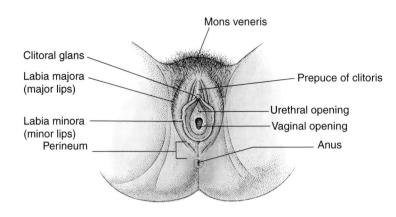

Mons veneris

Clitoral glans

Labia majora
(major lips)

Labia minora
(minor lips)

Perineum

Prepuce of clitoris

Urethral opening

Vaginal opening

Anus

figure 3.1

External Female Sex Organs. This figure shows the vulva with the labia opened to reveal the urethral and vaginal openings.

The Mons Veneris

The **mons veneris** consists of fatty tissue that covers the joint of the pubic bones in front of the body, below the abdomen and above the clitoris. At puberty, the mons becomes covered with pubic hair that is often thick and curly but varies from person to person in waviness, texture, and color. The pubic hair captures the chemical secretions that exude from the vagina during sexual arousal. Despite the preoccupation in the United States with chemicals that mask odors, these secretions produce a scent that may allure lovers.

The mons cushions a woman's body during sexual intercourse, protecting her and her partner from the pressure against the pubic bone that stems from thrusting motions. There is an ample supply of nerve endings in the mons, so caresses of the area can produce pleasurable sexual sensations.

The Labia Majora

The **labia majora** are large folds of skin that run downward from the mons along the sides of the vulva. The labia majora of some women are thick and bulging. In other

figure 3.2

Normal Variations in the Vulva. The features of the vulva show a great deal of variation. A woman's attitude toward her genitals is likely to reflect her general self-concept and early childhood messages rather than the appearance of her vulva per se.

Mons veneris A mound of fatty tissue that covers the joint of the pubic bones in front of the body, below the abdomen and above the clitoris. (The name is a Latin phrase meaning hill or "mount of Venus," the Roman goddess of love. Also known as the *mons pubis* or simply *mons*.)

Labia majora Large folds of skin that run downward from the mons along the sides of the vulva. (Latin for "large lips" or "major lips.")

women, they are thinner, flatter, and less noticeable. When close together, they hide the labia minora and the urethral and vaginal openings.

The outer surfaces of the labia majora, by the thighs, are covered with pubic hair and darker skin than that found on the thighs or labia minora. The inner surfaces of the labia majora are hairless and lighter in color. They are amply supplied with nerve endings that respond to stimulation and can produce sensations of sexual pleasure. The labia majora also shield the inner portion of the female genitals.

The Labia Minora

The **labia minora** are two hairless, light-colored membranes, located between the major lips. They surround the urethral and vaginal openings. The outer surfaces of the labia minora merge with the major lips. At the top, they join at the prepuce (hood) of the clitoris.

The labia minora differ markedly in appearance from woman to woman. The labia minora of some women form protruding flower shapes that are valued greatly in some cultures, such as that of the Hottentots of Africa. In fact, Hottentot women purposely elongate their labia minora by tugging at them.

Rich in blood vessels and nerve endings, the labia minora are highly sensitive to sexual stimulation. When stimulated, they darken and swell, indicating engorgement with blood.

The Clitoris

> What's the matter, papa? please don't stall.
> Don't you know I love it and want it all?
> I'm wild about that thing. Just give my bell a ring.
> You pressed my button. I'm wild about that thing.
> —"I'm Wild about That Thing," recorded by Bessie Smith, 1929

Worldwide, the clitoris is known by many names, from *bijou* (French for "jewel") to *pokhotnik* (Russian for "lust"). The Tuamotuan people of Polynesia have ten words for it, emblematic of their cultivated interest in female sexuality. By any name, however, the clitoris is the only sex organ whose only known function is the experiencing of pleasure.

Clitoris (Figure 3.1) derives from the Greek word *kleitoris*, meaning "hill" or "slope." The clitoris receives its name from the manner in which it slopes upward in the shaft and forms a mound of spongy tissue at the glans. The body of the clitoris, termed the clitoral shaft, is about 1 inch long and ¼ inch wide. The clitoral shaft consists of erectile tissue that contains two spongy masses called **corpora cavernosa** ("cavernous bodies") that fill with blood (become engorged) and become erect in response to sexual stimulation. The stiffening of the clitoris is less apparent than the erection of the penis, because the clitoris does not swing free from the body as the penis does. The **prepuce** (meaning "before a swelling"), or hood, covers the clitoral shaft. It is a sheath of skin formed by the upper part of the labia minora. The clitoral glans is a smooth, round knob or lump of tissue. It resembles a button and is situated above the urethral opening. The clitoral glans may be covered by the clitoral hood but is readily revealed by gently separating the labia minora and retracting the hood. It is highly sensitive to touch because of the rich supply of nerve endings.

The clitoris is the female sex organ that is most sensitive to sexual sensation. The size of the clitoris varies from woman to woman, just as the size of the penis varies among men. There is no known connection between the size of the clitoris and sensitivity to sexual stimulation. The clitoral glans is highly sensitive to touch. Women therefore usually prefer to be stroked or stimulated on the mons, or on the clitoral hood, rather than directly on the glans.

In some respects, the clitoris is the female counterpart of the penis. Both organs develop from the same embryonic tissue, which makes them similar in structure, or

Labia minora hairless, light-colored membranes, located between the labia majora. (Latin for "small lips" or "minor lips.")

Clitoris A female sex organ consisting of a shaft and glans located above the urethral opening. It is extremely sensitive to sexual sensations.

Corpora cavernosa Masses of spongy tissue in the clitoral shaft that become engorged with blood and stiffen in response to sexual stimulation. (Latin for "cavernous bodies.")

Prepuce The fold of skin covering the glans of the clitoris (or penis). (From Latin roots meaning "before a swelling.")

homologous. They are not fully similar in function, or **analogous,** however. Both organs receive and transmit sexual sensations, but the penis is directly involved in reproduction and excretion by serving as a conduit for sperm and urine, respectively. The clitoris, however, seems to be a unique sex organ. It serves no known purpose other than sexual pleasure. It is ironic that many cultures—including Victorian culture—have viewed women as unresponsive to sexual stimulation. It is ironic because women, not men, possess a sex organ that is apparently solely devoted to pleasurable sensations. The clitoris is the woman's most erotically charged organ, a fact that is borne out by the fact that women most often masturbate through clitoral stimulation, not vaginal insertion.

It is true that women, but not men, have a sex organ whose only known function is the experiencing of sexual pleasure. That organ is the clitoris. ■

Truth or Fiction?
REVISITED

    Surgical removal of the clitoral hood is common among Moslems in the Near East and Africa. As we see in the nearby A World of Diversity feature, this procedure aims to control female sexuality.

The Vestibule

The word *vestibule*, which means "entranceway," refers to the area within the labia minora that contains the openings to the vagina and the urethra. The vestibule is richly supplied with nerve endings and is very sensitive to tactile or other sexual stimulation.

The Urethral Opening

Urine passes from the female's body through the **urethral opening** (see Figure 3.1), which is connected by a short tube called the urethra to the bladder (see Figure 3.3), where urine collects. The urethral opening lies below the clitoral glans and above the vaginal opening. The urethral opening, urethra, and bladder are unrelated to the reproductive system. Many males (and even some females), however, believe erroneously that for women, urination and coitus occur through the same bodily opening. The confusion may arise from the fact that urine and semen both pass through the penis of the male or because the urethral opening lies near the vaginal opening.

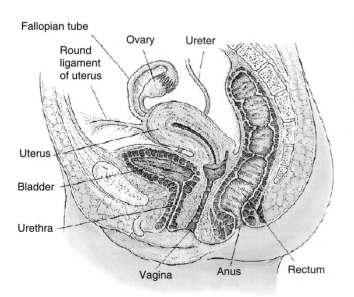

figure 3.3

The Female Reproductive System. This cross-section locates many of the internal sex organs that compose the female reproductive system. Note that the uterus is normally tipped forward.

Homologous Similar in structure; developing from the same embryonic tissue.

Analogous Similar in function.

Urethral opening The opening through which urine passes from the female's body.

CLITORIDECTOMY—RITUAL GENITAL MUTILATION

Despite hundreds of years of tradition, Hajia Zuwera Kassindja would not let it happen to her 17-year-old daughter, Fauziya. Hajia's own sister had died from it. So Hajia gave her daughter her inheritance from her deceased husband, which amounted to only $3,500 but left Hajia a pauper. Fauziya used the money to buy a phony passport and flee from the African country of Togo to the United States (Dugger, 1996a).

Upon arrival in the United States, Fauziya requested asylum from persecution. However, she was put into prison for more than a year. But then, in 1996, the Board of Immigration Appeals finally agreed that Fauziya was fleeing persecution, and she was allowed to remain in the United States. She now lives and studies near Washington, D.C.

From what had Hajia's sister died? From what was Fauziya escaping? *Ritual genital mutilation.*

Clitoridectomy

Cultures in some parts of Africa and the Middle East ritually mutilate or remove the entire clitoris, not just the clitoral hood. Removal of the clitoris, or **clitoridectomy,** is a rite of initiation into womanhood in many of these predominantly Islamic cultures. It is often performed as a puberty ritual in late childhood or early adolescence (not within a few days of birth, like male circumcision).

The clitoris gives rise to feelings of sexual pleasure in women. Its removal or mutilation represents an attempt to ensure the girl's chastity, since it is assumed that uncircumcised girls are consumed with sexual desires. Cairo physician Said M. Thabit says, "With circumcision we remove the external parts, so when a girl wears tight nylon underclothes she will not have any stimulation" (cited in MacFarquhar, 1996, p. A3). Some groups in rural Egypt and in the northern Sudan, however, perform clitoridectomies primarily because it is a social custom that has been passed down from ancient times. Some perceive it as part of their faith in Islam. However, the Koran—the Islamic bible—does not authorize it (Crossette, 1998). Ironically, many young women do not grasp that they are victims. They assume that clitoridectomy is part of being female.

Clitoridectomies are performed under unsanitary conditions without benefit of anesthesia. Medical complications are common, including infections, bleeding, tissue scarring, painful menstruation, and obstructed labor. The procedure is psychologically traumatizing. An even more radical form of clitoridectomy, called *infibulation* or Pharaonic circumcision, is practiced widely in the Sudan. Pharaonic circumcision involves complete removal of the clitoris along with the labia minora and the inner layers of the labia majora. After removal of the skin tissue, the raw edges of the labia majora are sewn together. Only a tiny opening is left to allow passage of urine and menstrual discharge. The sewing together of the vulva is intended to ensure the girls' chastity until marriage (Crossette, 1998). Medical complications are common, including menstrual and urinary problems and even death. After marriage, the opening is enlarged to permit intercourse. Enlargement is a gradual process that is often made difficult by scar tissue from the circumcision. Hemorrhaging and tearing of surrounding tissues are common consequences. It may take three months or longer before the opening is large enough to allow penile penetration. Mutilation of the labia is now illegal in the Sudan, although the law

---

The proximity of the urethral opening to the external sex organs may pose some hygienic problems for sexually active women. The urinary tract, which includes the urethra, bladder, and kidneys, may become infected from bacteria that are transmitted from the vagina or rectum. Infectious microscopic organisms may also pass from the male's sex organs to the female's urethral opening during sexual intercourse. Manual stimulation of the vulva with dirty hands may also transmit bacteria through the urethral opening to the bladder. Anal intercourse followed by vaginal intercourse may transfer microscopic organisms from the rectum to the bladder and cause infection. For similar reasons, women should first wipe the vulva, then the anus, when using the bathroom.

Cystitis is a bladder inflammation that may stem from any of these sources. Its primary symptoms are burning and frequent urination (also called *urinary urgency*). Pus or a bloody discharge is common, and there may be an intermittent or persistent ache just above the pubic bone. These symptoms may disappear after several days, but consultation with a **gynecologist** is recommended, because untreated cystitis can lead to serious kidney infections.

So-called honeymoon cystitis is caused by the tugging on the bladder and urethral wall that occurs during vaginal intercourse. It may occur upon beginning coital activity (though not necessarily on one's honeymoon) or upon resuming coital activity after lengthy abstinence. Figure 3.3 shows the close proximity of the urethra and vagina.

A few precautions may help women to prevent serious inflammation of the bladder:

- Drinking two quarts of water a day to flush the bladder.
- Drinking orange or cranberry juice to maintain an acid environment that discourages growth of infectious organisms.

Clitoridectomy Surgical removal of the clitoris.

Cystitis An inflammation of the urinary bladder. (From the Greek *kystis,* meaning "sac.")

Gynecologist A physician who treats women's diseases, especially of the reproductive tract. (From the Greek *gyne,* meaning "woman.")

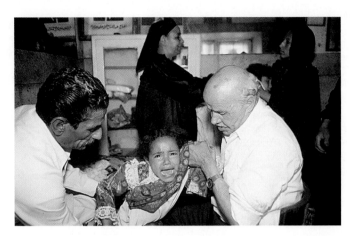

Ritual Genital Mutilation. Some predominantly Islamic cultures in Africa and the Middle East ritually mutilate or remove the clitoris as a rite of initiation into womanhood. Novelist Alice Walker drew attention to the practice in her novel *Possessing the Secret of Joy.* She has called for its abolition in her book and film, *Warrior Marks.*

of circumcision. Former Representative Patricia Schroeder of Colorado depicts the male equivalent of female genital mutilation as cutting off the penis (Dugger, 1996b). *The New York Times* columnist A. M. Rosenthal (1995) calls female genital mutilation the most widespread existing violation of human rights in the world. The Pulitzer Prize-winning African American novelist Alice Walker drew attention to the practice in her best-selling novel *Possessing the Secret of Joy* (1992). She called for its abolition in her book and movie *Warrior Marks.*

Outlawed

In 1996, the United States outlawed ritual genital mutilation within its borders. The government also directed U.S. representatives to world financial institutions to deny aid to countries that have not established educational programs to bring an end to the practice (Dugger, 1996b). But calls from Westerners to ban the practice in parts of Africa and the Middle East have sparked controversy on grounds of "cultural condescension"—that people in one culture cannot dictate the cultural traditions of another. But for Alice Walker, "torture is not culture." As the debate continues, some 2 million African girls are mutilated each year.

continues to allow removal of the clitoris. Some African countries, including Egypt, have outlawed clitoridectomies, although such laws might not be enforced.

More than 100 million women in Africa and the Middle East have undergone removal of the clitoris and the labia minora. Clitoridectomies remain common or even universal in nearly 30 countries in Africa, in many countries in the Middle East, and in parts of Malaysia, Yemen, Oman, Indonesia, and the India-Pakistan subcontinent (Rosenthal, 1995). Thousands of African immigrant girls living in European countries and the United States have also been mutilated (Crossette, 1998; Dugger, 1996b).

Do not confuse male circumcision with the maiming inflicted on girls in the name

- Decreasing use of alcohol and caffeine (from coffee, tea, or cola drinks) that may irritate the bladder.
- Washing the hands before masturbation or self-examination.
- Washing one's partner's and one's own genitals before and after intercourse.
- Preventing objects that have touched the anus (fingers, penis, toilet tissue) from subsequently coming into contact with the vulva.
- Urinating soon after intercourse to help wash away bacteria.

These measures do not guarantee protection against transmission of infectious organisms, but they may help.

The Vaginal Opening

> When I was five or six, my mother told me about sex. I remember that I was confused about what my mother said, because somehow I couldn't conceptualize what the female vagina looked like. I was curious to see an actual vagina and not just how it looked diagramed in a book. (Morrison et al., 1980, p. 35)

One does not see an entire vagina, but rather the vaginal opening, or **introitus,** when one parts the labia minora, or minor lips. The introitus lies below, and is larger than, the urethral opening. Its shape resembles that of the **hymen.**

The hymen is a fold of tissue across the vaginal opening that is usually present at birth and may remain at least partly intact until a woman engages in coitus. For this reason, the

Introitus The vaginal opening. (From the Latin for "entrance.")

Hymen A fold of tissue across the vaginal opening that is usually present at birth and remains at least partly intact until a woman engages in coitus. (Greek for "membrane.")

figure 3.4

Appearance of Various Types of Hymens and the Introitus (at Right) as It Appears after Delivery of a Baby.

hymen has been called the "maidenhead." Its presence has been taken as proof of virginity and its absence as evidence of coitus. However, some women are born with incomplete hymens, and other women's hymens are torn accidentally, such as during horseback riding, strenuous exercise, or gymnastics—or even when bicycle riding. A punctured hymen is therefore poor evidence of coital experience. A flexible hymen may also withstand many coital experiences, so its presence does not guarantee virginity. Some people believe incorrectly that virgins cannot insert tampons or fingers into their vaginas, but most hymens will accommodate these intrusions without great difficulty. Some hymens, however, are torn accidentally when tampons are inserted.

Truth or Fiction?
REVISITED

Contrary to myth, it is not true that one may determine whether or not a woman is a virgin by examination of the hymen. Examination of the hymen may yield false information. ■

Figure 3.4 illustrates various vaginal openings. The first three show common shapes of hymens among women who have not had coitus. The fifth drawing shows a *parous* ("passed through") vaginal opening, typical of a woman who has delivered a baby. Now and then the hymen consists of tough fibrous tissue and is closed, or *imperforate*, as in the fourth drawing. An imperforate hymen might not be discovered until after puberty, when menstrual discharges begin to accumulate in the vagina. In these rare cases, a simple surgical incision will perforate the hymen. A woman may also have a physician surgically perforate her hymen if she would rather forgo the tearing and discomfort that may accompany her initial coital experiences. This procedure is unnecessary, however, for the great majority of women. They experience little pain or distress during initial coitus, despite old horror stories. A woman may also stretch the vaginal opening in preparation for intercourse by inserting a finger and gently pressing downward toward the anus. After several repetitions, she may insert two fingers and repeat the process, spreading the fingers slightly after insertion. This procedure is sometimes followed over several days or weeks.

The hymen is found only in female horses and humans. It is not present in the animal species that are closest to humans on the evolutionary scale, such as chimps and gorillas. The hymen remains something of a biological mystery, since it serves no apparent biological function.

DEFLORATION   The hymen has been of great cultural significance because of the (erroneous) association between it and virginity. In some societies, its destruction, or **defloration,** is ritualized. For example, in some ancient religious rites, young girls were deflowered by sculpted phalluses in ceremonies conducted on the temple steps. In Europe, during the Middle Ages, the lord of the manor held the *droit du seigneur* (French for "right of the lord") to deflower (by means of intercourse) a maiden on her wedding night, after which she became her husband's sexual property. Among the Yungar of Australia, older women deflowered maidens before marriage. Girls who were found to have ruptured hymens might be tortured or killed. Since some girls are born with minimal hymens, many have probably been unjustly punished for purported sexual indiscretions.

Defloration Destruction of the hymen (especially as a cultural ritual).

The Perineum

The **perineum** incorporates the skin and underlying tissue between the vaginal opening and the anus. The perineum is rich in nerve endings. Stimulation of the area may heighten sexual arousal. Many physicians make a routine perineal incision during labor, called an **episiotomy,** to facilitate childbirth.

Structures That Underlie the External Sex Organs

Figure 3.5 shows what lies beneath the skin of the vulva. The vestibular bulbs and Bartholin's glands are active during sexual arousal and are found on both sides (shown on the right in Figure 3.5). Muscular rings **(sphincters)** that constrict bodily openings, such as the vaginal and anal openings, are also found on both sides.

The clitoral **crura** are wing-shaped, leglike structures that attach the clitoris to the pubic bone beneath. The crura contain corpora cavernosa, which engorge with blood and stiffen during sexual arousal.

The **vestibular bulbs** are attached to the clitoris at the top and extend downward along the sides of the vaginal opening. Blood congests them during sexual arousal, swelling the vulva and lengthening the vagina. This swelling contributes to coital sensations for both partners.

Bartholin's glands lie just inside the minor lips on each side of the vaginal opening. They secrete a couple of drops of lubrication just before orgasm. This lubrication is not

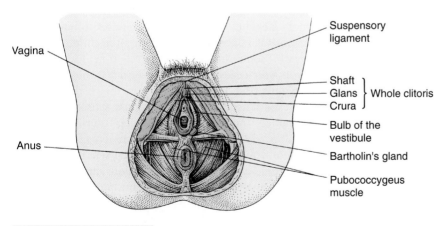

figure 3.5

Structures That Underlie the Female External Sex Organs. If we could see beneath the vulva, we would find muscle fibers that constrict the various body openings, plus the crura ("legs") of the clitoris, the vestibular bulbs, and Bartholin's glands.

Perineum The skin and underlying tissue that lie between the vaginal opening and the anus. (From Greek roots meaning "around" and "to empty out.")

Episiotomy A surgical incision in the perineum that may be made during childbirth to protect the vagina from tearing. (From the Greek roots *epision,* meaning "pubic region," and *tome,* meaning "cutting.")

Sphincters Ring-shaped muscles that surround body openings and open or close them by expanding or contracting. (From the Greek for "that which draws close.")

Crura Anatomical structures resembling legs that attach the clitoris to the pubic bone. (Singular: crus. A Latin word meaning "leg" or "shank.")

Vestibular bulbs Cavernous structures that extend downward along the sides of the introitus and swell during sexual arousal.

Bartholin's glands Glands that lie just inside the minor lips and secrete fluid just before orgasm.

69

a CLOSER look

Kegels

Kegel exercises are commonly used to help women heighten their awareness of vaginal sensations. They may also have a psychological benefit, because women who perform Kegel exercises assume a more active role in enhancing their genital sensations. Sex therapist Lonnie Barbach (1975) offers instructions for Kegel exercises:

1. Locate the P-C muscle by purposely stopping the flow of urine. The muscle you squeeze to stop the urine flow is the P-C muscle. (The P-C muscle acts as a sphincter for both the urethral and vaginal openings.)
2. To learn to focus consciously on contracting the P-C muscle, insert a finger into the vaginal opening and contract the muscle so that it can be felt to squeeze or contain the finger. (The P-C muscle can contract to contain objects as narrow as a finger. Therefore, men need not fear that a large penis is required to induce stimulating vaginal sensations in a woman.)
3. Remove your finger, squeeze the P-C muscle for 3 seconds, and then relax. Repeat several times. This part of the exercise may be performed while seated at a classroom or business desk. No one (except the woman herself) will be the wiser. Many women practice a series of Kegel exercises consisting of 10 contractions, 3 times a day.
4. The P-C muscle may also be tensed and relaxed in rapid sequence. Since this exercise may be more fatiguing than the above, women may choose to practice it perhaps 10 to 25 times, once a day.

essential for coitus. In fact, the fluid produced by the Bartholin's glands has no known purpose. If the glands become infected and clogged, however, a woman may notice swelling and local irritation. It is wise to consult a gynecologist if these symptoms do not fade within a few days.

It was once believed that the source of the vaginal lubrication or "wetness" that women experience during sexual arousal was produced by the Bartholin's glands. It is now known that engorgement of vaginal tissues during sexual excitement results in a form of "sweating" by the lining of the vaginal wall. During sexual arousal, the pressure from this engorgement causes moisture from the many small blood vessels that lie in the vaginal wall to be forced out and to pass through the vaginal lining, forming the basis of the lubrication. In less time than it takes to read this sentence (generally within 10 to 30 seconds), beads of vaginal lubrication appear along the interior lining of the vagina in response to sexual stimulation, in much the same way that rising temperatures cause water to pass through the skin as perspiration.

Pelvic floor muscles permit women to constrict the vaginal and anal openings. They contract automatically, or involuntarily, during orgasm, and their tone may contribute to coital sensations. Gynecologist Arnold Kegel (1952) developed exercises to build pelvic muscle tone in women who had problems controlling urination after childbirth. The stress of childbirth on the pelvic muscles sometimes reduces muscle tone, leading to an involuntary loss of urine when a woman sneezes or coughs. Kegel also observed that women with thin or weak **pubococcygeus (P-C) muscles** reported they had little or no vaginal sensations during coitus or experienced unpleasant vaginal sensations. Some women with weak P-C muscles complained, "I just don't feel anything" (during coitus) or "I don't like the feeling" (Kegel, 1952, p. 522). Kegel found that women who practiced his exercises improved their urinary control along with their genital sensations during coitus. He believed that many women could enhance vaginal sensations during coitus by exercising their P-C muscles through exercises that have since become known as "Kegels."

Reflections

Pubococcygeus muscle
The muscle that encircles the entrance to the vagina.

- What are your attitudes toward your own genital organs? Where do you think your attitudes come from?
- What are the roles of the female external sex organs in reproduction?

■ What are your attitudes toward female circumcision? Do you believe that disapproval of the practice by Americans and other Westerners shows cultural insensitivity? Why or why not?

■ What did the information in this section add to your knowledge of the female external sex organs? Did you have any erroneous beliefs about them before reading the section? What were they?

■ What measures can you take to ensure the health of your own sex organs and those of the people you care about? Are you doing everything you can? If not, why not?

INTERNAL SEX ORGANS

The internal sex organs of the female include the innermost parts of the vagina, the cervix, the uterus, and two ovaries, each connected to the uterus by a fallopian tube (see Figures 3.3 and 3.6). These structures comprise the female reproductive system.

The Vagina

The **vagina** extends back and upward from the vaginal opening (see Figure 3.3). It is usually 3 to 5 inches long at rest. Menstrual flow and babies pass from the uterus to the outer world through the vagina. During coitus, the penis is contained within the vagina.

The vagina is commonly pictured as a canal or barrel, but when at rest, it is like a collapsed muscular tube. Its walls touch like the fingers of an empty glove. The vagina expands in length and width during sexual arousal. The vagina can also expand to allow insertion of a tampon, as well as the passage of a baby's head and shoulders during childbirth.

The vaginal walls have three layers. The inner lining, or *vaginal mucosa*, is made visible by opening the labia minora. It is a mucous membrane similar to the skin that lines the inside of the mouth. It feels fleshy, soft, and corrugated. It may vary from very dry (especially if the female is anxious about something such as examinations) to very wet, in which case fingers slide against it readily. The middle layer of the vaginal wall is muscular. The outer or deeper layer is a fibrous covering that connects the vagina to other pelvic structures.

The vaginal walls are rich with blood vessels but poorly supplied with nerve endings. Unlike the sensitive outer third of the vaginal barrel, the inner two thirds are so insensitive to touch that minor surgery may sometimes be performed on those portions without anesthesia. The entire vaginal barrel is sensitive to pressure, however, which can be experienced as sexually pleasurable.

The vaginal walls secrete substances that help to maintain the vagina's normal acidity (pH 4.0 to 5.0). Normally, the secretions taste salty. The odor and taste of these secretions may vary during the menstrual cycle. Although the evidence is not clear, the

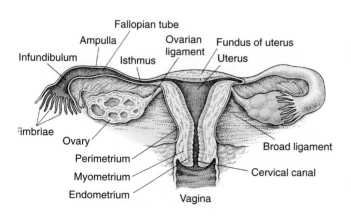

figure 3.6

Female Internal Reproductive Organs. This drawing highlights the relationship of the uterus to the fallopian tubes and ovaries. Note the layers of the uterus, the ligaments that attach the ovaries to the uterus, and the relationship of the ovaries to the fimbriae of the fallopian tubes.

Vagina The tubular female sex organ that contains the penis during sexual intercourse and through which a baby is born. (Latin for "sheath.")

secretions are thought to contain substances that may act as sexual attractants. Women who frequently **douche** or use feminine deodorant sprays may remove or mask substances that may arouse sex partners. Douching or spraying may also alter the natural chemical balance of the vagina, which can increase the risk of vaginal infections. Feminine deodorant sprays can also irritate the vagina and evoke allergic reactions. The normal, healthy vagina cleanses itself through regular chemical secretions that are evidenced by a mild white or yellowish discharge.

Vaginitis refers to any vaginal inflammation, whether it is caused by an infection, an allergic reaction, or chemical irritation. Vaginitis may also stem from use of birth-control pills or antibiotics that alter the natural body chemistry or from other factors, such as lowered resistance (from fatigue or poor diet). Changes in the natural body chemistry or lowered resistance permit microscopic organisms that are normally found in the vagina to multiply to infectious levels. Vaginitis may be recognized by abnormal discharge, itching, burning of the vulva, and, sometimes, urinary urgency. The causes and treatments of vaginitis are elaborated in Chapter 16. Women with vaginitis are advised to seek medical attention, but let us note some suggestions that may help to prevent vaginitis (Boston Women's Health Book Collective, 1992):

1. Wash your vulva and anus regularly with mild soap. Pat dry (taking care not to touch the vulva after dabbing the anus).
2. Wear cotton panties. Nylon underwear retains heat and moisture that cause harmful bacteria to flourish.
3. Avoid pants that are tight in the crotch.
4. Be certain that sex partners are well-washed. Condoms may also reduce the spread of infections from one's sex partner.
5. Use a sterile, water-soluble jelly such as K-Y jelly if artificial lubrication is needed for intercourse. Do *not* use Vaseline. Birth-control jellies can also be used for lubrication.
6. Avoid intercourse that is painful or abrasive to the vagina.
7. Avoid diets that are high in sugar and refined carbohydrates, since they alter the normal acidity of the vagina.
8. Women who are prone to vaginal infections may find it helpful to douche occasionally with plain water, a solution of 1 or 2 tablespoons of vinegar in a quart of warm water, or a solution of baking soda and water. Douches consisting of unpasteurized, plain (unflavored) yogurt may help to replenish the "good" bacteria that are normally found in the vagina and that may be destroyed by use of antibiotics. Be careful when douching, and do not douche when pregnant or when you suspect you may be pregnant. Consult your physician before deciding to douche or to apply any preparations to the vagina.
9. Watch your general health. Eating poorly or getting insufficient rest will reduce your resistance to infection.

The Cervix

> When someone first said to me two years ago, "You can feel the end of your own cervix with your finger," I was interested but flustered. I had hardly ever put my finger in my vagina at all, and felt squeamish about touching myself there, in that place "reserved" for lovers and doctors. It took me two months to get up nerve to try it, and then one afternoon, pretty nervously, I squatted down in the bathroom and put my finger in deep, back into my vagina. There it was, feeling slippery and rounded, with an indentation at the center through which, I realized, my menstrual flow came. It was both very exciting and beautifully ordinary at the same time. Last week I bought a plastic speculum so I can look at my cervix. Will it take as long this time? (Boston Women's Health Book Collective, 1992)

The **cervix** is the lower end of the uterus. Its walls, like those of the vagina, produce secretions that contribute to the chemical balance of the vagina. The opening in middle of the cervix, or **os,** is normally about the width of a straw, although it expands to permit

Douche Application of a jet of liquid to the vagina as a rinse. (From the Italian *doccia,* meaning "shower bath.")

Vaginitis Vaginal inflammation.

Cervix The lower end of the uterus. (Latin for "neck.")

Os The opening in middle of the cervix. (Latin for "mouth.")

passage of a baby from the uterus to the vagina during childbirth. Sperm pass from the vagina to the uterus through the cervical canal.

Cervical cancer is relatively uncommon in the United States, largely because of effective screening programs (Cannistra & Niloff, 1996). Nearly 16,000 new cases of cervical cancer are reported annually. Cervical cancer is more common among women who have had many sex partners, who became sexually active at a relatively early age, who come from lower socioeconomic status, and who smoke. All women are at risk, however.

A **Pap test** examines a sample of cervical cells that are smeared on a slide to screen for cervical cancer and other abnormalities. The American Cancer Society (1995) recommends annual Pap tests along with a pelvic examination for in women who are, or have been, sexually active or who have reached age 18. Most cases of cervical cancer can be successfully treated by surgery and **radiotherapy** if they are detected early. The five-year survival rate for women with cervical cancer patients is 67%. For women diagnosed with localized cancer, the survival rate is 90% (American Cancer Society, 1995). However, cervical cancer can also be prevented when precancerous changes are detected by a Pap test ("Panel says," 1996). There are nearly 5,000 deaths from cervical cancer a year in the United States. The mortality rate is more than twice as high for African American women as for White women (American Cancer Society, 1995).

The Uterus

The **uterus,** or womb (see Figures 3.3, 3.6), is the organ in which a fertilized ovum implants and develops until birth. The uterus usually slants forward (is *antroverted*), although about 10% of women have uteruses that tip backward (are *retroverted*). In most instances, a retroverted uterus causes no problems, but some women with retroverted uteruses find coitus in certain positions painful. (They quickly learn more comfortable positions by trial and error.) A retroverted uterus normally tips forward during pregnancy. This condition probably does not interfere with conception, although at one time it was thought that it might do so. The uterus is suspended in the pelvis by flexible ligaments. In a woman who has not given birth, the uterus is about 3 inches long, 3 inches wide, and 1 inch thick near the top. It expands to accommodate a fetus during pregnancy and shrinks after pregnancy, though not to its original size.

The uppermost part of the uterus is called the **fundus** (see Figure 3.6). The uterus is shaped like an inverted pear. If a ceramic model of a uterus were placed on a table, it would balance on the fundus. The central region of the uterus is called the body. The narrow lower region is the cervix, which leads downward to the vagina.

LAYERS OF THE UTERUS   Like the vagina, the uterus has three layers (also shown in Figure 3.6). The innermost layer, or **endometrium,** is richly supplied with blood vessels and glands. Its structure varies according to a woman's age and phase of the menstrual cycle. Endometrial tissue is discharged through the cervix and vagina at menstruation. For reasons that are not entirely understood, in some women, endometrial tissue may also grow in the abdominal cavity or elsewhere in the reproductive system. This condition is called **endometriosis,** and the most common symptom is menstrual pain. If left untreated, endometriosis may lead to infertility.

Cancer of the endometrial lining is called endometrial cancer. Risk factors include obesity, a diet that is high in fats, early menarche or late menopause, history of failure to ovulate, and estrogen-replacement therapy (Grodstein et al., 1997). For women who obtain hormone-replacement therapy, combining estrogen with progestin mitigates the risk of endometrial cancer (Grodstein et al., 1996; Rose, 1996). Endometrial cancer is symptomized by abnormal uterine staining or bleeding, especially after menopause. The most common treatment is surgery (Rose, 1996). The five-year survival rate for endometrial cancer is up to 95% if it is discovered early and limited to the endometrium (Rose, 1996). (Endometrial cancer is usually diagnosed early because women tend to quickly report

Pap test A test of a sample of cervical cells that screens for cervical cancer and other abnormalities. (Named after the originator of the technique, Dr. Papanicolaou.)

Radiotherapy Treatment of a disease by X-rays or by emissions from a radioactive substance.

Uterus The hollow, muscular, pear-shaped organ in which a fertilized ovum implants and develops until birth.

Fundus The uppermost part of the uterus. (*Fundus* is a Latin word meaning "base.")

Endometrium The innermost layer of the uterus. (From Latin and Greek roots meaning "within the uterus.")

Endometriosis A condition caused by the growth of endometrial tissue in the abdominal cavity or elsewhere outside the uterus and characterized by menstrual pain.

postmenopausal bleeding to their doctors.) The survival rate drops when the cancer invades surrounding tissues or metastasizes.

The second layer of the uterus, the **myometrium,** is well muscled. It endows the uterus with flexibility and strength, and it creates the powerful contractions that propel a fetus outward during labor. The third or outermost layer, the **perimetrium,** provides an external cover.

HYSTERECTOMY   One woman in three in the United States has a **hysterectomy** by the age of 60. Most women who obtain them do so between the ages of 35 and 45. The hysterectomy is now the second most commonly performed operation on women in this country. (Cesarean sections are the most common.) A hysterectomy may be performed when a woman develops cancer of the uterus, ovaries, or cervix or other diseases that cause pain or excessive uterine bleeding. A hysterectomy may be partial or complete. A **complete hysterectomy** involves the surgical removal of the ovaries, fallopian tubes, cervix, and uterus. It is usually performed to reduce the risk of cancer spreading throughout the reproductive system. A partial hysterectomy removes the uterus but spares the ovaries and fallopian tubes. Sparing the ovaries allows the woman to continue to ovulate and produce adequate quantities of female sex hormones.

The hysterectomy has become steeped in controversy. In many cases, it is possible that less radical medical interventions might successfully treat the problem. On the basis of a sample of more than 5,000 hysterectomies performed in seven health maintenance organizations (HMOs) across the country, a panel of experts in gynecology and obstetrics reported that 28% of these operations in younger women, and 16% in women overall, were inappropriate (Bernstein et al., 1993). We advise women whose physicians advise a hysterectomy to seek a second opinion before proceeding.

The Fallopian Tubes

Two uterine tubes, also called **fallopian tubes,** are about 4 inches in length and extend from the upper end of the uterus toward the ovaries (see Figure 3.6). The part of each tube nearest the uterus is the **isthmus,** which broadens into the **ampulla** as it approaches the ovary. The outer part, or **infundibulum,** has fringelike projections called **fimbriae** that extend toward, but are not attached to, the ovary.

Ova pass through the fallopian tubes on their way to the uterus. The fallopian tubes are not inert passageways. They help to nourish and conduct ova. These tubes are lined with tiny hairlike projections termed cilia ("lashes") that help to move ova through the tube. The exact mechanisms by which ova are guided are unknown, however. It is tempting to say that ova move at a snail's pace, but a snail would leave them far behind. They journey toward the uterus at about 1 inch per day. Since ova must be fertilized within a day or two after they are released from the ovaries, fertilization usually occurs in the infundibulum within a couple of inches of the ovaries. The form of sterilization called tubal ligation ties off the fallopian tubes so that ova cannot pass through them or become fertilized.

In an **ectopic pregnancy,** the fertilized ovum implants outside the uterus, most often in the fallopian tube where fertilization occurred. Ectopic pregnancies can eventually burst fallopian tubes, causing hemorrhaging and death. Ectopic pregnancies are therefore terminated before the tube ruptures. They are not easily recognized, however, because their symptoms—missed menstrual period, abdominal pain, irregular bleeding—suggest many conditions. Experiencing any these symptoms is an excellent reason for consulting a gynecologist. Women who have had pelvic inflammatory disease (PID), undergone tubal surgery, or used intrauterine devices (IUDs) are at increased risk of developing ectopic pregnancies (Marchbanks, 1988).

The Ovaries

The two **ovaries** are almond-shaped organs that are each about 1½ inches long. They lie on either side of the uterus, to which they are attached by ovarian ligaments. The ovaries

---

Myometrium The middle, well-muscled layer of the uterus. (*Myo-* stems from the Greek *mys,* meaning "muscle.")

Perimetrium The outer layer of the uterus. (From roots meaning "around the uterus.")

Hysterectomy Surgical removal of the uterus.

Complete hysterectomy Surgical removal of the ovaries, fallopian tubes, cervix, and uterus.

Fallopian tubes Tubes that extend from the upper uterus toward the ovaries and conduct ova to the uterus. (After the Italian anatomist Gabriel Fallopio, who is credited with their discovery.)

Isthmus The segment of a fallopian tube closest to the uterus. (A Latin word meaning "narrow passage.")

Ampulla The wide segment of a fallopian tube near the ovary. (A Latin word meaning "bottle.")

Infundibulum The outer, funnel-shaped part of a fallopian tube. (A Latin word meaning "funnel.")

Fimbriae Projections from a fallopian tube that extend toward an ovary. (Singular: fimbria. Latin for "fiber" or "fringe.")

Ectopic pregnancy A pregancy in which the fertilized ovum implants outside the uterus, usually in the fallopian tube. (*Ectopic* derives from Greek roots meaning "out of place.")

Ovaries Almond-shaped organs that produce ova and the hormones estrogen and progesterone.

produce ova (egg cells) and the female sex hormones **estrogen** and **progesterone.**

Estrogen is a generic term for several hormones (such as estradiol, estriol, and estrone) that promote the changes of puberty and regulate the menstrual cycle. Estrogen also helps older women to maintain cognitive functioning and feelings of psychological well-being (Sourander, 1994). Progesterone also has multiple functions, including regulating the menstrual cycle and preparing the uterus for pregnancy by stimulating the development of the endometrium (uterine lining). Estrogen and progesterone levels vary with the phases of the menstrual cycle.

The human female is born with all the ova she will ever have (about 2 million), but they are immature in form. Of these, about 400,000 survive into puberty, each of which is contained in the ovary within a thin capsule, or **follicle.** During a woman's reproductive years, from puberty to menopause, only 400 or so ripened ova, typically 1 per month, will be released by their rupturing follicles for possible fertilization. How these ova are selected is among the mysteries of nature.

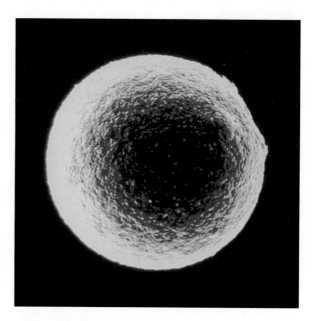

A Magnified Human Ovum (Egg Cell).

Each year, some 27,000 women in the United States are diagnosed with ovarian cancer, and 14,500 die from it (American Cancer Society, 1995; Altman, 1998d). It most often strikes women between the ages of 40 and 70 and ranks as the fourth leading cancer killer of women, behind lung cancer, breast cancer, and colon cancer. The women who are most at risk are those with blood relatives who had the disease, especially a first-degree relative (mother, sister, or daughter). Other risk factors are also important, since about 9 women in 10 who develop ovarian cancer do not have a family history of it. Researchers have identified several risk factors that increase the chances of developing the disease: never having given birth, prolonged use of talcum powder between the anus and the vagina, infertility, a history of breast cancer, and a diet that is rich in meat and animal fats. Questions have been raised as to whether the use of clomiphene, a fertility drug, increases the risk of ovarian cancer (Del Priore et al., 1995; Whittemore, 1994). On the other hand, use of acetaminophen (found in Tylenol and some other pain relievers—read the label) seems to cut the risk of ovarian cancer. Daniel Cramer and his colleagues (1998) studied the use of over-the-counter painkillers in 563 New England women who had ovarian cancer and 523 healthy New England women selected from the general population. They found that 8.8% of the healthy women used acetaminophen, compared with 4.6% of the women with ovarian cancer.

Early detection is the key to fighting ovarian cancer. When it is detected before spreading beyond the ovary, 90% of victims survive. However, the overall five-year survival rate is about 50% (Altman, 1998d). Unfortunately, ovarian cancer is often "silent" in the early stages, showing no obvious signs or symptoms. The most common sign is enlargement of the abdomen, which is caused by the accumulation of fluid. Periodic, complete pelvic examinations are important. The Pap test, which is useful in detecting cervical cancer, does not reveal ovarian cancer. The American Cancer Society (1995) advises women over the age of 40 to have a cancer-related checkup every year.

Surgery, radiation therapy, and drug therapy are treatment options. Surgery usually includes the removal of one or both ovaries, the uterus, and the fallopian tubes.

The Pelvic Examination

Women are advised to have an internal (pelvic) examination at least once a year by the time they reach their late teens (or earlier if they become sexually active) and twice yearly if they are over age 35 or use birth-control pills. The physician (usually a gynecologist) first examines the woman externally for irritations, swellings, abnormal vaginal discharges, and clitoral adhesions. The physician normally inserts a speculum to help inspect

Estrogen A generic term for female sex hormones (including estradiol, estriol, estrone, and others) or synthetic compounds that promote the development of female sex characteristics and regulate the menstrual cycle. (From the roots meaning "generating" [-*gen*] and "estrus.")

Progesterone A steroid hormone secreted by the corpus luteum or prepared synthetically that stimulates proliferation of the endometrium and is involved in regulation of the menstrual cycle.

Follicle A capsule within an ovary that contains an ovum. (From a Latin word meaning "small bag.")

figure 3.7

Use of the Speculum and Spatula During a Pelvic Examination. The speculum holds the vaginal walls apart while the spatula is used to gently scrape cells from the cervix. The Pap test screens for cervical cancer and other abnormalities.

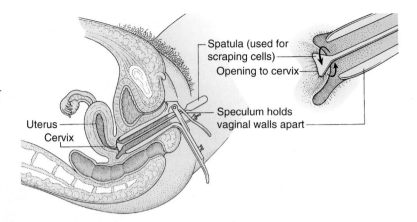

the cervix and vaginal walls for discharges (which can be signs of infection), discoloration, lesions, or growths. This examination is typically followed by a Pap test to detect cervical cancer. A sample of vaginal discharge may also be taken to test for the sexually transmitted disease gonorrhea.

To take a Pap smear, the physician will hold open the vaginal walls with a plastic or (hopefully prewarmed!) metal speculum so that a sample of cells (a smear) may be scraped from the cervix with a wooden spatula (see Figure 3.7). Women should not douche before Pap tests or schedule them during menstruation, since douches and blood confound analysis of the smear.

The speculum exam is normally followed by a bimanual vaginal exam in which the index and middle fingers of one hand are inserted into the vagina while the lower part of the abdomen is palpated (touched) by the other hand from the outside. The physician uses this technique to examine the location, shape, size, and movability of the internal sex organs, searching for abnormal growths and symptoms of other problems. Palpation may be somewhat uncomfortable, but severe pain is a sign that something is wrong. A woman should not try to be "brave" and hide such discomfort from the examiner. She may only be masking a symptom (that is, depriving the physician of useful information). Physical discomfort is usually mild, however, and psychological discomfort may often be relieved by discussing it frankly with the examiner.

Finally, the physician should do a recto-vaginal examination in which one finger is inserted into the rectum while another is inserted into the vagina. This procedure provides additional information about the ligaments of the uterus, the ovaries, and the fallopian tubes. The procedure also helps the physician to evaluate the health of the rectum.

Although it may be somewhat uncomfortable, the pelvic examination is not ordinarily painful. It is normal for a woman who has not had one, or who is visiting a new doctor, to be anxious about the exam. The doctor should be reassuring if the woman expresses concern. If the doctor is not, the woman should feel free to consult another doctor. She should not forgo the pelvic examination itself, however. It is essential for early detection of problems.

Reflections

- Are the female internal sex organs more complex than you had believed? If so, how?

- What are the risk factors for cancer of the female internal sex organs? What can be done to prevent them or to detect them early?

- According to a study by Bostick and his colleagues (1994), the best predictor concerning who will obtain screening for cancer is education. How will your own college education affect your own behavior? Are you sure?

- If you are a woman, would you prefer a female or male physician to conduct a pelvic exam? Why?

THE BREASTS

> The degree of attention which breasts receive, combined with the confusion about what the breast fetishists actually want, makes women unduly anxious about them. They can never be just right; they must always be too small, too big, the wrong shape, too flabby. The characteristics of the mammary stereotype are impossible to emulate because they are falsely simulated, but they must be faked somehow or another. Reality is either gross or scrawny.
>
> —Germaine Greer, *The Female Eunuch*

Some college women recall:

> I was very excited about my breast development. It was a big competition to see who was wearing a bra in elementary school. When I began wearing one, I also liked wearing see-through blouses so everyone would know. . . .

> My breasts were very late in developing. This brought me a lot of grief from my male peers. I just dreaded situations like going to the beach or showering in the locker room. . . .

> All through junior high and high school I felt unhappy about being "overendowed." I felt just too uncomfortable in sweaters—there was so much to reveal and I was always sure that the only reason boys liked me was because of my bustline. . . .

> By the time I was eleven I needed a bra. . . . The girls in my gym class in sixth grade laughed at me because my breasts were pretty big and I still didn't have a bra. It tried to cover myself up when I dressed and undressed. On my eleventh birthday my mom gave me a sailor blouse and inside was my first bra. . . . (It) was the best present I could have received. The bra made me feel a lot better about myself, but I was still unsure of my femininity for a long time. . . . (Morrison et al., 1980, pp. 66–70)

In some cultures, the breasts are viewed merely as biological instruments for feeding infants. In our culture, however, breasts have taken on such erotic significance that a woman's self-esteem may become linked to her bustline.

The breasts are **secondary sex characteristics.** That is, like the rounding of the hips, they distinguish women from men, but they are not directly involved in reproduction. Each breast contains 15 to 20 clusters of milk-producing **mammary glands** (see Figure 3.8). Each gland opens at the nipple through its own duct. The mammary glands are separated by soft, fatty tissue. It is the amount of this fatty tissue, not the amount of glandular tissue, that largely determines the size of the breasts. Women vary little in their amount of glandular tissue, so breast size does not determine the quantity of milk that can be produced.

It is not true that women with larger breasts produce more milk while nursing. It is the amount of fatty tissue, not the amount of glandular milk-producing tissue, that largely determines the size of the breasts. ■

Truth or Fiction? **REVISITED**

The nipple, which lies in the center of the **areola**, contains smooth muscle fibers that make the nipple become erect when they contract. The areola, or area surrounding the

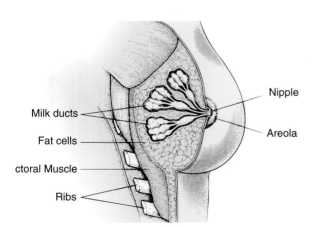

Milk ducts

Fat cells

ctoral Muscle

Ribs

Nipple

Areola

figure 3.8

A Breast of an Adult Woman. This drawing reveals the structures underlying the breast, including milk ducts and fat cells.

Secondary sex characteristics Traits that distinguish women from men but are not directly involved in reproduction.

Mammary glands Milk-secreting glands. (From the Latin *mamma*, which means both "breast" and "mother.")

Areola The dark ring on the breast that encircles the nipple.

f i g u r e 3 . 9

Normal Variations in the Size and Shape of the Breasts of Adult Women. The size and shape of the breasts have little bearing on ability to produce milk or on sensitivity to sexual stimulation. Breasts have become highly eroticized in our culture.

nipple, darkens during pregnancy and remains darker after delivery. Oil-producing glands in the areola help to lubricate the nipples during breast feeding. Milk ducts conduct milk from the mammary glands through the nipples. Nipples are richly endowed with nerve endings, so stimulation of the nipples heightens sexual arousal for many women. Male nipples are similar in sensitivity. Gay males often find nipple stimulation pleasurable. Male heterosexuals generally do not. Perhaps heterosexual men have learned to associate breast stimulation with the female sexual role. It is not that their nipples are less sensitive.

Figure 3.9 shows normal variations in the size and shape of the breasts of adult women. The sensitivity of the breasts to sexual stimulation is unrelated to their size. Small breasts may have as many nerve endings as large breasts, but they will be more densely packed. Women can prompt their partners to provide breast stimulation by informing them that their breasts are sensitive to stimulation. They can also guide a partner's hands in ways that provide the type of stimulation they desire. The breasts vary in sensitivity with the phases of the menstrual cycle, and some women appear to be less responsive to breast stimulation than others. However, some less sensitive women may learn to enjoy breast stimulation by focusing on breast sensations during lovemaking in a relaxed atmosphere.

Breast Cancer

In a recent year, it was estimated that breast cancer would strike about 178,000 women in the United States each year and take nearly 44,000 lives (Altman, 1998b, 1998d). (An estimated 240 men also die of breast cancer annually.) The disease takes the lives of nearly 3 of 10 women who develop it. It is not cancer in the breast that causes death, but rather its spread to vital body parts, such as the brain, the bones, the lungs, or the liver.

Despite the popular impression to the contrary, rates of breast cancer in the United States are not on the rise (American Cancer Society, 1995). Rather, more early cases of breast cancer are being detected because of an increased use of **mammography,** a kind of X-ray that detects cancerous lumps in the breast. Advances in early detection and treatment have led to increased rates of recovery. The five-year survival rate for women whose breast cancers have not metastasized—that is, spread beyond the breast—is near 93%, up from 78% in the 1940s (Miller et al., 1996). The five-year survival rate drops to 69% if the cancer has spread to the surrounding region and to 18% if it has spread to distant sites in the body. Overall, the five-year survival rate was about 85% in the 1990s, compared with 75% in the 1970s (Altman, 1998d).

It is not true that the incidence of breast cancer is on the rise in the United States. Instead, breast cancer is being detected earlier through means such as mammography. ■

RISK FACTORS   Breast cancer is rare in women under age 25. The risk increases sharply with age. The National Cancer Institute estimates that from birth to age 40, 1 in 217 women will develop breast cancer. By age 50, the risk rises to 1 in 50. By age 60, it rises to 1 in 24, and by age 70, to 1 in 14 (Ochs, 1993a).

The risk of breast cancer is higher among women with a family history of the disease (Slattery & Kerber, 1993). A study of more than 100,000 women nurses showed that those

Mammography A special type of X-ray test that detects cancerous lumps in the breast.

with mothers or sisters who had breast cancer had nearly twice the chance of developing the disease themselves (Colditz et al., 1993). Women who had both a mother and a sister with the disease had between two and three times greater risk. Still, about 80% of women with breast cancer have no family history of the disease. Only about 6% of the women with breast cancer in the nurses' study had either a mother or a sister with the disease (Johnson & Williams, 1993).

A key risk factor in breast cancer is prolonged exposure to estrogen, which stimulates breast development in young women and also the proliferation of breast cancer cells (Brody, 1998f). The following all heighten the risk of breast cancer because they increase the woman's exposure to estrogen: early onset of menstruation (before age 14), late menopause (after age 55), delayed childbearing (after age 30), and never giving birth (Brody, 1998f). Despite the fact that birth-control pills contain estrogen, a review of 54 studies involving more than 150,000 women concluded that there is no connection between using the pill and breast cancer (Gilbert, 1996). Exercise, by the way, appears to reduce the risk of breast cancer, apparently by decreasing the amount of fatty tissue in the body (Dreyfuss, 1998). Fat is connected with higher levels of estrogen production.

Heavy drinking of alcohol also heightens the risk of breast cancer (Brody, 1998b; Fuchs et al., 1995). It has *not* been shown that a diet that is high in fats contributes to breast cancer (Hunter et al., 1996). Nevertheless, higher amounts of fatty tissue in the body appear to be connected with breast cancer (Dreyfuss, 1998).

Does abortion increase a woman's risk of breast cancer? Some researchers have speculated that pregnancy would cause breast cells to proliferate and the abortion would prevent the cells from becoming specialized, allowing them to turn cancerous. However, carefully controlled studies do not find abortion to increase a woman's risk of breast cancer (Hartge, 1997; Melbye at al., 1997).

It is not true that women who have had abortions are at greater risk of breast cancer. ■

Truth or Fiction? REVISITED

DETECTION AND TREATMENT Women with breast cancer have lumps in the breast, *but most lumps in the breasts are not cancerous.* Most are either **cysts** or **benign** tumors called **fibroadenomas.** Breast cancer involves lumps in the breast that are **malignant.**

Early detection and treatment reduce the risk of mortality. The sooner cancer is detected, the less likely it is to have spread to critical organs.

Breast cancer may be detected in various ways, including breast self-examination, medical examination, and mammography. Through mammography, tiny, highly curable cancers can be detected—and treated—before they can be felt by touch (Brody, 1995a). By the time a malignant lump is large enough to be felt by touch, it already contains millions of cells. It may even have metastasized, that is, splintered off to form colonies elsewhere in the body. A mammography can detect tiny tumors before metastasis. One study found that 82% of women whose breast cancers were detected early by mammography survived for at least five years after surgery, compared to 60% of those whose cancers were discovered later.

Early detection may offer another benefit. Smaller cancerous lumps can often be removed by **lumpectomy,** which spares the breast. More advanced cancers are likely to be treated by **mastectomy**.

Many drugs are also used to treat breast cancer, and others are in the research pipeline. For example, *tamoxifen* locks into the estrogen receptors of breast cancer cells, thereby blocking the effects of estrogen that would otherwise stimulate the cells to grow and proliferate. The National Cancer Institute conducted experimental research with 13,338 women at high risk—because of either family history or the appearance of precancerous lesions in the breast (Altman, 1998b). However, tamoxifen increases the risks of uterine cancer and of blood clots in the lungs, along with some other side effects (see Figure 3.10 on page 80). The risks of these side effects were lowest among women below the age of 50. The drug raloxifene (sold under the brand name Evista), which is intended to treat osteoporosis and prevent heart problems in postmenopausal women (Nuland, 1998; "Study finds," 1998), has also been shown to dramatically reduce the risk of breast cancer

Cysts Saclike structures filled with fluid or diseased material.

Benign Doing little or no harm.

Fibroadenoma A benign, fibrous tumor.

Malignant Lethal; causing or likely to cause death.

Lumpectomy Surgical removal of a lump from the breast.

Mastectomy Surgical removal of the entire breast.

f i g u r e 3 . 1 0

Effects of Tamoxifen in the National Cancer Institute Study. Over the 3½ years of the study, tamoxifen reduced the risk of breast cancer by about 45%. However, it increased the risks of uterine cancer and blood clots in the lungs. The study included 13,338 women, about half of whom were assigned to tamoxifen, and half to a placebo.

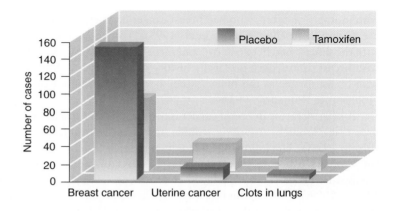

(Altman, 1998c). Moreover, raloxifene does not appear to have the side effects associated with tamoxifen. Other drugs including Taxol, which has already been approved by the Food and Drug Administration, Herceptin, and many others are also being studied for use against breast cancer (Altman, 1998d). Ask your gynecologist for the latest research results and which drugs, if any, are right for you, given your risk of breast cancer, your age, and other factors.

Many women who have had mastectomies have had surgical breast implants to replace the tissue that has been removed. Other women have breast implants to augment their breast size. Articles published in *The New England Journal of Medicine* and *The Journal of the American Medical Association* suggest that breast implants appear to have no effect on the probability of developing breast cancer (Bryant & Brasher, 1995), rheumatoid arthritis (Kolata, 1996a), and a number of other health problems (Sanchez-Guerrero et al., 1995), casting doubts on previous studies that had implicated them in the development of these problems. However, this issue remains quite controversial as this book goes to press. Readers are advised to consult their gynecologists for the latest research information.

The American Cancer Society recommends that women have a breast exam every three years when they are between 20 and 39 years of age, every one or two years between ages 40 and 49, and then annually thereafter ("Breast fears fade," 1993). They also recommend that young women receive a baseline mammogram for comparison with later tests. The mortality rate from breast cancer may be cut by 30% or more if women follow these guidelines (Brody, 1990b). Mammography is not foolproof, however. The chances of early detection are optimized through a combination of monthly breast self-examinations (see the nearby A Closer Look feature), annual breast examinations by a physician, and regular mammograms.

Questions have been raised about the recommendation that women in their 40s obtain regular mammograms. The results of a controversial 1992 Canadian study showed that women in their 40s who had received mammograms had the same death rates from breast cancer as women who did not (Kolata, 1993a, 1993c). Yet analysis of data from eight major studies, including the Canadian study, suggests that mammography in younger women can reduce their death rate from breast cancer by about 14% (Smart et al., 1995). When the results of the Canadian study are left out, analysis suggests that women of ages 40 to 49 can reduce their death rate from breast cancer by 23% (Smart et al., 1995). Mammograms reduce the death rate from breast cancer in women age 50 and above by 25% to 30%. Why the difference? It is possible that since younger women have denser breasts, mammograms in younger women are more difficult for doctors to read and so may be less reliable indicators of early cancers.

The decision as to whether a woman should have a mammogram rests with the woman and her doctor. We note, however, that only one study—the 1992 Canadian study—suggests that mammography is not of use in women under age 50. Moreover, the Canadian study has been criticized for relatively small sample size, relatively brief follow-

Good News About Breast Cancer

As we enter the new millennium, the National Cancer Institute estimates than one woman in eight will still eventually develop breast cancer (Altman, 1998b). Breast cancer remains the second leading cancer killer among women, behind lung cancer. Yet there is good news—very good news—about breast cancer. The five-year survival rate for women who develop breast cancer is now 85%, compared with 75% in the 1970s (Altman, 1998d). And if the cancer is deteced early—before it metastasizes—the five-year survival rate is about 93%, up from 78% in the 1940s (Miller et al., 1996).

More than ever is known about the development of breast cancer. Breast cancer that develops early, for example, is believed that be largely genetic, and genetic markers for early-onset breast cancer can indicate whether a particular woman is at risk (ask your gynecologist). Prolonged exposure to estrogen is a known risk factor because estrogen stimulates the proliferation of breast cancer cells as well as breast development in young women (Brody, 1998f). Exercise is believed to reduce the risk of breast cancer by decreasing the amount of fat in the body (Dreyfuss, 1998). (Estrogen is produced by fat cells as well as by the ovaries.)

Mammography also allows for the detection of tiny, highly curable cancers before they can be felt by clinical examination or touch (Brody, 1995a). Early detection allows many women to have small cancerous lumps removed by lumpectomy (surgical removal of the lump that contains the mass of cancer cells) rather than by mastectomy (removal of the entire breast).

An increasing arsenal of anti-breast-cancer medicines are also available or under development. For example, the drug *tamoxifen* locks into the estrogen receptors of breast cancer cells, thus blocking the effects of estrogen. Tamoxifen apparently reduces the probability of developing breast cancer by about 45% (Altman, 1998b). *Raloxifene* is used to treat osteoporosis and prevent heart problems in postmenopausal women (Nuland, 1998; "Study finds," 1998), but it also reduces the risk of breast cancer (Altman, 1998c). Other drugs, including *Taxol* and *Herceptin,* are being studied for use against breast cancer (Altman, 1998d).

Your gynecologist should have the latest research results. Be proactive. Seize the opportunity to evaluate whether or not you have breast cancer. There are more treatment options than ever; the survival rates are higher than ever; and earlier detection is often connected with less radical treatments.

Breast Cancer in the New Millennium. One woman in eight will eventually develop breast cancer, which remains the second leading cancer killer among women, behind lung cancer. Yet there is good news—very good news— about breast cancer. The five-year survival rate for women who develop breast cancer is now 85% as compared with 75% in the 1970s. And if the cancer is detected early— before it metastasizes—the 5-year survival rate is greater than 90%. There are more treatment options than ever before, but early detection remains the best key to survival.

ups of the women in the study, and failure to use the most up-to-date screening technology (Brody, 1995a). We therefore support the recommendations of the American Cancer Society that women of ages 40 to 50 have a mammogram every one to two years and that women age 50 and above have an annual mammogram.

The number of women who have had mammographies has risen dramatically in recent years. By 1990, three of four women over the age of 40 had at least one mammogram, up from 54% just three years earlier ("Mammograms on rise," 1992). Women who receive regular health care are more likely to also have mammograms (Siegler et al., 1995). A study of 670 Californian African American women found that women with more social ties were more likely to obtain mammograms (Kang et al., 1994). That is, people with concerned families and friends are more likely to take care of themselves.

Breast Self-Examination

Regular breast self-examination and regular visits to a physician provide the best protection against breast cancer, since they may lead to early detection and treatment. The woman should conduct a breast self-examination (see Figure 3.11) at least once a month, preferably about a week after her period ends (when the breasts are least influenced by hormones), so that any changes can be reported promptly to a physician.

The following instructions for breast self-examination are based on American Cancer Society guidelines. Additional material on breast self-examination may be obtained from the American Cancer Society by calling this toll-free number: (800) ACS-2345. However, women are advised to undertake their initial breast self-examinations with a physician to determine the degree of "lumpiness" that seems normal for them and to learn the proper technique. Breast self-examinations can be anxiety-provoking experiences, and it appears that using the proper method is essential (Zuger, 1998).

1. *In the shower.* Examine your breasts during your bath or shower; hands glide more easily over wet skin. Keep your fingers flat and move gently over every part of each breast. Use the right hand to examine the left breast and the left hand for the right breast. Check for any lump, hard knot, or thickening.
2. *Before a mirror.* Inspect your breasts with your arms at your sides. Next, raise your arms high overhead. Look for any changes in the contour of each breast, a swelling, dimpling of skin, or changes in the nipple. Then rest your palms on your hips and press down firmly to flex your chest muscles. Your left and right breasts will not exactly match—few women's breasts do. Regular inspection shows what is normal for you and will give you confidence in your examination.
3. *Lying down.* To examine your right breast, put a pillow or folded towel under your right shoulder. Place your right arm behind your head; this distributes breast tissue more evenly on the chest. With your left hand, fingers flat, press gently with the finger pads (the top thirds of the fingers) of the three middle fingers in small circular motions around an imaginary clock face. Begin at the outermost top of your right breast for 12 o'clock, then move to 1 o'clock, and so on around the circle back to 12. A ridge of firm tissue in the lower curve of each breast is normal. Then move in 1 inch, toward the nipple. Keep circling to examine *every part of your breast*, including the nipple. This requires at least three more circles. Now slowly repeat the procedure on your left breast. Place the pillow beneath your left shoulder, place your left arm behind your head, and use the finger pads on your right hand.

After you examine your left breast fully, squeeze the nipple of each breast gently between your thumb and index finger. Any discharge, clear or bloody, should be reported to your doctor immediately.

Research shows that many women who know how to do breast self-examinations do not do them regularly. Why? There are many reasons, including fear of what one will find and doubts as to whether self-examination will make a difference (Kash, 1998). But the most frequently mentioned reasons are being too busy and forgetting (Friedman et al., 1994).

figure 3.11

Woman Examining Her Breast for Lumps.

Nearly half (45%) of the women over age 40 who have not had mammograms explain that their doctors have not recommended it. Some women forgo mammograms because of the cost (Blustein, 1995). Some wonder whether their efforts at self-detection will actually be effective (Aiken et al., 1994). Others fear finding out that something is wrong. They might be encouraged to learn that more than 95% of women who receive a mammogram are given a clean bill of health. Most of the remaining 5%, moreover, show no evidence of cancer on follow-up tests. Even if cancer is present, it is best discovered and treated early.

Reflections

- Agree or disagree with the following statement and support your answer: The breasts are sex organs.
- How important is the size and shape of your breasts (or your partner's breasts) to you? Why?
- If you are a woman, what should you be doing at your age to prevent or detect breast cancer early? Are you doing everything you can? If not, why not?
- How do you believe you would react if you (or your partner) had a mastectomy? Why?

THE MENSTRUAL CYCLE

Menstruation is the cyclical bleeding that stems from the shedding of a woman's uterine lining (endometrium.) Menstruation takes place when a reproductive cycle has not led to the fertilization of an ovum. The word *menstruation* derives from the Latin *mensis*, meaning "month." The human menstrual cycle averages about 28 days in length.

The menstrual cycle is regulated by the hormones estrogen and progesterone and can be divided into four phases. During the first phase of the cycle, the *proliferative phase*, which follows menstruation, estrogen levels increase, causing the ripening of perhaps 10 to 20 ova (egg cells) within their follicles and the proliferation of endometrial tissue in the uterus. During the second phase of the cycle, estrogen reaches peak blood levels, and **ovulation** occurs. Normally, only one ovum reaches maturity and is released by an ovary during ovulation. Then the third phase—the *secretory*, or *luteal*, phase—of the cycle begins. The luteal phase begins right after ovulation and continues through the beginning of the next cycle.

The term *luteal phase* is derived from **corpus luteum,** the name given the follicle that releases an ovum. The corpus luteum functions as an **endocrine gland** and produces large amounts of progesterone and estrogen. Progesterone causes the endometrium to thicken so that it will be able to support an embryo if fertilization occurs. If the ovum goes unfertilized, however, estrogen and progesterone levels plummet. These falloffs provide the trigger for the fourth phase, the *menstrual phase*, which leads to the beginning of a new cycle.

Ovulation might not occur in every menstrual cycle. Anovulatory ("without ovulation") cycles are most common in the years just after **menarche.** They may become frequent again in the years before menopause, but they may also occur irregularly among women in their 20s and 30s.

Although the menstrual cycle averages about 28 days, variations among women, and in the same woman from month to month, are quite common. Girls' cycles are often irregular for a few years after menarche but later assume reasonably regular patterns. Variations from cycle to cycle tend to occur during the proliferative phase that precedes ovulation. That is, menstruation tends to reliably follow ovulation by about 14 days. Variations of more than 2 days in the postovulation period are rare.

Although hormones regulate the menstrual cycle, psychological factors can influence the secretion of hormones. Stress can delay or halt menstruation. Anxiety that she may be pregnant and thus miss her period may also cause a woman to be late. Many women who were in otherwise good health stopped menstruating during imprisonment in Nazi concentration camps during World War II.

Menstruation The cyclical bleeding that stems from the shedding of the uterine lining (endometrium).

Ovulation The release of an ovum from an ovary.

Corpus luteum The follicle that has released an ovum and then produces copious amounts of progesterone and estrogen during the luteal phase of a woman's cycle. (From Latin roots meaning "yellow body.")

Endocrine gland A ductless gland that releases its secretions directly into the bloodstream.

Menarche The first menstrual period.

Menstruation Versus Estrus

The menstrual cycle is found only in women, female apes, and female monkeys. It differs from an ovarian cycle, or **estrous cycle,** which occurs in "lower" mammals such as rodents, cats, and dogs. **Estrus** is the periodic sexual excitement (otherwise referred to as being "in heat") when the female is most receptive to the advances of the male. Estrus occurs when the animal is ovulating and hence most likely to conceive offspring. Women (and other female primates), however, ovulate about halfway through the cycle and may be interested in sexual activity at any time during their cycles. Estrous cycles, moreover, may be characterized by little bleeding ("spotting") or no bleeding. Menstruation typically involves a heavier flow of blood.

Regulation of the Menstrual Cycle

The menstrual cycle involves finely tuned relationships between structures in the brain—the **hypothalamus** and the **pituitary gland**—and the ovaries and uterus. All these structures are parts of the endocrine system, which means that they secrete chemicals directly into the bloodstream (see Figure 3.12). The ovaries and uterus are also reproductive organs. The chemicals secreted by endocrine glands are called **hormones.** (Other bodily secretions, such as milk, saliva, sweat, and tears, arrive at their destinations by passing through narrow, tubular structures in the body called ducts.)

Behavioral and social scientists are especially interested in hormones because of their behavioral effects. Hormones regulate bodily processes such as the metabolic rate, growth of bones and muscle, production of milk, metabolism of sugar, and storage of fats, among others. Several hormones play important roles in sexual and reproductive functions.

The gonads—the **testes** (or testicles) in the male and the ovaries in the female—secrete sex hormones directly into the bloodstream. The female gonads, the ovaries, pro-

Estrous cycle The female reproductive cycle of most mammals (other than primates), which is under hormonal control and includes a period of heat, followed by ovulation.

Estrus The periodic sexual excitement when female mammals (other than primates) are most receptive to the sexual advances of males.

Hypothalamus A bundle of neural cell bodies near the center of the brain that are involved in regulating body temperature, motivation, and emotion.

Pituitary gland The gland that secretes growth hormone, prolactin, oxytocin, and others.

Hormone A substance secreted by an endocrine gland that regulates various body functions. (From the Greek *horman,* meaning "to stimulate" or "to goad.")

Testes The male gonads.

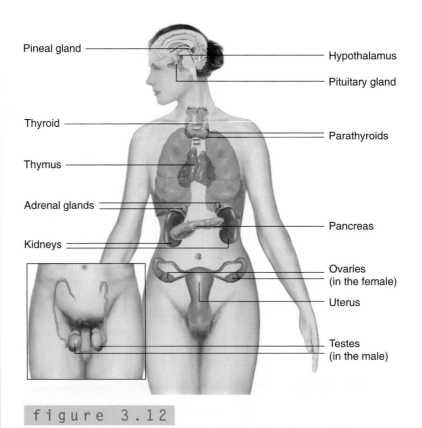

`figure 3.12`

Major Glands of the Endocrine System. The endocrine system consists of glands that secrete chemicals called hormones directly into the bloodstream.

duce the sex hormones estrogen and progesterone. The male gonads, the testes, produce the male sex hormone **testosterone.** Males and females also produce sex hormones of the other gender, but in relatively small amounts.

The hypothalamus is a pea-sized structure in the front part of the brain. It weighs about 4 to 5 grams and lies above the pituitary gland and below (hence the prefix *hypo-*, for "under") the thalamus. Despite its small size, it is involved in regulating many states of motivation, including hunger, thirst, aggression, and sex. For example, when the rear part of a male rat's hypothalamus is stimulated by an electric probe, the rat runs through its courting and mating sequence. It nibbles at a female's ears and at the back of her neck. When she responds, they copulate. Human sexuality is not so stereotyped or mechanical—although in the cases of some people who are highly routinized in their behavior, it might appear so.

The pituitary gland, which is about the size of a pea, lies below the hypothalamus at the base of the brain. Because many pituitary secretions regulate other endocrine glands, the pituitary has also been called the *master gland*. Pituitary hormones regulate bone and muscle growth and urine production. Two pituitary hormones are active during pregnancy and motherhood: **prolactin,** which stimulates production of milk; and **oxytocin,** which stimulates uterine contractions in labor and the ejection of milk during nursing. The pituitary gland also produces **gonadotropins** (literally, "that which feeds the gonads") that stimulate the ovaries: **follicle-stimulating hormone (FSH)** and **luteinizing hormone (LH).** These hormones play central roles in regulating the menstrual cycle.

The hypothalamus receives information about bodily events through the nervous and circulatory systems. It monitors the blood levels of various hormones, including estrogen and progesterone, and releases a hormone called **gonadotropin-releasing hormone (Gn-RH),** which stimulates the pituitary to release gonadotropins. Gonadotropins, in turn, regulate the activity of the gonads. It was once thought that the pituitary gland ran the show, but it is now known that the pituitary gland is regulated by the hypothalamus. Even the "master gland" must serve another.

Phases of the Menstrual Cycle

We noted that the menstrual cycle has four stages or phases: proliferative, ovulatory, secretory, and menstrual (see Figure 3.13). It might seem logical that a new cycle begins with the first day of the menstrual flow, since this is the most clearly identifiable event of

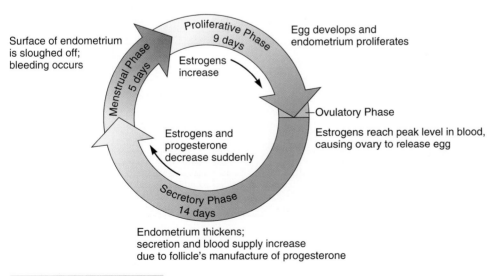

Surface of endometrium is sloughed off; bleeding occurs

Menstrual Phase 5 days

Proliferative Phase 9 days

Estrogens increase

Egg develops and endometrium proliferates

Ovulatory Phase

Estrogens reach peak level in blood, causing ovary to release egg

Estrogens and progesterone decrease suddenly

Secretory Phase 14 days

Endometrium thickens; secretion and blood supply increase due to follicle's manufacture of progesterone

figure 3.13

The Four Phases of the Menstrual Cycle. The menstrual cycle has proliferative, ovulatory, secretory (luteal), and menstrual phases.

Testosterone The male sex hormone that fosters the development of male sex characteristics and is connected with the sex drive.

Prolactin A pituitary hormone that stimulates production of milk.

Oxytocin A pituitary hormone that stimulates uterine contractions in labor and the ejection of milk during nursing.

Gonadotropins Pituitary hormones that stimulate the gonads. (Literally, "that which feeds the gonads").

Follicle-stimulating hormone (FSH) A gonadotropin that stimulates development of follicles in the ovaries.

Luteinizing hormone (LH) A gonadotropin that helps regulate the menstrual cycle by triggering ovulation.

Gonadotropin-releasing hormone (Gn-RH) A hormone secreted by the hypothalamus that stimulates the pituitary to release gonadotropins.

the cycle. Many women also count the days of the menstrual cycle beginning with the onset of menstruation. Biologically speaking, however, menstruation is really the culmination of the cycle. In fact, the cycle begins with the end of menstruation and the initiation of a series of biological events that lead to the maturation of an immature ovum in preparation for ovulation and possible fertilization.

figure 3.14

Changes That Occur during the Menstrual Cycle. This figure shows five categories of biological change: (a) changes in the development of the uterine lining (endometrium), (b) follicular changes, (c) changes in blood levels of ovarian hormones, (d) changes in blood levels of pituitary hormones, and (e) changes in basal temperature. Note the dip in temperature that is connected with ovulation.

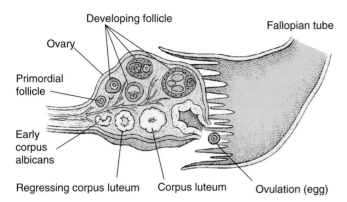

Developing follicle

Ovary

Primordial
follicle

Early
corpus
albicans

Regressing corpus luteum   Corpus luteum   Ovulation (egg)

Fallopian tube

figure 3.15

Maturation of an Ovarian Follicle. Many follicles develop
and produce estrogen during the proliferative phase of the
menstrual cycle. Usually only one, the graafian follicle, ruptures
and releases an ovum. The graafian follicle then develops into
the corpus luteum, which produces copious quantities of estrogen
and progesterone. When fertilization does not occur, the corpus
luteum decomposes.

THE PROLIFERATIVE PHASE   The first phase, or **proliferative phase,** begins with the
end of menstruation and lasts about 9 or 10 days in an average 28-day cycle (see Figures 3.13, 3.14). During this phase, the endometrium develops, or "proliferates." This
phase is also known as the *preovulatory* or *follicular* phase, because certain ovarian follicles
mature and the ovaries prepare for ovulation.

Low levels of estrogen and progesterone are circulating in the blood as menstruation
draws to an end. When the hypothalamus senses a low level of estrogen in the blood, it
increases its secretion of Gn-RH, which in turn triggers the pituitary gland to release
FSH. When FSH reaches the ovaries, it stimulates some follicles (perhaps 10 to 20) to begin to mature. As the follicles ripen, they begin to produce estrogen. Normally, however,
only one of them—called the *graafian follicle*—will reach full maturity in the days just preceding ovulation. As the graafian follicle matures, it moves toward the surface of the
ovary, where it will eventually rupture and release a mature egg (see Figures 3.14, 3.15).

Estrogen causes the endometrium in the uterus to thicken to about ⅛ inch. Glands
develop that would eventually nourish an embryo. Estrogen also stimulates the appearance of a thin cervical mucus. This mucus is alkaline and provides a hospitable, nutritious
medium for sperm. The chances are thus increased that sperm that enter the female reproductive system at the time of ovulation will remain viable.

THE OVULATORY PHASE   During ovulation, or the **ovulatory phase,** the graafian follicle ruptures and releases a mature ovum *near* a fallopian tube—not actually *into* a fallopian tube (see Figure 3.15). The other ripening follicles degenerate and are harmlessly
reabsorbed by the body. If two ova mature and are released during ovulation, which happens occasionally, and both are fertilized, fraternal (nonidentical) twins will develop.
Identical twins develop when one fertilized ovum divides into two separate **zygotes.**

Ovulation is set into motion when estrogen production reaches a critical level. The high
level of estrogen is detected by the hypothalamus, which triggers the pituitary to release copious amounts of FSH and LH (see Figure 3.14). The surge of LH triggers ovulation,
which usually begins 12 to 24 hours after the level of LH in the body has reached its peak.

The synthetic hormone **clomiphene** is chemically similar to LH and has been used
by women who ovulate irregularly to induce reliable ovulation. The induction and accurate prediction of the timing of ovulation increase the chances of conceiving.

A woman's *basal body temperature,* taken by oral or rectal thermometer, dips slightly
at ovulation (Figure 3.14) and rises by about 1 degree Fahrenheit on the day following
ovulation. Many women use this information to help them conceive or avoid conceiving.
Note, however, that Figure 3.14 is idealized. Many women show greater fluctuations in
daily temperature or gradual rises in temperature for about two days after ovulation.

Some women have discomfort or cramping during ovulation, termed **mittelschmerz.** Mittelschmerz is sometimes confused with appendicitis. Mittelschmerz, however, may occur on either side of the abdomen, depending on which ovary is releasing an
ovum. A ruptured appendix always causes pain on the right side.

THE SECRETORY PHASE   The phase following ovulation is called the postovulatory or
secretory phase. Some people refer to it as the *luteal phase,* which reflects the name

Proliferative phase The first
phase of the menstrual cycle,
which begins with the end
of menstruation and lasts
about nine or ten days. During
this phase, the endometrium
proliferates.

Ovulatory phase The second
stage of the menstrual cycle,
during which a follicle ruptures
and releases a mature ovum.

Zygote A fertilized ovum (egg
cell).

Clomiphene A synthetic hormone that is chemically similar
to LH and induces ovulation.

Mittelschmerz Pain that occurs
during ovulation. (German for
"middle pain," reflecting the
fact that the pain occurs midway
between menstrual periods).

Secretory phase The third
phase of the menstrual cycle,
which follows ovulation. Also
referred to as the *luteal phase,*
after the *corpus luteum,* which
begins to secrete large amounts
of progesterone and estrogen
following ovulation.

given the ruptured (graafian) follicle—the *corpus luteum*. Figures 3.14 and 3.15 show the transformation of the graafian follicle into the corpus luteum.

Under the influence of LH, the corpus luteum, which has remained in the ovary, begins to produce large amounts of progesterone and estrogen. Levels of these hormones peak at around the 20th or 21st day of an average cycle (see Figure 3.14). These hormones cause the glands in the endometrium to secrete nutrients to sustain a fertilized ovum that becomes implanted in the uterine wall.

If implantation does not occur, the hypothalamus responds to the peak levels of progesterone in the blood by signaling the pituitary to stop producing LH and FSH. Although certainly more complex, this feedback process is similar to that of a thermostat in a house reacting to rising temperatures by shutting down the furnace. The levels of LH and FSH decline rapidly, leading the corpus luteum to decompose. After its decomposition, levels of estrogen and progesterone fall precipitously. In this sense, the corpus luteum sows the seeds of its own destruction: Its hormones signal the brain to shut down secretion of substances that maintain it.

THE MENSTRUAL PHASE: AN END AND A BEGINNING   The **menstrual phase** is the sloughing off of the uterine lining (the endometrium) in the menstrual flow. Menstruation occurs when estrogen and progesterone levels decline to the point at which they can no longer sustain the uterine lining. The lining then disintegrates and is discharged from the body along with the menstrual flow. Menstruation itself is the passing of the lining through the cervix and vagina.

The low estrogen levels of the menstrual phase signal the hypothalamus to release Gn-RH, which in turn stimulates the pituitary to secrete FSH. FSH, in turn, prompts ovarian secretion of estrogen and the onset of another proliferative phase. Thus, a new cycle begins. The menstrual phase is a beginning as well as an end.

Menstrual flow contains blood from the endometrium (uterine lining), endometrial tissue, and cervical and vaginal mucus. Although the flow can appear persistent and last for five days or more, most women lose only a total of 2 or 3 ounces of blood (4 to 6 tablespoonfuls). A typical blood donor, by contrast, donates 16 ounces of blood at a sitting. A woman's blood loss through menstruation is therefore usually harmless. Extremely heavy or prolonged (over a week) menstrual bleeding may reflect health problems and should be discussed with a health care provider.

Before 1933, women generally used external sanitary napkins or pads to absorb the menstrual flow. In that year, however, **tampons** were introduced and altered the habits of millions of women. Women who use tampons can swim without concern while menstruating, wear more revealing or comfortable apparel, and feel generally less burdened.

Tampons are inserted into the vagina and left in place to absorb menstrual fluid. In recent years, questions have arisen about whether or not tampons cause or exacerbate infections. For example, tampon use has been linked to toxic shock syndrome (TSS), an infection that is sometimes fatal. Signs of TSS include fever, headache, sore throat, vomiting, diarrhea, muscle aches, rash, and dizziness. Peeling skin, disorientation, and a plunge in blood pressure may follow.

TSS is caused by the *Staphylococcus aureus* ("staph") bacterium. In 1980, the peak year for cases of TSS, there were 344 recorded cases of TSS and 28 fatalities. Procter & Gamble removed its "extra absorbent" tampon Rely from the market when it was discovered that 71% of these TSS victims had used the product. Plugging the vagina with a highly absorbent tampon that remains in place for six hours or more may create an ideal breeding ground for staph. The number of TSS cases has declined dramatically since then.

Some researchers believe that concern over TSS has been exaggerated. Nevertheless, many women now use regular rather than superabsorbent tampons to reduce the chance of creating a breeding ground for staph bacteria. Some women alternate tampons with sanitary napkins during each day of menstruation. Some change their tampons three or four times a day. These alternatives may also present problems, however. If more tampons are used, the increased number of insertions may increase the chances of transferring staph from the fingers or vaginal opening into the vagina. Other women have returned to

Menstrual phase The fourth phase of the menstrual cycle, during which the endometrium is sloughed off in the menstrual flow.

Tampon A cylindrical plug of cotton that is inserted into the vagina and left in place to absorb menstrual fluid. (A French word, meaning a gun barrel "plug.")

HISTORICAL AND CROSS-CULTURAL PERSPECTIVES ON MENSTRUATION

In Peru, they speak of a "visit from Uncle Pepe," whereas in Samoa, menstruation is referred to as "the boogie man." One of the more common epithets given to menstruation through the course of history is "the curse." The Fulani of Upper Volta in Africa use a term for it that translates "to see dirt." Nationalism also rises to the call, with some nations blaming "the curse" on their historical enemies. In earlier times, the French referred to menstruation as "the English" and to its onset as "the English are coming."

It is a common folk belief that menstruating women are contaminated. Men therefore avoid contact with menstruating women for fear of their lives. To prevent their contaminating others, menstruating women in tribal societies may be dispatched to special huts on the fringe of the village. In the traditional Navajo Indian culture, for instance, menstruating women would be consigned to huts that were set apart from other living quarters. In many Islamic societies, a menstruating woman is considered polluted and is not permitted either to pray or to enter a mosque.

Women in industrialized nations are not consigned to special huts, but throughout the history of Western culture, menstruation has been seen as unclean, contaminating, and even magical. In A.D. 77, the Roman historian Pliny summed up Roman misbeliefs about menstrual blood:

> Contact with it turns new wine sour, crops touched by it become barren, grafts die, seeds in gardens are dried up, the fruit of trees falls off. . . . [The] edge of steel and the gleam of ivory are dulled, hives of bees die, even bronze and iron are at once seized by rust, and a horrible smell fills the air; to taste it drives dogs mad and infects their bites with an incurable poison.

Truth or Fiction? REVISITED

Yes, the ancient Romans did believe that menstrual blood soured wine and killed crops. Negative views of menstruation and menstrual blood have persisted throughout history. ■

The Old Testament (Leviticus 15:19) warns against any physical contact with a menstruating woman, including, of course, coitus:

> And if a woman have an issue, and her issue in her flesh be blood, she shall be put apart seven days; and whosoever toucheth her shall be unclean.

Orthodox Jews still abstain from coitus during menstruation and the week afterward. Before resuming sexual relations, the woman must attend a *mikvah*—a ritual cleansing in which the genitals are washed and all foreign substances are removed. Such practices are grounded in religious tradition, not science. The attitudes of people in ancient and present-day preliterate societies toward menstruation should be understood in terms of their limited understanding of bodily processes. Because they lack knowledge that menstruation is a part of the woman's natural menstrual cycle, they may regard the flow of blood from a woman's loins as a sign of filth or contamination and believe that it is healthier for others to temporarily avoid physical contact with her. Science teaches that there is no medical basis to these fears and that there are no dangers in menstrual coitus—despite the persistence of superstition.

Fears of contamination by menstruating women are nearly universal across cultures and remain quite current in some circles. As late as the 1950s, women were not allowed in some European breweries for fear that the beer would turn sour. Some Indian castes still teach that a man who touches a woman during menses becomes contaminated and must be purified by a priest.

We might laugh off these misconceptions as folly and ignorance if it were not for their profound effect on women. Women who believe the myths about menstruation may see themselves as sources of pollution and endure anxiety, depression, and lowered self-esteem. Negative cultural beliefs concerning menstruation may also contribute to menstrual distress.

external sanitary napkins. Still others use natural sponges. Women are encouraged to consult their health care providers about TSS.

Coitus During Menstruation

Many couples continue to engage in coitus during menstruation, but others abstain. One study found that men and women are less likely to initiate sexual activity during menstruation than during any other phase of the woman's cycle (Harvey, 1987). Some people abstain because of religious prohibitions. Others express concern about the "fuss" or the "mess" of the menstrual flow. Despite traditional attitudes that associate menstruation with uncleanliness, there is no evidence that coitus during menstruation is physically harmful to either partner. Ironically, menstrual coitus may be helpful to the woman. The uterine contractions that occur during orgasm may help to relieve cramping by dispelling blood congestion. Orgasm achieved through masturbation may have the same effect.

Women may be sexually aroused at any time during the menstrual cycle. The preponderance of the research evidence, however, points to a peak in sexual desire in women around the time of ovulation (Kresin, 1993).

a CLOSER l o o k

Myths About Menopause

Menopause is certainly a major life change for most women. For many women, menopause symbolizes the many midlife issues they face, including changes in appearance, sexuality, and health (Jones, 1994). Yet exactly what types of changes do we find? Many of us harbor misleading ideas about menopause—ideas that can be harmful to women. Consider the following myths and the realities. To which myths have you fallen prey?

Myth 1: *Menopause is abnormal.* Of course not. Menopause is a normal development in women's lives.

Myth 2: *The medical establishment considers menopause a disease.* No longer. Menopause is described as a "deficiency syndrome" today, referring to the decline in secretion of estrogen and progesterone. Unfortunately, the term *deficiency* also has negative meanings.

Myth 3: *After menopause, women need complete replacement of estrogen.* Not necessarily. Some estrogen continues to be produced by the adrenal glands, fatty tissue, and the brain.

Myth 4: *Menopause is accompanied by depression and anxiety.* Not necessarily. Karen Matthews and her colleagues (1990) followed 541 healthy women through menopause and found that menopause was not significantly connected to depression, anxiety, stress, anger, or job dissatisfaction. (Outcomes may differ for women who have psychological problems before menopause.) Another group of researchers reported finding no overall relation-

ship between mental health symptoms and menopausal status in a sample of 522 African American women (Jackson et al., 1991).

Much of a woman's response to menopause reflects its meaning to her, not physical changes (Jones, 1994). Women who adopt the commonly held belief that menopause signals the beginning of the end of life may develop a sense of hopelessness about the future, which in turn can set the stage for depression. Women whose entire lives have centered on childbearing and childrearing are more likely to experience a sense of loss. Moreover, there is a cultural bias to explain depression and other problems of middle-aged women in terms of menopause, rather than to explore psychosocial factors.

Myth 5: *At menopause, women experience debilitating hot flashes.* Many women do not have hot flashes. Among those who do, the flashes are often relatively mild.

It is not necessarily true that women at menopause experience debilitating hot flashes. Many women have none at all. For most of those who do, hot flashes are mild. ■

Myth 6: *Menopause signals an end to a woman's sexual appetite.* Not at all. Many women feel liberated by the severing of the ties between sex and reproduction.

Human coital patterns during the phases of the menstrual cycle apparently reflect personal decisions, not hormone fluctuations. Some couples may decide to increase their frequency of coitus at ovulation to optimize the chances of conceiving or may abstain during menstruation because of religious beliefs or beliefs linking menses with uncleanliness. Some may also increase their coital activity preceding menstruation to compensate for anticipated abstinence during menses or increase coital activity afterwards to make up for deprivation. In contrast, females of other species that are bound by the estrous cycle respond sexually only during estrus, except in relatively rare cases in which the female submits to sexual advances to fend off attacks from an aggressive male.

Menopause

Menopause, or the "change of life," is the cessation of menstruation. Menopause is a process that most commonly occurs between the ages of 46 and 50 and lasts for about two years. However, it may begin any time between the ages of 35 and 60. There is at least one case of a woman who became pregnant at age 61.

Menopause is a specific event in a long-term process known as the **climacteric** ("critical period"), which refers to the gradual decline in the reproductive capacity of the ovaries. The climacteric generally lasts for about 15 years, from ages 45 to 60 or so. After about the age of 35, the menstrual cycles of many women shorten, from an average of 28 days to 25 days at age 40 and to 23 days by the mid-40s. By the end of her 40s, a woman's cycles often become erratic, with some periods close together and others missed.

Menopause The cessation of menstruation.

Climacteric A long-term process, including menopause, that involves the gradual decline in the reproductive capacity of the ovaries.

Menopause and Sexuality. Menopause does not mark the end of a woman's sex life. Many women, in fact, feel sexually liberated by the biological severing of the traditional link between sexual activity and reproduction.

Truth or Fiction? REVISITED

It is not true that menopause signals an end to a woman's sexual appetite. In fact, some women feel newly sexually liberated because of the separation of sex from reproduction. ■

Myth 7: *Menopause ends a woman's childbearing years.* Not necessarily! Postmenopausal women do not produce ova.

However, ova from donors have been fertilized in laboratory dishes, and the developing embryos have been implanted in the uteruses of postmenopausal women and carried to term (Bohlen, 1995; Sauer et al., 1990).

Myth 8: *A woman's general level of activity is lower after menopause.* Many postmenopausal women become peppier and more assertive

In menopause, the pituitary gland continues to pour normal levels of FSH and LH into the bloodstream, but for reasons that are not well understood, the ovaries gradually lose their capacity to respond. The ovaries no longer ripen egg cells or produce the sex hormones estrogen and progesterone.

The deficit in estrogen may lead to a number of unpleasant physical sensations, such as night sweats and hot flashes (suddenly feeling hot) and hot flushes (suddenly looking reddened). Hot flashes and flushes may alternate with cold sweats, in which a woman feels suddenly cold and clammy. Anyone who has experienced "cold feet" or cold hands from anxiety or fear will understand how dramatic the shifting patterns of blood flow can be. Hot flashes and flushes stem largely from "waves" of dilation of blood vessels across the face and upper body. All of these sensations reflect "vasomotor instability." That is, there are disruptions in the body mechanisms that dilate or constrict the blood vessels to maintain an even body temperature. Additional signs of estrogen deficiency include dizziness, headaches, pains in the joints, sensations of tingling in the hands or feet, burning or itchy skin, and heart palpitations. The skin usually becomes drier. There is some loss of breast tissue and decreased vaginal lubrication during sexual arousal. Women may also encounter sleep problems, such as awakening more frequently at night and having difficulty falling back to sleep.

Long-term estrogen deficiency has been linked to brittleness and porosity of the bones—a condition called **osteoporosis** (Delmas et al., 1997) Bones break more readily, and some women develop so-called dowager's hump. Osteoporosis can be severely handicapping, even life threatening. The increased brittleness of the bones increases the risk

Osteoporosis A condition caused by estrogen deficiency and characterized by a decline in bone density, such that bones become porous and brittle. (From the Greek *osteon*, meaning "bone," and the Latin *porus*, meaning "pore.")

of serious fractures, especially of the hip, and many older women never recover from these fractures (Eastell, 1998).

Estrogen deficiency also has psychological effects. It can impair cognitive functioning and feelings of psychological well-being (Sourander, 1994).

HORMONE-REPLACEMENT THERAPY (HRT)   Some women who experience severe physical symptoms have been helped by **hormone-replacement therapy (HRT),** which typically consists of synthetic estrogen and progesterone. These synthetic hormones are used to offset the losses of their naturally occurring counterparts. HRT may help reduce the hot flushes and other symptoms brought about by hormonal deficiencies during menopause. It is especially helpful in preventing the development of osteoporosis (Davidson, 1995; Delmas et al., 1997). Drinking milk, which is high in calcium, increases bone density among girls and is likely to help prevent osteoporosis later in life. Calcium supplements also seem to be helpful in decreasing the number of bone fractures among postmenopausal women (Eastell, 1998).

HRT is not without controversy. Although HRT has certainly been helpful to many menopausal women, exposure to estrogen increases the risk of some kinds of cancer, especially breast cancer (Brody, 1997c; Frank & Wenger, 1997). On the other hand, estrogen replacement lowers the woman's risk of cardiovascular disorders (heart and artery disease) (Grodstein et al., 1996), osteoporosis (Davidson, 1995; Eastell, 1998), colon cancer (Newcomb & Storer, 1995), and even Alzheimer's disease (Brody, 1997c). HRT may reduce the risk of cardiovascular disease by lowering cholesterol levels (Delmas et al., 1997). A study of 49,000 postmenopausal nurses found that HRT was connected with 44% fewer heart attacks and a reduced risk of death from heart disease of 39% (Stampfer et al., 1991). Estrogen remains beneficial for the heart even when it is combined with progestin (Grodstein et al., 1996).

Hormone-replacement therapy is usually not recommended for women who have a family history of breast cancer. On the other hand, researchers are attempting to develop estrogen compounds that will have the benefits of estrogen without the health risks (e.g., of uterine and breast cancer) (Brody, 1997b; Fuleihan, 1997). Women are advised to explore the health benefits and risks of HRT with their gynecologists.

Overall, only about one postmenopausal woman in four in the United States chooses to use HRT, and of these, only half will remain on HRT for more than a few years (Brody, 1997c; Frank & Wenger, 1997). In what could be considered a vote of confidence for HRT, it turns out that nearly half (47%) of postmenopausal women doctors use HRT—women gynecologists, who know the most about HRT, being the most likely subgroup to use it (Frank & Wenger, 1997). For women who do not receive replacement hormones, other drugs are available, when they are needed, to help them deal with menopausal problems, such as hot flashes.

MENSTRUAL PROBLEMS

Although menstruation is a natural biological process, the majority of women experience some discomfort before or during menstruation. Table 3.1 contains a list of commonly reported symptoms of menstrual problems. The problems we explore in this section include dysmenorrhea, mastalgia, menstrual migraine headaches, amenorrhea, and premenstrual syndrome (PMS).

Dysmenorrhea

Pain or discomfort during menstruation, or **dysmenorrhea,** is the most common type of menstrual problem. Most women at some time have at least mild menstrual pain or discomfort. Pelvic cramps are the most common manifestation of dysmenorrhea. They may be accompanied by headache, backache, nausea, or bloated feelings. Women who develop severe cases usually do so within a few years of menarche. **Primary dysmenorrhea** refers

Hormone-replacement therapy (HRT) Replacement of naturally occurring estrogen or estrogen and progesterone with synthetic equivalents, following menopause.

Dysmenorrhea Pain or discomfort during menstruation.

Primary dysmenorrhea Menstrual pain or discomfort that occurs in the absence of known organic problems.

Symptoms of menstrual problems	
Physical Symptoms	**Psychological Symptoms**
Swelling of the breasts	Depressed mood, sudden tearfulness
Tenderness in the breasts	Loss of interest in usual social or recreational activities
Bloating	Anxiety, tension (feeling "on edge" or "keyed up")
Weight gain	
Food cravings	Anger
Abdominal discomfort	Irritability
Cramping	Changes in body image
Lack of energy	Concern over skipping routine activities, school, or work
Sleep disturbance, fatigue	
Migraine headache	A sense of loss of control
Pains in muscles and joints	A sense of loss of ability to cope
Aggravation of chronic disorders such as asthma and allergies	

to menstrual pain or discomfort in the absence of known organic pathology. Women with **secondary dysmenorrhea** have identified organic problems that are believed to cause their menstrual problems. Their pain or discomfort is caused by, or *secondary to*, these problems. Endometriosis, pelvic inflammatory disease, and ovarian cysts are just a few of the organic disorders that can give rise to secondary dysmenorrhea. Yet evidence is accumulating that supposed primary dysmenorrhea is often *secondary* to hormonal changes, although the precise causes have not been delineated. For example, menstrual cramps sometimes decrease dramatically after childbirth as a result of the massive hormonal changes that occur with pregnancy.

Painful menstruation was reported by nearly 75% of the participants in a sample of college women (Wildman & White, 1986). The symptoms varied not only from person to person but also according to whether or not the women had been pregnant. Women who had been pregnant reported a lower incidence of menstrual pain but a higher incidence of premenstrual symptoms and menstrual discomfort.

BIOLOGICAL ASPECTS OF DYSMENORRHEA   Menstrual cramps appear to result from uterine spasms that may be brought about by copious secretion of hormones called **prostaglandins.** Prostaglandins apparently cause muscle fibers in the uterine wall to contract, as during labor. Most contractions go unnoticed, but powerful, persistent contractions are discomfiting in themselves and may temporarily deprive the uterus of oxygen, another source of distress. Women with more intense menstrual discomfort apparently produce higher quantities of prostaglandins. Prostaglandin-inhibiting drugs, such as ibuprofen, indomethacin, and aspirin are thus often of help. Menstrual pain may also be secondary to endometriosis.

Pelvic pressure and bloating may be traced to pelvic edema (Greek for "swelling")— the congestion of fluid in the pelvic region. Fluid retention can lead to a gain of several pounds, sensations of heaviness, and **mastalgia**—a swelling of the breasts that sometimes causes premenstrual discomfort. Masters and Johnson (1966) noted that orgasm (through coitus or masturbation) can help to relieve menstrual discomfort by reducing the pelvic congestion that spawns bloating and pressure. Orgasm may also increase the menstrual flow and shorten this phase of the cycle.

Headaches frequently accompany menstrual discomfort. Most headaches (in both sexes) stem from simple muscle tension, notably in the shoulders, the back of the neck, and the scalp. Pelvic discomfort may cause muscle contractions, thus contributing to the

Secondary dysmenorrhea Menstrual pain or discomfort that is caused by identified organic problems.

Prostaglandins Hormones that cause muscle fibers in the uterine wall to contract, as during labor.

Mastalgia A swelling of the breasts that sometimes causes premenstrual discomfort.

tension that produces headaches. Women who are tense about their menstrual flow are therefore candidates for muscle tension headaches. Migraine headaches may arise from changes in the blood flow in the brain, however. Migraines are typically limited to one side of the head and are often accompanied by visual difficulties.

Amenorrhea

Amenorrhea is the absence of menstruation and is a primary sign of infertility. **Primary amenorrhea** describes the absence of menstruation in a woman who has not menstruated at all by about the age of 16 or 17. **Secondary amenorrhea** describes delayed or absent menstrual periods in women who have had regular periods in the past. Amenorrhea has various causes, including abnormalities in the structures of the reproductive system, hormonal abnormalities, growths such as cysts and tumors, and psychological problems, such as stress. Amenorrhea is normal during pregnancy and after menopause. Amenorrhea is also a symptom of **anorexia nervosa,** an eating disorder characterized by an intense fear of putting on weight and a refusal to eat enough to maintain a normal body weight, which often results in extreme (and sometimes life-threatening) weight loss. Hormonal changes that accompany emaciation are believed to be responsible for the cessation of menstruation. Amenorrhea may also occur in women who exercise strenuously, such as competitive long-distance runners. It is unclear whether the cessation of menstruation in female athletes is due to the effects of strenuous exercise itself, to related physical factors such as low body fat, to the stress of intensive training, or to a combination of factors.

Premenstrual Syndrome (PMS)

The term **premenstrual syndrome (PMS)** describes the combination of biological and psychological symptoms that may affect women during the four- to six-day interval that precedes their menses each month (see Table 3.2). For many women, premenstrual symptoms persist during menstruation.

Nearly three women in four experience some premenstrual symptoms (Brody, 1996). The great majority of cases involve mild to moderate levels of discomfort. Only about 2.5% of women report menstrual symptoms severe enough to impair their social, academic, or occupational functioning (Mortola, 1998), and that is when the term *premenstrual syndrome* is usually applied.

PMS is not unique to our culture. Researchers find premenstrual symptoms to be equally prevalent among women studied in the United States, Italy, and the Islamic nation of Bahrain (Brody, 1992b).

Amenorrhea The absence of menstruation.

Primary amenorrhea Lack of menstruation in a woman who has never menstruated.

Secondary amenorrhea Lack of menstruation in a woman who has previously menstruated.

Anorexia nervosa A psychological disorder of eating characterized by intense fear of putting on weight and refusal to eat enough to maintain normal body weight.

Premenstrual syndrome (PMS) A combination of physical and psychological symptoms (e.g., anxiety, depression, irritability, weight gain from fluid retention, and abdominal discomfort) that regularly afflicts many women during the four- to six-day interval that precedes their menses each month.

t a b l e   3 . 2

Symptoms of PMS*	
Depression	Overeating or cravings for certain foods
Anxiety	Insomnia or too much sleeping
Mood swings	Feelings of being out of control or overwhelmed
Anger and irritability	
Loss of interest in usual activities	Physical problems such as headaches, tenderness in the breasts, joint or muscle pain, weight gain or feeling bloated (both from fluid retention)
Difficulty concentrating	
Lack of energy	

*Most women experience only a few of these symptoms, if they experience any at all.

Source of data: Jane E. Brody (1996, August 28). PMS need not be the worry it was just decades ago. *The New York Times,* p. C9.

The causes of PMS are unclear, but evidence is accumulating for a biological basis. Researchers are looking to possible relationships between menstrual problems, including PMS, and chemical imbalances in the body. Researchers have yet to find differences in levels of estrogen or progesterone between women with severe PMS and those with mild symptoms or no symptoms (Mortola, 1998; Rubinow & Schmidt, 1995). Research suggests that it is not the levels of these hormones themselves that contribute to PMS, but rather an abnormal response to the presence of these hormones (Schmidt et al., 1998). PMS also appears to be linked with imbalances in neurotransmitters such as serotonin (Mortola, 1998; Steiner et al., 1995). (Neurotransmitters are the chemical messengers in the nervous system.) Serotonin imbalances are also linked to changes in appetite. Women with PMS show greater increases of appetite during the luteal phase than other women do. Another neurotransmitter, gamma-aminobutyric acid (GABA), also appears to be involved in PMS, because medicines that affect the levels of GABA help many women with PMS (Mortola, 1998). Premenstrual syndrome may well be caused by a complex interaction between ovarian hormones and neurotransmitters (Mortola, 1998).

Only a generation ago, PMS was seen as something a woman must put up with. No longer. Today there are many treatment options. These include exercise, dietary control (for example, eating several small meals a day rather than two or three large meals; limiting salt and sugar; vitamin supplements), hormone treatments (usually progesterone), and medications that reduce anxiety or increase the amount of serotonin in the nervous system (Mortola, 1998). If you have PMS, get in touch with the kinds of symptoms that affect you most through use of a PMS calendar or simply paying close attention to what happens. Then check with your physician about the most up-to-date treatment approaches.

How to Handle Menstrual Discomfort

Most women experience some degree of menstrual discomfort. Women with persistent menstrual distress may profit from the suggestions listed below. Researchers are exploring the effectiveness of these techniques in controlled studies. For now, you might consider running a personal experiment. Adopt the techniques that sound right for you—all of them, if you wish. Try them out for a few months to find out whether you reap any benefits. Such personal experiments are uncontrolled, and it is scientifically difficult to pin down the reasons for results. (You might feel better simply because you *expect* to do so or because of overall improvements in health.) Still, the methods might enhance your comfort, your health, and your outlook on menstruation—not bad outcomes at all!

1. Don't blame yourself! Menstrual problems were once erroneously attributed to women's "hysterical" nature. This is nonsense. Menstrual problems appear, in large part, to reflect hormonal variations or chemical fluctuations in the brain during the menstrual cycle. Researchers have not yet fully identified all the causal elements and patterns, but their lack of knowledge does not mean that women who have menstrual problems are hysterical.

2. Keep a menstrual calendar so that you can track your menstrual symptoms systematically and identify patterns.

3. Develop strategies for dealing with days that you experience the greatest distress—strategies that will help to enhance your pleasure and minimize the stress affecting you on those days. Activities that distract you from your menstrual discomfort may be helpful. Go see a movie or get into that novel you've been meaning to read.

Exercise as a Strategy for Coping with Menstrual Discomfort. Some women find that vigorous exercise helps relieve menstrual discomfort.

4. Ask yourself whether you harbor any self-defeating attitudes toward menstruation that might be compounding distress. Do close relatives or friends see menstruation as an illness, a time of "pollution," a "dirty thing"? Have you adopted any of these attitudes—if not verbally, then in ways that affect your behavior, such as by restricting your social activities during your period?

5. See a doctor about your concerns, especially if you have severe symptoms. Severe menstrual symptoms are often secondary to medical disorders such as endometriosis and pelvic inflammatory disease (PID). Check it out.

6. Develop nutritious eating habits—and continue them throughout the entire cycle (that means always). Consider limiting intake of alcohol, caffeine, fats, salt, and sweets, especially during the days preceding menstruation.

7. Eat several smaller meals (or nutritious snacks) throughout the day, rather than a few highly filling meals.

8. Some women find that vigorous exercise—jogging, swimming, bicycling, fast walking, dancing, skating, even jumping rope—helps to relieve premenstrual and menstrual discomfort. Evidence suggests that exercise helps to relieve and possibly prevent menstrual discomfort (Choi, 1992). By the way, develop regular exercise habits—Don't seek to become solely a premenstrual athlete.

9. Check with your doctor about vitamin and mineral supplements (such as calcium and magnesium). Vitamin B_6 appears to have helped some women.

10. Ibuprofen (brand names: Medipren, Advil, Motrin, etc.) and other over-the-counter medicines may be helpful for cramping. Prescription drugs such as antianxiety drugs (e.g., alprazolam) and antidepressant drugs (serotonin-reuptake inhibitors) may also be of help (Mortola, 1998). Ask your doctor for a recommendation.

11. Remind yourself that menstrual problems are time limited. Don't worry about getting through life or a career. Just get through the next couple of days.

Reflections

■ What are the phases of the menstrual cycle?
■ Are any particular attitudes toward menstruation held by most people from your sociocultural background? What are they? Do you share these attitudes? Why or why not?
■ Would you engage in coitus during menstruation? Why or why not?
■ Do you connect menopause with a woman's femininity? Why or why not?
■ Do you (or your loved ones) experience menstrual problems? Have they been discussed with a health care specialist? If not, why not?

In this chapter, we have explored female sexual anatomy and physiology. In the following chapter, we turn our attention to those of the male.

s u m m i n g   u p

EXTERNAL SEX ORGANS

The female external sexual structures are collectively known as the vulva and consist of the mons veneris, labia majora and minora, the clitoris, the vestibule, and the vaginal opening.

The Mons Veneris
The mons veneris consists of fatty tissue that covers the joint of the pubic bones in front of the body.

The Labia Majora
The labia majora are large folds of skin that run downward from the mons along the sides of the vulva.

The Labia Minora
The labia minora are hairless, light-colored membranes that surround the urethral and vaginal openings.

The Clitoris
The clitoris is the female sex organ that is most sensitive to sexual sensation, but it is not directly involved in reproduction.

The Vestibule
The vestibule contains the openings to the vagina and the urethra.

The Urethral Opening
Urine passes from the female's body through the urethral opening.

The Vaginal Opening
The vaginal opening, or introitus, lies below the urethral opening.

The Perineum
The perineum is the area that lies between the vaginal opening and the anus.

Structures That Underlie the External Sexual Structures
These structures include the vestibular bulbs, Bartholin's glands, the sphincters, the clitoral crura, and the pubococcygeus (P-C) muscle.

INTERNAL SEX ORGANS
The internal female sex organs—or female reproductive system—include the innermost parts of the vagina, the cervix, the uterus, the ovaries, and the fallopian tubes.

The Vagina
Menstrual flow and babies pass from the uterus to the outer world through the vagina. During coitus, the vagina contains the penis.

The Cervix
The cervix is the lower end of the uterus.

The Uterus
The uterus or womb is the pear-shaped organ in which a fertilized ovum implants and develops until birth.

The Fallopian Tubes
Two fallopian tubes extend from the upper end of the uterus toward the ovaries. Ova pass through the fallopian tubes on their way to the uterus and are normally fertilized within these tubes.

The Ovaries
The ovaries lie on either side of the uterus and produce ova and the sex hormones estrogen and progesterone.

The Pelvic Examination
Regular pelvic examinations are essential for early detection of problems involving the reproductive tract.

THE BREASTS
In some cultures, a woman's breasts are viewed merely as biological instruments for feeding infants. In our culture, however, they have taken on erotic significance. The breasts are secondary sex characteristics that contain mammary glands.

Breast Cancer
Breast cancer is the second leading cancer killer in women, after lung cancer. Women with breast cancer will have lumps in the breast, but most lumps in the breasts are benign. Breast cancer may be detected in a number of ways, including breast self-examination, medical examinations, and mammography. Early detection yields the greatest chance of survival.

THE MENSTRUAL CYCLE
Menstruation is the cyclical bleeding that stems from the shedding of the endometrium when a reproductive cycle has not led to the fertilization of an ovum. The menstrual cycle is regulated by estrogen and progesterone.

Regulation of the Menstrual Cycle
The menstrual cycle involves finely tuned relationships between the hypothalamus, the pituitary gland, and the ovaries and uterus. Hormones produced by the hypothalamus regulate the pituitary, which in turn secretes hormones that regulate the secretions of the ovaries and uterus.

Phases of the Menstrual Cycle
The menstrual cycle has four stages or phases: proliferative, ovulatory, secretory, and menstrual. During the first phase of the cycle, which follows menstruation, ova ripen within their follicles and endometrial tissue proliferates. During the second phase, ovulation occurs. During the third phase, the corpus luteum produces copious amounts of progesterone and estrogen that cause the endometrium to thicken. If the ovum goes unfertilized, a plunge in estrogen and progesterone levels triggers the fourth, or menstrual, phase, which leads to the beginning of a new cycle.

Coitus During Menstruation
Couples are apparently less likely to initiate sexual activity during menstruation than during any other phase of the woman's cycle.

Menopause
Menopause is the cessation of menstruation, which most commonly occurs between the ages of 46 and 50. Estrogen deficiency in menopause may give rise to night sweats, hot flashes, hot flushes, cold sweats, dry skin, loss of breast tissue, and decreased vaginal lubrication. Long-term estrogen deficiency has been linked to osteoporosis. Hormone-replacement therapy can offset losses of estrogen and progesterone but has been linked to a slightly increased risk of breast and endometrial cancers, though also to a marked reduction in risk of cardiovascular disease and osteoporosis. For most women, menopausal problems are mild. Psychological problems can reflect the meaning of menopause to the individual.

MENSTRUAL PROBLEMS
Most women experience some discomfort before or during menstruation. Common menstrual problems include dysmenorrhea, amenorrhea, and premenstrual syndrome (PMS).

Dysmenorrhea
Dysmenorrhea is the most common menstrual problem, and pelvic cramps are the most common symptom. Dysmenorrhea can be caused by problems such as endometriosis, pelvic inflammatory disease, and ovarian cysts.

Amenorrhea
Amenorrhea can be caused by problems such as abnormalities in the structures of the reproductive system, hormonal abnormalities, cysts, tumors, and stress.

Premenstrual Syndrome (PMS)
As many as three women in four have some form of PMS. The causes of PMS are unclear, but most researchers look to potential links between menstrual problems and hormone levels.

How to Handle Menstrual Distress
Women with persistent menstrual problems may benefit from a number of active coping strategies for handling menstrual distress.

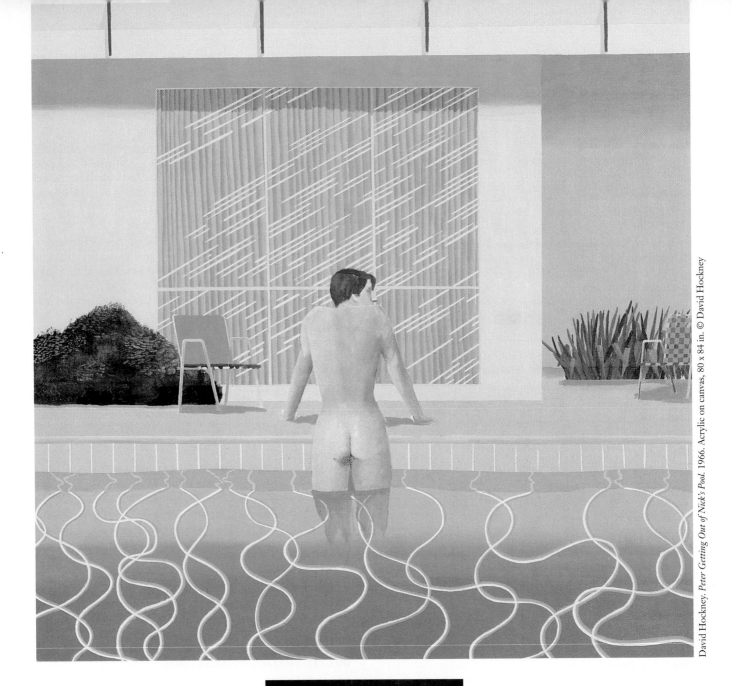

chapter

4

Male Sexual Anatomy

and Physiology

outline

TRUTH OR FICTION?

EXTERNAL SEX ORGANS

The Penis

The Scrotum

A CLOSER LOOK:
On Penis Size and Sexual Performance

INTERNAL SEX ORGANS

The Testes

A CLOSER LOOK:
Is There a Man*opause?*

A CLOSER LOOK:
Big

The Vas Deferens

The Seminal Vesicles

The Prostate Gland

Cowper's Glands

Semen

**DISEASES OF THE
UROGENITAL SYSTEM**

Urethritis

Cancer of the Testes

A CLOSER LOOK:
Self-Examination of the Testes

Disorders of the Prostate

IN THE NEW MILLENNIUM:
Good News About Prostate Cancer

MALE SEXUAL FUNCTIONS

Erection

Spinal Reflexes and Sexual Response

Ejaculation

SUMMING UP

Truth or Fiction?

_____ The penis contains bone and muscle.

_____ The father determines the baby's gender.

_____ The sperm of the tiny fruit fly are longer than human sperm.

_____ Morning erections reflect the need to urinate.

_____ Men can will themselves to have erections.

_____ The penis has a mind of its own.

_____ Many men who are paralyzed below the waist can attain erection, engage in sexual intercourse, and ejaculate.

_____ Men can have orgasms without ejaculating.

from the earliest foundations of Western civilization, male-dominated societies elevated men and exalted male genitalia. The ancient Greeks carried oversized images of fish as **phallic symbols** in their Dionysian processions, which celebrated the wilder and more frenzied aspects of human sexuality. In the murky predawn light of Western civilization, humankind engaged in phallic worship. Phallic symbols played roles in religious worship and became glorified in art in the form of ploughs, axes, and swords.

The tradition of phallic worship became raised to higher aesthetic levels. The ancient Greeks adorned themselves with phallic rings and necklaces. In ancient Rome, celebrations were held to honor Venus, the goddess of love. The Romans outfitted a float in the shape of a large phallus and paraded it through the streets. There were no tributes to the female genitals. Even though Venus was being honored, no artisans devoted themselves to creating floats in the likeness of the vulva or the clitoris.

Men held their own genitals in such high esteem that it was common courtroom practice for them to swear to tell the truth with their hands on their genitals—as we swear to tell the truth in the name of God or by placing our hands on the Bible. The words **testes** and **testicles** derive from the same Latin word as "testify." The Latin *testis* means "a witness."

Even today, we see evidence of pride—indeed veneration!—of the male genitalia. Men with large genitals are accorded respect from their male peers and sometimes adoration from female admirers. In *The Sun Also Rises*, Ernest Hemingway describes how matadors stuffed the front of their trousers with fabric. With their "manhood" fully packed, they plunged the sword into the poor animal's head before their adoring public. U.S. slang describes men with large genitals as "well-hung" or "hung like a bull" (or stallion).

Given these cultural attitudes, it is not surprising that young men (and some not-so-young men) belittle themselves if they feel, as many do, that they are little—that is, that their penises do not measure up to some ideal. Boys who mature late may be ridiculed by their peers for their small genitals. Their feelings of inadequacy may persist into adulthood. Adult men, too, may harbor doubts that their penises are large enough to satisfy their lovers. Or they may fear that their partners' earlier lovers had larger genitals.

In this chapter, we examine male sexual anatomy and physiology, and we attempt to sort out truth from fiction. We see, for example, that despite his lingering doubts, a man's capabilities as a lover do not depend on the size of his penis (at least within broad limits). For a man to judge his sexual prowess on the basis of locker-room comparisons makes about as much sense as choosing a balloon by measuring it when it is deflated.

In our exploration of male sexual anatomy and physiology, as in our exploration of female sexual physiology and anatomy, we begin with the external genitalia and then move inward. Once inside, we focus on the route of sperm through the male reproductive system.

EXTERNAL SEX ORGANS

The external male sex organs include the penis and the scrotum (see Figures 4.1, 4.2).

The Penis

> The penis mightier than the sword.
> —Mark Twain

> Is that a gun in your pocket, or are you just glad to see me?
> —Mae West

Phallic symbols Images of the penis that are usually suggestive of generative power.

Testes The male sex glands, suspended in the scrotum, that produce sperm cells and male sex hormones. Singular: *testis*.

Testicles Testes.

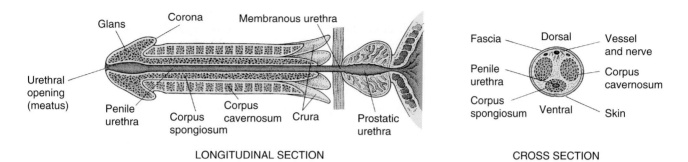

LONGITUDINAL SECTION   CROSS SECTION

figure 4.1

The Penis. During sexual arousal, the corpora cavernosa and corpus spongiosum become congested with blood, causing the penis to enlarge and stiffen.

At first glance, the **penis** may seem rather simple and obvious in its structures, particularly when compared to women's organs. This apparent simplicity may have contributed to cultural stereotypes that men are straightforward and aggressive, whereas women tend to be complicated and perhaps mysterious. Yet, as Figure 4.1 shows, the apparent simplicity of the penis is misleading. Much goes on below the surface. Gender stereotypes regarding anatomy are as misleading as those regarding personality (see Chapter 6).

The penis, like the vagina, is the sex organ used in sexual intercourse. Unlike the vagina, however, the penis serves as a conduit for urine. Semen and urine pass out of the penis through the urethral opening. The opening is called the urethral *meatus* (pronounced me-ATE-us), meaning "passage."

The penis arrived on the evolutionary scene some 100 million years ago. It was first found in reptiles—the ancestors of present-day crocodiles and lizards and of dinosaurs.

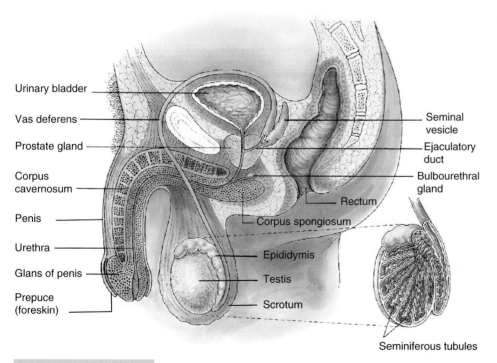

figure 4.2

The Male Reproductive System. The external male sex organs include the penis and the scrotum.

Penis The male organ of sexual intercourse. (From the Latin for "tail.")

Earlier in the evolutionary process, male and female animals each had a genital opening called a **cloaca.** The cloaca functioned as both an excretory and a sex organ. It took some fancy bodywork for couples to align their cloacae so that the male's sperm could find their way into the female's cloacal cavity. The penis has a more efficient shape—a shaft—for funneling sperm to the female. It gives them a head start on their journey toward the ovum.

Many mammals, including dogs, have penile bones that stiffen the penis to facilitate copulation. Despite the slang term "boner," the human penis contains no bones. Nor, despite another slang term, "muscle," does the penis contain muscle tissue. However, muscles at the base of the penis, like the muscles surrounding the vaginal and urethral openings in women, are involved in controlling urination and ejaculation.

Truth or Fiction?
REVISITED

Despite the slang terms, there is no bone or muscle tissue in the penis. ■

Rather than bones or muscles, the penis contains three cylinders of spongy material that run its length. The larger two of these cylinders, the **corpora cavernosa** (see Figure 4.1), lie side by side and function like the cavernous bodies in the clitoris. These cylinders fill up with blood and stiffen during sexual arousal. In addition, a **corpus spongiosum** (spongy body) runs along the bottom, or ventral, surface of the penis. It contains the penile urethra that conducts urine through the penis to the urinary opening (urethral meatus) at the tip. At the tip of the penis, the spongy body enlarges to become the glans, or head, of the penis.

All three cylinders consist of spongy tissue that swells (becomes engorged) with blood during sexual arousal, resulting in erection. The urethra is connected to the bladder, which is unrelated to reproduction, and to those parts of the reproductive system that transport semen.

The glans of the penis, like the clitoral glans, is extremely sensitive to sexual stimulation. Direct, prolonged stimulation can become irritating, even painful. Men generally prefer to masturbate by stroking the shaft of the penis rather than the glans, although some prefer the latter. The **corona,** or coronal ridge, separates the glans from the body of the penis. It is also quite sensitive to sexual stimulation. After the glans, the parts of the penis that men tend to find most sensitive are the corona and an area on the underside of the penis called the **frenulum.** The frenulum is a thin strip of tissue that connects the underside of the glans to the shaft. Most men find the top part of the penis to be the least sensitive part.

The base of the penis, called the **root,** extends into the pelvis. It is attached to pelvic bones by leglike structures, called crura, that are like those that anchor the female's clitoris. The body of the penis is called the penile **shaft.** The penile shaft, unlike the clitoral shaft, is free-swinging. Therefore, when sexual excitement engorges the penis with blood, the result—erection—is obvious. The expression "getting shafted," which means being taken advantage of, presumably refers to the penile shaft. Another phrase, "getting screwed," refers more directly to sexual intercourse.

The skin of the penis is hairless and loose, allowing expansion during erection. It is fixed to the penile shaft just behind the glans. Some of it, however, like the labia minora in the female, folds over to partially cover the glans. This covering is the prepuce, or **foreskin.** It covers part or all of the penile glans just as the clitoral prepuce (hood) covers the clitoral shaft. The prepuce consists of loose skin that freely moves over the glans. However, smegma—a cheeselike, foul-smelling secretion—may accumulate below the prepuce, causing the foreskin to adhere to the glans.

CIRCUMCISION **Circumcision** is the surgical removal of the prepuce (Figure 4.3). Advocates of circumcision believe that it is hygienic because it eliminates a site where smegma might accumulate and disease organisms might flourish. Opponents of circumcision believe that it is unnecessary because regular cleaning is sufficient to reduce the risk of these problems.

Cloaca The cavity in birds, reptiles, and many fish into which the genitourinary and intestinal tracts empty. (From the Latin *cluere,* meaning "to cleanse.")

Corpora cavernosa Cylinders of spongy tissue in the penis that become congested with blood and stiffen during sexual arousal.

Corpus spongiosum The spongy body that runs along the bottom of the penis, contains the penile urethra, and enlarges at the tip of the penis to form the glans.

Corona The ridge that separates the glans from the body of the penis. (From the Latin for "crown.")

Frenulum The sensitive strip of tissue that connects the underside of the penile glans to the shaft. (From the Latin *frenum,* meaning "bridle.")

Root The base of the penis, which extends into the pelvis.

Shaft The body of the penis, which expands as a result of vasocongestion.

Foreskin The loose skin that covers the penile glans. Also referred to as the *prepuce.*

Circumcision Surgical removal of the foreskin of the penis. (From the Latin *circumcidere,* meaning "to cut around.")

Normal Variations in the Male Genitals. The penis and scrotum vary a good deal in appearance from one man to another. The penis in the photo to the right is uncircumcised.

Male circumcision has a long history as a religious rite. Jews traditionally carry out male circumcision shortly after a baby is born. Circumcision is performed a sign of the covenant between God and the people of Abraham. Muslims also have ritual circumcisions for religious reasons.

According to the NHSLS study of 1410 men aged 18 to 59, circumcision is most common among non-Hispanic White men (81%) and men whose mothers graduated from college (87%) (Laumann et al., 1997). Figure 4.4 compares the circumcision rates among various ethnic groups in the United States. The groups have some overlap; the great majority of Jews—for whom circumcision is a religious rite—are also non-Hispanic White people.

Circumcision became widespread in the United States because medical research suggested that it prevented the transmission of sexually transmitted diseases, but the NHSLS study brought earlier findings into question. Edward O. Laumann, the lead researcher of the NHSLS study, explains the difference by saying that earlier studies used men who were being treated for STDs as their subjects (cited in Gilbert, 1998). The NHSLS study compared the rates of STDs in circumcised and uncircumcised men and considered factors that would predispose them to disease. Circumcised men in the NHSLS study were actually *more* likely to report having genital herpes and chlamydia infections. But we should note that other research reports that urinary tract infections are more common among uncircumcised male infants than among circumcised infants (Herzog, 1989). Emerging evidence also suggests that uncircumcised men may be at greater risk than circumcised men of becoming infected by the AIDS virus. Certain cells in the foreskin may be especially susceptible to it (Royce et al., 1997).

Questions have also been raised about the *sexual* effects of circumcision. According to the NHSLS study, there is a substantial relationship between circumcision and sexual activity. The study found that circumcised men engaged in a wider variety of sexual practices, including masturbation and oral and anal sex. As an example, 81% of circumcised men reported having experienced heterosexual fellatio, compared with 61% of

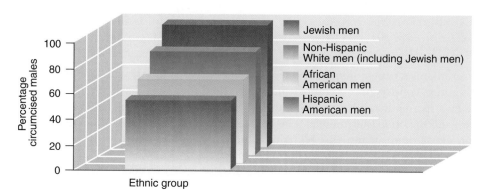

Who Is Circumcised? Circumcision was most common among Jewish men in the NHSLS study, for whom it is a religious rite, and among non-Hispanic White men in general, as compared with African American and Hispanic American men.
Source: Laumann et al. (1997).

uncircumcised men. Laumann offers possible explanations for the difference. One possibility is that uncircumcised men—in the minority in the United States—experience an inhibiting stigma. Another is that circumcision reduces the sensitivity of the penis, encouraging circumcised men to try a wider range of sexual activities.

The NHSLS study also found that circumcised men were less likely to have sexual dysfunctions such as lack of interest in sex, performance anxiety, or difficulty achieving or maintaining erections. Forty percent of the circumcised men reported sexual dysfunctions, compared with 58% of the uncircumcised men. Laumann speculated that feelings of stigma among uncircumcised men could be a factor here as well.

Physicians continue to debate the health benefits of circumcision. They do agree, however, that circumcision is the treatment of choice for **phimosis,** a condition in which it is difficult to retract the foreskin from the glans.

PENIS SIZE

> *Iras:* Am I not an inch of fortune better than she?
> *Charmian:* Well, if you were but an inch of fortune better than I, where would you choose it?
> *Iras:* Not in my husband's nose.
> —William Shakespeare, *Antony and Cleopatra*

In our culture, the size of the penis is sometimes seen as a measure of a man's masculinity and his ability to please his sex partner (see the nearby A Closer Look feature). Shakespeare and other writers inform us that men have looked down at themselves for centuries, sometimes in delight but more often in chagrin. Men who are heralded for their sexual or reproductive feats are presumed to have more prominent "testaments" to their manhood.

It may be of some comfort to note that even the smallest normal human penis is between three and four times the length of the phallus of the burly gorilla. Even so, the human penis does not merit comparison with the phallus of the blue whale. This ocean-dwelling mammal, the largest animal on earth, is about 100 feet from end to end and possesses a penis about 7 feet in length. When not in use, the whale's penis is cached in the male's abdomen, which is a fortunate thing. If it were to trail down permanently, it might act as a rudder and muddle the animal's internal navigational system.

Masters and Johnson (1966) reported that the penises of the 312 male subjects they studied generally ranged in length from 3½ inches to a little more than 4 inches when flaccid (soft). The average erect penis ranges from 5 to 7 inches in length (Reinisch, 1990). Erect penises differ less in size than flaccid penises do (Jamison & Gebhard, 1988). Penises that are small when flaccid tend to gain more size when they become erect. Larger flaccid penises gain relatively less. Size differences in flaccid penises may thus be largely canceled out by erection. Nor is there a relationship between penis size and body weight, height, or build (Money et al., 1984).

Even when flaccid, the same penis can vary in size. Factors such as cold air or water or emotions of fear or anxiety can cause the penis (along with the scrotum and testicles) to draw closer to the body, reducing its size. The flaccid penis may also grow in size in warm water or when the man is relaxed.

The Scrotum

The scrotum is a pouch of loose skin that becomes covered lightly with hair at puberty. The scrotum consists of two compartments that hold the testes. Each testicle is held in place by a spermatic cord, a structure that contains the vas deferens, blood vessels and nerves, and the cremaster muscle. The cremaster muscle raises and lowers the testicle within the scrotum in response to temperature changes and sexual stimulation. (The testes are drawn closer to the body during sexual arousal.)

Sperm production is optimal at a temperature that is slightly cooler than the 98.6 degrees Fahrenheit that is desirable for most of the body. Typically, scrotal temperature is 5

Phimosis An abnormal condition in which the foreskin is so tight that it cannot be withdrawn from the glans. (From the Greek *phimos,* meaning "muzzle.")

Scrotum The pouch of loose skin that contains the testes. (From the same linguistic root as the word *shred,* meaning "a long, narrow strip," and probably referring to the long furrows on the scrotal sac.)

Spermatic cord The cord that suspends a testicle within the scrotum and contains a vas deferens, blood vessels, nerves, and the cremaster muscle.

Vas deferens A tube that conducts sperm from the testicle to the ejaculatory duct of the penis. Plural: *vasa deferentia.*

Cremaster muscle The muscle that raises and lowers the testicle in response to temperature changes and sexual stimulation.

a CLOSER look

On Penis Size and Sexual Performance

Perhaps most men have had concerns about the size of their penises. As sex therapist Bernard Zilbergeld put it in his book *Male Sexuality*, "Women, we are given to believe, crave nothing so much as a penis that might be mistaken for a telephone pole" (1978, p. 27). Think critically about the belief that men with bigger penises make more effective lovers. What assumptions is it based upon? Is there supportive evidence?

The belief that the size of the man's penis determines his sexual prowess is based upon the assumption that men with bigger penises are better equipped to satisfy a woman sexually. Zilbergeld and others point out, however, that women rarely mention penis size as an important element in their sexual satisfaction. Quite regularly they *do* mention ability to communicate with partners, the emotional atmosphere of the relationship, and sensitivity to employing sexual techniques that enhance their partner's pleasure.

Does your knowledge of female sexual physiology support or challenge the assumption that bigger is necessarily better? From your reading of Chapter 3, what do you know about how the vagina accommodates the penis? What is the role of the P-C muscle? Which part of the vagina is most sensitive to tactile stimulation? What, if any, might be the relationships between the clitoris—the woman's most erotically sensitive organ—and the size of the penis? Which seems more crucial: sexual technique and the quality of the relationship or penis size? Why?

The diameter of the penis, rather than its length, may have a greater bearing on a partner's sexual sensations, since thicker penises may provide more clitoral stimulation during intercourse. Nonetheless, even though the inner vagina is relatively insensitive to touch, some women find the *pressure* of deeper penetration sexually pleasurable. Others, however, find deeper penetration to be uncomfortable or painful, especially if thrusting is too vigorous.

---

to 6 degrees lower than body temperature. The scrotum is loose-hanging and flexible. It permits the testes and nearby structures to escape the higher body heat, especially in warm weather. In the middle layer of the scrotum is the **dartos muscle,** which (like the cremaster) contracts and relaxes reflexively in response to temperature changes. In cold weather or when a man jumps into a body of cold water, it contracts to bring the testes closer to the body. In warm weather, it relaxes, allowing the testes to dangle farther from the body. The dartos muscle also increases or decreases the surface area of the scrotum in response to temperature changes. Smoothing allows greater dissipation of heat in hot weather. Tightening or constricting the skin surface helps to retain heat and gives the scrotum a wrinkled appearance in the cold.

The scrotum is developed from the same embryonic tissue that becomes the labia majora of the female. Therefore, like the labia majora, it is quite sensitive to sexual stimulation. It is somewhat more sensitive than the top side of the penis but less so than other areas of the penis.

Reflections

- Agree or disagree with the following statement and support your answer: Men with bigger penises make more effective lovers.
- Are you or are the men in your family circumcised? If so, why? If not, why not? Are you aware of any effects of circumcision? (Are you sure?)
- Were you knowledgeable about the penis and scrotum before reading this section? What was new to you? What mistaken ideas had you held?

INTERNAL SEX ORGANS

The male internal sex organs consist of the testes, the organs that manufacture sperm and the male sex hormone testosterone; the system of tubes and ducts that conduct sperm through the male reproductive system; and the organs that help to nourish and activate sperm and neutralize some of the acidity that sperm encounter in the vagina.

Dartos muscle The muscle in the middle layer of the scrotum that contracts and relaxes in response to temperature changes.

figure 4.5

Interstitial Cells. Testosterone is produced by the interstitial cells, which lie between the seminiferous tubules in each testis. Sperm (seen in the middle of the diagram) are produced within the seminiferous tubules.

The Testes

The testes (singular: testis) are the male gonads (*gonad* derives from the Greek *gone*, meaning "seed"). In slang, the testes are frequently referred to as "balls" or "nuts." These terms are considered vulgar, but they are reasonably descriptive. They also make it easier for many people to refer to the testes in informal conversation.

The testes serve two functions analogous to those of the ovaries. They secrete sex hormones and produce mature **germ cells.** In the case of the testes, the germ cells are **sperm** and the sex hormones are **androgens.** The most important androgen is testosterone.

TESTOSTERONE Testosterone is secreted by **interstitial cells,** which are also referred to as **Leydig's cells.** Interstitial cells lie between the seminiferous tubules and release testosterone directly into the bloodstream (see Figure 4.5). Testosterone stimulates prenatal differentiation of male sex organs, sperm production, and development of **secondary sex characteristics,** such as the beard, deep voice, and growth of the muscle mass.

In men, several endocrine glands—the hypothalamus, pituitary gland, and testes (see Figure 4.6)—keep blood testosterone levels at a more or less even level. This contrasts with the peaks and valleys in levels of female sex hormones during the phases of the menstrual cycle. Testosterone levels vary slightly with stress, time of day or month, and other factors, but a feedback loop among the endocrine glands keeps them relatively stable.

The same pituitary hormones, FSH and LH, that regulate the activity of the ovaries also regulate the activity of the testes. FSH regulates the production of sperm by the testes. LH stimulates secretion of testosterone by the interstitial cells. Low testosterone levels signal the hypothalamus to secrete a hormone, called LH-releasing hormone (LH-RH). Like dominoes falling in a line, LH-RH causes the pituitary gland to secrete LH, which in turn stimulates the testes to release testosterone into the blood system. LH is also referred to as *interstitial-cell stimulating hormone*, or ICSH.[1]

When the level of testosterone in the blood system reaches a certain peak, the hypothalamus directs the pituitary gland *not* to secrete LH. This system for circling information around these three endocrine glands is called a *feedback loop*. This feedback loop is *negative*. That is, increases in hormone levels in one part of the system trigger another part to shut down, and vice versa.

Germ cell A cell from which a new organism develops. (From the Latin *germen*, meaning "bud" or "sprout.")

Sperm The male germ cell. (From a Greek root meaning "seed.")

Androgens Male sex hormones. (From the Greek *andros*, meaning "man" or "males," and *-gene*, meaning "born.")

Testosterone A male steroid sex hormone.

Interstitial cells Cells that lie between the seminiferous tubules and secrete testosterone. (*Interstitial* means "set between.")

Leydig's cells Another term for *interstitial cells*.

Secondary sex characteristics Traits that distinguish the genders but are not directly involved in reproduction.

figure 4.6

Hormonal Control of the Testes. Several endocrine glands—the hypothalamus, the pituitary gland, and the testes—keep blood testosterone levels at a more or less constant level. Low testosterone levels signal the hypothalamus to secrete LH-releasing hormone (LH-RH). Like dominoes falling in line, LH-RH causes the pituitary gland to secrete LH, which in turn stimulates the testes to release testosterone. Follicle-stimulating hormone releasing hormone (FSH-RH) from the hypothalamus causes the pituitary to secrete FSH, which, in turn, causes the testes to produce sperm cells.

[1]We do not throw such terms at you willy-nilly or to complicate matters. In future years, you will be reading about the biology of sex in the popular media, and since it is unlikely that all commentators will agree on the terminology that is to be used, we want you to be able to recognize the meanings of various terms.

a CLOSER look

Is There a *Manopause?*

Men cannot undergo menopause; they have never menstruated. Yet one now and then hears of a so-called male menopause, occasionally referred to as "manopause." Some men during their later years are informally referred to as menopausal. Sadly, this description is usually meant to convey the negative, harmful stereotype of the aging person as crotchety and irritable. Such stereotypes of menopause are unfortunate reminders of sexism and ageism and are not necessarily consistent with the biology or psychology of aging.

The scientific jury is still out on the existence of the male menopause. Women encounter relatively sudden age-related declines in sex hormones and fertility during menopause. Men experience a gradual decline in testosterone levels as they age, but nothing like the sharp plunge in estrogen levels that women experience during menopause (Sheehy, 1998). Testosterone levels begin to fall at about age 40 or 50 and may decline to one-third or one-half of their peak levels by age 80 (Brody, 1995c).

The drop in testosterone levels that occurs as men age may be connected to a variety of age-related symptoms, including reduced muscle mass and strength, accumulation of body fat, reduced energy levels, lowered fertility, and reduced erectile ability. However, despite a decline in testosterone levels, most men remain potent throughout their lives. Little is known about the critical levels of testosterone that are needed to maintain erectile ability. Certain age-related changes, such as reduced muscle mass and strength and increased body fat, may be due to other factors associated with aging rather than to declining testosterone production, such as a gradual loss of *human growth hormone*, a hormone that helps to maintain muscle strength and that may prevent fat buildup. Some experts believe that testosterone replacement may help to avert erectile problems, bone loss, and frailty, in much the same way that estrogen replacement benefits postmenopausal women (Brody, 1995c). Others worry that excessive use of the hormone may increase the risks of prostate cancer and cardiovascular disease.

Although men do experience a gradual decline in the number and motility of sperm as they age, which reduces

Is There a *Manopause?* The term *menopause* is sometimes used to convey the negative. harmful stereotype of the aging person as crotchety and irritable. The scientific jury is still out on whether there is a "male menopause," but men do experience a gradual decline in testosterone levels as they age. The decline in testosterone is connected with age-related symptoms such as reduced muscle strength, accumulation of fat, reduced energy, lowered fertility, and reduced erectile ability. Nevertheless, most men maintain erectile ability throughout their lives.

their fertility, some viable sperm continue to be produced even into late adulthood (Sheehy, 1997, 1998). It is not surprising, from a physical standpoint, to find a man in his 70s or older fathering a child.

Men can remain sexually active and father children at advanced ages. For both genders, marital satisfaction and attitudes toward aging can affect sexual behavior as profoundly as physical changes can.

The testes usually range between 1 and 1¾ inches in length. They are about half as wide and deep. The left testicle usually hangs lower, because the left spermatic cord tends to be somewhat longer.

SPERM Each testicle is divided into many lobes. The lobes are filled with winding **seminiferous tubules** (see Figure 4.2). Although packed into a tiny space, these tubules, placed end to end, would span the length of several football fields. Through a process called **spermatogenesis,** these threadlike structures produce and store hundreds of billions of sperm through the course of a lifetime.

Seminiferous tubules Tiny, winding, sperm-producing tubes that are located within the lobes of the testes. (From Latin roots meaning "seed bearing.")

Spermatogenesis The process by which sperm cells are produced and developed.

**Human Sperm Cells
Magnified Many Times.**

Sperm cells develop through several stages. It takes about 72 days for the testes to manufacture a mature sperm cell (Leary, 1990). In an early stage, sperm cells are called **spermatocytes.** Each one contains 46 chromosomes, including one X and one Y sex chromosome. Each spermatocyte divides into two **spermatids,** each of which has 23 chromosomes. Half the spermatids have X sex chromosomes, and the other half have Y sex chromosomes. Looking something like tadpoles when examined under a microscope, mature sperm cells, called **spermatozoa,** each have a head, a cone-shaped midpiece, and a tail. The head is about 5 microns (1/50,000 of an inch) long and contains the cell nucleus that houses the 23 chromosomes. The midpiece contains structures that provide the energy that the tail needs to lash back and forth in a swimming motion. Each sperm cell is about 50 microns (1/5,000 of an inch) long, one of the smallest cells in the body (Thompson, 1993).

During fertilization, the 23 chromosomes from the father's sperm cell combine with the 23 chromosomes from the mother's ovum, furnishing the standard ensemble of 46 chromosomes in the offspring. Among the 23 chromosomes borne by sperm cells is one sex chromosome—an X sex chromosome or a Y sex chromosome. Ova contain X sex chromosomes only. The union of an X sex chromosome and a Y sex chromosome leads to the development of male offspring. Two X sex chromosomes combine to yield female offspring. So the presence of an X or Y sex chromosome from the father determines the baby's gender.

Truth or Fiction?

It is true that the father determines the baby's gender through the presence of an X or Y sex chromosome. If the fertilizing sperm has an X sex chromosome, the child will be a girl. If it has a Y sex chromosome, the child will be a boy. ■

The testes are veritable dynamos of manufacturing power, churning out about 1,000 sperm per second or about 30 billion—yes, *billion*—per year. Mathematically speaking, 10 to 20 ejaculations hold enough sperm to populate the earth. (Men are always so taken with themselves, notes the third author.)

Belgian researchers have discovered that sperm cells possess the same kind of receptors that the nose uses to sense odors (Angier, 1992). This discovery suggests that sperm may find their way to an egg cell by detecting its scent. Researchers at the Texas Southwestern Medical Center in Dallas had earlier discovered that the fertile egg cells emit a compound that attracts the interest of sperm cells. These odor receptors may be the

Spermatocyte An early stage in the development of sperm cells, in which each parent cell has 46 chromosomes, including one X and one Y sex chromosome.

Spermatids Cells formed by the division of spermatocytes. Each spermatid has 23 chromosomes.

Spermatozoa Mature sperm cells.

Chromosomes. The normal human cell contains 46 chromosomes which are arranged in pairs. When a sperm cell and ovum unite, 23 chromosomes from the father's sperm cell combine with 23 chromosomes from the mother's ovum, to form the normal complement of 46 chromosomes in the offspring. The presence of an X or Y sex chromosome from the father determines the baby's gender.

a CLOSER look

Big

Don't be fooled by his size. The tiny fruit fly, *Drosophila bifurca*, is only a fraction of an inch long. You can crush it easily with the tip of your finger. But this little insect holds the distinction of being number 1 in the *Guinness Book of Records* for length of sperm. He produces coiled sperm that stretch out to nearly 2½ inches, or 20 times the length of his own body! How does the fruit fly accomplish this feat? By devoting about 11% of his body weight to his testes.

This fruit fly's sperm are 1,000 times as long as human sperm (Pitnick, 1995). Remember that a human sperm cell is about 1/5,000 of an inch long and is one of the smallest cells in the body (Thompson, 1993). To match the achievement of *Drosophila*, a man would have to produce sperm that are 100 to 120 feet long (Leary, 1995).

Truth or Fiction? REVISITED

It is true that the sperm of the tiny fruit fly are longer than human sperm. In fact, they are longer than the sperm of any mammal. ■

There may be many more fruit flies than people, but fruit flies are no match for people in terms of numbers of sperm. Men can ejaculate several hundred million sperm at a time, whereas the fruit fly releases only about 50 (Pitnick, 1995). Moreover, human sperm are strong swimmers, whereas the rolled-up fruit fly sperm slowly unwinds in the female and apparently relies on transportation mechanisms within the female to reach its goal.

Why, the third author wishes to ask, must men be so competitive—even with fruit flies?

---

mechanism by which sperm recognize these attractants. If this turns out to be the case, it could lead to the development of contraceptives that prevent fertilization by blocking these receptors.

Sperm proceed from the seminiferous tubules through an intricate maze of ducts that converge in a single tube called the **epididymis.** The epididymis lies against the back wall of the testicle and serves as a storage facility for sperm. The epididymis, which is some 2 inches in length, consists of twisted passages that would be 10 to 20 feet in length if stretched end to end. Sperm are inactive when they enter the epididymis. They continue to mature as they slowly make their way through the epididymis for another two to four weeks.

The Vas Deferens

Each epididymis empties into a vas deferens (also called *ductus deferens*). The vas is a thin, cylindrical tube about 16 inches long that serves as a conduit for mature sperm. In the scrotum, the vas deferens lies near the skin surface within the spermatic cord. Therefore, a **vasectomy,** an operation in which the right and left vasa deferentia are severed, is a convenient means of sterilization. The tube leaves the scrotum and follows a circuitous path up into the abdominal cavity. Then it loops back along the rear surface of the bladder (see Figure 4.7 on page 110).

The Seminal Vesicles

The two **seminal vesicles** are small glands, each about 2 inches long. They lie behind the bladder and open into the **ejaculatory ducts,** where the fluids they secrete combine with sperm (see Figure 4.7). A vesicle is a small cavity or sac; the seminal vesicles were so named because they were mistakenly believed to be reservoirs for semen, rather than glands.

The fluid produced by the seminal vesicles is rich in fructose, a form of sugar, which nourishes sperm and helps them to become active, or motile. Sperm motility is a major factor in male fertility. Before reaching the ejaculatory ducts, sperm are propelled along

Epididymis A tube that lies against the back wall of each testicle and serves as a storage facility for sperm. (From Greek roots meaning "upon testicles.")

Vasectomy A sterilization procedure in which the vasa deferentia are severed, preventing sperm from reaching the ejaculatory duct.

Seminal vesicles Small glands that lie behind the bladder and secrete fluids that combine with sperm in the ejaculatory ducts.

Ejaculatory duct A duct formed by the convergence of a vas deferens with a seminal vesicle through which sperm pass through the prostate gland and into the urethra.

f i g u r e 4 . 7

Passage of Spermatozoa. Each testicle is divided into lobes that contain threadlike seminiferous tubules. Through spermatogenesis, the tubules produce and store hundreds of billions of sperm over the course of a lifetime. During ejaculation, sperm cells travel through the vas deferens, up and over the bladder, into the ejaculatory duct, and then through the urethra. Secretions from the seminal vesicles and the bulbourethral glands join with sperm to compose semen.

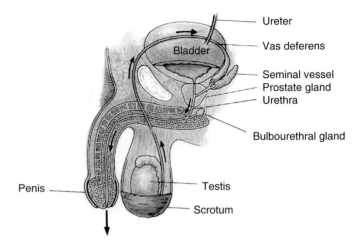

their journey by contractions of the epididymis and vas deferens and by **cilia** that line the walls of the vas deferens. Once they become motile, they propel themselves by whipping their tails.

At the base of the bladder, each vas deferens joins a seminal vesicle to form a short ejaculatory duct that runs through the middle of the prostate gland (see Figure 4.7). In the prostate, the ejaculatory duct opens into the urethra, which leads to the tip of the penis. The urethra carries sperm and urine out through the penis, but normally not at the same time.

The Prostate Gland

The **prostate gland** lies beneath the bladder and approximates a chestnut in shape and size (about ¾ inch in diameter). Note the spelling of the name of the gland—pros*tate*, not pros*trate*. (*Prostrate* means lying with one's face on the ground, as in some forms of prayer.) The prostate gland contains muscle fibers and glandular tissue that secrete prostatic fluid. Prostatic fluid is milky and alkaline. It provides the characteristic texture and odor of the seminal fluid. The alkalinity neutralizes some of the acidity of the vaginal tract, prolonging the life span of sperm as seminal fluid spreads through the female reproductive system. The prostate is continually active in mature males, but sexual arousal further stimulates secretions. Secretions are conveyed into the urethra by a sievelike duct system. There, the secretions combine with sperm and fluid from the seminal vesicles.

A vasectomy prevents sperm from reaching the urethra but does not cut off fluids from the seminal vesicles or prostate gland. A man who has had a vasectomy thus emits an ejaculate that appears normal but contains no sperm.

Cowper's Glands

The **Cowper's glands** are also known as the **bulbourethral glands**, in recognition of their shape and location. These two structures lie below the prostate and empty their secretions into the urethra. During sexual arousal, they secrete a drop or so of clear, slippery fluid that appears at the urethral opening. The functions of this fluid are not entirely understood. It may help to buffer the acidity of the male's urethra and lubricate the urethral passageway to ease the passage of seminal fluid. The fluid is not produced in sufficient amounts to play a significant role in lubricating the vagina during intercourse.

Fluid from the Cowper's glands precedes the ejaculate and often contains viable sperm. Therefore, coitus may lead to pregnancy even if the penis is withdrawn before ejaculation. This is one reason why people who practice the "withdrawal method" of birth control are frequently called "parents."

Cilia Hairlike projections from cells that beat rhythmically to produce locomotion or currents.

Prostate gland The gland that lies beneath the bladder and secretes prostatic fluid, which gives semen its characteristic odor and texture.

Cowper's glands Structures that lie below the prostate and empty their secretions into the urethra during sexual arousal.

Bulbourethral glands Another term for *Cowper's glands*.

Semen

Sperm and the fluids contributed by the seminal vesicles, the prostate gland, and the Cowper's glands make up **semen,** or whitish seminal fluid, which is expelled through the tip of the penis during ejaculation. The seminal vesicles secrete about 70% of the fluid that constitutes the ejaculate. The remaining 30% of seminal fluid consists of sperm and fluids produced by the prostate gland and the Cowper's gland. Sperm themselves account for only about 1% of the volume of semen. This is why men with vasectomies continue to ejaculate about as much semen as before, although their ejaculates are devoid of sperm.

Semen is the medium that carries sperm through much of the male's reproductive system and the reproductive tract of the female. Semen contains water, mucus, sugar (fructose), acids, and bases. It activates and nourishes sperm, and the bases help to shield sperm from vaginal acidity. The typical ejaculate contains between 200 million and 400 million sperm and ranges between 3 and 5 milliliters in volume. (Five milliliters is equal to about 1 tablespoon.) The quantity of semen decreases with age and with frequency of ejaculation.

Reflections

■ How are the testes analogous to the ovaries?
■ What are the components of semen? Where do they come from?
■ What is the evidence for the existence of "manopause"?

DISEASES OF THE UROGENITAL SYSTEM

Because the organs that make up the urinary and reproductive systems are near each other and share some "piping," they are referred to as the urinogenital or urogenital system. A number of diseases affect the urogenital system. The type of physician who specializes in their diagnosis and treatment is a **urologist.**

Urethritis

Men, like women, are subject to bladder and urethral inflammations, which are generally referred to as **urethritis.** The symptoms include frequent urination (urinary frequency), a strong need to urinate (urinary urgency), burning during urination, and a penile discharge. People with symptoms of urinary frequency and urinary urgency feel the pressing need to urinate repeatedly, even though they may have just done so and may have but another drop or two to expel. The discharge may dry on the urethral opening, in which case it may have to be peeled off or wiped away before it is possible to urinate. The urethra also may become constricted when it is inflamed, slowing or halting urination. It is a frightening sensation for a male to feel the urine rush from his bladder and then suddenly stop at the urethral opening!

Preventive measures for urethritis parallel those suggested for cystitis (bladder infection): drinking more water, drinking cranberry juice (4 ounces, two or three times a day), and lowering intake of alcohol and caffeine. Cranberry juice is highly acidic, and acid tends to eliminate many of the bacteria that can give rise to urethritis.

Cancer of the Testes

Cancer of the testicles remains a relatively rare form of cancer, accounting for about 6,000 new cases annually, or about 1% of all new cancers in men (American Cancer Society, 1991). It is the most common form of solid-tumor cancer to strike men between the ages

---

Semen The whitish fluid that constitutes the ejaculate, consisting of sperm and secretions from the seminal vesicles, prostate, and Cowper's glands.

Urologist A physician who specializes in the diagnosis and treatment of diseases of the urogenital system.

Urethritis An inflammation of the bladder or urethra.

Testicular Cancer. Professional figure skater and former Olympian Scott Hamilton was successfully treated for testicular cancer. As a spokesman for the American Cancer Society he brings attention to the need for early detection and treatment of the disease.

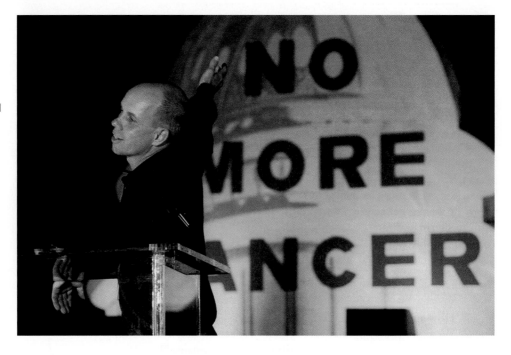

of 20 and 34, however (Vazi et al., 1989). It accounts for nearly 10% of all deaths from cancer among men in that age group.

There is no evidence that testicular cancer results from sexual overactivity or masturbation. Men who had **cryptorchidism** as children (a condition in which one or both testicles fail to descend from the abdomen into the scrotum) stand about a 40 times greater chance of contracting testicular cancer. Undescended testicles appear to occur more commonly in boys born to mothers who used the hormone diethylstilbestrol (DES) during pregnancy. In the 1940s and 1950s, pregnant women were often prescribed DES to help prevent miscarriages.

Although testicular cancer was generally fatal in earlier years, the prognosis today is quite favorable, especially for cases that are detected early. Treatments include surgical removal of the diseased testis, radiation, and chemotherapy. The survival rate among those cases whose cancer is detected early, before it has spread beyond the testes, is 96% (American Cancer Society, 1991). Delayed treatment markedly reduces the chances of survival, because survival is connected with the extent to which the cancer has spread.

The surgical removal of a testicle may have profound psychological implications. Some men who have lost a testicle feel less "manly." Fears related to sexual performance can engender sexual dysfunctions. From a physiological standpoint, sexual functioning should remain unimpaired, as adequate quantities of testosterone are produced by the remaining testis.

The early stages of testicular cancer usually produce no symptoms, other than the mass itself. Because early detection is crucial to survival, men are advised to examine themselves monthly following puberty (Reinisch, 1990) and to have regular medical checkups. Self-examination may also reveal evidence of sexually transmitted diseases and other problems.

Disorders of the Prostate

The prostate gland is tiny at birth and grows rapidly at puberty. It may shrink during adulthood but usually becomes enlarged past the age of 50.

BENIGN PROSTATIC HYPERPLASIA   The prostate gland becomes enlarged in about one quarter of men past the age of 60 (Walsh, 1996). When enlargement is due to hor-

Cryptorchidism A condition in which one of two testicles fails to descend from the abdomen into the scrotum.

a CLOSER look

Self-Examination of the Testes

Self-examination (see Figure 4.8) is best performed shortly after a warm shower or bath, when the skin of the scrotum is most relaxed. The man should exam the scrotum for evidence of pea-sized lumps. Each testicle can be rolled gently between the thumb and the fingers. Lumps are generally found on the side or front of the testicle. The presence of a lump is not necessarily a sign of cancer, but it should be promptly reported to a physician for further evaluation. The American Cancer Society (1990) lists these warning signals:

1. A slight enlargement of one of the testicles.
2. A change in the consistency of a testicle.
3. A dull ache in the lower abdomen or groin. (Pain may be absent in cancer of the testes, however).
4. Sensation of dragging and heaviness in a testicle.

figure 4.8

Self-Examination of the Testes.

monal changes associated with aging rather than other causes, such as inflammation from sexually transmitted diseases, it is referred to as **benign prostatic hyperplasia**. Because the prostate surrounds the upper part of the urethra (see Figure 4.2), enlargement constricts the urethra. Resultant symptoms include urinary frequency (including increased frequency of nocturnal urination), urinary urgency, and difficulty starting the flow of urine. Several treatments are available to relieve the pressure on the urethra and increase the flow of urine. They include medicines such as finasteride and alpha-adrenergic-agonist drugs ("alpha blockers") and surgical removal of part of the prostate (Wasson, 1998).

CANCER OF THE PROSTATE   A more serious and life-threatening problem is prostate cancer. The American Cancer Society estimates that about one man in eight in the United States will develop prostate cancer (Ochs, 1993b). Prostate cancer is the second most common form of cancer among men, after skin cancer, and the second leading cause of cancer deaths in men, after lung cancer (Morgan et al., 1996). Each year, there are about 185,000 new cases of prostate cancer in the United States, and nearly 40,000 men die from it (Altman, 1998d; Weinraub, 1998).

Prostate cancer involves the growth of malignant prostate tumors that can metastasize to bones and lymph nodes if not detected and treated early. African American men are one-third more likely than White men to develop prostate cancer (American Cancer Society, 1995). African American men may also have less access to routine medical evaluations than White men do, so that disease is diagnosed at a later stage. Researchers have identified intake of animal fat as a potential risk factor. Men whose diets are rich in animal fats, especially fats from red meat, have a substantially higher chance of developing advanced prostate cancer than do men with a low intake of animal fat. The incidence of prostate cancer also increases with age. Over 80% of all prostate cancers are diagnosed in men over the age of 65 (American Cancer Society, 1995). Genetic factors may also be involved (Wilson, 1995).

The early symptoms of cancer of the prostate may mimic those of benign prostate enlargement: urinary frequency and difficulty in urinating. Later symptoms include blood in the urine, pain or burning on urination, and pain in the lower back, pelvis, or upper thighs (American Cancer Society, 1995). Most cases occur without noticeable symptoms in the early stages.

Benign prostatic hyperplasia Enlargement of the prostate gland due to hormonal changes associated with aging and characterized by symptoms such as urinary frequency, urinary urgency, and difficulty starting the flow of urine.

Good News About Prostate Cancer

As we enter the new millennium, recently developed methods of detecting prostate cancer earlier are increasing the survival rate for men who develop the disease (Story, 1998). A blood test can detect evidence of prostate cancer even among men whose prostates feel normal upon physical examination. A study of more than 10,000 men found that the blood test was about twice as successful as physical examinations in early detection of prostate cancer (Cantalona et al., 1993). The blood test measures levels of prostate-specific antigen (PSA). PSA is a protein that helps to transform a gel-like substance in the prostate gland to a liquid that transports sperm when it is ejaculated. In the diseased or enlarged prostate, PSA seeps into the blood at higher levels, giving higher test readings. The five-year survival rate is 94% for prostate cancer that has *not* metastasized (American Cancer Society, 1995). By the time there are other symptoms or cancer is detected by means of rectal examination, the cancer may have already metastasized (Cantalona, 1998).

A Mayo Clinic Study reviewed medical records from the 1980s through the 1990s and found that the number of deaths from prostate cancer declined regularly as the use of PSA testing increased (Roberts, 1998). According to Dr. Steven Skates (1998) of Massachusetts General Hospital, PSA screening permits detection of prostate cancer an average of 11 years before other methods do. Dr. William Cantalona of at the Washington University School of Medicine predicts that by the year 2002 or 2003 PSA screening will be so widely used that it will reduce the number of deaths from prostate cancer by another 30% to 40%.

Researchers are currently investigating other possible markers for prostate cancer, such as high levels of insulin growth factor-I (Pollak et al., 1998). The American Cancer Society and other professional groups recommend that men of age 50 and above have an annual PSA blood test as well as a rectal examination (Morgan et al., 1996). African American men, who are more likely to develop and die from prostate cancer, are encouraged to begin such screening at the age of 40 (Morgan et al., 1996).

A Blood Test for Detection of Cancer of the Prostate. The PSA test assists in the early detection of prostate cancer.

The American Cancer Society (1995) recommends that men receive annual rectal examinations beginning at about age 40. The physician inserts a finger into the rectum and feels for abnormalities in the prostate gland. Unfortunately, many men are reluctant to undergo a rectal examination, even though it is only mildly uncomfortable and may save their lives. Some are embarrassed or reluctant to discuss urinary problems with their physicians. Some may resist the rectal examination because they associate rectal insertion with male-male sex. Still others fear that they may have cancer and choose to remain ignorant. Avoidance of, or ignorance of the need for, regular exams is a major contributor to the death rate from prostate cancer.

When a cancerous growth is suspected on the basis of a rectal examination or a PSA blood test, further testing is usually done via additional blood tests, ultrasound, or biopsy. Early detection is important because treatment is most effective before the cancer has spread ("Early prostate surgery," 1996). Fifty-eight percent of cases of prostate cancer are discovered while they are still localized. The survival rate drops dramatically if the cancer has metastasized. Still, the overall survival rate has improved in the past 30 years from 50% to 80% (American Cancer Society, 1995).

The most widely used treatment for prostate cancer is surgical removal of the prostate gland. However, surgical prostate removal may damage surrounding nerves, leading to problems in controlling the flow of urine or in erection or ejaculation. Recently introduced surgical techniques tend to spare the surrounding nerves and reduce, but not eliminate, the risk of complications. Other treatments include radiation, hormone treatment, and anticancer drugs. Hormone treatment and anticancer drugs may shrink the size of the tumor and relieve pain for long periods of time.

Among older men with slow-growing prostate cancer, physicians often prefer "watchful waiting" to surgery ("Early prostate surgery," 1996). The men frequently die first from causes other than cancer.

PROSTATITIS   Many infectious agents can inflame the prostate, causing **prostatitis.** The chief symptoms are an ache or pain between the scrotum and anal opening and painful ejaculation. Prostatitis is usually treated with antibiotics. Although aspirin and ibuprofen may relieve the pain, men with these symptoms should consult a physician. Painful ejaculation may discourage masturbation or coitus, which is ironic, since regular flushing of the prostate through ejaculation may be helpful in the treatment of prostatitis.

Reflections

- Why is it important for men to detect cancers of the testes and prostate early? What can men do to detect them early?
- A question to male readers: What are *you* doing to try to ensure the health of your sex organs?

MALE SEXUAL FUNCTIONS

The male sexual functions of erection and ejaculation provide the means for sperm to travel from the male's reproductive tract to the female's. There the sperm cell and ovum unite to conceive a new human being. Of course, the natural endowment of reproduction with sensations of pleasure helps to ensure that it will take place with or without knowledge of these biological facts.

Erection

Erection is caused by the engorgement of the penis with blood, such that the penis grows in size and stiffens. The erect penis is an efficient conduit, or funnel, for depositing sperm deep within the vagina.

In mechanical terms, erection is a hydraulic event. The spongy, cavernous masses of the penis are equipped to hold blood. Filling them with blood causes them to enlarge, much as a sponge swells as it absorbs water. This simple description belies the fact that erection is a remarkable feat of biological engineering (there they go again, notes the third author) that involves the cooperation of the vascular (blood) system and the nervous system.

In a few moments—as quickly as 10 or 15 seconds—the penis can double in length, become firm, and shift from a funnel for passing urine to one that expels semen. Moreover, the bladder is closed off when the male becomes sexually aroused, decreasing the likelihood that semen and urine will mix.

Yes, the blood that fills the penis during sexual arousal causes erectile tissue to expand. But what accounts for the firmness of an erection? A sponge that fills with water expands but does not grow hard. It happens that the corpora cavernosa are surrounded by a tough, fibrous covering called the *tunica albuginea*. As the rubber of a balloon resists the pressure of pumped-in air, this housing resists expansion, causing the penis to rigidify. The corpus spongiosum, which contains the penile urethra, also engorges with blood during erection. It does not become hard, however, since it lacks the fibrous casing. The penile glans, which is formed by the crowning of the spongiosum at the tip of the penis, turns a dark purplish hue as it becomes engorged, but it too does not stiffen.

Despite the advanced state of biological knowledge, some mechanics of erection are not completely understood. It is not entirely clear, for example, whether penile cavities

Prostatitis Inflammation of the prostate gland.

Erection The enlargement and stiffening of the penis as a consequence of engorgement with blood.

become engorged because the veins that carry blood away from the penis do not keep pace with the rapid flow of blood entering the penis or whether the returning blood flow is reduced by compression of the veins at the base of the penis (as stepping lightly on a garden hose slows the movement of water).

We do know that erection is reversed when more blood flows out of the erectile tissue than flows in, restoring the pre-erectile circulatory balance and shrinking the erectile tissue or spongy masses. The erectile tissue thus exerts less pressure against the fibrous covering, resulting in a loss of rigidity. Loss of erection occurs when sexual stimulation ceases or when the body returns to a (sexual) resting state following orgasm. Loss of erection can also occur in response to anxiety or perceived threats. Loss of erection in response to threat can be abrupt, as when a man in the "throes of passion" suddenly hears a suspicious noise in the adjoining room, suggestive of an intruder. Yet the "threats" that induce loss of erection are more likely to be psychological than physical. In our culture, men often measure their manhood by their sexual performance. A man who fears that he will be unable to perform successfully may experience **performance anxiety** that can prevent him from achieving erection or lead to a loss of erection at penetration.

The male capacity for erection quite literally spans the life cycle. Erections are common in babies, even within minutes after birth. Evidence from ultrasound studies shows that male fetuses may even have erections months before birth. Men who are well into their 80s and 90s continue to experience erections and engage in coitus.

Erections are not limited to the conscious state. Men have nocturnal erections every 90 minutes or so as they sleep. They generally occur during REM (rapid eye movement) sleep. REM sleep is associated with dreaming. It is so named because the sleeper's eyes dart about rapidly under the closed eyelids during this stage. Erections occur during most periods of REM sleep.

The mechanism of nocturnal erection appears to be physiologically based. That is, erections occur along with dreams that may or may not have erotic content. Morning erections are actually nocturnal erections. They occur when the man is awakened during REM sleep, as by an alarm clock. Men sometimes erroneously believe that a morning erection is caused by the need to urinate. When the man awakens with both an erection and the need to urinate, he may mistakenly assume that the erection was caused by the pressure of his bladder.

It is not true that morning erections reflect the need to urinate. Morning erections are actually a form of nocturnal erection. ■

Spinal Reflexes and Sexual Response

Men may become sexually aroused by a range of stimulation, including tactile stimulation provided by their partners, visual stimulation (such as from scanning photos of nude models in men's magazines), or even mental stimulation from engaging in sexual fantasies. Regardless of the source of stimulation, the man's sexual responses, erection and ejaculation, occur by **reflex.**

Erection and ejaculation are reflexes: automatic, unlearned responses to sexual stimulation. So too are vaginal lubrication and orgasm in women. We do not control sexual reflexes voluntarily, as we might control the lifting of a finger or an arm. We can set the stage for them to occur by ensuring the proper stimulation. Once the stage is set, the reflexes are governed by automatic processes, not by conscious effort. Efforts to control sexual responses consciously by "force of will" can backfire and make it more difficult to become aroused (for example, to attain erection or vaginal lubrication). We need not "try" to become aroused. We need only expose ourselves to effective sexual stimulation and allow our reflexes to do the job for us.

Performance anxiety Feelings of dread and foreboding experienced in connection with sexual activity (or any other activity that might be judged by another person).

Reflex A simple, unlearned response to a stimulus that is mediated by the spine rather than the brain.

It is not true that men can will themselves to have erections. Men can only set the stage for erections by providing physical or cognitive sexual stimulation. ■

The reflexes governing erection and ejaculation are controlled at the level of the spinal cord. Therefore, they are considered spinal reflexes. How does erection occur? Erections may occur in response to different types of stimulation. Some erections occur from direct stimulation of the genitals, as from stroking, licking, or fondling the penis or scrotum. Erectile responses to such direct stimulation involve a simple spinal reflex that does not require the direct participation of the brain.

Erections can also be initiated by the brain, without the genitals being touched or fondled at all. Such erections may occur when a man has sexual fantasies, when he views erotic materials, or when he catches a glimpse of a woman in a bikini on a beach. In the case of the "no-hands" type of erections, stimulation from the brain travels to the spinal cord, where the erectile reflex is triggered. To better understand how this reflex works, we need to first explain the concept of the reflex arc.

THE REFLEX ARC   When you withdraw your hand from a hot stove or blink in response to a puff of air, you do so before you have any time to think about it. These responses, like erection, are reflexes that involve sensory neurons and effector neurons (see Figure 4.9). In response to a stimulus such as a touch or a change in temperature, sensory neurons or receptors in the skin fire and thereby send messages to the spinal cord. The message is then transmitted to effector neurons that begin in the spinal cord and cause muscles to contract or glands to secrete chemical substances. So if you accidentally touched a hot stove, sensory neurons in your fingers or hand would deliver a message to the spinal cord, which would trigger effector neurons to contract muscles that pull your hand away from the stove. The brain does not control this spinal reflex arc. That is not to say that the brain fails to get the message shortly afterwards. Sensory messages usually rise from the spinal cord to the brain to make us aware of stimulation. (Awareness "dwells" within the nerve cells, or gray matter, of the brain.) The experience of pain occurs when a message travels from the site of the injury to the spinal cord and then to receiving stations in the brain that interpret the message to produce the sensation of pain. The withdrawal of your hand from a harmful object begins before your brain even gets the message.

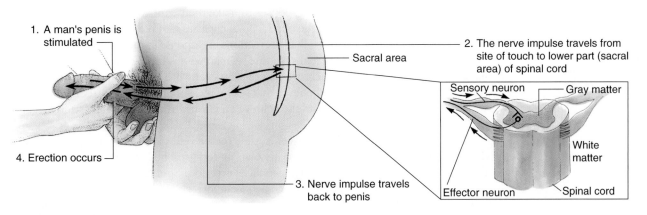

figure 4.9

Reflexes. Reflexes involve sensory neurons, effector neurons, and sometimes interneurons that connect the two in the spinal cord. Reflexes need not involve the brain, although messages to the brain may make us aware when reflexes are occurring. Reflexes are the product of "local government" in the spine.

THE ROLE OF THE SPINAL CORD   Let us look more closely at the spinal reflex that produces erection in response to tactile stimulation (touch). Tactile stimulation of the penis or nearby areas (lower abdomen, scrotum, inner thighs) causes sensory neurons to transmit nerve messages (signals) to an erection center in the lower back, in an area of the spinal cord called the **sacrum.** The sacral erection center controls reflexive erections—that is, erections occurring in response to direct stimulation of the penis and nearby areas (Spark, 1991). When direct penile stimulation occurs, messages in the form of nerve impulses are received by this erection center, which in turn sends impulses to the genitalia via nerves that service the penis. These impulses cause arteries carrying blood to the corpora cavernosa and corpus spongiosum to dilate, so more blood flows into these tissues; as these tissues expand, the penis becomes erect.

The existence of the sacral erection center makes it possible for men whose spinal cords have been injured or severed above the center to achieve erections (and ejaculate) in response to direct tactile stimulation of the penis. Erection occurs even though their injuries prevent nerve signals from reaching their brains. Because of the lack of communication between the genital organs and the brain, there are no sensations, no physical pleasure. Many spinal-injured men report that sex remains psychologically pleasurable and fulfilling nonetheless. They can observe the responses of their partners, and perhaps the brain fills in some sensations from memory or imagination.

THE ROLE OF THE BRAIN   If direct penile stimulation triggers erection at the spinal level, what is the role of the brain? Although it might seem that the penis sometimes has a mind of its own, the brain plays an important role in regulating sexual responses.

Tactile (touch) stimulation of the penis may trigger the erection reflex through a simple reflex arc in the spinal cord. Penile sensations are then normally relayed to the brain, which generally results in sensations of pleasure and perhaps in a decision to focus on erotic stimulation. The sight of one's partner, erotic fantasies, memories, and so forth can result in messages being sent by the brain through the spinal cord to the arteries servicing the penis, helping to maintain the erection.

The brain can also originate messages that trigger the erectile reflex. The "no-hands" type of erection can occur while recalling sexual memories, entertaining sexual fantasies, viewing erotic stimuli, or even while asleep. In such cases, the brain plays a more direct role in the erectile response by transmitting nerve impulses to a second and higher erection center located in the upper back in the lumbar region of the spinal cord. This higher spinal erection center serves as a "switchboard" between the brain and the penis, allowing perceptual, cognitive, and emotional responses to make their contributions. When the nerve pathways between the brain and the upper spinal cord are blocked or severed, men cannot achieve "psychogenic erections"—that is, erections in response to mental stimulation alone.

The brain can also stifle sexual response. A man who is highly anxious about his sexual abilities may be unable to achieve an erection even with the most direct, intense penile stimulation. Or a man who believes that sexual pleasure is sinful or dirty may be filled with anxiety and guilt and be unable to achieve erection when he is sexually stimulated by his partner.

In some males, especially adolescents, the erectile reflex is so easily tripped that incidental rubbing of the genitals against his own undergarments, the sight of an attractive passer-by, or a fleeting sexual fantasy produces erection. Spontaneous erections may occur under embarrassing circumstances, such as before classes change in junior or senior high school or on a public beach. In an effort to distract himself from erotic fantasies and to allow an erection to subside, many a male adolescent in the classroom has desperately renewed his interest in his algebra or foreign language textbook before the bell has rung. (A well-placed towel may serve in a pinch on a public beach.)

As men mature, they require more penile stimulation to achieve full erection. Partners of men in their 30s and 40s need not feel that their attractiveness has waned if their

Sacrum The thick, triangular bone located near the bottom of the spinal column.

lovers no longer have instant "no-hands" erections when they disrobe. It takes men longer to achieve erection as they age, and direct penile stimulation becomes a more critical source of arousal.

THE ROLE OF THE AUTONOMIC NERVOUS SYSTEM   Although stimulation that brings about an erection can originate in the brain, this does not mean that erection is a voluntary response, like raising your arm. Whatever the original or dominant source of stimulation—direct penile stimulation or sexual fantasy—erection remains an unlearned, automatic reflex.

Automatic responses, such as erection, involve the division of the nervous system called the **autonomic nervous system** (ANS). *Autonomic* means "automatic." The ANS controls automatic bodily processes such as heartbeat, pupil dilation, respiration, and digestion. In contrast, voluntary movement (such as raising an arm) is under the control of the *somatic* division of the nervous system.

The ANS has two branches, the **sympathetic** and the **parasympathetic.** These branches have largely opposing effects; when they are activated at the same time, their effects become balanced out to some degree. In general, the sympathetic branch is in command during processes that involve a release of bodily energy from stored reserves, such as during running, performing some other athletic task, or being gripped by fear or anxiety. The sympathetic branch also governs the general mobilization of the body, such as by increasing the heart rate and respiration rate in response to threat.

The parasympathetic branch is most active during processes that restore reserves of energy, such as digestion. When we experience fear or anxiety, the sympathetic branch of the ANS quickens the heart rate. When we relax, the parasympathetic branch curbs the heart rate. The parasympathetic branch activates digestive processes, but the sympathetic branch inhibits digestive activity. Since the sympathetic branch is in command when we feel fear or anxiety, such stimuli can inhibit the activity of the parasympathetic system, thereby slowing down the digestive process and possibly causing indigestion.

The divisions of the autonomic nervous system play different roles in sexual arousal and response. The nerves that cause penile arteries to dilate during erection belong to the parasympathetic branch of the autonomic nervous system. It is therefore the parasympathetic system that largely governs erection. The nerves governing ejaculation belong to the sympathetic branch, however. One implication of this division of neural responsibility is that intense fear or anxiety, which involves sympathetic nervous system activity, may inhibit erection by counteracting the activity of the parasympathetic nervous system. Since sympathetic arousal is involved in triggering the ejaculatory reflex, anxiety or fear may also accelerate ejaculation, causing premature ejaculation. Intense emotions such as fear and anxiety can thus lead to problems in achieving or maintaining erection as well as causing hasty ejaculation.

The connection between the emotions, sympathetic activity, and ejaculation can set up a vicious cycle. Anxiety in a sexual encounter may trigger premature ejaculation. During a subsequent sexual encounter, the man might fear a recurrence of premature ejaculation. This fear may engender the reality. He may thus face further sexual encounters with yet greater fear, possibly further hastening ejaculation—and possibly inhibiting erection itself. Methods for helping men with erectile dysfunction and premature ejaculation aim at reducing their levels of anxiety and thereby lessening sympathetic activity.

Because erections seem spontaneous at times and often occur when the man would rather not have them, it might seem to men that the penis has a mind of its own. Despite this common folk belief, however, the penis possesses no guiding intelligence. It consists of spongy masses of erectile tissue, not the lovely dense gray matter that renders your thought processes so incisive.

Autonomic nervous system
The division of the nervous system that regulates automatic bodily processes, such as heartbeat, pupil dilation, respiration, and digestion. Abbreviated *ANS*.

Sympathetic The branch of the ANS most active during emotional responses that spend the body's reserves of energy, such as fear and anxiety. The sympathetic ANS largely controls ejaculation.

Parasympathetic The branch of the ANS that is most active during processes that restore the body's reserves of energy, such as digestion. The parasympathetic ANS largely controls erection.

Truth or Fiction?
REVISITED

It is not true that the penis has a mind of its own. Although it may seem that the penis follows its own mind at times, it is governed by the autonomic (automatic) nervous system. ■

ERECTILE ABNORMALITIES   Some men find that their erect penises are slightly curved or bent. Some degree of curvature is perfectly normal, but men with **Peyronie's disease** have excessive curvature that can make erections painful or make it difficult to enjoy coitus. The condition is caused by buildup of fibrous tissue in the penile shaft. Although some cases of Peyronie's disease appear to clear up on their own, most require medical attention.

Some men experience erections that persist for hours or days. This condition is called *priapism*, after Priapus of Greek myth, the son of Dionysus and Aphrodite who personified male procreative power. Priapism is often caused by leukemia, sickle-cell anemia, or diseases of the spinal cord, although in some cases the cause remains unknown. Priapism occurs when the mechanisms that drain the blood that makes the penis erect are damaged and so cannot return the blood to the circulatory system. The name of the disorder is truly a misnomer, because Priapus had a voracious sexual appetite. Men with priapism instead suffer from a painful condition that should receive medical attention. Priapism may become a medical emergency, since erection prolonged beyond six hours can starve penile tissues of oxygen, leading to tissue deterioration. Immediate medical intervention in the form of drugs or even surgery may be required to reverse the condition and allow blood to drain from the penis (Spark, 1991).

Ejaculation

Ejaculation, like erection, is a spinal reflex. It is triggered when sexual stimulation reaches a critical point or threshold. Ejaculation generally occurs together with **orgasm,** the sudden muscle contractions that occur at the peak of sexual excitement and result in the abrupt release of sexual tension that had built up during sexual arousal. Orgasm is accompanied by subjective sensations that are generally intensely pleasurable. Ejaculation, however, refers only to the expulsion of semen from the tip of the penis. Orgasm and ejaculation are *not* synonymous, nor do they always occur simultaneously. For example, **paraplegics** can ejaculate if the area of the lower spinal cord that controls ejaculation is intact. They do not experience the subjective aspects of orgasm, however, since the sensations of orgasm do not reach the brain.

Truth or Fiction?
REVISITED

It is true that many men who are paralyzed below the waist can attain erection, engage in sexual intercourse, and ejaculate, if the spinal centers controlling erection and ejaculation remain intact. ■

Conversely, prepubertal boys may experience orgasms even though they emit no ejaculate. Orgasms without ejaculate are termed *dry orgasms*. Boys do not begin to produce seminal fluid (and sperm) until puberty. Mature men, too, can experience dry orgasms. They can take the form of "little orgasms" preceding a larger orgasm, or they can follow "wet orgasms" when sexual stimulation is continued but seminal fluids have not been replenished. These dry orgasms are perfectly normal. Dry orgasms can also be a result of retrograde ejaculation, however, as we shall see below.

Truth or Fiction?
REVISITED

It is true that men can have orgasms without ejaculating. Such orgasms are termed *dry orgasms.* ■

Ejaculation occurs in two stages. The first phase, often called the **emission stage,** involves contractions of the prostate, seminal vesicles, and the upper part of the vas deferens (the **ampulla**). The force of these contractions propels seminal fluid into the prostatic part of the urethral tract—a small tube called the **urethral bulb**—which balloons out as muscles close at either end, trapping the semen. It is at this point that the man perceives that orgasm is inevitable. Masters and Johnson term this feeling a sense of "ejaculatory inevitability" (Masters & Johnson, 1966). Men might colloquially describe the feeling as being about to "come." The man feels that a point of no return has been passed, that nothing can prevent ejaculation.

The second stage, which is often referred to as the **expulsion stage,** involves the propulsion of the seminal fluid through the urethra and out of the urethral opening at the tip of the penis. In this stage, muscles at the base of the penis and elsewhere contract rhythmically, forcefully expelling semen. The second stage is generally accompanied by the highly pleasurable sensations of orgasm.

In ejaculation, the seminal fluid is released from the urethral bulb and expelled by forceful contractions of the pelvic muscles that surround the urethral channel and the crura of the penis. The first few contractions are most intense and occur at 0.8-second intervals. Subsequent contractions lessen in intensity. The interval between them gradually increases. Seminal fluid is expelled in spurts during the first few contractions. The contractions are so powerful that seminal fluid may be propelled to distances of 12 to 24 inches, according to observations made by Masters and Johnson. Some men, however, report that semen travels but a few inches or just oozes from the penile opening. The force of the expulsion varies with the condition of the man's prostate, his general health, and his age. There is some correspondence between the force of the expulsion and the pleasure of orgasm. That is, more intense orgasms, psychologically speaking, often accompany more forceful ejaculations.

Like erection, ejaculation is regulated by two centers in the spinal cord, one in the sacral region and one in the higher lumbar region. When sexual arousal rises to a critical level—the point of ejaculatory inevitability—the lumbar ejaculatory center triggers the first stage of ejaculation, seminal emission. The lower, or sacral, ejaculatory center triggers the second stage of orgasm: the rhythmic muscle contractions that expel the ejaculate from the body.

Although ejaculation occurs by reflex, a man can delay ejaculation by maintaining the level of sexual stimulation below the critical threshold, or "point of no return." Men who suffer from **premature ejaculation** have been successfully treated in programs that train them to learn to recognize their "point of no return" and maintain sexual stimulation below it. (Issues concerning the definition and treatment of premature ejaculation are explored in Chapter 15 on sexual dysfunction.) Recognizing the point of no return and keeping stimulation beneath the critical level can also prolong coitus and enhance sexual pleasure for couples even when the man does not experience premature ejaculation.

RETROGRADE EJACULATION

Some men experience **retrograde ejaculation,** in which the ejaculate empties into the bladder rather than being expelled from the body. During normal ejaculation, an external sphincter opens, allowing seminal fluid to pass out of the body. Another sphincter, this one internal, closes off the opening to the bladder, preventing the seminal fluid from backing up into the bladder. In retrograde ejaculation, the actions of these sphincters are reversed. The external sphincter remains closed, preventing the expulsion of the seminal fluid, while the internal sphincter opens, allowing the ejaculate to empty into the bladder. The result is a dry orgasm. No ejaculate is apparent because semen has backed up into the bladder. Retrograde ejaculation condition may be caused by prostate surgery (much less so now than in former years), drugs such as tranquilizers, certain illnesses, and accidents. Retrograde ejaculation is usually harmless in itself, since the seminal fluid is later discharged with urine. Infertility can result, however, and there may be some changes in the sensations associated with orgasm.

Peyronie's disease An abnormal condition characterized by an excessive curvature of the penis that can make erections painful.

Orgasm The climax of sexual excitement.

Paraplegic A person with sensory and motor paralysis of the lower half of the body.

Emission phase The first phase of ejaculation, which involves contractions of the prostate gland, seminal vesicles, and the upper part of the vasa deferentia.

Ampulla A sac or dilated part of a tube or canal.

Urethral bulb The small tube that makes up the prostatic part of the urethral tract and that balloons out as muscles close at either end, trapping semen prior to ejaculation.

Expulsion stage The second stage of ejaculation, during which muscles at the base of the penis and elsewhere contract rhythmically, forcefully expelling semen and providing pleasurable sensations.

Premature ejaculation A sexual dysfunction in which the male persistently ejaculates too early to afford the couple adequate sexual gratification.

Retrograde ejaculation Ejaculation in which the ejaculate empties into the bladder. (From the Latin *retrogradi,* meaning "to go backward.")

Persistent dry orgasms should be medically evaluated, since their underlying cause may be a threat to health.

Reflections

■ Did you know how erection occurred before taking this course? Do the facts differ from your assumptions?

■ Since erection and ejaculation are reflexes, how is it that people can bring them about?

■ Agree or disagree with the following statement, and support your answer: The penis has a mind of its own.

■ What roles do the brain and spinal cord play in erection and ejaculation?

Male sexual functions, like female sexual functions, are incredibly complex. They involve the cooperation of the nervous system, the endocrine system, the cardiovascular system, and the musculoskeletal system. In Chapter 5, we learn more about how the female and male sex organs respond to sexual stimulation. In Chapter 6, we examine the similarities and differences between the genders with respect to sexual differentiation, behavior, and personality.

s u m m i n g   u p

EXTERNAL SEX ORGANS

The male external sex organs include the penis and the scrotum.

The Penis

Semen and urine pass out of the penis through the urethral opening. The penis contains cylinders that fill with blood and stiffen during sexual arousal. Circumcision—the surgical removal of the prepuce—has been carried out for religious and hygienic reasons. In our culture, the size of the penis is sometimes seen as a measure of a man's masculinity and his ability to please his sex partners, although there is little if any connection between the size of the penis and sexual performance.

The Scrotum

The scrotum is the pouch of loose skin that contains the testes. Each testicle is held in place by a spermatic cord, which contains the vas deferens and the cremaster muscle.

INTERNAL SEX ORGANS

The male internal sex organs consist of the testes, a system of tubes and ducts that conduct sperm, and organs that nourish and activate sperm.

The Testes

The testes serve two functions analogous to those of the ovaries. They secrete male sex hormones (androgens) and produce germ cells (sperm). The hypothalamus, pituitary gland, and testes keep blood testosterone levels at a more or less constant level through a hormonal negative feedback loop. Testosterone is produced by interstitial cells. Sperm are produced by seminiferous tubules. Sperm are stored and mature in the epididymis.

The Vas Deferens

Each epididymis empties into a vas deferens that conducts sperm over the bladder.

The Seminal Vesicles

The seminal vesicles are glands that open into the ejaculatory ducts where the fluids they secrete combine with and nourish sperm.

The Prostate Gland

The prostate gland secretes fluid that provides the characteristic texture and odor of semen.

Cowper's Glands

During sexual arousal, the Cowper's glands secrete a drop or so of clear, slippery fluid that appears at the urethral opening.

Semen

Sperm and the fluids contributed by the seminal vesicles, prostate gland, and Cowper's glands make up semen, the whitish fluid that is expelled through the tip of the penis during ejaculation.

DISEASES OF THE UROGENITAL SYSTEM

Urethritis

Men, like women, are subject to bladder and urethral inflammations, which are generally referred to as urethritis.

Cancer of the Testes

This is the most common form of solid-tumor cancer to strike young men between the ages of 20 and 34.

Disorders of the Prostate

The prostate gland generally becomes enlarged in men past the age of 50. Prostate cancer involves the growth of malignant prostate tumors that can metastasize to bones and lymph nodes. The chief symptoms of prostatitis are an ache or pain between the scrotum and anal opening and painful ejaculation.

MALE SEXUAL FUNCTIONS

Erection

Erection is the process by which the penis becomes engorged with blood, increases in size, and stiffens. Erection occurs in response to sexual stimulation but is also common during REM sleep.

Spinal Reflexes and Sexual Response

Erection and ejaculation occur by reflex. Reflexes involve sensory neurons and effector neurons, which meet in the spinal cord. There are two erection centers in the spinal cord. Although erection is a reflex, penile sensations are relayed to the brain, where they generally result in pleasure.

Erection and ejaculation also involve the autonomic nervous system (ANS). The parasympathetic branch of the ANS largely governs erection, whereas the sympathetic branch largely controls ejaculation.

Ejaculation

Ejaculation, like erection, is a reflex. It is triggered when sexual stimulation reaches a critical threshold. Ejaculation usually but not always occurs with orgasm, but the terms are not synonymous. The emission phase of ejaculation involves contractions of the prostate, seminal vesicles, and the upper part of the vas deferens. In the expulsion stage, semen is propelled through the urethra and out of the penis. In this stage, muscles at the base of the penis and elsewhere contract rhythmically, forcefully expelling semen. There are two ejaculation centers in the spinal cord. In retrograde ejaculation, the ejaculate empties into the bladder rather than being expelled from the body.

Theophilus Brown. *The Swing.* 1966. Acrylic on canvas, 52 x 56 in. Collection of Daniel and Virginia Mardesich. Photo by Ira Schrank

chapter

5

Sexual Arousal and Response

outline

TRUTH OR FICTION?

**MAKING SENSE OF SEX:
THE ROLE OF THE SENSES
IN SEXUAL AROUSAL**

Vision: The Better to See You With

Smell: Does the Nose Know Best?

IN THE NEW MILLENNIUM:
*Will We Finally Have "Love Potions"
in the New Millennium?*

The Skin Senses: Sex as a
Touching Experience

Taste: On Savory Sex

Hearing: The Better to Hear You With

**APHRODISIACS: OF SPANISH FLIES
AND RHINO HORNS**

Anaphrodisiacs

Psychoactive Drugs

**SEXUAL RESPONSE AND THE
BRAIN: CEREBRAL SEX?**

The Geography of the Brain

Brain Mechanisms in Sexual Functioning

On Pushing the Right Buttons:
Are There Pleasure Centers in the Brain?

**SEX HORMONES: DO THEY
"GOAD" US INTO SEX?**

Sex Hormones and Sexual Behavior:
Organizing and Activating Influences

Sex Hormones and Male Sexual Behavior

Sex Hormones and Female
Sexual Behavior

THE SEXUAL RESPONSE CYCLE

Excitement Phase

Plateau Phase

Orgasmic Phase

Resolution Phase

Kaplan's Three Stages of Sexual
Response: An Alternative Model

CONTROVERSIES ABOUT ORGASM

Multiple Orgasms: When You're Having
More Than One

How Many Kinds of Orgasms Do
Women Have? One, Two, or Three?

The G-Spot

SUMMING UP

Truth or Fiction **?**

_____ The menstrual cycles of women who live together
tend to become synchronized.

_____ The primary erogenous zone is the brain.

_____ "Spanish fly" will not turn your date on, but it might
cure his or her warts.

_____ Electrical stimulation of certain areas in the human
brain can yield sensations similar to those of sexual
pleasure and gratification.

_____ Normal men produce estrogen, and normal women
produce androgens.

_____ Written descriptions of men's and women's
experiences during orgasm cannot be differentiated.

_____ Orgasms attained through sexual intercourse are
more intense than those attained through
masturbation.

What turns you on? What springs your heart into your mouth, tightens your throat, and opens the floodgates into your genitals? The sight of your lover undressing, a photo of Denzel Washington or Cindy Crawford, a sniff of some velvety perfume, a sip of wine?

Many factors contribute to sexual arousal. Some people are aroused by magazines with photographs of nude or seminude models that have been airbrushed to perfection. Some need only to imagine Hollywood's latest sex symbol. Some become aroused by remembrances of past lovers. Some are stimulated by sexual fantasies of flings with strangers.

People vary greatly in the cues that excite them sexually and in the frequency with which they experience sexual thoughts and feelings. Some young people seem perpetually aroused or arousable. Some people rarely or never entertain sexual thoughts or fantasies.

In this chapter, we look at factors that contribute to sexual arousal and the processes that relate to sexual response. Since our experience of the world is initiated by our senses, we begin the chapter by focusing on the role of the senses in sexual arousal.

MAKING SENSE OF SEX: THE ROLE OF THE SENSES IN SEXUAL AROUSAL

We come to apprehend the world around us through our senses—vision, hearing, smell, taste, and the skin senses, which include that all-important sense of touch. Each of the senses plays a role in our sexual experience, but some senses play larger roles than others.

Vision: The Better to See You With

It was the face of Helen of Troy, not her scent or her melodic voice, that "launched a thousand ships." Men's and women's magazines are filled with pictures of comely members of the other gender, not with "scratch and sniff" residues of their scents (but wait, a new marketing idea dawns!).

In matters of sexual attraction, people seem to have more in common with birds than with fellow mammals such as dogs and cats. Birds identify prospective mates within their species on the basis of their plumage and other visual markings. People also tend to be visually oriented when it comes to sexual attraction. By contrast, dogs and cats are more attracted to each other on the basis of scents that signal sexual receptivity.

Visual cues can be sexual turn-ons. We may be turned on by the sight of a lover in the nude, disrobing, or dressed in evening wear. Lingerie companies hope to convince customers that they will enhance their sex appeal by wearing strategically concealing and revealing nightwear. Some couples find it arousing to observe themselves making love in an overhead mirror or on videotape. Some people find sexually explicit movies arousing. Others are bored or offended by them. Though both genders can be sexually aroused by visually mediated erotica (a technical term for "porn flicks"), men are more interested in them.

Smell: Does the Nose Know Best?

Although the sense of smell plays a lesser role in governing sexual arousal in humans than in lower mammals, odors can be sexual turn-ons or turn-offs. Perfume companies, for example, bottle fragrances that are purported to be sexually arousing.

Most Westerners prefer their lovers to be clean and fresh smelling. People in our society learn to remove or mask odors by the use of soaps, deodorants, and perfumes or colognes. The ancient Egyptians invented scented bathing to rid themselves of offensive odors (Ramirez, 1990). The ancient Romans had such a passion for perfume that they would bathe in fragrances and even dab their horses and household pets (Ackerman, 1990).

Inclinations to find underarm or genital odors offensive may reflect cultural conditioning and not biological predispositions. In some societies, genital secretions are considered **aphrodisiacs.**

Aphrodisiac Any drug or other agent that is sexually arousing or increases sexual desire. (From *Aphrodite*, the Greek goddess of love and beauty).

For centuries, people have searched for a love potion—a magical formula that could make other people fall in love with you or be strongly attracted to you. Some scientists suggest that such potions may already exist in the form of chemical secretions known as **pheromones.**

Pheromones are odorless chemicals that are detected through a "sixth sense": the *vomeronasal organ*. This organ, located in the nose, detects the chemicals and communicates information about them to the hypothalamus, where certain pheromones might affect sexual response (Azar, 1998). People may use pheromones in many ways. Infants may use them to recognize their mothers, and adults might respond to them in seeking a mate. Lower animals use pheromones to stimulate sexual response, organize food gathering, maintain pecking orders, sound alarms, and mark territories (Azar, 1998). Pheromones induce mating behavior in insects. Male rodents show less sexual arousal when their sense of smell is blocked, but the role of pheromones in sexual behavior becomes less vital as one moves upward through the ranks of the animal kingdom.

Only a few years ago, most researchers did not believe that pheromones played a role in human behavior. Today, however, it appears that people do possess vomeronasal organs (Bartoshuk & Beauchamp, 1994), and this field of research has attracted new interest. Some entrepreneurs have already formed companies that plan to commercialize the use of human pheromones—or shall we say "love potions"?—in the new millennium.

A Touching Experience. The sense of touch is intimately connected with sexual experience. The touch of a lover's hand on the cheek, or gentle massage, can be sexually stimulating. Certain parts of the body—called erogenous zones—have special sexual significance because of their response to erotic stimulation.

MENSTRUAL SYNCHRONY   Research by several investigators suggests that exposure to other women's sweat can modify a woman's menstrual cycle. In one study, women who were exposed to underarm secretions from other women, which may contain some as yet unidentified pheromones, showed converging shifts in their menstrual cycles (Bartoshuk & Beauchamp, 1994; Preti et al., 1986). Similar synchronization of menstrual cycles has also been observed among women who share dormitory rooms. In another study, 80% of the women who dabbed their upper lips with an extract of perspiration from other women began to menstruate in sync with the cycles of the donors after about three menstrual cycles (Cutler & Preti, 1986). A control group, who dabbed their lips with alcohol, showed no changes in their menstrual cycles. In yet another study from this research group, the length of the cycles of women with unusually short or long cycles began to normalize when they were exposed to an extract of *male* underarm perspiration (Preti et al., 1986).

The menstrual cycles of women who live together do tend to become synchronized, possibly in response to pheromones. ■

Truth or Fiction? **REVISITED**

The Skin Senses: Sex as a Touching Experience

Our skin senses enable us to sense pain, changes in temperature, and pressure (or touch). Whatever the roles of vision and smell in sexual attraction and arousal, the sense of touch has the most direct effects on sexual arousal and response. Any region of that sensitive layer we refer to as skin can become eroticized. The touch of your lover's hand on your cheek, or your lover's gentle massage of your shoulders or back, can be sexually stimulating.

Pheromones Chemical substances, secreted externally by certain animals, which convey information to, or produce specific responses in, other members of the same species. (From the Greek *pherien*, meaning "to bear [a message]" and *hormone*.)

127

EROGENOUS ZONES **Erogenous zones** are parts of the body that are especially sensitive to tactile sexual stimulation—to strokes and other caresses. **Primary erogenous zones** are erotically sensitive because they are richly endowed with nerve endings. **Secondary erogenous zones** are parts of the body that become erotically sensitized through experience.

Primary erogenous zones include the genitals; the inner thighs, perineum, buttocks, and anus; the breasts (especially the nipples); the ears (particularly the earlobes); the mouth, lips, and tongue; the neck; the navel; and, yes, the armpits. Preferences vary somewhat from person to person, reflecting possible biological, attitudinal, and experiential differences. Areas that are exquisitely sensitive for some people may produce virtually no reaction—or discomfort—in others. Many women, for example, report little sensation when their breasts are stroked or kissed. Many men are uncomfortable when their nipples are caressed. On the other hand (or foot), many people find the areas between their toes sensitive to erotic stimulation and enjoy keeping a toehold on their partners during coitus.

Secondary erogenous zones become eroticized through association with sexual stimulation. For example, a woman might become sexually aroused when her lover gently caresses her shoulders, because such caresses have been incorporated as a regular feature of the couple's lovemaking. A few of the women observed by Masters and Johnson (1966) reached orgasm when the smalls of their backs were rubbed.

People are also highly responsive to images and fantasies. This is why the brain is sometimes referred to as the primary sexual organ or an erogenous zone. Some women report reaching orgasm through fantasy alone (Kinsey et al., 1953). Men regularly experience erection and nocturnal emissions ("wet dreams") without direct stimulation of the genitals.

However, the brain is not an erogenous zone. It is not stimulated directly by touch. (The brain processes tactile information from the skin, but it does not have sensory neurons to directly gather this information itself.) Nevertheless, the etymology (word origins) of the term *erogenous* clearly applies to the brain. It *can* give birth to erotic sensations through production of fantasy, erotic memories, and other thoughts.

It is not true that the primary erogenous zone is the brain. The brain is not an erogenous zone in the strict sense of the term. Erogenous zones are directly sensitive to touch. However, the brain processes information received through erogenous zones and can have such an impact on sexual arousal that it has been dubbed an erogenous zone in recognition of its importance. ■

Taste: On Savory Sex

Taste appears to play a minor role in sexual arousal and response, unless we digress into puns and note that taste in the form of a zesty meal or a delicate wine may contribute to arousal. In any event, some people are sexually aroused by the taste of genital secretions, such as vaginal secretions or seminal fluid. We do not know, however, whether these secretions are laced with chemicals that have biologically arousing effects or whether arousal reflects the meaning that these secretions have to the individual. That is, we may learn to become aroused by, or to seek out, flavors or odors that have been associated with sexual pleasure. Others are turned off by them.

Hearing: The Better to Hear You With

The sense of hearing also provides an important medium for sexual arousal and response. Like visual and olfactory cues, sounds can be turn-ons or turn-offs. The sounds of one's lover, whether whispers, indications of pleasure, or animated sounds that may attend orgasm, may be arousing during the heat of passion. For some people, key words or vocal intonations may become as arousing as direct stimulation of an erogenous zone. Many

Erogenous zones Parts of the body that are especially sensitive to tactile sexual stimulation. (*Erogenous* is derived from roots meaning "giving birth to erotic sensations.")

Primary erogenous zones Erogenous zones that are particularly sensitive because they are richly endowed with nerve endings.

Secondary erogenous zones Parts of the body that become erotically sensitized through experience.

people are aroused when their lovers "talk dirty." Spoken vulgarities spur their sexual arousal. Others find vulgar language offensive.

The sultry voices of screen sirens Lauren Bacall and Kathleen Turner have aroused the ardor of many a moviegoer. Teenagers may thrill to the music of Metallica or Jewel, just as their parents (and grandparents) did when they heard the Beatles, Frank Sinatra, Johnny Mathis, or the King himself (Elvis, that is). Of course, the sex appeal of these performers goes beyond the sounds that they produce.

Music itself can contribute to sexual arousal. Music can relax us and put us "in the mood" or have associations ("They're playing our song!"). Many couples find background music "atmospheric"—a vital accouterment of lovemaking.

Sounds can also be sexual turn-offs. Most of us would find funeral music a damper on sexual arousal. We may also be inhibited by scratchy, unnerving voices. Heavy metal rock might be a sexual turn-off to many (are your authors showing their age?), but it could help to set the right tone for others.

Reflections

- Do you find photos of scantily clad or nude people to be sexually arousing? Why or why not?
- Do you find perfumes or colognes to enhance the attractiveness of other people? Why or why not?
- What kinds of touches do you find to be erotic? Do you have any secondary erogenous zones?

APHRODISIACS: OF SPANISH FLIES AND RHINO HORNS

The only known aphrodisiac is variety.
—Marc Connolly

An aphrodisiac is a substance that arouses or increases one's capacity for sexual pleasure or response. You may have heard of "Spanish fly," an alleged aphrodisiac that was once extracted from a Spanish beetle. (The beetle from which it was taken, *Lytta vesicatoria*, is near extinction.) A few drops in a date's drink was believed to make you irresistible. Spanish fly is but one of many purported aphrodisiacs. However, it is toxic, not sexually arousing. Spanish fly is now synthesized—but not as an aphrodisiac. The active ingredient, *cantharidin*, is a skin irritant that can burn off warts. If it can burn off warts, consider the damage it can do when taken internally. It irritates the urinary tract and can cause severe tissue damage or death. It inflames the urethra, producing a burning sensation in the penis that is sometimes misinterpreted as sexual feelings.

We should also be concerned about an expectancy, or placebo effect, when evaluating the effectiveness of a purported aphrodisiac (Brody, 1993). The belief that a substance has sexually stimulating effects may itself inspire sexual excitement. If a person tries a supposed aphrodisiac and feels sexually aroused, the person might well attribute the turn-on to the effects of the substance, even if the substance had no direct effect on sex drive.

It is true that "Spanish fly" might cure your date's warts (but not turn him or her on). Spanish fly contains cantharidin, a skin irritant that can in fact burn off warts. Cantharidin is not an aphrodisiac, but it can inflame the urethra, producing a burning sensation that could be misinterpreted as sexual feelings. ■

Truth or Fiction?
REVISITED

Foods that in some way resemble male genitals have now and then been considered aphrodisiacs. They include oysters, clams, bull's testicles ("prairie oysters"), tomatoes, and "phallic" items such as celery stalks, bananas, and even ground-up rhinoceros, reindeer, and elephant horns (which is one derivation of the slang term "horny").

Even potatoes have been held to be aphrodisiacs. Yes, potatoes. Shakespeare echoed this belief when he wrote, "Let the sky rain potatoes . . . ; let a tempest of provocation come." None of these foods or substances has been shown to be sexually stimulating, however—not even deep-fried potato skins with cheddar cheese and bacon. Sadly, myths about the sexually arousing properties of substances drawn from rhinoceroses or elephants may be contributing to the rapidly diminishing numbers of these animals.

Other drugs and psychoactive substances may have certain effects on sexual arousal and response. The drug *yohimbine*, an extract from the African yohimbe tree, does stimulate blood flow to the genitals (Brody, 1993). However, its effects are limited and unreliable (Morales, 1993). Yohimbine also happens to be toxic (Brody, 1993).

Amyl nitrate (in the form of "snappers" or "poppers") has been used mostly by gay men (and by some heterosexuals) in the belief that it heightens sensations of arousal and orgasm. Poppers dilate blood vessels in the brain and genitals, producing sensations of warmth in the pelvis and possibly facilitating erection and prolonging orgasm. Amyl nitrate does have some legitimate medical uses, such as helping to reduce heart pain (angina) among cardiac patients. It is inhaled from ampules that "pop" open for rapid use when heart pain occurs. Poppers can cause dizziness, fainting, and migraine-type headaches, however. They should be taken only under a doctor's care for a legitimate medical need, not to intensify sexual sensations.

The drug Viagra was originally developed as a treatment for angina (heart pain) because it was thought that it would increase the blood flow to the heart. It does so, modestly. However, it is more effective at dilating blood vessels in the genital organs, thereby facilitating vasocongestion and erection—and, according to some reports, sexual response in women as well. Viagra is marketed as a treatment for erectile dysfunction (also termed *impotence*). Is Viagra also an aphrodisiac? It is a matter of definition. Although Viagra facilitates erection, it still takes a sexual turn-on for erection to occur (Lewin, 1998). If an aphrodisiac is defined as a substance that is directly sexually arousing, Viagra is not an aphrodisiac.

But certain drugs do appear to have aphrodisiac effects, apparently because they act on the brain mechanisms that control the sex drive. For example, drugs that affect brain receptors for the neurotransmitter dopamine, such as the antidepressant drug *bupropion* (trade name Wellbutrin) and the drug L-dopa used in the treatment of Parkinson's disease, can increase the sex drive (Brody, 1993).

The most potent chemical "aphrodisiac" may be a naturally occurring substance in the body: the male sex hormone testosterone. It is the basic fuel of sexual desire in both genders (Brody, 1993).

The safest and perhaps most effective method for increasing the sex drive may not be a drug or substance, but exercise. Regular exercise not only enhances general health. It also boosts energy and increases the sex drive in both genders (Brody, 1993). Perhaps the most potent aphrodisiac of all is novelty. Partners can invent new ways of sexually discovering one another. They can make love in novel places, experiment with different techniques, wear provocative clothing, share or enact fantasies, or whatever their imaginations inspire.

Anaphrodisiacs

Some substances such as potassium nitrate (saltpeter) have been considered inhibitors of sexual response—**anaphrodisiacs.** Saltpeter, however, only indirectly dampens sexual arousal. As a diuretic that can increase the need for urination, it may make the thought of sex unappealing. It does not directly dampen sexual response.

Other chemicals do dampen sexual arousal and response. Tranquilizers and central nervous system depressants, such as barbiturates, can lessen sexual desire and impair sexual performance. These drugs may paradoxically enhance sexual arousal in some people, however, by lessening sexual inhibitions or fear of possible repercussions from sexual activity. Antihypertensive drugs, which are used in the treatment of high blood pressure,

Anaphrodisiacs Drugs or other agents whose effects are antagonistic to sexual arousal or sexual desire.

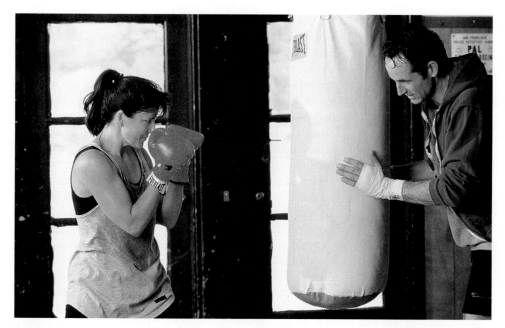

may produce erectile and ejaculatory difficulties in men and reduction of sexual desire in both genders. Certain antidepressant drugs, such as fluoxetine (brand name: Prozac), amitriptyline (brand name: Elavil), and imipramine (brand name: Tofranil) appear to dampen sex drive (Brody, 1993; Meston & Gorzalka, 1992). Antidepressants may also impair erectile response and delay ejaculation in men and orgasmic responsiveness in women (Meston & Gorzlaka, 1992). (Because they delay ejaculation, some of these drugs are being used to treat premature ejaculation.)

Nicotine, the stimulant in tobacco smoke, constricts the blood vessels. Thus, it can impede sexual arousal by reducing the capacity of the genitals to become engorged with blood. Chronic smoking can also reduce the blood levels of testosterone in men, which can in turn lessen sex drive or motivation.

Antiandrogen drugs may have anaphrodisiac effects. Their effectiveness in modifying deviant behavior patterns such as sexual violence and sexual interest in children is questionable.

Psychoactive Drugs

Psychoactive drugs, such as alcohol and cocaine, are widely believed to have aphrodisiac effects. Yet their effects may reflect our expectations of them, or their effects on sexual inhibitions, rather than direct stimulation of sexual response.

ALCOHOL: THE "GREAT PROVOKER OF THREE THINGS" In Shakespeare's *Macbeth*, the following exchange takes place between Macduff and a porter:

> PORTER: . . . drink, sir, is a great provoker of three things.
>
> MACDUFF: What three things does drink especially provoke?
>
> PORTER: Marry,[1] sir, nose-painting,[2] sleep, and urine. Lechery,[3] sir, it provokes, and unprovokes; it provokes the desire, but it takes away the performance.

---

[1]Contraction of the expression "By the Virgin Mary"; used by Elizabethans like Shakespeare to speak emphatically yet avoid disrespect to the Virgin Mary.

[2]The reddening of the nose that occurs in many chronic alcoholics as a result of the bursting of small blood vessels.

[3]Excessive indulgence of sexual desire. (Related to the German *lecken*, meaning "to lick.")

Antiandrogen A substance that decreases the levels of androgens in the bloodstream.

Effects of Alcohol on Sexual Behavior—A Complex Picture. Small doses of alcohol can be stimulating and induce feelings of euphoria, both of which would appear to be connected with sexual interest. Alcohol can also reduce fear of consequences of engaging in risky behavior—sexual and otherwise. Drinkers sometimes say, "It was the alcohol, not me." Alcohol is also expected to be sexually liberating, and people often live up to social and cultural expectations. Yet, as a depressant drug, alcohol biochemically dampens sexual response.

Small amounts of alcohol are stimulating, but large amounts curb sexual response. This fact should not be surprising because alcohol is a depressant. Alcohol reduces central nervous system activity. Large amounts of alcohol can severely impair sexual performance in both men and women.

People who drink moderate amounts of alcohol may feel more sexually aroused because of their expectations about alcohol, not because of its chemical properties. That is, people who expect alcohol to enhance sexual responsiveness may act the part. Expectations that alcohol serves as an aphrodisiac may lead men who have problems achieving erection to turn to alcohol as a cure (Roehrich & Kinder, 1991). The fact is, alcohol is a depressant and can reduce sexual potency rather than restore it.

Alcohol may also lower sexual inhibitions, because it allows us to ascribe our behavior to the effects of the alcohol rather than to ourselves (Crowe & George, 1989; Lang, 1985). Alcohol is connected with a liberated social role and thus provides an excuse for dubious behavior. "It was the alcohol," people can say, "not me." People may express their sexual desires and do things when drinking that they would not do when sober. For example, a person who feels guilty about sex may become sexually active when drinking because he or she can later blame the alcohol.

Consider a survey of 1,100 undergraduates taken at the University of Virginia (Grossman, 1991). Forty-three percent of the respondents were classified as "heavy drinkers." That is, they had had at least five alcoholic beverages in a row on one occasion within the two weeks preceding the survey. *More than half* of the heavy drinkers reported that under the influence of alcohol, they had engaged in sexual activity with someone they would not ordinarily have become involved with. All in all, between 20% and 25% of the total sample had engaged in sexual activity they deemed unwise when under the influence of alcohol!

In laboratory studies, men who were misled into believing that they had drunk alcohol spent more time lingering over pornographic pictures as researchers looked on than did men who thought they had not drunk alcohol. Did they believe that they would avert the censure of the onlookers because they could attribute their prurience to the alcohol? If so, perhaps alcohol provides an excuse for socially deviant behavior. The amount of time the men lingered over the pornographic material was unaffected by whether or not they had actually drunk alcohol (Lang et al., 1980; Lansky & Wilson, 1981).

Alcohol can also induce feelings of euphoria. Euphoric feelings may enhance sexual arousal and also wash away qualms about expressing sexual desires. Alcohol also appears to impair the ability to weigh information ("information processing") that might otherwise inhibit sexual impulses (Steele & Josephs, 1990). When people drink, they may be less able to foresee the consequences of misconduct and less likely to ponder their standards of conduct.

HALLUCINOGENICS There is no evidence that marijuana and other hallucinogenic drugs directly stimulate sexual response. However, fairly to strongly intoxicated marijuana users claim to have more empathy with others, to be more aware of bodily sensations, and to experience time as passing more slowly. These sensations could heighten subjective feelings of sexual response. Some marijuana users report that the drug inhibits their sexual responsiveness, however (Wolman, 1985). The effects of the drug on sexual response may depend upon the individual's prior experiences with the drug, attitudes toward the drug, and the amount taken.

Other hallucinogenics, such as LSD and mescaline, have also been reported by some users to enhance sexual response. Again, these effects may reflect dosage level, as well as expectations, user experiences, attitudes toward the drugs, and altered perceptions.

STIMULANTS   Stimulants such as amphetamines ("speed," "uppers," "bennies," "dexies") have been reputed to heighten arousal and sensations of orgasm. High doses can give rise to irritability, restlessness, hallucinations, paranoid delusions, insomnia, and loss of appetite. These drugs generally activate the central nervous system but are not known to have specific sexual effects. Nevertheless, arousing the nervous system can contribute to sexual arousal (Palace, 1995). The drugs can also elevate the mood, and perhaps sexual pleasure is heightened by general elation.

Cocaine is a natural stimulant that is extracted from the leaves of the coca plant—the plant from which the soft drink Coca-Cola obtained its name. In fact, Coca-Cola contained cocaine as part of its original formula. Cocaine was removed from the secret formula in 1906. Cocaine is ingested in various forms, snorted as a powder, smoked in hardened rock form ("crack" cocaine) or in a freebase form, or injected directly into the bloodstream in liquid form. Cocaine produces a euphoric rush, which tends to ebb quickly. Physically, cocaine constricts blood vessels (reducing the oxygen supply to the heart), elevates the blood pressure, and accelerates the heart rate.

Despite the popular belief that cocaine is an aphrodisiac, frequent use can lead to sexual dysfunctions, such as difficulty attaining erection and ejaculating among males, decreased vaginal lubrication in females, and sexual apathy in both men and women (Weiss & Mirin, 1987). Some people do report initial increased sexual pleasure with cocaine use; however, that increase may reflect cocaine's loosening of inhibitions. Over time, though, regular users may become dependent on cocaine for sexual arousal or lose the ability to enjoy sex (Weiss & Mirin, 1987).

Reflections

- What are the effects of alcohol on sexual arousal? Do the scientific "facts" contradict any beliefs you had held about alcohol?
- Have you done anything under the influence of alcohol or other drug that you otherwise would not have done? What role did the drug play?
- Before reading this section, did you believe that some substances serve as aphrodisiacs? What are they?

SEXUAL RESPONSE AND THE BRAIN: CEREBRAL SEX?

The brain may not be an erogenous zone, but it plays a central role in sexual functioning. Direct genital stimulation may trigger spinal reflexes that produce erection in the male and vaginal lubrication in the female without the direct involvement of the brain. The same reflexes may also be triggered by sexual stimulation that originates in the brain in the form of erotic memories, fantasies, visual images, and thoughts, however. The brain may also inhibit sexual responsiveness, as when we experience guilt or anxiety in a sexual situation or when we suddenly realize in the midst of a sexual encounter that we have left the car lights turned on. Let us explore the brain mechanisms that are involved in sexual functioning.

The Geography of the Brain

The brain consists of three major parts: the hindbrain, the midbrain, and the forebrain (see Figure 5.1 on page 134). The lower part of the brain, called the hindbrain, consists

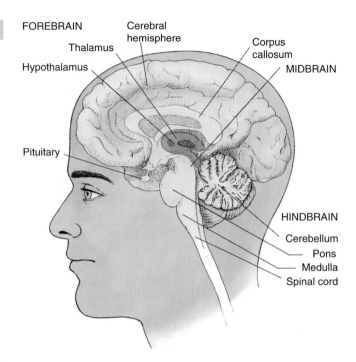

The Geography of the Brain. A view of the brain, split from top to bottom.

FOREBRAIN
Cerebral hemisphere
Thalamus
Corpus callosum
Hypothalamus
MIDBRAIN
Pituitary
HINDBRAIN
Cerebellum
Pons
Medulla
Spinal cord

Medulla An oblong area of the hindbrain that is involved in regulation of heartbeat and respiration.

Pons A structure of the hindbrain that regulates respiration, attention, sleep, and dreaming.

Cerebellum A part of the hindbrain that governs muscle coordination and balance.

Reticular activating system A part of the brain that is active during attention, sleep, and arousal.

Thalamus An area near the center of the brain that is involved in the relay of sensory information to the cortex and in the functions of sleep and attention.

Hypothalamus A brain structure below the thalamus that regulates body temperature, motivation, and emotion.

Limbic system A group of structures active in memory, motivation, and emotion; the structures that are part of this system form a fringe along the inner edge of the cerebrum.

Cerebrum The large mass of the forebrain, which consists of two hemispheres.

Cerebral cortex The wrinkled surface area (gray matter) of the cerebrum.

of the **medulla,** the **pons,** and the **cerebellum.** The medulla plays a role in regulating vital functions such as heart rate, respiration, and blood pressure. The pons relays information about body movement and plays a role in states or functions such as attention, sleep, and respiration. The cerebellum is involved in balance and coordination. Rising from the hindbrain into the forebrain is the **reticular activating system** (RAS), which is involved in attention, arousal, and sleep.

Key areas in the forebrain, or frontal part of the brain, are the **thalamus, hypothalamus, limbic system,** and **cerebrum.** The thalamus, which lies in the center of the brain, plays a role in regulating sleep and attention and relays sensory information to the cerebral cortex. Sensory information from the eyes, for example, is relayed by the thalamus to the visual areas of the cerebral cortex, where the information is processed. The hypothalamus lies between the thalamus and the pituitary gland and is involved in motivation and emotion; in body functions such as control of body temperature, concentration of fluids, and storage of nutrients; and in regulation of the menstrual cycle.

The limbic system consists of parts of the hypothalamus and contains other structures such as the hippocampus and the septum (see Figure 5.2). The limbic system is involved in memory and in regulation of hunger, aggression, and sexual behavior.

Your cerebrum is your crowning glory. The large mushroom-shaped outer surface of the cerebrum, convoluted with ridges and valleys, is called the **cerebral cortex.** It has two hemispheres and is involved in thinking, language, memory, and fantasy.

Brain Mechanisms in Sexual Functioning

Parts of the brain, in particular the cerebral cortex and the limbic system, play key roles in sexual functioning. Cells in the cerebral cortex fire (transmit messages) when we experience sexual thoughts, images, wishes, fantasies, and the like. Cells in the cerebral cortex interpret sensory information as sexual turn-ons or turn-offs. The sight of your lover disrobing, the anticipation of a romantic kiss, a passing sexual fantasy, or the viewing of an erotic movie can trigger the firing of cortical cells. These cells, in turn, transmit messages through the spinal cord that send blood rushing to the genitals, causing erection or vaginal lubrication. The cortex also provides the conscious sense of self. The

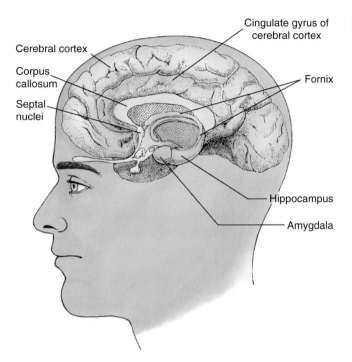

Cerebral cortex

Corpus callosum

Septal nuclei

Cingulate gyrus of cerebral cortex

Fornix

Hippocampus

Amygdala

figure 5.2

The Limbic System. The limbic system lies along the inner edge of the cerebrum.

cortex judges sexual behavior to be proper or improper, moral or immoral, relaxing or anxiety- or guilt-provoking.

Areas of the brain below the cortex, especially the limbic system, also play roles in sexual processes (Everitt, 1990; Kimble, 1992). For example, when the rear part of a male rat's hypothalamus is stimulated by an electrical probe, the animal mechanically runs through its courting and mounting routine. It nibbles at the ears and the back of the neck of a female rat and mounts her when she responds. People, of course, are influenced by learning, fantasy, and values as well as simple brain (or spinal) stimulation.

The importance of the limbic system in the sexual behavior in animals was demonstrated in experiments by Heinrich Klüver and Paul Bucy of the University of Chicago in 1939. Klüver and Bucy reported that destruction of areas of the limbic system triggered persistent sexual behaviors that included masturbation and male-female and male-male mounting attempts. The monkeys even tried to mount the experimenters. For obvious ethical reasons, researchers have not injured or destroyed parts of people's brains to observe the effects on humans.

Electrical stimulation of the hippocampus and septum of the limbic system has also been found to produce erections in laboratory monkeys (McLean, 1976). Electrical stimulation of a pathway in the thalamus, moreover, produced a seminal discharge in these monkeys—without erection. Stimulation of certain areas in the thalamus and hypothalamus may induce ejaculation. Still, the precise relationships among brain structures that regulate erection and ejaculation in animals or humans have not been fully mapped out.

On Pushing the Right Buttons: Are There Pleasure Centers in the Brain?

Research with electrical probes suggests that "pleasure centers" may exist in and near the hypothalamus in other animals and perhaps even in people. When electrodes are implanted in certain parts of the limbic system, investigators find that laboratory animals such as rats (Olds, 1956; Olds & Milner, 1954) will repeatedly press controls to receive bursts of electricity. Of course, we cannot know what the rats experience, but people report that stimulation of these so-called pleasure centers led to feelings of sexual arousal and gratification.

Heath (1972) found that electrical stimulation of the septal region of the limbic system resulted in orgasmlike sensations in two people. Delgado (1969) reported that two female epileptic patients who received limbic stimulation as part of a diagnostic evaluation became sexually aroused by the stimulation:

> [One] reported a pleasant tingling sensation in the left side of her body "from my face down to the bottom of my legs." She started giggling and . . . [stated] that she enjoyed the sensation "very much." Repetition of these stimulations made the patient more communicative and flirtatious, and she ended by openly expressing her desire to marry the therapist. [The other patient reported] a pleasant sensation of relaxation and considerably increased her verbal output, which took on a more intimate character. [She] expressed her fondness for the therapist [whom she had just met], kissed his hands, and talked about her immense gratitude. (p. 145)

Truth or Fiction?
REVISITED

It is true that electrical stimulation of certain areas in the human brain can yield sensations similar to those of sexual pleasure and gratification. Electrical stimulation of certain parts of the limbic system yielded sensations similar to those of sexual gratification—at least in the relatively small number of people who have been studied. ■

We cannot say whether specific "pleasure centers" in the brain are responsible for sexual pleasure. We might wonder, however, whether we would bother to develop sexual relationships if pleasure centers could be accessed through direct stimulation. Before you run to the store for electrodes, you should note that very few researchers suggest that we may someday replace our lovers with battery-powered kits.

Reflections

- What are the roles of the limbic system and cerebral cortex in sexual behavior?
- If you could electrically stimulate a pleasure center in your brain and find as much pleasure as you do in sexual activity with another person, do you think you would bother to form romantic relationships? Why or why not?

SEX HORMONES: DO THEY "GOAD" US INTO SEX?

In a TV situation comedy, a male adolescent was described as a "hormone with feet." Ask parents why teenagers act the way they do, and you are likely to hear a one-word answer: hormones! **Hormones** are chemical substances that are secreted by the ductless glands of the endocrine system and discharged directly into the bloodstream. The word *hormone* derives from the Greek *horman*, meaning "to stimulate" or "to goad." And we could say that they very much goad us into sexual activity. Hormones also regulate various bodily functions, including growth and resistance to stress as well as sexual functions.

Both men and women produce small amounts of the sex hormones of the other gender in their bodies. Testosterone, the major form of androgen, or male sex hormone, is secreted in small amounts by the adrenal glands (located above the kidneys) in both genders, but in much larger amounts by the testes. The ovaries produce small amounts of androgens but much larger amounts of the female sex hormones, estrogen and progesterone. The testes similarly produce small amounts of estrogen and progesterone.

Truth or Fiction?
REVISITED

It is true that normal men produce estrogen and normal women produce androgens. However, men do not produce as much estrogen as women do, and women do not produce as much of the male sex hormones as men do. ■

The hypothalamus and pituitary gland regulate gonadal secretion of sex hormones, specifically testosterone in males and estrogen and progesterone in females. At puberty a surge of sex hormones causes the blossoming of reproductive maturation: the sperm-producing ability of the testes in males and the maturation of ova and ovulation in females.

Hormone A substance secreted by an endocrine gland that regulates various body functions. (From the Greek *horman*, meaning "to stimulate" or "to goad.")

Sex hormones released at puberty also cause the flowering of **secondary sex characteristics.** In males, these include the lengthening of the vocal cords (and consequent lowering of the voice) and the growth of facial and pubic hair. In females, the breasts and hips become rounded with fatty tissue, and pubic hair grows.

Sex Hormones and Sexual Behavior: Organizing and Activating Influences

Sex hormones have organizing and activating effects on behavior. That is, they exert an influence on the type of behavior that is expressed (an *organizing* effect) and the frequency or intensity of the drive that motivates the behavior and the ability to perform the behavior (*activating* effects). For example, sex hormones predispose lower animals and possibly people toward stereotypical masculine or feminine mating behaviors (an organizing effect). They also facilitate sexual response and influence sexual desire (activating effects).

Though sex hormones clearly determine the sexual orientations and drives of many lower animals, their roles in human sexual behavior may be relatively more subtle and are not as well understood. Much of our knowledge of the organizing and activating effects of sex hormones comes from research with other species in which hormone levels were manipulated by castration or injection. Ethical standards prohibit such research with human infants, for obvious reasons.

Are Adolescents "Hormones with Feet"? Research shows that levels of androgens are connected with sexual interest in both male and female adolescents. Hormone levels are more likely to predict sexual behavior in adolescent males, however, perhaps because society places greater restraints on female sexuality.

The activating effects of testosterone can be clearly observed among male rats. For example, males who are castrated in adulthood and thus deprived of testosterone discontinue sexual behavior. If they are given injections of testosterone, however, they resume stereotypical male sexual behaviors, such as attempting to mount receptive females.

In rats, testosterone organizes or differentiates the brain in the masculine direction. As a result, adult male rats display stereotypical masculine behaviors upon activation by testosterone. Male fetuses and newborns normally have sufficient amounts of testosterone in their blood systems to organize their brains in the masculine direction. Female fetuses and newborns normally have lesser amounts of testosterone. Their brains thus become organized in a feminine direction. When female rats are prenatally exposed to large doses of testosterone, their sexual organs became somewhat masculinized, and they are predisposed toward masculine mating behaviors in adulthood (Kimble, 1992).

In rats and other rodents, sexual differentiation of the brain is not complete at birth. Female rodents who are given testosterone injections shortly before or shortly after birth (depending on the species) show typical masculine sexual patterns in adulthood, attempting to mount other females and resisting mounting by males (Ellis & Ames, 1987).

Questions remain about the organizing effects of sex hormones on human sexual behavior. Prenatal sex hormones are known to play a role in the sexual differentiation of the genitalia and of the brain structures, such as the hypothalamus. Their role in patterning sexual behavior in adulthood remains unknown, however. Researchers have speculated that the brains of **transsexual** individuals may have been prenatally sexually differentiated in one direction while their genitals were being differentiated in the other (Money, 1994). It has been speculated that prenatal sexual differentiation of the brain may also be connected with sexual orientation.

What of the activating effects of sex hormones on human sex drive and behavior? Though the countless attempts to extract or synthesize aphrodisiacs have failed to produce the real thing, men and women normally produce a genuine aphrodisiac: testosterone.

Secondary sex characteristics Physical traits that differentiate males from females but are not directly involved in reproduction.

Transsexual A person with a gender-identity disorder who feels that he or she is really a member of the other gender and is trapped in a body of the wrong gender.

Whatever the early organizing effects of sex hormones in humans, testosterone activates the sex drives of both men and women.

Sex Hormones and Male Sexual Behavior

Evidence of the role for hormones in sex drive is found among men who have declines in testosterone levels as the result of chemical or surgical castration. Surgical castration (removal of the testes) is sometimes performed as a medical treatment for cancer of the prostate or other diseases of the male reproductive tract, such as genital tuberculosis. But some convicted sex offenders have voluntarily undergone castration as a condition of release.

Regardless of the reason for castration, men who are surgically or chemically castrated usually exhibit a gradual decrease in the incidence of sexual fantasies and loss of sexual desire (Bradford, 1998; Gijs & Gooren, 1996; Rösler & Witztum, 1998). They also gradually tend to lose the capacities to attain erection and to ejaculate—an indication that testosterone is important in maintaining sexual functioning as well as drive, at least in males. Castrated men show great variation in their sexual interest and functioning, however. Some continue to experience sexual desires and are able to function sexually for years, even decades. Learning appears to play a large role in determining continued sexual response following castration. Males who were sexually experienced before castration show a more gradual decline in sexual activity. Those who were sexually inexperienced at the time show relatively little or no interest in sex. Male sexual motivation and functioning thus involve an interplay of hormonal influences and experience.

Further evidence of the relationship between hormonal levels and male sexuality is found in studies of men with **hypogonadism,** a condition marked by abnormally low levels of testosterone production. Hypogonadal men generally suffer loss of sexual desire and a decline in sexual activity (Carani et al., 1990). Here again, hormones do not tell the whole story. Hypogonadal men are capable of erection, at least for a while, even though their sex drives may wane (Bancroft, 1984). The role of testosterone as an activator of sex drives in men is further supported by evidence of the effects of testosterone replacement in hypogonadal men. When such men obtain testosterone injections, their sex drives, fantasies, and activity are often restored to former levels (Cunningham et al., 1989; Goleman, 1988).

Though minimal levels of androgens are critical to male sexuality, there is no one-to-one correspondence between hormone levels and the sex drive or sexual performance in adults. In men who have ample supplies of testosterone, sexual interest and functioning depend more on learning, fantasies, attitudes, memories, and other psychosocial factors than on hormone levels. At puberty, however, hormonal variations may play a more direct role in stimulating sexual interest and activity in males. Udry and his colleagues (Udry et al., 1985; Udry et al., 1986; Udry & Billy, 1987) found, for example, that testosterone levels predicted sexual interest, masturbation rates, and the likelihood of engaging in sexual intercourse among teenage boys. A positive relationship also has been found between testosterone levels in adult men and frequency of sexual intercourse (Dabbs & Morris, 1990; Knussman et al., 1986). Moreover, drugs that reduce the levels of androgen in the blood system, called *antiandrogens*, lead to reductions in the sex drive and in sexual fantasies (Bradford, 1998).

Sex Hormones and Female Sexual Behavior

The female sex hormones estrogen and progesterone play prominent roles in promoting the changes that occur during puberty and in regulating the menstrual cycle. Female sex hormones do not appear to play a direct role in determining sexual motivation or response in human females, however.

Hypogonadism An abnormal condition marked by abnormally low levels of testosterone production.

In most mammals, females are sexually receptive only during estrus. Estrus is a brief period of fertility that corresponds to time of ovulation, and during estrus, females are said to be "in heat." Estrus occurs once a year in some species; in others, it occurs periodically during the year in so-called sexual or mating seasons. Estrogen peaks at time of ovulation, so there is a close relationship between fertility and sexual receptivity in most female mammals. Women's sexuality is not clearly linked to hormonal fluctuations, however. Unlike females of most other species of mammals, the human female is sexually responsive during all phases of the reproductive (menstrual) cycle—even during menstruation, when ovarian hormone levels are low—and after menopause.

There is some evidence, however, that sexual responsiveness in women is influenced by the presence of circulating androgens, or male sex hormones, in their bodies. The adrenal glands of women produce small amounts of androgens, just as they do in males. The fact that women normally produce smaller amounts of androgens than men does not mean that they necessarily have weaker sex drives. Rather, women appear to be more sensitive to smaller amounts of androgens (Bancroft, 1984). For women, it seems that less is more.

Women who receive **ovariectomies,** which are sometimes carried out when a hysterectomy is performed, no longer produce female sex hormones. Nevertheless, they continue to experience sex drives and interest as before. Loss of the ovarian hormone estradiol may cause vaginal dryness and make coitus painful, but it does not reduce sexual desire. (The dryness can be alleviated by a lubricating jelly or by estrogen-replacement therapy.) However, women whose adrenal glands *and* ovaries have been removed (so that they no longer produce androgens) gradually lose sexual desire. An active and enjoyable sexual history seems to ward off this loss, however, providing further evidence of the impact of cognitive and experiential factors on human sexual response.

Research provides further evidence on the links between androgens and women's sex drives. Levels of testosterone in the bloodstream have been associated with increased sexual interest in women (Johannes, 1998). In the studies by Udry and his colleagues mentioned earlier, androgen levels were also found to predict sexual interest among teenage girls. In contrast to boys, however, girls' androgen levels were unrelated to the likelihood of coital experience. Androgens apparently affect sexual desire in both genders, but sexual interest may be more likely to be directly translated into sexual activity in men than in women (Bancroft, 1990). This gender difference may be explained by society's placement of greater restraints on adolescent female sexuality.

Other researchers report that women's sexual activity increases at points in the menstrual cycle when levels of androgens in the bloodstream are high (Morris et al., 1987). Another study was conducted with women whose ovaries had been surgically removed ("surgical menopause") as a way of treating disease. The ovaries supply major quantities of estrogen. Following surgery, the women in this study were treated either with estrogen-replacement therapy (ERT), with ERT *plus* androgens, or with a placebo (an inert substance made to resemble an active drug) (Sherwin et al., 1985). This was a double-blind study. Neither the women nor their physicians knew which drug the women were receiving. The results showed that the combination of androgens and ERT heightened sexual desire and sexual fantasies more than ERT alone or the placebo.

Androgens thus play a more prominent role than ovarian hormones in activating and maintaining women's sex drives. As with men, however, women's sexuality is too complex to be explained fully by hormone levels. For example, an active and enjoyable sexual history seems to ward off the loss of sexual interest that generally follows the surgical removal of the adrenal glands and ovaries.

Reflections

- What are the organizing and activating effects of sex hormones?
- Do you know people who have taken testosterone or estrogen for medical or other reasons? What were the reasons for using hormones? What were their effects?

Ovariectomy Surgical removal of the ovaries.

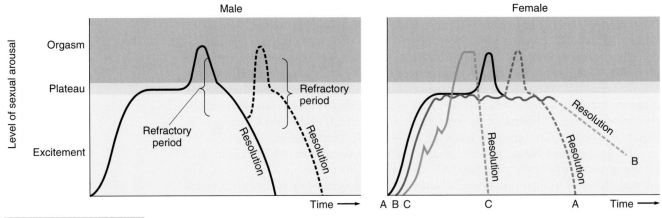

figure 5.3

Levels of Sexual Arousal during the Phases of the Sexual Response Cycle. Masters and Johnson divide the sexual response cycle into four phases: excitement, plateau, orgasm, and resolution. During the resolution phase, the level of sexual arousal returns to the prearoused state. For men, there is a refractory period after orgasm. As shown by the broken line, however, men can become rearoused to orgasm once the refractory period is past and their levels of sexual arousal have returned to preplateau levels. Pattern A for women shows a typical response cycle, with the broken line suggesting multiple orgasms. Pattern B shows the cycle of a woman who reaches the plateau phase but for whom arousal is resolved without reaching the orgasmic phase. Pattern C shows the possibility of orgasm in a highly aroused woman who passes quickly through the plateau phase.

THE SEXUAL RESPONSE CYCLE

Although we may be culturally attuned to focus on gender differences rather than similarities, Masters and Johnson (1966) found that the physiological responses of men and women to sexual stimulation (whether from coitus, masturbation, or other sources) are quite alike. The sequence of changes in the body that takes place as men and women become progressively more aroused is referred to as the **sexual response cycle.** Masters and Johnson divided the cycle into four phases: *excitement, plateau, orgasm,* and *resolution.* Figure 5.3 suggests the levels of sexual arousal associated with each phase.

Both males and females experience **vasocongestion** and **myotonia** early in the response cycle. Vasocongestion is the swelling of the genital tissues with blood, which causes erection of the penis and engorgement of the area surrounding the vaginal opening. The testes, nipples, and even earlobes become engorged as blood vessels in these areas dilate.

Myotonia refers to muscle tension. Myotonia causes voluntary and involuntary muscle contractions, which produce facial grimaces, spasms in the hands and feet, and eventually, the spasms of orgasm. Let us follow these and the other bodily changes that constitute the sexual response cycle.

Excitement Phase

In younger men, vasocongestion during the **excitement phase** produces penile erection as early as 3 to 8 seconds after stimulation begins. Erection may occur more slowly in older men, but the responses are essentially the same. Erection may subside and return as stimulation varies. The scrotal skin thickens, losing its baggy appearance. The testes increase in size. The testes and scrotum become elevated.

In the female, vaginal lubrication may start 10 to 30 seconds after stimulation begins. Vasocongestion swells the clitoris, flattens the labia majora and spreads them apart, and increases the size of the labia minora. The inner two thirds of the vagina expand. The

Sexual response cycle Masters and Johnson's model of sexual response, which consists of four phases.

Vasocongestion The swelling of the genital tissues with blood, which causes erection of the penis and engorgement of the area surrounding the vaginal opening.

Myotonia Muscle tension.

Excitement phase The first phase of the sexual response cycle, which is characterized by erection in the male, vaginal lubrication in the female, and muscle tension and increases in heart rate in both males and females.

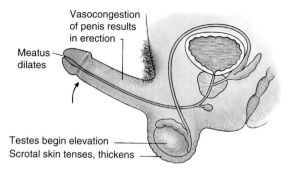

1. EXCITEMENT PHASE

Vasocongestion of penis results in erection

Meatus dilates

Testes begin elevation

Scrotal skin tenses, thickens

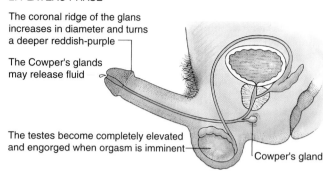

2. PLATEAU PHASE

The coronal ridge of the glans increases in diameter and turns a deeper reddish-purple

The Cowper's glands may release fluid

The testes become completely elevated and engorged when orgasm is imminent

Cowper's gland

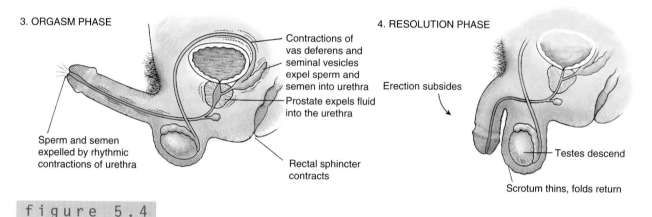

3. ORGASM PHASE

Contractions of vas deferens and seminal vesicles expel sperm and semen into urethra

Prostate expels fluid into the urethra

Sperm and semen expelled by rhythmic contractions of urethra

Rectal sphincter contracts

4. RESOLUTION PHASE

Erection subsides

Testes descend

Scrotum thins, folds return

figure 5.4

The Male Genitals during the Phases of the Sexual Response Cycle.

vaginal walls thicken and, because of the inflow of blood, turn from their normal pink to a deeper hue. The uterus becomes engorged and elevated. The breasts enlarge, and blood vessels near the surface become more prominent.

The skin may take on a rosy **sex flush** late in this phase. It varies with intensity of arousal and is more pronounced in women. The nipples may become erect in both genders, especially in response to direct stimulation. Men and women show some increase in myotonia, heart rate, and blood pressure.

Plateau Phase

A plateau is a level region, and the level of arousal remains somewhat constant during the **plateau phase** of sexual response. Nevertheless, the plateau phase is an advanced state of arousal that precedes orgasm. Men in this phase show a slight increase in the circumference of the coronal ridge of the penis. The penile glans turns a purplish hue, a sign of vasocongestion. The testes are elevated further into position for ejaculation and may reach one and a half times their unaroused size. The Cowper's glands may secrete a few droplets of fluid that are found at the tip of the penis (see Figure 5.4).

In women, vasocongestion swells the tissues of the outer third of the vagina, contracting the vaginal opening (thus preparing it to "grasp" the penis) and building the **orgasmic platform** (see Figure 5.5 on pages 142 and 143). The inner part of the vagina expands fully. The uterus becomes fully elevated. The clitoris withdraws beneath the clitoral hood and shortens. Therefore, a women (or her partner) may feel that the clitoris

Sex flush A reddish rash that appears on the chest or breasts late in the excitement phase of the sexual response cycle.

Plateau phase The second phase of the sexual response cycle, which is characterized by increases in vasocongestion, muscle tension, heart rate, and blood pressure in preparation for orgasm.

Orgasmic platform The thickening of the walls of the outer third of the vagina, due to vasocongestion, that occurs during the plateau phase of the sexual response cycle.

The Female Genitals during the Phases of the Sexual Response Cycle.

1. EXCITEMENT PHASE

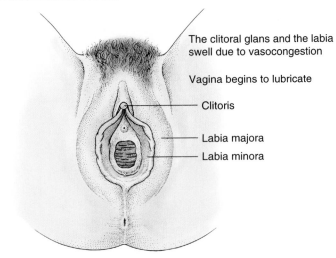

The clitoral glans and the labia swell due to vasocongestion

Vagina begins to lubricate

Clitoris

Labia majora

Labia minora

3. ORGASM PHASE

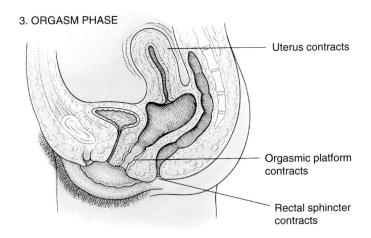

Uterus contracts

Orgasmic platform contracts

Rectal sphincter contracts

has become lost. This may be mistaken as a sign that the woman's sexual arousal is waning, although it is actually increasing.

Coloration of the labia minora appears, which is referred to as the **sex skin.** The labia minora become a deep wine color in women who have borne children and bright red in women who have not. Further engorgement of the areolas of the breasts might make it seem that the nipples have lost part of their erection (see Figure 5.6). The Bartholin's glands secrete a fluid that resembles mucus.

About one man in four, and about three women in four, show a sex flush, which often does not appear until the plateau phase. Myotonia may cause spasmodic contractions in the hands and feet and facial grimaces. Breathing becomes rapid, like panting, and the heart rate may increase to 100 to 160 beats per minute. Blood pressure continues to rise. The increase in heart rate is usually less dramatic with masturbation than during coitus.

Orgasmic Phase

The orgasmic phase in the male consists of two stages of muscular contractions. In the first stage, contractions of the vas deferens, the seminal vesicles, the ejaculatory duct, and the prostate gland cause seminal fluid to collect in the urethral bulb at the base of the penis (see Figure 5.4). The bulb expands to accommodate the fluid. The internal sphincter of the urinary bladder contracts, preventing seminal fluid from entering the bladder in a backward, retrograde ejaculation. The normal closing off of the bladder also serves to

Sex skin Reddening of the labia minora that occurs during the plateau phase.

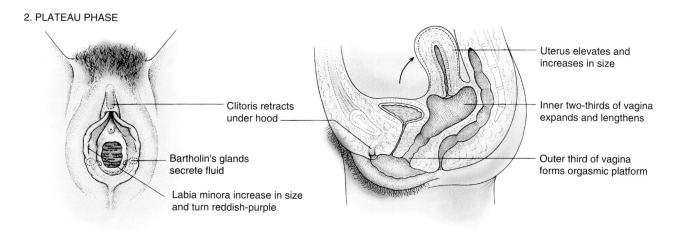

2. PLATEAU PHASE

Clitoris retracts under hood

Bartholin's glands secrete fluid

Labia minora increase in size and turn reddish-purple

Uterus elevates and increases in size

Inner two-thirds of vagina expands and lengthens

Outer third of vagina forms orgasmic platform

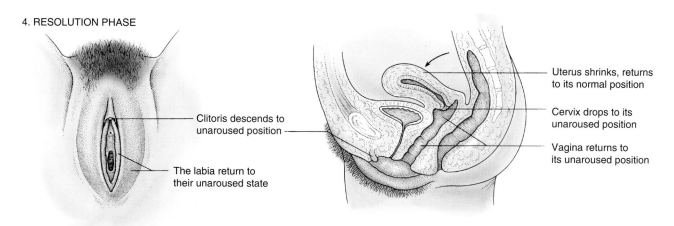

4. RESOLUTION PHASE

Clitoris descends to unaroused position

The labia return to their unaroused state

Uterus shrinks, returns to its normal position

Cervix drops to its unaroused position

Vagina returns to its unaroused position

prevent urine from mixing with semen. The collection of semen in the urethral bulb produces feelings of ejaculatory inevitability—the sensation that nothing will stop the ejaculate from "coming." This sensations lasts for about 2 to 3 seconds.

In the second stage, the external sphincter of the bladder relaxes, allowing the passage of semen. Contractions of muscles surrounding the urethra and urethral bulb

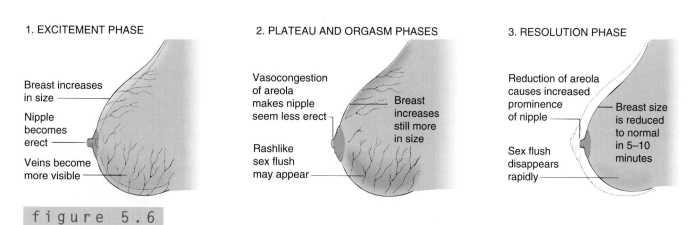

1. EXCITEMENT PHASE

Breast increases in size

Nipple becomes erect

Veins become more visible

2. PLATEAU AND ORGASM PHASES

Vasocongestion of areola makes nipple seem less erect

Breast increases still more in size

Rashlike sex flush may appear

3. RESOLUTION PHASE

Reduction of areola causes increased prominence of nipple

Breast size is reduced to normal in 5–10 minutes

Sex flush disappears rapidly

figure 5.6

The Breast during the Phases of the Sexual Response Cycle.

and the base of the penis propel the ejaculate through the urethra and out of the body. Sensations of pleasure tend to be related to the strength of the contractions and the amount of seminal fluid. The first 3 to 4 contractions are generally most intense and occur at 0.8-second intervals (5 contractions every 4 seconds). Another 2 to 4 contractions occur at a somewhat slower pace. Rates and patterns vary somewhat from man to man.

Orgasm in the female is manifested by 3 to 15 contractions of the pelvic muscles that surround the vaginal barrel. The contractions first occur at 0.8-second intervals, producing, as in the male, a release of sexual tension. Another 3 to 6 weaker and slower contractions follow. The spacing of these contractions is generally more variable in women than in men. The uterus and the anal sphincter also contract rhythmically. Uterine contractions occur in waves from the top to the cervix. In both genders, muscles go into spasm throughout the body. Blood pressure and heart rate reach a peak, the heart beating up to 180 times per minute. Respiration may increase to 40 breaths per minute.

SUBJECTIVE EXPERIENCE OF ORGASM   The sensations of orgasm have challenged the descriptive powers of poets. Words like "rush," "warmth," "explosion," and "release" do not adequately capture them. We may assume (rightly or wrongly) that others of our gender experience pretty much what we do, but can we understand the sensations of the other gender?

Several studies suggest that the orgasms of both genders might feel quite similar. In one, 48 men and women provided written descriptions of orgasms. The researchers (Proctor et al., 1974) modified the language (for example, changing "penis" to "genitals") so that the authors' genders would not be apparent. They then asked 70 "experts" (psychologists, gynecologists, etc.) to indicate the gender of each author. The ratings were no more reliable than guesswork.

Truth or Fiction?
~~REVISITED~~

It is true that written descriptions of men's and women's experiences during orgasm cannot be differentiated—at least when they are altered to exclude language that gives away exactly which anatomic features are involved. Therefore, this Truth-or-Fiction item is only qualifiedly "true." (Listen: Life is complex. Be tolerant.) ■

Resolution Phase

The period following orgasm, in which the body returns to its prearoused state, is called the **resolution phase.** After ejaculation, the man loses his erection in two stages. The first occurs in about a minute. Half the volume of the erection is lost as blood from the corpora cavernosa empties into the other parts of the body. The second stage occurs over a period of several minutes: The remaining tumescence subsides as the corpus spongiosum empties. The testes and scrotum return to normal size, and the scrotum regains its wrinkled appearance.

In women, orgasm also triggers release of blood from engorged areas. In the absence of continued stimulation, swelling of the areolas decreases; then the nipples return to normal size. The sex flush lightens rapidly. In about 5 to 10 seconds, the clitoris descends to its normal position. The clitoris, vaginal barrel, uterus, and labia gradually shrink to their prearoused sizes. The labia minora turn lighter (the "sex skin" disappears) in about 10 to 15 seconds.

Most muscle tension (myotonia) tends to dissipate within 5 minutes after orgasm in both men and women. Blood pressure, heart rate, and respiration may also return to their prearousal levels within a few minutes. About 30% to 40% of men and women find their palms, the soles of their feet, or their entire bodies covered with a sheen of perspiration. Both men and women may feel relaxed and satiated. However, . . .

Although the processes by which the body returns to its prearousal state are similar in men and women, there is an important gender difference during the resolution phase. Unlike women, men enter a **refractory period** during which they are physiologically incapable of experiencing another orgasm or ejaculation (in much the same way that the

Resolution phase The fourth phase of the sexual response cycle, during which the body gradually returns to its prearoused state.

Refractory period A period of time following a response (e.g., orgasm) during which an individual is no longer responsive to stimulation (e.g., sexual stimulation).

flash attachment to a camera cannot be set off again immediately after it is used—it has to be recharged). The refractory period of adolescent males may last only minutes, whereas that of men age 50 and above may last from several minutes to a day. Women do not undergo a refractory period and so can become quickly rearoused to the point of repeated (multiple) orgasm if they desire and receive continued sexual stimulation (see Figure 5.3).

Myotonia and vasocongestion may take an hour or more to dissipate in people who are aroused but who do not reach orgasm. Persistent pelvic vasocongestion may cause "blue balls" in males—the slang term for a throbbing ache. Some men insist that their dates should consent to coitus, since it is unfair to stimulate them to the point where they have this condition. This condition can be relieved through masturbation as well as coitus, however—or allowed to dissipate naturally. Although it may be uncomfortable, it is not dangerous and should not be an excuse to pressure or coerce another person into any sexual activity. "Blue" sensations are not limited to men. Women, too, may experience unpleasant pelvic throbbing if they have become highly aroused and do not find release (Barbach, 1975). Women, too, can relieve pelvic throbbing through masturbation.

Kaplan's Three Stages of Sexual Response: An Alternative Model

Helen Singer Kaplan was a prominent sex therapist and author of several professional books (1974, 1979, 1987) on sex therapy. Whereas Masters and Johnson had proposed a four-stage model of sexual response, Kaplan developed a three-stage model consisting of (1) desire, (2) excitement, and (3) orgasm. Kaplan's model is an outgrowth of her clinical experience in working with people with sexual dysfunctions. She believes that their problems can best be classified according to these three phases. Kaplan's model makes it convenient for clinicians to classify sexual dysfunctions involving desire (low or absent desire), excitement (such as problems with erection in the male or lubrication in the female), and orgasm (such as premature ejaculation in the male or orgasmic dysfunction in the female).

Masters and Johnson focus on physiological changes that occur during sexual stimulation. Kaplan's model includes two phases that are primarily physiological (*excitement*, consisting of initial vasocongestion of the genitals, resulting in erection in the male and vaginal lubrication in the female, and *orgasm*, marked by pelvic muscular contractions) and one that is primarily psychological (*desire*). Kaplan's stages of excitement and orgasm are clearly differentiated along physiological lines. (Masters and Johnson's excitement and plateau stages are less clearly differentiated in terms of differences in biological processes. Both primarily involve vasocongestion.)

Masters and Johnson view sexual response as being composed of *successive* stages; the order is crucial and invariant. Kaplan treats her phases as relatively independent components of sexual response whose sequence is somewhat variable. For example, a person may experience sexual excitement and even orgasm, though sexual desire remains low. Excitement may also precede desire in some situations. For example, people with low sexual desire may find their sexual appetites sparked as their bodies respond to their partners' sexual stimulation. A person who lacks desire might not be motivated to seek sexual stimulation or be able to respond adequately to sexual stimuli, however.

Kaplan's model is noteworthy for designating desire as a separate phase of sexual response. Problems in lack of sexual interest or desire are among the most common brought to the attention of sex therapists.

Reflections

- How do you know when you are becoming sexually aroused? Do the phases of the sexual response cycle describe your reactions to sexual stimulation?
- Were you surprised to learn that the sensations of orgasm are apparently quite similar among women and men? Why or why not?

CONTROVERSIES ABOUT ORGASM

Are women capable of experiencing multiple orgasms? Are men? Physiologically speaking, is there but one type of orgasm? Or are there different types of orgasm, depending on the site of stimulation? Do women ejaculate during orgasm? If so, what fluid do they emit?

Few other topics in human sexuality have aroused more controversies over the years than orgasm. We do not have all the answers, but some intriguing research findings have shed light on some of these continuing controversies.

Multiple Orgasms: When You're Having More Than One

Kinsey's report (Kinsey et al., 1953) that 14% of his female respondents regularly had **multiple orgasms** sent shock waves through the general community and even surprised his fellow scientists. Many people were aghast that women could have more than one orgasm at a time. There were comments (mostly by men, of course!) that the women in the Kinsey surveys must be "nymphomaniacs" who were incapable of being satisfied with the "normal" complement of one orgasm per occasion. However, only 13 years later, Masters and Johnson (1966) reported that most, if not all, women are capable of multiple orgasms. Though all women may have a biological capability for multiple orgasm, not all women report them. A recent survey of 720 nurses showed that only 43% reported experiencing multiple orgasms (Darling et al., 1991).

It is difficult to offer a precise definition of multiple orgasm. In Masters and Johnson's view, multiple orgasm involves the occurrence of one or more *additional* orgasms following the first, within a short period of time and before the body has returned to a preplateau level of arousal. By this definition, a person would not have experienced a multiple orgasm if he or she had two or more successive orgasms that were separated by a return to a prearoused state or a preplateau (excitement stage) level of arousal. (Note that the pattern shown by the broken line for the male in Figure 5.3 does *not* constitute a multiple orgasm, even if it occurs reasonably rapidly after the first orgasm, because he *does* return to a preplateau level of sexual arousal between orgasms.) The lines of demarcation between the excitement and plateau stages of arousal are not very obvious, however. Therefore, a person may experience two or more successive orgasms within a short time but not know whether these are, technically speaking, "multiple orgasms." Whether or not the orgasm fits the definition does not diminish the experience, but it does raise the question of whether both men and women are capable of multiple orgasm.

By Masters and Johnson's definition, men are not capable of achieving multiple orgasms, because they enter a refractory period following ejaculation during which they are physiologically incapable of achieving another orgasm or ejaculation for a time. Put more simply, men who want more than one orgasm during one session may have to relax for a while and allow their sexual arousal to subside. Yet women can maintain a high level of arousal between multiple orgasms and have them in rapid succession.

Women do not enter a refractory period. Women can continue to have orgasms if they continue to receive effective stimulation (and, of course, are interested in continuing). Some men therefore refrain from reaching orgasm until their partners have had the desired number. The differential capacity for multiple orgasms is one of the major gender differences in sexual response.

Some men have two or more orgasms without ejaculation ("dry orgasms") preceding a final ejaculatory orgasm. These men might not enter a refractory period following their initial dry orgasms and might therefore be able to maintain their level of stimulation at near-peak levels. Some men report multiple orgasms in which dry orgasms follow an ejac-

Multiple orgasms One or more additional orgasms following the first, which occur within a short period of time and before the body has returned to a preplateau level of arousal.

ulatory orgasm, with little or no loss of erection between orgasms (Dunn & Trost, 1989). Some men report more varied patterns, with ejaculatory orgasms and dry orgasms preceding or following each other in different sequences.

Men who report multiple orgasms indicate that if they are highly aroused following an initial orgasm, and if sexual stimulation continues, they can achieve one or more subsequent orgasms before losing their erections (Dunn & Trost, 1989). Still, the evidence for multiple orgasm in men is largely anecdotal and limited to a relatively few case examples. Nor is it known whether such "multiple" orgasms meet the technical definition given by Masters and Johnson of two or more orgasms in rapid succession without a return to a *preplateau* stage of arousal in between. Nor do we know what percentage of men might be multiply orgasmic (Dunn & Trost, 1989).

Masters and Johnson found that some women experienced 20 or more orgasms by masturbating. Still, few women have multiple orgasms during most sexual encounters, and many are satisfied with just one per occasion. Some women who have read or heard about female orgasmic capacity wonder what is "wrong" with them if they are content with just one. Nothing is wrong with them, of course: A biological capacity does not create a behavioral requirement.

"Front desk? Look, I hate to sound like a prude, but the folks in room 614 seem to be having an excessive number of orgasms."

How Many Kinds of Orgasms Do Women Have? One, Two, or Three?

Until Masters and Johnson published their laboratory findings, many people believed that there were two types of female orgasm, as proposed by the psychoanalyst Sigmund Freud: the *clitoral orgasm* and the *vaginal orgasm*. Clitoral orgasms were achieved through direct clitoral stimulation, such as by masturbation. Clitoral orgasms were seen by psychoanalysts (mostly male psychoanalysts, naturally) as emblematic of a childhood fixation—a throwback to an erogenous pattern acquired during childhood masturbation.

The term *vaginal orgasm* referred to an orgasm achieved through deep penile thrusting during coitus and was theorized to be a sign of mature sexuality. Freud argued that women achieve sexual maturity when they forsake clitoral stimulation for vaginal stimulation. This view would be little more than an academic footnote but for the fact that some adult women who continue to require direct clitoral stimulation to reach orgasm, even during coitus, have been led by traditional (generally male) psychoanalysts to believe that they are sexually "fixated" at an immature stage or are, at least, sexually inadequate.

Despite Freudian theory, Masters and Johnson (1966) were able to find only one kind of orgasm, physiologically speaking, regardless of the source of stimulation (manual-clitoral or penile-vaginal). By monitoring physiological responses to sexual stimulation, they found that the female orgasm involves the same biological events whether it is reached through masturbation, petting, coitus, or just breast stimulation. All orgasms involve spasmodic contractions of the pelvic muscles surrounding the vaginal barrel, leading to a release of sexual tension. Gertrude Stein wrote, "Rose is a rose is a rose." Biologically speaking, the same principle can be applied to orgasm: "An orgasm is an orgasm is an orgasm." In men, it also matters not how orgasm is achieved—through masturbation, petting, oral sex, coitus, or by fantasizing about a fellow student in chem lab. Orgasm still involves the same physiological processes: Involuntary contractions of the pelvic muscles at the base of the penis expel semen and release sexual tension. A woman or a man might prefer one source of orgasm to another—she or he might prefer achieving orgasm with a lover rather than by masturbation or with one person rather than another, but the biological events that define orgasm remain the same.

Though orgasms attained through coitus or masturbation may be physiologically alike, there are certainly key psychological or subjective differences. (Were it not so, there would be fewer sexual relationships.) The coital experience, for example, is often accompanied by feelings of attachment, love, and connectedness toward one's partner. Masturbation, by contrast, is more likely to be experienced solely as a sexual release.

Orgasms that are experienced through different means may also vary in physiological and subjective intensity. Masters and Johnson (1966) found that orgasms experienced during masturbation were generally more physiologically intense than those experienced during intercourse, perhaps because masturbation allows one to focus only on one's own pleasure and on ensuring that one receives effective stimulation to climax. This does not mean that orgasms during masturbation are more enjoyable or gratifying than those experienced through coitus, however. Given the emotional connectedness we may feel toward our lovers, we are unlikely to break off our relationships in favor of masturbation. Thus, "physiological intensity," as measured by laboratory instruments, does not translate directly into subjective pleasure or fulfillment.

Truth or Fiction?
REVISITED

Actually, orgasms attained through masturbation appear to be more intense than those attained through coitus—at least in terms of physiological measurements. (That does not mean that they are more enjoyable.) ▪

The purported distinction between clitoral and vaginal orgasms also rests on an assumption that the clitoris is not stimulated during coitus. Masters and Johnson showed this to be a *false* assumption. Penile coital thrusting draws the clitoral hood back and forth against the clitoris. Vaginal pressure also heightens blood flow in the clitoris, further setting the stage for orgasm (Lavoisier et al., 1995).

One might think that Masters and Johnson's research settled the question of whether or not there are different types of female orgasm. Other investigators, however, have proposed that there are distinct forms of female orgasm, yet not those suggested by psychoanalytic theory. For example, Singer and Singer (1972) suggested that there are three types of female orgasm: *vulval, uterine,* and *blended.* According to the Singers, the vulval orgasm represents the type of orgasm described by Masters and Johnson (1966) that involves *vulval* contractions; that is, contractions of the vaginal barrel. Consistent with the findings of Masters and Johnson (1966), they note that the vulval orgasm remains the same regardless of the source of stimulation, clitoral or vaginal.

According to the Singers, the uterine orgasm does not involve vulval contractions. It occurs only in response to deep penile thrusting against the cervix. This thrusting slightly displaces the uterus and stimulates the tissues that cover the abdominal organs. The uterine orgasm is accompanied by a certain pattern of breathing: gasping or gulping of air is followed by an involuntary holding of the breath as orgasm approaches. When orgasm is reached, the breath is explosively exhaled. The uterine orgasm is accompanied by deep feelings of relaxation and sexual satisfaction.

The third type, or blended orgasm, is described as combining features of the vulval and uterine orgasms. It involves both an involuntary breath-holding response and contractions of the pelvic muscles. The Singers note that the type of orgasm a woman experiences—vulval, uterine, or blended—depends on factors such as the parts of the body that are stimulated and the duration of stimulation. Each produces its own kind of satisfaction, and no one type is necessarily better or preferable to any other.

The Singers' hypothesis of three distinct forms of female orgasm remains controversial. Researchers initially scoffed at the idea that orgasms could arise from vaginal stimulation alone. The vagina, after all, especially the inner two thirds of the vaginal cavity, is relatively insensitive to stimulation (erotic or otherwise). Proponents of the Singers' model counter that the type of uterine orgasm that the Singers described is induced more by pressure resulting from deep pelvic thrusting than by touch.

The G-Spot

A part of the vagina, notably a bean-shaped area within the anterior wall, may have special erotic significance. This area is believed to lie about 1 to 2 inches from the vaginal entrance and to consist of a soft mass of tissue that swells from the size of a dime to a half dollar when stimulated (Davidson et al., 1989). It has been called the **Grafenberg spot**—the "G-spot" for short (see Figure 5.7). The spot can be directly stimulated by the woman's or her partner's fingers or by penile thrusting in the rear entry or the female-superior positions. Some researchers suggest that stimulation of the spot produces intense erotic sensations and that with prolonged stimulation, a distinct form of orgasm occurs. This orgasm is characterized by intense pleasure and, in some cases, by a biological event that was earlier thought to be exclusively male in nature: ejaculation (Perry & Whipple, 1981; Whipple & Komisaruk, 1988). These claims, as with other claims of distinct forms of female orgasm, have been steeped in controversy.

The G-spot was named after a gynecologist, Ernest Grafenberg, who first suggested the erotic importance of this area. Grafenberg observed that orgasm in women could be induced by stimulating this area. He also claimed that such orgasms may be accompanied by the discharge of a milky fluid or "ejaculate" from the urethra. In a laboratory experiment, Zaviacic and his colleagues (1988a, 1988b) found evidence of an ejaculate in 10 of 27 women studied. Some researchers believe that this fluid is urine that some women release involuntarily during orgasm (Alzate, 1985). Other researchers believe that it differs from urine (Zaviacic & Whipple, 1993). The nature of this fluid and its source remain a source of controversy, but Zaviacic and Whipple (1993) suggest that it may represent a fluid that is released during sex by a "female prostate," a system of ducts and glands called *Skene's glands*, in much the same way that semen is released by the prostate gland in men. Zaviacic and Whipple suggest that "many women who felt that they may be urinating during sex . . . [may be helped by] the knowledge that the fluid they expel may be different from urine and a normal phenomenon that occurs during sexual response" (1993, p. 149). Some women, however, may expel urine during sex, perhaps because of urinary stress incontinence (Zaviacic & Whipple, 1993). Zaviacic and Whipple also note that stimulation of the G-spot may be related to ejaculation in some women but not in others.

Even proponents of the existence of the G-spot recognize that it is difficult to locate, since it is not apparent to the eye (Ladas et al., 1982). Perry and Whipple (1981) suggest that women may try to locate the spot either by self-exploration or with the assistance of a partner. In either case, two fingers should be used to press deeply but gently into the front, or anterior, wall of the vagina to locate the spot, which may feel like a small lump

figure 5.7

The Grafenberg Spot.

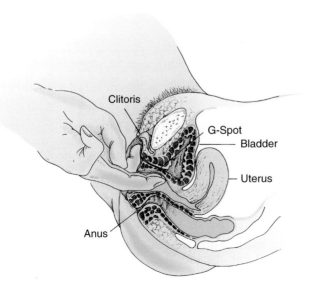

Grafenberg spot A part of the anterior wall of the vagina, whose prolonged stimulation is theorized to cause particularly intense orgasms and a female ejaculation. Abbreviated *G-spot*.

within the anterior wall (see Figure 5.7). When the spot is stimulated by stroking, the woman may initially experience an urge to urinate, perhaps because the sensitive area lies close to the bladder and urethra. A few minutes of continued stimulation lead to strong sensations of sexual pleasure in some women, which is accompanied by vasocongestion that swells the area. More prolonged stimulation may lead to an intense orgasm; however, fear of loss of urinary control leads some women to avoid such prolonged stimulation (Ladas et al., 1982).

Perry and Whipple (1981) relate the G-spot to the Singers' model of three kinds of orgasm. They suggest that sustained stimulation of the G-spot can produce a uterine orgasm that is characterized by deeper sensations than those that occur during the vulval orgasm that is produced by clitoral stimulation. The connection between the G-spot and the Singers' model is controversial.

The very existence of the G-spot remains debatable. Ladas, Whipple, and Perry (1982) reported locating the G-spot in every one of more than 400 women they examined. Zaviacic and his colleagues (1988b) reported finding the spot in each of 27 women they examined. Other researchers have been unable to find an area of heightened sensitivity corresponding to the G-spot, however (Alzate & Londono, 1984; Masters et al., 1989). Some researchers (e.g., Hock, 1983) deny the existence of the G-spot as a distinct anatomical structure. They argue that the entire anterior wall of the vagina, and not any one spot or area, is richly supplied with nerve endings and sensitive to erotic stimulation.

Although the existence of the G-spot continues to be debated among researchers, a recent survey of 1,289 professional women in the health and counseling professions revealed that a majority believe that the G-spot exists and that they have experienced sexual pleasure when it has been stimulated (Davidson et al., 1989). Still, there was considerable confusion among these women as to the precise location of this sensitive area. About three out of four women reported experiencing an orgasm from stimulation of this area, most frequently from manual stimulation.

More research is needed to determine the scientific basis of the claims for different kinds of orgasm in women and whether there are specific sites in the vagina, such as the G-spot, that may be especially sensitive to erotic stimulation.

Reflections

- Have you ever felt pressured to have multiple orgasms? If so, why?
- Do you believe that you have experienced more than one kind of orgasm? Do your own experiences coincide with any of the descriptions of orgasm in the text?
- Do you believe that women have a G-spot? Why or why not?

s u m m i n g   u p

MAKING SENSE OF SEX: THE ROLE OF THE SENSES IN SEXUAL AROUSAL

Each sense plays a role in sexual experience, but some play more of a role than others.

Vision: The Better to See You With

Visual information plays a major role in human sexual attraction. Visual cues can be sexual turn-ons or turn-offs.

Smell: Does the Nose Know Best?

Although the sense of smell plays a lesser role in governing sexual arousal in humans than in lower mammals, particular odors can be sexual turn-ons or turn-offs. Many organisms are sexually aroused by naturally produced chemicals called pheromones, but their role in human sexual behavior remains unclear.

The Skin Senses: Sex as a Touching Experience

The sense of touch has the most direct effects on sexual arousal and response. Erogenous zones are especially sensitive to tactile sexual stimulation.

Taste: On Savory Sex

Taste appears to play only a minor role in sexual arousal and response.

Hearing: The Better to Hear You With

Like visual and olfactory cues, sounds can be turn-ons or turn-offs.

APHRODISIACS: OF SPANISH FLIES AND RHINO HORNS

Alleged aphrodisiacs such as Spanish fly and foods that in some way resemble the genitals have not been shown to contribute to sexual arousal or response.

Anaphrodisiacs

Anaphrodisiacs, such as central nervous system depressants, dampen sexual arousal.

Psychoactive Drugs

The alleged aphrodisiac effects of psychoactive drugs, such as alcohol and cocaine, may reflect our expectations of them or their effects on sexual inhibitions, rather than direct stimulation of sexual response. Alcohol is also connected with a liberated social role and thus provides an external excuse for dubious behavior. Some people report initial increased sexual pleasure with cocaine use, but frequent use can lead to sexual dysfunctions.

SEXUAL RESPONSE AND THE BRAIN: CEREBRAL SEX?

The brain plays a central role in sexual functioning.

The Geography of the Brain

The brain consists of three major parts: the hindbrain, the midbrain, and the forebrain.

Brain Mechanisms in Sexual Functioning

The cerebral cortex interprets sensory information as sexual turn-ons or turn-offs. The cortex transmits messages through the spinal cord that cause vasocongestion. Direct stimulation of parts of the limbic system may cause erection and ejaculation in male animals.

On Pushing the Right Buttons: Are There Pleasure Centers in the Brain?

Electrical stimulation of certain parts of the limbic system apparently yields sensations similar to those of sexual gratification.

SEX HORMONES: DO THEY "GOAD" US INTO SEX?

Sex hormones have organizing and activating effects on behavior. Men and women normally produce one genuine aphrodisiac: testosterone. Female sex hormones do not appear to play a direct role in determining sexual motivation or response in human females. Yet levels of testosterone in the bloodstream have been associated with sexual interest in women.

THE SEXUAL RESPONSE CYCLE

Masters and Johnson found that the physiological responses of men and women to sexual stimulation are quite alike. Both experience vasocongestion and myotonia early in the response cycle.

Excitement Phase

Sexual excitement is characterized by erection in the male and vaginal lubrication in the female.

Plateau Phase

The plateau phase is an advanced state of arousal that precedes orgasm.

Orgasmic Phase

The third phase of the sexual response cycle is characterized by orgasmic contractions of the pelvic musculature. Orgasm in the male occurs in two stages of muscular contractions. Orgasm in the female is manifested by contractions of the pelvic muscles that surround the vaginal barrel.

Resolution Phase

During the resolution phase, the body returns to its prearoused state.

Kaplan's Three Stages of Sexual Response: An Alternative Model

Kaplan developed a three-stage model of sexual response consisting of desire, excitement, and orgasm. Kaplan's model makes it more convenient for clinicians to classify and treat sexual dysfunctions.

CONTROVERSIES ABOUT ORGASM

Multiple Orgasms: When You're Having More Than One

Multiple orgasm is the occurrence of one or more additional orgasms following the first, within a short period of time and before the body has returned to a preplateau level of arousal. Most women, but not most men, are capable of multiple orgasms.

How Many Kinds of Orgasms Do Women Have? One, Two, or Three?

Freud theorized the existence of two types of orgasm in women: clitoral and vaginal. Masters and Johnson found only one kind of orgasm among women. Singer and Singer suggested that there are three types of female orgasm: vulval, uterine, and blended.

The G-Spot

The G-spot—an allegedly distinct area of the vagina within the anterior wall—may have special erotic significance. Some researchers suggest that prolonged stimulation of the spot produces an orgasm that is characterized by intense pleasure and, in some women, by a type of ejaculation. The nature of this ejaculate remains in doubt.

Emil Nolde. *Young Couple (Junges Paar).* 1913. Lithograph, printed in color, composition: 24-7/16 x 20 in. The Museum of Modern Art, New York. Purchase. Photograph © 1999 The Museum of Modern Art

c h a p t e r

6

Gender Identity and Gender Roles

outline

TRUTH OR FICTION?

**PRENATAL SEXUAL
DIFFERENTIATION**
The Role of Sex Hormones in
Sexual Differentiation
Descent of the Testes and the Ovaries
Sex Chromosomal Abnormalities
Prenatal Sexual Differentiation
of the Brain

GENDER IDENTITY
Nature and Nurture in Gender Identity
Hermaphroditism
Transsexualism

A CLOSER LOOK:
Jayne Thomas, Ph.D.—In Her Own Words

GENDER ROLES AND STEREOTYPES

A WORLD OF DIVERSITY:
Machismo/Marianismo *Stereotypes and
Hispanic Culture*

SEXISM

A WORLD OF DIVERSITY:
Mom the Breadwinner

**GENDER DIFFERENCES:
VIVE LA DIFFÉRENCE OR
VIVE LA SIMILARITÉ?**
Differences in Cognitive Abilities
Differences in Personality

IN THE NEW MILLENNIUM:
*Will We See Differences in Fitness
Evaporate in the New Millennium?*

**ON BECOMING A MAN OR A
WOMAN: GENDER TYPING**
Biological Perspectives
Cross-Cultural Perspectives
Psychological Perspectives

**GENDER ROLES AND
SEXUAL BEHAVIOR**
Men as Sexually Aggressive, Women
as Sexually Passive
Men as Overaroused, Women
as Underaroused

**PSYCHOLOGICAL ANDROGYNY:
THE MORE TRAITS, THE MERRIER?**
Psychological Androgyny, Psychological
Well-Being, and Personal Development
Psychological Androgyny and
Sexual Behavior

SUMMING UP

Truth or Fiction?

_____ If male sex hormones were not present during critical stages of prenatal development, we would all develop female sexual organs.

_____ The sex of a baby crocodile is determined by the temperature at which the egg develops.

_____ Thousands of people have changed their genders through gender-reassignment surgery.

_____ Men act more aggressively than women do.

_____ A 2½-year-old child might know that he is a boy but think that he can grow up to be a mommy.

_____ Adolescent girls who show a number of masculine traits are more popular than girls who thoroughly adopt the traditional feminine gender role.

We're halfway there. We've begun to raise our daughters more like sons—so now women are whole people. But fewer of us have the courage to raise our sons more like daughters. Yet until men raise children as much as women do—and are raised to raise children, whether or not they become fathers—they will have a far harder time developing in themselves those human qualities that are wrongly called "feminine," but are really those necessary to raise children: empathy, flexibility, patience, compassion, and the ability to let go.

—Gloria Steinem, graduation speech at Smith College, 1995

Whatever women do they must do twice as well as men to be thought half as good. Luckily, this is not difficult.

—Charlotte Whitton

I like men to behave like men—strong and childish.

—French author Françoise Sagan

These remarks from war correspondents in the battle of the genders signify key issues in the study of gender: gender roles, the actual differences between the genders, and the enduring problem of sexism. This chapter addresses the biological, psychological, and sociological aspects of gender. First we focus on sexual differentiation: the process by which males and females develop distinct reproductive anatomy. We then turn to gender roles: the complex behavior patterns that are deemed "masculine" or "feminine" in a particular culture. The chapter examines empirical findings on actual gender differences, which may challenge some of the preconceptions that many of us hold regarding the differences between men and women. We next consider gender typing: the processes by which boys come to behave in line with what is expected of men (most of the time) and girls with what is expected of women (most of the time). We shall also explore the concept of psychological androgyny, which applies to people who display characteristics associated with both genders.

PRENATAL SEXUAL DIFFERENTIATION

Over the years, many ideas have been proposed to account for **sexual differentiation,** such as the belief that sperm from the right testicle make females and sperm from the left testicle make males (Angier, 1990). If this were so, males would indeed be sinister, because *sinister* means "left-hand" or "unlucky side" in Latin.

According to the Bible, Adam was created first, and Eve issued forth from one of his ribs. From the standpoint of modern biological knowledge, however, it would be more accurate to say that "Adams" (that is, males) develop from "Eves" (females). Let us trace the development of sexual differentiation.

When a sperm cell fertilizes an ovum, 23 **chromosomes** from the male parent normally combine with 23 chromosomes from the female parent. The **zygote,** the beginning of a new human being, is only $1/175$ of an inch long. Yet on this tiny stage, one's stamp as a unique individual has already been ensured—whether one will have black or blond hair, grow bald or develop a widow's peak, or become male or female.

The chromosomes from each parent combine to form 23 pairs. The 23rd pair are the sex chromosomes. An ovum carries an X sex chromosome, but a sperm carries either an X or a Y sex chromosome. If a sperm with an X sex chromosome fertilizes the ovum, the newly conceived individual will normally develop as a female, with an XX sex chromosomal structure. If the sperm carries a Y sex chromosome, the individual will normally develop as a male (XY).

After fertilization, the zygote divides repeatedly. After a few short weeks, one cell has become billions of cells. At about 3 weeks, a primitive heart begins to drive blood through the embryonic bloodstream. At about 5 to 6 weeks, when the **embryo** is only ¼ to ½ inch

Sexual differentiation The process by which males and females develop distinct reproductive anatomy.

Chromosome One of the rodlike structures, found in the nucleus of every living cell, that carry the genetic code in the form of genes.

Zygote A fertilized ovum (egg cell).

Embryo The stage of prenatal development that begins with implantation of a fertilized ovum in the uterus and concludes with development of the major organ systems at about two months after conception.

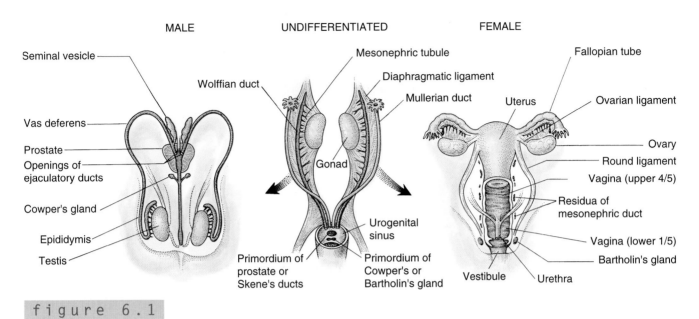

MALE   UNDIFFERENTIATED   FEMALE

figure 6.1

Development of the Internal Sexual Organs from an Undifferentiated Stage at about 5 or 6 Weeks after Conception.

long, primitive gonads, ducts, and external genitals whose gender cannot be distinguished visually have formed (see Figure 6.1 and Figure 6.2 on page 156). Each embryo possesses primitive external genitals, a pair of sexually undifferentiated gonads, and two sets of primitive duct structures, the Müllerian (female) ducts and the Wolffian (male) ducts.

During the first 6 weeks or so of prenatal development, embryonic structures of both genders develop along similar lines and resemble primitive female structures. At about the seventh week after conception, the genetic code (XX or XY) begins to assert itself, causing changes in the gonads, genital ducts, and external genitals. The Y sex chromosome causes the testes to begin to differentiate. Ovaries begin to differentiate if the Y chromosome is absent. Some rare individuals who have only one X sex chromosome instead of the typical XY or XX arrangement also become females, since they too lack the Y chromosome (Angier, 1990).

Thus, the basic blueprint of the human embryo is female. The genetic instructions in the Y sex chromosome cause the embryo to deviate from the female developmental course. "Adams" develop from embryos that otherwise would become "Eves."

By about the seventh week of prenatal development, the Y sex chromosome stimulates the production of *H-Y antigen,* a protein that fosters the development of testes. Strands of tissue begin to organize into seminiferous tubules. Female gonads begin to develop somewhat later than male gonads. The forerunners of follicles that will bear ova are not found until the fetal stage of development, about 10 weeks after conception. Ovaries begin to form at 11 or 12 weeks.

The Role of Sex Hormones in Sexual Differentiation

Without the influence of male sex hormones, or **androgens,** we would all develop into females (Federman, 1994). Once the testes develop in the embryo, they begin to produce androgens. The most important androgen, **testosterone,** spurs differentiation of the male (Wolffian) duct system (see Figure 6.1). Each Wolffian duct develops into an epididymis, vas deferens, and seminal vesicle. The external genitals, including the penis, begin to take shape at about the eighth week of development under the influence of another androgen, *dihydrotestosterone* (DHT). Yet another testicular hormone, one secreted during the fetal stage, prevents the Müllerian ducts from developing into the female duct system. It is appropriately termed the Müllerian inhibiting substance (MIS).

Androgens Male sex hormones.

Testosterone The male sex hormone that fosters the development of male sex characteristics and is connected with the sex drive.

figure 6.2

Development of the External Sexual Organs from an Undifferentiated Stage at about 5 or 6 Weeks after Conception.

UNDIFFERENTIATED

Glans area
Urethral fold
Urethral groove
Lateral buttress
Anal pit
Anal tubercle

Genital tubercle

45–50 mm

MALE   Glans   FEMALE
Site of future origin of prepuce
Urethral fold
Urogenital groove
Lateral buttress (corpus or shaft)
Labioscrotal swelling
Urethral folds partly fused (perineal raphé)
Anal tubercle
Anus

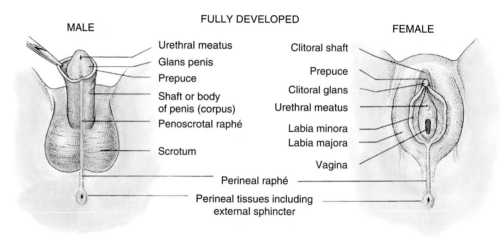

FULLY DEVELOPED

MALE   FEMALE

Urethral meatus   Clitoral shaft
Glans penis   Prepuce
Prepuce   Clitoral glans
Shaft or body of penis (corpus)   Urethral meatus
Penoscrotal raphé   Labia minora
                                   Labia majora
Scrotum   Vagina

Perineal raphé
Perineal tissues including external sphincter

Small amounts of androgens are produced in female fetuses, but they are not normally sufficient to cause male sexual differentiation. In female fetuses, the relative absence of androgens causes degeneration of the Wolffian ducts and prompts development of female sexual organs. The Müllerian ducts evolve into fallopian tubes, the uterus, and the upper two thirds of the vagina. These developments occur even in the absence of female sex hormones. Although female sex hormones are crucial in puberty, they are not involved in fetal sexual differentiation. If a fetus with an XY sex chromosomal structure failed to produce testosterone, it would develop female sexual organs.

Truth or Fiction?
REVISITED

It is true that we would all develop female sexual organs if male sex hormones were not present during critical stages of prenatal development. Embryos develop female sexual organs in the absence of male sex hormones. ■

Descent of the Testes and the Ovaries

The testes and ovaries develop from slender structures high in the abdominal cavity. By about 10 weeks after conception, they have descended so that they are almost even with the upper edge of the pelvis. The ovaries remain there for the rest of the prenatal period.

Later, they rotate and descend farther to their adult position in the pelvis. About four months after conception, the testes normally descend into the scrotal sac through the **inguinal canal.** After their descent, this passageway is closed.

In a small percentage of males, one or both testes remain undescended. They remain in the abdomen at birth. The condition is termed **cryptorchidism.** In most cases of cryptorchidism, the testes migrate to the scrotum during infancy. In still other cases, the testes descend by puberty. Men with undescended testes are usually treated through surgery or hormonal therapy, since they are at higher risk for cancer of the testes. Sperm production is also impaired because the undescended testes are subjected to a higher-than-optimal body temperature, causing sterility.

Sex Chromosomal Abnormalities

Abnormalities of the sex chromosomes can have profound effects on sexual characteristics, physical health, and psychological development. **Klinefelter syndrome,** a condition that affects about 1 in 500 males, is caused by an extra X sex chromosome, so the man has an XXY rather than an XY pattern. Men with this pattern fail to develop appropriate secondary sex characteristics. They have enlarged breasts and poor muscular development, and because they fail to produce sperm, they are infertile. They also tend to be mildly retarded.

Turner syndrome, found only in women, occurs in 1 in 2,000–5,000 girls. It is caused by the loss of some X sex chromosome material. These girls develop typical external genital organs, but they are short in stature and their ovaries do not develop or function normally. Girls with Turner syndrome have abnormal hairlines and tend to be involved in fewer social activities than other girls (Rovet & Ireland, 1994). However, they are not retarded (Saenger, 1996).

Prenatal Sexual Differentiation of the Brain

The brain, like the genital organs, undergoes prenatal sexual differentiation. Testosterone causes cells in the hypothalamus of male fetuses to become insensitive to the female sex hormone estrogen. In the absence of testosterone, as in female fetuses, the hypothalamus does develop sensitivity to estrogen.

Sensitivity to estrogen is important in the regulation of the menstrual cycle of women after puberty. The hypothalamus detects low levels of estrogen in the blood at the end of each cycle and initiates a new cycle by stimulating the pituitary gland to secrete FSH. FSH, in turn, stimulates estrogen production by the ovaries and the ripening of an immature follicle in an ovary. Sexual differentiation of the hypothalamus most likely occurs during the second trimester of fetal development (Pillard & Weinrich, 1986).

Reflections

- What is the relationship between sex chromosomes and anatomic sex? Do you know anyone with one of the chromosomal abnormalities discussed in this section? How did it affect her or him?
- What is the role of sex hormones in sexual differentiation?

GENDER IDENTITY

Our awareness of being male or being female—our **gender identity**—is one of the most obvious and important aspects of our self-concepts. Gender identity is not an automatic extension of our anatomic gender. Gender identity is psychological—a sense of being male or being female. **Gender assignment** reflects the child's anatomic gender and

Inguinal canal A fetal canal that connects the scrotum and the testes, allowing their descent. (From the Latin *inguinus,* meaning "near the groin.")

Cryptorchidism The condition defined by undescended testes. (From roots meaning "hidden testes.")

Klinefelter's syndrome A sex-chromosomal disorder caused by an extra X sex chromosome.

Turner syndrome A sex-chromosomal disorder caused by loss of some X chromosome material.

Gender identity The psychological sense of being male or female.

Gender assignment The labeling of a newborn as a male or female.

figure 6.3

A True Hermaphrodite. This
genetic (XX) female has one
testicle and one ovary and
the gender identity of a male.

usually occurs at birth. Gender identity is so important to parents that they might want
to know "Is it a boy or a girl?" before they begin to count fingers and toes.

Most children first become aware of their anatomic gender by about the age of 18
months. By 36 months, most children have acquired a firm sense of gender identity
(Etaugh & Rathus, 1995).

Nature and Nurture in Gender Identity

What determines gender identity? Are our brains biologically programmed along masculine or feminine lines by prenatal sex hormones? Does the environment, in the form of
postnatal learning experiences, shape our self-concepts as males or females? Or does gender identity reflect an intermingling of biological and environmental influences?

Gender identity is almost always consistent with chromosomal gender. Such consistency does not certify that gender identity is biologically determined, however. We also
tend to be reared as males or females, according to our anatomic genders. How, then,
might we sort out the roles of nature and nurture, of biology and the environment?

Clues may be found in the experiences of rare individuals, **pseudohermaphrodites,** who possess the gonads of one gender but external genitalia that are ambiguous or typical of the other gender. Pseudohermaphrodites are sometimes reared as
members of the other gender (the gender other than their chromosomal gender). Researchers wondered whether the gender identity of these children reflects their chromosomal and gonadal gender or the gender according to which they were reared. Before
going further with this, let us distinguish between true hermaphroditism and pseudohermaphroditism.

Hermaphroditism

Hormonal errors during prenatal development produce various congenital defects. Some
individuals are born with both ovarian and testicular tissue. They are called **hermaphrodites,** after the Greek myth of the son of Hermes and Aphrodite, whose body became
united with that of a nymph while he was bathing. True hermaphrodites may have one gonad of each gender (a testicle and an ovary) or gonads that combine testicular and ovarian tissue.

Regardless of their genetic gender, hermaphrodites usually assume the gender identity and gender role of the gender assigned at birth. Figure 6.3 shows a genetic female
(XX) with a right testicle and left ovary. This person married and became a stepfather with
a firm male identity. The roles of biology and environment remain tangled, however,
since true hermaphrodites have gonadal tissue of both genders.

True hermaphroditism is extremely rare. More common is pseudohermaphroditism,
which occurs in perhaps 1 infant in 1,000. The occurrence of pseudohermaphroditism has
given scientists an opportunity to examine the roles of nature (biology) and nurture (environmental influences) in the shaping of gender identity.

PSEUDOHERMAPHRODITISM   *Pseudohermaphrodites* ("false" hermaphrodites) have
testes or ovaries but not both. Unlike true hermaphrodites, their gonads (testes or
ovaries) match their chromosomal gender. Because of prenatal hormonal errors, however, their external genitals and sometimes their internal reproductive anatomy are ambiguous or resemble those of the other gender.

The most common form of female pseudohermaphroditism is **androgenital syndrome,** in which a genetic (XX) female has female internal sexual structures (ovaries) but
masculinized external genitals (see Figure 6.4). The clitoris is so enlarged that it may resemble a small penis. The syndrome occurs as a result of excessive levels of androgens. In
some cases, the fetus's own adrenal glands produce excess androgen (the adrenal glands
usually produce low levels of androgen). In other cases, mothers may have received synthetic androgens during their pregnancies. In the 1950s and 1960s, before these side

Pseudohermaphrodites People
who possess the gonads of one
gender but external genitalia that
are ambiguous or typical of the
other gender.

Hermaphrodites People who
possess both ovarian and testicular tissue. (From the names of
the male and female Greek gods
Hermes and *Aphrodite*.)

Androgenital syndrome
A form of pseudohermaphroditism in which a genetic female has internal female sexual
structures but masculinized external genitals.

effects were known, synthetic androgens were sometimes prescribed to help prevent miscarriages in women with histories of spontaneous abortions.

Another type of pseudohermaphroditism, **androgen-insensitivity syndrome,** describes genetic (XY) males who had lower-than-normal prenatal sensitivity to androgens. As a result, their genitals did not become normally masculinized. At birth, their external genitals are feminized, including a small vagina, and their testes are undescended. Because of insensitivity to androgens, the male duct system (epididymis, vas deferens, seminal vesicles, and ejaculatory ducts) fails to develop. Nevertheless, the fetal testes produce Müllerian inhibiting substance, preventing the development of a uterus or fallopian tubes.

A third type of pseudohermaphroditism is named **Dominican Republic syndrome** because it was first documented in a group of 18 affected boys in two rural villages in that nation (Imperato-McGinley et al., 1974). Dominican Republic syndrome is a genetic enzyme disorder that prevents testosterone from masculinizing the external genitalia. The boys were born with normal testes and internal male reproductive organs, but their external genitals were malformed. Their penises were stunted and resembled clitorises. Their scrotums were incompletely formed and resembled female labia. They also had partially formed vaginas.

PSEUDOHERMAPHRODITISM AND GENDER IDENTITY The experiences of pseudohermaphrodites provide insights into the origins of gender identity. The genitals of girls with androgenital syndrome are normally surgically feminized in infancy. The girls also receive hormone treatments to correct excessive adrenal output of androgens. As a result, they usually acquire a feminine gender identity and develop physically as normal females.

What if the syndrome is not identified early in life, however? Consider the cases of two children who were treated at Johns Hopkins University Hospital. The children both had androgenital syndrome, but their treatments and the outcomes were very different. Each child was genetically female (XX). Each had female internal sex organs. Because of prenatal exposure to synthetic male sex hormones, however, each developed masculinized external sex organs (Money & Ehrhardt, 1972).

The problem was identified in one child (let's call her Abby) in infancy. Her masculinized sex organs were removed surgically when she was age 2. Like many other girls, Abby was tomboyish during childhood, but she was always feminine in appearance and had a female gender identity. She began to develop breasts by the age of 12 but did not begin to menstruate until age 20. She dated boys, and her fantasy life centered around marriage to a man.

The other child (let's call him James) was initially mistaken for a genetic male with stunted external sex organs. The error was discovered at the age of 3½. By then, he had a firm male gender identity, so surgeons further masculinized his external sex organs rather than remove them. At puberty, hormone treatments stoked the development of body hair, male musculature, and other male secondary sex characteristics.

As an adolescent, James did poorly in school. Possibly in an effort to compensate for his poor grades, he joined a gang of semidelinquents. He became "one of the boys." In contrast to Abby, James was sexually attracted to women.

Both children were pseudohermaphrodites. Both had internal female sexual organs and masculinized external organs, but they were treated and reared differently. In Abby's case, the newborn was designated female, surgically altered to remove the masculinized genitals, and reared as a girl. In James's case, the infant was labeled and reared as a boy. Each child acquired the gender identity of the assigned gender. Environmental influences appeared to play the critical role in shaping the gender identity of these children.

Further evidence for a role for psychosocial influences on gender identity is found in studies of genetic (XY) males with androgen-insensitivity syndrome. They possess testes but are born with feminine-appearing genitals and are typically reared as girls. They develop a female gender identity and stereotypical feminine interests. They show as much interest in dolls, dresses, and future roles as mothers and housewives as do genetic (XX) girls of the same ages and social class (Brooks-Gunn & Matthews, 1979; Money & Ehrhardt, 1972).

figure 6.4

Pseudohermaphroditism. In androgenital syndrome, a genetic (XX) female has female internal sexual structures (ovaries) but masculinized external genitals.

Androgen-insensitivity syndrome A form of pseudohermaphroditism in which a genetic male is prenatally insensitive to androgens. As a result, his genitals do not become normally masculinized.

Dominican Republic syndrome A form of pseudohermaphroditism in which a genetic enzyme disorder prevents testosterone from masculinizing the external genitalia.

The boys with Dominican Republic syndrome also resembled girls at birth and were reared as females. At puberty, however, their testes swung into normal testosterone production, causing startling changes: their testes descended, their voices deepened, their musculature filled out, and their "clitorises" expanded into penises. Of the 18 boys who were reared as girls, 17 shifted to a male gender identity. Sixteen of the 18 assumed a stereotypical masculine gender role. Of the remaining two, one adopted a male gender identity but continued to maintain a feminine gender role, including wearing dresses. The other maintained a female gender identity and later sought a gender-reassignment surgery to "correct" the pubertal masculinization.

The Dominican transformations suggest that gender identity is malleable. What of the roles of nature and nurture in the formation of gender identity, however? If environmental forces (nurture) were predominant, gender identity would be based on the gender in which the person is reared, regardless of biological abnormalities. With the Dominicans, however, pubertal biological changes led to changes in both gender identity and gender roles. Is nature (biology) then the primary determinant of gender identity? Unfortunately, the Dominican study does not allow clear separation of the effects of nature and nurture. It is possible that the pubertal surges of testosterone activated brain structures that were masculinized during prenatal development. Prenatal testosterone levels in these boys were presumably normal and could have affected the sexual differentiation of brain tissue, even though the genetic defect prevented the hormone from masculinizing the external genitalia.

Consider some other possibilities: Did the children, seeing themselves transforming into men, begin to change their self-concepts to be consistent with their bodily changes? Did the children choose to assume male gender identities because the masculine gender role was positively valued in their culture? Either possibility permits a psychological or cultural explanation of gender identity.

What, then, can we conclude from studies of pseudohermaphrodites? For one thing, gender identity and the assumption of gender roles are strongly influenced by psychosocial factors. Pseudohermaphrodites can acquire the gender identity of the other chromosomal gender when they are reared as members of that gender. The genetic (XX) females—Abby and James—were reared as members of different genders and acquired the gender identity in which they were reared. Yet both were treated with sex hormones appropriate to their assigned gender. Therefore, we cannot be certain that sex hormones did not influence their subsequent gender identity. The Dominican study also suggests that gender identity might not be fixed by early learning influences but may be subject to subsequent biological and/or psychosocial influences.

We should also recognize that the experiences of people who are affected by these hormonal errors might not generalize to others. Perhaps the brains of these children had not been clearly gender-typed prenatally and were therefore capable of an unusual degree of postnatal flexibility in the assumption of gender identity. Perhaps in normal people, the brain is more clearly differentiated prenatally, so that gender identity is not so readily influenced by experience.

Most scientists conclude that gender identity is influenced by complex interactions between biological and psychosocial factors. Some place relatively greater emphasis on psychosocial factors (Money, 1987a; Money & Ehrhardt, 1972). Others emphasize the role of biological factors (Collaer & Hines, 1995). The debate over the relative contributions of nature and nurture is likely to continue.

In case you have had enough discussion of the complex issues surrounding the origins of gender in human beings, consider the crocodile. Crocodile eggs do not carry sex chromosomes. The baby's sex is determined, instead, by the temperature at which the eggs develop (Ackerman, 1991). Some (males) like it hot (at least in the mid-90s Fahrenheit), and some (females) like it not cold, perhaps, but under the mid-80s Fahrenheit.

Truth or Fiction?
REVISITED

It is true that the sex of a baby crocodile is determined by the temperature at which the egg develops. ■

Transsexualism

In 1953, an ex-GI who journeyed to Denmark for a "sex-change operation" made headlines. She became known as Christine (formerly George) Jorgensen. Since then, thousands of **transsexuals** have undergone gender-reassignment surgery. Among the better known is the tennis player Dr. Renée Richards, formerly Dr. Richard Raskin.

Gender-reassignment surgery cannot implant the internal reproductive organs of the other gender. Instead, it generates the likeness of external genitals typical of the other gender. This can be done more precisely with male-to-female than female-to-male transsexuals. After such operations, people can participate in sexual activity and even attain orgasm, but they cannot conceive or bear children.

It is not true that people have changed their genders through gender-reassignment surgery. Gender-reassignment surgery cannot implant the internal reproductive organs of the other gender. It only generates the appearance of the external genitals typical of the other gender. ■

Truth or Fiction?
REVISITED

Transsexuals experience **gender dysphoria.** That is, according to John Money (1994), they have the subjective experience of incongruity between their genital anatomy and their gender identity or role. They have the anatomic sex of one gender but feel that they are members of the other gender. As a result of this discrepancy, they wish to be rid of their own primary sex characteristics (their external genitals and internal sex organs) and to live as members of the other gender. A male transsexual perceives himself to be a female who, through some quirk of fate, was born with the wrong genital equipment. A female transsexual perceives herself as a man trapped in a woman's body. Although the prevalence of transsexualism remains unknown, it is thought to be rare. Pauly (1974) estimated the prevalence at 1 in 100,000 males and 1 in 130,000 females. Experts estimate the number of transsexuals in the United States to be about 25,000. Perhaps 6,000 to 11,000 of them have undergone gender-reassignment surgery (Selvin, 1993).

Patterns of sexual attraction do not appear to be central in importance. Some transsexuals report never having had strong sexual feelings. Others are attracted to members of their own (anatomic) gender. They are unlikely to regard themselves as gay or lesbian, however. From their perspective, their lovers are members of the other gender. Still others are attracted to members of the other anatomic gender. Nonetheless, they all want to be rid of their own sex organs and to live as members of the other gender.

Transsexualism is not to be confused with a gay male or lesbian sexual orientation. Gay males and lesbians are erotically attracted to members of their own gender. A gay man may desire another man as a lover; a lesbian may sexually desire another woman. Gay men and lesbians perceive their gender identities to be consistent with their anatomic gender, however. They would no more want to be rid of their own genitals than would heterosexuals. As one gay man put it, "Just because I'm turned on by other men doesn't make me feel less like a man."

Transsexuals usually show cross-gender preferences in play and dress in early childhood. Many report that they felt they belonged to the other gender for as long as they can remember. Only a few were unaware of their transsexual feelings until adolescence. Male transsexuals generally recall that as children they preferred playing with dolls, enjoyed wearing frilly dresses, and disliked rough-and-tumble play. They were often perceived by their peers as "sissy boys." Female transsexuals usually report that as children they disliked dresses and acted much like "tomboys." They also preferred playing "boys' games" and doing so with boys. Female transsexuals appear to have an easier time adjusting than male transsexuals (Selvin, 1993). "Tomboys" generally find it easier to be accepted by their peers than "sissy boys." Even in adulthood, it may be easier for a female transsexual to don men's clothes and "pass" as a slightly built man than it is for a brawnier man to "pass" for a tall woman.

The transition to adolescence is particularly difficult for transsexuals. They find their bodies changing in ways that evoke their disgust. Female transsexuals abhor the onset of

Transsexuals People who have a gender-identity disorder in which they feel trapped in the body of the wrong gender.

Gender dysphoria The subjective experience of incongruity between genital anatomy and gender identity or role.

menstruation and the development of breasts. They might seek to disguise their budding breasts by binding them or wearing loose clothing. Some have mastectomies at the age of consent to remove the obvious reminder of what they perceive as "nature's mistake."

THEORETICAL PERSPECTIVES   No clear understanding of the nature or causes of transsexualism has emerged (Money, 1994). Views on its origins somewhat parallel those on the origins of a gay male or lesbian sexual orientation, which is surprising, given the fundamental differences that exist between the two.

Psychoanalytic theorists have focused on early parent-child relationships. Male transsexuals, in this view, may have had "close-binding mothers" (extremely close mother-son relationships) and "detached-hostile fathers" (fathers who were absent or disinterested) (Stoller, 1969). Such family circumstances may have fostered intense **identification** with the mother, to the point of an inversion of typical gender roles and identity. Girls with weak, ineffectual mothers and strong, masculine fathers may identify with their fathers, rejecting their own female identities.

There is some evidence that male transsexuals tend to have had unusually close relationships with their mothers during childhood. Female transsexuals tend to have identified more with their fathers and to have perceived their mothers as cold and rejecting (Pauly, 1974). Yet one problem with the psychoanalytic view is that the roles of cause and effect may be reversed. It could be that in childhood, transsexuals gravitate toward the parent of the other gender and reject the efforts of the parent of the same gender to reach out to them and engage them in gender-typed activities. These views also do not account for the many transsexuals whose family backgrounds fail to match these patterns. Moreover, these views lack predictive power. Most children—in fact, the vast majority!—with such family backgrounds do *not* become transsexuals.

The early onset of transsexual feelings suggests that critical early learning experiences, if they exist, might occur in the preschool years. Transsexuals may also be influenced by prenatal hormonal imbalances. The brain is in some ways "masculinized" or "feminized" by sex hormones during prenatal development. Researchers in the Netherlands have discovered that a small region of the hypothalamus is about 50% larger in men than in women and nearly 60% larger in men than in male-to-female transsexuals (Angier, 1995). It is possible that the brain could be influenced in one direction, even as the genitals are being differentiated in the other direction.

GENDER REASSIGNMENT   Gender reassignment for transsexuals has been controversial since its inception. Yet psychotherapy is not considered a reasonable alternative, because it has been generally unsuccessful in helping transsexuals to accept their anatomic genders (Roberto, 1983; Tollison & Adams, 1979).

Surgery is one element of gender reassignment. Since the surgery is irreversible, health professionals conduct careful evaluations to determine that people seeking reassignment are competent to make such decisions and have thought through the consequences. They usually require that the transsexual live openly as a member of the other gender for a trial period of at least a year before surgery.

Once the decision is reached, a lifetime of hormone treatments is begun. Male-to-female transsexuals receive estrogen, which fosters the development of female secondary sex characteristics. It causes fatty deposits to develop in the breasts and hips, softens the skin, and inhibits growth of the beard. Female-to-male transsexuals receive androgens, which promote male secondary sex characteristics. The voice deepens, hair becomes distributed according to the male pattern, muscles enlarge, and the fatty deposits in the breasts and hips are lost. The clitoris may also grow more prominent.

Gender-reassignment surgery is largely cosmetic. Medical science cannot construct internal genital organs or gonads. Male-to-female surgery is generally more successful. The penis and testicles are first removed. Tissue from the penis is placed in an artificial vagina so that sensitive nerve endings will provide sexual sensations. A penis-shaped form of plastic or balsa wood is used to keep the vagina distended during healing.

Identification In psychoanalytic theory, the process of incorporating within ourselves our perceptions of the behaviors, thoughts, and feelings of others.

In female-to-male transsexuals, the internal sex organs (ovaries, fallopian tubes, uterus) are removed, along with the remaining fatty tissue in the breasts. The nipples are moved to keep them at the proper height on the torso. The urethra is rerouted through the enlarged clitoris, or an artificial penis and scrotum are constructed from tissue from the abdomen, the labia, and the perineum through a series of operations. In either case, the patient can urinate while standing, which appears to provide psychological gratification. Although the artificial penis does not stiffen and become erect naturally, a variety of methods, including implants, can be used to allow the artificial penis to approximate erection.

Some transsexuals hesitate to undertake surgery because they are repulsed by the prospect of such extreme medical intervention. Others forgo surgery so as not to jeopardize high-status careers or family relationships (Kockott & Fahrner, 1987). Such people continue to think of themselves as members of the other gender, however, even without surgery.

OUTCOMES OF GENDER-REASSIGNMENT SURGERY   Following the introduction of gender-reassignment surgery in the United States in 1960s, most reports of postoperative adjustment were positive (Pauly & Edgerton, 1986). An influential study in the 1970s conducted at the Gender Identity Clinic at Johns Hopkins University was quite negative, however (Meyer & Reter, 1979). The study included a control group of transsexuals who did not receive gender-reassignment surgery. Psychological adjustment was more positive among transsexuals in the control group than among those who had undergone surgery.

Other reviews report more positive outcomes for gender-reassignment surgery (Kockott & Fahrner, 1987; Lundstrom et al., 1984; Pauly & Edgerton, 1986). One study of 42 postoperative male-to-female transsexuals found that all but one would repeat the surgery and that the great majority found sexual activity more pleasurable as a "woman" (Bentler, 1976).

Reviewers of the international literature reported in 1984 that about 90% of transsexuals who undergo gender-reassignment surgery experience positive results (Lundstrom et al., 1984). In Canada, a follow-up study of 116 transsexuals (female-to-male and male-to-female) at least one year after surgery found that most of them were content with the results and were reasonably well adjusted (Blanchard et al., 1985). Positive results for surgery were also reported in a study of 141 Dutch transsexuals (Kuiper & Cohen-Kettenis, 1988). Nearly 9 of 10 male-to-female and female-to-male transsexuals in a study of 23 transsexuals reported they were very pleased with the results of their gender-reassignment surgery (Lief & Hubschman, 1993). Still another study (Abramowitz, 1986) reported that about two out of three cases showed at least some postoperative improvement in psychological adjustment. These favorable results do not mean that postoperative transsexuals were ecstatic about their lives. In many cases, it meant that they were less unhappy. Most transsexuals are socially maladjusted before gender reassignment, and many remain lonely and isolated afterward. Moreover, about half incur postoperative medical complications (Lindermalm et al., 1986).

Male-to-female transsexuals whose surgery permitted them to pass as members of the other gender showed better adjustment than those whose surgery left telltale signs (such as breast scarring and leftover erectile tissue) that they were not "real" women (Ross & Need, 1989). Social and family support also contributed to postsurgical adjustment (Ross & Need, 1989).

Male-to-female transsexuals outnumber female-to-males, but postoperative adjustment is apparently more favorable for female-to-males. Nearly 10% of male-to-female cases, compared to 4% to 5% of female-to-males, have had disturbing outcomes, such as severe psychological disorders, hospitalization, requests for reversal surgery, and even suicide (Abramowitz, 1986). One reason for the relatively better postoperative adjustment of the female-to-male transsexuals may be society's more accepting attitudes toward women who desire to become men (Abramowitz, 1986). Female-to-male transsexuals tend to be better adjusted socially before surgery as well (Kockott & Fahrner,

a CLOSER look

Jayne Thomas, Ph.D.— In Her Own Words

The "Glass Ceiling," male bashing, domestic violence, nagging, PMS, Viagra—these are but a few of the important issues examined in the Human Sexuality classes I instruct. As a participant-observer in my field, I see many of these topics aligning themselves as masculine/feminine or male/female. Ironically, I can both see and not see such distinctions. Certainly women have bumped up against, smudged (and in some cases even polished) this metaphorical limitation of women's advancement in the workplace (i.e., that "Glass Ceiling"). And most assuredly men have often found themselves "bashed" by angry women intent upon extracting a pound of flesh for centuries of felt unjust treatment. As previously mentioned, these distinctions between masculine and feminine, for me often become blurred; I must add that, having lived my life in both the roles of man and woman, I offer a rather unique perspective of masculinity and femininity.

Gender Identity Disorder

Gender Identity Disorder (GID) is defined by the American Psychiatric Association (1994) as a "strong and persistent cross-gender identification [accompanied by] a persistent discomfort with his or her sex or sense of appropriateness in the gender role of that sex" (p. 537). All of my life, I harbored the strongest conviction that I was inappropriately assigned to the wrong gender—that of a man—when inside I knew myself to be a woman. Even so (and like so many other GID's) I continued a life-long struggle with this deeply felt mistake; I was successful in school, became a national swimming champion, received my college degrees, married twice (fathering children in both marriages) and was respected as a competent and good man in the workplace. However, the persistently unrelenting wrongfulness of my life continued. Not until my fourth decade was I truly able to address my gender issue.

Jay Thomas, Ph.D. underwent gender reassignment and officially became Jayne Thomas, Ph.D. in November of 1985, and what has transpired in the ensuing years has been the most enlightening of glimpses into the plight of humankind.

Jayne Thomas, Ph.D. Psychologist Jayne Thomas teaches courses in human sexuality in Southern California. She offers a unique perspective on masculinity and feminity because she has lived as both a man and a woman.

As teachers, we are constantly being taught by those we purport to instruct. My students, knowing my background (I share who I am when it is appropriate to do so), find me accessible in ways that many professors are not. Granted, I am continually asked the titillating questions that one watching *Geraldo* might ask and we do have fun with the answers (several years ago I even appeared on a few of the *Geraldo* shows). My students, however, are able to take our discussions beyond the sensational and superficial, and we enter into meaningful dialogue regarding gender differences in society and the workplace, sexual harassment, power and control issues in relationships, and what it really means to be a man or a woman.

Challenging Both the Masculine and the Feminine

Iconoclastically, I try to challenge both the masculine and feminine. "I know something none of you women know or

1987; Pauly, 1974), so their superior postoperative adjustment might be nothing more than a selection factor.

Programs across the country help transsexuals to come to terms with themselves and adjust to living in a society in which they rarely feel welcome (Selvin, 1993). One example is the Gender Identity Project in New York City's Greenwich Village, which sponsors meetings at which transsexuals get together and share common concerns. Such programs help to create a sense of community for a group of people who feel alienated from the larger society.

will ever know in your lifetime," I can provocatively address the females in my audiences as Jayne. "I once lived as a man and have been treated as an equal. You never have nor will you experience such equality." Or, when a male student once came to my assistance in a classroom, fixing an errant video playback device and then strutting peacock-like back to his seat as only a satisfied male can, I teasingly commented to a nearby female student, "I use to be able to do that."

Having once lived as a man and now as a woman, I can honestly state that I see profound differences in our social/psychological/biological being as man and woman. I have now experienced many of the ways in which women are treated as less than men. Jay worked as a consultant to a large banking firm in Los Angeles and continued in that capacity as a woman following her gender shift. Amazingly the world presented itself in a different perspective. As Jay, technical presentations to management had generally been received in a positive manner and credit for my work fully acknowledged. Jayne now found management less accessible, credit for her effort less forthcoming and, in general, found herself working harder to be well prepared for each meeting than she ever had as a male. As a man, her forceful and impassioned presentations were an asset; as a woman they definitely seemed a liability. On one occasion, as Jayne, when I passionately asserted my position regarding what I felt to be an important issue, my emotion and disappointment in not getting my point across (my voice showed my frustration) was met with a nearby colleague (a man) reaching to touch my arm with words of reassurance, "There, there, take it easy, it will be all right." Believe me; that never happened to Jay. There was also an occasion when I had worked most diligently on a presentation to management only to find the company vice president more interested in the fragrance of my cologne than my technical agenda.

Certainly there are significant difference in the treatment of men and women, and yet I continue to be impressed with how similar we two genders really are. Although I have made this seemingly enormous change in lifestyle (and it is immense in so many ways), I continue as the same human being, perceiving the same world through these same sensory neu-

rons. The difference—I now find myself a more comfortable and serene being, than the paradoxical woman in a man's body, with anatomy and gender have attained congruence.

Adjusting the Shifting Gender Roles

Does the shifting of gender role create difficulties in the GID's life? Most assuredly it does. Family and intimate relationships rank highest among those issues most problematic for the transitioning individual to resolve. When one shifts gender role the effects of such a change are global; as ripples in a pond, the transformation radiates outward impacting all that have significantly touched the GID's life. My parents had never realized that their eldest son was dealing with such a life-long problem. Have they accepted or do they fully understand the magnitude of my issue? I fear not. After almost fifteen years of having lived as a female, my father continues to call me by my male name. I do not doubt my parents' or children's love for me, but so uninformed are we of the true significance of gender identity that a clear understanding seems light years away. Often I see my clients losing jobs, closeness with family members, visitation rights with children and generally becoming relegated to the role of societal outcast. Someone once stated that "Everybody is born unique, but most of us die copies"—a great price my clients often pay for personal honesty and not living their lives a version of how society deems they should.

Having lived as man and woman in the same lifetime one personal truth seems clear. Rather than each gender attempting to change and convert the other to their own side, as I often see couples undertaking to accomplish (women need be more logical and men more sharing of their emotions), we might more productively come together in our relationships building upon our gender uniqueness and strengths. Men and women have different perspectives, which can be used successfully to address life's issues.

Dr. Thomas teaches and lectures at colleges and universities on the West Coast, sharing her views of masculine and feminine with her students, conducting workshops, and continuing her experiment or *experience* of life.

Reflections

- What is your gender identity? What is the relationship between your anatomic sex and your gender identity?
- Had you heard of transsexualism before taking this course? How do the facts on transsexualism differ from what you had heard?
- What is the difference between transsexualism and a gay male or lesbian sexual orientation?

GENDER ROLES AND STEREOTYPES

"Why can't a woman be more like a man?" You might recall this lyric from the song that Professor Henry Higgins sings in the musical *My Fair Lady*. In the song, the professor laments that women are emotional and fickle, whereas men are logical and dependable. The "emotional woman" is a **stereotype**—a fixed, oversimplified, and sometimes distorted idea about a group of people. The "logical man" is also a stereotype—albeit a more generous one. Gender roles are stereotypes in that they evoke fixed, conventional expectations of men and women.

Our gender identities—our identification of ourselves according to our concepts of masculinity and femininity—do not determine the roles or behaviors that are deemed masculine or feminine in our culture. Cultures have broad expectations of men and women that are termed **gender roles.**

Some might think that people "play" gender roles in the same way that many actors play roles. That is, they sense that they are pretending, and they conform to what the director wants. (The "director" here may be society at large.) John Money, however, writes that gender roles are very much a part of the person:

> In the language of the theater, a gender role is not a script handed to an actor but a role incorporated into the actor, who, [changed] by it, manifests it in person. An actor does not simply learn a role, he or she assimilates and lives it. So also with gender role: a child assimilates and lives it, is inhabited by it, has it as a belonging, and manifests it to others . . . in word and deed. There is no one cause of a gender role. It develops under the influence of multiple factors, sequentially over time, from prenatal life onwards. Nature alone is not responsible, nor is nurture alone. They work together, hand in glove. (Money, 1994, p. 166)

Stereotype A fixed, conventional idea about a group of people.

Gender roles Complex clusters of ways in which males and females are expected to behave.

An Elementary School Teacher. If you think there is something wrong with this picture, it is because you have fallen prey to traditional gender-role stereotypes. Tradition has prevented many women from seeking jobs in "male" preserves such as construction work, the military, and various professions. Tradition has also prevented many men from obtaining work in "female" domains such as secretarial work, nursing, and teaching at the elementary level.

t a b l e   6 . 1

Gender role stereotypes in 30 nations from around the world

Stereotypes of Males		Stereotypes of Females	
Active	Opinionated	Affectionate	Nervous
Adventurous	Pleasure-seeking	Appreciative	Patient
Aggressive	Precise	Cautious	Pleasant
Arrogant	Quick	Changeable	Prudish
Autocratic	Rational	Charming	Self-pitying
Capable	Realistic	Complaining	Sensitive
Course	Reckless	Complicated	Sentimental
Conceited	Resourceful	Confused	Sexy
Confident	Rigid	Dependent	Shy
Courageous	Robust	Dreamy	Softhearted
Cruel	Sharp-witted	Emotional	Sophisticated
Determined	Show-off	Excitable	Submissive
Disorderly	Steady	Fault-finding	Suggestible
Enterprising	Stern	Fearful	Superstitious
Hardheaded	Stingy	Fickle	Talkative
Individualistic	Stolid	Foolish	Timid
Inventive	Tough	Forgiving	Touchy
Loud	Unscrupulous	Frivolous	Unambitious
Obnoxious		Fussy	Understanding
		Gentle	Unstable
		Imaginative	Warm
		Kind	Weak
		Mild	Worrying
		Modest	

Source of data: Williams & Best, 1994, p. 193, Table 1.
Psychologists John Williams and Deborah Best (1994) found that people in 30 countries largely agreed on what constituted masculine and feminine gender-role stereotypes.

The stereotypical female exhibits traits such as gentleness, dependency, kindness, helpfulness, patience, and submissiveness. The masculine gender-role stereotype is one of toughness, gentlemanliness, and protectiveness. Females are generally seen as warm and emotional; males as independent, assertive, and competitive. The times are a-changing—somewhat. Women, as well as men, now bring home the bacon, but women are still more often expected to fry it in the pan and bear the primary responsibility for childrearing (Deaux & Lewis, 1983). A survey of 30 countries confirmed that these gender-role stereotypes are widespread (Williams & Best, 1994), as shown in Table 6.1. In some cultures, however, women are reared to be the hunters and food gatherers while men stay close to home and tend the children.

Reflections

- Agree or disagree with the following statement, and support your answer: A woman's place is in the home.
- How do most people from your sociocultural background feel about traditional gender roles? Why?

Machismo/Marianismo Stereotypes and Hispanic Culture

The term *Hispanic* is generally used to describe Spanish-speaking peoples of Latin America whose cultures were influenced by a mixture of Spanish, African, and Native American (Indian) cultures. Although Hispanic peoples share some common cultural traditions, most notably the Spanish language and devotion to Christianity, each Spanish-speaking nation in Latin America has its own cultural tradition, as well as distinct subcultures. The differences among the peoples of Latin America can be seen in their dress styles, their use of language, and their musical and literary traditions. Argentinians, for example, tend to be more Europeanized in their style of dress and tastes in music. In the Dominican Republic and Puerto Rico, the influence of African and native Carib Indian cultures blossoms forth in the colorful style of dress and in the use of percussion instruments in music.

The *machismo* tradition should be evaluated in this light. *Machismo* is a cultural stereotype that defines masculinity in terms of an idealized view of manliness. To be *macho* is to be strong, virile, and dominant. Each Hispanic culture puts its own particular cultural stamp on the meaning of *machismo*, however. In the Spanish-speaking cultures of the Caribbean and Central America, the macho code encourages men to restrain their feelings and maintain an emotional distance. In my travels in Argentina and some other Latin American countries, however, I have observed that men who are sensitive and emotionally expressive are not perceived as compromising their macho code.

Marianismo

In counterpoint to the macho ideal among Hispanic peoples is the cultural idealization of femininity embodied in the concept of *marianismo*. The *marianismo* stereotype, which derives its name from the Virgin Mary, refers to the ideal of the virtuous woman as one who "suffers in silence," submerging her needs and desires to serve those of her husband and children. With the *marianismo* stereotype, the image of a woman's role as a martyr is raised to the level of a cultural ideal. According to this cultural stereotype, a woman is expected to demonstrate her love for her husband by waiting patiently at home and having dinner prepared for him at any time of day or night he happens to come home, to have his slippers ready for him, and so on. The feminine ideal is one of suffering in silence and being the provider of joy, even in the face of pain. Strongly influenced by the patriarchal Spanish tradition, the *marianismo* stereotype has historically been used to maintain women in a subordinate position in relation to men.

Acculturation: When Traditional Stereotypes Meet the Financial Realities of Life in the United States

Acculturation—the merging of cultures that occurs when immigrant groups become assimilated into the mainstream culture—has challenged this traditional *machismo/marianismo* division of marital roles among Hispanic couples in the United States. I have seen in my own work in treating Hispanic couples in therapy that marriages are under increasing strain from the conflict between traditional and modern expectations about marital roles. Hispanic American women have been entering the workforce in increasing numbers, usually in domestic or child-care positions, but they are still expected to assume responsibility for tending their own children, keeping the house, and serving their husbands' needs when they return home. In many cases, a reversal of traditional roles occurs, in which the wife works and supports the family while the husband remains at home because he is unable to find or maintain employment.

It is often the Hispanic American husband who has the greater difficulty accepting a more flexible distribution of roles within the marriage and giving up a rigid set of expectations tied to traditional *machismo/marianismo* gender expectations. Although some couples manage to reshape their expectations and marital roles in the face of changing conditions, many relationships buckle under the strain and are terminated in divorce. While I do not expect either the *machismo* or *marianismo* stereotype to disappear entirely, I would not be surprised to find a greater flexibility in gender-role expectations as a product of continued acculturation.

Source: This "World of Diversity" feature was written by Rafael Art Javier, Ph.D. Dr. Javier is Associate Clinical Professor of Psychology and Director of the Center for Psychological Services and Clinical Studies at St. John's University in Jamaica, New York. All rights are reserved by Dr. Javier.

SEXISM

We have all encountered the effects of **sexism**—the prejudgment that because of gender, a person will possess certain negative traits. These negative traits are assumed to disqualify the person for certain vocations or prevent him or her from performing adequately in these jobs or in some social situations.

Sexism may even lead us to interpret the same behavior in prejudicial ways when performed by women or by men. We might see the man as "self-assertive" but the woman as "pushy." We might look upon *him* as flexible but brand *her* fickle and indecisive. *He* may be rational, whereas *she* is cold. *He* is tough when necessary, but *she* is bitchy. When the businesswoman engages in stereotypical masculine behaviors, the sexist reacts negatively by branding her abnormal or unhealthy.

Sexism The prejudgment that because of gender, a person will possess negative traits.

MOM THE BREADWINNER

Why do women work? To buy the family a second car? To provide vacation money? To send the kids to camp? According to a poll by Louis Harris and Associates (1995), these stereotypes no longer hold water. Women's work is no longer supplemental. Women, like men, work to support the family.

Yes, we are all familiar with the high-powered mothers like Demi Moore, Hillary Clinton, and Katie Couric, who outearn their husbands or support their children on their own. But out of the spotlight, the earning power of the ordinary woman has been growing by leaps and bounds. Ac-

cording to the Harris poll, wives share about equally with their husbands in supporting their families. Nearly half of them—48%—reported that they provided at least half of their family's income, not just vacation money: half the mortgage, the clothing, medical bills, Reeboks and mountain bikes (Lewin, 1995).

Why do we still think of women as primarily mothers? Why haven't we paid more attention to their new roles as providers? Perhaps it is because working mothers continue to do what mothers in general have done. That is, 9 of 10 working mothers still bear the primary responsibility for the children, cooking, and cleaning

(Lewin, 1995). Are they overburdened? Perhaps. The survey reveals that working mothers are pressed for time. They are worried about not having enough time with their families and about balancing the demands of work and a home life. Nevertheless, when they were asked whether they would like to surrender some of their responsibilities, 53% of working women said no. Even more ironic, full-time working mothers reported that they felt more likely to feel valued for their contributions at home than full-time homemakers were.

So Mom is still doing what mom has been expected to do. She is still looking after the house and kids. But now she also pays half the bills.

Sexism may make it difficult for men to act in ways that are stereotyped as feminine. A "sensitive" woman is simply sensitive, but a sensitive man may be seen as a "sissy." A woman might be perceived as polite, whereas a man showing the same behavior seems passive or weak. Only recently have men begun to enter occupational domains that were previously restricted largely to women, such as secretarial work, nursing, and teaching in the primary grades. Only recently have the gates opened for women into traditionally masculine professions such as engineering, law, and medicine.

Although children of both genders have about the same general learning ability, stereotypes limit their horizons. Children tend to show preferences for gender-typed activities and toys as early as 2 or 3 years of age. If they should stray from these, their peers are sure to remind them of the "errors of their ways." How many little girls are discouraged from considering professions such as architecture and engineering because they are handed dolls, not blocks and fire trucks? How many little boys are discouraged from pursuing child care and nursing professions because of the disapproving looks they get from others when they reach for dolls?

Children not only develop stereotyped attitudes about play activities; they also develop stereotypes about the differences between "man's work" and "woman's work." Women have been historically excluded from "male occupations," and stereotypical expectations concerning "men's work" and "women's work" filter down to the primary grades. For example, according to traditional stereotypes, women are *not expected* to excel in math. Exposure to such negative expectations may discourage women from careers in science and technology.

Reflections

▪ Have you encountered sexism? Under what circumstances? What was its effect on you?
▪ Have you been guilty of sexism? (Are you sure?) What are you going to do about it?

GENDER DIFFERENCES: *VIVE LA DIFFÉRENCE* OR *VIVE LA SIMILARITÉ?*

If the genders were not anatomically different, this book would never have been written. How do the genders differ in cognitive abilities and personality, however?

Are There Gender Differences in Cognitive Abilities? The physical differences between females and males are well established—and well celebrated! But are there cognitive differences between the genders? If so, what are they? How large are they? Are they the result of nature (heredity) or nurture (environmental influences such as educational experiences and cultural expectations)?

Differences in Cognitive Abilities

A classic review by Eleanor Maccoby and Carol Nagy Jacklin (1974) found persistent evidence that females are somewhat superior to males in verbal ability. But a more recent review of the accumulated evidence found no overall gender differences in verbal abilities, with the exception that boys are more often slower to develop language skills (Hyde & Linn, 1988). Far more boys than girls have reading problems, ranging from reading below grade level to severe disabilities.

Males generally exceed females in visual-spatial abilities (Voyer et al., 1995). Visual-spatial skills include the ability to follow a map when traveling to an unfamiliar location, to construct a puzzle or assemble a piece of equipment, and to perceive relationships between figures in space.

Differences in math are small and narrowing at all ages (Hyde et al., 1990). Females excel in computational ability in elementary school. However, males excel in mathematical problem solving in high school and in college (Hyde et al., 1990). Differences in problem solving are reflected on the mathematics test of the Scholastic Aptitude Test (SAT). The mean score is 500, and about two-thirds of the test takers receive scores between 400 and 600. Boys outperform girls on SAT math items (Byrnes & Takahira, 1993). Twice as many boys as girls attain scores over 500. According to Byrnes and Takahira (1993), boys' superiority in math does not reflect gender per se. Instead, boys do well because of prior knowledge of math and their strategies for approaching math problems.

In our culture, then, girls are somewhat advanced in their development of verbal abilities. Boys apparently show greater math ability, beginning in adolescence. Three factors should caution us not to attach too much importance to these gender differences, however:

1. In most cases, the differences are small (Hyde & Plant, 1995). Differences in verbal, mathematical, and spatial abilities are also getting smaller (Hyde et al., 1990; Maccoby, 1990; Voyer et al., 1995).
2. These gender differences are *group* differences. Variation in ability on tests of verbal or math skills is larger *within* the genders than between them (Maccoby, 1990).

Despite differences between groups of boys and girls, millions of boys exceed the "average" girl in writing and spelling skills. Likewise, millions of girls outperform the "average" boy in problem solving and spatial tasks. The male gender has produced its Shakespeares and the female gender its Madame Curies.

3. The small differences that may exist may largely reflect environmental influences and cultural expectations (Tobias, 1982). Spatial and math skills are stereotyped in our culture as masculine, whereas reading skills are stereotyped as feminine. In one study, however, female introductory psychology students who were given but three hours of training in performing visual-spatial skills such as rotating geometric figures performed these tasks as well as men (Stericker & LeVesconte, 1982).

Differences in Personality

There are also many gender differences in personality. According to a meta-analysis of the research literature, females exceed males in extraversion, anxiety, trust, and nurturance (Feingold, 1994). Males exceed females in assertiveness, tough-mindedness, and self-esteem. The assertiveness is connected with aggressiveness, as we see below. The tough-mindedness has unfortunate implications for men's health, as we also see. Your third author notes, with some displeasure, two factors that may largely account for the relatively lower self-esteem of females:

- Parents, on the average, prefer to have boys.
- Society has created an unlevel playing field in which females have to perform better than males to be seen as doing equally well.

DIFFERENCES IN COMMUNICATION STYLES: "HE'S JUST AN OLD CHATTERBOX"
We have been inundated with cartoons of suburban housewives gossiping across the fence or pouring endless cups of coffee when the "girls" drop by for a chat. Research has shown, however, that in many situations, men spend more time talking than women do. Men are also more likely to introduce new topics and interrupt others (Brooks, 1982; Deaux, 1985; Hall, 1984). Girls tend to be more talkative during early childhood than boys. By the time they enter school, however, boys dominate classroom discussions (Sadker & Sadker, 1994). As girls mature, it appears that they learn to defer to boys and let the boys do most of the talking when they are in mixed-gender groups (Hall, 1984).

Women are more willing than men to disclose their feelings and personal experiences, however (Dindia & Allen, 1992). The stereotype of the "strong and silent" male might not discourage men from hogging the conversation, but it might inhibit them from expressing their personal feelings.

DIFFERENCES IN AGGRESSIVENESS   In almost all cultures (Ford & Beach, 1951; Mead, 1935), it is the males who march off to war and who battle for fame, glory, and shaving cream commercial contracts in stadiums and arenas. In most psychological studies on aggression, males have been found to behave more aggressively than females (White, 1983).

It is true that men act more aggressively, on the whole, than women do. The question remains, *why?* ■

Truth or Fiction?
REVISITED

DIFFERENCES IN WILLINGNESS TO SEEK HEALTH CARE   Men's life expectancies are seven years shorter, on the average, than women's. Part of the difference, according to surveys of physicians ("Doctors tie male mentality," 1995) and of the general population (Brody, 1998d), is due to women's greater willingness to seek health care. Men often let symptoms go until a problem that could have been prevented or readily treated becomes serious or life threatening. For example, women are much more likely to check themselves for breast cancer than men are to even recognize the symptoms of prostate cancer. Many men, according to the survey, have a "bulletproof mentality." They are too strong to see the doctor in their 20s, too busy in their 30s, and too frightened later on.

Will We See Gender Differences in Fitness Evaporate in the New Millennium?

Not so long ago, women who were interested in athletics were not taken seriously or were perceived as unfeminine. If they did take up a sport, such as tennis, they were expected to approach it in a "ladylike" way, which meant that they weren't expected to compete too hard, let alone to grunt when serving the ball, as many male players do. Today, though women athletes are accorded greater respect than in the past, they still have to fight for parity with their male counterparts. With the exception of figure skating and perhaps professional tennis, the rule still holds that male athletes are awarded more lucrative contracts and endorsements and receive the lion's share of television exposure.

The belief that competitive sports are male preserves, especially sports that demand muscle strength and physical endurance, reflects an underlying premise that women are not strong enough or fit enough to compete. But is it so?

ARE MEN NATURALLY STRONGER?

In muscle strength, especially upper body strength, the average man does have an advantage over the average women (Wells, 1991; Wilmore, 1991). This is not surprising when you consider that the average man is 35 pounds heavier, has more muscle mass, has less body fat, and is 5 inches taller than the average woman. Men also have broader shoulders, slimmer hips, and slightly longer legs proportionally to their height. Before puberty (beginning around age 12 or 13), boys and girls are well matched in physical strength and ability. Girls can run just as fast, lift as much, and otherwise match boys in physical strength. Differences begin to emerge, however, as children pass through puberty.

Hormonal influences play a large role in accounting for growth differences between males and females during puberty. At the onset of puberty, males experience a steep rise in testosterone production, the so-called male sex hormone ("so-called" because females also have testosterone, although in far lesser amounts). This leads to a number of changes in males, not the least of which is a growth spurt lasting about two years longer than in females. The result is greater height, denser bones, and larger muscles.

Females also undergo many changes during puberty. These are caused by a surge in estrogen and other female hormones. One effect of these hormones is to increase body fat—which is why women taking birth control pills or estrogen supplements often experience a weight gain. Some of this fat directly prepares the body for reproduction (for instance, fat around internal organs and in the breasts). A greater amount of fat becomes stored in the buttocks, hips, and thighs, giving women a more rounded shape.

Even if women manage to reduce the amount of stored fat to levels comparable to those of males—and it's harder to do this, since estrogen slows the metabolism of stored fat—they are left with a minimum of 10% more fat than men. This means that a woman's body has proportionately less muscle than it did before puberty and proportionately less muscle mass than a man's. The female's pelvis also broadens during puberty in preparation for childbearing; this, along with shorter thigh bones, results in a greater inward sloping of the upper leg (causing knock-knees in some women).

Given the fact that the average man has greater muscle mass, greater body weight, and a lower percentage of body fat, is it fair to compare men and women directly in terms of muscle strength? In professional boxing, we hardly would expect a 155-pound middleweight to go head to head with a 215-pound heavyweight. On the football field, we're not likely to see any 150-pound defensive linemen. If we just compare men and women of the same age, the average woman has about half the upper body strength and about three quarters of the lower body strength of the average man. However, if we take into account body weight and composition, men and women are actually quite similar in lower body strength, though men still retain an advantage in upper body strength. Consider, too, that with weight training, women can develop upper body strength that is similar to that of men of the same weight and body composition whose muscles are similarly trained. Yes, there may be some male bodybuilders who have not (not yet at least) met their match in women competitors. But when we look more broadly at the general population, differences in strength relate more to the use to which we put our muscles than to our gender.

ARE MEN NATURALLY MORE FIT?

Fitness is the body's ability to withstand stress and sustain physically demanding work. One measure of fitness is cardiorespiratory fitness: the body's ability to pump oxygen-rich blood to the muscles to sustain vigorous physical activity. Here, men do have an advantage. The typical male heart beats at a slower rate because it can pump out a greater amount of blood per beat (Wells, 1991; Wilmore, 1991). Men also have a higher concentration of hemoglobin-rich (oxygen-carrying) red blood cells in their bloodstream. The smaller heart volumes and lower hemoglobin levels in women mean that the female heart must beat faster to provide the same amount of blood and oxygen. At rest, the female heart beats about 7 to 10 beats per minute faster than males of comparable age and fitness levels. At a given level of exercise, the female heart is working harder. So female joggers, for instance, work their hearts harder to run a 10-minute mile than do their male counterparts. These cardiovascular differences account for the fact that cardiorespiratory endurance, measured by maximum oxygen uptake relative to body weight, is 28% higher in men than women.

Once again, however, to accurately assess the differences in cardiorespiratory endurance between males and females, we need to compare males and females with both similar-sized hearts (and bodies) and who also carry around the same body fat. When this is done—by adding weight to males to simulate extra body fat—it turns out that body fat accounts for about one-third of the differences between men and women in cardiorespiratory endurance. Nonetheless, even when body fat is taken into account, males still have greater cardiorespiratory endurance (about 16% more than that of comparable females). This 16% advantage appears to be due to the fact that males are born with higher hemoglobin levels. Hemoglobin is the part of blood that carries oxygen, so males can use oxygen more efficiently than females.

END OF THE STORY?

Across the board, women athletes are narrowing the gender gap in sports achievement. The reason is their rigorous training schedules. Elite female athletes of today have body fat levels between

10% and 15%—the same as or lower than those of male athletes—and cardiorespiratory fitness greater than that of most men. Elite female runners have been steadily closing the gap between their marathon times and those of male athletes (Whipp & Ward, 1992). In 1971, for instance, the women's marathon record was 38 minutes slower than the men's record. In 1981, this difference was 21.5 minutes. In the 1990s, a mere 15 minutes has separated the fastest male and female marathon runners. This rapid rate of improvement indicates that women athletes are on their way to "catching up" to their male counterparts.

But what of the great majority of us who aren't elite athletes? The fact is that differences in fitness, like differences in muscle strength, are largely a function of training. Sedentary people of either gender are less fit when it comes to cardiorespiratory fitness, muscle strength, and ability to endure hard physical activity like running or swimming laps than are those who regularly train. When it comes to muscle strength and fitness, the issue is not so much which gender you are, but how well conditioned you are.

Are Gender Differences in Fitness on the Way Out in the New Millennium? Are men naturally more fit than women? If so, why? Can training eliminate differences in fitness?

ON BECOMING A MAN OR A WOMAN: GENDER TYPING

We have chronicled the biological process of sexual differentiation, and we have explored some gender differences in cognitive abilities and behavior. In this section, we consider various explanations of **gender typing.**

Biological Perspectives

Biological views on gender typing tend to focus on the roles of genetics and prenatal influences in predisposing men and women to gender-linked behavior patterns. Biological perspectives have also focused on the possible role of hormones in sculpting the brain during prenatal development.

SOCIOBIOLOGY: IT'S ONLY NATURAL   To the sociobiologist, the story of the survival of our ancient ancestors is etched in our genes. Sociobiologists propose that the genes that bestow attributes that increase an organism's chances of surviving to produce viable offspring are most likely to be transmitted to future generations. We thus possess the

Gender typing The process by which children acquire behavior that is deemed appropriate to their gender.

173

genetic remnants of traits that helped our ancestors survive and reproduce (Bjorklund & Kipp, 1996). This heritage, according to sociobiologists, influences our social and sexual behavior as well as our anatomic features.

According to sociobiologists, men's traditional roles as hunters and warriors and women's roles as caregivers and gatherers of fruits and vegetables are bequeathed to us in our genes. Men are better suited to war and the hunt because of physical attributes that have been passed along since ancestral times. Upper-body strength, for example, would have enabled them to throw spears and overpower adversaries. Men also possess perceptual-cognitive advantages, such as superior visual-motor skills that favor aggression. Visual-motor skills would have enabled men to aim spears or bows and arrows.

Women, it is argued, are genetically predisposed to be empathic and nurturant because these traits enabled ancestral women to respond to children's needs and enhance the likelihood that their children would flourish and eventually reproduce, thereby transmitting their own genetic legacy to future generations. Prehistoric women therefore tended to stay close to home, care for the children, and gather edible plants, whereas men ventured from home to hunt and raid their neighbors' storehouses.

Sociobiology is steeped in controversy. Although scientists do not dispute the importance of evolution in determining physical attributes, many are reluctant to attribute complex social behaviors, such as aggression and gender roles, to heredity. The sociobiological argument implies that stereotypical gender roles—men as breadwinners and women as homemakers, for example—reflect the natural order of things. Critics contend that biology is not destiny, that our behavior is not dictated by our genes.

PRENATAL BRAIN ORGANIZATION   Researchers have sought the origins of gender-typed behavior in the organization of the brain. Is it possible that the cornerstone of gender-typed behavior is laid in the brain before the first breath is taken?

The hemispheres of the brain are specialized to carry out certain functions. In most people, the right hemisphere ("right brain") appears to be specialized to perform visual-spatial tasks. The "left brain" appears to be more essential to verbal functions, such as speech, in most people.

We know that sex hormones are responsible for prenatal sexual differentiation of the genitals and for the gender-related structural differences in the hypothalamus of the developing prenatal brain. Sexual differentiation of the brain may also partly explain men's (slight!) superiority at spatial-relations tasks, such as interpreting road maps and visualizing objects in space. Testosterone in the brains of male fetuses spurs greater growth of the right hemisphere and slows the rate of growth of the left hemisphere. This difference may be connected with the ability to accomplish spatial-relations tasks.

Might boys' inclinations toward aggression and rough-and-tumble play also be prenatally imprinted in the brain? Some theorists argue that prenatal sex hormones may masculinize or feminize the brain by creating predispositions that are consistent with gender-role stereotypes, such as rough-and-tumble play and aggressive behavior in males (Collaer & Hines, 1995). Money (1988) allows a role for prenatal dispositions but argues that social learning plays a stronger role in gender typing. He claims that social learning is even potent enough to counteract prenatal predispositions.

Cross-Cultural Perspectives

Sociobiology cannot account for differences in gender roles that exist across cultures, especially neighboring cultures. The anthropologist Margaret Mead (1935) lived among several tribes on the South Pacific island of New Guinea and found that gender roles in these tribes differed not only from those of Western culture, but also from one another.

Among the Mundugumor, a tribe of headhunters and cannibals, both men and women were warlike and aggressive. The women disdained bearing and rearing children because it interrupted participation in warring parties against neighboring villages. The men and women of the Arapesh tribe were gentle and peaceful, by contrast. Both genders nurtured the children. The Tchambuli were even more unusual in terms of what we consider stereotypical behavior in our society. The men spent most of their time caring for children, gossiping, bickering, primping and applying makeup, and haggling over prices. Fish was the staple diet of the Tchambuli, and women brought home the daily catch. Women kept their heads shaven, disdained ornaments, and were more highly sexed and aggressive than men.

Whatever the influence of biology on behavior, biological factors alone do not make men aggressive or independent or make women passive or submissive (Havemann & Lehtinen, 1990). Cultural expectations and learning play a large role.

GENDER ROLES AS A CULTURAL ADAPTATION The Mundugumor, Arapesh, and Tchambuli peoples of New Guinea—and members of modern industrialized societies—all share the same biological makeup. Within each gender, the same sex hormones pulse through the arteries of the peoples of New Guinea as through the arteries of stockbrokers on Wall Street. (Yes, even stockbrokers are warm-blooded.) Yet despite this common biological makeup, wide cultural variations exist with respect to gender roles.

Anthropologists believe that cultural differences in gender roles can be explained in terms of the adaptations that cultures make to their social and natural environments (Werner & Cohen, 1990). Consider differences in gender roles between the Sambian people of New Guinea and the !Kung people of Africa. The Sambians have rigidly defined gender roles. Boys are socialized to become warriors. Women tend the children and keep a discreet distance from men (Herdt, 1987). Among the !Kung people, however, women play a more active role in tribal affairs and are permitted more autonomy (Drapers, 1975).

How might such differences arise? The Sambians, until recently, were subject to repeated attacks from enemies and could survive only by rearing their sons as warriors (Werner & Cohen, 1990). Sambians' rigid gender roles may be seen as an adaptation to these onslaughts. The !Kung live in small scattered groups and forage for their food. Both genders make substantial contributions to the food supply. In this egalitarian society, gender roles are more flexible. Both men and women enjoy considerable autonomy and influence.

Psychological Perspectives

Children acquire awareness of gender-role stereotypes by the tender ages of 2½ to 3½ (Etaugh & Rathus, 1995). Both boys and girls generally agree, when asked to describe the differences between the genders, that boys build things, play with transportation toys such as cars and fire trucks, enjoy helping their fathers, and hit other children. Both boys and girls also agree that girls enjoy playing with dolls and helping their mothers cook and clean and are talkative, dependent on others for help, and nonviolent. They perceive the label "cruel" to be a masculine trait, whereas "cries a lot" is perceived as a feminine trait. By the time they are age 3, most children have become aware of the different stereotypical ways in which men and women dress and the types of occupations that are considered appropriate for each gender (Etaugh & Rathus, 1995). Psychologists have attempted to explain how children acquire such knowledge and adopt stereotypical behavior patterns in terms of psychodynamic, social-learning, and cognitive-developmental theories.

PSYCHODYNAMIC THEORY Sigmund Freud explained gender typing in terms of identification. Appropriate gender typing, in Freud's view, requires that boys come to identify with their fathers and girls with their mothers. Identification is completed, in Freud's view, as children resolve the **Oedipus complex** (sometimes called the *Electra complex* in girls).

According to Freud, the Oedipus complex occurs during the phallic period of psychosexual development, from the ages of 3 to 5. During this period, the child develops incestuous wishes for the parent of the other gender and comes to perceive the parent of the same gender as a rival. The complex is resolved by the child's forsaking incestuous wishes for the parent of the other gender and identifying with the parent of the same gender. Through identification with the same-gender parent, the child comes to develop gender-typed behaviors that are typically associated with that gender. Children display stereotypical gender-typed behaviors earlier than Freud would have predicted, however. Even during the first year, boys are more independent than girls. Girls are more quiet and restrained. Girls show preferences for dolls and soft toys, and boys for hard transportation toys, by the ages of 1½ to 3.

SOCIAL-LEARNING THEORY Social-learning theorists explain the development of gender-typed behavior in terms of processes such as observational learning, identification, and socialization. Children can learn what is deemed masculine or feminine by observational learning, as suggested by the results of an experiment by Perry and Bussey (1979). In this study, 8- and 9-year-old boys and girls watched adult role models indicate their preferences for each of 16 pairs of items—pairs such as toy cows versus toy horses and oranges versus apples. What the children didn't know was that the expressed preferences were made arbitrarily. The children then were asked to indicate their own preferences for the items represented in the pairs. The boys' choices agreed with the adult men's an average of 14 out of 16 times. Girls chose the pair item selected by the men, on the average, only 3 out of 16 times.

In social-learning theory, identification is viewed as a continuing and broadly based learning process in which rewards and punishments influence children to imitate adult models of the same gender—especially the parent of the same gender (Storms, 1980). Identification is more than imitation, however. In identification, the child not only imitates the behavior of the model, but also tries to become like the model in broad terms.

Socialization also plays a role in gender typing. Almost from the moment a baby comes into the world, it is treated according to its gender. Parents tend to talk more to baby girls, and fathers especially engage in more roughhousing with boys (Jacklin et al., 1984). When children are old enough to speak, parents and other adults—even other children—begin to instruct children in how they are expected to behave. Parents may reward children for behavior they consider gender-appropriate and punish (or fail to reinforce) them for behavior they consider inappropriate for their gender. Girls are encouraged to practice caretaking behaviors, which are intended to prepare them for traditional feminine adult roles. Boys are handed Legos or doctor sets to help prepare them for traditional masculine adult roles.

Fathers generally encourage their sons to develop assertive, instrumental behavior (that is, behavior that gets things done or accomplishes something) and their daughters to develop nurturant, cooperative behavior. Fathers are likely to cuddle their daughters gently. They are likely to carry their sons like footballs or toss them into the air. Fathers also tend to use heartier and harsher language with their sons, such as "How're yuh doin', Tiger?" and "Hey you, get your keester over here" (Jacklin et al., 1984). Being a nontraditionalist, your first author made sure to toss his young daughters into the air, raising immediate objections from the relatives, who chastised him for being too rough. This, of course, led him to modify his behavior. He learned to toss his daughters into the air when the relatives were not around.

Generally speaking, from an early age, boys are more likely to receive toy cars and guns and athletic equipment and to be encouraged to compete aggressively. Even rela-

Oedipus complex A conflict of the phallic stage in which the boy wishes to possess his mother sexually and perceives his father as a rival in love.

Socialization The process of guiding people into socially acceptable behavior patterns by means of information, rewards, and punishments.

tively sophisticated college students are likely to select traditionally masculine toys as gifts for boys and traditionally feminine toys for girls (Fisher-Thompson, 1990). Girls are spoken to more often, whereas boys are handled more frequently and more roughly. Whatever the biological determinants of gender differences in aggressiveness and verbal skills, early socialization experiences clearly contribute to gender typing.

Parental roles in gender typing are apparently changing. With more mothers working outside the home, daughters today are exposed to more women who represent career-minded role models than was the case in earlier generations. More parents today are encouraging their daughters to become career-minded and to engage in strenuous physical activities, such as organized sports. Many boys today are exposed to fathers who take a larger role than men used to in child care and household responsibilities.

Schools are also important socialization influences. Schools have been slow to adapt to recent changes in gender roles (Sadker & Sadker, 1994). They may be exposing children to masculine and feminine images that are even more rigid and polarized than those currently held in society at large. Teachers often expect girls to perform better than boys in reading and language arts and have higher expectations of boys in math and science. These expectations may be conveyed to children, patterning their choices of careers.

Sexism in America's schools is widespread. Many tests remain biased against girls, reducing their chances of obtaining scholarships and gaining admission to more competitive colleges (Chira, 1992). Many science teachers and some math teachers tend to ignore girls in favor of boys. Such biases may discourage young women with aptitude in math and science from pursuing careers in these areas. Yet the report highlighted some promising developments. The traditional gender gap in math scores is narrowing; girls have made significant gains in catching up to boys. Moreover, special programs in math and science for girls held after school and in the summer have helped to bolster the girls' confidence and interest in these subjects.

The popular media—books, magazines, radio, film, and especially television—also convey gender stereotypes (Remafedi, 1990). The media, by and large, portray men and women in traditional roles (Signorielli, 1990). Male actors more often play doctors, attorneys, and police officers. Female actors more often play nurses, secretaries, paralegals, and teachers. Even when women portray attorneys or police officers, they are more likely than men to handle family disputes. The male police officer is more likely to be shown in action roles; the male holds the court spellbound with a probing cross-examination. Working women are also more likely than men to be portrayed as undergoing role conflict—being pulled in opposite directions by job and family. One study reported that despite current awareness of sexism, "Women are often still depicted on television as half-clad and half-witted, and needing to be rescued by quick-thinking, fully clothed men" (Adelson, 1990). Ageism buttresses sexism in that female characters age 40 and above are only rarely depicted in roles other than mothers and grandmothers.

Social-learning theorists believe that aggression is largely influenced by learning. Boys are permitted, even encouraged, to engage in more aggressive behavior than girls. Nonetheless, females are likely to act aggressively under certain conditions. Ann Frodi and her colleagues (1977) reviewed 72 studies that examined gender differences in aggression. All in all, females acted as aggressively as men when they were given the physical means to do so and believed that aggression was justified. In an influential review article, Maccoby and Jacklin commented on the socialization influences that discourage aggression in girls:

> Aggression in general is less acceptable for girls, and is more actively discouraged in them, by either direct punishment, withdrawal of affection, or simply cognitive training that "that isn't the way girls act." Girls then build up greater anxieties about aggression, and greater inhibitions against displaying it. (1974, p. 234)

Social-learning theorists have made important contributions to our understanding of how rewards, punishments, and modeling influences foster gender-typed behavior patterns. How do children integrate gender-role expectations within their self-concepts?

Gender Typing. According to cognitive theories of gender typing, children are motivated to behave in ways that are consistent with their genders. Children seek information as to what behaviors are deemed appropriate for people of their gender.

And how do their concepts concerning gender influence their development of gender-typed behavior? Let us consider two cognitive approaches to gender typing that shed light on these matters: cognitive-developmental theory and gender schema theory.

COGNITIVE-DEVELOPMENTAL THEORY Psychologist Lawrence Kohlberg (1966) proposed a cognitive-developmental view of gender typing. From this perspective, gender typing is not the product of environmental influences that mechanically "stamp in" gender-appropriate behavior. Rather, children themselves play an active role. They form concepts, or **schemas,** about gender and then conform their behavior to their gender concepts. These developments occur in stages and are entwined with general cognitive development.

According to Kohlberg, gender typing entails the emergence of three concepts: *gender identity*, *gender stability*, and *gender constancy*. Gender identity is usually acquired by the age of 3. By the age of 4 or 5, most children develop a concept of **gender stability**—the recognition that people retain their genders for a lifetime. Before this age, boys may think that they will become mommies when they grow up, and girls, daddies.

Truth or Fiction?
REVISITED

It is true that a 2½-year-old child might know that he is a boy but think that he can grow up to be a mommy. Children at this age have not yet developed gender stability. ■

The more sophisticated concept of **gender constancy** develops in most children by the age of 7 or 8. They recognize that gender does not change, even if people alter their dress or behavior. So gender remains constant even when appearances change. A woman who wears her hair short (or shaves it off) remains a woman. A man who dons an apron and cooks dinner remains a man.

According to cognitive-developmental theory, children are motivated to behave in gender-appropriate ways once they have established the concepts of gender stability and gender constancy. They then make an active effort to obtain information as to which behavior patterns are considered "masculine" and which "feminine" (Perry & Bussey, 1979). Once they obtain this information, they imitate the "gender-appropriate" pattern. So boys and girls who come to recognize that their genders will remain a fixed part of their identity will show preferences for "masculine" and "feminine" activities, respectively.

Schema Concept; way of interpreting experience or processing information.

Gender stability The concept that people retain their genders for a lifetime.

Gender constancy The concept that people's genders do not change, even if they alter their dress or behavior.

Researchers find, for instance, that boys who had achieved gender constancy played with an uninteresting gender-typed toy for a longer period of time than did boys who hadn't yet achieved gender constancy (Frey & Ruble, 1992). Both groups of boys played with an interesting gender-typed toy for about an equal length of time.

Cross-cultural studies of the United States, Samoa, Nepal, Belize, and Kenya find that the concepts of gender identity, gender stability, and gender constancy emerge in the order predicted by Kohlberg. However, gender-typed play often emerges at an earlier age than would be predicted by the cognitive-developmental theory. Many children make gender-typed choices of toys by the age of 2. Children as young as 18 months are likely to have developed a sense of gender identity, but gender stability and constancy are some years off. Gender identity alone therefore seems sufficient to prompt children to assume gender-typed behavior patterns. Psychologist Sandra Bem (1983) also notes that Kohlberg's theory does not explain why the concept of gender plays such a prominent role in children's classification of people and behavior. Another cognitive view, gender schema theory, attempts to address these concerns.

GENDER SCHEMA THEORY: AN INFORMATION-PROCESSING APPROACH   Gender schema theory proposes that children develop a **gender schema** as a means of organizing their perceptions of the world (Bem, 1981, 1985; Martin & Halverson, 1981). A gender schema is a cluster of mental representations about male and female physical qualities, behaviors, and personality traits. Gender gains prominence as a schema for organizing experience because of society's emphasis on it. Even young children start to mentally group people of the same gender according to the traits that represent that gender.

Children's gender schemas determine how important gender-typed traits are to them. Consider the dimension of *strength-weakness.* Children may learn that strength is connected with maleness and weakness with femaleness. (Other dimensions, such as *light-dark,* are not gender-typed and therefore may fall outside children's gender schemas.) Children also gather that some dimensions, such as strong-weak, are more important to one gender (in this case, male) than the other.

Once children acquire a gender schema, they begin to judge themselves according to traits considered relevant to their genders. In doing so, they blend their developing self-concepts with the prominent gender schema of their culture. The gender schema furnishes standards for comparison. Children with self-concepts that are consistent with the prominent gender schema of their culture are likely to develop higher self-esteem than children whose self-concepts are inconsistent. Jack learns that muscle strength is a characteristic associated with "manliness." He is likely to think more highly of himself if he perceives himself as embodying this attribute than if he does not. Barbara is likely to discover that the dimension of kindness-cruelty is more crucial than strength-weakness to the way in which women are perceived in society.

According to gender schema theory, gender identity itself is sufficient to inspire gender-appropriate behavior. Once children develop a concept of gender identity, they begin to seek information concerning gender-typed traits and strive to live up to them. Jack will retaliate when provoked, because boys are expected to do so. Barbara will be "sugary and sweet" if such is expected of little girls. Thus, gender-typed behavior emerges earlier than would be proposed by cognitive-developmental theory. Jack and Barbara's self-esteem depends in part on how they measure up to the gender schema.

Research suggests that children do process information according to a gender schema (Levy & Carter, 1989; Stangor & Ruble, 1989). Objects and activities that are pertinent to a child's own gender are better retained in memory. Boys, for example, do a better job of remembering transportation toys they have been shown previously, whereas girls are better at recalling dolls and other "feminine" objects (Bradbard & Endsley, 1984). In another study, Martin and Halverson (1983) showed elementary school children pictures of children involved in "gender-consistent" or "gender-inconsistent" activities. Gender-consistent pictures showed boys doing things like sawing wood and playing with trains. Girls were shown doing things like cooking and cleaning. Gender-inconsistent

Gender schema A cluster of mental representations about male and female physical qualities, behaviors, and personality traits.

pictures showed models of the other gender involved in gender-typed endeavors. A week later, the children were asked whether boys or girls had engaged in each activity. Boys and girls both made errors recalling the genders of the models shown engaging in "gender-inconsistent" behavior.

Once established, gender schemas resist change, even when broad social changes occur. For this reason, many parents cannot accept their sons' wearing ("feminine") earrings. A generation earlier, parents had similar difficulty accepting daughters in jeans or sons in long hair.

Reflections

■ Summarize gender differences in cognitive functioning and personality. Do research findings on the nature of gender differences fit your own ideas about gender differences? How or how not?

■ What biological and psychological factors contribute to gender differences?

■ How would you explain gender differences in aggressive behavior? Do you know some men who are aggressive and some who are not? How would you explain the differences from person to person?

GENDER ROLES AND SEXUAL BEHAVIOR

Gender roles have had a profound influence on dating practices and sexual behavior. Children learn at an early age that men usually make dates and initiate sexual interactions, whereas women usually serve as the "gatekeepers" in romantic relationships. In their traditional role as gatekeepers, women are expected to wait to be asked out and to screen suitors. Men are expected to make the first (sexual) move and women to determine how far advances will proceed. Regrettably, some men refuse to take no for an answer. They feel that they have the right to force their dates into sexual relations.

Men as Sexually Aggressive, Women as Sexually Passive

The cultural expectation that men are initiators and women are gatekeepers is embedded within the larger stereotype that men are sexually aggressive and women are sexually passive. Men not only initiate sexual encounters; they are expected to dictate all the "moves" thereafter, just as they are expected to take the lead on the dance floor. According to the stereotype, women are to let men determine the choice, timing, and sequence of sexual positions and techniques. Unfortunately, the stereotype favors men's sexual preferences, denying women the opportunity to give and receive their preferred kinds of stimulation.

A woman may more easily reach orgasm in the **female-superior position,** but her partner may prefer the **male-superior position.** If the man is calling the shots, she may not have the opportunity to reach orgasm. Even the expression of her preferences may be deemed "unladylike."

The stereotypical masculine role also imposes constraints on men. Men are expected to take the lead in bringing their partners to orgasm, but they should not ask their partners what they like because they are expected to be natural experts. ("Real men" not only don't eat quiche; they also need not ask women how to make love.)

Fortunately, more flexible attitudes are emerging. Women are becoming more sexually assertive, and men are becoming more receptive to expressing tenderness and gentleness. Still, the roots of traditional gender roles run deep. A recent survey of students in human sexuality classes in colleges in the New York–New Jersey area showed that males

Female-superior position
A coital position in which the woman is on top.

Male-superior position.
A coital position in which the man is on top.

reported more instances of women initiating sex than women reported initiating (Anderson & Aymami, 1993). Who got it right? Are women who initiate sex less willing to admit they do so, perhaps even to themselves, because they hold to the stereotypical expectation that "nice girls don't"? Are men so taken with themselves that they believe that women can't help pursuing them for sexual relations? Perhaps a combination of factors is involved in explaining this discrepancy. What do you think?

Men as Overaroused, Women as Underaroused

According to another stereotype, men become sexually aroused at puberty and remain at the ready throughout adulthood. Women, however, do not share men's natural interests in sex, and a woman discovers her own sexuality only when a man ignites her sexual flame. Men must continue to stoke women's sexual embers, lest they die out. The stereotype denies that "normal" women have spontaneous sexual desires or are readily aroused.

It was widely believed in the Victorian period (even by so-called sex experts!) that women are naturally asexual and "unbothered" by sexual desires. The contemporary residues of this stereotype hold that women do not enjoy sex as much as men and that women who openly express their sexual desires are "whores" or "sluts." The stereotype that women are undersexed also supports the traditional double standard: it is natural for men to sow their wild oats, but women who are sexually active outside of committed relationships are sluts or *nymphomaniacs*.

Despite the stereotype, women are no less arousable than men. Nor do they wait for men to discover their sexuality. Children of both genders routinely discover that touching their genitals produces pleasurable sensations long before they have intimate relationships.

Reflections

- Are the men you know sexually aggressive? Are the women you know sexually passive? How do you account for differences in sexual aggressiveness and sexual passivity among the people you know?
- Do you notice gender differences in sexual arousability? If so, what are they? How do you account for them?
- Which do you find to be more noticeable among the people you know: gender differences in sexual arousability or individual differences in sexual arousability? Explain.

PSYCHOLOGICAL ANDROGYNY: THE MORE TRAITS, THE MERRIER?

Most people think of masculinity and femininity as opposite ends of one continuum (Storms, 1980). People tend to assume that the more masculine a person is, the less feminine he or she must be, and vice versa. So a man who exhibits stereotypical feminine traits of nurturance, tenderness, and emotionality is often considered less masculine than other men. Women who compete with men in business are perceived not only as more masculine but also as less feminine than other women.

Some behavioral scientists, such as Sandra Bem, argue that masculinity and femininity comprise separate personality dimensions. A person who is highly masculine, whether male or female, may also possess feminine traits—and vice versa. People who exhibit "masculine" assertiveness and instrumental skills (skills in the sciences and business, for example) along with "feminine" nurturance and cooperation fit both the masculine and feminine gender-role stereotypes. They are said to show **psychological androgyny**

Psychological androgyny Possession of stereotypical masculine traits, such as assertiveness and instrumental skills, along with stereotypical feminine traits, such as expressiveness, nurturance, and cooperation.

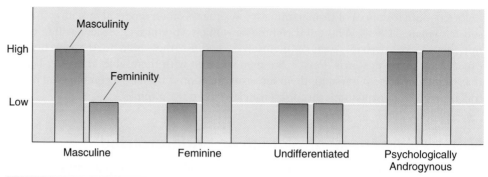

figure 6.5

A Model of Psychological Androgyny. Some behavioral scientists argue that masculinity and femininity are independent personality dimensions. People who exhibit "masculine" assertiveness and instrumental skills along with "feminine" nurturance and cooperation are said to be psychologically androgynous. People who are high in assertiveness and instrumental skills fit only the masculine stereotype. People who are high in traits such as nurturance and cooperation fit only the feminine stereotype. People who are low in the stereotypical masculine and feminine patterns are considered undifferentiated.

(see Figure 6.5). People who are high in assertiveness and instrumental skills fit only the masculine stereotype. People who are high in traits such as nurturance and cooperation fit only the feminine stereotype. People who are low in the stereotypical masculine and feminine patterns are considered "undifferentiated" according to gender-role stereotypes.

People who are psychologically androgynous may be capable of summoning a wider range of masculine and feminine traits to meet the demands of various situations and to express their desires and talents. For example, researchers have found psychologically androgynous individuals of both genders to show "masculine" independence under group pressures to conform and "feminine" nurturance in interactions with a kitten or baby (Bem, 1975; Bem et al., 1976). Androgynous men and women are more apt to share leadership responsibilities in mixed-gender groups (Porter et al., 1985). By contrast, "masculine" men and women tend to dominate such groups, whereas "feminine" men and women are likely to take a back seat.

Many people who oppose the constraints of traditional gender roles may perceive psychological androgyny as a desirable goal. Some feminist writers, however, criticize psychological androgyny on grounds that the concept is defined in terms of, and thereby perpetuates, belief in the existence of masculine and feminine gender roles (Lott, 1985).

Psychological Androgyny, Psychological Well-Being, and Personal Development

Psychologically androgynous people tend to have higher self-esteem and to be generally better adjusted psychologically than people who are feminine or undifferentiated. Yet it appears that these benefits are more strongly related to the presence of masculine traits than to the combination of masculine and feminine traits (Whitley, 1983; Williams & D'Alessandro, 1994). That is, masculine traits such as assertiveness and independence may be related to psychological well-being, whether or not they are combined with feminine traits such as warmth, nurturance, and cooperation.

There is also evidence that feminine traits, such as nurturance and sensitivity, appear to predict success in intimate relationships—in *men* as well as in women. Marital happiness as rated by husbands is positively related to femininity in the wives (Antill, 1983). More interestingly, perhaps, ratings of marital happiness from the wives were also positively correlated with their husbands' femininity. Androgynous men are more likely to express tender feelings of love toward their partners and to be more accepting of their partner's faults than are masculine-typed ("macho") men (Coleman & Ganong, 1985). It seems that both genders appreciate spouses who are sympathetic, able to express warmth and tenderness, and nurturant toward children.

Masculine and androgynous adolescents of both genders tend to be more popular and to have higher self-esteem than other adolescents (Lamke, 1982b). We might not be surprised, given the prevalence of sexism, that adolescent boys fare better if they possess stereotypical masculine traits. What is more surprising is that adolescent girls also fare better when they exhibit stereotypical masculine traits, such as assertiveness and independence. It seems that young women do not risk having others question their femininity if they exhibit masculine traits, a finding that provides more evidence that the constellations of traits we call masculinity and femininity are independent clusters.

It is true that adolescent girls who show a number of masculine traits are more popular than girls who thoroughly adopt the traditional feminine gender role. Masculine traits such as independence and assertiveness apparently do not compromise their friends' perceptions of their femininity. ■

Psychological Androgyny and Sexual Behavior

Some evidence shows psychologically androgynous men and women to be more comfortable with their sexuality than are masculine men and feminine women (Walfish & Mayerson, 1980). Perhaps they can draw upon a broader repertoire of sexual behaviors. They may be comfortable with cuddling and tender holding and also with initiating and directing sexual interactions. Researchers also find that androgynous women experience orgasm more frequently (Radlove, 1983) and express greater sexual satisfaction (Kimlika et al., 1983) than feminine women do.

In this chapter, we have focused on the biology and psychology of gender. Our gender, both anatomically and psychologically, is a primary aspect of our sexuality. In the next chapter, we begin to explore how we express our sexuality through intimate relationships with others.

Reflections

- Would you consider yourself to be a highly masculine man? A highly feminine woman? Why or why not?
- How is your masculinity or femininity related to your sense of who you are and to your self-esteem? Explain.
- Would most people from your sociocultural background believe that psychological androgyny is desirable? Why or why not?

s u m m i n g   u p

PRENATAL SEXUAL DIFFERENTIATION

During the first six weeks or so of prenatal development, embryonic structures of both genders develop along similar lines and resemble primitive female structures. At about the seventh week after conception, the genetic code (XX or XY) begins to assert itself, causing changes in the gonads, genital ducts, and external genitals.

The Role of Sex Hormones in Sexual Differentiation
Testosterone spurs differentiation of the male (Wolffian) duct system. In the absence of testosterone, the Wolffian ducts degenerate, and female sex organs develop.

Descent of the Testes and the Ovaries
The testes and ovaries develop in the abdominal cavity. About four months after conception, the testes descend into the scrotal sac.

Sex Chromosomal Abnormalities

Abnormalities of the sex chromosomes can have profound effects on sexual characteristics, physical health, and psychological development. Examples include Klinefelter syndrome and Turner syndrome.

Prenatal Sexual Differentiation of the Brain

Gender-specific changes occur in the hypothalamus during prenatal development. Testosterone causes cells in the hypothalamus of male fetuses to become insensitive to estrogen.

GENDER IDENTITY

One's gender identity is one's sense of being male or being female.

Nature and Nurture in Gender Identity

Gender identity is almost always consistent with anatomic gender.

Hermaphroditism

Some individuals—hermaphrodites—are born with both ovarian and testicular tissue. Hermaphrodites usually assume the gender identity and gender role of the gender that is assigned at birth. Pseudohermaphrodites can acquire the gender identity of the other chromosomal gender when they are reared as members of that gender.

Transsexualism

Transsexuals harbor a deep sense of discomfort about their anatomic gender. Hormone treatments and gender-reassignment surgery provide transsexuals with many of the characteristics of the other gender.

GENDER ROLES AND STEREOTYPES

Cultures have broad expectations of men and women that are termed *gender roles*. In our culture the stereotypical female is seen as gentle, dependent, kind, helpful, patient, and submissive. The stereotypical male is tough, competitive, gentlemanly, and protective.

SEXISM

Sexism is the prejudgment that because of gender, a person will possess certain negative traits that disqualify him or her for certain vocations or prevent him or her from performing adequately in these jobs or in some social situations. Women have been historically excluded from "male occupations," and stereotypical expectations concerning "men's work" and "women's work" filter down to the primary grades.

GENDER DIFFERENCES: *VIVE LA DIFFÉRENCE* OR *VIVE LA SIMILARITÉ?*

Differences in Cognitive Abilities

Boys have historically been seen as excelling in math and spatial-relations skills, whereas girls have been viewed as excelling in language skills. Gender differences in these areas are small, however, and cultural expectations play a role in them.

Differences in Personality

Stereotypical gender preferences for toys and play activities are in evidence at an early age. Males are more aggressive than females, but the question is *why?*

ON BECOMING A MAN OR A WOMAN: GENDER TYPING

Biological Perspectives

Biological views on gender typing focus on the roles of genetics and prenatal influences in predisposing men and women to gender-linked behavior patterns. Testosterone in the brains of male fetuses spurs greater growth of the right hemisphere, which may be connected with the ability to manage spatial-relations tasks.

Cross-Cultural Perspectives

Anthropologists have found that differences in gender roles exist among preliterate cultures, and even between neighboring cultures.

Psychological Perspectives

Psychologists have attempted to explain gender typing in terms of psychodynamic, social-learning, and cognitive-developmental theories. Freud explained gender typing in terms of identification with the parent of the same gender through resolution of the Oedipus complex.

Social-learning theorists explain the development of gender-typed behavior in terms of processes such as observational learning, identification, and socialization.

According to the cognitive-developmental view, children form concepts about gender and then make their behavior conform to their gender concepts. According to Kohlberg, gender typing entails the emergence of three concepts: gender identity, gender stability, and gender constancy.

Gender schema theory proposes that children develop a gender schema as a means of organizing their perceptions of the world. Once children acquire a gender schema, they begin to judge themselves according to traits that are considered appropriate to their genders. In doing so, they blend their developing self-concepts with the prominent gender schema of their culture.

GENDER ROLES AND SEXUAL BEHAVIOR

Stereotypical gender-role expectations affect dating practices and sexual behavior.

Men as Sexually Aggressive, Women as Sexually Passive

According to this stereotype, men are sexual initiators and women are sexual gatekeepers. Men not only initiate sexual encounters; they are expected to initiate all the "moves."

Men as Overaroused, Women as Underaroused
According to another stereotype, women do not share men's interests in sex and discover their own sexuality only when a man ignites their sexual flame.

PSYCHOLOGICAL ANDROGYNY: THE MORE TRAITS, THE MERRIER?

Masculinity and femininity may comprise two independent personality dimensions. People who combine stereotypical masculine and feminine behavior patterns are psychologically androgynous.

Psychological Androgyny, Psychological Well-Being, and Personal Development
Masculine and androgynous people of both genders tend to be better psychologically adjusted than people who are feminine or undifferentiated.

Psychological Androgyny and Sexual Behavior
Psychologically androgynous men and women are more comfortable with their sexuality than masculine men and feminine women are.

chapter

7

Attraction and Love

outline

TRUTH OR FICTION?

ATTRACTION

Physical Attractiveness: How Important
Is Looking Good?

IN THE NEW MILLENNIUM:
*How Do We Compete with "Cyberbabes"
and "CyberHunks"?*

A WORLD OF DIVERSITY:
Wide-Eyed with . . . Beauty?

A WORLD OF DIVERSITY:
*Gender Differences in Preferences in Mates
across 37 Cultures*

The Matching Hypothesis: Who Is
"Right" for You?

Similarity in Attitudes:
Do Opposites Attract?

Reciprocity: If You Like Me, You Must
Have Excellent Judgment

LOVE

The Greek Heritage

Romantic Love in Contemporary
Western Culture

QUESTIONNAIRE:
*Are You a Romantic or a Realist?
The Love Attitude Scale*

Contemporary Models of Love:
Dare Science Intrude?

QUESTIONNAIRE:
Sternberg's Triangular Love Scale

SUMMING UP

Truth or Fiction?

_____ Beauty is in the eye of the beholder.

_____ College men would like women to be thinner than the women want to be.

_____ People are regarded as more attractive when they are smiling.

_____ Women who are randomly assigned names such as Kathy and Jennifer are rated as more attractive than women who are assigned names such as Harriet and Gertrude.

_____ Physical appeal is the most important trait we seek in partners for long-term relationships.

_____ "Opposites attract." That is, we are more apt to be attracted to people who disagree with our views and tastes than to people who share them.

_____ It is possible to be in love with someone who is not also a friend.

Candy and Stretch. A new technique for controlling weight gain? No, these are the names of a couple who have just met at a camera club that doubles as a meeting place for singles.

Candy and Stretch stand above the crowd—literally. She is almost 6 feet tall, an attractive woman in her early 30s. He is more plain looking but "wholesome." He is in his late 30s and 6 feet 5 inches tall. Stretch has been in the group for some time. Candy is a new member. Let us follow them as they meet during a coffee break. As you will see, there are some differences between what they say and what they think.[1]

They Say	*They Think*
STRETCH: Well, you're certainly a welcome addition to our group.	(Can't I ever say something clever?)
CANDY: Thank you. It certainly is friendly and interesting.	(He's cute.)
STRETCH: My friends call me Stretch. It's left over from my basketball days. Silly, but I'm used to it.	(It's safer than saying my name is David Stein.)
CANDY: My name is Candy.	(At least my nickname is. He doesn't have to hear Hortense O'Brien.)
STRETCH: What kind of camera is that?	(Why couldn't a girl named Candy be Jewish? It's only a nickname, isn't it?)
CANDY: Just this old German one of my uncle's. I borrowed it from the office.	(He could be Irish. And that camera looks expensive.)
STRETCH: May I? (He takes her camera, brushing her hand and then tingling with the touch.) Fine lens. You work for your uncle?	(Now I've done it. Brought up work.)
CANDY: Ever since college.	(Okay, so what if I only went for a year?)
It's more than being just a secretary. I get into sales, too.	(If he asks what I sell, I'll tell him anything except underwear.)
STRETCH: Sales? That's funny. I'm in sales, too, but mainly as an executive. I run our department.	(Is there a nice way to say used cars? I'd better change the subject.)
I started using cameras on trips. Last time I was in the Bahamas, I took—	(Great legs! And the way her hips move—)
CANDY: Oh! Do you go to the Bahamas, too? I love those islands.	(So I went just once, and it was for the brassiere manufacturers' convention At least we're off the subject of jobs.)
STRETCH:	(She's probably been around. Well, at least we're off the subject of jobs.)
I did a little underwater work there last summer. Fantastic colors. So rich in life.	(And lonelier than hell.)
CANDY:	(Look at that build. He must swim like a fish. I should learn.)
I wish I'd had time when I was there. I love the water.	(Well, I do. At the beach, anyway, where I can wade in and not go too deep.)

---

[1]Bach and Deutsch (1970).

188

So begins a relationship. Candy and Stretch have a drink and talk, talk, talk—sharing their likes and dislikes. Amazingly, they seem to agree on everything, from clothing to cars to politics. The attraction they feel is very strong, and neither of them is willing to turn the other off by disagreeing.

They fall in love. Weeks later, they still agree on everything, even though there is one topic that they avoid scrupulously: religion. Their different backgrounds became apparent once they exchanged last names. That doesn't mean they have to talk about it, however.

They delay introductions to their parents. The O'Briens and the Steins are narrow-minded about religion. If the truth be known, so are Candy and Stretch. Candy errs by telling Stretch, "You're not like other Jews I know." Stretch also voices his feelings now and then. After Candy has nursed him through a cold, he remarks, "You know, you're very Jewish." Candy and Stretch play the games required to maintain the relationship. They tell themselves that their remarks were mistakes, and, after all, anyone can make mistakes. They were meant as compliments, weren't they? Yet each is becoming isolated from family and friends.

One of the topics they ignore is birth control. As a Catholic, Candy does not take oral contraceptives. (Stretch later claims that he had assumed she did.) Candy becomes pregnant, and they get married. Only through professional help do they learn each other's genuine feelings. And on several occasions, the union comes close to dissolving.

How do we explain the goings-on in this tangled web of deception? Candy and Stretch felt strongly attracted to each other. What determines who is attractive? Why did Candy and Stretch pretend to agree on everything? Why did they put off introductions to their parents?

Two possible consequences of attraction are friendship and love. Candy and Stretch "fell in love." What *is* love? When the first author was a teenager, the answer was, "Five feet of heaven in a ponytail." However, this answer may lack scientific merit. We see that there are different forms of love and that our concepts of love are far from universal.

ATTRACTION

Let us explore some of the factors that determine interpersonal attraction.

Physical Attractiveness: How Important Is Looking Good?

We might like to think of ourselves as so sophisticated that physical attractiveness does not move us. We might like to claim that sensitivity, warmth, and intelligence are more important to us. However, we might never learn about other people's personalities if they do not meet our minimal standards for physical attractiveness. Research shows that physical attractiveness is a major determinant of interpersonal and sexual attraction (Hensley, 1992). In fact, physical appearance is the key factor in consideration of partners for dates, sex, and marriage (Hatfield & Sprecher, 1986).

IS BEAUTY IN THE EYE OF THE BEHOLDER? What determines physical attractiveness? Are our standards fully subjective, or is there broad agreement on what is attractive?

Cross-cultural studies show that people universally want physically appealing partners (Ford & Beach, 1951). However, is that which appeals in one culture repulsive in others?

In certain African tribes, long necks and round, disklike lips are signs of feminine beauty. Women therefore stretch their necks and lips to make themselves more appealing. Women of the Nama tribe persistently tug at their labia majora to make them "beautiful"—that is, prominent and elongated (Ford & Beach, 1951).

Truth or Fiction?
~~REVISITED~~

Beauty might not be completely in the eye of the beholder. Although personal tastes may vary within and across cultures, there are cultural standards for physical attractiveness. ∎

In our culture, women consider taller men to be more attractive (Hensley, 1994; Sheppard & Strathman, 1989). Undergraduate women prefer their dates to be about 6 inches taller than themselves. Undergraduate men, on the average, prefer women who are about 4½ inches shorter than themselves. (Gillis & Avis, 1980). Tall women are not viewed as positively. Shortness, though, is perceived to be a liability for both men and women (Jackson & Ervin, 1992).

Some women of Candy's stature find that shorter men are discouraged from asking them out. Some tall women walk with a hunch, as if to minimize their height. A neighbor of the first and third authors refers to herself as "5 feet 13 inches tall."

Female plumpness is valued in many, perhaps most, preliterate societies (Anderson et al., 1992; Frayser, 1985). Wide hips and a broad pelvis are widely recognized as sexually appealing. In our culture, however, slenderness is in style. Some young women suffer from an eating disorder called **anorexia nervosa,** in which they literally starve themselves to conform to the contemporary ideal. Both genders find slenderness (though not anorexic thinness) attractive, especially for females (Fallon & Rozin, 1985; Franzoi & Herzog, 1987; Rozin & Fallon, 1988).

The hourglass figure is popular in the United States. In one study, 87 African American college undergraduates—both male and female—rated women of average weight with a waist-to-hip ratio of 0.7 to 0.8 as most attractive and desirable for long-term relationships (Singh, 1994a). Neither very thin nor obese women were found to be as attractive, regardless of the waist-to-hip ratio. Findings were similar for a sample of 188 White students (Singh, 1994b).

Do men idealize the *Penthouse* centerfold? What size busts do men prefer? Women's beliefs that men prefer large breasts may be somewhat exaggerated. The belief that men want women to have bursting bustlines leads many women to seek breast implants in the attempt to live up to an ideal that men themselves don't generally hold (Rosenthal, 1992). Researchers in one study showed young men and women (ages 17 to 25 years) a continuum of male and female figures that differed only in the size of the bust for the female figures and of the pectorals for the male figures (Thompson & Tantleff, 1992). The participants were asked to indicate the ideal size for their own gender and the size that they believed the average man and woman would prefer.

The results show some support for the "big is better" stereotype—for both men and women. Women's conception of ideal bust size was greater than their actual average size. Men preferred women with still larger busts, but not nearly as large as the busts women *believed* that men prefer. Men believed that their male peers preferred women with much bustier figures than their peers themselves said they preferred. Ample breast or chest sizes may be preferred by the other gender, but people seem to have an exaggerated idea of the sizes the other gender actually prefers.

Both genders find obese people to be unattractive, but there are gender differences in impressions of the most pleasing body shape. On the average, college men think that their present physiques are close to ideal and appealing to women (Fallon & Rozin, 1985). College women generally see themselves as much heavier than the figure that is most alluring to men and heavier still than the figure that they perceive as the ideal feminine form. Both genders are wrong about the preferences of the other gender, however. Men

Anorexia nervosa A potentially life-threatening eating disorder characterized by refusal to maintain a healthy body weight, intense fear of being overweight, a distorted body image, and, in females, lack of menstruation (amenorrhea.)

Beauty and Culture. Can you find Mr. or Ms. Right among these people? Are your judgments of physical beauty based on universal standards or on your cultural experiences?

actually prefer women to be somewhat heavier than the women imagine they would. Women prefer their men to be a bit leaner than the men would have expected.

It is not true that college men would like women to be thinner than the women want to be. College men actually prefer women who are heavier, though still slender, than the women expect. On the other hand, college women prefer men who are thinner than the men imagine. ■

Truth or Fiction?
REVISITED

HOW TRAITS AND NAMES AFFECT PERCEPTIONS OF PHYSICAL ATTRACTIVENESS: ON THE IMPORTANCE OF *NOT* BEING ERNEST   Both genders rate the attractiveness of faces higher when they are shown smiling in photographs than when they are shown in a nonsmiling pose (Mueser et al., 1984). (Photographers are not ignorant of this fact.) So there is reason to "put on a happy face" when you meet people socially or ask someone out on a date. Context is important, however. It may be more appropriate in a business context to maintain a more serious countenance. The effects of a smile may also be a greater determinant of attractiveness in women than in men (Deutsch et al., 1987).

How Do We Compete with "Cyberbabes" and "CyberHunks"?

Many women in the United States find themselves competing against the ideal of the tall, slender, "buffed" woman (Williams, 1992). The image of the ideal has sent millions of women, young and older, to their mirrors, searching out any extra ounces of fat. It has given rise to an epidemic of eating disorders, as women take drastic measures—including self-starvation and purging—to shed pounds.

Men, too, feel the pressure to slim down and get pumped up. Many dancers, wrestlers, and male models have also developed eating disorders (DeAngelis, 1997a; Gilbert 1996b).

It is tough enough to compete against the flesh-and-blood models people see in the popular media. But what of the virtual models that will soon be assaulting them? A case in point is Lara Croft. She is a 29-year-old epitome of female perfection. She's tall (5 feet 9 inches), slim (110 pounds), and pumped up. If all that sounds a little bit "unreal," perhaps it's because Lara *is* unreal. Lara is a "cyberbabe," not a flesh-and-blood "babe," and you'll find her starring in videogames and commercials:

Her name is Lara Croft, and she seems to be everywhere.

Her image is popping up in magazines, on television and computer screens, even on pinup posters like the one in the [January 1998] issue of *PC Games* magazine, which shows her reclining in a bikini, a handgun resting suggestively on her hip.

And she's not even real. Lara is a digitized female image from one of the hottest-selling video games of [1998], Tomb Raider 2, which is published by Eidos Interactive, based in London.

But that has not stopped Lara—whose tanned, voluptuous cyberframe is the equivalent of 34–24–34—from becoming a popular female icon. She is a far cry from Betty Boop, and she is no Barbie doll. She is more like a female Indiana Jones, but pumped up, vertically and horizontally, in the fashion of the 1990s.

Her fans say she is gritty, sexy, sassy, smart and, well, virtually real. And that's exactly what her British creators were hoping for.

"It's really a strange phenomenon because people talk about her as if she's a real person," said Cindy Church, a spokeswoman for Eidos. "A lot of people who play video games fantasize about her."

Unsure of just how to portray the silicon icon, Church went on, "She's not overly sexual," then paused. "OK, she is physically sexual, but she has a personality behind her."

Because of those attributes, Eidos executives are being flooded with gifts and presents for the silicon princess. There are flowers, Christmas gifts, even vows from young boys and men. "People all over the world have sent in their pictures," said Tricia Gray at the Eidos office in San Francisco. "She's had dozens of marriage proposals and all these cheesy letters."

Indeed, in Britain, only the bubbly Spice Girls are said to be more popular. And in the United States, her Indiana Jones–like video exploits are being sold in large quantities to game players who are well into their 30s.

Lara's first game, Tomb Raider, was released in November 1996 and sold about 3.5 million copies worldwide. Tomb Raider 2, which came out [in November of 1997], has sold several million, according to Eidos.

As a result, just about every game and computer magazine wants to reprint Lara's sexy image. There are even entire World Wide Web sites devoted to her and sites created by

---

Truth or Fiction?
REVISITED

It is true that people are regarded as more attractive when they are smiling. Therefore, it might make sense to "put on a happy face" when meeting people. ■

Gender-role expectations may affect perceptions of attractiveness. Women who viewed videos of prospective dates found men who acted outgoing and self-expressive more appealing than men who were passive (Riggio & Woll, 1984). Another study found that highly feminine women are more likely to be attracted to dominant "macho" men than less feminine women are (Maybach & Gold, 1994). Yet men who viewed videos in the Riggio and Woll (1984) study were put off by outgoing, self-expressive behavior in women. In yet another study, women rated videos of dominant college men (defined in this study as social control over a troublesome interaction with an instructor) as more appealing than submissive men. Again, male viewers were put off by similarly dominant women (Sadalla et al., 1987). Despite recent changes in traditional gender-role stereotypes, many men in the United States still prefer demure women. This is not to suggest that dominant, self-expressive women should stifle themselves to attract traditional men; the relationships would probably rub them both the wrong way.

Names also may affect perceptions of physical appeal. In one study, women who were randomly assigned names such as Kathy, Jennifer, and Christine were rated more attractive than women who were assigned the names Harriet, Gertrude, and Ethel (Garwood et al., 1980). Seems silly, does it not? After all, our parents name us, and there need be no relationship between our names and our physical appeal. On the other hand, we may individuals who even take the liberty of posing the digital Lara in the nude.

"The most obvious reason Lara Croft is so popular is that 99.5 percent of the gaming population is young men," says Steve Klett, editor of *PC Games* magazine, which has Lara gracing its cover this month. "And it doesn't hurt that she's so outrageously proportioned."

Indeed, the craze surrounding Lara (there is also an online newspaper dedicated to chronicling her life) might be yet another sign that technological advances in human imagery are creating lifelike portraits that further blur the line between reality and fantasy.

Devoted fans, who see a three-dimensional image and hear a real British voice projecting out of their computer speakers, have dubbed Lara a "cyberbabe" and the "silicon chick."

And to bolster such realism, Lara has her own biography and a rebellious past. Born into an aristocratic family in Wimbledon, England, Lara Croft—whose given age is 29—grew up in a world of private tutors, boarding schools and a Swiss finishing school.

But on a skiing trip to the Himalayas, her plane crashed. Lara, who was the sole survivor, soon realized that she could not stand the "suffocating atmosphere of the upper-class British society" and preferred a new adventurous life. Thus she began searching for ancient artifacts and fighting villains and a zoo of animals, like tigers and wolves.

But her creators say that Lara's future is not about slaying dragons but winning eyeballs. "The digital Lara is going to sign a modeling contract with a big agency," Church boasts. "She'll become a supermodel, like Naomi Campbell and Linda Evangelista."

Even her creators think she's real.

Source: Reprinted with permission from Barboza, D. (1998, January 19). Video world is smitten by a gun-toting, tomb-raiding sex symbol. *The New York Times,* p. D3.

Cyberbabe Lara Croft and a Flesh-and-Blood Copy (Model Nell McAndrew). It is difficult enough for us average folks to compete against the flesh-and-blood models we find in the popular media. But what of the virtual models that will be assaulting us more and more in the new millennium? Tombraider Lara Croft is more than perfect—she's "unreal" in the realest sense of the term. At 5'9" tall, 110 lbs in weight, and all pumped up, she creates even a more difficult standard for normal people to live up to.

choose to keep our names or to use nicknames. So if you are unhappy with your name, why not assume a more popular nickname? Beginning college or a new job is an ideal time for doing so. Men, too, can doff their Sylvesters and Ernests if they prefer. If you have an unusual name and are content with it, however, be yourself.

It is true that women who are randomly assigned names such as Kathy and Jennifer are rated as more attractive than women who are assigned names such as Harriet and Gertrude. Perhaps observers thought that the Harriets and Gertrudes of the world would use more contemporary nicknames if they were "with it." ■

WHAT DO YOU LOOK FOR IN A LONG-TERM, MEANINGFUL RELATIONSHIP? Your second author conducted a survey of college men and women in the early 1980s and found that psychological characteristics such as warmth, fidelity, honesty, and sensitivity were rated higher in importance than physical attractiveness as desirable qualities in a prospective partner for a meaningful, long-term relationship (Nevid, 1984). Physical attractiveness won out when students were asked to consider the qualities that are most important in a partner for a sexual relationship. Overall, however, men placed greater emphasis on the physical characteristics of their partners for both types of relationships than did women. Women placed more value on qualities such as warmth, assertiveness, wit, and ambition. The single most highly desired quality that students wanted in long-term partners was honesty. Honestly.

WIDE-EYED WITH . . . BEAUTY?

Some aspects of beauty seem to be largely cross-cultural. Research suggests that White people, African Americans, Asian Americans, and Hispanic Americans tend to agree on the facial features that they find to be attractive (Cunningham et al., 1995). They all prefer female faces with large eyes, greater distance between the eyes, small noses, narrower faces with smaller chins, high, expressive eyebrows, larger lower lips, and a well-groomed, full head of hair.

Consider the methodology of a study that compared the facial preferences of people in Japan and England. Perrett (1994) created computer composites of the faces of 60 women. Part A of Figure 7.1 is a composite of the 15 women who were rated the most attractive. He then used computer enhancement to exaggerate the differences between the composite of the 60—that is, the average face—and the composite of the 15 most attractive women. He found that both Japanese and British men deemed women with large eyes, high cheekbones, and narrow jaws to be the most attractive (Perret, 1994). Computer enhancement resulted in the image shown in Part B of Figure 7.1. The enhanced composite has still higher cheekbones and a narrower jaw than Part A. Part B was then rated as the most attractive image. Similar results were found for the image of a Japanese woman.

Cunningham and his colleagues (1995) reported historical anecdotes that suggest that the facial preferences of people as diverse as Europeans, Black Africans, Native Americans, Indians (in India, that is), and Chinese are quite consistent. They quoted from Charles Darwin's 1871 treatise, *The Descent of Man, and Selection in Relation to Sex:*

Mr. Winwood Reade . . . who has had ample opportunities for observation [with Black Africans] who have never associated with Europeans is convinced that their ideas of beauty are, on the whole, the same as ours; and Dr. Rohlfs writes to me the same effect with respect to Borneo and the countries inhabited by the Pullo tribes. . . . Capt. Burton believes that a woman whom we consider beautiful is admired throughout the world.

Darwin believed that our physical preferences were largely inborn and related to survival of our species. What do you think? Do you believe that "their ideas of beauty are, on the whole, the same as ours"? Or do you think that research hasn't yet ferreted out significant cultural or ethnic differences that might exist? If there is ethnic consistency in these preferences, how would you explain them? For example, do you believe

- that they are coincidental?
- that there has been more exchange of ideas among cultures than has been believed?
- that there is something instinctive about them?

figure 7.1

What Features Contribute to Facial Attractiveness? In both England and Japan, features such as large eyes, high cheekbones, and narrow jaws contribute to perceptions of the attractiveness of women. Part A is a computer composite of the faces of 15 women rated as the most attractive of a group of 60. Part B is a computer composite that exaggerates the features of these 15 women. That is, they are developed further in the direction that separates them from the average of the full group.

(a)

(b)

Truth or Fiction **REVISITED**

It is not true that physical appeal is the most important trait we seek in partners for long-term relationships. According to the results of one study, honesty was reported to be more vital in partners for long-term relationships. ▪

Although personal qualities may assume more prominent roles in determining partner preferences in long-term relationships, physical appeal probably plays a "filtering" role. Unless a prospective date meets minimal physical standards, we might not look beneath the surface for "more meaningful" traits.

Nevid's results have been replicated in studies on initial attraction and on choice of mates. Women place relatively greater emphasis than men on traits such as vocational status, earning potential, expressiveness, kindness, consideration, dependability, and fondness for children. Men give relatively more consideration to youth, physical attractiveness, cooking ability (can't they switch on the microwave by themselves?), and frugality (Howard et al., 1987; Sprecher et al., 1994). When it comes to mate selection, females in a sample of students from Germany and the Netherlands also emphasized the financial prospects and status of a potential mate, whereas males emphasized the importance of physical attractiveness (de Raad & Doddema-Winsemius, 1992). A study of more than 200 Korean college students found that in mate selection, women placed relatively more emphasis on education, jobs, and family of origin than men did (Brown, 1994). Men placed relatively more emphasis on physical attractiveness and affection. (Yes, men were more "romantic." Women were more pragmatic.)

Susan Sprecher and her colleagues (1994) surveyed a national probability sample of 13,017 English- or Spanish-speaking people, age 19 or above, living in households in the United States. In one section of their questionnaire, they asked respondents how willing they would be to marry someone who was older, younger, of a different religion, not likely to hold a steady job, not good-looking, and so forth. Each item was followed by a seven-point scale in which 1 meant "not at all" and 7 meant "very willing." As shown in Table 7.1, women were more willing than men to marry someone who was not good-looking. On the other hand, women were less willing to marry someone who was not likely to hold a steady job.

ARE ATTRACTIVENESS PREFERENCES INHERITED? On the surface, gender differences in perceptions of attractiveness seem unbearably sexist—and perhaps they are. Yet some sociobiologists believe that evolutionary forces favor the continuation of gender differences in preferences for mates because certain preferred traits provide reproductive advantages (Bjorklund & Kipp, 1996). Some physical features, such as cleanliness, good

table 7.1

Gender differences in mate preferences		
How willing would you be to marry someone who . . .	**Men**	**Women**
was not "good-looking"?	3.41	4.42*
was older than you by 5 or more years?	4.15	5.29*
was younger than you by 5 or more years?	4.54	2.80*
was not likely to hold a steady job?	2.73	1.62*
would earn much less than you?	4.60	3.76*
would earn much more than you?	5.19	5.93*
had more education than you?	5.22	5.82*
had less education than you?	4.67	4.08*
had been married before?	3.35	3.44
already had children?	2.84	3.11†
was of a different religion?	4.24	4.31
was of a different race?	3.08	2.84*

Source: Based on information in Susan Sprecher, Quintin Sullivan, & Elaine Hatfield (1994). Mate Selection Preferences: Gender Differences Examined in a National Sample. *Journal of Personality and Social Psychology, 66*(6), 1074–1080.

*Difference statistically significant at the .001 level of confidence.

†Difference statistically significant at the .01 level of confidence.

GENDER DIFFERENCES IN PREFERENCES IN MATES ACROSS 37 CULTURES

What do men in Nigeria, Japan, Brazil, Canada, and the United States have in common? For one thing, men in these countries report that they prefer mates who are younger than themselves. Buss (1994) reviewed survey evidence on the preferred age difference between oneself and one's mate in 37 cultures (representing 33 countries) in Europe, Africa, Asia, Australia, New Zealand, and North and South America. In every culture, men preferred younger mates (the range was from 0.38 year to 6.45 years). Women, however, preferred older mates (the range was from 1.82 years to 5.1 years).

Gender differences in the preferred age of mates paralleled actual differences in age of men and women at the time of marriage. Men were between two and five years older, on the average, than their brides at the time of marriage. The smallest average age difference at marriage, 2.1 years, was found in Poland. The largest average difference, 4.92 years, was found in Greece. Men in the mainland United States are 2.71 years older than women at the time of marriage. In Canada, men are 2.51 years older than their mates, on the average.

Buss finds that in all 37 cultures, men placed greater value on a prospective partner's "good looks" than women did. On the other hand, women in 36 of 37 cultures placed greater value on prospectivemates' "good earning capacity."

The consistency of Buss's findings lends credence to the notion that there are widespread gender differences in preferences with respect to age, physical characteristics, and financial status of prospective mates. Generally speaking, men place greater value on the physical attractiveness and relative youth of prospective mates. Women place relatively greater value on the earning capacity of prospective mates. Buss interprets women's preferences for relatively older mates as additional evidence that women appraise future mates on the basis of their ability to provide for a wife and family, since age and income tend to be linked among men.

Despite these gender differences in preferences for mates, Buss finds that both men and women placed greater weight on personal qualities than on looks or income potential of prospective mates. In *all* 37 cultures, the characteristics "kind, understanding" and "intelligent" were rated higher than earning power or physical attractiveness.

---

complexion, clear eyes, good teeth, good hair, firm muscle tone, and a steady gait are universally appealing to both genders (Ford & Beach, 1951). Perhaps they are markers of reproductive potential (Symons, 1995). Age and health may be relatively more important to a woman's appeal, since these characteristics tend to be associated with her reproductive capacity: the "biological clock" limits her reproductive potential. Physical characteristics associated with a woman's youthfulness, such as smooth skin, firm muscle tone, and lustrous hair, may thus have become more closely linked to a woman's appeal (Buss, 1994). A man's reproductive value, however, may depend more on how well he can provide for his family than on his age or physical appeal. The value of men as reproducers, therefore, is more intertwined with factors that contribute to a stable environment for childrearing—such as economic status and reliability. Sociobiologists argue that these gender differences in mate preferences may have been passed down through the generations as part of our genetic heritage (Buss, 1994; Symons, 1995).

Men's interest in younger women occurs in both preliterate and industrialized societies (Buss, 1994). Female jealousy of younger women is another thread that spans cultures. Sexual competition, according to Margaret Mead, generally involves

the struggle between stronger older men and weaker younger men or between more attractive younger women and more entrenched older ones. (Mead, 1967, p. 198)

Sociobiological views of gender differences in mate preferences are largely speculative and not fully consistent with the evidence. Despite gender differences, both men and women report that they place greater weight on personal characteristics than on physical features in judging prospective mates (Buss, 1994). Many women, like men, still prefer physically appealing partners. Women also tend to marry men who are similar to themselves in physical attractiveness as well as socioeconomic standing. Note also that older men are more likely than younger men to die from natural causes. From the standpoint of reproductive advantages, women would therefore achieve greater success by marrying fit, younger males who are likely to survive during the childrearing years than by marrying older, higher-status males. Moreover, similar cultural influences, rather than inherited dispositions, may explain commonalities across cultures in gender differences in mate preferences. For example, in societies in which women are economically dependent on men, a man's appeal may depend more on his financial resources than on his physical appeal.

The Matching Hypothesis: Who Is "Right" for You?

Do not despair if you are less than exquisite in appearance, along with most of us mere mortals. You may be saved from permanently blending in with the wallpaper by the effects of the **matching hypothesis.** This concept holds that people tend to develop romantic relationships with people who are similar to themselves in physical attractiveness rather than the local Will Smith or Cindy Crawford look-alike.

Researchers have found that people who are dating steadily, engaged, or married tend to be matched in physical attractiveness (Kalick, 1988). Young married couples even tend to be matched in weight (Schafer & Keith, 1990). The central motive for seeking "matches" seems to be fear of rejection by more appealing people (Bernstein et al., 1983).

There are exceptions to the matching hypothesis. Now and then we find a beautiful woman married to a plain or ugly man (or vice versa). How do we explain it? What, after all, would *she* see in *him*? According to one study (Bar-Tal &

Who Is Right for You? Research shows that people tend to pair off with others who are similar in physical characteristics and personality traits. Do you agree?

Saxe, 1976), people judging "mismatched" pairs may tend to ascribe wealth, intelligence, or success to the man. We seek an unseen factor that will balance the physical attractiveness of one partner. For some mismatched couples, similarities in attitudes and personalities may balance out differences in physical attractiveness.

MORE THAN BEAUTY   Matching applies not only to physical appeal. Our sex and marital partners tend to be like us in race and ethnicity, age, level of education, and religion. Consider some findings of the NHSLS study (Michael and others, 1994):

- The sex partners of nearly 94% of unmarried White men are White women. About 2% of single White men are partnered with Hispanic American women, 2% with Asian American women, and less than 1% with African American women.
- The sex partners of nearly 82% of African American men are African American women. Nearly 8% of African American men are partnered with White women. Under 5% are partnered with Hispanic American women.
- About 83% of the women and men in the study chose partners within five years of their own age and of the same or a similar religion.
- Of all the women in the study, *not one* with a graduate college degree had a partner who had not finished high school.
- Men with a college degree almost never had sexual relationships with women who had much more or much less education than they had.

Similarity in Attitudes: Do Opposites Attract?

Why do the great majority of us have partners from our own backgrounds? One reason is that marriages are made in the neighborhood and not in heaven (Michael et al., 1994). That is, we tend to live among people who are similar to us in background and thus come into contact with them. Another is that we are drawn to people who are similar in their attitudes. People who are similar in background are more likely to be similar in their attitudes. Similarity in attitudes and tastes is a key contributor to attraction, friendships, and love relationships (Cappella & Palmer, 1990; Griffin & Sparks, 1990; Laumann et al., 1994).

Matching hypothesis The concept that people tend to develop romantic relationships with people who are similar to themselves in attractiveness.

Let us also note a gender difference. Evidence shows that women place greater weight on attitude similarity as a determinant of attraction to a stranger of the other gender than do men, whereas men place more value on physical attractiveness (Feingold, 1991). We also tend to *assume* that people we find attractive share our attitudes (Dawes, 1989; Marks et al., 1981). The physical attraction between Candy and Stretch motivated them to pretend that their preferences, tastes, and opinions coincided. They entered into an unspoken agreement not to discuss their religious differences. When sexual attraction is strong, perhaps we want to think that the kinks in the relationship will be small or that we can iron them out. Let us also note that though similarity may be important in determining initial attraction, compatibility appears to be an even stronger determinant of maintaining an enduring intimate relationship (Vinacke et al., 1988).

Truth or Fiction?
REVISITED

Actually, it is not true that "opposites attract." That is, we are actually *less* apt to be attracted to people who disagree with our views and tastes than to people who share them. ■

Reciprocity: If You Like Me, You Must Have Excellent Judgment

Has anyone told you that you are good-looking, brilliant, and emotionally mature? That your taste is elegant? Ah, what superb judgment!

When we feel admired and complimented, we tend to return these feelings and behaviors. This is called **reciprocity.** Reciprocity is a potent determinant of attraction (Condon & Crano, 1988). We tend to be much more warm, helpful, and candid when we are with strangers who we believe like us (Clark et al., 1989; Curtis & Miller, 1986). We even tend to welcome positive comments from others when we know these comments to be inaccurate (Swann et al., 1987).

Perhaps the power of reciprocity has enabled many couples to become happy with one another and reasonably well adjusted. By reciprocating positive words and actions, a person can perhaps stoke neutral or mild feelings into robust, affirmative feelings of attraction.

Reflections

■ How important is physical attractiveness to you in your evaluation of partners for dating, sex, and marriage? (Are you being truthful?)
■ What personality traits are most important to you in your evaluation of partners for dating, sex, and marriage?
■ Would you date someone of another race? Of another religion? Why or why not? What would be the response of your parents or other members of your sociocultural group if you did?

Attraction can lead to feelings of love. Let us now turn to that most fascinating topic.

LOVE

For thousands of years, poets have sought to capture love in words. A seventeenth-century poet wrote that his love was like "a red, red rose." In Sinclair Lewis's novel *Elmer Gantry*, love is "the morning and the evening star." Love is beautiful and elusive. It shines, brilliant and heavenly. Passion and romantic love are also earthy and sexy, brimming with sexual desire.

Romantic love is hardly unique to our culture. Researchers report finding evidence of romantic love in 147 of the 166 different cultures they studied in a recent cross-cultural comparison (Jankowiak & Fischer, 1992). Romantic love occurs even in most preliterate societies. The absence of romantic love in the remaining 19 cultures, the investigators suspect, was most probably due to the limitations of their study methods (Gelman, 1993).

Our culture idealizes the concept of romantic love. We readily identify with the plight of the "star-crossed" lovers in *Romeo and Juliet* and *West Side Story*, who sacrificed

Reciprocity Mutual exchange.

themselves for love. We learn that "love makes the world go round" and that "love is everything." Virtually all of the participants in the Janus and Janus nationwide survey (96% of the men and 98% of the women) reported that love is important to them (Janus & Janus, 1993). Like other aspects of sexual and social behavior among humans, the concept of love must be understood within a cultural context. Luckily (or miserably), we have such a context in Western culture.

The Greek Heritage

The concept of love can be traced back at least as far as the classical age of Greece. The Greeks distinguished four concepts related to the modern meanings of love: *storge, agape, philia,* and *eros.*

Storge is loving attachment, deep friendship, or nonsexual affection. It is the emotion that binds friends and parents and children. Some scholars believe that even romantic love is a form of attachment that is similar to the types of attachments infants have to their mothers (Hazan & Shaver, 1987).

Agape is similar to generosity and charity. It implies the wish to share one's bounty and is epitomized by anonymous donations of money. In relationships, it is characterized by selfless giving (Lee, 1988). Agape, according to Lee's research, is the kind of love that is least frequently found between adults in committed relationships.

Philia is closest in meaning to friendship. It is based on liking and respect rather than sexual desire. It involves the desire to do and enjoy things with the other person and to see him or her when one is lonely or bored.

Eros is closest in meaning to our concept of passion. Eros was a character in Greek mythology (transformed in Roman mythology into Cupido, now called Cupid) who would shoot unsuspecting people with his love arrows, causing them to fall madly in love with the person who was nearest to them at the time. Erotic love embraces sudden passionate desire: "love at first sight" and "falling head over heels in love." Passion can be so gripping that one is convinced that life has been changed forever. This feeling of sudden transformation was captured by the Italian poet Dante Alighieri (1265–1321), who exclaimed upon first beholding his beloved Beatrice, "*Incipit vita nuova,*" which can be translated as "My life begins anew." Romantic love can also be earthy and sexy. In fact, sexual arousal and desire may be the strongest component of passionate or romantic love (Berscheid, 1988). Romantic love begins with a powerful physical attraction or feelings of passion and is associated with strong physiological arousal (Lee, 1988).

Unlike the Greeks, we tend to use the word *love* to describe everything from feelings of affection toward another to romantic ardor to sexual intercourse ("making love"). Still, different types or styles of love are recognized in our own culture, as we shall see.

Romantic Love in Contemporary Western Culture

The experience of *romantic love,* as opposed to loving attachment or sexual arousal per se, occurs within a cultural context in which the concept is idealized. Western culture has a long tradition of idealizing the concept of romantic love, as represented, for instance, by romantic fairy tales that have been passed down through the generations. In fact, our exposure to the concept of romantic love may begin with hearing the fairy tales of Sleeping Beauty, Cinderella, and Snow White—along with their princes charming. Later perhaps, the concept of romantic love blossoms with exposure to romantic novels, television and film scripts, and the heady tales of friends and relatives.

During adolescence, strong sexual arousal along with an idealized image of the object of our desires leads us to label our feelings as love. We may learn to speak of "love" rather than "lust," because sexual desire in the absence of a committed relationship might be viewed as primitive or animalistic. Being "in love" ennobles attraction and sexual arousal, not only to society but also to oneself. Unlike lust, love can be discussed even at the dinner table. If others think we are too young to experience "the real thing"—which

Storge (STORE-gay) Loving attachment and nonsexual affection; the type of emotion that binds parents to children.

Agape (AH-gah-pay) Selfless love; a kind of loving that is similar to generosity and charity.

Philia (FEEL-yuh) Friendship love, which is based on liking and respect rather than sexual desire.

Eros The kind of love that is closest in meaning to the modern-day concept of passion.

presumably includes knowledge of and respect for the other person's personality traits—our feelings may be called "puppy love" or a "crush."

Western society maintains much of the double standard toward sexuality. Therefore, women are more often expected to justify sexual experiences as involving someone they love. Young men usually need not attribute sexual urges to love, so men are more apt to deem love a "mushy" concept. The vast majority of people in the United States nonetheless believe that romantic love is a prerequisite for marriage. Young people rate romantic love as the single most important reason for marriage (Roper Organization, 1985). Over 80% of college men and women subscribe to the belief that "being in love" is a precondition for marriage (Berscheid, 1988; Simpson et al., 1986). More than half also believe that falling out of love justifies divorce.

questionnaire

Are You a Romantic or a Realist? The Love Attitudes Scale

David Knox of East Carolina University contrasts romantic love with *realistic love*—the kind of love that is maintained across the years. Partners who share a realistic love have the blinders off. They accept and cherish each other, warts and all.

Knox (1983) developed the Love Attitudes Scale to evaluate the degree to which people hold a romantic or realistic view of love. How about you? Are you a realist or a romantic when it comes to matters of the heart? To find out, complete the scale, and then turn to the scoring key in the Appendix.

Directions: Circle the number that best represents your opinion on each item according to the following code. Add up your scores to arrive at a total score.

1 = Strongly agree (SA)
2 = Mildly agree (MA)
3 = Undecided (U)
4 = Mildly disagree (MD)
5 = Strongly disagree (SD)

1. Love doesn't make sense. It just is.

   1 2 3 4 5

2. When you fall "head over heels" in love, it's sure to be the real thing.

   1 2 3 4 5

3. To be in love with someone you would like to marry but can't is a tragedy.

   1 2 3 4 5

4. When love hits, you know it.

   1 2 3 4 5

5. Common interests are really unimportant; as long as each of you is truly in love, you will adjust.

   1 2 3 4 5

6. It doesn't matter if you marry after you have known your partner for only a short time as long as you know you are in love.

   1 2 3 4 5

7. If you are going to love a person, you will "know" after a short time.

   1 2 3 4 5

8. As long as two people love each other, the educational differences they have really do not matter.

   1 2 3 4 5

9. You can love someone even though you do not like any of that person's friends.

   1 2 3 4 5

10. When you are in love, you are usually in a daze.

    1 2 3 4 5

11. Love "at first sight" is often the deepest and most enduring type of love.

    1 2 3 4 5

12. When you are in love, it really does not matter what your partner does because you will love him or her anyway.

    1 2 3 4 5

13. As long as you really love a person, you will be able to solve the problems you have with that person.

    1 2 3 4 5

Which is the more romantic gender? Although the question may well incite an argument in mixed company, the Janus and Janus (1993) nationwide survey of adult Americans found that a slightly greater percentage of the single men (82%) perceived themselves as being romantic than did single women (77%). Yet among married people, the figures were reversed, with 79% of the women describing themselves as romantic, compared to 72% of the men. Perhaps there is some truth to the stereotype that men are more romantic during the courtship stage of relationships than the marriage stage. Then again, maybe self-perceptions of being romantic don't quite jibe with the reality. In any event, you can explore self-perceptions of being a romantic or a realist when it comes to love by completing the nearby questionnaire on love attitudes.

14. Usually you can really love and be happy with only one or two people in the world.

    1 2 3 4 5

15. Regardless of other factors, if you truly love another person, that is a good enough reason to marry that person.

    1 2 3 4 5

16. It is necessary to be in love with the one you marry to be happy.

    1 2 3 4 5

17. Love is more of a feeling than a relationship.

    1 2 3 4 5

18. People should not get married unless they are in love.

    1 2 3 4 5

19. Most people truly love only once during their lives.

    1 2 3 4 5

20. Somewhere there is an ideal mate for most people.

    1 2 3 4 5

21. In most cases, you will "know it" when you meet the right partner.

    1 2 3 4 5

22. Jealousy usually varies directly with love; that is, the more you are in love, the greater your tendency to become jealous will be.

    1 2 3 4 5

23. When you are in love, you are motivated by what you feel rather than by what you think.

    1 2 3 4 5

24. Love is best described as an exciting rather than a calm thing.

    1 2 3 4 5

25. Most divorces probably result from falling out of love rather than failing to adjust.

    1 2 3 4 5

26. When you are in love, your judgment is usually not too clear.

    1 2 3 4 5

27. Love often comes only once in a lifetime.

    1 2 3 4 5

28. Love is often a violent and uncontrollable emotion.

    1 2 3 4 5

29. When selecting a marriage partner, differences in social class and religion are of small importance compared with love.

    1 2 3 4 5

30. No matter what anyone says, love cannot be understood.

    1 2 3 4 5

Total Score on the Love Attitudes Scale: _____

Source: Knox, D. (1983). *The Love Attitudes Inventory* (rev. ed.). Saluda, NC: Family Life Publications. Reprinted with permission.

When reciprocated, romantic love is usually a source of deep fulfillment and ecstasy (Hatfield, 1988). How wonderful when love meets its match. When love is unrequited, however, it can lead to emptiness, anxiety, or despair. Romantic love can thus teeter between states of ecstasy and misery (Hatfield, 1988). Perhaps no other feature of our lives can lift us up as high or plunge us as low as romantic love.

INFATUATION VERSUS "TRUE LOVE": WILL TIME TELL? Perhaps you first noticed each other when your eyes met across a crowded room, like the star-crossed lovers in *West Side Story*. Or perhaps you met when you were both assigned to the same Bunsen burner in chemistry lab—less romantic but closer to the flame. However it happened, the meeting triggered such an electric charge through your body that you could not get him (or her) out of your mind. Were you truly in love, however, or was it merely a passing fancy? Was it infatuation or the "real thing"—a true, lasting, and mutual love? How do you tell them apart?

Perhaps you don't, at least not at first. **Infatuation** is a state of intense absorption in or focusing on another person. It is usually accompanied by sexual desire, elation, and general physiological arousal or excitement. Some refer to passion as infatuation. Others dub it a "crush." Both monikers suggest that it is a passing fancy. In infatuation, your heart may pound whenever the other person draws near or enters your fantasies.

For the first month or two, infatuation and the more enduring forms of romantic love are essentially indistinguishable (Gordon & Snyder, 1989). At first, both may be characterized by intense focusing or absorption. Infatuated people may become so absorbed that they cannot sleep, work, or carry out routine chores. Logic and reason are swept aside. Infatuated people hold idealized images of their love objects and overlook their faults. Caution may be cast to the winds. In some cases, couples in the throes of infatuation rush to get married, only to find a few weeks or months later that they are not well suited.

As time goes on, signs that distinguish infatuation from a lasting romantic love begin to emerge. The partners begin to view each other more realistically and determine whether or not the relationship should continue.

Infatuation has been likened to a state of passionate love (Sternberg, 1986) that is based on intense feelings of passion but not on the deeper feelings of attachment and caring that typify a more lasting mutual love. Although infatuation may be a passing fancy, it can be supplanted by the deeper feelings of attachment and caring that characterize more lasting love relationships.

Note, too, that infatuation is not a necessary first step on the path to a lasting mutual love. Some couples develop deep feelings of love without ever experiencing the fireworks of infatuation (Sternberg, 1986). Or sometimes one partner is infatuated while the other manages to keep his or her head below the clouds.

Contemporary Models of Love: Dare Science Intrude?

Despite the importance of love, scientists have historically paid little attention to it. Some people believe that love cannot be analyzed scientifically. Love, they maintain, should be left to the poets, philosophers, and theologians. Yet researchers are now applying the scientific method to the study of love. They recognize that love is a complex concept, involving many areas of experience—emotional, cognitive, and motivational (Sternberg & Grajek, 1984). They have reinforced the Greek view that there are different kinds and styles of love. Let us consider some of the views of love that have emerged from modern theorists and researchers.

LOVE AS APPRAISAL OF AROUSAL Social psychologists Ellen Berscheid and Elaine Hatfield (Berscheid & Walster, 1978; Walster & Walster, 1978) define **romantic love** in terms of a state of intense physiological arousal and the cognitive appraisal of that arousal

Infatuation A state of intense absorption in or focus on another person, which is usually accompanied by sexual desire, elation, and general physiological arousal or excitement; passion.

Romantic love A kind of love characterized by feelings of passion and intimacy.

as love. The physiological arousal may be experienced as a pounding heart, sweaty palms, and butterflies in the stomach when one is in the presence of, or thinking about, one's love interest. Cognitive appraisal of the arousal means attributing it to some cause, such as fear or love. The perception that one has fallen in love is thus derived from several simultaneous events: (1) a state of intense physiological arousal that is connected with an appropriate love object (that is, a person, not an event such as a rock concert), (2) a cultural setting that idealizes romantic love, and (3) the attribution of the arousal to feelings of love toward the person.

STYLES OF LOVE   Some psychologists speak in terms of *styles* of love. Clyde and Susan Hendrick (1986) developed a love attitude scale that suggests the existence of six styles of love among college students. The following is a list of the styles. Each one is exemplified by statements similar to those on the original scale. As you can see, the styles owe a debt to the Greeks:

1. *Romantic love (eros):* "My lover fits my ideal." "My lover and I were attracted to one another immediately."
2. *Game-playing love (ludus):* "I keep my lover up in the air about my commitment." "I get over love affairs pretty easily."
3. *Friendship (storge, philia):* "The best love grows out of an enduring friendship."
4. *Logical love (pragma):* "I consider a lover's potential in life before committing myself." "I consider whether my lover will be a good parent."
5. *Possessive, excited love (mania):* "I get so excited about my love that I cannot sleep." "When my lover ignores me, I get sick all over."
6. *Selfless love (agape):* "I would do anything I can to help my lover." "My lover's needs and wishes are more important than my own."

Most people who are "in love" experience a number of these styles, but the Hendricks (1986) found some interesting gender differences in styles of love. College men are significantly more likely to develop game-playing and romantic love styles. College women are more apt to develop friendly, logical, and possessive love styles. (There were no gender differences in selfless love.) The Hendricks (1988b) have also found that romantically involved couples tend to experience the same kinds of love styles. They also showed that couples with romantic and selfless styles of love are more likely to remain together. A game-playing love style leads to unhappiness, however, and is one reason that relationships come to an end.

STERNBERG'S TRIANGULAR THEORY OF LOVE   Psychologist Robert Sternberg (1986, 1987, 1988) offers a triangular theory of love. In his view, love has three distinct components:

1. *Intimacy:* the experience of warmth toward another person that arises from feelings of closeness, bondedness, and connectedness to the other. Intimacy also involves the desire to give and receive emotional support and to share one's innermost thoughts with the other.
2. *Passion:* an intense romantic or sexual desire for another person, which is accompanied by physiological arousal.
3. *Commitment:* a component of love that involves *commitment* to maintain the relationship through good times and bad.

According to Sternberg's model, love can be conceptualized in terms of a triangle in which each vertex represents one of these basic elements of love (see Figure 7.2 on page 204). The way the components are balanced can be represented by the shape of the triangle. For example, a love in which all three components were equally balanced would be represented by an equilateral triangle, as in Figure 7.2.

figure 7.2

The Triangular Model of Love. According to psychologist Robert Sternberg, love consists of three components, as shown by the vertices of this triangle. Various kinds of love consist of different combinations of these components. Romantic love, for example, consists of passion and intimacy. Consummate love—the cultural ideal—consists of all three.

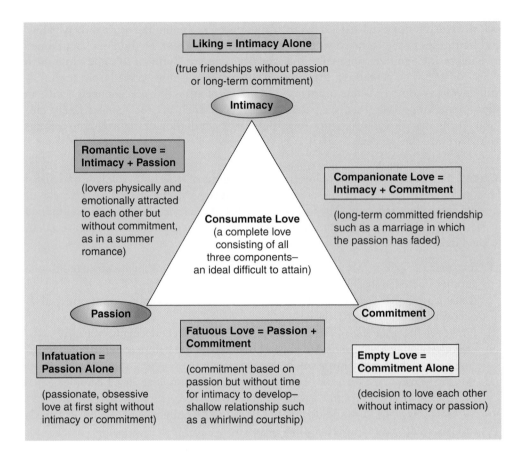

Sternberg believes that couples are well matched if they possess corresponding levels of passion, intimacy, and commitment. Compatibility can be represented visually in terms of the congruence of the love triangles. Figure 7.3(a) shows a perfect match, in which the triangles are congruent. Figure 7.3(b) depicts a good match; the partners are similar in the three dimensions. Figure 7.3(c) shows a mismatch; major differences exist between the partners on all three components. Relationships may run aground when partners are mismatched. A relationship may fizzle, rather than sizzle, when one partner experiences more passion than the other or when one wants a long-term commitment when the other's idea of commitment is to stay all night.

According to the Sternberg model, various combinations of the three elements of love characterize different types of love relationships (Sternberg, 1986, 1988) (see Figure 7.3 and Table 7.2). For example, *infatuation* (passionate love) is typified by strong sexual desire but not by intimacy and commitment. The partners may each feel passionate love for the other, or, as in the case of Tom, such feelings may go unrequited:

Tom sat behind Lisa in physics class. Tom hated physics, but he could not say the same for Lisa. One look at her was enough to change his life. He had fallen madly in love with her. Instead of listening to the teacher or looking at the blackboard, he would gaze at Lisa throughout the class. Lisa was aware of this and was not happy about it. She did not much care for Tom, and when he tried to start a conversation with her, she moved on as quickly as possible. Tom's staring and his awkwardness in talking to her made her feel uncomfortable. Tom, on the other hand, could think of little else besides Lisa, and his grades began to suffer as he spent the time he should have been devoting to his homework thinking about her. He was a man obsessed. The obsession might have gone on for quite some time had not both Tom and Lisa graduated that June and gone to different colleges. Tom never saw Lisa again, and after several unanswered love letters, he finally gave up on her.

—(Sternberg, 1988, p. 123)

Liking is a basis for friendship. It consists of feelings of closeness and emotional warmth without passion or commitment. Liking is not felt toward passing acquaintances. It is reserved for people to whom one feels close enough to share one's innermost feelings and thoughts. We sometimes develop these intimate relationships without making the commitment to maintaining a long-term relationship that typifies other types of love, however. Liking may develop into a passionate love, however, or into a more committed form of friendship (called *companionate love* in Sternberg's model).

Should lovers also be friends, or are lovers and friends part of the twain that never meet? Candy and Stretch's relationship lacked the quality that is most often associated with true friendship: the willingness to share confidences. Despite their physical intimacy, their relationship remained so superficial that they couldn't even share information about their religious backgrounds.

Perfectly matched involvements
(a)

Closely matched involvements
(b)

Severely mismatched involvements
(c)

table 7.2

Types of love according to Sternberg's triangular model	
1. Nonlove	A relationship in which all three components of love are absent. Most of our personal relationships are of this type—casual interactions or acquaintances that do not involve any elements of love.
2. Liking	A loving experience with another person or a friendship in which intimacy is present but passion and commitment are lacking.
3. Infatuation	A kind of "love at first sight" in which one experiences passionate desires for another person in the absence of both intimacy and commitment components of love.
4. Empty love	A kind of love characterized by commitment (to maintain the relationship) in the absence of either passion or intimacy. Stagnant relationships that no longer involve the emotional intimacy or physical attraction that once characterized them are of this type.
5. Romantic love	A loving experience characterized by the combination of passion and intimacy but without commitment.
6. Companionate love	A kind of love that derives from the combination of intimacy and commitment components of love. This kind of love often occurs in marriages in which passionate attraction between the partners has died down and has been replaced by a kind of committed friendship.
7. Fatuous love	The type of love associated with whirlwind romances and "quickie marriages" in which the passion and commitment components of love are present but intimacy is not.
8. Consummate love	The full or complete measure of love involving the combination of passion, intimacy, and commitment. Many of us strive to attain this type of complete love in our romantic relationships. Maintaining it is often harder than achieving it.

Source: Adapted from Sternberg, 1988.

figure 7.3

Compatibility and Incompatibility, According to the Triangular Model of Love. Compatibility in terms of Sternberg's types of love can be represented as triangles. Part A shows a perfect match in which triangles are congruent. Part B depicts a good match; the partners are similar according to the three dimensions. Part C shows a mismatch. Major differences exist between the partners on all three components.

Sternberg's Triangular Love Scale

Which are the strongest components of your love relationship? Intimacy? Passion? Commitment? All three components? Two of them?

To complete the following scale, fill in the blank spaces with the name of one person you love or care about deeply. Then rate your agreement with each of the items by using a nine-point scale in which 1 = "not at all," 5 = "moderately," and 9 = "extremely." Use points in between to indicate intermediate levels of agreement between these values. Then consult the scoring key in the Appendix.

Intimacy Component

_____ 1. I am actively supportive of _____'s well-being.

_____ 2. I have a warm relationship with _____.

_____ 3. I am able to count on _____ in times of need.

_____ 4. _____ is able to count on me in times of need.

_____ 5. I am willing to share myself and my possessions with _____.

_____ 6. I receive considerable emotional support from _____.

_____ 7. I give considerable emotional support to _____.

_____ 8. I communicate well with _____.

_____ 9. I value _____ greatly in my life.

_____ 10. I feel close to _____.

_____ 11. I have a comfortable relationship with _____.

_____ 12. I feel that I really understand _____.

_____ 13. I feel that _____ really understands me.

_____ 14. I feel that I can really trust _____.

_____ 15. I share deeply personal information about myself with _____.

Passion Component

_____ 16. Just seeing _____ excites me.

_____ 17. I find myself thinking about _____ frequently during the day.

_____ 18. My relationship with _____ is very romantic.

_____ 19. I find _____ to be very personally attractive.

_____ 20. I idealize _____.

Truth or Fiction?
REVISITED

It is indeed possible to be in love with someone who is not also a friend. Being in love can refer to states of passion or infatuation, whereas friendship is usually based on shared interests, liking, and respect. ▪

Candy and Stretch were "in love," although they were far from friends. Friendship and passionate love do not necessarily overlap. There is nothing that prevents people in love from becoming good friends, however—perhaps even the best of friends. Sternberg's model recognizes that the intimacy we find in true friendships and the passion we find in love are blended in two forms of love: romantic love and consummate love. These love types differ along the dimension of commitment, however.

Romantic love has both passion and intimacy but lacks commitment. Romantic love may burn brightly and then flicker out. Or it may develop into a more complete love, called *consummate love*, in which all three components flower. Desire is accompanied by a deeper intimacy and commitment. The flames of passion can be stoked across the years, even if they do not burn quite as brightly as they once did. Consummate love is most special—and certainly an ideal toward which many Westerners strive. In *empty love*, by contrast, there is nothing but commitment. Neither the warm emotional embrace of intimacy nor the flame of

_____ 21. I cannot imagine another person making me as happy as _____ does.

_____ 22. I would rather be with _____ than anyone else.

_____ 23. There is nothing more important to me than my relationship with _____.

_____ 24. I especially like physical contact with _____.

_____ 25. There is something almost "magical" about my relationship with _____.

_____ 26. I adore _____.

_____ 27. I cannot imagine life without _____.

_____ 28. My relationship with _____ is passionate.

_____ 29. When I see romantic movies and read romantic books, I think of _____.

_____ 30. I fantasize about _____.

Commitment Component

_____ 31. I know that I care about _____.

_____ 32. I am committed to maintaining my relationship with _____.

_____ 33. Because of my commitment to _____, I would not let other people come between us.

_____ 34. I have confidence in the stability of my relationship with _____.

_____ 35. I could not let anything get in the way of my commitment to _____.

_____ 36. I expect my love for _____ to last for the rest of my life.

_____ 37. I will always feel a strong responsibility for _____.

_____ 38. I view my commitment to _____ as a solid one.

_____ 39. I cannot imagine ending my relationship with _____.

_____ 40. I am certain of my love for _____.

_____ 41. I view my relationship with _____ as permanent.

_____ 42. I view my relationship with _____ as a good decision.

_____ 43. I feel a sense of responsibility toward _____.

_____ 44. I plan to continue my relationship with _____.

_____ 45. Even when _____ is hard to deal with, I remain committed to our relationship.

Source: Sternberg, 1988. Reprinted by permission of Basic Books, Inc., Publishers, New York.

passion exists. With empty love, one's lover is a person whom one tolerates and remains with because of a sense of duty.

Sometimes a love relationship has both passion and commitment but lacks intimacy. Sternberg calls this _fatuous (foolish) love._ Fatuous love is associated with whirlwind courtships that burn brightly but briefly as the partners come to the realization that they are not well matched. Intimacy can develop in such relationships, but couples who rush into marriage often find that the realities of marriage give the lie to their expectations:

> They expect a marriage made in heaven, but do not realize what they must do truly to maintain such a marriage. They base the relationship on passion and are disappointed when the passion starts to fade. They feel shortchanged—they have gotten much less than they bargained for. The problem, of course, is that they bargained for too much of one thing [passion] and not enough of another [intimacy]. (Sternberg, 1988, p. 128)

Consummate Love. According to Sternberg, romantic love may develop into a more complete love, called consummate love, in which desire is accompanied by deep intimacy and commitment. Consummate love is the special ideal toward which many Westerners strive.

In *companionate love*, finally, intimacy and commitment are strong but passion is lacking. This form of love typifies long-term (so-called platonic) friendships and marriages in which passion has ebbed but a deep and abiding friendship remains. Berscheid and Walster defined companionate love as "the affection we feel for those with whom our lives are deeply entwined" (1978, p. 9).

Although romantic love may become transformed into companionate love, the process by which this transformation takes place remains vague (Shaver et al., 1988). Companionate love need not be sexless or lacking in romance, however. Although passion may have ebbed, the giving and receiving of sexual pleasure can help to strengthen bonds. Partners may feel that their sex lives have even become more deeply satisfying as they seek to please each other by practicing what they have learned about each other's sexual needs and wants.

The balance among Sternberg's three aspects of love is likely to shift through the course of a relationship. A healthful dose of all three components—found in consummate love—typifies, for many of us, an ideal marriage. At the outset of marriage, passions may be strong but intimacy weak. Couples may only be starting to get to know each other's innermost thoughts and feelings. Time alone does not cause intimacy and commitment to grow, however. Some couples are able to peer into each other's deeper selves and form meaningful commitments at relatively early stages in their relationships. Yet some long-married couples may remain distant or waver in their commitment. Some couples experience only a faint flickering of passion early in the relationship. Then it becomes quickly extinguished. For some, the flames of passion burn ever brightly. Yet many married couples find that passion tends to fade while intimacy and commitment grow stronger.

Knowing about these components of love can help couples to avoid pitfalls. Couples who recognize that passion exerts a strong pull early in a relationship may be less likely to let passion rush them into marriage. Couples who recognize that it is normal for passions to fade might avoid assuming that their love is at an end when it may, in fact, be changing into a deeper, more intimate and committed form of love. This knowledge might also encourage couples to focus on finding ways of rekindling the embers of romance, rather than looking to escape at the first signs that the embers have cooled.

Researchers have tested some facets of the triangular model. One study reported mixed results. As the model would predict, married adults reported higher levels of commitment to their relationships than did unmarried adults (Acker & Davis, 1992). Yet the expected decline in passion over time was found only for women. Critics contend that Sternberg's model does not account for all the nuances and complexities of love (Murstein, 1988). The model tells us little, for example, about the *goals* of love or the *sources* of love. In fairness, Sternberg's model is a major contribution to the scientific study of love, which is only now beginning. Poets, philosophers, and theologians, by comparison, have been writing about love for millennia.

Reflections

▓ Have you been in romantic love? How did you know you were in love?

▓ Consider the kinds of love discussed in this chapter. What kind of love have you felt for family members? For friends? For people with whom you have had romantic relationships? Has one kind of love ever changed into another?

In this chapter, we have discussed interpersonal attraction—the force that initiates social contact. In the next chapter, we follow the development of social contacts into intimate relationships.

summing up

ATTRACTION

A number of factors determine interpersonal attraction.

Physical Attractiveness: How Important Is Looking Good?

Physical attractiveness is a major determinant of sexual attraction. In our culture, slenderness is in style. Both genders consider smiling faces more attractive. Socially dominant men, but not dominant women, are usually found to be attractive. Women place relatively greater emphasis on traits such as vocational status and earning potential, whereas men give relatively more consideration to physical attractiveness. Some sociobiologists believe that evolutionary forces favor the continuation of such gender differences in preferred traits because certain preferred traits provide reproductive advantages.

The Matching Hypothesis: Who Is Right for You?

According to the matching hypothesis, people tend to develop romantic relationships with people who are similar to themselves in attractiveness.

Similarity in Attitudes: Do Opposites Attract?

Similarity in attitudes and tastes is a strong contributor to attraction, friendships, and love relationships.

Reciprocity: If You Like Me, You Must Have Excellent Judgment

Through the reciprocation of positive words and actions, neutral or mild feelings may be stoked into feelings of attraction.

LOVE

In our culture, we are brought up to idealize the concept of romantic love.

The Greek Heritage

The Greeks had four concepts related to the modern meanings of love: storge, agape, philia, and eros.

Romantic Love in Contemporary Western Culture

Western culture has a long tradition of idealizing the concept of romantic love. Most people in the United States see romantic love as prerequisite to marriage. At first, infatuation and more enduring forms of romantic love may be indistinguishable.

Contemporary Models of Love: Dare Science Intrude?

Researchers are now applying the scientific method to the study of love.

Berscheid and Hatfield define romantic love in terms of intense physiological arousal and cognitive appraisal of that arousal as love.

Hendrick and Hendrick suggest that there are six styles of love among college students: romantic love, game-playing love, friendship, logical love, possessive love, and selfless love.

Sternberg suggests that there are three distinct components of love: intimacy, passion, and commitment. Various combinations of these components typify different kinds of love. Romantic love is characterized by the combination of passion and intimacy.

Francesco Clemente. Untitled. 1992. Watercolor on paper, 9-1/8 x 11-3/4 in. Courtesy of Gagosian Gallery, New York

8

Relationships and Communication

o u t l i n e

TRUTH OR FICTION?

THE ABC(DE)S OF ROMANTIC RELATIONSHIPS

The A's—Attraction

The B's—Building

IN THE NEW MILLENNIUM:
Modem Matchmaking

WHAT DO YOU SAY NOW:
How to Improve Date-Seeking Skills

The C's—Continuation

A WORLD OF DIVERSITY:
Self-Disclosure: East May Be East and West May Be West, but Here, Perhaps, the Twain Do (Almost) Meet

The D's—Deterioration

The E's—Ending

LONELINESS: "ALL THE LONELY PEOPLE, WHERE DO THEY ALL COME FROM?"

Causes of Loneliness

Coping with Loneliness

INTIMACY

Knowing and Liking Yourself

Trusting and Caring

Being Honest

Making a Commitment

Maintaining Individuality When the *I* Becomes *We*

Communicating

COMMUNICATION SKILLS FOR ENHANCING RELATIONSHIPS AND SEXUAL RELATIONS

Common Difficulties in Sexual Communication

Getting Started

Listening to the Other Side

Learning About Your Partner's Needs

Providing Information

Making Requests

Delivering Criticism

Receiving Criticism

When Communication Is Not Enough: Handling Impasses

SUMMING UP

Truth or Fiction?

_____ Small talk is an insincere method of opening a relationship.

_____ Only phonies practice opening lines.

_____ Swift self-disclosure of intimate information is the best way to deepen a new relationship.

_____ Many people remain lonely because they fear being rejected by others.

_____ People can have intimate relationships without being sexually intimate.

_____ "Love is all you need." That is, when partners truly love one another, they instinctively know how to satisfy each other sexually.

_____ If you are criticized, the best course is to retaliate.

_____ Relationships come to an end when the partners cannot resolve their differences.

_____ Disagreement is destructive to a relationship.

Will you, won't you, will you, won't you, will you join the dance?

—From Lewis Carroll's *Alice in Wonderland*

No man is an island, entire of itself.

—John Donne

"One, two. One, two." A great opening line? In the film *Play It Again, Sam*, Woody Allen plays the role of Allan Felix, a social klutz who has just been divorced. Diane Keaton plays his platonic friend Linda. At a bar one evening with Linda and her husband, Allan Felix spots a young woman on the dance floor who is so attractive that he wishes *he* could have *her* children.

The thing to do, Linda prompts him, is to begin dancing, then dance over to her and "say something." With a bit more prodding, Linda convinces Allan to dance. It's so simple, she tells him. He need only keep time—"One, two, one, two."

"One, two," repeats Allan. Linda shoves him off to his dream woman.

Hesitantly, Allan dances up to her. Working up courage, he says, "One, two. One, two, one, two." He is ignored and finds his way back to Linda.

"Allan, try something more meaningful," Linda implores.

Once more, Allan dances nervously back toward the woman of his dreams. He stammers, "Three, four, three, four."

"*Speak* to her, Allan," Linda insists.

He dances up to her again and tries, "You interested in dancing at all?"

"Get lost, creep," she replies.

Allan dances rapidly back toward Linda. "What'd she say?" Linda asks.

"She'd rather not," he shrugs.

So much for "One, two, one, two" and, for that matter, "Three, four, three, four." Striking up a relationship requires some social skills, and the first few conversational steps can be big ones.

In this chapter, we first define the stages that lead to intimacy in relationships. We define intimacy and see that not all relationships achieve this level of interrelatedness, even some supposedly deep and permanent relationships such as marriage. Moreover, we do not all have partners with whom we can develop intimate relationships; some of us remain alone and, perhaps, lonely. There are steps that we can take to overcome loneliness, however, as we illustrate in the pages ahead. Finally, we discuss the ways in which communication contributes to relationships and sexual satisfaction, and we enumerate ways of enhancing communication skills.

THE ABC(DE)S OF ROMANTIC RELATIONSHIPS

Social-exchange theory The view that the development of a relationship reflects the unfolding of social exchanges—that is, the rewards and costs of maintaining the relationship as opposed to ending it.

Romantic relationships, like people, undergo stages of development. According to **social-exchange theory,** the development reflects the unfolding of social exchanges, which involve the rewards and costs of maintaining the relationship as opposed to dissolving it. During each stage, positive factors sway partners toward maintaining and enhancing their relationship. Negative factors incline them toward letting it deteriorate and end (Karney & Bradbury, 1995).

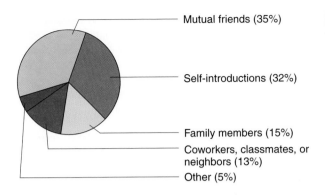

Mutual friends (35%)

Self-introductions (32%)

Family members (15%)

Coworkers, classmates, or neighbors (13%)

Other (5%)

figure 8.1

How Married People Meet Their Partners. Data from the NHSLS study (Michael et al., 1994).

George Levinger (1980) proposes an **ABCDE model** to describe the stages of romantic relationships: (1) *A*ttraction, (2) *B*uilding, (3) *C*ontinuation, (4) *D*eterioration, and (5) *E*nding.

The A's—Attraction

Attraction occurs when two people become aware of each other and find one another appealing or enticing. We may find ourselves attracted to an enchanting person "across a crowded room," in a nearby office, or in a new class. We may meet others through blind dates, introductions by mutual friends, computer match-ups, or by "accident." Initial feelings of attraction are largely based on visual impressions, though we may also form initial impressions by overhearing people speak or hearing others talk about them.

According to the NHSLS study (Michael et al., 1994), married people are most likely to have met their spouses through mutual friends (35%) or by self-introductions (32%) (see Figure 8.1). Other sources of introductions are family members (15%) and coworkers, classmates, or neighbors (13%). Mutual friends and self-introductions are also the most common ways of meeting for unmarried couples (Michael et al., 1994). As we see in the In the New Millennium feature on pages 214–215, more and more couples are also meeting online.

The B's—Building

Building a relationship follows initial attraction. Factors that motivate us to try to build relationships include similarity in the level of physical attractiveness, similarity in attitudes, and mutual liking and positive evaluations. Factors that may deter us from trying to build relationships include lack of physical appeal, dissimilarity in attitudes, and negative mutual evaluations.

NOT-SO-SMALL TALK: AN AUDITION FOR BUILDING A RELATIONSHIP   In the early stages of building a relationship, we tend to probe each other with **surface contact:** We typically look for common ground in the form of overlapping attitudes and interests, and we check out our feelings of attraction. At this point, the determination of whether to strive to develop the relationship is often made, at least in part, on the basis of **small talk.** Small talk allows an exchange of information but stresses breadth of topic coverage rather than in-depth discussion. Engaging in small talk may seem "phony," but premature self-disclosure of intimate information may repel the other person, as we shall see.

Small talk is a trial balloon for friendship. Successful small talk encourages a couple to venture beneath the surface. At a cocktail party, people may flit about from person to person, exchanging small talk, but now and then a couple finds common ground and pairs off.

ABCDE model Levinger's view, which approaches romantic relationships in terms of five stages: attraction, building, continuation, deterioration, and ending.

Surface contact A probing phase of building a relationship in which people seek common ground and check out feelings of attraction.

Small talk A superficial kind of conversation that allows exchange of information but stresses breadth of topic coverage rather than in-depth discussion.

Modem Matchmaking

Maybe they're not matches made in heaven—but close.

Loveseekers are swarming into cyberspace.

Online has become the hot new place for finding sweethearts.

"The Net is what singles bars and mixers used to be," says Stanford University psychologist Al Cooper. "It's turning into the place for smart, eligible people to meet."

Bill Stanfield, 47, says he can't imagine marrying a woman after dating for only a few months. But he and his wife Jacqueline wed "and I've never regretted it. There were no surprises."

Of course, they didn't really date. They met online. "We spent hundreds and hundreds of hours communicating. There were no distractions. . . . I knew my first wife for three years before we got married, but I didn't know her as well as I knew Jackie."

The Stanfields' courtship, peculiar as it sounds, is hardly unique. Love at AOL, an area on America Online designed for searching singles, began in February 1996 with 50 "personal photo ads" posted; now there are 30,000, with more than 700,000 visits to the area monthly. It's the service's most heavily used content area, says Anne Bentley of AOL.

Match.Com, largest independent dating service on the Web, offers 85,000 member "profiles," adding about 6,000 new faces weekly, corporate vice-president Fran Maier reports.

Why such a crowd?

Surveys show Net traffic is dominated by affluent, educated 20- to 40-somethings, often overworked professionals for whom "dating isn't so great," Cooper says. Many are "solid people, good long-term prospects but not good 'daters.' The guys may be a little shy, they're not adept at small talk and don't have great pickup lines."

Finding someone online with similar interests and values can feel a lot easier than hitting bars or "meat market" clubs, Cooper says.

Net liaisons can be "female-friendly" too, he adds: Communication is queen; sex stays off the front burner (at least for a while); and guys don't snub women if they're not 10-pluses.

A feeling of intimacy often develops quickly. Online talk lacks nonverbal cues that can put the brakes on romantic encounters, says Santa Clara, Calif., psychologist Coralie Scherer. Disapprov-ing glances, tone of voice changes, hesitance and breaks in eye contact aren't there. "All you know is what they tell you," says Scherer, so honesty can't make or break the deal.

The Stanfields, who married three months after meeting on-line, quickly realized they shared a passionate interest in hiking, camping and outdoor beauty. "We were really honest with each other about our personal likes and dislikes, what we want out of life," he says.

But honesty can also be elusive online. "Gender-bending" is so common that experts estimate that two out of three "women" in many chat rooms, particularly the sex-oriented ones, are men.

Changing or omitting other truths is common. San Diego psychologist Marlene Maheu tells about one client, "an intelligent, sophisticated professional woman," who recently flew hundreds of miles to meet a Net boyfriend and found "not only was he obese, but he looked considerably older than he claimed to be."

Women play that game, too. New York psychologist Judy Kuriansky, host of a nationally syndicated radio call-in show, [took one] frantic call from a lady about to meet her longtime online sweetheart. She'd neglected to mention she weighed 350 pounds and wondered what to do next.

"Omissions" can be more diabolical—even dangerous. Kuriansky recently heard a self-satisfied Michigan woman describe her "hobby": She's traveled coast to coast visiting cities she'd always wanted to see, at male expense, after feigning online interest in a string of men.

Maheu tells of one client recently stalked after giving her phone number to an e-mail friend who used it to find her address. "I've heard of similar situations quite often," Maheu reports.

Several new "Netiquette" books advise how to bring cyberspace romantic encounters safely down to earth. *Looking for Love Online* by Richard Rogers (Macmillan, $12.95) suggests ways to sniff out phonies and crazies, and how to surround in-person meetings with safety nets and escape hatches.

Denise Beaupre, an Attleboro, Mass., single mother, was pretty sure after three months of constant contact that her online friend, Scott Arena, was a wonderful guy. Still, she brought two friends to her first meeting (and one friend brought a taser gun).

"He was a sweetheart from the beginning though. . . . Look, I've been followed home from bars. Online is much safer, if you're careful about it."

Net romance may be most threatening to addicts, those online for many hours a week. And addicts may also behave most deceptively to would-be partners.

Truth or Fiction? REVISITED

It is not true that small talk is an insincere method of opening a relationship. Actually, small talk is a realistic way to begin a relationship. It allows couples to search for common ground and test feelings of attraction. ▪

THE "OPENING LINE": HOW DO YOU GET THINGS STARTED? One kind of small talk is the greeting, or opening line. We usually precede verbal greetings with eye contact and decide to begin talking if eye contact is reciprocated. Avoidance of eye contact might mean that the person is shy, but it could also signify lack of interest. If you would like to progress from initial attraction to surface contact, try a smile and direct eye contact. If the eye contact is reciprocated, choose an opening line, or greeting. Since your opening line can be important, you may prefer to say something more meaningful than "One, two, one, two."

Consider some greetings, or opening lines:

Verbal salutes, such as "Good morning."
Personal inquiries, such as "How are you doing?"

University of Pittsburgh psychologist Kimberly Young [reports a link] between Net addiction and clinical depression. Addicts may be "very vulnerable. They're quick to jump into relationships but sensitive to rejection."

Net addicts are also prone to donning online "personas" different from their everyday selves, her research shows.

"The chat rooms now are crowded with people who change their name daily. Who knows who they really are?" grumbles Joan Bousacos. She and husband George met online in 1990, "the good old days," married two years later and know a number of happily married couples matched years ago in cyberspace.

"Too many strange people are online now," Bounacos says, "and they want things to happen quick. . . . We were just good friends for a long time. What you bring to it is what you're going to get out of it."

That's exactly the point, argues psychologist Sherry Turkle, an MIT professor and author of *Life on the Screen* (Simon & Schuster, $25). She's studied several hundred adults who pursued relationships online.

"It's like a living Rorschach test," Turkle says. The absent nonverbal cues and isolation make Net encounters akin to [traditional] psychoanalysis in which patients "projected their greatest desires and fears" onto remote analysts. "They'll tell me, 'I was deceived,' and there is some deception. But when I look at their e-mail transcripts, I see less deception and more projection. These transcripts are often thin, people fill in the gaps as they wish."

How the gaps are filled in is the real tale. It's often a positive one. She's seen people use online encounters "as an occasion for self-reflection. They can learn a lot about themselves."

New York writer Sally Banks says she did just that. And Banks, alumna of several online liaisons, author of *Love Online* (Career Press, $12.99), is a bit embarrassed to admit she met her sweetheart, "the best relationship I've ever had," walking their dogs in Central Park. Her romantic forays on the Net harvested the self-revealing fodder for a real-world love.

"All those online relationships made me realize what I needed, what I was really looking for. I'll tell you what happened—I met myself online."

Reprinted with permission from Marilyn Elias, "Modem matchmaking." *USA Today,* August 14, 1997, pp. 1D, 2D.

Matchmaking in the New Millennium? In the new millennium, matches are more likely to be made by modem than in heaven. For example, nearly one million people visit Love at AOL each month, an area on America Online that is designed to help searching singles find their matches. You can check out people online—including their photos and their interests—before taking the plunge and meeting them in person. E-mail can take the place of small talk. For many people, it's a lot less threatening than bars or "meat market" clubs.

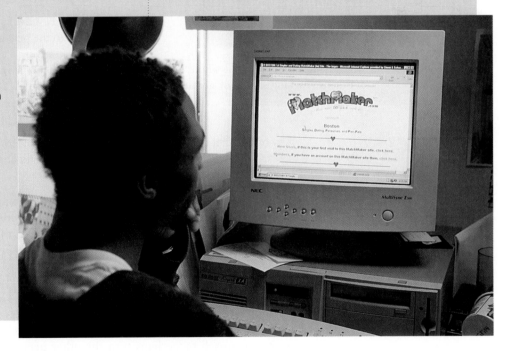

Compliments, such as "I like your outfit."

References to your mutual surroundings, such as "What do you think of that painting?" or "This is a nice apartment house, isn't it?"

References to people or events outside the immediate setting, such as "How do you like this weather we've been having?"

References to the other person's behavior, such as "I couldn't help noticing you were sitting alone" or "I see you out on this track every Saturday morning."

References to your own behavior or to yourself, such as "Hi, my name is Allan Felix" (feel free to use your own name if you prefer).

The simple "Hi" or "Hello" is very useful. A friendly glance followed by a cheerful hello ought to give you some idea of whether the attraction is reciprocated. If the hello is returned with a friendly smile and inviting eye contact, follow it up with another greeting, such as a reference to your surroundings, the other person's behavior, or your name.

what do you say now?

How to Improve Date-Seeking Skills

All right, so you think you have found Mr. or Ms. Right. So what do you do? How do you go about making a date?

Psychologists have learned that we can enhance our social skills, including our date-seeking skills, through the technique of *successive approximations*. (The third author interjects: "See here, you two psychologists, if you *mean* building skills step by step, why not just *say* 'step by step'?") That means that we can practice a series of tasks that are *graded in difficulty*. (The third author surrenders!) We can hone our social skills and gain self-confidence at each step. We can try out some of our skills on friends. Friends can role-play the prospective date and give honest feedback about our behavior.

Here is an example of a series of graduated (*step-by-step*)[1] tasks that may help you to sharpen your own date-seeking skills:

Easy Practice Level

Select a person with whom you are friendly but whom you have no desire to date. Practice making small talk about the weather, new films, TV shows, concerts, museum shows, political events, and personal hobbies.

Select a person you might have some interest in dating. Smile when you pass this person at work, school, or elsewhere, and say, "Hi." Engage in this activity with other people of both genders to increase your skills at greeting others.

Speak into your mirror, using behavior rehearsal and role playing. Pretend you are in the process of sitting next to the person you would like to date, say, at lunch or in the laundry room. Say "Hello" with a broad smile, and introduce yourself. Work on the smile until it looks inviting and genuine. Make some comment about the food or the setting—the cafeteria, the office, whatever. Use a family member or confidant to obtain feedback about the effectiveness of the smile, your tone of voice, posture, and choice of words.

Medium Practice Level

Sit down next to the person you want to date, and engage in small talk. If you are in a classroom, talk about a homework assignment, the seating arrangement, or the instructor (be kind). If you are at work, talk about the building or some re-

---

Truth or Fiction? REVISITED

It is not true that only phonies practice opening lines. Actually, it can be helpful for everyone to practice them. People are social beings, and opening lines help us to initiate social relationships—with new friends as well as dates. ∎

EXCHANGING "NAME, RANK, AND SERIAL NUMBER" Early exchanges are likely to include name, occupation, marital status, and hometown. This has been likened to exchanging "name, rank, and serial number" with the other person. Each person seeks a sociological profile of the other to discover common ground that might provide a basis for pursuing the conversation. An unspoken rule seems to be at work: "If I provide you with some information about myself, you will reciprocate by giving me an equal amount of information about yourself. Or . . . 'I'll tell you my hometown if you tell me yours' " (Knapp, 1978, p. 114). If the other person is unresponsive, she or he might not be attracted to you, and you might wish to try someone else. But you might also be awkward in your approach or perhaps turn the other person off by disclosing too much about yourself at once. The nearby What Do You Say Now? feature suggests ways of improving date-seeking skills.

SELF-DISCLOSURE: YOU TELL ME AND I'LL TELL YOU . . . CAREFULLY Opening up, or **self-disclosure,** is central to building intimate relationships. But just what sort of information is safe to disclose upon first meeting someone? If you refuse to go beyond name, rank, and serial number, you might look uninterested or, as if you are trying to keep things under wraps. If, on the other hand, you spill out the fact that you have a terrible rash on your thigh, it's likely that you have disclosed too much too soon.

If the surface contact provided by small talk and initial self-disclosure has been mutually rewarding, partners in a relationship tends to develop deeper feelings of liking for each other (Collins & Miller, 1994). Self-disclosure may continue to build gradually through the course of a relationship as partners come to trust each other enough to share confidences and more intimate feelings.

Self-disclosure The revelation of personal, perhaps intimate, information.

cent interesting event in the neighborhood. Ask your intended date how he or she feels about the situation. If you are at a group meeting, such as Parents Without Partners, tell the other person that you are there for the first time and ask for advice on how to relate to the group.

Engage in small talk about the weather and local events. Channel the conversation into an exchange of personal information. Give your "name, rank, and serial number"—who you are, your major field or your occupation, where you're from, why or how you came to the school or company. The other person is likely to reciprocate and provide equivalent information. Ask how he or she feels about the class, place of business, city, hometown, and so on.

Rehearse asking the person out before your mirror, a family member, or a confidant. You may wish to ask the person out for a cup of coffee or to a film. It is somewhat less threatening to ask someone out to a gathering at which "some of us will be getting together." Or you may rehearse asking the person to accompany you to a cultural event, such as an exhibition at a museum or a concert—it's "sort of" a date, but also less anxiety inducing.

Target Behavior Level

Ask the person out on a date in a manner that is consistent with your behavior rehearsal. If the person says he or she has a previous engagement or can't make it, you might wish to say something like, "That's too bad" or "I'm sorry you can't make it" and add something like, "Perhaps another time." You should be able to get a feeling for whether the person you asked out was just seeking an excuse or has a genuine interest in you and, as claimed, could not in fact accept the specific invitation.

Before asking the date out again, pay attention to his or her apparent comfort level when you return to small talk on a couple of occasions. If there is still a chance, the person should smile and return your eye contact. The other person might also offer you an invitation. In any event, if you are turned down twice, do not ask a third time. And don't make a catastrophe out of the refusal. Look up. Note that the roof hasn't fallen in. The birds are still chirping in the trees. You are still paying taxes. Then give someone else a chance to appreciate your fine qualities.

[1]Happy now?

GENDER DIFFERENCES IN SELF-DISCLOSURE   A woman complains to a friend, "He never opens up to me. It's like living with a stone wall." Women commonly declare that men are loath to express their feelings (Tannen, 1990). Researchers find that men tend to be less willing to disclose their feelings, perhaps in adherence to the traditional "strong and silent" male stereotype.

Yet gender differences in self-disclosure tend to be small. Overall, researchers find that women are only slightly more revealing about themselves than men are (Dindia & Allen, 1992). We should therefore be careful not to rush to the conclusion that men are always more "tight-lipped." The belief that there are large gender differences in self-disclosure appears to be something of a myth.

Stereotypes are also a-changing—somewhat. We now see depictions in the media of the "new" man as someone who is able to express feelings without compromising his masculinity. We shall have to wait to see whether this "new" sensitive image replaces the rugged, reticent stereotype or is a passing fancy.

MUTUALITY: WHEN THE "WE," NOT THE "I'S," HAVE IT   When feelings of attraction and the establishment of common ground lead a couple to regard themselves as "we"—not two "I's" who happen to be in the same place at the same time—they have attained what Levinger terms **mutuality.** Mutuality favors continuation and further deepening of the relationship.

The C's—Continuation

Once a relationship has been established, the couple embarks upon the stage of continuation. Factors that encourage continuation include seeking ways to introduce variety and maintain interest (such as trying out new sexual practices and social activities), showing evidence of caring and positive evaluation (such as sending birthday or Valentine's Day

Mutuality A phase in building a relationship in which members of a couple come to regard themselves as "we," no longer two "I's" who happen to be in the same place at the same time.

SELF-DISCLOSURE: East May Be East and West May Be West, but Here, Perhaps, the Twain Do (Almost) Meet

Research suggests that we should refrain from disclosing certain types of information too rapidly if we want to make a good impression. In one study, confederates of the experimenters (Wortman et al., 1976) engaged in 10-minute conversations with study participants. Some confederates were "early disclosers," who shared intimate information early. Others, "late disclosers," shared intimate information toward the end of the conversation only. In either case, the information was identical. Study participants then rated the disclosers. Early disclosers were rated less mature, secure, well adjusted, and genuine than the late disclosers. Study participants also preferred to continue relationships with the late disclosers. We may say we value "openness" and "honesty" in our relationships, but it may be a social mistake to open up too soon.

Truth or Fiction?
REVISITED

It is not true that swift self-disclosure of intimate information is the best way to deepen a new relationship. Actually, swift or premature self-disclosure can make one seem distraught or awkward and can turn people off. ■

A Japanese study showed similar results. Japanese college students rated actors in a mock conversation more favorably when they disclosed less about themselves (Nakanishi, 1986). Chinese people also responded negatively to others who are prone to early self-disclosure.

Despite such cross-cultural similarities, self-disclosure in general may be viewed less favorably in Eastern cultures. In Japanese society, for example, self-disclosure is often seen as inappropriate in social relationships (Nakanishi, 1986). Not surprisingly, researchers find that people in the United States tend to disclose much more about themselves in social interactions than do the Japanese (Gudykunst & Nishida, 1984).

Do You Dare Let It All Hang Out? Despite the common belief that one should be honest and open, research suggests that people who self-disclose too much too soon are seen as socially inept. Researchers find that people in Japan tend to disclose less personal information in social interactions than people in the United States do.

---

cards), showing lack of jealousy, perceiving fairness in the relationship, and experiencing mutual feelings of general satisfaction.

Factors in this stage that can throw the relationship into a downward spiral include boredom (e.g., falling into a rut in leisure activities or sexual practices), displaying evidence of negative evaluation (such as bickering and forgetting anniversaries and other important dates or pretending that they do not exist), perceiving a lack of fairness in the relationship (such as one partner's always deciding how the couple will spend their free time), or experiencing feelings of jealousy and general dissatisfaction.

JEALOUSY

> O! beware, my lord, of jealousy; It is the green-ey'd monster . . .
> —William Shakespeare, *Othello*

Thus was Othello, the Moor of Venice, warned of jealousy in the Shakespearean play that bears his name. Yet Othello could not control his feelings and killed his beloved wife, Desdemona. The English poet John Dryden labeled jealousy a "tyrant of the mind." Anthropologists find evidence of jealousy in all cultures, although it may vary in amount and intensity across and within cultures. It appears to be more common and intense among cultures with a stronger *machismo* tradition, in which men are expected to display their virility.

Sexual jealousy is aroused when we suspect that an intimate relationship is threatened by a rival. Lovers can become jealous when others show sexual interest in their partners or when their partners show an interest (even a casual or nonsexual interest) in another. Jealousy can impair a relationship and produce feelings of mistrust of one's partner or toward potential rivals.

Sexual jealousy may be associated with a range of negative emotions, including fear of losing the loved one and anger toward the rival, the loved one, or both. Feelings of possessiveness, which are related to jealousy, can also stress a relationship. In extreme cases jealousy can cause depression or give rise to spouse abuse, suicide, or, as with Othello, murder. But milder forms of jealousy are not necessarily destructive to a relationship. They may even serve the positive function of revealing how much one cares for one's partner.

How common is sexual jealousy? Common. In a survey of 103 women at various stages of involvement in an intimate relationship, 3 out of 4 reported feelings of jealousy (Pines & Aronson, 1983). Fifty-four percent described themselves as jealous. Women who were in nonmonogamous relationships or were dissatisfied with their relationships were more likely to describe themselves as jealous. A typical situation that prompted jealousy was a party at which the woman's partner spent time talking to, or dancing or flirting with, other women.

What causes jealousy? In some cases, people become mistrustful of their current partners because their former partners had cheated. Jealousy may also derive from low self-esteem or a lack of self-confidence. People with low self-esteem may experience sexual jealousy because they become overly dependent on their partners. They may also fear that they will not be able to find another partner if their present lover leaves.

White (1981) has concluded from his research on jealousy that feelings of inadequacy lead to jealousy in women. In men, the reverse seems to be the case. For men, that is, feelings of jealousy tend to give rise to feelings of inadequacy. It is as though jealousy leads them to question whether they are worthy of their partners' affections. For both men and women, however, feelings of jealousy can lead to perceiving anyone as a rival, which can make them continually mistrustful.

Unfortunately, many lovers—including many college students—play jealousy games. They let their partners know that they are attracted to other people. They flirt openly and even manufacture tales to make their partners pay more attention to them, to test the relationship, to inflict pain, or to take revenge for a partner's disloyalty.

The D's—Deterioration

Deterioration is the fourth stage of a relationship. It is not necessarily a stage that we seek, and it is certainly not an inevitability. Positive factors that can deter or slow deterioration include putting time and energy into the relationship, striving to cultivate the relationship, and showing patience—for example, giving the relationship a reasonable opportunity to improve. Negative factors that foster deterioration include failure to invest time and energy in the relationship, deciding to put an end to it, or simply permitting deterioration to proceed unchecked.

A relationship begins to deteriorate when one or both partners deem the relationship to be less enticing or rewarding than it had been. Couples who work toward maintaining and enhancing their relationships may find that the relationship becomes stronger and more meaningful.

ACTIVE AND PASSIVE RESPONSES TO DETERIORATION   When a couple perceives their relationship to be deteriorating, they can respond in active or passive ways. Active means of response include doing something that may enhance the relationship (such as

Will They Allow Their Relationship to Deteriorate?
Deterioration is the fourth stage in a relationship. We can deter or slow deterioration in our relationships by putting time and energy into them and giving them a reasonable opportunity to improve. We can hasten deterioration by refusing to invest the necessary time and energy, by deciding to end the relationship, or by simply allowing the deterioration to proceed without making an effort to stop it.

working on improving communication skills, negotiating differences, or seeking professional help) or making a decision to end the relationship. Passive methods of responding are basically characterized by waiting for something to happen, by just doing nothing. People can sit back passively and wait for the relationship to improve on its own (once in a great while, it does) or for the relationship to deteriorate to the point at which it ends. ("Don't look at me; these things happen.")

It is irrational (and damaging to a relationship) to assume that suitable relationships require no investment of time and effort. No two people are matched perfectly. Unless one member of a couple does double duty as a doormat, inevitable frictions will surface. When problems arise, it is better to work to resolve them than to act as if they don't exist and hope that they will disappear of their own accord.

The E's—Ending

Ending is the fifth and final stage of a relationship. Although it may be the ultimate stage of development, like deterioration, it need not be inevitable or desirable. Various factors can prevent a deteriorating relationship from ending. For example, people who continue to find some sources of satisfaction, who are committed to maintaining the relationship, or who believe that they will eventually be able to overcome their problems are more likely to invest what they must to prevent the collapse.

According to social-exchange theory, relationships draw to a close when negative forces are in sway—when the partners find little satisfaction in the affiliation, when the barriers to leaving the relationship are low (that is, the social, religious, and financial constraints are manageable), and especially when alternative partners are available (Karney & Bradbury, 1995).

The swan song of a relationship is not always a bad thing. When people are definitely incompatible, and when genuine attempts to preserve the relationship have faltered, ending the relationship can offer each partner a chance for happiness with someone else.

Reflections

■ What opening lines, if any, have you used to begin relationships? Do you find it difficult to make small talk? Why or why not?

■ Have you ever had trouble deciding how much intimate information to disclose to a dating partner? What are the dangers in disclosing too much too soon to a partner? Are there some things that you believe you should never share with a partner?

■ Have you ever experienced feelings of jealousy? How did they affect your relationship? Your self-esteem? Did you handle the feelings well? Why or why not?

LONELINESS: "ALL THE LONELY PEOPLE, WHERE DO THEY ALL COME FROM?"

Many people start relationships because of loneliness. Loneliness and being alone are not synonymous. Loneliness is a state of painful isolation, of feeling cut off from others. Being alone, a state of solitude, can be quite desirable, since it allows us to work, study, or reflect on the world around us. Solitude is usually a matter of choice; loneliness is not.

Lonely people tend to spend a lot of time by themselves, eat dinner alone, spend weekends alone, and participate in few social activities. They are unlikely to date. Some lonely people report having many friends, but a closer look suggests that these "friendships" are shallow. Lonely people are unlikely to share confidences. Loneliness tends to peak during adolescence. This is when most young people begin to supplant family ties with peer relationships. Loneliness is often connected with feelings of depression and with feelings of being "sick at heart."

Loneliness is even reported among some married people. In one study (Sadava & Matejcic, 1987), lonely wives tended to feel less liking and love for their partners and expressed less marital satisfaction. Lonely husbands reported less liking for their wives and less intimacy in their relationships.

Causes of Loneliness

The causes of loneliness are many and complex. Lonely people tend to have several of the following characteristics:

1. *Lack of social skills.* Lonely people often lack the interpersonal skills needed to make friends or to cope with disagreements.
2. *Lack of interest in other people.*
3. *Lack of empathy.*
4. *Fear of rejection.* This fear is often connected with self-criticism of social skills and expectations of failure in relating to others (Schultz & Moore, 1984).
5. *Failure to disclose personal information to potential friends* (Solano et al., 1982).
6. *Cynicism about human nature* (e.g., seeing people as being only out for themselves).
7. *Demanding too much too soon.* They perceive other people as cold and unfriendly in the early stages of a relationship.
8. *General pessimism.* When we expect the worst, we often get . . . you guessed it.
9. *An external locus of control.* That is, they do not see themselves as being capable of taking their lives into their own hands and achieving their goals.

It is true that many people remain lonely because they fear being rejected by others. ■

Truth or Fiction?
REVISITED

Coping with Loneliness

Psychologists have helped people to cope with loneliness by fostering more adaptive ways of thinking and behaving. Lonely people often have distorted views of other people. They may have one or two unfortunate experiences and jump to the conclusion that people are generally selfish and not worth the effort of getting involved. Let's face it: Some people *are* basically out for themselves, but the expectation that everyone is can perpetuate loneliness by motivating avoidance of social activities.

What can you do to deal with loneliness in your own life? We are all different, and the methods that might help one person might not aid another. But here is a list of suggestions compiled by Rathus and Fichner-Rathus (1997):

1. *Challenge your feelings of pessimism.* Adopt the attitude that things happen when you make them happen.
2. *Challenge your cynicism about human nature.* Yes, lots of people are selfish and not worth knowing, but if you assume that all people are like that, you can doom yourself to a lifetime of loneliness. Your task is to find people who possess the qualities that you value.
3. *Challenge the idea that failure in social relationships is awful and is therefore a valid reason for giving up on them.* Sure, social rejection can be painful, but unless you happen to be Brad Pitt or Kate Winslet, you might not appeal to everyone. We must all learn to live with some rejection. But keep looking for the people who possess the qualities you value and who will find things of equal value in you.
4. *Follow the suggestions for improving your date-seeking skills spelled out in the What Do You Say Now? feature.* Sit down at a table with people in the cafeteria, not off in a corner by yourself. Smile and say hi to people who interest you. Practice opening lines for different occasions—and a few follow-up lines. Try them out in the mirror.
5. *Make numerous social contacts.* Join committees for student activities. Try intramural sports. Join social-action groups, such as environmental groups and community betterment groups. Join clubs, such as the photography club or the ski club. Get on the school yearbook or newspaper staff.
6. *Be assertive.* Express your genuine opinions.
7. *Become a good listener.* Ask people how they're doing. Ask them for their opinions about classes, politics, or the campus events of the day. Then actually *listen* to what they have to say. Tolerate diverse opinions; remember that no two of us are identical in our outlooks (not even your "perfectly" matched first and third authors). Maintain eye contact. Keep your face friendly. (No, you don't have to remain neutral and friendly if someone becomes insulting toward a religious or ethnic group.)
8. *Give people the chance to know you.* Exchange opinions and talk about your interests. Yes, you'll turn some people off—who doesn't?—but how else will you learn whether you and another person share common ground?
9. *Fight fair.* Friends will inevitably disappoint you, and you'll want to tell them about it. Do so, but fairly. You can start by asking whether it's okay to be open about something. Then say, "I feel upset because you. . . ." You can ask your friend whether he or she realized that his or her behavior upset you. Try to work together to find a way to avoid recurrences. Finish by thanking your friend for helping you to resolve the problem.
10. *Remember that you're worthy of friends.* It's true—warts and all. None of us is perfect. We're all unique, but you might connect with more people than you imagine. Give people a chance.
11. *Use your college counseling center.* Many thousands of students are lonely but don't know what to do about it. Others just cannot find the courage to approach others. College counseling centers are very familiar with the problem of loneliness, and you should consider them a valuable resource. You might even ask whether there's a group at the center for students seeking to improve their dating or social skills.

Reflections

■ What is the difference between loneliness and solitude?
■ Have you ever been lonely? What were the reasons for it?
■ Did you do anything to overcome your loneliness? What? Would you now do anything differently?

Trusting and Caring. Trusting and caring are key ingredients of an intimate relationship. Trust gives partners the security they need to disclose intimate feelings. Caring is an emotional connection that allows intimacy to develop.

INTIMACY

Intimacy involves feelings of emotional closeness and connectedness with another person and the desire to share each other's inmost thoughts and feelings. Intimate relationships are also characterized by attitudes of mutual trust, caring, and acceptance.

Sternberg's (1986) triangular theory of love (see Chapter 7) regards intimacy as a basic component of romantic love. But people can be intimate and not in love, at least not in romantic love. Close friends and family members become emotionally intimate when they care deeply for each other and share their private feelings and experiences. It is not necessary for people to be *sexually* intimate to have an emotionally intimate relationship. Nor does sexual intimacy automatically produce emotional intimacy. People who are sexually involved may still fail to touch each other's lives in emotionally intimate ways. Even couples who fall in love may not be able to forge an intimate relationship because of unwillingness or inability to exchange inmost thoughts and feelings. Sometimes, husbands or wives share greater emotional intimacy with friends than with their spouses.

It is true that people can have intimate relationships without being sexually intimate. Close friends and relatives can have nonsexual but intimate relationships. ■

Truth or Fiction?
REVISITED

Let us now consider some of the factors that are involved in building and maintaining intimate relationships.

Knowing and Liking Yourself

Some social scientists suggest that an initial step toward intimacy with others is getting to know and like yourself. By coming to know and value yourself, you identify your inmost feelings and needs and develop the security to share them.

Trusting and Caring

Two of the most important ingredients of an intimate relationship are trust and caring. When trust exists in a relationship, partners feel secure that disclosing intimate feelings will not lead to ridicule, rejection, or other kinds of harm. Trust usually builds gradually

Intimacy Feelings of closeness and connectedness that are marked by sharing of inmost thoughts and feelings.

as partners learn whether or not it is safe to share confidences. Caring is an emotional bond that allows intimacy to develop. In caring relationships, partners seek to gratify each other's needs and interests.

Tenderness is expressed by putting one's arm around a partner's shoulder to offer support or by verbalizations of love, caring, and appreciation. In romantic relationships, tenderness also takes the form of kissing, hugging, cuddling, and holding hands.

Being Honest

Since intimacy involves the sharing of one's inmost thoughts and feelings, honesty is a core feature of intimacy. Without honesty, partners see only each other's facades. A person need not be an "open book" to develop and maintain intimacy, however. Some aspects of experience are kept even from one's most intimate partners, for they may be too embarrassing or threatening to reveal (Kammeyer et al., 1990). For example, we would not expect partners to disclose every passing sexual fantasy.

Intimate relationships thus usually involve balances in which some things are revealed and others are not. Total honesty could devastate a relationship. It would not be reasonable, for example, to expect intimate partners to divulge the details of past sexual experiences. The recipient might wonder, "Why is Kimball telling me this? Am I as good a lover as _____? Is Kimball still in love with _____? What else did Kimball do with _____?" Discretion thus also buttresses intimate relationships. As Gordon and Snyder (1989) put it, "Honesty means *saying what you mean*, not revealing every detail" (p. 24). Nor is intimacy established by frank but brutal criticism, even if it is honest.

Making a Commitment

Have you ever noticed that people may open up to strangers on airplanes or trains yet find it hard to talk openly with people to whom they are closest? An intimate relationship involves more than the isolated act of baring one's soul to a stranger. Truly intimate relationships are marked by commitment or resolve to maintain the relationship through thick and thin. When we open up to strangers on a plane, we know that it is unlikely that we will have to face them again.

This does not mean that intimate relationships require indefinite or lifelong commitments. A commitment, however, carries an obligation that the couple will work to overcome problems in the relationship rather than run for the exit at the first sign of trouble.

Maintaining Individuality When the *I* Becomes *We*

In committed relationships, a delicate balance exists between individuality and mutuality. In healthy unions, a strong sense of togetherness does not eradicate individuality. Partners in such relationships remain free to be themselves. Neither seeks to dominate or submerge himself or herself into the personality of the other. Each partner maintains individual interests, likes and dislikes, needs and goals.

Communicating

Good communication is another hallmark of an intimate relationship. Partners are able to share their most personal thoughts and feelings clearly and honestly. Communication is a two-way street. It embraces sending and receiving messages. The good communicator is therefore a skilled listener as well as a clear speaker (Tannen, 1990). We generally associate communication with *talk*, which involves the use of verbal messages to convey a thought or a feeling. Through talk, the speaker *encodes* a thought or a feeling into words. The listener *decodes* the words to extract the meaning of the message. Problems in verbal communication can arise at several levels:

1. *The speaker might use words differently than the listener, leading to misunderstandings or miscommunication.* For example, the speaker might say, "You look really cute tonight." The listener might object, saying, "You think I look *cute*? What's wrong with the way I look?" The speaker protests, "No, I didn't mean it that way. I meant you look good. Yes, good."

2. *The speaker's words might not match his or her tone of voice, facial expression, or body gestures.* For example, the speaker says, "Darling, I really *don't mind* if we visit your mother this weekend." But the speaker did not say, "I really *want* to visit your mother," and the words "don't mind" come across as a kind of snarl. In such cases, the listener is likely to place greater weight on *how* something is said than on *what* is said.

3. *The speaker might not be able to put into words what he or she truly means or feels.* Sometimes, we grasp for words to express our feelings, but they do not come, or those that do come miss the mark.

NONVERBAL COMMUNICATION: THE BODY SPEAKS   Though the spoken word is a primary form of communication, we often express our feelings through nonverbal channels as well, such as by tone of voice, gestures, body posture, and facial expressions (Tannen, 1990). People may place more weight on how words are said than on their denotative meaning. People also accentuate the meaning of their words through gestures, raising or lowering their voices, or using a sterner or softer tone of voice.

Nonverbal communication is used not only to accentuate the spoken word, but also to directly express feelings. We sometimes are better able to convey our feelings through body language than by the use of words. A touch or a gaze into someone's eyes may express more about our feelings than words can. Parents express feelings of tenderness and caring toward infants by hugging, holding, and caressing them and by speaking in a gentle and soothing tone of voice, even though the meanings of the words cannot yet be grasped.

Let us examine some aspects of nonverbal communication:

Communicating. Good communication is an aspect of an intimate relationship. Partners share their most personal thoughts and feelings by communicating. We generally associate communication with talking, but we also express our feelings through nonverbal channels as well, including our tone of voice, our gestures, our body posture, and facial expressions. Sometimes the ways in which we express our words are as important, or more important, than the words themselves.

On Being Uptight and Hanging Loose   The ways in which people carry themselves offer cues about their feelings and potential actions. People who are emotionally uptight often stand or sit rigidly and straight-backed. People who feel relaxed more literally "hang loose."

People who face us and lean toward us are in effect saying that they like us or care about what we are saying. If we overhear a conversation between a couple and see that the woman is leaning toward the man but he is leaning back and playing with his hair, we tend to infer that he is not accepting what she is saying or has lost interest.

Touching   Touching is a powerful form of communication. Women are more apt than men to touch the people with whom they interact. When touching suggests too much intimacy, however, it can be annoying. Touching may also establish "property rights" over one's partner. People may touch their partners in public or hold their hands, not as a sign of affection, but as a signal to others that their partners are taken and that others should keep a respectful distance. Similarly, the wearing of an engagement or wedding ring signals unavailability.

Gazing and Staring: The Look of Love? We gather information about the motives, feelings, and attitudes of others through eye contact. In Western culture, looking other people "squarely in the eye"—at least among men—is positively valued. People who do so appear self-assertive, direct, and candid. When people look away, they may be perceived as shy, deceitful, or depressed. In some Asian cultures, however, looking other people directly in the eye might seem to be an aggressive invasion.

Unaggressive gazing into another person's eyes—especially the eyes of a person whom one considers attractive—can create deep feelings of intimacy in our culture. In a laboratory study, couples who had just met were instructed to gaze into each other's eyes for two minutes. Afterward, many reported experiencing feelings of passion (Kellerman et al., 1989). Is this what is meant by "the look of love"?

All in all, there are many ways in which we communicate with others through verbal and nonverbal channels. Let us now look at ways in which partners can learn to communicate better with each other, especially about sex. Many couples, even couples who are able to share deepest thoughts and feelings, may flounder at communicating their sexual needs and preferences. Couples who have lived together for decades may know each other's tastes in food, music, and movies about as well as they know their own but still be hesitant to share their sexual likes and dislikes (Havemann & Lehtinen, 1990). They may also be reluctant, for fear of opening wounds in the relationship, to exchange their feelings about other aspects of their relationship, including each other's habits, appearance, and gender-stereotypical attitudes.

Reflections

- What are the various meanings of *intimacy*? Are you or have you been involved in an intimate relationship?
- Do you touch people when you are communicating with them? How do you touch them? What does the touching mean?
- Have you ever stared at anyone you disliked? What was the message of your eye contact? Have you ever gazed into the eyes of someone who appealed to you? What was the message of this eye contact?

COMMUNICATION SKILLS FOR ENHANCING RELATIONSHIPS AND SEXUAL RELATIONS

Marital counselors and sex therapists might be as busy as the proverbial Maytag *repairperson*[2] if more couples communicated with each other about their sexual feelings. Unfortunately, when it comes to sex, *talk* may be the most overlooked four-letter word.

Many couples suffer for years because one or both partners are unwilling to speak up. Or problems arise when one partner misinterprets the other. One partner might interpret the other's groans or grimaces of pleasure as signs of pain and pull back during sex, leaving the other frustrated. Improved communication may be no panacea, but it helps. Clear communication can take the guesswork out of relationships, avert misunderstandings, relieve resentments and frustrations, and increase both sexual and general satisfaction with the relationship.

---

[2]"A bow in the direction of political correctness?" asks the third author.

Common Difficulties in Sexual Communication

Why is it so difficult for couples to communicate about sex? Here are some possibilities:

ON "MAKING WHOOPIE"—IS SEX TALK VULGAR? Vulgarity, like beauty, is to some degree in the eye (or ear) of the beholder. One couple's vulgarity may be another couple's love talk. Some people may maintain a Victorian belief that any talk about sex is not fit for mixed company, even between intimate partners. Sex, that is, is something you may do, but not something to be talked about. Other couples may be willing in principle to talk about sex but find the reality difficult because of the lack of an agreeable, common language.

How, for example, are they to refer to their genitals or to sexual activities? One partner might prefer to use coarse four-letter (or five-letter) words to refer to them. The other might prefer more clinical terms. A partner who prefers slang for the sexual organs might be regarded by the other as vulgar or demeaning. (But as the forbidden fruit is often the sweetest, some people feel sexually aroused when they or their partners "talk dirty.") One who uses clinical terms, such as fellatio or coitus, might be regarded as, well, clinical. Some couples try to find a common verbal ground, one that is not vulgar at one extreme or clinical at the other. They might speak, for example, of "doing it" rather than "engaging in sexual intercourse." (The title of the Eddie Cantor musical of the 1930s suggests that some people once spoke of "making whoopie.") Or they might speak of "kissing me down there" rather than practicing fellatio or cunnilingus.

In some cases of gross mismatch in partners' choices for the language of love, the differences run much deeper than choice of words.

ON IRRATIONAL BELIEFS Many couples also harbor irrational beliefs about relationships and sex, such as the notion that people should somehow *know* what their partners want, without having to ask. The common misconception that people should know what pleases their partners undercuts communication. Men, in particular, seem burdened with the stereotype that they should have a natural expertise at sex. Women might think that it is "unladylike" to talk openly about their sexual needs and feelings. Both partners might hold the idealized romantic notion that "love is all you need" to achieve sexual happiness. But such knowledge does not arise from instinct nor love. It is learned—or it remains unknown.

A related irrational belief is that "my partner will read my mind." We might erroneously assume that if our partners truly loved us, they would somehow instinctively know what types of sexual stimulation we desire. Unfortunately, or fortunately, others cannot read our minds. We must assume the responsibility for communicating our preferences.

It is not true that "love is all you need." Even when partners truly love each other, they do not instinctively know how to satisfy each other sexually. Communication is required. ■

Truth or Fiction?
REVISITED

Some people communicate more effectively than others, perhaps because they are more sensitive to others' needs or because their parents served as good models as communicators. But communication skills can be acquired at any time. Learning takes time and work, but the following guidelines should prove helpful if you want to enhance your communication skills. The skills discussed can also be used to improve communication in areas of intimate relationships other than the sexual.

Getting Started

How do you broach tough topics? Here are some ideas.

TALKING ABOUT TALKING You can start by talking about talking. You can inform your partner that it is difficult for you to talk about problems and conflicts: "You know, I've always found it awkward to find a way of bringing things up" or "You know, I think other people have an easier time than I do when it comes to talking about some things." You can allude to troublesome things that happened in the past when you attempted to resolve conflicts. This approach encourages your partner to invite you to proceed.

Broaching the topic of sex is perhaps the most difficult step in communicating with your partner. Couples who gab endlessly about their finances, their children, their work, and their hobbies suddenly clam up when sex comes up. So it might be helpful for you and your partner to first agree to talk about talking about sex. You can begin by admitting that it is hard or embarrassing for you to talk about sex. You can say that your sexual relationship is important to you and that you want to do everything you can to enhance it. Gently probe your partner's willingness to set aside time to talk about sex, preferably when you can dim the lights and not be interrupted.

The "right time" may be when you are both relaxed, rested, and unpressed for time. The "right place" can be any place where you can enjoy privacy and go undisturbed. Sex talk need not be limited to the bedroom. Couples may feel more comfortable talking about sex over dinner, when cuddling on the sofa, or when just relaxing together.

REQUESTING PERMISSION TO BRING UP A TOPIC Another possibility is to request permission to raise an issue. You can say something like this: "There's something on my mind. Do you have a few minutes? Is now a good time to tell you about it?" Or you can say, "There's something that we need to talk about, but I'm not sure how to bring it up. Can you help me with it?"

GIVING YOUR PARTNER PERMISSION TO SAY SOMETHING THAT MIGHT BE UPSETTING TO YOU You can tell your partner that it is okay to point out ways in which you can become a more effective lover. For example, you can say, "I know that you don't want to hurt my feelings, but I wonder if I'm doing anything that you'd rather I didn't do?"

Active Listening. Effective communication requires listening to the other person's side. We can listen actively rather than passively by maintaining eye contact and showing that we understand the other person's feelings and ideas.

Listening to the Other Side

Skilled listening involves such skills as active listening, paraphrasing, the use of reinforcement, and valuing your partner even when the two of you disagree.

LISTENING ACTIVELY To listen actively rather than passively, first adopt the attitude that you may actually learn something—or perceive things from another vantage point—by listening. Second, recognize that even though the other person is doing the talking, you need not sit back passively. In other words, it is not helpful to stare off into space while your partner is talking or to offer a begrudging "Mm-hmm" now and then to be polite. Instead, you can listen actively by maintaining eye contact and modifying your facial expression to show that you understand his or her feelings and ideas. For example, nod your head when appropriate.

Listening actively also involves asking helpful questions, such as "Would you please give me an example?" or "Was that good for you?"

An active listener does not simply hear what the other person is saying, but also focuses attentively on the speaker's words and gestures to grasp meaning. Nonverbal cues may reveal more about the speaker's inner feelings than the spoken word. Good listeners do not interrupt, change the topic, or walk away when their partners are speaking.

PARAPHRASING Paraphrasing shows that you understand what your partner is trying to say. In paraphrasing, you recast or restate the speaker's words to confirm your comprehension. For example, if your partner says, "You hardly ever say anything when we're making love. I don't want you to scream or make obligatory grunts, or do something silly, but sometimes I wonder if I'm trying to make love to a brick wall." You can paraphrase it by saying something like this: "So it's sort of hard to know if I'm really enjoying it."

REINFORCING THE OTHER PERSON FOR COMMUNICATING   Even when you disagree with what your partner is saying, you can maintain good relations and keep channels of communication open by saying something like "I really appreciate your taking the time to try to work this out with me" or "I hope you'll think it's okay if I don't see things entirely in the same way, but I'm glad that we had a chance to talk about it."

SHOWING THAT YOU VALUE YOUR PARTNER, EVEN WHEN THE TWO OF YOU DIS-AGREE   When you disagree with your partner, do so in a way that shows that you still value your partner as a person. In other words, say something like "I love you very much, but it annoys me when you. . . ." rather than "You're really contemptible for doing . . . ." By doing so, you encourage your partner to disclose sensitive material without fear of personal attack or the risk of losing your love or support.

Learning About Your Partner's Needs

Listening is basic to learning about another person's needs, but sometimes it helps to go a few steps further.

ASKING QUESTIONS TO DRAW THE OTHER PERSON OUT   You can ask open-ended questions that allow for a broader exploration of issues, such as these:

"What do you like best about the way we make love?"
"Do you think that I do things to bug you?"
"Does it bother you that I go to bed later than you do?"
"Does anything disappoint you about our relationship?"
"Do you think that I do things that are inconsiderate when you're studying for a test?"

Closed-ended questions that call for a limited range of responses would be most useful when you're looking for a simple yes-or-no type of response, such as "Would you rather make love with the stereo off?"

USING SELF-DISCLOSURE   Self-disclosure is essential to developing intimacy. You can also use self-disclosure to learn more about your partner's needs, because communicating your own feelings and ideas invites reciprocation. For example, you might say, "There are times when I feel that I disappoint you when we make love. Should I be doing something differently?"

GRANTING PERMISSION FOR THE OTHER PERSON TO SAY SOMETHING THAT MIGHT UPSET YOU   You can ask your partner to level with you about an irksome issue. You can say that you recognize that it might be awkward to discuss it but that you will try your best to listen conscientiously and not get too disturbed. You can also limit communication to one such difficult issue per conversation. If the entire emotional dam were to burst, the job of mopping up could be overwhelming.

Providing Information

There are many skillful ways of communicating information, including accentuating the positive and using verbal and nonverbal cues. When you want to get something across, remember that it is irrational to expect that your partner can read your mind. He or she can tell when you're wearing a grumpy face, but your expression does not provide much information about your specific feelings. When your partner asks, "What would you like me to do?" responding with "Well, I think you can figure out what I want" or "Just do whatever you think is best" is not very helpful. Only you know what pleases you. Your partner is not a mind reader.

ACCENTUATING THE POSITIVE   Let your partner know when he or she is doing something right! Speak up or find another way to express your appreciation. Accentuating the positive is rewarding and also informs your partner about what pleases you. In other words, don't just wait around until your partner does something wrong and then seize the opportunity to complain!

USING VERBAL CUES   Sexual activity provides an excellent opportunity for direct communication. You can say something like "Oh, that's great" or "Don't stop." Or you can ask for feedback, as in "How does that feel?"

Feedback provides direct guidance about what is pleasing. Partners can also make specific requests and suggestions.

USING NONVERBAL CUES   Sexual communication also occurs without words. Couples learn to interpret each other's facial expressions as signs of pleasure, boredom, even disgust. Our body language also communicates our likes and dislikes. Our partners might lean toward us or away from us when we touch them, or they might relax or tense up; in any case, they speak volumes in silence.

The following exercises can help couples to use nonverbal cues to communicate their sexual likes and dislikes. Sex therapists use similar exercises to help couples with sexual dysfunctions.

1. *Taking turns petting.* Taking turns petting can help partners to learn what turns one another on. Each partner takes turns caressing the other, stopping frequently enough to receive feedback by asking questions like "How does that feel?" The recipient is responsible for giving feedback, which can be expressed either verbally ("Yes, that's it—yes, just like that" or "No, a little lighter than that") or nonverbally, as by making certain appreciative or disapproving sounds. Verbal feedback is usually more direct and less prone to misinterpretation. The knowledge that is gained through this exercise can be incorporated into the couple's regular pattern of lovemaking.
2. *Directing your partner's hand.* Gently guiding your partner's hand—to show your partner where and how you like to be touched—is a most direct way of communicating sexual likes. While taking turns petting, and during other acts of lovemaking, one partner can gently guide the other's fingers and hands through the most satisfying strokes and caresses. Women might show partners how to caress the breasts or clitoral shaft in this manner. Men might cup their partners' hands to show them how to stroke the penile shaft or caress the testes.
3. *Signaling.* Couples can use agreed-upon nonverbal cues to signal sexual pleasure. For example, one partner might rub the other in a certain way or tap the other to signal that something is being done right. The recipient of the signal takes mental notes and incorporates the pleasurable stimulation into the couple's lovemaking. This is a sort of hit-or-miss technique, but even near misses can be rewarding.

Making Requests

A basic part of improving relationships or lovemaking is asking partners to change their behavior—to do something differently or to stop doing something that hurts or is ungratifying. The skill of making requests now comes to the fore.

BEING SPECIFIC   Be specific in requesting changes. Telling your partner something like "I'd like you to be nicer to me" might accomplish little. Your partner might not know that his or her behavior is *not* nice and might not understand how to be "nicer." It is better to say something like "I would appreciate it if you would get coffee for yourself, or at least ask me in a more pleasant way" or "I really have a hard time with the way you talk to me in front of your friends. It's as if you're trying to show them that you have control over me or something." Similarly, it may be less effective to say, "I'd like you to be more loving" than to say, "When we make love, I'd like you to kiss me more and tell me how you care about me."

Of course, you can precede your specific requests with openers such as "There's something on my mind. Is this a good time for me to bring it up with you?"

USING "I-Talk" Using the word *I* is an excellent way of expressing your feelings. Psychologists who help people to become more assertive often encourage them to use the words *I*, *me*, and *my* in their speech, not just to express their feelings, but to buttress their sense of self-worth.

You are more likely to achieve desired results by framing requests in *I*-talk than by heaping criticisms on your partner. For example, "I would like it if we spent some time cuddling after sex" is superior to "You don't seem to care enough about me to want to hold me after we make love." Saying "I find it very painful when you use a harsh voice with me" is probably more effective than "Sometimes people's feelings get hurt when their boyfriends [girlfriends] speak to them harshly in front of their friends or families."

You might find it helpful to try out *I*-talk in front of a mirror or with a confidant before using it with your partner. In this way, you can see whether your facial expression and tone of voice are consistent with what you are saying. Friends may also provide pointers on the content of what you are saying.

Delivering Criticism

Delivering criticism effectively is a skill. It requires focusing partners' attention on the problem without inducing resentment or defensiveness or reducing them to trembling masses of guilt or fear.

EVALUATING YOUR MOTIVES First, weigh your goals forthrightly. Is your primary intention to punish your partner, or are you more interested in gaining cooperation? If your goal is punishment, you may as well be coarse and disparaging, but expect reprisals. If your goal is to improve the relationship, however, a tactful approach is in order.

PICKING THE RIGHT TIME AND PLACE Deliver criticism privately—not in front of friends or family. Your partner has a right to be upset when you make criticism public. Making private matters public induces indignation and cuts off communication.

BEING SPECIFIC   Being specific may be even more important when delivering criticism than when making requests. By being specific about the *behavior* that disturbs you, you bypass the trap of disparaging your partner's personality or motives. For example, it is probably more effective to say, "I could lose this job because you didn't write down the message" than to say, "You're completely irresponsible" or "You're a flake." Similarly, you might achieve better results by saying "The bathroom looks and smells dirty when you throw your underwear on the floor" rather than "You're a filthy pig." It is more to the point (and less intimidating) to complain about specific, modifiable behavior than to try to overhaul another person's personality.

EXPRESSING DISPLEASURE IN TERMS OF YOUR OWN FEELINGS   Your partner is likely to feel less threatened if you express displeasure in terms of your own feelings than if you directly attack his or her personality. Attacks often arouse defensive behavior, and sometimes retaliation, rather than enhance relationships. In confronting your partner for failing to be sensitive to your sexual needs when making love, it is likely to be more effective to say, "You know, it really upsets me that you don't seem to care about my feelings when we make love" than to say, "You're so wrapped up in yourself that you never think about anyone else."

KEEPING CRITICISM AND COMPLAINTS TO THE PRESENT   How many times have you been in an argument and heard things like "You never appreciated me!" or "Last summer you did the same thing!" Bringing up the past during conflicts muddles current issues and heightens resentments. When your partner forgets to jot down the details of the telephone message, it is more useful to note that "This was a vital phone call" than "Three weeks ago you didn't tell me about the phone call from Chris, and as a result I missed out on seeing *Home Alone: The College Years*." It's better to leave who did what to whom last year (or even last week) alone. Focus on the present.

EXPRESSING CRITICISM CONSTRUCTIVELY   Be sensitive to your partner's needs by avoiding blunt criticisms or personal attacks and by suggesting constructive alternatives. Avoid saying things like "You're really a lousy lover." Say instead, "Can I take your hand and show you what I'd like?" As a rule of thumb, unless you can criticize your partner constructively, it may be best not to criticize at all.

EXPRESSING CRITICISM POSITIVELY   Whenever possible, express criticism positively, and combine it with a concrete request. When commenting upon the lack of affection your partner displays during lovemaking, say, "I love it when you kiss me. Please kiss me more" rather than "You never kiss me when we're in bed and I'm sick of it."

Receiving Criticism

> Honest criticism is hard to take, particularly from a relative, a friend, an acquaintance, or a stranger.
> —Franklin P. Jones

Delivering criticism can be tricky, especially when you want to inspire cooperation. Receiving criticism can be even trickier. Nevertheless, the following suggestions offer some help.

CLARIFYING YOUR GOALS   When you hear "It's time you did something about . . . ," it would be understandable if the hair on the backs of your arms did a headstand. After all, it's a blunt challenge. When we are confronted harshly, we are likely to become defensive and think of retaliating. But if your objective is to enhance the relationship, take a few moments to stop and think. To resolve conflicts, we need to learn about the other person's concerns, keep lines of communication open, and find ways of changing problem behavior.

So when your partner says, "It's about time you did something about the bathroom," stop and think before you summon up your most menacing voice and say, "Just what the hell is that supposed to mean?" Ask yourself what you want to find out.

ASKING CLARIFYING QUESTIONS   Just as it's important to be specific when delivering criticism, it helps if you encourage the other person to be specific when you are on the receiving end of criticism. In the example of the complaint about the bathroom, you can help your partner to be specific and can, perhaps, avert the worst by asking clarifying questions such as "Can you tell me exactly what you mean?" or "The bathroom?"

Consider a situation in which a lover says something like "You know, you're one of the most irritating people I know." Rather than retaliate and perhaps hurt the relationship further, you can say something like "How about forgoing the character assassination and telling me what I did that's bothering you?" This response assertively requests an end to insults and asks that your partner be specific.

ACKNOWLEDGING THE CRITICISM   Even when you disagree with a criticism, you can keep lines of communication open and show some respect for your partner's feelings by acknowledging and paraphrasing the criticism.

On the other hand, if you are at fault, you can acknowledge that forthrightly. For example, you can say, "You're right. It was my day to clean the bathroom and it totally slipped my mind" or "I was so busy, I just couldn't get to it." Now the two of you should look for a way to work out the problem. When you acknowledge criticism, you cue your partner to back off a bit and look for ways to improve the situation. But what if your partner then becomes abusive and says something like "So you admit you blew it?" You might then try a little education in conflict resolution. You could say, "I admitted that I was at fault. If you're willing to work with me to find a way to handle it, great. But I'm not going to let you pound me into the ground over it."

REJECTING THE CRITICISM   If you think that you were not at fault, express your feelings. Use *I*-talk and be specific. Don't seize the opportunity to angrily point out your partner's shortcomings. By doing so, you may shut down lines of communication.

NEGOTIATING DIFFERENCES   Negotiate your differences if you feel that there is merit on both sides of the argument. You might want to say something like "Would it help if I . . . ?" And if there's something about your obligation to clean the bathroom that seems totally out of place, perhaps you and your partner can work out an exchange—that is, you get relieved of cleaning the bathroom in exchange for tackling a chore that your partner finds equally odious.

If none of these approaches helps to resolve the conflict, consider the possibility that your partner is using the comment about the bathroom as a way of expressing anger over other issues. You might find out by saying something like "I've been trying to find a way to resolve this thing, but nothing I say seems to be helping. Is this really about the bathroom, or are there other things on your mind?"

Notice that we haven't suggested that you seize the opportunity to strike back by saying, "Who're you to complain about the bathroom? What about your breath and that pigsty you call your closet?" Retaliation is tempting and might make you feel good in the short run, but it can do a relationship more harm than good in the long run.

It is not true that retaliation is the best course of action if you are criticized. Retaliation is an inferior way to handle criticism—that is, if your goal is to resolve conflict. ■

Truth or Fiction?
REVISITED

When Communication Is Not Enough: Handling Impasses

Communication helps to build and maintain relationships, but sometimes partners have profound, substantial disagreements. In fact, it is normal to have disagreements from time to time. Even when their communication skills are superbly tuned, partners now and then reach an impasse.

Opening the lines of communication may also elicit hidden frustrations. These frustrations can lead partners to seriously question the value of continuing the relationship or to agree to consult a helping professional. Though some people believe that it is best to "let sleeping dogs lie," the *skillful* airing of dissatisfactions can be healthful for a relationship. Couples who reach an impasse can follow several courses of action that might be helpful:

LOOKING AT THE SITUATION FROM THE OTHER PERSON'S PERSPECTIVE   Some of the conflict may be resolved by (honestly!) saying something like "I still disagree with you, but I can understand why you take your position." In this way, you recognize your partner's goodwill and perhaps lessen tensions.

SEEKING VALIDATING INFORMATION   On the other hand, if you do not follow your partner's logic, you can say something like "Please believe me: I'm trying very hard to look at this from your point of view, but I can't follow your reasoning. Would you try to help me understand your point of view?"

TAKING A BREAK   Sometimes when you reach a stalemate, it helps to allow the problem to "incubate" for a while. If you and your partner put the issue aside for a while, perhaps a resolution will dawn on one of you later on. If you wish, schedule a follow-up discussion so that the issue won't be swept under the rug.

TOLERATING DIFFERENTNESS   Although we tend to form relationships with people who share similar attitudes, there is never a perfect overlap. A partner who pretends to be your clone will most likely become a bore. If your relationship is generally rewarding and pleasurable, you might find it possible to tolerate certain differences between yourself and your partner. Respecting other people in part means allowing them to be who they are. When we have a solid sense of who we are as individuals and what we stand for, we are more apt to tolerate differentness in our partners.

Truth or Fiction?
REVISITED

Many relationships do come to an end when the partners cannot resolve their differences. However, it is possible for relationships to continue and improve even when we reach impasses. We need to be able to tolerate differentness in other people if relationships are to improve. ■

AGREEING TO DISAGREE   When all else fails, you can agree to disagree on various issues. You can remain a solid, respected individual, and your partner can remain a worthwhile, effective person even if the two of you disagree from time to time.

Disagreement is not necessarily destructive to a relationship—unless you are convinced that it must be. Two people cannot see everything in the same way. Failure to ever disagree will have to leave at least one partner feeling frustrated now and then.

Truth or Fiction?
REVISITED

It is not true that disagreement is destructive to a relationship. Everyone disagrees with her or his partner now and then (whether or not disagreements are expressed). The important thing is to try to resolve disagreements and, when they cannot be resolved, to handle the impasse productively. ■

You can handle an impasse by focusing on the things that you and your partner have in common. Presumably, there will be a number of them—some of them with little feet.

Reflections

- Have you had arguments with dates or lovers? Was part of the problem difficulty in communicating? What methods of communication discussed in this chapter might have been of help to you?
- Do you have difficulty criticizing another person or accepting criticism? Why? How can you become better at delivering or receiving criticism?
- Have you ever arrived at an impasse in a disagreement with a partner? What did you do about it? How did it work out?

THE ABC(DE)S OF ROMANTIC RELATIONSHIPS

Levinger proposes an ABCDE model of romantic relationships, which refers to five stages: attraction, building, continuation, deterioration, and ending.

The A's—Attraction
The major promoter of attraction is propinquity.

The B's—Building
Similarity in the level of physical attractiveness, similarity in attitudes, and liking motivate us to build relationships.

The C's—Continuation
Factors such as variety, caring, positive evaluations, lack of jealousy, perceived fairness in the relationship, and mutual feelings of satisfaction encourage us to continue relationships.

The D's—Deterioration
Factors that foster deterioration include failure to invest time and energy in the relationship, deciding to put an end to it, or simply permitting deterioration to proceed unchecked.

The E's—Ending
Relationships tend to end when the partners find little satisfaction in the affiliation, when alternative partners are available, when couples are not committed to preserving them, and when they expect them to falter.

LONELINESS: "ALL THE LONELY PEOPLE, WHERE DO THEY ALL COME FROM?"

Loneliness is a state of painful isolation, of feeling cut off from others.

Causes of Loneliness
The causes of loneliness include lack of social skills, lack of interest in other people, lack of empathy, fear of rejection, lack of self-disclosure, cynicism about human nature, demanding too much too soon, general pessimism, and an external locus of control.

Coping with Loneliness
People are helped to overcome loneliness by challenging self-defeating attitudes and social-skills training.

INTIMACY

Intimacy involves feelings of emotional closeness with another person and the desire to share each other's inmost thoughts and feelings.

Knowing and Liking Yourself
An initial step toward intimacy with others is getting to know and like yourself so that you can identify your inmost feelings and develop the security to share them.

Trusting and Caring
Intimate relationships require trust, caring, and tenderness.

Being Honest
Honesty is a core feature of intimacy.

Making a Commitment
Truly intimate relationships are marked by commitment, a resolve to maintain the relationship through thick and thin.

Maintaining Individuality When the *I* Becomes *We*
In healthy unions, a strong sense of togetherness does not eradicate individuality.

Communicating
Communication is a two-way street. It embraces sending and receiving messages. We often express feelings through nonverbal channels such as tone of voice, gestures, body posture, and facial expressions.

COMMUNICATION SKILLS FOR ENHANCING RELATIONSHIPS AND SEXUAL RELATIONS

Common Difficulties in Sexual Communication
Couples may find it difficult to talk about sex because of the lack of an agreeable common language. Many couples also harbor irrational beliefs about relationships and sex.

Getting Started
Ways of getting started in communicating include talking about talking, requesting permission to raise an issue, and granting one's partner permission to say things that might be upsetting.

Listening to the Other Side
Skilled listening involves elements such as active listening, paraphrasing, the use of reinforcement, and valuing your partner even when the two of you disagree.

Learning About Your Partner's Needs
You can learn about your partner's needs by asking questions, using self-disclosure, and asking your partner to level with you about an irksome issue.

Providing Information
You can provide information by "accentuating the positive" and using verbal and nonverbal cues.

Making Requests
In making requests, it is helpful to take responsibility for what happens, to be specific, to be assertive, and to use "I-talk."

Delivering Criticism
In delivering criticism, it is helpful to evaluate your motives, pick a good time and place, be specific, express displeasure in terms of your own feelings, keep complaints to the present, and express criticism constructively and positively.

Receiving Criticism
To receive criticism effectively, it is helpful to clarify goals, ask clarifying questions, acknowledge the criticism, reject inappropriate criticisms, and negotiate differences.

When Communication Is Not Enough: Handling Impasses
Partners can help to manage impasses by trying to see things from the partner's perspective, seeking validating information, taking a break, tolerating differentness, and, when necessary, agreeing to disagree.

Ekatherina Savtchenko. *Dance of Love.* 1999. Oil on canvas, 100 x 120 cm. Courtesy of Gallery Stendhal

chapter

9

Sexual Techniques and Behavior Patterns

outline

TRUTH OR FICTION?

SOLITARY SEXUAL BEHAVIOR

Masturbation

Sexual Fantasy

SEX WITH OTHERS

Foreplay

Kissing

Touching

IN THE NEW MILLENNIUM:
Sex Becomes "Interactive"

Breast Stimulation

Oral-Genital Stimulation

A WORLD OF DIVERSITY:
Sociocultural Factors and Oral Sex

Sexual Intercourse:
Positions and Techniques

A WORLD OF DIVERSITY:
*Are African Americans Sexually Permissive?
Cultural Mythology versus Some Facts*

SUMMING UP

Truth or Fiction?

_____ Married people rarely if ever masturbate.

_____ White men are more likely to masturbate than African American men are.

_____ Women who masturbate during adolescence are less likely to find gratification in marital coitus than women who do not.

_____ Women are more likely to reach orgasm through sexual intercourse than masturbation.

_____ Most women masturbate by inserting a finger or other object into the vagina.

_____ Heterosexual people do not fantasize about sexual activity with people of their own gender.

_____ Statistically speaking, oral sex is the norm for today's young married couples.

_____ African Americans are more likely than White Americans to engage in oral sex.

_____ When lovers fantasize about other people, the relationship is in trouble.

_____ Anal sex is more common among less well educated people.

t his is the chapter that describes sexual techniques and statistical breakdowns of "who does what with whom." There is great variety in human sexual expression. Some of us practice few, if any, of the techniques in the chapter. Some of us practice most or all of them. Some of us practice some of them some of the time. Our knowledge of the prevalence of these techniques comes from sex surveys that began with Kinsey and have continued with the work of Hunt, the University of Chicago group, and others. Of course, surveys are plagued by problems such as nonrepresentative sampling, social desirability, and volunteer bias. Therefore, we must be cautious in generalizing their results. Surveys provide our best "guesstimate" of the prevalence of sexual behaviors. They do not provide precise figures.

Readers of this textbook are as varied in their sexual values, preferences, and attitudes as is society in general. Some of the techniques discussed might therefore strike some readers as indecent. Our aim is to provide information about the diversity of sexual expression. We are not seeking common ground as to what is acceptable. Nor do we pass judgments or encourage readers to expand their sexual repertoires.

The human body is sensitive to many forms of sexual stimulation. Yet we reiterate the theme that biology is not destiny: A biological capacity does not impose a behavioral requirement. Cultural expectations, personal values, and individual experience— not only our biological capacities—determine our sexual behavior. What is right for you is right for you—not necessarily for your neighbor.

We begin by reviewing the techniques that people practice by themselves to derive sexual pleasure: masturbation and sexual fantasy. We then consider techniques that involve a partner.

SOLITARY SEXUAL BEHAVIOR

Various forms of sexual expression do not require a partner or are not generally practiced in the presence of a partner. Masturbation is one of the principal forms of one-person sexual expression. Masturbation involves direct stimulation of the genitals. Other forms of individual sexual experience, such as sexual fantasy, may or may not be accompanied by genital stimulation.

Masturbation

> In solitude he pollutes himself, and with his own hand blights all his prospects for both this world and the next. Even after being solemnly warned, he will often continue this worse than beastly practice, deliberately forfeiting his right to health and happiness for a moment's mad sensuality.
> —J. H. Kellogg, M.D., *Plain Facts for Old and Young*, 1888

The word *masturbation* derives from the Latin *masturbari*, from the roots for "hand" and "to defile." The derivation provides clues to historical cultural attitudes toward the practice. **Masturbation** may be practiced by manual stimulation of the genitals, perhaps with the aid of artificial stimulation, such as a vibrator. It may employ an object, such as a pillow or a **dildo**, that touches the genitals. Even before we conceive of sexual experiences with others, we may learn early in childhood that touching our genitals can produce pleasure.

Pleasure is not the only reason that people masturbate. Table 9.1 lists reasons for masturbation, according to the findings of the NHSLS study.

Within the Judeo-Christian tradition, masturbation has been strongly condemned as sinful. Early Judeo-Christian attitudes toward masturbation reflected the censure that was applied toward nonprocreative sexual acts. In the Judeo-Christian tradition, masturbation

Masturbation Sexual self-stimulation.

Dildo A penis-shaped object used in sexual activity.

t a b l e   9 . 1

Reasons for masturbation (percentage of respondents who report reason), according to the NHSLS study		
Reasons for Masturbation	**Men (%)**	**Women (%)**
To relax	26	32
To relieve sexual tension	73	63
Partners are unavailable	32	32
Partner does not want to engage in sexual activity	16	6
Boredom	11	5
To obtain physical pleasure	40	42
To help get to sleep	16	12
Fear of AIDS and other STDs	7	5
Other reasons	5	5

Source: Adapted from Laumann, E. O., Gagnon, J. H., Michael, R. T., & Michaels, S. (1994). *The social organization of sexuality: Sexual practices in the United States.* Chicago: University of Chicago Press, Table 3.3, p. 86.

has been referred to as "onanism," a name that is derived from the biblical story of Onan. According to the Book of Genesis (38:9–11), Onan was the secondborn son of Judah. Judah's first son, Er, had died without an heir. Biblical law required that if a man died without leaving a male heir, his brother must take the widow as a wife (a union called a levirate marriage) and rear their first son as his brother's heir. Judah therefore directed Onan to "Go in unto thy brother's wife, and perform the duty of a husband's brother unto her, and raise up seed to thy brother." But Onan "spilled [his seed] upon the ground" during relations with his deceased brother's wife and was struck down by God for his deed.

Though "onanism" has come to be associated with Judeo-Christian condemnation of masturbation, Onan's act was one of **coitus interruptus,** not masturbation. Both acts, however, involve nonprocreative sex—spilling the seed. Moreover, Onan's punishment seems to have more to do with his failure to fulfill his lawful obligations than with spilling his seed. Whatever its biblical origins, masturbation is prohibited under Jewish law. Historians speculate that Jews and Christians in ancient times condemned sexual practices that did not lead to pregnancy because of the need for an increase in their numbers. The need for progeny is also linked to the widespread view that coitus in marriage is the only morally acceptable avenue of sexual expression.

The history of cultural attitudes toward masturbation in Western society has been, until very recently, one of almost continual condemnation of the practice on moral and religious grounds—even on medical grounds.

HISTORICAL MEDICAL VIEWS OF MASTURBATION   Until recent years, masturbation was thought to be physically and mentally harmful, as well as degrading. The eighteenth-century physicians S. A. D. Tissot and Benjamin Rush (a signer of the Declaration of Independence) believed that masturbation caused tuberculosis, "nervous diseases," poor eyesight, memory loss, and epilepsy.

Many clergy and medical authorities of the nineteenth century were persuaded that certain foods had a stimulating effect on the sex organs. So one form of advice to parents focused on modifying their children's diets to eliminate foods that were believed to excite the sexual organs, notably meat, coffee, tea, and chocolate, and to substitute "unstimulating" foods in their place, most notably grain products. In the 1830s, the Reverend Sylvester Graham developed a cracker, now called the graham cracker, to help people control their sexual impulses.

Coitus interruptus The practice of withdrawing the penis before ejaculation during sexual intercourse.

figure 9.1

Devices Designed to Curb Mastur-bation. Because of widespread beliefs that masturbation was harmful, various contraptions were introduced in the nineteenth century to prevent the practice in children. Some of the devices were barbarous.

Yet another household name belongs to a man who made his mark by introducing a bland diet that was also intended to help people, especially youngsters, control their sexual impulses. In the nineteenth-century United States, medical advice was disseminated to the general public largely through pamphlets and guides written by leading medical authorities. One of the more influential writers was the superintendent of the Battle Creek Sanatorium in Michigan, Dr. J. H. Kellogg (1852–1943), better known to you as the creator of the modern breakfast cereal. Kellogg identified 39 signs of masturbation, including acne, paleness, heart palpitations, rounded shoulders, weak backs, and convulsions. Kellogg, like Graham, believed that sexual desires could be controlled by a diet of simple foods, especially grains, including the corn flakes that have since borne his name. (We wonder how Kellogg would react to the energizing, sugarcoated cereals that now bear his name.)

Many nineteenth-century physicians also advised parents to take measures to prevent their children from masturbating. Kellogg suggested that parents bandage or cage their children's genitals or tie their hands. Some of the contraptions that were devised to prevent masturbation were barbarous (see Figure 9.1).

Several nineteenth-century scholars of sexuality joined the crusade against masturbation. Richard von Krafft-Ebing (in *Psychopathia Sexualis*, 1886) and Havelock Ellis (in *Studies in the Psychology of Sex*, 1900) condemned masturbation as psychologically dangerous. Krafft-Ebing linked masturbation to sexual orientation. Male masturbation, or so it was mistakenly believed, arrested the development of normal erotic instincts and led to **impotence** with women. Thus, it encouraged male-male sexual activity.

MASTURBATION TODAY   Despite this history, there is no scientific evidence that masturbation is harmful. Masturbation does not cause insanity, grow hair on the hands, or cause warts or any of the other psychological and physical ills that were ascribed to it in the past. Masturbation is physically harmless, except for rare injuries to the genitals due to rough stimulation. Nor is masturbation in itself psychologically harmful, although it may be a sign of an adjustment problem if people use masturbation as an exclusive sexual outlet when opportunities for sexual relationships are available. Sex therapists have even found therapeutic benefits in masturbation. It has emerged as a treatment for women who have difficulty reaching orgasm (Kay, 1992) (see Chapter 15).

Of course, people who consider masturbation wrong, harmful, or sinful may experience anxiety or guilt if they masturbate or wish to masturbate. These negative emotions are linked to their attitudes toward masturbation, not to masturbation per se (Michael et al., 1994).

Despite the widespread condemnation of masturbation in our society, surveys indicate that most people masturbate at some time. The incidence of masturbation is generally greater among men than among women. However, there are women who masturbate frequently and men who rarely, if ever, do so (Michael et al., 1994).

Nearly all of the adult men and about two-thirds of the adult women in Kinsey's samples (Kinsey et al., 1948, 1953) reported that they had masturbated at some time. In a study of students in an urban university, 85% of the women and 95% of the men reported that they had masturbated (Person et al., 1989). Seventy-one percent of the women and 83% of the men reported having masturbated during the previous three months.

Not all researchers find that the gender gap has narrowed to such an extent. A survey of students in a New England college found nearly twice as many men (81%) as women (45%) reporting some experience with masturbation (Leitenberg et al., 1993).

Impotence Recurrent difficulty in achieving or sustaining an erection sufficient to successfully engage in sexual intercourse. (The term has been replaced by the terms *male erectile disorder* or *erectile dysfunction,* as discussed in Chapter 15.)

About three in four men, compared to only one in three women, reported having masturbated during the previous year.

The NHSLS study also found a notable gender gap in reported frequencies of masturbation (Laumann et al., 1994). Table 9.2 shows how the sample group reported the frequency of masturbation during the preceding 12 months, broken down according to gender, age, marital status, level of education, religion, and race/ethnicity.

t a b l e   9 . 2

Sociocultural factors and frequency of masturbation
during past 12 months, as found in the NHSLS study

| | | FREQUENCY OF MASTURBATION | | | |
| | | Not at All | | At Least Once a Week | |
	Sociocultural Characteristics	Men (%)	Women (%)	Men (%)	Women (%)
Total population		36.7	58.3	26.7	7.6
Age	18–24	41.2	64.4	29.2	9.4
	25–29	28.9	58.3	32.7	9.9
	30–34	27.6	51.1	34.6	8.6
	35–39	38.5	52.3	20.8	6.6
	40–44	34.5	49.8	28.7	8.7
	45–49	35.2	55.6	27.2	8.6
	50–54	52.5	71.8	13.9	2.3
	55–59	51.7	77.6	10.3	2.4
Marital Status	Never married (not cohabiting)	31.8	51.8	41.3	12.3
	Married	42.6	62.9	16.5	4.7
	Formerly married (not cohabiting)	30.2	52.7	34.9	9.6
Education	Less than high school	54.8	75.1	19.2	7.6
	High school graduate	45.1	68.4	20.0	5.6
	Some college	33.2	51.3	30.8	6.9
	College graduate	24.2	47.7	33.2	10.2
	Advanced degree	18.6	41.2	33.6	13.7
Religion	None	32.6	41.4	37.6	13.8
	Liberal, moderate Protestant	28.9	55.1	28.2	7.4
	Conservative Protestant	48.4	67.3	19.5	5.8
	Catholic	34.0	57.3	24.9	6.6
Race/Ethnicity	White (non-Hispanic)	33.4	55.7	28.3	7.3
	African American	60.3	67.8	16.9	10.7
	Hispanic American	33.1	65.5	24.4	4.7
	Asian American	38.7	—*	31.3	—*
	Native American	—*	—*	—*	—*

Source: Adapted from Laumann, E. O., Gagnon, J. H., Michael, R. T., & Michaels, S. (1994). *The social organization of sexuality: Sexual practices in the United States.* Chicago: University of Chicago Press, Table 3.1, p. 82.

*Sample sizes too small to report findings.

Overall, 37% of the men and 58% of the women sampled reported that they had *not* masturbated during the preceding 12 months. Within every social category, men reported masturbating more frequently than women did. Despite the sexual revolution, women might still find masturbation less pleasurable or acceptable than men do (Leitenberg et al., 1993). Women might still be subject to traditional socialization pressures that teach that sexual activity for pleasure's sake is more of a taboo for women than for men. Then, too, women are more likely to pursue sexual activity within the context of a relationship.

Married people are less likely to have masturbated during the past 12 months than never-married and formerly married people. Nevertheless, only 43% of the married men and 63% of the married women sampled said that they had not masturbated at all during the preceding year.

Truth or Fiction?
REVISITED

It is not true that married people rarely if ever masturbate. The majority of married men and a sizable minority of married women in the United States report masturbating at least occasionally. ■

Education appears to be a clear liberating influence on masturbation. For both genders, people with more education reported more frequent masturbation. Perhaps better-educated people are less likely to believe the old horror stories about masturbation or to be subject to traditional social restrictions. Conservative religious beliefs appear to constrain masturbation. Conservative Protestants are apparently less likely to masturbate than liberal and moderate Protestants are. African Americans are notably less likely to report masturbating over a 12-month period than are other ethnic groups.

Truth or Fiction?
REVISITED

It is true that White men are more likely to masturbate than African American men are. Perhaps African American men are relatively more likely to adhere to traditional views concerning masturbation. ■

There appears to be a link between attitudes toward masturbation and orgasmic potential. A study of women revealed more negative attitudes toward masturbation among a group of 21- to 40-year-olds who had never achieved orgasm than among a comparison group of women who had (Kelly et al., 1990). Kinsey and his colleagues had reported links between prior masturbation and sexual satisfaction in marriage. Women who had masturbated during adolescence were more likely to find gratification in marital coitus than women who did not (Kinsey et al., 1953).

This evidence does not suggest that adolescents should be encouraged to masturbate to enhance the likelihood of sexual fulfillment as adults. A selection factor probably explains the link (see Figure 9.2). That is, people who masturbate early are probably generally more open to exploring their sexuality and learning about the types of stimulation that arouse them. These attitudes would carry over into marriage and increase the likelihood that women would seek the coital stimulation they need to achieve sexual gratification. Nevertheless, adolescent masturbation probably does also set the stage for marital

---

figure 9.2

What Are the Connections between Masturbation during Adolescence and Sexual Satisfaction in Marriage? There is a positive correlation between masturbation during adolescence and sexual satisfaction in marriage. What hypotheses can we make about the causal connections? Does experience with masturbation teach people about their sexual needs so that they are more likely to obtain adequate sexual stimulation in marriage? Are people who masturbate early generally more open to exploring their sexuality and learning about the types of stimulation that arouse them? Such attitudes might also increase the likelihood that people would seek the coital stimulation they need to achieve sexual gratification in marriage.

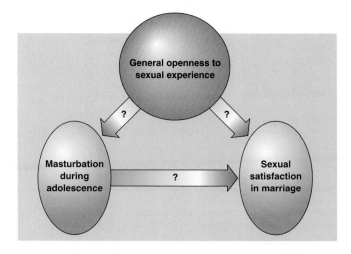

sexual satisfaction by yielding information about the types of stimulation people need to obtain sexual gratification.

Actually, women who masturbate during adolescence are *more* likely to find gratification in marital coitus than women who do not. ■

Truth or Fiction? REVISITED

Other researchers find that women achieve orgasm more reliably through masturbation than through coitus. On the basis of her magazine survey, Hite (1977) reported that 92% of her sample could reliably achieve orgasm through masturbation. Only 30% regularly did so through coitus. Masters and Johnson (1966) also found that masturbation was a more reliable means for women to achieve orgasm than coitus, at least for women who accept masturbation as a sexual outlet.

Women are actually *more* likely to reach orgasm through masturbation than through sexual intercourse. ■

Truth or Fiction? REVISITED

In our efforts to correct misinformation about masturbation, we do not wish to leave the impression that there is anything wrong with people who choose *not* to masturbate. Nor do we wish to imply that people should masturbate. Although we may all be able to experience pleasure from self-stimulation, let us say once more that biology is not destiny. It is illogical to transform a biological capacity into a behavioral requirement.

TECHNIQUES OF MALE MASTURBATION

Sex is like bridge—if you don't have a good partner, you'd better have a good hand.

—Contemporary bathroom graffito

Although masturbation techniques vary widely, most men report that they masturbate by manual manipulation of the penis (see Figure 9.3). Typically they take one or two minutes to reach orgasm (Hite, 1981; Kinsey et al., 1948). Men tend to grip the penile shaft with one hand, jerking it up and down in a milking motion. Some men move the whole hand up and down the penis; others use just two fingers, generally the thumb and index finger. Men usually shift from a gentler rubbing action during the flaccid or semi-erect state of arousal to a more vigorous milking motion once full erection takes place. Men are also likely to stroke the glans and frenulum lightly at the outset, but their grip tightens and their motions speed up as orgasm nears. At orgasm, the penile shaft may be

figure 9.3

Male Masturbation. Masturbation techniques vary widely, but most men report that they masturbate by manual manipulation of the penis. They tend to grip the penile shaft with one hand and jerk it up and down in a milking motion.

gripped tightly, but the glans has become sensitive, and contact with it is usually avoided. (Likewise, women usually avoid stimulating the clitoris directly during orgasm because of increased sensitivity.)

Some men use soapsuds (which may become irritating) as a lubricant for masturbation during baths or showers. Other lubricants, such as petroleum jelly or K-Y jelly, may also be used to reduce friction and to simulate the moist conditions of coitus.

A few men prefer to masturbate by rubbing the penis and testicles against clothing or bedding (Kinsey et al., 1948). A very few men rub their genitals against inflatable dolls sold in sex shops. These dolls may come with artificial mouths or vaginas that can be filled with warm water to mimic the sensations of coitus. Artificial vaginas are also for sale.

Some men strap vibrators to the backs of their hands. Electrical vibrators save labor but do not simulate the type of up-and-down motions of the penis that men favor. Hence, they are not used very often. Most men rely heavily on fantasy or erotic photos or videos but do not use sex shop devices.

TECHNIQUES OF FEMALE MASTURBATION   Techniques of female masturbation also vary widely. In fact, Masters and Johnson reported never observing two women masturbate in precisely the same way. Even when the general technique was similar, women varied in the tempo and style of their self-caresses. But some general trends have been noted. Most women masturbate by massaging the mons, labia minora, and clitoral region with circular or back-and-forth motions (Hite, 1976; Kinsey et al., 1953). They may also straddle the clitoris with their fingers, stroking the shaft rather than the glans (see Figure 9.4). The glans may be lightly touched early during arousal, but because of its exquisite sensi-

figure 9.4

Female Masturbation. Techniques of female masturbation vary so widely that Masters and Johnson reported never observing two women masturbating in precisely the same way. Most women masturbate by massaging the mons, labia minora, and clitoral region, either with circular or back-and-forth motions.

figure 9.5

Electric Vibrators and Other Devices.

tivity, it is rarely stroked for any length of time during masturbation. Women typically achieve clitoral stimulation by rubbing or stroking the clitoral shaft or pulling or tugging on the vaginal lips. Some women also massage other sensitive areas, such as their breasts or nipples, with the free hand. Many women, like men, fantasize during masturbation (Leitenberg & Henning, 1995).

In contrast to the male myth (Kinsey and his colleagues [1953] describe it as a "male conceit") that women usually masturbate by simulating penile thrusting through the insertion of fingers or phallic objects into their vaginas, relatively few women actually do (Hite, 1976; Kinsey et al., 1953). Hite reported that only 1.5% of her respondents exclusively relied on vaginal insertion as a means of masturbation. Kinsey and his colleagues found that only one in five women had sometimes used vaginal insertions of objects during masturbation. Some women first experimented with the technique of vaginal insertions but then gave it up as they became more familiar with their sexual anatomy and capabilities. Others practiced the technique because their male partners found it sexually stimulating to watch them engage in this type of activity. Still, some women reported experiencing erotic pleasures from deep vaginal penetration.

It is not true that most women masturbate by inserting a finger or other object into the vagina. Most women rely on clitoral stimulation. ■

Truth or Fiction?
REVISITED

Even when women do use insertion, they usually precede or combine it with clitoral stimulation. Sex shops sell dildos, which women can use to rub their vulvas or to insert them vaginally. Penis-shaped vibrators may be used in a similar fashion. Many women masturbate during baths, some by spraying their genitals with water-massage showerheads.

Handheld electrical vibrators (see Figure 9.5) provide a constant massaging action against the genitals that can be erotic. Some women find this type of stimulation too intense, however, and favor vibrators that strap to the back of the hand and cause the fingers to vibrate during manual stimulation of the genitals. This type of vibration may numb the hand that is attached to the vibrator, however. Women who use vibrators often experiment with different models to find one with the shape and intensity of vibration that suits them.

Sexual Fantasy

Sexual fantasies are sexual experiences that can occur without a partner, but many people also fantasize during lovemaking (Leitenberg & Henning, 1995). Some couples find it sexually arousing to share their fantasies or to enact them with their partners. Strictly speaking, however, a fantasy is a private mental experience involving thoughts or images that are sexually arousing to the individual. Sexual fantasies may be experienced without sexual behavior, as in erotic dreams or daydreams. Sexual fantasies can also be use to heighten sexual response during masturbation or sexual activity with another person. Masturbators often require some form of cognitive stimulation, such as fantasy or reading or viewing erotica, to increase their arousal to the point of orgasm.

How common are sexual fantasies? It is a popular belief that only people with deficient sex lives engage in sexual fantasies. However, evidence shows that the majority of men and women engage in sexual fantasies from time to time, especially during masturbation (Reinisch, 1990). Men fantasize more often than women do (Hsu et al., 1994). In their national survey, Laumann and his colleagues (1994) found that 54% of men and 19% of women said that they thought about sex at least once a day.

A study of 212 married college women found that 88% of them reported having erotic fantasies. Most of them fantasized both during masturbation and coitus (Davidson & Hoffman, 1986). Another study showed that sexual daydreaming or fantasy in women was associated with a greater sex drive, more sexual activity, and a more positive attitude toward sex (Purifoy et al., 1992). We would hardly expect to find such a pattern among people with deficient sex lives.

Sexual fantasies may be reasonably realistic, such as imagining sexual activity with an attractive classmate. They may involve flights of fancy, such as making love to a movie star. The most common fantasy theme reported among women involves someone they are or have been involved with (Leitenberg & Henning, 1995). In contrast to men's fantasies, women are more likely to focus on the partner's feelings, touching, their own responses to what is happening, and the general feeling tone of the sexual encounter (Leitenberg & Henning, 1995).

The most common masturbation fantasy reported by both genders in the *Playboy* sample was "having intercourse with a loved one" (Hunt, 1974). But note some interesting gender differences: Men are more likely to assume aggressive, dominant roles. Women are more apt to enact passive, submissive roles (Leitenberg & Henning, 1995; Person et al., 1989). Women are more likely to connect sexual activity to relationships and emotional involvement than men are (Barbach, 1995; Leitenberg & Henning, 1995).

Fantasy themes apparently parallel traditional gender stereotypes but may also reflect deeper currents. Sociobiologists might conjecture that women are relatively more likely to fantasize about the images of familiar lovers because female reproductive success in ancestral times was more likely to depend on a close, protective relationship with a stable partner (Symons, 1995). Women can bear and rear relatively few offspring. Therefore, they would have had (and might still have) a relatively greater genetic investment in each reproductive opportunity.

Whether or not the wellspring of sexual fantasy themes lies in our genetic heritages, we should not confuse sexual fantasies with behavior. Fantasies are imaginary. Most people do not intend to act out their fantasies. They use them as a means of inducing or enhancing sexual pleasure (Reinisch, 1990). As one woman noted,

> My fantasies are so personal, and the pleasure I get from them derives so much, I think, from the fact that they are private and locked away in my imagination, that I wouldn't dream of trying to make them come true. . . . But act my fantasies out? Make them come true? No, absolutely not. My real life's not what they're about; I don't want those things to really happen to me, I simply want to imagine what it would be like. So that's where they'll stay. (Friday, 1973, p. 288)

What Friday says here of women's fantasies also applies to men:

> For many women, fantasy is a way of exploring, safely, all the ideas and actions which might frighten them in reality. In fantasy they can expand their reality, play out certain sexual variables and images in much the same way that children enter into fantasy as a form of play, of trying out desires, releasing energies for which they have no outlet in reality. Thinking about it, even getting excited over the image doesn't mean you want it as

your reality . . . or else we all, night dreamers that we are, would be suppressed robbers, bisexuals, murderers, or even inanimate objects. (p. 41)

Fantasizing about forcing someone into sexual activity or about being victimized does not mean that one wants these events to occur (Leitenberg & Henning, 1995; Reinisch, 1990). Women who imagine themselves being sexually coerced remain in control of their fantasies. Real assault victims are not. Nor is it unusual for heterosexual people to have episodic fantasies about sexual activity with people of their own gender or for gay males or lesbians to fantasize about sexual activity with people of the other gender. In neither case does the person necessarily intend to carry out the fantasy.

Heterosexual people may in fact fantasize about sexual activity with people of their own gender. People do not necessarily express their fantasies in their behavior. ■

Truth or Fiction?
REVISITED

Why do people fantasize when they masturbate? Masturbation fantasies serve several functions. For one, they increase or facilitate sexual arousal. Sex therapists encourage clients to use sexual fantasies to enhance sexual arousal (e.g., Heiman & LoPiccolo, 1987). Sexual fantasies are highly arousing, in part because fantasizers can command the imagined sexual encounter. They might imagine that people who will not give them the time of day find them irresistible and are willing to fulfill their sexual desires. Or fantasizers might picture improbable or impossible arousing situations, such as sexual activity on a commercial airliner or while skydiving. Some masturbation fantasies may be arousing because they permit us to deviate from traditional gender roles. Women might fantasize about taking an aggressive role or forcing someone into sexual activity. Men, by contrast, might imagine being overtaken by a horde of sexually aggressive women. Other fantasies involve sexual transgressions or "forbidden" behaviors, such as exposing oneself, doing a striptease before strangers, engaging in sexual activity with strangers, or sadomasochistic sex (S&M).

Masturbation fantasies can also allow people to rehearse sexual encounters. We might envision the unfolding of an intended sexual encounter, from greeting a date at the door, through dinner and a movie, and finally to the bedroom. We can mentally rehearse what we would say and do as a way of preparing for the date. Finally, masturbation fantasies may fill in the missing love object when we are alone or our partners are away.

Reflections

- ■ What are the beliefs of most people from your sociocultural group about masturbation? Do you share these beliefs? Why or why not?
- ■ What misinformation, if any, did you receive about masturbation as you were growing up? What was the source of the misinformation?
- ■ Do you have sexual fantasies? What do you fantasize about? Do you—or did you—wonder whether your fantasies are "normal"? If so, why?

SEX WITH OTHERS

Partners' feelings for one another and the quality of their relationships may be stronger determinants of their sexual arousal and response than the techniques that they employ. Partners are most likely to experience mutually enjoyable sexual interactions when they are sensitive to each other's sexual needs and incorporate techniques with which they are both comfortable. As with other aspects of sharing relationships, communication is the most important "sexual" technique.

Foreplay

Various forms of noncoital sex, such as cuddling, kissing, petting, and oral-genital contact, are used as **foreplay.** The pattern and duration of foreplay vary widely within and across cultures. Broude and Greene (1976) found that prolonged foreplay was the norm

Foreplay Physical interactions that are sexually stimulating and set the stage for intercourse.

in about half of the societies in their cross-cultural sample. Foreplay was minimal in one in ten societies and virtually absent in about one-third of them.

Within the United States, there is a gender difference in the amount of foreplay desired. A survey of college students revealed that women wanted longer periods of foreplay (and "afterplay") than men did (Denny et al., 1984). Since women usually require a longer period of stimulation during sex with a partner to reach orgasm, increasing the duration of foreplay may increase female coital responsiveness.

Foreplay is not limited to the human species. Virtually all species of mammals, from horses and sheep to dogs and chimpanzees, engage in some kind of foreplay. Depending on the particular species, mating pairs may rub, playfully nip, lick, or nuzzle each other's genitals for minutes or hours preceding coitus (Geer et al., 1984).

Kissing, genital touching, and oral-genital contact may also be experienced as ends in themselves, not as preludes to coitus. Yet some people object to petting for petting's sake, equating it with masturbation as a form of sexual activity without a "product." Many people behave as though all sexual contact must lead to coitus, perhaps because of the importance that our culture places on it.

Kissing

Kissing is almost universal in our culture, but it occurs less often among the world's cultures than manual or oral stimulation of the genitals (Frayser, 1985). Kissing is unknown in some cultures, such as among the Thonga of Africa and the Siriono of Bolivia. Variations in styles of kissing also exist across cultures (Ford & Beach, 1951). Kissing is now becoming practiced in Japan because of the influence of Western culture but was previously unknown there. Instead of kissing, the Balinese of the South Pacific bring their faces close enough to each other to smell each other's scent and feel the warmth of each other's skin. This practice has been wrongly dubbed "rubbing noses" by Europeans. Among some preliterate societies, kissing consists of sucking the partner's lips and tongue and allowing saliva to pass from one mouth to the other.

Couples may kiss for its own enjoyment or as a prelude to intercourse, in which case it is a part of foreplay. In *simple kissing*, the partners keep their mouths closed. Simple kissing may develop into caresses of the lips with the tongue or into nibbling of the lower lip. In what Kinsey called *deep kissing*, which is also called French kissing or soul kissing, the partners part their lips and insert their tongues into each other's mouths. Some prefer the lips parted slightly. Others open their mouths widely.

Kissing may also be an affectionate gesture without erotic significance, as in kissing someone good-night. Some people are accustomed to kissing relatives and close friends affectionately on the lips. Others limit kissing relatives to the cheek. Sustained kissing on the lips and deep kissing are almost always erotic gestures.

Kissing is not limited to the partner's mouth. Kinsey found that more than nine husbands in ten kissed their wives' breasts. Women usually prefer several minutes of body contact and gentle caresses before desiring to have their partner kiss their breasts or suck or lick their nipples. Women also usually do not prefer a hard sucking action unless they are highly aroused. Many women are reluctant to tell their partners that sucking hurts because they do not want to interfere with their partner's pleasure.

Other parts of the body are also often kissed, including the hands and feet, the neck and earlobes, the insides of the thighs, and the genitals themselves.

Touching

Touching or caressing erogenous zones with the hands or other parts of the body can be highly arousing. Even simple hand-holding can be sexually stimulating for couples who are sexually attracted to one another. The hands are very rich in nerve endings.

Sex Becomes "Interactive"

There's nothing new about pulling down the curtains so that sex remains a private matter. But a new wrinkle has been added by the black curtains at the computer expositions at the turn of the new millennium. The curtains shield high-tech peep shows that feature nude models on CD-ROMs produced by *Penthouse* and other purveyors of multimedia erotica. Sex has always followed hard on the heels of the technological innovations of the day. Four thousand years ago, the Sumerians celebrated the pleasures of sex in their early cuneiform writing on clay tablets. Shortly after Gutenberg invented the printing press, a volume of erotic engravings appeared. (The year was A.D. 1524, and the work was soon suppressed by the Pope.)

Today, we have multimedia interactivity. One could argue, of course, that sex has always been about as interactive a sphere of activity as one could have. But only now has a *Penthouse* model saying, "Let's get interactive" become available for your computer.

In one program produced by the CD-ROM company Interotica, entitled *Interactive Adventures,* a narrator introduces himself to a young woman in Los Angeles. The action soon comes to a halt with her face frozen on the monitor. The screen presents the computer operator with a menu of choices: retreating, asking the woman out to dinner, and inviting her to enjoy a sojourn in a hot tub. Retreating and the hot tub proposition offer no rewards. (The hot tub invitation is judged premature by this socially sophisticated program.) But the dinner invitation, followed up by additional "correct" choices, leads to a CD-ROM-mediated "sexual encounter."

Social critics point out that the advanced technology that makes such interactive adventures possible serves to maintain men's lowtech sexist illusions about women. As in pornographic books, films, and videocassettes, women are portrayed as objects whose function is to serve the cruder wishes of men. In such works, "love" is reduced to anonymous encounters in which women seek to fulfill men's sexual desires, not to develop relationships.

Businesspeople are already contemplating new ways of raking in the dollars from interactive erotica. Pay-per-view video sex over modems is likely to replace telephone sex, especially as modems become able to transmit torrents of information faster. Today, socalled "hot chats" are popular with computer online services. The services allow people who have unusual sexual interests to conduct conversations with people who share their interests any place in the country by typing their comments onto their screens. Video versions of the hot chat are also becoming common as we enter the new millennium. If one wishes to remain anonymous during an interactive session, one can assume the identity of a makebelieve character known as an "avatar." No doubt we will soon be donning the computer-generated screen images of, say, Brad Pitt or Uma Thurman.

Or consider what some futurists refer to as *cybersex* or *virtual sex.* You don headphones, 3-D glasses, and a light bodysuit with miniature detectors that follow your movements and tiny stimulators for your skin. The detectors and stimulators are connected to computers that record your responses and create the impression of being touched by textures such as virtual satin, virtual wool, or virtual skin. The information superhighway allows you either to interact with another online person who is outfitted with similar gear or to be connected with a canned program.

What are some of the psychological implications of such new forms of interactive sex? If we could electronically dress up as movie stars, would our sense of self and our dignity as individuals suffer?

If we could, at a moment's notice, access a satisfying virtual sexual encounter with an appealing person (or program) who was concerned only about meeting our needs, would we become less sensitive to the needs of our real-life romantic partners? Would virtual sex provide additional outlets for people whose needs were not being fully met by others? Or would they become the preferred sexual outlets? If they did become preferred outlets, what would be the implications for the family? For children?

Would a virtual sex interaction be grounds for divorce?

Let us note that traditional family life remains a popular ideal despite provocative cuneiform writings on clay tablets, despite arousing engravings (and photographs) in printed media, despite adult films and videotapes, even despite telephone sex and the Internet. On the other hand, we have not yet witnessed the most titillating interactions of the new millennium.

Virtual Sex. Consider what futurists refer to as *cybersex* or *virtual sex.* In the new millennium, you may don headphones, 3-D glasses, and a bodysuit with skin stimulators that create the impression of being touched by virtual satin or virtual skin. There's no chance of unwanted pregnancy or STIs and no need to form a relationship—but then, there's no relationship.

How Touching? Touching is a common form of foreplay. Most men and women like manual or oral stimulation of the genitals as a prelude to intercourse.

Touching is a common form of foreplay. Both men and women generally prefer manual or oral stimulation of the genitals as a prelude to intercourse. Women generally prefer that direct caressing of the genitals be focused around the clitoris but not directly on the extremely sensitive clitoral glans. Men sometimes assume (often mistakenly) that their partners want them to insert their finger or fingers into the vagina as a form of foreplay. But not all women enjoy this form of stimulation. Some women go along with it because it's what their partners want or something they think their partners want. Ironically, men may do it because they assume that their partners want it. When in doubt, it would not hurt to *ask.* If you are not sure what to say, you can always blame us: "Listen, I read this thing in my human sexuality text, and I was wondering. . . ."

Masters and Johnson (1979) noted gender differences with respect to preferences in foreplay. Men typically prefer direct stroking of their genitals by their partner early in lovemaking. Women tend to prefer that their partners caress their genitals after a period of general body contact that includes holding, hugging, and nongenital massage. This is not a hard and fast (or slow) rule, but it concurs with other observations that men tend to be more genitally oriented than women. Women are more likely to view sex within a broader framework of affection and love.

TECHNIQUES OF MANUAL STIMULATION OF THE GENITALS   Here again, variability in technique is the rule, so partners need to communicate their preferences. The man's partner may use two hands to stimulate his genitals. One may be used to fondle the scrotum, by gently squeezing the skin between the fingers (taking care not to apply pressure to the testes themselves). The other hand may circle the coronal ridge and engage in gentle stroking of the penis, followed by more vigorous up-and-down movements as the man becomes more aroused.

The penis may also be gently rolled back and forth between the palms as if one were making a ball of clay into a sausage—increasing pressure as arousal progresses. Note that men who are highly aroused or who have just had an orgasm might find direct stimulation of the penile glans uncomfortable.

The woman might prefer that her partner approach genital stimulation gradually, following stimulation of other body parts. Genital stimulation may begin with light, stroking motions of the inner thighs and move on to the vaginal lips (labia) and the clitoral area. Women may enjoy pressure against the mons pubis from the heel of the hand or tactile stimulation of the labia, which are sensitive to stroking motions. Clitoral stimulation can focus on the clitoral shaft or the region surrounding the shaft, rather than the clitoris itself, because of the extreme sensitivity of the clitoral glans to touch.

Moreover, the clitoris should not be stroked if it is dry, lest it become irritated. Since the clitoris produces no lubrication of its own, a finger may enter the outer portion of the vagina to apply some vaginal lubrication to the clitoral region.

Some, but not all, women enjoy having a finger inserted into the vagina, which can stroke the vaginal walls or simulate thrusting of the penis. Vaginal insertion is usually not preferred, if at all, until the woman has become highly aroused. Many women desire that their partners discontinue stroking motions while they are experiencing orgasm, but others wish stimulation to continue. Men and women woman may physically guide their partners' hands or otherwise express their preferences as to the types of strokes they find most pleasurable.

If a finger is to be inserted into the vagina, it should be clean. Fingernails should be well trimmed. Inserting fingers that have been in the anus into the vagina is dangerous.

The fingers may transfer microbes from the woman's digestive tract, where they do no harm, to the woman's reproductive tract, where they can cause serious infections.

Breast Stimulation

Men are more likely to stimulate women's breasts than to have their own breasts fondled, even though the breasts (and especially the nipples) are erotically sensitive in both genders. Most, but not all, women enjoy breast stimulation. Masters and Johnson report that some women are capable of achieving orgasm from breast stimulation alone.

The hands and the mouth can be used to stimulate the breasts and the nipples. Since the desired type and intensity of breast stimulation vary from person to person, partners need to communicate their preferences.

Masters and Johnson (1979) find that gay men frequently stroke their partners' nipples before stimulating the penis. Although some heterosexual men enjoy having their breasts and nipples stimulated by their partners, many, if not most, do not. Many men are simply unaware that their breasts are erotically sensitive. Cultural conditioning may also play a major part in men's reluctance to having their breasts stimulated: Men may feel uncomfortable receiving a form of stimulation that they have learned to associate with the stereotypical feminine sexual role.

Oral-Genital Stimulation

Oral stimulation of the male genitals is called **fellatio.** Fellatio is referred to by slang terms such as "blow job," "sucking," "sucking off," or "giving head." Oral stimulation of the female genitals is called **cunnilingus,** which is referred to by slang expressions such as "eating" (a woman) or "going down" on her.

The popularity of oral-genital stimulation has increased dramatically since Kinsey's day, especially among young married couples. Kinsey and his colleagues (1948, 1953) found that at least 60% of married, *college-educated* couples had experienced oral-genital contact. Such experiences were reported by only about 20% of couples who had only a high school education and 10% who had only a grade school education.

The incidence of oral sex may have peaked during the sexual revolution. The *Playboy* survey in the early 1970s found that more than 90% of the married couples under 25 years of age—*across all educational levels*—reported that they had engaged in oral-genital sex (Hunt, 1974). But remember that 80% of the people who were approached by Hunt refused to participate in the survey. Therefore, there is likely to be a volunteer bias in his statistics. (The researchers who conducted the NHSLS study are less kind in discussion of the representativeness of Hunt's sample.)

According to the NHSLS study, the incidence of oral sex was somewhat lower in the 1990s (Laumann et al., 1994). About three of four men (77%) and two of three women (68%) reported playing the active role in oral sex during their lifetimes. Nearly four men in five (79%) and three of four women (73%) reported having been the recipients of oral-genital sex during their lifetimes. Among married couples, 80% of the men and 71% of the women have performed oral sex. Eighty percent of the men and 74% of the women have received oral sex. These are dramatic increases since Kinsey's day. Among young White women (ages 18 to 36) in Kinsey's sample, 48% reported ever engaging in fellatio. Fifty-one percent of their partners had engaged in cunnilingus.

It is true that oral sex is the norm for today's young married couples, statistically speaking. A majority of them report participating in this form of sexual expression. ■

As with touching, oral-genital stimulation can be used as a prelude to intercourse or as a sexual end in itself. If orgasm is reached through oral-genital stimulation, a woman might be concerned about tasting or swallowing a man's ejaculate. There is a lack of scientific evidence that swallowing semen is harmful to one's health, unless the man is infected with a sexually transmitted disease for which semen can act as a conduit of infection (Reinisch, 1990). Note that oral-genital contact with the genitals of an infected partner,

 Truth or Fiction? REVISITED

Fellatio Oral stimulation of the male genitals.

Cunnilingus Oral stimulation of the female genitals.

A World of Diversity

SOCIOCULTURAL FACTORS AND ORAL SEX

Table 9.3 shows the incidence of oral sex among men and women with various levels of education and from different racial/ethnic backgrounds in the NHSLS survey. As with masturbation, the incidence of oral sex correlates with level of education. That is, more highly educated individuals are more likely to have practiced oral sex. Why? Perhaps education encourages experimentation. Perhaps education dispels myths that nontraditional behavior patterns are necessarily harmful. Note also that African American men and women are less likely to have engaged in oral sex than are people from other racial/ethnic backgrounds. African American men and women were also less likely than other ethnic groups to report masturbating during the past 12 months. African Americans

table 9.3

		PERFORMED ORAL SEX (%)		RECEIVED ORAL SEX (%)	
		Men (%)	Women (%)	Men (%)	Women (%)
Education	Less than high school	59.2	42.1	60.7	49.6
	High school graduate	75.3	59.6	76.6	67.1
	Some college	80.0	78.2	84.0	81.6
	College graduate	83.7	78.9	84.6	83.1
	Advanced college degree	80.5	79.0	81.4	81.9
Race/Ethnicity	White	81.4	75.3	81.4	78.9
	African American	50.5	34.4	66.3	48.9
	Hispanic American	70.7	59.7	73.2	63.7
	Asian American	63.6	—*	72.7	—*

Percentages of NHSLS study respondents who report experience with oral sex

Source: Adapted from Laumann, E. O., Gagnon, J. H., Michael, R. T., & Michaels, S. (1994). *The social organization of sexuality: Sexual practices in the United States.* Chicago: University of Chicago Press, Table 3.6, p. 98.

*There were not enough Asian American women in the sample to allow for the reporting of meaningful findings.

even without contact with semen, may transmit harmful organisms. Couples are therefore advised to practice "safer sex" techniques (see Chapters 16 and 17) unless they know that they and their partners are free of sexually transmitted diseases (Reinisch, 1990).

TECHNIQUES OF FELLATIO   Although the word *fellatio* is derived from a Latin root meaning "to suck," a sucking action is generally not highly arousing. The up-and-down movements of the penis in the partner's mouth or the licking of the penis is generally the most stimulating. Gentle licking of the scrotum may also be highly arousing.

The mouth is stimulating to the penis because it contains warm, moist mucous membranes, as does the vagina. Muscles of the mouth and jaw can create varied pressure and movements. Erection may be stimulated by gently pulling the penis with the mouth (being careful never to touch the penis with the teeth) and simultaneously providing manual stimulation, as described earlier.

Higher levels of sexual arousal or orgasm can be promoted by moving the penis in and out of the mouth, simulating the motion of the penis in the vagina during intercourse. The speed of the motions can be varied, and manual stimulation near the base of the penis (firmly encircling the lower portion of the penis or providing pressure behind the scrotum) can also be stimulating.

might adhere more strictly to traditional ideas about what kinds of sexual behavior are and are not proper.

Findings from a national survey of more than 3,000 sexually active men between the ages of 20 and 39 conducted by the Battelle Human Affairs Research Center in Seattle are consistent with the NHSLS findings. Seventy-five percent of the men reported performing oral sex. Seventy-nine percent reported receiving oral sex (Billy et al., 1993). Mirroring the racial differences observed by Laumann and his colleagues (1994), African American men in the Battelle survey were also much less likely than their White counterparts to have performed or received oral sex.

The results of a 1980s survey of college students are also consistent with the NHSLS data. Eighty-one percent of White females reported they had engaged in fellatio, compared to 47% of African American females (Belcastro, 1985). Seventy-two percent of White males had performed cunnilingus, compared to 50% of African American males. Although the prevalence of oral-genital sex since Kinsey's time has increased for both African Americans and White Americans, African Americans remain relatively less likely than White Americans to engage in oral sexual activity.

Truth or Fiction? REVISITED

It is not true that African Americans are more likely than White Americans to engage in oral sex. A review of the available survey evidence shows that White Americans are more likely than African Americans to engage in oral-genital sexual activity. ■

Ethnicity and Oral Sex. According to the NHSLS study and others, African Americans report that they are less likely than people from other racial/ethnic backgrounds to engage in oral sex. Why do you think that this is so?

Some people may gag during fellatio, a reflex that is triggered by pressure of the penis against the back of the tongue or against the throat. Gagging may be avoided if the man's partner grasps the shaft of the penis with one hand and controls the depth of penetration. Gagging is less likely to occur if the partner who is performing fellatio is on the top, rather than below, or if there is verbal communication about how deep the man may comfortably penetrate. Gagging may also be overcome by allowing gradually deeper penetrations of the penis over successive occasions while keeping the throat muscles relaxed.

TECHNIQUES OF CUNNILINGUS Women can be highly aroused by their partner's tongue because it is soft, warm, and well lubricated. In contrast to a finger, the tongue can almost never be used too harshly. A woman may thus be more receptive to direct clitoral contact by a tongue. Cunnilingus provides such intense stimulation that many women find it to be the best means for achieving orgasm. Some women cannot reach orgasm in any other way (Hite, 1976).

In performing cunnilingus, the partner may begin by kissing and licking the woman's abdomen and inner thighs, gradually nearing the vulva. Gentle tugging at or sucking of the labia minora can be stimulating, but the partner should take care not to bite. Many women enjoy licking of the clitoral region, and others desire sucking of the

figure 9.6

Simultaneous Oral-Genital Contact. The "69" position allows partners to engage in simultaneous oral-genital stimulation.

clitoris itself. The tongue may also be inserted into the vagina, where it may imitate the thrusts of intercourse.

"69"   The term *sixty-nine*, or *soixante-neuf* in French (pronounced swah-sahnt nuff), describes simultaneous oral-genital stimulation (see Figure 9.6). The numerals *6* and *9* are used because they resemble two partners who are facing each other upside-down.

The "69" position has the psychologically positive feature of allowing couples to experience simultaneous stimulation, but it can be an awkward position if two people are not similar in size. Some couples avoid "69" because it deprives each partner of the opportunity to focus fully on receiving or providing sexual pleasure. A person may find it distracting when receiving stimulation to have to focus on stimulating someone else.

The "69" technique may be practiced side by side or with one partner on top of the other. But here again, there are no strict rules, and couples often alternate positions.

ABSTAINING FROM ORAL SEX   Despite the popularity of oral sex among couples today, those who desire to abstain from it have no reason to consider themselves abnormal.

People offer various reasons for abstaining from oral sex. Although natural body odors may be arousing to some people, others are disturbed by the genital odors to which they are exposed. Some people object on grounds of cleanliness. They view the genitals as "dirty" because of their proximity to the urinary and anal openings. Concerns about offensive odors or cleanliness may be relieved by thoroughly washing the genitals beforehand.

Some women prefer not to taste or swallow semen because they find it to be "dirty," sinful, or repulsive. Others are put off by the taste or texture. Semen has a salty taste and a texture similar to the white of an egg. If couples are to engage in unprotected oral sex, open discussion of feelings can enhance pleasure and diminish anxiety. For example, the man can be encouraged to warn his partner or remove his penis from her mouth when he is nearing ejaculation.

Let us dispel a couple of myths about semen. For one thing, it is impossible to become pregnant by swallowing semen. For another, semen is not fattening. The average amount of semen expelled in the ejaculate contains only about 5 calories. On the other hand, it is not our intention to encourage swallowing of semen. The aesthetics of swallowing semen have little or nothing to do with concerns about pregnancy or weight. They involve the preferences of the individual.

Some of the objections expressed by people who are reluctant to engage in oral sex may be overcome. Others, such as beliefs that oral-genital contact is offensive or repulsive, are more deeply rooted. Shyness and embarrassment may also deter oral sex. A survey of college students found that shyness and embarrassment were the two most frequent reasons given for not engaging in oral sex (Gagnon & Simon, 1987). In one respect, oral sex is one of the most intimate types of lovemaking. After all, it provides a direct view of parts of the body that we have been reared to keep private.

People may also object to oral sex because it is condemned by Judeo-Christian moral codes. In the Judeo-Christian tradition, any sexual contact that does not lead to procreation has been considered sinful. Couples may also be deterred from oral sex because it illegal in many states, even for married couples. Some people object to oral sex on grounds that it is unnatural, even though many other species practice some form of oral-genital contact (Ford & Beach, 1951).

Sexual Intercourse: Positions and Techniques

Sexual intercourse, or *coitus* (from the Latin *coire*, meaning "to go together"), is sexual activity in which the penis is inserted into the vagina. Intercourse may take place in many different positions. Each position, however, must allow the genitals to be aligned so that the penis is contained by the vagina. In addition to varying positions, couples also vary the depth and rate of thrusting (in-and-out motions) and sources of additional sexual stimulation.

Though the number of possible coital positions is virtually endless, we will focus on four of the most commonly used positions: the male-superior (man-on-top) position, the female-superior (woman-on-top) position, the lateral-entry (side-entry) position, and the rear-entry position. Although not properly fitting the definition of sexual intercourse, we shall discuss anal intercourse as well, a sexual technique that both male-female and male-male couples use.

THE MALE-SUPERIOR (MAN-ON-TOP) POSITION   The male-superior position ("superiority" is used purely in relation to body position but has sometimes been taken as a symbol of male domination) has also been called the **missionary position.** In this position, the partners face one another. The man lies above the woman, perhaps supporting himself on his hands and knees rather than applying his full weight against his partner (see Figure 9.7 on page 256). Movement is easier for the man than for the woman, a fact that suggests that he is responsible for directing their activity.

Many students of human sexuality suggest that it is preferable for the woman to guide the penis into the vagina, rather than having the man do so. The idea is that the woman can feel the location of the vaginal opening and determine the proper angle of entry. To accomplish this, the woman must feel comfortable "taking charge" of the couple's lovemaking. With the breaking down of the traditional stereotype of the female as passive, women are feeling more comfortable taking this role. On the other hand, if the couple prefers that the man guide his penis into his partner's vagina, the slight loss of efficiency need not trouble them, as long as he moves prudently to avoid hurting his partner.

Missionary position The coital position in which the man is on top. Also termed the *male-superior position.*

figure 9.7

The Male-Superior Coital Position. In this position, the couple face one another. The man lies above the woman, perhaps supporting himself on his hands and knees rather than allowing his full weight to press against his partner. The position is also referred to as the *missionary position*.

The male-superior position has the advantage of permitting the couple to face one another so that kissing is easier. The woman may run her hands along her partner's body, stroking his buttocks and perhaps cupping a hand beneath his scrotum to increase stimulation as he reaches orgasm.

But the male-superior position makes it difficult for the man to caress his partner while simultaneously supporting himself with his hands. So the position might not be favored by women who enjoy having their partners provide manual clitoral stimulation during coitus. This position can be highly stimulating to the man, possibly making it difficult for him to delay ejaculation. The position also limits the opportunity for the woman to control the angle, rate, and depth of penetration. It might therefore be more difficult for her to attain the type of stimulation she may need to achieve orgasm, especially if she favors combining penile thrusting with manual clitoral stimulation. Finally, this position is not advisable during the late stages of pregnancy. At that time, the woman's distended abdomen would force the man to arch severely above her, lest he place undue pressure on her abdomen.

THE FEMALE-SUPERIOR (WOMAN-ON-TOP) POSITION In the female-superior position, the couple face one another with the woman on top. The woman straddles the male from above, controlling the angle of penile entry and the depth of thrusting (see Figure 9.8). Some women maintain a sitting position; others lie on top of their partners. Many women vary their position.

figure 9.8

The Female-Superior Coital Position. The woman straddles the male from above, controlling the angle of penile entry and the depth of thrusting. The female-superior position puts the woman psychologically and physically in charge. The woman can ensure that she receives adequate clitoral stimulation from the penis or the hand. The position also tends to be less stimulating for the male and may thus help him to control ejaculation.

In the female-superior position, the woman is psychologically, and to some degree physically, in charge. She can move as rapidly or as slowly as she wishes with little effort, adjusting her body to vary the angle and depth of penetration. She can reach behind her to stroke her partner's scrotum or lean down to kiss him.

As in the male-superior position, kissing is relatively easy. This position has additional advantages. The man may readily reach the woman's buttocks or clitoris to provide manual stimulation. Assuming that the woman is shorter than he is, it is rather easy for him to stimulate her breasts orally (a pillow tucked behind his head may help). The woman can, in effect, guarantee that she receives adequate clitoral stimulation, either by the penis or manually by his hand or her own. This position thus facilitates orgasm in the

figure 9.9

The Lateral-Entry Coital Position. In this position, the couple face each other side by side. Each partner has relatively free movement and easy access to the other. Because both partners rest easily on the bedding, it is an excellent position for prolonged coitus or for coitus when couples are fatigued.

woman. As it tends to be less stimulating for the male, it can help him to control ejaculation. For these reasons, this position is commonly used by couples who are learning to overcome sexual difficulties.

THE LATERAL-ENTRY (SIDE-ENTRY) POSITION In the lateral-entry position, the man and woman lie side by side, facing one another (see Figure 9.9). This position has the advantages of allowing each partner relatively free movement and easy access to the other. The man and woman may kiss freely, and they can stroke each other's bodies with a free arm. The position is not physically taxing, because both partners are resting easily on the bedding. Therefore, it is an excellent position for prolonged coitus or for coitus when couples are somewhat fatigued.

Let us note some disadvantages to this position. First, inserting the penis into the vagina while lying side by side might be awkward. Many couples therefore begin coitus in another position and then change into the lateral-entry position—often because they wish to prolong coitus. Second, one or both partners might have an arm lying beneath the other that will "fall asleep" or become numb because of the constricted blood supply. Third, women might not receive adequate clitoral stimulation from the penis in this position. Of course, such stimulation may be provided manually (by hand) or by switching to another position after a while. Fourth, it might be difficult to achieve deeper penetration of the penis. The lateral position is useful during pregnancy (at least until the final stages, when the distension of the woman's abdomen may make lateral entry difficult).

figure 9.10

The Rear-Entry Coital Position. The rear-entry position is highly erotic for men who enjoy viewing and pressing their abdomens against their partners' buttocks. Some couples feel uncomfortable about the position because of its association with animal mating patterns. The position is also impersonal in that the partners do not face one another. Moreover, some couples dislike the feeling that the man is psychologically in charge because he can see his partner but she cannot readily see him.

THE REAR-ENTRY POSITION In the rear-entry position, the man faces the woman's rear. In one variation (see Figure 9.10), the woman supports herself on her hands and knees while the man supports himself on his knees, entering her from behind. In another, the couple lie alongside one another, and the woman lifts one leg, draping it backward over her partner's thigh. The latter position is particularly useful during the later stages of pregnancy.

The rear-entry position may be highly stimulating for both partners. Men may enjoy viewing and pressing their abdomens against their partner's buttocks. The man can reach around or underneath to provide additional clitoral or breast stimulation, and the woman may reach behind (if she is on her hands and knees) to stroke or grasp her partner's testicles.

Potential disadvantages of this position include the following: First, this position is the mating position that most other mammals use, which is why it is sometimes referred to as *doggy style*. Some couples might feel uncomfortable about using the position because of its association with animal mating patterns. The position is also impersonal in the sense

ARE AFRICAN AMERICANS SEXUALLY PERMISSIVE? CULTURAL MYTHOLOGY VERSUS SOME FACTS

African Americans have long been stereotyped as more sexually permissive than White Americans (Wyatt, 1989). The perpetuation of this stereotype is based more on cultural biases than on scientific evidence. Evidence from Kinsey's time through the 1980s has shown that African American teenagers begin intercourse at earlier ages, on the average, than White teenagers (Wyatt, 1989). Such research has largely failed to control for socioeconomic (social class) differences between the groups, however.

Researchers have begun to critically examine existing stereotypes of African American sexuality. The 1988 National Survey of Family Growth, which surveyed nearly 8,500 American women ages 15 to 44, found that White women were more likely to have had 10 or more sex partners than either African American or Hispanic women (Lewin, 1992).

Gail Wyatt (1989) used Kinsey-style interviews to examine various aspects of sexual behavior among 126 African American and 122 White American women, ages 18 to 36, from Los Angeles County. Wyatt's study is noteworthy for balancing White and African American samples with respect to sociodemographic factors such as income level, education, and marital status. Wyatt reported no significant differences in age of first intercourse between the African American and White American women in her sample. The average age at first intercourse was 16.6 years for the total sample—16.5 years for African American women and 16.7 years for White women, respectively—an insignificant difference. Factors that predicted age of first intercourse were similar across groups. For both groups, perceptions that one's parents were more influential than one's friends during adolescence and the eventual attainment of higher educational levels were associated with a delay in the age of first intercourse.

All in all, results of the Wyatt survey fail to support the stereotype of African American sexual permissiveness. The similarities between the races overshadowed their differences. We should caution, however, that the sample was not a national probability sample. The results therefore may not generalize to all African Americans or White Americans. Although more interracial research would be of interest, an even richer understanding of sexual behavior patterns might be gained by examining variability within racial groups according to factors such as socioeconomic status and family background.

---

that the partners do not face one another, which might create a sense of emotional distance. Since the man is at the woman's back, the couple might feel that he is very much in charge—he can see her, but she cannot readily see him. Physically, the penis might not provide adequate stimulation to the clitoris. The penis also tends to pop out of the vagina from time to time. Finally, air tends to enter the vagina during rear-entry coitus. When it is expelled, it can sound as though the woman has passed air through the anus—a possibly embarrassing though harmless occurrence.

USE OF FANTASY DURING COITUS As with masturbation, mental excursions into fantasy during coitus may be used to enhance sexual arousal and response (Davidson & Hoffman, 1986). In a sense, coital fantasies allow couples to inject sexual variety and even offbeat sexual escapades into their sexual activity without being unfaithful. Fantasies were historically viewed as evil. People believed that fantasies, like dreams, were placed in the mind by agents of the Devil. Despite this tradition, researchers find that most married people have engaged in coital fantasies (Davidson & Hoffman, 1986). In one study, 71% of the men and 72% of the women reported engaging in coital fantasies to enhance their sexual arousal (Zimmer et al., 1983). A more recent survey of a sample of 178 students, faculty, and staff members at a college in Vermont found that 84% reported fantasizing at least occasionally during intercourse (Cado & Leitenberg, 1990). Nor does there appear to be any connection between sexual dissatisfaction with one's relationship and the use of coital fantasies (Davidson & Hoffman, 1986). Therefore, coital fantasies are not a form of compensation for an unrewarding sexual relationship.

Lest you think that coital fantasies arise only out of sexual monotony in marriage, many, if not most, unmarried people also fantasize during sexual relations. In one study of sexually experienced, single undergraduates, Sue (1979) found that virtually the same percentages of men (58.6%) and women (59.4%) reported "sometimes" or "almost always" fantasizing during coitus.

Coital fantasies, like masturbation fantasies, run a gamut of themes. They include making love to another partner, group sex, orgies, images of past lovers or special erotic experiences, and making love in fantastic and wonderful places, among others.

Table 9.4 shows the coital fantasies that were reported to Hariton and Singer (1974) by a sample of married women from an affluent New York City suburb. The women included PTA members and regular churchgoers. Yet 65%—a strong majority—used coital fantasies. The use of fantasies was not a sign of marital difficulty. In fact, women who fantasized reported *better* sexual relations with their partners than did those who did not. The content of these fantasies suggests that they serve to introduce novelty or variety into their sexual relationships.

RELATIONSHIP ISSUES AND COITAL FANTASIES   Studies of coital fantasies by Hariton and Singer (1974) and Sue (1979), among others, find that sexual fantasies during intercourse are common among couples with close relationships and are a means of facilitating sexual arousal. By facilitating sexual arousal, coital fantasies may help to strengthen the intimate bond between the partners. Evidence does not show coital fantasies to be a sign of a troubled relationship.

Evidence fails to show that coital fantasies are a sign of a troubled relationship. ■

Truth or Fiction?
REVISITED

Partners are often reluctant to share their coital fantasies or even to admit to them. This is especially true when the fantasy is about someone other than the partner. The fan-

table 9.4

Coital fantasies of married women	
Fantasy	**Women Reporting Fantasy (%)**
Thoughts of an imaginary romantic lover enter my mind.	56
I relive a previous sexual experience.	52
I enjoy pretending that I am doing something forbidden.	50
I imagine that I am being overpowered or forced to surrender.	49
I am in a different place, like a car, motel, beach, woods, etc.	47
I imagine myself delighting many men.	43
I pretend that I struggle and resist before being aroused to surrender.	40
I imagine that I am observing myself or others having sex.	38
I pretend that I am another irresistibly sexy female.	38
I daydream that I am being made love to by more than one man at a time.	36
My thoughts center about feelings of weakness or helplessness.	33
I see myself as a striptease dancer, harem girl, or other performer.	28
I pretend that I am a whore or a prostitute.	25
I imagine that I am being forced to expose my body to a seducer.	19
My thoughts center around urination or defecation.	2

Source: Hariton & Singer, 1974.

tasizer might fear being accused of harboring extramarital desires. Or the fantasizer might fear that the partner will interpret fantasies as a sign of rejection: "What's the matter, don't I turn you on anymore?" The advisability of self-disclosure is best weighed against one's partner's potential reactions to coital fantasies.

ANAL INTERCOURSE Anal intercourse can be practiced by male-female couples and male-male couples. It involves insertion of the penis into the rectum. The rectum is richly endowed with nerve endings and is therefore highly sensitive to sexual stimulation. Anal intercourse is also referred to as "Greek culture" or lovemaking in the "Greek style" because of bisexuality in ancient Greece among males. It is also the major act that comes under the legal definition of sodomy. Both women and men may reach orgasm through receiving the penis in the rectum and thrusting.

In anal intercourse, the penetrating male usually situates himself behind his partner. (He can also lie above or below his partner in a face-to-face position.) The receiving partner can supplement anal stimulation with manual stimulation of the clitoral region or penis to reach orgasm.

Women often report wanting their partner's fingers in the anus at the height of passion or at the moment of orgasm. A finger in the rectum at the time of orgasm can heighten sexual sensation because the anal sphincters contract during orgasm. Although some men also want a finger in the anus, many resist because they associate anal penetration with the female role or with male-male sexual activity. However, the desire to be entered by one's partner is not necessarily connected with sexual orientation. A gay male or lesbian sexual orientation refers to the eroticization of members of one's own gender, not the desire to penetrate or be penetrated.

Many couples are repulsed by the idea of anal intercourse. They view it as unnatural, immoral, or risky. Others find anal sex to be an enjoyable sexual variation, though perhaps not a regular feature of their sexual diet.

The NHSLS survey found that one man in four (26%) and one woman in five (20%) reported having engaged in anal sex at some time during their lives (Laumann et al., 1994). Yet only about one person in ten (10% of the men and 9% of the women) had engaged in anal sex during the past year. As with oral sex, there was a higher incidence of anal sex among more highly educated people in the NHSLS survey. For example, about 30% of the male college graduates had engaged in anal sex, compared with 23% of male high school graduates. About 29% of the women with advanced college degrees had engaged in anal sex, compared with about 17% of the women who had graduated only from high school (Laumann et al., 1994). Education appears to be a liberating experience in sexual experimentation. About one in five men in the Battelle sample reported having engaged in anal intercourse (Billy et al., 1993). As in the NHSLS survey, anal intercourse was more commonly reported among better-educated men.

Truth or Fiction?
REVISITED

Anal sex actually turns out to be *less* common among less well educated people. Perhaps education is a liberating influence on sexual experimentation. ■

Religion appears to be a restraining influence on anal sex. About 34% of the men and 36% of the women in the NHSLS survey who said that they had no religion reported engaging in anal sex during their lifetimes. Percentages for male Christians ranged from the lower to upper 20s, and those for female Christians ranged from the midteens to the lower 20s (Laumann et al., 1994, p. 99). There were too few Jews in the sample to report meaningful figures for Jewish men and women.

Many couples kiss or lick the anus in their foreplay. This practice is called **anilingus.** Oral-anal sex carries a serious health risk, however, because microorganisms that cause intestinal diseases and various sexually transmitted diseases can be spread through oral-anal contact.

Many couples today hesitate to engage in anal intercourse because of the fear of AIDS and other sexually transmitted infections (STIs). The AIDS virus and other

Anilingus Oral stimulation of the anus.

microorganisms causing STIs such as gonorrhea, syphilis, and hepatitis can be spread by anal intercourse, because small tears in the rectal tissues may allow the microbes to enter the recipient's bloodstream. Women also incur a greater risk of contracting HIV, the virus that causes AIDS, from anal intercourse than from vaginal intercourse—just as receptive anal intercourse in gay men carries a high risk of infection (Voeller, 1991). However, partners who are both infection-free are at no risk of contracting STIs through any sexual act.

Reflections

- How do our attitudes and values influence the kinds of foreplay and sexual techniques we will enjoy?
- What is the connection between level of education and sexual practices such as oral sex? Do you believe that your college experience will have any effects on your own sexual behavior? Explain.
- Do the "missionary," female-superior, or rear-entry positions for intercourse seem to you to express any political attitudes concerning male-female relationships? Explain.

In this chapter, we have observed many of the variations in human sexual expression. No other species shows such diversity in sexual behavior. People show diversity not only in sexual behavior, but also in sexual orientation—which is the focus of the following chapter.

summing up

SOLITARY SEXUAL BEHAVIOR

Masturbation
Masturbation may be practiced by means of manual stimulation of the genitals, perhaps with the aid of an electric vibrator or object that provides tactile stimulation. Within the Judeo-Christian tradition, masturbation has been condemned as sinful. Until recent years, masturbation was thought to be physically and mentally harmful, yet contemporary scholars see masturbation as harmless. Surveys indicate that most people have masturbated at some point in their lives.

Sexual Fantasy
Sexual fantasies are often incorporated with masturbation or with sex with another person to heighten sexual response. Sexual fantasies range from the realistic to flights of fancy. Many people fantasize about sexual activities in which they would not actually engage.

SEX WITH OTHERS

Foreplay
The pattern and duration of foreplay vary widely within and across cultures. Women usually desire longer periods of foreplay than men do.

Kissing
Couples kiss for its own enjoyment or as a prelude to intercourse.

Touching
Touching or caressing erogenous zones with the hands or other parts of the body can be highly arousing. Men typically prefer direct stroking of their genitals by their partner early in lovemaking. Women tend to prefer that their partners caress their genitals after a period of general body contact.

Breast Stimulation
Most, but not all, women enjoy breast stimulation. The hands and the mouth can be used to stimulate the breasts.

Oral-Genital Stimulation
The popularity of oral-genital stimulation has increased dramatically since Kinsey's day, but survey researchers find persistent differences in the frequency of these activities between African and White Americans.

Sexual Intercourse: Positions and Techniques
Couples today use a greater variety of coital positions than couples in Kinsey's time. Four of the most commonly used coital positions are the male-superior position, the female-superior position, the lateral-entry position, and the rear-entry position.

Charles Demuth. *Dancing Sailors.* 1917. Watercolor, 20.4 x 25.7 cm. © The Cleveland Museum of Art, 1999, Mr. and Mrs. William H. Marlatt Fund, 1980.9

chapter

10

Sexual Orientation

o u t l i n e

TRUTH OR FICTION?

SEXUAL ORIENTATION

Coming to Terms with Terms

Sexual Orientation and Gender Identity

Classification of Sexual Orientation

Bisexuality

PERSPECTIVES ON GAY MALE AND LESBIAN SEXUAL ORIENTATIONS

Historical Perspectives

Cross-Cultural Perspectives

A WORLD OF DIVERSITY:
Ethnicity and Sexual Orientation: A Matter of Belonging

Cross-Species Perspectives

Attitudes Toward Sexual Orientation in Contemporary Society

Biological Perspectives

Psychological Perspectives

Gender Nonconformity

ADJUSTMENT OF GAY MALES AND LESBIANS

Treatment of Gay Male and Lesbian Sexual Orientations

COMING OUT: COMING TO TERMS WITH BEING GAY

Coming Out to Oneself

Coming Out to Others

IN THE NEW MILLENNIUM:
Out into the "Gay Global Village" of Cyberspace

PATTERNS OF SEXUAL ACTIVITY AMONG GAY MALES AND LESBIANS

Sexual Techniques

GAY LIFESTYLES

Lifestyle Differences Between Gay Males and Lesbians

Variations in Gay Lifestyles

SUMMING UP

Truth or Fiction?

_____ A lesbian lost custody of her daughter to the girl's father, even though he had served a prison term for murdering his first wife.

_____ Gay males and lesbians would prefer to be members of the other gender.

_____ Gay males and lesbians suffer from hormonal imbalances.

_____ Gay males unconsciously fear women's genitals because they associate them with castration.

_____ The American Psychiatric Association considers homosexuality to be a mental disorder.

_____ Many gay couples have lifestyles similar to those of married heterosexual couples and are as well adjusted.

John, a nurse, was awarded custody of his 7-year-old son, Jacob, after a divorce. John's companion, Don, often picks Jacob up after school. "Who is that?" a teacher unfamiliar with the situation asked Jacob one day.

"That's my father's husband," Jacob replied matter-of-factly. (Gross, 1991)

Alyson Publications, a Boston publisher, added two titles to its children's list: *Heather Has Two Mommies* and *Daddy's Roommate*. (Gross, 1991)

A Florida mother—a lesbian—lost custody of her 12-year-old daughter to the girl's father, even though he had served 8 years in prison for murdering his first wife. (Navarro, 1996)

Over a cup of coffee one blustery afternoon, Deidra Mack confessed to feeling the jitters about entering the stately brick church nearby, standing before a minister and making vows of lifetime commitment. But minutes later, there she was, in First Unitarian Universalist Society's austerely elegant sanctuary, facing her partner, Barbara Dolores. At the Rev. Gary Kowalski's invitation, the two women, both 28, spoke their vows and exchanged rings. "You have made for yourselves a marriage," the minister said. "Your lives are now joined." Family members and friends applauded. (Niebuhr, 1998)

This chapter is about **sexual orientation.** Sexual orientation concerns the *direction* of one's romantic interests and erotic attractions—toward members of the same gender, the other gender, or both.

As the news clips at the beginning of the chapter suggest, many children are reared by gay male or lesbian couples. In most states, a gay male or lesbian sexual orientation is no longer grounds for parents to lose custody of their children (Dunlap, 1995). States have become generally more accepting of this living arrangement because there is no evidence that children who are reared by gay male and lesbian parents are less well adjusted than other children (Allen & Burrell, 1996; Patterson, 1995). Still there are exceptions, as indicated by the Florida case in which custody of a girl was transferred from the girl's mother—a lesbian—to the father, even though the father had served a prison term for murdering his first wife. Nor is there evidence that being reared by a parent with a gay male or lesbian sexual orientation causes children to develop such sexual orientations or gender identity confusion (Allen & Burrell, 1996; Patterson, 1995).

It is true that a lesbian lost custody of her daughter to the girl's father, even though he had served a prison term for murdering his first wife. It happened in Florida in 1996. ■

Truth or Fiction?
REVISITED

In the chapter, we see that gay people, like heterosexual people, struggle to incorporate their sexuality within their personal identity, to find lovers, and to establish satisfying lifestyles. In fact, gay marriages are now permitted in a number of states. In 1996, however, the U.S. Senate voted 85–14 that one state would not have to recognize a gay marriage that was permitted in another state (Schmitt, 1996). Unlike heterosexual people, gay people in our culture face a backdrop of social intolerance, even if they commit themselves to "traditional" long-term relationships such as marriage.

Sexual orientation The directionality of one's sexual interests—toward members of the same gender, the other gender, or both genders.

Heterosexual orientation Erotic attraction to, and preference for developing romantic relationships with, members of the other gender.

SEXUAL ORIENTATION

Sexual orientation refers to one's erotic attractions toward, and interests in developing romantic relationships with, members of one's own or the other gender (American Psychological Association, 1998b). A **heterosexual orientation** refers to an erotic attraction to, and preference for developing romantic relationships with, members of the other gender. (Many gay people refer to heterosexual people as being *straight* or as *straights.*) Notice that we say "other gender," not "opposite gender." Social critics note that many of the prob-

Terminology of Sexual Orientation. Are these women homosexuals, homophiles, or lesbians, or do they have a lesbian sexual orientation? Many gay people object to the term *homosexual* because it focuses on sexual behavior rather than relationships. Because the Greek root *philia* refers to love or friendship and not to sexual behavior, perhaps the most appropriate term is *homophile*.

lems that arise between men and women are based on the notion that men and women are polar opposites (Bem, 1993). Research and common sense both support the view that men and women are more alike in personality and behavior than they are different, however.

A **homosexual orientation** refers to an erotic attraction to, and interest in forming romantic relationships with, members of one's own gender. The term *homosexuality* denotes sexual interest in members of one's own gender and applies to both men and women. Homosexual men are often referred to as **gay males.** Homosexual women are also called **lesbians** or *gay women*. Gay males and lesbians are also referred to collectively as "gays" or "gay people." The term **bisexuality** refers to an orientation in which one is sexually attracted to, and interested in forming romantic relationships with, both males and females.

Coming to Terms with Terms

Now that we have defined the term *homosexuality*, let us note that we will use it only sparingly. Many gay people object to the term *homosexual* because they believe that it draws too much attention to sexual behavior. Moreover, the term bears a social stigma. Many gays would prefer terms such as *gay male* or *lesbian sexual orientation* or a term such as *homophile* if a term must be used to set them apart. The Greek root *philia* suggests love and friendship rather than sexual behavior. Therefore, a homophile is a person who develops romantic love and emotional commitment to members of her or his own gender. Sexual activity is secondary.

We therefore use the terms *gay male* and *lesbian* instead of *homosexual* when we refer to sexual orientation. As was noted by the American Psychological Association's (1991) Committee on Lesbian and Gay Concerns, the word *homosexual* has also been historically associated with concepts of deviance and mental illness. It perpetuates negative stereotypes of gay people. Also, the term is often used to refer to men only. It thus renders lesbians invisible.

Then, too, the word *homosexual* is ambiguous in meaning—that is, does it refer to sexual behavior or sexual orientation (Suppe, 1994)? In this book, your authors speak of male-female sexual behavior (not *heterosexual* behavior), male-male sexual behavior, and female-female sexual behavior.

Homosexual orientation Erotic attraction to, and preference for developing romantic relationships with, members of one's own gender. (From the Greek *homos*, meaning "same," not the Latin *homo*, which means "man").

Gay males Males who are erotically attracted to and desire to form romantic relationships with other males.

Lesbians Females who are erotically attracted to, and desire to form romantic relationships with, other females. (After *Lesbos*, the Greek island on which, legend has it, female-female sexual activity was idealized).

Bisexuality Erotic attraction to, and interest in developing romantic relationships with, males and females.

Sexual Orientation and Gender Identity

Since gay people are attracted to members of their own gender, some people assume that they would prefer to be members of the other gender. Like heterosexual people, however, gay people have a gender identity that is consistent with their anatomic gender. Unlike transsexuals, gay people do not see themselves as being trapped in the body of the other gender.

It is not true that gay males and lesbians would prefer to be members of the other gender. Their gender identity is consistent with their anatomic gender. ■

Heterosexuals tend to focus almost exclusively on sexual aspects of male-male and female-female relationships. But the love relationships of gay people, like those of heterosexual people, involve more than sex. Gay people, like heterosexual people, spend only a small proportion of their time in sexual activity. More basic to a gay male or lesbian sexual orientation is the formation of romantic attachments with members of one's own gender. These attachments, like male-female attachments, provide a framework for love and intimacy. Although sex and love are common features of relationships, neither is a *necessary* prerequisite for a relationship. Sexual orientations are not defined by sexual activity per se, but rather by the *direction* of one's romantic interests and erotic attractions.

Classification of Sexual Orientation

Determining a person's sexual orientation might seem to be a clear-cut task. Some people are exclusively gay and limit their sexual activities to partners of their own gender. Others are strictly heterosexual and limit their sexual activities to partners of the other gender. Many people fall somewhere in between, however. Where might we draw the line between a gay male or lesbian sexual orientation, on the one hand, and a heterosexual orientation, on the other? Where do we draw the line between these orientations and bisexuality?

It is possible, indeed not unusual, for heterosexual people to have had some sexual experiences with people of their own gender. Consider a survey of more than 7,000 male readers of *Playboy* magazine. Among those reporting sexual experiences with both men and women in adulthood, more than two out of three perceived themselves to be heterosexual rather than bisexual (Lever et al., 1992). For many of these men, sexual experiences with other men were limited to a brief period of their lives and did not alter their sexual orientations. Lacking heterosexual outlets, prison inmates may have sexual experiences with people of their own gender while they maintain their heterosexual identities. Inmates would form sexual relationships with people of the other gender if they were available, and they return to male-female sexual behavior upon release from prison. Physical affection also helps some prisoners, male and female, to cope with loneliness and isolation. Males who engage in prostitution with male clients may separate their sexual orientation from their "trade." Many fantasize about a female when permitting a client to fellate them. The behavior is male-male. The person's sexual *orientation* may be heterosexual.

Gay males and lesbians, too, might engage in male-female sexual activity while maintaining a gay sexual orientation. Some gay males and lesbians marry members of the other gender but continue to harbor unfulfilled desires for members of their own gender. Then, too, some people are bisexual but might not have acted upon their attraction to members of their own gender.

Sexual orientation is not necessarily expressed in sexual behavior. Many people come to perceive themselves as gay or heterosexual long before they ever engage in sex with members of their own gender. Some people, gay and heterosexual alike, adopt a celibate lifestyle for religious or ascetic reasons and abstain from sexual relationships. Some remain celibate not by choice but because of lack of partners.

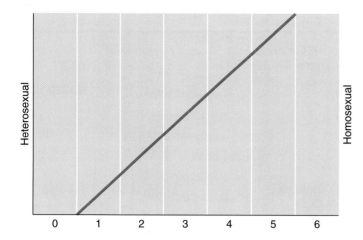

figure 10.1

The Kinsey Continuum. Kinsey and his colleagues conceived a seven-point heterosexual-homosexual continuum that classifies people according to their homosexual behavior and the magnitude of their attraction to members of their own gender. People in category 0, who accounted for most of Kinsey's study participants, were considered exclusively heterosexual. People in category 6 were considered exclusively homosexual.

People's erotic interests and fantasies may also shift over time. Gay males and lesbians may experience sporadic **heteroerotic** interests. Heterosexual people may have occasional **homoerotic** interests. Many heterosexual people report fantasies about sexual activity with people of their own gender. Many gay people have fantasies about sex with people of the other gender (Masters & Johnson, 1979). About 50% of one sample of lesbians reported that they are sometimes attracted to men (Bell & Weinberg, 1978).

Attraction to people of the other gender and people of one's own gender may therefore not be mutually exclusive. People may have various degrees of sexual interest in, and sexual experience with, people of either gender. Kinsey and his colleagues recognized that the boundaries between gay male and lesbian sexual orientations, on the one hand, and a heterosexual orientation, on the other, are sometimes blurry. They therefore proposed a continuum of sexual orientation rather than two poles.

THE KINSEY CONTINUUM Before Kinsey, scientists generally viewed gay and heterosexual orientations as separate categories. People were viewed as either gay or heterosexual in their psychological makeup and erotic interests. However, Kinsey and his colleagues (1948, 1953) found evidence of degrees of gay and heterosexual orientations among people he surveyed, with bisexuality representing a midpoint between the two. As Kinsey and his colleagues noted,

> The world is not to be divided into sheep and goats. . . . Only the human mind invents categories and tries to force facts into separated pigeonholes. The living world is a continuum in each and every one of its aspects. (1948, p. 639)

Kinsey and his colleagues (1948, 1953) conceived a seven-point "heterosexual-homosexual continuum" (see Figure 10.1). People are located on the continuum according to their patterns of sexual attraction and behavior. People in category 0 are considered exclusively heterosexual. People in category 6 are considered exclusively gay.

PICKING CRITERIA What percentage of the population, then, is gay? The percentages depend on the criteria that one uses. Kinsey and his colleagues reported that about 4% of men and 1% to 3% of women in their samples were exclusively gay (6 on their scale). A larger percentage of people were considered predominantly gay (scale points 4 or 5) or predominantly heterosexual (1 or 2 on their scale). Some were classified as equally gay and heterosexual in orientation and could be labeled bisexual (scale point 3). Most people were classified as exclusively heterosexual (scale point 0). Table 10.1 on page 270 indicates the percentage of people who were classified according to the seven categories in Figure 10.1. Percentages varied according to marital status, age, level of education, and other factors. This particular table is based on people ages 20 to 35.

Heteroerotic Of an erotic nature and involving members of the other gender.

Homoerotic Of an erotic nature and involving members of one's own gender.

table 10.1

Percentages of respondents ages 20 to 35 at each level of the Kinsey Continuum of Sexual Orientation		
Rating Category	**Females (%)**	**Males (%)**
0: Entirely heterosexual experience		
Single	61–72	53–78
Married	89–90	90–92
Previously married	75–80	
1–6: At least some sexual experience with people of one's own gender	11–20	18–42
2–6: More than incidental sexual experience with people of one's own gender	6–14	13–38
3–6: Homosexual as much or more than heterosexual	4–11	9–32
4–6: Mostly homosexual	3–8	7–26
5–6: Almost exclusively homosexual	2–6	5–22
6: Exclusively homosexual	1–3	3–16

Source: Adapted from Kinsey, A. C., et al. (1953). *Sexual behavior in the human female.* Philadelphia: W. B. Saunders, p. 488. Reprinted by permission of the Kinsey Institute for Research in Sex, Gender, and Reproduction, Inc.

Married people were more likely than single people to be classified as exclusively heterosexual. During Kinsey's day, single young people had fewer heterosexual outlets, which could have encouraged them to seek partners of their own gender. A gay male or lesbian sexual orientation might have influenced some to delay marriage, however. Men, overall, were more likely than women to report sexual experiences with people of their own gender.

Between the poles of the continuum lie people with various degrees of sexual interest in, and sexual experience with, people of their own gender. Thirty-seven percent of men and 13% of the women told interviewers that they had reached orgasm through sexual activity with someone of their own gender at some time after puberty. Fifty percent of men who remained single until age 35 reported that they had reached orgasm through sexual activity with other males.

Many people in Kinsey's day were startled by these figures. They meant that sexual activity with people of one's own gender, especially among males, was more widespread than had been believed. But Kinsey's figures for male-male sexual activity might have been exaggerated. For instance, his finding that 37% of males had reached orgasm through sexual activity with other males was based on a sample that included a high proportion of former prisoners. Findings might also have been distorted by the researchers' efforts to recruit known gay people into their samples. Once these sources of possible bias are corrected, the incidence of male-male sexual activity drops from 37% to about 25%. (Even this percentage is much higher than people suspected at the time.) Because Kinsey's sample was not drawn at random, however, we cannot say whether it represented the general population.

A 1970 nationwide survey conducted by the Kinsey Institute obtained results (published in 1989) that were strikingly similar to Kinsey's early (adjusted) estimates. At least 20% of the randomly selected adult men in the United States had reached orgasm through male-male sexual activity at some point in their lives (Fay et al., 1989). Between 1% and 2% of men in the United States reported male-male sexual experiences within the past year. A 1993 Louis Harris poll found that 4.4% of men and 3.6% of women reported sexual activity with a member of their own gender within the past five years (Barringer, 1993b). Kinsey Institute director June Reinisch (1990) examined the available evidence and estimated that more than 25% of men in the United States have had a male-male sexual experience in their teens or adult years.

Statistics concerning *past* sexual activity with a member of one's own gender can be misleading. They may represent a single episode or a brief period of adolescent experimentation. Half of the men who reported male-male sexual activity in Kinsey's sample had limited their experiences to the ages of 12 to 14. Another third had male-male sexual experience by the age of 18 but not again.

Kinsey's research also showed that sexual behavior patterns could shift during a person's lifetime, sometimes dramatically (Sanders et al., 1990). Sexual experiences or feelings involving people of one's own gender are common, especially in adolescence, and do not mean that one will engage in sexual activity exclusively with people of one's own gender in adulthood (Bullough, 1990).

What did Kinsey find with respect to more enduring patterns of male-male and female-female sexual activity? Estimates based on an analysis of Kinsey's data (Gebhard, 1977) suggest that 13% of the men and 7% of the women, or 10% for both genders combined, were either predominantly or exclusively interested in, and sexually active with, people of their own gender for at least three years between the ages of 16 and 55.

Lately, there has been considerable controversy concerning the percentages of people who are believed to be gay. Current estimates generally find lower percentages of gay people in the population than Kinsey did. Considering data drawn from studies conducted in the United States, Asia, and Pacific Island countries, Milton Diamond (1993) estimates that only about 5% of men and 2% to 3% of women across different cultures have engaged in sexual activity with someone of their own gender on at least one occasion since adolescence. No cross-cultural studies show rates of sexual activity with people of the same gender to reach Kinsey's often-cited figure of 10% of predominant or exclusive sexual behavior with partners of one's own gender. Diamond also finds fewer people to have a bisexual orientation than a gay male or lesbian sexual orientation.

Research in the United States, Britain, France, and Denmark finds that about 3% of men surveyed *identify* themselves as gay (Hamer et al., 1993; Laumann et al., 1994). About 2% of the U.S. women surveyed *identify* themselves as lesbians (Janus & Janus, 1993; Laumann and others, 1994). Surveys in the United States, Britain, and France find that larger numbers of men (5% to 11%) and women (2% to 4%) report *engaging in sexual behavior* with members of their own gender within the past five years (Sell et al., 1995). Surveys show that still larger numbers of men (8% to 9%) and women (8% to 12%) report some *sexual attraction* to members of their own gender but no sexual interaction since the age of 15 (Sell et al., 1995).

Sex surveys reveal the percentages only of people who are *willing to admit* to certain behaviors or sexual orientations (Cronin, 1993; Isay, 1993). "We can't count people who simply don't want to be counted" (Cronin, 1993). Surveys may omit gay people who hesitate to proclaim their sexual orientation because of social stigma or repression of their sexual feelings.

Keep in mind that the following factors affect survey results:

- The ways in which the questions are phrased (for example, do they look into sexual identity, sexual behavior, or sexual attraction—and over what period of time?)
- The social desirability of the professed behavior
- The gender of the interviewer
- The manner in which the survey was conducted, such as by means of personal interviews, phone calls, or written surveys
- The biases of respondents, such as volunteer bias

CHALLENGES TO THE KINSEY CONTINUUM   Although the Kinsey continuum has been widely adopted by sex researchers, it is not universally accepted. Kinsey believed that exclusive heterosexual and gay sexual orientations lay at opposite poles of one continuum. Therefore, the more heterosexual a person is, the less gay that person is, and vice versa (Sanders et al., 1990).

Viewing gay and heterosexual orientations as opposite poles of one continuum is akin to the traditional view of masculinity and femininity as opposite poles of one continuum, such that the more masculine one is, the less feminine, and vice versa. Viewing men and women as opposites has led to misunderstandings, even hostility, between the genders (Bem, 1993). But we may also regard masculinity and femininity as independent personality dimensions. Similarly, the view of gay people and heterosexuals as opposites had also led to misunderstandings and hostility (Katz, 1995). Yet these sexual orientations may also be separate dimensions, rather than polar opposites.

Psychologist Michael Storms (1980) suggests that gay and heterosexual orientations are independent dimensions. Thus, one can be high or low on both dimensions simultaneously. Storms (1980) suggests that there are separate dimensions of responsiveness to male-female stimulation (heteroeroticism) and sexual stimulation that involves someone of the same gender (homoeroticism), as shown in Figure 10.2. According to this model, bisexuals are high in both dimensions, whereas people who are low in both are essentially asexual. According to Kinsey, bisexual individuals would be *less* responsive to stimulation by people of the other gender than heterosexual people are but *more* responsive to stimulation by people of their own gender. According to the two-dimensional model, however, bisexual people may be as responsive to stimulation by people of the other gender as heterosexual people are and as responsive to stimulation by people of their own gender as gay people are.

FANTASY AS THE MEASURE   Kinsey had argued that the content of erotic fantasies was an excellent gauge of sexual orientation. To test this formulation, Storms (1980) investigated the erotic fantasies of heterosexual, gay, and bisexual people. Kinsey might have predicted that bisexual individuals would have *fewer* heteroerotic fantasies than heterosexual people, and *more* homoerotic fantasies than heterosexual people. But Storms predicted that "bisexuals will report as *much* heteroerotic fantasy as heterosexual people and as much homoerotic fantasy as homosexuals" (p. 786).

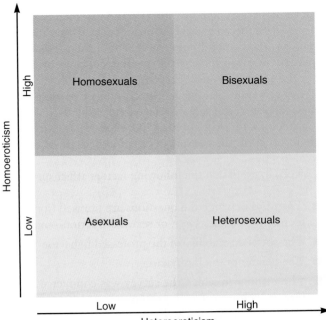

figure 10.2

Heterosexuality and Homosexuality as Separate Dimensions.
According to this model, homosexuality and heterosexuality are independent dimensions. One can thus be high or low on both dimensions at the same time. Most people are high in one dimension. Bisexuals are high in both dimensions. People who are low in both are considered *asexual*.

Storms found that heterosexual students reported significantly more fantasies about the other gender than about their own gender. Gay students reported more frequent fantasies about their own gender. Bisexuals, as predicted, reported a high level of both kinds of fantasies. Gay students were also more likely to have fantasies about the other gender than heterosexual students were to have fantasies about their own gender. Given the stigma attached to homosexuality, it may be that heterosexual people are less likely to admit to fantasies about their own gender (even to themselves). It may also be that gay males and lesbians are influenced by the media and the culture at large, which, of course, continually portray socially desirable male-female interactions.

Whatever the reasons, Storms did find that many bisexual people show a high level of sexual interest, as measured by erotic fantasies, in both men and women. Therefore, it may be that sexual interest in the other gender and in one's own gender are independent dimensions rather than opposite poles of one continuum. Yet most sex researchers continue to use the Kinsey scale, or some derivative of it, for classifying sexual orientation (Sanders et al., 1990).

Bisexuality

To me, I never felt like I had a stronger attraction to men or women. I didn't have a problem identifying myself as gay, but I knew that wasn't the whole picture.

—A 29-year-old social worker from North Carolina who fell in love with a woman and then had a sexual relationship with his male roommate

I don't limit myself to a guy or a girl. Whoever comes into my life, if we hit it off, great. That's happened with a lot of people I know. They'll say, "Guess what happened last night." It's very accepted.

—A 22-year-old political science major

She finally came out of the closet and said, "Mom, there's this girl and she's the most gorgeous girl you've ever seen." I said, "You're only for girls?" She said, "No, it's not just the girls. I can see a really good-looking guy, too."

—The mother of a 19-year-old woman who uses a computer bulletin board to meet other bisexuals

(Adapted from Gabriel, 1995b)

Bisexual people are sexually attracted to both males and females. Many bisexual people have somewhat stronger attraction to one gender than the other, yet they remain bisexual (Weinberg et al., 1994). Kinsey and his colleagues considered people rated as 3s to be bisexual (see Figure 10.1).

Depending on how one defines bisexuality, perhaps 1% to 4% of the population is bisexual. About 1% of the people (0.8% of the men and 0.9% of the women) surveyed in the NHSLS study (Laumann et al., 1994) reported having a bisexual *identity*. However, about 4% (3.9% of the men and 4.1% of the women) reported that they were sexually attracted to both women and men.

Bisexual people are sometimes said to "swing both ways," or to be "AC-DC" (as in "alternating current" and "direct current"). Some gay people (and some heterosexual people) believe that claims to bisexuality are a "cop-out" that people use to deny being gay. Perhaps they fear leaving their spouses or "coming out" (declaring their gay male or lesbian sexual orientation publicly). Others view bisexuality as a form of sexual experimentation with people of one's own gender by people who are predominantly heterosexual. But many avowed bisexual people disagree. They report that they can maintain erotic interests in, and romantic relationships with, members of both genders. Some authors (e.g., Garber, 1995; Weinberg et al., 1994) insist that bisexuality is an authentic sexual orientation and not simply a cover for a gay male or lesbian sexual orientation.

Some bisexual people follow lifestyles that permit them to satisfy their dual inclinations. Others feel pressured by heterosexual and gay people alike to commit themselves one way or the other (Garber, 1995; Weinberg et al., 1994). Some gay people also mask their sexual orientation by adopting a bisexual lifestyle. That is, they get married but also enter into clandestine sexual liaisons with members of their own gender.

Reflections

- ▨ Agree or disagree with the following statement and support your answer: Gay males and lesbians should be permitted to adopt children.
- ▨ We prefer to use the terms *gay males* and *lesbians* rather than *homosexuals*. Do you endorse the use of our terminology? Why or why not?
- ▨ Does it make sense to you to distinguish between one's sexual orientation and one's sexual behavior? For example, do you believe that males may engage in sexual activity with other males and maintain a heterosexual orientation? Why or why not?

PERSPECTIVES ON GAY MALE AND LESBIAN SEXUAL ORIENTATIONS

Gay male and lesbian sexual orientations have existed throughout history. Attitudes toward them have varied widely. They have been tolerated in some societies, openly encouraged in others, but condemned in most (Bullough, 1990). In this section, we review historical and other perspectives on gay male and lesbian sexual orientations.

Historical Perspectives

In Western culture, few sexual practices have met with such widespread censure as sexual activities with members of one's own gender. Throughout much of history, male-male and female-female sexual behavior were deemed sinful and criminal—an outrage against God and humanity. Within the Judeo-Christian tradition, male-male sexual activity was regarded as a sin so vile that no one dared speak its name. Our legal system, grounded in this religious tradition, maintains criminal penalties for sexual practices commonly associated with male-male and female-female sex, such as anal and oral sex. Much of the criminalization of male-male and female-female sex has been directed against men (Bullough, 1990; Katz, 1995).

Jews and Christians have traditionally referred to male-male sexual activity as the sin of Sodom. Hence the origin of the term *sodomy*, which generally alludes to anal intercourse (and sometimes to oral-genital contact). According to the Book of Genesis, the city of Sodom was destroyed by God. Yet it is unclear what behavior incurred God's wrath. Pope Gregory III was not ambiguous, however, in his eighth-century account of the city's obliteration as a punishment for sexual activity with members of one's own gender.

The Book of Leviticus was also clear in its condemnation:

> If a man lies with a man as with a woman, both of them have committed an abomination; they shall be put to death, their blood is upon them. (Leviticus 20:13)

Sexual activity with members of one's own gender was not the only sexual act that the early Christians considered sinful. Any nonprocreative sexual act was considered sinful, even within marriage. With the fall of the Roman Empire, the influence of Christianity spread across Western Europe. Christian beliefs were eventually encoded into secular law. By the late Middle Ages, most civil statutes throughout Western Europe contained penalties for nonprocreative sexual acts involving the discharge of semen, including oral or anal sex, masturbation, male-male sexual behavior, and bestiality (Boswell, 1990). Male-male and female-female sexual practices continue to be condemned by most Christian and Jewish denominations and by Islam.

The Roman Catholic Church draws a distinction between a gay male or lesbian sexual orientation, on the one hand, and male-male or female-female sexual behavior on the other, however (Donoghue, 1995; Sullivan, 1995). The behavior is the sin, not the orientation. The church sees sin as a temporary state from which a sinner, including a gay male or lesbian sinner, can be freed by behavioral change, contrition, and repentance.

Despite the history of opposition to gay male and lesbian sexual orientations, some churches today are performing marriages of gay couples—or, if marriage itself remains illegal, they are at least "blessing" their relationships. The St. Paul–Reformation Lutheran Church in St. Paul, Minnesota, has even written a theological statement to explain why it blesses the relationships of gay couples. The church interprets the biblical creation story to mean that God did not intend for people to live alone and "that all human creatures are created for the sake of mutual companionship on this earth" (in Niebuhr, 1998). The Reverend Gary Kowalski, who blesses some three gay unions a year at the First Unitarian Universalist Society (while performing about 20 traditional weddings), says, "The reason I perform same-sex ceremonies is I think churches and other social institutions should be in the business of encouraging long-term relationships" (Niebuhr, 1998).

Cross-Cultural Perspectives

Male-male sexual behavior has been practiced in many preliterate societies. In their review of the literature on 76 preliterate societies, Ford and Beach (1951) found that in 49 societies (64%), male-male sexual interactions were viewed as normal and deemed socially acceptable for some members of the group. The other 27 societies (36%) had sanctions against male-male sexual behavior. Nevertheless, male-male sexual activity persisted. In another cross-cultural analysis, Broude and Greene (1976) found that male-male sexual behavior was present but uncommon in 41% of a sample of 70 of the world's non-European societies. It was rare or absent in 59% of these societies. Broude and Greene also found evidence of societal disapproval and punishment of male-male sexual activity in 41% of a sample of 42 societies for which information was available.

Sexual behavior between adult males appears to be more common in societies that highly value female virginity before marriage and segregate young men and women (Davenport, 1977). Such factors may increase juvenile male-male sexual experimentation, which may then persist into adulthood.

Some societies permit or require some forms of male-male sexual activity. In some societies, sexual activities are acceptable between older and younger males or between adolescents but not between adult men. At the turn of the century, the Swans of North Africa expected all juvenile males to engage in sexual relations with older men. Fathers arranged for unmarried sons to be given to older men. Almost all men were reported to have had such sexual relationships as boys. Later, between the ages of 16 and 20, they all married women.

Sexual activities between males are sometimes limited to rites that mark the young male's initiation into manhood. In some preliterate societies, semen is believed to boost strength and virility. Older males therefore transmit semen to younger males through oral or anal sexual activities. Among the Sambian people of New Guinea, a tribe of warlike headhunters, 9- to 12-year-old males leave their parents' households and live in a "clubhouse" with other prepubertal and adolescent males. There, they undergo sexual rites of passage. To acquire the fierce manhood of the headhunter, they perform fellatio on older males and drink "men's milk" (semen) (Herdt, 1981; Money, 1990; Stoller & Herdt, 1985). The initiate is enjoined to ingest as much semen as he can, "as if it were breast milk or food" (Herdt, 1981, p. 235). Ingestion of semen is believed to give rise to puberty. Following puberty, adolescents are fellated by younger males (Baldwin & Baldwin, 1989). By the age of 19, however, young men are expected to take brides and enter exclusively male-female sexual relationships.

ETHNICITY AND SEXUAL ORIENTATION: A Matter of Belonging

Lesbians and gay men frequently suffer the slings and arrows of an outraged society. Because of societal prejudices, it is difficult for many young people to come to terms with an emerging lesbian or gay male sexual orientation. You might assume that people who have been subjected to prejudice and discrimination—members of ethnic minority groups in the United States—would be more tolerant of a lesbian or gay male sexual orientation. However, according to psychologist Beverly Greene (1994) of St. John's University, such an assumption might not be warranted.

In an article that addresses the experiences of lesbians and gay men from ethnic minority groups, Greene (1994) notes that it is difficult to generalize about ethnic groups in the United States. For example, African Americans may find their cultural origins in the tribes of West Africa, but they have also been influenced by Christianity and the local subcultures of their North American towns and cities. Native Americans represent hundreds of tribal groups, languages, and cultures. By and large, however, a lesbian or gay male sexual orientation is rejected by ethnic minority groups in the United States. Lesbians and gay males are pressured to keep their sexual orientations a secret or to move to communities where they can live openly without sanction.

Within traditional Hispanic American culture, the family is the primary social unit. Men are expected to support and defend the family, and women are expected to be submissive, respectable, and deferential to men (Morales, 1992). Because women are expected to remain virgins until marriage, men sometimes engage in male-male sexual behavior without considering themselves gay (Greene, 1994). Hispanic American culture frequently denies the sexuality of women. Thus, women who label themselves lesbians are doubly condemned—because they are lesbians and because they are confronting others with their sexuality. Because lesbians are independent of men, most Hispanic American heterosexual people view Hispanic American lesbians as threats to the tradition of male dominance (Trujillo, 1991).

Asian American cultures emphasize respect for one's elders, obedience to parents, and sharp distinctions in masculine and feminine gender roles (Chan, 1992). The topic of sex is generally taboo within the family. Asian Americans, like Hispanic Americans, tend to assume that sex is unimportant to women. Women are also considered to be less important than men. Open admission of a lesbian or gay male sexual orientation is seen as a rejection of one's traditional cultural roles and a threat to the continuity of the family line (Chan, 1992; Garnets & Kimmel, 1991).

Because many African American men have had difficulty finding jobs, gender roles among African Americans have been more flexible than those found among White Americans and most other ethnic minority groups (Greene, 1994). Nevertheless, the African American community appears to strongly reject gay men and lesbians, pressuring them to remain secretive about their sexual orientations (Gomez & Smith, 1990; Poussaint, 1990). Greene (1994) hypothesizes a number of factors that influence African Americans to be hostile toward lesbians and gay men. One is strong allegiance to Christian beliefs and biblical scripture. Another is internalization of the dominant culture's stereotyping of African Americans as highly sexual beings. That is, many African Americans may feel a need to assert their

These practices of Sambian culture might seem to suggest that the sexual orientations of males are fluid and malleable. The practices involve *behavior*, however, and not *sexual orientation*. Male-male sexual behavior among Sambians takes place within a cultural context that bears little resemblance to consensual male-male sexual activity in Western society. The prepubertal Sambian male does not *seek* sexual liaisons with other males. He is removed from his home, by force if necessary, and thrust into male-male sexual encounters by older males (Baldwin & Baldwin, 1989).

Little is known about female-female sexual activity in non-Western cultures. Ford and Beach found evidence of female-female sexual behavior in only 17 of the 76 societies they studied. Perhaps it was more difficult to acquire data about female sexuality. Perhaps female sexual behavior in general, not just sexual activity with other females, was more likely to be repressed. Of course, it is also possible that women are less likely than men to develop sexual interests in, or romantic relationships with, members of their own genders. Whatever the reasons, this cross-cultural evidence is consistent with data from our own culture. Here, too, males are more likely than females to develop sexual interests in, or romantic relationships with, members of their own genders (Katz, 1995; Laumann et al., 1994).

Cross-Species Perspectives

Many of us have observed pets and other animals engaging in sexual behaviors that resemble male-male or female-female contacts among humans, such as attempting to

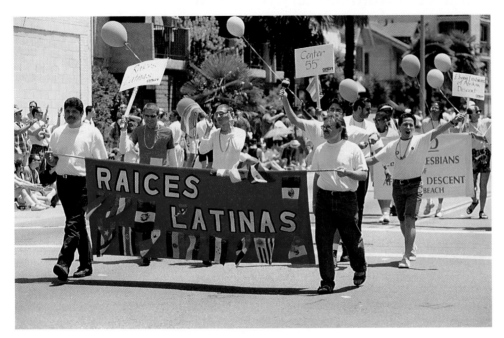

Ethnicity and Sexual Orientation. The experiences of lesbians and gay men can differ according to their ethnicity. For example, traditional Hispanic American culture supports strong differences in gender roles. Men are expected to support and defend the family, and women are expected to be submissive, respectable, and deferential to men. Hispanic American culture also often denies the sexuality of women. Thus, Hispanic American lesbians are multiply condemned—because they are lesbians, because they confront others with their sexuality, and because their independence from men is perceived as a threat to the tradition of male dominance.

sexual "normalcy" or even a sense of sexual superiority.

Before the European conquest, Native Americans might not have discussed sex openly, but it was generally seen as a natural part of life. Individuals who incorporated both traditional feminine and masculine styles were generally accepted and even admired. The influence of the colonists' religions led to greater rejection of lesbians and gay men and pressure to move off the reservation to the big city (Greene, 1994). Native American lesbians and gay men, like Asian American lesbians and gay men, thus often feel doubly removed from their families.

If any generalization is possible, it may be that lesbians and gay men find more of a sense of belonging in the gay community than in their ethnic communities.

mount others of their own sex. We should be careful, though, about drawing comparisons between the behavior of people and lower animals. Superficially similar behaviors might not have the same function in other species.

A male baboon might present his rear and allow himself to be mounted by another male. This behavior might resemble anal intercourse among gay men. Is the behavior sexually motivated, however? Mounting behavior among male baboons could represent a type of dominance ritual in which lower-ranking males adopt a submissive (feminine) posture to ward off attack from dominant males (Nadler, 1990). (Some male-male acts among people also involve themes of dominance, as in the case of a dominant male prisoner forcing a less dominant one to submit to anal intercourse.) In other cases, male baboons might be seeking favors or protection from more dominant males (Nadler, 1990). Among juvenile animals, male-male behaviors may also be a form of play. Females might also attempt to mount other females, but here too, the motivations may not be the same as those of humans.

Sexual motivation appears to play a role in some, but not all, male-male and female-female sexual interactions among animals. Fellatio and anal intercourse to ejaculation among juvenile male orangutans may be cases in point, as may be thrusting by one adult female gorilla against another. Some male-male encounters among rhesus monkeys also appear to be sexually motivated. However, researchers have not found evidence among nonhuman primates of the prolonged, exclusive male-male sexual activity found among humans that occurs when male-female opportunities are available.

Attitudes Toward Sexual Orientation in Contemporary Society

> Toni, a 20-year-old lesbian college student, was incredulous that her parents believed she had *chosen* her sexual orientation. They saw her lesbianism as linked to the general rebelliousness that had been stirred by attending a school known for its "radical" image. Toni was infuriated that they believed that she would "get over" her lesbian sexual orientation once she decided to accept adult responsibilities. (the authors' files)

Historically speaking, negative attitudes toward gay people have pervaded our society (Katz, 1995). Male-male and female-female sexual behavior has, at worst, been viewed as a crime against God or against "nature." A national survey of males in their late teens (aged 15 to 19) showed that 9 of 10 thought that sex between men was "disgusting." Three of five could not even see themselves being friends with a gay man (Marsiglio, 1993b). Young males tend to be the harshest group in their judgments of gay people. Yet a national poll conducted in June 1998 found that 59% of American adults believe that homosexuality is morally wrong, compared to 35% who say that it is not wrong (Berke, 1998). (The remaining 6% had no answer or said they didn't know.)

Still, there are strong signs that Americans have grown more tolerant of gay people over the past few decades. For example, a poll conducted in June 1977 found that 56% of Americans said that gay people should have equal rights in terms of job opportunities (33% said that they should not). In October 1989, 71% said that gay people should have equal rights (compared to 18% who said they should not). By November 1996, 84% of Americans endorsed equal rights for gay people, and only 12% were opposed (Berke, 1998).

Although most Americans believe that gay people should have equal access to jobs, some would bar them from teaching and similar activities because they believe that gay people, given the chance, will seduce and recruit children into a gay lifestyle. Such beliefs have been used to prevent gay couples from becoming adoptive or foster parents and to deny them custody or visitation rights to their own children after divorce. Some people who would bar gay people from interactions with children fear that the children will be molested. Yet more than 90% of cases of child molestation involve heterosexual male assailants (Gelles & Cornell, 1985; Gordon & Snyder, 1989). Nor are children who are reared or taught by gay men or lesbians more likely to become gay themselves. One study found that 36 of 37 children who were reared by lesbian or transsexual couples developed a heterosexual orientation (Green, 1978). Nor has it been shown that children who are reared by gay parents are more likely to encounter gender identity conflicts (Allen & Burrell, 1996; Patterson, 1995). Nonetheless, a nationwide poll taken in June 1997 found that 56% of respondents believed that it was a "bad thing" for gay couples to raise children (Berke, 1998). (Thirty-one percent believed that the sexual orientation of the parents made no difference in childrearing.)

We began this section with the case of Toni, whose parents assumed that she would change her lesbian sexual orientation once she "outgrew" her rebelliousness. Like many people, Toni's parents assumed that Toni had *chosen* to be gay. As we will see in the section on biological perspectives, research evidence is accumulating to support the view that inborn biological factors play a strong role in the development of sexual orientation. Interestingly, people who believe that sexual orientation is biologically determined and inborn are more tolerant of gay people than are those who see sexual orientation as stemming from upbringing or other environmental factors. Over the years, more people have believed in environmental rather than biological causes of sexual orientation (Berke, 1998), but the trend seems to favor the inborn, biological point of view.

For example, a nationwide poll conducted in June 1977 found that only 13% of Americans believed that gay people were "born with" their sexual orientation, compared to 56% who favored environmental causes. In October 1989, 18% of Americans said that gay people were born with their orientation, compared to 48% who favored an environmental explanation. By June 1998, 31% of Americans believed that gay people were born with their sexual orientations (Berke, 1998). Forty-seven percent still favored the envi-

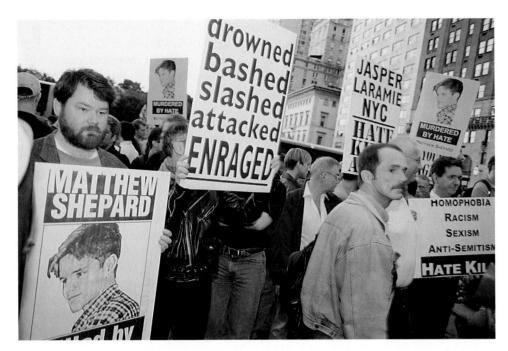

Protesting Homophobia. Gay men and lesbians are frequently assaulted because of their sexual orientation. Hatred of gays is termed *homophobia*, although the roots of the word mean *fear* of gays. Why do some people hate gay men and lesbians? Why was a college student, Matthew Shepard, killed by homophobes?

ronmental approach. Nonetheless, the trend seems clear: More and more people are coming to look upon sexual orientation as something that one is born with. Fewer and fewer people are likely to believe that young people can be "seduced" into one sexual orientation or another.

HOMOPHOBIA   **Homophobia** takes many forms, including

- Use of derogatory names (such as *queer*, *faggot*, and *dyke*)
- Telling disparaging "queer jokes"
- Barring gay people from housing, employment, or social opportunities
- Taunting (verbal abuse)
- **Gay bashing** (physical abuse)

Homophobia derives from root words meaning "fear of homosexuals." Although homophobia is more common among heterosexual people, gay people themselves can be homophobic. Homophobia among gay people is called *internalized homophobia*. It is believed to stem from the internalization of negative societal attitudes toward gay people (Gonsiorck, 1988).

Although some psychologists link homophobia to fears of a gay male or lesbian sexual orientation within oneself, homophobic attitudes may also be embedded within a cluster of stereotypical gender-role attitudes toward family life (Kerns & Fine, 1994). These attitudes support male dominance and the belief that it is natural and appropriate for women to sacrifice for their husbands and children (Katz, 1995; Marsiglio, 1993b). People who have a strong stake in maintaining stereotypical gender roles might feel more readily threatened by the existence of the gay male or lesbian sexual orientation, since gay people appear to confuse or reverse these roles.

Homophobic attitudes are more common among males who identify with a traditional male gender role and those who hold a fundamentalist religious orientation (Kerns & Fine, 1994; Marsiglio, 1993b). Similarly, researchers find that college students who hold a conservative political orientation tend to be more accepting of negative attitudes toward gay people than are liberal students (Lottes & Kuriloff, 1992). Another university sample found male students to be more homophobic than women in their attitudes (Kunkel & Temple, 1992).

Homophobia A cluster of negative attitudes and feelings toward gay people, including intolerance, hatred, and fear. (From Greek roots meaning "fear" [of members of the] "same" [gender]).

Gay bashing Violence against homosexuals.

Generally speaking, heterosexual men are relatively less tolerant of gay people than are heterosexual women (Kerns & Fine, 1994; Seltzer, 1992; Whitley & Kite, 1995). Perhaps some heterosexual men are threatened by the possibility of discovering male-male sexual impulses within themselves (Freiberg, 1995). Consistent with this view, heterosexual males tend to hold more negative attitudes toward gay men than toward lesbians (Kite, 1992).

At least some homophobic men may have homoerotic impulses of which they are unaware. Denial of these impulses might be connected with their fear and disapproval of gay males. Henry Adams and his colleagues (1996) showed men sexually explicit videotapes of male-female, female-female, and male-male sexual activity and measured their sexual response by means of the penile plethysmograph. The plethysmograph measures penile circumference (size of erection). Participants were also asked to report how sexually aroused they felt in response to the videos. The men were also evaluated for their attitudes toward gay males. Men who were not homophobic were sexually aroused, according to their penile circumference, only by videos of male-female and female-female sexual activity. The homophobic viewers were also aroused in terms of penile circumference by the video of male-male sexual activity. However, the homophobic men also reported that they did not *feel* aroused by the male-male sexual activity, a finding suggesting that they were out of touch with their biological response.

GAY BASHING AND THE AIDS EPIDEMIC   Although strides toward social acceptance of gay people have been made since Kinsey's day, the advent of AIDS has added fuel to the fire of hatred and prejudice. When AIDS first appeared, it primarily struck the gay male community. Some people in the larger society believed that the epidemic was a God-sent plague intended to punish gay people for sinful behavior.

The advent of the epidemic has been accompanied by a dramatic rise in the incidence of gay bashing (Freiberg, 1995). Perhaps the epidemic has served as a pretext for some people to attack gay males, whom they blame for spreading the disease (Katz, 1995).

Gay bashing also occurs on college campuses. A large percentage (77%) of 121 lesbian and gay male undergraduate students in one survey at Pennsylvania State University reported that they had been verbally insulted. Nearly one in three (31%) reported being chased or followed (D'Augelli, 1992a). Nearly 20% said they had been physically assaulted. Most of the victimizers were fellow students. Few of these incidents were reported to the authorities.

Students also tend to hold gay men more responsible for behaviors that put themselves at risk of contracting AIDS. One study found that students assigned a greater amount of blame to a hypothetical person who had contracted AIDS when the person was identified as a gay male than when the person was identified as a heterosexual male (Anderson, 1992).

Ironically, the percentage of gay men who account for new cases of AIDS has been steadily declining (see Chapter 17). By contrast, the percentages of people who contract AIDS by sharing contaminated hypodermic syringes while injecting drugs, and by male-female sexual intercourse, have been on the upswing.

SEXUAL ORIENTATION AND THE LAW   During the past generation, gay people have organized effective political groups to fight discrimination and to overturn the sodomy laws that have traditionally targeted them. Despite their success, sodomy laws are still on the books in about half of our states. Sodomy laws prohibit "unnatural" sexual acts, even between consenting adults. A gay male or lesbian sexual orientation is not illegal in itself. However, certain sexual acts in which many gay people (and heterosexual people) participate, such as anal intercourse and oral-genital contact, fall under the legal definition of sodomy in many states. Sodomy laws also typically prohibit sexual contacts with animals. Although sodomy laws are usually intended to apply equally to all adults, married or unmarried, heterosexual or gay, the vast majority of prosecutions have been directed against gay people.

A 1986 Supreme Court decision (*Hardwick* v. *Bowers*) let stand a Georgia sodomy law that makes oral-genital or anal-genital sexual contact crimes punishable by up to 20 years in prison. Whether the acts occur between consenting adults is irrelevant. The decision was a blow to gay rights organizations, which had looked to the Supreme Court to overturn sodomy laws nationwide. Instead, the court held that states retain the right to enact sodomy laws and impose criminal penalties.

Many other countries, including Mexico, Holland, Italy, Spain, England, France, and the Scandinavian countries have decriminalized male-male and female-female sexual activity (Carrera, 1981). In Canada, a consensual sexual act is prosecutable under sodomy laws only if one of the participants is under 21 years of age or the act is performed in public.

GAY ACTIVISM   Nowhere in the United States have gay people been more politically effective than in San Francisco. They are well represented on the city police force and in other public agencies. The coming out of many gay people and their flocking to more tolerant urban centers have rendered them formidable political forces in these locales.

The Mattachine Society, named after gay medieval court jesters, was the first powerful gay rights organization. At first, membership was kept secret to protect members' social standing in the community. Today, however, members' names are published, and many heterosexual supporters are listed in their ranks. Founded in Los Angeles in 1950, the Mattachine Society now has chapters in most metropolitan areas. The society publishes the *Mattachine Newsletter* and *Homosexual Citizen*. Another newsletter, the *Advocate*, has become the nation's best-known gay newsletter.

The largest lesbian organization is the Daughters of Bilitis, named after the Greek courtesan who was loved by the lesbian poet Sappho. Founded in 1956, the group provides a forum for sharing social experiences and pursuing equal rights. The organization's newsletter is the *Ladder*.

The AIDS epidemic has had a profound effect on the political agenda of gay rights organizations. These organizations have mounted a vigorous effort to combat the AIDS epidemic on several fronts:

1. To lobby for increased funding for AIDS research and treatment
2. To educate the gay and wider communities of the dangers associated with high-risk sexual behavior
3. To encourage gay men and others to adopt safer sex practices, including the use of latex condoms (see Chapter 17)
4. To protect the civil rights of people with AIDS and carriers of the virus that causes AIDS (the *human immunodeficiency virus [HIV]*) with respect to employment, housing, medical and dental treatment, and medical insurance
5. To provide counseling and support services for people with AIDS and those infected with HIV

Some gay rights organizations work within the mainstream political process. Others, such as the militant Act-Up organization, have taken a more strident and confrontational stance to secure more funding for AIDS research and treatment.

Some militant gay groups have resorted to the method of **outing** to combat discrimination. In this method, gay people unmask other gay people without their consent, forcing them "out of the closet." Many gay people protest this practice vehemently, terming it a "gay witch hunt."

STEREOTYPES AND SEXUAL BEHAVIOR   Among heterosexual people, sexual aggressiveness is linked to the masculine gender role. Sexual passivity is linked to the feminine role. Some heterosexual people assume (often erroneously) that in gay male and lesbian relationships, one partner consistently assumes the masculine role in sexual relations and the other assumes the feminine role.

Many gay couples vary the active and passive roles, however. Among gay male couples, for example, roles in anal intercourse (*inserter* versus *insertee*) and in fellatio are of-

Outing The revelation of the identities of gay people by other gay people. The method is intended to combat discrimination against gay people by forcing individuals out of the closet and into the fray.

ten reversed. Contrary to popular assumptions, sexual behavior between lesbians seldom reflects distinct **butch** and **femme** gender roles. Most lesbians report providing and receiving oral-genital stimulation. Typically, partners alternate roles or simultaneously perform and receive oral stimulation. Many gay people claim that the labels of *masculine* and *feminine* only represent the "straight community's" efforts to pigeonhole them in terms that "straights" can understand.

Biological Perspectives

Is sexual orientation an *inborn* trait that is transmitted genetically, like eye color or height? Does it reflect hormonal influences? Biological perspectives focus on the role of genetics and hormonal influences in shaping sexual orientation.

GENETICS AND SEXUAL ORIENTATION   Considerable evidence exists that gay male and lesbian sexual orientations run in families (Bailey et al., 1993; Pillard, 1990). In one study, for example, 22% of the brothers of a sample of 51 predominantly gay men were either gay or bisexual themselves. This is nearly four times the proportion expected in the general population (Pillard & Weinrich, 1986). Although such evidence is consistent with a genetic explanation, families also share a common environment.

Twin studies also shed light on the possible role of heredity (Rose, 1995). **Monozygotic (MZ) twins,** or identical twins, develop from a single fertilized ovum and share 100% of their heredity. **Dizygotic (DZ) twins,** or fraternal twins, develop from two fertilized ova. Like other brothers and sisters, DZ twins share only 50% of their heredity. Thus, if a gay male or lesbian sexual orientation were transmitted genetically, it should be found about twice as often among identical twins of gay people as among fraternal twins. Since MZ and DZ twins who are reared together share similar environmental influences, differences in the degree of **concordance** for a given trait between the types of twin pairs are further indicative of genetic origins.

Several studies have identified gay men who had either identical (MZ) or fraternal (DZ) twin brothers to examine the prevalence of a gay male sexual orientation in their twin brothers (Rose, 1995). In an early study, Kallmann (1952) found 100% concordance for a gay male sexual orientation among the identical twin brothers of gay men, compared to 12% concordance for fraternal twin pairs in which one of the brothers was identified as gay. This seemed strong evidence indeed of genetic factors in sexual orientation. However, later studies have found much lower concordance rates among MZ twins (Bailey & Pillard, 1991; Eckert et al., 1986; McConaghy & Blaszczynski, 1980). These studies found many instances of MZ twins in which one identical twin member was gay and the other in the pair was not. Still, MZ twins do appear to have a higher concordance rate for a gay male sexual orientation than DZ twins. Bailey and Pillard (1991) reported a 52% concordance rate among MZ twin pairs versus a 22% rate among DZ twin pairs in their sample. In another study, researchers reported a concordance rate for a gay sexual orientation of 66% in MZ twins, compared to 30% among DZ twins (Whitam et al., 1993).

Bear in mind that MZ twins are more likely to be dressed alike and treated alike than DZ twins. Therefore, their greater concordance for a gay sexual orientation might at least in part reflect environmental factors. The greater concordance between MZ twins might signify only that MZ twins are likely to react more similarly than DZ twins to the same *environmental* influences (Bancroft, 1990).

Researchers at the National Cancer Institute have found evidence linking a region on the X sex chromosome to a gay male sexual orientation (Hamer et al., 1993). The researchers found that gay males in a sample of 114 gay men were more likely to have gay male relatives on their mothers' side of the family than would be expected on the basis of the prevalence of a gay male sexual orientation in the general population. Yet they did not have a greater-than-expected number of gay male relatives on their paternal side of the family. This pattern of inheritance is consistent with genetic traits, such as hemophilia, that are linked to the X sex chromosome, which men receive from their mothers.

Butch A lesbian who assumes a traditional masculine gender role.

Femme A lesbian who assumes a traditional feminine gender role.

Monozygotic (MZ) twins Twins who develop from the same fertilized ovum. Identical twins.

Dizygotic (DZ) twins Twins who develop from different fertilized ova. Fraternal twins.

Concordance Agreement.

The researchers then went on to examine the X sex chromosome in 40 pairs of gay male, non-twin brothers. In 33 of the pairs, the brothers had identical DNA markers on the end tip of the X chromosome. For brothers overall in the general population, about half would be expected to have inherited this chromosomal structure. It is suspected, therefore, that this chromosomal region might hold a gene that predisposes men to a gay male sexual orientation.

The researchers cautioned that they had not found a particular gene linked to sexual orientation, just a general location of where the gene may be found. Nor do scientists know how such a gene, or combination of genes, might account for sexual orientation. Perhaps a particular gene or gene governs the development of proteins that sculpt parts of the brain in ways that favor the development of a gay male sexual orientation. On the other hand, a number of the gay brothers, 7 of the 40 pairs, did *not* share the chromosomal marker.

Sexologist John Money (1994) agrees that genetic factors might play a role in the development of sexual orientation but that they do not fully govern it. Most researchers believe that sexual orientation is affected by a complex interplay of biological and psychosocial influences (Barlow & Durand, 1995).

HORMONAL INFLUENCES AND SEXUAL ORIENTATION   Sex hormones strongly influence the mating behavior of other species (Crews, 1994). Researchers have therefore looked into possible hormonal factors in determining sexual orientation in humans.

Testosterone is essential to male sexual differentiation. Therefore, the levels of testosterone and its by-products in the blood and urine have been suspected as a possible influence on sexual orientation, at least in males. Research has failed to connect sexual orientation in either gender with differences in the levels of either male or female sex hormones in adulthood (Friedman & Downey, 1994). In adulthood, testosterone appears to have **activating effects.** That is, it affects the intensity of sexual desire but not the preference for partners of the same or the other gender (Whalen et al., 1990).

What of the possible *prenatal* effects of sex hormones? Experiments have been performed in which pregnant rats were given antiandrogen drugs that block the effects of testosterone. When the drugs were given during critical periods in which the fetuses' brains were becoming sexually differentiated, male offspring were likely to show feminine mating patterns as adults (Ellis & Ames, 1987). The adult males became receptive to mounting attempts by other males and failed to mount females.

Do prenatal sex hormones play a similar role in determining sexual orientation in people? There is suggestive evidence. For example, Meyer-Bahlburg and his colleagues (1995) interviewed groups of women who had been exposed prenatally to DES, a synthetic estrogen. They found that these women were more likely to be rated as lesbian or bisexual than women who were not exposed to DES. We do know that the genitals of gay people differentiate prenatally in accord with their chromosomal gender (Whalen et al., 1990). It remains possible that imbalances in prenatal sex hormones may cause brain tissue to be sexually differentiated in one direction even though the genitals are differentiated in the other (Collaer & Hines, 1995).

It is not true that gay males and lesbians suffer from hormonal imbalances. Gay males and lesbians do not show imbalances of sex hormones in adulthood. However, the role of prenatal hormonal factors in the development of sexual orientation remains an open question. ▪

Truth or Fiction?
REVISITED

THE STRUCTURE OF THE BRAIN   Evidence suggests that there may be structural differences between the brains of heterosexual and gay men. In 1991, Simon LeVay, a neurobiologist at the Salk Institute in La Jolla, California, carried out autopsies on the brains of 35 AIDS victims—19 gay men and 16 (presumably) heterosexual men. He found that a segment of the hypothalamus—specifically, a cell group called the third interstitial nucleus of the anterior hypothalamus—in the brains of the gay men was less than half the size of the same segment in the heterosexual men. The same brain segment was larger in the brain tissues of heterosexual men than in brain tissues obtained from a comparison

Activating effects Those effects of sex hormones that influence the level of the sex drive but not sexual orientation.

group of six presumably heterosexual women. No significant differences in size were found between the brain tissues of the gay men and the women, however.

LeVay's findings are intriguing, but they are preliminary. We do not know, for example, whether the structural differences found by LeVay are innate. Nor should LeVay's findings be taken to mean that biology is destiny. As Richard Nakamura, a scientist with the National Institute of Mental Health, commented, "This [LeVay's findings] shouldn't be taken to mean that you're automatically [gay] if you have a structure of one size versus a structure of another size" (Angier, 1991).

The belief that sexual orientation is innate or inborn has many adherents, in both the scientific and general communities. Support for the possible influences of prenatal hormonal factors in "sculpting" the brain in a masculine or feminine direction is based largely on animal studies, however. Direct evidence with people is lacking. We must also be careful in generalizing results from other species to our own.

Psychological Perspectives

Do family relationships play a role in the origins of sexual orientation? What are the effects of childhood sexual experiences? Psychoanalytic theory and learning theory provide two of the major psychological approaches to understanding the origins of sexual orientation.

PSYCHOANALYTIC VIEWS   Sigmund Freud, the originator of psychoanalytic theory, believed that children enter the world **polymorphous perverse.** That is, before internalizing social inhibitions, children are open to all forms of sexual stimulation. However, through proper resolution of the Oedipus complex, a boy will forsake his incestuous desires for his mother and come to identify with his father. As a result, his erotic attraction to his mother will eventually be transferred, or **displaced,** onto more appropriate *female* partners. A girl, through proper resolution of her Electra complex, will identify with her mother and seek erotic stimulation from men when she becomes sexually mature.

In Freud's view, a gay male or lesbian sexual orientation results from failure to successfully resolve the Oedipus complex by identifying with the parent of the same gender. In men, faulty resolution of the Oedipus complex is most likely to result from the so-called classic pattern of an emotionally "close-binding" mother and a "detached-hostile" father. A boy who is reared in such a family may come to identify with his mother and even to "transform himself into her" (Freud, 1922/1959, p. 40). He may thus become effeminate and develop sexual interests in men.

Freud believed that the mechanism of unresolved **castration anxiety** plays a role in a gay male sexual orientation. By the time the Oedipus complex takes effect, the boy will have learned from self-stimulation that he can obtain sexual pleasure from his penis. In his youthful fantasies, he associates this pleasure with mental images of his mother. Similarly, he is likely to have learned that females do not possess a penis. Somewhere along the line the psychoanalyst theorizes that the boy might also have been warned that his penis will be removed if he plays with himself. From all this, the boy might surmise that females—including his mother—once had penises but that they were removed.

During the throes of the Oedipus complex, the boy unconsciously comes to fear that his father, his rival in love for the mother, will retaliate by removing the organ that the boy has come to associate with sexual pleasure. His fear causes him to repress his sexual desire for his mother and to identify with the potential aggressor—his father. The boy thus overcomes his castration anxiety and is headed along the path of adult heterosexuality.

If the Oedipus complex is not successfully resolved, castration anxiety may persist. When sexually mature, the man will not be able to tolerate sex with women. Their lack of a penis will arouse unconscious castration anxiety within himself. According to psy-

Polymorphous perverse In psychoanalytic theory, being receptive to all forms of sexual stimulation.

Displacement In psychoanalytic theory, a defense mechanism that allows one to transfer unacceptable wishes or desires onto more appropriate or less threatening objects.

Castration anxiety In psychoanalytic theory, a man's fear that his genitals will be removed. Castration anxiety is an element of the Oedipus complex and is implicated in the directionality of erotic interests.

choanalytic theory, the boy might unconsciously associate the vagina with teeth, or other sharp instruments, and be unable to perform sexually with a woman.

The Electra complex in little girls follows a somewhat different course. Freud believed that little girls become envious of boys' penises, since they lack their own. This concept of **penis envy** was one of Freud's most controversial beliefs. In Freud's view, jealousy leads little girls to resent their mothers, whom they blame for their anatomic "deficiency," and to turn from their mothers to their fathers as sexual objects. They now desire to possess the father, because the father's penis provides what they lack. But incestuous desires bring the girl into competition with her mother. Motivated by fear that her mother will withdraw her love if the desires persist, the girl normally represses them and identifies with her mother. She then develops traditional feminine interests and eventually seeks erotic stimulation from men. She supplants her childhood desire for a penis with a desire to marry a man and bear children. The baby, emitted from between her legs, serves as the ultimate penis substitute.

A girl who does not resolve her penis envy in childhood may "manifest homosexuality, . . . exhibit markedly masculine traits in the conduct of her later life, choose a masculine vocation, and so on" (Freud, 1922/1959, p. 50). The residue of this unresolved complex is continued penis envy, the striving to become a man by acting like a man and seeking sexual satisfaction with women: lesbianism.

In Freud's view, a gay male or lesbian sexual orientation is one result of assuming the gender role that is normally taken up by the other gender. The gay male is expected to be effeminate; the lesbian, masculine. But, as is noted in research into gender-typed behavior and sexual orientation, this stereotypical view of gay people is far from universal. Nor do the behaviors stereotypical of the other gender that are found in some adult gay men or women necessarily derive from Oedipal problems. Biological and other psychosocial factors may be involved.

A nagging problem of Freudian theory is that many of its concepts, such as castration anxiety and penis envy, are believed to operate at an unconscious level. As such, they lie beyond the scope of scientific observation and measurement. We cannot learn whether boys experience castration anxiety by asking them, since the theory claims that **repression** will keep such anxieties out of awareness. Nor can we directly learn about penis envy by interviewing girls.

Actually, the idea that "castration anxiety" in gay males is aroused by heterosexual intercourse has not been scientifically demonstrated and remains speculative. ■

Truth or Fiction? REVISITED

RESEARCH ON PSYCHOANALYTIC THEORIES OF SEXUAL ORIENTATION   Psychoanalysts—psychotherapists who are trained in the Freudian tradition—have researched sexual orientation largely through case studies. These studies have been carried out almost exclusively with gay males who were in therapy at the time.

In 1962, psychoanalyst Irving Bieber reported the results of questionnaires filled out by 77 psychiatrists on 106 gay male clients. In 1976, he reported the results of similar surveys of gay men in therapy.

Bieber claimed to find the "classic pattern" among gay males: Their orientation was determined by having a dominant, "smothering" mother and a passive, detached father. As the clients described them, the mothers were overprotective, seductive, and jealous of their sons. The fathers were aloof, unaffectionate, and hostile toward them. The father, being detached, might have failed to buffer the close mother-son relationship. The mother's relationship with the father was typically disturbed, and the mother might have substituted a "close-binding" relationship with her son. This classic pattern was believed to result in the boy's developing a fear of sexual contacts with women. Though he would be unconscious of this dynamic, for him, any female partner would unconsciously represent his mother. Desire for her would stir unconscious fears of retaliation by the father— that is, castration anxiety.

Penis envy   In psychoanalytic theory, the girl's wish to have a penis.

Repression   In psychoanalytic theory, the most basic defense mechanism through which threatening ideas and impulses are ejected from conscious awareness.

Father–Son Relationship. Does the father-son relationship play a role, as some theorists suspect, in the development of homosexuality in men? According to a recent study, gay men perceived themselves as having been more distant from their fathers during childhood than did heterosexual men. The question is, why?

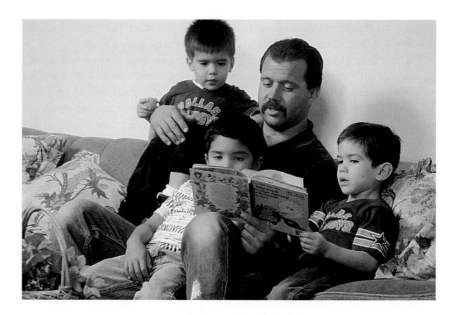

Bieber's findings may be criticized on several grounds:

1. The study participants were all in analysis, and many wanted to become heterosexual. Therefore, we cannot generalize the results to well-adjusted gay men.
2. The analysts might have chosen cases that confirmed their theoretical perspectives. Or perhaps over the course of analysis, clients were subtly encouraged to provide "evidence" that was consistent with psychoanalytic theory.
3. No clear evidence exists that gay males either fear or are repulsed by female genitalia. On the contrary, many gay males have successfully, and often repeatedly, engaged in coitus with women. They might simply not be sexually attracted to women or might find relationships with men more satisfying.
4. Many *hetero*sexual men have family backgrounds that fit the classic pattern, and the families of many gay men do *not* fit the pattern. Researchers from the Kinsey Institute found that heterosexual males identified with their mothers as often as gay males did. A seductive mother-son relationship had little if any bearing on sexual orientation (Bell et al., 1981). Parent-child relations were only weakly linked to lesbianism as well.
5. Retrospective accounts of childhood relationships with parents are subject to gaps in memory and distortions.

More recent evidence has brought the issue of familial closeness between gay men and their parents into closer perspective. Richard Pillard and his colleagues (Pillard & Weinrich, 1986; Pillard, 1990) found that gay males described themselves as more distant from their fathers during childhood than did either heterosexual controls or the gay men's own heterosexual brothers. The gay men in their sample also reported greater closeness to their mothers. Still, the father's psychological distance from the son might have reflected the *son's* alienation from him, not the reverse. That is, the son might have been so attached to his mother, or so uninterested in traditional masculine activities, that he rebuffed paternal attempts to engage him in conventional father-son activities.

In sum, family characteristics could play a role in the development of sexual orientation. However, there is great variation among the families of gay males and lesbians. No one pattern applies in all cases (Isay, 1990). Family dynamics might be one of many factors that shape sexual orientation.

LEARNING THEORIES   Learning theorists agree with Freud that early experiences play an important role in the development of sexual orientation. They focus on the role of reinforcement of early patterns of sexual behavior, however, rather than on the resolution of unconscious conflicts. People generally repeat pleasurable activities and discontinue painful ones. Thus, people may learn to engage in sexual activity with people of their own gender if childhood sexual experimentation with them is connected with sexual pleasure.

If sexual motivation is high, as it tends to be during adolescence, and the only outlets are with others of one's own gender, adolescents might experiment sexually with them. If these encounters are pleasurable and heterosexual experiences are unpleasant, a firmer gay male or lesbian sexual orientation might develop (Gagnon & Simon, 1973). Conversely, pain, anxiety, or social disapproval might be connected with early contacts with people of one's own gender. In such cases, the child might learn to inhibit feelings of attraction to people of one's own gender and develop a firmer heterosexual orientation.

Although learning might play a role in the development of a gay male or lesbian sexual orientation, learning theorists have not identified specific learning experiences that would lead to these orientations. Moreover, most adolescent encounters with people of the same gender, even if pleasurable, do not lead to an adult gay male or lesbian sexual orientation. Many heterosexual people have had adolescent encounters with members of their own gender without swaying their adult orientations. This is true even of people whose early sexual interactions with the other gender were fumbling and frustrating. Moreover, the overwhelming majority of gay males and lesbians were aware of sexual interest in people of their own gender *before* they had sexual encounters with them, pleasurable or otherwise (Bell et al., 1981).

Gender Nonconformity

Stereotypes of the effeminate gay male and the masculine lesbian are exaggerated. Nevertheless, research finds that gay males and lesbians are more likely than heterosexuals to report childhood behavior that is stereotypical of the other gender (Bailey & Zucker, 1995; Friedman & Downey, 1994). Many gay males and lesbians have childhood recollections of acting and feeling "different" from their peers from a young age. Some gay males can recall feeling different as early as age 3 or 4 (Isay, 1990). Feelings of differentness were often related to behavior that is stereotypical of the other gender.

It would appear that the majority of gay males perceive themselves to have been effeminate during childhood (Bailey & Zucker, 1995). Gay males from various groups, such as prisoners, psychiatric patients, and members of gay rights organizations, more often reported that they avoided participating in competitive sports as children, were more fearful of physical injury, and were more likely to avoid getting into fights than did heterosexual males (McConaghy, 1987).

Gay males are also more likely to recall feeling more sensitive than their peers during childhood (Isay, 1990). They cried more easily. Their feelings were more readily hurt. They had more artistic interests. They had fewer male buddies but more female playmates. Gay males were also more likely than their heterosexual counterparts to have preferred "girls' toys." They preferred playing with girls to playing with trucks or guns or engaging in rough-and-tumble play. Their preferences often led to their being called "sissies" (Bell et al., 1981; Green, 1987). Gay men also recall more cross-dressing during childhood. They preferred the company of older women to older men and engaged in childhood sex play with other boys rather than with girls (Whitam, 1977).

There is also evidence of masculine-typed behavior among lesbians as children (Bailey & Zucker, 1995). Lesbians were more likely than heterosexual women to perceive themselves as having been "tomboys" as children. They were more likely to have preferred rough-and-tumble games to playing with dolls and to have enjoyed wearing boy's clothing rather than "cutesy" dresses.

How might extreme childhood effeminacy lead to a gay male sexual orientation? Green (1987) speculates that the social detachment of these boys from male peers and role models (especially fathers) creates strong, unfulfilled cravings for male affection. This craving then leads them to seek males as partners in sex and love relationships in adolescence and adulthood.

Alan Bell of the Kinsey Institute offers a different explanation. He believes that self-perceptions of differentness and social distance from other males during childhood lead these boys to develop erotic attractions that are also different from the other boys'. These are erotic attractions toward members of their own gender.

Bear in mind that not all of these highly effeminate boys turned out to be gay. Note, too, that these studies followed only boys who were stereotypically effeminate in childhood. Thus, it failed to address the development of gay males who do *not* show behavior that is stereotypical of the other gender as children. Some gay men report engaging in few if any gender-conforming behaviors in childhood. Others report as many typically masculine behaviors and as few feminine behaviors in childhood as heterosexual men. Moreover, perhaps 5% of heterosexual males cross-dressed as children (Carrier, 1986). Still, there appears to be a general connection between excessive behavior stereotypical of the other gender and the development of a gay male sexual orientation in some cases (McConaghy, 1987). It remains unclear whether early effeminacy reflects genetic factors, prenatal influences (such as hormonal imbalances), early experiences, or some combination of these.

All in all, the origins of a gay male or lesbian sexual orientation remain mysterious and complex, just as mysterious as the origins of heterosexuality. In reviewing theories and research, we are left with the impression that sexual orientation is unlikely to have a single cause. Sexual orientation appears to spring from multiple origins, including biological and psychosocial factors (Strickland, 1995). Genetic and biochemical factors (such as hormone levels) might affect the prenatal organization of the brain (Money, 1994). These factors might predispose people to a certain sexual orientation. But it could be that early socialization experiences are also required to give rise to a gay male, lesbian, heterosexual, or bisexual sexual orientation. The precise influences and interactions of these factors have so far eluded researchers.

Reflections

- What are the attitudes of people from your sociocultural group toward gay males and lesbians? Do you share these attitudes? Why or why not?
- In your opinion, why do men tend to be more homophobic than women?
- Evaluate the evidence for biological and psychological theories of sexual orientation.

ADJUSTMENT OF GAY MALES AND LESBIANS

Despite the widespread belief that there is something wrong with gay men and lesbians, evidence has failed to show that they are more emotionally unstable or more subject to psychological disorders (such as anxiety and depression) than other people (Reiss, 1980). Nor have researchers been able to distinguish between gay and heterosexual people on the basis of psychological tests (Reiss, 1980). A gay male or lesbian sexual orientation is no longer itself considered a form of mental illness. In 1973, the American Psychiatric Association voted to drop gay male and lesbian sexual orientations from its list of mental disorders, although a diagnostic category remains for people with persistent and marked distress about their sexual orientation (American Psychiatric Association, 1994, p. 538).

Truth or Fiction? REVISITED

It is not true that the American Psychiatric Association considers homosexuality to be a mental disorder. The American Psychiatric Association has not considered a gay male or lesbian sexual orientation to be a mental disorder since 1973. ■

Gay men, lesbians, and bisexuals occupy all socioeconomic and vocational levels and follow a variety of lifestyles. Researchers find gay men and lesbians overall to be more highly educated than most Americans (Cronin, 1993). Bell and Weinberg (1978) found

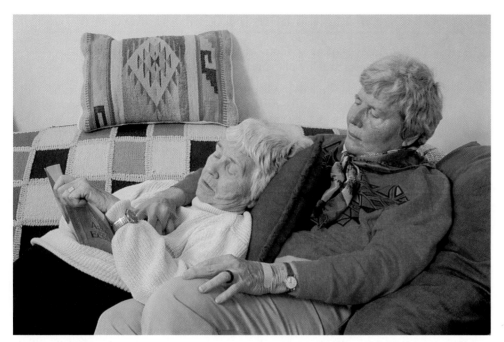

Adjustment and Sexual Orientation. Overall, gay males and lesbians are about as well adjusted (or poorly adjusted) as their heterosexual counterparts. One's adjustment is connected with one's lifestyle, regardless of one's sexual orientation. For example, gay males and lesbians in stable, long-term relationships are about as well adjusted as married heterosexuals.

variations in adjustment in the gay community that seem to mirror the variations in the heterosexual community. Gay people who lived with partners in stable, intimate relationships—so-called close couples—were about as well adjusted as married people. Older gay people who lived alone and had few sexual contacts were more poorly adjusted. So, too, are many heterosexual people who have similar lifestyles. All in all, differences in adjustment seem more likely to reflect the lifestyle than the sexual orientation.

Most gay males and lesbians who share close relationships with their partners are satisfied with the quality of their relationships. Researchers find that heterosexual and gay couples report similar levels of satisfaction with their relationships (Kurdek & Schmitt, 1986a; Peplau & Cochran, 1990). Gay males and lesbians who are in enduring relationships generally report high levels of love, attachment, closeness, caring, and intimacy (Peplau & Cochran, 1980).

As with heterosexual people, not all of the relationships of gay people are satisfying. Among both groups, satisfaction is higher when both partners feel that the benefits they receive from the relationship outweigh the costs (Duffy & Rusbult, 1985/1986). Like heterosexual people, gay men and lesbians are happier in relationships in which they share power and make joint decisions (Kurdek & Schmitt, 1986b). In sum, researchers have not found that gay men and lesbians suffer from more psychological distress than heterosexual people.

Much of the research on gay lifestyles has focused on the younger gay male and lesbian population. We do not know very much about the adjustment of gay people as they grow older. Still, research indicates that aging gay men and lesbians (50 to 73 years of age) who are active in the gay community generally report high levels of life satisfaction and acceptance of aging (Quam & Whitford, 1992). Developing and maintaining a sense of belonging or group identification among gay people may be helpful in navigating life's passages—just as they are in the general population.

Treatment of Gay Male and Lesbian Sexual Orientations

Despite the judgment of the American Psychiatric Association, some people still view a gay male or a lesbian sexual orientation as an illness. If it is an illness, then it is something to be "cured," perhaps by medical or psychological means. However, the great majority

t a b l e   1 0 . 2

	White Males (%)	African American Males (%)	White Females (%)	African American Females (%)
Percentages of gay people who wish they had received a "magic heterosexuality pill" at birth or could receive one today				
Desire magic pill at birth?	28	23	16	11
Desire magic pill today?	14	13	5	6

Source: Reprinted by permission of Simon & Schuster from Bell, A.P., & Weinberg, M.S. (1978). *Homosexualities: A study of diversity among men and women.* New York: Simon & Schuster, p. 339.

of gay men and lesbians do not seek professional assistance to change their sexual orientations. Most see their sexual orientations as integral parts of their personal identities. Bell and Weinberg (1978) found only a few gay people who were interested in changing their sexual orientation—even if a "magic pill" were available to bring about the change (see Table 10.2). Only a minority of Bell and Weinberg's sample had *ever* considered discontinuing male-male or female-female sexual activity.

A few gay men and women do express an interest in changing their orientations, however. Helping professionals have tried to help them do so in a variety of ways. At one time, when it was commonly believed that hormonal imbalances influenced one's sexual orientation, hormone treatments were in vogue. There is no evidence that they were effective.

A few psychotherapists have reported changing the sexual orientations of some individuals. For example, Bieber (1976) claimed that about one in four clients changed his or her sexual orientation through psychoanalytic psychotherapy. But critics charge that these clients were highly motivated to change. Moreover, some of them began therapy as bisexuals. Their change in lifestyle may be attributable to their initial motivation to change and not to the therapy itself.

Masters and Johnson (1979) employed methods used to treat sexual dysfunctions (see Chapter 15) to "reverse" patients' gay male or lesbian sexual orientations. For example, they involved gay males in a graded series of pleasurable activities with women, such as massage and genital stimulation. Masters and Johnson reported a failure rate of 20% for the gay men and 23% for the lesbians they treated in their therapy program. At a five-year follow-up, more than 70% of the clients continued to engage in male-female sexual activity (Schwartz & Masters, 1984). For many reasons, however, these patients do not seem to represent the general gay population:

- Most of them were bisexuals. Only about one in five engaged exclusively in male-male or female-female sexual activities.
- More than half were married.
- All were motivated to switch their sexual orientations.

Regardless of these people's changes in sexual behavior, remember that sexual behavior is not the equivalent of sexual orientation. (It was therefore inaccurate for Masters and Johnson to claim that they had reversed an individual's sexual *orientation*.) That is, many gay people engage in sexual activities with people of the other gender. Nevertheless, they still prefer to have such relationships with people of their own gender.

Critics of this kind of therapy argue that gay men and women often enter therapy because of conflicts that arise from social pressure and prejudice. Such pressures can create problems in the acceptance of one's gay male or lesbian sexual orientation. The role of the therapist, he argues, should be to help unburden the client of conflict and promote a more gratifying life as a gay person (Sleek, 1997).

Reflections

- Agree or disagree with the following statement, and support your answer: Gay males and lesbians are maladjusted.
- Agree or disagree with the following statement, and support your answer: We should help gay males and lesbians to change their sexual orientation whenever possible.

COMING OUT: COMING TO TERMS WITH BEING GAY

You must worship rugby and beer. And if you don't, God help you.
—A Roman Catholic priest in New Zealand (cited in Shenon, 1995)

Because of the backdrop of social condemnation and discrimination, gay males and lesbians in our culture often struggle to come to terms with their sexual orientation. Gay men and lesbians usually speak of the process of accepting their sexual orientation as "coming out" or "coming out of the closet." Coming out is a two-pronged process: coming out to oneself (recognizing one's gay male or lesbian sexual orientation) and coming out to others (declaring one's orientation to the world). Coming out can create a sense of pride in one's sexual orientation and foster the ability to form emotionally and sexually satisfying relationships with gay male or lesbian partners.

Coming Out to Oneself

Many gay people have a difficult time coming to recognize, let alone accept, their sexual orientation. Some have even considered or attempted suicide because of problems in self-acceptance:

It (suicidal thinking) was because of my homosexuality. I was completely depressed that my homosexuality was leading me nowhere. My life seemed to be going around in a circle. I was still fighting against recognition of my homosexuality. I knew what I was but I didn't want to be.

[I had] the feeling that homosexuality was a hopeless existence. I felt there was no future in it, that I was doomed to be alone. And from my Catholic background, I felt that homosexuality was very evil. (Bell & Weinberg, 1978, p. 202)

Consider the experience of a New Zealand gay adolescent who was subjected to merciless taunting until his parents pulled him out of school. "He threw a ball like a girl does," said a hot-line worker (cited in Shenon, 1995), "and the hassling just wouldn't stop. He was hassled nonstop from the day he got to that school until the day he left."

"You're judged constantly on your maleness," adds a Roman Catholic priest in New Zealand (cited in Shenon, 1995). "It can be a very intolerant country. You must worship rugby and beer. And if you don't, God help you. I think we've just been dreadful about this macho-ness."

For some people, coming to recognize and accept a gay male or lesbian sexual orientation involves gradually stripping away layers of denial. For others, it can be a sudden awakening. Longstanding sexual interests in members of one's own gender might rush into focus on a particular person, as happened with a graduate student named David:

> In college [David's] closest friend was gay. Although this friend had wanted to have sex with David and the attraction was mutual, David still could not associate this attraction with a sexuality that was acceptable to him. In his first year of graduate school, when he was about 23, he fell in love and then suddenly and with a great sense of relief recognized and acknowledged to himself that he was homosexual. He then had sex for the first time and has subsequently been . . . open about his sexuality. (Isay, 1990, p. 295)

Recognition of a gay sexual orientation might be only the first step in a lifelong process of sexual identity formation. Acceptance of being gay becomes part of one's self-definition (Isay, 1990). The term *gay identity* or *homosexual identity* refers to the subjective or psychological sense of being gay.

Some gay men and lesbians who have not yet come to recognize or accept their gay sexual orientation get married. For some, marriage is a means of testing feelings toward people of the other gender. For others, marriage represents an attempt to conceal or overcome their sexual orientation (Buxton, 1994; Gabriel, 1995a). Perhaps 20% of gay males and a higher percentage of lesbians get married at least once (Bell & Weinberg, 1978). But such marriages tend to be unhappy and short-lived. They might be strained by one partner's concealing her or his gay sexual orientation. Alternatively, they might buckle from the open acknowledgment of being gay. Virtually all such marriages in Bell and Weinberg's study eventually ended in separation or divorce.

In the 1990s, many American couples have a gay or lesbian spouse. Thousands of gay men and lesbians who had conformed to social pressures by getting married are now coming out of the closet and sometimes leaving home (Buxton, 1994; Gabriel, 1995a).

Coming Out to Others

There are different patterns of coming out to others. Coming out occasionally means an open declaration to the world. More often, a person may inform only one or a few select people. The person might tell friends but not family members.

Many gay men and lesbians remain reluctant to declare their sexual orientation, even to friends and family. Disclosure is fraught with the risk of loss of jobs, friendships, and social standing (Padesky, 1988). A social worker who counsels lesbians described some fears of coming out to others expressed by her clients:

> Will I lose my job, will I lose my house, will I lose my children, will I be attacked? I've seen people lose a job. Even if you don't lose it, you become marginal, excluded either actively or through uncomfortable vibes. (cited in Barrett, 1990, p. 470)

Gay men and lesbians often anticipate negative reactions from informing family members, including denial, anger, and rejection. Family members and loved ones might refuse to hear or be unwilling to accept reality, as Martha Barron Barrett notes in her book *Invisible Lives*, which chronicles the lives of a sample of lesbians in the United States:

> Parents, children, neighbors, and friends of lesbians deny, or compartmentalize, or struggle with their knowledge in the same way the women themselves do. "My parents know I've lived with my partner for six years. She goes home with me. We sleep in the same bed there. The word *lesbian* has never been mentioned." "I told my mother and she said, 'Well, now that's over with. We don't need to mention it again.' She never has, and that was ten years ago. I don't know if she ever told my father." A husband may dismiss it as "just a phase," a boyfriend may interpret it as a sexual tease, a straight woman may believe "she's just saying that because she couldn't get a man."

> The strong message is, "Keep it quiet." Many lesbians do that by becoming invisible. . . . They (lesbians) leave their lesbian persona at home when they go to work on Monday morning. On Friday they don it again. That weekend at home, the flip side of the double life, is what most of heterosexual society never sees. (Barrett, 1990, p. 52)

The gay community has been active online for quite some time. An *Out* magazine survey shows that gay men and lesbians are more likely than the general population to use personal computers, modems, and online services. In an average month in the 1990s, 40,000 gay people spent more than 100,000 hours online with America Online's Gay and Lesbian Community Forum.

Planet Out (http://www.planetout.com), the electronic media company, has become a sort of "gay global village" in cyberspace. It has received the endorsement of virtually all the leading gay organizations. The Human Rights Campaign Fund, the National Gay and Lesbian Task Force, Parents and Friends of Lesbians and Gays, the Gay and Lesbian Victory Fund, Digital Queers, and the Gay and Lesbian Alliance Against Defamation all provide information on the service.

Planet Out is also a meeting place for millions of gay men, lesbians, bisexuals, and others who might be reluctant to associate with one another in public. A creative director of Netscape and the former head of design at Apple Computer said that chatting electronically with gay men and lesbians on America Online had given him the courage to discuss his gay sexual orientation openly. "It's something that would have been unthinkable for me even a year or two ago," he said. "If I had relied on more traditional ways of meeting people, like going to bars, or going to meetings of various organizations, or picking up gay publications, it never would have happened" (Lewis, 1995).

Some families are more accepting. They might in fact have had suspicions and prepared themselves for such news. Then, too, many families are initially rejecting but often eventually come to at least grudging acceptance that a family member is gay.

Reflections

- Do you know any gay males or lesbians? Have they shared with you their experiences in coming out? What did they go through? Why?
- Are you a gay male or lesbian? If so, have you come out? If so, what was the experience like? If not, why not?

PATTERNS OF SEXUAL ACTIVITY AMONG GAY MALES AND LESBIANS

Heterosexual people are often confused about the sexual practices of gay couples. They might wonder, "Just what do they do?" Generally speaking, gay couples express themselves sexually through as wide a range of activities as heterosexual couples, with the exception of vaginal intercourse. But there are shades of difference between gay and heterosexual couples in sexual techniques.

Sexual Techniques

Gay male couples tend to engage in sexual activities such as kissing, hugging, petting, mutual masturbation, fellatio, and anal intercourse. Laboratory observations of sexual relations between gay males by Masters and Johnson (1979) showed that gay males spent a good deal of time caressing their partners' bodies before approaching the genitals. After hugging and kissing, 31 of 42 gay male couples observed by Masters and Johnson used oral or manual nipple stimulation.

Not all gay males enjoy or practice anal intercourse. Of those who do, most alternate between being the inserter and the insertee. The frequency of anal intercourse among gay males is apparently declining in the face of the AIDS epidemic (Catania et al., 1991; Sonenstein et al., 1989).

Risks of infection and of injury to the rectum or anus are associated with another sexual practice called "fisting." Fisting is the insertion of the fist or hand into the rectum, usually after the bowels have been evacuated with an enema.

Sex and Sexual Orientation. Like heterosexual women, lesbians are less genitally oriented and less fixated on orgasm than men. The emotional aspects of lovemaking—gentle touching, cuddling, and hugging—are key features of sexual sharing in lesbian relationships.

Sexual techniques practiced by lesbians vary. Lesbian couples report kissing, manual and oral breast stimulation, and manual and oral stimulation of the genitals (Kinsey et al., 1953). Manual genital stimulation is the most common and frequent sexual activity among lesbian couples (Bell & Weinberg, 1978). Most lesbian couples also engage in genital apposition. That is, they position themselves so as to rub their genitals together rhythmically (Kinsey et al., 1953). Like gay males, lesbians spend a good deal of time holding, kissing, and caressing each other's bodies before they approach the breasts and genitals. By contrast, heterosexual males tend to move quickly to stimulate their partners' breasts or start directly with genital stimulation (Masters & Johnson, 1979).

Like heterosexual women, lesbians are less genitally oriented and less fixated on orgasm than men. Lesbians generally begin stimulating their partners with more general genital stimulation rather than direct clitoral stimulation, whereas heterosexual males often begin by stimulating the clitoris (Masters & Johnson, 1979). Nor do lesbian couples generally engage in deep penetration of the vagina with fingers. Rather, they might use more shallow vaginal penetration, focusing stimulation on the vaginal lips and entrance. Images of lesbians strapping on dildos for vaginal penetration exist more in the imagination of uninformed heterosexual people than in the sexual repertoire of lesbian couples (Masters & Johnson, 1979). The emotional components of lovemaking—gentle touching, cuddling, and hugging—are important elements of sexual sharing in lesbian relationships.

Reflections

- Agree or disagree with the following statement, and support your answer: The sexual practices of gay males and lesbians are more similar to, than different from, the sexual practices of heterosexuals.

GAY LIFESTYLES

One of the mistakes that laypeople (and some researchers) make is to treat gay people as if they were all the same. According to Bell and Weinberg (1978), gay people do not adopt a single, stereotypical lifestyle. That is why the authors termed their report *Homosexualities: A Study of Diversity among Men and Women.* Variations in sexual expression exist within and across sexual orientations. Descriptions of gay and heterosexual lifestyles must consider individual differences.

Gay men and lesbians in larger U.S. urban centers can usually look to gay communal structures to provide services and support. These include gay rights organizations and gay-oriented newspapers, magazines, bookstores, housing cooperatives, medical services, and other support services (Gagnon, 1990). The gay community provides a sense of acceptance and belonging that gay people do not typically find in society at large. Gay people still encounter discrimination in the workplace, in housing, and in the military.

Restrictions on gay males participating in the armed services has been a continuing controversy. In 1993, President Clinton encountered stiff opposition when he sought to follow through on his campaign pledge to permit openly gay men and women to serve in the military. As a compromise measure, he instituted a "don't ask, don't tell" policy. It permits gay males and lesbians to serve as long as they do not publicly express or reveal their sexual orientation. Moreover, military officials are prohibited from inquiring about the sexual orientation of recruits or initiating investigations in the absence of a public display or

Sexual Orientation and Lifestyle. Gay people, like heterosexuals, have a variety of lifestyles. Some go from partner to partner. Others form stable relationships. Some avoid sexual intimacy and committed relationships altogether. As Alexandre Dumas once said, "All generalizations are dangerous. Even this one."

disclosure of a gay male or lesbian sexual orientation ("Defense dept. suspends," 1993). The constitutionality of this policy has been challenged, since it may restrict freedom of speech.

Gay rights organizations fight for rights for gay people to participate fully in society—to teach in public schools, to adopt children, to live together in sanctioned relationships, and to serve openly and proudly in the military. Cafés and social clubs provide places where gay men and lesbians can socialize and be open about their sexual orientations. Many such establishments also serve as meeting places for casual sexual pickups, although the advent of AIDS might have curtailed such activity. Organizations such as New York's Gay Men's Health Crisis (GMHC) provide medical, social, and psychological assistance to gay males who have been afflicted by AIDS.

Not all gay people feel that they are a part of the "gay community" or participate in gay rights organizations, however. For many, their sexual orientation is a part of their identity but not a dominant theme that governs their social and political activities.

Lifestyle Differences Between Gay Males and Lesbians

Much of our knowledge of lifestyle patterns among gay males and lesbians comes from research that predates the AIDS epidemic. Researchers in the 1970s found that gay males were more likely than lesbians to engage in casual sex with many partners. Lesbians more often confined their sexual activity to a committed, affectionate relationship (Bell & Weinberg, 1978). Bell and Weinberg reported that 84% of gay males, compared to about 7% of lesbian women, reported having more than 50 partners in their lifetimes. Seventy-nine percent of gay males in their study, compared to only 6% of lesbians, reported that more than half of their partners had been strangers.

Even in this age of AIDS, a recent survey found that only about half of gay men (40% to 60%), but about three in four lesbians, are currently involved in a steady relationship (Peplau & Cochran, 1990). Even gay males within committed relationships have more permissive attitudes toward extracurricular sexual activity than lesbians do (Blumstein & Schwartz, 1990; Peplau & Cochran, 1990).

Traditionally, the gay bar was an arena for making sexual contacts (Bell & Weinberg, 1978). **Cruising** is the name gay people give to searching for a sex partner, principally for casual sex. One can "cruise," and one can "be cruised." Gay males were more likely than lesbians to cruise in public places such as gay bars. Lesbians were more likely to find partners among friends, at work, and at informal social gatherings.

Today, with the threat of AIDS hanging over every casual sexual encounter, cruising has lost popularity. Many gay bathhouses, long a setting for casual sexual contacts, have

Cruising The name homosexuals give to searching for a sex partner.

closed down—or been closed down by authorities—because of AIDS. These closings are but one sign of changes in gay communities that have occurred since the advent of AIDS. Many gay males have changed their behavior to prevent contracting or spreading AIDS. Evidence shows that as a group, gay males have become more likely to limit or avoid anal and oral sex, especially with new partners. They are now more likely to use latex condoms when they do practice these techniques, to limit their sexual contacts to partners they know, and to rely more on masturbation as a sexual outlet (Centers for Disease Control, 1990; Siegel et al., 1988). Despite the advent of AIDS, some gay men, like some heterosexual people, continue high-risk behavior. For example, they engage in unprotected anal intercourse and sexual activity with multiple partners.

Research also shows that extracurricular sexual activity continues to be commonplace among gay male couples. One study surveyed 943 gay males and 1,510 married heterosexual males who had been living with a partner for 2 to 10 years. Four of five (79%) of the gay males reported sex with another partner during the preceding year, compared to only 11% of the heterosexual males (Blumstein & Schwartz, 1990). Among couples who had been together for longer than 10 years, 94% of gay men reported extracurricular activity at some time during their primary relationships.

Variations in Gay Lifestyles

Bell and Weinberg (1978) found that about three out of four gay couples they studied could be classified according to one of five lifestyles: *close couples*, *open couples*, *functionals*, *dysfunctionals*, and *asexuals*. **Close couples** strongly resembled married couples. They evidenced deep emotional commitment and few outside sexual relationships. Almost three times as many lesbians (28%) as gay males (10%) lived in such committed, intimate relationships. Gay people living in close relationships showed fewer social and psychological problems than those with any other lifestyle.

Truth or Fiction?
REVISITED

It is true that many gay couples have lifestyles similar to those of married heterosexual couples and are as well adjusted. They are referred to as *close couples* by Bell and Weinberg. ■

Partners in **open couples** lived together but engaged in clandestine affairs. Gay people in open couples were not as well adjusted as those in close couples. Nevertheless, their overall adjustment was similar to that of heterosexual people. Still other gay people lived alone and had sexual contacts with numerous partners—a kind of "swinging singles" gay lifestyle. Some of those who lived alone, **functionals,** appeared to have adapted well to their swinging lifestyle and were sociable and well adjusted. Others, called **dysfunctionals,** had sexual, social, or psychological problems. Dysfunctionals were often anxious and unhappy and found it difficult to form intimate relationships. **Asexuals** also lived alone but were distinguished by having few sexual contacts. Asexuals tended to be older than gay people in the other groups. Although they did not have the adjustment problems of dysfunctionals, they too did not form intimate relationships. Despite being largely asexual in terms of their behavior, their sexual orientation was clearly gay.

The Bell and Weinberg study described diversity of lifestyles in the gay community in the 1970s, before the AIDS epidemic struck. Although such lifestyles continue today to a certain extent, the AIDS epidemic has inhibited promiscuous sex within the gay community. The specter of AIDS has had a more profound effect on the lifestyles and sexual practices of gay males than on any other group in society.

Reflections

■ Agree or disagree with the following statement, and support your answer: Gay males and lesbians lead a wild, swinging sexual lifestyle. (Hint: Critical thinkers avoid overgeneralizations.)

■ What did you learn about gay males and lesbians from this chapter? What misinformation has been corrected? What is completely new to you?

■ Do you believe that the information in this chapter has been presented in a straightforward or a biased manner? Explain.

Close couples Bell and Weinberg's term for gay couples whose relationships resemble marriage in their depth of commitment and exclusiveness.

Open couples Bell and Weinberg's term for gay couples who live together but engage in secret affairs.

Functionals Bell and Weinberg's term for gay people who live alone, have adapted well to a swinging lifestyle, and are sociable and well adjusted.

Dysfunctionals Bell and Weinberg's term for gay people who live alone and have sexual, social, or psychological problems.

Asexuals Bell and Weinberg's term for gay people who live alone and have few sexual contacts.

summing up

SEXUAL ORIENTATION

Coming to Terms with Terms
Sexual orientation describes the directionality of one's sexual and romantic interests—toward members of the same gender, the other gender, or both. Gay male and lesbian sexual orientations denote sexual and romantic interest in members of one's own gender.

Sexual Orientation and Gender Identity
Gay males and lesbians have a gender identity that is consistent with their chromosomal and anatomic sex.

Classification of Sexual Orientation
Kinsey and his colleagues found evidence of degrees of homosexuality and heterosexuality, with bisexuality representing a midpoint between the two. Heterosexuality and homosexuality may be separate dimensions rather than polar opposites, however.

PERSPECTIVES ON GAY MALE AND LESBIAN SEXUAL ORIENTATIONS

Historical Perspectives
Throughout much of Western history, gay people have been deemed sinful and criminal.

Cross-Cultural Perspectives
Male-male sexual behavior is practiced by at least some members of many preliterate societies.

Cross-Species Perspectives
Many animals engage in behaviors that resemble male-male contacts among humans, but we must be cautious in ascribing motives to animals.

Attitudes Toward Sexual Orientation in Contemporary Society
The majority of people in our society view gay people negatively. During the past generation, gay males and lesbians have organized effective political groups to fight discrimination and overturn antisodomy laws that have traditionally targeted them.

Biological Perspectives
Evidence of a genetic contribution to sexual orientation is accumulating. Research has failed to connect sexual orientation with differences in current (adult) levels of sex hormones. Prenatal sex hormones may play a role in determining sexual orientation in humans, however.

Psychological Perspectives
Psychoanalytic theory connects sexual orientation with unconscious castration anxiety and improper resolution of the Oedipus complex. Learning theorists focus on the role of reinforcement of early patterns of sexual behavior.

Gender Nonconformity
Although only a few gay people fit the stereotypes of swishy men and butch women, research finds that homosexuals report a greater incidence of behavior stereotypical of the other gender as children than do heterosexual reference groups.

ADJUSTMENT OF GAY MALES AND LESBIANS

Evidence has failed to show that gay males, lesbians, and bisexuals are more emotionally unstable or more subject to psychiatric disorders than heterosexual people are.

COMING OUT: COMING TO TERMS WITH BEING GAY

Gay people in our culture struggle to come to terms with their sexual orientation against a backdrop of social condemnation and antagonism. Coming out is a two-pronged process: coming out to oneself and coming out to others. Coming to recognize and accept one's gay sexual orientation may occur as a gradual process or a sudden awakening.

PATTERNS OF SEXUAL ACTIVITY AMONG GAY MALES AND LESBIANS

Gay people generally express themselves sexually through as wide a range of activities as heterosexual people do, with the exception of vaginal intercourse.

GAY LIFESTYLES

Gay people do not adopt a single, stereotypical lifestyle.

Lifestyle Differences Between Gay Males and Lesbians
Gay males are more likely than lesbians to engage in casual sex with many partners. Lesbians more often confine sexual activity to a committed, affectionate relationship. Many gay males have changed their sexual behavior to prevent contracting or spreading AIDS.

Variations in Gay Lifestyles
The majority of gay people studied by Bell and Weinberg could be classified according to one of five lifestyles: close couples, open couples, functionals, dysfunctionals, and asexuals.

Charleen Touchette. *We Are the Same But We Are Different.* Mixed media on paper, 30 x 22 in. © 1987. Courtesy of the artist

chapter

11

Conception, Pregnancy, and Childbirth

o u t l i n e

TRUTH OR FICTION?

CONCEPTION: AGAINST ALL ODDS
Optimizing the Chances of Conception

IN THE NEW MILLENNIUM:
Two Views of Parenting in the New Millennium: Childfree by Choice and Pushing the Biological Clock

IN THE NEW MILLENNIUM:
Selecting the Gender of Your Child

A CLOSER LOOK:
Sex and the Single Lizard

INFERTILITY AND ALTERNATIVE WAYS OF BECOMING PARENTS
Male Fertility Problems
Female Fertility Problems

IN THE NEW MILLENNIUM:
Sperm and Egg Donations for Overnight Delivery?

PREGNANCY
Early Signs of Pregnancy

QUESTIONNAIRE:
Should You Have a Child?

Pregnancy Tests
Early Effects of Pregnancy
Miscarriage (Spontaneous Abortion)
Sex During Pregnancy
Psychological Changes During Pregnancy

PRENATAL DEVELOPMENT
The Germinal Stage
The Embryonic Stage
The Fetal Stage
Environmental Influences on
    Prenatal Development
Chromosomal and Genetic
    Abnormalities

CHILDBIRTH
The Stages of Childbirth
Methods of Childbirth
Alternatives to the Hospital:
    Where Should a Child Be Born?

BIRTH PROBLEMS
Anoxia

A WORLD OF DIVERSITY:
Ethnicity and Infant Mortality
Preterm and Low-Birthweight Children

THE POSTPARTUM PERIOD
Maternal Depression
Breast-Feeding Versus Bottle-Feeding
Resumption of Ovulation
    and Menstruation
Resumption of Sexual Activity

SUMMING UP

Truth or Fiction?

_____ There is an all-female species of lizard that lays unfertilized eggs that develop into identical females, generation after generation.

_____ Prolonged athletic activity can decrease fertility in the male.

_____ A "test-tube baby" is grown in a large laboratory dish throughout the nine-month gestation period.

_____ For the first week after conception, a fertilized egg cell is not attached to its mother's body.

_____ Pregnant women can have one or two alcoholic beverages a day without harming their babies.

_____ A baby signals its mother when it is ready to be born.

_____ One U.S. birth in five is by cesarean section.

_____ Couples should abstain from sexual activity for at least six weeks after childbirth.

On a balmy day in October, Elaine and her husband Dennis rush to catch the train to their jobs in the city. Elaine's workday is outwardly much the same as any other. Within her body, however, a drama is unfolding. Yesterday, hormones had caused a follicle in her ovary to rupture, releasing its egg cell, or ovum. Like all women, Elaine possessed at birth all the ova she would ever have, each encased in a sac or follicle. How this particular follicle was selected to mature and release its ovum this month remains a mystery. For the next day or so, however, Elaine will be capable of conceiving.

When Elaine used her ovulation-timing kit the previous morning, it showed that she was about to ovulate. So later that night, Elaine and Dennis had made love, hoping that Elaine would conceive. When Dennis ejaculated, hundreds of millions of sperm were deposited within Elaine's vagina. Only a few thousand survived the journey through the cervix and uterus to the fallopian tube that contained the ovum, released just hours earlier. Of these, a few hundred remained to bombard the ovum. Only one succeeded in penetrating the ovum's covering, resulting in conception. From a single cell formed by the union of sperm and ovum, a new life begins to form. The **zygote** is but $1/175$ of an inch across—a tiny beginning. But Elaine must wait a few weeks before a pregnancy test will reveal that she is pregnant.

Elaine is 37 years old. Four months into her pregnancy, Elaine obtains **amniocentesis** to check for the presence of chromosomal abnormalities, such as **Down syndrome.** (Down syndrome is more common among children born to women in their late 30s and older.) Amniocentesis also indicates the gender of the fetus. Although many parents prefer to know the gender of their baby before it is born, Elaine and Dennis ask their doctor not to inform them. "Why ruin the surprise?" Dennis explains to his friends. So Elaine and Dennis are left to debate boys' names and girls' names for the next few months.

CONCEPTION: AGAINST ALL ODDS

Conception is the union of a sperm cell and an ovum. On one hand, conception is the beginning of a new human life. Conception is also the end of a fantastic voyage, however, in which a viable ovum, one of only several hundred that will mature and ripen during a woman's lifetime, unites with one of several hundred *million* sperm produced by the man in the average ejaculate.

Ova carry X sex chromosomes. Sperm carry either X or Y sex chromosomes. Girls are conceived from the union of an ovum and an X-bearing sperm, boys from the union of an ovum and a Y-bearing sperm. Sperm that bear Y sex chromosomes appear to be faster swimmers than those bearing X sex chromosomes. This is one of the reasons that between 120 and 150 boys are conceived for every 100 girls. What seem to be natural balancing factors favor the survival of female fetuses, however. Male fetuses are more likely to be lost in a **spontaneous abortion,** which often occurs during the first month of pregnancy. In many cases of early spontaneous abortion, the woman never realizes that she had been pregnant. Despite spontaneous abortions, boys still outnumber girls at birth. Boys suffer from a higher incidence of infant mortality, however. Therefore, the numbers of boys and girls in the population are further equalized by the time they mature to the point of pairing off.

The 200 million to 400 million sperm in an average ejaculate might seem excessive, since only 1 can fertilize an egg. Only 1 in 1,000 will ever arrive in the vicinity of an ovum, however. Millions deposited in the vagina simply flow out of the woman's body because of gravity, unless she remains prone for quite some time. Normal vaginal acidity kills

Zygote A fertilized ovum.

Amniocentesis A procedure for drawing off and examining fetal cells in the amniotic fluid to determine the presence of various disorders in the fetus.

Down syndrome A chromosomal abnormality that leads to mental retardation, caused by an extra chromosome on the twenty-first pair.

Spontaneous abortion The sudden, involuntary expulsion of the embryo or fetus from the uterus before it is capable of independent life.

many more. Many surviving sperm swim against the current of fluid coming from the cervix, through the os and into the uterus. Surviving sperm may reach the fallopian tubes 60 to 90 minutes after ejaculation. About half the sperm end up in the wrong tube—that is, the one that does not contain the egg. Perhaps some 2,000 sperm find their way into the right tube. Fewer still manage to swim the final 2 inches against the currents generated by the cilia that line the tube.

The journey of sperm might not be random or blind. Fertile ova secrete a compound that appears to attract sperm cells (Angier, 1992). Sperm cells contain odor receptors of a type that was once thought to be found only in the nasal cavity. It is therefore conceivable (pardon the pun) that sperm cells are attracted to ova through a variation of the sense of smell.

Fertilization normally occurs in a fallopian tube. (Figure 11.1 shows sperm swarming around an egg in a fallopian tube.) Ova contain chromosomes, proteins, fats, and nutritious fluid and are surrounded by a gelatinous layer called the **zona pellucida.** This layer must be penetrated if fertilization is to occur. Sperm that have completed their journey secrete the enzyme **hyaluronidase,** which briefly thins the zona pellucida, enabling one sperm to penetrate. Once a sperm has entered, the zona pellucida thickens, locking other sperm out. The corresponding chromosomes in the sperm and ovum line up opposite each other. Conception occurs as the chromosomes from the sperm and ovum combine to form 23 new pairs, which carry a unique set of genetic instructions.

Optimizing the Chances of Conception

Some couples wish to optimize their chances of conceiving during a particular month so that birth occurs at a desired time. Others have difficulty conceiving and wish to maximize their chances for a few months before consulting a fertility specialist. Some fairly simple procedures can dramatically increase the chances of conceiving for couples without serious fertility problems.

The ovum can be fertilized for about 4 to 20 hours after ovulation. Sperm are most active within 48 hours after ejaculation. So one way of optimizing the chances of conception is to engage in coitus within a few hours of ovulation. There are a number of ways to predict ovulation.

figure 11.1

Human Sperm Swarming Around an Ovum in a Fallopian Tube. Fertilization normally occurs in a fallopian tube, not in the uterus.

Zona pellucida A gelatinous layer that surrounds an ovum. (From roots meaning "zone through which light can shine.")

Hyaluronidase An enzyme that briefly thins the zona pellucida, enabling one sperm to penetrate. (From roots meaning "substance that breaks down a glasslike fluid.")

Two Views of Parenting in the New Millennium: Childfree by Choice and Pushing the Biological Clock

CHILDFREE BY CHOICE

As we approached the new millennium, the first wave of the baby boomers reached the age of menopause. For many of them, the biological clock that so many had anxiously watched wound down forever. Perhaps one woman in six had been infertile. But another 15% of them had chosen not to bear children. They were childfree by choice.

To many, the decision not to have children still violates norms of feminine conduct. Little girls are still given dolls and baby carriages as toys. Religious traditionalists still view motherhood as a woman's obligation and primary source of fulfillment. Traditional psychologists and psychiatrists have also believed in the psychological value of motherhood. Erik Erikson wrote, "A woman who does not fulfill her innate need to fill her uterus with embryonic tissue is likely to be frustrated or neurotic."

According to psychoanalyst Jeanne Safer (1996), the conventional wisdom and traditional teachings are all wrong. Women who chose to remain childfree feel fully womanly in their menopausal years. Many believe that they have pioneered new psychological territory for women to come. They have shown that women can make psychologically healthy informed choices about reproduction. Women are free to see motherhood as a way of life that might or might not suit them. Women can find fulfillment regardless of whether they choose motherhood.

Safer bases her conclusions on her own experience and on interviews with 50 women who, like her, had made conscious decisions to remain childfree. She found that most of the women had few regrets. Most of them were excited about the future. Most had never been happier. Consider some vignettes:

Jane was a dancer who at the age of 35 married a man who did not want children. At 40, she went to medical school. She now has a child psychiatry practice and has repaid her loans. "I make a difference in children's lives and still go out at night," she explained.

Then there's Anna, an accupuncturist. "My life is really beginning at 50," Anna said, as she and her bridegroom prepared for a trip around the world.

One woman, unnamed, spent ten years as a war correspondent in the Middle and Far East. "I've had such an eventful time," she told Safer, "I wouldn't mind dying now. Would I have been able to go into Afghanistan with the rebels if I'd had a child waiting at home?"

Robin is a secretary in a Long Island suburb. She is surrounded by other people's children. Yet she says, "There's no gene for motherhood. I'm happy with my life. I feel no need to undo what I didn't do—and I will leave lots of love behind me."

Lauren is a housewife and community activist. She admits that she has not experienced the "kind of self-knowledge you only get from having kids." On the other hand, she has gained "time to reflect that most people don't have."

Leslie, a gallery owner, is also approaching 50. Yet only recently has she been able to tell acquaintances that she chose to remain childfree. "I felt a stigma in my earlier years," she explained. "I was afraid people would judge me or feel sorry for me, because I mis-

trusted my decision to be different. Now I know that I made that choice out of strength."

Many of the women attributed their happiness to the opportunities for self-expression and community service that remaining childfree has provided. They are the centers of their own attention. Yet they are not selfish or cold. Rather, they have made the decision that it is all right for them to focus on their own lives.

All of the 50 women said that they felt proud that they actively grappled with their motherhood dilemma. They hadn't just fallen into motherhood as had so many of their peers. They did not regret remaining childfree, even though many wondered what motherhood would have been like. Still others saw themselves as permanent outsiders to the core concern of most other women. Yet they enjoyed their unconventional lives, the intimacy of their marriages, and their freedom and privacy.

And then there were those who decided to have children later on.

PUSHING THE BIOLOGICAL CLOCK

At the beginning of the new millennium, we also find more and more parents with gray hair at Little League games and PTA meetings—even while most of the other parents are still trying to cope with their acne (Matus, 1996). As we enter the new millennium, bearing children is no longer defined as an event of young adulthood. Although fertility declines with age, fathers have traditionally had children in middle and late adulthood. But today, increasing numbers of women in the United States are bearing children in middle age. The birthrate for women aged 40 to 44 doubled be-

Pushing the Biological Clock. People in the United States are having and rearing babies at later ages than ever before. Part of the delay is due to advances in medicine. One can now conceive and carry a baby safely to term at more advanced ages. Part of the delay is due to lifestyle. Many people spend much of their early adulthoods establishing themselves in the career world. By the time they get around to having children, they are approaching middle age.

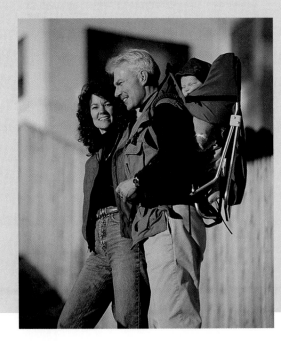

tween 1974 and 1994 (Clay, 1996a). In 1997, a 63-year-old woman gave birth. The trend to bear children at later ages continues.

Mothers in Their Forties

What kinds of mothers do middle-aged women make? According to Los Angeles psychologist Renee Cohen (1996), they make good ones. These mothers are usually settled in their work and marriage. Their decisions to bear children are well thought out. Because they have usually completed their education, established their career, and traveled, they are less likely to resent children for interfering with their lives.

"By the time older people decide to become parents," notes Cohen (1996, p. 37), "nothing is haphazard. Everything is planned. By having a baby, they're opening a new chapter in their lives."

Older Fathers

Older men also tend to be more involved as fathers, whether they are having their first child or parenting a second family (Clay, 1996b). Younger fathers tend to get embroiled in power struggles and physical discipline with their children, but "All of the studies on parenting show that the older the parent, the more nurturing, laid back, flexible, and supportive they are" (Pollack, 1996, p. 37).

Unlike younger men, men who choose fatherhood in their 40s are less likely to view themselves as distant breadwinners whose major role in the home is to provide discipline. More mature fathers are more likely to see themselves as "team players" who share parenting with their wives. Moreover, they are likely to have more time and patience for fatherhood because they have already established themselves in their careers.

Childfree by Choice. Many people remain childfree by choice. Deciding against having children was once seen as blasphemous, aberrant, selfish, or just plain weird. But many people today decide that they can lead fulfilling lives without reproducing. Many prefer the personal freedom that goes with remaining childfree.

USING THE BASAL BODY TEMPERATURE CHART   Few women have perfectly regular cycles, so they can only guess when they are ovulating. A basal body temperature (BBT) chart (Figure 11.2) may help provide a more reliable estimate.

As shown in the figure, body temperature is fairly even before ovulation, and early morning body temperature is generally below 98.6 degrees Fahrenheit. But just before

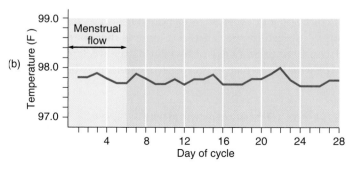

figure 11.2

A Basal Body Temperature (BBT) Chart. Because most women have somewhat irregular menstrual cycles, they may not be able to perfectly predict ovulation. The basal body temperature (BBT) chart helps them to do so. Body temperature dips slightly just prior to ovulation, rises about 0.4 to 0.8 of a degree following ovulation, and remains elevated through the course of the cycle. Part (a) represents a cycle in which a sustained elevation in temperature occurred following ovulation on day 15. Part (b) shows no sustained temperature rise, which is indicative of an absence of ovulation in this cycle.

Source: Adapted from Kolodny, R. C., Masters, W. H., and Johnson, V. E. (1979). *Textbook of sexual medicine.*

Selecting the Gender of Your Child

For thousands of years, parents have wished that they could select the gender of their children. In many cultures, one gender—usually male—has been preferred over the other. In other cases, parents who already have girls (or boys) would like to be able to "balance" their family by having a boy (or girl). Then, too, there are a number of sex-linked diseases—diseases that show up only in sons, for example. In such cases, parents would feel more secure if they could elect to have only daughters (Bennett, 1998).

But how would one select the gender of one's children? Folklore is replete with methods. Some cultures have advised coitus under the full moon to conceive boys. The Greek philosopher Aristotle suggested that making love during a north wind would beget sons. Making love during a south wind would produce daughters. Sour foods were once suggested for parents desirous of having boys. Those who wanted girls were advised to consume sweets. Husbands who yearned to have boys might be advised to wear their boots to bed. The thesis that the right testicle was responsible for seeding boys was popular at one time. Eighteenth-century French noblemen were advised to have their left testicles removed if they wanted to sire sons. It should go without saying that none of these methods worked.

These methods (or, should we say, non-methods?) would supposedly lead to the conception of children of the desired gender. However, methods after conception have also been used, such as the abortion of fetuses because of their gender. Infanticide has also been used in many cultures. Because boys have usually been considered more desirable than girls, female infanticide has been more common than male infanticide.

As we stand on the edge of the new millennium, more reliable methods seem to be in the offing.

SHETTLES'S APPROACH

Sperm bearing the Y sex chromosome are smaller than those bearing the X sex chromosome and are faster swimmers. But sperm with the X sex chromosome are more durable. From these assumptions, Shettles (1982) derived a number of strategies for choosing the gender of one's children. For example, to increase the chances of having a boy, the couple should engage in coitus on the day of ovulation, and the man should be penetrating deeply at the moment of ejaculation. To increase the chances of having a girl, the couple should engage in coitus two days or more before ovulation, and the man should ejaculate at a shallow depth of penetration. However, other researchers have not found these methods to be effective (Rawlins, 1998; Wilcox et al., 1995).

SPERM SEPARATION PROCEDURES

Several sperm separation procedures have also been used. One is based on the relative swimming rates of Y- and X-bearing sperm. Another relies on the differences in electrical charges of the two types of sperm to separate them.

A more current and promising sperm separation method relies on the fact that sperm carrying the Y sex chromosome have about 2.8% less genetic material (DNA) than sperm carrying the X sex chromosome (Kolata, 1998c). Edward Fugger (1998) and his colleagues have managed to pass the some 200 million human sperm in an ejaculation through a "DNA detector" and sort them on this basis. The cell sorter lined up the sperm individually in a stream, and then they were separated according to the amount of DNA they contained. Mothers were then artificially inseminated with the "proper" sperm. The results: The method may be able to create a female baby on about 85% of attempts and a male baby on about 65% of attempts. The method is more effective with cows and

---

ovulation, basal temperature dips slightly. Then, on the day after ovulation, temperature tends to rise by about 0.4 to 0.8 degree and to remain higher until menstruation. In using the BBT method, a woman attempts to detect these temperature changes by tracking her temperature just after awakening each morning but before rising from bed. Thermometers that provide finely graded readings, such as electronic digital thermometers, are best suited for determining these minor changes. The couple record the woman's temperature and the day of the cycle (as well as the day of the month) and indicate whether they have engaged in coitus. With regular charting for six months, the woman can learn to predict the day of ovulation more accurately—assuming that her cycles are fairly regular.

Opinion is divided as to whether it is better for couples to have coitus every 24 hours or every 36 to 48 hours for the several-day period during which ovulation is expected. More frequent coitus around the time of ovulation could increase the chances of conception. Relatively less frequent coitus (that is, every 36 to 48 hours) leads to a higher sperm count during each ejaculation. Most fertility specialists recommend that couples seeking to conceive a baby have intercourse once every day or two during the week in which the woman expects to ovulate. Men with lower-than-normal sperm counts may be advised to wait 48 hours between ejaculations.

ANALYZING URINE OR SALIVA FOR LUTEINIZING HORMONE   Over-the-counter kits are more accurate than the BBT method and predict ovulation by analyzing the woman's horses, because there is a larger difference (one of about 4%) in the amount of DNA between male and female sex-chromosome bearing sperm among these animals (Kolata, 1998c).

Should this method and others prove to be reliable and affordable, they raise many moral and ethical questions. Many individuals will wonder, for example, whether people have the right to select the gender of their children. In some cases, the word *right* will have a religious meaning. That is, some believe that only God should be able to determine the gender of a child. Others might think of the word *right* in terms of gender balancing within a culture. Since male children tend to be preferred, gender-selection could lead quickly to an overabundance of males within a society. Some social critics consider the very concept or availability of gender-selection methods to be sexist. But many believe that selecting the gender of one's children is a purely personal matter: "By what authority," they challenge, "do some decide whether the rest of us have acceptable reasons for selecting the sex of our children?" (Holmes-Farley, 1998).

The new millennium is likely to bring yet more efficient and affordable methods of the gender selection of infants. For that reason, we are very likely to have to cope with these moral and ethical questions—sooner rather than later.

Selecting the Gender of Your Child. Various approaches are available for selecting the gender of one's children, some of which are more reliable than others. If you could choose, would you prefer to have girls or boys? Do you believe that it is ethical to select the gender of your children? Why or why not?

urine or saliva for the surge in luteinizing hormone (LH) that precedes ovulation by about 12 to 24 hours.

TRACKING VAGINAL MUCUS Women can track the thickness of their vaginal mucus during the phases of the menstrual cycle by rolling it between their fingers and noting changes in texture. The mucus is thick, white, and cloudy during most phases of the cycle. It becomes thin, slippery, and clear for a few days preceding ovulation. A day or so after ovulation, the mucus again thickens and becomes opaque.

ADDITIONAL CONSIDERATIONS Coitus in the male-superior position allows sperm to be deposited deeper in the vagina and minimizes leakage of sperm out of the vagina due to gravity. Women may improve their chances of conceiving by lying on their backs and drawing their knees close to their breasts after ejaculation. This position, perhaps aided by the use of a pillow beneath the buttocks, may prevent sperm from dripping out quickly and elevates the pool of semen in relation to the cervix. It thus makes gravity work for, rather than against, conception. Women can also avoid standing and may lie as still as possible for about 30 to 60 minutes following ejaculation to help sperm move toward the cervical opening.

Women with severely retroverted or "tipped" uteruses may profit from supporting themselves on their elbows and knees and having their partners enter them from behind. Again, this position helps to prevent semen from dripping out of the vagina.

a **CLOSER** l o o k

Sex and the Single Lizard

Some years back, a scandalous book emerged on the scene: *Sex and the Single Girl.* A somewhat different scandal has now emerged in the animal world. It could be dubbed "Sex and the Single Lizard."

National Geographic reports the discovery of a most un-usual all-female species of lizard found in South America and the West Indies. At time for reproduction, no males need ap-ply. With no male contact, the lizards lay unfertilized eggs. The hatchlings develop into identical females, generation af-ter generation (Cole, 1995). Why? They derive all of their hereditary material from their mothers. The scientific name of the species is *Gymnophthalmus underwoodi.* (We include the scientific name so that you will think that there is some value to this A Closer Look feature.)

The lizards are hybrids of two species of lizard, each of which reproduces normally—that is, by having male lizards fertilize the females' eggs.

Truth or Fiction ? REVISITED

It is true that there is an all-female species of lizard that lays unfertilized eggs that develop into identical females, genera-tion after generation. ▪

The third author notes that she has three perfect daugh-ters and no sons. The first author does not wish to discuss the matter further.

The man should penetrate the woman as deeply as possible just before ejaculation, hold still during ejaculation, then withdraw slowly in a straight line to avoid dispersing the pool of semen.

Reflections

▪ Where does conception normally take place? Did you know this?
▪ Agree or disagree with the following statement, which is based on the remarks of a social critic: "Gender selection technology is sexist."

INFERTILITY AND ALTERNATIVE WAYS OF BECOMING PARENTS

For couples who want children, few problems are more frustrating than inability to con-ceive. Physicians often recommend that couples try to conceive on their own for six months before seeking medical assistance. The term **infertility** is usually not applied un-til the failure to conceive has persisted for more than a year.

Infertility concerns millions of Americans. Because the incidence of infertility in-creases with age, it is partially the result of a rise in couples who postpone childbearing un-til their 30s and 40s (Sheehy, 1995). All in all, about 15% of American couples have fertility problems (Howards, 1995). However, about half of them eventually succeed in conceiving a child (Jones & Toner, 1993). Many treatment options are available, ranging from drugs that stimulate ovulation to newer reproductive technologies, such as in vitro fertilization.

Male Fertility Problems

Although most concerns about fertility have traditionally centered on women, the prob-lem lies with the man in about 30% of cases (Howards, 1995). In about 20% of cases, problems are found in both partners (Hatcher et al., 1998; Howards, 1995).

Infertility Inability to conceive a child.

Fertility problems in the male reflect abnormalities such as these:

1. Low sperm count
2. Irregularly shaped sperm—for example, malformed heads or tails
3. Low sperm **motility**
4. Chronic diseases such as diabetes, as well as infectious diseases such as sexually transmitted diseases
5. Injury to the testes
6. An **autoimmune response,** in which antibodies produced by the man deactivate his own sperm
7. A pituitary imbalance and/or thyroid disease

Problems in producing normal, abundant sperm may be caused by genetic factors, advanced age, hormonal problems, diabetes, injuries to the testes, varicose veins in the scrotum, drugs (alcohol, narcotics, marijuana, tobacco), antihypertensive medications, environmental toxins, excess heat, and emotional stress. Sperm production gradually declines with age, but normal aging does not produce infertility. Men in late adulthood father children, even though conception can require more attempts.

Low sperm count (or the absence of sperm) is the most common problem. Sperm counts of 40 million to 150 million sperm per milliliter of semen are considered normal. A count of fewer than 20 million is generally regarded as low. Sperm production may be low among men with undescended testes that were not surgically corrected before puberty. Frequent ejaculation can reduce sperm counts. Sperm production may also be impaired in men whose testicles are consistently 1 or 2 degrees above the typical scrotal temperature of 94 to 95 degrees Fahrenheit (Leary, 1990). Frequent hot baths and tight-fitting underwear can also reduce sperm production, at least temporarily. Some men may encounter fertility problems from prolonged athletic activity, use of electric blankets, or even long, hot baths. In such cases, the problem can be readily corrected. Male runners with fertility problems are often counseled to take time off to increase their sperm counts. Interestingly, the small amounts of estrogen that men produce might help to keep sperm counts high ("Estrogen," 1997).

Sometimes, the sperm count is adequate, but prostate, hormonal, or other factors deprive sperm of motility or deform them. Motility can also be hampered by scar tissue from infections. Scarring can prevent sperm from passing through parts of the male reproductive system, such as the vas deferens. To be considered normal, sperm must be able to swim for at least two hours after coitus and most (60% or more) must be normal in shape.

It is true that prolonged athletic activity can decrease fertility in the male. Such activity can raise the temperature of the scrotum, providing a less-than-optimal environment for sperm. ■

Truth or Fiction?
REVISITED

Sperm counts have been increased by surgical repair of the varicose veins in the scrotum. Microsurgery can open blocked passageways that prevent the outflow of sperm (Howards, 1995). Researchers are also investigating the effects on sperm production of special cooling undergarments. One device, a kind of athletic supporter that is kept slightly damp with distilled water, has been approved by the Federal Drug Administration. Seventy percent of the men whose infertility is due to higher-than-normal scrotal temperatures show increased sperm count and quality with the wearing of cooling undergarments (Leary, 1990; Silber, 1991).

ARTIFICIAL INSEMINATION   The sperm of men with low sperm counts can be collected and quick-frozen. The sperm from multiple ejaculations can then be injected into a woman's uterus at the time of ovulation. This is one kind of **artificial insemination.** The sperm of men with low sperm motility can also be injected into their partners' uteruses, so the sperm begin their journey closer to the fallopian tubes. Sperm from a

Motility Self-propulsion. A measure of the viability of sperm cells.

Autoimmune response The production of antibodies that attack naturally occurring substances that are (incorrectly) recognized as being foreign or harmful.

Artificial insemination The introduction of sperm in the reproductive tract through means other than sexual intercourse.

donor can be used to artificially inseminate a woman whose partner is completely infertile or has an extremely low sperm count. The child then bears the genes of one of the parents—the mother. A donor can be chosen who resembles the man in physical traits and ethnic background.

A variation of artificial insemination has been used with some men with very low (or zero!) sperm counts in the semen, immature sperm, or immotile sperm. Immature sperm can be removed from a testicle by a thin needle and then directly injected into an egg in a laboratory dish (Brody, 1995b). The method has even been successful with a few men who only have tailless spermatids in the testes.

Female Fertility Problems

Major causes of infertility in women include the following:

1. Irregular ovulation, including failure to ovulate
2. Obstructions or malfunctions of the reproductive tract, which are often caused by infections or diseases involving the reproductive tract
3. Endometriosis
4. Declining hormone levels of estrogen and progesterone that occur with aging and may prevent the ovum from becoming fertilized or remaining implanted in the uterus

Ten percent to 15% of female infertility problems stem from failure to ovulate. Many factors can play a role in failure to ovulate, including hormonal irregularities, malnutrition, genetic factors, stress, and chronic disease. Failure to ovulate may occur in response to low levels of body fat, as in the cases of women with eating disorders and athletes (Frisch, 1997).

Ovulation may often be induced by the use of fertility drugs such as *clomiphene* (Clomid). Clomiphene stimulates the pituitary gland to secrete FSH and LH, which in turn stimulates maturation of ova. Clomiphene leads to conception in the majority of cases of infertility that are due *solely* to irregular or absent ovulation (Reinisch, 1990). But since infertility can have multiple causes, only about 50% of women who use clomiphene become pregnant. Another infertility drug, Pergonal, contains a high concentration of FSH, which directly stimulates maturation of ovarian follicles. Like clomiphene, Pergonal has high success rates with women whose infertility is due to lack of ovulation. Clomiphene and Pergonal have been linked to multiple births, including quadruplets and even quintuplets. However, fewer than 10% of such pregnancies result in multiple births.

Local infections that scar the fallopian tubes and other organs impede the passage of sperm or ova. Such infections include pelvic inflammatory disease—an inflammation of the woman's internal reproductive tract that can be caused by various infectious agents, such as the bacteria responsible for gonorrhea and chlamydia (see Chapter 16).

In **endometriosis,** cells break away from the uterine lining (the endometrium) and become implanted and grow elsewhere. When they develop on the surface of the ovaries or fallopian tubes, they may block the passage of ova or impair conception. About one case in six of female sterility is believed to be due to endometriosis. Hormone treatments and surgery sometimes reduce the blockage to the point at which women can conceive. A physician may suspect endometriosis during a pelvic exam, but it is diagnosed with certainty by **laparoscopy.** A long, narrow tube is inserted through an incision in the navel, permitting the physician to inspect the organs in the pelvic cavity visually. The incision is practically undetectable.

Suspected blockage of the fallopian tubes may also be checked by a **Rubin test** or a **hysterosalpingogram** (sometimes shortened to "hysterogram"). In a Rubin test, carbon dioxide gas is blown through the cervix. Its pressure is then monitored to determine whether it flows freely through the fallopian tubes into the abdomen or is trapped in the

Endometriosis An abnormal condition in which endometrial tissue is sloughed off into the abdominal cavity rather than out of the body during menstruation. The condition is characterized by abdominal pain and may cause infertility.

Laparoscopy A medical procedure in which a long, narrow tube (laparoscope) is inserted through an incision in the navel, permitting the visual inspection of organs in the pelvic cavity. (From the Greek *lapara,* meaning "flank.")

Rubin test A test in which carbon dioxide gas is blown through the cervix and its progress through the reproductive tract is tracked to determine whether or not the fallopian tubes are blocked.

Hysterosalpingogram A test in which a dye is injected into the reproductive tract and its progress is tracked by X-rays to determine whether or not the fallopian tubes are blocked. (From roots meaning "uterus," "fallopian tubes," and "record of.")

Intracytoplasmic Sperm Injection. This method of conception is sometimes used when the man has too few sperm for in vitro fertilization (IVF), or when IVF fails. As shown in the photograph, a micro-needle injects a single sperm directly into an ovum.

uterus. In the more common hysterosalpingogram, the movement of an injected dye is monitored by X-rays. This procedure may be uncomfortable.

Several new methods help many couples with problems such as blocked fallopian tubes to bear children.

IN VITRO FERTILIZATION   When Louise Brown was born in England in 1978 after being conceived by the method of **in vitro fertilization (IVF),** the event made headlines around the world. Louise was dubbed the world's first "test-tube baby." However, conception took place in a laboratory dish (not a test tube), and the embryo was implanted in the mother's uterus, where it developed to term. Before the in vitro fertilization, fertility drugs stimulate ripening of ova. Ripe ova are then surgically removed from an ovary and placed in a laboratory dish along with the father's sperm. Fertilized ova are then injected into the mother's uterus to become implanted in the uterine wall.

It is not true that a "test-tube baby" is grown in a large laboratory dish throughout the nine-month gestation period. A test-tube baby is actually conceived in a laboratory dish (which is similar to a test tube, perhaps), but the fertilized egg is then placed in the mother's uterus, where it must become implanted if it is to develop to term. ■

GIFT   In **gamete intrafallopian transfer (GIFT),** sperm and ova are inserted together into a fallopian tube for fertilization. Unlike in vitro fertilization, conception occurs in a fallopian tube rather than a laboratory dish.

ZIFT   **Zygote intrafallopian transfer (ZIFT)** involves a combination of IVF and GIFT. Sperm and ova are combined in a laboratory dish. After fertilization, the zygote is placed in the mother's fallopian tube to begin its journey to the uterus for implantation. ZIFT has an advantage over GIFT in that the fertility specialists can ascertain that fertilization has occurred before insertion is performed.

DONOR IVF   "I tell her Mommy was having trouble with, I call them ovums, not eggs," says a 50-year-old female therapist in Los Angeles (cited in Stolberg, 1998a). "I say that I needed these to have a baby, and there was this wonderful woman and she was willing to give me some, and that was how she helped us. I want to be honest that we got pregnant in a special way."

That special way is termed **donor IVF.** It is a variation of the IVF procedure in which the ovum is taken from another woman, fertilized, and then injected into the uterus or fallopian tube of the intended mother. The procedure is used when the intended mother does not produce ova. The number of births using this method has been mushrooming in recent years (Stolberg, 1998a).

Truth or Fiction?
REVISITED

In vitro fertilization (IVF) A method of conception in which mature ova are surgically removed from an ovary and placed in a laboratory dish along with sperm.

Gamete intrafallopian transfer (GIFT) A method of conception in which sperm and ova are inserted into a fallopian tube to encourage conception.

Zygote intrafallopian transfer (ZIFT) A method of conception in which an ovum is fertilized in a laboratory dish and then placed in a fallopian tube.

Donor IVF A variation of in vitro fertilization in which the ovum is taken from one woman, fertilized, and then injected into the uterus or fallopian tube of another woman.

Sperm and Egg Donations for Overnight Delivery?

Ellen is a 34-year-old Australian whose ovaries were ravaged by cancer treatments. She tried without luck to find an Australian woman who would donate eggs to her for two years. Then she learned about the Los Angeles Egg Donor Program, which advertised that it had access to "extremely bright, attractive and kind-hearted" women who would donate eggs. Oh, yes, their intelligence test scores were on file.

So Ellen selected a donor from a file that included photos and data on her personality, education, family history—even her special talents. Then Ellen and her husband flew to Los Angeles. The eggs were fertilized in a laboratory dish by her husband's sperm and implanted in Ellen's uterus. The first attempt did not work, but a later attempt with a frozen embryo from the program did, and Ellen's daughter was born nine months later.

NOT UNUSUAL

Ellen's case is not unusual. The United States has become a center for infertile foreigners who are seeking sperm or egg donors. Some would-be parents want babies with an "American look," but nearly all prefer to have children of their own race. In the case of sperm donors, the American look translates into a tall man with brown or blond hair, blue or green eyes, and—of course—dimples. Of course, there are no guarantees that donors come as advertised. There have even been cases of consumer fraud.

Many foreigners turn to the United States because other countries, including England and Australia, do not permit payments to egg donors. Most countries also place limits on donation of sperm. But in the United States, there are few restrictions on the buying and selling of sperm and eggs.

Donation is easy for a man: He just ejaculates into a container. Then his sperm is frozen and medically tested for health problems. Egg donors take powerful hormone to stimulate their ovaries to produce upwards of 10 eggs, and then the eggs are surgically removed. Many women who seek egg donors are women whose ovaries are not producing viable eggs. An egg from a donor is fertilized in a laboratory, and then the embryo is implanted in the recipient's uterus or frozen for future use.

In the United States, commercial sperm banks advertise that they have sperm that are free of HIV and other sexually transmitted diseases. They offer to ship frozen semen around the world overnight. Donated eggs are available from centers that advertise hundreds of donors, with no waiting lists. Enthusiastic customers typically fork over between $100 and $200 for sperm and about $5,000 for eggs. Catalogues of American donors, complete with color photos, are posted on the Internet for prospective customers.

"There was no delay," Ellen said (Kolata, 1998c). "We ordered it. It was like ordering a hamburger. [In Australia] it's like getting blood from a stone."

WEB SITES

Prospective customers can go to Web sites, such as those of Cryobank and of the Beverly Hills Center for Surrogate Parenting and Egg Donation, and click on traits they want in donors, in categories such as religion, ethnic background, height, weight, color of eyes or hair, hair texture, blood type, education, and occupation. Some centers even allow customers to check out donors' favorite books and movies and their philosophies of life. Donors who meet the criteria pop up. How many of us will be surfing the Web to find parents for our children in the new millennium?

EMBRYONIC TRANSFER   A similar method for women who do not produce ova of their own is **embryonic transfer.** In this method, a woman volunteer is artificially inseminated by the male partner of the infertile woman. Five days later, the embryo is removed from the volunteer and inserted within the uterus of the mother-to-be, where it is hoped that it will become implanted.

In vitro and transfer methods are costly. Success with in vitro fertilization drops from nearly 30% in women in their mid-20s to 10% to 15% in women in their late 30s (Toner et al., 1991).

INTRACYTOPLASMIC SPERM INJECTION   **Intracytoplasmic sperm injection** has been used when the man has too few sperm for IVF or when IVF fails (Howards, 1995). In this method, a single sperm is injected directly into an ovum. To date, the method has resulted in pregnancy in about 35% of cases (Van Steirteghem et al., 1993). However, research with Belgian and Australian children who were conceived by this methods suggests that it may be associated with an increase in the risk of birth defects. These defects include heart, stomach, kidney, and bladder problems, along with cleft palates and hernias ("New fertility treatment," 1997). Couples who are considering using the procedure are advised to inquire as to the latest research concerning the possibility of birth defects.

SURROGATE MOTHERHOOD   A **surrogate mother** is artificially inseminated by the husband of the infertile woman and carries the baby to term. The surrogate signs a con-

Embryonic transfer A method of conception in which a woman volunteer is artificially inseminated by the male partner of the intended mother, after which the embryo is removed from the volunteer and inserted within the uterus of the intended mother.

Intracytoplasmic sperm injection A method of conception in which a single sperm is injected directly into an ovum.

Surrogate mother A woman who is impregnated through artificial insemination with the sperm of a prospective father, carries the embryo and fetus to term, and then gives the child to the prospective parents.

tract to turn the baby over to the infertile couple. Such contracts have been invalidated in some states, however, so surrogate mothers in these states cannot be compelled to hand over the babies.

ADOPTION   Adoption is yet another way for people to obtain children. Despite the occasional conflicts in which adoptive parents are pitted against biological parents who change their minds about giving their children up for adoption, most adoptions result in the formation of loving new families. Many people in the United States find it easier to adopt infants from other countries, infants with special needs, or older children.

Reflections

▪ Do you know of any couples who have had difficulty conceiving a child? Did they consult a health professional about the problem? What was recommended? How did it work out? What did the couple experience during the process?

▪ Today's reproductive technologies make it possible for women to have babies after menopause (by receiving donor eggs) or to become mothers to their own grandchildren (by using eggs donated by their daughters). It may even become possible for a woman to receive a transplanted ovary from an aborted fetus and later give birth to a child whose biological mother is the aborted fetus. These reproductive technologies have leapfrogged ahead of society's efforts to grapple with their ethical, moral, and legal implications. Where should the line be drawn in determining how far medical science should go in providing reproductive alternatives to infertile people?

PREGNANCY

People react to becoming pregnant in different ways. For those who are psychologically and economically prepared, pregnancy may be greeted with joyous celebration. Some women feel that pregnancy helps to fulfill their sense of womanhood:

> Being pregnant meant I was a woman. I was enthralled with my belly growing. I went out right away and got maternity clothes.

> It gave me a sense that I was actually a woman. I had never felt sexy before . . . I felt very voluptuous.
> —Boston Women's Health Book Collective, *The New Our Bodies, Ourselves,* 1992

On the other hand, an unwanted pregnancy may evoke feelings of fear and hopelessness, as occurs with many teenagers.

In this section, we examine biological and psychological aspects of pregnancy: signs of pregnancy, prenatal development, complications, effects of drugs and sex, and the psychological experiences of pregnant women and fathers. The nearby questionnaire invites you to consider whether you should have a child.

Early Signs of Pregnancy

For many women, the first sign of pregnancy is missing a period. But some women have irregular menstrual cycles or miss a period because of stress. Missing a period is therefore not a fully reliable indicator. Some women also experience cyclic bleeding or spotting during pregnancy, although the blood flow is usually lighter than normal. If a woman's basal body temperature remains high for about three weeks after ovulation, there is reason to suspect pregnancy even if she spots two weeks after ovulation.

Should *You* Have a Child?

Whether or not to have children is one of the most significant life decisions you will face. Children have a way of needing a generation (or a lifetime) of love and support. We have no simplistic answers to this question, no standardized questionnaire that yields a score for a "Go."

Instead, we offer the following questionnaire to help you consider some of the reasons to have or not to have children. This listing of reasons may offer you some insight into your own motives. You can check the blank spaces to see how many pros you come up with and how many cons. The items are not intended to be equal in weight. Nor should your total score govern your decision. You be the judge. It's your life and your choice.

Reasons to Have Children

Couples offer reasons such as the following for having children. Check those that seem to apply to you:

_____ 1. *Personal experience.* Having children is a unique experience. To many people, no other experience compares with having the opportunity to love children, experience their love, help shape their lives, and watch them develop.

_____ 2. *Personal pleasure.* There is fun and pleasure in playing with children, taking them to the zoo and the circus, and viewing the world through their fresh, innocent eyes.

_____ 3. *Personal extension.* Children carry on our family heritage and some of our own wishes and dreams beyond the confines of our own mortality. We name them after ourselves or others in our families and see them as extensions of ourselves. We identify with their successes.

_____ 4. *Loving relationship.* Parents have the opportunity to establish extremely close and cherished bonds with other human beings.

_____ 5. *Personal status.* Within our culture, parents are afforded respect *just because* they are parents. Consider the commandment "Honor thy father and thy mother."

_____ 6. *Personal competence.* Parenthood is a challenge. Competence in the social roles of mother or father is a potential source of gratification to many people.

_____ 7. *Personal responsibility.* Parents have the opportunity to be responsible for the welfare and education of their children.

Pregnancy Tests

You may have heard your parents say that they learned your mother was pregnant by means of the "rabbit test," in which a sample of the woman's urine was injected into a laboratory animal. This procedure, which was once commonly used to confirm pregnancy, relied on the fact that women produce **human chorionic gonadotropin** (HCG) shortly after conception. HCG causes rabbits, mice, or rats to ovulate.

Today, pregnancy can be confirmed in minutes by tests that directly detect HCG in the urine as early as the third week of pregnancy. A blood test—the *beta subunit HCG radioimmunoassay* (RIA)—can detect HCG in the woman's blood as early as the eighth day of pregnancy, about five days preceding her expected period.

Over-the-counter home pregnancy tests are also available. They too test the woman's urine for HCG and are intended to be used as early as one day after a missed period. Laboratory-based tests are considered 98% or 99% accurate. Home-based tests performed by laypeople are somewhat less accurate. Women are advised to consult their physicians if they suspect that they are pregnant or wish to confirm a home pregnancy test result.

About a month after a woman misses her period, a health professional may be able to confirm pregnancy by pelvic exam. Women who are pregnant usually show **Hegar's sign.** Hegar's sign is softness of a section of the uterus between the uterine body and the cervix, which may be palpated (felt) by the woman's physician by placing a hand on the abdomen and two fingers in the vagina.

Human chorionic gonadotropin A hormone produced by women shortly after conception that stimulates the corpus luteum to continue to produce progesterone. The presence of HCG in a woman's urine indicates that she is pregnant.

Hegar's sign Softness of a section of the uterus between the uterine body and the cervix, which indicates that a woman is pregnant.

8. *Companionship for the later years.* Many people expect that their children will provide them with comfort, companionship, and perhaps crucial aid in their later years.

9. *Moral worth.* Some people feel that having children provides the opportunity for a moral, selfless act in which they place the needs of others—their children—ahead of their own.

10. *Religious beliefs.* The biblical injunction to "be fruitful and multiply" is followed by many people across a range of religious affiliations.

Reasons Not to Have Children
Many couples who decide not to have children cite reasons such as the following. Check those that you endorse:

1. *Strain on the earth's resources.* Because the world is overpopulated, it is wrong to place additional strain on limited resources. More children will only geometrically increase the problem of overpopulation.

2. *Time together.* Childfree couples may be able to spend more time together as a couple and develop a more intimate relationship.

3. *Freedom.* Children have a way of erasing leisure time. They may also make it more difficult to pursue educational and vocational advancement. Childfree couples may be more able to live spontaneously, to go where they please and do as they please.

4. *Dual careers.* Both members of childfree couples may pursue careers without distraction.

5. *Financial drain.* Children are a financial burden, especially considering the costs of child care and education.

6. *Difficulty.* Parenthood is demanding. It requires sacrifices of time, money, and energy, and not everyone makes a good parent.

7. *Irrevocable decision.* Once you have children, the decision cannot be changed.

8. *Failure.* Some people fear that they will not be good parents. People with poor relationships with their own parents might fear that they will repeat the same mistakes their parents made with them.

9. *Other children.* People can enjoy children other than their own, such as nieces and nephews, or become "Big Brothers" or "Big Sisters" without assuming the full burden of parental responsibility.

10. *Sense of danger.* The world is perceived to be a dangerous place, with the threats, for example, of crime, environmental destruction, and nuclear war. It is better not to bring children into such a world.

Early Effects of Pregnancy

Just a few days after conception, a woman may note tenderness of the breasts. Hormonal stimulation of the mammary glands may make the breasts more sensitive and cause sensations of tingling and fullness.

Morning sickness, which may actually occur throughout the day, refers to the nausea, food aversions, and vomiting that many women experience during pregnancy. About half of all pregnant women experience morning sickness during the first few months of pregnancy (Thompson, 1993). In some cases, morning sickness is so severe that the woman cannot eat regularly and must be hospitalized to ensure that she and the fetus receive adequate nutrition. Morning sickness usually subsides by about the twelfth week of pregnancy. Pregnant women may also experience greater-than-normal fatigue during the early weeks, so they sleep longer and fall asleep more readily than usual. Frequent urination, which may also be experienced, is caused by pressure from the swelling uterus on the bladder.

Miscarriage (Spontaneous Abortion)

Miscarriages have many causes, including chromosomal defects in the fetus and abnormalities of the placenta and uterus. About three in four miscarriages occur in the first 16 weeks of pregnancy, and the great majority of these occur in the first 7 weeks. Some miscarriages occur so early that the woman is not aware that she was pregnant.

Morning sickness Symptoms of pregnancy, including nausea, aversions to specific foods, and vomiting.

Miscarriage A spontaneous abortion.

After a miscarriage, a couple might feel a deep sense of loss and undergo a period of mourning. Emotional support from friends and family often helps the couple to cope with the loss. In most cases, women who miscarry can carry subsequent pregnancies to term.

Sex During Pregnancy

Most health professionals concur that coitus is safe throughout the course of pregnancy until the start of labor, provided that the pregnancy is developing normally and the woman has no history of miscarriages. Women who experience bleeding or cramps during pregnancy may be advised by their obstetricians not to engage in coitus.

Masters and Johnson (1966) reported an initial decline in sexual interest among pregnant women during the first trimester. There is increased interest during the second trimester and another decline in interest during the third. Many women show declines in sexual interest and activity during the first trimester because of fatigue, nausea, or misguided concerns that coitus will harm the embryo or fetus. Also during the first trimester, vasocongestion may cause tenderness of the breasts, discouraging fondling and sucking. Researchers in Israel reported a gradual decline in sexual interest and frequency of intercourse and orgasm during pregnancy among a sample of 219 women. The greatest decline occurred during the third trimester (Hart et al., 1991). Pain during intercourse is also commonly reported, especially in the third trimester.

As the woman's abdominal region swells, the popular male-superior position becomes unwieldy. The female-superior, lateral-entry, and rear-entry positions are common alternatives. Manual and oral sex can continue as usual.

Some women are concerned that the uterine contractions of orgasm may dislodge an embryo. Such concerns are usually unfounded unless the woman has a history of miscarriage or is currently at risk of miscarriage. Women and their partners are advised to consult their obstetricians for the latest information.

Psychological Changes During Pregnancy

A woman's psychological response to pregnancy reflects her desire to be pregnant, her physical changes, and her attitudes toward these changes. Women with the financial, social, and psychological resources to meet the needs of pregnancy and childrearing may welcome pregnancy. Some describe it as the most wondrous experience of their lives. Other women might question their ability to handle their pregnancies and childbirth. Or they might fear that pregnancy will interfere with their careers or their mates' feelings about them. In general, women who want to have a baby and choose to become pregnant are better adjusted during their pregnancies.

The first trimester can be difficult for women who are ambivalent about pregnancy. At that stage, symptoms such as morning sickness are most pronounced, and women must come to terms with being pregnant. The second trimester is generally less tempestuous. Morning sickness and other symptoms have largely vanished. It is not yet difficult to move about, and the woman need not yet face the delivery. Women first note fetal movement during the second trimester, and for many, the experience is stirring:

> I was lying on my stomach and felt—something, like someone lightly touching my deep insides. Then I just sat very still and . . . felt the hugeness of having something living growing in me. Then I said, No, it's not possible, it's too early yet, and then I started to cry. . . . That one moment was my first body awareness of another living thing inside me. (*The New Our Bodies, Ourselves,* 1992)

During the third trimester, it is normal, especially for first-time mothers, to worry about the mechanics of delivery and whether the child will be normal. The woman becomes increasingly heavy and literally "bent out of shape." It might become difficult to get up from a chair or out of bed. She must sit farther from the steering wheel when driving. Muscle tension from supporting the extra weight in her abdomen may cause backaches. She may feel impatient in the days and weeks just before delivery.

Men, like women, respond to pregnancy according to the degree to which they want the child. Many men are proud and look forward to the child with great anticipation. In such cases, pregnancy may bring parents closer together. But fathers who are financially or emotionally unprepared might consider the pregnancy a "trap." Now and then, an expectant father experiences some signs of pregnancy, including morning sickness and vomiting. This reaction is termed a **sympathetic pregnancy.**

Reflections

- How did people in your life react on learning that they were pregnant? Why?
- Has anyone you know had a miscarriage? How did she react?
- Do you believe that it is appropriate to engage in sexual activity during pregnancy? Why or why not?

PRENATAL DEVELOPMENT

We can date pregnancy from the onset of the last menstrual cycle before conception, which makes the normal gestation period 280 days. We can also date pregnancy from the date at which fertilization was assumed to have taken place, which normally corresponds to two weeks after the beginning of the woman's last menstrual cycle. In this case, the normal gestation period is 266 days.

Once pregnancy has been confirmed, the delivery date may be calculated by *Nagele's rule:*

- Jot down the date of the first day of the last menstrual period.
- Add seven days.
- Subtract three months.
- Add one year.

For example, if the last period began on November 12, 2001, adding seven days yields November 19, 2001. Then subtracting three months yields August 19, 2001. Adding one year gives a "due date" of August 19, 2002. Few babies are born exactly when they are due,[1] but the great majority are delivered during a ten-day period that spans the date.

Shortly after conception, the single cell that results from the union of sperm and egg begins to multiply—becoming two cells, then four, then eight, and so on. During the weeks and months that follow, tissues, structures, and organs begin to form, and the fetus gradually takes on the shape of a human being. By the time the fetus is born, it consists of hundreds of billions of cells—more cells than there are stars in the Milky Way galaxy. Prenatal development can be divided into three periods: the *germinal stage*, which corresponds to about the first two weeks; the *embryonic stage*, which coincides with the first two months; and the *fetal stage*. We also commonly speak of prenatal development in terms of three trimesters of three months each.

---

[1]The first and third authors wish to boast, however, that their daughters Allyn and Jordan were born precisely on their due dates. At least one of them has been just as compulsive ever since. The second author adds that he and his wife Judy had their son Michael within one day of the due date. (Close, but no cigar, notes the first author.)

Sympathetic pregnancy The experiencing of a number of signs of pregnancy by the father.

Prenatal Development. The rates of human growth and development are most dramatic prior to birth. Within a few months, a human fetus advances from weighing a fraction of an ounce to several pounds, and from one cell to billions of cells.

The Germinal Stage

Within 36 hours after conception, the zygote divides into 2 cells. It then divides repeatedly, becoming 32 cells within another 36 hours as it continues its journey to the uterus. It takes the zygote perhaps three or four days to reach the uterus. This mass of dividing cells then wanders about the uterus for perhaps another three or four days before it begins to become implanted in the uterine wall. The process of implantation takes about another week. This period from conception to implantation is termed the **germinal stage,** or the **period of the ovum** (see Figure 11.3).

Truth or Fiction?
REVISITED

It is true that for the first week after conception, a fertilized egg cell is not attached to its mother's body. Later, it becomes implanted in the uterine wall. ■

Several days into the germinal stage, the cell mass takes the form of a fluid-filled ball of cells, which is called a **blastocyst.** Already, some cell differentiation has begun. Cells begin to separate into groups that will eventually become different structures. Within a thickened mass of cells that is called the **embryonic disk,** two distinct inner layers of cells are beginning to form. These cells will become the embryo and eventually the fetus. The outer part of the blastocyst, called the **trophoblast,** consists of several membranes from which the amniotic sac, placenta, and umbilical cord eventually develop.

Implantation may be accompanied by some bleeding, which results from the usual rupturing of some small blood vessels that line the uterus. Bleeding can also be a sign of a miscarriage—though most women who experience implantation bleeding do not miscarry but go on to have normal pregnancies and deliver healthy babies.

Germinal stage The period of prenatal development before implantation in the uterus.

Period of the ovum The germinal stage.

Blastocyst A stage within the germinal stage of prenatal development at which the embryo is a sphere of cells surrounding a cavity of fluid.

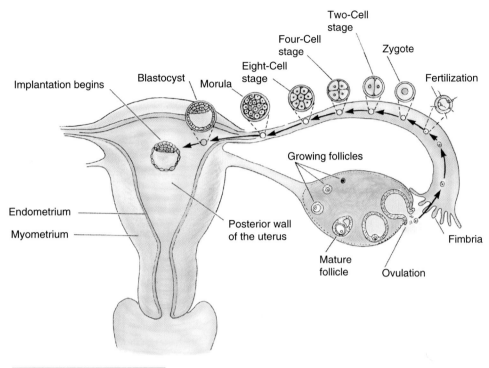

figure 11.3

The Ovarian Cycle, Conception, and the Early Days of the Germinal Stage. The zygote first divides about 36 hours after conception. Continuing division creates the hollow sphere of cells termed the blastocyst. The blastocyst normally becomes implanted in the wall of the uterus.

The Embryonic Stage

The period from implantation to about the eighth week of development is called the **embryonic stage.** The major organ systems of the body begin to differentiate during this stage.

Development of the embryo follows two trends—**cephalocaudal** and **proximodistal.** The apparently oversized heads depicted in Figure 11.4 on page 318 represent embryos and fetuses at various stages of prenatal development. Growth of the head (the cephalic region) takes precedence over growth of the lower parts of the body. You can also think of the body as containing a central axis that coincides with the spinal cord. The growth of the organ systems that lie close to this axis (that is, *proximal* to the axis) takes precedence over the growth of those that lie farther away toward the extremities (that is, *distal* to the axis). Relatively early maturation of the brain and organ systems that lie near the central axis allows these organs to facilitate further development of the embryo and fetus.

As the embryonic stage unfolds, the nervous system, sensory organs, hair, nails, and teeth and the outer layer of skin begin to develop from the outer layer of cells, or **ectoderm,** of the embryonic disk. By about three weeks after conception, two ridges appear in the embryo. The ridges fold together to form the **neural tube.** This tube develops into the nervous system. The inner layer of the embryonic disk is called the **endoderm.** From this layer develop the respiratory and digestive systems and organs such as the liver and the pancreas. A short time later in the embryonic stage, the middle layer of cells, or **mesoderm,** differentiates and develops into the reproductive, excretory, and circulatory systems, as well as the skeleton, the muscles, and the inner layer of the skin.

During the third week of development, the head and blood vessels begin to form. By the fourth week, a primitive heart begins to beat and pump blood in an embryo that measures but a fifth of an inch in length. The heart will normally continue to beat without

Embryonic disk The platelike inner part of the blastocyst, which differentiates into the ectoderm, mesoderm, and endoderm of the embryo.

Trophoblast The outer part of the blastocyst, from which the amniotic sac, placenta, and umbilical cord develop.

Embryonic stage The stage of prenatal development that lasts from implantation through the eighth week and is characterized by the differentiation of the major organ systems.

Cephalocaudal From the head downward. (From Latin roots meaning "head" and "tail.")

Proximodistal From the central axis of the body outward. (From Latin roots meaning "near" and "far.")

Ectoderm The outermost cell layer of the newly formed embryo, from which the skin and nervous system develop.

Neural tube A hollow area in the blastocyst from which the nervous system will develop.

Endoderm The inner layer of the newly formed embryo, from which the lungs and digestive system develop.

Mesoderm The central layer of the embryo, from which the bones and muscles develop.

figure 11.4

Human Embryos and Fetuses.
Development is cephalocaudal and proximodistal. Growth of the head takes precedence over the growth of the lower parts of the body.

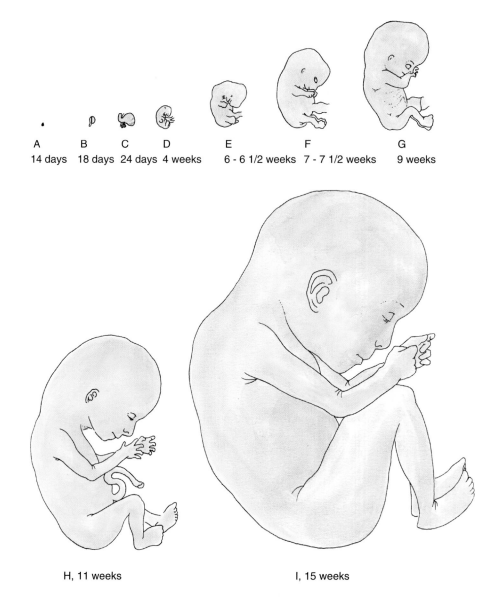

A	B	C	D	E	F	G
14 days	18 days	24 days	4 weeks	6 - 6 1/2 weeks	7 - 7 1/2 weeks	9 weeks

H, 11 weeks   I, 15 weeks

rest for every minute of every day for the better part of a century. By the end of the first month of development, we can see the beginnings of the arms and legs—"arm buds" and "leg buds." The mouth, eyes, ears, and nose begin to take shape. The brain and other parts of the nervous system begin to develop.

The arms and legs develop in accordance with the proximodistal principle. First the upper arms and legs develop, then the forearms and lower legs. Then the hands and feet form, followed by webbed fingers and toes about six to eight weeks into development. The webbing is gone by the end of the second month. By this time, the head has become rounded, and the limbs have elongated and separated. Facial features are visible. All this has occurred in an embryo that is about 1 inch long and weighs 1/30 of an ounce. During the second month, nervous impulses also begin to travel through the developing nervous system.

THE AMNIOTIC SAC   The embryo—and later on the fetus—develops within a protective environment in the mother's uterus called the **amniotic sac,** which is surrounded by a clear membrane. The embryo and fetus are suspended within the sac in **amniotic fluid.** The amniotic fluid acts like a shock absorber. It cushions the embryo from damage that might result from the mother's movements. The fluid also helps to maintain a steady temperature.

Amniotic sac The sac containing the fetus.

Amniotic fluid Fluid within the amniotic sac that suspends and protects the fetus.

THE PLACENTA   Nutrients and waste products are exchanged between mother and embryo (or fetus) through a mass of tissue called the **placenta.** The placenta is unique in origin. It develops from material supplied by both mother and embryo. Toward the end of the first trimester, it becomes a flattish, round organ about 7 inches in diameter and 1 inch thick—larger than the fetus itself. The fetus is connected to the placenta by the **umbilical cord.** The mother is connected to the placenta by the system of blood vessels in the uterine wall. The umbilical cord develops about five weeks after conception and reaches 20 inches in length. It contains two arteries through which maternal nutrients reach the embryo. A vein transports waste products back to the mother.

The circulatory systems of mother and embryo do not mix. A membrane in the placenta permits only certain substances to pass through, such as oxygen (from the mother to the fetus); carbon dioxide and other wastes (from the embryo or fetus to the mother, to be eliminated by the mother's lungs and kidneys); nutrients; some microscopic disease-causing organisms; and some drugs, including aspirin, narcotics, alcohol, and tranquilizers.

The placenta is also an endocrine gland. It secretes hormones that preserve the pregnancy, stimulate the uterine contractions that induce childbirth, and help to prepare the breasts for breast-feeding. Some of these hormones may also cause the signs of pregnancy. HCG (human chorionic gonadotropin) stimulates the corpus luteum to continue to produce progesterone. The placenta itself secretes increasing amounts of estrogen and progesterone. Ultimately, the placenta passes from the woman's body after delivery. For this reason, it is also called the "afterbirth."

The Fetal Stage

The fetal stage begins by the ninth week and continues until birth. By about the ninth or tenth week, the fetus begins to respond to the outside world by turning in the direction of external stimulation. By the end of the first trimester, the major organ systems, the fingers and toes, and the external genitals have been formed. The gender of the fetus can be determined visually. The eyes have become clearly distinguishable.

During the second trimester, the fetus increases dramatically in size, and its organ systems continue to mature. The brain now contributes to the regulation of basic body functions. The fetus increases in weight from 1 *ounce* to *2 pounds* and grows from about 4 to 14 inches in length. Soft, downy hair grows above the eyes and on the scalp. The skin turns ruddy because of blood vessels that show through the surface. (During the third trimester, layers of fat beneath the skin will give the red a pinkish hue.)

FETAL MOVEMENTS   Usually, by the middle of the fourth month, the mother can feel the first fetal movements. By the end of the second trimester, the fetus moves its limbs so vigorously that the mother may complain of being kicked—often at 4:00 A.M. It opens and shuts its eyes, sucks its thumb, alternates between periods of wakefulness and sleep, and perceives lights and sounds. The fetus also does somersaults, which the mother will definitely feel. Fortunately, the umbilical cord will not break or strangle the fetus, no matter what acrobatic feats the fetus performs.

Near the end of the second trimester, the fetus approaches the **age of viability.** Still, only a minority of babies born at the end of the second trimester who weigh under 2 pounds will survive—even with intense medical efforts.

During the third trimester, the organ systems continue to mature and enlarge. The heart and lungs become increasingly capable of maintaining independent life. Typically, during the seventh month, the fetus turns upside down in the uterus so that it will be headfirst, or in a **cephalic presentation,** for delivery. But some fetuses do not turn during this month. If such a fetus is born prematurely, it can have either a **breech presentation** (bottom first) or a shoulder-first presentation, which can complicate problems of prematurity. The closer to term (the full nine months) the baby is born, the more likely it is that the presentation will be cephalic. If birth occurs at the end of the eighth month, the odds are overwhelmingly in favor of survival.

Placenta An organ connected to the fetus by the umbilical cord. The placenta serves as a relay station between mother and fetus, allowing the exchange of nutrients and wastes.

Umbilical cord A tube that connects the fetus to the placenta.

Age of viability The age at which a fetus can sustain independent life.

Cephalic presentation Emergence of the baby headfirst from the womb.

Breech presentation Emergence of the baby feetfirst from the womb.

During the final months of pregnancy, the mother may become concerned that the fetus seems to be less active than before. Most of the time, the change in activity level is normal. The fetus has grown so large that it is cramped, and its movements are restricted.

Environmental Influences on Prenatal Development

Advances in scientific knowledge have made us more aware of the changes that take place during prenatal development. They have also heightened our awareness of the problems that can occur and what might be done to prevent them. We focus in this next section on the environmental factors that affect prenatal development. These include the mother's diet, maternal diseases and disorders, and the mother's use of drugs.

THE MOTHER'S DIET   It is a common misconception that the fetus will take what it needs from its mother. Actually, malnutrition in the mother can adversely affect fetal development. Women who are too slender risk preterm deliveries and having babies who are low in birthweight (Cnattingius, 1998). Pregnant women who are adequately nourished are more likely to deliver babies of average or above-average size. Their infants are also less likely to develop colds and serious respiratory disorders. However, maternal *obesity* is linked with a higher risk of stillbirth (Cnattingius, 1998).

A woman can expect to gain at least 20 pounds during pregnancy because of the growth of the placenta, amniotic fluid, and the fetus itself. Most women will gain about 25 pounds or so (Thompson, 1993). Overweight women often gain less. Slender women might gain 30 pounds. Regular weight gains are most desirable, about half a pound a week during the first half of pregnancy and about 1 pound a week during the second half.

MATERNAL DISEASES AND DISORDERS   Environmental influences or agents that can harm the embryo or fetus are called **teratogens.** These include drugs taken by the mother, such as alcohol and even aspirin, as well as substances produced by the mother's body, such as Rh-positive antibodies. Other teratogens include the metals lead and mercury, radiation, and disease-causing organisms such as viruses and bacteria. Although many disease-causing organisms cannot pass through the placenta to infect the embryo or fetus, some extremely small organisms, such as those causing syphilis, measles, mumps, and chicken pox, can. Some disorders such as toxemia are not transmitted to the embryo or fetus but can adversely affect the environment in which it develops.

CRITICAL PERIODS OF VULNERABILITY   The times at which exposure to particular teratogens can cause the greatest harm are termed **critical periods of vulnerability.** Critical periods correspond to the times at which the structures most affected by the teratogens are developing (see Figure 11.5). The heart, for example, develops rapidly from the third to the fifth week after conception. It may be most vulnerable to certain teratogens at this time. The arms and legs, which develop later, are most vulnerable from the fourth through the eighth week of development. Since the major organ systems differentiate during the embryonic stage, the embryo is most vulnerable to the effects of teratogens during this stage (Koren et al., 1998).

Let us now consider some of the most damaging effects of specific maternal diseases and disorders.

RUBELLA (GERMAN MEASLES)   **Rubella** is a viral infection. Women who contract rubella during the first month or two of pregnancy, when rapid differentiation of major organ systems is taking place, may bear children who are deaf or who develop mental retardation, heart disease, or cataracts. Risk of these defects declines as pregnancy progresses.

Nearly 85% of women in the United States had rubella as children and so acquired immunity. Women who do not know whether they have had rubella may be tested. If they are not immune, they can be vaccinated *before pregnancy.* Inoculation during pregnancy is considered risky because the vaccine causes a mild case of the disease in the mother, which can affect the embryo or fetus. Increased awareness of the dangers of rubella during preg-

Teratogens Environmental influences or agents that can damage an embryo or fetus. (From the Greek *teras,* meaning "monster.")

Critical period of vulnerability A period of time during which an embryo or fetus is vulnerable to the effects of a teratogen.

Rubella A viral infection that can cause mental retardation and heart disease in an embryo. Also called *German measles.*

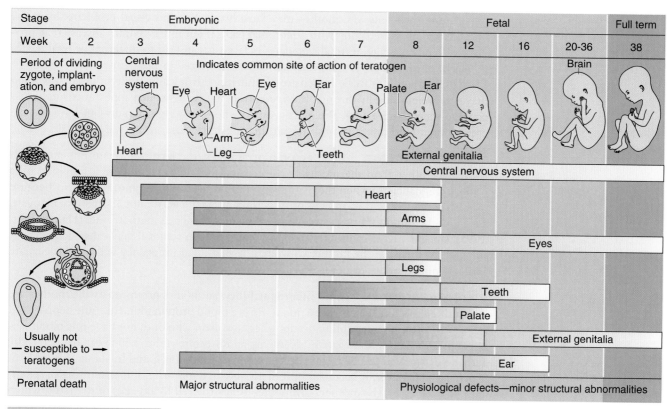

figure 11.5

Critical Periods in Prenatal Development. The developing embryo is most vulnerable to teratogens when the organ systems are taking shape. The periods of greatest vulnerability of organ systems are shown in blue. Periods of lesser vulnerability are shown in yellow.

nancy, and of the preventive effects of inoculation, has led to a dramatic decline in the number of children who are born in the United States with defects caused by rubella.

SYPHILIS   Maternal **syphilis** may cause miscarriage or **stillbirth** or be passed along to the child in the form of congenital syphilis. Congenital syphilis can impair the vision and hearing, damage the liver, or deform the bones and teeth.

Routine blood tests early in pregnancy can diagnose syphilis and other problems. Because the bacteria that cause syphilis do not readily cross the placental membrane during the first months of pregnancy, the fetus will probably not contract syphilis if an infected mother is treated successfully with antibiotics before the fourth month of pregnancy.

ACQUIRED IMMUNODEFICIENCY SYNDROME (AIDS)   **Acquired immunodeficiency syndrome (AIDS)** is caused by the *human immunodeficiency virus* (HIV). HIV is bloodborne and is sometimes transmitted through the placenta to infect the fetus. The rupturing of blood vessels in mother and baby during childbirth provides another opportunity for transmission of HIV (Peckham & Gibb, 1995). *However, the majority of babies born to mothers who are infected with HIV do not become infected themselves.* Using antiviral medication can also minimize the probability of transmission (see Chapter 16). HIV can also be transmitted to children by breast-feeding (Meier, 1997).

TOXEMIA   **Toxemia** is a life-threatening condition characterized by high blood pressure that may afflict women late in the second or early in the third trimester of pregnancy. The first stage is termed *preeclampsia*. It is diagnosed by protein in the urine, swelling from fluid retention, and high blood pressure and may be relatively mild. As

Syphilis A sexually transmitted infection caused by a bacterial infection.

Stillbirth The birth of a dead fetus.

Acquired immunodeficiency syndrome (AIDS) A sexually transmitted infection that destroys white blood cells in the immune system, leaving the body vulnerable to various opportunistic diseases.

Toxemia A life-threatening condition that is characterized by high blood pressure.

preeclampsia worsens, the mother may have headaches and visual problems from the raised blood pressure, along with abdominal pain. If left untreated, the disease may progress to the final stage, termed *eclampsia*. Eclampsia can lead to maternal or fetal death. Babies born to women with toxemia are often undersized or premature.

Toxemia appears to be linked to malnutrition. Ironically, undernourished women may gain weight rapidly through fluid retention, but their swollen appearance might discourage them from eating. Pregnant women who gain weight rapidly but have not increased their food intake should consult their obstetricians.

ECTOPIC PREGNANCY   In an **ectopic pregnancy,** the fertilized ovum implants itself someplace other than the uterus. Most ectopic pregnancies occur in a fallopian tube ("tubal pregnancies") when the ovum is prevented from moving into the uterus because of obstructions caused by infections. If ectopic pregnancies do not abort spontaneously, they must be removed by surgery or use of medicines such as methotrexate (Hausknecht, 1995), since the fetus cannot develop to term. Delay in removal may cause hemorrhaging and the death of the mother. A woman with a tubal pregnancy will not menstruate but may notice spotty bleeding and abdominal pain.

RH INCOMPATIBILITY   In **Rh incompatibility,** antibodies produced by the mother are transmitted to a fetus or newborn infant. *Rh* is a blood protein found in some people's red blood cells. Rh incompatibility occurs when a woman who does not have this blood factor, and is therefore *Rh-negative*, is carrying an *Rh-positive* fetus, which can happen if the father is Rh-positive. The negative-positive combination is found in about 10% of U.S. marriages. However, it becomes a problem only in a minority of the resulting pregnancies. In such cases, the mother's antibodies attack the red blood cells of the fetus, which can cause brain damage or death. Rh incompatibility does not usually adversely affect a first child because women will usually not yet have formed antibodies to the Rh factor.

Since mother and fetus have separate circulatory systems, it is unlikely that Rh-positive fetal red blood cells will enter the Rh-negative mother's body. The probability of an exchange of blood increases during childbirth, however, especially when the placenta becomes detached from the uterine wall. If an exchange of blood occurs, the mother will then produce antibodies to the baby's Rh-positive blood. The mother's antibodies may enter the fetal bloodstream and cause a condition called *fetal erythroblastosis*, which can result in anemia, mental deficiency, or even the death of the fetus or newborn infant.

Fortunately, blood-typing of pregnant women significantly decreases the threat of uncontrolled erythroblastosis. If an Rh-negative mother is injected with the vaccine RhoGAM within 72 hours after delivery of an Rh-positive baby, she will not develop the dangerous antibodies and thus will not pass them on to the fetus in a subsequent pregnancy. A fetus or newborn child who is at risk for erythroblastosis may also receive a preventive blood transfusion to remove the mother's Rh-positive antibodies from its blood.

DRUGS TAKEN BY THE MOTHER (AND THE FATHER)   Some widely used drugs, including nonprescription drugs, are linked with birth abnormalities (Koren et al., 1998). In the 1960s the drug thalidomide was marketed to pregnant women as a presumably safe treatment for nausea and insomnia. However, the drug caused birth deformities, including stunted or missing limbs (Koren et al., 1998). Maternal use of illegal drugs such as cocaine and marijuana may also place the fetus at risk.

Paternal use of certain drugs also may endanger the fetus. One question is whether drugs alter the genetic material in the father's sperm. The use of certain substances by those who come into contact with a pregnant woman can harm the fetus. For example, the mother's inhalation of secondhand tobacco or marijuana smoke can hurt the fetus.

Several antibiotics may harm a fetus, especially if they are taken during certain periods of fetal development. Tetracycline may yellow the teeth and deform the bones (Koren et al., 1998). Other antibiotics have been implicated in deafness and jaundice.

Acne drugs such as Accutane can cause physical and mental handicaps in the children of women who use them during pregnancy. Antihistamines, used commonly for allergies, may deform the fetus.

Ectopic pregnancy   A pregnancy in which the fertilized ovum becomes implanted someplace other than the uterus.

Rh incompatibility   A condition in which antibodies produced by a pregnant woman are transmitted to the fetus and may cause brain damage or death.

If you are pregnant or suspect that you are, it is advisable to consult your obstetrician before taking any and all drugs, not just prescription drugs. Your obstetrician can usually direct you to a safe and effective substitute for a drug that could harm a fetus.

HORMONES   The hormones progestin and DES have sometimes been used to help women who are at risk of miscarriage to maintain their pregnancies. When taken at about the time that sex organs differentiate, progestin—which is similar in composition to male sex hormones, can masculinize the external sex organs of embryos with female (XX) sex chromosomal structures. Progestin taken during the first trimester has also been linked to increased levels of aggressive behavior during childhood.

DES (short for *diethylstilbestrol*), a powerful estrogen, was given from the 1940s through the 1960s to many women who were at risk of miscarriage to help maintain their pregnancies. DES is suspected of causing cervical and testicular cancer in some of the children whose mothers used it when pregnant (Koren et al., 1998). Other problems have been reported as well. Daughters whose mothers used DES during their pregnancies have a higher-than-expected rate of miscarriages and premature deliveries. It was once suspected that men who were exposed prenatally to DES had higher-than-expected rates of infertility. However, research reveals no connection between in utero exposure to DES and male infertility (Wilcox et al., 1995). DES users themselves appear to be at high risk of some serious medical problems, such as breast cancer (Greenberg et al., 1984).

VITAMINS   Many pregnant women are prescribed daily doses of multivitamins to maintain their own health and to promote the development of a healthy pregnancy. "Too much of a good thing" may be hazardous, however. High doses of vitamins such as A, B_6, D, and K have been linked to birth defects. Vitamin A excesses have been linked with cleft palate and eye damage; excesses of vitamin D are linked to mental retardation.

NARCOTICS   Narcotics such as heroin and methadone can readily pass from mother to fetus through the placental membrane. Narcotics are addictive. Fetuses of mothers who use them regularly during their pregnancies can become addicted in utero. At birth, such babies may undergo withdrawal and show muscle tension and agitation. Women who use narcotics are advised to notify their obstetricians so that measures can be taken to aid the infants before and after delivery.

TRANQUILIZERS AND SEDATIVES   The tranquilizers Librium and Valium cross the placental membrane and may cause birth defects such as harelip. Sedatives, such as the barbiturate *phenobarbital*, are suspected of decreasing testosterone production and causing reproductive problems in the sons of women who use them during pregnancy.

HALLUCINOGENICS   Use of hallucinogenic drugs such as marijuana and LSD during pregnancy has been linked to chromosomal damage in fetuses (National Academy of Sciences, 1982). The active ingredient in marijuana, THC, readily crosses the placenta, as does LSD. Use of marijuana can lead to decreased androgen production in male fetuses, which can interfere with the process of sexual differentiation. Research provides evidence that preschoolers whose mothers used marijuana during their pregnancies suffered more neurological and visual problems than did children of nonusers (Fried, 1986).

ALCOHOL   Mothers who drink heavily during pregnancy expose the fetus to greater risk of birth defects, infant mortality, sensory and motor problems, and mental retardation (Barr et al., 1990; Coles, 1994). Nearly 40% of children whose mothers drank heavily during pregnancy develop **fetal alcohol syndrome** (FAS). FAS is a cluster of symptoms typified by developmental lags and characteristic facial features, such as an underdeveloped upper jaw, a flattened nose, and widely spaced eyes. Infants with FAS are often smaller than average and have smaller-than-average brains. They may be mentally retarded, lack coordination, and have deformed limbs and heart problems.

Although research suggests that light drinking is unlikely to harm the fetus in most cases (Jacobson & Jacobson, 1994), FAS has been found even among the children of mothers who drank only 2 ounces of alcohol a day during the first trimester (Astley et al., 1992).

DES Diethylstilbestrol: an estrogen that was once given to women at risk for miscarriage to help maintain pregnancy.

Fetal alcohol syndrome A cluster of symptoms caused by maternal drinking, in which the child shows developmental lags and characteristic facial features such as an underdeveloped upper jaw, a flattened nose, and widely spaced eyes.

Moreover, individual sensitivities to alcohol may vary widely (Jacobson & Jacobson, 1994). The critical period for the development of the facial features associated with FAS seems to be the first two months of prenatal development, when the head is taking shape (Coles, 1994).

Truth or Fiction?
REVISITED

It is not true that pregnant women can have one or two alcoholic beverages a day without harming their babies. No safe minimal amount of drinking for pregnant women has been established. Therefore, pregnant women are advised to abstain from alcohol completely. ∎

CIGARETTE SMOKING Cigarette smoke contains chemicals such as carbon monoxide and the stimulant nicotine that are transmitted to the fetus. Maternal smoking increases the risk of spontaneous abortion and complications during pregnancy such as premature rupturing of the amniotic sac, stillbirth, premature birth, low birthweight and early infant mortality (English & Eskenazi, 1992; Floyd et al., 1993; USDHHS, 1992). The health risks generally increase with the amount smoked.

Maternal smoking may also impair intellectual development. In one study, women who smoked during pregnancy were 50% more likely than women who did not to have children whose intelligence test scores placed them in the mentally retarded range (that is, beneath an IQ score of 70) when the children were 10 years old (Drews et al., 1996).

Low birthweight is the most common risk factor for infant disease and mortality (USDHHS, 1992). Maternal smoking during pregnancy more than doubles the risk of low birthweight (Mayer et al., 1990). The combination of smoking and drinking alcohol places the child at greater risk of low birthweight than either practice alone (Day & Richardson, 1994). As many as one in four cases of low birthweight could be prevented if mothers-to-be quit smoking during pregnancy (USDHHS, 1990). The earlier the pregnant smoker quits, the better for the baby (and herself!). Simply cutting down on smoking during pregnancy might not offer much protection in preventing low birthweight, however (USDHHS, 1990).

Maternal smoking also has important acute effects on fetal heart rate (Graca et al., 1991) and increases the risk of sudden infant death syndrome (SIDS) (Feng, 1993; Haglund & Cnattingius, 1990; Malloy et al., 1992; Schoendorf & Kiely, 1992; Zhang & Fried, 1992). Maternal smoking has also been linked to reduced lung function in newborns (Hanrahan et al., 1992) and asthma in childhood (Martinez et al., 1992). Evidence also points to reduced attention spans, hyperactivity, and lower IQs and achievement test scores in children who are exposed to maternal smoking during and after pregnancy (Barr et al., 1990).

Don't Do It! Smoking cigarettes and pregnancy do not mix. Maternal smoking has been shown to increase the risk of spontaneous abortion and complications during pregnancy. It is connected with premature rupturing of the amniotic sac, stillbirth, premature birth, low birthweight, early infant mortality, and even with delayed intellectual development.

Smoking by the father (or other household members) can be dangerous to a fetus because secondary smoke (smoke exhaled by the smoker or emitted from the tip of a lit cigarette) might be absorbed by the mother and passed along to the fetus. Passive exposure to secondhand smoke during infancy is also linked to increased risk of SIDS (Schoendorf & Kiely, 1992).

The majority of women in the United States of reproductive age drink alcohol, at least occasionally. More than one in four smoke cigarettes. Many of them do not suspend drug use until they learn that they are pregnant. Unfortunately, this knowledge might not be obtained until a woman is weeks into the pregnancy. By this time, damage to the fetus might already have occurred. Many women are unwilling or unable to change their drug use habits even after learning that they are pregnant. Among women who smoke, only one in five quits smoking when she becomes pregnant (Floyd et al., 1993).

Our clinical experience suggests that it might be easier for women to quit if they conceptualize their quitting as limited in time to the terms of their pregnancies rather than as permanent. Then, of course, if they should remain abstinent after delivery, perhaps they will not be disappointed.

OTHER AGENTS X-rays increase the risk of malformed organs in the fetus, especially within a month and a half following conception. (Ultrasound has *not* been shown to harm the embryo or fetus.)

Chromosomal and Genetic Abnormalities

Not all of us have the normal complement of chromosomes. Some of us have genes that threaten our health or our existence (see Table 11.1).

table 11.1

Some chromosomal and genetic abnormalities	
Health Problem	**Characteristics**
Cystic fibrosis	A genetic disease in which the pancreas and lungs become clogged with mucus, which impairs the processes of respiration and digestion.
Down syndrome	A condition characterized by a third chromosome on the twenty-first pair. The child with Down syndrome has a characteristic fold of skin over the eye and mental retardation. The risk of having a child with the syndrome increases as parents increase in age.
Hemophilia	A sex-linked disorder in which the blood fails to clot properly.
Huntington's chorea	A fatal neurological disorder whose onset occurs in middle adulthood.
Neural tube defects	Disorders of the brain or spine, such as *anencephaly,* in which part of the brain is missing, and *spina bifida,* in which part of the spine is exposed or missing. Anencephaly is fatal shortly after birth, but some spina bifida victims survive for a number of years, albeit with severe handicaps.
Phenylketonuria	A disorder in which children cannot metabolize phenylalanine, which builds up in the form of phenylpyruvic acid and causes mental retardation. The disorder can be diagnosed at birth and controlled by diet.
Retinoblastoma	A form of blindness caused by a dominant gene.
Sickle-cell anemia	A blood disorder that mostly afflicts African Americans, in which deformed blood cells obstruct small blood vessels, decreasing their capacity to carry oxygen and heightening the risk of occasionally fatal infections.
Tay-Sachs disease	A fatal neurological disorder that primarily afflicts Jews of European origin.

Source: Etaugh & Rathus (1995).

DOWN SYNDROME   Children with Down syndrome have characteristic round faces; wide, flat noses; and protruding tongues. They often suffer from respiratory problems and heart malformations, problems that tend to claim their lives by middle age—the "prime of life" when most of us are reaching our vocational heights. People with Down syndrome are also moderately mentally retarded, but they usually can learn to read and write. With a little help from family and social agencies, they may hold jobs and lead largely independent lives.

The risk of a child's having Down syndrome increases with the mother's age (see Table 11.2). Down syndrome is usually caused by an extra chromosome on the twenty-first pair. In about 95% of cases, Down syndrome is transmitted by the mother (Antonarakas et al., 1991). The inner corners of the eyes of people with the syndrome have a downward-sloping crease of skin that gives them a superficial likeness to Asians. This is why the syndrome was once dubbed *mongolism*, a moniker that has since been rejected because of its racist overtones.

SICKLE-CELL ANEMIA AND TAY-SACHS DISEASE   Sickle-cell anemia and Tay-Sachs disease are genetic disorders that are most likely to afflict certain racial and ethnic groups. Sickle-cell anemia is most prevalent in the United States among African Americans. One of every 375 African Americans is affected by the disease, and 8% are carriers of the sickle-cell trait (Leary, 1993). In sickle-cell anemia, the red blood cells assume a sickle shape—hence the name—and they form clumps that obstruct narrow blood vessels and diminish the supply of oxygen. As a result, victims can suffer problems ranging from swollen, painful joints to potentially lethal problems such as pneumonia and heart and kidney failure. Infections are a leading cause of death among those with the disease (Leary, 1993).

Tay-Sachs disease is a fatal neurological disease of young children. Only 1 in 100,000 people in the United States is affected, but among Jews of Eastern European background, the figure rises steeply to 1 in 3,600 (Hubbard & Wald, 1993). The disease is characterized by degeneration of the central nervous system and gives rise to retardation, loss of muscle control, paralysis, blindness, and deafness. Victims seldom live beyond the age of 5.

SEX-LINKED GENETIC ABNORMALITIES   Some genetic defects, such as hemophilia, are sex linked, in that they are carried only on the X sex chromosome. They are trans-

t a b l e   1 1 . 2

Risk of giving birth to an infant with Down syndrome, according to age of the mother			
Age of Mother	**Probability of Down Syndrome**	**Age of Mother**	**Probability of Down Syndrome**
30	1/885	40	1/109
31	1/826	41	1/85
32	1/725	42	1/67
33	1/592	43	1/53
34	1/465	44	1/41
35*	1/365	45	1/32
36	1/287	46	1/25
37	1/225	47	1/20
38	1/176	48	1/16
39	1/139	49	1/11

*Age at which testing for Down syndrome is usually first recommended.

Source: Adapted from Samuels & Samuels, 1986, p. 240. Reprinted with permission.

mitted from generation to generation as **recessive traits.** Females, each of whom has two X sex chromosomes, are less likely than males to be afflicted by sex-linked disorders, because the genes that carry the disorder would have to be present on both of their sex chromosomes for the disorder to be expressed. Sex-linked disorders are more likely to afflict sons of female carriers because they have only one X sex chromosome, which they inherit from their mothers. England's Queen Victoria was a hemophilia carrier and transmitted the condition to many of her children, who in turn carried it into several ruling families of Europe. For this reason, hemophilia has been dubbed the "royal disease."

AVERTING CHROMOSOMAL AND GENETIC ABNORMALITIES   On the basis of information about a couple's medical background and family history of genetic defects, genetic counselors help couples to appraise the risks of passing along genetic defects to their children. Some couples who face a high risk of passing along genetic defects to their children decide to adopt. Other couples decide to have an abortion if the fetus is determined to have certain abnormalities.

Various medical procedures are used to detect the presence of these disorders in the fetus. *Amniocentesis* is usually performed about four months into pregnancy but is sometimes done earlier. Fluid is drawn from the amniotic sac (or "bag of waters") with a syringe. Fetal cells in the fluid are grown in a culture and examined under a microscope for the presence of biochemical and chromosomal abnormalities. *Chorionic villus sampling (CVS)* is performed several weeks earlier. A narrow tube is used to snip off material from the chorion, which is a membrane that contains the amniotic sac and fetus. The material is analyzed. CVS is somewhat riskier than amniocentesis, so most obstetricians prefer to use the latter. The tests detect Down syndrome, sickle-cell anemia, Tay-Sachs disease, spina bifida, muscular dystrophy, Rh incompatibility, and other conditions. The tests also identify the gender of the fetus.

In ultrasound, high-pitched sound waves are bounced off the fetus, like radar, revealing a picture of the fetus on a TV monitor and allowing the obstetrician to detect certain abnormalities. Obstetricians also use ultrasound to locate the fetus during amniocentesis to lower the probability of injuring it with the syringe.

Parental blood tests can suggest the presence of problems such as sickle-cell anemia, Tay-Sachs disease, and neural tube defects. Still other tests examine fetal DNA and can indicate the presence of Huntington's chorea, cystic fibrosis, and other disorders. Blood tests also now allow detection of Down syndrome during the first trimester (Haddow et al., 1998).

An Ultrasound Image. An ultrasound image of the second author's son, Michael, at 12 weeks following conception. The head and upper torso (facing upwards) can be seen in the upper middle section of the picture. He was handsome even then, his perfectly objective father points out.

Reflections

■ Have you been with anyone during a pregnancy? (Don't exclude yourself!) How did she react when she first detected fetal movements?

■ Do you know anyone who drank alcohol or smoked during pregnancy? Would she talk about her drinking or smoking? What did she say?

■ Do you know of anyone who has been tested to learn whether her or his child is likely to have a genetic or chromosomal abnormality? Which test was used? Why?

CHILDBIRTH

Early in the ninth month of pregnancy, the fetus's head settles in the pelvis. This shift is called "dropping" or "lightening." The woman may actually feel lighter because of lessened pressure on the diaphragm. About a day or so before the beginning of labor, the woman might notice blood in her vaginal secretions because fetal pressure on the pelvis might rupture superficial blood vessels in the birth canal. Tissue that had plugged the

Recessive trait A trait that is not expressed when the gene or genes involved have been paired with dominant genes. Recessive traits are transmitted to future generations, however, and are expressed if they are paired with other recessive genes.

cervix, possibly preventing entry of infectious agents from the vagina, becomes dislodged. There is a resultant discharge of bloody mucus. At about this time, one woman in ten also has a rush of warm "water" from the vagina. The "water" is amniotic fluid, and it means that the amniotic sac has burst. Labor usually begins within a day after rupture of the amniotic sac. For most women, the amniotic sac does not burst until the end of the first stage of childbirth. Other signs of impending labor include indigestion, diarrhea, abdominal cramps, and an ache in the small of the back. Labor begins with the onset of regular uterine contractions.

The first uterine contractions are relatively painless and are called **Braxton-Hicks contractions** or false labor contractions. They are false because they do not widen the cervix or advance the baby through the birth canal. They tend to increase in frequency but are less regular than labor contractions. Real labor contractions, by contrast, become more intense when the woman moves around or walks.

The initiation of labor may involve the secretion of hormones by the fetal adrenal and pituitary glands that stimulate the placenta and mother's uterus to secrete **prostaglandins.** Prostaglandins stimulate the uterine musculature to contract. It would make sense for the fetus to have a mechanism for signaling the mother that it is mature enough to sustain independent life. The mechanisms that initiate and maintain labor are not fully understood, however. Later in labor the pituitary gland releases **oxytocin,** a hormone that stimulates contractions strong enough to expel the baby.

Truth or Fiction?

It is probably true that a baby signals its mother (chemically) when it is ready to be born (that is, to sustain independent life). ■

The Stages of Childbirth

Childbirth begins with the onset of labor and progresses through three stages.

THE FIRST STAGE   In the first stage, uterine contractions **efface** and **dilate** the cervix to about 4 inches (10 centimeters) in diameter so that the baby may pass. Stretching of the cervix causes most of the pain of childbirth. A woman may experience little or no pain if her cervix dilates easily and quickly. The first stage may last from a couple of hours to more than a day. Twelve to 24 hours of labor is considered about average for a first pregnancy. In later pregnancies, labor takes about half this time.

The initial contractions are usually mild and spaced widely, at intervals of 10 to 20 minutes. They may last 20 to 40 seconds. As time passes, contractions become more frequent, long, strong, and regular.

Transition is the process that occurs when the cervix becomes nearly fully dilated and the baby's head begins to move into the vagina, or birth canal. Contractions usually come quickly during transition. Transition usually lasts about 30 minutes or less and is often accompanied by feelings of nausea, chills, and intense pain.

THE SECOND STAGE   The second stage of childbirth follows transition and begins when the cervix has become fully dilated and the baby begins to move into the vagina and first appears at the opening of the birth canal (see Figure 11.6). The woman may be taken to a delivery room for the second stage of childbirth. The second stage is shorter than the first stage. It lasts from a few minutes to a few hours and ends with the birth of the baby.

Each contraction of the second stage propels the baby farther along the birth canal (vagina). When the baby's head becomes visible at the vaginal opening, it is said to have *crowned.* The baby typically emerges fully a few minutes after crowning.

An **episiotomy** may be performed on the mother when the baby's head has crowned. Episiotomies are controversial, however. The incision can cause infection, be painful, and cause discomfort and itching as it heals. In some cases, the discomfort interferes with

Braxton-Hicks contractions
So-called false labor contractions that are relatively painless.

Prostaglandins Uterine hormones that stimulate uterine contractions.

Oxytocin A pituitary hormone that stimulates uterine contractions.

Efface To become thin.

Dilate To open or widen.

Transition The process during which the cervix becomes nearly fully dilated and the head of the fetus begins to move into the birth canal.

Episiotomy A surgical incision in the perineum that widens the birth canal, preventing random tearing during childbirth.

1. The second stage of labor begins

2. Further descent and rotation

3. The crowning of the head

4. Anterior shoulder delivered

5. Posterior shoulder delivered

6. The third stage of labor begins with separation of the placenta from the uterine wall

figure 11.6

The Stages of Childbirth. In the first stage, uterine contractions efface and dilate the cervix to about 4 inches so that the baby may pass. The second stage begins with movement of the baby into the birth canal and ends with birth of the baby. During the third stage the placenta separates from the uterine wall and is expelled through the birth canal.

coitus for months. Many obstetricians no longer perform episiotomies routinely. However, most health professionals concur that an episiotomy is preferable to the random tearing that can occur if the tissues of the **perineum** become extremely effaced.

With or without an episiotomy, the baby's passageway to the external world is a tight fit at best. As a result, the baby's facial features and the shape of its head might be temporarily distended. The baby might look as if it has been through a prizefight. Its head might be elongated, its nose flattened, and its ears bent. Although parents might be concerned about whether the baby's features will assume a more typical shape, they almost always do.

Perineum The area between the vulva and the anus.

Coming into the World. Childbirth progresses through three stages. In the first stage, uterine contractions efface and dilate the cervix so that the baby may pass. The second stage lasts from a few minutes to a few hours and ends with the birth of the baby. During the third stage the placenta is expelled.

THE THIRD STAGE The third, or placental, stage of childbirth may last from a few minutes to an hour or more. During this stage, the placenta is expelled. Detachment of the placenta from the uterine wall can cause some bleeding. The uterus begins the process of contracting to a smaller size. The attending physician sews up the episiotomy or any tears in the perineum.

IN THE NEW WORLD As the baby's head emerges, mucus is cleared from its mouth by means of suction aspiration to prevent the breathing passageway from being obstructed. Aspiration is often repeated after the baby is fully delivered. (Newly delivered babies are no longer routinely held upside down to help expel mucus. Nor is the baby slapped on the buttocks to stimulate breathing, as in old films.)

Once the baby is breathing adequately, the umbilical cord is clamped and severed about 3 inches from the baby's body. (After the birth of your first and third authors' third child, the obstetrcian invited your first author to cut the umbilical cord—but the third author seized the scissors and cut the umbilical cord herself, squirting blood on the obstetrician's glasses. "Who gave the obstetrician the right to determine who would cut the umbilical cord!" she wanted to know.) The stump of the umbilical cord dries and falls off in its own time, usually in seven to ten days.

While the mother is in the third stage of labor, the nurse may perform procedures on the baby, such as placing drops of silver nitrate or an antibiotic ointment into the eyes. This procedure is required by most states to prevent bacterial infections in the newborn's eyes. Typically, the baby is also footprinted and (if the birth has taken place in a hospital) given an identification bracelet. Since neonates do not manufacture vitamin K on their own, the baby may also receive an injection of the vitamin to ensure that her or his blood will clot normally in case of bleeding.

Methods of Childbirth

Until this century, childbirth was usually an event that happened at home and involved the mother, a midwife, family, and friends. These days, women in the United States and Canada typically give birth in hospitals attended by obstetricians who use surgical instruments and anesthetics to protect mothers and children from infection, complications, and pain. Medical procedures save lives but also make childbearing more impersonal. Social critics argue that these procedures have medicalized a natural process. They have usurped control over women's bodies and, through the use of drugs, denied many women the experience of giving birth.

ANESTHETIZED CHILDBIRTH

> In sorrow thou shalt bring forth children.
> (Genesis 3:16)

The Bible suggests that the ancients saw suffering as a woman's lot. But during the past two centuries, science and medicine have led to the expectation that women should experience minimal discomfort during childbirth. Today, some anesthesia is used to minimize or eliminate pain in most U.S. deliveries.

General anesthesia first became popular when Queen Victoria of England delivered her eighth child under chloroform in 1853. General anesthesia, like the chloroform of old, induces unconsciousness. The drug sodium pentothal, a barbiturate, induces general

General anesthesia The use of drugs to put people to sleep and eliminate pain, as during childbirth.

anesthesia when it is injected into a vein. Barbiturates may also be taken orally to reduce anxiety while the woman remains awake. Women may also receive tranquilizers such as Valium or narcotics such as Demerol to help them relax and to blunt pain without inducing sleep.

Anesthetic drugs, as well as tranquilizers and narcotics, decrease the strength of uterine contractions during delivery. They may thus delay the process of cervical dilation and prolong labor. They also weaken the woman's ability to push the baby through the birth canal. Because they cross the placental membrane, they also lower the newborn's overall responsiveness.

Regional or **local anesthetics** block pain in parts of the body without generally depressing the mother's alertness or putting her to sleep. In a *pudendal block*, the external genitals are numbed by local injection. In an *epidural block* and a *spinal block*, an anesthetic is injected into the spinal canal, temporarily numbing the mother's body below the waist. To prevent injury, the needles that are used for these injections do not come into contact with the spinal cord itself. Although local anesthesia decreases the responsiveness of the newborn baby, there is little evidence that medicated childbirth has serious, long-term consequences on children (Ganitsch, 1998).

NATURAL CHILDBIRTH   Partly as a reaction against the use of anesthetics, English obstetrician Grantly Dick-Read endorsed **natural childbirth** in his 1944 book *Childbirth without Fear*. Dick-Read argued that women's labor pains were heightened by their fear of the unknown and resultant muscle tensions. Many of Dick-Read's contributions came to be regarded as accepted practice in modern childbirth procedures, such as the emphasis on informing women about the biological aspects of reproduction and childbirth, the encouragement of physical fitness, and the teaching of relaxation and breathing exercises.

PREPARED CHILDBIRTH: THE LAMAZE METHOD   The French obstetrician Fernand Lamaze visited the Soviet Union in 1951 and found that many Russian women bore babies without anesthetics and without reporting a great deal of pain. Lamaze returned to Western Europe with some of the techniques the women used; they are now usually termed the **Lamaze method,** or *prepared childbirth*. Lamaze (1981) argued that women can learn to conserve energy during childbirth and reduce the pain of uterine contractions by associating the contractions with other responses, such as thinking of pleasant mental images such as beach scenes or engaging in breathing and relaxation exercises.

A pregnant woman typically attends Lamaze classes with a "coach"—usually the father—who will aid her in the delivery room by timing contractions, offering emotional support, and coaching her in the breathing and relaxation exercises. The woman and her partner also receive more general information about childbirth. The father is integrated into the process, and many couples report that their marriages are strengthened as a result.

The Lamaze method is flexible about the use of anesthetics. Many women report some pain during delivery and obtain anesthetics. However, the Lamaze method appears to help women to gain a greater sense of control over the delivery process.

CESAREAN SECTION   In a **cesarean section,** the baby is delivered through surgery rather than naturally through the vagina. The term *section* is derived from the Latin for "to cut." Julius Caesar is said to have been delivered in this way, but health professionals believe this to be unlikely (Brody, 1989). In a cesarean section (C-section for short), the woman is anesthetized, and incisions are made in the abdomen and uterus so that the surgeon can remove the baby. The incisions are then sewn up and the mother can begin walking, often on the same day, although generally with some discomfort for a while. While most C-sections are without complications, some cause urinary tract infections, inflammation of the wall of the uterus, blood clots, or hemorrhaging (Gilbert, 1998).

Local anesthesia Anesthesia that eliminates pain in a specific area of the body, as during childbirth.

Natural childbirth A method of childbirth in which women use no anesthesia but are given other strategies for coping with discomfort and are educated about childbirth.

Lamaze method A childbirth method in which women learn about childbirth, learn to relax and to breathe in patterns that conserve energy and lessen pain, and have a coach (usually the father) present at childbirth. Also termed *prepared childbirth*.

Cesarean section A method of childbirth in which the fetus is delivered through a surgical incision in the abdomen.

Cesarean Section. In a cesarean section (C-section for short), the baby is delivered through surgery rather than the vagina. The woman is anesthetized, and incisions are made in the abdomen and uterus so that the baby can be removed. The incisions are then sewn up. C-sections are usually advised when normal delivery is difficult or threatening to the health of the mother or child. In the United States nearly 1 birth in 5 is by C-section.

C-sections are most likely to be advised when normal delivery is difficult or threatens the health of the mother or child. Vaginal deliveries can become difficult if the baby is large, the mother's pelvis is small or misshapen, or the mother is overly tired or weakened. Herpes and HIV infections in the birth canal can be bypassed by C-section. C-sections are also likely to be performed if the baby presents for delivery in the breech position (feet downward) or the **transverse position** (lying crosswise) or if the baby is in distress.

Use of the C-section has mushroomed. Nearly one of every five births (21%) is now by C-section (Gilbert, 1998). The peak year was 1988, when about 25% of births were by C-section. Compare this figure to about 1 in 20 births in 1965. Much of the increase in the rate of C-sections reflects advances in medical technology, such as use of fetal monitors that allow doctors to detect fetal distress, fear of malpractice suits, financial incentives for hospitals and physicians, and, simply, current medical practice patterns (DiMatteo et al., 1996). Yet some women request C-sections to avoid the discomforts of vaginal delivery or to control the timing of the delivery (Gilbert, 1998). Critics claim that many C-sections are unnecessary, and the U.S. Department of Health and Human Services hopes to lower the rate to 15 per 100 births by the year 2000 (Paul, 1996). However, Dr. Charles Lockwood, a member of the committee of obstetrical practice of the American College of Obstetricians and Gynecologists, is concerned that the effort to lower the C-section rate to 15% is based on "zero data" and could be dangerous (in Gilbert, 1998).

Truth or Fiction?
REVISITED

It is true that one U.S. birth in five is by cesarean section. The use of cesarean section mushroomed in the latter part of the twentieth century, to a peak of about 25% in 1988. ■

Some negative emotional consequences are connected with C-sections. For example, women who have C-sections report being less satisfied with the birth process, are less likely to breast-feed, and interact somewhat less with their infants in the hospital and upon arrival back home (DiMatteo et al., 1996).

Medical opinion once held that once a woman had a C-section, subsequent deliveries also had to be by C-section. Otherwise, uterine scars might rupture during labor. Research has shown that rupture is rare, however. In one study, only 10 of 3,249 women who chose to try vaginal delivery after a previous C-section had a uterine rupture (McMahon et al., 1996). Moreover, there were no maternal deaths.

Transverse position A crosswise birth position.

Alternatives to the Hospital: Where Should a Child Be Born?

In the United States, most births occur in hospitals. Medical equipment and personnel are thus available to handle complications. But hospital deliveries have their disadvantages. Hospitals are often impersonal and very expensive, although the costs may be offset by medical insurance. Giving birth in a hospital tends to instill the perception that pregnancy is an illness rather than a healthy, natural process. In addition, the hospital environment tends to encourage mothers to assume a passive role and surrender responsibility for their care to the doctor. For various reasons, then, many pregnant women and their partners have sought alternative places to deliver their children.

BIRTH CENTERS   Birth centers seek to provide the atmosphere associated with home delivery. Birth centers typically have some medical equipment available and are frequently located within or adjacent to medical centers to permit immediate access to medical facilities (e.g., if an emergency C-section is needed). Such centers are intended for women who are deemed to be at low risk for birth complications.

The birthing room itself is typically decorated and furnished cheerfully, like a bedroom. Family members, friends, and siblings of the baby may be present to share the experience. Women in labor can move about the room freely and eat, drink, rest, or chat with friends and family as they wish. After the birth, the family generally remains together in the room, sharing what for most is a loving and joyous experience. These days, even maternity wards in U.S. hospitals seem to be assuming much of the comforting ambience of birthing centers.

HOME BIRTHS   Home birth provides familiar surroundings and the psychological sense that the woman and her family are more in control. Some advocates of home childbirth argue that it is safe enough for women who have been medically screened for potential complications and who have a history of normal births. Critics charge that it is not possible to screen women for every possible complication, however, and that home delivery exposes the mother and child to unnecessary risks, especially if unexpected complications occur. Many physicians refuse to deliver babies in the home.

Reflections

- Do you know anyone who has used the Lamaze method? What does she or he say about it?
- Do you know anyone who had a cesarean section? What was the reason for it? What are the mother's feelings about it? Did the C-section affect subsequent deliveries?
- Where were you born? Who was present during delivery? Why?

BIRTH PROBLEMS

Most deliveries are uncomplicated, or "unremarkable" in the medical sense—although childbirth is the most remarkable experience of many parents' lives. Problems can and do occur, however. Some of the most common birth problems are anoxia and the birth of preterm and low-birthweight babies.

Anoxia

Prenatal **anoxia** can cause various problems in the neonate and affect later development. It leads to complications such as brain damage and mental retardation. Prolonged anoxia during delivery can also result in cerebral palsy and possibly death.

Anoxia Oxygen deprivation.

ETHNICITY AND INFANT MORTALITY

Back in 1950, there were more than 25 infant deaths per 1,000 live births in the United States. Because the United States now has some of the world's most sophisticated medical technology, that number has been dropping sharply, to 8.5 in 1992 and 7.9 in 1994. Yet within the United States, there are also dramatic ethnic differences in rates of infant mortality. Infant mortality rates are lowest for Chinese Americans and Japanese Americans (Singh & Yu, 1995). The infant mortality rate for African Americans is about twice that for non-Hispanic White Americans (Singh & Yu, 1995). In the year 1992, African Americans made up about 12% of the U.S. population. However, they accounted for about 17% of the live births and one third of the infant deaths in the nation (Singh & Yu, 1995).

Much of the ethnic difference in infant mortality can apparently be attributed to differences in prenatal health care.

Prenatal Care. The incidence of low-birthweight babies is clearly connected to the quality of prenatal care. Many women in the United States—especially women from minority groups—do not receive adequate prenatal care. Some receive no prenatal care at all.

Table 11.3 shows infant health statistics obtained from public records in New York City. Residents of the affluent White Kips Bay–Yorkville area had healthier newborns than residents of East Harlem (a low-income neighborhood made up mostly of African Americans) or of middle-income and mainly White Astoria–Long Island City. East Harlem mothers, like other low-income mothers (McLaughlin et al., 1992), were more likely than their middle- and upper-income counterparts to have babies with low birthweights and babies who died

---

The baby is supplied with oxygen through the umbilical cord. Passage through the birth canal squeezes the umbilical cord. Temporary squeezing, like holding one's breath for a moment, is unlikely to cause problems. (In fact, slight oxygen deprivation at birth is not unusual because the transition from receiving oxygen through the umbilical cord to breathing on its own may not happen immediately after the baby emerges.) Anoxia can result if constriction of the cord is prolonged, however. Prolonged constriction is more likely to occur with a breech presentation, because the baby's head presses the umbilical cord against the birth canal during delivery. Fetal monitoring can help detect anoxia early, however, before damage occurs. A C-section can be performed if the fetus appears to be in distress.

Preterm and Low-Birthweight Children

A neonate is considered to be premature, or **preterm,** if it is born before 37 weeks of gestation. The normal period of gestation is 40 weeks. Prematurity is generally linked with low birthweight, since the fetus normally makes dramatic gains in weight during the last weeks of pregnancy. Regardless of the length of its gestation period, a newborn baby is considered to have a low birthweight if it weighs less than 5 pounds (about 2,500 grams). Preterm and low-birthweight babies face a heightened risk of infant mortality (Singh & Yu, 1995).

Preterm babies are relatively thin because they have not yet formed the layer of fat that accounts for the round, robust appearance of most full-term babies. Their muscles are immature, weakening their sucking and breathing reflexes. Also, in the last weeks of pregnancy, fetuses secrete **surfactant** that prevent the walls of their airways from sticking together. Muscle weakness and incomplete lining of the airways with surfactant can cause

Preterm Born prior to 37 weeks of gestation.

Surfactant Substance that prevent the walls of the airways from sticking together.

table 11.3

Infant Health Statistics	East Harlem	Astoria–Long Island City	Kips Bay–Yorkville
Infant deaths per 1,000 live births	23.4	14.9	7.3
Low-birthweight babies per 100 live births (less than 5.5 pounds)	18.5	6.1	6.0
Very low-birthweight babies per 100 live births (less than 3.3 pounds)	3.8	0.98	0.87
Live births per 100 in which mothers received late or no prenatal care	35.8	10.4	6.1

Infant health statistics for three New York City neighborhoods

This table shows infant health statistics for three New York City neighborhoods. East Harlem is a heavily studied inner-city area characterized by poverty, a high proportion of minority residents, and many teenage pregnancies. The Astoria–Long Island City area is populated by middle-income residents. Kips Bay–Yorkville is a high-income area.
Source: Department of Health, City of New York, 1990.

during infancy. Maternal malnutrition and use of chemical substances such as alcohol and tobacco during pregnancy have all been linked to low birthweights and increased mortality during the first year of life (Barr et al., 1990; McLaughlin et al., 1992).

The differences in infant health shown in the table are also connected with the incidence of prenatal care received by the mothers in the three neighborhoods. According to 1990 New York City Department of Health records, nearly 36% of East Harlem mothers received either late prenatal care or none, compared with about 6% in Kips Bay–Yorkville and about 10% in Astoria–Long Island City. Research has shown that comprehensive prenatal care is connected with higher birthweights (McLaughlin et al., 1992).

a cluster of problems known as **respiratory distress syndrome,** which is responsible for many neonatal deaths. Preterm babies may also suffer from underdeveloped immune systems, which leave them more vulnerable to infections.

Preterm infants usually remain in the hospital for a time. There they can be monitored and placed in incubators that provide a temperature-controlled environment and offer some protection from disease. If necessary, they may also receive oxygen.

Reflections

- Do you know of anyone who experienced birth problems such as anoxia or low birthweight? What was the outcome?

THE POSTPARTUM PERIOD

The weeks following delivery are called the **postpartum** period. The first few days postpartum are frequently happy ones. The long wait is over, as are the discomforts of childbirth. A sizable number of women experience feelings of depression, however, in the days and sometimes weeks and months following childbirth.

Maternal Depression

Mood changes following childbirth are experienced by many new mothers. During the days or weeks after the delivery of their babies, anywhere from 50% to 80% of new mothers (Harding, 1989) experience periods of sadness, tearfulness, and irritability that are

Respiratory distress syndrome
A cluster of breathing problems, including weak and irregular breathing, to which preterm babies are especially vulnerable.

Postpartum Following birth.

commonly called the "postpartum blues," the "maternity blues," or the "baby blues." This downswing in mood typically occurs around the third day after delivery (Samuels & Samuels, 1986). The baby blues usually last about 48 hours and are generally believed to be a normal response to hormonal and psychological changes that attend childbirth (Harding, 1989; Samuels & Samuels, 1986).

Some mothers experience more persistent and severe mood changes, called **postpartum depression** (PPD) (Whiffen, 1992). PPD may last a year or even longer. PPD can involve extreme sadness or despair, apathy, changes in appetite and sleep patterns, low self-esteem, and difficulty concentrating. A study of 1033 married, middle-class, first-time mothers from the Pittsburgh area who had full-term, healthy infants found that 9.3% of them had experienced PPD (Campbell & Cohn, 1991). Some researchers (e.g., Gitlin & Pasnau, 1989) estimate that PPD affects up to 15% of new mothers.

Like the "maternity blues," PPD may reflect a combination of physiological and psychological factors. Hormonal changes may play a role in PPD, but women with PPD are more likely than those with the maternity blues to have been susceptible to depression before and during their pregnancies (O'Hara et al., 1984). Psychosocial factors such as stress, a troubled marriage, or the need to adjust to an unwanted or sick baby may all increase a woman's susceptibility to PPD (Gitlin & Pasnau, 1989; O'Hara et al., 1984, 1991). Adjusting to a new baby imposes inevitable changes on parents, and change is usually stressful in itself. Depression is likely to be prolonged in women who feel helpless in meeting the demands they face (Cutrona, 1983). First-time mothers, single mothers, and mothers who lack social support from their partners or family members face the greatest risk of PPD (Gitlin & Pasnau, 1989).

New fathers may also have bouts of depression. New mothers are not the only ones who must adjust to the responsibilities of parenthood. Fathers too may feel overwhelmed or unable to cope. Perhaps more fathers might experience the "paternity blues" but for the fact that mothers generally shoulder the lion's share of childrearing chores.

Breast-Feeding Versus Bottle-Feeding

Only a minority of U.S. women breast-feed their children. One reason is that many women return to the workforce shortly after childbirth. Some choose to share feeding chores with the father, who is equally equipped to prepare and hold a bottle but not to breast-feed. Other women find breast-feeding inconvenient or unpleasant. Long-term comparisons of breast-fed and bottle-fed children show few, if any, significant differences. Breast-feeding does reduce the general risk of infections to the baby, however, by transmitting the mother's antibodies to the baby. Breast-feeding also reduces the incidence of allergies in babies, particularly in allergy-prone infants (Barisic, 1998; Nevid et al., 1998). On the other hand, HIV (the AIDS virus) can be transmitted to infants by means of breast milk. According to United Nations estimates, one third of the infants with HIV around the world were infected via breast milk (Meier, 1997).

The hormones prolactin and oxytocin are involved in breast-feeding. **Prolactin** stimulates production of milk, or **lactation,** two to three days after delivery. Oxytocin causes the breasts to eject milk and is secreted in response to suckling. When an infant is weaned, secretion of prolactin and oxytocin is discontinued, and lactation comes to an end.

Uterine contractions that occur during breast-feeding help to return the uterus to its typical size. Breast-feeding also delays resumption of normal menstrual cycles. Breast-feeding is not a perfectly reliable birth-control method, however. (But nursing women are advised not to use birth-control pills, since the hormone content of the pills is passed to the infant through the milk.)

Should a woman breast-feed her baby? Although breast-feeding has benefits for both mother and infant, each woman must weigh these benefits against the difficulties breast-

Postpartum depression Persistent and severe mood changes during the postpartum period, involving feelings of despair and apathy and characterized by changes in appetite and sleep, low self-esteem, and difficulty concentrating.

Prolactin A pituitary hormone that stimulates production of milk. (From roots meaning "for milk.")

Lactation Production of milk by the mammary glands.

feeding might pose for her. These include assuming the sole responsibility for nighttime feedings, the physical demands of producing and expelling milk, tendency for soreness in the breasts, and the inconvenience of being continually available to meet the infant's feeding needs. Women should breast-feed because they want to, not because they feel that they must.

Resumption of Ovulation and Menstruation

For close to a month after delivery, women experience a reddish vaginal discharge called **lochia.** A nonnursing mother does not resume actual menstrual periods until two to three months postpartum. The first few cycles are likely to be irregular. Many women incorrectly assume that they will resume menstruating after childbirth by first having a menstrual period and then ovulating two weeks later. In most cases, the opposite is true. Ovulation precedes the first menstrual period after childbirth. Therefore, a woman can become pregnant before the menstrual phase of her first postpartum cycle. Some women, but not all, who suffered premenstrual syndrome before their pregnancies find that their periods give them less discomfort after the birth of their children.

Resumption of Sexual Activity

The resumption of coitus depends on a couple's level of sexual interest, the healing of episiotomies or other injuries, fatigue, the recommendations of obstetricians, and, of course, tradition. Obstetricians usually advise a six-week waiting period for safety and comfort.

It is true that couples should abstain from coitus for at least six weeks after childbirth. However, many other kinds of sexual activities are safe and do not cause discomfort. (Check with your obstetrician.) ■

Truth or Fiction?
REVISITED

Women will typically prefer to delay coitus until it becomes physically comfortable, generally when the episiotomy or other lacerations have healed and the lochia has ended. This can take several weeks. Women who breast-feed might also find that they have less vaginal lubrication, and the dryness can cause discomfort during coitus. K-Y jelly or other lubricants can help in such cases.

The return of sexual interest and resumption of sexual activity take longer for some couples than for others. Sexual interest depends more on psychological than on physical factors. Many couples encounter declining sexual interest and activity in the first year after childbirth, generally because child care can sap energy and limit free time. Generally speaking, couples whose sexual relationships were satisfying before the baby arrived tend to show greater sexual interest and to resume sexual activity earlier than those who had less satisfying relationships beforehand. (No surprise.)

Reflections

- Do you know of anyone who was depressed after delivering a baby? How serious was the depression? Do you have any idea what caused it? Was it treated? If so, how? How long did the depression last?
- Would you prefer that your children be breast-fed or bottle-fed? (Or, if you have had children, were they breast-fed or bottle-fed?) Why?
- Do you have any opinion as to how long after delivery a woman should wait to resume sexual activity? Explain.

Lochia A reddish vaginal discharge that may persist for a month after delivery. (From the Greek *lochios,* meaning "of childbirth.")

summing up

CONCEPTION: AGAINST ALL ODDS

Conception is the union of a sperm cell and an ovum. Fertilization normally occurs in a fallopian tube.

Optimizing the Chances of Conception

Optimizing the chances of conception means engaging in coitus at the time of ovulation. Ovulation can be predicted by calculating the woman's basal body temperature, analyzing the woman's urine for luteinizing hormone, or tracking the thickness of vaginal mucus.

INFERTILITY AND ALTERNATIVE WAYS OF BECOMING PARENTS

Male Fertility Problems

Fertility problems in the male include low sperm count, irregularly shaped sperm, low sperm motility, certain chronic or infectious diseases, trauma to the testes, an autoimmune response to sperm, and pituitary imbalances and/or thyroid disease.

Female Fertility Problems

The major causes of infertility in women include irregular ovulation, obstructions or malfunctions of the reproductive tract, endometriosis, and the decline of hormone levels with age. Failure to ovulate can often be overcome by fertility drugs. Methods for overcoming other female fertility problems include in vitro fertilization, GIFT, ZIFT, donor IVF, embryonic transfer, and surrogate motherhood.

PREGNANCY

Early Signs of Pregnancy

Early signs include a missed period, presence of HCG in the blood or urine, and Hegar's sign.

Pregnancy Tests

Pregnancy tests detect the presence of human chorionic gonadotropin (HCG) in the woman's urine or blood.

Early Effects of Pregnancy

Early effects include tenderness in the breasts and morning sickness.

Miscarriage (Spontaneous Abortion)

Miscarriages have many causes, including chromosomal defects in the fetus and abnormalities of the placenta and uterus.

Sex During Pregnancy

Most health professionals concur that in most cases coitus is safe until the start of labor.

Psychological Changes during Pregnancy

A woman's psychological response to pregnancy reflects her desire to be pregnant, her physical changes, and her attitudes toward these changes. Men, like women, respond to pregnancy according to the degree to which they want the child.

PRENATAL DEVELOPMENT

The Germinal Stage

The germinal stage is the period from conception to implantation.

The Embryonic Stage

The embryonic stage begins with implantation and extends to about the eighth week of development and is characterized by differentiation of the major organ systems.

The Fetal Stage

The fetal stage begins by the ninth week and continues until the birth of the baby. The fetal stage is characterized by continued maturation of the fetus's organ systems and dramatic increases in size.

Environmental Influences on Prenatal Development

Environmental factors that affect prenatal development include the mother's diet, maternal diseases and disorders, and drugs. Maternal malnutrition has been linked to low birthweight and infant mortality. Exposure to particular teratogens causes the greatest harm during critical periods of vulnerability.

Chromosomal and Genetic Abnormalities

Chromosomal and genetic abnormalities can lead to cystic fibrosis, Down syndrome, hemophilia, Huntington's chorea, neural tube defects, phenylketonuria, retina blastoma, sickle-cell anemia, and Tay-Sachs disease. Parental blood tests, amniocentesis, and ultrasound allow parents to learn whether the fetus has, or is at risk for, many such disorders.

CHILDBIRTH

The Stages of Childbirth

In the first stage, uterine contractions efface and dilate the cervix so that the baby may pass. The first stage may last from a couple of hours to more than a day. The second stage lasts from a few minutes to a few hours and ends with the birth of the baby. During the third stage, the placenta is expelled.

Methods of Childbirth

Contemporary methods for facilitating childbirth include anesthetized childbirth, natural childbirth, the Lamaze method, and cesarean section.

Alternatives to the Hospital: Where Should a Child Be Born?

In the United States, most births occur in hospitals. Some parents, however, seeking more intimate arrangements, opt for a birth center or home delivery.

BIRTH PROBLEMS

Anoxia
Prenatal anoxia can cause brain damage and mental retardation in the child.

Preterm and Low-Birthweight Children
Preterm and low birthweight babies have a heightened risk of infant mortality.

THE POSTPARTUM PERIOD

Maternal Depression
Many new mothers experience transient mood changes after childbirth. Women with postpartum depression experience lingering depressions after childbirth.

Breast-Feeding Versus Bottle-Feeding
Breast-feeding is connected with fewer infections and allergic reactions in the baby than bottle-feeding. Long-term studies show few differences between children whose parents used one or the other feeding method, however.

Resumption of Ovulation and Menstruation
The first few menstrual cycles after childbirth are likely to be irregular.

Resumption of Sexual Activity
Obstetricians usually advise a six-week waiting period following childbirth before resuming coitus. Couples need not wait this long to enjoy other forms of sexual activity.

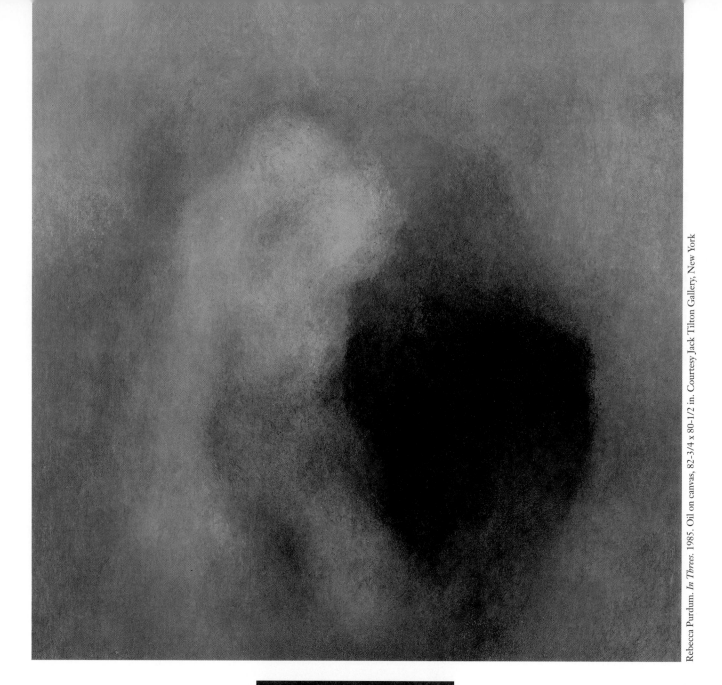

Rebecca Purdum. *In Threes*. 1985. Oil on canvas, 82-3/4 x 80-1/2 in. Courtesy Jack Tilton Gallery, New York

chapter

12

Contraception and Abortion

outline

TRUTH OR FICTION?

CONTRACEPTION

Contraception in the United States:
The Legal Battle

WHAT DO YOU SAY NOW?
*Talking with Your Partner
about Contraception*

Selecting a Method of Contraception

METHODS OF CONTRACEPTION

Oral Contraceptives ("the Pill")

Norplant

A CLOSER LOOK:
Congratulations, Wheat Ridge, It's a . . . !

Intrauterine Devices (IUDs)

The Diaphragm

Spermicides

The Cervical Cap

Condoms

Douching

Withdrawal (Coitus Interruptus)

Fertility Awareness Methods
(Rhythm Methods)

Sterilization

IN THE NEW MILLENNIUM:
The Search Goes On

ABORTION

When Does Human Life Begin?

QUESTIONNAIRE:
*Pro-Choice or Pro-Life? Where Do
You Stand?*

Historical and Legal Perspectives
on Abortion

Methods of Abortion

A CLOSER LOOK:
Partial-Birth Abortion

Psychological Consequences of Abortion

A WORLD OF DIVERSITY:
*Japan's Abortion Agony: In a Country
That Prohibits the Pill, Reality Collides
with Religion*

SUMMING UP

Truth or Fiction **?**

_____ Ancient Egyptians used crocodile dung as a contraceptive substance.

_____ Contraceptives not only prevent conception; they also prevent sexually transmitted infections.

_____ There are oral contraceptives that can be taken the morning after unprotected intercourse.

_____ Sterilization operations can be surgically reversed.

_____ Testosterone can be used as a male contraceptive device.

_____ Abortions were legal in the newly founded United States.

_____ The D&C is the most widely used abortion method in the United States.

it was a stifling day in July 1912. Margaret Sanger (1883–1966), a nurse-practitioner, was summoned to the house of a woman who was near death from a botched self-induced abortion. Her husband had called a doctor, and the doctor sent for Sanger. Together, doctor and nurse worked feverishly through the days and nights that followed to stem an infection that had taken hold in the woman. Sanger later commented,

> Never had I worked so fast, never so concentratedly. The sultry days and nights were melted into a torpid inferno. It did not seem possible there could be such heat, and every bit of food, ice, and drugs had to be carried up three flights of stairs. (Sanger, 1938)

After two interminable weeks, the woman began to recover. Her neighbors, who had feared the worst, came to express their joy. But the woman, who smiled wanly at those who came to see her, appeared more depressed and anxious than would be expected of someone who was recovering from a grave illness. By the end of the third week, when Sanger prepared to leave her patient, the woman, Mrs. Sachs, voiced the fear that was haunting her. Her face registered deep despair as she explained to Sanger that she dreaded becoming pregnant again and facing a choice between attempting another abortion, which she feared might kill her, and bearing a baby whose care it was beyond her means to support. She pleaded for information about contraception but Sanger could offer none. In 1912, it was a crime even for health professionals like Margaret Sanger to dispense information about contraceptives. Abortions, too, were illegal. Sanger tried to comfort her and promised to return to talk again.

Three months later, she received another urgent call. It was Mr. Sachs. His wife was sick again—from the same cause. As Sanger recalled,

> For a wild moment I thought of sending someone else, but actually, of course, I hurried into my uniform, caught up my bag, and started out. All the way I longed for a subway wreck, an explosion, anything to keep me from having to enter that home again. But nothing happened, even to delay me. I turned into the dingy doorway and climbed the familiar stairs once more. The children were there, young little things.

> Mrs. Sachs was in a coma and died within ten minutes. I folded her still hands across her breast, remembering how they had pleaded with me, begging so humbly for the knowledge which was her right. I drew a sheet over her pallid face. Jake was sobbing, running his hands through his hair and pulling it out like an insane person. Over and over again he wailed, "My God! My God! My God!" (Sanger, 1938)

Today, partly because of the work of Margaret Sanger, who went on to become a key advocate for birth control, information about contraceptives is disseminated freely throughout the United States.

Methods of birth control include contraception and abortion. The term *contraception* refers to techniques that prevent conception. The term *abortion* refers to the termination of a pregnancy before the embryo or fetus is capable of surviving outside the womb.

CONTRACEPTION

People have been devising means of contraception since they became aware of the relationship between coitus and conception. Ironically, the safest and most effective method of contraception is also the least popular: abstinence. The Bible contains many references to contraceptive techniques, including vaginal sponges and contraceptive concoctions. It

Margaret Sanger. Sanger was a key advocate for birth control in the United States. She established the National Birth Control League and a birth-control clinic in Brooklyn, New York. She was instrumental in the dismantling of the Comstock law, which prevented physicians from disseminating information about birth control and prevention of sexually transmitted diseases.

also refers to **coitus interruptus,** or withdrawal. The story of Onan, for example, implies knowledge of the withdrawal method.

Ancient Egyptian methods of birth control included douching with wine and garlic after coitus and soaking crocodile dung in sour milk and stuffing the mixture deep within the vagina. The dung blocked the passage of many—if not all—sperm through the cervix and also soaked up sperm. The dung may also have done its job through a social mechanism. It may have discouraged all but the most ardent suitors.

It is true that ancient Egyptians used crocodile dung as a contraceptive substance. ■

Greek and Roman women placed absorbent materials within the vagina to absorb semen. The use of sheaths or coverings for the penis has a long history. Sheaths worn over the penis as decorative covers can be traced to ancient Egypt (1350 B.C.). Sheaths of linen were first described in European writings in 1564 by the Italian anatomist Fallopius (from whom the name of the fallopian tube is derived). Linen sheaths were used, without success, as a barrier against syphilis. The term **condom** was not used to describe penile sheaths until the eighteenth century. At that time, sheaths made of animal intestines became popular as a means of preventing sexually transmitted infections and unwanted pregnancies. Among the early advocates of condoms as a method of contraception was the Italian adventurer and writer Giovanni Casanova (1725–1798). We now associate his name with men who are known for their amorous adventures. James Boswell (1740–1795), the biographer of Samuel Johnson, described his use of "armor," or condoms, in his graphic *London Journal.* On one occasion, however, he was so enamored of a street prostitute that he neglected to use his armor and contracted gonorrhea. Condoms made of rubber (hence the slang "rubbers") were introduced shortly after Charles Goodyear invented vulcanization of rubber in 1843. Many other forms of contraception were also used widely in the nineteenth century, including withdrawal, vaginal sponges, and douching.

Contraception in the United States: The Legal Battle

As methods of contraception grew more popular in the nineteenth century, opponents waged a battle to make contraception illegal. One powerful opponent of contraception was Anthony Comstock, who served for a time as the secretary of the New York Society

Coitus interruptus A method of contraception in which the penis is withdrawan from the vagina before ejaculation. Also referred to as the *withdrawal method.*

Condom A sheath made of animal membrane or latex that covers the penis during coitus and serves as a barrier to sperm following ejaculation.

for the Suppression of Vice. Comstock lobbied successfully for passage of a federal law in 1873—the Comstock law—that prohibited the dissemination of birth-control information through the mail on the grounds that it was "obscene and indecent." Many states passed even more restrictive laws. They outlawed passage of information from one person to another, even from physician to patient.

Consider the resistance that Margaret Sanger met when she challenged the laws restricting information about contraception. In 1914, she established the National Birth Control League, which published the magazine *The Woman Rebel.* The magazine did not publish birth-control information but challenged the view that it was obscene. Nevertheless, charges were brought against Sanger, and she fled to Europe before her trial. During her self-imposed exile, she visited birth-control clinics in the Netherlands. When the charges against her in the United States were dropped in 1916, Sanger returned and established a birth-control clinic in Brooklyn, New York. The clinic was closed by the police, and Sanger was arrested. Released on bail, she reopened the clinic and was thereupon sentenced to 30 days in jail. She successfully appealed the sentence. In 1918, the courts ruled that physicians must be allowed to disseminate information that might aid in the cure and prevention of disease. Dismantling of the Comstock law

what do you say now?

Talking with Your Partner about Contraception

When is the right time to discuss contraception? On a first date? When you are invited to meet your partner's family? When you are lost in amorous embraces? Broaching the topic can be awkward. *Not* broaching it can be disastrous. Often, a man responds to news that his partner is pregnant by saying something like this: "But I thought you were using *something!*"

Technically speaking, the right time to discuss birth control is *anytime* that allows your contraceptive to become effective before you engage in coitus. That can mean weeks or months before, if you decide to use a prescription contraceptive such as the birth-control pill, the IUD, the diaphragm, or the cervical cap. Or it can mean a few moments before coitus, if you decide to use a condom and have one ready. Despite the obvious advantage to deciding upon contraception before coitus, the issue is often broached, if it is broached at all, only after the partners become sexually intimate.

Practically speaking, it is awkward—and perhaps presumptuous!—to discuss contraception when you meet or are on a first date. But at the very least, it is advisable to prepare oneself for the possibility of coitus. The man or woman can bring along a condom. The woman might already be on the pill, have an IUD in place, or have a diaphragm.

Talking about contraception helps many couples to make the transition from a casual relationship to an intimate one. Talking enables partners to share responsibility for their behavior. As a result, the woman is less likely to be resentful that the responsibility rests entirely on her.

Yes, it can be awkward or difficult to raise the topic. Couples might not feel that their relationship is secure enough. They might think, "We'll cross that bridge when we come to

it." Not planning ahead, however, prevents the effective use of contraceptives that require advance planning.

Couples who choose to discuss contraception before engaging in coitus may benefit from these communication guidelines:

1. *Pick a strategic time and place.* Choose a time when the two of you are alone and are free of distractions. Pick a place that is comfortable and private.
2. *Couch your discussion in terms of your feelings about your partner and your relationship.* Talk about your general feelings toward your partner and your general relationship before you narrow in on contraception.
3. *Don't apologize for raising the topic.* You might feel embarrassed talking about sensitive topics such as birth control. But you need not apologize for bringing up the subject. Apologizing suggests that you think you are doing something wrong.
4. *Raise the subject in a way that encourages candid discussion.* Use open-ended questions to explore your partner's attitudes. Say something like "I think our relationship has reached the point where we need to talk about contraception. I know we're not sleeping together yet, but some forms of contraception require advanced planning. Have you been thinking about it?"
5. *Explore options.* Don't make demands of your partner. Don't say, "Since we may start sleeping together, I think you should go on the pill." Rather, say something like "I know that many different types of contraceptives are available. Why don't we discuss which method might be best for us if we become intimate?" Use the opportunity to explore each other's views about birth control in general and specific techniques in particular.

had begun. With the financial support of a wealthy friend, Katherine Dexter McCormack, Sanger spurred research into the use of hormones as one approach to contraception. In 1960, only six years before Sanger's death, oral contraception—"the pill"—was finally marketed in the United States. In 1965, the Supreme Court struck down the last impediment to free use of contraception: a law preventing the sale of contraceptives in Connecticut (*Griswold* v. *Connecticut*, 1965). In 1973, abortion was in effect legalized by the Supreme Court in the case of *Roe* v. *Wade*, permitting women to terminate unwanted pregnancies.

Today, contraceptives are advertised in popular magazines and sold through vending machines in college dormitories. The U.S. history of birth control is not a one-way road to unrestricted use, however. Recent Supreme Court decisions have set aside bits and pieces of *Roe* v. *Wade*, giving the states more discretion over the regulation of abortion and restricting access to abortions for minors. Many groups, including the Roman Catholic Church, continue to oppose the use of **artificial contraception.** Yet many individual Catholics, including many priests, hold liberal attitudes toward contraception.

Selecting a Method of Contraception

If you believe that you and your partner should use contraception, how will you determine which method is right for you? There is no simple answer. What is right for your friends might be wrong for you. You and your partner will make your own selections, but there are some issues you might want to consider:

1. *Convenience*. Is the method convenient? The convenience of a method depends on a number of factors: Does it require a device that must be purchased in advance? If so, can it be purchased over the counter as needed, or are a consultation with a doctor and a prescription required? Will the method work at a moment's notice, or, as with the birth-control pill, will it require time to reach maximum effectiveness? Some couples feel that few things dampen ardor and spontaneity more quickly than the need to pay attention to a contraceptive device in the heat of passion. Use of contraceptives such as the condom and the diaphragm need not interrupt sexual activity, however. Both partners can share in applying the device. Some couples find that this becomes an erotic aspect of their lovemaking.
2. *Moral acceptability*. A method that is morally acceptable to one person might be objectionable to another. For example, some oral contraceptives prevent fertilization; others allow fertilization to occur but then prevent implantation of the fertilized ovum in the uterus. In the second case, the method of contraception might be considered to produce a form of early abortion, which is likely to concern people who object to abortion no matter how soon after conception it occurs. Yet the same people might have no moral objection to preventing fertilization.
3. *Cost*. Methods vary in cost. Some more costly methods involve devices (such as the diaphragm, the cervical cap, and the IUD) or hormones (pills or Norplant) that require medical visits in addition to the cost of the devices themselves. Other methods, such as rhythm methods, are essentially free.
4. *Sharing responsibility*. Most forms of birth control place the burden of responsibility largely, if not entirely, on the woman. The woman must consult with her doctor to obtain birth-control pills or other prescription devices such as diaphragms, cervical caps, Norplant, and IUDs. The woman must take birth-control pills reliably or check to see that her IUD remains in place.

   Some couples prefer methods that allow for greater sharing of responsibility, such as alternating use of the condom and diaphragm. A man can also share the responsibility for the birth-control pill by accompanying his partner on her medical visits, sharing the expense, and helping her to remember to take her pill.
5. *Safety*. How safe is the method? What are the side effects? What health risks are associated with its use? Can your partner's health or comfort be affected by its use?

Artificial contraception A method of contraception that applies a human-made device.

6. *Reversibility.* Reversibility refers to the effects of a birth-control technique or device. In most cases, the effects of birth-control methods can be fully reversed by discontinuing their use. In other cases, reversibility might not occur immediately, as with oral contraceptives. One form of contraception, sterilization, should be considered irreversible, although many attempts at reversal have been successful.

7. *Protection against sexually transmitted infections.* Birth-control methods vary in the degree of protection they afford against sexually transmitted infections (STIs), such as gonorrhea, chlamydia, and AIDS. This is especially important to people who are sexually active with one or more partners who are *not known* to be free of infectious diseases.

Some contraceptives prevent sexually transmitted infections as well as conception. Most methods, however, offer no protection against STIs. Therefore, this Truth or Fiction item is too broad to be true. ■

table 12.1

	PERCENTAGE OF WOMEN EXPERIENCING AN ACCIDENTAL PREGNANCY WITHIN THE FIRST YEAR OF USE		Percentage of Women Continuing Use at One Year [3]		Protection against Sexually Transmitted Infections (STIs)
Method	**Typical Use[1]**	**Perfect Use[2]**		**Reversibility**	
Chance[4]	85	85		Yes (unless fertility has been impaired by exposure to an STI)	No
Spermicides[5]	21	6	43	Yes	Unclear
Periodic abstinence	20		67	Yes	No
Calendar		9			
Ovulation method		3			
Sympto-thermal[6]		2			
Post-Ovulation		1			
Withdrawal	19	4		Yes	No
Cervical cap[7]					
Parous women*	36	26	45	Yes	Some
Nulliparous[†] women	18	9	58	Yes	Some
Diaphragm[7]	18	6	58	Yes	Some

Approximate failure rates of various methods of birth control (in percentages of women using the method who become pregnant within the first year of use)

[1]Among typical couples who initiate use of a method (not necessarily for the first time), the percentage who experience an accidental pregnancy during the first year if they do not stop use for any other reason.

[2]Among couples who initiate use of a method (not necessarily for the first time) and who use it perfectly (both consistently and correctly), the percentage who experience an accidental pregnancy during the first year if they do not stop use for any other reason.

[3]Among couples attempting to avoid pregnancy, the percentage who continue to use a method for one year.

[4]The percentages failing in columns 2 and 3 are based on data from populations where contraception is not used and from women who cease using contraception in order to become pregnant. Among such populations, about 89% become pregnant within one year. This estimate was lowered slightly (to 85%) to represent the percentage who would become pregnant within one year among women now relying on reversible methods of contraception if they abandoned contraception altogether.

[5]Foams, creams, gels, vaginal suppositories, and vaginal film.

8. *Effectiveness.* Techniques and devices vary widely in their effectiveness in actual use. Despite the widespread availability of contraceptives, about two of three pregnancies in the United States are unplanned, and of these, about half result from contraceptive failures (Angier, 1993a). The failure rate for a particular method refers to the percentage of women who become pregnant when using the method for a given period of time, such as during the first year of use. Most contraceptive methods are not used correctly all or even much of the time. Therefore, it is instructive to compare the failure rate among people who use a particular method or device *perfectly* (consistently and correctly) with the failure rate among *typical* users. Failure rates among typical users are often considerably higher because of incorrect, unreliable, or inconsistent use. Table 12.1 shows the failure rates, continuation rates, reversibility, and degree of protection against STIs associated with various contraceptive methods.

| Method | PERCENTAGE OF WOMEN EXPERIENCING AN ACCIDENTAL PREGNANCY WITHIN THE FIRST YEAR OF USE | | Percentage of Women Continuing Use at One Year [3] | Reversibility | Protection against Sexually Transmitted Infections (STIs) |
	Typical Use [1]	Perfect Use [2]			
Condom alone					
Female (Reality)	21	5	56	Yes	Yes
Male	12	3	63	Yes	Yes
Pill	3		72	Yes	No, and may reduce the risk of PID[8]
Progestin only		0.5			
Combined		0.1			
IUD					
Progesterone T	2.0	1.5	81	Yes, except if fertility is impaired	No, and may increase the risk of PID
Copper T 380A	0.8	0.6	78		
LNg 20	0.1	0.1	81		
Depo-Provera	0.3	0.3	70	Yes	No
Norplant (6 capsules)	0.09	0.09	85	Yes	No
Female sterilization	0.4	0.4	100	Not usually	No
Male sterilization	0.15	0.10	100	Not usually	No

[6]Cervical mucus (ovulation) method supplemented by calendar in the pre-ovulatory and basal body temperature in the post-ovulatory.

[7]With spermicidal cream or jelly.

[8]Pelvic inflammatory disease.

*Women who have borne children.

[†]Women who have not borne children.

Sources: For failure rates and percentages of women discontinuing use, adapted from Hatcher et al. (1994, 1998).

For reversibility and protection against sexually transmitted infections, adapted from Reinisch (1990).

Selecting a Method of Contraception. If you and your partner use contraception, how can you determine which method is right for you? Issues you may want to consider include convenience, effectiveness, moral acceptability, safety, reversibility, and cost. Other issues include whether the method allows you and your partner to share the responsibility, and whether it also affords protection from STIs.

Reflections

▓ What is your personal reaction to the true story told by Margaret Sanger? Why?

▓ What problems would you anticipate in trying to discuss contraception with a partner? Why?

▓ Which of the factors in selecting a method of contraception are most important to you? Explain.

METHODS OF CONTRACEPTION

There are many methods of contraception, including oral contraceptives (the pill), Norplant, intrauterine devices (IUDs), diaphragms, cervical caps, spermicides, condoms, douching, withdrawal (coitus interruptus), timing of ovulation (rhythm), and some devices that are under development.

Oral Contraceptives ("the Pill")

An **oral contraceptive** is commonly referred to as a birth-control pill, or simply "the pill." However, there are many kinds of birth-control pills that vary in the type and dosages of hormones they contain. Birth-control pills fall into two major categories: combination pills and minipills.

Combination pills (such as Ortho-Novum, Ovcon, and Loestrin) contain a combination of synthetic forms of the hormones estrogen and progesterone (progestin). Most combination pills provide a steady dose of synthetic estrogen and progesterone. Other combination pills, called *multiphasic* pills, vary the dosage of these hormones across the menstrual cycle to reduce the overall dosages to which the woman is exposed and possible side effects. The **minipill** contains synthetic progesterone (progestin) only.

Available only by prescription, oral contraceptives are used by 28% of women in the United States who use reversible (nonsterilization) forms of contraception, or some 19 million women (Angier, 1993a). Birth-control pills are the most popular forms of contraception among single women of reproductive age (Gilbert, 1996).

Oral contraceptive A contraceptive, consisting of sex hormones, that is taken by mouth.

Combination pill A birth-control pill that contains synthetic estrogen and progesterone.

Minipill A birth-control pill that contains synthetic progesterone but no estrogen.

HOW THEY WORK   Women cannot conceive when they are already pregnant because their bodies suppress maturation of egg follicles and ovulation. The combination pill fools the brain into acting as though the woman is already pregnant, so no additional ova mature or are released. If ovulation does not take place, a woman cannot become pregnant.

In a normal menstrual cycle, low levels of estrogen during and just after the menstrual phase stimulate the pituitary gland to secrete FSH, which in turn stimulates the maturation of ovarian follicles. The estrogen in the combination pill inhibits FSH production, so follicles do not mature. The progesterone (progestin) inhibits the pituitary's secretion of LH, which would otherwise lead to ovulation. The woman continues to have menstrual periods, but there is no unfertilized ovum to be sloughed off in the menstrual flow.

The combination pill is taken for 21 days of the typical 28-day cycle. Then, for 7 days, the woman either takes no pill at all or takes an inert placebo pill to maintain the habit of taking a pill a day. The sudden drop in hormone levels causes the endometrium to disintegrate and menstruation to follow three or four days after the last pill has been taken. Then the cycle is repeated.

The progestin in the combination pill also increases the thickness and acidity of the cervical mucus. The mucus thus becomes a more resistant barrier to sperm and inhibits development of the endometrium. Therefore, even if an egg were somehow to mature and become fertilized in a fallopian tube, sperm would not be likely to survive the passage through the cervix. Even if sperm were somehow to succeed in fertilizing an egg, the failure of the endometrium to develop would mean that the fertilized ovum could not become implanted in the uterus. Progestin may also impede the progress of ova through the fallopian tubes and make it more difficult for sperm to penetrate ova.

The minipill contains progestin but no estrogen. Minipills are taken daily through the menstrual cycle, even during menstruation. They act in two ways. They thicken the cervical mucus to impede the passage of sperm through the cervix, and they render the inner lining of the uterus less receptive to a fertilized egg. Thus, even if the woman does conceive, the fertilized egg will pass from the body rather than becoming implanted in the uterine wall. Since it contains no estrogen, the minipill does not usually prevent ovulation. The combination pill, by contrast, works directly to prevent ovulation. Since ovulation and fertilization can occur in women who use the minipill, some people see use of the minipill as an early abortion method. Others reserve the term "abortion" for methods of terminating pregnancy after successful implantation.

EFFECTIVENESS OF BIRTH-CONTROL PILLS   The failure rate of the birth-control pill associated with perfect use is very low—0.5% or less, depending on the type of pill (see Table 12.1). The failure rate increases to 3% in typical use. Failures can occur when women forget to take the pill for two days or more, when they do not use backup methods when they first go on the pill, and when they switch from one brand to another. But forgetting to take the pill even for one day can alter the woman's hormonal balance, allowing ovulation—and fertilization.

REVERSIBILITY   Use of oral contraceptives might temporarily reduce fertility after they are discontinued but is not associated with permanent infertility (Mishell, 1989). Nine of ten women begin ovulating regularly within three months of suspending use (Reinisch, 1990). Users of the pill who frequently start and stop usage might later incur fertility problems, however (Reinisch, 1990). When a woman appears not to be ovulating after going off the pill, a drug such as clomiphene is often used to induce ovulation.

ADVANTAGES AND DISADVANTAGES   The great advantage of oral contraception is that, when used properly, it is nearly 100% effective. Unlike many other forms of contraception, such as the condom or diaphragm, its use does not interfere with sexual spontaneity or diminish sexual sensations. The sex act need not be interrupted, as it would be by use of a condom.

Birth-control pills might also have some *healthful* side effects. They appear to reduce the risk of pelvic inflammatory disease, benign ovarian cysts, and fibrocystic (benign) breast growths (Gilbert, 1996). The pill regularizes menstrual cycles and reduces menstrual cramping and premenstrual discomfort. The pill can also be helpful in the treatment of iron-deficiency anemia and facial acne. The combination pill reduces the risks of ovarian and endometrial cancer, even for a number of years after the woman has stopped taking it (Gilbert, 1996; Hatcher & Guillebaud, 1998; Narod et al., 1998). The pill's protective effects against invasive ovarian cancer increase with the length of use (Whittemore et al., 1992).

The pill does have some disadvantages. It confers no protection against STIs. Moreover, it can reduce the effectiveness of antibiotics that are used to treat STIs. Going on the pill requires medical consultation, so a woman must plan to begin using the pill at least several weeks before becoming sexually active or before discontinuing the use of other contraceptives and must incur the expense of medical visits.

The main drawbacks of birth-control pills are potential side effects and possible health risks. The estrogen in combination pills can produce side effects such as nausea and vomiting, fluid retention (feeling bloated), weight gain, increased vaginal discharge, headaches, tenderness in the breasts, and dizziness. Many of these side effects are temporary. When they persist, women may be switched from one pill to another, perhaps to one with lower doses of hormones. Pregnant women produce high estrogen levels in the corpus luteum and placenta. The combination pill artificially raises levels of estrogen, so it is not surprising that some women who use it have side effects that mimic the early signs of pregnancy, such as weight gain or nausea ("morning sickness"). Weight gain can result from estrogen (through fluid retention) or progestin (through increased appetite and development of muscle). Oral contraceptives can also increase blood pressure in some women, but clinically significant elevations are rare in women using the low-dose pills that are available today (Hatcher et al., 1998). Still, it is wise for women who use the pill to have their blood pressure checked regularly (Mishell, 1989). Women who encounter problems with high blood pressure from taking the pill are usually advised to switch to another form of contraception.

Many women have avoided using the pill because of the risk of blood clots. The lower dosages of estrogen that are found in most types of birth-control pills today are associated with much lower risk of blood clots than was the case in the 1960s and 1970s, when higher dosages were typically used (Gilbert, 1996). Still, women who are at increased risk for blood clotting problems, such as those with a history of circulatory problems or stroke, are typically advised not to use the pill.

Women who are considering using the pill need to weigh the benefits and risks with their health care providers. For the great majority of young, healthy women in their 20s and early 30s, there is very little chance of developing blood clots or other cardiovascular problems from using the pill (Hatcher & Guillebaud, 1998). Women who use the pill are no more likely than nonusers to develop cardiovascular problems later in life—even women who had used the pill for more than ten years (Stampfer et al., 1988).

Some women should not be on the pill at all (Calderone & Johnson, 1989; Hatcher et al., 1998; Reinisch, 1990). These include women who have had circulatory problems or blood clots and those who have suffered a heart attack or stroke or have a history of coronary disease, breast or uterine cancer, undiagnosed genital bleeding, liver tumors, or sickle-cell anemia (because of associated blood-clotting problems). Because of their increased risk of cardiovascular problems, caution should be exercised when women over 35 years of age who are heavy smokers (15 or more cigarettes daily) use the combination pill (Hatcher et al., 1998). Nursing mothers should also avoid using the pill, as the hormones may be passed to the baby in the mother's milk.

Since the risks of cardiovascular complications generally increase with age, many women over the age of 35 have been encouraged by their gynecologists to use other forms of birth control. Recent studies, however, show no increased risk of serious cardiovascular disease among healthy, nonsmoking women up to the age of 45 who use oral contraceptives containing lower dosages of estrogen (Mishell, 1989). Many health professionals, including the American College of Obstetricians and Gynecologists, believe that healthy nonsmokers age 35 to 44 can continue to use oral contraceptives safely (Mishell, 1989).

The pill may also have psychological effects. Some users report depression or irritability. Switching brands or altering doses might help. Evidence is lacking concerning the effects of lower-estrogen pills on sexual desire.

Progestin fosters male secondary sex characteristics, so women who take the minipill might develop acne, facial hair, thinning of scalp hair, reduction in breast size, vaginal dryness, and missed or shorter periods. Irregular bleeding, or so-called breakthrough bleeding, between menstrual periods is a common side effect of the minipill (Reinisch, 1990). Irregular bleeding should be brought to the attention of a health professional. Because they can produce vaginal dryness, minipills can hinder vaginal lubrication during intercourse, decreasing sexual sensations and rendering sex painful.

Researchers have also examined suspected links between the use of the pill and certain forms of cancer, especially breast cancer, since breast cancer is sensitive to hormonal changes. Results from several large-scale studies show no overall increase in the rates of breast cancer among pill users, but it remains possible that some subgroups of women who use the pill are at increased risk (Hatcher et al., 1998). The evidence linking use of the pill with increased risk of cervical cancer is mixed, with some studies showing such a link and others showing none (Hatcher et al., 1998).

Women who are considering the pill are advised to have a thorough medical evaluation to rule out contraindications (reasons for *not* using the pill). The evaluation should include a detailed medical and family history and a physical exam including a Pap smear, assessment of blood pressure, screening for STIs, urinalysis, breast and pelvic exam, and possibly an EKG (electrocardiogram). Women who begin to use the pill, regardless of their age or risk status, should pay attention to changes in their physical condition, have regular checkups, and promptly report any physical complaints or unusual symptoms to their physicians.

"MORNING-AFTER" PILLS The so-called morning-after pill, or postcoital contraceptive, actually refers to several types of pills that have high doses of estrogen and progestin. Since they are not taken regularly, they do not prevent ovulation from occurring. Instead, they stop fertilization from taking place or prevent the fertilized egg from implanting itself in the uterus. In that respect, then, they represent an early abortion technique. However, 65% of the respondents in a national poll taken by *The New York Times* said that they would consider morning-after pills to be a form of birth control, and fewer than 20% considered them to be an abortion method (Goldberg & Elder, 1998).

Morning-after pills are most effective when taken within 72 hours after ovulation. Women who wait to see whether they have missed a period are no longer candidates for the morning-after pill. Depending on the brand, four, six, or eight pills are prescribed.

It is true that there are effective oral contraceptives that can be taken the morning after unprotected intercourse. They are termed "morning-after" pills. ■

Truth or Fiction?
REVISITED

Morning-after pills have a higher hormone content than most birth-control pills. For this reason, nausea is a common side effect, occurring in perhaps 70% of users. Nausea is usually mild and passes within a day or two after treatment; it can be treated with anti-nausea medication (Hatcher et al., 1998). Vomiting should be brought to the attention of a physician, since the woman might need to take additional pills to make up for ones possibly lost in vomiting (Hatcher et al., 1998).

Because of the strength of the dosage, the morning-after pill is not recommended as a regular form of birth control. We also know little about possible long-term health complications. Morning-after pills are *one-time* forms of emergency protection (Hatcher et al., 1998), which might be most appropriate to use after rape or when regular contraceptive devices fail (for example, if a condom breaks or a diaphragm becomes dislodged). The morning-after pill is generally effective in preventing implantation of a fertilized ovum, but health professionals caution that when it fails, the fetus might be damaged by exposure to the hormones that the pill contains.

Norplant. Norplant uses the female sex hormone progestin to suppress fertility. This contraceptive implant consists of small silicone tubes containing progestin that are surgically embedded in the woman's arm. The tubes release a small, steady dose of progestin into the bloodstream. Progestin suppresses ovulation and thickens the cervical mucus so that sperm cannot pass.

Norplant

The contraceptive implant Norplant consists of six matchstick-size silicone tubes that contain progestin and are surgically embedded in a woman's upper arm. More than 1 million women in the United States have received Norplant since FDA approval in 1990 (Kolata, 1995).

HOW IT WORKS   Norplant, like the pill, relies on female sex hormones to suppress fertility. But rather than taking a pill once a day, tubes implanted in the woman's body release a small, steady dose of progestin into her bloodstream, providing continuous contraceptive protection for as long as five years (Hatcher, 1998). The progestin in the Norplant system suppresses ovulation and thickens the cervical mucus so that sperm cannot pass. The contraceptive effect occurs within 24 hours of insertion. After five years, the spent tubes are replaced. An alternative implant, Norplant-2, consists of two hormone-releasing tubes that provide at least three years of protection.

HOW IT IS USED   Implantation takes a few minutes in a doctor's office and is carried out under local anesthesia.

EFFECTIVENESS   Norplant is reported to have an extremely low failure rate of less than 1% per year across five years (see Table 12.1). The failure rate approximates that of surgical sterilization.

REVERSIBILITY   Although the failure rate of Norplant approximates that of sterilization, Norplant is fully reversible. Removal restores a normal likelihood of pregnancy.

ADVANTAGES AND DISADVANTAGES   The key advantage of Norplant is its convenience. The hormone is dispensed automatically. The woman need not remember to take a pill each day, insert a device before coitus, or check that an IUD is in place. The most commonly reported side effect is abnormal menstrual bleeding (Hatcher, 1998; Mishell, 1989).

a CLOSER look

Many health professionals who are concerned about finding ways to reduce teenage pregnancy rates are enthusiastic about Norplant. School-based programs have been initiated to make Norplant available to young women, which has fueled the debate over whether schools should be involved in distributing contraceptives to minors (see Chapter 13). The nearby A Closer Look feature recounts another use of Norplant.

Intrauterine Devices (IUDs)

Camel drivers setting out on long desert journeys once placed round stones in the uteruses of female camels to prevent them from becoming pregnant and lost to service. The stones may have acted as primitive **intrauterine devices** (IUDs). IUDs are small objects of various shapes that are inserted into the uterus. Humans have used IUDs since Greek times. Today, IUDs are inserted in the uterus by a physician or nurse-practitioner are and usually left in place for a year or more. Fine plastic threads or strings hang down from the IUD into the vagina so that the woman can check to make sure that it remains in place.

IUDs are used by about 1.5 million women in the United States and more than 80 million women around the world (Altman, 1991). Nearly 60 million IUD users are in China, where nearly one in three married women uses an IUD during her childbearing years. By contrast, IUDs are used by only about 3% of married women of childbearing age in the United States. Married women in the United States are more than twice as likely as single women to use an IUD (U.S. Bureau of the Census, 1990).

IUDs achieved their greatest popularity in the United States in the 1960s and 1970s. Then there was a sharp drop-off in their use during the 1980s after use of a popular model, the Dalkon Shield, was linked to a high incidence of pelvic infections and tubal infertility (Darling et al., 1992).

Figure 12.1 on page 354 shows two IUDs: the Progestasert T, which releases small quantities of progesterone (progestin) daily, and the Copper T 380A (ParaGard), a T-shaped, copper-based device. Because the Progestasert T must be replaced annually and any insertion carries some risk of infection, health authorities recommend the use of the ParaGard device, which can be used for upward of eight years, unless the woman is allergic to copper (Stewart, 1998).

HOW THEY WORK We do not know exactly how IUDs work. A foreign body, such as the IUD, apparently irritates the uterine lining. This irritation gives rise to mild

Intrauterine device A small object that is inserted into the uterus and left in place to prevent conception. Abbreviated *IUD*.

Two IUDs: The Progestasert T and the Copper T 380A (ParaGard). The Progestasert T releases small quantities of progesterone (progestin) daily. The Copper T 380A is a T-shaped, copper-based device.

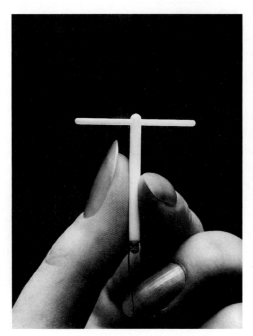

inflammation and the production of antibodies that might be toxic to sperm or to fertilized ova and/or may prevent fertilized eggs from becoming implanted. Inflammation might also impair proliferation of the endometrium—another impediment to implantation. Progestin released by the Progestasert T also has effects like the progestin-only minipill: It lessens the likelihood of fertilization and implantation. Action on fertilized ova might be considered to constitute an early abortion. Since IUDs might not prevent fertilization, people who oppose abortion, regardless of how soon it occurs after conception, also oppose the IUD.

EFFECTIVENESS The failure rate associated with typical use of the Progestasert T is about 2% (see Table 12.1). Most failures occur within three months of insertion, often because the device shifts position or is expelled. ParaGard is the most effective IUD. The first-year failure rate in typical use is 0.8%.

The IUD might irritate the muscular layer of the uterine wall, causing contractions that expel it through the vagina. The device is most likely to be expelled during menstruation, so users are advised to check their sanitary napkins or tampons before discarding them. Women who use IUDs are advised to check the string several times a month to ensure that the IUD is in place. Spontaneous expulsions occur in 2% to 10% of users within the first year of use (Stewart, 1998). Women who have not borne children have a higher expulsion rate (about 7%) than women who have (3%) (Reinisch, 1990). Some family-planning clinics advise women to supplement their use of IUDs with other devices for the first three months, when the risks of a shift in position or expulsion are greatest.

Anti-inflammatory drugs, such as aspirin, and antibiotics can also decrease IUD effectiveness. Since many physicians recommend an aspirin every other day as a way of helping to prevent certain kinds of cancer (Marcus, 1995), women are advised to discuss these issues with their gynecologists.

REVERSIBILITY IUDs can be removed readily by professionals. Nine out of ten former IUD users who wish to do so become pregnant within a year (Reinisch, 1990).

ADVANTAGES AND DISADVANTAGES   The IUD has three major advantages: (1) it is highly effective; (2) it does not diminish sexual spontaneity or sexual sensations; and (3) once in place, the woman need not do anything more to prevent pregnancy (other than check that it remains in place). The small risk of failure is reduced in effect to zero if the couple also use an additional form of birth control, such as the diaphragm or condom.

The IUD also does not interfere with the woman's normal hormonal production. Users continue to produce pituitary hormones that stimulate ovarian follicles to mature and rupture, thereby releasing mature ova and producing female sex hormones.

If IUDs are so effective and relatively "maintenance free," why are they not more popular? One reason is that insertion can be painful. Another reason is side effects. The most common side effects are excessive menstrual cramping, irregular bleeding (spotting) between periods, and heavier than usual menstrual bleeding (Reinisch, 1990). These usually occur shortly after insertion and are among the primary reasons women ask to have the device removed. A more serious concern is the possible risk of pelvic inflammatory disease (PID), a serious disease that can become life threatening if left untreated (Stewart, 1998). Women who use the IUD may have an increased risk of PID (Cates, 1998). The risk of infection is associated more with the insertion of the device (bacteria may enter the woman's reproductive tract during insertion) than with use of the device itself (Cates, 1998).

PID can produce scar tissue that blocks the fallopian tubes, causing infertility. Women with pelvic infections should not use an IUD (Stewart, 1998). Women who have risk factors for PID might also wish to consider the advisability of an IUD. Risk factors include a recent episode of gonorrhea or chlamydia, recurrent episodes of these STIs, sexual contact with multiple partners, or sexual contact with a partner who has had multiple sexual partners. All in all, the IUD might be best suited to women who have completed their families and are advised not to use oral contraceptives (Mishell, 1989).

Another risk in using an IUD is that the device might perforate (tear) the uterine or cervical walls, which can cause bleeding, pain, and adhesions and become life threatening. Perforations are usually caused by improper insertion and occur in perhaps 1 case in 1,000 (Reinisch, 1990). IUD users are also at greater risk for ectopic pregnancies, both during and after usage, and for miscarriage. Ectopic pregnancies occur in about 5% of women who become pregnant while using an IUD (Cole, 1989). IUD use is not recommended for women with a history of ectopic pregnancy (Cole, 1989). Women who become pregnant while using the IUD stand about a 50–50 chance of miscarriage (Stewart, 1998).

Despite the fact that the IUD irritates uterine tissues, there is no evidence that IUD users run a greater risk of cancer. Long-term data on the health effects of IUD use are limited, however.

Another drawback to the IUD is its cost. The typical cost of an IUD insertion in family planning clinic is a few hundred dollars. Potential expulsion of the IUD presents yet another disadvantage. Moreover, the IUD, like the pill, offers no protection against STIs. Finally, like the pill, the IUD places the burden of contraception entirely on the woman.

The Diaphragm

Diaphragms were once used by about one third of U.S. couples who practiced birth control. When invented in 1882, they were a breakthrough. Their popularity declined only in the 1960s with the advent of the pill and the IUD. Today, only 1 married White woman in 20 and 1 married African American woman in 50 under the age of 44 regularly use the diaphragm (U.S. Bureau of the Census, 1990). Overall, 3% of U.S. women using reversible forms of contraception use the diaphragm (Angier, 1993b).

Diaphragm A shallow rubber cup or dome, fitted to the contour of a woman's vagina, that is coated with a spermicide and inserted before coitus to prevent conception.

Rubber dome

Coil spring

Spermicide

Diaphragm

figure 12.2

A Diaphragm. The diaphragm is a shallow cup or dome made of latex. Diaphragms must be fitted to the contour of the vagina by a health professional. The diaphragm forms a barrier to sperm but should be used in conjunction with a spermicidal cream or jelly.

The diaphragm is a shallow cup or dome made of thin latex rubber (see Figure 12.2). The rim is a flexible metal ring covered with rubber. Diaphragms come in different sizes to allow a precise fit.

Diaphragms are available by prescription and must be fitted to the contour of the vagina by a health professional. Several sizes and types of diaphragms may be tried during a fitting. Women practice insertion in a health professional's office so that they can be guided as needed.

HOW IT WORKS The diaphragm is inserted and removed by the woman, much like a tampon. It is akin to a condom in that it forms a barrier against sperm when placed snugly over the cervical opening. Yet it is unreliable as a barrier alone. Therefore, the diaphragm should be used in conjunction with a spermicidal cream or jelly. The diaphragm's main function is to keep the spermicide in place.

HOW IT IS USED The diaphragm should be inserted no more than two hours before coitus, since the spermicides that are used may begin to lose effectiveness beyond this time. Though some health professionals suggest that the diaphragm may be inserted up to six hours before intercourse, it seems reasonable to err on the side of caution and assume that there is a two-hour time limit. The woman or her partner places a tablespoonful of spermicidal cream or jelly on the inside of the cup and spreads it inside the rim. (Cream spread outside the rim might cause the diaphragm to slip.) The woman opens the inner lips of the vagina with one hand and folds the diaphragm with the other by squeezing the ring. She inserts the diaphragm against the cervix, with the inner side facing upward (see Figure 12.3). Her partner can help to insert the diaphragm, but the woman is advised to check its placement. Some women prefer a plastic insertion device, but most find it easier to insert the diaphragm without it. The diaphragm should be left in place *at least six hours* to allow the spermicide to kill any remaining sperm in the vagina (Hatcher et al., 1998). It should not be left in place for longer than 24 hours, to guard against toxic shock syndrome (TSS).

After use, the diaphragm should be washed with mild soap and warm water and stored in a dry, cool place. When cared for properly, a diaphragm can last about two years. Women might need to be refitted after pregnancy or a change in weight of about ten pounds or more.

EFFECTIVENESS If the diaphragm is used consistently and correctly, its failure rate is estimated to be 6% during the first year of use (see Table 12.1). In typical use, however, the failure rate is believed to be three times as high—18%. Some women become pregnant because they do not use the diaphragm during every coital experience. Others insert it too early or do not leave it in long enough. The diaphragm might not fit well, or it might slip—especially if the couple is acrobatic. A diaphragm can develop tiny holes or cracks. Women are advised to inspect the diaphragm for signs of wear and consult their health professionals when in doubt. Effectiveness also is seriously compromised when the diaphragm is not used along with a correctly applied spermicide (Trussell et al., 1993).

REVERSIBILITY The effects of the diaphragm are fully reversible. To become pregnant, the woman simply stops using it. The diaphragm has not been shown to influence subsequent fertility.

ADVANTAGES AND DISADVANTAGES The major advantage of the diaphragm is that when used correctly, it is a safe and effective means of birth control and does not alter the woman's hormone production or reproductive cycle. The diaphragm can be used as needed, whereas the pill must be used daily and the IUD remains in place whether or not the woman engages in coitus. Another advantage is the virtual absence of side effects. The few women who are allergic to the rubber in the diaphragm can switch to a plastic

figure 12.3

Insertion and Checking of the Diaphragm. Women are instructed in insertion of the diaphragm by a health professional. In practice, a woman and her partner might find joint insertion an erotic experience.

Uterus

Cervix

Vagina

Diaphragm

Insertion of diaphragm

model. Some writers have argued that that spermicides that contain nonoxynol-9 could provide some protection against STIs, including HIV/AIDS, genital herpes, trichomoniasis ("trich"), syphilis, and chlamydia (Reinisch, 1990). Yet a recent controlled experiment in Africa did not find that nonoxynol-9 afforded any protection against disease-causing agents (Roddy et al., 1998).

The major disadvantage is the high pregnancy rate associated with typical use. Nearly one in five typical users (18%) of the diaphragm combined with spermicidal cream or jelly becomes pregnant during the first year of use (Hatcher et al., 1998). Another disadvantage is the need to insert the diaphragm before intercourse, which the couple might find disruptive. Another disadvantage is that the woman's partner might find the taste of the spermicides used in conjunction with the diaphragm to be unpleasant during oral sex. The pressure exerted by the diaphragm against the vaginal and cervical walls can also irritate the urinary tract and cause urinary or even vaginal infections. Switching to a different size of diaphragm or one with a different type of rim might help to alleviate this problem. About 1 woman or man in 20 develops allergies to the particular spermicide that is used, which can lead to irritation of the genitals. This problem can also be alleviated by switching to another brand.

Spermicides

Spermicides are chemical agents that kill sperm. They come in different forms, including jellies and creams, suppositories, aerosol foam, and a contraceptive film. Spermicides should be left in place in the vagina (no douching) for *at least six to eight hours* after coitus (Cates & Raymond, 1998).

figure 12.4

The Application of Spermicidal Foam. Spermicidal jellies and creams come in tubes with plastic applicators. Spermicidal foam comes in a pressurized can and is applied with a plastic applicator in much the same way as spermicidal jellies and creams.

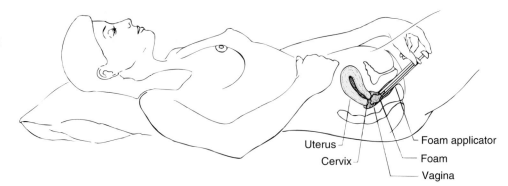

Uterus — ⌐ Foam applicator
Cervix — — Foam
— Vagina

HOW THEY ARE USED   Spermicidal jellies, creams, foam, and suppositories should be used no more than 60 minutes before coitus to provide for maximum effectiveness (Cates & Raymond, 1998). Spermicidal jellies and creams come in tubes with plastic applicators that introduce the spermicide into the vagina (see Figure 12.4). Spermicidal foam is a fluffy white cream with the consistency of shaving cream. It is contained in a pressurized can and is introduced with a plastic applicator in much the same way as spermicidal jellies and creams.

Vaginal suppositories are inserted into the upper vagina, near the cervix, where they release spermicide as they dissolve. Unlike spermicidal jellies, creams, and foam, which become effective immediately when applied, suppositories must be inserted no less than 10 to 15 minutes before coitus so that they have sufficient time to dissolve (Cates & Raymond, 1998).

Spermicidal film consists of thin, two-inch-square sheets that are saturated with spermicide. When placed in the vagina, they dissolve into a gel and release the spermicide. The spermicidal film should be inserted at least five minutes before intercourse to allow it time to melt and for the spermicide to be dispersed. It remains effective for upwards of one hour. One disadvantage of the film that some users have noted is a tendency for it to adhere to the fingertips, which makes it difficult to insert correctly.

HOW THEY WORK   Spermicides coat the cervical opening, blocking the passage of sperm and killing sperm by chemical action.

EFFECTIVENESS   In typical use, the first-year failure rate of spermicides used alone is 21 pregnancies per year per 100 users (Cates & Raymond, 1998; Reinisch, 1990). When used correctly and consistently, the failure rate is estimated to drop to about 6 pregnancies per 100 users in the first year. All forms of spermicide are more effective when they are combined with other forms of contraception, such as the condom.

REVERSIBILITY   Spermicides have not been linked with any changes in reproductive potential. So couples who wish to become pregnant simply stop using them.

ADVANTAGES AND DISADVANTAGES   The major advantages of spermicides are that they do not alter the woman's natural biological processes and are applied only as needed. Unlike a diaphragm, they do not require a doctor's prescription or a fitting. They can be bought in virtually any drugstore, and the average cost per use of the foam variety is modest—about 50 cents.

The major disadvantage is the high failure rate among typical users. Foam often fails when the can is not shaken enough, when too little is used, when it is not applied deeply enough within the vagina near the cervix, or when it is used after coitus had begun.

Spermicides are generally free of side effects but occasionally cause vaginal or penile irritation. Irritation is sometimes alleviated by changing brands. Some partners find the taste of spermicides unpleasant. (Couples can engage in oral sex before applying spermicides.) Spermicides can pose a danger to an embryo, so women who suspect that they are pregnant are advised to suspend use of spermicides until they find out for certain.

The Cervical Cap

The cervical cap, like the diaphragm, is a dome-shaped rubber cup. It comes in different sizes and must be fitted by a health professional. It is smaller than the diaphragm, however—about the size of a thimble—and is meant to fit snugly over the cervical opening.

HOW IT IS USED   Like the diaphragm, the cap is intended to be used with a spermicide applied inside it (Hatcher et al., 1998). When inserting it, the woman (or her partner) fills the cap about a third full of spermicide. Then, squeezing the edges together, the woman inserts the cap high in the vagina so that it presses firmly against the cervix. The woman can test the fit by running a finger around the cap to ensure that the cervical opening is covered. It should be left in place for at least 8 hours after intercourse. The cap provides continuous protection for upwards of 48 hours without the need for additional spermicide. To reduce the risk of toxic shock syndrome, the cap should not be left in place longer than 48 hours. Like the diaphragm, the cap should be cleaned after use and checked for wear and tear. When cared for properly, the cap should last for at least three years.

HOW IT WORKS   Like the diaphragm, the cervical cap forms a barrier and also holds spermicide in place against the cervix. It prevents sperm from passing into the uterus and fallopian tubes and kills sperm by chemical action.

EFFECTIVENESS   The failure rate of the cervical cap in typical use is estimated to be high, ranging from 18% in women who have not borne children to 36% in women who have (Hatcher et al., 1998). Failures may be attributed, at least in part, to the cap's becoming dislodged and to changes in the cervix during the menstrual cycle, which can cause the cap to fit less snugly over the cervix.

REVERSIBILITY   There is no evidence that the cervical cap affects fertility.

ADVANTAGES AND DISADVANTAGES   Like the diaphragm, the cap is a mechanical device that does not affect the woman's hormonal production or reproductive cycle. The cap might be especially suited to women who cannot support a diaphragm because of lack of vaginal muscle tone. Because of concern that the cap may irritate cervical tissue, however, Mishell (1989) recommends that repeat Pap tests be performed on users.

Some women find the cap uncomfortable. The cap can also become dislodged during sexual activity or lose its fit as the cervix changes during the menstrual cycle. Reported side effects include urinary tract infections and allergic reactions or sensitivities to the rubber or spermicide. Other potential disadvantages include the expense and inconvenience of being fitted by a health professional. Moreover, some women are shaped so that the cap does not remain in place. For these reasons, and because they may be hard to obtain, cervical caps are not very popular in the United States (Reinisch, 1990).

The effectiveness of the cervical cap is considerably greater among women who have not given birth (Trussell et al., 1993). Women who have given birth might wish to consult their gynecologists concerning the suitability of the cap.

Condoms

Condoms are also called "rubbers," "safes," **prophylactics** (because latex condoms protect against STIs), and "skins" (referring to those that are made from lamb intestines). Condoms lost popularity with the advent of the pill and the IUD. They are less effective

Prophylactic An agent that protects against disease.

than the pill or IUD, may disrupt sexual spontaneity, and can decrease coital sensations because they prevent the penis from actually touching the vaginal wall.

Condoms have been making a comeback, however, because those made of latex rubber can help to prevent the spread of the AIDS virus (the *human immunodeficiency virus* [HIV]) and other STIs and, to a lesser extent, because of concerns about side effects of the pill and the IUD. Largely because of concerns about AIDS and other STIs, use of condoms among unmarried women jumped from 18% in 1987 to 33% in 1992 (Forrest & Fordyce, 1993). Unmarried women are more likely to report using condoms than are married women (33% versus 19%). Overall, 17% of U.S. women who use reversible forms of contraception use condoms (Angier, 1993b).

Condom advertisements have appeared in mainstream media, including magazines such as *People* and *Cosmopolitan*, and on major TV networks. In a TV commercial, a man and a woman are shown hurriedly undressing. The man tells the woman that he forgot to bring a condom with him. She then tells him that he'd best forget it (making love, that is). Whether the media campaign will increase condom usage remains to be seen.

The renewed popularity of condoms has also been spurred by the increased assertiveness of contemporary women. They make the point (which should be obvious, but all too often is not) that contraception is as much the man's responsibility as the woman's. Condoms alter the psychology of sexual relations. By using a condom, the man assumes much of the responsibility for contraception. Condoms are the only contraceptive device worn by men and the only readily reversible method of contraception that is available to men. Condoms are inexpensive and can be obtained without prescription from pharmacies, family-planning clinics, rest rooms, and even vending machines in some college dormitories.

Some condoms are made of latex rubber. Thinner, more expensive condoms ("skins") are made from the intestinal membranes of lambs. The latter allow greater sexual sensation but do not protect as well against STIs. Only latex condoms are effective against the tiny AIDS virus. Condoms made of animal intestines have pores that are large enough to permit the AIDS virus and other viruses, such as the one that causes hepatitis B, to slip through (Consumer's Union, 1995). A few condoms are made from other materials, such as plastic (polyurethane). Questions remain about the effectiveness of polyurethane condoms (Consumer's Union, 1995). Some condoms have plain ends. Others have nipples or reservoirs (see Figure 12.5) that catch semen and may help to prevent the condom from bursting during ejaculation.

HOW THEY WORK   A condom is a cylindrical sheath that serves as a barrier, preventing the passage of sperm and disease-carrying microorganisms from the man to his partner. It also helps to prevent infected vaginal fluids (and microorganisms) from entering the man's urethral opening or from penetrating through small cracks in the skin of the penis.

figure 12.5

Condoms. Some condoms are plain-tipped; others have nipples or reservoirs that catch semen and may help to prevent the condom from bursting during ejaculation. Latex condoms form effective barriers to the tiny AIDS virus.

HOW THEY ARE USED   The condom is rolled onto the penis once erection is achieved and before contact between the penis and the vagina (see Figure 12.6). If the condom is *not* used until moments before the point of ejaculation, sperm-carrying fluid from the Cowper's glands or from preorgasmic spasms might already have passed into the vagina. Nor does the condom afford protection against STIs if it is fitted after penetration.

Condoms sometimes fall off or break. Between 1% and 2% of condoms break or fall off during intercourse or during withdrawal of the penis afterward (Warner & Hatcher, 1998). Condoms also sometimes slip down the shaft of the penis without falling off. To use a condom most effectively and to help prevent it from either breaking or falling off, a couple should observe the following guidelines:[1]

■ Use a condom each and every time you have intercourse. Inexperienced users should also practice putting on a condom before they have the occasion to use one with a partner.

■ Handle the condom carefully, making sure not to damage it with your fingernail, teeth, or sharp objects.

■ Place the condom on the erect penis before it touches the vulva.

■ Uncircumcised men should pull back the foreskin before putting on the condom.

■ If you use a spermicide, place some inside the tip of the condom before placing the condom on the penis. You might also wish to use an applicator to insert additional spermicide inside the vagina to provide extra protection, especially in the event of breakage of the condom.

■ Do not pull the condom tightly against the tip of the penis.

■ For a condom without a reservoir tip, leave a small empty space—about a half-inch—at the end of the condom to hold semen, but do not allow any air to be trapped at the tip. Some condoms come equipped with a reservoir (nipple) tip that will hold semen.

■ Unroll the condom all the way to the base of the penis.

■ Ensure that adequate vaginal lubrication during intercourse is present, possibly using lubricants if necessary. But use only water-based lubricants such as contraceptive jelly or K-Y jelly. Never use an oil-based lubricant that can weaken the latex material, such as petroleum jelly (Vaseline), cold cream, baby oil or lotion, mineral oil, massage oil, vegetable oil, Crisco, hand or body lotions, and most skin creams. Do not use saliva as a lubricant because it might contain infectious organisms, such as viruses.

■ If the condom breaks during intercourse, withdraw the penis immediately, put on a new condom, and use more spermicide.

■ After ejaculation, carefully withdraw the penis while it is still erect.

■ Hold the rim of the condom firmly against the base of the penis as the penis is withdrawn, to prevent the condom from slipping off.

■ Remove the condom carefully from the penis, making sure that semen doesn't leak out.

■ Check the removed condom for tears or cracks. If any are found, immediately apply a spermicide containing nonoxynol-9 directly to the penis and within the vagina. Wrap the used condom in a tissue, and discard it in the garbage. (Condoms can be hard to flush down the toilet.) Wash your hands thoroughly with soap and water.

figure 12.6

Applying a Condom. First the rolled-up condom is placed on the head of the penis, and then it is rolled down the shaft of the penis. If a condom without a reservoir tip is used, a half-inch space should be left at the tip for the ejaculate to accumulate.

---

[1]Adapted from the Centers for Disease Control pamphlet, *Condoms and Sexually Transmitted Diseases . . . Especially AIDS* (HHS Publication FDA 90–4329) and other sources.

Since condoms can be eroded by exposure to body heat or other sources of heat, they should not be kept for any length of time in a pocket or the glove compartment of a car. Nor should a condom be used more than once. Here are some other things that you should *never* do with a condom:

- Never use teeth, scissors, or sharp fingernails to open a package of condoms. Open the condom package carefully to avoid tearing or puncturing the condom.
- Never test a condom by inflating it or stretching it.
- Never use a condom after its expiration date.
- Never use damaged condoms. Condoms that are sticky, gummy, discolored, or brittle, that appear otherwise damaged, or that show signs of deterioration should be considered damaged.
- Never use a condom if the sealed packet containing the condom is damaged, cracked, or brittle, as the condom itself may be damaged or defective.
- Do not open the sealed packet until you are ready to use the condom. A condom contained in a packet that has been opened can become dry and brittle within a few hours, causing it to tear more easily. The box that contains the condom packets, however, may be opened at any time.
- Never use the same condom twice. Use a new condom if you switch the site of intercourse, such as from the vagina to the anus or from the anus to the mouth, during a single sexual act.
- If you want to carry a condom with you, place it in a loose jacket pocket or purse, not in your pants pocket or in a wallet held in your pants pocket, where it might be exposed to body heat.
- Never buy condoms from vending machines that are exposed to extreme heat or placed in direct sunlight.

EFFECTIVENESS In typical use, the failure rate of the male condom is estimated at 12% (see Table 12.1). That is, 12 women out of 100 whose partners rely on condoms alone for contraception can expect to become pregnant during the first year of use. This rate drops dramatically if the condom is used correctly and combined with the use of a spermicide (Warner & Hatcher, 1998). The effectiveness of a condom and spermicide combined rivals that of the birth-control pill when they are used correctly and consistently.

REVERSIBILITY The condom is simply a mechanical barrier to sperm and does not compromise fertility. Therefore, a couple who wish to conceive a child simply discontinue its use.

ADVANTAGES AND DISADVANTAGES Condoms have the advantage of being readily available. They can be purchased without prescription. They require no fitting and can remain in sealed packages until needed. They are readily discarded after use. The combination of condoms and spermicides containing the ingredient nonoxynol-9 increases contraceptive effectiveness. Some condoms contain this spermicidal agent as a lubricant. When in doubt, ask a pharmacist.

Condoms do not affect production of hormones, ova, or sperm. Women whose partners use condoms ovulate normally. Men who use them produce sperm and ejaculate normally. With all these advantages, why are condoms not more popular?

One disadvantage of the condom is that it can render sex less spontaneous. The couple must interrupt lovemaking to apply the condom. Condoms can also lessen sexual sensations, especially for the man. Latex condoms do so more than animal membrane sheaths. Condoms also sometimes slip off or tear, allowing sperm to leak through.

On the other hand, condoms are almost entirely free of side effects (an advantage reported by 70% of female respondents [Consumer's Union, 1995]). They offer protection against STIs that is unparalleled among contraceptive devices. They can also be used without prior medical consultation. Both partners can share putting on the condom, making it an erotic part of their lovemaking, not an intrusion. The use of textured or ultrathin condoms can increase sensitivity, especially for the male. Therefore, many couples find that advantages outweigh disadvantages. Sex in the age of AIDS has given condoms a new respectability, even a certain trendiness. Notice, for example, the new "designer colors" and styles on display at your local pharmacy. Advertisers now also target women in their ads, suggesting that women, like men, can come prepared with condoms.

It is tempting to claim that the condom has a perfect safety record and no side effects. Let us settle for "close to perfect." Some people have allergic reactions to the spermicides with which some lubricated condoms are coated or that the woman may apply. In such cases, the couple might need to use a condom without a spermicidal lubricant or stop using supplemental spermicides. Some people are allergic to latex.

Women have an absolute right to insist that their male sex partners wear latex condoms if their partners are not latex-sensitive. STIs such as gonorrhea and chlamydia (see Chapter 16) do far more damage to a woman's reproductive tract than to a man's. Condoms can help to protect women from vaginitis, pelvic inflammatory disease (PID), infections that can harm a fetus or cause infertility, and most important, AIDS.

Douching

Many couples believe that if a woman **douches** shortly after coitus, she will not become pregnant. Women who douche for contraceptive purposes often use syringes to flush the vagina with water or a spermicidal agent. The water is intended to wash sperm out; the spermicides, to kill them. Douching is ineffective, however, because large numbers of sperm move beyond the range of the douche seconds after ejaculation. In addition, squirting a liquid into the vagina might even propel sperm *toward* the uterus. Douching has a failure rate among typical users of 40% at best (Reinisch, 1990), too high to be considered reliable.

Regular douching might also alter the natural chemistry of the vagina, increasing the risk of vaginal infection. In short, douching is a "nonmethod" of contraception.

Withdrawal (Coitus Interruptus)

Withdrawal means that the man removes his penis from the vagina before ejaculating. Withdrawal has a first-year failure rate among typical users of about 20% (Kowal, 1998; Reinisch, 1990). There are several reasons for these failures. The man might not withdraw in time. Even if the penis is withdrawn just before ejaculation, some ejaculate might still fall on the vaginal lips, and sperm might find their way to the fallopian tubes. Active sperm can also be present in the *pre*-ejaculatory secretions of fluid from the Cowper's glands, a discharge of which the man is usually unaware and cannot control. These sperm are capable of fertilizing an ovum even if the man withdraws before orgasm. Because of its unreliability and high failure rate, withdrawal, like douching, is a nonmethod of contraception.

Fertility Awareness Methods (Rhythm Methods)

Fertility awareness, or *rhythm*, methods rely on awareness of the fertile segments of the woman's menstrual cycle. Terms such as *natural birth control* and *natural family planning* also refer to these methods. The essence of such methods is that coitus is avoided on days when conception is most likely. Fertility awareness methods are used by about 3% of married women ages 15 to 44 but by less than 1% of single women (U.S. Bureau of the Census, 1990). Women between the ages of 25 and 44 are more than twice as likely as 15- to 24-year-olds to use rhythm methods. Since the rhythm method does not employ artificial devices, it is acceptable to the Roman Catholic Church.

Douche To rinse or wash the vaginal canal by inserting a liquid and allowing it to drain out.

HOW THEY WORK   A number of rhythm methods are used to predict the likelihood of conception. They are the mirror images of the methods that couples use to increase their chances of conceiving (see Chapter 11). Methods for enhancing the chances of conception seek to predict the time of ovulation so that the couple can arrange to have sperm present in the woman's reproductive tract at about that time. As methods of *birth control*, rhythm methods seek to predict ovulation so that the couple can *abstain* from coitus when the woman is fertile.

THE CALENDAR METHOD   The **calendar method** assumes that ovulation occurs 14 days before menstruation. The couple abstains from intercourse during the period that begins three days prior to day 13 (because sperm are unlikely to survive for more than 72 hours in the female reproductive tract) and ends two days after day 15 (because an unfertilized ovum is unlikely to remain receptive to fertilization for longer than 48 hours). The period of abstention thus covers days 10 to 17 of the woman's cycle.

When a woman has regular 28-day cycles, predicting the period of abstention is relatively straightforward. Women with irregular cycles are generally advised to chart their cycles for 10 to 12 months to determine their shortest and longest cycles. The first day of menstruation counts as day 1 of the cycle. The last day of the cycle is the day preceding the onset of menstruation.

Consider a woman whose cycles vary from 23 to 33 days. In theory, she will ovulate 14 days before menstruation begins. (To be safe, she should assume that ovulation will take place anywhere from 13 to 15 days before her period.) Applying the rule of "three days before and two days after," she should avoid coitus from day 5 of her cycle, which corresponds to three days before her earliest expected ovulation (computed by subtracting 15 days from the 23 days of her shortest cycle and then subtracting 3 days), through day 22, which corresponds to two days after her latest expected ovulation (computed by subtracting 13 days from the 33 days of her longest cycle and then adding 2 days). Another way of determining this period of abstention would be to subtract 18 days from the woman's shortest cycle to determine the start of the "unsafe" period and 11 days from her longest cycle to determine the last "unsafe" day. The woman in the example has irregular cycles. She thus faces an 18-day abstention period each month—quite a burden for a sexually active couple.

Most women who follow the calendar method need to abstain from coitus for at least 10 days during the middle of each cycle (Reinisch, 1990). Moreover, the calendar method cannot ensure that the woman's longest or shortest menstrual cycles will occur during the 10- to 12-month period of baseline tracking. Some women, too, have such irregular cycles that the range of "unsafe" days cannot be predicted reliably even if baseline tracking is extended.

THE BASAL BODY TEMPERATURE (BBT) METHOD   In the **basal body temperature (BBT) method,** the woman tracks her body temperature upon awakening each morning to detect the small changes that occur directly before and after ovulation. A woman's basal body temperature sometimes dips slightly just before ovulation and then tends to rise between 0.4 and 0.8 degree Fahrenheit just before, during, and after ovulation. It remains elevated until the onset of menstruation. (The rise in temperature is caused by the increased production of progesterone by the corpus luteum during the luteal phase of the cycle.) Thermometers that provide finely graded readings, such as electronic thermometers, are best suited for determining minor changes. A major problem with the BBT method is that it does not indicate the several *unsafe* preovulatory days during which sperm deposited in the vagina can remain viable. Rather, the BBT method indicates when a woman *has* ovulated. Therefore, many women use the calendar method to predict the number of "safe" days before ovulation and the BBT method to determine the number of "unsafe" days after. A woman would avoid coitus during the "unsafe" preovulatory period (as determined by the calendar method) and then for three days when her temperature rises and remains elevated. A drawback of the BBT method is that changes in body temperature may also result from factors unrelated to ovulation, such as infections, sleep-

Calendar method A fertility awareness (rhythm) method of contraception that relies on prediction of ovulation by tracking menstrual cycles, typically for a 10- to 12-month period, and assuming that ovulation occurs 14 days before menstruation.

Basal body temperature (BBT) method A fertility awareness method of contraception that relies on prediction of ovulation by tracking the woman's temperature during the course of the menstrual cycle.

lessness, or stress. So some women triple-check themselves by also tracking their cervical mucus.

THE CERVICAL MUCUS (OVULATION) METHOD   The **ovulation method** tracks changes in the **viscosity** of the cervical mucus. After menstruation, the vagina feels rather dry. There is also little or no discharge from the cervix. These dry days are relatively safe. Then a mucous discharge appears in the vagina that is first thick and sticky and is white or cloudy in color. Coitus (or unprotected coitus) should be avoided at the first sign of any mucous. As the cycle progresses, the mucus discharge thins and clears, becoming slippery or stringy, like raw egg white. These are the **peak days.** This mucus discharge, called the *ovulatory mucus,* may be accompanied by a feeling of vaginal lubrication or wetness. Ovulation takes place about a day after the last peak day (about four days after this ovulatory mucus first appears). Then the mucus becomes cloudy and tacky once more. Intercourse may resume four days after the last peak day.

One problem with the mucus method is that some women have difficulty detecting changes in the mucus discharge. Such changes may also result from infections, certain medications, or contraceptive creams, jellies, or foam. Sexual arousal may also induce changes in viscosity.

OVULATION PREDICTION KITS   Predicting ovulation is more accurate with an ovulation prediction kit. Kits allow women to test their urine daily for the presence of luteinizing hormone (LH). LH levels surge about 12 to 24 hours before ovulation. Ovulation prediction kits are more accurate than the BBT method. Some couples use the kits to enhance their chances of conceiving a child by engaging in coitus when ovulation appears imminent. Others use them as a means of birth control to find out when to avoid coitus. When used correctly, ovulation prediction kits are between 95% to 100% accurate (Reinisch, 1990).

Ovulation kits are expensive and require that the woman's urine be tested each morning. Nor do they reveal the full range of the unsafe *pre*ovulatory period during which sperm may remain viable in the vagina. A couple might therefore choose to use the kits to determine the unsafe period following ovulation and the calendar method to determine the unsafe period preceding ovulation.

EFFECTIVENESS   The estimated first-year failure rate in typical use is 20%, which is high but no higher than the use of contraceptive devices such as the cervical cap or the female condom (see Table 12.1). Still, perhaps one in five typical users will become pregnant during the first year of use. (You might have heard the joke "What do you call people who use the rhythm method? Parents!") Fewer failures occur when these methods are applied conscientiously, when a combination of rhythm methods is used, and when the woman's cycles are quite regular. Restricting coitus to the postovulatory period can reduce the pregnancy rate to 1% (Jennings et al., 1998). The trick is to determine when ovulation occurs. The pregnancy rate can be reduced to practically zero if rhythm methods are used with other forms of birth control, such as the condom or diaphragm.

ADVANTAGES AND DISADVANTAGES   Because they are a natural form of birth control, rhythm methods appeal to many people who, for religious or other reasons, prefer not to use artificial means. Since no devices or chemicals are used, there are no side effects. Nor do they cause any loss of sensation, as condoms do. Nor is there disruption of lovemaking, as with condoms, diaphragms, or foam, although lovemaking could be said to be quite disrupted during the period of abstention. Rhythm methods are inexpensive, except for ovulation prediction kits. Both partners can share the responsibility for rhythm methods. The man, for example, can take his partner's temperature or assist with the charting. All rhythm methods are fully reversible.

A disadvantage is the fact that the reliability of rhythm methods is low. Rhythm methods may be unsuitable for women who have irregular cycles. Women with irregular cycles

---

Ovulation method A fertility awareness method of contraception that relies on prediction of ovulation by tracking the viscosity of the cervical mucus.

Viscosity Stickiness, consistency.

Peak days The days during the menstrual cycle during which a woman is most likely to be fertile.

who ovulate as early as a week after their menstrual flows can become pregnant even if they engage in unprotected intercourse only when they are menstruating, since some sperm remaining in a woman's reproductive tract may survive for up to eight days and fertilize an ovum that is released at that time (Reinisch, 1990). Moreover, the rhythm method requires abstaining from coitus for several days, or perhaps weeks, each month. Rhythm methods also require that records of the menstrual cycle be kept for many months before implementation. Unlike diaphragms, condoms, or spermicides, rhythm methods cannot be used at a moment's notice. Finally, rhythm methods do not offer any protection against STIs.

Sterilization

Many people decide to be sterilized when they plan to have no children or no more children. With the exception of abstinence, sterilization is the most effective form of contraception. Yet the prospect of **sterilization** arouses strong feelings because a person is transformed all at once, and presumably permanently, from someone who might be capable of bearing children to someone who cannot. This transformation often involves a profound change in self-concept. These feelings are especially strong in men and women who link fertility to their sense of masculinity or femininity.

Still, more than a million sterilizations are performed in the United States each year. Sterilization is the most widely used form of birth control among married couples age 30 and above (Reinisch, 1990). In a 1992 national sample of nearly 7,000 women ages 15 to 50, 19% of the respondents reported being sterilized; 12% reported having partners who had undergone a vasectomy. Married women were far more likely to rely on a permanent method of contraception (tubal sterilization or vasectomy) than were single women (48% versus 11%).

MALE STERILIZATION   The male sterilization procedure that is used today is the **vasectomy.** About 500,000 vasectomies are performed each year in the United States (Altman, 1993). More than 15% of men in the United States have had vasectomies.

A vasectomy is usually carried out in a doctor's office, under local anesthesia, in 15 to 20 minutes. Small incisions are made in the scrotum. Each vas is cut, a small segment of each is removed, and the ends are tied off or cauterized (to prevent them from growing back together) (see Figure 12.7). Now sperm can no longer reach the urethra. Instead, they are harmlessly reabsorbed by the body.

The man can usually resume sexual relations within a few days. Since some sperm may be present in his reproductive tract for a few weeks, however, he is best advised to use an additional contraceptive method until his ejaculate shows a zero sperm count. Some health professionals recommend that the man have a follow-up sperm count a year after his vasectomy to ensure that the cut ends of each vas deferens have not grown together—a complication that occurs in about 1% of cases (Reinisch, 1990).

Vasectomy does not diminish sex drive or result in any change in sexual arousal, erectile or ejaculatory ability, or sensations of ejaculation. The testes still produce male sex hormones and sperm. Without a passageway to the urethra, however, sperm are no longer expelled with the ejaculate. Since sperm account for only about 1% of the ejaculate, the volume of the ejaculate is not noticeably different.

Though there are no confirmed long-term health risks of vasectomy (Reinisch, 1990), two recent studies of more than 73,000 men who had undergone vasectomies raise concerns that the procedure might not be as risk-free as people generally believe. The studies showed that men who had had vasectomies more than 20 years earlier faced a slightly increased risk of prostate cancer (Altman, 1993a; Giovannucci et al., 1993a, 1993b). The studies found a correlation between vasectomies and the risk of prostate cancer but did not establish a causal connection. It is possible that other factors may explain the greater risk faced by vasectomized men than the vasectomy itself. The results also conflict with earlier studies showing either no link between vasectomies and the risk of prostate cancer or even a *lower* risk among vasectomized men. More research is needed to

Sterilization Surgical procedures that render people incapable of reproduction without affecting sexual activity.

Vasectomy The surgical method of male sterilization in which sperm are prevented from reaching the urethra by cutting each vas deferens and tying it back or cauterizing it.

1. Location of vas deferens

2. Injection of local anesthetic

3. Incision over vas deferens

4. Isolation of vas from surrounding tissue

5. Removal of segment of vas; tying of ends

6. Return of vas to position; incision is closed and process is repeated on the other side

figure 12.7

Vasectomy. The male sterilization procedure is usually carried out in a doctor's office, using local anesthesia. Small incisions are made in the scrotum. Each vas deferens is cut, and the ends are tied off or cauterized to prevent sperm from reaching the urethra. Sperm are harmlessly reabsorbed by the body after the operation.

clarify the relationship between vasectomy and prostate cancer. In the meantime, medical experts recommend that men who have had vasectomies get annual checkups for signs of prostate cancer (Altman, 1993).

The vasectomy is nearly 100% effective. Fewer than 2 pregnancies occur during the first year among 1,000 couples in which the man has undergone a vasectomy (see Table 12.1). The few failures stem from sperm remaining in the male's genital tract shortly after the operation, or the growing together of the segments of a vas deferens.

Reversibility is simple in concept but not in practice. Therefore, vasectomies should be considered permanent. In an operation to reverse a vasectomy, called a **vasovasostomy**, the ends of the vas deferens are sewn together, and in a few days, they grow together. Estimates of success at reversal, as measured by subsequent pregnancies, range from 16% to 79% (Hatcher et al., 1998). Some vasectomized men develop antibodies that attack their own sperm. The production of antibodies does not appear to endanger the man's health (Hatcher et al., 1998), but it might contribute to infertility following reconnection (Reinisch, 1990).

Major studies conducted over a 15-year period revealed no deaths due to vasectomy in the United States (Reinisch, 1990). Few documented complications of vasectomies have been reported in the medical literature. Minor complications are reported in 4% or 5% of cases, however. They typically involve temporary local inflammation or swelling after the operation. Ice packs and anti-inflammatory drugs, such as aspirin, may help to reduce swelling and discomfort. More serious but rarer medical complications include infection of the epididymis (Reinisch, 1990).

Vasovasostomy The surgical method of reversing vasectomy in which the cut or cauterized ends of each vas deferens are sewn together.

The Search Goes On

The search continues—the search for the perfect contraceptive. It is difficult to say precisely what that contraceptive will look like, but it will be safe and effective, and it will not interfere at all with sexual spontaneity or sexual pleasure.

As we cross over into the new millennium, that contraceptive does not yet seem to be within our grasp. However, it does appear that we will be making new advances in mechanical and chemical barrier methods, systems for delivering hormones, intrauterine devices (IUDs), and systemic methods for men (such as a male pill) (Gabelnick, 1998).

MECHANICAL BARRIER METHODS

Mechanical barriers have the advantage of not introducing chemicals into people's circulatory systems. On the other hand, they have sometimes been cumbersome and, in the case of the male condom, can reduce sexual sensations and spontaneity. Moreover, the male condom is "male controlled," and there is the desire for more female-controlled devices. One, the female condom, is already on the market.

The Female Condom

The female condom consists of a polyurethane (plastic) sheath that lines the vagina during intercourse. It is held in place at each end by a flexible plastic ring. The female condom provides a secure but flexible shield that barricades against sperm but allows the penis to move freely within the vagina during coitus. It can be inserted as long as eight hours before intercourse but should be removed immediately afterward (Hatcher et al., 1998). A new one must be used for each act of intercourse.

Like the male condom, the female condom may offer some protection against STIs. Dr. Mary E. Guinan (1992) of the Centers for Disease Control points out that women can use the female condom if their partners refuse to wear a male condom. Cynthia Pearson (1992) of the National Women's Health Network notes that the female condom "for the first time [gives] women control over exposure to sexually transmitted disease, including AIDS."

The female condom (brand name: Reality) carries a warning label that it appears to be less effective than the male latex condom in preventing pregnancies and transmission of STIs. During test trials, the pregnancy rate was estimated to range between 21% and 26% but is estimated to be as low as 5% among cautious users (Hatcher et al., 1998). Evidence on the effectiveness of the female condom in providing protection against STIs is scarce.

Many women complain that the female condom is bulky and difficult to insert (Stewart, 1992). Still, it is the first barrier method of contraception that women control themselves. Naming the device "Reality" suggests that it might be used most widely by women faced with the reality of male partners who refuse to use condoms themselves or who fail to use them consistently or properly. The female condom costs several times as much as the male condom.

Lea's Shield

This diaphragm-like device fits all women. It has a valve that allows air to escape when it it put in place, creating suction that keeps it in close contact with the cervix. The valve permits uterine and cervical fluid to drain but prevents the passage of sperm. It is already being marketed in Canada and Europe.

The Silicone Diaphragm

A diaphragm made of silicone is under development. It promises to be more user-friendly than earlier models—more comfortable and easier to use.

Nonlatex Male Condoms

The latex condom is often not used because it interferes with sexual spontaneity and pleasure. Condoms made of animal intestine provide more sexual sensations but permit the passage of some infectious organisms, including HIV. A polyurethane condom that allows more sexual sensations but prevents passage of HIV is currently on the market, and other nonlatex condoms are under development.

CHEMICAL BARRIER METHODS

New spermicides are under development—chemical barriers that will adhere better to the vaginal wall but provide less irritation. Such devices will take the form of contraceptive film, sponges, and so on. One sponge that is now available in Canada, Protectaid, uses low levels of active ingredients to avoid irritating the woman.

Let us note parenthetically that the search is on for chemical barriers that will kill disease organisms, such as HIV, but not harm sperm. To date, however, the search for a "microbicide" (which kills microorganisms) that does not damage sperm has been elusive.

HORMONAL METHODS

Hormonal methods have excellent track records for women in terms of efficacy and safety. Therefore, there is not much incentive to change them dramatically. Norplant and Depo-Provera have been quite successful with women who might find it burdensome to take a daily pill. New hormone preparations are also under development that take the form of vaginal rings, subdermal implants (like Norplant), suppositories, long-acting injections (like Depo-Provera), and hormone pills or injections for men.

The Vaginal Ring

The vaginal ring can be worn in the vagina for three months before replacement. Shaped like a diaphragm, the ring contains either a combination of estrogen and progestin or progestin only. The hormones are slowly released and pass into the bloodstream through the mucousal lining of the vagina. The vaginal ring is a convenient means of receiving a continuous dose of hormones without having to remember to take a pill. Research on the effectiveness of the vaginal ring is underway.

Improved Implants

Implanon is a single implant containing a progestin that would remain effective for three to four years. Improved versions of Norplant will necessitate fewer rods.

Depo-Provera

Depo-Provera (medroxyprogesterone acetate) is a long-acting, synthetic form of progesterone that works as a contraceptive by inhibiting ovulation. The progesterone signals the pituitary gland in the brain to stop producing hormones that would lead to the release of mature ova by the ovaries. Administered by injection once every three months, Depo-Provera is an effective form of contraception, with reported failure rates of less than 1 pregnancy per 100 women during the first year of use (Hatcher et al., 1998). A World Health Organization study of 12,000 women found no links between the drug and the risk of ovarian or cervical cancer (Walt, 1993). Yet the drug may produce side effects such as weight gain, menstrual irregularity, and spotting between periods (Hatcher et al., 1998). Use of Depo-

Provera has also been linked to osteoporosis, a condition involving bone loss that can cause bones to become brittle and fracture easily.

Designer Hormones

Research is under way to find "designer" hormone preparations that act more specifically to prevent conception without acting on other bodily systems. Designer hormones would have fewer side effects and would carry less risk of fostering the growth of cancerous cells.

Hormonal Methods for Men

The male sex hormone testosterone has shown promise in reducing sperm production ("Male birth control," 1995). The pituitary gland normally stimulates the testes to produce sperm. Testosterone suppresses the pituitary, in turn suppressing sperm production. Men who have received testosterone injections have shown declines in sperm production. Potential complications include an increased risk of prostate cancer. Testosterone also appears to increase cholesterol levels in the bloodstream, which may heighten the risk of cardiovascular disease.

Nevertheless, testosterone delivery systems for men are under development. Eventually, they will provide protection by reducing the sperm count for months or years. Methods that are now being tested in pilot studies involve drawbacks such as long induction periods that require supplementary contraception and also weekly injections—certainly not very user-friendly.

Truth or Fiction?
REVISITED

It is true that testosterone can be used as a male contraceptive. However, side effects and other questions have prevented testosterone from being marketed for such use. ■

One "male pill" that is under development includes testosterone and another hormone called progestogen (Cohen, 1998). This pill is 95% effective in reducing the sperm counts to levels at which impregnation is highly unlikely, and it may be available within a few years. In a University of Edinburgh study, about two of three men said that they would use such a pill is if were safe and effective (Cohen, 1998). Yet a survey of college men in the United States found that only one in five expressed willingness to take a male pill (Laird, 1994). The men believed that taking a male pill would be more of a bother than having one's partner take a female pill and more "contrary to nature"!

OTHER METHODS FOR MEN

Another approach to male contraception was suggested when investigators in China found extremely low birth rates in communities in which cottonseed oil was used in cooking. They extracted a drug from the cotton plant, *gossypol,* which shows promise as a male contraceptive. Chinese studies reveal the drug to be nearly 100% effective in preventing pregnancies. The drug appears to nullify sperm production without affecting hormone levels or the sex drive. However, toxic effects of gossypol have limited its acceptability as a male contraceptive.

Some men are infertile because they produce antibodies that destroy their own sperm. It is also speculated that vasectomy causes some men's bodies to react to their own sperm as foreign substances and produce antibodies. This is an immunological response to sperm. Some researchers have suggested that it might be possible to develop ways to induce the body to produce such antibodies. Ideally, this procedure would be reversible.

Applying ultrasound waves to the testes has been shown to produce reversible sterility in laboratory rats, dogs, and monkeys. No one is quite certain how ultrasound works in inducing temporary sterilization. Moreover, its safety has not been demonstrated. A Chinese researcher has developed an electronic device that emits impulses that kill sperm and make a man sterile for up to a month ("China develops," 1998). The device is gaining some followers in China. It remains to be seen whether interest will spread to the West.

INTRAUTERINE DEVICES (IUDS)

Use of existing IUDs has been connected with problems such as expulsion, cramping, and irritation or perforation of the uterus. Under development is a "frameless" IUD that would eliminate pressure against the uterus (Gabelnick, 1998), thus minimizing cramping. The copper-releasing sleeves would be anchored by a polypropylene thread rather than by a frame.

Mirena, an IUD that is available in Europe, releases the chemical levonorgestrel. It is highly effective and proves up to a decade of protection against conception. Mirena is less likely than other IUDs in use to cause bleeding, and it may be helpful in avoiding PID. Its main disadvantage is that it is much more expensive than copper devices, but it may become available in the United States.

IMMUNOCONTRACEPTIVES

Many chemicals are under development that will cause the body's immune system to prevent fertilization. For example, antigens may be developed for use with women that act on sperm or the zona pellucida of ova.

"Vaccines" are under development for men that shut down production of both sperm and testosterone, or sperm alone. A vaccine that shut down testosterone production would have to be used in conjunction with testosterone supplements, and therefore it would be better to just shut down sperm production. A vaccine based on follicle-stimulating hormone (FSH) might do the job.

THE ULTIMATE CONTRACEPTIVE DEVICE

Wouldn't it be wonderful if people—female or male—could take a pill that would suspend fertility, with no side effects, until they took another pill that reversed the situation and made it possible for them to conceive again? It would be perfectly effective and perfectly safe. It would not interfere with sexual spontaneity. It would be quickly reversible if and when couples changed their minds about conceiving.

That pill is a long way off, but researchers are thinking about it.

A Birth Control Pill for Men. Most current methods of contraception, including "the pill," place the burden of contraception on the woman. One of the "male pills" under development contains the hormones testosterone and progestogen.

In a laparoscopy or so-called "belly-button" operation, the incision is made through the abdomen, usually at the navel.

Laparoscope — Cut tube — Tied or cauterized tube

Fallopian tube

Ovary
Uterus

figure 12.8

Laparoscopy. In this method of female sterilization, the surgeon approaches the fallopian tubes through a small incision in the abdomen just below the navel. A narrow instrument called a laparoscope is inserted through the incision, and a small section of each fallopian tube is cauterized, cut, or clamped to prevent ova from joining with sperm.

Tubal sterilization The most common method of female sterilization, in which the fallopian tubes are surgically blocked to prevent the meeting of sperm and ova. Also called *tubal ligation.*

Minilaparotomy A kind of tubal sterilization in which a small incision is made in the abdomen to provide access to the fallopian tubes.

Laparoscopy Tubal sterilization by means of a *laparoscope,* which is inserted through a small incision just below the navel and used to cauterize, cut, or clamp the fallopian tubes. Sometimes referred to as "belly button surgery."

Culpotomy A kind of tubal sterilization in which the fallopian tubes are approached through an incision in the back wall of the vagina.

Hysterectomy Surgical removal of the uterus. (*Not* appropriate as a method of sterilization.)

FEMALE STERILIZATION Nearly four in ten (39%) married women under the age of 45 have been surgically sterilized (U.S. Bureau of the Census, 1990). **Tubal sterilization,** also called *tubal ligation,* is the most common method of female sterilization. Tubal sterilization prevents ova and sperm from passing through the fallopian tubes. About 650,000 tubal sterilizations are performed each year in the United States (Altman, 1993).

The two main surgical procedures for tubal sterilization are *minilaparotomy* and *laparoscopy.* In a **minilaparotomy,** a small incision is made in the abdomen, just above the pubic hairline, to provide access to the fallopian tubes. Each tube is cut and either tied back or clamped with a clip. In a **laparoscopy** (see Figure 12.8), sometimes called "belly button surgery," the fallopian tubes are approached through a small incision in the abdomen just below the navel. The surgeon uses a narrow, lighted viewing instrument called a *laparoscope* to locate the tubes. A small section of each of the tubes is cauterized, cut, or clamped. The woman usually returns to her daily routine in a few days and can resume coitus when it becomes comfortable. In an alternative sterilization procedure, a **culpotomy,** the fallopian tubes are approached through an incision in the back wall of the vagina.

None of these methods disrupts sex drive or sexual response. Surgical sterilization does not induce premature menopause or alter the woman's production of sex hormones. The menstrual cycle is undisturbed. The unfertilized egg is simply reabsorbed by the body, rather than being sloughed off in the menstrual flow.

A **hysterectomy** also results in sterilization. A hysterectomy is a major operation that is commonly performed because of cancer or other diseases of the reproductive tract; it is inappropriate as a method of sterilization. Hysterectomy carries the risks of major surgery, and when the ovaries are removed along with the uterus, it induces a "surgical menopause" because the woman no longer produces female sex hormones.

Female sterilization is highly effective in preventing pregnancy, although slightly less effective than male sterilization. Overall, about 1 women in 200 (0.4%) is likely to become pregnant in the first year following a tubal sterilization (Hatcher et al., 1998), most likely the result of a failed surgical procedure or an undetected pregnancy at the time of the procedure. Like vasectomy, tubal ligation should be considered irreversible. Reversals are successful, as measured by subsequent pregnancies, in 43% to 88% of cases (Hatcher et al., 1998). Reversal is difficult and costly, however.

Truth or Fiction?
REVISITED

Not all sterilization operations can be surgically reversed; therefore, the Truth-or-Fiction item is too broad to be true. Sterilization is not advised for individuals who believe that they might later change their minds about becoming pregnant. ■

About 2% to 11% of women incur medical complications (Reinisch, 1990). The most common complications are abdominal infections, excessive bleeding, inadvertent punctures of nearby organs, and scarring. The use of general anesthesia (typical in laparoscopies and in some minilaparotomies) poses additional risks, as in any major operation. (Most of the deaths that are attributed to tubal sterilization actually result from the anesthesia [Reinisch, 1990]. The overall death rate is quite small, however: 2 to 5 deaths per 100,000 operations.)

ADVANTAGES AND DISADVANTAGES OF STERILIZATION   The major advantages of sterilization are effectiveness and permanence. Sterilization is nearly 100% effective. After surgery, the couple need not do anything more to prevent conception. The permanence is also its major drawback, however. People sometimes change their minds about wanting to have children.

Sterilization procedures create varying risks of complications following surgery, with women generally incurring greater risks than men. Another disadvantage of sterilization is that it affords no protection against STIs. People who are sterilized might still wish to use condoms and spermicides for protection against STIs.

Reflections

- ■ Have you discussed methods of contraception with your peers? If so, what factors account for your peers' choices?
- ■ Are some or all of the methods of contraception morally or ethically unacceptable to you? Explain.
- ■ Do you believe that your views on contraception are consistent with those of most people from your sociocultural background? Explain.

ABORTION

"When I was young, I felt it myself, that it was wrong to kill a baby," said Maria (cited in Lewin, 1998a). Maria is a 17-year-old Hispanic American high school student who lives in Houston. She is waiting to be seen at an abortion clinic. "But when I got to be a teenager, and started having sex, things looked different. It's more complicated when it's your own life. I want to go to college, and I know that having a baby now, without a husband or anything, would make that very hard."

Maria is not all that unusual among young people in the United States today. Abortion has little to do with politics to her. The *Roe* v. *Wade* decision occurred eight years before Maria was born. Like half the adults in the United States, Maria believes that abortion is murder (Goldberg & Elder, 1998). But like one third of the Americans who say that abortion is murder, Maria believes that abortion is an acceptable solution to a very bad situation.

An **induced abortion** (in contrast to a spontaneous abortion, or miscarriage) is the purposeful termination of a pregnancy. Perhaps more than any other contemporary social issue, induced abortion (hereafter referred to simply as abortion) has divided neighbors and family members into opposing camps.

Induced abortion The purposeful termination of a pregnancy before the embryo or fetus is capable of sustaining independent life. (From the Latin *abortio,* meaning "that which is miscarried.")

Thirty-seven million abortions worldwide are performed each year. In the United States, the abortion rate increased steadily from the early 1970s through 1980, leveled off somewhat in the 1980s, reached a peak in about 1990, when there were about 1.4 million abortions, and has declined to about 1.2 million abortions per year more recently (Smolowe, 1993; Lewin, 1998a). The great majority of abortions in the United States—nearly 90%—occur during the first trimester. This is when they are safest to the woman and least costly.

Some 80% of the women in the United States who have abortions are unmarried (Lewin, 1998a). Nearly half of them have had a previous abortion. Nearly half are mothers who already bear family responsibilities (Russo et al., 1992). They are young: Nearly three-quarters of them are under 30. Sixty percent of them are White. About one in three (35%) is African American. Nearly one in six is Hispanic American.

Abortion is practiced widely in Canada, Japan, Russia, and many European nations. It is less common in developing nations, largely because of sparse medical facilities. Abortion is rarely used as a primary means of birth control. It usually comes into play when other methods have failed.

There are many reasons why women have abortions, including psychological factors as well as external circumstances. Abortion is often motivated by a desire to reduce the risk of physical, economic, psychological, and social disadvantages that the woman perceives for herself and her present and future children if she takes the pregnancy to term (Russo et al., 1992).

The national debate over abortion has been played out in recent years against a backdrop of demonstrations, marches, and occasional acts of violence, such as firebombing of abortion clinics and even murder. The right-to-life (pro-life) movement asserts that human life begins at conception and therefore views abortion as the murder of an unborn child (Sagan & Dryan, 1990). Some in the pro-life movement brook no exception to their opposition to abortion. Others would permit abortion to save the mother's life or when a pregnancy results from rape or incest.

The pro-choice movement contends that abortion is a matter of personal choice and that the government has no right to interfere with a woman's right to terminate a pregnancy. Pro-choice advocates argue that women are free to control what happens within their bodies, including pregnancies.

When Does Human Life Begin?

Moral concerns about abortion often turn on the question of when human life begins. For some Christians, the matter revolves around when they believe the fetus obtains a soul.

In his thesis on *ensoulment*, the thirteenth-century Christian theologian Saint Thomas Aquinas wrote that a male fetus does not acquire a human soul until 40 days after conception. A female fetus does not acquire a soul until after 80 days. Scientists, too, have attempted to define when human life can be said to begin. Astronomer Carl Sagan, for example, wrote that fetal brain activity can be considered a scientific marker of human life (Sagan & Dryan, 1990). Brain activity is needed for thought, the quality that many people consider most "human." Brain wave patterns that are typical of children do not begin until about the thirtieth week of pregnancy. Before then, the human fetus lacks the brain architecture to begin thinking (Sagan & Dryan, 1990). Of course, this line of thinking raises the question of whether fetal brain wave activity can be equated with thought. (What would a fetus "think" about?) Moreover, some people argue that a newly fertilized ovum carries the *potential* for human thought in the same way that the embryonic or fetal brain does. It could even be argued that sperm cells and ova are living things in that they carry out the biological processes characteristic of cellular life. All in all, the question of when *human* life begins is a matter of definition that is apparently unanswerable by science.

Pro-Choice or Pro-Life? Where Do You Stand?

What does it mean to be "pro-life" on the abortion issue? What does it mean to be "pro-choice"? Which position is closer to your own views on abortion?

The *Reasoning About Abortion Questionnaire (RAQ)* (Parsons et al., 1990) assesses agreement with pro-life or pro-choice lines of reasoning about abortion. To find out which position is closer to your own, indicate your level of agreement or disagreement with each of the following items by circling the number that most closely represents your feelings. Then refer to the key in the appendix to interpret your score.

5 = Strongly agree
4 = Agree
3 = Mixed feelings
2 = Disagree
1 = Strongly disagree

1. Abortion is a matter of personal choice.

   5 4 3 2 1

2. Abortion is a threat to our society.

   5 4 3 2 1

3. A woman should have control over what is happening to her own body by having the option to choose abortion.

   5 4 3 2 1

4. Only God, not people, can decide if a fetus should live.

   5 4 3 2 1

5. Even if one believes that there may be some exceptions, abortion is still basically wrong.

   5 4 3 2 1

6. Abortion violates an unborn person's fundamental right to life.

   5 4 3 2 1

7. A woman should be able to exercise her rights to self-determination by choosing to have an abortion.

   5 4 3 2 1

8. Outlawing abortion could take away a woman's sense of self and personal autonomy.

   5 4 3 2 1

9. Outlawing abortion violates a woman's civil rights.

   5 4 3 2 1

10. Abortion is morally unacceptable and unjustified.

    5 4 3 2 1

11. In my reasoning, the notion that an unborn fetus may be a human life is not a deciding issue in considering abortion.

    5 4 3 2 1

12. Abortion can be described as taking a life unjustly.

    5 4 3 2 1

13. A woman should have the right to decide to have an abortion based on her own life circumstances.

    5 4 3 2 1

14. If a woman feels that having a child might ruin her life, she should consider an abortion.

    5 4 3 2 1

15. Abortion could destroy the sanctity of motherhood.

    5 4 3 2 1

16. An unborn fetus is a viable human being with rights.

    5 4 3 2 1

17. If a woman feels she can't care for a baby, she should be able to have an abortion.

    5 4 3 2 1

18. Abortion is the destruction of one life for the convenience of another.

    5 4 3 2 1

19. Abortion is the same as murder.

    5 4 3 2 1

20. Even if one believes that there are times when abortion is immoral, it is still basically the woman's own choice.

    5 4 3 2 1

Historical and Legal Perspectives on Abortion

Societal attitudes toward abortion have varied across cultures and times in history. Abortion was permitted in ancient Greece and Rome, but women in ancient Assyria were impaled on stakes for attempting abortion. The Bible does not specifically prohibit abortion (Sagan & Dryan, 1990). For much of its history, the Roman Catholic Church held to Thomas Aquinas's belief that ensoulment of the fetus did not occur for at least 40 days after conception. In 1869, Pope Pius IX declared that human life begins at conception. Thus, an abortion at any stage of pregnancy became murder in the eyes of the church and grounds for excommunication. The Roman Catholic Church has since opposed abortion during any stage of pregnancy.

Abortion was legal in the United States from 1607 to 1828 (Hitt, 1998). Women were permitted to terminate a pregnancy until "quickening" occurred (the point at which the woman was first able to feel the fetus stirring within her) (Sagan & Dryan, 1990). More restrictive abortion laws emerged because of a national desire to increase the population and because of concerns voiced by physicians about protecting women from botched abortions (Hitt, 1998). By 1900, virtually all states in the union had enacted legislation banning abortion *at any point* during pregnancy, except when necessary to save the woman's life.

Truth or Fiction?
REVISITED

It is true that abortions were legal in the newly founded United States—until the point in the pregnancy at which the woman sensed fetal movements. ■

Abortion laws remained essentially unchanged until the late 1960s, when some states liberalized their abortion laws under mounting public pressure. Then, in 1973, the U.S. Supreme Court in effect legalized abortion nationwide in the landmark *Roe* v. *Wade* decision.

Roe v. *Wade* held that a woman's right to an abortion was protected under the right to privacy guaranteed by the Constitution. The decision legalized abortions for any reason during the first trimester, leaving the decision to have an abortion entirely in the hands of the woman. In its ruling, the Court also noted that a fetus is not considered a person and is therefore not entitled to constitutional protection. The Court ruled that states may regulate a woman's right to have an abortion during the second trimester to protect her health, such as by requiring her to obtain an abortion in a hospital rather than a doctor's office. The Court also held that when a fetus becomes viable, its rights override the mother's right to privacy. Because the fetus may become viable early in the third trimester, states may prohibit third-trimester abortions, except in cases in which an abortion is necessary to protect a woman's health or life.

In 1977, Congress enacted the Hyde Amendment, which denies Medicaid funding for abortions except in cases in which the woman's life is endangered. In *Harris* v. *McRae* (1980), the U.S. Supreme Court essentially upheld the Hyde Amendment (and similar state legislation) by ruling that federal and state governments are not required to pay for abortions for poor women who are receiving public assistance.

Since *Roe* v. *Wade*, most states have also enacted laws requiring parental consent or notification before a minor may have an abortion (Carlson, 1990). Sixty-nine percent of adults in the United States believe that parental permission should be required before teenage girls can have abortions (Carlson, 1990). Many pregnant teenage girls, however, especially those living in families with alcoholic or abusive parents, fear telling their parents that they are pregnant. In 1990 rulings involving state laws in Ohio and Minnesota, the U.S. Supreme Court upheld the rights of states to require that a minor seeking an abortion notify at least one parent and wait 48 hours before an abortion can be performed. The Court provided an "escape clause," however: The minor girl may go before a judge instead. Carlson (1990) notes that many pregnant teenagers who are reluctant to reveal pregnancies to their parents also hesitate to reveal them to authority figures such as judges. A 1993 U.S. Supreme Court ruling let stand a Mississippi law requiring minors to obtain approval either from both parents or from a judge.

Parental consent laws have widespread popular support. Four out of five adults support such provisions, including many abortion rights supporters (Goldberg & Elder, 1998). Yet, with or without the rules, the majority of girls who seek abortions do consult their parents before going through with their plans. One of the arguments favoring parental approval is the belief that parents know what is best for their children. However, opponents say that parental consent laws only serve to delay girls from getting safer early abortions and force them to postpone abortions until the second trimester, when the risks are greater (Pliner & Yates, 1992).

ATTITUDES TOWARD LEGALIZED ABORTION   National public opinion polls taken since *Roe* v. *Wade* have consistently shown that a majority of people in the United States support the decision legalizing abortion (Goldberg & Elder, 1998). There is little difference in support for abortion among Catholics, Jews, and Protestants (Goldberg & Elder, 1998; Gordon & Snyder, 1989). On the other hand, African Americans are less likely than White Americans to support abortion. Researchers find that higher levels of education are associated with pro-choice attitudes. Reduced support for legal abortion is associated with religious commitment, conservative attitudes on premarital sex, and a belief in having large families (Lynxwiler & Gay, 1994).

Most people in the United States favor legalized abortion, but not under all circumstances. A national poll conducted by *The New York Times* found that 61% of Americans believe that abortion should be permitted during the first trimester (see Figure 12.9), but 70% said that abortion was unacceptable if the purpose was to prevent the child from interfering with the woman's career (Goldberg & Elder, 1998). Only 42% believed that abortion was justified to prevent interference with a teenage girl's education. But there was strong support for abortion when the woman was raped, when her health was endangered, or when there was the strong possibility of a deformity in the baby. Half (50%) of the respondents said that abortion was the same thing as murdering a child; 38% said abortion was not murder because a fetus is not the same thing as a child. Not only are people in conflict with other people about abortion; they are also in conflict within themselves: One third (32%) of those who said that abortion was murder still agreed that abortion was sometimes the best course in a bad situation! Although some consider abortion a "women's issue," there were no differences between men's and women's attitudes among the respondents to *The New York Times* poll. Nor did the pollsters find that the age of the respondent was related to attitudes toward abortion. However, people with more years of education were more accepting of abortion (see Figure 12.10 on page 376), and people who said that religion was extremely important to them were less tolerant of abortion than were those who said that religion was not so important. Elizabeth Cook (1998), author of a book about abortion entitled *Between Two Absolutes*, suggests that a consensus

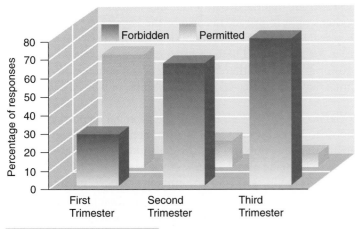

figure 12.9

Responses to the Question "Should a Woman Be Permitted or Forbidden to Have an Abortion During . . . " the Three Trimesters of Pregnancy. As you can see, respondents to *The New York Times* poll were less permissive of abortion during the later stages of pregnancy.

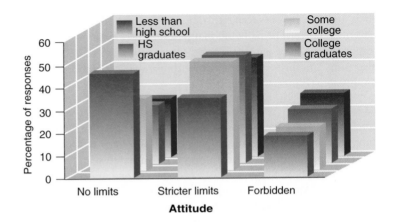

figure 12.10

Attitudes toward Abortion by Level of Education.
Respondents to *The New York Times* poll with more years of education were more likely to say that abortion should be generally available (with no limits). People with fewer years of education were more likely to say that abortion should not be permitted (forbidden).

about abortion may be emerging—that abortion should be allowed under some circumstances but is not to be taken lightly. Three quarters of the sample opposed a constitutional amendment that would ban abortion. Most Americans clearly want the individual to have the right to an abortion, even if they disapprove of abortion.

The controversy over abortion has led to a decline in the numbers of abortion providers. Nearly three of five (59%) of doctors who perform abortions are 65 years of age or older (Hitt, 1998). The percentage of obstetricians who are willing to perform abortions dropped from 42% in 1983 to 33% in 1995 (Hitt, 1998). Only about one family practitioner in six has experience with any abortion method. Nationwide, five out of six counties have no abortion provider. Many women who seek abortions at abortion clinics must navigate past pro-life picketers to gain entrance. Many doctors who perform abortions believe that their lives are in jeopardy (Hitt, 1998). Consider the commentary of one young doctor who was considering learning abortion methods: "But then I started to think, well, gosh," said the doctor, "I don't want to end up being known as the abortion person. Do you know what I mean?" (Hitt, 1998, p. 22). Yet doctors who perform abortions say that it eliminates the butchery that would otherwise go on in the back alleys, provides poor women with the same access that affluent women have always managed to find, and raises general awareness of the need for contraception (Hitt, 1998).

Many people in the pro-choice movement argue that if abortions were to be made illegal again, thousands of women, especially poor women, would die or suffer serious physical consequences from botched or nonsterile abortions. People in the pro-life movement counter that alternatives to abortion such as adoption are available to pregnant women. Pro-choice advocates argue that the debate about abortion should be framed not only by notions of the mother's right to privacy but also by the issue of the quality of life of an unwanted child. They argue that minority and physically or mentally disabled children are often hard to place for adoption. These children often spend their childhoods being shuffled from one foster home to another. Pro-life advocates counter that killing a fetus eliminates any potential that it might have, despite hardships, of living a fruitful and meaningful life.

As Tamar Lewin (1998a) noted, *Roe* v. *Wade* is not in the personal memories of most individual women who choose to have abortions in the United States today. Many of them have a hard time recognizing that abortion was ever illegal and cannot imagine what it would mean if abortion were to be made illegal again.

Says a 19-year-old woman from Chicago who is waiting in an abortion clinic:

I've never heard anything about Roe vs. Wade. I know there is tension between different groups and that there are people who are really, really against abortion. My mom is totally against it. If she knew I was here, Wow! I can't even imagine what it was like when abortion was illegal. I just opened up the phone book. People definitely take it for granted today. I think of the movie 'Dirty Dancing.' I never understood why she was so sick, but it was because she got an illegal abortion." (Lewin, 1998a)

Says Sirena, a 24-year-old woman from Brooklyn who has two young children and has had three abortions:

I don't think there could ever be a time when abortion would be illegal. No one would let that happen. There would be too many girls throwing babies in the garbage or abusing their kids. But there's always going to be people who are against abortion, like my sister, and people who are pro-choice, like me. It's always been the same and it's always going to be. (Lewin, 1998a)

Methods of Abortion

Regardless of the moral, legal, and political issues that surround abortion, many abortion methods are in use today.

VACUUM ASPIRATION   **Vacuum aspiration,** or suction curettage, is the safest and most common method of abortion. It accounts for more than 90% of abortions in the United States. It is relatively painless and inexpensive. It can be done with little or no anesthesia in a medical office or clinic, but only during the first trimester. Later, thinning of the uterine walls increases the risks of perforation and bleeding.

In the procedure, the cervix is usually dilated first by insertion of progressively larger curved metal rods, or "dilators," or by insertion, hours earlier, of a stick of seaweed called *Laminaria digitata. Laminaria* expands as it absorbs cervical moisture, providing a gentler means of opening the os. Then an angled tube connected to an aspirator (suction machine) is inserted through the cervix into the uterus. The uterine contents are then evacuated (emptied) by suction (see Figure 12.11). Possible complications include perforation of the uterus, infection, cervical lacerations, and hemorrhaging, but these are rare.

It is not true that the D&C is the most widely used abortion method in the United States today. Vacuum aspiration is the most widely used abortion method. ∎

Truth or Fiction?
REVISITED

DILATION AND CURETTAGE (D&C)   The **D&C** was once the customary method of performing abortions. It now accounts for only a small number of abortions in the United States. It is usually performed 8 to 20 weeks after the last menstrual period. Once the cervix has been dilated, the uterine contents are scraped from the uterine lining with a blunt scraping tool.

D&Cs are carried out in a hospital, usually under general anesthesia. The scraping increases the chances of hemorrhaging, infection, and perforation. Because of these

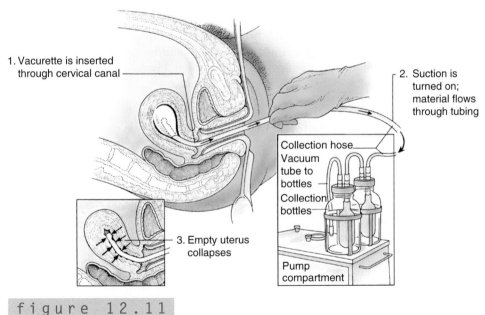

1. Vacurette is inserted through cervical canal
2. Suction is turned on; material flows through tubing
Collection hose
Vacuum tube to bottles
Collection bottles
3. Empty uterus collapses
Pump compartment

figure 12.11

Vacuum Aspiration. This is the safest and most common method of abortion, but it can be performed only during the first trimester. An angled tube is inserted through the cervix into the uterus, and the uterine contents are then evacuated (emptied) by suction.

Vacuum aspiration Removal of the uterine contents by suction. An abortion method that is used early in pregnancy. (From the Latin *aspirare,* meaning "to breathe upon.")

D&C Abbreviation for *dilation and curettage,* an operation in which the cervix is dilated and uterine contents are then gently scraped away.

risks, D&Cs have largely been replaced by the vacuum aspiration method. D&Cs are still used to treat various gynecological problems, however, such as abnormally heavy menstrual bleeding.

DILATION AND EVACUATION (D&E) The **D&E** is used most commonly during the second trimester, when vacuum aspiration alone would be too risky. The D&E combines suction and the D&C. First the cervix is dilated. The cervix must also be dilated more fully than with vacuum aspiration to allow for passage of the larger fetus. Then a suction tube is inserted to remove some of the contents of the uterus. But suction alone cannot safely remove all uterine contents. So the remaining contents are removed with forceps. A blunt scraper might also be used to scrape the uterine wall to make sure that the lining has been removed fully. Like the D&C, the D&E is usually performed in the hospital under general anesthesia. Most women recover quickly and relatively painlessly. In rare instances, however, complications can arise. These include excessive bleeding, infection, and perforation of the uterine lining (Thompson, 1993).

INDUCING LABOR BY INTRA-AMNIOTIC INFUSION Second-trimester abortions are sometimes performed by chemically inducing premature labor and delivery. The procedure, which must be performed in a hospital, is called instillation, or **intra-amniotic infusion.** It is usually performed when fetal development has progressed beyond the point at which other methods are deemed safe. A saline (salt) solution or a solution of prostaglandins (hormones that stimulate uterine contractions during labor) is injected into the amniotic sac. Prostaglandins may also be administered by vaginal suppository. Uterine contractions (labor) begin within a few hours after infusion. The fetus and placenta are expelled from the uterus within the next 24 or 48 hours.

Intra-amniotic infusion accounts for only a small number of abortions. Medical complications, risks, and costs are greater with this procedure than with other methods of abortion. Overly rapid labor can tear the cervix, but previous dilation of the cervix with *Laminaria* lessens the risk. Perforation, infection, and hemorrhaging are rare if prostaglandins are used, but about half the recipients experience nausea and vomiting, diarrhea, or headaches. Saline infusion can cause shock and even death if the solution is carelessly introduced into the bloodstream.

HYSTEROTOMY The **hysterotomy** is, in effect, a cesarean section. Incisions are made in the abdomen and uterus, and the fetus and uterine contents are removed. Hysterotomy may be performed during the late second trimester, between the sixteenth and twenty-fourth weeks after the last menstrual period. It is performed very rarely, usually only when intra-amniotic infusion is not advised. A hysterotomy is major surgery that must be carried out under general anesthesia in a hospital. Hysterotomy involves risks of complications from the anesthesia and the surgery itself.

ABORTION DRUGS Most early abortions are accomplished by vacuum aspiration, which is a surgical technique. Although vacuum aspiration is safe enough for the woman, 60% to 70% of women in the United States would prefer a drug-induced abortion if it were available (Population Council, 1995).

RU-486 is an abortion pill that was given a "tentative seal of approval" by the U.S. Food and Drug Administration in September 1996 (Reuter, 1996). It contains *mifepristone*, a chemical that induces early abortion by blocking the effects of progesterone. Progesterone is the hormone that stimulates proliferation of the endometrium, allowing implantation of the fertilized ovum and, subsequently, development of the placenta. The pill was developed in France. Today, nearly half of French women seeking abortion prefer RU-486 to surgical methods, including vacuum aspiration. Similarly, half of the respondents to *The New York Times* poll said that they would favor use of RU-486 over surgical abortion (Goldberg & Elder, 1998).

Supporters of RU-486 argue that it offers a safe, noninvasive substitute for more costly and unpleasant abortion procedures (Reuter, 1996). Moreover, use of RU-486 means that a woman need not run a gauntlet of demonstrators to visit an abortion clinic

D&E Abbreviation for *dilation and evacuation,* an abortion method in which the cervix is dilated before vacuum aspiration.

Intra-amniotic infusion An abortion method in which a substance is injected into the amniotic sac to induce premature labor. Also called *instillation.*

Hysterotomy An abortion method in which the fetus is removed by cesarean section.

or hospital. Supporters also note that RU-486 could reduce the numbers of women who die each year from complications from self-induced abortions. Such women are usually too poor to avail themselves of legally sanctioned abortion facilities, or they live in third world countries that lack adequate medical services.

RU-486 might make abortion physically easier, but not necessarily psychologically easier. The developer of the RU-486, Dr. Étienne-Émile Baulieu, remarks, "It's insulting to women to say that abortion now will be as easy as taking aspirins. . . . It is always difficult, psychologically and physically, sometimes tragic" (Smolowe, 1993, p. 51). Then, too, there are side effects, including heavy menstrual bleeding and cramping.

RU-486's introduction in the United States was delayed largely because of opposition by pro-life groups (Hausknecht, 1998). Opponents argue that RU-486 makes abortions more accessible and difficult to regulate (Smolowe, 1993). Pro-life groups consider abortion to be murder, whether it is induced by surgery or by a pill. In any event, as of this writing, RU-486 remains hard to get for most people (Hausknecht, 1998).

As the abortion debate continues, so does research into the use of other drugs. A combination of the cancer drug *methotrexate* and the ulcer drug *misoprostol*, for example, can be used to terminate early pregnancy. Methotrexate is toxic to the trophoblastic tissue of the embryo, and misoprostol causes uterine contractions. Hausknecht (1995) reported a pilot study in which an injection of methotrexate followed by a vaginal suppository with misoprostol led to successful abortions in 171 of 178 women. (The remaining seven subsequently underwent aspiration.) Moreover, it appears that the combination of methotrexate and misoprostol has fewer side effects than RU-486. Another effective drug combination is mifepristone (used in RU-486) and misoprostol. One study found that the combination terminated pregnancy in 92% of women who were pregnant for 49 days or less (Spitz et al., 1998). The combination was less effective later in pregnancy.

It seems likely that additional methods of chemical induction of abortion will become available as the years go on. None of them is likely to defuse the abortion debate, however. As noted by journalist Jack Hitt, "the moral debate plays out like an unending episode of 'Crossfire,' almost reassuring in the way anti-abortion and abortion-rights positions rerun on a continuous tape loop" (1998, p. 22).

a CLOSER look

Partial-Birth Abortion

Most Americans believe that early abortions should be permitted, although not without some limits (Goldberg & Elder, 1998). Moreover, the Supreme Court does not show signs of overturning the outcome of *Roe* v. *Wade*. Therefore, much of the recent battle over abortion has focused on more specific issues, such as whether parents should have the right to know or to approve if an underage daughter wants to have an abortion, or on the availability of specific methods, such as RU-486 or the "partial-birth abortion." The latter is a late-term surgical abortion method that is referred to, medically, as an "intact dilation and extraction" or "intact D and X" (Hitt, 1998).

In a partial-birth abortion, the cervix is dilated, and then a fetus that may be 10 inches long is extracted from the mother through the birth canal. Measures that will not be described here are then taken rapidly to terminate any life functions in the fetus (refer to Hitt, 1998, if you wish).

Remember that support of abortion rights drops off rapidly as the stages of pregnancy progress (Figure 12.9). Therefore, most individuals who support early first-trimester abortions will oppose the partial-birth abortion because of its timing. Others will oppose it because of the nature of the disposal of the fetus. However, many pro-choice people argue in favor of partial-birth abortions for at least two reasons. One is that they are relatively rare and usually performed when the health of the mother is at stake. Another is the "slippery slope" argument—that is, the fear that surrendering a woman's right to have a partial-birth abortion could eventually lead to surrendering her rights to have other kinds of abortions.

The general attitudes of the medical profession toward the partial-birth abortion may be expressed in the fact that the procedure is not to be found in medical books. Neither is the more technical term "intact dilation and extraction" (Hitt, 1998).

Psychological Consequences of Abortion

The woman who faces an unwanted pregnancy may experience a range of negative emotions, including

> fear ("What will I do now?"), self-anger ("How could I let this happen?"), guilt ("What would my parents think if they knew I was pregnant?"), ambivalence ("Will I be sorry if I have an abortion? Will I be sorry if I don't?"), and sometimes desperation ("Is suicide a way out?")
>
> (Knox, 1988, p. 455)

Consider the comments of Yardena, a 22-year-old woman who is the mother of a 3-year-old, had an abortion at the age of 16, and was waiting to be seen at the Planned Parenthood clinic when she learned that she was pregnant again: "I'm not pro-choice—I'm anti-abortion. I still have negative feelings about abortion, and I love children, but this is something I have to do at this point in my life" (Lewin, 1998a).

A 19-year-old college student says, "I don't like the idea of abortion being used as birth control. This is my first time [at the clinic] and my last. If I get pregnant again, which I won't, I'm having the child. That will mean I was stupid twice. Once is all right, but not the same mistake twice."

Whether to have an abortion is typically a painful decision—perhaps the most difficult decision a woman will ever make. Even women who apparently make the decision without hesitation may later have feelings of guilt, remorse, anger, and sadness. Although the woman's partner is often overlooked in the research on abortion, he may encounter similar feelings.

Women's reactions depend on various factors, including the support they receive from others (or the lack thereof) and the strength of their relationships with their partners. Women with greater support from their male partners or parents tend to show a more positive emotional reaction after an abortion (Armsworth, 1991). Generally speaking, the sooner the abortion occurs, the less stressful it is. Women who have a difficult time reaching an abortion decision, who blame the pregnancy on their character, who have lower coping ability, and who have less social support experience more distress following abortion (Major & Cozzarelli, 1992).

Many men are very concerned and supportive of their partners. Others seek to detach themselves from the situation. And of course there are some cases in which the identity of the father is unknown. Some men consider pregnancy the woman's responsibility: "She's the one who let herself get pregnant." Some men reproach the woman for failing to take precautions. No wonder feminists insist that men share full responsibility for pregnancies.

Pro-life advocates such as Wanda Franz, the president of the National Right to Life Committee, have argued that having an abortion triggers negative emotional reactions such as depression and post-traumatic stress disorder (cited in Brody, 1997a). However, a study of more than 700 women who had had abortions, which included questionnaires and annual interviews, did not find any lasting relationship between having had an abortion, depression, post-traumatic stress disorder, or other measures of psychological well-being, such as self-esteem (Russo & Marin, 1997). Catholic women who had had abortions also had the lowest self-esteem, but the researchers found that this group also had the lowest self-esteem *before* they had the abortions. High self-esteem was connected with being employed, having higher incomes and more years of education, and bearing fewer children, but the researchers found no effect for having had an abortion. In sum, argue the researchers, a woman's emotional state before pregnancy is the best predictor of her feelings after having an abortion. Neither her religious affiliation nor her involvement in religion seems to make a difference.

The nearby World of Diversity feature provides some perspective on the ways in which some citizens of one of the wealthiest nations on the Pacific Rim cope with their feelings about abortion.

JAPAN'S ABORTION AGONY: In a Country That Prohibited the Pill, Reality Collided with Religion

Yuka Sugimoto winds her way among thousands of miniature stone statues in a hillside Buddhist temple (WuDunn, 1996). She finds the one she is seeking—the proper *mizuko jizo*—and lingers to ponder the clandestine act that resulted in this.

Buddhists come to the temples to pray for health, wealth, or a wife or husband. Not Ms. Sugimoto. She comes to this ancient temple once a month as a way of making amends with the fetus she aborted two years earlier, when she was an unmarried student.

Japan may be one of the richest, most technologically advanced nations in the world, but until the birth-control pill was allowed in 1999, it depended on an antiquated system of birth control that forced women to rely heavily on abortion in a society that at the same time disapproved of it.

Japan's abortion rate has been one of the highest among the world's industrialized nations. One reason for this has been the lack of birth-control alternatives. The government banned the use of the birth-control pill as a contraceptive until 1999, and doctors did not encourage sterilization, IUDs, or diaphragms. Most Japanese people were in the habit of using condoms and rhythm methods despite their high failure rate.

Over the years Japanese officials defended the ban against the pill by arguing that oral contraceptives are unsafe and would promote promiscuity (Fukuyama, 1999; 1992). In 1992, a review by the Health and Welfare Ministry found birth-control pills to be safe, but decided to uphold the ban because of concerns about AIDS. Though Japan had relatively few AIDS cases by international standards (about 500 by 1991), the health ministry feared that lifting the ban on the pill might discourage condom use and lead to an epidemic of AIDS.

In part because of limited contraceptive options, the Japanese have used condoms more than any other people in the world. Condoms are widely available in drugstores, supermarkets, and vending machines; embarrassed housewives can buy them from door-to-door saleswomen. Abortion is the widely used backup for failed contraception.

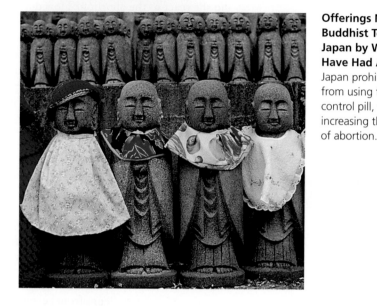

Offerings Made at a Buddhist Temple in Japan by Women Who Have Had Abortions. Japan prohibits women from using the birth-control pill, thereby increasing the incidence of abortion.

Yet, while abortions have been legal and easily accessible in Japan for over 40 years, women who have them feel stigmatized because many Japanese, even those who accept it, regard abortion as killing a baby.

The majority of Japanese draw little distinction between a fetus and an infant. According to Samuel Coleman, the author of *Family Planning in Japanese Society*, the reasons lie at least partially in Shinto and Buddhism, Japan's two major religions. Although neither religion promotes active opposition to abortion, Buddhism is based on the ideal of overcoming one's sense of ego. In this context, a woman who aborts wrongly puts her ego before her fetus. Shinto, an ancient religion based on ancestor and nature worship, holds that an aborted fetus can place a curse on the woman who aborts.

Offerings at the Temple

Hiroshi Hihara, a gynecologist in Tokyo, makes his living on infertility work and abortions, many of them for married women whose method of contraception has failed. Although Hihara is a member of a Buddhist temple, he does not consider himself religious. But he is not comfortable with abortion. "Abortion is legal and approved of by the government, and if a patient wants it, I can't turn her down," he said. "She's entitled to it. But I am not happy to do it." Yet prior to the availability of the pill, he was performing some 200 abortions a year and quietly admitted, when asked, that his fees from abortion represented "a large portion of my income."

Caught in this moral and economic trap, he resolved his feelings in a uniquely Japanese way. First, he told each abortion patient to make an offering after the operation at any of the Buddhist temples selling statuettes, or *mizuko jizo*, which women can buy in memory of an aborted fetus. Thousands of such statues stand on display at temples these days; although some are for miscarriages and stillborn children, the vast majority are for abortions. Many of the statues are decorated with crocheted hats, plastic bibs, and little pinwheels, all put there by women to keep the soul of the aborted fetus warm and amused.

As the birth-control pill becomes more widely used in Japan, some social critics still fear dire consequences, including explosions in the divorce rate and freeing men from having to deal with the consequences of sex (Fukuyama, 1999). The extent to which Japanese women will use the pill remains an open question. Most Japanese women still report preferring child-rearing to careers, and the majority say they will not use the pill even though it is available (Fukuyama, 1999).

Source: Fukuyama, F. (1999, June 9). At last, Japan gets the pill. Is this good news? *The New York Times*, p. A29.

Reflections

■ Do you know anyone who has had an abortion? What motivated the abortion? How did she react to the abortion? How did you feel at the time?

■ One of the issues concerning abortion is whether it is the taking of a human life. How do *you* define *human life*? When do *you* believe human life begins? At conception? When the embryo becomes implanted in the uterus? When the fetus begins to assume a human shape or develops human facial features? When the fetus is capable of sustaining independent life? Explain.

■ What are your own views on abortion? Are some abortion methods more acceptable to you than others? Why or why not?

summing up

Birth control methods include contraception and induced abortion.

CONTRACEPTION

Contraception in the United States: The Legal Battle

In the United States, Anthony Comstock lobbied successfully for passage of a federal law in 1873 that prohibited the dissemination of birth-control information through the mail on the grounds that it was obscene and indecent. In 1918, the courts ruled that physicians must be allowed to disseminate information that might aid in the cure and prevention of disease. Dismantling of the Comstock law had begun.

Selecting a Method of Contraception

Issues surrounding the choice of a method of contraception involve their convenience, moral acceptability, cost, sharing of responsibility between the partners, safety, reversibility, the protection they afford from STIs, and effectiveness.

METHODS OF CONTRACEPTION

Oral Contraceptives ("the Pill")

Birth-control pills include combination pills and minipills. Combination pills contain estrogen and progestin and fool the brain into acting as though the woman is already pregnant, so no additional ova mature or are released. Minipills contain progestin, thicken the cervical mucus to impede the passage of sperm through the cervix, and render the inner lining of the uterus less receptive to a fertilized egg. Oral contraception is nearly 100% effective. The main drawbacks are side effects and potential health risks.

"Morning-after" pills prevent implantation of a fertilized ovum in the uterus.

Norplant

Norplant consists of tubes containing progestin that are surgically embedded under the skin of the woman's upper arm. Norplant provides continuous contraceptive protection for as long as five years.

Intrauterine Devices (IUDs)

The IUD apparently irritates the uterine lining, causing inflammation and the production of antibodies that may be toxic to sperm or fertilized ova and/or may prevent fertilized eggs from becoming implanted. The IUD is highly effective, but there are possible troublesome side effects and the potential for serious health complications.

The Diaphragm

The diaphragm covers the cervix and should be used with a spermicidal cream or jelly. It must be fitted by a health professional.

Spermicides

Spermicides block the passage of sperm and kill sperm. Their failure rate is high.

The Cervical Cap

Like the diaphragm, the cap covers the cervix and is most effective when used with a spermicide.

Condoms

Latex condoms afford protection against STIs. Condoms are the only contraceptive device worn by men and the only readily reversible method of contraception that is available to men.

Douching

Douching is ineffective as a contraceptive because large numbers of sperm may pass beyond the range of the douche within seconds after ejaculation.

Withdrawal (Coitus Interruptus)

Withdrawal requires no special equipment but has a high failure rate.

Fertility Awareness Methods (Rhythm Methods)

Rhythm methods rely on awareness of the fertile segments of the woman's menstrual cycle. Rhythm methods include the calendar method, the basal body temperature method, and the cervical mucus method. Their failure rate is high in typical use.

Sterilization
Sterilization methods should be considered permanent, although they may be reversed in many cases. The vasectomy is usually carried out under local anesthesia in 15 to 20 minutes. Female sterilization methods prevent ova and sperm from passing through the fallopian tubes.

ABORTION

Historical and Legal Perspectives on Abortion
In colonial times and through the early to mid-nineteenth century, women in the United States were permitted to terminate a pregnancy until "quickening" occurred. More restrictive abortion laws came into being after the Civil War. In 1973, the U.S. Supreme Court in effect legalized abortion nationwide in the landmark *Roe* v. *Wade* decision.

Methods of Abortion
Abortion methods that are in use today include vacuum aspiration, D&C, D&E, induction of labor by intra-amniotic infusion, hysterotomy, and drugs.

Psychological Consequences of Abortion
Although choosing to have an abortion is typically a painful decision, women who are interviewed about a year after an abortion generally show good psychological adjustment.

Balthus. *Figure in Front of a Mantel (Nu Devant La Cheminée).* 1975. Oil on canvas, 75 x 64.5 in. The Metropolitan Museum of Art, Robert Lehman Collection

13

Sexuality in Childhood
and Adolescence

outline

TRUTH OR FICTION?

**INFANCY (0 TO 2 YEARS):
THE SEARCH FOR THE ORIGINS
OF HUMAN SEXUALITY**

The Infant's Capacity for
   Sexual Response

Masturbation

A WORLD OF DIVERSITY:
*Cross-Cultural Perspectives on
Childhood Sexuality*

Genital Play

EARLY CHILDHOOD (3 TO 8 YEARS)

Masturbation

WHAT DO YOU SAY NOW?
*How Should a Parent React to
Childhood Masturbation?*

Male-Female Sexual Behavior

Male-Male and Female-Female
   Sexual Behavior

**PREADOLESCENCE
(9 TO 13 YEARS)**

Masturbation

Male-Female Sexual Behavior

Male-Male and Female-Female
   Sexual Behavior

Sex Education and Miseducation

WHAT DO YOU SAY NOW?
Talking with Your Children about Sex

ADOLESCENCE

Puberty

A WORLD OF DIVERSITY:
Menarche in Cross-Cultural Perspective

Masturbation

Male-Female Sexual Behavior

IN THE NEW MILLENNIUM:
Teenagers and Sex: Where Do We Stand?

A WORLD OF DIVERSITY:
*Ethnic Differences in Premarital Intercourse,
Adolescent Use of Contraception, and
Resolution of Unwanted Pregnancies*

A CLOSER LOOK:
The First Time

Male-Male and Female-Female
   Sexual Behavior

TEENAGE PREGNANCY

Contraceptive Use among Sexually
   Active Teens

A CLOSER LOOK:
*Should Public Schools Provide Students
with Contraceptives?*

SUMMING UP

Truth or Fiction?

Truth or Fiction?

_____ Many boys are born with erections.

_____ Infants often engage in pelvic thrusting at 8 to 10 months of age.

_____ Most children learn the facts of life from parents or from school sex education programs.

_____ Sex education encourages sexual activity among children and adolescents.

_____ Nocturnal emissions in boys accompany erotic dreams.

_____ Nearly 1 million adolescent girls in the United States become pregnant each year.

_____ In some school districts, condoms are distributed to adolescents without parental consent.

m y heart leaps up when I behold
        A rainbow in the sky:
So it was when my life began;
So it is now I am a man;
So be it when I shall grow old,
        Or let me die!
The Child is father of the Man;
And I could wish my days to be
Bound each to each by natural piety.
    —William Wordsworth, "My Heart Leaps Up"

What a life it would be, indeed, were our hearts to swell with the wonders of the world throughout our lives. In this chapter, we begin our chronicle of sexual behavior across the life span, and we see the ways in which the child is father of the man. Within children's personal and social experiences lie the seeds of later sexual competence and self-esteem—or the seeds of incompetence, guilt, and shame. In the next chapter, we shall see that our sexuality remains an integral part of our lives throughout our lives—one that has the potential to help our hearts leap up for all our days.

INFANCY (0 TO 2 YEARS): THE SEARCH FOR THE ORIGINS OF HUMAN SEXUALITY

Fetuses not only have erections, they also suck their fingers. The sucking reflex allows babies to gain nourishment, which is necessary for survival. But as Sigmund Freud hypothesized, infants also seem to reap sensual pleasure from sucking fingers, pacifiers, nipples, or whatever else fits into the mouth. This is not surprising, given the sensitivity of the mouth's mucosal lining.

Stimulation of the genitals in infancy might also produce sensations of pleasure. Parents who touch their infants' genitals while changing or washing them might discover the infants smiling or becoming excited. Infants discover the pleasure of self-stimulation (masturbation) for themselves when they gain the capacity to manipulate their genitals with their hands.

The Infant's Capacity for Sexual Response

Boys are often born with erections. Most have erections during the first few weeks.

It is true that many boys are born with erections. Ultrasound has revealed erections even in fetuses. ∎

Signs of sexual arousal in infant girls, such as vaginal lubrication, are less readily detected. Yet evidence of lubrication and genital swelling has been reported (Martinson, 1976).

Do not interpret children's responses according to adult concepts of sexuality, however. Lubrication and erection are reflexes, not necessarily signals of "interest" in sex. Infants have the biological capacity for these reflexes, but we cannot say what, if anything, the reflexes "mean" to them.

Parent-Child Bonding. Parents who form warm and affectionate relationships with their children may help them develop the ability to form loving attachments later in life.

PELVIC THRUSTING   Pelvic thrusting is observed in infant monkeys, apes, and humans. These observations led ethologist John Bowlby (1969) to suggest that infantile sexual behavior might be the rule in mammals, not the exception. Thrusting has been observed in humans at 8 to 10 months of age and might be an expression of affection. Typically, the infant clings to the parent, nuzzles, and thrusts and rotates the pelvis for several seconds.

It is true that infants often engage in pelvic thrusting at 8 to 10 months of age. However, there is no reason to believe that thrusting means the same thing to infants that it does to adults. ▪

Truth or Fiction?
REVISITED

ORGASM   At least some infants seem capable of sexual responses that closely resemble orgasm. Kinsey and his colleagues (1953) noted that baby boys show behaviors that resemble adult orgasm by as early as 5 months; baby girls, as early as 4 months. Orgasmic responses in boys are similar to those in men—but without ejaculation. Ejaculation occurs only after puberty.

Masturbation

Masturbation is typical for infants and young children and tends to start between 6 and 12 months. At early ages, children usually masturbate by rubbing the genitals against a soft object, such as a towel, bedding, or a doll. As the child matures and becomes capable of more coordinated hand movements, direct manual stimulation of the genitals often becomes preferred.

Masturbation to orgasm is rare until the second year, however (Reinisch, 1990). Some children begin masturbating to orgasm later. Some never do. All in all, however, an orgasmic response from masturbation is common among children, as it is among adults (Reinisch, 1990).

A World of Diversity

CROSS-CULTURAL PERSPECTIVES ON CHILDHOOD SEXUALITY

Though we are born with the capacity for sexual response, our expression of sexuality largely reflects the culture in which we are reared. Every culture encourages people to conform to socially acceptable behavior. Most people in a given culture develop similar behavior patterns and attitudes.

Cultures vary in their attitudes and practices concerning human sexuality—in particular, childhood and adolescent sexuality. Some may be characterized as sexually permissive, others as sexually restrictive. Broude and Greene (1976) analyzed attitudes toward, and frequency of, premarital sex among 114 of the world's societies. Most societies (55%) either disapproved of or disallowed premarital sex among females. About one in four societies (24%) permitted girls to engage in premarital sex. Another 21% tolerated discreet premarital sex for females. Despite societal prohibitions, premarital sex among females was common or universal in two-thirds of the societies sampled. Female premarital sex was uncommon or absent in the other third. Premarital sex among males was even more common. Among 107 societies in their cross-cultural sample, male premarital sex was universal or typical in 78%. It was atypical in the other 22%.

Sexually Permissive Societies

Ford and Beach (1951) noted that when masturbation was permitted in a society, children progressed from occasional genital touching to more purposeful masturbation by about 6 to 8 years of age. Sexually permissive cultures also permit sexual expression among peers. Among the Seniang people of Oceania, boys and girls publicly simulate coitus without fear of reproach by adults (Ford & Beach, 1951). The Lesu of Oceania believe that it is normal for children to imitate coital positions. The Chewu people of Africa believed that childhood sexual experimentation is necessary for adult fertility.

The Lecha people of the Himalayas believed that girls do not attain physical maturity unless they engage in early sexual intercourse. During early childhood, Lecha children engaged in mutual masturbation and attempted copulation. Girls began to engage in regular sexual intercourse by age 11 or 12. Among the Trobrianders of the South Pacific, girls were usually initiated into sexual intercourse by 6 or 8 years of age, boys by age 10 or 12. Among the Muria Gond of India, boys and girls as young as 10 lived together in dormitories and spent their evenings dancing, singing, and pairing off for sex.

Societies that permit sex play among children also tend to encourage open discussion of sex and to allow children to observe sexual behavior among adults. Among the Trukese of the South Pacific, children learned about sex by observing and asking adults. Lesu children, too, would observe adults, but there was at least one taboo: They were not to watch their own mothers.

Sexually Restrictive Societies

Ford and Beach (1951) found that only a minority of preliterate societies were sexually restrictive. The Apinaye people of South America warned their children not to masturbate and thrashed them if they were suspected of doing so. The Kwoma of New Guinea warned boys never to touch their genitals, even when urinating. They risked having their penises beaten with a stick if they touched them.

Sexually restrictive societies discourage masturbation and sex play among children. Children who disobey are punished. Such societies also tend to be closed-lipped about sex. Parents try to keep their children ignorant about reproduction. Premarital sex and watching adults engage in sex are also restricted.

Many societies hold to a sexual double standard by which boys are allowed greater sexual freedom than girls.

Genital Play

Children in the United States typically do not engage in genital play with others until about the age of 2. Then, as an expression of their curiosity about their environment and other people, they may investigate other children's genitals; or hug, cuddle, kiss; or climb on top of them. None of this need cause concern. Spiro (1965) describes 2-year-olds at play in an Israeli kibbutz:

> Ofer [a boy] and Pnina [a girl] sit side by side on chamber pots. . . . Ofer puts his foot on Pnina's foot, she then does the same—this happens several times. . . . Finally, Pnina shifts her pot away, then moves back, then away . . . they laugh. . . . Pnina stands up, lies on the table on her stomach, . . . Ofer pats her buttocks. . . . Ofer kicks Pnina gently, and they laugh . . . Pnina touches and caresses Ofer's leg with her foot . . . says "more more" . . . Ofer stands, then Pnina stands, both bounce up and down . . . both children are excited, bounce, laugh together . . . Pnina grabs Ofer's penis, and he pushes her away . . . she repeats, he pushes her away, and turns around . . . Pnina touches his buttocks. (p. 225)

There is no reason to infer that Ofer and Pnina were seeking sexual gratification. Rough-and-tumble play, including touching the genitals, is common among children.

Reflections

- How did you feel when you saw that we were covering sexuality during infancy? Did it seem to you that we ought not be discussing sexuality during infancy (or childhood)? Why or why not?

- Was any of the information about infant sexuality surprising to you? If so, what?

- Would you characterize your own sociocultural background as sexually permissive or restrictive? Why?

EARLY CHILDHOOD (3 TO 8 YEARS)

SUSAN: Once my younger sister and I were over at a girl friend's house playing in her bedroom. For some reason she pulled her pants down and exposed her rear to us. We were amazed to see she had an extra opening down there we didn't know about. My sister reciprocated by pulling her pants down so we could see if she had the same extra opening. We were amazed at our discovery, our mothers not having mentioned to us that we had a vagina!

CHRISTOPHER: Nancy was a willing playmate, and we spent many hours together examining each other's bodies as doctor and nurse. We even once figured out a pact that we would continue these examinations and watch each other develop. That was before we had started school. (Morrison et al., 1980, p. 19)

These recollections of early childhood show children's interest in sexual anatomy and sexual behavior. Children often show each other their bodies. The unwritten rule seems to be "I'll show you mine if you'll show me yours."

Masturbation

KIM: I began to masturbate when I was 3 years old. My parents . . . tried long and hard to discourage me. They told me it wasn't nice for a young lady to have her hand between her legs.

When I was five I remember my mother discovering that I masturbated with a rag doll I slept with. She was upset, but she didn't make a big deal about it. She just told me in a matter-of-fact way, "Do you know that what you're doing is called masturbating?" That didn't make much sense to me, except I got the impression she didn't want me to do it. (Morrison et al., 1980, pp. 4, 5)

Because of the difficulties in conducting such research, statistics concerning the incidence of masturbation in children is largely speculative. Parents might not wish to respond to questions about the sexual conduct of their children. Or if they do, they might have a tendency to present their children as little "gentlemen" and "ladies" and perhaps underreport their sexual activity. Their biases could also lead them not to perceive their children's genital touching as masturbation. Many parents will not even permit their adolescents to be interviewed about their sexual behavior (Fisher & Hall, 1988), let alone younger children. When we are asked to look back as adults, our memories may be less than accurate.

One recent study by psychologist William Friedrich (1998) of the Mayo Institute relied on interviews with the mothers of more than 1,100 children. The goal of the study was to establish what kinds of sexual behaviors can normally be expected in childhood to help educators and other professionals determine when sexual behavior might be suggestive of childhood sexual abuse. The study did not provide data about masturbation per se,

what do you say now?

How Should a Parent React to Childhood Masturbation?

Few parents today believe that childhood masturbation sets the stage for physical and mental maladies. Still, some parents react with concern, disgust, or shock when their children masturbate.

Parents who are unaware that masturbation is commonplace among children might erroneously assume that children who masturbate are oversexed or aberrant. The parent might pull a child's hands away and scold her or him. Some may even slap the child's hand. Once the child is capable of understanding speech, the parent might say things like "Don't touch down there! That's a bad thing to do. Stop doing that." Threats and punishments might be used. Or parents might fail to acknowledge the behavior openly but move the hands away from the genitals or pick up the child whenever he or she is discovered masturbating.

Sex educators Mary Calderone and Eric Johnson (1989) argue that punishment will not stop children from masturbating. It could cause them to become secretive and guilty about it, however. Sex guilt tends to persist and can impede sexual pleasure in marriage. June Reinisch (1990), director of the Kinsey Institute, notes that

> Parents who scowl, scold, or punish in response to a child's exploring his or her genitals may be teaching the child that this kind of pleasure is wrong and that the *child* is "bad" for engaging in this kind of behavior. This message may hinder the ability to give and receive erotic pleasures as an adult and ultimately interfere with the ability to establish a loving and intimate relationship. (p. 248)

Calderone, Johnson, and Reinisch concur that children need to learn that masturbation in public is not acceptable in our culture, however. Calderone and Johnson suggest that the

Childhood Sexuality? Children are naturally inquisitive about sexual behavior and anatomy.

child who masturbates in front of others can be told something like this:

> I'm glad you've found your body feels good, but when you want to touch your body that way, it's more private to be in your room by yourself. (p. 138)

Reinisch adds that parents are important shapers of their children's sexuality and, more broadly, of their self-esteem. Acknowledging the child's sexuality, rather than rejecting and discouraging it, can strengthen children's self-esteem, build a positive body image, and encourage competence and assertiveness.

Not all authorities, and certainly not all parents, endorse such views. Some object to masturbation on religious or moral grounds. Others feel uncomfortable or conflicted about masturbation themselves. Parents must decide for themselves how best to react when they discover their children masturbating.

---

but as you can see in Table 13.1, it did offer some insight into how many children touch their "private parts." Friedrich suggests that behavior that occurs in at least 20% of children can be considered normal from a statistical point of view.

Male-Female Sexual Behavior

> ALICIA: On my birthday when I was in the second grade, I remember a classmate, Tim, walked home with a friend and me. He kept chasing me to give me kisses all over my face, and I acted like I didn't want him to do it, yet I knew I liked it a lot; when he would stop, I thought he didn't like me anymore. (Morrison et al., 1980, pp. 21, 29)

Three- and 4-year-olds commonly express affection through kissing. Curiosity about the genitals may also occur by this stage. Sex games like "show" and "playing doctor" might begin earlier but become common between the ages of 6 and 10 (Reinisch, 1990). Much of this sexual activity takes place in same-gender groups, although mixed-gender sex

table 13.1

Some normal sexual behaviors in childhood		
Ages 2–5	**Boys %**	**Girls (%)**
Touches or tries to touch mother's or other women's breasts	42.4	43.7
Touches private parts when at home	60.2	43.8
Tries to look at people when they are nude or undressing	26.8	26.9
Ages 6–9		
Touches private parts when at home	39.8	20.7
Tries to look at people when they are nude or undressing	20.2	20.5
Ages 10–12		
Is very interested in the opposite sex	24.1	28.7

Source of data: William M. Friedrich. Cited in Susan Gilbert (1998, April 7). "New light shed on normal sexual behavior in a child." *The New York Times,* p. F7.

games are not uncommon. Children might exhibit their genitals to each other, touch each other's genitals, or even masturbate together.

Male-Male and Female-Female Sexual Behavior

> ARNOLD: When I was about 5, my cousin and I . . . went into the basement and dropped our pants. We touched each other's penises, and that was it. I guess I didn't realize the total significance of the secrecy in which we carried out this act. For later . . . my parents questioned me . . . and I told them exactly what we had done. They were horrified and told me that that was definitely forbidden. (Morrison et al., 1980, p. 24)

Despite Arnold's parents' horror, same-gender sexual play in childhood does not presage adult sexual orientation (Reinisch, 1990). It might, in fact, be more common than heterosexual play. It typically involves handling the other child's genitals, although it might include oral or anal contact. It might also include an outdoor variation of the game of "show" in which boys urinate together and see who can reach farthest or attain the highest trajectory.

We will end this section with the memories of a woman when she was on the edge of preadolescence.

> When I was 8 and had just learned about menstruation, I fashioned a small sanitary napkin for [my Barbie doll] out of neatly folded tissues. Rubber bands held it in place. "Look," said my bemused mother, "Barbie's got her little period. Now she can have a baby."[1] I was disappointed, but my girlfriends snickered in a way that satisfied me. You see, we all wanted Barbie to be, well. Dirty.
>
> Our Barbies had sex, at least our childish version of it. They hugged and kissed the few available boy dolls we had—clean-cut and oh-so-square Ken, the more relaxed and sexy Allan. Our Barbies also danced, pranced and strutted, but mostly they stripped. An adult friend tells me how she used to put her Barbie's low-backed bathing suit on backward, so the doll's breasts were exposed. I dressed mine in her candy-striped baby-sitter's apron—and nothing else. Girls respond intuitively to the doll's sexuality, and it lets them play out those roles in an endlessly compelling and yet ultimately safe manner. (McDonough, 1998, p. 70)

---

[1]Yes, we know that the first several cycles of most girls are anovulatory (so they cannot get pregnant), but we are recounting what someone *said*. As far as we know, it is difficult for Barbie dolls to get pregnant under the best of circumstances.

Reflections

- Have you ever discussed masturbation with your friends? At what age did your friends or you begin to masturbate? Did you know what you were doing (that is, that you were masturbating)? How did you feel about it? Why?
- Did you ever play "show" or "doctor" as a child? What were your feelings about it?
- Did your parents or other adults find you masturbating or playing "doctor"? What was their response? Has their response contributed to your own attitudes? If so, how?

PREADOLESCENCE (9 TO 13 YEARS)

During preadolescence, children typically form relationships with a close "best friend" that enable them to share secrets and confidences. The friends are usually peers of the same gender. Preadolescents also tend to socialize with larger networks of friends in gender-segregated groups. At this stage, boys are likely to think that girls are "dorks." To girls at this stage, "dork" is too nice an epithet to apply to most boys.

Preadolescents grow increasingly preoccupied with and self-conscious about their bodies. Their peers pressure preadolescents to conform to dress codes, standards of "correct" slang, and group standards concerning sex and drugs. Peer disapproval can be an intense punishment.

Sexual urges are experienced by many preadolescents, but they may not emerge until adolescence. Sigmund Freud had theorized that sexual impulses are hidden, or latent, during preadolescence, but many preadolescents are quite active sexually during the so-called latency period.

Masturbation

> PAUL: When I was about 10, stories about masturbation got me worried. A friend and I went to a friend's older brother whom we respected and asked, "Is it really bad?" His reply stuck in my mind for years. "Well, it's like a bottle of olives—every time you take one out, there is one less in there." We were very worried because we thought we'd run out before we got to girls. (Morrison et al., 1980, pp. 6, 7, 8)

Kinsey and his colleagues (1948, 1953) reported that masturbation is the primary means of achieving orgasm during preadolescence for both genders. They found that 45% of males and 15% of females masturbated by age 13.

Male-Female Sexual Behavior

Preadolescent sex play often involves mutual display of the genitals, with or without touching. Such sexual experiences are quite common and do not appear to impair future sexual adjustment (Leitenberg et al., 1989).

Although preadolescents tend to socialize in same-gender groups, interest in the other gender among heterosexuals tends to gradually increase as they approach puberty. Group dating and mixed-gender parties often provide preadolescents with their first exposure to heterosexual activities. Couples might not begin to pair off until early or middle adolescence.

Male-Male and Female-Female Sexual Behavior

Much preadolescent sexual behavior among members of the same gender is simply exploration. Some incidents reflect lack of availability of partners of the opposite gender. As with younger children, experiences with children of the same gender during preadolescence might be more common than heterosexual experiences (Leitenberg et al., 1989). These activities are usually limited to touching of each other's genitals or mutual masturbation. Since preadolescents generally socialize within their genders, it is not surprising that their sexual explorations are also often within their genders. Most same-gender sexual experiences involve single episodes or short-lived relationships and are not signs of a budding gay orientation.

Sex Education and Miseducation

> Imagine teaching driving the same way sex education is taught. You'd be told never to drive or ride as a passenger because you could be injured and go to the hospital. No one would ever take a car out.
> —Mark Miller (1998)

Mark Miller is a graduate of Brown University's program in sexuality and society. He and other scholars of human sexuality lament the approaches of most sex education programs. Says Anke Ehrhardt (1998), a psychiatry professor at Columbia University, "In other countries, sex education is put in a positive context of loving relationships, but here we spread fear. And it hasn't worked. We have a much higher rate of teen pregnancy."

Yet fewer than 10% of American children receive a comprehensive sex education in school (Bronner, 1998). Studies have consistently shown that peers are the main source of sexual information for both genders. According to an ABC News *Nightline* poll (1995), 53% of American adults had learned about sex from their friends. Thirty percent had learned from their parents. When asked where teenagers today learn about sex, five of six (83%) said they had learned from friends.

It is not true that most children learn the facts of life from parents or from school sex education programs. Most children learn about sex from peers. Is the lamp on the street corner the key guiding light for U.S. youth? ■

Truth or Fiction?
REVISITED

School-based sex education programs were relatively rare as late as the early 1970s, despite the fact that an overwhelming majority of parents supported sex education in the schools (Norman & Harris, 1981). Sex education programs became more common in the 1970s and 1980s. By the late 1980s, about six in ten teenagers received some form of sex education in the schools (Kenney et al., 1989).

The ABC News *Nightline* poll (1995) found that most American adults believe that sex education programs should teach students to use contraceptives if they are going to engage in premarital sexual activity (91%), that condoms can prevent AIDS (85%), and that early sex is a bad idea (80%). On the other hand, there is great disagreement as to whether school sex education programs should discuss masturbation, abortion, and sexual orientation.

Today, nearly all states mandate or recommend sex education programs. The content and length of sex education programs vary widely. Most programs emphasize the biological aspects of puberty and reproduction (Haffner, 1993). In keeping with parents' preferences, few focus on abortion, masturbation, or sexual orientation. Sexual pleasure is rarely mentioned.

Sex education in the schools, especially about value-laden topics, remains a source of controversy. Some people argue that sex education ought to be left to parents and religious authorities. But the data suggest that the real alternatives to the schools are peers and the corner newsstand, which sells more copies of "adult" magazines than of textbooks. Many parents are also concerned that teaching subjects such as sexual techniques and contraception encourages sexual experimentation. Yet the research does not show that sex education increases sexual experimentation (Eisen & Zellman, 1987; Kolbe, 1998; Richardson, 1997).

what do you say now?

Talking with Your Children about Sex

"Daddy, where do babies come from?"

"What are you asking me for? Go ask your mother."

Most children do not find it easy to talk to their parents about sex (Coles & Stokes, 1985). The parents might not find it any easier. Nearly half (47%) of the teens who were polled in a national survey said that they would ask their friends, siblings, or sex partners if they wanted information about sex. Only about a third (36%) would turn to their parents (Coles & Stokes, 1985). Three out of four said that it is hard to talk about sex with their fathers. More than half (57%) found it difficult to approach their mothers. Regrettably, information received from peers is likely to be strewn with inaccuracies. Misinformed teenagers run a higher risk of unwanted pregnancies and STIs.

Yet most young children are curious about where babies come from, about what makes little girls different from little boys, and so on. Parents who avoid answering such questions convey their own uneasiness about sex and might teach children that sex is something to be ashamed of, not something they should discuss openly.

Some parents resist talking about sex with their children because they are insecure in their own knowledge. Reinisch (1990) argues that parents need not be sex experts to talk to their children about sex, however. Parents can turn to books in the local bookstore to fill in gaps in knowledge or to books that are intended for parents to read to their children. They can also admit that they do not know the answer to a particular question. Reinisch suggests that children will respect parents who display such honesty.

In answering children's questions, parents need to be sensitive to what their children can understand. The 4-year-old who wants to know where babies come from is probably not interested in detailed biological information. It might be sufficient to say, "From Mommy's uterus" and then point to the mother's abdominal region. Why say "tummy"? "Tummy" is wrong and confusing.

In their *Family Book about Sexuality*, Calderone and Johnson (1989) offer parents some pointers:

1. *Be willing to answer your child's questions about sex.* Parents who respond to their children's questions about sex by saying, "Why do you want to know that?" squelch further questioning. The child is likely to interpret the parent's response as meaning "You shouldn't be interested in that."
2. *Use appropriate language.* As children develop awareness of their sexuality, they need to learn the names of their sex organs. They also need to learn that the "dirty words" that others use to refer to the sexual parts of the body are not acceptable in most situations, since they carry emotional connotations that can arouse negative feelings.

Nor should parents use "silly words" to describe sexual organs. As June Reinisch (1990) notes,

Another way parents send out negative messages about sexuality is by using silly words (or no words at all) to describe

---

Truth or Fiction?
REVISITED

There is no evidence that sex education encourages sexual activity among children and adolescents. ∎

Many school programs that offer information about contraception and other sensitive topics are limited to high school juniors and seniors. Sexual experimentation often begins earlier, however (Ehrhardt, 1998). Most sexually active teens in Coles and Stokes's (1985) sample began engaging in intercourse by age 15. Fifty percent of the sexually active teenage boys and 18% of the sexually active teenage girls began by age 13.

Accurate information in preadolescence might prevent various sexual mishaps (Coles & Stokes, 1985). Many teens, for example, erroneously believe that a female cannot get pregnant from her first coital experience. Others believe that douching protects them from sexually transmitted diseases (STDs) or unwanted pregnancies.

Reflections

∎ How old were you when you learned "the facts of life"? What was your reaction?
∎ How did you learn about reproduction and sexuality? What inaccuracies were there in your early sources of information?
∎ Do you support sex education in the schools? If so, what topics should be covered? Which should not? Why?

sexual anatomy. Whether they call genitals "pee-pee" or "privates" or nothing at all, parents are telling children that these body parts are significantly different, embarrassing, mysterious, or taboo compared to such other body parts as the eyes, nose, and knees, which have names openly used in conversation. (p. 248)

3. *Give advice in the form of information that the child can use to make sound decisions, not as an imperial edict.* State your own convictions, but label your beliefs as your own, rather than as something you are trying to impose on your child. Parents are not as likely to be effective by "laying down the law" as by relating convictions in firm but loving ways—by providing information and encouraging discussion. Reinisch (1990) suggests combining information about sex with expressions of the parents' values and beliefs.

   Parents of teenage children often react to sexual experimentation with threats or punishments, which might cause adolescents to rebel or tune them out. Or the adolescent might learn to associate sex with fear and anger, which may persist even in adult relationships. Parents might find it more constructive to convey concern about the consequences of children's actions in a loving and nonthreatening way that invites an open response. Say, for example, "I'm worried about the way you are experimenting, and I'd like to give you some information that you may not have. Can we talk about it?" (Calderone & Johnson, 1989, p. 141).

4. *Share information in small doses.* Pick a time and place that feels natural for such discussions, such as when the child is preparing for bed or when you are riding in the car.

5. *Encourage the child to talk about sex.* Children might feel embarrassed about talking about sex, especially with family members. Make the child aware that you are always available to answer questions. Be "askable." But let the child postpone talking about a sensitive topic until the two of you are alone or the child feels comfortable. Books about sexuality might help a child to open up. They can be left lying around or given to the child with a suggestion such as "This is a good book about sex, or at least I thought so. If you read it, then maybe we can talk about it" (Calderone & Johnson, 1989, p. 136).

6. *Respect privacy rights.* Most of us, parents and children alike, value our privacy at certain times. A parent who feels uncomfortable sharing a bathroom with a child can simply tell the child that Daddy or Mommy likes to be alone when using the bathroom. Or the parent might explain, "I like my privacy, so please knock and I'll tell you if it's okay to come in. I'll do the same for you" (Calderone & Johnson, 1989, p. 137). This can be said without a scolding or harsh tone. Privacy rights in the bedroom can be established by saying in a clear and unthreatening way, "Please knock when the door's closed and wait to be invited in" (Calderone & Johnson, 1989, p. 138). But it is just as important for the parent to respect the child's rights to privacy. The child is likely to feel grateful for the respect and to show respect in return.

ADOLESCENCE

Adolescence is bounded by the advent of puberty at the lower end and the capacity to take on adult responsibilities at the upper end. In our society, adolescents are "neither fish nor fowl," as the saying goes—neither children nor adults. Adolescents may be able to reproduce and be taller than their parents, but they might not be allowed to get driver's licenses or attend R-rated films. They are prevented from working long hours and must usually stay in school until age 16. They cannot marry until they reach the "age of consent." The message is clear: Adults see adolescents as impulsive and needing to be restricted for "their own good." Given these restrictions, a sex drive that is heightened by surges of sex hormones, and media inundation with sexual themes, it is not surprising that many adolescents are in conflict with their families about going around with certain friends, sex, and using the family car.

Puberty The stage of development during which reproduction first becomes possible. Puberty begins with the appearance of secondary sex characteristics and ends when the long bones make no further gains in length. (From the Latin *puber,* meaning "of ripe age.")

Secondary sex characteristics Physical characteristics that differentiate males and females and that usually appear at puberty but are not directly involved in reproduction, such as the bodily distribution of hair and fat, development of the muscle mass, and deepening of the voice.

Puberty

Puberty begins with the appearance of **secondary sex characteristics** and ends when the long bones make no further gains in length (see Table 13.2 on pages 396 and 397). The appearance of strands of pubic hair is often the first visible sign of puberty. Pubic hair

t a b l e   1 3 . 2

Stages of pubertal development

In Females

Beginning sometime between ages 8 and 11	Pituitary hormones stimulate ovaries to increase production of estrogen. Internal reproductive organs begin to grow.
Beginning sometime between ages 9 and 15	First the areolas (the darker area around the nipples) and then the breasts increase in size and become more rounded. Pubic hair becomes darker and coarser. Growth in height continues. Body fat continues to round body contours. A normal vaginal discharge becomes noticeable. Sweat and oil glands increase in activity, and acne may appear. Internal and external reproductive organs and genitals grow, making the vagina longer and the labia more pronounced.
Beginning sometime between ages 10 and 16	Areolas and nipples grow, often forming a second mound sticking out from the rounded breast mound. Pubic hair begins to grow in a triangular shape and to cover the center of the mons. Underarm hair appears. Menarche occurs. Internal reproductive organs continue to develop. Ovaries may begin to release mature eggs capable of being fertilized. Growth in height slows.
Beginning sometime between ages 12 and 19	Breasts near adult size and shape. Pubic hair fully covers the mons and spreads to the top of the thighs. The voice may deepen slightly (but not as much as in males). Menstrual cycles gradually become more regular. Some further changes in body shape may occur into the young woman's early 20s.

This table is a general guideline. Changes may appear sooner or later than shown and do not always appear in the indicated sequence.

Primary sex characteristics
Physical characteristics that differentiate males and females and are directly involved in reproduction, such as the sex organs.

Menarche The onset of menstruation; first menstruation. (From Greek roots meaning "month" [*men*] and "beginning" [*arche*].)

tends to be light colored, sparse, and straight at first. Then it spreads and grows darker, thicker, and coarser. Puberty also involves changes in **primary sex characteristics.** Once puberty begins, most major changes occur within three years in girls and within four years in boys (Etaugh & Rathus, 1995).

Toward the end of puberty, reproduction becomes possible. The two principal markers of reproductive potential are **menarche** in the girl and the first ejaculation in the boy. But these events do not generally herald immediate fertility.

Girls typically experience menarche between the ages of 10 and 18. In the mid-1800s, European girls typically achieved menarche by about age 17 (see Figure 13.1 on page 398). The age of menarche has declined sharply since then among girls in Western nations, most likely because of improved nutrition and health care. In the United States, the

In Males

Beginning sometime between ages 9 and 15	The testicles begin to grow. The skin of the scrotum becomes redder and coarser. A few straight pubic hairs appear at the base of the penis. Muscle mass develops, and the boy begins to grow taller.
Beginning sometime between ages 11 and 16	The areolas grow larger and darker. The penis begins to grow longer. The testicles and scrotum continue to grow. Pubic hair becomes coarser and more curled and spreads to cover the area between the legs. The body gains in height. The shoulders broaden. The hips narrow. The larynx enlarges, resulting in a deepening of the voice. Sparse facial and underarm hair appears.
Beginning sometime between ages 11 and 17	The penis begins to increase in circumference as well as in length (though more slowly). The testicles continue to increase in size. The texture of the pubic hair is more like an adult's. Growth of facial and underarm hair increases. Shaving may begin. First ejaculation occurs. In nearly half of all boys, gynecomastia (breast enlargement) occurs, which then decreases in a year or two. Increased skin oils may produce acne.
Beginning sometime between ages 14 and 18	The body nears final adult height, and the genitals achieve adult shape and size, with pubic hair spreading to the thighs and slightly upward toward the belly. Chest hair appears. Facial hair reaches full growth. Shaving becomes more frequent. For some young men, further increases in height, body hair, and muscle growth and strength continue into their early 20s.

Source: Copyright © 1990 by the Kinsey Institute for Research in Sex, Gender, and Reproduction. From THE KINSEY INSTITUTE NEW REPORT ON SEX.

average age of menarche by the 1960s and 1970s had dropped to between 12½ and 13 (Etaugh & Rathus, 1995).

The **critical fat hypothesis** suggests that girls must reach a certain body weight (perhaps 103 to 109 pounds) to trigger pubertal changes such as menarche, and children today do tend to achieve larger body sizes sooner. Body fat would play a crucial role because fat cells secrete leptin. Leptin is a chemical that would then signal the body to secrete a cascade of hormones that increases the levels of estrogen in the body. It is known that menarche comes later to girls who have a lower percentage of body fat, such as athletes (Frisch, 1997). Injections of leptin also cause laboratory animals to reach sexual maturity early (Angier, 1997). Whatever the exact triggering mechanism, the average age at which girls experience menarche has leveled off in recent years.

Critical fat hypothesis The view that girls must reach a certain body weight to trigger pubertal changes such as menarche.

figure 13.1

Age at Menarche. The age at menarche has been declining since the mid-1800s among girls in Western nations, apparently because of improved nutrition and health care. Menarche might be triggered by the accumulation of a critical percentage of body fat.

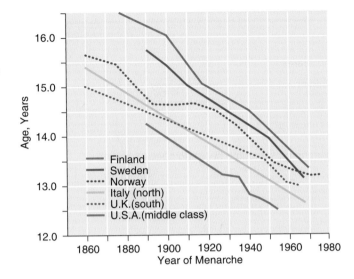

PUBERTAL CHANGES IN THE FEMALE   First menstruation, or menarche, is the most obvious sign of puberty in girls. Yet other, less obvious changes have already taken place that have set the stage for menstruation. Between 8 and 14 years of age, release of FSH by the pituitary gland causes the ovaries to begin to secrete estrogen. Estrogen has several major effects on pubertal development. For one, it stimulates the growth of breast tissue ("breast buds"), perhaps as early as age 8 or 9. The breasts usually begin to enlarge during the tenth year.

Estrogen also promotes the growth of the uterus and the thickening of the vaginal lining. It also stimulates growth of fatty and supporting tissue in the hips and buttocks. This tissue and the widening of the pelvis cause the hips to become rounded and permit childbearing. But growth of fatty deposits and connective tissue varies considerably. Some women may have pronounced breasts; others may have relatively large hips.

Small amounts of androgens produced by the female's adrenal glands, along with estrogen, stimulate development of pubic and underarm hair, beginning at about age 11. Excessive androgen production can darken or thicken facial hair.

Estrogen causes the labia to grow during puberty, but androgens cause the clitoris to develop. Estrogen stimulates growth of the vagina and uterus. Estrogen typically brakes the female growth spurt some years before that of the male. Girls who are deficient in estrogen during their late teens may grow quite tall, but most tall girls reach their heights because of normal genetically determined variations, not estrogen deficiency.

Estrogen production becomes cyclical in puberty and regulates the menstrual cycle. Following menarche, a girl's early menstrual cycles are typically **anovulatory.** Girls cannot become pregnant until ovulation occurs, which may lag behind menarche by as much as two years. At first, ovulation might not be reliable, so a girl might be relatively infertile. Some teenagers are highly fertile soon after menarche, however (Reinisch, 1990).

PUBERTAL CHANGES IN THE MALE   At puberty, the hypothalamus signals the pituitary to increase production of FSH and LH. These releasing hormones stimulate the testes to increase their output of testosterone. Testosterone prompts growth of the male genitals: the testes, scrotum, and penis. It fosters differentiation of male secondary sex characteristics: the growth of facial, body, and pubic hair and the deepening of the voice. Testicle growth, in turn, accelerates testosterone production and pubertal changes. The testes continue to grow, and the scrotal sac becomes larger and hangs loosely from the body. The penis widens and lengthens, and pubic hair appears.

Anovulatory Without ovulation.

By age 13 or 14, erections become frequent. Indeed, many junior high school boys dread that they may be caught between classes with erections or asked to stand before the class. Under the influence of testosterone, the prostate and seminal vesicles—the organs that produce semen—increase in size, and semen production begins. Boys typically experience their first ejaculation by age 13 or 14, most often through masturbation. There is much variation, however. First ejaculations might occur as early as age 8 or not until the early 20s (Reinisch, 1990). Mature sperm are not usually found in the ejaculate until about a year after the first ejaculation, at age 14 on the average (Kulin et al., 1989). But sperm may be present in the first ejaculate (Reinisch, 1990), so pubertal boys should not assume that they have an infertile "grace period" following first ejaculation. About a year after first ejaculation, boys may also begin to experience **nocturnal emissions,** which are also called "wet dreams" because of the belief that nocturnal emissions accompany erotic dreams—which need not be so.

Despite the term "wet dreams," nocturnal emissions in boys need not accompany erotic dreams. ■

Underarm hair appears at about age 15. Facial hair is at first a fuzz on the upper lip. A beard does not appear for another two or three years. Only half of U.S. boys shave (of necessity) by age 17. The beard and chest hair continue to develop past the age of 20. At age 14 or 15 the voice deepens because of the growth of the **larynx** and the lengthening of the vocal cords. Development is gradual, and the voices of adolescent boys sometimes crack embarrassingly.

Boys and girls undergo general growth spurts during puberty. Girls usually shoot up before boys. Individuals differ, however, and some boys spurt sooner than some girls.

Increases in muscle mass produce increases in weight. The shoulders and the circumference of the chest widen. At the age of 18 or so, men stop growing taller because estrogen prevents the long bones from making further gains in length (Smith et al., 1994). Males normally produce some estrogen in the adrenal glands and testes. Nearly one in two boys experiences temporary enlargement of the breasts, or **gynecomastia,** during puberty (this is also caused by estrogen).

Nocturnal emission Involuntary ejaculation of seminal fluid while asleep. Also referred to as a "wet dream," although the individual need not be dreaming about sex, or dreaming at all, at the time.

Larynx A structure of muscle and cartilage at the upper end of the trachea that contains the vocal cords; the voice box.

Gynecomastia Overdevelopment of a male's breasts. (From Greek roots meaning "woman" [*gyne*] and "breast" [*mastos*].)

MENARCHE IN CROSS-CULTURAL PERSPECTIVE

I'll never forget seventh grade when it seemed all my friends were menstruating but me. At first I was thinking of coming to school one day and telling them I had gotten my first period but I was afraid that they'd know I was lying so I didn't. Pretty soon no one talked about it much so by the time I did get my first period no one really cared—except my mother who told me I was now a woman.

I began menstruating when I was twelve. I remember feeling great ambivalence about it. I was a little frightened by the blood, and resented having to wear a "diaper." I was sure everyone would be able to tell I had a belt and pad on! On the other hand, I was excited to know that I could become pregnant—that I had become a woman.

My mother showed me how to roll up and wrap a used sanitary napkin in Kleenex. I really did it perfectly my first try and went out to show my mother, who had company in the living room.

They giggled, though I got no negative messages about it, I felt embarrassed. (Morrison et al., 1980, pp. 70–73)

These recollections of college women reflect common attitudes toward menstruation. Some pubescent girls see it as a sign of "becoming a woman." They anxiously await menarche. They compete with friends to see who will be first to arrive on the doorstep of adulthood. The second quotation shows that many people mistakenly believe that menstruation signals reproductive capacity. Yet such capacity might lag behind menarche by more than a year.

Girls tend to be more likely to share news of first menstruation with friends than boys are to tell other boys of their first ejaculation (Brooks-Gunn et al., 1986; Gaddis & Brooks-Gunn, 1985). Menstruation is perceived as a biological event that signals a passage to womanhood. Ejaculation is perceived as a sexual event, however. Boys might also feel embarrassed to disclose the experience to friends because it typically occurs during masturbation.

In different times, in different places, menarche has had different meanings. The Thais view menarche as transforming a girl into a complete woman (Gardiner & Gardiner, 1991). The Kurtatchi, who live on an island off the green coast of New Guinea, greet menarche with an elaborate ceremony (Matlin, 1996). The girl's mother announces the event to friends and relatives, who go into seclusion with the girl. They paint their bodies in preparation for public ceremonies. The girl and her entourage emerge from seclusion, perform a dance, and blow on a conch shell. The girl parades among the rejoicing villagers. Then there is a feast.

Among Hindu families in India, the onset of menstruation signifies the loss of the girl's purity (Kumar, 1991). During menstruation, she is expected to abstain from cooking food for the family or participating in religious ceremonies. A menstruating girl might be expected to cease daily activities and spend time alone in her room, a practice of isolation that may continue even into her marriage.

Masturbation

Masturbation is a major sexual outlet during adolescence. About half of the adolescent boys (46%) in Coles and Stokes's (1985) national survey of 1,067 teenagers and about a quarter of the girls (24%) reported masturbating. The average age at which teenagers in the Coles and Stokes survey reported they started to masturbate was 11 years, 8 months.

A southern California survey of 641 teenagers showed that boys who masturbate do so two to three times a week, on the average, compared to about once a month for girls (Hass, 1979). Researchers find no links between adolescent masturbation and early sexual activity (for example, frequency of intercourse, number of different partners, or age upon first intercourse) and sexual adjustment during young adulthood (Leitenberg et al., 1993).

Many teens still think of masturbation as shameful (Coles & Stokes, 1985). Only about one in three (31%) of the teens surveyed by Coles and Stokes reported feeling completely free of guilt over masturbation. One in five felt a "large amount" or "a great deal" of guilt. The others felt a "small" or "medium" amount of guilt.

Male-Female Sexual Behavior

Young people today start dating and "going steady" earlier than in past generations. These changes have implications for teenage pregnancy. Teens who date earlier (by age 14) are more likely to engage in coitus during high school (Miller et al., 1986). Teens who initiate sexual intercourse earlier are also less likely to use contraception and more likely to incur an unwanted pregnancy. If the young woman decides to keep her baby, she is also more likely to have to leave school and scuttle educational and vocational plans. Early dating does not always lead to early coitus, however. Nor does early coitus always lead to unwanted pregnancies. Still, some young women find their options in adulthood restricted by a chain of events that began in early adolescence.

PETTING Many adolescents use petting to express affection, satisfy their curiosities, heighten their sexual arousal, and reach orgasm while avoiding pregnancy and maintaining virginity.

An overwhelming majority (97%) of teenagers sampled in the Coles and Stokes (1985) survey had engaged in kissing (a form of light petting) by the age of 15. Girls tended to engage in kissing earlier than boys, perhaps because girls tend to mature faster. By age 13, 73% of the girls and 66% of the boys had engaged in kissing.

ORAL SEX The incidence of premarital oral sex has increased twofold to threefold since Kinsey's time. About four in ten (41%) of the 17- and 18-year-old girls in the Coles and Stokes (1985) survey of the 1980s reported that they had performed fellatio. About a third of the boys reported performing cunnilingus. Many girls reported that they had engaged in fellatio for the partner's pleasure, not their own.

A 1982 survey of 16-year-old high school students revealed even higher rates of oral sex (Newcomer & Udry, 1985). Fifty-three percent of the 256 boys sampled and 42% of the 289 girls reported having engaged in oral sex. More students had engaged in oral sex than in coitus. Some couples maintain *technical virginity* by substituting oral sex for intercourse (Gagnon & Simon, 1987). This seems to represent a reversal of the traditional sexual script in which couples do not engage in oral sex until after they have begun to engage in coitus, if at all.

Some adolescent couples use oral sex as a means of birth control. As one 17-year-old New York girl put it, "That's what we used to do before we could start having sex, because we didn't have protection and stuff" (Coles & Stokes, 1985, p. 60).

PREMARITAL INTERCOURSE As we enter the new millennium, a federal survey found that about half of the high school students in the United States are sexually active (Kolbe, 1998). No statistics were available for high school dropouts, who make up about 5% of the teenage population. Many young people feel as if they are caught betwixt and between. On the one hand, adults tell them to wait until they're older, to "just say no." On the other hand, the movies and television programs they see and the stories they hear from their peers reinforce the belief that everybody's "doing it."

Premarital Intercourse. Surveys show that about half of the high school students in the United States are sexually active. The incidence of premarital intercourse, especially for females, increased dramatically during the twentieth century, but seems to have leveled off. Sexually active adolescents incur the risks of unwanted pregnancy and STIs.

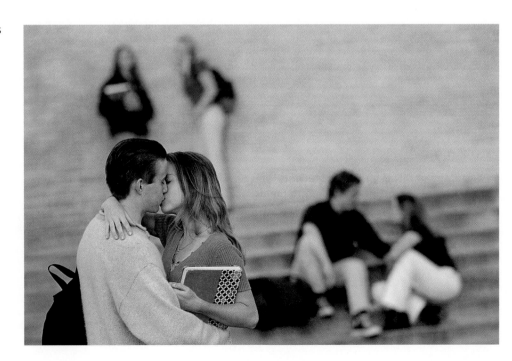

Teenagers and Sex: Where Do We Stand?

By the turn of the millennium, the American public seemed to have had its fill of sex scandals in Washington, Hollywood, and other "happening" places. But the nation had barely begun to face an even more serious "sex scandal"—the young ages at which boys and girls were engaging in sexual intercourse, often risking pregnancy and sexually transmitted infections.

Yet there were some positive signs. A federal survey of more than 16,000 high school students found that in 1997, 48% of students reported that they had become sexually active, compared with 54% in 1991 (Kolbe, 1998). Sixteen percent of the respondents reported having sex with four or more partners, down from the 19% reported in 1991. Why the decline? Figure 13.2 shows ethnic differences among students in 1991 and 1997. It reveals that the percentage of African American students who had become sexually active fell by about 8 points from 1991 to 1997, from 81% to 73%. The percentage for non-Hispanic White American students fell about 6%, from 50% to 44%. For Hispanic American students, the rate dropped about 1%, from 53% to 52%. Lloyd Kolbe (1998), director of the CDC's Division of Adolescent and School Health (which released the report), speculated that efforts by school and parents to instruct high school students about the risks of pregnancy and sexually transmitted infections had begun to pay off.

The 1990s also saw a decline in the teenage pregnancy rate because of increased use of contraception as well as the leveling off of sexual activity among teenagers (Kolbe, 1998; Meckler, 1998). Still, the rate of teenage pregnancy remains much higher in the United States than in many other developed countries. For example, the U.S. rate is twice as high as the comparable rate in England and Canada. It is nine times as high as the rate in Japan (Brody, 1998e).

Adolescent girls, by and large, obtain little advice at home or in school about how to resist sexual pressures. Nor do most of them have ready access to effective contraception. According to the Alan Guttmacher Institute (1998), fewer than half of the adolescents who are sexually active report using contraceptives consistently. As a result, about 1 million teenage girls get pregnant each year (Meckler, 1998). More than 200,000 of them have abortions (Shalala, 1998). This figure includes nearly 20% of the sexually active girls aged 15 through 19. Nearly 3 million teenagers in the United States also obtain a sexually transmitted infection each year. One-fifth of the Americans who are diagnosed with AIDS are in their 20s, and most of them were infected as adolescents.

WHY SO YOUNG?

According to a study published in the *British Medical Journal,* there are many reasons for the young age of first intercourse. For example, "Children are exposed to sexual images through the media. . . . Social and peer pressure may arise from the portrayal of sex as glamorous, pleasurable and adult, while negative consequences and the responsibilities involved in sexual relationships are seldom portrayed" (cited in Brody, 1998e). For example, in a popular movie, *Slums of Beverly Hills,* a 13-year-old decides to engage in sexual intercourse with an older boy "just to get it over with."

The New York Times columnist Jane Brody (1998e) asks, "Is this the message we want to convey to American youth—that sex is something you try, like rollerblading or water skiing, to see what it's like or to add to your roster of achievements?"

Remaining a virgin until married is no longer as important as it was early in the twentieth century. Nor does becoming a single mother or having an abortion carry the stigma it once had. Nevertheless, there are problems. A study published in *Family Planning Perspectives* found that girls who had first intercourse at an early age, especially those who became pregnant and had children, tended to have low self-esteem and to be depressed (cited in Brody, 1998e).

RESISTING SEXUAL PRESSURE

Programs like those developed by Girls Inc., Growing Together, and Will Power/Won't Power, seem to be helpful in delaying sexual activity among adolescent girls. Growing Together involves mother-daughter workshops that enhance communication about sex and other sensitive matters. Will Power/Won't Power is an assertiveness training program that helps teenagers to resist sexual pressure without jeopardizing their relationships with their peers. Both programs provide information about the problems that adolescent girls encounter when they become pregnant. For information about the programs, contact Girls Inc. at (212) 509–2000 or see the Web site at http://www.girlsinc.org.

figure 13.2

Percentage of U.S. High School Students Who Have Become Sexually Active, According to Ethnicity.
A poll by the Centers for Disease Control and Prevention found that fewer U.S. high school students were sexually active in 1997 than in 1991. African American students were most likely to be sexually active.

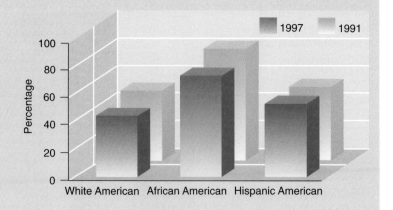

The incidence of premarital intercourse, especially for females, has increased dramatically since Kinsey's day. In Kinsey's time, the sexual double standard held firm. Women were expected to remain virgins until marriage, but society looked the other way for men. Not surprisingly, Kinsey and his colleagues found a much greater incidence of premarital coitus among men. By the age of 20, 77% of the single men but only 20% of the single women reported that they had engaged in premarital coitus. Of those who were still single by age 25, the figures rose to 83% for men but only 33% for women. The discrepancy between the genders is partly explained by the fact that men were often sexually initiated by prostitutes (Hunt, 1974). Rates of premarital coitus among young women should not be confused with sexual promiscuity. Kinsey found that 53% of the females who had engaged in premarital coitus had done so with one partner only (Kinsey et al., 1953).

Sexual activity among adolescents in the United States has increased since the 1970s. Surveys in the early 1970s found that about half (46% to 57% across studies) of the women sampled had engaged in premarital sex by the age of 19 (Kantner & Zelnik, 1972; Sorensen, 1973). This figure compares to fewer than 20% in Kinsey's day. By 1979, 65%—nearly two out of three—young, never-married women 19 years of age who lived in metropolitan areas of the United States had engaged in sexual intercourse (Zeman, 1990). By 1988, among 19-year-old, never-married adolescents living in metropolitan areas of the United States, 78% of the girls and 86% of boys had become sexually active (Zeman, 1990).

The Janus and Janus nationwide sample taken during the late 1980s and early 1990s found that even among adults today who identify themselves as very religious, seven in ten reported having had premarital sexual experiences (Janus & Janus, 1993). Young people today are also initiating sexual intercourse at younger ages. Kinsey found that 7% of White females had engaged in intercourse by the age of 16. By 1979, 22% of 15-year-old girls in U.S. metropolitan areas had engaged in coitus; by 1988, the figure had risen to 27% (Zeman, 1990). By 1988, about one in three 15-year-old boys also reported coital experiences (Zeman, 1990). The average age of first intercourse among girls in the United States is about 16; for boys, 15.5 (USDHHS, 1990).

In sum, the incidence of premarital sex has increased since Kinsey's day, dramatically so among females. Rates of premarital sex among young men have traditionally been higher, but the gender gap has narrowed considerably.

MOTIVES FOR INTERCOURSE   Premarital intercourse is motivated by a number of factors. Sex hormones, especially testosterone, activate sexual arousal. Thus, the pubertal surge of hormones directly activates sexual arousal, at least among boys (Brooks-Gunn & Furstenberg, 1989). Hormonal changes might also have indirect effects on sexual experimentation (Brooks-Gunn & Furstenberg, 1989). About half of the men (51%) and one quarter of the women (24%) in the NHSLS study reported that their primary reason for the first coital experience was curiosity or "readiness for sex" (Michael et al., 1994, p. 93).

Hormonal changes stoke the development of secondary sex characteristics. Adolescents whose secondary sex characteristics develop early might begin dating earlier, which might increase the likelihood of progressing toward sexual intercourse at an earlier age. Some early maturers are pressured into dating or sex—whether they are psychologically ready or not.

Some adolescents perceive sexual intercourse as the natural outgrowth of love (Thompson, 1995). The NHSLS study found that affection for the partner was the primary reason for first intercourse among nearly half (48%) of the women and one quarter (25%) of the men sampled (Michael et al., 1994). Betsy believed that she was in love:

> I was seventeen when I had my first sexual experience. I had been going out with my boyfriend for about five months, during which time he had been continually pressuring me to have sex. He made it seem as though I had to comply or he would end the relationship. Because I was deeply in love with him (or so I thought), I allowed it to happen. (Copyright © 1991 by Osterhout, Formichella, and McIntyre by arrangement with AVON BOOKS, p. 64)

Adolescents might consider intercourse a sign of maturity, a way for girls to reward a boyfriend for remaining loyal, or a means of punishing parents (Thompson, 1995).

ETHNIC DIFFERENCES IN PREMARITAL INTERCOURSE, ADOLESCENT USE OF CONTRACEPTION, AND RESOLUTION OF UNWANTED PREGNANCIES

African American teenagers become sexually active two years earlier, on the average, than White teenagers. They are more likely in dating relationships to progress directly from light petting to intercourse (Brooks-Gunn & Furstenberg, 1989). Earlier initiation to coitus and more rapid progression from petting to intercourse could place African American females at greater risk of unwanted pregnancies (Brooks-Gunn & Furstenberg, 1989; Smith & Udry, 1985).

A review of the research on ethnicity and sexual behavior in college students shows Asian American and Hispanic American students to be somewhat more conservative sexually than their African American or (non-Hispanic) White American counterparts (Baldwin et al., 1992; Padilla & O'Grady, 1987). A survey of 114 Chinese American students attending the University of California at Berkeley showed that more than 60% approved of premarital intercourse for couples who are in love or engaged to be married (Huang & Uba, 1992). Four in ten reported engaging in premarital intercourse themselves. By contrast, a much lower proportion (fewer than one in ten) of the respondents in a survey of Chinese students in Hong Kong reported having premarital intercourse (Chan, 1990). The experience of living in a sexually permissive culture like the United States seems to liberalize the sexual behavior and attitudes of young Chinese Americans. Lending support to this interpretation is the finding from the Berkeley survey that the level of acculturation to the United States was associated with both greater sexual experience and more permissive attitudes. Still, the prevalence of premarital sex among Asian American students, including the Chinese American students in the Berkeley sample, is low by comparison with the general U.S. college population.

There are also informative ethnic group differences in the use of contraception. Hispanic American adolescents, for example, are less likely than non-Hispanics to use contraception (Darabi et al., 1986). Horowitz (1983) attributes the low rate of use of contraceptives by Hispanic American teens not to lack of knowledge about birth control but to conflict between sexual activity and the conservative sexual values with which they are reared. The use of contraception might be a nagging reminder that one's sexual behavior is inconsistent with one's sexual values. A survey of Mexican American and Anglo undergraduates at a southern California state university with a large Mexican American enrollment found that Mexican American students were more conservative and traditional in their sexual attitudes and reported *less* sexual experience than their Anglo counterparts (Padilla & O'Grady, 1987). Another researcher reports that Mexican American women tend to delay first intercourse in comparison to non-Hispanic White women (Slonim-Nevo, 1992). Yet other research shows that the more often Hispanic American adolescent females engage in intercourse, the more likely they are to use effective contraception (DuRant et al., 1990). Perhaps it becomes more difficult to maintain a veneer of denial of sexual activity as the young woman becomes more sexually active.

The survey by Padilla and O'Grady (1987) also revealed that Mexican American students held more conservative attitudes than Anglo students about masturbation, abortion, and premarital and extramarital relationships. Mexican American students less frequently engaged in sexual intercourse, had fewer coital partners, and reported masturbating less often than their Anglo counterparts. They also identified more strongly than Anglo students with a traditional Judeo-Christian value system. The Padilla and O'Grady survey was based on one college sample of 165 Mexican American students (86 male, 79 female) and 99 Anglo students (47 male, 52 female). They might not represent the Mexican American community at large.

A longitudinal study in Houston, Texas, sheds light on some ethnic differences in the resolution of teenage pregnancies (Buchanan & Robbins, 1990). The data shown in Table 13.3 are based on a sample of more than 2,000 males from the Houston school district who were first evaluated in seventh grade and then ten years later. By age 21, rates of adolescent pregnancies among the sexual partners of these young men were greater among African Americans (24%)

Some adolescents engage in coitus in response to peer pressure, especially from close friends. Adolescents whose friends have engaged in sexual intercourse are more likely to engage in intercourse themselves. Coles and Stokes (1985) found that for 78% of the virgins in their national sample, few if any of their friends had engaged in intercourse. This was true of only 28% of the nonvirgins.

Sometimes the pressure comes from dating partners. About one quarter (24%) of the women sampled in the NHSLS study said that they went along with intercourse only for the sake of their partners (Michael et al., 1994):

MEGAN (18, California): I have felt pressure before. My first boyfriend pressured me because he knew I loved him and that he could take advantage of my feelings. I was blinded by my feelings and I had sex with him. I hated it.

AMY (18, Washington, D.C.): I was sexually pressured by my second boyfriend. He didn't love me, but he did want to have sex. I helped him sneak into my room in the middle

table 13.3

Resolution of adolescent pregnancies by racial/ethnic group

	Percentage Whose Partners Experienced Pregnancy by Age 21	OF THOSE WHOSE PARTNERS EXPERIENCED PREGNANCY		
		Percentage Whose Partners Had Abortions	Percentage Whose Partners Had the Child; Couple Did Not Marry or Cohabit	Percentage Whose Partners Had the Child; Couple Married or Cohabited
African American (*N* = 627)	24	16	56	28
White American (*N* = 1666)	12	58	8	34
Hispanic American (*N* = 240)	16	29	16	55
Total (*N* = 2533)	15	38	28	34

Source: Adapted from Buchanan, M., & Robbins, C. (1990). Early adult psychological consequences for males of adolescent pregnancy and its resolution. *Journal of Youth and Adolescence, 19,* 413–424. Reprinted with permission.

than White Americans (12%) or Hispanic Americans (16%).

Abortions were more often used as a means for resolving adolescent pregnancies among White teenagers in this sample than among African Americans or Hispanic Americans. Among African Americans and Hispanic Americans, adolescent pregnancies were more often carried to term, with a greater percentage of adolescent fathers among the Hispanics either marrying or living with the mothers.

Teen pregnancy cuts across all ethnic, religious and socioeconomic groupings and is a major social problem in our society. Although almost everyone agrees with the need to prevent teens from becoming pregnant, how to accomplish this goal has become the subject of a major national debate.

Other researchers focus on relationships between family factors and premarital intercourse. Children whose parents are separated or divorced are more likely than those from intact homes to engage in premarital intercourse (Coles & Stokes, 1985). Perhaps parents who have "failed" in their marital relationships lack credibility in advising their adolescent children (Coles & Stokes, 1985). Perhaps divorced mothers communicate more permissive attitudes than married mothers (Thornton & Camburn, 1987). Single parents, because of time constraints, might also be less capable of supervising their children (Newcomer & Udry, 1987). So teenagers from single-parent homes may have greater opportunities for privacy, especially when the parent is employed outside the home (Coles & Stokes, 1985). Moreover, a teenager might interpret a single parent's becoming sexually active with dates as tacit approval of premarital sex.

of the night. Just before we were about to have sex, I realized that it wasn't something I wanted to do. I wanted my first time to be with someone I loved and who loved me. I stopped him, although he tried everything to get me to say yes. The next day we broke up, and I couldn't have been happier.
(Copyright © 1991 by Osterhout, Formichella, and McIntyre by arrangement with AVON BOOKS, pp. 4–6)

About 8% of the men in the NHSLS study say they went along with intercourse for the sake of their partners (Michael et al., 1994). As one young man describes it:

MATT (18, New York): My girlfriend pressured me and I didn't handle it very well. I submitted so she wouldn't be mad or disappointed.
(Copyright © 1991 by Osterhout, Formichella, and McIntyre by arrangement with AVON BOOKS, p. 65)

a CLOSER look

The First Time

MARK: As we had no place to go, we went out into the woods with several blankets and made love. It was like something out of a Woody Allen movie. I couldn't get my pants off because I was shaking from nerves and from the cold. The nerves and cold made it all but impossible for me to get an erection and then after I had and we made love I couldn't find the car keys.

AMY: My first sexual experience occurred after the Junior Prom in high school in a car at the drive-in. We were both virgins, very uncertain, but very much in love. We had been going together since eighth grade. The experience was somewhat painful. I remember wondering if I would look different to my mother the next day. I guess I didn't because nothing was said. (Morrison et al., 1980, p. 608)

For those who do not remain celibate, there must be a first time. Given the inexperience and awkwardness of at least one member of the couple and frequent feelings of guilt and fear, it is not surprising that most people, like Mark and Amy, don't get it quite right the first time. Adolescent boys and girls often report different concerns about first intercourse. The girl is more likely to be concerned about whether she is doing the right thing. The boy is more likely to be concerned about whether he is doing the thing right. Women are more likely than men to be physically and psychologically disappointed with the experience and to feel guilty afterward (Darling et al., 1992; Sprecher et al., 1995). One study of 300 sexually experienced college students found that only 28% of the women considered their first encounter physically or psychologically satisfying. Yet 81% of college men were physically satisfied, and 67% were psychologically satisfied (Darling & Davidson, 1986).

Negative attitudes among women toward their first coital experience might have cultural roots. A comparison between American and Swedish women showed that American women reported more negative emotional experiences of their first premarital coitus (Schwartz, 1993). In general, the Swedish have more permissive attitudes about sex than do people in the United States. Negative emotional consequences of first intercourse reflect cultural norms or standards as well as the act itself. Of course, it is also possible that Swedish men are also be more responsive to their partners' needs.

Coles and Stokes (1985) found that most adolescent boys (60%) reported feeling "glad" after their first intercourse (see Table 13.4). Most adolescent girls (61%) expressed ambivalence. One in ten girls (11%) reported feeling "sorry," compared to only 1% of boys. Some females feel guilty about ending their virginity. Others find first intercourse painful or uncomfortable, in part because of the tearing of the hymen, in part because penetration might have been rushed or forced. The pain was more than one 15-year-old New York girl had anticipated:

[I] wasn't expecting it to hurt that much. It was like total pain. Even after the first minutes of pain, it's still like you're too sore to enjoy anything. I didn't expect that at all. (Coles & Stokes, 1985, p. 74)

Yet for some, the quality of the relationship tempered pain:

We were both so excited. We hadn't been able to sleep the night before. I can't remember that much leading up to it, but we had sex a few times—I guess about three times—that night. He really enjoyed it; I found it emotionally nice, but painful. It was like a *good* hurt, but still it hurt; it was

FACTORS IN PREMARITAL INTERCOURSE Many young people abstain from premarital coitus for religious or moral reasons (Coles & Stokes, 1985; Miller & Bingham, 1989). Family influences and religious values are important determinants of adolescent sexual experience (White & DeBlassie, 1992). Other reasons include fear of being caught, of pregnancy, or of disease.

A study of 142 low-income, African American adolescent females (ages 13–18) at an inner-city health clinic in Dallas found that girls who were not sexually active tended to be younger and more career oriented, to have a father at home, to hold more conservative values about sexuality, and to be more influenced by family values, than sexually active girls (Keith et al., 1991).

Teens who have higher educational goals and do better in school are less likely to engage in coitus than less academically oriented teens (Brooks-Gunn & Furstenberg, 1989; Hofferth & Hayes, 1987). The causal connection between school performance and premarital sex is difficult to discern, because adolescents who do well in school are also more likely to come from better-functioning families.

Not surprisingly, older teens are more likely than younger ones to engage in premarital intercourse (Miller & Bingham, 1989). The likelihood of premarital intercourse

table 13.4

	Sorry (%)	Ambivalent (%)	Glad (%)	No Feelings (%)
		Feelings about first intercourse		
Males	1	34	60	5
Females	11	61	23	4

Source: From SEX AND THE AMERICAN TEENAGER by R. Coles and G. Stokes. Copyright © 1985 by Rolling Stone Press. Reprinted by permission of HarperCollins Publishers.

uncomfortable. But it was something we both felt really good about. (Coles & Stokes, 1985, p. 74)

Young women are more likely to find their first coital experience satisfying when their partners are loving, gentle, and considerate (Weiss, 1983).

First intercourse is often awkward, even fumbling. The partners are still learning about their own sexual responses and how to please each other:

KAREN (23, New York): I had sexual intercourse for the first time at age 18. My boyfriend and I had been going out for a year. For several months before we had intercourse we engaged in a lot of petting but not much genital contact. I was the more aggressive partner and I was the one who suggested we have intercourse. It was very awkward; the first time we tried, he couldn't get in. (Copyright © 1991 by Osterhout, Formichella, and McIntyre by arrangement with AVON BOOKS, pp. 50–51)

Let us note some gender differences in choice of first partners. For first-time intercourse, survey evidence shows that females are more likely than males to report having been in a committed relationship with their partners (Darling et al., 1992; Sprecher et al., 1995). In the study of some 1,600 college students by Susan Sprecher and her colleagues (1995), 60% of the women reported that their first partner was someone they were dating seriously, compared to 36% of the men. Men were more likely than women (23% versus 8%) to engage in first intercourse with someone they had been seeing for less than a week. Men experienced more pleasure, largely because they were more likely to reach orgasm. Women experienced more guilt. These gender differences are consistent with the traditional double standard that accords greater sexual freedom to men. Men are expected to "sow their wild oats" with casual partners. Women are expected to save themselves for a man with whom they share strong emotional ties and an enduring relationship.

is also linked to early dating, especially early steady dating (Brooks-Gunn & Furstenberg, 1989; Miller et al., 1986). Adolescents who begin dating earlier might be more likely to progress through stages of petting to coitus.

The quality of the relationship between teens and their parents can also be important (Brooks-Gunn & Furstenberg, 1989). Teens who feel that they can talk to their parents are less likely to engage in coitus than those who describe communication with their parents as poor. Adolescents whose parents are permissive and impose few rules and restrictions are more likely to engage in premarital intercourse (Hogan & Kitigawa, 1985; Miller et al., 1986). Parents who show interest in their children's behavior and communicate their concerns and expectations with understanding and respect may best influence their children to show sexual restraint.

TEENAGERS' VALUES AND THE SEXUAL DOUBLE STANDARD   Do young people today subscribe to the traditional double standard that allows greater sexual freedom for men than for women? It might be premature to drive the nails into the coffin of the sexual double standard, but a common standard for judging acceptability of premarital sex could be emerging. A study of 666 undergraduate students in a midwestern university showed no evidence of the double standard; students were not differently disposed toward the acceptability of premarital sex for one gender or the other (Sprecher, 1989). According to the Coles and Stokes (1985) national survey, teenagers express only slightly more approval of casual sex for boys than for girls.

Male-Male and Female-Female Sexual Behavior

About 5% of the adolescents in the Coles and Stokes (1985) national survey reported sexual experiences with people of their own gender. More than nine out of ten experiences among adolescents of the same gender are between peers (Sorensen, 1973). Seduction of adolescents by gay male and lesbian adults is relatively rare. Most adolescent sexual encounters with people of the same gender are transitory. They most often include mutual masturbation, fondling, and genital display.

Many gay males and lesbians, of course, develop a firm sense of being gay during adolescence. Coming to terms with adolescence is often a difficult struggle, but it is often more intense for gay people (Baker, 1990) (see Chapter 10). Adolescents can be particularly cruel in their stigmatization, referring to gay peers as "homos," "queers," "faggots," and so on. Many adolescent gays therefore feel isolated and lonely and decide to cloak their sexual orientation. Many do not express their sexual orientation at all until after their high school years.

Adding to the strain of developing a gay identity in a largely hostile society is the threat of AIDS, which is all the more pressing a threat to young gay males because of the toll that AIDS has inflicted on the gay male community (Baker, 1990).

TEENAGE PREGNANCY

About 10% of American girls of ages 15 to 19 become pregnant each year ("Rate of births," 1995). This amounts to one in five sexually active girls and nearly 1 million pregnancies a year. More than 200,000 of the pregnancies end in abortion.

Truth or Fiction?
REVISITED

It is true that nearly 1 million adolescent girls in the United States become pregnant each year. ■

Although these figures are cause for concern, the rate of births for teenagers was actually dropping modestly during the 1990s (Meckler, 1998). The proportion of out-of-wedlock births among teenagers shot up during the 1970s and 1980s. Among young women 15 to 17 years of age in the period 1985–1989, 81% of births occurred out of wedlock, compared to 41% in 1965–1969 and 59% in 1975–1979 (Pear, 1991). Two of three teenage mothers in the 1990s are unmarried, compared to 15% in 1960. Among African American teenage mothers, 92% are unmarried (National Research Council, 1993).

Some pregnant teenagers plan their pregnancies, but the great majority do not. Nine in ten pregnancies among unmarried teenagers are unplanned (Alan Guttmacher Institute, 1991).

The consequences of unplanned teenage pregnancies can devastate young mothers, their children, and society at large. Even young people themselves perceive teenage parenthood to be disastrous (Moore & Stief, 1992). Teenage mothers are more likely to live in poverty and to receive welfare than their peers (Grogger & Bronars, 1993). Poverty, joblessness, and lack of hope for the future are recurrent themes in adolescent pregnancy (Desmond, 1994). Half of teenage mothers quit school and go on public assistance (Kantrowitz, 1990a). Few receive consistent emotional or financial help from the fathers, who generally cannot support themselves, much less a family. Working teenage mothers earn just half as much as those who give birth in their 20s (National Research Council, 1993). Barely able to cope with one baby, many young mothers who give birth at age 15 or

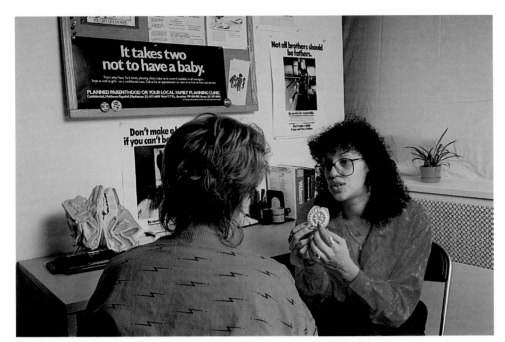

Teenage Pregnancy. About 10% of American girls aged 15 to 19—1 million girls—become pregnant each year. Teenage mothers are more likely to live in poverty and to receive welfare than other girls their age. Half of them quit school and rely on public assistance. Few receive meaningful help from the fathers. There is intense public debate over whether schools should provide teenagers with contraceptives to help stem the tide of teenage pregnancy.

16 have at least one more baby by the time they are 20. Among teenage girls who become pregnant, nearly one in five will become pregnant again within a year. More than 31% will have a repeat pregnancy within two years (Alan Guttmacher Institute, 1991). Undereducated, unskilled, and overburdened, these young mothers face a constant uphill struggle.

Medical complications associated with teenage childbearing are highest of any group of fertile women except for those in their late 40s (Hess et al., 1993). In addition to high rates of miscarriage and stillbirths, children who are born to teenagers are at greater risk of prematurity, birth complications, and infant mortality (Fraser et al., 1995; Goldenberg & Klerman, 1995). These problems are often the result of inadequate prenatal care. However, even when prenatal care is taken into consideration, the children of teenagers are at greater risk than those of women in their 20s (Fraser et al., 1995; Goldenberg & Klerman, 1995).

Children of teenage mothers are at greater risk of physical, emotional, and intellectual problems in their preschool years, owing to poor nutrition and health care, family instability, and inadequate parenting (Furstenberg et al., 1989; Hechtman, 1989). They are more aggressive and impulsive as preschoolers than are children of older mothers (Furstenberg et al., 1989). They do more poorly in school. They are also more likely to suffer maternal abuse or neglect (Felsman et al., 1987; Kinard & Reinherz, 1987).

A number of factors have contributed to the increase in teenage pregnancy, including a loosening of traditional taboos on adolescent sexuality (Hechtman, 1989). Impaired family relationships, problems in school, emotional problems, misunderstandings about reproduction or contraception, and lack of contraception also play roles (Hechtman, 1989). Some adolescent girls believe that a baby will elicit a commitment from their partners or fill an emotional void. Some become pregnant as a way of rebelling against parents. Some poor teenagers view early childbearing as the best of the severely limited options they perceive for their futures. But the largest number become pregnant because of misunderstandings about reproduction and contraception or miscalculations about the odds of conception. Even many teens who are relatively well informed about contraception fail to use it consistently (Hechtman, 1989).

More attention has been focused on teenage mothers, but young fathers bear an equal responsibility for teenage pregnancies. A survey based on a nationally representative sample of 1,880 young men ages 15 through 19 showed that socioeconomically

table 13.5

Type of birth control used by sexually active teenagers		
	First Time (%)	Most Recent Time (%)
Rhythm	3	4
Withdrawal	18	17
Condom	62	54
The pill	11	45
Diaphragm	3	4
Foam	1	4
IUD	0	2

Source: From SEX AND THE AMERICAN TEENAGER by R. Coles and G. Stokes. Copyright © 1985 by Rolling Stone Press. Reprinted by permission of HarperCollins Publishers.

disadvantaged young men, in particular, appeared to view paternity as a source of self-esteem and were consequently more likely than more affluent young men to say that fathering a child would make them feel like a real man and that they would be pleased, or at least not as upset, with an unplanned pregnancy (Marsiglio, 1993a). Consistent with these attitudes, young men living in poorer conditions were less likely to have used an effective contraceptive method during their most recent sexual experience.

Teenage fathers are more likely to have problems in school—both behavioral and academic—and to hold more pessimistic attitudes toward the future than their peers (Hanson et al., 1989). Steady dating also increased the risk of teenage fatherhood.

Contraceptive Use among Sexually Active Teens

Sexually active teenagers use contraception inconsistently, if at all. Contraception is most likely to be used by teens who are in stable, monogamous relationships (Baker et al., 1988). Even teens in monogamous relationships tend to use ineffective methods of contraception or to use effective methods inconsistently, however (Polit-O'Hara & Kahn, 1985). About one in five sexually active teens in the Coles and Stokes (1985) national sample relied on withdrawal or the rhythm method the first and most recent times they engaged in intercourse (see Table 13.5).

Various factors determine use of contraceptives (Beck & Davies, 1987). Teenage girls who engage in more frequent intercourse are more likely to use contraception and to use more effective methods (DuRant & Sanders, 1989). Teens whose peers use contraceptives are more likely to use them themselves (Jorgensen et al., 1980). Older teenagers are more likely than younger ones to use contraception (Mosher & Bachrach, 1987). Younger teens who are sexually active might be less likely to use contraception because they lack information about contraception and because they do not always perceive the repercussions of their actions (Handler, 1990). Younger teens might also have less access to contraceptives.

Teenage boys are more likely than teenage girls to know how to obtain and use condoms correctly, according to the results of a California survey of more than 1,000 high school students (Leland & Barth, 1992). Boys are also more likely to have used birth control during their first or most recent sexual experience. It appears that girls are more uncomfortable than boys in obtaining or using contraception, especially condoms (Leland & Barth, 1992).

Poor family relationships and communication with parents are associated with inconsistent contraceptive use (Brooks-Gunn & Furstenberg, 1989). Poor performance in school and low educational ambitions predict irregular contraceptive use, as they also predict early sexual initiation.

When asked to explain why they don't use contraceptives, sexually active teens often cite factors such as sexual infrequency ("don't have intercourse often enough to use it") and disruption of sexual spontaneity ("interferes with sex") (Coles & Stokes, 1985). Some teenagers get "carried away" and do not wish to disrupt sex by applying birth-control devices. For others, coitus is an unplanned, spur-of-the-moment experience.

Myths also decrease the likelihood of using birth control. Some adolescents believe that they are too young to become pregnant. Others believe that pregnancy results only from repeated coitus or will not occur if they are standing up. Still other adolescents simply do not admit to themselves that they are engaging in coitus. Concerns about side effects are also given as reasons for failure to use contraception (Washington et al., 1983).

Teenagers who focus on the long-term consequences of their actions are more likely to use contraceptives. The quality of the relationship is also a factor. Satisfaction with the relationship is associated with more frequent intercourse *and* more consistent use of contraception (Jorgensen et al., 1980). More consistent contraceptive use is found in relationships in which the young woman takes the initiative in making decisions and resolving conflicts.

Let us note that many adolescents today who use condoms do so more because of fear of AIDS than to protect themselves against unwanted pregnancies (Lewin, 1991). A reduction in teenage pregnancies might be a side effect of this trend.

COMBATING TEENAGE PREGNANCY: A ROLE FOR THE SCHOOLS?   Various means have been recommended to combat the problem of teenage pregnancy, including universal sex education, free contraceptive services for teenagers, open discussion of sex between parents and children, and dissemination of information about responsible sex practices and contraception through the media. Given the effects of sex education in other industrialized countries, many helping professionals believe that the rate of teenage pregnancy and the spread of sexually transmitted diseases in the United States could be curtailed through sex education about contraception and provision of contraceptives.

Pregnancy prevention programs in the schools range from encouraging teens to delay sex ("saying no to early sex") to providing information about contraception to distributing condoms or referring students to contraceptive clinics (Furstenberg et al., 1989; Richardson, 1997). The vast majority of sex educators (86%) recommend abstinence to their students as the best way to prevent pregnancy and AIDS (Kantrowitz, 1990b). Fewer than half inform their students about how to obtain contraceptives. Three out of four large school districts in the United States provide some instruction about the methods of contraception and the use of condoms to prevent the spread of AIDS and other sexually transmitted diseases.

Evidence supports the effectiveness of programs that counsel abstinence, at least among younger teens. A school-based sex education program that focused on the development of skills needed to resist social and peer pressure to initiate sexual activity encouraged younger (junior high school) teens to postpone sexual involvement (Howard & McCabe, 1990). Program participants also had fewer pregnancies than students who did not participate in the program. However, programs that rely on the "just say no" model to encourage abstinence are less effective in persuading high school students to abstain from sexual activity (Wilson & Sanderson, 1988).

Because many teenagers are or will become sexually active, our society faces the question of whether the public schools should make contraceptive services or contraceptives themselves available to sexually active teens. This issue is the focus of heated debate among parents, educators, health officials, and other public officials in various communities in the United States and Canada. We explore this question further in the A Closer Look feature on pages 412 and 413.

Reflections

- At what ages did you experience the changes of puberty? Were you early or late compared with your friends? Did it matter? If so, how?
- At what ages did you or your friends become sexually active? What were your or their motives for becoming sexually active? Were your or their early sexual experiences as exciting or pleasurable as expected?
- What are the attitudes of most people from your sociocultural background toward premarital sexuality? Do you share their attitudes? Why or why not?

In this chapter, we have chronicled sexuality in childhood and adolescence. In the next chapter, we continue our journey through the life span.

a CLOSER look

Should Public Schools Provide Students with Contraceptives?

Alarmed by the threat of AIDS and the epidemic of teenage pregnancy, some school districts distribute contraceptives, such as condoms, to students (Richardson, 1997). Most school districts require parental consent. Others, such as the New York City school system, do not. Clinics that protect the confidentiality of their teenage clients often attempt to involve the parents in some way, usually by providing opportunities for family counseling, parent advisory groups, and parent-child communication training (Beck & Davies, 1987).

Truth or Fiction? REVISITED

It is true that condoms are distributed to adolescents without parental consent in some school districts. They are not distributed without controversy, however. ■

Adults voice hope that sex education will prevent teenage pregnancies. According to the ABC News (1995) poll, nine Americans in ten say that sex education classes should teach pupils to practice birth control if they engage in sexual activity. However, 80% favor teaching that sex at an early age is a bad idea. A small majority (59%) say that school health clinics should provide students with condoms and other forms of contraceptives. However, about the same number (58%) say that students who use this service should be required to get parental permission. Many parents oppose programs that do not require parental consent for fear that they compromise family cohesiveness and parental authority.

Of course, many parents believe that they, not the schools, should dispense information to their children about contraception and that they should be the ones who decide whether their children are given contraceptives. Many oppose giving adolescents contraceptives on moral and religious grounds. They argue that the emphasis should be on abstinence rather than on contraception. Some opponents believe that distributing contraceptives to teens encourages premarital sex.

Advocates of these programs argue that requiring parental consent would discourage participation by large numbers of sexually active teens. They note that many teens become sexually active despite educators' encouragement to abstain. Given this reality, they argue, society has a responsibility to help protect sexually active teens from unwanted pregnancies and AIDS.

Handing out condoms is not likely to reduce teenage pregnancy or the spread of sexually transmitted diseases unless the handouts are accompanied by counseling that focuses on their proper use. Sexually active teenagers also need to learn how to communicate the need for contraception to their partners. More comprehensive reproductive health care clinics have been established in some schools that combine condom distribution with counseling about sex. But are they effective in lowering the rates of teenage pregnancy? Thus far, these programs have failed to dent schoolwide pregnancy rates (Kirby et al., 1992, 1993).

There is a question as to whether making condoms available to students increases the prevalence of sexual activity. A Los Angeles study (Schuster et al., 1998) suggests that distributing free condoms to teenage boys does not increase the incidence of their sexual activity but makes it more likely that they will use the condoms when they have sex. In this study, which followed more than 1,000 students for a year:

- The percentage of sexually active boys who reported using a condom every time they had sex increased to 50% from 37%.
- The percentage of boys who reported using a condom during their first coital experience increased to 80% from 65%.
- There was no change in the percentage of boys who reported being sexually active.

Enter Norplant

The introduction of the contraceptive device Norplant has added a new wrinkle to the debate over distributing contraceptives in the schools. The advantage of Norplant is that once implanted, it offers around-the-clock protection against unwanted pregnancies for several years. Baltimore, which is beset with one of the highest teen pregnancy rates in the United States, became the first city in the nation to offer Norplant to teenage girls in a school-based clinic in the attempt to combat teenage pregnancies (Kantrowitz, 1992; Lewin, 1992b). In Baltimore, 1 in 10 girls of ages 15 to 17 were having babies ("For high school girls," 1993). Most lived in poverty. Until the experimental program, Norplant was too expensive for most teens. The Norplant program was located in a school in an impoverished, inner-city community, where the problem of teenage pregnancy was most acute. This is how a 16-year-old teenage mother in Baltimore expressed her hopes that Norplant will enable her to finish high school and pursue a college education without becoming pregnant again:

> I don't know what I would do if I had another baby. . . . I share a crowded bedroom with two younger sisters, and it's so small and cluttered with bunk beds and cribs. I've tried to find a job, but there aren't any, and my stepfather is out of work. I want to go to art school, and I always dreamed of having fun on a college campus. . . . I wanted Norplant to help me finish school. (*The New York Times*, March 7, 1993, p. 28)

The Baltimore Norplant program sparked considerable controversy. Although some proponents hail Norplant as a "silver bullet" against teen pregnancies, others believe that it will encourage teenage promiscuity. As one local clergyman put it, "Norplant sends a message that it is O.K. to have sex as long as you don't get pregnant" ("Plan for wider use of Norplant," 1993). Norplant also does not offer protection against sexually transmitted infections. Some opponents consider the use of Norplant in inner-city schools to be a racist tool. Some worry about potential side effects or medical risks, especially in a population of inner-city teens who might not see a physician regularly. Proponents argue that Norplant is needed because teens fail to use other forms of contraception consistently or at all, even if they are made available to them.

s u m m i n g   u p

INFANCY (0 TO 2 YEARS): A SEARCH FOR THE ORIGINS OF HUMAN SEXUALITY

The Infant's Capacity for Sexual Response
Fetuses have been found to have erections and suck their fingers. Stimulation of the genitals in infancy might produce sensations of pleasure. Pelvic thrusting has been observed in humans as early as 8 months of age. Masturbation might begin as early as 6 to 12 months. Some infants seem capable of sexual responses that closely resemble orgasm.

Masturbation
Self-stimulation for pleasure (masturbation) typically occurs among children as young as 6 to 12 months of age.

Genital Play
U.S. children typically do not engage in genital play with others until about the age of 2.

EARLY CHILDHOOD (3 TO 8 YEARS)

Masturbation
Statistics concerning the incidence of masturbation at ages 3 to 8 is speculative.

Male-Female Sexual Behavior
In early childhood, children show curiosity about the genitals and may play "doctor."

Male-Male and Female-Female Sexual Behavior
Same-gender sexual play might be more common than heterosexual play and does not presage adult sexual orientation.

PREADOLESCENCE (9 TO 13 YEARS)

Preadolescents tend to socialize with best friends and with large groups and to become self-conscious about their bodies.

Masturbation
Masturbation is apparently the primary means of achieving orgasm during preadolescence for both genders.

Male-Female Sexual Behavior
Preadolescent sex play often involves mutual display of the genitals, with or without touching. Group dating and mixed-gender parties often provide preadolescents with their first exposure to heterosexual activities.

Male-Male and Female-Female Sexual Behavior
Much preadolescent same-gender sexual behavior involves sexual exploration and is short-lived.

Sex Education and Miseducation
Despite the increased availability of sex education programs, peers apparently remain the major source of sexual information.

ADOLESCENCE

Adolescence is bounded by the advent of puberty at the lower end and the capacity to take on adult responsibilities at the upper. The conflicts and distress that many adolescents experience apparently reflect the cultural expectations to which they are exposed.

Puberty
Pubertal changes are ushered in by sex hormones. Puberty begins with the appearance of secondary sex characteristics and ends when the long bones make no further gains in length. Once puberty begins, most major changes in primary sex characteristics occur within three years in girls and within four years in boys.

Masturbation
Masturbation is a major sexual outlet during adolescence.

Male-Female Sexual Behavior
Adolescents today date and "go steady" earlier than in past generations, a change that has apparently increased the incidence of teenage pregnancy. Many adolescents use petting as a way of achieving sexual gratification without becoming pregnant or ending one's virginity. The incidence of premarital intercourse, especially for females, has increased dramatically since Kinsey's day.

Male-Male and Female-Female Sexual Behavior
Most adolescent same-gender sexual encounters are transitory. Coming to terms with adolescence is often more intense for gay males and lesbians, largely because gay male and lesbian sexual orientations are stigmatized in our society.

TEENAGE PREGNANCY

Nearly 1 million adolescents in the United States become pregnant each year. Rates of teenage pregnancy are connected with socioeconomic status.

Contraceptive Use among Sexually Active Teenagers
Sexually active teenagers use contraception inconsistently, if at all. Thus, more than 1 million teenage girls in the United States become pregnant each year.

Pablo Picasso. *The Three Dancers.* 1925. Tate Gallery, London. Art Resource, New York

chapter

14

Sexuality in Adulthood

outline

TRUTH OR FICTION?

SINGLEHOOD

A WORLD OF DIVERSITY:
*Snug in Their Beds for Christmas Eve—
In Japan, December 24 Has Become the
Hottest Night of the Year*

**COHABITATION: DARLING, WOULD
YOU BE MY POSSLQ?**

Who Are the Cohabitors?

Reasons for Cohabitation

Cohabitation and Later Marriage:
A Benefit or a Risk?

MARRIAGE

Historical Perspectives

Why Do People Marry?

Types of Marriage

Whom Do We Marry:
Are Marriages Made in Heaven
or in the Neighborhood?

MARITAL SEXUALITY

The Sexual Revolution Hits Home

Sexual Satisfaction

EXTRAMARITAL SEX

Patterns of Extramarital Sex

Attitudes Toward Extramarital Sex

Effects of Extramarital Sex

Swinging

DOMESTIC VIOLENCE

DIVORCE

The Cost of Divorce

**ALTERNATIVE FORMS
OF MARRIAGE**

Open Marriage

Group Marriage

SEX IN THE LATER YEARS

Physical Changes

IN THE NEW MILLENNIUM:
Trends in Adult Sexuality

Patterns of Sexual Activity

SEX AND DISABILITY

Physical Disabilities

Psychological Disabilities

SUMMING UP

Truth or Fiction **?**

_____ "Singlehood" (forgive the word) has become a more common U.S. lifestyle over the past few decades.

_____ Cohabitation is most common among college students.

_____ In the ancient Hebrew and Greek civilizations, wives were viewed as their husbands' property.

_____ Men are more romantic than women.

_____ Most of today's sophisticated young people see nothing wrong with an occasional extramarital fling.

_____ Few women can reach orgasm after the age of 70.

_____ People who are paralyzed because of spinal cord injuries cannot become sexually aroused or engage in coitus.

americans entering adulthood today face a wider range of sexual choices and lifestyles than those of earlier generations. The sexual revolution loosened traditional constraints on sexual choices, especially for women. Couples experiment with lifestyles that would have been unthinkable in earlier generations. An increasing number of young people choose to remain single as a way of life, not merely as a way station preceding the arrival of Mr. or Ms. Right.

In this chapter, we discuss diverse forms of adult sexuality in the United States today, including singlehood, marriage, and alternative lifestyles such as cohabitation, open marriage, and group marriage. Let us begin as people begin—with singlehood.

SINGLEHOOD

Recent years have seen a sharp increase in the numbers of single young people in our society. "Singlehood," not marriage, is now the most common lifestyle among people in their early 20s. Though marriages may be made in heaven, many Americans are saying heaven can wait. By the early 1990s, one in four people in the United States 18 years of age and older had never married, compared to about one in six in 1970 and one in five in 1980 (Barringer, 1992a, 1992b). The rate of marriages had also fallen off. The proportion of people tying the knot reached a 25-year low (Barringer, 1992b). Nearly 80% of single men in the 20-to-24 age range were unmarried, up from 55% in 1970 (U.S. Bureau of the Census, 1990). The percentage of single women in this age group grew from 36% in 1970 to 61%. About one in four U.S. households consisted of a single adult. This represented a threefold increase since 1960.

Although most people do get married by their late 20s, never-married singles still account for some 43% of the men and 30% of the women in the 25-to-29 age group (U.S. Bureau of the Census, 1990). In fact, the proportion of people who remain single into their late 20s and early 30s has more than doubled since 1970 (U.S. Bureau of the Census, 1990).

Truth or Fiction?
REVISITED

It is true that "singlehood" has become a more common U.S. lifestyle over the past few decades. More people are remaining single into their 20s and 30s than was the case a generation or two ago. ■

Singles. There is no one "singles scene" today. While some singles meet in singles' bars, many singles meet in more casual settings, such as the neighborhood laundromat. Some singles advertise in newspapers and magazines, or online.

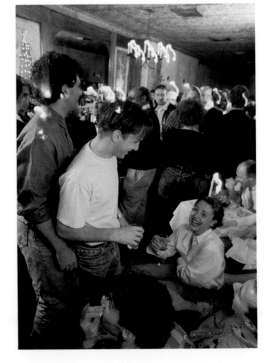

SNUG IN THEIR BEDS FOR CHRISTMAS EVE:
In Japan, December 24 Has Become the Hottest Night of the Year

For young people all over the Christian world, Christmas Eve is a night of magic and wonder. In Japan as well, Christmas Eve has become immensely important—but for rather different reasons.

It has become the sexiest night of the year.

Japanese popular culture has made Christmas Eve a night, similar to our New Year's Eve, when unmarried people are expected to have a date. It has now come to be expected that the date include an overnight stay. For weeks before this night, TV shows, magazines, and *manga* (adult comic books) are full of reports and advice on which hotels are best for young couples to stay in on Christmas Eve, what each partner should wear, and where the pair should have breakfast the following morning.

"Christmas Eve is now important as a night for making love," complains poet and social critic Hazuki Kajiwara. This is such a widely accepted aspect of the day here known as *eebu*, the Japanese pronunciation of "eve," that December 24 is frequently referred to as "H-day." The letter *H*, taken from the English word "hormone," is a common symbol here for sex.

The *eebu* phenomenon is carried out in an intensely materialistic, free-spending atmosphere, reflecting the commercial nature of the Christmas season in Japan. In a country less than 1% Christian, December 25 is just another working day. Yet stores and restaurants here have more Christmas trees, wreaths, and reindeer on display than most places in the United States.

For a couple's Christmas Eve fling, the man is expected to bear all costs. Many "salary men" save all year for this one date. The news magazine *Asahi Journal* printed a breakdown of a fairly standard "Eve course": When the man arrives to pick up his date, he should present her with a $215 silver heart pendant from Tiffany's and then take her out for an evening at Tokyo Disneyland, where admission and extras will cost $100 or so. Then it's on to dinner for two at a French or American restaurant

Eebu. Japanese popular culture has made Christmas Eve into a night similar to our New Year's Eve. Unmarried people are expected to have a date, and that date is usually expected to include an overnight stay.

($385) and a room for the night overlooking Tokyo Bay at the Hilton or the Sheraton Grande ($300, or $650 for a suite). Breakfast in the hotel coffee shop should cost only $35, but a rental limousine to take the couple to their homes so they can quickly change and go to work will cost another $150.

But *eebu* is hardly a free ride for Japanese women. They must pay the emotional cost.

Women between college age and their mid-30s have more money and more independence today than ever before in Japanese history. But they are losing their connection to family and peer groups and are struggling to survive on their own.

"Behind the traditional Japanese groupism is a fear of being alone," says Hikaru Hayashi, senior research director at the Hakuhodo Institute, a sociological think tank. For single women, "Christmas Eve enhances the fear that they are not rooted in society."

With virtually everyone making elaborate plans for *eebu*, it has become something of a social necessity for single men and women to have a date that night. The tribulations of those who don't have one become the subject of enormous media attention.

A travel agency has been advertising excursion trips for singles under the headline

"Find a Boyfriend by Christmas!" The Tokyo Broadcasting System ran a miniseries called "Christmas Eve." The story concerned a young "office lady" who listened to her friends chattering about the fancy restaurants and hotels they were going to for *eebu* but was ashamed to admit she had no date. In the final episode, a young man called her at the last minute. The two walked off happily into the night, presumably in search of a hotel with a vacant room.

The idea that it might be shameful for a single woman to spend the night with her date is less commonly expressed, but it does occur. Sampei Sato, the editorial cartoonist for the newspaper *Asahi Shimbun*, devoted his space one day to an appeal to young unmarried women to sleep at home rather than in a hotel on Christmas Eve.

The new view of *eebu* has increased the Japanese people's belief that they are unique. "In all the world," said the lead-in to a TV talk show, "only Japan has turned the day before Christmas into a day for sex."

Source: Adapted from Reid, T. R. (1990, December 24). Snug in their beds for Christmas Eve: In Japan, Dec. 24 has become the hottest night of the year. *The Washington Post.*

Several factors contribute to the increased proportion of singles. For one thing, more people are postponing marriage to pursue educational and career goals (Barringer, 1991). Many young people are deciding to "live together" (cohabit), at least for a while, rather than get married. Also, people are getting married at later ages (Kornblum, 1994). The increased prevalence of divorce also swells the ranks of single adults.

Less social stigma is attached to remaining single today. Though single people are less likely today to be perceived as socially inadequate or as failures, some unmarried people still encounter stereotypes. Men who have never married may be suspected of being gay. Single women might feel that men perceive them as "loose."

Many single people do not choose to be single. Some remain single because they have not yet found Mr. or Ms. Right. Many young people, however, see singlehood as an alternative, open-ended way of life—not just a temporary stage that precedes marriage. As career options for women have expanded, they are not as financially dependent on men as their mothers and grandmothers were. A number of career women, like young career-oriented men, choose to remain single (at least for a time) to focus their energies on their careers.

Singlehood is not without its problems. Many single people are lonely. Some singles express concerns about a lack of a steady, meaningful social relationship. Others, usually women, worry about their physical safety. Some people living alone find it difficult to satisfy their needs for intimacy, companionship, sex, and emotional support. Despite these concerns, most singles are well adjusted and content. Singles who have a greater number of friends and a supportive social network tend to be more satisfied with their lifestyles.

There is no single "singles scene." Single people differ in their sexual interests and lifestyles. Many achieve emotional and psychological security through a network of intimate relationships with friends. Most are sexually active and practice **serial monogamy.** Other singles have a primary sexual relationship with one steady partner but occasional brief flings. A few, even in this age of AIDS, are "swinging singles." That is, they pursue casual sexual encounters, or "one-night stands."

Some singles remain celibate, either by choice or for lack of opportunity. People choose **celibacy** for a number of reasons. Nuns and priests do so for religious reasons. Others believe that celibacy allows them to focus their energies and attention on work or to commit themselves to an important cause. They see celibacy as a temporary accommodation to other pursuits. Others remain celibate because they view sex outside of marriage as immoral. Still others remain celibate because they find the prospects of sexual activity aversive or unalluring or because of fears of STIs.

Reflections

- At what age do most of your peers plan to get married? (Or at what age *did* most of your peers get married?) Why?
- Is remaining single an option for you? Why or why not?

COHABITATION: DARLING, WOULD YOU BE MY POSSLQ?

There is nothing I would not do
If you would be my POSSLQ

—Charles Osgood

POSSLQ? This unromantic abbreviation was introduced by the U.S. Bureau of the Census to refer to **cohabitation.** It stands for People of Opposite Sex Sharing Living Quarters and applies to unmarried couples who live together.

Some social scientists believe that cohabitation has become accepted within the social mainstream (Bumpass, 1995). Whether or not this is so, society in general has become

Serial monogamy A pattern of involvement in one exclusive relationship after another, as opposed to engaging in multiple sexual relationships at the same time.

Celibacy Complete sexual abstinence. (Sometimes used to describe the state of being unmarried, especially in the case of people who take vows to remain single.)

Cohabitation Living together as though married but without legal sanction.

more tolerant of it. We seldom hear cohabitation referred to as "living in sin" or "shacking up" as we once did. People today are more likely to refer to cohabitation with value-free expressions such as "living together."

Perhaps the current tolerance reflects societal adjustment to the increase in the numbers of cohabiting couples. Or perhaps the numbers of cohabiting couples have increased as a consequence of tolerance. The numbers of households consisting of an unmarried adult male and female couple living together in the United States doubled between 1980 and the early 1990s (Steinhauer, 1995). They grew from 1.6 million couples in 1980 to 2.9 million couples in 1990 and 3.3 million in 1992.

Who Are the Cohabitors?

Much of the attention on cohabitation has been focused on college students living together, but cohabitation is more prevalent among the less well educated and less affluent classes (Willis & Michael, 1994). The cohabitation rate is about twice as high among African American couples as White couples. Fifty-five percent of male cohabitors and 41% of female cohabitors have never been married (U.S. Bureau of the Census, 1990). Children live with about one cohabiting couple in three (Saluter, 1992).

It is not true that cohabitation is most common among college students. Cohabitation is actually more prevalent among the less well educated and less affluent. ■

Truth or Fiction?
REVISITED

About one cohabitor in three is divorced. Divorced people are more likely than people who have never married to enter cohabiting relationships. Apparently, the experience of divorce makes some people more willing to share their lives than their bank accounts—the second or third time around (Steinhauer, 1995).

Willingness to cohabit is related to more liberal attitudes toward sexual behavior, less traditional views of marriage, and less traditional views of gender roles (Huffman et al., 1994). Cohabitors are less likely than noncohabitors to attend church regularly (Laumann et al., 1994). Six out of ten male cohabitors and nearly seven out of ten female cohabitors are under 35 years of age (U.S. Bureau of the Census, 1990). Yet the greatest increase since 1980 in the numbers of people cohabiting has not been among young romantics, but among people age 35 and above (Bumpass, 1995).

Reasons for Cohabitation

Why do people cohabit? Cohabitation, like marriage, is an alternative to the loneliness that can accompanying living alone. Romantic partners might have deep feelings for each other but not be ready to get married. Some couples prefer cohabitation because it provides a consistent relationship without the legal entanglements of marriage (Steinhauer, 1995).

Many cohabitors feel less commitment toward their relationships than married people do (Nock, 1995). Ruth, an 84-year-old woman, has been living with her partner, age 85, for four years. "I'm a free spirit," she says. "I need my space. Sometimes we think of marriage, but then I think that I don't want to be tied down" (cited in Steinhauer, 1995, p. C7).

Ruth's comments are of interest because they counter stereotypes of women and older people. However, it is more often the man who is unwilling to make a marital commitment (Yorburg, 1995), as in the case of Mark. Mark, a 44-year-old computer consultant, lives with Nancy and their 7-year-old daughter, Janet. Mark says, "We feel we are not primarily a couple but rather primarily individuals who happen to be in a couple. It allows me to be a little more at arm's length. Men don't like committing, so maybe this is just some sort of excuse" (cited in Steinhauer, 1995, p. C7).

Economic factors come into play as well. Emotionally committed couples might decide to cohabit because of the economic advantages of sharing household expenses.

Cohabitation. Cohabitation was once referred to as "living in sin," but it has become an increasingly common lifestyle. Some sociologists predict that cohabitation will replace marriage as the nation's most popular lifestyle sometime during the first century of the new millennium. Why do people cohabit? Cohabitation is an alternative to the loneliness of living by oneself. It also allows for the experience of an intimate relationship without some of the obligations of marriage. Men are more likely than women to want to cohabit rather than get married.

Cohabiting individuals who receive public assistance (social security or welfare checks) risk losing support if they get married (Steinhauer, 1995). Some older people live together rather than marry because of resistance from adult children (Yorburg, 1995). Some children fear that a parent will be victimized by a needy senior citizen. Others might not want their inheritances to come into question or might not want to decide where to bury the remaining parent. Younger couples might cohabit secretly to maintain parental support that they might lose if they were to get married or openly reveal their living arrangements.

Cohabitation and Later Marriage: Benefit or Risk?

Cohabiting couples may believe that cohabitation will strengthen eventual marriage by helping them iron out the kinks in their relationship. Yet cohabitors who later marry might run a greater—not lesser—risk of divorce than noncohabitors. Statistics from a national survey of households reveal that the likelihood of divorce within ten years of marriage is nearly twice as great among married couples who cohabited before marriage (Riche, 1988). A Swedish study found that the likelihood of marital dissolution was 80% greater among women who had cohabited before a first marriage than among women who had not (Bennett et al., 1988).

We must be cautious about drawing causal conclusions from correlational data, however. None of the couples in these studies were *randomly assigned* to cohabitation or noncohabitation. Therefore, *selection factors*—the factors that lead some couples to cohabit and others not to cohabit—may explain the results (see Figure 14.1). Cohabitors tend to be more committed to personal independence (Bumpass, 1995). They also tend to be less traditional and less religious than noncohabitors. All in all, people who cohabit before marriage tend to be less committed to the values and interests that are traditionally associated with the institution of marriage. The attitudes of cohabitors, not cohabitation itself, could thus account for their higher rates of marital dissolution.

About 40% of cohabiting couples eventually marry (Laumann et al., 1994). The majority of cohabiting couples break up within three years. Termination of the relationship, not marriage, is the more likely outcome of cohabitation (Willis & Michael, 1994).

figure 14.1

Does Cohabitation before Marriage Increase the Risk of Eventual Divorce? There is a correlational relationship between cohabitation before marriage and the risk of divorce later on. Does cohabitation increase the risk of divorce, or do other factors—such as a commitment to personal independence—contribute to both the likelihood of cohabitation and eventual divorce?

Reflections

■ Do you know people who are living together without being married? What is their motivation for doing so? How do most people from their sociocultural background feel about cohabitation? Why?

■ Agree or disagree with the following statement and support your answer: Cohabitation helps couples to determine whether they are compatible before they get married.

■ Agree or disagree with the following statement and support your answer: Cohabitation is a normal variation in lifestyle.

MARRIAGE

Marriage is found in all human societies. Most people in every known society, sometimes nearly all, get married at least once (Ember & Ember, 1990; Kammeyer, 1990).

Marriage is our most common lifestyle. In some cultures, such as among the Hindu of India, marriage is virtually universal, with more than 99% of the females eventually marrying. In the United States, most people still get married, but today, one in four people of age 18 and above has never married (Steinhauer, 1995). In 1970, the number of never-married adults was only one in six (Steinhauer, 1995). However, cohabitation is becoming widespread in the United States as well. University of Wisconsin researcher Larry Bumpass has been following 10,000 people since the late 1980s. In 1995, he reported that 49% of people ages 35 to 39 were cohabiting, compared to 34% in the late 1980s. Bumpass estimates that nationwide, half of the adult population under age 40 is cohabiting. In 1995, he estimated that in ten years, half of the adult population under the age of 50 would be cohabiting.

In the United States, about 65% of the adult men and 60% of the adult women are married and living with their spouses (U.S. Bureau of the Census, 1990). With more people delaying marriage in favor of pursuing educational and career goals, the average (median) age of first marriage has been rising steadily over the past few decades and is now 26.5 years for men and 24.4 years for women (Saluter, 1992). This represents an increase of three years for both men and women since 1975.

Historical Perspectives

Marriage in Western culture has a long and varied history. Among the ancient Hebrews, men dominated most aspects of life. This system was known as **patriarchy.** The man of the house had the right to choose wives for his sons and could himself take concubines or

Patriarchy A form of social organization in which the father or eldest male runs the group or family; government, rule, or domination by men. (From the Greek *pater,* meaning "father," and *archein,* meaning "to rule.")

Marriage. Marriage is the most common lifestyle in the United States. Nearly 65% of adult men and 60% of adult women are married and living with their spouses. Some married couples still adhere to traditional gender roles in which the man is the breadwinner and the woman is the homemaker. However, increasing numbers of couples in the United States share or reverse marital roles.

additional wives. He alone could institute divorce—a practice that is still found among Orthodox Jews. Although he could dally, his wife had to be scrupulous in the maintenance of her virtue. Failure to bear children was grounds for divorce. The wife was clearly considered to be part of the property of the man of the house: a **chattel.**

In classical Greece, women were also viewed as the property of men. Their central purposes were to care for the household and to bear children. Rarely were they viewed as suitable companions for men. During the golden age of Greece, men would turn to high-class prostitutes for sensual sex and sophisticated conversation—not to their wives.

Truth or Fiction?
REVISITED

It is true that in the ancient Hebrew and Greek civilizations, wives were viewed as their husbands' property. The women's movement has fought to throw off the weight of millennia of such oppressive practices. ■

The Romans also had a powerful patriarchy. The oldest man directed family life and could, if he wished, sell his children into slavery and arrange their marriages and divorces. Marriages were typically arranged for financial or political gain. Women were in effect given by their fathers to their husbands.

The Christian tradition also has a strong patriarchal foundation. Male dominance was legitimized by biblical scripture, as we can see in this passage from the New Testament: "Wives, submit to your own husbands, as unto the Lord. For the husband is the head of the wife, as Christ is the head of the church" (Ephesians 5:23–24).

Patriarchal traditions in Western culture gradually weakened with time, and women came to be viewed as loving companions rather than mere chattels. They gradually gained more household responsibilities and were recognized as being capable of profiting from education. The notion that a married woman might rightfully seek personal fulfillment through a career unrelated to her husband's needs is a relatively recent development, however. The perception that married women have a right to sexual fulfillment is also new. As late as the nineteenth century, sex in marriage was seen largely as a means for bearing children and satisfying the husband's sexual needs. Although there were some caring and sensitive husbands, typical nineteenth-century sexual relations between husbands and wives were brief and brutal. Women derived little pleasure from them. Sex was viewed, even among educated classes, as a husband's right and a wife's

Chattel A movable piece of personal property, such as furniture or livestock. (From the Old French word meaning "cattle.")

table 14.1

A comparison of traditional and modern marriages	
Traditional Marriage	**Modern Marriage**
The emphasis is on ritual and traditional roles.	The emphasis is on companionship.
Couples do not live together before marriage.	Couples may live together before marriage.
The wife takes the husband's last name.	The wife may choose to keep her maiden name.
The husband is dominant; the wife is submissive.	Neither spouse is dominant or submissive.
The roles for the husband and the wife are specific and rigid.	Both spouses have flexible roles.
There is one income (the husband's).	There may be two incomes; that is, the couple may share the breadwinning role. In many cases, the woman is the breadwinner.
The husband initiates sexual activity; the wife complies.	Either spouse may initiate (or refuse) sex.
The wife cares for the children.	The parents share childrearing chores.
Education is considered important for the husband, not for the wife.	Education is considered equally important for both spouses.
The husband's career decides the location of the family residence.	The career of either spouse may determine the location of the family residence.

Source: Adapted by permission from CHOICES IN RELATIONSHIPS by D. Knox; Copyright © 1988 by West Publishing Company. All rights reserved.

duty. Marriage manuals of the time held that a woman's role was to submit to her husband's advances in order to please him. Women were assumed to be motivated sexually only by the desire for children.

Marital roles in modern society have changed and are changing still. Some couples still adhere to traditional gender roles that ascribe breadwinning responsibilities to the husband and child care and homemaking roles to the wife. U.S. couples today are more likely to share or even reverse marital roles, however. Table 14.1 lists some of the discriminating features of traditional and so-called modern marriages.

Why Do People Marry?

Marriage meets personal and cultural needs. It legitimizes sexual relations and provides a legal sanction for deeply committed relationships. It permits the maintenance of a home life and provides an institution in which children can be supported and socialized into adopting the norms of the family and the culture at large. Marriage restricts sexual relations so that a man can be assured—or at least can assume—that his wife's children are his. Marriage also permits the orderly transmission of wealth from one family to another and from one generation to another. As late as the seventeenth and eighteenth centuries, most European marriages were arranged by the parents of the bride and groom, generally on the basis of how the marriage would benefit the families.

Notions such as romantic love, equality, and the very radical concept that men as well as women would do well to aspire to the ideal of faithfulness are recent additions to the structure of marriage in Western society. Not until the nineteenth century did the notion of love as a basis for marriage become widespread in Western culture. In some preliterate societies, the very idea of being in love is considered a laughable concept—hardly a basis for marriage.

Today, because more people believe that premarital sex is acceptable between two people who feel affectionate toward each other, the desire to engage in sexual intercourse is less likely to motivate marriage. Marriage provides a sense of emotional and psychological security, however, and opportunities to share feelings, experiences, and ideas with someone with whom one forms a special attachment. Desires for companionship and intimacy are central goals in contemporary marriages. Even in these more liberated times, young people (ages 17 to 23) today strongly endorse the traditional ideal that marriage is a lifetime commitment (Moore & Stief, 1992).

Types of Marriage

There are two major types of marriage: monogamy and polygamy. In **monogamy,** a husband and wife are wed only to each other. But let us not confuse monogamy, which is a form of matrimony, with sexual exclusivity. People who are monogamously wedded often do have extramarital affairs, as we shall see, but are considered to be married to only one person at a time. In **polygamy,** a person has more than one spouse and is permitted sexual access to each of them.

Polygyny is by far the most prevalent form of polygamy among the world's preliterate societies (Ford & Beach, 1951; Frayser, 1985). **Polyandry** is practiced only rarely (see Chapter 1). In polygynous societies, men are permitted to have multiple wives if they can support them; more rarely, a man will have one wife and one or more concubines. The man's first wife typically has higher status than the others. Economic factors and the availability of prospective mates usually limit the opportunities for men to wed more than one woman at a time, however. In many cases, only wealthy men can afford to support multiple wives and the children of these unions. In addition, few if any societies have enough women to allow most men to have two or more wives (Ember & Ember, 1990). For these reasons, even in societies that prefer polygyny, fewer than half of the men at any given time actually have multiple mates (Ford & Beach, 1951).

Whom Do We Marry: Are Marriages Made in Heaven or in the Neighborhood?

Most preliterate societies regulate the selection of spouses in some way. The universal incest taboo proscribes matings between close relatives. Societal rules and customs also determine which persons are desirable mates and which are not.

In Western cultures, mate selection is presumably free. Parents today seldom arrange marriages, although they might still encourage their child to date that wonderful son or daughter of the solid churchgoing couple who live down the street. Nevertheless, factors such as race, social class, and religion often determine the categories of people within which we seek mates (Laumann et al., 1994). People in our culture tend to marry others from the same geographical area and social class. Since neighborhoods are often made up of people from a similar social class, storybook marriages like Cinderella's are the exception to the rule.

Because we make choices, we tend to marry people who attract us. These people are usually similar to us in physical attractiveness and attitudes, even minute details. We are more often than not similar to our mates in characteristics such as height, weight, personality traits, and intelligence (Buss, 1994; Lesnik-Oberstein & Cohen, 1984; Schafer & Keith, 1990). The people we marry also seem likely to meet our material, sexual, and psychological needs.

The concept of "like marrying like" is termed **homogamy.** We usually marry people of the same racial/ethnic background, educational level, and religion. Interracial marriages account for fewer than 1 in every 100 marriages (U.S. Bureau of the Census, 1998).

Monogamy Marriage to one person.

Polygamy Simultaneous marriage to more than one person.

Polygyny A form of marriage in which a man is married to more than one woman at the same time.

Polyandry A form of marriage in which a woman is married to more than one man at the same time.

Homogamy The practice of marrying people who are similar in social background and standing. (From Greek roots meaning "same" [*homos*] and "marriage" [*gamos*].)

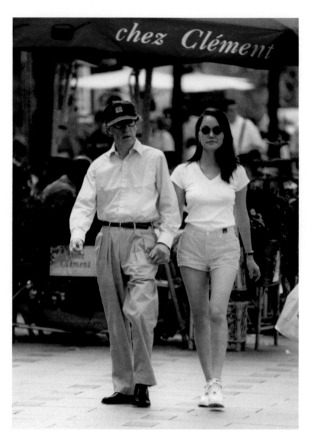

Whom Do We Marry? The marriage of Woody Allen and Soon-Yi is typical in some ways, and atypical in others. It is common for the man to be older than the woman. When there is a great disparity of ages, as there is here, the man is frequently well established and the woman is usually very attractive. But Allen and Soon-Yi are of different races, which remains uncommon in the United States. Moreover, Soon-Yi is the adopted daughter of Allen's ex-wife, Mia Farrow, which makes the union quite unusual.

Moreover, more than nine of ten marriages are between people of the same religion. Marriages between individuals who are alike may stand a better chance of survival, since the partners are more likely to share their values and attitudes (Michael et al., 1994). Dissimilar couples, however, can work to overcome the barriers that divide them by developing shared interests and mutual respect for their differences.

We also tend to follow *age homogamy* (Michael et al., 1994). Age homogamy—the selection of a partner who falls in one's own age range—might reflect the tendency to marry early in adulthood. Persons who marry late or who remarry tend not to select partners who are as close in age. Bridegrooms tend to be two to five years older than their wives, on the average, in European, North American, and South American countries (Buss, 1994).

Some marriages also show a **mating gradient.** The stereotype has been that an economically established older man would take an attractive, younger woman as his wife. But by and large, with boring predictability, we are attracted to and marry the boy or girl (almost) next door. Most marriages seem to be made not in heaven, but in the neighborhood.

WHO HAS HIS HEAD IN THE CLOUDS? (HINT: THE QUESTION IS *NOT* PHRASED IN SEXIST LANGUAGE)   When it comes to picking a mate, men tend to be the romantics; women, the pragmatists. Men are more likely to believe that each person has one true love whom he or she is destined to find (Peplau & Gordon, 1985). Men are more likely to believe in love at first sight. Women, on the other hand, are more likely to value financial security as much as passion. Women are more likely to believe that they could form a loving relationship with many individuals. Women are also less likely to believe that love conquers all—especially economic problems.

Mating gradient The tendency for women to "marry up" (in social or economic status) and for men to "marry down."

It is true that men are more romantic than women—when we define being romantic as believing in love at first sight or that there is one person who is right for oneself. (Who is more "romantic" if we define romantic to mean that one wishes to confine sexual activity to a romantic relationship?) ▪

Reflections

- ▪ Agree or disagree with the following statement and support your answer: There is a right person for everyone, and they are destined to meet.
- ▪ Agree or disagree with the following statement and support your answer: Marriage is an old-fashioned, outdated lifestyle that has become irrelevant for today's sophisticated young people.
- ▪ Agree or disagree with the following statement, and support your answer: Children are best reared by married parents.

MARITAL SEXUALITY

Patterns of marital sexuality vary across cultures, yet anthropologists have noted some common threads (Ember & Ember, 1990). Privacy for sexual relations is valued in almost all cultures. Most cultures also place restrictions on coitus during menstruation, during at least some stages of pregnancy, and for a time after childbirth.

Until the sexual revolution of the 1960s and 1970s, Western culture could have been characterized as sexually restrictive, even toward marital sex. Hunt noted that "Western civilization has long had the rare distinction of contaminating and restricting the sexual pleasure of married couples more severely than almost any other" (1974, p. 175).

The Sexual Revolution Hits Home

We usually think of the sexual revolution in terms of the changes in sexual behaviors and attitudes that occurred among young, unmarried people. It also ushered in profound changes in marital sexuality, however. Compared to Kinsey's "prerevolution" samples from the late 1930s and 1940s, married couples today engage in coitus more frequently, with greater variety, and for longer durations of time. They report higher levels of sexual satisfaction.

The sexual revolution also helped to dislodge traditional male dominance in sexual behavior. In essence, male dominance is the view that sexual pleasure is meant for men but not women and that it is the duty of women to satisfy their husbands' sexual needs and serve as passive "receptacles." Assumptions of male dominance are found even in the writing of the (for his time) liberated Kinsey. Nowhere are they more evident than in his (and his colleagues') comment that men, who have the biological capacity to ejaculate a few moments after entry, need not feel bound to "wait" for women to reach orgasm (Kinsey et al., 1948, p. 580).

People who are caught up in social revolutions may not perceive themselves as revolutionaries. They might not even be aware that a "revolution" is taking place. The sexual revolution was not heralded by parades or massive demonstrations. There was no "storming of the Bastille" to proclaim sexual freedom. Organizations promoting "free love" did not attract large followings. Even the most famous slogan of the sexual revolution— "Make love, not war"—was more an indictment of the Vietnam War than a call for free love. Moreover, social movements are begun by a few but are spread by the perception that they define popular trends. Married people, as well as singles, thus made sexual decisions not only on the basis of their religious teachings and personal values, but also on their perceptions of the norm.

Liberalizing trends were communicated through popular media. Hundreds if not-thousands of books and magazines with sexual content crammed bookstore shelves and supermarket display cases. During Kinsey's day, books such as Henry Miller's *Tropic of Cancer* and D. H. Lawrence's *Lady Chatterley's Lover* were censored in the United States. Now they are readily available but so tame when compared to today's explicit books and magazines that they barely raise an eyebrow. Similarly, since the late 1960s, pornographic films have been shown in adult theaters across the nation. In many places, the audiences include middle-class couples and college students, not just "dirty old men." The VCR has brought sexually explicit films into middle-class suburban homes.

Scientific findings were also liberalizing influences. Kinsey's and Masters and Johnson's findings that normal women were capable not only of orgasm but also of multiple orgasms punctured traditional beliefs that sexual gratification was the birthright of men alone. TV shows, films, and radio talk shows began to portray women as sexual initiators who enjoy sex. All of these influences have encouraged U.S. women to forgo the traditional passive approach to sexuality.

The affluence of the post–World War II years also encouraged more young people to pursue a college education and live away from home. College liberates not only through exposure to great books and scientific knowledge, but also through challenging students' attitudes by bright, knowledgeable peers from different backgrounds. Prejudice and myth are often analyzed and discarded.

Americans have also become more mobile. Jobs carry young people thousands of miles from home. Their sexual attitudes are influenced by new acquaintances from many parts of the country and by people from other nations, not just by a few people from "the neighborhood."

The development of effective contraceptives also separated sex from reproduction. Motives for sexual pleasure became more open. The term *recreational sex* came into play. All these liberalizing forces have led to changes in the frequency of marital sex and in techniques of foreplay and coitus since Kinsey's day.

CHANGES IN DURATION AND TECHNIQUES OF FOREPLAY   Married women in Kinsey's sample reported an average (median) length of foreplay of about 12 minutes. This figure rose to nearly 15 minutes among the wives in the Playboy survey (Hunt, 1974). Kinsey found that men at lower educational levels engaged in briefer periods of foreplay, generally lasting but a minute or two before penetration. The length of foreplay rose to 5 to 15 minutes among college-educated men. In a dramatic shift in sophistication since Kinsey's day, Hunt found that the typical duration of foreplay in the 1970s was 15 minutes for college-educated and noncollege males alike. Foreplay was relatively longer in duration among younger married couples than their elders, however.

Marital foreplay has also become more varied since Kinsey's day. Couples in more recent surveys report using a wider variety of foreplay techniques, including oral stimulation of the breasts and oral-genital contact (Blumstein & Schwartz, 1983; Hunt, 1974).

CHANGES IN FREQUENCY OF MARITAL COITUS   How frequently do married couples engage in coitus? A comparison of the reports from Kinsey's couples and the Playboy survey couples (Table 14.2) shows increases in coital frequency at every age level. However, keep in mind that because 80% of those contacted by the Playboy survey refused to participate, the figures in the table might have a strong volunteer bias. Because volunteers tend to be more open about their sexuality than people who refuse to divulge information about sex, this bias would tend to inflate the statistical results (Laumann et al., 1994).

table 14.2

Median weekly frequency of marital coitus, male and female estimates combined (Kinsey and Playboy surveys)			
KINSEY (1948, 1953)		**PLAYBOY (1974)**	
Age	**Frequency**	**Age**	**Frequency**
16–25	2.45	18–24	3.25
26–35	1.95	25–34	2.55
36–45	1.40	35–44	2.00
46–55	.85	45–54	1.00
55–60	.50	55 & over	1.00

Source: Hunt, M. (1974). *Sexual behavior in the 1970's.* New York: Dell Books, p. 191.

table 14.3

Frequency of marital sexual relations during the past year, according to NHSLS study		
Frequency of Sexual Relations	**Men (%)**	**Women (%)**
Not at all	1.3	3.0
A few times per year	12.8	11.9
A few times per month	42.5	46.5
Two to three times a week	36.1	31.9
Four or more times a week	7.3	6.6

Source: Adapted from Laumann, E. O., Gagnon, J. H., Michael, R. T., & Michaels, S. (1994). *The social organization of sexuality: Sexual practices in the United States.* Chicago: University of Chicago Press, Table 3.4, pp. 88–89.

The data reported by the NHSLS study do not allow a direct comparison with the Kinsey and Playboy figures. As shown in Table 14.3, however, the overwhelming majority of married men and women in the United States now report engaging in sexual relations either a few times per month or two to three times a week (Laumann et al., 1994). The average is seven times a month (Michael et al., 1994, p. 136). These figures are somewhat more in keeping with Kinsey's than with the Playboy survey's, which might cast doubt on the Playboy survey's statistics.

Kinsey and the University of Chicago group (who conducted the NHSLS study) did not find strong links between coital frequency and educational level. Studies consistently find that the frequency of sexual relations declines with age, however (Call et al., 1995; Laumann et al., 1994). At the ages of 50–59, for example, people reported an average of four to five times per month (Laumann et al., 1994). Regardless of a couple's age, sexual frequency also appears to decline with years of marriage (Blumstein & Schwartz, 1990).

CHANGES IN TECHNIQUES AND DURATION OF COITUS   In coitus, as in foreplay, the marital bed since Kinsey's day has become a stage on which the players act more varied roles. Today's couples use greater variety in coital positions.

Kinsey's study participants mainly limited coitus to the male-superior position. As many as 70% of Kinsey's males used the male-superior position exclusively (Kinsey et al., 1948). Perhaps three couples in ten used the female-superior position frequently. One in four or five used the lateral-entry position frequently, and about one in ten use the rear-entry position. Younger and more highly educated men showed greater variety, however. Hunt (1974), by comparison, found that three quarters of the married couples in the Playboy survey used the female-superior position at least occasionally. More than half had used the lateral-entry position, and about four in ten had used the rear-entry position.

An often overlooked but important difference between Kinsey's and current samples involves the length of intercourse. In Kinsey's time, it was widely believed that the "virile" man ejaculated rapidly during intercourse. Kinsey estimated that most men reached orgasm within 2 minutes after penetration, many within 10 or 20 seconds. Kinsey recognized that women usually took longer to reach orgasm through coitus and that some clinicians were already asserting that a man's ejaculation was "premature" unless he delayed it until "the female (was) ready to reach orgasm" (1948, p. 580).

Even today's less-educated couples appear to be more sophisticated than Kinsey's in their recognition of the need for sexual variety and their focus on exchanging sexual pleasure rather than rapidly reaching orgasm (Michael et al., 1994). According to the NHSLS study, the "duration of the last sexual event" of three out of four married couples was 15 minutes to an hour. Eight percent to 9% of couples exceeded an hour (Michael et al.,

1994). (About one unmarried, noncohabiting couple in three made love for an hour or more, suggesting that novelty and youth have their motivational aspects.)

Sexual Satisfaction

One index by which researchers measure sexual satisfaction is orgasmic consistency. Men tend to reach orgasm more consistently than women do. After 15 years of marriage, 45% of the wives in Kinsey's study reported reaching orgasm 90% to 100% of the time. After 15 years of marriage, 12% of the wives in Kinsey's study had not experienced orgasm.

Orgasmic consistency now seems higher than in Kinsey's day. The NHSLS study found that more than 90% of the men and about 70% of women reported reaching orgasm "always" or "usually" with their primary partner during the 12 months prior to the survey (Laumann et al., 1994; Michael et al., 1994) (see Table 14.4). Three of four men (75%) and nearly three women in ten (28.6%) reported reaching orgasm on every occasion (not shown in Table 14.4). Only 2% of the married women reported never reaching orgasm with their husbands during the past year (not shown).

Women in their 40s were somewhat more likely to reach orgasm consistently than younger and older women. Perhaps women in their 40s have had more time to get in touch with their sexuality and may be more secure in their relationships than younger women are. The falloff for women and men in their 50s may be biologically related.

t a b l e   1 4 . 4

Sociocultural factors and sexual satisfaction in primary relationship during last year						
Sociocultural Characteristics	**ALWAYS OR USUALLY HAD AN ORGASM WITH PARTNER**		**HAS BEEN EXTREMELY PHYSICALLY SATISFIED WITH PARTNER**		**HAS BEEN EXTREMELY EMOTIONALLY SATISFIED WITH PARTNER**	
	Men (%)	**Women (%)**	**Men (%)**	**Women (%)**	**Men (%)**	**Women (%)**
Age						
18–24	92	61	44	44	41	39
25–29	94	71	50	39	46	40
30–39	97	70	45	41	39	38
40–49	97	78	44	42	38	42
50–59	91	73	53	32	52	32
Marital Status						
Noncohabiting	94	62	39	40	32	31
Cohabiting	95	68	44	46	35	44
Married	95	75	52	41	49	42
Race/Ethnicity*						
White (non-Hispanic)	96	70	47	40	43	38
African American	90	72	43	44	43	38
Hispanic American	96	68	51	39	43	39

*The numbers of Asian Americans and Native Americans were too small to report reliable statistics.

Source: Combined from Laumann, E. O., Gagnon, J. H., Michael, R. T., & Michaels, S. (1994). *The social organization of sexuality: Sexual practices in the United States.* Chicago: University of Chicago Press, Table 3.7, pp. 116–117, and Michael, R. T., Gagnon, J. H., Laumann, E. O., & Kolata, G. (1994). *Sex in America: A definitive survey.* Boston: Little, Brown, Table 9, pp. 128–129.

The nature of the relationship is a factor for women. Married women were most likely to reach orgasm consistently, followed by cohabiting women, and then noncohabiting women. Security in the relationship apparently promotes orgasmic consistency. There do not seem to be notable racial or ethnic differences.

Orgasm is not the only criterion for measuring pleasure or satisfaction in marital sex. The NHSLS study asked participants whether they had been extremely physically satisfied with their primary partners during the past year. It is apparent, from Table 14.4, that men's and women's general physical satisfaction is comparable—about 47% and 41%, respectively. Orgasm, then, is not a guarantee of satisfaction. And lack of orgasm is not necessarily a sign of dissatisfaction.

The emotional satisfaction in a marital relationship is also linked to sexual satisfaction. Table 14.4 shows that about 40% of men and women report being extremely emotionally satisfied with their primary partners. Closer relationships are connected with more consistent orgasm.

Other researchers have found that wives who talk openly to their husbands about their sexual feelings and needs report higher levels of sexual satisfaction (Banmen & Vogel, 1985; Tavris & Sadd, 1977). Women respondents to the *Redbook* survey who took an active role during sex were more satisfied with their sex lives than were those who assumed the traditional passive female role (Tavris & Sadd, 1977).

Reflections

■ Agree or disagree with the following statement and support your answer: Sexual pleasure is meant for men but not women, and it is the duty of women to satisfy their husbands' sexual needs.

■ What has been the role of contraceptives as a liberating force in the expression of human sexuality?

■ Agree or disagree with the following statement and support your answer: Marital sex tends to become routine, repetitious, and unexciting.

EXTRAMARITAL SEX

Women seek soul mates; men seek playmates. Women believe that their affair is justified when it is for love; men, when it's *not* for love.

—Janis Abrahms Spring (1997)

It's next door and it's in the White House—Bill Clinton and Gennifer Flowers, Bill Clinton and Monica Lewinsky. Journalist Eric Alterman (1997) writes that adultery is everywhere today. When French President François Mitterand died, his wife, his mistress, and his illegitimate daughter were numbered among the mourners. Alterman mentions the examples of Kelly Flinn (who was forced to resign from the armed services), Frank Gifford (who retired from *Monday Night Football* in 1998), Bill Cosby (who admitted to an affair but denied that the woman's daughter was his child), and actor Eddie Murphy.

Why do people engage in extramarital sex? What does it mean? What are its effects on a marriage?

Some people engage in extramarital sex for variety (Lamanna & Riedmann, 1997). Some have affairs to break the routine of a confining marriage. Others enter affairs for reasons similar to the nonsexual reasons adolescents often have for sex: as a way of expressing hostility toward a spouse or retaliating for injustice. Husbands and wives who engage in affairs often report that they are not satisfied with, or fulfilled by, their marital relationships. Curiosity and desire for personal growth are often more prominent motives than marital dissatisfaction. Middle-aged people might have affairs to boost their self-esteem or to prove that they are still attractive.

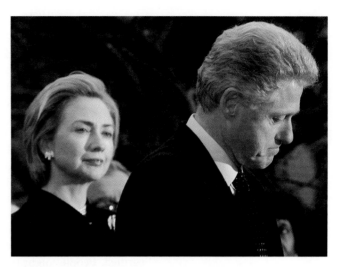

Convicted! Acquitted! Airwoman Kelly Flinn and many other officers in the military have been court martialed for having adulterous affairs. Yet, is it an example of a double standard when others who commit similar acts receive little or no punishment? President Bill Clinton remained in office despite reports of extramarital affairs. Clinton's statements about his affair with White House intern Monica Lewinsky led him down the path to impeachment by the House of Representatives on charges of perjury and obstruction of justice. However, he was acquitted of these charges by the Senate.

Many times, the sexual motive is less pressing than the desire for emotional closeness. Some women say that they are seeking someone whom they can talk to or communicate with (Lamanna & Riedmann, 1997). There is a notable gender difference here. According to Janis Abrahms Spring, author of *After the Affair* (a self-help book designed to help people save their marriages after an affair), men might be seeking sex in affairs. Women, however, are usually seeking "soul mates" (while men are seeking "playmates"). Spring (1997) notes that "Women believe that their affair is justified when it is for love; men, when it's *not* for love." (Seventy-seven percent of women who have had affairs, compared to 43% of the men, cite love as their justification [Townsend, 1995]). Men who have had affairs are more likely to cite a need for sexual excitement as a justification than women are—75% versus 55% (Glass & Wright, 1992).

These data support the view, expressed repeatedly throughout this text, that women are less accepting of sex without emotional involvement (Townsend, 1995). Men are more likely than women to "separate sex and love; women appear to believe that love and sex go together and that falling in love justifies sexual involvement" (Glass & Wright, 1992, p. 361). Men (whether single, married, or cohabiting) are also generally more approving of extramarital affairs than women are (Glass & Wright, 1992). But note that these are all *group* differences. Many individual men are interested primarily in the extramarital relationship rather than the sex per se. Similarly, many women are out for the sex and not the relationship.

Patterns of Extramarital Sex

Let is begin with a few definitions. **Extramarital sex** (an "affair") is usually conducted without the spouse's knowledge or approval. Secret affairs are referred to as **conventional adultery,** infidelity, or simply "cheating." Conventional adultery runs the gamut from the "one-night stand" to the affair that persists for years. (Bill Clinton's affair with Gennifer Flowers allegedly persisted for a dozen years.) In **consensual adultery,** extramarital

Extramarital sex Sexual relations between a married person and someone other than his or her spouse.

Conventional adultery Extramarital sex that is kept clandestine (hidden) from one's spouse.

Consensual adultery Extramarital sex that is engaged in openly with the knowledge and consent of one's spouse.

relationships are conducted openly—that is, with the partner's knowledge and consent. In what is called **swinging**, or *mate-swapping*, the partner participates.

How many people "cheat" on their spouses? Viewers of TV talk shows might get the impression that everyone cheats, but surveys paint a different picture. In surveys conducted between 1988 and 1996 by the respected National Opinion Research Center, about one husband in four or five, and one wife in eight, admitted to marital infidelity (Alterman, 1997; "Cheating," 1993). Similarly, more than 90% of the married women and 75% of the married men in the NHSLS study reported remaining loyal to their spouses (Laumann et al., 1994). The vast majority of people who were cohabiting also reported that they were sexually faithful to their partners while they were living together (Laumann et al., 1994). What can we conclude? Perhaps two things: One is that men are about twice as likely as women to admit to affairs. The other is that only a minority of married people admit to affairs.

Those are the conclusions, but note that we said *"admit* to affairs." Having presented the percentages of reported extramarital sex, we point out that these reports cannot be verified. People might be reluctant to reveal they have "cheated" on their spouses even when they are assured of anonymity. There is likely to be an overall tendency to underreport the incidence of extramarital sex.

Attitudes Toward Extramarital Sex

The sexual revolution does not seem to have changed attitudes toward extramarital sex. About nine out of ten Americans say that affairs are "always wrong" or "almost always wrong" (Alterman, 1997). Three out of four Americans say that extramarital sex is "always wrong" (Berke, 1997). Another one in seven say that it is "almost always wrong." Only about 1% say that extramarital sex is "not at all wrong." Most married couples embrace the value of monogamy as the cornerstone of their marital relationship (Blumstein & Schwartz, 1990).

Truth or Fiction?
REVISITED

It is not true that most of today's sophisticated young people see nothing wrong with an occasional extramarital fling. The sexual revolution never extended itself to extramarital affairs—at least among the majority of married people. ■

CROSS-CULTURAL PERSPECTIVES ON EXTRAMARITAL SEX Most preliterate societies prohibit extramarital relationships for one or both spouses (Frayser, 1985). In cultures in which extramarital sex is permitted, husbands are typically allowed greater sexual freedom than wives. Frayser could find no societies that allowed extramarital sex for wives but not husbands.

Slightly more than half (54%) of the preliterate societies around the world permit men to have extramarital partners (Ember & Ember, 1990). Only 11% allow women the same opportunity. In some societies, extramarital affairs are formalized within rules of social conduct. Among the Aleut people of Alaska's Aleutian Islands, for example, men may offer visitors the opportunity to sleep with their wives as a gesture of hospitality. Among the Chukchee of Siberia, who often travel long distances from their homes, a married man is allowed to engage in sexual activity with his host's wife. The understanding is that he would reciprocate when the host visited him (Ford & Beach, 1951).

Kinship ties often determine sexual access to extramarital partners (Frayser, 1985). Among the people of the Marshall Islands in the Pacific, a woman is allowed to have a sexual relationship with her sister's husband. Among the Native American Comanches, a man is permitted to have intercourse with his brother's wife if his brother consents. Customs sometimes limit extramarital intercourse to ceremonial occasions. The Fijians of Oceania, for example, engage in extramarital relationships only after the return of their men from warfare. In Western society, Mardi Gras and some out-of-town conventions represent ceremonial occasions for extramarital liaisons that might not be tolerated otherwise.

Swinging A form of consensual adultery in which both spouses share extramarital sexual experiences. Also referred to as *mate-swapping*.

Effects of Extramarital Sex

The discovery of infidelity can evoke a range of emotional responses. The spouse might be filled with anger, jealousy, even shame. Feelings of inadequacy and doubts about one's attractiveness and desirability might surface. The betrayed spouse might see infidelity as a serious breach of trust and intimacy. Marriages that are not terminated in the wake of the disclosure might survive in a damaged condition (Charny & Parnass, 1995).

The harm that an affair does to a marriage might reflect the meaning of the affair to the individual and his or her spouse. Deborah Lamberti, director of a counseling and psychotherapy center in New York City, points again to women's traditional intertwining of sex with relationships and argues that "Men don't view sex with another person as a reason to leave a primary relationship" (1997, pp. 131–132). Women might recognize this and be able to tell themselves that their husbands are sleeping with someone else just for physical reasons. But women are more concerned about remaining monogamous. Therefore, if a woman is sleeping with another man, she might already have a foot out the door, so to speak. Alterman (1997) also notes that a wife's affair might be an unforgivable blow to the husband's ego or pride. A woman might be more likely to see the transgression as a threat to the structure of her life.

If a person has an affair because the marriage is deeply troubled, the affair could be one more factor that speeds its dissolution. The effects on the marriage might depend on the nature of the affair. It might be easier to understand that a spouse has fallen prey to an isolated, unplanned encounter than to accept an extended affair (Charny & Parnass, 1995). In some cases, the discovery of infidelity stimulates the couple to work to improve their relationship. If the extramarital activity continues, however, it could undermine the couple's efforts to restore their relationship.

Swinging

Swinging—also called "mate-swapping" or **comarital sex**—is a form of consensual adultery in which both partners openly share sexual experiences with other people. Most swingers seek to avoid emotional entanglements with their swinging partners, but they might fail to separate their emotions from their sexual activity. Emotional intimacy between swinging partners can be even more threatening to the swingers' primary relationships than sexual intimacy. For various reasons, most swinging couples drop out after a short period of experimentation.

Swingers tend to be White, fairly affluent, and well educated and to have only nominal religious affiliations (Jenks, 1985). Solid statistics on the prevalence of swinging are lacking, however. Observers of sexual trends suggest that swinging, like other nontraditional forms of matrimony, seems to have largely vanished from the social scene (Havemann & Lehtinen, 1990). Concern over AIDS, coupled with the more conservative social climate of recent years, seems to have restricted swinging to a few devotees. Even during the heyday of the sexual revolution, only 2% of married males and fewer than 2% of married females in the Playboy survey had "swung," and many of these individuals had tried it just once (Hunt, 1974).

Reflections

- Why do you think that even the majority of "sexually liberated" people draw the line at extramarital sex?
- Agree or disagree with the following statement and support your answer: Extramarital sex is more exciting and satisfying than marital sex.
- How would you account for gender differences in the incidence of extramarital sex?

Comarital sex Swinging; mate-swapping.

DOMESTIC VIOLENCE

Although the O.J. Simpson case might have brought the problem of domestic violence into the public eye, such battering is a national epidemic. At least one woman in eight is subjected to violence at the hands of her partner each year, and about 2,000 women die from it (Nevid et al., 2000).

Women are more likely to be raped, injured, or killed by their current or former partners than by other types of assailants (Nevid et al., 2000). Yet women are as likely as men to be violent (Magdol et al., 1997). In about half of the couples in which domestic violence occurs, both partners are guilty of physical abuse. However, women are more likely than men to sustain physical injuries such as broken bones and other internal damage (Magdol et al., 1997).

It also appears that men are more likely to act, or go on the attack, whereas women are more likely to *react*. That is, male violence toward women often stems from factors that threaten men's traditional dominance in relationships, such as unemployment and substance abuse. Women are often violent because of the stress of coping with an abusive partner (Magdol et al., 1997).

Domestic violence cuts across all strata of our society, but it is reported more commonly among people of lower socioeconomic levels. This difference might reflect the greater amount of stress experienced by people who are struggling financially. In many cases, a disparity in income between partners such that the woman earns more than the man, not poverty per se, seems to contribute to domestic violence (McCloskey, 1996).

Ethnic or racial group differences are unrelated to the risk of domestic violence when we consider socioeconomic level and other demographic factors (Nevid et al., 2000). Generally speaking, lack of opportunity and alienation from the larger society increase the potential for mental health problems and violence and abuse within relationships (Nevid et al., 2000). These factors tend to be found more often among members of ethnic minority groups.

Domestic violence often follows a triggering event such as criticism or rejection by one's partner or incidents that cause the man to feel trapped, insecure, or threatened (Nevid et al., 2000). The use of alcohol or other drugs is also heavily connected with battering (Brookoff et al., 1997). Male batterers often have low self-esteem and a sense of personal inadequacy (Nevid et al., 2000). They might become dependent on their partners for emotional support and feel threatened if they perceive their partners becoming more independent or developing separate interests.

Feminist theorists look upon domestic violence as a product of the power relationships that exist between men and women in our society. Men are socialized into dominant roles in which they expect women to be subordinate to their wishes (Wilson & Daly, 1996). Men learn that aggressive displays of masculine power are socially sanctioned and even glorified in some settings, such as in the athletic arena. These role expectations, together with a willingness to accept interpersonal violence as an appropriate means of resolving differences, create a context for domestic violence when the man perceives his partner to be threatening his sense of control or failing to meet his needs or respect his wishes. Men who batter might also have less power in their relationships and be attempting to make up for it through the use of force.

Domestic Violence. Former Boston Red Sox outfielder Wilfredo Cordero pleaded guilty to charges of beating his wife. He received a suspended sentence and was ordered to attend counseling for batterers. Was his arrest a signal that the justice system is now more willing to prosecute alleged batterers, or was the suspended sentence a message that domestic violence is still considered a "family affair"?

Feminist theorists argue further that our society supports domestic violence by appearing to condone it (Nevid et al., 2000). The man who beats his wife might be taken aside and "talked to" by a police officer, rather than arrested on the spot. Even if he is arrested and convicted, his punishment is likely to be less severe (sometimes just a "slap on the wrist") than if he had assaulted a stranger.

Reflections

- How common is domestic violence?
- Can you explain the feminist argument that our society socializes men into engaging in domestic violence?

DIVORCE

My wife and I were considering a divorce, but after pricing lawyers we decided to buy a new car instead.
—Henny Youngman

Whenever I date a guy, I think, is this the man I want my children to spend their weekends with?
—Rita Rudner

Nearly half of the marriages in the United States end in divorce (Kirn, 1997; Laumann et al., 1994). The divorce rate in the United States rose steadily through much of the twentieth century (see Figure 14.2) before leveling off in the 1980s. About one quarter (26%) of children below the age of 18 live in single-parent households (Barringer, 1991). Divorced women outnumber divorced men, in part because men are more likely to remarry after divorce (Saluter, 1992).

The relaxation of legal restrictions on divorce, especially the introduction of the so-called no-fault divorce, has made divorces easier to obtain. Until the mid-1960s, adultery was the only legal grounds for divorce in New York State. Other states were equally strict. But no-fault divorce laws have now been enacted in nearly every state, allowing a divorce to be granted without a finding of marital misconduct. The increased economic independence of women has also contributed to the rising divorce rate. More women today have the economic means of breaking away from a troubled marriage. Today, more people consider marriage an alterable condition than in prior generations.

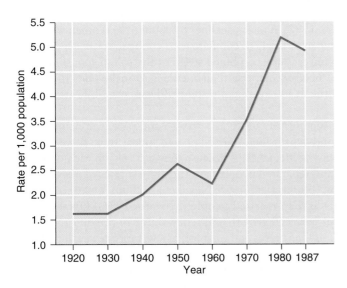

figure 14.2

Divorce Rates in the United States. The divorce rate in the United States rose steadily through much of the twentieth century before leveling off in the 1980s.

table 14.5

The main reason for the increase in the number of divorces in the United States, according to a *Time*/CNN poll	
Reason	**Respondents Citing Reason as Main Reason (%)**
Marriage is not taken seriously by the couples	45
Society has become more accepting of divorced people	15
It is easier to get divorced than it used to be	10
People who get divorced are selfish	9
Changes in the earning power of women and men	7
All of the above	9

Source of data: Kirn, Walter. (1997, August 18). The ties that bind. *Time*, pp. 48–50.

People today hold higher expectations of marriage than their parents or grandparents did. They expect marriage to be personally fulfilling as well as meet the traditional expectation of marriage as an institution for rearing children. Many demand the right to be happy in marriage. The most common reasons given for a divorce today are problems in communication and a lack of understanding. Years ago, it was more likely to be lack of financial support.

Why do Americans believe that the divorce rate has risen so high? A *Time*/CNN Poll asked a national sample "Which is the main reason for the increase in the number of divorces?" Answers are shown in Table 14.5. Respondents were almost equally split in their answer to the question, "Do you believe it should be harder than it is for married couples to get a divorce?" Half (50%) said yes, and 46% said no.

The Cost of Divorce

Divorce often causes financial and emotional problems. When a household splits, the resources often cannot maintain the earlier standard of living for each partner. Financially speaking, divorce hits women harder than men. According to the Population Reference Bureau report, *Women, Work and Family in America*, a woman's household income drops by about 24% (Bianchi & Spain, 1997). A man's declines by about 6%. Women who have not pursued a career might have to struggle to compete with younger, more experienced workers. Divorced mothers often face the combined stress of the sole responsibility for rearing their children and the need to increase their incomes to make ends meet. Divorced fathers might find it difficult to pay alimony and child support while attempting to establish a new lifestyle.

Divorce can also prompt feelings of failure as a spouse and parent, loneliness and uncertainty about the future, and depression. Married people appear to be better able to cope with the stresses and strains of life, perhaps because they can rely on each other for emotional support. Divorced and separated people have the highest rates of physical and mental illness in the population (Bloom et al., 1978; Nevid et al., 2000). Divorced people also have higher rates of suicide than married people (Trovato, 1986). On the other hand, divorce may be a time of personal growth and renewal. It can provide an opportunity for people to take stock of themselves and establish a new, more rewarding life for themselves.

Children also suffer in a divorce. On the other hand, marital conflict or fighting is connected with the same kinds of problems (Amato & Keith, 1991; Davies & Cummings,

1994). Marital conflict causes psychological distress in children and adolescents (Erel & Burman, 1995; Harold et al., 1997). Boys have greater problems adjusting to conflict or divorce, such as conduct problems at school and increased anxiety and dependence (Grych & Fincham, 1993; Holden & Ritchie, 1991).

Wallerstein and Blakeslee (1989) reported that about four out of ten children in their case studies showed problems such as anxiety, academic underachievement, decreased self-worth, and anger ten years after the divorce. A "sleeper effect" was also described. Apparently well-adjusted children of divorce developed problems in early adulthood, especially difficulties trusting that their partners in intimate relationships would make lasting commitments. Researchers attribute children's problems after divorce not only to the divorce itself, but also to a subsequent decline in the quality of parenting. Children's adjustment is enhanced when parents maintain their parenting responsibilities and set aside their differences long enough to agree on childrearing practices (Wallerstein & Blakeslee, 1989). Children of divorce also benefit when divorced parents encourage each other to continue to play important roles in their children's lives and avoid saying negative things about each other in their children's presence.

Despite the difficulties in adjusting to a divorce, most divorced people eventually bounce back. The majority remarry. Among older people, divorced men are more likely than divorced women to remarry—in part because men usually die earlier than women (and so fewer prospective husbands are available), in part because older men tend to remarry younger women.

Remarriages are even more likely than first marriages to end in divorce (Lown & Dolan, 1988). One reason is the selection factor. That is, divorced people are a subgroup of people who get married who are relatively less inclined than others to persist in a troubled marriage. Many divorced people who remarry are also encumbered with alimony and child support payments that strain their new marriages. Many bring children from their earlier marriages to their new ones.

The stepfamily could soon be the most common family unit in the United States (CBS News, 1991). Six of ten stepfamilies eventually disband, often under the weight of the financial and emotional pressures of coping with the demands of a reconstituted family (CBS News, 1991). However, among remarriages that survive, the level of personal happiness in spouses is as high as among spouses in first marriages and much higher than the level among divorced people (Weingarten, 1985).

What of the long-term consequences of divorce? In one study, only one person in five reported that divorce had been a mistake five years after the fact (Wallerstein & Kelly, 1980). Most felt that the divorce had enhanced their lives. Most, however, also reported that they had underestimated the emotional pain they would encounter.

Reflections

- Agree or disagree with the following statement and support your answer: Falling out of love is sufficient reason for a divorce.
- Do you think that parents should remain together "for the sake of the children," regardless of the nature of the marital relationship? Explain.
- Do most people from your sociocultural background approve or disapprove of divorce as a remedy for an unhappy marriage? Do you agree with their beliefs? Why or why not?

ALTERNATIVE FORMS OF MARRIAGE

Marriages are generally based on the expectation of sexual exclusivity. Alternative or nontraditional marital styles, however, such as open marriages and group marriages, permit intimate relationships with people outside the marriage. Such alternative lifestyles attracted a flurry of attention during the heyday of the sexual revolution in the 1970s but were even then more often talked about than practiced (Havemann & Lehtinen, 1990). Today, they find still fewer adherents.

Open Marriage

Open marriage is based on the view that people's needs for intimacy are unlikely to be gratified through one relationship. Proponents argue that the core marriage can be enhanced if the partners have the opportunity to develop emotionally intimate relationships with others (O'Neill & O'Neill, 1972).

The prevalence of open marriages, like that of swinging, remains unknown. Nor are there much data upon which to base conclusions about the success of open marriages. Rubin found no meaningful differences in marital adjustment between 130 couples with sexually open marriages and 130 couples who maintained sexual exclusivity. Still another study found no differences in the longevity of sexually open and sexually exclusive marriages over a five-year period (Rubin & Adams, 1986).

Group Marriage

Group marriage also attracted some adherents during the sexual revolution of the 1960s and 1970s. In a group marriage, three or more people share an intimate relationship, although they are not legally married. Each member feels committed or married to at least two others. The major motive for group marriage is extension of intimacy beyond one spouse to increase personal fulfillment (Constantine & Constantine, 1973). Members of eight out of nine group marriages surveyed by the Constantines also admitted interest in a variety of sexual partners, however.

Group marriages differ from swinging in that participants share their innermost thoughts and feelings and expect their bonds to be permanent. Group marriages, therefore, are not perceived merely as vehicles for legitimizing mate-swapping. Adherents expect children to profit by observing several adult role models and by escaping the "smothering" possessiveness of exclusive parent-child relationships.

Although they provide sexual variety, group marriages require adjustment to at least two other people—not just one. Moreover, legal and social problems can arise with respect to issues such as paternity and inheritance. Managing money may also be stressful, with arguments arising over joint accounts and who can spend how much for what. Sexual jealousies often arise as well. Given these problems, it is not surprising that group marriages are rare and have a high failure rate.

Group marriages are not unique to our culture. Although rare, other cultures have developed analogous marital customs (Werner & Cohen, 1990). Among the Chukchee people of Siberia, for example, group marriages sometimes involved as many as 10 couples. The men in such marriages, who considered themselves "companions-in-wives," had sexual rights to each wife.

All in all, the ideal of the traditional marriage remains strong in our culture. Men are somewhat more likely than women to participate or express an interest in lifestyles that permit greater sexual freedom and, perhaps, less personal responsibility (Knox, 1988). (Why is the third author not surprised?) But even most of those who have tried alternative lifestyles such as cohabitation, open marriage, or group marriage enter into traditional marriages at some time.

All in all, most adults in the United States still seem to feel about marriage the way Winston Churchill felt about democracy: It's flawed, laden with problems, and frustrating—but preferable to the alternatives.

Reflections

■ Can you imagine yourself in an open marriage or a group marriage? Why or why not?

Open marriage A marriage that is characterized by the personal privacy of the spouses and the agreed-upon liberty of each spouse to form intimate relationships, which may include sexually intimate relationships, with people other than the spouse.

Group marriage A social arrangement in which three or more people share an intimate relationship. Group marriages are illegal in the United States.

SEX IN THE LATER YEARS

Which is the fastest-growing segment of the U.S. population? People age 65 and above. More than 30 million people in the United States are senior citizens, and their number is growing fast. This "graying" of the United States could have a profound effect on our views of older people, especially concerning their sexuality. Many people in our culture see sexual activity as appropriate only for the young (Reiss, 1988). This belief falls within a constellation of unfounded cultural myths about sexuality among older people, which includes the notions that older people are sexless, older people with sexual urges are abnormal, and older men with sexual interests are "dirty old men."

Researchers find that sexual daydreaming, sex drive, and sexual activity tend to decline with age, whereas negative sexual attitudes tend to increase (Purifoy et al., 1992). However, research does not support the belief that people lose their sexuality as they age. Nearly all (95%) of the older people in one sample reported that they liked sex, and 75% reported that orgasm was essential to their sexual fulfillment (Starr & Weiner, 1981). People who are exposed to cultural views that sex among older people is deviant might renounce sex as they age, however. Those who remain sexually active might be bothered by guilt (Reiss, 1988).

Sexual activity among older people, as among other groups, is influenced not only by physical structures and changes, but also by psychological well-being, feelings of intimacy (Shaw, 1994), and cultural expectations.

Physical Changes

Although many older people retain the capacity to respond sexually, physical changes do occur as the years pass (see Table 14.6). If we are aware of them, we will not view them as abnormal or find ourselves unprepared to cope with them. Many potential problems can be averted by changing our expectations or making some changes to accommodate the aging process.

CHANGES IN THE FEMALE   Many of the physical changes in women stem from decline in the production of estrogen around the time of menopause. The vaginal walls lose much elasticity and the thick, corrugated texture of the childbearing years. They grow paler and thinner. Coitus might therefore become irritating. The thinning of the walls can also place greater pressure against the bladder and urethra during coitus, leading in some cases to symptoms of urinary urgency and burning urination. The condition might persist for days.

The vagina also shrinks in size. The labia majora lose much of their fatty deposits and become thin. The introitus becomes relatively constricted, and penile entry might

t a b l e   1 4 . 6

Changes in sexual arousal often associated with aging	
Changes in the Female	**Changes in the Male**
Reduced myotonia (muscle tension)	Longer time to erection and orgasm
Reduced vaginal lubrication	Need for more direct stimulation for erection and orgasm
Reduced elasticity of the vaginal walls	Less semen emitted during ejaculation
Smaller increases in breast size during sexual arousal	Erections might be less firm
Reduced intensity of muscle spasms at orgasm	Testicles might not elevate as high into scrotum
	Less intense orgasmic contractions
	Lessened feeling of a need to ejaculate during sex
	Longer refractory period

Source: Copyright © 1990 by The Kinsey Institute for Research in Sex, Gender, and Reproduction. From THE KINSEY INSTITUTE NEW REPORT ON SEX. Reprinted with permission from St. Martin's Press, New York, NY.

Trends in Adult Sexuality

What are adults doing and what do they believe as we turn the corner into the new millennium? In some ways, such as in the continuation of marriage as a highly popular lifestyle and in the continued widespread disapproval of extramarital affairs, the majority of American adults tend to remain traditional. In some other ways, such as the numbers of people who are choosing to remain single and those who are getting divorces, the times have changed. Here are some trends in adult sexuality as we enter the new millennium:

- More people in the United States are remaining single. Whereas "singlehood" was once seen as a way station on the path to marriage, more people are choosing to remain single as a way of life.
- More people are cohabiting. Cohabitation was once dubbed "living in sin." Now some researchers believe that the numbers of cohabiting couples might approach those of married couples in the United States of the new millennium.
- Marriage remains a highly popular—in fact, the *most* popular—lifestyle in the United States and in the world at large. Marital sex has become more varied, and there is wider recognition of the role of foreplay in helping couples reach orgasm.
- Most Americans cite love as the main reason for getting married, and many Americans see falling out of love as a valid reason for getting a divorce.
- Despite the sexual revolution, most people in the United States remain morally opposed to extramarital sex. Only a minority of married people *admit* to engaging in extramarital sex—about one husband in four or five and one wife in eight to ten.
- The divorce rate in the United States seems to have leveled off at about 50%. Reasons for the high divorce rate at turn of millennium include the relaxation of legal restrictions against divorce and the increased economic independence of women.
- Alternatives to marriage such as open marriage and group marriage have all but disappeared. The main alternative to marriage in the new millennium is cohabitation.
- Because of advances in health care and because of the belief that sex is still an important part of life for them, Americans are remaining sexually active at advanced ages.

become somewhat difficult. This "problem" has a positive aspect: Increased friction between the penis and vaginal walls might heighten sexual sensations. The uterus decreases in size after menopause and no longer becomes as congested during sexual arousal. After menopause, women also produce less vaginal lubrication, and the lubrication that is produced might take minutes, not seconds, to appear. Lack of adequate lubrication is also a major reason for painful coitus.

Many of these changes may be slowed or reversed through estrogen-replacement therapy (see Chapter 3). Natural lubrication can also be increased through more elaborate foreplay. The need for more foreplay might encourage the man to become a more considerate lover. (Older men too will likely need more time to become aroused.) An artificial lubricant can also ease problems posed by difficult entry or painful thrusting.

Women's breasts show smaller increases in size with sexual arousal as they age, but the nipples still become erect. Because the muscle tone of the urethra and anal sphincters decreases, the spasms of orgasm become less powerful and fewer in number. Therefore, orgasms might feel less intense. The uterine contractions that occur during orgasm might become discouragingly painful for some postmenopausal women. Despite these changes, women can retain their ability to achieve orgasm well into their advanced years. The subjective experience of orgasm also remains highly satisfying, despite the lessened intensity of muscular contractions.

It is not true that few women can reach orgasm after the age of 70. Actually, healthy women can retain the capacity for orgasm well into their advanced years. ◼

CHANGES IN THE MALE Age-related changes tend to occur more gradually in men than in women and are not clearly connected with any one biological event, as they are with menopause in the woman. Male adolescents might achieve erection in a matter of seconds through sexual fantasy alone. After about age 50, men take progressively longer to achieve erection. Erections become less firm, perhaps because of lowered testosterone production. Older men might require minutes of direct stimulation of the penis to achieve an erection. Couples can adjust to these changes by extending the length and variety of foreplay.

Most men remain capable of erection throughout their lives. Erectile dysfunction is not inevitable with aging. Men generally require more time to reach orgasm as they age, however, which may also reflect lowered testosterone production. In the eyes of their sex partners, however, delayed ejaculation might make them better lovers.

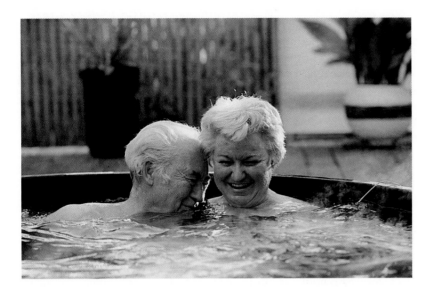

Sexuality and Aging. Despite stereotypes that stigmatize older people who are sexually active as abnormal or deviant, it is normal for older people to have sexual urges and maintain an active sex life.

The testes often decrease slightly in size and produce less testosterone with age. Testosterone production usually declines gradually from about age 40 to age 60 and then begins to level off. However, the decline is not inevitable and may be related to the man's general health. Sperm production tends to decline as the seminiferous tubules degenerate, but viable sperm may be produced quite late in life. Men in their 70s, 80s, and even 90s have fathered children.

Nocturnal erections tend to diminish in intensity, duration, and frequency as men age, but they do not normally disappear in healthy men (Reinisch, 1990; Schiavi et al., 1990). The refractory period tends to lengthen with age. An adolescent might require only a few minutes to regain erection and ejaculate again after a first orgasm, whereas a man in his 30s might require half an hour. Past age 50, the refractory period might increase to several hours.

Older men produce less ejaculate, and it might seep rather than shoot out. Though the contractions of orgasm still begin at 0.8-second intervals, they become weaker and fewer. Still, the number and strength of spasms do not translate precisely into subjective pleasure. An older male might enjoy orgasm as thoroughly as he did at a younger age. Attitudes and expectations can be as important as the contractions themselves.

An 82-year-old man commented on his changing sexual abilities:

> I come maybe once in every three sexual encounters these days with my wife. My erection comes and goes, and it's not a big concern to us. I get as much pleasure from touching and thrusting as I do from an ejaculation. When I was younger it was inconceivable to me that I might enjoy sex without an orgasm, but I can see now that in those days I missed out on some pleasure by making orgasm such a focus. (Gordon & Snyder, 1989, p. 153)

After orgasm, erection subsides more rapidly than it does in a younger man. A study of 65 healthy men ages 45 to 74 showed an age-related decline in sexual desire, arousal, and activity. Yet there were no differences between younger and older men in level of sexual satisfaction or enjoyment (Schiavi et al., 1990).

In sum, most physical changes do not bring a man's or a woman's sex life to a grinding halt. People's attitudes, sexual histories, and partners are usually more important factors in sexual behavior and enjoyment.

Patterns of Sexual Activity

Despite the decline in certain physical functions, older people can continue to lead a vibrant, fulfilling sex life. In fact, years of sexual experience might more than compensate for any diminution of physical responsiveness (Hodson & Skeen, 1994). A Roper Starch poll of 1,292 people in the United States aged 60 and above found that 74% of the men and 70% of the women who had remained sexually active said that they were as satisfied or *more* satisfied with sex than they were in their 40s (Leary, 1998). Unfortunately, people who overreact to expected changes in sexual response might conclude that their sex lives are over and give up on sexual activity or even on expressing any physical affection (Dunn, 1998).

Ninety-four percent of the men and 84% of the women in Kinsey's samples remained sexually active at the age of 60. In a survey of 800 people between the ages of 60 and 91, half of the respondents reported sexual relations on a regular basis, and half of these had sex at least once a week (Starr & Weiner, 1981). A study of 200 healthy 80- to 102-year olds reported that 30% of the women and 62% of the men still engaged in intercourse (Bretschneider & McCoy, 1988). A study of 100 older men in England found that the key factor in whether they continued to engage is sexual activity was the availability of a partner, not physical condition (Jones et al., 1994). Sex therapist Helen Singer Kaplan (1990) concluded:

> The loss of sexuality is not an inevitable aspect of aging. . . . The results of these studies are remarkable in their consensus: Without exception, each investigator found that, providing they are in good health, the great majority of people remain sexually functional and active on a regular basis until virtually the end of life. Or, to put it more succinctly, 70% of healthy 70-year-olds remain sexually active, and are having sex at least once a week, and typically more often than that. . . .
>
> Although it is widely believed that sex no longer matters after middle age, the opposite is true, and sex often becomes *more* and not *less* important as a person grows older. Because sex is among the last pleasure-giving biological processes to deteriorate, it is potentially an enduring source of gratification at a time when these are becoming fewer and fewer, and a link to the joys of youth. These are important ingredients in the [older] person's emotional well-being. (pp. 185, 204)

Coital frequency tends to decline with age (Laumann et al., 1994). One study of people who had been married for more than 50 years showed that nearly half (47%) had discontinued intercourse, and 92% reported a decline over the years (Ade-Ridder, 1985). Several factors played a role in declining activity, including physical problems, boredom, and cultural attitudes toward sex among the aging. Despite general trends, sexuality among older people is variable (Knox, 1988). Many older people engage in intercourse, oral sex, and masturbation at least as often as they did when younger; some become disgusted by sex; others simply lose interest. A six-year longitudinal study of older married couples found that one in five actually increased their coital frequency over time (Palmore, 1981).

Coital frequency, however, is not synonymous with sexual satisfaction. In a Canadian study of 215 married people who were middle-aged and older (51 to 81 years of age), those aged 65 or above showed lower coital frequency than did younger respondents (Libman, 1989). No sizable differences emerged in the level of sexual satisfaction between older and younger groups, however.

The frequency of masturbation also generally declines with age for both men and women, although an increase might occur after a marital separation, divorce, or death of a spouse (Hegeler & Mortensen, 1977). Still, continued masturbation was reported by nearly half (46%) among a sample of people ages 60 to 91 (Starr & Weiner, 1981). This is a high level of acceptance among people who were reared during a time when masturbation was generally viewed as harmful (Kammeyer, 1990).

Couples might accommodate to the physical changes of aging by broadening their sexual repertoire to include more diverse forms of stimulation. Many respondents to a *Consumer Reports* survey reported using oral-genital stimulation, sexual fantasy, sexually explicit materials, anal stimulation, vibrators, and other sexual techniques to offset problems in achieving lubrication or erection (Brecher, 1984). Sexual satisfaction may be derived from manual or oral stimulation, cuddling, caressing, and tenderness, as well as from intercourse to orgasm.

The availability of a sexually interested and supportive partner may be the most important determinant of continued sexual activity. Many women discontinue sexual activity because of the death of their husbands. Women's life expectancy exceeds men's by an average of seven years.

Reflections

- Did any of the information presented about sexuality among older people surprise you? What was it? Why was it a surprise?
- What stereotypes of older people do you hold? Do you believe that sexual activity is proper for people in their 60s or older? Why or why not?

SEX AND DISABILITY

Like older people, people with disabilities (especially those whose physical disabilities render them dependent on others) are often seen as sexless and childlike (Nosek et al., 1994). Such views are based on misconceptions about the sexual functioning of people with disabilities. Some of these myths and stereotypes may be eroding, however, in part because of the success of the civil and social rights movements of the disabled in the 1970s and the attention focused on the sexuality of people with disabilities in films such as *Coming Home*, *Born on the Fourth of July*, and *My Left Foot*.

A person may have been born with or acquire a bodily impairment or suffer a loss of function or a disfiguring change in appearance. Although the disability might require the person to make adjustments to perform sexually, most people with disabilities have the same sexual needs, feelings, and desires as people without disabilities. Their ability to express their sexual feelings and needs depends on the physical limitations imposed by their disabilities, their adjustment to their disabilities, and the availability of partners. The establishment of mature sexual relationships generally demands some distance from one's parents. Therefore, people with disabilities who are physically dependent on their parents might find it especially difficult to develop sexual relationships (Knight, 1989). Parents who acknowledge their children's sexual development can be helpful by facilitating dating. Far too often, parents become overprotective:

> Adolescent disabled girls have the same ideas, hopes, and dreams about sexuality as able-bodied girls. They will have learned the gender role expectations set for them by the media and others and may experience difficulty if they lack more substantive educational information about sexuality and sex function. In addition their expectations may come in conflict with the family which may have consistently protected or overindulged the child and not permitted her to "grow up." . . . In many cases the families are intensely concerned about the sexual and emotional vulnerability of the daughter and hope that "nothing bad" will happen to her. They may, therefore, encourage her to wear youthful clothing and to stay a safe little girl. The families can mistakenly assume there may be no sexual life ahead of her and protect her from this perceived bitter reality with youthful clothing and little-girlish ways. The result can be, of course, that the young emerging woman may become societally handicapped in learning how to conduct herself as a sexual woman. She will be infantilized. (Cole, 1988, pp. 282–283)

In such families, young people with disabilities get the message that sex is not for them. As they mature, they might need counseling to help them recognize the normalcy of their sexual feelings and to help them make responsible choices for exploring their sexuality.

Physical Disabilities

According to Margaret Nosek and her colleagues (1994), sexual wellness, even among the disabled, involves five factors:

- Positive sexual self-concept; seeing oneself as valuable sexually and as a person
- Knowledge about sexuality
- Positive, productive relationships
- Coping with barriers to sexuality (social, environmental, physical, and emotional)
- Maintaining the best possible general and sexual health, given one's limitations

Sex and Disabled People. Most people with disabilities have the same sexual needs, feelings, and desires as people without disabilities. They are capable of expressing their sexuality in ways that can be pleasurable for themselves and their partners.

This model applies to all of us, of course. Let us now consider aspects of specific physical disabilities and human sexuality.

CEREBRAL PALSY   **Cerebral palsy** does not generally impair sexual interest, capacity for orgasm, or fertility (Reinisch, 1990). Depending on the nature and degree of muscle spasticity or lack of voluntary muscle control, however, afflicted people might be limited to certain types of sexual activities and coital positions.

The importance of sex education for disabled people is highlighted by a case of a man with cerebral palsy:

> A 40-year-old man with moderate cerebral palsy came to see me for sexual counseling. When asked why he came for counseling, he said, "I think I'm old enough to learn about sex." He was college educated, fully employed, and had been living by himself, away from his parents, for three years. In questioning him further, I found that the extent of his sexual knowledge was he knew he had a penis but knew nothing about the human sexual response or about female anatomy. When I asked him if any "white, sticky stuff" ever came out of his penis, he replied, "Yes, and doesn't that have something to do with my cerebral palsy?" (Knight, 1989, p. 186)

People with disabilities such as cerebral palsy often suffer social rejection during adolescence and perceive themselves as unfit or unworthy of intimate sexual relationships, especially with people who are not disabled. They are often socialized into an asexual role. Sensitive counseling can help them to understand and accept their sexuality, promote a more positive body image, and provide the social skills to establish intimate relationships (Edmonson, 1988).

SPINAL CORD INJURIES   People who suffer physical disabilities as the result of traumatic injuries or physical illness must not only learn to cope with their physical limitations, but also adjust to a world designed for nondisabled people (Trieschmann, 1989). Spinal cord injuries affect about 6,000 to 10,000 people annually in the United States (Seftel et al., 1991). The majority of persons who suffer disabling spinal cord injuries are young, active males. Automobile or pedestrian accidents account for about half of these cases. Other common causes include stabbing or bullet wounds, sports injuries, and falls. Depending on the location of the injury to the spinal cord, a loss of voluntary control (paralysis) can occur in either the legs (*paraplegia*) or all four limbs (*quadriplegia*). A loss of sensation may also occur in parts of the body that lie beneath the site of injury. Most people who suffer such injuries have relatively normal life spans, but the quality of their lives is profoundly affected.

The effect of spinal cord injuries on sexual response depends on the site and severity of the injury. Men have two erection centers in the spinal cord: a higher center in the lumbar region that controls psychogenic erections and a lower one in the sacral region that controls reflexive erections. When damage occurs at or above the level of the lumbar center, men lose the capacity for psychogenic erections, the kinds of erections that occur in response to mental stimulation alone, such as when viewing erotic films or fantasizing. They may still be able to achieve reflexive erections from direct stimulation of the penis, as these erections are controlled by the sacral erection center located in a lower portion of the spinal cord. However, they cannot feel any genital sensations because the nerve connections to the brain are severed. Men with damage to the sacral erection center lose the capacity for reflexive erections but can still achieve psychogenic erections so long as their upper spinal cords remains intact (Spark, 1991). Overall, researchers find that about three of four men with spinal cord injuries are able to achieve erections, but only about one in ten continues to ejaculate naturally (Geiger, 1981; Spark, 1991). Others can be helped to ejaculate with the aid of a vibrator (Szasz & Carpenter, 1989). Their brains might help to fill in some of the missing sensations associated with coitus and even orgasm. When direct stimulation does not cause erection, the woman can insert the limp penis into the vagina and gently thrust her hips, taking care not to dislodge the penis.

Although the frequency of sexual activity among spinal-cord-injured men tends to decline after the injury (Alexander et al., 1993), a study of almost 1,300 men with these injuries found that about one out of three (35%) continued to engage in sexual inter-

Cerebral palsy   A muscular disorder that is caused by damage to the central nervous system (usually before or during birth) and characterized by spastic paralysis.

course (Spark, 1991). Only about one in five of the men received any kind of sexual counseling to help them adjust sexually to their disability. The men typically reported increased interest in alternative sexual activities, especially those involving areas above the level of the spinal injury, such as the mouth, lips, neck, and ears.

Retention of sexual response depends on the site and severity of the injury (Seftel et al., 1991). Women might lose the ability to experience genital sensations or to lubricate normally during sexual stimulation. However, breast sensations might remain intact, making this area even more erotogenic. Most women with spinal cord injuries can engage in coitus, become impregnated, and deliver vaginally. A survey of 27 spinal-cord-injured women showed that about half were able to experience orgasm (Kettl et al., 1991). Some also report "phantom orgasms" that provide intense psychological pleasure and that are accompanied by nongenital physical sensations that are similar to those experienced by nondisabled women (Perduta-Fulginiti, 1992). Spinal-cord-injured women can heighten their sexual pleasure by learning to use fantasized orgasm, orgasmic imagery, and amplification of their physical sensations (Perduta-Fulginiti, 1992).

Actually, people who are paralyzed because of spinal cord injuries usually *can* become sexually aroused and engage in coitus. Most spinal-cord-injured women can become impregnated and bear healthy children. ■

Truth or Fiction?
REVISITED

Couples facing the challenge of spinal cord injury might expand their sexual repertoire to focus less on genital stimulation (except to attain the reflexes of erection and lubrication) and more on the parts of the body that retain sensation. Stimulation of some areas of the body, such as the ears, the neck, and the breasts (in both men and women), can yield pleasurable erotic sensations (Knight, 1989; Seftel et al., 1991).

SENSORY DISABILITIES Sensory disabilities, such as blindness or deafness, do not directly affect genital responsiveness. Still, sexuality may be affected in many ways. A person who has been blind since birth or early childhood might have difficulty understanding a partner's anatomy. Sex education curricula have been designed specifically to enable visually impaired people to learn about sexual anatomy via models. Anatomically correct dolls can be used to simulate positions of intercourse.

Deaf people, too, often lack knowledge about sex. Their ability to comprehend the social cues involved in forming and maintaining intimate relationships may also be impaired. Sex education programs based on sign language are helping many hearing-impaired people become more socially perceptive as well as knowledgeable about the physical aspects of sex. People with visual and hearing impairments often lack self-esteem and self-confidence, problems that make it difficult for them to establish intimate relationships. Counseling might help them to become more aware of their sexuality and develop social skills.

OTHER PHYSICAL DISABILITIES AND IMPAIRMENTS Specific disabilities pose particular challenges to, and limitations on, sexual functioning. **Arthritis** can make it difficult or painful for sufferers to bend their arms, knees, and hips during sexual activity. Coital positions that minimize discomfort and the application of moist heat to the joints before sexual relations may be helpful.

A male amputee might find that he is better balanced in the lateral-entry or female-superior position than in the male-superior position (Knight, 1989). A woman with limited hand function might find it difficult or impossible to insert a diaphragm and might need to request assistance from her partner or switch to another contraceptive (Cole, 1988). Sensitivity to each other's needs is as vital to couples in which one member has a disability as it is to nondisabled couples.

Psychological Disabilities

People with psychological disabilities, such as mental retardation, are often stereotyped as incapable of understanding their sexual impulses. Retarded people are sometimes assumed to maintain childlike innocence through their lives or to be devoid of sexuality.

Arthritis A progressive disease that is characterized by inflammation or pain in the joints.

Some stereotype retarded people in the opposite direction: as having stronger-than-normal sex drives and being incapable of controlling them (Reinisch, 1990). Some mentally retarded people do act inappropriately—by masturbating publicly, for example. The stereotypes are exaggerated, however, and even many mentally retarded people who act inappropriately can be trained to follow social rules (Reinisch, 1990).

Parents and caretakers often discourage retarded people from learning about their sexuality or teach them to deny or suppress their sexual feelings. Although the physical changes of puberty might be delayed in mentally retarded people, most develop normal sexual needs (Edmonson, 1988). Most are capable of learning about their sexuality and can be guided into rewarding and responsible intimate relationships.

One of the greatest impediments to sexual fulfillment among people with disabilities is finding a loving and supportive partner. Some people engage in sexual relations with people with disabilities out of sympathy. By and large, however, the partners are other people with disabilities or nondisabled people who have overcome stereotypes that portray disabled people as undesirable. Many partners have had some prior positive relationship with a person with a disability, usually during childhood (Knight, 1989). Experience facilitates acceptance of the idea that a disabled person can be desirable. Depending on the nature of the disability, the nondisabled partner might need to be open to assuming a more active sexual role to compensate for the limitations of the partner with the disability. Two partners with disabilities need to be sensitive to each other's needs and physical limitations. People with disabilities and their partners might also need to expand their sexual repertoires to incorporate ways of pleasuring each other that are not as fixated on genital stimulation.

The message is simple: Sexuality may enrich the lives of nearly all adults at virtually any age.

Reflections

- Do you know anyone with one of the disabilities discussed in the chapter? What do you know of the role of sexuality in that individual's life? What are your thoughts on the subject? Why?
- Why do you think that people with disabilities tend to be stereotyped as asexual?
- Why do you think parents and caretakers discourage retarded people from learning about their sexuality or teach them to suppress their sexual feelings?

summing up

SINGLEHOOD

Recent years have seen a sharp increase in the numbers of single young people in our society. Reasons include increased permissiveness toward premarital sex and, particularly for women, the desire to become established in a career. No one lifestyle characterizes single people.

COHABITATION: DARLING, WOULD YOU BE MY POSSLQ?

Who Are the Cohabitors?
Cohabitation is more prevalent among less well educated and less affluent people.

Reasons for Cohabitation
Some couples prefer cohabitation because it provides a consistent intimate relationship without the legal and economic entanglements of marriage. Some emotionally committed couples cohabit because of the economic advantages of sharing household expenses.

Cohabitation and Later Marriage: A Benefit or a Risk?
Cohabitors who later marry might run a greater risk of divorce than noncohabitors who marry, perhaps because cohabitors are a more liberal group.

MARRIAGE

Marriage is found in all human societies and is our most common lifestyle.

Historical Perspectives
In historical patriarchies, the man of the house had the right to choose wives for his sons and could himself take concubines or additional wives.

Why Do People Marry?

Throughout Western history, marriages have legitimized sexual relations, sanctioned the permanence of a deeply committed relationship, and provided for the orderly transmission of wealth and a setting for childrearing. In Western society today, romantic love is seen as an essential aspect of marriage.

Types of Marriage

The major types of marriage are monogamy and polygamy. Polygamy includes polygyny and polyandry.

Whom Do We Marry: Are Marriages Made in Heaven or in the Neighborhood?

People in the United States tend to marry within their geographical area and social class. They tend to marry people who are similar in physical attractiveness, who share similar attitudes, and who seem likely to meet their material, sexual, and psychological needs.

MARITAL SEXUALITY

Western culture before the sexual revolution could be characterized as sexually restrictive, even in its attitudes toward marital sex.

The Sexual Revolution Hits Home

Married couples today engage in coitus more frequently and for longer durations of time than those in Kinsey's day. They report higher levels of sexual satisfaction and engage in a greater variety of sexual activities.

Sexual Satisfaction

U.S. women today are more likely to reach orgasm through marital sex than those in Kinsey's day. Wives take more active sexual roles than in Kinsey's day.

EXTRAMARITAL SEX

In most cases, extramarital relationships are conducted without the spouse's knowledge or approval. People might have affairs for sexual variety, to punish their spouses, to achieve emotional closeness, or to prove that they are attractive.

Patterns of Extramarital Sex

Precise figures on the prevalence of extramarital sex are lacking.

Attitudes Toward Extramarital Sex

Extramarital sex continues to be viewed negatively by the majority of married people in our society.

Effects of Extramarital Sex

The discovery of infidelity can evoke anger, jealousy, even shame. Affairs often, but not always, damage marriages.

Swinging

Only a small minority of married couples engage in swinging.

DOMESTIC VIOLENCE

Women and men are equally likely to engage in domestic violence, but women are more likely to sustain injury. Domestic violence is frequently connected with threats to men's dominance in relationships.

DIVORCE

About half the marriages in the United States end in divorce. Reasons include relaxed restrictions on divorce, greater financial independence among women, and the idea that marriages should be happy.

The Cost of Divorce

Divorce is often associated with financial and emotional problems, however. Divorce can give rise to feelings of failure and depression and make it difficult to rear children.

ALTERNATIVE FORMS OF MARRIAGE

Alternative marital styles such as open marriages and group marriages permit intimate relationships with people outside the marriage.

Open Marriage

Open marriages allow each partner open companionship and personal privacy, which may allow sexual intimacy with others.

Group Marriage

In a group marriage, three or more people share an intimate relationship, although they are not legally married.

SEX IN THE LATER YEARS

There are a number of unfounded cultural myths about the sexuality of older people, including the stereotypes that older people are sexless and that older people with sexual urges are abnormal.

Physical Changes

Physical changes as the years pass can impair sexual activity. Many potential problems can be averted by changing our expectations and making changes to accommodate the aging process.

Patterns of Sexual Activity

Sexual activity tends to decline with age, but continued sexual activity can boost self-esteem and be an important source of gratification.

SEX AND DISABILITY

People with disabilities can suffer from prejudice that depicts them as sexless or as lacking the means to express their sexual needs or feelings.

Physical Disabilities

Cerebral palsy does not usually impair sexual interest, capacity for orgasm, or fertility, but afflicted people might be limited to certain types of sexual activities and coital positions. People with spinal cord injuries might be paralyzed and lose sensation below the waist. They often respond reflexively to direct genital stimulation. Sensory disabilities do not directly affect sexual response but may impair sexual knowledge and social skills.

Psychological Disabilities

Most mentally retarded people can learn the basics of their own sexuality and develop responsible intimate relationships.

Elmer Bischoff. *Two Figures at the Seashore.* 1957. Oil on canvas, 56-7/8 x 56-7/8 in. Collection of the Orange County Museum of Art; Museum purchase with additional funds provided by the National Endowment of the Arts, a federal agency

chapter

15

Sexual Dysfunctions

outline

TRUTH OR FICTION?

TYPES OF SEXUAL DYSFUNCTIONS

Sexual Desire Disorders

Sexual Arousal Disorders

Orgasmic Disorders

Sexual Pain Disorders

A WORLD OF DIVERSITY:
Inis Beag and Mangaia—Worlds Apart

ORIGINS OF SEXUAL DYSFUNCTIONS

Organic Causes

Psychosocial Causes

A WORLD OF DIVERSITY:
An Odd Couple: Koro and Dhat Syndromes

TREATMENT OF SEXUAL DYSFUNCTIONS

The Masters and Johnson Approach

The Helen Singer Kaplan Approach

Sexual Desire Disorders

Sexual Arousal Disorders

IN THE NEW MILLENNIUM:
The Brave New World of Viagra

Orgasmic Disorders

IN THE NEW MILLENNIUM:
The "Orgasm Pill" for Women

Sexual Pain Disorders

Evaluation of Sex Therapy

HOW DO YOU FIND A QUALIFIED SEX THERAPIST?

SUMMING UP

Truth or Fiction?

_____ Sexual dysfunctions are rare occurrences.

_____ The most common cause of painful intercourse in women is vaginal infection.

_____ During the 1980s, 2,000 people fell prey to the belief that their genitals were shrinking and retracting into their bodies.

_____ Sex therapy teaches a man with erectile disorder how to will an erection.

_____ A doctor made a somewhat unusual presentation to a medical convention by dropping his pants to reveal an erection.

_____ Many sex therapists recommend masturbation as the treatment for women who have never been able to reach orgasm.

_____ A man can be prevented from ejaculating by squeezing his penis when he feels that he is about to ejaculate.

d erek Jones, 39, and his wife Pam, 37, had not attempted coitus for five years. Their sexual relations had been limited to fondling and caressing each other and to occasional oral-genital contact. They had given up at coitus because of Derek's persistent difficulty in attaining and sustaining erections. But recently, they had begun trying again. Some nights Derek would have an erection enabling him to penetrate, only to find that he ejaculated too rapidly. Many nights he was unable to perform at all. Each failure was yet another blow to Derek's self-esteem. Pam kept secret her belief that he could not perform because he was no longer sexually attracted to her.

Terry, 24, has decided she is built differently from friends and women she reads about. They all reach orgasm, it seems, at the drop of a hat. But she has never managed "one of those things." Her husband David, also 24, is considerate, but Terry knows that he, too, is frustrated and feels guilty with every ejaculation. Why should he enjoy sex if Terry cannot? Sex has become a chore rather than a source of pleasure, and David has been having some difficulty attaining erection. Terry wonders whether she should try to fake orgasm to hold on to him. But she is too embarrassed to ask a friend how to act. (the authors' files)

Derek and Terry have **sexual dysfunctions.** That is, they have difficulties in becoming sexually aroused or reaching orgasm. Many of us are troubled by sexual problems from time to time. Men occasionally have difficulty achieving an erection or ejaculate more rapidly than they would like. Most women occasionally have difficulty achieving orgasm or becoming sufficiently lubricated. People are not considered to have a sexual dysfunction unless the problem is persistent and causes distress, however.

Although there are different types of sexual dysfunctions, they share some features. People with sexual dysfunctions might avoid sexual opportunities for fear of failure. They might anticipate that sex will result in frustration or physical pain rather than pleasure and gratification. Because of the emphasis that our culture places upon sexual competence, people with sexual dysfunctions might feel inadequate or incompetent, feelings that diminish their self-esteem. They might experience feelings such as guilt, shame, frustration, depression, and anxiety.

Many people with sexual dysfunctions find it difficult to talk about them, even with their spouses or helping professionals. A woman who cannot reach orgasm with her husband might fake orgasms rather than "make a fuss." A man might find it difficult to admit erectile problems to his physician during a physical. Many physicians are also uncomfortable talking about sexual matters. They might never inquire about sexual problems.

Because many people are reluctant to admit to sexual problems, we do not have precise figures on their frequencies. The best current information that we have may be based on the National Health and Social Life Survey (Laumann et al., 1994) (see Table 15.1). The NHSLS group asked respondents for a yes-or-no answer to the question "During the last 12 months has there ever been a period of several months or more when you lacked interest in having sex; were unable to come to a climax; came to a cli-

t a b l e   15.1

Current sexual dysfunctions according to the NHSLS study (respondents reporting the problem within the past year)		
	Men (%)	Women (%)
Pain during sex	3.0	14.4
Sex not pleasurable	8.1	21.2
Unable to reach orgasm	8.3	24.1
Lack of interest in sex	15.8	33.4
Anxiety about performance*	17.0	11.5
Reaching climax too early	28.5	10.3
Unable to keep an erection	10.4	—
Having trouble lubricating	—	18.8

*Anxiety about performance is not itself a sexual dysfunction. However, it figures prominently in sexual dysfunctions.

Source: Adapted from Tables 10.8A and 10.8B, pages 370 and 371, in Laumann, E. O., Gagnon, J. H., Michael, R. T., & Michaels, S. (1994). *The social organization of sexuality: Sexual practices in the United States.* Chicago: University of Chicago Press.

max too quickly; experienced physical pain during intercourse; did not find sex pleasurable; felt anxious about your ability to perform sexually; or (for men) had trouble achieving or maintaining an erection or (for women) had trouble lubricating?" Overall, women reported more problems than men in the areas of painful sex, lack of pleasure, inability to reach orgasm, and lack of interest in sex. Men were more likely than women to report reaching climax too early and being anxious about their performance. Difficulty keeping an erection (erectile disorder) increases with age from about 6% in the 18- to 24-year-old age group to about 20% in the 55- to 59-year-old age group. (But note that urologist Irwin Goldstein [1998] of the Boston University School of Medicine found that nearly *half* the men aged 40 to 70 in a Massachusetts survey reported problems in obtaining and maintaining erections!) The NHSLS figures represent persistent current problems. The incidences of occasional problems and of lifetime problems would be higher.

It is not true that sexual dysfunctions are rare. On the contrary, they are quite common. ■

Truth or Fiction?
REVISITED

TYPES OF SEXUAL DYSFUNCTIONS

The most widely used system of classification of sexual dysfunctions is based on the American Psychiatric Association's *Diagnostic and Statistical Manual of Mental Disorders* (the DSM) of 1994. The DSM, which is now in its fourth edition, groups sexual dysfunctions into four categories:

1. **Sexual desire disorders.** These involve dysfunctions in sexual desire, interest, or drive, in which the person experiences a lack of sexual desire or an aversion to genital sexual contact.

2. **Sexual arousal disorders.** Sexual arousal is principally characterized by erection in the male and vaginal lubrication and swelling of the external genitalia in the female. In men, sexual arousal disorders involve recurrent difficulty in achieving or sustaining erections that are sufficient to successfully engage in sexual intercourse. In women, they typically involve failure to become sufficiently lubricated.

3. **Orgasmic disorders.** Men or women may encounter difficulties in achieving orgasm or may reach orgasm more rapidly than they would like. Women are more likely to encounter difficulties reaching orgasm; men are more likely to experience overly rapid orgasm (premature ejaculation). But some men inhibit orgasm during coitus, and a few women complain of overly rapid orgasms.

4. **Sexual pain disorders.** Both men and women may suffer from **dyspareunia** (painful intercourse). Women may experience **vaginismus,** which prevents penetration by the penis or renders penetration painful.

Sexual dysfunctions can also be classified as either lifelong or acquired. *Lifelong* dysfunctions have existed throughout the person's lifetime. *Acquired* dysfunctions develop after a period of normal functioning. They also can be classified as generalized or situational. *Generalized* dysfunctions affect a person's general sexual functioning. *Situational* dysfunctions affect sexual functioning only in some sexual situations (such as during coitus but not during masturbation) or occur with some partners but not with others. Consider, for example, a man who has never been able to achieve or maintain an erection during sexual relations with a partner but can do so during masturbation. His dysfunction would be classified as lifelong and situational.

Sexual dysfunctions Persistent or recurrent difficulties in becoming sexually aroused or reaching orgasm.

Sexual desire disorders Sexual dysfunctions in which people have persistent or recurrent lack of sexual desire or aversion to sexual contact.

Sexual arousal disorders Sexual dysfunctions in which people persistently or recurrently fail to become adequately sexually aroused to engage in or sustain sexual intercourse.

Orgasmic disorders Sexual dysfunctions in which people persistently or recurrently have difficulty reaching orgasm or reach orgasm more rapidly than they would like, despite attaining a level of sexual stimulation of sufficient intensity to normally result in orgasm.

Sexual pain disorders Sexual dysfunctions in which people persistently or recurrently experience pain during coitus.

Dyspareunia A sexual dysfunction characterized by persistent or recurrent pain during sexual intercourse. (From roots meaning "badly paired.")

Vaginismus A sexual dysfunction characterized by involuntary contraction of the muscles surrounding the vaginal barrel, preventing penile penetration or rendering penetration painful.

Sexual Desire Disorders

Sexual desire disorders involve lack of sexual desire or interest and/or aversion to genital sexual activity. Although the prevalence of these disorders in the general population is not known, sex therapists report an increase in their frequency over the past generation (Schmidt, 1994).

LACK OF SEXUAL DESIRE   People who have little or no sexual interest or desire are said to have *hypoactive sexual desire disorder*. They also often report an absence of sexual fantasies. According to the NHSLS Study (Laumann et al., 1994), the problem is more common among women than men. Nevertheless, the belief that men are always eager and willing to engage in sexual activity is no more than a myth.

Lack of sexual desire does not imply that a person is unable to achieve erection, lubricate adequately, or reach orgasm. Some people with low sexual desire do have such problems. Others can become sexually aroused and reach orgasm when stimulated adequately. Many enjoy sexual activity, even if they are unlikely to initiate it. Many appreciate the affection and closeness of physical intimacy but have no interest in genital stimulation.

Hypoactive sexual desire is one of the most commonly diagnosed sexual dysfunctions (Letourneau & O'Donohue, 1993). Yet there is no clear consensus among clinicians and researchers concerning the definition of low sexual desire. How much sexual interest or desire is "normal"? There is no standard level of sexual desire—no 98.6 degree reading on the "sexual thermometer." Lack of desire is usually considered a problem when couples recognize that their level of sexual interest has gotten so low that little remains. Sometimes, the lack of desire is limited to one partner. When one member of a couple is more interested in sex than the other, sex therapists often recommend that the couple try to reach a compromise. They also try to uncover and resolve problems in the relationship that might dampen the sexual ardor of one or both partners.

Biological and psychosocial factors—hormonal deficiencies, depression, marital dissatisfaction, and so on—contribute to lack of desire. Among the medical conditions that diminish sexual desire are testosterone deficiencies, thyroid overactivity or underactivity, and temporal lobe epilepsy (Kresin, 1993). Sexual desire is stoked by testosterone, which is produced by men in the testes and by both genders in the adrenal glands. Women may experience less sexual desire when their adrenal glands are surgically removed. Low sexual interest, along with erectile difficulties, are also common among men with **hypogonadism**. (Hypogonadism is treated with testosterone [Brody, 1995c; Carani et al., 1990].) Women with inhibited sexual desire usually have normal levels of the hormones testosterone, estrogen, and progesterone (Schreiner-Engle & Schiavi, 1986). The role of hormones in lack of desire among physically healthy men and women remains unclear.

Researchers find men with hypoactive sexual desire disorder to be older than women with the disorder (Segraves & Segraves, 1993). A gradual decline in sexual desire, at least among men, might be explained in part by the reduction in testosterone levels that occurs in middle and later life (Brody, 1995c). Abrupt changes in sexual desire, however, are more often explained by psychological and interpersonal factors such as depression, emotional stress, and problems in the relationship (Leiblum & Rosen, 1991; Schreiner-Engle & Schiavi, 1986).

Psychological problems can contribute to low sexual desire (Letourneau & O'Donohue, 1993). Anxiety is the most commonly reported factor. Various types of anxiety may be involved in dampening sexual desire, including performance anxiety (anxiety over being evaluated negatively), anxiety involving fears of pleasure or loss of control, and deeper sources of anxiety relating to fears of castration or injury. Depression is also a common cause of inhibited desire. A history of sexual assault has also been linked to low sexual desire.

Some medications, including those used to control anxiety or hypertension, can also reduce desire. Changing medications or dosage levels might return the person's previous level of desire.

Hypogonadism An endocrine disorder that reduces the output of testosterone.

SEXUAL AVERSION DISORDER   People with low sexual desire might have little or no interest in sex, but they are not repelled by genital contact. Some people, however, find sex disgusting or aversive and avoid genital contact.

Sexual aversions are less common than lack of desire and remain poorly understood (Spark, 1991). Some researchers consider sexual aversion to be a *sexual phobia* or *sexual panic state* with intense, irrational fears of sexual contact and a pressing desire to avoid sexual situations (Kaplan, 1987). A history of erectile problems can cause sexual aversion in men (Spark, 1991). Men with such histories might be anxious in sexual situations because they trigger feelings of failure and shame. Their partners might also develop an aversion to sexual contact because of this anxiety and because of their own frustration. A history of sexual trauma, such as rape or childhood sexual abuse or incest, often figures prominently in cases of sexual aversion, especially in women.

Sexual Arousal Disorders

When we are sexually stimulated, our bodies normally respond with **vasocongestion,** which produces erection in the male and vaginal lubrication in the female. People with sexual arousal disorders, however, fail to achieve or sustain the lubrication or erection that is necessary to facilitate sexual activity. Or they lack the subjective feelings of sexual pleasure or excitement that normally accompany sexual arousal (American Psychiatric Association, 1994).

Problems of sexual arousal have sometimes been labeled *impotence* in the male and *frigidity* in the female. But these terms are pejorative, so many professionals prefer to use less threatening, more descriptive labels.

MALE ERECTILE DISORDER   Sexual arousal disorder in the male is called **male erectile disorder** or *erectile dysfunction*. It is characterized by persistent difficulty in achieving or maintaining an erection that is sufficient to allow the completion of sexual activity. In most cases, the failure is limited to sexual activity with partners or with some partners and not others. It can therefore be classified as *situational*. In rare cases, the dysfunction is found during any sexual activity, including masturbation. In such cases, it is considered *generalized*. Some men with erectile disorder are unable to attain an erection with their partners. Others can achieve erection but not sustain it (or recover it) long enough for penetration and ejaculation.

As many as 30 million men in the United States experience some degree of erectile dysfunction (Goldstein et al., 1998). The incidence of erectile disorder increases with age and is believed to affect as many as one men in two over the age of 40—at least intermittently. Men with *lifelong* erectile disorder (formerly called *primary* erectile dysfunction) never had adequate erectile functioning. Erectile disorder far more commonly develops after a period of normal functioning and is classified as *acquired erectile disorder* (formerly called *secondary* erectile dysfunction). Many such men engaged in years of successful coitus before the problem began.

Occasional problems in achieving or maintaining erection are quite common. Fatigue, alcohol, anxiety over impressing a new partner, and other factors might account for a transient episode. Even an isolated occurrence can lead to a persistent problem if the man fears recurrence, however. The more anxious and concerned the man becomes about his sexual ability, the more likely he is to suffer **performance anxiety.** This anxiety can contribute to repeated failure, and a vicious cycle of anxiety and failure might develop.

A man with erectile problems might try to "will" an erection, which can compound the problem. Each failure might further demoralize and defeat him. He might ruminate about his sexual inadequacy, setting the stage for yet more anxiety. His partner might try to comfort and support him by saying things like "It can happen to anyone," "Don't worry

Vasocongestion Engorgement of blood vessels with blood, which swells the genitals and breasts during sexual arousal.

Male erectile disorder Persistent difficulty in achieving or maintaining an erection sufficient to allow the man to engage in or complete sexual intercourse. Also termed *erectile dysfunction*.

Performance anxiety Anxiety about one's ability to perform behaviors, especially behaviors that might be evaluated by other people.

Sexual Arousal Disorders. It is not unusual for couples to experience some degree of sexual dysfunction. In fact, results of recent studies out of the University of Chicago and published in the *Journal of the American Medical Association* indicate that the number of people reporting some type of sexual dysfunction is much higher than previously thought.

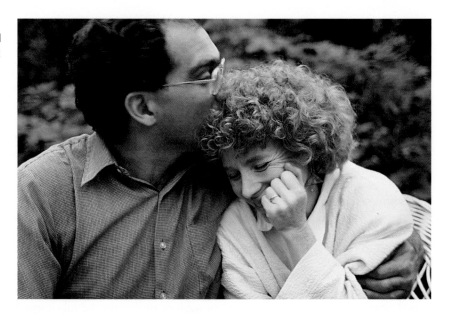

about it," or "It will get better in time." But attempts at reassurance might be to no avail. As one client put it,

> I always felt inferior, like I was on probation, having to prove myself. I felt like I was up against the wall. You can't imagine how embarrassing this (erectile failure) was. It's like you walk out in front of an audience that you think is a nudist convention and it turns out to be a tuxedo convention. (from the authors' files)

The vicious cycle of anxiety and erectile failure can be interrupted if the man recognizes that occasional problems are normal and does not overreact. The emphasis in our culture on men's sexual prowess might spur them to view occasional failures as catastrophes rather than transient disappointments, however. Viewing occasional problems as an inconvenience, rather than a tragedy, might help to avert the development of persistent erectile difficulties.

Performance anxiety is a prominent cause of erectile disorder. So are other psychological factors such as depression, lack of self-esteem, and problems in the relationship. Biological factors can also play a causal role, as we shall see.

FEMALE SEXUAL AROUSAL DISORDER   Women might encounter persistent difficulties becoming sexually excited or sufficiently lubricated in response to sexual stimulation. In some cases, these difficulties are lifelong. In others, they develop after a period of normal functioning. In some cases, difficulties are pervasive and occur during both masturbation and sex with a partner. More often, they occur in certain situations. For example, they occur with some partners and not with others or during coitus but not during oral-genital sex or masturbation.

Female sexual arousal disorder often accompanies other sexual disorders such as hypoactive sexual desire disorder and orgasmic disorders (Segraves & Segraves, 1993). Despite problems in becoming sexually aroused, women with sexual arousal disorders can often engage in coitus. Vaginal dryness might produce discomfort, however.

Female sexual arousal disorder, like its male counterpart, can have physical causes (Graber, 1993). A thorough evaluation by a medical specialist (a urologist in the case of a male, a gynecologist in the case of a female) is recommended. Any neurological, vascular, or hormonal problem that interferes with the lubrication or swelling response of the vagina to sexual stimulation can contribute to female sexual arousal disorder. For example, diabetes mellitus might lead to diminished sexual excitement in women because of the degeneration of the nerves servicing the clitoris and the blood vessel (vascular) damage it causes. Reduced estrogen production can also result in vaginal dryness.

Female sexual arousal disorder more commonly has psychological causes, however. In some cases, women harbor deep-seated anger and resentment toward their partners and find it difficult to turn off these feelings when they go to bed. In other cases, sexual trauma is implicated. Survivors of sexual abuse often find it difficult to respond sexually to their partners. Childhood sexual abuse is especially prevalent in cases of female sexual arousal disorder (Morokoff, 1993). Feelings of helplessness, anger, or guilt, or even flashbacks of the abuse, might surface when the woman begins sexual activity, dampening her ability to become aroused. Other psychosocial causes include anxiety or guilt about sex and ineffective stimulation by the partner (Morokoff, 1993).

Orgasmic Disorders

Three disorders concern the orgasm phase of the sexual response cycle: (1) female orgasmic disorder, (2) male orgasmic disorder, and (3) premature ejaculation.

In female or male orgasmic disorder, the woman or man is persistently delayed in reaching orgasm or does not reach orgasm at all, despite achieving sexual stimulation of sufficient intensity to normally result in orgasm. The problem is more common among women than men. In some cases, a person can reach orgasm without difficulty while engaging in sexual relations with one partner but not with another.

MALE ORGASMIC DISORDER   Male orgasmic disorder has also been termed *delayed ejaculation, retarded ejaculation,* or *ejaculatory incompetence.*[1] The problem may be lifelong or acquired, generalized or situational. There are very few cases of men who have never ejaculated. In most cases, the disorder is limited to coitus. The man might be capable of ejaculating during masturbation or oral sex but find it difficult, if not impossible—despite high levels of sexual excitement—to ejaculate during intercourse. There is a myth that men with male orgasmic disorder and their female partners enjoy his condition, because it enables him to "go on forever" (Dekker, 1993). Actually, the experience is frustrating for both partners.

Male orgasmic disorder is relatively infrequent in the general population and in clinical practice, where it is among the least frequently diagnosed disorders (Dekker, 1993). Research on the problem has been scarce (Dekker, 1993), and only a few individual or multiple case reports have appeared in the literature (e.g., Masters & Johnson, 1970; Rathus, 1978).

Male orgasmic disorder can be caused by physical problems such as multiple sclerosis (Kedia, 1983) or neurological damage that interferes with neural control of ejaculation. It can also be a side effect of certain drugs. Various psychological factors may also play a role, including performance anxiety, sexual guilt, and hostility toward the partner. Helen Singer Kaplan (1974) suggests that some men with male orgasmic disorder might be unconsciously "holding back" their ejaculate from their partners because of underlying hostility or resentment. Masters and Johnson (1970) found that men with this problem frequently have strict religious backgrounds that might leave a residue of unresolved guilt about sex, which inhibits ejaculation. Emotional factors such as fears of pregnancy and anger toward one's partner can also play a role.

As with other sexual dysfunctions, men with male orgasmic disorder and their partners might "try harder." But trying harder often compounds rather than alleviates sexual problems. Sexual relations become a job to get done, a chore rather than an opportunity for pleasure and gratification.

---

[1]Just as we find terms such as *impotence* and *frigidity* unnecessarily pejorative, we prefer to use the more clinical-sounding but less offensive *male orgasmic disorder* or *delayed ejaculation* rather than "retarded" ejaculation or ejaculatory "incompetence."

FEMALE ORGASMIC DISORDER   Women with female orgasmic disorder are unable to reach orgasm or have difficulty reaching orgasm after what would usually be an adequate amount of sexual stimulation. Women who have never achieved orgasm through any means are sometimes labeled **anorgasmic** or *preorgasmic.*

A woman who reaches orgasm through masturbation or oral sex might not necessarily reach orgasm dependably during coitus with her partner (Stock, 1993). Penile thrusting during coitus might not provide sufficient clitoral stimulation to facilitate orgasm. An orgasmic disorder might be diagnosed, however, if orgasm during coitus was impaired by factors such as sexual guilt or performance anxiety. Women who try to force an orgasm might also find themselves unable to do so. They might assume a **spectator role** and observe rather than fully participate in their sexual encounters. "Spectatoring" might further decrease the likelihood of orgasm.

PREMATURE EJACULATION   A second type of male orgasmic disorder, premature ejaculation, was the most common male sexual dysfunction reported in the NHSLS study (see Table 15.1). Men with **premature ejaculation** ejaculate too rapidly to permit their partners or themselves to fully enjoy sexual relations. The degree of prematurity varies. Some men ejaculate during foreplay, even at the sight of their partner disrobing. But most ejaculate either just before or immediately upon penetration or after a few coital thrusts (Kaplan, 1974).

Just what constitutes *prematurity?* Some definitions focus on a particular time period during which a man should be able to control ejaculation. Is ejaculation within 30 seconds of intromission premature? Within one minute? Ten minutes? There is no clear cutoff. Some scholars argue that the focus should be on whether the couple is satisfied with the duration of coitus rather than on a specific time period.

Helen Singer Kaplan (1974) suggested that the label "premature" should be applied to cases in which men persistently or recurrently lack voluntary control over their ejaculations. This might sound like a contradiction in terms, since ejaculation is a reflex and reflexes need not involve thought or conscious control. However, Kaplan means that a man can control his ejaculation by learning to regulate the amount of sexual stimulation he experiences so that it remains below the threshold at which the ejaculation reflex is triggered.

RAPID FEMALE ORGASM: CAN WOMEN REACH ORGASM TOO QUICKLY?   The female counterpart to premature ejaculation, *rapid orgasm*, is so rarely recognized as a problem that it is generally ignored by clinicians and is not classified as a sexual dysfunction in the DSM system. Still, some women experience orgasm rapidly and show little interest in continuing sexual activity so that their partners can achieve gratification. Many women who reach orgasm rapidly are open to continued sexual stimulation and capable of experiencing successive orgasms, however.

Sexual Pain Disorders

For most of us, coitus is a source of pleasure. For some of us, however, coitus gives rise to pain and discomfort.

DYSPAREUNIA   Dyspareunia, or painful coitus, can afflict men or women. Dyspareunia is one of the most common sexual dysfunctions and is also a common complaint of women seeking gynecological services (Quevillon, 1993).

Pain is a sign that something is wrong—physically or psychologically. Dyspareunia may result from physical causes, emotional factors, or an interaction of the two (Meana & Binik, 1994). The most common cause of coital pain in women is inadequate lubrication. In such a case, additional foreplay or artificial lubrication may help. Vaginal infections or sexually transmitted diseases (STDs) may also produce coital pain, however. Allergic reactions to spermicides, even the latex material in condoms, can give rise to coital pain or irritation. Pain during deep thrusting might be caused by endometriosis or pelvic inflammatory disease (PID), by other diseases or structural disorders of the reproductive organs, or by penile contact with the cervix.

Anorgasmic Never having reached orgasm. (Literally, "without orgasm.")

Spectator role A role, usually taken on because of performance anxiety, in which people observe rather than fully participate in their sexual encounters.

Premature ejaculation A sexual dysfunction in which ejaculation occurs with minimal sexual stimulation and before the man desires it.

The most common cause of painful intercourse in women is not vaginal infection. Lack of adequate lubrication is the most common cause of coital pain in women. ■

Truth or Fiction?
REVISITED

Psychological factors such as unresolved guilt or anxiety about sex or the lingering effects of sexual trauma might also be involved. These factors can inhibit lubrication and cause involuntary contractions of the vaginal musculature, making penetration painful or uncomfortable.

Painful intercourse is less common in men and is generally associated with genital infections that cause burning or painful ejaculation. Smegma under the penile foreskin of uncircumcised men can also irritate the penile glans during sexual contact.

VAGINISMUS Vaginismus involves an involuntary contraction of the pelvic muscles that surround the outer third of the vaginal barrel. Vaginismus occurs reflexively during attempts at vaginal penetration, making entry by the penis painful or impossible. These reflexive contractions are accompanied by a deep-seated fear of penetration (Beck, 1993). Some women with vaginismus are unable to tolerate penetration by any object, including a finger, a tampon, or a physician's speculum. The prevalence of vaginismus is unknown.

The woman with vaginismus usually is not aware that she is contracting her vaginal muscles. In some cases, husbands of women with vaginismus develop erectile disorder after repeated failures at penetration (Masters & Johnson, 1970; Speckens et al., 1995).

Vaginismus is caused by a psychological fear of penetration rather than by a physical injury or defect (LoPiccolo & Stock, 1986). Women with vaginismus often have histories of sexual trauma, rape, or botched abortions that resulted in vaginal injuries. They might desire sexual relations. They might be capable of becoming sexually aroused and achieving orgasm. However, fear of penetration triggers an involuntary spasm of the vaginal musculature at the point of penile insertion. Vaginismus can also be a cause or an effect of dyspareunia. Women who experience painful coitus might develop a fear of penetration. Fear then leads to the development of involuntary vaginal contractions. Women with vaginismus might also experience pain during coital attempts if the couple tries to force penetration. Vaginismus and dyspareunia can also give rise to, or result from, erectile disorder in men (Speckens et al., 1995). Feelings of failure and anxiety come to overwhelm both partners.

Table 15.2 shows differences in the incidences of current sexual dysfunctions and other problems between White Americans and African Americans, according to the NHSLS study (Laumann et al., 1994). The African American men report a higher incidence than White men of each of the sexual dysfunctions surveyed. African American women report a higher incidence of most sexual dysfunctions, with the exceptions of painful sex and trouble lubricating.

table 15.2

White and African American differences in the incidence of current sexual problems (respondents reporting the problem within the past year)				
	White Men (%)	**African American Men (%)**	**White Women (%)**	**African American Women (%)**
Pain during sex	3.0	3.3	14.7	12.5
Sex not pleasurable	7.0	15.2	19.7	30.0
Unable to reach orgasm	7.4	9.9	23.2	29.2
Lack of interest in sex	14.7	20.0	30.9	44.5
Anxiety about performance	16.8	23.7	10.5	14.5
Reaching climax too early	27.7	33.8	7.5	20.4
Unable to keep an erection	9.9	14.5	—	—
Having trouble lubricating	—	—	20.7	13.0

Source: Adapted from Tables 10.8A and 10.8B, pages 370 and 371, in Laumann, E. O., Gagnon, J. H., Michael, R. T., & Michaels, S. (1994). *The social organization of sexuality: Sexual practices in the United States.* Chicago: University of Chicago Press.

INIS BEAG AND MANGAIA— WORLDS APART

Let us invite you on a journey to two islands that are a world apart—sexually as well as geographically. The sexual attitudes and practices within these societies will shed some light on the role of cultural values in determining what is sexually normal and what is sexually dysfunctional.

Our first stop was the island of Inis Beag, which lies off the misty coast of Ireland. From the air, Inis Beag was a green jewel, fertile and inviting. At ground level, things did not appear quite so warm, however.

The residents of this Irish community did not believe that it was normal for women to experience orgasm. Anthropologist John Messenger (1971), who visited Inis Beag in the 1950s and 1960s, reported that any woman who found pleasure in sex—especially the intense waves of pleasure that can accompany orgasm—was viewed as deviant. *Should women on Inis Beag, then, be diagnosed as orgasmically impaired?*

Premarital sex was all but unknown on Inis Beag. Before marriage, men and women socialized apart. Marriage came relatively late, usually in the middle 30s for men and the middle 20s for women. Mothers taught their daughters that they would have to submit to their husbands' animal cravings to obey God's injunction to "be fruitful and multiply." *After this indoctrination, women showed little interest in sex. Should they be diagnosed as having hypoactive sexual desire disorder?*

The women of Inis Beag did not need to be overly concerned about frequent sexual intercourse, however, since the men of the island believed, erroneously, that sexual activity would drain their strength. Consequently, men avoided sex on the eve of sporting activity or strenuous work. Because of taboos against nudity, married couples engaged in intercourse with their underclothes on. Intercourse took place in the dark—literally as well as figuratively.

During intercourse, the man took the male-superior position. The male was always the initiator. Foreplay was brief, rarely involving manual stimulation of the breasts and never including oral stimulation of the genitals. *Should people who have difficulty becoming sexually aroused under these circum-*

stances be diagnosed as having sexual arousal disorders? The man ejaculated as rapidly as he could, in the belief that he was the only partner with sexual needs and to spare his wife as best he could. Then he turned over and rapidly fell asleep. Once more, the couple had done their duty. *Since the man ejaculated rapidly, should he be diagnosed as having premature ejaculation?*

Our next stop was Mangaia, a Polynesian pearl of an island. It lifts languidly out of the blue waters of the Pacific. It lies on the other side of the world from Inis Beag—in more ways than one.

From an early age, Mangaian boys and girls were encouraged to get in touch with their own sexuality through sexual play and masturbation (Marshall, 1971). At about the age of 13, Mangaian boys were initiated into manhood by adults who instructed them in sexual techniques. Mangaian males were taught the merit of bringing their female partners to multiple orgasms before ejaculating. *Were Mangaian males who ejaculated before their partners had multiple orgasms suffering from premature ejaculation?*

Boys practiced their new techniques with girlfriends on secluded beaches or beneath the listing fronds of palms. They may have visited girlfriends in the evening in the huts where they slept with their families.

Parents often listened for their daughters to laugh and gasp so that they would know that they had reached orgasm with a visiting young man, called a "sleepcrawler." Usually, they pretended to be asleep so as not to interfere with courtship and impede their daughters' chances of finding a suitable mate. Daughters may have received a nightly succession of sleepcrawlers.

Girls, too, learned techniques of coitus from their elders. Typically, they were initiated by an experienced male relative. Mangaians looked on virginity with disdain, because virgins did not know how to provide sexual pleasure. Thus, the older relative made his contribution to the family by initiating the girl.

Mangaians, by the way, expressed concern when they learned that many European and U.S. women did not regularly experience orgasm during coitus. Orgasm was apparently universal among Mangaian women. Therefore, Mangaians could only assume that Western women suffered from some abnormality of the sex organs. *Do they?*

All in all, the sharp contrasts between Inis Beag and Mangaia illustrate how concepts of normality are embedded within a cultural context. Behavior that is judged to be normal in one culture may be regarded as abnormal in another. How might our own cultural expectations influence our judgments about sexual dysfunction?

Polynesia. Cultural expectations affect our judgments as to what kinds of sexual behavior are functional and dysfunctional. Some Polynesian cultures are sexually permissive. They encourage children to explore their sexuality. Men may be expected to bring their partners to orgasm several times before ejaculating. In such cultures, should men who ejaculate before their partners have multiple orgasms be diagnosed with premature ejaculation?

Reflections

- Why do you think so many people have difficulty talking about sexual problems or sexual dysfunctions? Why do you think men have more difficulty talking about them than women do?
- The text notes that there is no consensus among clinicians and researchers concerning the definition of low sexual desire. How much sexual interest or desire would seem to be normal to you? Why?
- How would *you* define "premature" ejaculation? Explain.

ORIGINS OF SEXUAL DYSFUNCTIONS

Since sexual dysfunctions involve the sex organs, it was once assumed that they stemmed largely from organic or physical causes. Today, it is widely believed that many cases reflect psychosocial factors such as sexual anxieties, lack of sexual knowledge, or marital dissatisfaction. Many cases also involve a combination of organic and psychological factors (Meisler & Carey, 1990; Mohr & Beutler, 1990).

Organic Causes

Physical factors, such as fatigue and lowered testosterone levels, can dampen sexual desire and reduce responsiveness. Fatigue can lead to male erectile disorder and male orgasmic disorder and to female orgasmic disorder and inadequate lubrication. But these will be isolated incidents unless the person attaches too much meaning to them and becomes concerned about future performances. Painful coitus, however, often reflects organic factors such as underlying infections. Various medical conditions can affect orgasmic functioning in both men and women, including diabetes mellitus, multiple sclerosis, spinal cord injuries, complications from certain surgical procedures (such as removal of the prostate in men), endocrinological problems, and use of some pharmacological agents, such as drugs used to treat hypertension and psychiatric disorders (Segraves & Segraves, 1993).

It was once believed that the great majority of cases of erectile disorder had psychological causes (Masters & Johnson, 1970). It is now known that organic factors are involved in as many as 80% of cases (Brody, 1998c). But psychological factors such as anxiety or depression can perpetuate or exacerbate the problem even when there are underlying organic causes.

Organic causes of erectile disorder involve the flow of blood to and through the penis—a problem that becomes more common as men age—or damage to nerves involved in erection (Goldstein, 1998; Leland, 1997). Erectile problems can arise when clogged or narrow arteries leading to the penis deprive the penis of oxygen (Lipshultz, 1996). For example, erectile disorder is common among men with diabetes mellitus, a disease that can damage blood vessels and nerves. Nerve damage resulting from prostate surgery can also impair erectile response. Former senator and presidential candidate Bob Dole encountered erectile problems after removal of his prostate gland in 1991. Erectile disorder can also result from multiple sclerosis (MS), a disease in which nerve cells lose the protective coatings that facilitate transmission of neural messages. MS has also been implicated in male orgasmic disorder (Kedia, 1983).

Syphilis, a sexually transmitted disease, can result in erectile failure if the bacteria that cause the disease invade the spinal cord and affect the cells that control erection (Spark, 1991). Chronic kidney disease, hypertension, cancer, emphysema, and heart disease can all impair erectile response. So too can endocrine disorders that impair testosterone production.

Many cases of erectile disorder involve failure of the body to produce enough nitric oxide (Rajfer et al., 1992). When nitric oxide comes into contact with the muscles encircling blood vessels in the penis, the muscles relax, allowing vasocongestion to occur and causing the penis to swell. Lack of nitric oxide allows blood to leak out of the penis and be reabsorbed by the body, thereby preventing the degree of engorgement necessary for erection.

Women might also encounter vascular or nerve disorders that impair genital blood flow, reducing lubrication and sexual excitement, rendering intercourse painful, and reducing their ability to reach orgasm. As with men, these problems become more likely as women age.

People with sexual dysfunctions are generally advised to undergo a physical examination to determine whether their problems are biologically based. Men with erectile disorder may be evaluated in a sleep center to determine whether they attain erections while asleep. Healthy men usually have erections during rapid-eye-movement (REM) sleep, which occurs every 90 to 100 minutes. Men with organically based erectile disorder often do not have nocturnal erections. However, this technique, called nocturnal penile **tumescence** (NPT), can lead to misleading results in perhaps 20% of cases (Meisler & Carey, 1990). NPT might thus be helpful but not definitive in suggesting whether erectile disorder is organically based (Mohr & Beutler, 1990).

Prescription drugs and illicit drugs are believed to account for one in four cases of erectile disorder (Leary, 1992). Antidepressant medication and antipsychotic drugs might impair erectile functioning and cause orgasmic disorders (Segraves, 1988b; Spark, 1991). Tranquilizers like Valium and Xanax can cause orgasmic disorder in either gender (Segraves, 1988b). Antihypertensive drugs can lead to erectile failure (Segraves, 1988b). Switching to hypertension drugs that do not impair sexual response or adjusting dosage levels might help (Spark, 1991).

Central nervous system depressants such as alcohol, heroin, and morphine can reduce sexual desire and impair sexual arousal (Segraves, 1988a). Regular marijuana use has also been associated with reduced sexual desire and performance (Nelson, 1988). Heavy drinking can damage the nerves that control erection and ejaculation (Spark, 1991). Narcotics also depress testosterone production, which can further reduce sexual desire and lead to erectile failure (Spark, 1991).

It is commonly believed that cocaine is an aphrodisiac. However, regular use can cause erectile disorder or male orgasmic disorder and can reduce sexual desire in both genders (Weiss & Mirin, 1987). Some people report increased sexual pleasure from the initial use of cocaine, but repeated use can lead to dependency on the drug for sexual arousal. Long-term use might compromise the ability to experience sexual pleasure (Weiss & Mirin, 1987).

Occasional use of alcohol and other drugs can also lead to sexual difficulties when people misattribute their sexually dampening effects to causes within themselves. If you are unable to perform sexually when you have had a few drinks and do not recognize that alcohol can depress your performance, you might believe that something else is wrong with you. This belief can create anxiety at your next sexual opportunity, which can prevent normal functioning. A second failure might set off a vicious cycle in which self-doubts prompt more anxiety, leading to repeated failure and further heightened anxiety.

Psychosocial Causes

Psychosocial factors are connected with sexual dysfunctions. These include—but are not necessarily limited to—cultural influences, psychosexual trauma, a gay sexual orientation, ineffectual sexual techniques, emotional factors, problems in the relationship, psychological conflict, lack of sexual skills, irrational beliefs, and performance anxiety.

CULTURAL INFLUENCES   Children who are reared in sexually repressive cultural or home environments might learn to respond to sex with feelings of anxiety and shame, rather than sexual arousal and pleasure. People whose parents instilled in them a sense of guilt over touching their genitals might find it difficult to accept their sex organs as sources of pleasure.

In Western cultures, sexual pleasure has traditionally been a male preserve. Young women might be reared to believe that sex is a duty to be performed for their husbands,

Tumescence Swelling; erection. (From the Latin *tumere,* meaning "to swell." *Tumor* has the same root.)

A World of Diversity

AN ODD COUPLE: Koro and Dhat Syndromes

Many men in the United States are concerned that their penises are too small. However, they are not usually concerned that their genitals will retract into their bodies. Some people in the United States also still believe that men should avoid sex on the eve of an athletic event, because sex saps the body of strength. This belief has a counterpart in India.

Let us consider two Far Eastern sexual disorders: Koro and Dhat syndromes.

Koro Syndrome

Koro syndrome is found primarily in China and some other Far Eastern countries. People with Koro syndrome fear that their genitals are shrinking and retracting into the body, a problem that they believe will be fatal. Koro syndrome has been identified mainly in young men, although some cases have also been reported in women. People with Koro syndrome show signs of acute anxiety, including profuse sweating, breathlessness, and heart palpitations. Men with the disorder have been known to use mechanical devices, such as chopsticks, to try to prevent the penis from retracting into the body.

Koro syndrome has been traced as far back as 3000 B.C. Epidemics involving hundreds or thousands of people have been reported in parts of Asia such as China, Singapore, Thailand, and India (Tseng et al., 1992). In Guangdong Province in China, an epidemic involving more than 2,000 people occurred during the 1980s. Guangdong residents who did not fall victim to Koro were less superstitious and more intelligent than those who fell victim to the epidemic of fear (Tseng et al., 1992).

Reassurance by a health professional that fears that the genitals will retract into the body are unfounded often put an end to Koro episodes. In any event, Koro episodes tend to pass with time.

Truth or Fiction? REVISITED

It is true that during the 1980s, 2,000 people fell prey to the belief that their genitals were shrinking and retracting into their bodies. The syndrome is known as Koro and is found in the Far East. ■

Dhat Syndrome

Dhat syndrome, found among young Asian Indian males, involves excessive fears over the loss of seminal fluid during nocturnal emissions (Akhtar, 1988). Some men with Dhat syndrome also believe (incorrectly) that semen mixes with urine and is excreted by urinating.

There is a widespread belief within Indian culture (and other Near and Far Eastern cultures) that the loss of semen is harmful because it depletes the body of physical and mental energy (Chadda & Ahuja, 1990). Therefore, men with Dhat syndrome might visit physician after physician to find help in preventing nocturnal emissions or the imagined loss of semen mixed with urine. Dhat syndrome can best be understood within its cultural context:

> In India, attitudes toward semen and its loss constitute an organized, deep-seated belief system that can be traced back to the scriptures of the land . . . [even as far back as the classic Indian sex manual, the *Kama Sutra*, which was believed to be written by the sage Vatsayana between the third and fifth centuries A.D.]. . . . Semen is considered to be the elixir of life, in both a physical and mystical sense. Its preservation is supposed to guarantee health and longevity. (Akhtar, 1988, p. 71)

It is a commonly held Hindu belief that it takes "40 meals to form one drop of blood; 40 drops of blood to fuse and form one drop of bone marrow, and 40 drops of this produce one drop of semen" (Akhtar, 1988, p. 71). Some Indian males therefore experience great anxiety over the involuntary loss of the fluid through nocturnal emissions (Akhtar, 1988). Dhat syndrome has also been associated with difficulty in achieving or maintaining erection, apparently due to excessive concern about loss of seminal fluid through ejaculation.

---

not a source of personal pleasure. Although the traditional double standard may have diminished in the United States in recent years, girls might still be exposed to relatively more repressive attitudes. Women are more likely than men in our culture to be taught to repress their sexual desires and even to fear their sexuality (Nichols, 1990). Self-control and vigilance—not sexual awareness and acceptance—become identified as feminine virtues. Women who are reared with such attitudes might be less likely to learn about their sexual potentials or express their erotic preferences to their partners. Compared with women who readily reach orgasm, sexually active but anorgasmic women report more negative attitudes toward masturbation, greater sexual guilt, and greater discomfort in talking with their partners about sexual activities that involve direct clitoral contact (cunnilingus and manual stimulation) (Kelly et al., 1990).

Many women who are exposed to negative attitudes about sex during childhood and adolescence find it difficult to suddenly view sex as a source of pleasure and satisfaction once they are married. The result of a lifetime of learning to turn themselves off sexually might lead to difficulties in experiencing the full expression of sexual arousal and enjoyment when an acceptable opportunity arises (Morokoff, 1993).

PSYCHOSEXUAL TRAUMA   Learning theorists focus on the role of conditioned anxiety in explaining sexual dysfunctions. Sexual stimuli come to elicit anxiety when they have been paired with physically or psychologically painful experiences, such as rape, incest, or sexual molestation. Strong conditioned anxiety can stifle sexual arousal. Unresolved anger and misplaced guilt can also make it difficult for victims of rape and other sexual traumas to respond sexually, even years afterward. People who have been sexually victimized might harbor feelings of disgust and revulsion toward sex or deep-seated fears of sex that make it difficult for them to respond sexually, even with loving partners.

SEXUAL ORIENTATION   Some gay males and lesbians test their sexual orientation by developing heterosexual relationships, even marrying and rearing children with partners of the other gender. Others might wish to maintain the appearance of heterosexuality to avoid the social stigma that society attaches to a gay sexual identity. In such cases, problems in arousal or performance with heterosexual partners can be due to a lack of heteroerotic interests. A lack of heterosexual response is not a problem for people who are committed to a gay lifestyle, however. Sexual dysfunctions may also occur in gay relationships, as they do in heterosexual relationships.

INEFFECTIVE SEXUAL TECHNIQUES   In some marriages, couples practice a narrow range of sexual techniques because they have fallen into a certain routine or because one partner controls the timing and sequence of sexual techniques. A woman who remains unknowledgeable about the erotic importance of her clitoris might be unlikely to seek direct clitoral stimulation. The man who responds to a temporary erectile failure by trying to force an erection might be unintentionally setting himself up for repeated failure. The couple who fail to communicate their sexual preferences or to experiment with altering their sexual techniques might find themselves losing interest. Brevity of foreplay and coitus might contribute to female orgasmic disorder.

EMOTIONAL FACTORS   Orgasm involves a sudden loss of voluntary control. Fear of losing control or "letting go" might block sexual arousal. Other emotional factors, especially depression, are often implicated in sexual dysfunctions (Beck, 1988). Women with hypoactive sexual desire are more likely to report a history of depressive episodes (Schreiner-Engle & Schiavi, 1986). People who are depressed frequently report lessened sexual interest and might find it difficult to respond sexually. People who are exposed to a high level of emotional stress might also experience an ebbing of sexual interest and response.

PROBLEMS IN THE RELATIONSHIP   Problems in the relationship are important and often pivotal factors in sexual dysfunctions (Catalan et al., 1990; Fish et al., 1994; Leiblum & Rosen, 1991). Problems in a relationship are not easily left at the bedroom door. Couples usually find that their sexual relationships are no better than the other facets of their relationships. Couples who harbor resentments toward one another might make sex their arena of combat. They might fail to become aroused by their partners or "withhold" orgasm to make their partners feel guilty or inadequate.

Problems in communication can also play a role. Troubled relationships are usually characterized by poor communication. Partners who have difficulty communicating about other matters might be unlikely to communicate their sexual desires to each other.

The following case highlights how sexual dysfunctions can develop against the backdrop of a troubled relationship:

After living together for six months, Paul and Petula are contemplating marriage. But a problem has brought them to a sex therapy clinic. As Petula puts it, "For the last two months he hasn't been able to keep his erection after he enters me." Paul is 26, a lawyer; Petula, 24, is a buyer for a large department store. They both grew up in middle-class, suburban families, were introduced through mutual friends and began having intercourse, without difficulty, a few months into their relationship. At Petula's urging, Paul moved into her apartment, although he wasn't sure he was ready for such a step. A week later he began to have difficulty maintaining his erection during intercourse, although he felt strong desires for his partner. When his erection waned, he would try again, but would lose his desire and be unable to achieve another erection. After a few times like this, Petula would become so angry that she began striking Paul in the chest and screaming at him. Paul, who at 200 pounds weighed more than twice as much as Petula, would just walk away, which angered Petula even more.

It became clear that sex was not the only trouble spot in their relationship. Petula complained that he preferred to be with his friends and go to baseball games than to spend time with her. When they were together at home, he would become absorbed in watching sports events on television, and showed no interest in activities she enjoyed— attending the theater, visiting museums, etc. Since there was no evidence that the sexual difficulty was due to either organic problems or depression, a diagnosis of male erectile disorder was given. Neither Paul nor Petula was willing to discuss their nonsexual problems with a therapist. While the sexual problem was treated successfully with a form of sex therapy modeled after techniques developed by Masters and Johnson [see discussion later in the chapter] and the couple later married, Paul's ambivalence continued well into their marriage, and there were future recurrences of sexual problems as well. (Adapted from Spitzer et al., 1989, pp. 149–150)

Though couples with strongly committed and supportive relationships can generally develop effective coping strategies for overcoming even the most severe sexual problems, couples in relationships with unresolved conflicts might derive little if any benefit from even the most advanced psychological, medical, or surgical treatments of sexual dysfunctions (Leiblum & Rosen, 1991).

Parents as Models. Parental examples are important modeling influences in shaping a child's development. Parents who are warm and affectionate toward each other model loving interactions which can help children develop positive attitudes toward intimate relationships.

PSYCHOLOGICAL CONFLICTS   Within Freud's psychoanalytic theory, sexual dysfunctions are rooted in the failure to successfully resolve the Oedipus or Electra complexes of early childhood. Sexual encounters in adulthood arouse unconscious anxieties and hostilities that are believed to reflect unresolved conflicts, thereby inhibiting sexual response.

A modern psychoanalytic theorist, Helen Singer Kaplan (1974), believes that sexual dysfunctions represent an interaction of *immediate* causes (such as poor techniques, marital conflict, performance anxiety, and lack of effective communication) and deep-seated or *remote* causes (such as unresolved childhood conflicts that predispose people to encounter sexual anxiety and hostility in adulthood). Kaplan believes that there is value in combining direct behavioral techniques, which deal with the immediate causes of sexual dysfunctions, with psychoanalytic (insight-oriented) techniques that deal with the remote causes.

LACK OF SEXUAL SKILLS   Sexual competency involves the acquisition of sexual knowledge and skills and is based largely on learning. We generally learn what makes us and others feel good through trial and error and by talking and reading about sex. Some people might not develop sexual competency because of a lack of opportunity to acquire knowledge and experience—even within marriage. People with sexual dysfunctions might have been reared in families in which discussions of sexuality were off limits and early sexual experimentation was harshly punished. Such early influences might have squelched the young person's sexual learning and experimentation or led her or him to associate anxiety or guilt with sex.

Helen Singer Kaplan (1974) notes that premature ejaculators might have failed to learn to recognize the level of sexual arousal that directly precedes their ejaculatory threshold—the level of stimulation that triggers the ejaculatory reflex. As a result, they might be less able to employ self-control strategies to delay ejaculation such as temporarily halting genital stimulation when they approach their "point of no return." Men with limited sexual experience are particularly unlikely to recognize their ejaculatory threshold and to regulate sexual stimulation so that it remains below this triggering point. Some men might try to delay ejaculation by keeping their minds blank or diverting their attention from sex (as by thinking about their forthcoming calculus exam). In so doing, they ignore their own sexual stimulation and do not learn "when to say when."

Although some men with premature ejaculation might have difficulty gauging their level of sexual arousal, research fails to show that premature ejaculators in general are less accurate than other men in making such judgments (Kinder & Curtiss, 1988; Strassberg et al., 1990). It might be that premature ejaculators are more physiologically sensitive to sexual stimulation, not that they are less capable of assessing their sexual arousal (Strassberg et al., 1990). Perhaps premature ejaculators simply require less stimulation to achieve orgasm. Though this might be the case, it does not account for the factors explaining these differences in sensitivity levels (O'Donohue et al., 1993).

IRRATIONAL BELIEFS   Psychologist Albert Ellis (1962, 1977) points out that irrational beliefs and attitudes might contribute to sexual dysfunctions. Negative feelings such as anxiety and fear, Ellis submits, do not stem directly from the events we experience, but rather from our interpretations of these events. If a person encounters a certain event such as an erectile or orgasmic disorder on a given day and then *believes* that the event is awful or catastrophic, he or she will exaggerate feelings of disappointment and set the stage for future problems.

PERFORMANCE ANXIETY   Anxiety—especially performance anxiety—plays important roles in the development of sexual dysfunctions. Performance anxiety occurs when a person becomes overly concerned with how well he or she performs a certain act or task. Performance anxiety can place a dysfunctional individual in a spectator rather than a performer role. Rather than focusing on erotic sensations and allowing involuntary responses such as erection, lubrication, and orgasm to occur naturally, he or she focuses on self-doubts and fears and thinks, "Will I be able to do it this time? Will this be another failure?"

Performance anxiety can set the stage for a vicious cycle in which a sexual failure increases anxiety. Anxiety then leads to repeated failure and so on. Sex therapists emphasize the need to break this vicious cycle by removing the need to perform.

In men, performance anxiety can inhibit erection while also triggering a premature ejaculation. (Erection, mediated by the parasympathetic nervous system, can be blocked by activation of the sympathetic nervous system in the form of anxiety. Since ejaculation, like anxiety, is mediated by the sympathetic nervous system, arousal of this system in the form of anxiety can increase the level of stimulation and thereby heighten the potential for premature ejaculation.)

In women, performance anxiety can reduce vaginal lubrication and contribute to orgasmic disorder. Women with performance anxieties might try to force an orgasm, only to find that the harder they try, the more elusive it becomes.

Reflections

- Do you know of anyone who has sexual problems or dysfunctions that are apparently related to traumatic sexual experiences as a child or an adult? Explain.
- Are there any sexual attitudes common to people of your sociocultural background that can give rise to sexual problems or dysfunctions? What are the attitudes? Do you share these attitudes? Why or why not?
- What kinds of vicious cycles characterize sexual problems and feelings of anxiety? Have you known anyone with similar concerns about taking tests in college? How does anxiety interact with test performance for them?

TREATMENT OF SEXUAL DYSFUNCTIONS

When Kinsey conducted his surveys in the 1930s and 1940s, there was no effective treatment for sexual dysfunctions. At the time, the predominant model of therapy for sexual dysfunctions was long-term psychoanalysis. Psychoanalysts believed that the sexual problem would abate only if the presumed unconscious conflicts that lay at the root of the problem were resolved through long-term therapy. Evidence of the effectiveness of psychoanalysis in treating sexual dysfunctions is still lacking, however.

Since that time, behavioral models of short-term treatment, collectively called **sex therapy,** have emerged. These models aim to modify the dysfunctional behavior as directly as possible. Sex therapists also recognize the roles of childhood conflicts, self-defeating attitudes, and the quality of the partners' relationship. Therefore, they draw upon various forms of therapy, as needed (LoPiccolo, 1994; Rosen et al., 1994).

Although the particular approaches vary, sex therapies aim to:

1. Change self-defeating beliefs and attitudes
2. Teach sexual skills
3. Enhance sexual knowledge
4. Improve sexual communication
5. Reduce performance anxiety

Sex therapy usually involves both partners, although individual therapy is preferred in some cases. Therapists find that granting people "permission" to sexually experiment or discuss negative attitudes about sex helps many people to overcome sexual problems without the need for more intensive therapy.

Today, biological treatments have also been emerging for various sexual dysfunctions. In 1998, practically all public attention was focused on Viagra, a drug that is helpful in most cases of erectile dysfunction. But biological treatments are also emerging for premature ejaculation, female orgasmic dysfunction, and lack of sexual desire.

Sex therapy A collective term for short-term behavioral models for treatment of sexual dysfunctions.

In this section, we will explore both psychological and behavioral approaches to the treatment of sexual dysfunctions. Let us begin with the groundbreaking work of Masters and Johnson.

The Masters and Johnson Approach

Masters and Johnson pioneered the use of direct behavioral approaches to treating sexual dysfunctions (Masters & Johnson, 1970). A female-male therapy team focuses on the couple as the unit of treatment during a two-week residential program. Masters and Johnson consider the couple, not the individual, dysfunctional. A couple might describe the husband's erectile disorder as the problem, but this problem is likely to have led to problems in the couple by the time they seek therapy. Similarly, a man whose wife has an orgasmic disorder is likely to be anxious about his ability to provide effective sexual stimulation.

The dual-therapist team permits each partner to discuss problems with someone of his or her own gender. It reduces the chance of therapist bias in favor of the female or male partner. It allows each partner to hear concerns expressed by another member of the other gender. Anxieties and resentments are aired, but the focus of treatment is behavioral change. Couples perform daily sexual homework assignments, such as **sensate focus exercises,** in the privacy of their own rooms.

Sensate focus sessions are carried out in the nude. Partners take turns giving and receiving stimulation in nongenital areas of the body. Without touching the breasts or genitals, the giver massages or fondles the receiving partner to provide pleasure under relaxing and nondemanding conditions. Since genital activity is restricted, there is no pressure to "perform." The giving partner is freed to engage in trial-and-error learning about the receiving partner's sensate preferences. The receiving partner is also freed to enjoy the experience without feeling rushed to reciprocate or obliged to perform by becoming sexually aroused. The receiving partner's only responsibility is to direct the giving partner as needed. In addition to these general sensate focus exercises, Masters and Johnson used specific assignments designed to help couples overcome particular sexual dysfunctions.

Masters and Johnson were pioneers in the development of sex therapy. Yet many sex therapists have departed from the Masters and Johnson format. Many do not treat clients in an intensive residential program. Many question the necessity of female-male therapist teams. Researchers find that one therapist is about as effective as two, regardless of her or his gender (Libman et al., 1985). Nor does the therapeutic benefit seem to depend to any great extent on whether the sessions are conducted within a short period of time, as in the Masters and Johnson approach, or spaced over time (Libman et al., 1985). Some success has also been reported in minimal contact programs in which participants are given written instructions rather than live therapy sessions (Mohr & Beutler, 1990). Therapists have also departed from the Masters and Johnson approach by working individually with preorgasmic women rather than the couple. Group treatment programs have also been used successfully in treating female orgasmic disorder (Killmann et al., 1987).

The Helen Singer Kaplan Approach

Kaplan (1974) calls her approach *psychosexual therapy*. Psychosexual therapy combines behavioral and psychoanalytic methods. Kaplan, as has been noted, believes that sexual dysfunctions have both *immediate* causes and *remote* causes (underlying intrapsychic conflicts that date to childhood). Kaplan begins therapy with the behavioral approach. She focuses on improving the couple's communication, eliminating performance anxiety, and fostering sexual skills and knowledge. She uses a brief form of insight-oriented therapy when it appears that remote causes impede response to the behavioral program. In so doing, she hopes to bring to awareness unconscious conflicts that are believed to have stifled the person's sexual desires or responsiveness. Although Kaplan reports a number of successful case studies, there are no controlled studies demonstrating that the combination of behavioral and insight-oriented, or psychoanalytic, techniques is more effective than the behavioral techniques alone.

Sensate focus exercises Exercises in which sex partners take turns giving and receiving pleasurable stimulation in nongenital areas of the body.

Let us now consider some of the specific techniques that sex therapists have introduced in treating several of the major types of sexual dysfunction.

Sexual Desire Disorders

Some sex therapists help to kindle the sexual appetites of people with hypoactive sexual desire by prescribing self-stimulation exercises combined with erotic fantasies (LoPiccolo & Friedman, 1991). Sex therapists might also assist dysfunctional couples by prescribing sensate focus exercises, enhancing communication, and expanding the couple's repertoire of sexual skills. Sex therapists recognize that hypoactive sexual desire is often a complex problem that requires more intensive treatment than do problems of the arousal or orgasm phases (Leiblum & Rosen, 1991). Helen Singer Kaplan (1987) argues that insight-oriented approaches are especially helpful in the treatment of hypoactive sexual desire and sexual aversion to uncover and resolve deep-seated psychological conflicts.

Some cases of hypoactive sexual desire in men involve hormonal deficiencies, especially deficiencies in testosterone. But testosterone replacement therapy is believed to be successful only in the relatively few cases of bona fide testosterone deficiencies (Spark, 1991). Among women, as among men, lack of sexual desire can be connected with low levels of androgens, and testosterone shows promise in heightening desire. For example, Solvay Pharmaceuticals is developing an oral hormone pill, Estratest, which is intended to stoke sexual desire in menopausal women. Another company, TheraTech, is developing a testosterone patch for women (Johannes, 1998).

When lack of desire is connected with depression, sexual interests might rebound when the depression lifts. Treatment in such cases might involve psychotherapy or chemotherapy, not sex therapy per se. When problems in the relationship are involved, marital or couples therapy might be indicated to improve the relationship. Once interpersonal problems are ironed out, sexual interest might return.

Treatment of sexual aversion disorder might involve a multifaceted approach, including biological treatments such as the use of medications to reduce anxiety and psychological treatments designed to help the individual overcome the underlying sexual phobia. Couples therapy might be used in cases in which sexual aversions arise from problems in relationships (Gold & Gold, 1993). Sensate focus exercises might be used to lessen generalized anxiety about sexual contact. But fears of specific aspects of the sexual act might need to be overcome through behavioral exercises in which the client learns to manage the stimuli that evoke fears of sexual contact:

Bridget, 26, and Bryan, 30, were married for four years but had never consummated their relationship because Bridget would panic whenever Bryan attempted coitus with her. While she enjoyed foreplay and was capable of achieving orgasm with clitoral stimulation, her fears of sexual contact were triggered by Bryan's attempts at vaginal penetration. The therapist employed a program of gradual exposure to the feared stimuli to allow Bridget the opportunity to overcome her fears in small, graduated steps. First she was instructed to view her genitals in a mirror when she was alone—this in order to violate her long-standing prohibition against looking at and enjoying her body. While this exercise initially made her feel anxious, with repeated exposure she became comfortable performing it and then progressed to touching her genitals directly. When she became comfortable with this step, and reported experiencing pleasurable erotic sensations, she was instructed to insert a finger into the vagina. She encountered intense anxiety at this step and required daily practice for two weeks before she could tolerate inserting her finger into her vagina without discomfort. Her husband was then brought into the treatment process. The couple was instructed to have Bridget insert her own finger in her vagina while Bryan watched. When she was comfortable with this exercise, she then guided his finger into her vagina. Later he placed one and then two fingers into her vagina, while she controlled the depth, speed and duration of penetration. When she felt ready, they proceeded to attempt penile penetration in the female superior position, which allowed her to maintain control over penetration. Over time, Bridget became more comfortable with penetration to the point that the couple developed a normal sexual relationship. (Adapted from Kaplan, 1987, pp. 102–103)

Sexual Arousal Disorders

Men with chronic erectile disorder might believe that they have "forgotten" how to have an erection. They might ask their therapists to "teach" them or "show them" how. Some of our clients have asked us to tell them what they should think or picture in their minds to achieve an erection or how they should touch their partners or be touched. Erection is an involuntary reflex, however, not a skill. A man need not learn how to have an erection any more than he needs to learn how to breathe.

In sex therapy, women who have trouble becoming lubricated and men with erectile problems learn that they need not "do" anything to become sexually aroused. As long as their problems are psychologically based, not organically based, they need only receive sexual stimulation under relaxed circumstances so that anxiety does not inhibit their natural reflexes.

Truth or Fiction?
REVISITED

It is not true that sex therapy teaches a man with erectile disorder how to will an erection. Men with erectile disorder are actually taught that it is not possible to will an erection. One can only set the stage for erection (or vaginal lubrication) to occur and then allow it to happen reflexively. ■

To reduce performance anxiety, the partners engage in nondemanding sexual contacts: contacts that do not demand lubrication or erection. They might start with nongenital sensate focus exercises in the style of Masters and Johnson. After a couple of sessions, sensate focus extends to the genitals. The position shown in Figure 15.1 allows the woman easy access to her partner's genitals. She repeatedly "teases" him to erection and allows the erection to subside. Thus, she avoids creating performance anxiety that could lead to loss

figure 15.1

The Training Position Recommended by Masters and Johnson for Treatment of Erectile Disorder and Premature Ejaculation.
By lying in front of her partner, who has his legs spread, the woman has ready access to his genitals. In one part of a program designed to overcome erectile disorder, she repeatedly "teases" him to erection and allows the erection to subside. Thus, she avoids creating performance anxiety that could lead to loss of erection. Through repeated regaining of erection, the man loses the fear that loss of erection means that it will not return.

of erection. By repeatedly regaining his erection, the man loses the fear that loss of erection means it will not return. He learns also to focus on erotic sensations for their own sake. He experiences no demand to perform, as the couple is instructed to refrain from coitus.

When the dysfunctional partner can reliably achieve sexual excitement (denoted by erection in the male and lubrication in the female), the couple does not immediately attempt coitus, since this might rekindle performance anxiety. Rather, the couple engages in a series of nondemanding, pleasurable sexual activities, eventually culminating in coitus.

In Masters and Johnson's approach, the couple begin coitus after about 10 days of treatment. The woman teases the man to erection while she is sitting above him, straddling his thighs. When he is erect, *she* inserts the penis—to avoid fumbling attempts at entry—and moves slowly back and forth in a *nondemanding way*. Neither person attempts to reach orgasm. If erection is lost, teasing and coitus are repeated. Once the couple become confident that erection can be retained—or reinstated if lost—they may increase coital thrusting gradually to reach orgasm.

BIOLOGICAL APPROACHES TO TREATMENT OF ERECTILE DISORDER

As this book is being written, the world's attention is focused on biological approaches to treating erectile disorder. Perhaps the opening shot in the biological war against erectile disorder was heard in 1983, when a speaker made a somewhat unusual presentation to his audience at a medical convention. He dropped his trousers to reveal an erection. The erection was the result not of sexual stimulation or sexual fantasies, but of an injection of a drug called *alprostadil* directly into his penis. The drug relaxed muscles surrounding the blood vessels in the penis, allowing the vessels to bring more blood into the penis, thereby increasing vasocongestion and causing erection. The speaker—a urologist—was giving a "live" demonstration of a biological method of treating erectile disorder.

It is true that a doctor dropped his pants to reveal an erection at a medical convention. He was demonstrating the effects of alprostadil. ■

Biological or biomedical approaches are helpful in treating erectile disorder, especially when organic factors are involved. Treatments include surgery, medication, and vacuum pumps (see Table 15.3 on page 470).

SURGERY   There are two main types of surgery: vascular surgery and the installation of penile implants. *Vascular surgery* can help in cases in which the blood vessels that supply the penis are blocked or in which structural defects in the penis restrict blood flow (Cowley & Rogers, 1997). An arterial bypass operation reroutes vessels around the blockage.

A *penile implant* may be used when other treatments fail. Implants are either malleable (semirigid) or inflatable. The semirigid implant is made of rods of silicone rubber that remain in a *permanent* semirigid position. It is rigid enough for intercourse but permits the penis to hang reasonably close to the body at other times. The inflatable type requires more extensive surgery. Cylinders are implanted in the penis. A fluid reservoir is placed near the bladder, and a tiny pump is inserted in the scrotum. To attain erection, the man squeezes the pump, releasing fluid into the cylinders. When the erection is no longer needed, a release valve returns the fluid to the reservoir, deflating the penis. The inflatable implant more closely duplicates the normal processes of tumescence and detumescence. Some adverse side effects of penile implants have been reported, including destruction of erectile tissue, impairing the man's ability to have normal erections. Penile implants do not affect sex drive, sexual sensations, or ejaculation.

Implant surgery is irreversible (Padma-Nathan et al., 1997). Therefore, the National Institutes of Health recommend that penile implants be used only when less invasive techniques, such as sex therapy and medication, are unsuccessful.

MEDICATION   There are several ways in which medication can be used to help men with erectile problems. For example, *hormone (testosterone) treatments* might help to restore the sex drive and erectile ability in men who have abnormally low levels of testosterone

Truth or Fiction?
REVISITED

Penile Implants. This implant consists of cylinders which are implanted in the penis. A fluid reservoir (top left) is placed near the bladder. A pump (lower middle) is typically inserted in the scrotum. Squeezing the pump forces fluid into the cylinders, inflating the penis. A release valve returns the fluid to the reservoir, deflating the penis.

table 15.3

Biological treatments of erectile problems	
Surgery	
Vascular surgery	Helps when blood vessels that supply the penis are blocked.
Penile implants	May be used when other treatments fail due to biological problems.
Medication	
Hormone therapy	Helps men and women with abnormally low levels of male sex hormones.
Injections	Muscle relaxants such as *alprostadil* and *phentolamine* are injected into the corpus cavernosum of the penis, relaxing the muscles that surround the small blood vessels in the penis, allowing the vessels to dilate and blood to flow into them more freely
Suppository	Alprostadil is inserted into the tip of the penis in gel form.
Oral medication	The oral form of sildenafil (Viagra) and the oral form of phentolamine (Vasomax) relax the muscles that surround the small blood vessels in the penis, allowing them to dilate so that blood can flow into them more freely. Apomorphine (Spontane) affects the part of the brain that triggers erections. Sexual stimulation is required to achieve erection with these pills.
Vacuum Pump	
Vacuum pump	A *vacuum constriction device* creates a vacuum when it is held over the penis. The vacuum induces erection by increasing the flow of blood into the penis. Rubber bands around the base of the penis maintain the erection.

(Bagatell & Bremner, 1996; Carani et al., 1990; Spark, 1991). There is no evidence that hormone therapy helps men who already have normal hormone levels. Testosterone does not help women who complain of lack of sexual desire unless their problem follows a surgically induced menopause in which the testosterone-producing adrenal glands were removed along with the ovaries (Bagatell & Bremner, 1996).

The muscle relaxants *alprostadil* (brand names Caverject and Edex) and *phentolamine* (Invicorp) can be injected into the corpus cavernosum of the penis. These chemicals relax the muscles that surround the small blood vessels in the penis. The vessels dilate and allow blood to flow into the penis more freely. In the case of alprostadil, erections last for an hour or more and occur whether or not there is sexual stimulation. A physician teaches the man how to inject himself. Phentolamine is used along with the protein VIP, and erection occurs only when sexual stimulation is applied.

Injections are most effective for men with problems in the transmission of nerve signals that regulate erection (Altman, 1995c). They are less effective for men with vascular problems that restrict the flow of blood into the penis (Spark, 1991). Injections are also helpful with most men whose erectile problems are psychologically based (Linet & Ogrinc, 1996).

Penile injections can have side effects, including pain from the injection itself and prolonged, painful erections (*priapism*) (Linet & Ogrinc, 1996; Lipshultz, 1996). Many men find the idea of penile injections distasteful and reject them out of hand or drop out after a trial (Lipshultz, 1996).

Alprostadil is also available as a suppository in gel form (brand name MUSE), which is inserted into the tip of the penis by an applicator. The suppository helps men get to around the "wince" factor that many experience with injections (Leland, 1997; Padma-Nathan et al., 1997).

Medications are also available in pill form. The oral form of sildenafil is sold as Viagra, and the oral form of phentolamine will be marketed as Vasomax (Vasomax is currently under review by the FDA [Leland, 1997].) The drug apomorphine (Spontane) apparently affects the part of the brain that triggers erections. Sexual stimulation is required to achieve erection with these pills.

Viagra was hailed as a miracle drug when it hit the market in early 1998. It sold faster than any new drug had ever sold. Bob Dole said on the Larry King show that he had participated in the clinical trials of Viagra a couple of years earlier and found it to be effective ("Cancer survivor Bob Dole," 1998). At a press interview, Dole's wife, Elizabeth Dole, who is president of the American Red Cross, echoed his view that Viagra is a "great drug" ("Mrs. Dole," 1998). The stock of Pfizer Company, which produces Viagra, shot up after the drug came on the market. A study published in *The New England Journal of Medicine* tested the effects of Viagra on more than 800 men with erectile dysfunction due both to psychological and to a number of organic causes (Goldstein et al., 1998). Men with extreme physical problems, such as serious anatomical defects and spinal cord injury, were not included. In one phase of the study, 69% of attempts to engage in sexual intercourse were successful for men taking Viagra, compared to 22% for men taking a placebo.

VACUUM PUMPS   Sounding like something from the "what will they think of next" category, a *vacuum constriction device* helps men to achieve erections through vacuum pressure. The device (brand name: ErecAid) consists of a cylinder that is connected to a hand-operated vacuum pump. It creates a vacuum when it is held over the limp penis. The vacuum induces erection by increasing the flow of blood into the penis. Rubber bands around the base of the penis can maintain the erection for as long as 30 minutes.

The device has been used successfully by men with both organically and psychologically based erectile failure. However, side effects such as pain and black-and-blue marks are common. The rubber bands prevent normal ejaculation, so semen remains trapped in the urethra until the bands are released. The quality of the erections that the device produces is also considered inferior to spontaneous erections (Spark, 1991).

WHERE DO WE GO FROM HERE?   It appears that oral medications (pills) will be the most popular biological treatment of erectile problems. They are helpful with the majority of men treated and surmount the "wince factor." Viagra has side effects such as headaches, flushing, indigestion, nasal congestion, and distorted color vision, however (Goldstein et al., 1998). The likelihood of side effects increases with the dose. For example, about 20% of men taking the 50-mg pill have headaches (dubbed "Vigraines"), compared with about 30% of men using the 100-mg pill (Goldstein et al., 1998). Five to ten percent of users see things with a blue tinge for up to a few hours. Given one of the slang meanings of the word "blue," this side effect might not be inappropriate. However, the visual problems are no laughing matter—they have apprently caused crashes of some small aircraft.

Spontane is most helpful with men who have mild erectile problems. Vasomax promises to have fewer side effects than Viagra. Given the rapid development of these medications, within a few years most men with erectile problems will probably have effective oral medications available with few if any side effects.

The Brave New World of Viagra

Many think that drugs such as Viagra enhance sexual pleasure among people who do not have sexual dysfunctions—people who are looking to heighten normal sexual experience (Kolata, 1998a). It might be that in future years, people will be popping pills left and right to increase their sexual arousal and response. At that time, we will have many issues to consider. Some people will certainly argue that people do not have the right to toy with what is "normal." Others will doubtlessly counter that one could extend the argument to outlaw perfume, R-rated movies, sips of wine, and coffee—all of which can enhance sexual arousal and response in one way or another.

We must also wonder what effects Viagra will have on marriages, especially those in which couples have been together for many decades. It might seem that Viagra would usually be a "home saver." However, Viagra can now and then be a "home wrecker." Let us see how:

For a former New England auto dealer, years of retirement to Florida brought two major changes: His golf scores improved as his sexual powers declined. Both seemed to him, at 67, to be in the natural order of things.

"To tell the truth, I was more concerned about my putting than playing around," said the man, a Palm Beach-area resident, who spoke only on condition of anonymity. "But my wife was unhappy," he continued. "She wanted me to see a doctor because I no longer had erections." He saw a urologist, who prescribed an injectable, anti-impotence drug. "It worked great," the man recalled. "My wife was very happy."

That was 10 months ago. Today, the man has separated from his wife of 46 years and lives with a woman half his age. It was the return of his sexual vigor, he said, that gave him "the confidence to see other women," which precipitated the breakup of his marriage.

For countless men who suffer from erectile dysfunction, which was treated until recently primarily with penile injections or implants and now with the wonder pill Viagra, restored sexual function can seem nothing short of a miracle. It can be a boon as well to the woman who has shared the physical and emotional frustration caused by her partner's condition. But it is also becoming clear that reawakened sexual vigor can have unforeseen and sometimes devastating side effects for some relationships. Marriage counselors, sex therapists, and physicians caution that some women may not be thrilled by having a born-again lover around the house.

Women who suffer medical afflictions associated with age or a severely reduced sex drive might be disturbed by a husband's restored potency and cool to his advances, experts said. Moreover, when other problems have derailed a relationship, they said, no little blue pill is going to make them magically disappear.

"I'd say that for 80 percent of men in a monogamous, stable relationship with a wife over many years, Viagra will bring relief and happiness," said Dr. Ira Sharlip, a San Francisco urologist and a founder of the Society for the Study of Impotence, a national organization that studies male sexual dysfunction. "As to what happens to the other 20 percent, nothing will surprise me," he added with a wry smile. For some men, Sharlip and others said, restored sexual function can create issues of fidelity that previously had been moot. A man suddenly empowered sexually after years of inactivity may go flying out the door looking for someone else if his partner doesn't share his enthusiasm or flatly rejects him. Or, as in the case of the retired auto dealer, even a spouse's enthusiasm and support might not satisfy a wanderlust penned up by years of self-doubt and frustration.

In Florida, with its high ratio of elderly men and women, retirement communities are buzzing with speculation on Viagra and its restorative promise. Just as in younger communities elsewhere, men are consulting doctors who are writing prescriptions for Viagra after a cursory medical checkup. But marriage and sex counselors are uneasy that men, whatever their age, are overhauling their sex lives without any guidelines to the possible earthquake they may introduce into their emotional lives.

Older married couples who have settled for intimacy without intercourse may represent a fairly wide population, experts say. Though it is considered normal and healthy for couples to remain sexually intimate long into their older years, it is not always possible to do so. A study of male impotence several years ago suggested that perhaps as many as one out of two American men over 40 experiences problems attaining or sustaining erections.

Some loving couples find sexual joy even when penetration is difficult or impossible. For them, Viagra is a virtual fountain of youth. "My husband took Viagra last night for the first time, and when my friends saw me this morning, they said I was positively sparkling," Dr. Marilyn Volker of Miami said. But Dr. Volker is a sex therapist, whose training and experience had already helped guide her husband, David, 56, to self-esteem and a sex life that was satisfying to them both after diabetes and a heart condition left him partly impotent. She conceded, however, that not all women have the skills to traverse the "eggshells" of male egos made fragile by impotence problems.

Orgasmic Disorders

Women who have never experienced orgasm often harbor negative sexual attitudes that cause anxiety and inhibit sexual response. Treatment in such cases might first address these attitudes.

Masters and Johnson use a couples-oriented approach in treating anorgasmic women. They begin with sensate focus exercises. Then, during genital massage and later during coitus, the woman guides her partner in the caresses and movements that she finds sexually exciting. Taking charge helps to free the woman, psychologically speaking, from the traditional stereotype of the passive, subordinate female role.

Masters and Johnson recommend a training position (see Figure 15.2 on page 474) that gives the man access to his partner's breasts and genitals. She can guide his hands to

"Many elderly couples are very active sexually, but there are those who have lost interest and haven't been intimate for years," said Dr. Elliot Klorfein, a Florida urologist, who has many retirees as patients. He said he has written "a zillion" prescriptions for Viagra in the last few weeks, and much of the demand is coming from retirees he's never treated before. "Typically, an older man is still interested in sex, and he jumps at an idea that here's a pill he can take orally that will make him a new man," Klorfein said. "The trouble is his wife is no longer interested. She may have problems that make intercourse uncomfortable for her, like a lack of lubrication or some ailment like arthritis. So her husband is all dressed up with nowhere to go."

Even middle-aged women might not be receptive to the sexual blandishments of a Viagra-assisted man looking to make up for lost time. Debbie Walker, 44, a divorced woman who manages the Turtle Bay Golf Club in West Palm Beach, bluntly said that she placed a low premium on sex and preferred men who shared her feelings. "A candlelight dinner with no sex afterward puts a big smile on my face," she said proudly. "I think a lot of women who feel comfortable with not having sex with their partners are going to be crushed when their man pops a pill and begins to demand it again."

A Miami man who also refused to be identified said that the injections he started last year gave him a new sexual lease on life. "It really hurt that my wife didn't share my excitement," he related. "Before, she complained about me starting. Now, she complains about me not finishing quickly enough."

Experts in the field also cautioned that men who have known years of anxiety and perhaps self-loathing because of inability to perform may enter the Viagra age with unrealistic expectations that an erection alone can transform them as lovers. Erections obviously make intercourse easier, physicians pointed out, but they do not guarantee sexual satisfaction. Older men who have not had intercourse for many years might be disappointed that orgasm lacks the punch it once had for them. "An older man can still ejaculate, but it is less explosive and much lower in volume than when he was younger," Dr. Harold M. Reed, a Miami urologist, explained.

Dr. Carlos Nazir, a urologist in Coral Gables, who says that his patients are Latin Americans with impotence problems, said that most men he treats are interested in improving their own sex life but not necessarily that of their wives. In many cases the men have not even confided to their spouses that they were seeking medical help. "This Viagra is going to cause a revolution because men who couldn't perform before are now not going to be content with handholding and cuddling," he said. He and others said that many impotent men compensated in the past for their perceived failings by becoming very attentive lovers. If they now turn sex into prolonged athletic contests, their partners might quickly rebel, they said.

"There are a lot of so-called happy marriages that have held together because he could not get an erection and couldn't wander," Nazir said. "Now, he suddenly doesn't have that problem holding him back." Nazir said he performed a penile implant on his father several years ago, an event that directly led to the breakup of his parents' marriage. "My father told me he had wanted a divorce for years, but his inability to perform with another woman kept him home," he said. "He's now married to a much younger woman and very happy."

Most therapists interviewed said that they were concerned that physicians appeared to be dispensing prescriptions for Viagra without giving patients guidance about how it may change their lives. "With or without an erection, the level of intimacy between partners often determines the level of satisfaction," remarked James H. Pitisci, a Miami psychologist and family therapist. "If the relationship is in trouble already, Viagra is not going to change much and may become just another area of conflict."

Source: Adapted from Jon Nordheimer (1998, May 10). Some couples may find Viagra a home wrecker. *The New York Times*, Section 9, p. 2.

Treating Erectile Disorder in the New Millennium.
Viagra and other drugs can help men with erectile disorder obtain and sustain erections that are adequate for sexual intercourse. Viagra has been a boon to their self-esteem as well as to their sex life.

show him the types of stimulation she enjoys. The genital play is *nondemanding.* The goals are to learn to provide and enjoy effective sexual stimulation, not to reach orgasm. The clitoris is not stimulated early, since doing so might produce a high level of stimulation before the woman is prepared.

After a number of occasions of genital play, the couple undertake coitus in the female-superior position (see Figure 15.3 on page 475). This position allows the woman freedom of movement and control over her genital sensations. She is told to regard the penis as her "toy." The couple engages in several sessions of deliberately slow thrusting to sensitize the woman to sensations produced by the penis and break the common counterproductive pattern of desperate, rapid thrusting.

Orgasm cannot be willed or forced. When a woman receives effective stimulation, feels free to focus on erotic sensations, and feels that nothing is being demanded of her,

figure 15.2

The Training Position for Nondemanding Stimulation of the Female Genitals. This position gives the man access to his partner's breasts and genitals. She can guide his hands to show him the types of stimulation she enjoys.

she will generally reach orgasm. Once the woman is able to attain orgasm in the female-superior position, the couple may extend their sexual repertoire to other positions.

Masters and Johnson prefer working with the couple in cases of anorgasmia, but other sex therapists prefer to begin working with the woman individually through masturbation (Barbach, 1975; Heiman & LoPiccolo, 1987). This approach assumes that the woman accepts masturbation as a therapy tool. Masturbation provides women with opportunities to learn about their own bodies at their own pace. It frees them of the need to rely on partners or to please partners. The sexual pleasure that they experience helps to counter lingering sexual anxieties. Although there is some variation among therapists, the following elements are commonly found in directed masturbation programs:

1. *Education.* The woman and her sex partner (if she has one) are educated about female sexuality.
2. *Self-exploration.* Self-exploration is encouraged as a way of increasing the woman's sense of body awareness. She might hold a mirror between her legs to locate her sexual anatomic features. Kegel exercises might be prescribed to help tone and strengthen the pubococcygeus (PC) muscle that surrounds the vagina and increase her awareness of genital sensations and sense of control.

figure 15.3

Coitus in the Female-Superior Position. In treatment of female orgasmic disorder, the couple undertake coitus in the female-superior position after a number of occasions of genital play. This position allows the woman freedom of movement and control over her genital sensations. She is told to regard the penis as her "toy." The couple engages in several sessions of deliberately slow thrusting to sensitize the woman to sensations produced by the penis and break the common counterproductive pattern of desperate, rapid thrusting.

3. *Self-massage.* Once the woman feels comfortable about exploring her body, she creates a relaxing setting for self-massage. She chooses a time and place where she is free from external distractions. She begins to explore the sensitivity of her body to touch, discovering and then repeating the caresses that she finds pleasurable. At first, self-massage is not concentrated on the genitals. It encompasses other sensitive parts of the body. She might incorporate stimulation of the nipples and breasts and then direct genital stimulation, focusing on the clitoral area and experimenting with hand movements. Nonalcohol-based oils and lotions may be used to enhance the sensuous quality of the massage and to provide lubrication for the external genitalia. Kegel exercises may also be performed during self-stimulation to increase awareness of vaginal sensations and increase muscle tension. Some women use their dominant hand to stimulate their breasts while the other hand massages the genitals. No two women approach masturbation in quite the same way. During the first few occasions, to prevent performance anxiety, the woman does not attempt to reach orgasm.

4. *Giving oneself permission.* The woman might be advised to practice assertive thoughts to dispel lingering guilt and anxiety about masturbation. For example, she might repeat to herself, "This is my body. I have a right to learn about my body and receive pleasure from it."

5. *Use of fantasy.* Arousal is heightened through the use of sexual images, fantasies, and fantasy aids, such as erotic written or visual materials.

6. *Allowing, not forcing, orgasm.* It might take weeks of masturbation to reach orgasm, especially for women who have never achieved orgasm. By focusing on her erotic sensations and fantasies, but not demanding orgasm, the woman lowers performance anxiety and creates the stimulating conditions needed to reach orgasm.

7. *Use of a vibrator.* A vibrator might be recommended to provide more intense stimulation, especially for women who find that manual stimulation is insufficient.

8. *Involvement of the partner.* Once the woman is capable of regularly achieving orgasm through masturbation, the focus might shift to the woman's sexual relationship with her partner. Nondemanding sensate focus exercises might be followed by nondemanding coitus. The female-superior position is often used. It enables the woman to control the depth, angle, and rate of thrusting. She thus ensures that she receives the kinds of stimulation she needs to reach orgasm.

The "Orgasm Pill" for Women

Erectile disorder in men may be seen as a vascular problem or disease (Goldstein, 1998). As women get older, they too experience a reduced flow of blood to the genital region, which means that the clitoris becomes less engorged during sexual arousal and may be connected with feelings of lessened sexual arousal overall. About 50% of adult women say that they have lost interest in sex or have difficulty becoming aroused (Kolata, 1998b).

Some researchers (and many women) have asked whether Viagra or similar drugs that enhance the flow of blood might also enhance the sexual experiences of women—when taken by the women, that is (Kolata, 1998a, 1998b). Some women report experiencing greater vaginal lubrication and stronger orgasms as a result of using Viagra. It turns out that a number of pharmaceutical companies are developing Viagra-like drugs for women. Pilot studies with 500 European women found the approach to be "remarkably effective" ("Women might mark millennium," 1998). The drugs promise not only to help trigger orgasm, but also to increase general sexual pleasure and enjoyment in women.

Truth or Fiction?
REVISITED

It is true that many sex therapists recommend masturbation as the treatment for women who have never been able to reach orgasm. Masturbation allows women (and men) to get in touch with their own sexual responses without relying on a partner. ■

Kaplan (1974) suggests a bridge maneuver to assist couples who are interested in making the transition from a combination of manual and coital stimulation to coital stimulation alone as a means for reaching orgasm. Manual stimulation during coitus is used until the woman senses that she is about to reach orgasm. Manual stimulation is then stopped, and the woman thrusts with her pelvis to provide the stimulation necessary to reach orgasm. Over time, the manual clitoral stimulation is discontinued earlier and earlier. Although some couples might prefer this "hands-off" approach to inducing orgasm, Kaplan points out that there is nothing wrong with combining manual stimulation and penile thrusting. There is no evidence that reliance on clitoral stimulation means that women are sexually immature. (Evidence has not borne out the theoretical psychoanalytic distinction between clitoral and vaginal orgasms.)

Our focus has been on sexual techniques, but it is worth noting that a combination of approaches that focus on sexual techniques and underlying interpersonal problems might be more effective than focusing on sexual techniques alone, at least for couples whose relationships are troubled (Killmann et al., 1987; LoPiccolo & Stock, 1986).

MALE ORGASMIC DISORDER Treatment of male orgasmic disorder generally focuses on increasing sexual stimulation and reducing performance anxiety (LoPiccolo & Stock, 1986). Masters and Johnson instruct the couple to practice sensate focus exercises for several days, during which the man makes no attempt to ejaculate. The couple is then instructed to bring the man to orgasm in any way they can, usually by the woman's stroking his penis. Once the husband can ejaculate in the woman's presence, she brings him to the point at which he is about to ejaculate. Then, in the female-superior position, she inserts the penis and thrusts vigorously to bring him to orgasm. If he loses the feeling that he is about to ejaculate, the process is repeated. Even if ejaculation occurs at the point of penetration, it often helps to break the pattern of inability to ejaculate within the vagina.

PREMATURE EJACULATION In the Masters and Johnson approach, sensate focus exercises are followed by practice in the training position shown in Figure 15.1. The woman teases her partner to erection and uses the **squeeze technique** when he indicates that he is about to ejaculate. She squeezes the tip of the penis, which temporarily prevents ejaculation. This process is repeated three or four times in a 15- to 20-minute session before the man purposely ejaculates.

In using the squeeze technique (which should be used only after personal instruction from a sex therapist), the woman holds the penis between the thumb and first two fingers of the same hand. The thumb presses against the frenulum. The fingers straddle the coronal ridge on the other side of the penis. Squeezing the thumb and forefingers together fairly hard for about 20 seconds (or until the man's urge to ejaculate passes) prevents

Squeeze technique A method for treating premature ejaculation whereby the tip of the penis is squeezed temporarily to prevent ejaculation.

476

ejaculation. The erect penis can withstand fairly strong pressure without discomfort, but the erection might be partially lost.

It is true that a man can be prevented from ejaculating by squeezing his penis when he feels that he is about to ejaculate. This is the so-called squeeze technique. ■

Truth or Fiction?
REVISITED

After two or three days of these sessions, Masters and Johnson have the couple begin coitus in the female-superior position because it creates less pressure to ejaculate. The woman inserts the penis. At first, she contains it without thrusting, allowing the man to get used to intravaginal sensations. If he signals that he is about to ejaculate, she lifts off and squeezes the penis. After some repetitions, she begins slowly to move backward and forward, lifting off and squeezing as needed. The man learns gradually to tolerate higher levels of sexual stimulation without ejaculating.

The alternate "stop-start" method for treating premature ejaculation was introduced by urologist James Semans (1956). The method can be applied to manual stimulation or coitus. For example, the woman can manually stimulate her partner until he is about to ejaculate. He then signals her to suspend sexual stimulation and allows his arousal to subside before stimulation is resumed. This process enables the man to recognize the cues that precede his point of ejaculatory inevitability, or "point of no return," and to tolerate longer periods of sexual stimulation. When the stop-start technique is applied to coitus, the couple begin with simple vaginal containment with no pelvic thrusting, preferably in the female-superior position. The man withdraws if he feels that he is about to ejaculate. As the man's sense of control increases, thrusting can begin, along with variations in coital positions. The couple again stop when the man signals that he is approaching ejaculatory inevitability.

BIOLOGICAL APPROACHES TO TREATMENT OF PREMATURE EJACULATION   Pilot studies have recently appeared in which drugs usually used for psychological problems have been helpful in treating premature ejaculation. One, clomipramine, is normally used to treat people with obsessive-compulsive disorder or schizophrenia. However, in a pilot study with 15 couples, low doses of clomipramine helped men to engage in coitus five times longer than usual without ejaculating (Althof, 1994). So-called antidepressant drugs have also been helpful in treatment of premature ejaculation (Forster & King, 1994; Waldinger et al., 1994; Wise, 1994).

Why do drugs that are used to treat psychological problems help with premature ejaculation? The psychological problems are frequently connected with imbalances in body chemistry, such as **neurotransmitters**—the chemical messengers of the brain. Neurotransmitters are also involved in other bodily functions, including ejaculation. The antidepressant drugs (fluoxetine, paroxetine, and sertraline) all work by increasing the action of the neurotransmitter serotonin. Serotonin, in turn, might inhibit the ejaculatory reflex (Assalian, 1994). It remains to be seen whether medications continue to show positive effects and compare their effectiveness with psychological sex therapy techniques.

Sexual Pain Disorders

DYSPAREUNIA   Dyspareunia, or painful intercourse, generally calls for medical intervention to ascertain and treat any underlying physical problems, such as genital infections, that might give rise to pain. When dyspareunia is caused by vaginismus, treatment of vaginismus through a behavioral approach, described below, may eliminate pain.

VAGINISMUS   Vaginismus is generally treated with behavioral exercises in which plastic vaginal dilators of increasing size are inserted to help relax the vaginal musculature. A gynecologist may first demonstrate insertion of the narrowest dilator. Later, the woman

Neurotransmitter A chemical that transmits messages from one brain cell to another.

herself practices insertion of wider dilators at home. The woman increases the size of the dilator as she becomes capable of tolerating insertion and containment (for 10 or 15 minutes) without discomfort or pain. The woman herself—not her partner or therapist—controls the pace of treatment (LoPiccolo & Stock, 1986). The woman's or her partner's fingers (first the littlest finger, then two fingers, and so on) can be used in place of the plastic dilators, with the woman controlling the speed and depth of penetration. When the woman is able to tolerate dilators (or fingers) that are equivalent in thickness to the penis, the couple may attempt coitus. Still, the woman should control insertion. Circumstances should be relaxed and nondemanding. The idea is to avoid resensitizing her to fears of penetration. Since vaginismus often occurs among women with a history of sexual trauma, such as rape or incest, treatment for the psychological effects of these experiences might also be in order (LoPiccolo & Stock, 1986).

Evaluation of Sex Therapy

Masters and Johnson (1970) reported an overall success rate of about 80% in treating sexual dysfunctions in their two-week intensive program. Some dysfunctions proved more difficult to treat than others. An analysis of treatment results from 1950 to 1977 showed success rates ranging from 67% for primary erectile disorder to 99% for vaginismus (Kolodny, 1981) (see Table 15.4). A follow-up of 226 initial successes after a five-year period showed that 16 people, or 7%, experienced a "treatment reversal."

Masters and Johnson's critics note that they followed up on a disappointingly small percentage (29%) of their sample over a five-year period. Thus, they may have seriously underestimated the actual number of treatment reversals (Adams, 1980; Zilbergeld & Evans, 1980). Zilbergeld and Evans (1980) also challenged their outcome measures. They argued that Masters and Johnson used a global measure of success that was not tied to specific criteria.

t a b l e   1 5 . 4

Outcomes of sex therapy at the Masters and Johnson Institute (1959–1977)			
Variables	**N**	**Failures**	**Successes**	**Success Rate (%)**
Primary (lifelong) erectile disorder	51	17	34	67
Secondary (acquired) erectile disorder	501	108	393	78
Premature ejaculation	432	17	415	96
Male orgasmic disorder	75	18	57	76
Male totals	1,059	160	899	85
Primary female orgasmic disorder	399	84	315	79
Secondary female orgasmic disorder	331	96	235	71
Vaginismus	83	1	82	99
Female totals	813	181	632	78
Combined totals	1,872	341	1531	82

Source: Adapted from Kolodny, R. C. (1981). Evaluating Sex Therapy: Process and Outcome at the Masters & Johnson Institute. *Journal of Sex Research, 17,* 301–318. Reprinted from *The Journal of Sex Research,* a publication of The Society for the Scientific Study of Sex; Mount Vernon, Iowa 42315 USA.

Masters and Johnson's sample might also have been biased in at least two ways. It consisted only of people who were willing and could afford to spend two weeks at their institute for full-time therapy. These people were better educated and more affluent than the general population. Masters and Johnson also denied treatment to a number of people whom they considered not "really interested" in changing. Thus, their final sample might have been limited to people who were highly motivated. So some of the success of treatment might have been due to the clients' high level of motivation rather than to the treatment they received. Finally, the absence of a control group prevents us from knowing whether factors extraneous to the treatment itself might have been responsible for the apparent success.

Other researchers have reported more modest levels of success in treating erectile disorder than those reported at the Masters and Johnson Institute (Barlow, 1986). Nevertheless, long-term follow-up evaluations support the general effectiveness of sex therapy for erectile disorder (Everaerd, 1993). Yet problems do recur in some cases and are not always easily overcome (Everaerd, 1993). Some couples cope with recurring problems by using the techniques that they learned during treatment, such as sensate focus exercises. The addition of biological treatments to the arsenal of treatments for erectile disorder has improved success rates to the point at which virtually all erection problems can be successfully treated in one way or another (Reinisch, 1990).

We lack controlled studies of treatments of male orgasmic disorder (Dekker, 1993). Other than the original Masters and Johnson studies, results have been generally disappointing, with most people showing only modest if any improvement (Dekker, 1993). New techniques in treating low sexual desire are also needed because the available techniques are often inadequate (Hawton, 1991).

Sex therapy approaches to treating vaginismus and premature ejaculation have produced more consistent levels of success (Beck, 1993; O'Donohue et al., 1993). Reported success in treating vaginismus has ranged as high as 80% (Hawton & Catalan, 1990) to 100% in Masters and Johnson's (1970) original research. Treatment of premature ejaculation has resulted in success rates above 90% using the squeeze technique or the stop-start method (Killmann & Auerbach, 1979). But there are few data on the long-term results of treatment for premature ejaculation (LoPiccolo & Stock, 1986). Nor do we know why these techniques are effective (Kinder & Curtiss, 1988). Because the squeeze technique carries with it some risk of discomfort, many therapists prefer using the stop-start method.

LoPiccolo and Stock (1986) found that 95% of a sample of 150 previously anorgasmic women were able to achieve orgasm through a directed masturbation program. About 85% of these women were able to reach orgasm through manual stimulation by their partners. Only about 40% were able to achieve orgasm during coitus, however. Christensen (1995) argues that prescribing masturbation in sex therapy can have the side effect of damaging the trust and openness that couples need for sexually rewarding relationships.

Generally speaking, couples-oriented treatment helps to facilitate orgasm during coitus but is no guarantee that women will become orgasmic during coitus (Heiman & LoPiccolo, 1987; LoPiccolo & Stock, 1986). Nevertheless, the goal of achieving orgasm through some form of genital stimulation with a cooperative partner, as through oral sex or by direct manual clitoral stimulation, is realistic for most women (LoPiccolo & Stock, 1986). Many couples who believe that it is important for the woman to reach orgasm during coitus are able to accomplish this end by combining direct clitoral stimulation with coital stimulation (LoPiccolo & Stock, 1986).

Researchers have come to understand some of the factors that predict success in sex therapy. Couples are generally more likely to benefit from sex therapy if they have good relationships and are highly motivated (Killmann et al., 1987; McCabe & Delaney, 1992). It should come as little surprise that the success of treatment often depends on the quality of the relationship. Nor is it surprising that people are generally more successful when they are more motivated to take full advantage of the treatments that they receive. It also appears that partners who acquire coping skills from therapy that they can use later, such as learning to respond to problems that arise by discussing them openly and by reinstating techniques learned in therapy, are generally better able to overcome recurrences of the problem. Sex therapy techniques might not be appropriate for people in whom profound personal problems or problems in the relationship underlie sexual dysfunctions (Pryde, 1989).

HOW DO YOU FIND A QUALIFIED SEX THERAPIST?

How would you find a sex therapist if you had a sexual dysfunction? You might find advertisements for "sex therapists" in the Yellow Pages. But beware. Most states do not restrict use of the term "sex therapist" to recognized professionals. In these states, anyone who wants to use the label may do so, including quacks and prostitutes.

Therefore, it is essential to determine that a sex therapist is a member of a recognized profession (such as psychology, social work, medicine, or marriage and family counseling) with training and supervision in sex therapy. Professionals are usually licensed or certified by their states. All states require licensing of psychologists and physicians, but some states do not license social workers or marriage counselors. If you have questions about the license laws in your state, contact your state's professional licensing board. The ethical standards of these professions prohibit practitioners from claiming expertise in sex therapy without suitable training.

If you are uncertain how to locate a qualified sex therapist in your area, you can obtain names of local practitioners from various sources, such as your university or college psychology department, health department, or counseling center; a local medical or psychological association; a family physician; or your instructor. You might also seek services from a sex therapy clinic affiliated with a local medical center or medical school in your area, many of which charge for services on a sliding scale, depending on your income level. You can also contact the American Association of Sex Educators, Counselors, and Therapists (AASECT), a professional organization that certifies sex therapists. They can provide you with the names of certified sex therapists in your area. They are located at 11 Dupont Circle, N.W., Washington, DC.

Ethical professionals are not annoyed or embarrassed if you ask them (1) what their profession is, (2) where they earned their advanced degree, (3) whether they are licensed or certified by the state, (4) their fees, (5) their plans for treatment, and (6) the nature of their training in human sexuality and sex therapy. If the therapist hems and haws, asks why you are asking such questions, or fails to provide a direct answer, beware.

Professionals are also restricted by the ethical principles of their professions from engaging in unethical practices, such as sexual relations with their clients. The nature of therapy creates an unequal power relationship between the therapist and the client. The therapist is perceived as an expert whose suggestions are likely to carry great authority. Clients may thus be vulnerable to exploitation by therapists who misuse their therapeutic authority. Let's be absolutely clear here: There is no therapeutic justification for a therapist to engage in sexual activity with a client. Any therapist who makes a sexual overture toward a client or tries to persuade a client to engage in sexual relations is acting unethically.

Reflections

■ How do sex therapy programs help people to deal with pressure to perform? How can you adapt this knowledge to enhance your own sexual pleasure?

■ If you had a sexual dysfunction, do you think you would be willing to participate in sex therapy? Why or why not? Do some techniques seem more acceptable to you than others? Explain.

■ How would you go about finding a qualified sex therapist if you needed one?

TYPES OF SEXUAL DYSFUNCTIONS

Sexual dysfunctions are difficulties in becoming sexually aroused or reaching orgasm.

Sexual Desire Disorders

These disorders involve dysfunctions in sexual desire, interest, or drive, in which the person experiences a lack of sexual desire or an aversion to genital sexual contact.

Sexual Arousal Disorders

In men, sexual arousal disorders involve recurrent difficulty in achieving or sustaining erections sufficient to successfully engage in sexual intercourse. In women, they typically involve failure to become sufficiently lubricated.

Orgasmic Disorders

Women are more likely to encounter difficulties reaching orgasm. Men are more likely to have premature ejaculation.

Sexual Pain Disorders

These disorders include dyspareunia and vaginismus.

ORIGINS OF SEXUAL DYSFUNCTIONS

Many sexual dysfunctions involve the interaction of organic and psychological factors.

Organic Causes

Fatigue can lead to erectile disorder in men and to orgasmic disorder and dyspareunia in women. Dyspareunia often reflects vaginal infections and STDs. Organic factors are believed to be involved in more than 50% of cases of erectile disorder. Medications and other drugs can also impair sexual functioning.

Psychosocial Causes

Psychosocial factors that are connected with sexual dysfunctions include cultural influences, psychosexual trauma, a gay sexual orientation, ineffectual sexual techniques, emotional factors, problems in the relationship, psychological conflict, lack of sexual skills, irrational beliefs, and performance anxiety. Children who are reared in sexually repressive cultural or home environments might learn to respond to sex with feelings of anxiety and shame, rather than sexual arousal and pleasure. Many people do not acquire sexual competencies because of a lack of opportunity to acquire knowledge and experience, even within marriage. Irrational beliefs and attitudes such as excessive needs for approval and perfectionism can also contribute to sexual problems. Performance anxiety might place a dysfunctional individual in a spectator rather than performer role.

TREATMENT OF SEXUAL DYSFUNCTIONS

Sex therapy aims to directly modify dysfunctional behavior by changing self-defeating beliefs and attitudes, fostering sexual skills and knowledge, enhancing sexual communication, and suggesting behavioral exercises to enhance sexual stimulation while reducing performance anxiety.

The Masters and Johnson Approach

Masters and Johnson pioneered the direct, behavioral approach to treating sexual dysfunctions. They employ a male-female therapy team during an in-residence program, which focuses on the couple as the unit of treatment. Sensate focus exercises are used to enable the partners to give each other pleasure in a nondemanding situation.

The Helen Singer Kaplan Approach

Kaplan's psychosexual therapy combines behavioral and psychoanalytic methods.

Sexual Desire Disorders

Some sex therapists help to kindle the sexual appetites of people with inhibited sexual desire by prescribing self-stimulation exercises combined with erotic fantasies.

Sexual Arousal Disorders

Men and women with impaired sexual arousal receive sexual stimulation from their partners under relaxed circumstances so that anxiety does not inhibit their natural reflexes. Biological treatments such as the drug Viagra are also used to treat male erectile disorder.

Orgasmic Disorders

Masters and Johnson use a couples-oriented approach in treating anorgasmic women. Other sex therapists prefer a program of directed masturbation to enable women to learn about their own bodies at their own pace and free them of the need to rely on partners or please partners. Premature ejaculation is usually treated with the squeeze technique or the stop-start method. Biological treatment methods for female orgasmic disorder and premature ejaculation are under development.

Sexual Pain Disorders

Dyspareunia or painful intercourse is generally treated with medical intervention. Vaginismus is generally treated with plastic vaginal dilators of increasing size.

Evaluation of Sex Therapy

The success of sex therapy has varied with the type of sexual dysfunction treated.

chapter

16

Sexually Transmitted Infections

outline

TRUTH OR FICTION?

AN EPIDEMIC

WHAT DO YOU SAY NOW?
Talking with Your Partner about STIs

QUESTIONNAIRE:
STI Attitude Scale

BACTERIAL INFECTIONS

Gonorrhea

Syphilis

Chlamydia

Other Bacterial Infections

VAGINAL INFECTIONS

Bacterial Vaginosis

Candidiasis

Trichomoniasis

VIRAL INFECTIONS

HIV Infection and AIDS

A WORLD OF DIVERSITY:
Ethnicity and AIDS in the United States

IN THE NEW MILLENNIUM:
HIV Infection and AIDS—A Mixed Picture

Herpes

Viral Hepatitis

Genital Warts

Molluscum Contagiosum

ECTOPARASITIC INFESTATIONS

Pediculosis

Scabies

PREVENTION OF STIs: IT'S MORE THAN SAFER SEX

A CLOSER LOOK:
Sources of Help

SUMMING UP

Truth or Fiction **?**

_____ Most women who contract gonorrhea do not develop symptoms.

_____ Christopher Columbus brought more than beads, blankets, and tobacco back to Europe from the New World: He also brought syphilis.

_____ Gonorrhea and syphilis can be contracted from toilet seats in public rest rooms.

_____ If a syphilitic chancre (sore) goes away by itself, the infection does not require medical treatment.

_____ Men too can develop vaginal infections.

_____ As you are reading this page, you are engaged in search-and-destroy missions against foreign agents within your body.

_____ Most people who are infected by HIV remain symptom-free and appear healthy for years.

_____ Sub-Saharan Africa accounts for about 90% of the world's deaths from AIDS.

_____ Genital herpes can be transmitted only during flare-ups of the infection.

harold and Carin, both 20, have been dating for several months. They feel strong sexual attraction toward each other but have hesitated to become sexually intimate because of fears about AIDS. Harold believes that using condoms is no guarantee against infection and wants the two of them to be tested for HIV, the virus that causes AIDS. Carin has resisted undergoing an HIV test, partly because she feels insulted that Harold fears that she may be infected and, frankly, partly in fear of the test results. She has heard that symptoms might not develop for years after infection. She wonders whether she might have been infected by one of the men with whom she had slept in the past.

Keisha has genital herpes. A 19-year-old pre-law student, she has had no recurrences since the initial outbreak two years earlier. But she knows that herpes is a lifelong infection and may recur periodically from time to time. She also knows that she may inadvertently pass the herpes virus along to her sex partners, even to the man she eventually marries. She has begun thinking seriously about Steve, a man she has been dating for the past month. She would like to tell him that she has herpes before they become sexually intimate. Yet she fears that telling him might scare him off.

José, 21, a math and computer science major, is planning a career in computer operations, hoping one day to run the computer systems for a large corporation. He lives off-campus with several of his buddies in a run-down house they've dubbed the "Nuclear Dumpsite." He has been dating Maria, a theater major, for several months. They have begun having sexual relations and have practiced "safer sex"—at least most of the time. During the past week he noticed a burning sensation while urinating. It seems to have passed now, so he figures that it was probably nothing to worry about. But he's not sure and wonders whether he should see a doctor.

Harold, Carin, Keisha, and José express some of the fears and concerns of a generation of young people who are becoming sexually active at a time when the threat of AIDS and other STIs (**sexually transmitted infections**) hangs over every sexual decision.

AIDS is indeed a scary thing, a very scary thing. But AIDS is only one of many STIs, though certainly the most deadly and frightening. Nearly every time you pick up a newspaper or turn on the radio or TV, you hear about AIDS, yet other STIs pose much wider threats (Stolberg, 1998b). In a study of more than 16,000 students on 19 U.S. college campuses, HIV (the virus that causes AIDS) was found in 30 blood samples (Gayle et al., 1990), or 0.2% of the students in the sample. *Chlamydia trachomatis* (the bacterium that causes chlamydia) was found in 1 sample in 10, or 10% of the college population! *Human papilloma virus* (HPV) (the organism that causes genital warts) is estimated to be present in 20% of Americans over the age of 12 and in at least one-third of college women (Cannistra & Niloff, 1996). A study at Rutgers University found HPV among *60%* of female students (Ho, 1998; Stolberg, 1998b).

College students have become reasonably well versed about AIDS. However, many are unaware that chlamydia can go undetected for years. Moreover, if it is left untreated, it can cause pelvic inflammation and infertility. Many, perhaps most, students are ignorant about HPV,

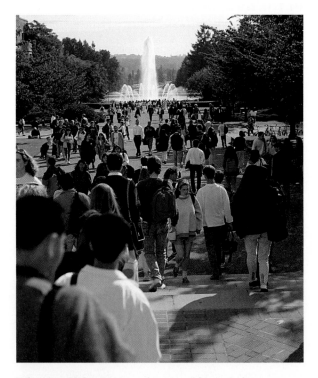

Who's at Risk? More and more evidence today suggests that young people are more sexually active than ever before, making it more important than ever that they be aware of their risks and take responsibility for their sexual health.

which is linked to cervical cancer (Cannistra & Niloff, 1996; Ho, 1998). Yet the Federal Centers for Disease Control and Prevention (CDC) estimate that as many as 1 million new cases of HPV infection occur each year in the United States—more than syphilis, genital herpes, and AIDS combined (Penn, 1993). Whereas about 1 million Americans are thought to be infected with HIV, about 56 million are infected with other STI-causing viruses, such as those causing genital warts, herpes, and hepatitis (Barringer, 1993a; "Huge gains," 1998). *None of this is intended to downplay the threat of AIDS. AIDS is lethal, and one case is one case too many.*

STIs are transmitted through sexual means, such as vaginal or anal intercourse or oral sex. They were formerly called *sexually transmitted diseases* (STDs) and, before that, *venereal diseases* (VDs)—after Venus, the Roman goddess of love.

Some STIs can be spread (and often are) through nonsexual contact as well. For example, AIDS and viral hepatitis may be spread by sharing contaminated needles. And yes, a few STIs (such as "crabs") may be picked up from bedding or other objects, such as moist towels, that harbor the infectious organisms that cause these STIs.

AN EPIDEMIC

STIs are rampant. The World Health Organization (WHO) estimates that at least 333 million people around the world are stricken with curable STIs each year (WHO, 1995). The United States is believed to have the highest rate of infection by STIs in the industrialized world ("CDC tackles surge," 1998). In a recent year, for example, 150 cases of gonorrhea were reported per 100,000 people in the United States, compared with 18.6 per 100,000 in Canada and 3 per 100,000 in Sweden.

In the United States, 10 to 12 million new cases of STIs are reported to disease control centers each year (Stolberg, 1998b), including 2.5 million adolescents (about one in six). At least one in four Americans is likely to contract an STI at some point in life (Barringer, 1993a). Two cases in three occur in people under the age of 25. Yet many young people remain largely uninformed about the dangers of STIs.

Some readers have STIs and do not realize it. Ignorance is not bliss, however. Some STIs might not produce noticeable symptoms, but they can be harmful if left untreated. STIs can also be painful and, in the cases of AIDS and advanced syphilis, lethal. An estimated 100,000 to 150,000 women become infertile each year because of STIs that are spreading through the reproductive system (Barringer, 1993a). Overall, STIs are believed to account for 15% to 30% of cases of infertility among women. In addition to their biological effects, STIs exact an emotional toll and strain relationships to the breaking point.

Why the surge in the incidence of STIs? One reason is the increased numbers of young people who engage in coitus. Many of them fail to use latex condoms consistently, if at all (Kamb et al., 1998). Some people do not use condoms because the woman is on the pill. Although birth-control pills are reliable methods of contraception, they do not prevent the spread of STIs. Another reason is that some infections, such as chlamydia, often have no symptoms. Therefore, some infected individuals unwittingly pass them along to others. Other risk factors include early sexual involvement and sex with multiple partners. Drug use is also associated with an increased risk of STIs. People who abuse drugs are more likely than others to engage in risky sexual practices (Lowry et al., 1994). Moreover, certain forms of drug use, such as needle sharing, can directly transmit infectious organisms such as HIV.

Education is critical to curtailing the STI epidemic among young people (Kamb et al., 1998). STI instruction is intended to promote responsible sexual decision making and to alter risky behavior patterns. However, education might not be enough.

Sexually transmitted infections (STIs) Infections that are communicated through sexual contact. Some, such as HIV/AIDS, can also be transmitted in other ways.)

what do you say now?

Talking with Your Partner about STIs

Many people find it hard to talk about STIs with their partners. As one young woman explained:

It's one thing to talk about being responsible . . . and a much harder thing to do it at the very moment. It's just plain hard to say to someone I am feeling very erotic with, "Oh, yes, before we go any further, can we have a conversation about STI?" It's hard to imagine murmuring into someone's ear at a time of passion, "Would you mind slipping on this condom or using this cream just in case one of us has STI?" Yet it seems awkward to bring it up any sooner if it's not clear between us that we want to make love. (Boston Women's Health Book Collective, 1992)

Because talking about STIs with sex partners can be awkward, many people wing it. They assume that their partners are free of STIs and hope for the best. Some people act as if not talking about AIDS and other STIs will cause these problems to go away. But the microbes that cause AIDS, herpes, chlamydia, genital warts, and other STIs will not simply go away by ignoring them.

Imagine yourself in this situation: You've gone out with Chris a few times, and you're keenly attracted. Chris is attractive, bright, and witty; shares some of your attitudes; and, all in all, is a powerful turn-on. Now the evening is winding down. You've been cuddling, and you think you know where things are heading.

Something clicks in your mind! You realize that as wonderful as Chris is, you don't know every place Chris has "been." As healthy as Chris looks and acts, you don't know what's swimming around in Chris's bloodstream. Chris might not know either. In a moment of pent-up desire, Chris might also (how should we put this delicately?) lie about not being infected or about past sexual experiences.

What do you say now? How do you protect yourself without turning Chris off? Write some possible responses in the spaces provided and then keep reading for more.

1. _____
_____
_____

2. _____
_____

3. _____
_____

Ah, the clumsiness! If you ask about condoms or STIs, it is sort of making a verbal commitment to have sexual relations, and perhaps you're not exactly sure that's what your partner intends. Even if it's clear that's where you're heading, will you seem too straightforward? Will you kill the romance? The spontaneity of the moment? Sure you might—Life has its risks. But which is riskier: an awkward moment or being infected with a fatal illness?

Let's put it another way: Are you *really* willing to die for sex? Given that few verbal responses are perfect, here are some things you can try:

1. You might say something like this: "I've brought something, and I'd like to use it . . . " (referring to a condom).
2. Or you can say, "I know this is a bit clumsy [you are assertively expressing a feeling and asking permission to pursue a clumsy topic; Chris is likely to respond with "That's okay" or "Don't worry—what is it?"] but the world isn't as safe as it used to be, and I think we should talk about what we're going to do."

The point is that your partner hasn't been living in a cave. Your partner is also aware of the dangers of STIs, especially of AIDS, and ought to be working with you to make things safe and unpressured. If your partner is pressing for unsafe sex and is inconsiderate of your feelings and concerns, you need to reassess whether you want to be with this person. We think you can do better.

Young people must also want to practice prevention and risk-reduction strategies if education is to have a meaningful effect on their behavior (Yarber & Parillo, 1992).

Reflections

■ Does concern about STIs play a role in your life? If not, why not? (Are you fooling yourself?) If so, how?
■ What problems would you anticipate in discussing concern over STIs with a dating partner? Would these concerns prevent you from talking about STIs? Why or why not?
■ Would you be insulted if a partner asked you whether you were infected with any STIs? Why or why not?

STI Attitude Scale

Do your attitudes toward sexually transmitted infections lead you to take risks that increase the chances of contracting one? The STI Attitude Scale (Yarber et al., 1989) was constructed to measure the attitudes of young adults toward STIs and to provide to insight into these questions.

To complete the questionnaire, read each statement carefully. Record your reactions by circling the letters according to this code:

SA = Strongly Agree
A = Agree
U = Undecided
D = Disagree
SD = Strongly Disagree

Interpret your responses by referring to the scoring key in the Appendix.

1. How one uses her or his sexuality has nothing to do with STI.

   SA A U D SD

2. It is easy to use the prevention methods that reduce one's chances of getting an STI.

   SA A U D SD

3. Responsible sex is one of the best ways of reducing the risk of STI.

   SA A U D SD

4. Getting early medical care is the main key to preventing harmful effects of STI.

   SA A U D SD

5. Choosing the right sex partner is important in reducing the risk of getting an STI.

   SA A U D SD

6. A high rate of STI should be a concern for all people.

   SA A U D SD

7. People with an STI have a duty to get their sex partners to medical care.

   SA A U D SD

8. The best way to get a sex partner to STI treatment is to take him or her to the doctor with you.

   SA A U D SD

9. Changing one's sex habits is necessary once the presence of an STI is known.

   SA A U D SD

10. I would dislike having to follow the medical steps for treating an STI.

    SA A U D SD

11. If I were sexually active, I would feel uneasy doing things before and after sex to prevent getting an STI.

    SA A U D SD

12. If I were sexually active, it would be insulting if a sex partner suggested we use a condom to avoid STI.

    SA A U D SD

13. I dislike talking about STI with my peers.

    SA A U D SD

14. I would be uncertain about going to the doctor unless I was sure I really had an STI.

    SA A U D SD

15. I would feel that I should take my sex partner with me to a clinic if I thought I had an STI.

    SA A U D SD

16. It would be embarrassing to discuss STI with one's partner if one were sexually active.

    SA A U D SD

17. If I were to have sex, the chance of getting an STI makes me uneasy about having sex with more than one person.

    SA A U D SD

18. I like the idea of sexual abstinence (not having sex) as the best way of avoiding STI.

    SA A U D SD

19. If I had an STI, I would cooperate with public health persons to find the sources of STI.

    SA A U D SD

20. If I had an STI, I would avoid exposing others while I was being treated.

    SA A U D SD

21. I would have regular STI checkups if I were having sex with more than one partner.

    SA A U D SD

22. I intend to look for STI signs before deciding to have sex with anyone.

    SA A U D SD

(continued)

STI Attitude Scale *(continued)*

23. I will limit my sex activity to just one partner because of the chances I might get an STI.

    SA A U D SD

24. I will avoid sexual contact any time I think there is even a slight chance of getting an STI.

    SA A U D SD

25. The chance of getting an STI would not stop me from having sex.

    SA A U D SD

26. If I had a chance, I would support community efforts toward controlling STI.

    SA A U D SD

27. I would be willing to work with others to make people aware of STI problems in my town.

    SA A U D SD

Source: Yarber, W. L., Torabi, M. R., & Veenker, C. H. (1989). Development of a three-component sexually transmitted diseases attitude scale. *Journal of Sex Education & Therapy, 15,* 36–49. Reprinted with permission.

BACTERIAL INFECTIONS

Without the one-celled microorganisms that we call **bacteria,** there would be no wine. Bacteria are essential to fermentation. They also play vital roles in our bodies' digestive systems. Unfortunately, bacteria also cause many diseases, such as pneumonia, tuberculosis, and meningitis—along with the common STIs gonorrhea, syphilis, and chlamydia.

Gonorrhea

Gonorrhea—also known as "the clap" or "the drip"—was once the most widespread STI in the United States, but the rate of infection declined substantially during the 1980s. About 800,000 new cases of gonorrhea are now reported each year ("CDC tackles surge," 1998). Most new cases are contracted by people between the ages of 20 and 24.

Gonorrhea is caused by the gonococcus bacterium (see Table 16.1). A penile discharge that was probably gonorrhea is described in ancient Egyptian and Chinese writings and is mentioned in the Old Testament (Leviticus 15). Ancient Jews and Greeks assumed that the discharge was an involuntary loss of seminal fluid. In about 400 B.C., the Greek physician Hippocrates suggested that the loss stemmed from excessive sex or "worship" of Aphrodite (whom the Romans would later rename Venus). The term *gonorrhea* is credited to the Greek physician Galen, who lived in the second century A.D. In 1879, Albert L. S. Neisser identified the gonococcus bacterium that bears his name: *Neisseria gonorrhoeae.*

TRANSMISSION Gonococcal bacteria require a warm, moist environment like that found along the mucous membranes of the urinary tract in both genders or the cervix in women. Outside the body, they die in about a minute. There is no evidence that gonorrhea can be picked up from public toilet seats or by touching dry objects. In rare cases, gonorrhea is contracted by contact with a moist, warm towel or sheet that had been used immediately beforehand by an infected person. Gonorrhea is almost always transmitted by unprotected vaginal, oral, or anal sexual activity or from mother to newborn during delivery.

Bacteria Plural of *bacterium,* a class of one-celled microorganisms that have no chlorophyll and can give rise to many illnesses. (From the Greek *baktron,* meaning "stick," referring to the fact that many bacteria are rod-shaped.)

Gonorrhea An STI that is caused by the *Neisseria gonorrhoeae* bacterium and characterized by a discharge and burning urination. Left untreated, gonorrhea can give rise to pelvic inflammatory disease (PID) and infertility. (From the Greek *gonos,* meaning "seed," and *rheein,* meaning "to flow," referring to the fact that in ancient times, the penile discharge characteristic of the illness was erroneously interpreted as a loss of seminal fluid.)

t a b l e   1 6 . 1

Causes, modes of transmission, symptoms, diagnosis, and
treatment of major sexually transmitted infections (STIs)

STI and Pathogen	Modes of Transmission	Symptoms	Diagnosis	Treatment
Bacterial Diseases				
Gonorrhea ("clap," "drip"): Gonococcus bacterium (*Neisseria gonorrhoeae*)	Transmitted by vaginal, oral, or anal sexual activity or from mother to newborn during delivery.	In men, yellowish, thick penile discharge, burning urination. In women, increased vaginal discharge, burning urination, irregular menstrual bleeding (most women show no early symptoms).	Clinical inspection, culture of sample discharge.	Antibiotics: ceftriaxone, ciprofloaxin, cefixime, ofloxacin
Syphilis: *Treponema pallidum*	Transmitted by vaginal, oral, or anal sexual activity or by touching an infectious chancre.	In primary stage, a hard, round painless chancre or sore appears at site of infection within 2 to 4 weeks. May progress through secondary, latent, and tertiary stages, if left untreated.	Primary-stage syphilis is diagnosed by clinical examination and by examination of fluid from a chancre in a dark-field test. Secondary-stage syphilis is diagnosed by blood test (the VDRL).	Penicillin, or doxycycline, tetracycline, or erythromycin for nonpregnant penicillin-allergic patients
Chlamydia and non-gonococcal urethritis (NGU): *Chlamydia trachomatis* bacterium; NGU in men may also be caused by *Ureaplasma urealyticum* bacterium and other pathogens	Transmitted by vaginal, oral, or anal sexual activity; to the eye by touching one's eyes after touching the genitals of an infected partner; or to newborns passing through the birth canal of an infected mother.	In women, frequent and painful urination, lower abdominal pain and inflammation, and vaginal discharge (but most women are symptom-free). In men, symptoms are similar to but milder than those of gonorrhea—burning or painful urination, slight penile discharge (most men are also asymptomatic). Sore throat may indicate infection from oral-genital contact.	The Abbott Testpack analyzes a cervical smear in women; in men, an extract of fluid from the penis is analyzed.	Antibiotics: azithromycin, doxycycline, ofloxacin, amoxicillin
Vaginitis				
Bacterial vaginosis: *Gardnerella vaginalis* bacterium and others	Can arise by overgrowth of organisms in vagina, allergic reactions, etc.; also transmitted by sexual contact.	In women, thin, foul-smelling vaginal discharge. Irritation of genitals and mild pain during urination. In men, inflammation of penile foreskin and glans, urethritis, and cystitis. May be asymptomatic in both genders.	Culture and examination of bacterium.	Metronidazole, clindamycin

(continued)

t a b l e　1 6 . 1　*(c o n t i n u e d)*

Causes, modes of transmission, symptoms, diagnosis, and treatment of major sexually transmitted infections (STIs)

STI and Pathogen	Modes of Transmission	Symptoms	Diagnosis	Treatment
Candidiasis (moniliasis, thrush, "yeast infection"): *Candida albicans*—a yeast-like fungus	Can arise by over-growth of fungus in vagina; may also be transmitted by sexual contact or by sharing a washcloth with an infected person.	In women, vulval itching; white, cheesy, foul-smelling discharge; soreness or swelling of vaginal and vulval tissues. In men, itching and burning on urination, or a reddening of the penis.	Diagnosis usually made on basis of symptoms.	Single dose oral fluconazole, or suppositories of miconazole, clotrimazole, or butaconazole; modification of use of other medicines and chemical agents; keeping infected area dry
Trichomoniasis ("trich"): *Trichomonas vaginalis*—a protozoan (one-celled animal)	Almost always transmitted sexually.	In women, foamy, yellowish, odorous vaginal discharge; itching or burning sensation in vulva. Many women are asymptomatic. In men, usually asymptomatic, but mild urethritis is possible.	Microscopic examination of a smear of vaginal secretions or of culture of the sample (latter method preferred).	Metronidazole
Viral Diseases				
Oral herpes: Herpes simplex virus–type 1 (HSV-1)	Touching, kissing, sexual contact with sores or blisters; sharing cups, towels, toilet seats.	Cold sores or fever blisters on the lips, mouth, or throat; herpetic sores on the genitals.	Usually clinical inspection.	Over-the-counter lip balms, cold-sore medications; check with your physician, however.
Genital herpes: Herpes simplex virus–type 2 (HSV-2)	Almost always by means of vaginal, oral, or anal sexual activity; most contagious during active outbreaks of the disease.	Painful, reddish bumps around the genitals, thighs, or buttocks; in women, may also be in the vagina or on the cervix. Bumps become blisters or sores that fill with pus and break, shedding viral particles. Other possible symptoms: burning urination, fever, aches and pains, swollen glands; in women, vaginal discharge.	Clinical inspection of sores; culture and examination of fluid drawn from the base of a genital sore.	There is no cure, but the antiviral drugs acyclovir, famciclovir, valacyclovir may provide relief and prompt healing over; people with herpes often profit from counseling and group support as well.
Viral Hepatitis: hepatitis A, B, C, and D type viruses	Sexual contact, especially involving the anus (especially hepatitis A); contact with infected fecal matter; transfusion of contaminated blood (especially hepatitis B and C).	Ranges from being asymptomatic to mild flulike symptoms and more severe symptoms, including fever, abdominal pain, vomiting, and "jaundiced" (yellowish) skin and eyes.	Examination of blood for hepatitis antibodies; liver biopsy.	Treatment usually involves bed rest, intake of fluids, and, sometimes, antibiotics to ward off bacterial infections that might take hold because of lowered resistance. Alpha interferon is sometimes used in treating hepatitis C.

STI and Pathogen	Modes of Transmission	Symptoms	Diagnosis	Treatment
Acquired immunodeficiency syndrome (AIDS): Human immunodeficiency virus (HIV)	HIV is transmitted by sexual contact; by infusion with contaminated blood; from mother to fetus during pregnancy, or through childbirth or breast-feeding.	Infected people may initially be asymptomatic or develop mild flulike symptoms, which may then disappear for many years before the development of full-blown AIDS. Full-blown AIDS is symptomized by fever, weight loss, fatigue, diarrhea, and opportunistic infections such as rare forms of cancer (Kaposi's sarcoma) and pneumonia (PCP).	Blood, saliva, or urine tests detect HIV antibodies. More expensive tests confirm the presence of the virus (HIV) itself. The diagnosis of AIDS is usually made on the basis of antibodies, a low count of CD4 cells, and/or the presence of indicator diseases.	There is no cure for HIV infection or AIDS. Treatment is a combination of antiviral drugs including a protease inhibitor and nucleoside analogues such as AZT.
Genital warts (venereal warts): Human papilloma virus (HPV)	Transmission is by sexual and other forms of contact, such as with infected towels or clothing	Appearance of painless warts, often resembling cauliflowers, on the penis, foreskin, scrotum, or internal urethra in men or on the vulva, labia, wall of the vagina, or cervix in women. May occur around the anus and in the rectum of both genders.	Clinical inspection	Methods include cryotherapy (freezing), podophyllin, trichloroacetic acid (TCA) or bichloroacetic acid (BCA), burning, surgical removal.

Ectoparasitic Infestations

STI and Pathogen	Modes of Transmission	Symptoms	Diagnosis	Treatment
Pediculosis ("crabs"): *Phthirus pubis* (pubic lice)	Transmission is by sexual contact, or by contact with an infested towel, sheet, or toilet seat	Intense itching in pubic area and other hairy regions to which lice can attach.	Clinical examination	Lindane (brand name: Kwell)—a prescription shampoo; nonprescription medications containing pyrethrins or piperonal butoxide (brand names: RID, Triple X)
Scabies: *Sarcoptes scabiei*	Transmission is by sexual contact or by contact with infested clothing or bed linen, towels, and other fabrics.	Intense itching; reddish lines on skin where mites have burrowed in; welts and pus-filled blisters in affected areas.	Clinical inspection	Lindane (Kwell)

Source: Adapted from Rathus, S. A. (1999). *Psychology in the new millennium,* 7th ed. Fort Worth, TX: Harcourt Brace College Publishers.

figure 16.1

Gonorrheal Discharge.
Gonorrhea in the male often causes a thick, yellowish, pus-like discharge from the penis.

A person who performs fellatio on an infected man may develop **pharyngeal gonorrhea,** which produces a throat infection. Mouth-to-mouth kissing and cunnilingus are less likely to spread gonorrhea. The eyes provide a good environment for the bacterium. Therefore, a person whose hands come into contact with infected genitals and who inadvertently touches his or her eyes afterward may infect them. Babies have contracted gonorrhea of the eyes **(ophthalmia neonatorum)** when passing through the birth canals of infected mothers. This disorder can cause blindness but has become rare because the eyes of newborns are treated routinely with silver nitrate or penicillin ointment, which are toxic to gonococcal bacteria.

A gonorrheal infection may be spread from the penis to the partner's rectum during anal intercourse. A cervical gonorrheal infection can be spread to the rectum if an infected woman and her partner follow vaginal intercourse with anal intercourse. Gonorrhea is less likely to be spread by vaginal discharge than by penile discharge.

Gonorrhea is highly contagious. Women stand nearly a 50% chance of contracting gonorrhea after one exposure. Men have a 25% risk of infection (Cates, 1998). The risks to women are apparently greater because women retain infected semen in the vagina. The risk of infection increases with repeated exposure.

SYMPTOMS   Most men experience symptoms within two to five days after infection. Symptoms include a penile discharge that is clear at first. Within a day, it turns yellow to yellow-green, thickens, and becomes puslike (see Figure 16.1). The urethra becomes inflamed, and urination is accompanied by a burning sensation. Thirty percent to 40% of males have swelling and tenderness in the lymph glands of the groin. Inflammation and other symptoms may become chronic if left untreated.

The initial symptoms of gonorrhea usually abate within a few weeks without treatment, leading people to think of gonorrhea as being no worse than a bad cold. However, the gonococcus bacterium will usually continue to damage the body even though the early symptoms fade.

In women, the primary site of the infection is the cervix, where it causes **cervicitis.** Cervicitis may cause a yellowish to yellow-green puslike discharge that irritates the vulva. If the infection spreads to the urethra, women may also note burning urination. *About 80% of the women who contract gonorrhea are* **asymptomatic** *during the early stages of the disease, however.* Unfortunately, therefore, many infected women do not seek treatment until more serious symptoms develop. They may also innocently infect another sex partner.

When gonorrhea is not treated early, it may spread through the urogenital systems in both genders and strike the internal reproductive organs. In men, it can lead to **epididymitis,** which can cause fertility problems. Swelling and feelings of tenderness or pain in the scrotum are the principal symptoms of epididymitis. Fever may also be present. Occasionally, the kidneys are affected.

In women, the bacterium can spread through the cervix to the uterus, fallopian tubes, ovaries, and other parts of the abdominal cavity, causing **pelvic inflammatory disease (PID).** Symptoms of PID include cramps, abdominal pain and tenderness, cervical tenderness and discharge, irregular menstrual cycles, coital pain, fever, nausea, and vomiting. PID may also be asymptomatic. Whether or not women experience symptoms, PID can cause scarring that blocks the fallopian tubes, leading to infertility. PID is a serious illness that requires aggressive treatment with antibiotics. Surgery might be needed to remove infected tissue. Unfortunately, many women become aware of a gonococcal infection only when they develop PID. These consequences are all the more unfortunate because gonorrhea, when diagnosed and treated early, clears up rapidly in over 90% of cases.

Truth or Fiction?
REVISITED

It is true that most women who contract gonorrhea do not develop symptoms. However, they may develop quite serious health problems later on. ■

DIAGNOSIS AND TREATMENT   Diagnosis of gonorrhea involves clinical inspection of the genitals by a physician (e.g., a family practitioner, urologist, or gynecologist) and the culturing and examination of a sample of genital discharge.

Antibiotics are the standard treatment for gonorrhea. Penicillin was once the favored antibiotic, but the rise of penicillin-resistant strains of *Neisseria gonorrhoeae* has required that alternative antibiotics be used (Cates, 1998). An injection of the antibiotic ceftriaxone is often recommended. Other antibiotics that are used to treat gonorrhea include ciprofloxaxin, cefixime, and ofloxacin. Since gonorrhea and chlamydia often occur together, people who are infected with gonorrhea are usually also treated for chlamydia through the use of another antibiotic (Cates, 1998). Sex partners of people with gonorrhea should also be examined.

Syphilis

No society wanted to be associated with the origins of **syphilis.** In Naples, they called it "the French disease." In France, it was "the Neapolitan disease." Many Italians called it "the Spanish disease," but in Spain, they called it "the disease of Española" (modern Haiti).

In 1530, the Italian physician Girolamo Fracastoro wrote a poem about Syphilus, a shepherd boy. Syphilus was afflicted with the disease as retribution for insulting the sun god Apollo. In 1905, the German scientist Fritz Schaudinn isolated the bacterium that causes syphilis (see Figure 16.2). It is *Treponema pallidum* (*T. pallidum*, for short). The name contains Greek and Latin roots meaning a "faintly colored (pallid) turning thread"—a good description of the corkscrewlike shape of the microscopic organism. Because of the spiral shape, *T. pallidum* is also called a *spirochete*, from Greek roots meaning "spiral" and "hair."

THE ORIGINS OF SYPHILIS   The origins of syphilis are controversial. The Columbian theory holds that Christopher Columbus returned to Spain from his first voyage to the West Indies (1492–1493) with more than beads, blankets, and tobacco. Then, from Spain, Spanish mercenaries might have carried the disease to Naples when they were hired to protect that city from French invaders. Then the French army might have contracted syphilis from prostitutes, who also practiced their profession with the Spaniards and Neapolitans. Sailors might have eventually spread syphilis to the East.

figure 16.2

Treponema Pallidum. *Treponema pallidum* is the bacterium that causes syphilis. Because of its spiral shape, *T. pallidum* is also called a *spirochete*.

Pharyngeal gonorrhea A gonorrheal infection of the pharynx (the cavity leading from the mouth and nasal passages to the larynx and esophagus) that is characterized by a sore throat.

Ophthalmia neonatorum A gonorrheal infection of the eyes of newborn children, who contract the disease by passing through an infected birth canal. (From the Greek *ophthalmos*, meaning "eye.")

Cervicitis Inflammation of the cervix.

Asymptomatic Without symptoms.

Epididymitis Inflammation of the epididymis.

Pelvic inflammatory disease Inflammation of the pelvic region—possibly including the cervix, uterus, fallopian tubes, abdominal cavity, and ovaries— that can be caused by organisms such as *Neisseria gonorrhoeae*. Its symptoms are abdominal pain, tenderness, nausea, fever, and irregular menstrual cycles. The condition may lead to infertility. Abbreviated *PID*.

Syphilis An STI that is caused by the *Treponema pallidum* bacterium, which may progress through several stages of development—often from a chancre to a skin rash to damage to the cardiovascular or central nervous systems. (From the Greek *siphlos*, meaning "maimed" or "crippled.")

It is generally accepted that Columbus exhibited symptoms of advanced syphilis when he died in 1506. However, evidence reported in 1992 shows that syphilis existed in Europe before the voyages of Columbus ("Disease discovered Europe first?," 1992; Wilford, 1992).

Truth or Fiction?
REVISITED

It is not true that Christopher Columbus brought syphilis back to Europe from the New World. One theory of the origins of syphilis was that Christopher Columbus brought it back to Europe from the New World. Evidence unearthed in the 1990s refutes this theory, however. ■

The incidence of syphilis decreased in the United States with the introduction of penicillin. But despite the availability of penicillin, there was a resurgence in rates of syphilis during the 1980s (Rolfs & Nakashima, 1990), to about 50,000 a year by 1990 (Stolberg, 1998b). However, during the 1990s, syphilis rates plunged to the lowest on record, to about 8,500 cases a year by 1997 (Bynum, 1998).

Researchers believe that the incidence of syphilis is linked to the use of cocaine (Minkoff et al., 1990; Rolfs et al., 1990). Cocaine users risk contracting syphilis through sex with multiple partners or with prostitutes, not through cocaine use per se (Rolfs et al., 1990). Syphilis and other STIs are often spread among drug users, prostitutes (many of whom abuse drugs themselves), and their sex partners (Farley et al., 1990).

Although syphilis is less widespread than it has been, its effects can be extremely harmful. They can include heart disease, blindness, gross confusion, and death. Syphilis killed the painter Paul Gauguin.

TRANSMISSION Syphilis, like gonorrhea, is most often transmitted by vaginal or anal intercourse or oral-genital or oral-anal contact with an infected person. The spirochete is usually transmitted when open lesions on an infected person come into contact with the mucous membranes or skin abrasions of the partner's body during sexual activity. The chance of contracting syphilis from one sexual contact with an infected partner is estimated to be 1 in 3 (Reinisch, 1990). Syphilis can also be contracted by touching an infectious **chancre,** but not from using the same toilet seat as an infected person.

Truth or Fiction?
REVISITED

It is not true that gonorrhea and syphilis can be contracted from toilet seats in public rest rooms. Pubic lice can be contracted in this manner, however, as we will see later. ■

Pregnant women can transmit syphilis to their fetuses, because the spirochete can cross the placental membrane. Miscarriage, stillbirth, or **congenital syphilis** might result. Congenital syphilis can impair vision and hearing or deform bones and teeth. Blood tests are administered routinely during pregnancy to diagnose syphilis in the mother so that congenital problems in the baby may be averted. The fetus will probably not be harmed if an infected mother is treated before the fourth month of pregnancy.

SYMPTOMS AND COURSE OF ILLNESS Syphilis develops through several stages. In the first stage, or *primary stage*, of syphilis, a painless chancre (a hard, round, ulcerlike lesion with raised edges) appears at the site of infection two to four weeks after contact (see Figure 16.3). When women are infected, the chancre usually forms on the vaginal walls or the cervix. It may also form on the external genitalia, most often on the labia. When men are infected, the chancre usually forms on the penile glans. It can also form on the scrotum or penile shaft. If the mode of transmission is oral sex, the chancre may appear on the lips or tongue. If the infection is spread by anal sex, the rectum may serve as the site of the chancre. The chancre disappears within a few weeks, but if the infection remains untreated, syphilis will continue to work within the body.

The *secondary stage* begins a few weeks to a few months later. A skin rash develops, consisting of painless, reddish, raised bumps that darken after a while and burst, oozing a discharge. Other symptoms include sores in the mouth, painful swelling of joints, a sore throat, headaches, and fever. A person with syphilis might wrongly assume that he or she has the flu.

These symptoms also disappear. Syphilis then enters the *latent stage* and may lie dormant for 1 to 40 years. But spirochetes continue to multiply and burrow into the circula-

Chancre A sore or ulcer.

Congenital syphilis A syphilis infection that is present at birth.

figure 16.3

Syphilis Chancre. The first, or primary, stage of a syphilis infection is marked by the appearance of a painless sore or chancre at the site of infection.

tory system, central nervous system (brain and spinal cord), and bones. The person might no longer be contagious to sex partners after several years in the latent stage, but a pregnant woman can pass along the infection to her newborn at any time (Wooldridge, 1991).

In many cases, the disease eventually progresses to the late stage, or *tertiary stage*. A large ulcer might form on the skin, muscle tissue, digestive organs, lungs, liver, or other organs. This destructive ulcer can often be successfully treated, but still more serious damage can occur as the infection attacks the central nervous system or the cardiovascular system (the heart and the major blood vessels). Either outcome can be fatal. **Neurosyphilis** can cause brain damage, resulting in paralysis or the mental illness called **general paresis.**

The primary and secondary symptoms of syphilis inevitably disappear. Infected people might therefore be tempted to believe that they are no longer at risk and fail to see a doctor. This is unfortunate, because failure to eradicate the infection through proper treatment can eventually lead to dire consequences.

It is not true that if a syphilitic chancre (sore) goes away by itself, the infection does not require medical treatment. The belief that medical treatment is unnecessary if the symptoms of an STI disappear by themselves is unfounded. Gonorrhea and syphilis, for example, both can damage the body even when their early symptoms have abated. ■

Truth or Fiction?

DIAGNOSIS AND TREATMENT   Primary-stage syphilis is diagnosed by clinical examination. If a chancre is found, fluid drawn from it can be examined under a microscope. The spirochetes are usually quite visible. Blood tests are not definitive until the secondary stage begins. The most frequently used blood test is the **VDRL.** The VDRL tests for the presence of **antibodies** to *Treponema pallidum* in the blood.

Penicillin is the treatment of choice for syphilis, although for people who are allergic to penicillin, doxycycline and some other antibiotics can be used (Cates, 1998). Sex partners of people who are infected with syphilis should also be evaluated by a physician.

Chlamydia

Although you might be more familiar with gonorrhea and syphilis, chlamydia, another bacterial STI, is actually more common in the United States (Cates, 1998). Chlamydia infections are caused by the *Chlamydia trachomatis* bacterium, a parasitic organism that can survive only within cells. This bacterium can cause several different types of infection, including *nongonococcal urethritis (NGU)* in men and women; *epididymitis* (infection of the epididymis) in men; and *cervicitis* (infection of the cervix), *endometritis* (infection of the endometrium), and PID in women (Cates, 1998).

Neurosyphilis Syphilitic infection of the central nervous system, which can cause brain damage and death.

General paresis A progressive form of mental illness caused by neurosyphilis and characterized by gross confusion.

VDRL The test named after the Venereal Disease Research Laboratory of the U.S. Public Health Service that tests for the presence of antibodies to *Treponema pallidum* in the blood.

Antibodies Specialized proteins produced by the white blood cells of the immune system in response to disease organisms and other toxic substances. Antibodies recognize and attack the invading organisms or substances.

A Silent Disease. There are millions of new cases each year in the United States, and many—perhaps most—of them go undiagnosed and untreated. For young men, certain chlamydial infections pose a greater risk than do others.

Nearly 4 million new chlamydia infections occur each year ("CDC tackles surge," 1998). The incidence of chlamydia infections is especially high among teenagers and college students (Burstein et al., 1998; Shafer et al., 1993). Researchers estimate that between 8% and 40% of teenage women become infected (Yarber & Parillo, 1992).

TRANSMISSION *Chlamydia trachomatis* is usually transmitted through sexual intercourse—vaginal or anal. *Chlamydia trachomatis* can also cause an eye infection if a person touches his or her eyes after handling the genitals of an infected partner. Oral sex with an infected partner can infect the throat. Newborns can acquire potentially serious chlamydia eye infections as they pass through the cervix of an infected mother during birth. Even newborns delivered by cesarean section may be infected if the amniotic sac breaks before delivery (Reinisch, 1990). Evidence from several studies suggests that between 2% and 26% of pregnant women in the United States carry the *Chlamydia trachomatis* bacterium in the cervix (Reinisch, 1990). Each year, more than 100,000 infants are infected with the bacterium during birth (Graham & Blanco, 1990). Of these, about 75,000 develop eye infections, and 30,000 develop pneumonia.

SYMPTOMS Chlamydia infections usually produce symptoms that are similar to, but milder than, those of gonorrhea. In men, *Chlamydia trachomatis* can lead to nongonococcal urethritis (NGU). *Urethritis* is an inflammation of the urethra. NGU refers to forms of urethritis that are not caused by the gonococcal bacterium. (NGU is generally diagnosed only in men. In women, an inflammation of the urethra caused by *Chlamydia trachomatis* is called a chlamydia infection or simply chlamydia.) NGU was formerly called nonspecific urethritis (NSU). Many organisms can cause NGU. *Chlamydia trachomatis* accounts for about half of the cases among men (Cates, 1998).

NGU in men may give rise to a thin, whitish discharge from the penis and some burning or other pain during urination. These contrast with the yellow-green discharge and more intense pain produced by gonorrhea. There may be soreness in the scrotum and feelings of heaviness in the testes. NGU is about two to three times as prevalent among American men as gonorrhea (Cates, 1998). Men in the 20- to 24-year age range are most at risk of contracting gonorrhea and NGU, presumably because of their high levels of sexual activity (Bowie, 1990).

In women, chlamydial infections usually give rise to infections of the urethra or cervix. Women, like men, may experience burning when they urinate, genital irritation, and a mild (vaginal) discharge. Women are also likely to encounter pelvic pain and irregular menstrual cycles. The cervix might look swollen and inflamed.

Yet as many as 25% of men and 70% of women who are infected with chlamydia are asymptomatic (Cates, 1998). For this reason, chlamydia has been dubbed the "silent disease." People without symptoms may go untreated and unknowingly pass along their infections to their partners. In women, an untreated chlamydial infection can spread throughout the reproductive system, leading to PID and to scarring of the fallopian tubes, resulting in infertility (Garland et al., 1990; Hodgson et al., 1990). About half of the more than 1 million annual cases of PID are attributed to chlamydia (Cates, 1998). Women with a history of exposure to *Chlamydia trachomatis* also stand twice the normal chance of incurring an ectopic (tubal) pregnancy (Sherman et al., 1990).

Untreated chlamydial infections can also damage the internal reproductive organs of men. About 50% of cases of epididymitis are caused by chlamydial infections (Cates, 1998). Yet only about 1% or 2% of men with untreated NGU caused by *Chlamydia trachomatis* go on to develop epididymitis. The long-term effects of untreated chlamydial infections in men remain undetermined.

Chlamydial infections also frequently occur together with other STIs, most often gonorrhea. Nearly half of cases of gonorrhea involve coexisting chlamydial infections (Cates, 1998).

DIAGNOSIS AND TREATMENT   The Abbott Testpack permits physicians to verify a diagnosis of chlamydia in women. The test analyzes a cervical smear (like a Pap smear) and identifies 75% to 80% of infected cases. In men, a swab is inserted through the penile opening, and the extracted fluid is analyzed to detect the presence of *Chlamydia trachomatis.*

Antibiotics other than penicillin are highly effective in eradicating chlamydia infections. These include azithromycin, doxycycline, ofloxacin, and amoxicillin (Cates, 1998). (Penicillin, effective in treating gonorrhea, is ineffective against *Chlamydia trachomatis.*) Treatment of sex partners is considered critical regardless of whether the partner shows symptoms, to prevent the infection from bouncing back and forth (Cates, 1998). Moreover, a woman whose sex partner develops NGU should be examined for a chlamydial infection herself. At least 30% of these women will test positive for chlamydia even though they (and their partners) may be free of symptoms (Stamm & Holmes, 1990). Likewise, men whose sex partners develop urethral or cervical infections should be medically evaluated, whether or not they notice any symptoms. With chlamydia, both partners might be unaware that they are infected and be oblivious to the internal damage the infection is causing. Because of the risks posed by untreated chlamydial infections, especially to women, and the high rate of asymptomatic infections, many physicians perform diagnostic tests on young women to detect chlamydia during regular checkups.

Other Bacterial Infections

Several other types of bacterial STIs occur less commonly in the United States and Canada. These include chancroid, shigellosis, granuloma inguinale, and lymphogranuloma venereum.

CHANCROID   **Chancroid,** or "soft chancre," is caused by the bacterium *Hemophilus ducreyi.* It is more commonly found in the tropics and Eastern nations than in Western countries. The chancroid sore consists of a cluster of small bumps or pimples on the genitals, the perineum (the area of skin that lies between the genitals and the anus), or the anus itself. These lesions usually appear within seven days of infection. Within a few days, the lesion ruptures, producing an open sore or ulcer. Several ulcers may merge with other ulcers, forming giant ulcers (Ronald & Albritton, 1990). There is usually an accompanying swelling of a nearby lymph node. In contrast to the syphilis chancre, the chancroid ulcer has a soft rim (hence the name) and is painful in men. Women frequently do not experience any pain and may be unaware of being infected (Ronald & Albritton, 1990). The bacterium is typically transmitted through sexual or bodily contact with the lesion or its discharge. Diagnosis is usually confirmed by culturing the bacterium, which is found in pus from the sore, and examining it under a microscope. Antibiotics (azithromycin, ciprofloaxin, erythromycin) are usually effective in treating the disease (Cates, 1998).

SHIGELLOSIS   **Shigellosis** is caused by the *Shigella* bacterium and is characterized by fever and severe abdominal symptoms, including diarrhea and inflammation of the large intestine. About 25,000 cases of shigellosis are reported each year in the United States. Shigellosis can result from food poisoning, but it is also often contracted by oral contact

Chancroid An STI caused by the *Hemophilus ducreyi* bacterium. Also called *soft chancre.*

Shigellosis An STI caused by the *Shigella* bacterium.

with infected fecal material, which may stem from oral-anal sex. Shigellosis often resolves itself, but people with the disease may become severely dehydrated from the diarrhea. Severe cases are usually treated with antibiotics, such as tetracycline or ampicillin.

GRANULOMA INGUINALE Rare in the United States, **granuloma inguinale,** like chancroid, is more common in tropical regions. It is caused by the bacterium *Calymmatobacterium granulomatis* and is not as contagious as many other STIs. Primary symptoms are painless red bumps or sores in the groin area that ulcerate and spread. Like chancroid, it is usually spread by intimate bodily or sexual contact with a lesion or its discharge. Diagnosis is confirmed by microscopic examination of tissue of the rim of the sore. The antibiotics trimethoprim-sulfamethoxazole, doxycycline, ciprofloxin, and erythromycin are effective in treating this disorder (Cates, 1998). If left untreated, however, the disease may lead to the development of fistulas (holes) in the rectum or bladder, destruction of the tissues or organs that underlie the infection, or scarring of skin tissue that is reminiscent of a condition called *elephantiasis,* which is characterized by gross enlargements of various body parts.

LYMPHOGRANULOMA VENEREUM (LGV) **Lymphogranuloma venereum** (LGV) is another tropical STI that occurs only rarely in the United States and Canada. Some U.S. soldiers returned home from Vietnam with cases of LGV. It is caused by several strains of the *Chlamydia trachomatis* bacterium. LGV usually enters the body through the penis, vulva, or cervix, where a small, painless sore may form. The sore might go unnoticed, but a nearby lymph gland in the groin swells and grows tender. Other symptoms mimic those of flu: chills, fever, and headache. Other symptoms that can occur include backache (especially in women) and arthritic complaints (painful joints). If LGV is untreated, complications such as growths and fistulas in the genitals and elephantiasis of the legs and genitals may occur. Diagnosis is made by skin tests and blood tests. The antibiotics doxycycline or erythromycin are the usual treatment (Cates, 1998).

Reflections

- If you have no symptoms of any STI, do you think it would be wise to have your physician check out your status anyway? Why or why not?
- Agree or disagree with the following statement and support your answer: Gonorrhea is no worse than a bad cold.
- Does it seem that this textbook's presentation of information about STIs is straightforward, or do you think that it uses some scare tactics? Explain.

VAGINAL INFECTIONS

Vaginitis refers to any kind of vaginal infection or inflammation. Women with vaginitis may encounter genital irritation or itching and burning during urination, but the most common symptom is an odorous discharge.

Most cases of vaginitis are caused by organisms that reside in the vagina or by sexually transmitted organisms. Organisms that reside in the vagina may overgrow and cause symptoms when the environmental balance of the vagina is upset by factors such as birth-control pills, antibiotics, dietary changes, excessive douching, or nylon underwear or pantyhose. (See Chapter 3 for suggestions to help reduce the risk of vaginitis.) Still other cases are caused by sensitivities or allergic reactions to various chemicals.

The great majority of vaginal infections (Sobel, 1997) involve bacterial vaginosis (BV), candidiasis (commonly called a "yeast" infection), or trichomoniasis ("trich"). Bacterial vaginosis is the most common form of vaginitis, followed by candidiasis, then by trichomoniasis, but some cases involve combinations of the three.

The microbes causing vaginal infections in women can also infect the man's urethral tract. A "vaginal infection" can be passed back and forth between sex partners (Sobel, 1997).

Granuloma inguinale A tropical STI caused by the *Calymmatobacterium granulomatis* bacterium.

Lymphogranuloma venereum A tropical STI caused by the *Chlamydia trachomatis* bacterium.

Vaginitis Any type of vaginal infection or inflammation.

It is not literally true that men can develop vaginal infections. Only women have vaginas. However, the microbes that cause these infections in women can also cause problems for men. ■

Bacterial Vaginosis

Bacterial vaginosis (BV), formerly called *nonspecific vaginitis*, is most often caused by overgrowth of the bacterium *Gardnerella vaginalis* (Sobel, 1997). The bacterium is transmitted primarily through sexual contact. The most characteristic symptom in women is a thin, foul-smelling vaginal discharge, but infected women are often asymptomatic. Accurate diagnosis requires culturing the bacterium in the laboratory (Reinisch, 1990). Besides causing troublesome symptoms in some cases, BV may increase the risk of various gynecological problems, including infections of the reproductive tract (Hillier & Holmes, 1990). Oral treatment with metronidazole (brand name: Flagyl) is recommended and is effective in about 90% of cases (Sobel, 1997). Topical treatments with metronidazole or clindamycin are also effective. Recurrences are common, however.

Questions remain about whether the male partner should also be treated. The bacterium can usually be found in the male urethra but does not generally cause symptoms (Reinisch, 1990). Lacking symptoms, the male partner might unknowingly transmit the bacterium to others. There is no evidence that treating the male with metronidazole benefits either him or the female patient, however (Sobel, 1997).

Candidiasis

Also known as *moniliasis*, *thrush*, or, most commonly, a yeast infection, **candidiasis** is caused by a yeastlike fungus, *Candida albicans*. Candidiasis commonly produces soreness, inflammation, and intense (sometimes maddening) itching around the vulva that is accompanied by a white, thick, curdlike vaginal discharge (see Figure 16.4). Yeast generally produces no symptoms when the vaginal environment is normal. Yeast infections can also occur in the mouth in both men and women and in the penis in men.

figure 16.4

Candidiasis. The soreness, inflammation, and intense itching around the vulva is accompanied by a thick white vaginal discharge.

Bacterial vaginosis A form of vaginitis usually caused by the *Gardnerella vaginalis* bacterium.

Candidiasis A form of vaginitis caused by a yeastlike fungus, *Candida albicans*.

Infections most often arise from changes in the vaginal environment that allow the fungus to overgrow. Factors such as the use of antibiotics, birth-control pills, intrauterine devices (IUDs), pregnancy, and diabetes can alter the vaginal balance, allowing the fungus that causes yeast infections to grow to infectious levels (Sobel, 1997). Wearing nylon underwear and tight, restrictive, poorly ventilated clothing can also set the stage for a yeast infection.

Diet may play a role in recurrent yeast infections. Reducing one's intake of substances that produce excessive excretion of urinary sugars (such as dairy products, sugar, and artificial sweeteners) apparently reduces the frequency of recurrent yeast infections. The daily ingestion of one pint of yogurt containing active bacterial (*Lactobacillus acidophilus*) cultures helped to reduce the rate of recurrent infections in one sample of women (Hilton et al., 1992).

Candidiasis can be passed back and forth between sex partners through vaginal intercourse. It may also be passed back and forth between the mouth and the genitals through oral-genital contact and infect the anus through anal intercourse. However, most infections in women are believed to be caused by an overgrowth of "yeast" that is normally found in the vagina, not by sexual transmission. Still, it is advisable to evaluate both partners simultaneously. Whereas most men with *Candida* are asymptomatic, some may develop NGU or a genital thrush that is accompanied by sensations of itching and burning during urination or a reddening of the penis. Candidiasis can also be transmitted by nonsexual means, as between women who share a washcloth.

About 75% of women will have at least one episode of candidiasis during their reproductive years (Sobel, 1997). About half of them will have recurrent infections. A single dose of oral fluconazole or vaginal suppositories or creams containing miconazole, clotrimazole, or butaconazole are recommended for treatment (Cates, 1998; Sobel, 1997). Many of these treatments are sold over the counter. Ask the pharmacist which preparations contain these medicines (or read the labels). We also recommend that women with vaginal complaints consult their physicians before taking any of these medications to ensure that they receive the proper diagnosis and treatment.

Trichomoniasis

Trichomoniasis ("trich") is caused by *Trichomonas vaginalis*. *Trichomonas vaginalis* is a one-celled parasite. Trichomoniasis is the most common parasitic STI. It accounts for 2 million to 3 million cases a year among women in the United States (Sobel, 1997). Symptoms in women include burning or itching in the vulva, mild pain during urination or coitus, and an odorous, foamy, whitish to yellowish-green discharge. Lower abdominal pain is reported by 5% to 12% of infected women (Rein & Muller, 1990). Many women notice symptoms appearing or worsening during or just after their menstrual periods. Trichomoniasis facilitates the transmission of HIV (Sobel, 1997) and is also linked to the development of tubal adhesions that can result in infertility (Grodstein et al., 1993). As with many other STIs, about half of infected women have no symptoms (Reinisch, 1990).

Candidiasis most often reflects an overgrowth of organisms that are normally found in the vagina. However, trichomoniasis is almost always sexually transmitted. Because the parasite can survive for several hours on moist surfaces outside the body, trich can be communicated from contact with infected semen or vaginal discharges on towels, washcloths, and bedclothes. This parasite is one of the few disease agents that can be picked up from a toilet seat, but it would have to directly touch the penis or vulva (Reinisch, 1990).

Trichomonas vaginalis can cause NGU in the male, which can be asymptomatic or cause a slight penile discharge that is usually noticeable only upon awakening, before one first urinates in the morning. There might be tingling, itching, and other irritating sensations in the urethral tract. Yet most infected men are symptom free. Therefore, they can unwittingly transfer the organism to their sex partners. Perhaps three or four in ten male

Trichomoniasis A form of vaginitis caused by the protozoan *Trichomonas vaginalis*.

partners of infected women are found to harbor *Trichomonas vaginalis* themselves (Reinisch, 1990). Diagnosis is frequently made by microscopic examination of a smear of a woman's vaginal fluids in a physician's office. Diagnosis based on examination of cultures grown from the vaginal smear is considered more reliable, however.

Except during the first three months of pregnancy, trichomoniasis is usually treated in both genders with metronidazole (brand name: Flagyl). Both partners are treated, whether or not they report symptoms. When both partners are treated simultaneously, the success rate approaches 100% (Cates, 1998; Sobel, 1997).

Reflections

- ▪ What can women do to prevent vaginal infections?
- ▪ If a woman suspects that she has a vaginal infection, should she attempt a cure with an over-the-counter medicine or see her physician? Explain.
- ▪ How would you feel if you had been infected with an STI by a partner? What precautions would you expect the partner to have taken? Would you take such precautions yourself?

AIDS Virus (HIV) Attacking a White Blood Cell.

VIRAL INFECTIONS

Viruses are tiny particles of DNA surrounded by a protein coating. They are incapable of reproducing on their own. When they invade a body cell, however, they can direct the cell's own reproductive machinery to spin off new viral particles that spread to other cells, causing infection. In this chapter, we discuss several viral STIs: HIV/AIDS, herpes, viral hepatitis, genital warts, and molluscum contagiosum.

HIV Infection and AIDS

AIDS is the acronym for **acquired immunodeficiency syndrome.** AIDS is a fatal syndrome that is caused by the **human immunodeficiency virus** (HIV). HIV attacks and disables the immune system, the body's natural line of defense, stripping it of its ability to fend off disease-causing organisms (see Figure 16.5). No one knows where HIV originated, but some investigators suspect that it may be a variant of viruses found in monkeys and chimpanzees.

PREVALENCE OF HIV INFECTION AND AIDS   AIDS was first described in the medical journals only 20 years ago—in 1981 (Gottlieb, 1991). As we enter the new millennium, nearly 600,000 Americans have been diagnosed with AIDS (CDC, 1996, 1998). About 400,000 Americans have died from it (CDC, 1996, 1998). AIDS has become the leading killer of Americans of ages 25 to 44. The incidence of AIDS is increasing most rapidly among women, people of color, people who share needles when they inject drugs, and people who engage in unprotected, male-female sex.

About 1 million people in the United States are infected with HIV (CDC, 1998). About 40 million people worldwide are infected with HIV (Burns, 1997).

In the United States, AIDS predominantly affects men who engage in sexual activity with other men (about 40% to 50%) or share needles when injecting drugs (25% to 30%) (CDC, 1996, 1998). The rate of new cases of AIDS in gay men has been declining—in part because of more widespread use of safer sex practices by gay males, including increased use of condoms and reduced numbers of sex partners.

Male-female sexual contact is the fasting-growing exposure category. Among women, however, male-female sexual contact now accounts for nearly 40% of cases. Bear in mind that it is a person's behavior, not the groups to which the person belongs, that determines her or his relative risk of infection. Therefore, we speak in terms of high-risk *behaviors* (such as unprotected intercourse) rather than high-risk *groups.*

Acquired immunodeficiency syndrome (AIDS) A condition caused by the human immunodeficiency virus (HIV) and characterized by destruction of the immune system so that the body is stripped of its ability to fend off life-threatening diseases.

Human immunodeficiency virus (HIV) A sexually transmitted virus that destroys white blood cells in the immune system, leaving the body vulnerable to life-threatening diseases.

ETHNICITY AND AIDS IN THE UNITED STATES

Disproportionately high numbers of African Americans and Hispanic Americans have contracted AIDS (CDC, 1996, 1998). Nearly half of the men and three quarters of the women with AIDS in the United States are African American or Hispanic American (CDC, 1996, 1998). Yet these groups make up only 22% of the population. Death rates due to AIDS are much higher among African Americans and Hispanic Americans (especially Hispanic people of Puerto Rican origin) than among White Americans (CDC, 1996, 1998).

Ethnic differences in rates of transmission of HIV appear to be linked to injecting illicit drugs. People who share needles with HIV-infected people when they inject drugs can become infected themselves. They can then also transmit the virus to their sex partners. People who share needles now account for one in four AIDS cases. African Americans constitute more than half of the people who apparently became infected with HIV by injecting drugs (CDC, 1996, 1998). Hispanic Americans account for another case in every five (CDC, 1996, 1998). Drug abuse and the related problem of prostitution occur disproportionately in poor, urban communities with large populations of people of color. Therefore, it is not surprising that HIV infection and AIDS have affected these groups disproportionately.

THE IMMUNE SYSTEM AND AIDS   AIDS is caused by a virus that attacks the body's **immune system**—the body's natural line of defense against disease-causing organisms. The immune system combats disease in a number of ways. It produces white blood cells that envelop and kill **pathogens** such as bacteria, viruses, and funguses; worn-out body cells; and cancer cells. White blood cells are referred to as **leukocytes.** Leukocytes engage in microscopic warfare. They undertake search-and-destroy missions. They identify and eradicate foreign agents and debilitated cells.

Truth or Fiction?
REVISITED

It is true that as you read this page, you are engaged in search-and-destroy missions against foreign agents within your body. The white cells in your immune system continuously seek and destroy foreign pathogens within your body. ■

Leukocytes recognize foreign agents by their surface fragments. The surface fragments are termed **antigens** because the body reacts to their presence by developing specialized proteins, or antibodies. Antibodies attach themselves to the foreign bodies, inactivate them, and mark them for destruction. (Infection by HIV can be determined by examining the blood or saliva for the presence of antibodies to the virus.)

Rather than mark pathogens for destruction or war against them, special "memory lymphocytes" are held in reserve. Memory lymphocytes can remain in the bloodstream for years, and they form the basis for a quick immune response to an invader the second time around.[1]

Another function of the immune system is to promote **inflammation.** When you suffer an injury, blood vessels in the region initially contract to check bleeding. Then they dilate. Dilation expands blood flow to the injured region, causing the redness and warmth that identify inflammation. The elevated blood supply also brings in an army of leukocytes to combat invading microscopic life forms, such as bacteria, that might otherwise use the local injury to establish a beachhead into the body.

EFFECTS OF HIV ON THE IMMUNE SYSTEM   Spikes (technically known as "gpl20" spikes) on the surface of HIV allow it to bind to sites on cells in the immune system (Sodroski et al., 1998). Like other viruses, HIV uses the cells that it invades to spin off copies

---

Immune system A term for the body's complex of mechanisms for protecting itself from disease-causing agents such as pathogens.

Pathogen An agent, especially a microorganism, that can cause a disease. (From the Greek *pathos,* meaning "suffering" or "disease," and *genic,* meaning "forming" or "coming into being.")

Leukocytes White blood cells that are essential to the body's defenses against infection. (From the Greek *leukos,* meaning "white," and *kytos,* meaning "a hollow," and used in combination with other word forms to mean *cell.*)

Antigen A protein, toxin, or other substance to which the body reacts by producing antibodies. (Combined word formed from *anti*body *gen*erator.)

---

[1]Vaccination is the placement of a weakened form of an antigen in the body, which activates the creation of antibodies and memory lymphocytes. Smallpox has been annihilated by vaccination, and researchers are trying to develop a vaccine against the virus that causes AIDS.

of itself. HIV uses the enzyme *reverse transcriptase* to cause the genes in the cells it attacks to make proteins that the virus needs to reproduce.

HIV directly attacks the immune system by invading and destroying a type of lymphocyte called the CD4 cell (or helper T-cell).[2] The CD4 cell is the "quarterback" of the immune system. CD4 cells "recognize" invading pathogens and signal B-lymphocytes or B-cells—another kind of white blood cell—to produce antibodies that inactivate pathogens and mark them for annihilation. CD4 cells also signal another class of T-cells, called killer T-cells, to destroy infected cells. By attacking and destroying helper T-cells, HIV disables the very cells on which the body relies to fight off this and other diseases. As HIV cripples the body's defenses, the individual is exposed to serious infections that would not otherwise take hold. Cancerous cells might also proliferate. Although the CD4 cells appear to be its main target, HIV also attacks other types of white blood cells.

The blood normally contains about 1,000 CD4 cells per cubic millimeter. The numbers of CD4 cells may remain at about this level for years after HIV infection. Many people show no symptoms and appear healthy while CD4 cells remain at this level. Then, for reasons that are not clearly understood, the levels of CD4 cells begin to drop off, although symptoms might not appear for a decade or more. As the numbers of CD4 cells decline, symptoms generally increase, and people fall prey to diseases that their weakened immune systems are unable to fight off. People become most vulnerable to opportunistic infections when the level of CD4 cells falls below 200 per cubic millimeter.

PROGRESSION OF HIV INFECTION AND AIDS   HIV follows a complex course once it enters the body. Shortly after infection, the person might experience mild flulike symptoms—fatigue, fever, headaches and muscle pain, lack of appetite, nausea, swollen glands, and possibly a rash. Such symptoms usually disappear within a few weeks. People might dismiss them as a passing case of flu. People who enter this asymptomatic or carrier state generally look and act well and do not realize that they are infectious. Thus, they can unwittingly pass along the virus to others.

Most people who are infected with HIV remain asymptomatic for years. Some enter a symptomatic state (previously labeled *AIDS-related complex*, or ARC) that is typically denoted by symptoms such as chronically swollen lymph nodes and intermittent weight loss, fever, fatigue, and diarrhea. This symptomatic state does not constitute full-blown AIDS but shows that HIV is undermining the integrity of the immune system.

It is true that most people who are infected by HIV remain symptom-free and appear healthy for years. ■

Truth or Fiction?
REVISITED

Even during the years when HIV appears to be lying dormant in the body, billions of viral particles are being spun off. In a seesaw battle, the great majority of them are wiped out by the immune system. Eventually, in almost all cases, the balance tips in favor of HIV. Then the virus's numbers swell. Perhaps a decade or more after the person is infected with HIV, and for reasons that remain unclear, the virus begins to overtake the immune system. It obliterates the cells that house it and spreads to other immune system cells, eventually destroying or disabling the body's ability to defend itself from disease. About half of people with HIV develop AIDS within 10 years of initial infection. For this reason, people who know that they are infected with HIV might feel that they are carrying time bombs within them. AIDS is classified as a *syndrome* because it is characterized by a variety of different symptoms. The beginnings of full-blown cases of AIDS are often marked by such symptoms as swollen lymph nodes, fatigue, fever, night sweats, diarrhea, and weight loss that cannot be attributed to dieting or exercise.

AIDS is connected with the appearance of diseases such as *Pneumocystis carinii pneumonia* (PCP), Kaposi's sarcoma (a form of cancer), toxoplasmosis of the brain (an in-

Inflammation Redness and warmth that develop at the site of an injury, reflecting dilation of blood vessels that permits the expanded flow of leukocytes to the region.

---

[2]CD4 cells are also known as T4 cells.

Could This Couple Be Transmitting HIV? Transmission of HIV through kissing, even prolonged kissing or "French" kissing, is considered unlikely. According to the Centers for Disease Control, HIV is not found in infectious amounts in saliva.

fection of parasites), or herpes simplex with chronic ulcers. These diseases are termed **opportunistic diseases** because they are not likely to emerge unless a disabled immune system provides the opportunity.

About 10% of people with AIDS have a wasting syndrome. Wasting is the unintentional loss of more than 10% of a person's body weight and is connected with AIDS, some other infections, and cancer (Grunfeld, 1995). It appears that people with AIDS who waste away do so because they take in less energy, not because they burn more calories (Macallan et al., 1995).

As AIDS progresses, the individual grows thinner and more fatigued. He or she becomes unable to perform ordinary life functions and falls prey to opportunistic infections. If left untreated, AIDS almost always results in death within a few years.

TRANSMISSION HIV can be transmitted by certain contaminated bodily fluids—blood, semen, vaginal secretions, or breast milk. The first three of these fluids may enter the body through vaginal, anal, or oral-genital intercourse with an infected partner. Other avenues of infection include sharing a hypodermic needle with an infected person (as do many people who inject drugs), transfusion with contaminated blood, transplants of organs and tissues that have been infected with HIV, artificial insemination with infected semen, or being stuck by a needle used previously on an infected person. HIV may enter the body through tiny cuts or sores in the mucosal lining of the vagina, the rectum, and even the mouth. These cuts or sores can be so tiny that you are not aware of them.

When a person injects drugs, a small amount of his or her blood remains inside the needle and syringe. If the person is HIV-infected, the virus may be found in the blood remaining in the needle or syringe. When others use the same needle, they inject the infected blood into their bloodstream. HIV can also be spread by sharing needles used for other purposes, such as injecting steroids, ear piercing, or tattooing. If you are interested in having your ears pierced or getting a tattoo, insist upon seeing a qualified person who uses new or sterilized equipment. Ask questions about the safety measures that are followed before undergoing any such procedure.

HIV may also be transmitted from mother to fetus during pregnancy or from mother to child through childbirth or breast-feeding (Peckham & Gibb, 1995). Transmission is most likely to occur during childbirth.

Male-to-female transmission through vaginal intercourse is about twice as likely as female-to-male transmission (Allen & Setlow, 1991), partly because more of the virus is found in the ejaculate than in vaginal secretions. A man's ejaculate might also remain for many days in the vagina, providing greater opportunity for infection to occur. Male-female or male-male anal intercourse is especially risky, particularly to the recipient, since it often tears or abrades rectal tissue, facilitating entry of the virus into the bloodstream (Caceres & van Griensven, 1994).

Male-female transmission via sexual intercourse is the primary route of HIV infection in Africa, Latin America, and Asia (Specter, 1998). Worldwide, male-female sexual intercourse accounts for 75% of cases of HIV infection (Novello, 1991). Many cases of male-female transmission occur within the community of people who inject drugs and their sex partners.

In the early years of the AIDS epidemic, HIV spread rapidly among hemophiliacs who had unknowingly been transfused with contaminated blood. Tennis great Arthur Ashe, who died of complications from AIDS in 1993, believed that he had contracted HIV during a blood transfusion. But blood supplies are now routinely screened for HIV. Medical authorities now consider the risk of HIV transmission through transfusion of screened blood to be negligible (Lackritz et al., 1995; Schreiber et al., 1996; Vyas et al., 1996).

HIV can also be spread by donor semen, such as that used in artificial insemination. Many sperm banks do not test donors for STIs. Cases have been reported of women who

Opportunistic diseases Diseases that take hold only when the immune system is weakened and unable to fend them off. Kaposi's sarcoma and pneumocystis carinii pneumonia (PCP) are examples of opportunistic diseases found in people with AIDS.

have become infected with hepatitis B, gonorrhea, trichomoniasis ("trich"), chlamydia, and even HIV via insemination with donor semen (Meyer, 1994).

Factors Affecting the Risk of Sexual Transmission Some people seem more likely to communicate HIV, and others seem to be especially vulnerable to HIV infection. Why, for instance, are some people infected by one sexual contact with an infected partner, whereas others are not infected during months or years of unprotected sex? Several factors appear to affect the risk of HIV infection and development of AIDS:

- The probability of sexual transmission rises with the number of sexual contacts with an infected partner.
- The probability of transmission is also affected by the type of sexual activity. Anal intercourse, for example, provides a convenient port of entry for HIV because it often tears or abrades the rectal lining.
- The amount of virus in semen also affects the probability of infection. The quantity of HIV in the semen peaks shortly after initial infection and when full-blown AIDS develops.
- STIs such as genital warts, gonorrhea, trichomoniasis, and chlamydia inflame the genital region, heightening the risk of sexual transmission of other STIs (Stolberg, 1998b). STIs that produce genital ulcers, such as syphilis and genital herpes, may heighten vulnerability to HIV infection by allowing the virus to enter the circulatory system through the ulcers.
- Circumcision apparently lowers the risk of infection because circumcised men are less likely to have genital ulcers. Moreover, HIV cannot accumulate under the folds of the foreskin in men who have been circumcised. Cells in the foreskin might also be particularly vulnerable to HIV infection (Royce et al., 1997).
- Genetic factors might also be at work. About 1% of people of Western European descent have inherited a gene that prevents HIV from entering cells in the immune system from both parents and are apparently immune to HIV infection. Perhaps 20% of individuals of Western European descent have inherited the gene from one parent; HIV disease appears to progress more slowly in these people. Some prostitutes in Thailand and Africa, where HIV infection has been running rampant, also appear to be immune to HIV infection (Royce et al., 1997).

How HIV Is Not Transmitted There is much misinformation about the transmission of HIV. Let us consider some of the ways in which HIV is *not* transmitted:

1. *HIV is not transmitted from donating blood.* AIDS cannot be contracted by donating blood because needles are discarded after a single use. Unfortunately, many people have avoided donating blood because of unfounded fears of HIV transmission.
2. *HIV is not transmitted through casual, everyday contact.* There is no evidence of transmission of HIV through hugging someone, shaking hands, bumping into strangers on buses and trains; handling money, doorknobs, or other objects that have been touched by infected people; sharing drinking fountains, public telephones, public toilets, or swimming pools; or trying on clothing that has been worn by an infected person. Nor is HIV known to be transmitted by contact with urine, feces, sputum, sweat, tears, or nasal secretions, unless blood is clearly visible in these fluids. (Still, should you need to clean up someone's urine, feces, nasal secretions, and especially blood, it would be wise to use rubber gloves and wash your hands thoroughly immediately afterwards.)
3. *HIV is not transmitted by insect bites.* HIV is not transmitted by mosquito bites or from bites by other insects such as bedbugs, lice, or flies (CDC, 1992). Nor can you get HIV from contact with animals.
4. *HIV is not transmitted by airborne germs or contact with contaminated food.* People do not contract HIV from contact with airborne germs, as by sneezing or coughing, or by contact with contaminated food or eating food prepared by a person infected with HIV.

5. *HIV is not transmitted through sharing work or home environments.* HIV has not been shown to be transmitted from infected people to family members or others they live with through any form of casual contact, such as hugging or touching, or through sharing bathrooms, food, or eating utensils, as long as there is no exchange of blood or genital secretions. There are some isolated reports of nonsexual transmission of HIV between children living together in the same household. Investigators suspect that the route of transmission in these cases involved blood contact, such as the sharing of razor blades in one of the two reported cases and the sharing of a toothbrush in the other (the infected child in this case had bleeding gums) ("AIDS without needles or sex," 1993). No cases of HIV transmission have been documented that were based on nonsexual contact in schools or in the workplace.

DIAGNOSIS OF HIV INFECTION AND AIDS   The most widely used test for HIV infection is the enzyme-linked immunosorbent assay (ELISA, for short). ELISA does not directly detect HIV in the blood. Instead, it reveals HIV antibodies. People may show an antibody response to HIV long before they develop symptoms of infection. A positive **(seropositive)** test result means that antibodies were found and usually[3] indicates that the person is infected with HIV. A negative **(seronegative)** outcome means that antibodies to HIV were not detected.

ELISA can be performed on samples of blood, saliva, or urine. A saliva test is not quite as accurate as a blood test, but it is less expensive and might encourage people who avoid blood tests to be tested. Although HIV antibodies can be detected in saliva, HIV itself is not found in measurable quantities. This is why kissing is not considered an avenue of transmission of HIV. The saliva is absorbed by a cotton pad on a stick that is placed between the lower gum and the cheek. The saliva in the cotton, like blood, undergoes ELISA in a laboratory.

The urine test is also not quite as accurate as the blood test. Yet the test does not require specially trained health workers for administration. Nor does it use needles, which can pose hazards to health care professionals. Luc Montagnier (1996), one of the discoverers of HIV, notes that the ease of use of the urine test could be of particular advantage in identifying HIV infection in people in developing countries.

When people receive positive ELISA results, the Western blot test or PCR (polymerase chain reaction) test can be performed to confirm the findings. The PCR test is expensive but detects the virus itself. It can take many months for people who have been exposed to HIV to develop antibodies. For this reason, repeated tests over a six-month or even longer period of time from the date of possible exposure may be in order.

TREATMENT OF HIV INFECTION AND AIDS

> We can really say "Get tested, get into care." We have more to offer people, so the concept of getting into care and getting treatment becomes more important.
> —Margaret Chesney, Center for AIDS Prevention Studies, University of California–San Francisco (cited in Freiberg, 1996)

For many years, researchers were frustrated by failure in the effort to develop effective vaccines and treatments for HIV infection and AIDS. There is still no safe, effective vaccine, but recent developments in drug therapy have raised hopes in the area of treatment.

Vaccines   A number of experimental AIDS vaccines are being tested on people and animals ("FDA allows large-scale AIDS vaccine trial," 1998). Several vaccines have proved somewhat effective in animal trials (Ho, 1995). Yet the development of an ideal vaccine

Seropositive Having a pathogen or antibodies to that pathogen in the bloodstream.

Seronegative Lacking a pathogen or antibodies to that pathogen in the bloodstream.

---

[3]But not always! Fetuses, for example, might receive antibodies from infected mothers but not the virus itself. Some fetuses, however, do become infected with the virus.

against AIDS—one that would be safe and inexpensive and would render lifetime protection against all strains of the disease with a single dose—might be years away.

The mutability of HIV has thus far stymied efforts to find a cure or an effective vaccine. HIV can mutate into forms that resist particular antiviral drugs or vaccines (Ho, 1995). The genes that make up HIV mutate a million times more rapidly than human genes, leading scientists on wild goose chases as they try to eradicate a killer that keeps changing its form. A vaccine that might protect against one strain or a drug that could render a death blow might have no value against another strain. Moreover, whenever the body's own immune system or a drug is initially successful in attacking a particular HIV variant, a mutated form that is capable of resisting the attack can arise and takes it place (Ho, 1995).

Drug Therapy Today, many drugs are used to combat HIV infection and AIDS. They offer a good deal of hope for people with HIV infection and AIDS, including pregnant women who are infected with HIV.

Zidovudine (AZT) has been the most widely used HIV/AIDS drug. AZT is one of a number of so-called nucleoside analogues that inhibit replication (reproduction) of HIV by targeting the enzyme called reverse transcriptase. Other nucleoside analogues include ddI, ddC, d4T, and

Treatment for HIV/AIDS. The standard treatment for HIV/AIDS is a combination of antiviral drugs including a protease inhibitor. The drug "cocktail" reduces HIV to blood levels that are undetectable in many patients, but is not known to eradicate the infection.

3TC. AZT has in many cases delayed the progression of infection from the asymptomatic to the symptomatic state and increased the blood count of CD4 cells. AZT administered to HIV-infected pregnant women has also reduced the rate of HIV infection in their newborns by two thirds (Connor et al., 1994). AZT helps to prevent transmission during childbirth by reducing the amount of the virus in the mother's bloodstream (Meyer, 1998). Only 8% of the babies who are born to the AZT-treated women became infected with HIV, compared to 25% of the babies born to women in the placebo group. For this purpose, AZT is usually used for 26 weeks before childbirth. However, using AZT for even the final few weeks cuts the transmission rate of HIV from mother to child by half (Meyer, 1998). Since AZT is expensive, the briefer treatment might be of most help in developing nations or in cases in which the mother has not sought prenatal treatment early in pregnancy.

Although AZT is helpful, it seems eventually to lose effectiveness. Researchers have therefore also studied the effectiveness of combining AZT with other antiviral drugs, such as didanosine (ddI) and zalcitabine (ddC). AZT in combination with either ddI or ddC is more effective in delaying the progression of HIV infection to AIDS than is AZT alone.

A new generation of drugs that block the replication of HIV, called *protease inhibitors*, are more effective treatments for HIV infection and AIDS (Flexner, 1998; Palella et al., 1998). Protease inhibitors block reproduction of HIV particles by targeting the protease enzyme. A combination, or "cocktail," of antiviral drugs including AZT, another nucleoside analogue, and a protease inhibitor has become the standard treatment of HIV infection and AIDS (Flexner, 1998). This combination decreases the likelihood that HIV will develop resistance to treatment (Hirsch et al., 1998). It has reduced HIV below detectable levels in many infected people (Altman, 1998a). It has created hope that AIDS will become "increasingly manageable, a chronic disease as opposed to a terminal illness" (Chesney, 1996). However, combination drug therapy is expensive, and many people who could benefit from it cannot afford it. Many pills must be taken at precise intervals, such that many people with HIV/AIDS find it difficult to adhere to the schedule (Hirsch et al.,

HIV Infection and AIDS— A Mixed Picture

As the last decade of the twentieth century drew to a close, there was finally some good news about HIV infection and AIDS. As *The New York Times* noted, people who had believed that they were doomed were given a new lease on life ("Huge gains," 1998). Only a few years earlier, infection with HIV was considered a death sentence. It might take a decade or more for the virus to devastate the body's immune system, but eventually, almost everyone who was infected developed symptoms, grew progressively weaker and sicker, and died. Then came along powerful new combinations of drugs that not only attacked HIV itself but also effectively treated the pneumonias and other health problems that typically administered the coup de grace.

The death rate from AIDS was suddenly on the decline in the United States. Yet the rate of new infections with HIV was remaining more or less stable at about 40,000 cases per year ("Huge gains," 1998). "This is a case of the glass [being] half full," commented Cornelius Baker of the National Association of People with AIDS (cited in "HIV infection rate in U.S.," 1998). "People are living longer. That's great. But with a steady infection rate, it means the epidemic isn't going away."

While the overall rate of infection by HIV in the United States is not changing dramatically, there is some change in terms of *who* gets infected. Whereas HIV infection and AIDS were once considered a problem of gay men, the numbers of gay men and injecting drugs users who are being infected have been on the decline, while the rate of transmission through male-female sexual activity has been increasing, especially in minority groups (Rosenberg & Biggar, 1998).

Moreover, the good news about treatment in the United States did not extend to all parts of the world. At the 1998 world conference on AIDS, the disparity was considered a "North-South" problem—a world North-South problem that promised to make the million deaths that resulted from the U.S. North-South problem (that is, the Civil War) seem like a small number. The rate of HIV infection is increasing faster in areas of the former Soviet Union and many developing countries in Asia, Latin America, and Africa than it is in the United States and other industrialized nations (WHO, 1995).

Consider some facts about the spread of HIV infection and AIDS in sub-Saharan Africa, the region that accounts for about 90% of the world's deaths from AIDS (Specter, 1998b). Sex with prostitutes is the most important factor in the male-female transmission of HIV in Africa, where the infection is spread predominantly via male-female sexual intercourse. Prostitutes incur a greater risk of HIV transmission because they have sexual relations with a great many partners, often without protection. HIV may be spread by unprotected sex from prostitutes to customers, then to the customers' wives or lovers. As a result, most of the infected people in Africa are women (Bogert et al., 1995; Lorch, 1993a). The economic and social costs of AIDS have been staggering, especially to some of the developing nations in Africa. One quarter to two-fifths of the adults in some countries are believed to be infected with HIV (Specter, 1998b). In Uganda, deaths from AIDS have touched virtually every family. AIDS has decimated the population of young adults and family breadwinners and left other family members to care for the children.

Truth or Fiction? REVISITED

It is true that sub-Saharan Africa accounts for about 90% of the world's deaths from AIDS. ■

Among women in the United States today, the risks of HIV infection and deaths from AIDS fall most heavily on poor women, mostly African American or Hispanic American, who live in urban areas (Amaro, 1995). Overall, African American and Hispanic American women account for nearly three quarters of women

1998). The side effects of these medicines can be unpleasant, including nausea and, in the case of protease inhibitors, unusual accumulations of fat, such as "buffalo humps" in the neck (Altman, 1998b). But other drugs (Sustiva is one) are coming into use that do not require use of as many pills and that appear to have milder side effects ("FDA approves an AIDS drug," 1998).

Combination therapy has worked many wonders to date (Flexner, 1998; Hirsch et al., 1998). It cut the U.S. death rate from AIDS-related causes by 26% from 1995 to 1996 and by 44% from 1996 to 1997 (Altman, 1998a; Irvine, 1998). It cut the California and New York death rates from AIDS-related causes by 60% and 48%, respectively, from 1996 to 1997 (Altman, 1998a; Irvine, 1998). Yet even when HIV has been reduced to "undetectable levels" by ordinary means, scientists have been able to use methods of close scrutiny to locate it in "resting" (non-replicating) CD4 cells ("U.S. scientists admit," 1997). Therefore, combination drug therapy cannot be considered a cure. It might even be that strains of HIV will arise that replicate rapidly even when they are bombarded by combination therapy (Irvine, 1998). Moreover, there is some danger that the public will assume that AIDS is no longer a threat and funding of research will decline.

Promising results are also reported in treating the opportunistic infections, such as PCP (Bozzette et al., 1995) and fungal infections (Powderly et al., 1995), that take hold in people with weakened immune systems (Clumeck, 1995).

with AIDS in the United States, although they make up less than one quarter of the female population (CDC, 1996, 1998).

Here, then, are some predictions—based on the facts today—about further developments in the war against HIV infection and AIDS that we are likely to witness in the early years of the new millennium. It remains very much a mixed picture:

- We are likely to see further developments in antiviral therapy that help many people with HIV infection and AIDS to live for many years, perhaps indefinitely. New classes of antiviral drugs will be made available, and existing forms of drug therapy—specifically, the combination therapy that uses a protease inhibitor along with other antiviral agents—will be packaged in forms that are easier to take and have fewer side effects.
- We are likely to see further development in vaccines against HIV infection and AIDS. Some vaccines might help to prevent people from being infected with HIV; others might be of help to people who are already infected. These vaccines might even-tually eradicate AIDS in the same way that smallpox was erad-icated by vaccination.

- We are likely to see continued ravages by HIV infection and AIDS across sub-Saharan Africa and in some other developing areas of the world. In the foreseeable future, many developing nations are likely to be unable to afford the antiviral therapies that are being used in the United States and other developed countries. Unless developed nations make these therapies avail-able to the rest of the world, vaccination (which does not yet exist) and improved education about prevention may be the only real hopes of developing countries.
- Although the United States and Canada have some of the most advanced health care in the world, it is not equally available to all people in these nations. Therefore, we are likely to see some remaining social class differences in the transmission of HIV and the treatment of HIV infection and AIDS in the United States. Again, vaccination and education (about prevention and about the availability of treatment) might remain the best hopes of some people in the United States for years to come.

Caring for People with AIDS. People with AIDS need love and support, but are often rejected by others, even family members, who fear contracting the disease by touch-ing or hugging them. However, HIV is not transmitted by hugging or touching an infected person, or by being in the same room.

PREVENTION   What can we do to curb the spread of AIDS? Given that there is no vac-cine or cure, prevention is our best hope. Our discussion of prevention will focus on sex-ual transmission, but other efforts have been made to prevent transmission of HIV from mother to child, through injection of drugs, and through blood transfusions. For exam-ple, HIV-infected women are advised to avoid breast-feeding. AZT and other measures, such as cesarean section, decrease the probability of transmission through childbirth. The screening of potential donors has reduced the probability of donating infected blood to about one in half a million (Schreiber et al., 1996). We have been less successful in re-ducing the risk of infection through unsafe sexual contact.

Most prevention efforts focus on education. Sexually active people have been advised to alter their sexual behavior either by practicing abstinence, by limiting their sexual ex-periences to a lifelong monogamous relationship, or by practicing "safe sex"—which, as we shall see, could be more accurately dubbed "safer sex."

TARGETING SPECIAL POPULATIONS   Some AIDS experts believe that AIDS preven-tion programs should be aimed at the communities that have been hardest hit (St. Lawrence et al., 1995). It is possible, these experts believe, that the epidemic can be all but wiped out if prevention efforts were focused on the communities, especially poor communities, that have been ravaged by the epidemic (Kolata, 1993b; "Research panel," 1993). A 1993 report by the National Research Council lends support to the targeted approach. The council found that AIDS was devastating a handful of communities while leaving much of the nation virtually untouched. As one of the members of the council committee that drafted the report framed the issue, "If we want to really deal with the epidemic, we have to go where the epidemic is" (p. 26). Proponents of this approach point to the city of Tacoma, Washington, which concentrated its prevention efforts on promoting safer injection and sexual practices in people who inject drugs and managed to keep its infection rates in these groups under 5%, compared to the skyrocketing rates found in other cities like New York, where infection rates in people who inject drugs now range between 50% and 80%. AIDS experts do not universally support the belief that AIDS prevention efforts should be narrowly but intensively focused on hard-hit communities. Some believe that since the virus has spread into the more general population, a broader prevention effort is needed. Health officials also fear that the general public might largely ignore AIDS if it becomes perceived as a problem that is endemic to socially disadvantaged groups in our society rather than to the society at large.

Some AIDS researchers argue that people who inject drugs should be given sterile needles as well as easier access to drug treatment programs. In 1995, some 75 needle-exchange programs were operating in 55 U.S. cities. A study by the National Academy of Sciences (1995) concluded that these programs slow the spread of HIV without increasing drug abuse. Many political and religious leaders oppose government distribution of condoms or clean-needle programs on moral grounds, however. Meanwhile, many drug treatment programs have long waiting lists. As a result, some infected addicts spread the virus through needle sharing and sexual contact while awaiting entry.

The lack of Spanish-language AIDS education materials and bilingual treatment providers has handicapped efforts to stem the spread of AIDS in the Hispanic community (Fuentes, 1993). Recognizing that drug use is often implicated in the transmission of HIV among Hispanic Americans, the National Latino Coalition on AIDS has called for expanding the availability of drug treatment programs and expanding AIDS prevention efforts in the Hispanic community.

The advent of AIDS presents the medical, mental health, and educational communities with an unparalleled challenge in developing programs to contain the spread of AIDS and for compassionate treatment of people with HIV and AIDS. As frightening as AIDS might be, it is preventable. For the latest information on HIV/AIDS, call the government AIDS hotline: 1–800-342-AIDS. The call is free, and you will not be asked to identify yourself. We expand our discussion of prevention of HIV/AIDS in the section entitled "Prevention of STIs: It's More Than Safer Sex."

Herpes

The hysteria that surrounded the rapid spread of genital herpes in the 1970s and 1980s has died down since the advent of AIDS. Nevertheless, there are 200,000 to 500,000 new cases of genital herpes each year ("CDC tackles surge," 1998).

Once you get herpes, it's yours for life. After the initial attack, it remains an unwelcome guest in your body. It finds a cozy place to lie low until it stirs up trouble again. It causes recurrent outbreaks that often happen at the worst times, such as around final exams. This is not just bad luck. Stress can depress the functioning of the immune system and heighten the likelihood of outbreaks.

Not only are you stuck with the virus. You can also pass it along to sex partners for the rest of your life. Flare-ups might continue to recur, sometimes with annoying frequency. On the other hand, some people have no recurrences. Still others have mild, brief recurrences that become less frequent over time.

In the wake of the AIDS epidemic, the threat of genital herpes has not received much attention. Yet the viruses that cause herpes are alive and well. There are actually different

figure 16.6

Herpes Lesion on the Male Genitals.
Herpes lesions or sores can appear on the genitals in women or men and be associated with flulike symptoms.

types of herpes that are caused by variants of the *herpes simplex* virus. The most common type, **herpes simplex virus type 1** (HSV-1 virus) causes oral herpes. Oral herpes is characterized by cold sores or fever blisters on the lips or mouth. It can also be transferred to the genitals by the hands or by oral-genital contact (Mertz et al., 1992). **Genital herpes** is caused by a related but distinct virus, the **herpes simplex virus type 2** (HSV-2). This virus produces painful shallow sores and blisters on the genitals (see Figure 16.6). HSV-2 can also be transferred to the mouth through oral-genital contact. Both types of herpes can be transmitted sexually. Another type of herpes virus (type 8) is also transmitted sexually and is connected with Kaposi's sarcoma, a kind of cancer that is found frequently in men with HIV/AIDS (Martin et al., 1998).

Physicians are not required to report cases of herpes to public health officials, so there are no precise statistics on its prevalence. It is estimated that more than 100 million people in the United States are infected with oral herpes and perhaps 30 million with genital herpes (Brody, 1993a).

TRANSMISSION Herpes can be transmitted through oral, anal, or vaginal sexual activity with an infected person (Martin et al., 1998; Mertz et al., 1992; Wald et al., 1995). The herpes viruses can also survive for several hours on toilet seats or other objects, where they can be picked up by direct contact. Oral herpes is easily contracted by drinking from the same cup as an infected person, by kissing, even by sharing towels. But genital herpes is generally spread by coitus or by oral or anal sex.

One problem is that many people do not realize that they are infected. They can thus unknowingly transmit the virus through sexual contact. And many of the people who know that they are infected don't realize that they can pass along the virus even when they have no noticeable outbreak (Mertz et al., 1992; Wald et al., 1995). Though genital herpes is most contagious during active flare-ups, it can also be transmitted when an infected partner has no symptoms (genital sores or feelings of burning or itching in the genitals). Any intimate contact with an infected person carries some risk of transmission of the virus, even if the infected person never has another outbreak. People may also be infected with the virus and have no outbreaks yet pass the virus along to others.

Herpes simplex virus type 1
The virus that causes oral herpes, which is characterized by cold sores or fever blisters on the lips or mouth. Abbreviated HSV-1.

Genital herpes An STI caused by the herpes simplex virus type 2 and characterized by painful shallow sores and blisters on the genitals.

Herpes simplex virus type 2
The virus that causes genital herpes. Abbreviated HSV-2.

Truth or Fiction?
REVISITED

It is not true that genital herpes can be transmitted only during flare-ups of the infection. Genital herpes can be transmitted between flare-ups, although people are most contagious during outbreaks of the disease. ■

Herpes can also be spread from one part of the body to another by touching the infected area and then touching another body part. One potentially serious result is a herpes infection of the eye: **ocular herpes.** Thorough washing with soap and water after touching an infected area might reduce the risk of spreading the infection to other parts of the body. Still, it is best to avoid touching the infected area altogether, especially if there are active sores.

Women with genital herpes are more likely than the general population to have miscarriages. Passage through the birth canal of an infected mother can infect babies with genital herpes, damaging or killing them (Whitley et al., 1991). Obstetricians therefore often perform cesarean sections if the mother has active lesions or **prodromal symptoms** at the time of delivery (Osborne & Adelson, 1990). Herpes can also place women at greater risk of genital cancers, such as cervical cancer. (All women, not just women with herpes, are advised to have regular pelvic examinations, including Pap tests for early detection of cervical cancer.)

SYMPTOMS   Genital lesions or sores appear about six to eight days after infection with genital herpes. At first, they appear as reddish, painful bumps, or papules, along the penis or the vulva. They may also appear on the thighs or buttocks, in the vagina, or on the cervix. These papules turn into groups of small blisters that are filled with fluid containing infectious viral particles. The blisters are attacked by the body's immune system (white blood cells). They fill with pus, burst, and become extremely painful, shallow sores or ulcers that are surrounded by a red ring. People are especially infectious during such outbreaks, as the ulcers shed millions of viral particles. Other symptoms may include headaches and muscle aches, swollen lymph glands, fever, burning urination, and a vaginal discharge. The blisters crust over and heal within one to three weeks. Internal sores in the vagina or on the cervix may take 10 days longer than external (labial) sores to heal completely. Physicians therefore advise infected women to avoid unprotected intercourse for at least 10 days after the healing of external sores.

Although the symptoms disappear, the disease does not. The virus remains in the body permanently, burrowing into nerve cells in the base of the spine, where it may lie dormant for years or a lifetime. The infected person is least contagious during this dormant stage. For reasons that remain unclear, the virus becomes reactivated and gives rise to recurrences in most cases.

Recurrences may be related to factors such as infections (as in a cold), stress, fatigue, depression, exposure to the sun, and hormonal changes, such as those that occur during pregnancy or menstruation. Recurrences tend to occur within 3 to 12 months of the initial episode and to affect the same part of the body.

About 50% of people with recurrent herpes experience prodromal symptoms before an active outbreak (Reinisch, 1990). These warning signs may include feelings of burning, itching, pain, tingling, or tenderness in the affected area. These symptoms may be accompanied by sharp pains in the lower extremities, groin, or buttocks. People with herpes may be more infectious when prodromal symptoms appear. They are advised to avoid unprotected sex until the flare-up subsides.

Symptoms of oral herpes include sores or blisters on the lips, the inside of the mouth, the tongue, or the throat. Fever and feelings of sickness may occur. The gums may swell and redden. The sores heal over in about two weeks, and the virus retreats into nerve cells at the base of the neck, where it lies dormant between flare-ups. About 90% of people with oral herpes experience recurrences. About half of them have five or more recurrences during the first two years after the initial outbreak (Reinisch, 1990).

Ocular herpes A herpes infection of the eye, usually caused by touching an infected area of the body and then touching the eye.

Prodromal symptoms Warning symptoms that signal the onset or flare-up of a disease. (From the Greek *prodromos,* meaning "forerunner.")

DIAGNOSIS AND TREATMENT   Genital herpes is first diagnosed by clinical inspection of herpetic sores or ulcers in the mouth or on the genitals. A sample of fluid may be taken from the base of a genital sore and cultured in the laboratory to detect the growth of the virus.

There is no cure or safe, effective vaccine for herpes. Viruses, unlike the bacteria that cause gonorrhea or syphilis, do not respond to antibiotics. Antiviral drugs such as acyclovir (brand name: Zovirax), famciclovir (Diaz-Mitoma et al., 1998), and valacyclovir can relieve pain, speed healing, and reduce the duration of viral shedding (Cates, 1998). Acyclovir can be applied directly to the sores in ointment form but must be taken orally, in pill form, to help combat internal lesions in the vagina or on the cervix. Oral administration of antiviral drugs may reduce the severity of the initial episode and, if taken regularly, the frequency and duration of recurrent outbreaks (Cates, 1998).

Warm baths, loose-fitting clothing, aspirin, and cold, wet compresses may relieve pain during flare-ups. People with herpes are advised to maintain regular sleeping habits and to learn to manage stress.

COPING WITH GENITAL HERPES   The psychological problems connected with herpes can be more distressing than the physical effects of the illness. The prospects of a lifetime of recurrences and concerns about infecting one's sex partners exacerbate the emotional impact of herpes. A "herpes syndrome" has been described that involves feelings of anger, depression, isolation, and shame—even thoughts of being tainted, ugly, or dangerous (Mirotznik et al., 1987).

An anonymous survey of Brooklyn College students suggests the emotional toll being exacted by the herpes epidemic. Fifty-five percent of people with herpes reported strong emotional responses to it. Twenty-eight percent reported moderate reactions. Only 17% reported mild reactions (Mirotznik et al., 1987). The majority reported feelings of fear and anger. Half indicated feeling "damaged." Most also believed that herpes had affected their sexual behavior. Seventy-five percent said that they had avoided sex for "a long time" because of herpes. Although most had resumed sexual activity, many sought partners who were also infected so that they would not have to explain the disease, or risk transmitting it, to uninfected people. Given the consequences of herpes, you might think that students would be concerned about contracting the disease. Another survey at Brooklyn College revealed that most sexually active, uninfected students perceived herpes as having serious consequences. However, about three of four were not fearful of contracting the disease, and nearly half had not changed their dating behavior because of it (Mirotznik, 1991).

People with herpes often feel angry, especially toward those who transmitted the disease to them. They might feel anxious about making a long-term commitment or bearing children:

> After the first big episode of herpes, I felt distant from my body. When we began lovemaking again, I had a hard time having orgasms or trusting the rhythm of my responses. I shed some tears over that. I felt my body had been invaded. My body feels riddled with it; I'm somehow contaminated. And there is always that lingering anxiety: is my baby okay? It's unjust that the birth of my child may be affected. (Boston Women's Health Book Collective, 1992)

Most people with herpes learn to cope. Some are helped by support groups that share ways of living with the disease. A caring and trusting partner is important. Joanne, a 26-year-old securities analyst, kept her herpes a secret from Jonathan during the first month they were dating. But when they approached the point of becoming sexually intimate, she felt obligated to tell him that she carried the virus:

> I feared that telling him would scare him off. After all, who wants to have a relationship with someone who can give them herpes? After the first few dates I felt that this was the

person I could spend the rest of my life with. I knew he also felt the same way. I had to tell him before things became too intense between us. Believe me, it wasn't easy blurting it out. He wasn't shocked or anything, although he did ask me all kinds of questions about it. I remember telling him that I got recurrences about once a year or so for about a week at a time. I told him that there was always the potential that I could infect him but that we would play it safe and avoid having sex whenever I had an outbreak. I also told him that even at other times I couldn't guarantee that it would be perfectly safe. He said at first that he needed some time to think about it. But later, that very night in fact, he called to tell me that he didn't want this to come between us and that we should try to make our relationship work.

(Joanne and Jonathan were married about six months later. A year after that their daughter Andrea was born. Jonathan remains uninfected. Joanne's occasional outbreaks are treated with acyclovir ointment and pass within a week or so.) (from the authors' files)

The attitudes of people with herpes also play a role in adjusting. People who view herpes as a manageable illness or problem, not as a medical disaster or character deficit, seem to find it easier to cope.

Viral Hepatitis

Hepatitis is an inflammation of the liver that may be caused by such factors as chronic alcoholism and exposure to toxic materials. Viral hepatitis refers to several different types of hepatitis caused by related, but distinct, viruses. The major types are *hepatitis A* (formerly called infectious hepatitis), *hepatitis B* (formerly called serum hepatitis), *hepatitis C* (formerly called hepatitis non-A, non-B), and *hepatitis D*.

Most people with acute hepatitis have no symptoms (CDC, 1989b). When symptoms do appear, they often include **jaundice,** feelings of weakness and nausea, loss of appetite, abdominal discomfort, whitish bowel movements, and brownish or tea-colored urine. The symptoms of hepatitis B tend to be more severe and long-lasting than those of hepatitis A or C. In about 10% of cases, hepatitis B can lead to chronic liver disease. Hepatitis C tends to have milder symptoms but often leads to chronic liver disease such as cirrhosis or cancer of the liver. Hepatitis D—also called *delta hepatitis* or type D hepatitis—occurs only in the presence of hepatitis B. Hepatitis D, which has symptoms similar to those of hepatitis B, can produce severe liver damage and often leads to death.

The hepatitis A virus is transmitted through contact with infected fecal matter found in contaminated food or water and by oral contact with fecal matter, as through oral-anal sexual activity (licking or mouthing the partner's anus). (It is largely because of the risk of hepatitis A that restaurant employees are required to wash their hands after using the toilet.) Ingesting uncooked infested shellfish is also a frequent means of transmission of hepatitis A (Lemon & Newbold, 1990).

Hepatitis B can be transmitted sexually through anal, vaginal, or oral intercourse with an infected partner; through transfusion with contaminated blood supplies; by the sharing of contaminated needles or syringes; and by contact with contaminated saliva, menstrual blood, nasal mucus, or semen (Lemon & Newbold, 1990). Sharing razors, toothbrushes, or other personal articles with an infected person can also transmit hepatitis B. Hepatitis C and hepatitis D can also be transmitted sexually or through contact with contaminated blood. A person can transmit the viruses that cause hepatitis even if he or she is unaware of having any symptoms of the disease.

Hepatitis is usually diagnosed by testing blood samples for the presence of hepatitis antigens and antibodies. There is no cure for viral hepatitis. Bed rest and fluids are usually recommended until the acute stage of the infection subsides, generally in a few weeks. Full recovery might take months. A vaccine provides protection against hepatitis B and also against hepatitis D, since hepatitis D can occur only if hepatitis B is present (Cates, 1998).

Hepatitis An inflammation of the liver. (From the Greek *hepar,* meaning "liver.")

Jaundice A yellowish discoloration of the skin and the whites of the eyes. (From the Old French *jaune,* meaning "yellow.")

Genital Warts

The *human papilloma virus* (HPV) causes **genital warts** (formerly termed *venereal warts*). HPV is the world's most common sexually transmitted infection, with signs of infection found in nearly half of the adult women in some countries (Ho and others, 1998). There are 800,000 new diagnosed infections each year in the United States. It also appears that more than half of the sexually active college women in the United States are infected with HPV. Though the warts may appear in visible areas of the skin, in perhaps 7 of 10 cases they appear in areas that cannot be seen, such as on the cervix in women or in the urethra in men (Reinisch, 1990). They occur most commonly among people in the 20- to 24-year-old age range (Reinisch, 1990). Within a few months after infection, the warts are usually found in the genital and anal regions. Women are more susceptible to HPV infection because cells in the cervix divide swiftly, facilitating the multiplication of HPV (Blakeslee, 1992). Women who initiate coitus before the age of 18 and who have many sex partners are particularly susceptible to infection (Blakeslee, 1992). Similarly, it is estimated that nearly half of the sexually active teenage women in some U.S. cities are infected with HPV (Blakeslee, 1992).

Genital warts are similar to common plantar warts—itchy bumps that vary in size and shape (see Figure 16.7). Genital warts are hard and yellow-gray when they form on dry skin. They take on pink, soft, cauliflower shapes in moist areas such as the lower vagina. In men, they appear on the penis, foreskin and scrotum, and within the urethra. They appear on the vulva, along the vaginal wall, and on the cervix in women. They can occur outside the genital area in either gender—for example, in the mouth; on the lips, eyelids, or nipples; around the anus; or in the rectum.

Genital warts might not cause any symptoms, but those that form on the urethra can cause bleeding or painful discharges. HPV has been implicated in cancers of the genital organs, particularly cervical cancer and penile cancer (Koutsky et al., 1992). Ninety percent of cases of cervical cancer are linked to certain strains of HPV (Cannistra & Niloff, 1996; Reaney, 1998). Researchers in one study found that women who had a history of HPV infection were 11 times more likely than other women to develop cervical cancer during the two-year study period (Koutsky et al., 1992). Moreover, women whose husbands visit prostitutes or have many sex partners are 5 to 11 times as likely as other married women to develop cervical cancer ("Roving mates," 1996). All in all, it would seem wise for women to safeguard themselves from HPV-related cervical cancer by limiting their number of sex partners (to reduce their risk of exposure to HPV), thinking about the extracurricular sexual activities of their mates, and having regular Pap smears.

HPV can be transmitted sexually through skin-to-skin contact during vaginal, anal, or oral sex. It can also be transmitted by other forms of contact, such as touching infected towels or clothing. The incubation period may vary from a few weeks to a couple of years.

Freezing the wart *(cryotherapy)* with liquid nitrogen is a preferred treatment. One alternative treatment involves painting or coating the warts over several days with podofilox solution or gel, imiquimod cream, trichloroacetic acid (TCA), or bichloroacetic acid (BCA) (Cates, 1998). An alcohol-based podophyllin solution causes the warts to dry up and fall off. Unfortunately, though the warts themselves may be removed, treatment does not rid the body of the virus (Cates, 1998). There may thus be recurrences. Podophyllin is not recommended for use with pregnant women or for treatment of warts that form on the cervix. The warts can also be treated by a doctor with electrodes (burning) or surgery (by laser or surgical removal).

Researchers are attempting to develop a vaccine for HPV, based on the discovery of molecules that inform the immune system that that virus is present (Reaney, 1998). For the time being, however, prevention means using latex condoms, which help to reduce the risk of contracting HPV. They do not eliminate the risk entirely because the virus can be transmitted from areas of the skin that are not protected by condoms, such as the scrotum (Ochs, 1994). People with active warts should probably avoid sexual contact until the warts are removed and the area heals completely.

f i g u r e   16.7

Genital Warts. Genital warts are caused by the human papilloma virus (HPV) and often have a cauliflower appearance.

Genital warts An STI that is caused by the human papilloma virus and takes the form of warts that appear around the genitals and anus.

Molluscum Contagiosum

Molluscum contagiosum is caused by a pox virus that can be spread sexually. The virus causes painless raised lesions to appear on the genitals, buttocks, thighs, or lower abdomen. Pinkish in appearance with a waxy or pearly top, they usually appear within two or three months of infection. Most infected people have between 10 and 20 lesions, although the number of lesions can range from 1 to perhaps 100 or more (Douglas, 1990). The lesions are generally not associated with serious complications and often disappear on their own within six months. Or they can be treated by squeezing them (like "popping" a blackhead) to exude the whitish center plug. Solutions of podophyllin, trichloroacetic acid (TCA), or silver nitrate are also used. Freezing with liquid nitrogen (cryotherapy) can also be used to remove the lesions. However, do not try to treat any lesions on your own. See your doctor.

Reflections

- Do you think that AIDS is something for you to be concerned about or something that affects "other people"? Explain.
- Why do you think knowledge about the deadliness of AIDS and modes of transmission of HIV does not translate into people's ceasing risky behavior?
- Do you favor distribution of condoms in the public schools as a means of attempting to prevent transmission of HIV? Do you support the distribution of free hypodermic needles to people who inject drugs? Why or why not?
- Many people with genital herpes feel "damaged" and avoid sex. How do you believe that you would feel if you had genital herpes? Why?
- How might you discuss a herpes infection with a prospective lover or mate?

ECTOPARASITIC INFESTATIONS

Ectoparasites, as opposed to *endoparasites*, live on the outer surfaces of animals (*ecto* means "outer"). *Trichomonas vaginalis*, which causes trichomoniasis, is an endoparasite (*endo* means "inner"). Ectoparasites are larger than the agents that cause other STIs. In this section, we consider two types of STIs caused by ectoparasites: pediculosis and scabies.

Pediculosis

Pediculosis is the name given to an infestation of a parasite whose proper Latin name, *Phthirus pubis* (pubic lice), sounds rather too dignified for these bothersome (dare we say ugly?) creatures that are better known as "crabs." Pubic lice are commonly called "crabs" because, under the microscope, they are somewhat similar in appearance to crabs (see Figure 16.8). They belong to a family of insects called biting lice. Another member of the family, the human head louse, is an annoying insect that clings to hair on the scalp and often spreads among schoolchildren.

Truth or Fiction? **REVISITED**

It is not true that pubic lice are of the same family of animals as crabs. Viewed under a microscope, however, they look somewhat similar to crabs. ■

In the adult stage, pubic lice are large enough to be seen with the naked eye. They are spread sexually but can also be transmitted by contact with an infested towel, sheet, or—yes—toilet seat. They can survive for only about 24 hours without a human host, but they may deposit eggs that can take up to seven days to hatch in bedding or towels (Reinisch, 1990). Therefore, all bedding, towels, and clothes that have been used by an infested person must be washed in hot water and dried on the hot cycle or dry-cleaned to ensure that they are safe. Fingers may also transmit the lice from the genitals to other

Molluscum contagiosum An STI caused by a pox virus that causes painless raised lesions to appear on the genitals, buttocks, thighs, or lower abdomen.

hair-covered parts of the body, including the scalp and armpits. Sexual contact should be avoided until the infestation is eradicated.

Itching, ranging from the mildly irritating to the intolerable, is the most prominent symptom of a pubic lice infestation. The itching is caused by the "crabs" attaching themselves to the pubic hair and piercing the skin to feed on the blood of their hosts. (Yecch!) The life span of these insects is only about one month, but they are prolific egg-layers and may spawn several generations before they die. An infestation can be treated effectively with a prescription medication, a 1% solution of lindane (brand name: Kwell), which is available as a cream, lotion, or shampoo. Nonprescription medications containing pyrethrins or piperonyl butoxide (brand names: RID, Triple X, and others) will also do the job (Reinisch, 1990). Kwell is not recommended for use by pregnant or lactating women (CDC, 1989b). A careful reexamination of the body is necessary after four to seven days of treatment to ensure that all lice and eggs were killed (Reinisch, 1990).

figure 16.8

Pubic Lice. Pediculosis is an infestation by such pubic lice (*Phthirus pubis.*) Pubic lice are commonly called "crabs" because of their appearance under a microscope.

Scabies

Scabies (short for *Sarcoptes scabiei*) is a parasitic infestation caused by a tiny mite that may be transmitted through sexual contact or contact with infested clothing, bed linen, towels, and other fabrics. The mites attach themselves to the base of pubic hair and burrow into the skin, where they lay eggs and subsist for the duration of their 30-day life span. Like pubic lice, scabies are often found in the genital region and cause itching and discomfort. They are also responsible for reddish lines (created by burrowing) and sores, welts, or blisters on the skin. Unlike lice, they are too tiny to be seen by the naked eye. Diagnosis is made by detecting the mite or its by-products on microscopic examination of scrapings from suspicious-looking areas of skin (Levine, 1991). Scabies are most often found on the hands and wrists, but they may also appear on the genitals, buttocks, armpits, and feet (Reinisch, 1990). They do not appear above the neck—thankfully!

Scabies, like pubic lice, may be treated effectively with 1% lindane (Kwell). The entire body from the neck down must be coated with a thin layer of the medication, which should not be washed off for eight hours (CDC, 1989b). But lindane should not be used by women who are pregnant or lactating. To avoid reinfection, sex partners and others in close bodily contact with infected individuals should also be treated. Clothing and bed linen that the infected person has used must be washed and dried on the hot cycle or dry-cleaned. As with "crabs," sexual contact should be avoided until the infestation is eliminated.

Reflections

■ Had you ever heard of "crabs"? What had you imagined the word meant? Were you correct?

PREVENTION OF STIs: IT'S MORE THAN SAFER SEX

Prevention is the best way to control the spread of STIs, especially those for which there is no cure or vaccine. Prevention of even one case of an STI can prevent its spread to others—and perhaps eventually to you.

Prevention Strategies

There are many things that you can do to lower the risk of contracting STIs. As you will see, safer sex is only one aspect of prevention.

Ectoparasites Parasites that live on the outside of the host's body—in contrast to *endoparasites*, which live within the body. (From the Greek *ektos*, meaning "outside.")

Pediculosis A parasitic infestation by pubic lice (*Phthirus pubis*) that causes itching.

Scabies A parasitic infestation caused by a tiny mite (*Sarcoptes scabiei*) that causes itching.

CONSIDER ABSTINENCE OR MONOGAMY

> I don't even masturbate anymore. I'm so afraid I'll give myself something. I just want to be friends with myself.
> —Richard Lewis

The only fully effective strategies to prevent the sexual transmission of STIs are abstinence or maintaining a monogamous sexual relationship with an uninfected partner. If you are celibate or if you and your sex partner are not infected and neither of you engages in sexual activity with anyone else, you have little to be concerned about. Many people are sexually active and have not committed themselves to a monogamous relationship, however. Even for those who seek monogamous relationships, there must always be that "first time."

BE KNOWLEDGEABLE ABOUT THE RISKS   Be aware of the risks of STIs. Many of us try to put the dangers of STIs out of our minds—especially in moments of passion. Make a pact with yourself to refuse to play the dangerous game of pretending that the dangers of STIs do not exist or that you are somehow immune.

Prevention programs are apparently raising public awareness of HIV/AIDS. Seventy-nine percent of respondents to a 1993 *The New York Times*/CBS News national poll correctly recognized that one cannot be infected with HIV by sharing a drinking glass with a person with AIDS, up from 34% in 1985. Eighty-nine percent recognized that you cannot be infected by a toilet seat, up from 49% in 1985. Nearly everyone knew that HIV can be transmitted by male-female sex (96%) and blood transfusions (98%). More people today are also personally acquainted with a person with AIDS. One-third of those polled know someone who has died of AIDS or has either HIV infection or AIDS.

Knowledge about HIV transmission does not always translate into behavioral change, such as increased use of latex condoms (which can block the transmission of HIV) and other safer sex practices. In fact, knowledge about transmission of HIV and other STIs is not clearly related to condom use (Geringer et al., 1993; Klepinger et al., 1993; Rotheram-Borus & Koopman, 1991a, 1991b). Despite widespread efforts to educate the public about the dangers of unprotected sex, negative attitudes toward using condoms persist, especially among males (Fisher et al., 1995). Consider the litany of complaints we come across: "They reduce sexual pleasure. . . . They're a nuisance to put on. . . . They cost too much. . . . They interrupt sex," and so on.

Virtually all young people are similarly aware of the sexual transmission of HIV (Wulfert & Wan, 1993). Why, then, do so many of them continue to engage in risky sexual behavior?

For one thing, teenagers do not perceive risky behavior to be as dangerous as adults do. This generalization extends to drinking, smoking, failure to use seat belts, and drag racing, as well as sexual behavior (Cohn et al., 1995). Young people also profit from being taught specific skills to protect themselves from engaging in risky behaviors, such as communication skills for discussing safer sex options with their partners, assertiveness skills for ensuring that their needs and interests are respected by their partners, social skills to resist peer pressures, and correct use of condoms (Kamb et al., 1998; St. Lawrence et al., 1995). Greater efforts are needed to reverse peer norms that discourage condom use. For example, it might be advisable for adolescents themselves to support and teach condom use to their peers (Hodges et al., 1992).

Researchers have identified several factors underlying risky sexual behavior among young people:

1. *Perceived low risk of infection.* One of the major stumbling blocks in promoting safer sex practices is that many young heterosexuals perceive a low risk of contracting HIV (Nadeau et al., 1993; Oswalt & Matsen, 1993). People who perceive themselves as being at low risk are less likely to alter their behavior.

   Given the current low rate of known infections among heterosexuals who do not inject drugs, many heterosexuals may perceive risky sexual practices to be a reasonable gamble (Pinkerton & Abramson, 1992). Heterosexuals who have never had a friend or relative with HIV or AIDS might dismiss HIV infection and AIDS as problems that affect other types of people. Even gay men might operate under the "I'm not the type" fallacy and underestimate their personal risks. According to Pinkerton & Abramson (1992),

the frightening picture that emerges is one in which it is only the *other guy* (or gal) who gets AIDS: To the heterosexual who does not inject drugs, it's just gays and "druggies" that get AIDS; to the "average" gay man, it's those gay men who are overly promiscuous; and to the bath house participant, it's those who aren't "careful." (pp. 564–565)

2. *Negative attitudes toward condom use.* Many factors discourage condom use. Some people feel embarrassed to buy them. For others, the risk of being infected with HIV seems to fly out of their minds whenever the opportunity for sex arises. Some claim that a condom dampens romantic ardor in moments of passion by requiring an interruption of the sexual act to apply one. Some people just regard them as too much of a fuss. Many men say that condoms deprive them of sexual pleasure. Unless such obstacles to using condoms are overcome, efforts to stem the tide of HIV infection might be thwarted.

3. *Myth of personal invulnerability.* Another factor underlying risky sexual behaviors is that some people subscribe to a myth of personal invulnerability and believe that they are somehow immune to AIDS and other diseases. Even students who are generally well informed about STIs might perceive themselves as personally immune. One junior at the University of Miami (Ohio) explained to an interviewer why she did not insist that her partners use a condom: "I have an attitude—it may be wrong—that any guy I would sleep with would not have AIDS" (Johnson, 1990, p. A18). The adventurous spirit that we often associate with youth might confer a dangerous sense of immortality and a greater willingness to take risks (Johnson, 1990). Perceptions of personal invulnerability help to explain why AIDS education does not always translate into behavioral change (Rosenthal et al., 1992).

Making Sex Safe(r). There are many ways to protect oneself and one's partner from STIs. The first step is recognizing that STIs exist and that everyone is vulnerable to them.

Even people who do not believe themselves to be immune might underestimate their risk of being infected with HIV (van der Velde et al., 1994). This finding holds true for impoverished inner-city residents (Hobfoll et al., 1993) as well as college students (Goldman & Harlow, 1993). People tend to view themselves as luckier than the norm. (After all, don't you believe that you alone hold the winning lottery ticket?) Moreover, since the transmission of HIV infection through casual male-female sexual encounters is an infrequent event, people who regularly engage in risky sexual practices and so far have remained uninfected might be lulled into a false sense of security.

REMAIN SOBER Alcohol and other drugs increase the likelihood of engaging in risky sexual behavior.

INSPECT YOURSELF AND YOUR PARTNER Inspect yourself for a discharge, bumps, rashes, warts, blisters, chancres, sores, lice, or foul odors. Do not expect to find telltale signs of an HIV infection, but infected people often have other STIs. Check out any unusual feature with a physician before you engage in sexual activity.

You might be able to work an inspection of your partner into foreplay—a reason for making love the first time with the lights on. In particular, a woman can hold her partner's penis firmly, pulling the loose skin up and down, as if "milking" it. Then she can check for a discharge at the penile opening. The man can use his fingers to detect any sign of a vaginal discharge. Other visible features of STIs include herpes blisters, genital warts, syphilitic chancres or rashes, and pubic lice.

If you find anything that doesn't look, feel, or smell right, bring it to your partner's attention. Treat any unpleasant odor as a warning sign. Your partner might not be aware of the symptom and might be carrying an infection. If you notice any suspicious signs, refrain from further sexual contact until your partner has the chance to seek a medical evaluation. It is advisable to be informed about the common signs and symptoms of STIs, but you need not become a medical expert. Even if your concerns prove groundless, you can resume sexual relations without the uncertainty that you would have had if you had ignored them.

Of course, your partner might become defensive or hostile if you express a concern that he or she may be carrying an STI. Try to be empathetic. The social stigma that is attached to people with STIs makes it difficult to accept the possibility of infection. It might be appropriate to point out that STIs are quite common (among college students, bank officers, military personnel, or . . . fill in the blanks) and that many people are unaware that they carry them.

But for your sake as well as your partner's, if you are not sure that sex is safe, stop. Think carefully about the risks and seek expert advice.

USE LATEX CONDOMS   Latex condoms are effective in blocking nearly all sexually transmissible organisms (Hatcher et al., 1998). In regular use, condoms reduce the rate of STI infections by about 50%, on the average (Hatcher et al., 1998). Improper use or inconsistent use is a common reason for failures in using condoms to prevent STI transmission (Hatcher et al., 1998). Yet even when used properly, condoms may be of limited or no value against disease-causing organisms that are transmitted externally, such as those causing herpes, genital warts, and ectoparasitic infestations.

Condoms that are made from animal membranes ("skins") are less effective as barriers against STI-causing organisms (they contain pores that allow tiny microbes, including HIV, to penetrate). Even latex condoms are not 100% effective in preventing the transmission of HIV and other STIs. Condoms (and the people who use them) are fallible. Condoms can break or slip off.

USE BARRIER DEVICES WHEN PRACTICING ORAL SEX (FELLATIO OR CUNNILINGUS)
If you decide to practice oral sex, use a condom before practicing fellatio and a dental dam (a square piece of latex rubber used by dentists during oral surgery) to cover the vagina before engaging in cunnilingus (Reinisch, 1990).

AVOID HIGH-RISK SEXUAL BEHAVIORS   Avoid unprotected vaginal intercourse (intercourse without the use of a latex condom). Unprotected anal intercourse is one of riskiest practices. Other high-risk behaviors include unprotected oral-genital activity, oral-anal activity, insertion of a hand or fist ("fisting") into someone's rectum or vagina, or any activity in which you or your partner would come into contact with the other's blood, semen, or vaginal secretions. If you do engage in anal-genital sex and are uncertain as to whether you or your partner is infected, use a latex condom and spermicide. Oral-anal sex, or anilingus (sometimes called *rimming*), should be avoided because of the potential of transmitting microbes between the mouth and the anus.

Also avoid sexual contact with people with STIs, people who practice high-risk sexual behaviors, people who inject drugs, and prostitutes or people who frequent prostitutes.

WASH THE GENITALS BEFORE AND AFTER SEX   Washing the genitals before and after sex removes a quantity of potentially harmful agents. Washing together can be incorporated into erotic foreplay. Right after intercourse, a thorough washing with soap and water might help to reduce the risk of infection. Do not, however, deceive yourself into believing that washing your genitals is an effective substitute for safer sex. Most STIs are transmitted internally. Washing is of no avail against them.

Douching right after coitus might have some limited benefits for women. But frequent douching should be avoided, since it may change the vaginal flora and encourage the growth of infectious organisms. Nor is immediate douching possible for women who use a diaphragm and spermicide that must remain in the vagina for at least six to eight hours after intercourse. But such women might profit from washing the external genitals immediately after coitus.

HAVE REGULAR MEDICAL CHECKUPS   A sexually active person should have health examinations regularly, at least once a year. Many community clinics and family-planning centers scale their charges to ability to pay. Checkups are a small investment to make in one's own health. Many people are symptomless carriers of STIs, especially of chlamydial infections. Medical checkups enable them to learn about and receive treatment for disorders that might otherwise go unnoticed. Many physicians advise routine testing of asymptomatic young women for chlamydial infections to prevent the hidden damage that can occur if the infection goes untreated (Buhaug et al., 1990).

DISCUSS WHETHER YOU AND YOUR PARTNER SHOULD UNDERGO TESTING BEFORE INITIATING SEXUAL RELATIONS   Some couples reach a mutual agreement to be tested for HIV and other STIs before they initiate sexual relations. (Some people simply insist that their prospective partners be tested before they initiate sexual relations.) But many people resist testing or feel insulted when their partners raise the issue. People usually assume that they are free of STIs if they are symptom-free and have been reasonably selective in their choice of partners. But STIs happen to the "nicest people," and the absence of symptoms is no guarantee of freedom from infection. Unless you have been celibate or involved in a monogamous relationship with an uninfected partner, you should consider yourself at risk of carrying or contracting an infectious STI.

ENGAGE IN NONCOITAL SEXUAL ACTIVITIES   Other forms of sexual expression, such as hugging, massage, caressing, mutual masturbation, and rubbing bodies together without vaginal, anal, or oral contact, are low-risk ways of finding sexual pleasure, as long as semen or vaginal fluids do not come into contact with mucous membranes or breaks in the skin. Many sexologists refer to such activities as **outercourse** to distinguish them from sexual intercourse. Sharing sexual fantasies can be very titillating, as can taking a bath or shower together. Vibrators, dildos, and other "sex toys" may also be erotically stimulating and carry a low risk of infection if they are washed thoroughly with soap and water before use and between uses by two people. If used for penetration, they should be used gently and with plenty of lubricant to avoid irritating or breaking vaginal or rectal tissues (Reinisch, 1990).

CONSULT YOUR PHYSICIAN IF YOU SUSPECT THAT YOU HAVE BEEN EXPOSED TO AN STI   If you think that you may have been exposed to an STI, such as HIV, see a doctor as soon as possible. Many STIs are detectable in the early stages of development and can be successfully treated. If HIV is in your bloodstream, there is some chance that it can be eradicated before it infects cells in the immune system. If you are infected with HIV, early treatment may keep virus levels low and prevent you from developing AIDS. Early intervention may also prevent the damage of an STI from spreading to vital body organs. Be sensitive to any physical changes that may be symptomatic of STIs. Talk to a health professional when in doubt.

GET TO KNOW YOUR PARTNER BEFORE INITIATING SEXUAL RELATIONS   Be selective in your choice of sex partners. Having sex with multiple partners—especially "one-night stands"—increases your risk of sexual contact with an infected person. It also lessens the opportunity to get to know your partner well enough to know whether he or she has participated in high-risk sexual practices or has had sex partners in the past who practiced high-risk behaviors.

Outercourse Forms of sexual expression, such as massage, hugging, caressing, mutual masturbation, and rubbing bodies together that do not involve the exchange of body fluids. (Contrast with *intercourse*.)

a CLOSER look

Sources of Help

Do you have questions about the signs and symptoms of STIs? Do you need assistance in coping with an STI? A number of organizations have established telephone hotlines that provide anonymous callers with information. Some organizations publish newsletters and other material to help people with particular diseases to cope more effectively.

National Toll-Free Hotlines for Information about AIDS and Other STIs

These hotlines provide information about AIDS and other STIs, as well as referral sources. You needn't give your name or identify yourself to obtain information.

National AIDS Hotline, Centers for Disease Control AIDS Hotline: (800) 342-AIDS: Information and referral resources nationwide, 24 hours a day.

National STI Hotline: (800) 227-8922 (in California, 800-982-5883) (A hotline sponsored by the American Social Health Association that dispenses information about STI symptoms and refers callers to local STI clinics that provide confidential, minimum or no cost treatment.)

Spanish AIDS/SIDA Hotline: (800) 344-7432

AIDS Hotline for Teens: (800) 234-TEEN

AIDS Hotline for the Hearing Impaired: (800) 243-7889

Canadian Toll-Free Hotline (Toll-free in Canada): AIDS Committee of Toronto: (800) 267-6600

Where to Obtain Help or Information about Herpes

National Herpes Hotline: (919) 361-8488

The Helper is a newsletter published by HELP (Herpetics Engaged in Living Productively), an organization that helps people who have herpes cope with the disease. For copies of the newsletter and for the address of the HELP chapter closest to you, either call the National STI Hotline (800-227-8922) or write to HELP, Herpes Resource Center, P.O. Box 13827, Research Triangle Park, NC 27709.

Herpes Resource Center, Box 100, Palo Alto, CA 94302

AVOID OTHER HIGH-RISK BEHAVIORS   Avoid contact with bodily substances (blood, semen, vaginal secretions, fecal matter) from other people. Do not share hypodermic needles, razors, cuticle scissors, or other implements that could contain another person's blood. Be careful when handling wet towels, bed linen, or other material that might contain bodily substances.

Reflections

- Which methods of preventing STIs seem workable to you? Why? Which seem unworkable? Explain.
- Will reading this chapter lead to any changes in your behavior? Why or why not?
- Agree or disagree with the following statement and support your answer: My partner and I should undergo testing before initiating sexual relations.

summing up

AN EPIDEMIC

More than 13 million people in the United States contract a sexually transmitted infection (STI) each year. Although public attention has been riveted on AIDS for a decade, other STIs such as chlamydia and genital warts pose wider threats.

BACTERIAL INFECTIONS

Bacteria are one-celled microorganisms that cause many illnesses.

Gonorrhea

Gonorrhea is caused by the gonococcus bacterium. For men, symptoms include a penile discharge and burning urination. Most women are asymptomatic. If left untreated, gonorrhea can attack the internal reproductive organs and lead to PID in women. Gonorrhea is treated with antibiotics.

Syphilis

Syphilis is caused by the *Treponema pallidum* bacterium. Syphilis undergoes several stages of development. Although it can lie dormant for many years, it may also be lethal. Syphilis is treated with antibiotics.

Chlamydia

Chlamydia or chlamydial infections are caused by the *Chlamydia trachomatis* bacterium. The symptoms of chlamydial infections resemble those of gonorrhea but tend to be milder. Chlamydial infections also respond to antibiotics.

VAGINAL INFECTIONS

Vaginitis is usually known by a foul-smelling discharge, genital irritation, and burning during urination. Most cases involve bacterial vaginosis, candidiasis, or trichomoniasis.

Bacterial Vaginosis

Bacterial vaginosis is usually caused by the *Gardnerella vaginalis* bacterium.

Candidiasis

Candidiasis is caused by a yeastlike fungus, *Candida albicans*. Infections usually arise from changes in the vaginal environment that allow the fungus to overgrow.

Trichomoniasis

"Trich" is caused by a protozoan called *Trichomonas vaginalis*.

VIRAL INFECTIONS

Viruses are particles of DNA that reproduce by invading a body cell and directing the cell's own reproductive machinery to spin off new viral particles.

HIV Infection and AIDS

The number of people worldwide who are infected with HIV (human immunodeficiency virus) stands at about 40 million. AIDS is caused by HIV, which attacks the body's immune system. As HIV disables the body's natural defenses, the person becomes vulnerable to opportunistic diseases—such as serious infections and cancers—that are normally held in check. HIV is a blood-borne virus that is also found in semen, vaginal secretions, and breast milk. Common avenues of transmission include sexual intercourse, transfusion with contaminated blood, sharing a hypodermic needle with an infected person, childbirth, and breast-feeding. HIV infection is usually diagnosed through blood, saliva, and urine tests that detect HIV antibodies. There is neither a cure for AIDS nor an effective, safe vaccine. The most effective form of treatment as this book goes to press is combination drug therapy, which uses a protease inhibitor along with other antiviral agents.

Herpes

Oral herpes is caused by the herpes simplex virus type 1 (HSV-1). Genital herpes is caused by the herpes simplex virus type 2 (HSV-2), which produces painful shallow sores and blisters on the genitals. There is no cure or vaccine for herpes, but antiviral drugs can relieve pain and speed healing during flare-ups.

Viral Hepatitis

There are several types of hepatitis, and they are caused by different hepatitis viruses. Most cases of hepatitis are transmitted sexually or by contact with contaminated blood or fecal matter.

Genital Warts

Genital warts are caused by the human papilloma virus (HPV). HPV has been linked to cancers of the genital tract. Freezing the wart is a preferred treatment for removal of the wart, but the virus remains in the body afterward.

Molluscum Contagiosum

This viral STI, caused by a pox virus, brings about an outbreak of painless raised lesions on the genitals, buttocks, thighs, or lower abdomen. The lesions usually disappear on their own without serious complications within six months.

ECTOPARASITIC INFESTATIONS

Pediculosis

Pediculosis ("crabs") is caused by pubic lice (*Phthirus pubis*). Pubic lice attach themselves to pubic hair and feed on the blood of their hosts, which often causes itching. Infestations can be treated with a prescription medication, lindane, or with nonprescription medications containing pyrethrins or piperonal butoxide.

Scabies

Scabies (*Sarcoptes scabiei*) is a parasitic infestation caused by a tiny mite that causes itching. Scabies, like pubic lice, is treated with lindane.

PREVENTION OF STIs: IT'S MORE THAN SAFER SEX

Strategies for preventing STIs include abstinence, monogamy, inspecting oneself and one's partner, using latex condoms, avoiding high-risk sex, washing the genitals before and after sex, having regular medical checkups, and getting to know one's partner before engaging in sexual activity.

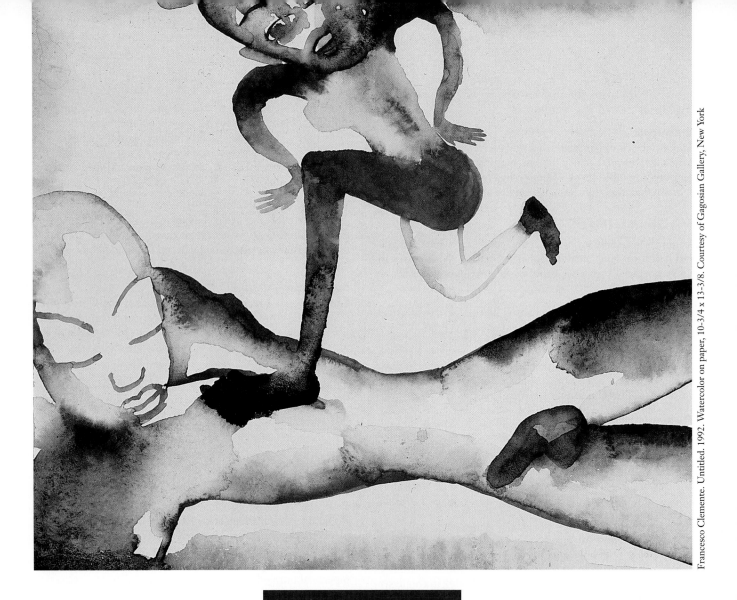

Francesco Clemente. Untitled. 1992. Watercolor on paper, 10-3/4 x 13-3/8. Courtesy of Gagosian Gallery, New York

chapter

17

Atypical Sexual Variations

outline

TRUTH OR FICTION?

NORMAL VERSUS DEVIANT SEXUAL BEHAVIOR

THE PARAPHILIAS

Fetishism

Transvestism

A CLOSER LOOK:
A Case of Transvestism

Exhibitionism

WHAT DO YOU SAY NOW?
How to Respond to an Exhibitionist

Obscene Telephone Calling

Voyeurism

IN THE NEW MILLENNIUM:
Exhibitionism, Voyeurism, and Videophones:
Videoconferencing's Killer App May Be Sex

Sexual Masochism

Sexual Sadism

Frotteurism

Other Paraphilias

A CLOSER LOOK:
Paraphilias as Sexual Addictions

A WORLD OF DIVERSITY:
Nymphomania, Satyriasis, and the Sexual
Double Standard

THEORETICAL PERSPECTIVES

Biological Perspectives

Psychoanalytic Perspectives

Learning Perspectives

Sociological Perspectives

An Integrated Perspective:
The "Lovemap"

TREATMENT OF THE PARAPHILIAS

Psychotherapy

Behavior Therapy

Biochemical Approaches

SUMMING UP

Truth or Fiction?

_____ King Henry III of France insisted on being considered a woman and addressed as "Her Majesty."

_____ Nude sunbathers are exhibitionists.

_____ People who enjoy watching their mates undress are voyeurs.

_____ Exhibitionists and voyeurs are never violent.

_____ Some people cannot become sexually aroused unless they are bound, flogged, or humiliated by their sex partners.

_____ It is considered normal to enjoy some mild forms of pain during sexual activity.

_____ There is a subculture in the United States in which sexual sadists and sexual masochists form liaisons to inflict and receive pain and humiliation during sexual activity.

t he following incident took place in New York City. It could have happened anyplace where windows of residences face one other across yards, alleyways, and narrow streets.

A newly married couple were in their apartment, and the wife walked over to the window, which looked into the window of another apartment, and as she put it when recalling the story, "I just couldn't believe my eyes." The couple across the way, who had not pulled down a shade, and who had no curtain on the window, were relaxing on the bed. At least it seemed as if they were relaxing, but soon they became active and energetic, going through all the motions of discovery and exploration, no doubt precoital. There stood the watcher at the window, safe in a perch where she could remain undetected. "Disgusting," she murmured under her breath, but the spectacle held her in fascination. . . . She could not move herself from the window. She did, however, become fearful that the couple might look up and see her, so she stepped inside, and continued to watch by peering out from behind the wall. Still they continued, still she watched. Finally, she called her husband. He too watched, his eyes glued on what had become by then the primal scene. Then he walked away, went to the bedroom, and returned, a pair of opera glasses in his hand.

"No, you will not look with those glasses," the wife indignantly said. "What are you, anyway, a voyeur?"

"But you've been standing over here, watching, all this time, and you called me over," he protested.

"Yes, I called you to see what's going on, but not to get your glasses. I have a right to look out of my own window, and it's their problem if they don't have the decency to pull down a shade. But when you get a telescope, well, that's going too far!" And she insisted at this point that she and her husband, the peepers, pull down the shades. (Sagarin, 1973, p. 5)

The incident raises questions about our labels for sexual behavior—particularly about the boundaries between what is normal and what is deviant or abnormal. One couple clearly created conditions under which their sexual activity might become public. Another couple became spellbound by what they were doing. The exposed couple were in their own home, but could they be considered *exhibitionists*? And were the observers *voyeurs*? The observing wife became indignant when her husband brought out opera glasses. Perhaps she could justify her own "peeping" by thinking that she had stumbled across the other couple. Using opera glasses would transform her accidental discovery into a purposeful act, however. Then, perhaps, she could no longer regard watching as "normal."

What is normal and what is abnormal or deviant sexual behavior? In this chapter we explore a number of sexual behaviors that deviate from the norm in one sense or another.

NORMAL VERSUS DEVIANT SEXUAL BEHAVIOR

One common approach to defining normality is based on a statistical norm. From this perspective, rare or unusual sexual behaviors are considered abnormal or deviant. The statistical approach might seem value-free, since the yardstick of normality is based on the frequency of behavior, not on judgment of its social acceptability. Engaging in coitus while standing or more than seven times a week might be considered deviant by this yardstick. The choice of behaviors that we subject to statistical comparison is not divorced from our underlying values, however. Sexual practices such as humming tunes from Rodgers and Hammerstein musicals while making love might be statistically infrequent (at least for people born after 1960) but would not be considered aberrant. Statistical infrequency, then, is not a sufficient criterion for classifying behavior as abnormal or deviant. We must also consider whether the sexual practice deviates from a social norm.

What is considered normal in one culture or at a particular time may be considered abnormal in other cultures and at other times. A gay male or lesbian sexual orientation was considered abnormal throughout most of Western history and was labeled a mental disorder by the American Psychiatric Association. But in 1973, a gay male or lesbian sexual orientation was dropped as a mental disorder from the association's official diagnostic manual. What is "normal" behavior for the female adolescent Trobriand islander (see Chapter 1) might be considered deviant—even *nymphomaniacal*—by the standards of Western culture.

In our own culture, sexual practices such as oral sex and masturbation were once considered to be deviant or abnormal. Today, however, they are practiced so widely in our society that few people would label them as deviant practices. Concepts of "normalcy" and "deviance," then, reflect the mores and customs of a particular culture at a given time.

Another basis for determining sexual deviance is to classify sexual practices as deviant when they involve the persistent preference for nongenital sexual outlets. If a man prefers fondling a woman's panties to engaging in sexual relations with her or prefers to masturbate against her foot rather than engage in coitus, his behavior is likely to be labeled deviant.

Because of the confusing array of meanings of the terms *deviant* and *abnormal*, we prefer to speak about unusual patterns of sexual arousal or behavior as "atypical variations" in sexual behavior rather than as "sexual deviations." Atypical patterns of sexual arousal or behavior that become problematic in the eyes of the individual or society are labeled *paraphilias* by the American Psychiatric Association (1994). Clinicians consider paraphilias to be mental disorders. But milder forms of these behaviors may be practiced by many people and fall within the normal spectrum of human sexuality (Brody, 1990a).

THE PARAPHILIAS

Paraphilias involve sexual arousal in response to unusual stimuli such as children or other nonconsenting persons (such as unsuspecting people whom one watches or to whom one exposes one's genitals), nonhuman objects (such as shoes, leather, rubber, or undergarments), or pain or humiliation. The psychiatric diagnosis of paraphilia requires that the person has acted on the urges or is distinctly distressed by them.

People with paraphilias usually feel that their urges are insistent, demanding, or compulsory (Money, 1988). They might describe themselves as overcome by these urges now and then (Brody, 1990a). People with paraphilias tend to experience their urges as beyond their control, as drug addicts or compulsive gamblers see themselves as helpless to avert irresistible urges. For these reasons, theorists have speculated that paraphilias may represent a type of sexual compulsion or an addiction.

Paraphilias vary in severity. In some cases, the person can function sexually in the absence of the unusual stimuli and seldom if ever acts upon his or her deviant urges. In other cases, the person resorts to paraphilic behavior only in times of stress. In more extreme forms, the person repeatedly engages in paraphilic behavior and might become preoccupied with thoughts and fantasies about these experiences. In such cases, the person might not be able to become sexually aroused without either fantasizing about the paraphilic stimulus or having it present. For some people, paraphilic behavior is the only means of attaining sexual gratification.

The person with a paraphilia typically replays the paraphilic act in sexual fantasies to stimulate arousal during masturbation or sexual relations. It is as if he or she is mentally replaying a videotape of the paraphilic scene. The scene grows stale after a while, how-

Paraphilia A diagnostic category used by the American Psychiatric Association to describe atypical patterns of sexual arousal or behavior that become problematic in the eyes of the individual or society, such as fetishism or exhibitionism. The urges are recurrent and either are acted on or are distressing to the individual. (From Greek roots meaning "to the side of" [*para-*] and "loving" [*philos*].)

ever. According to sex researcher John Money, "the tape wears out and he has to perform another paraphilic act, in effect, to create a new movie" (quoted in Brody, 1990a, p. C12).

Some paraphilias are generally harmless and victimless, such as *fetishism* and cross-dressing to achieve sexual arousal (*transvestic fetishism*). Even being humiliated by one's partner might be relatively harmless if the partner consents. Other paraphilic behaviors, such as exposing oneself in public or enticing children into sexual relations, do have victims and can cause harm, sometimes severe physical or psychological harm. They are also against the law. Sexual sadism, in which sexual arousal is connected to hurting or humiliating another person, can be a most harmful paraphilia when it is forced upon a nonconsenting person. Some brutal rapes involve sexual sadism.

Except in the case of sexual masochism, paraphilias are believed to occur almost exclusively among men (Money & Wiedeking, 1980). The prevalence of paraphilias in the general population remains unknown, because people are generally unwilling to talk about them. Much of what we have learned about paraphilias derives from the reported experiences of people who have been apprehended for performing illegal acts (such as exposing themselves in public) and the few who have voluntarily sought help. The characteristics of people who have not been identified or studied remain virtually unknown.

We discuss the major types of paraphilia in this chapter, with the exception of *pedophilia*. In pedophilia, children become the objects of sexual arousal. Pedophilia often takes the form of sexual coercion of children, as in incest or sexual molestation. It is discussed in Chapter 18 as a form of sexual coercion.

Fetishism

The roots of the word *fetish* come from the French *fétiche*, which is thought to derive from the Portuguese *feitico*, meaning "magic charm." The "magic" in this case lies in an object's ability to arouse a person sexually. In **fetishism,** an inanimate object elicits sexual arousal. Articles of clothing (for example, women's panties, bras, lingerie, stockings, gloves, shoes, or boots) and materials made of rubber, leather, silk, or fur are among the more common fetishistic objects. Leather boots and high-heeled shoes are popular ones.

Fetishism A paraphilia in which an inanimate object such as an article of clothing or items made of rubber, leather, or silk elicit sexual arousal.

Fetishism. In fetishism, inanimate objects such as leather shoes or boots elicit sexual arousal. Fetishists may derive sexual gratification by fondling, manipulating, or fantasizing about the object during masturbation. They may want the object to be present during sexual activity with, or to be worn by, their partners.

The fetishist might act on the urges to engage in fetishistic behavior, such as by masturbating by stroking an object or while fantasizing about it, or he might be distressed about such urges or fantasies but not act upon them. In a related paraphilia, **partialism,** people are excessively aroused by a particular body part, such as the feet, breasts, or buttocks.

Most fetishes and partialisms are harmless. Fetishistic practices are almost always private and involve masturbation or are incorporated into coitus with a willing partner. Only rarely have fetishists coerced others into paraphilic activities. Yet some partialists have touched parts of women's bodies in public, and some fetishists have committed burglaries to acquire the fetishistic objects (Sargent, 1988).

Transvestism

Transvestism may be viewed as a type of fetish. Whereas other fetishists become sexually aroused by handling the fetishistic object while they masturbate, transvestites become excited by wearing articles of clothing—the fetishistic objects—of the other gender. A fetishist might find the object or sex involving the object to be erotically stimulating. For the transvestite, the object is sexually alluring only when it is worn. Transvestites are almost always males. True transvestism has only been described among heterosexual males, although such men may occasionally engage in male-male sexual activity. Most are married and otherwise masculine in behavior and style of dress.

Transvestism is often confused with transsexualism, but there are important differences between them. Transvestites cross-dress because they find it sexually arousing. Most transvestites have masculine gender identities and do not seek to change their anatomic sex. Some male transvestites show some aspects of a feminine gender identity, however (Doorn et al., 1994). Transsexuals, by contrast, cross-dress because they are uncomfortable with the attire associated with their anatomic sex.

Like fetishism in general, the origins of transvestism remain obscure. There is no evidence of biological abnormalities in transvestism (Buhrich et al., 1979). Family relationships appear to play a role, however. Transvestites are more likely than other people to be oldest children or only children (Schott, 1995). They also report closer relationships with their mothers than their fathers (Schott, 1995). Some transvestites report a history of "petticoat punishment" during childhood. That is, they were humiliated by being dressed in girl's attire. Some authorities have speculated that the adult transvestite might be attempting psychologically to convert humiliation into mastery by achieving an erection

Transvestism. Transvestites cross-dress for the purpose of sexual gratification. Some transvestites sport feminine attire in public. Others cross-dress only in the privacy of their own homes.

Partialism A paraphilia related to fetishism in which sexual arousal is exaggeratedly associated with a particular body part, such as feet, breasts, or buttocks.

Transvestism A paraphilia in which a person repeatedly cross-dresses to achieve sexual arousal or gratification, or is troubled by persistent, recurring urges to cross-dress. (From the Latin roots *trans-,* meaning "cross," and *vestis,* meaning "garment.") Also known as *transvestic fetishism*.

and engaging in sexual activity despite being attired in female clothing (Geer et al., 1984). Transvestism can also be looked at as an attempt by males to escape the narrow confines of the masculine role (Bullough, 1991).

Cross-dressing is common in other cultures and has been reported in historical accounts of figures such as King Henry III of France. This sixteenth-century monarch wanted to be considered a woman and to be addressed as "Her Majesty" (Geer et al., 1984). But cross-dressing can occur in other cultures for reasons other than sexual arousal. In the case of Henry III, it appears that transsexualism, not transvestism, was involved.

Truth or Fiction?
REVISITED

It is true that King Henry III of France insisted on being considered a woman and addressed as "Her Majesty." The king appears to have been transsexual. ∎

Some men cross-dress for reasons other than sexual arousal and so are not "true transvestites." Some men make a living by impersonating women such as Marilyn Monroe and Madonna on stage and are not motivated by sexual arousal. Among some segments of the gay male community, it is fashionable to masquerade as women. Gay men do not usually cross-dress to become sexually stimulated, however.

Transvestism behaviors may range from wearing a single female garment when alone to sporting dresses, wigs, makeup, and feminine mannerisms at a transvestite club. Some transvestites become sexually aroused by masquerading as women and attracting the interest of unsuspecting males. They sometimes entice these men or string them along until they find some excuse to back out before their anatomic sex is revealed. The great majority of transvestites do not engage in antisocial or illegal behavior. Most practice their sexual predilection in private and would be horrified or embarrassed to be discovered by associates while dressed in female attire.

a **CLOSER** l o o k

A Case of Transvestism

Most transvestites are married and engage in sexual activity with their wives. Yet they seek additional sexual gratification through dressing as women, as in the case of Archie.

Archie was a 55-year-old plumber who had been cross-dressing for many years. There was a time when he would go out in public as a woman, but as his prominence in the community grew, he became more afraid of being discovered in public. His wife Myrna knew of his "peccadillo," especially since he borrowed many of her clothes. She urged him to stay at home, offering to help him with his "weirdness." For many years, his paraphilia had been restricted to the home.

The couple came to the clinic at the urging of the wife. Myrna described how Archie had imposed his will on her for 20 years. Archie would wear her undergarments and masturbate while she told him how disgusting he was. (The couple also regularly engaged in "normal" sexual intercourse, which Myrna enjoyed.) The cross-dressing had come to a head because a teenage daughter had almost walked into the couple's bedroom while they were acting out Archie's fantasies.

With Myrna out of the consulting room, Archie explained how he grew up in a family with several older sisters. He described how underwear had been perpetually hanging to dry in the one bathroom. As an adolescent, Archie experimented

with rubbing against articles of underwear, then with trying them on. On one occasion, a sister walked in while he was modeling panties before the mirror. She told him he was a "dredge to society," and he straightaway experienced unparalleled sexual excitement. He masturbated when she left the room, and his orgasm was the strongest of his young life.

Archie did not think that there was anything wrong with wearing women's undergarments and masturbating. He was not about to give it up, regardless of whether it destroyed his marriage. Myrna's main concern was finally separating herself from Archie's "sickness." She didn't care what he did any more, as long as he did it by himself. "Enough is enough," she said.

That was the compromise the couple worked out. Archie would engage in his fantasies by himself. He would choose times when Myrna was not at home, and she would not be informed of his activities. He would also be very, very careful to choose times when the children would not be around.

Six months later, the couple were together and content. Archie had replaced Myrna's input into his fantasies with transvestic-sadomasochistic magazines. Myrna said, "I see no evil, hear no evil, smell no evil." They continued to have sexual intercourse. After a while, Myrna forgot to check to see which underwear had been used.

Although some transvestites persuade their female partners to permit them to wear feminine attire during their sexual activities, most keep their transvestic urges and activities to themselves. A survey of 504 transvestite men showed that most had kept their transvestism a secret from their wives-to-be, hoping that they would not be bothered by their urge to cross-dress once they were married (Weinberg & Bullough, 1986, 1988). The urges continued into their marriages and the wives eventually discovered their husbands' secrets, however. Seventy of the wives were interviewed (Bullough & Weinberg, 1989). The wives tended to react with confusion, surprise, or shock to discovering their husbands' cross-dressing. Most tried to be understanding at first. Some assisted their husbands in their cross-dressing, such as by helping them apply makeup. Yet the longer the women were married, the more negative their attitudes tended to become toward their husbands' cross-dressing. Over time, wives generally learned to be tolerant, though not supportive, of their husbands' cross-dressing.

Exhibitionism

Exhibitionism ("flashing") involves persistent, powerful urges and sexual fantasies involving exposing one's genitals to unsuspecting strangers for the purpose of achieving sexual arousal or gratification. The urges either are acted upon or are disturbing to the individual. Exhibitionists are almost always males.

What we know of exhibitionists, as with most other people with paraphilias, is almost entirely derived from studies of men who have been apprehended or treated by mental health professionals. Such knowledge might yield a biased picture of exhibitionists. Although about one in three arrests for sexual offenses involves exhibitionism, relatively few reported incidents result in apprehension and conviction (Cox, 1988). Studies in England, Guatemala, the United States, and Hong Kong have shown that fewer than 20% of occurrences are reported to the police (Cox, 1988). The characteristics of most perpetrators may therefore differ from those of people who have been available for study.

The prevalence of exhibitionism in the general population is unknown, but a survey of 846 college women at nine randomly selected U.S. universities found exposure to exhibitionism to be widespread. A third of the women reported that they had run into a "flasher" (Cox, 1988). A majority of the women had been approached for the first time (some had been approached more than once) by 16 years of age. Only 15 of the women had reported these incidents to the police. The clinical definition of exhibitionism involves exposure to a stranger, but about a third (36%) of the incidents among the college women were committed by acquaintances, relatives, or "good friends."

The archetypal exhibitionist is young, unhappily married, and sexually repressed. An exhibitionist might claim that marital coitus is reasonably satisfactory but that he also experiences the compulsion to expose himself to strangers. Many exhibitionists are single, however. They typically have difficulties relating to women and have been unable to establish meaningful heterosexual relationships.

Exhibitionism usually begins before age 18 (American Psychiatric Association, 1994). The urge to exhibit oneself, if not the actual act, usually begins in early adolescence, generally between the ages of 13 and 16 (Freund et al., 1988). The frequency of exhibitionism declines markedly after the age of 40 (American Psychiatric Association, 1994). The typical exhibitionist does not attempt further sexual contact with the victim. Therefore, he does not usually pose a physical threat (American Psychiatric Association, 1994).

The police sometimes trivialize exhibitionism as a "nuisance crime," but the psychological consequences among victims, especially young children, indicate that exhibitionism is not victimless. Victims might feel violated and be bothered by recurrent images or nightmares. They might harbor misplaced guilt that they had unwittingly enticed the exhibitionist. They might blame themselves for reacting excessively or for failing to apprehend the perpetrator. They might also develop fears of venturing out on their own.

Exhibitionism A paraphilia characterized by persistent, powerful urges and sexual fantasies involving exposing one's genitals to unsuspecting strangers for the purpose of achieving sexual arousal or gratification.

Geer and his colleagues (1984) see exhibitionism as an indirect means of expressing hostility toward women. Exposure might be an attempt by the exhibitionist to strike back at women because of a belief that women have wronged him or damaged his self-esteem by failing to notice him or take him seriously. The direct expression of anger might be perceived as too risky, so the exhibitionist vents his rage by humiliating a defenseless stranger. The urge to expose oneself almost always follows a situation in which the exhibitionist feels that his masculinity has been insulted. Some evidence suggests that exhibitionists might be attempting to assert their masculinity by evoking a response from their victims. A number of exhibitionists have reported that they hoped that the women would enjoy the experience and be impressed with the size of their penises (Langevin et al., 1979).

Other studies show exhibitionists to be shy, dependent, passive, lacking in sexual and social skills, even inhibited (Dwyer, 1988). They tend to be self-critical, to have doubts about their masculinity, and to suffer from feelings of inadequacy and inferiority (Blair & Lanyon, 1981; Dwyer, 1988). Many have had poor relationships with their fathers and have overprotective mothers (Dwyer, 1988). Exhibitionists who are socially shy or inadequate might be using exhibitionism as a substitute for the intimate relationships they cannot develop.

The preferred victims are typically girls or young women (Freund & Blanchard, 1986). The typical exhibitionist drives up to, or walks in front of, a stranger and exposes his penis. In one sample of 130 exhibitionists, about 50% reported that they always or nearly always had erections when they exposed themselves (Langevin et al., 1979). After his victim has registered fear, disgust, confusion, or surprise, an exhibitionist will typically cover himself and flee. He usually masturbates, either while exposing himself or shortly afterward while thinking about the act and the victim's response (American Psychiatric Association, 1994; Blair & Lanyon, 1981). Some exhibitionists ejaculate during the act. Most of the 238 exhibitionists in a Canadian study reported masturbating to orgasm while exposing themselves or afterward while fantasizing about it (Freund et al., 1988).

Exhibitionists might also need to risk being caught to experience a heightened erotic response (Stoller, 1977). The exhibitionist might even situate himself to increase the risk. For example, he might expose himself in the same location or while sitting in his own easily identifiable car.

Courts nowadays tend to be hard on exhibitionists, partly because of evidence that shows that some exhibitionists progress to more serious crimes of sexual aggression. In one sample, about 10% of rapists and child molesters had begun their "sexual careers" by exposing themselves to strangers (Abel et al., 1984). This does not mean that exhibitionists inevitably become rapists and child molesters. Most do not.

Definitions of exhibitionism also bring into focus the boundaries between normal and abnormal behavior. Are exotic dancers (stripteasers) or nude sunbathers exhibitionists? After all, aren't they also exposing themselves to strangers? But exotic dancers—male or female—remove their clothes to sexually excite or entertain an audience that is paying to watch them. Their motive is (usually) to earn a living. Sunbathers in their "birthday suits" might also seek to sexually arouse others, not themselves. Of course, they might also be seeking an all-over tan or trying to avoid feeling encumbered by clothing. In any case, stripteasers and sunbathers do not expose themselves to unsuspecting others. Therefore, these behaviors are not regarded as exhibitionistic.

Truth or Fiction? REVISITED

It is not true that nude sunbathers are exhibitionists—at least not in terms of the clinical definition of the disorder. Exhibitionists seek to become sexually aroused by exposing themselves to unsuspecting victims, not to show off their physical attractiveness. ■

It is also normal to become sexually excited while stripping before one's sex partner. Such stripping is done to sexually excite a willing partner, not to surprise or shock a stranger.

what do you say now?

How to Respond to an Exhibitionist

It is understandable that an unsuspecting woman who is exposed to an exhibitionist might react with shock, surprise, or fear. Unfortunately, her display of shock or fear might reinforce the flasher's tendencies to expose himself. She might fear that the flasher, who has already broken at least one social code, is likely to assault her physically as well. Fortunately, most exhibitionists do not seek actual sexual contact with their victims and run away before they can be apprehended by the police or passers-by.

Some women respond with anger, insults, or even arguments that the offender should feel ashamed. A display of anger might reinforce exhibitionism. We do not recommend that the victim insult the flasher, lest it provoke a violent response. Although most exhibitionists are nonviolent, about one in ten has considered or attempted rape (Gebhard et al., 1965).

When possible, showing no reaction or simply continuing on one's way might be the best response. If women do desire to respond to the flasher, they might calmly say something like "You really need professional help. You should see a professional to help you with this problem." They should promptly report the incident to police so that authorities can apprehend the offender.

Obscene Telephone Calling

Like exhibitionists, obscene phone callers (almost all of whom are male) seek to become sexually aroused by shocking their victims. Whereas an exhibitionist exposes his genitals to produce the desired response, the obscene phone caller exposes himself verbally by uttering obscenities and sexual provocations to a nonconsenting person. Because of such similarities, obscene telephone calling is sometimes considered a subtype of exhibitionism. The American Psychiatric Association (1994) labels this type of paraphilia **telephone scatologia** (lewdness).

Relatively few obscene callers are women (Matek, 1988). Women who are charged with such offenses are generally motivated by rage for some actual or fantasized rejection rather than by the desire for sexual arousal. They use the phone to hurl sexual invective against men who they feel have wronged them. By contrast, male obscene phone callers are generally motivated by a desire for sexual excitement and usually choose their victims randomly from the phone book or by chance dialing. They typically masturbate during the phone call or shortly afterward. Despite the offensiveness of their actions, most obscene phone callers are not dangerous. Nor do most make repeat calls to the same person (Reinisch, 1990).

There are many patterns of obscene phone calling (Matek, 1988). Some callers limit themselves to obscenities. Others make sexual overtures. Some just breathe heavily into the receiver. Others describe their masturbatory activity to their victims. Some profess to have previously met the victim at a social gathering or through a mutual acquaintance. Some even present themselves as "taking a sex survey" and ask a series of personally revealing questions.

The typical obscene phone caller is a socially inadequate heterosexual male who has had difficulty forming intimate relationships with women. The relative safety and anonymity of the telephone might shield him from the risk of rejection. A reaction of shock or fright from his victims might fill him with feelings of power and control that are lacking in his life, especially in his relationships with women. The obscenities might vent the rage that he holds against women who have rejected him.

Obscene phone calls are illegal, but it has been difficult for authorities to track down perpetrators (Matek, 1988). Call tracing can help police to track obscene or offending phone callers. Call tracing works in different ways in different locales. *Caller ID*, which shows the caller's telephone number on a display panel on the receiving party's telephone, is available in many locales. Though this service might deter some obscene callers, others might use public phones instead of their home phones. Callers might also be able to

Telephone scatologia A paraphilia characterized by the making of obscene telephone calls. (From the Greek *skatos*, meaning "excrement.")

Is This True Voyeurism? Voyeurs are frequently called "peepers," and so-called peep shows are found in this business establishment. However, voyeurs seek out unsuspecting victims. The women in the peep show are paid for their services; they are anything but unsuspecting.

electronically block the display of their telephone numbers. Check with your local telephone company if you are interested in these services.

What should a woman do if she receives an obscene phone call? Advice generally parallels that given to women who are victimized by exhibitionists. Above all, women are advised to remain calm and not reveal shock or fright, since such reactions tend to reinforce the caller and increase the probability of repeat calls. Women might be best advised to say nothing at all and gently hang up the receiver. A woman might alternatively offer a brief response that alludes to the caller's problems before hanging up. She might say in a calm but strong voice, "It's unfortunate you have this problem. I think you should seek professional help." If she should receive repeated calls, the woman might request an unlisted number or contact the police about tracing the calls. Many women list themselves only by their initials in the phone directory so as to disguise their gender. But since this practice is so widespread, obscene callers might surmise that people listed by initials are women living alone.

Voyeurism

Voyeurism involves strong, repetitive urges to observe unsuspecting strangers who are naked, disrobing, or engaged in sexual relations (American Psychiatric Association, 1994). The voyeur becomes sexually aroused by the act of watching and typically does not seek sexual relations with the observed person. Like fetishism and exhibitionism, voyeurism is found almost exclusively among males. It usually begins before the age of 15 (American Psychiatric Association, 1994).

The voyeur might masturbate while peeping or afterward while replaying the incident in his imagination or engaging in voyeuristic fantasies. The voyeur might fantasize about making love to the observed person but have no intention of actually doing so.

Are people voyeurs who become sexually aroused by the sight of their lovers undressing? What about people who enjoy watching pornographic films or stripteasers? No, no, and no. The people being observed are not unsuspecting strangers. The lover knows that his or her partner is watching. Porn actors and strippers know that others will be viewing them. They would not be performing if they did not expect or have an audience.

It is perfectly normal for men and women to be sexually stimulated by the sight of other people who are nude, undressing, or engaged in sexual relations. Voyeurism is characterized by urges to peep on *unsuspecting* strangers.

It is not true that people who enjoy watching their mates undress are voyeurs. In such cases, the person who is disrobing is knowingly and willingly observed, and the watcher's enjoyment is completely normal. Voyeurs target unsuspecting victims. ■

Voyeurs are also known as "peepers," or *peeping Toms*. Why "peeping Toms"? According to an old English legend, Lady Godiva asked the townspeople not to look upon her while she rode horseback in the nude to protest the oppressive tax that her husband, a landowner, had imposed on them. A tailor named Tom of Coventry was the only townsperson not to grant her request.

Voyeurs often put themselves in risky situations in which they face the prospect of being discovered or apprehended. They might risk physical injury by perching themselves in trees or otherwise assuming precarious positions to catch a preferred view of their target. They will occupy rooftops and fire escapes in brutal winter weather. Peepers can be

Voyeurism A paraphilia characterized by strong, repetitive urges and related sexual fantasies of observing unsuspecting strangers who are naked, disrobing, or engaged in sexual relations. (From the French verb *voir,* meaning "to see.")

in.the.new.millennium

Exhibitionism, Voyeurism, and Videophones: Videoconferencing's Killer App May Be Sex

Videophones add a new dimension of anxiety to the familiar problem of the phone ringing while you are in the bathtub. It turns out, however, that thousands of people actually look forward to video calls while they, and their callers, are undressed. In fact, as is typically the case with a new technology, early adopters of videoconferencing have discovered that the so-called killer app is sex. From Kansas to Kiev, Internet users are enthusiastically embracing Net-based videoconferencing that allows them to play show-and-tell with other uninhibited souls.

The Microsoft Corporation and other companies that make videoconferencing products say that while sex-related applications are a very visible use of the new technology, the most common applications are indeed for business: conducting meetings, collaborating on work projects and telecommuting, for example. But there are also some people—thousands, actually—who use the technology to exhibit themselves, in real time, without clothes and to watch others doing the same.

All it takes is a recent-model personal computer, an Internet connection, conferencing software, a microphone and a video camera. For voyeurs, even less equipment is needed. Thousands of commercial sex sites on the Internet offer live video to customers. But for two-way video and audio, it gets a bit more complicated. One of the most popular software packages for Internet videoconferencing is Net Meeting, which is free from Microsoft. To make it easy for software users to find one another, Microsoft has set up a half-dozen Internet Locator Server computers. There are probably 200 public locator servers on the Net. There may be thousands more on private networks.

One morning . . . the Adults Only directory on a server run by Microsoft was fully populated with users who had registered their home countries as Canada, China, Germany, Italy, Portugal, Taiwan, Korea and Turkey, among others. Users from the United States accounted for about half of the connections. Net Meeting users register to be included in a directory that displays names, e-mail addresses, home locations and special interests. On the Adults Only directory, very few people use their real names or e-mail addresses.

Tom Laemmel, a product manager for Net Meeting, said Microsoft did not encourage the use of its products for what he called risque activities. "We're looking for technology to solve the problem," he said. But he added, "We're not in the business of trying to police the stuff." Laemmel said users could screen out other directory entries and get an unlisted number.

Source: Reprinted from Lewis, P. H. (1998, July 16). Videoconferencing's killer app may be sex. *The New York Times*; America Online.

exceedingly patient in their outings. They might wait hour after hour, night after night, for a furtive glimpse of an unsuspecting person. One 25-year-old recently married man secreted himself in his mother-in-law's closet, waiting for her to disrobe. Part of the sexual excitement seems to stem from the risks that voyeurs run. The need for elements of risk in their voyeurism might explain why voyeurs are not known to frequent nude beaches or nudist camps where it is acceptable to look (though not to stare) at others.

Although most voyeurs are nonviolent, some commit violent crimes such as assault and rape (Langevin et al., 1985). Voyeurs who break into and enter homes or buildings, or who tap at windows to gain the attention of victims, are among the more dangerous.

Truth or Fiction? **REVISITED**

It is incorrect to say that exhibitionists and voyeurs are *never* violent. Exhibitionistic and voyeuristic activities per se do not involve outright violence, but some exhibitionists and voyeurs have been known to be violent, and they may, if provoked or angered, react violently. ■

Compared to other types of sex offenders, voyeurs tend to be less sexually experienced and are less likely to be married (Gebhard et al., 1965). Like exhibitionists, voyeurs tend to harbor feelings of inadequacy and to lack social and sexual skills (Dwyer, 1988). They may therefore have difficulty forming romantic relationships with women. For this shy and socially inadequate type of voyeur, "peeping" affords sexual gratification without risk of rejection. Yet not all voyeurs are socially awkward and inept with women.

Sexual Masochism

Although pleasure and pain might seem like polar opposites, some people experience sexual pleasure through having pain or humiliation inflicted on them by their sex partners. People who associate the receipt of pain or humiliation with sexual arousal are called **sexual masochists.** A sexual masochist either acts upon or is distressed by persistent urges and sexual fantasies involving the desire to be bound, flogged, humiliated, or made to suffer in some way by a sexual partner so as to achieve sexual excitement. In extreme cases,

Sexual masochism A paraphilia characterized by the desire or need for pain or humiliation to enhance sexual arousal so that gratification may be attained. (From the name of Leopold von Sacher-Masoch.)

535

the person is incapable of becoming sexually aroused unless pain or humiliation is incorporated into the sexual act.

It is true that some sexual masochists cannot become sexually aroused unless they are bound, flogged, or humiliated by their sex partners. ■

Sexual masochism is the only paraphilia that is found among women with some frequency (American Psychiatric Association, 1994). Even sexual masochism is much more prevalent among men than women, however. Male masochists may outnumber females by a margin of 20 to 1 (American Psychiatric Association, 1994).

The word *masochism* is derived from the name of the Austrian storyteller Leopold von Sacher-Masoch (1835–1895). He wrote tales of men who derived sexual satisfaction from having a female partner inflict pain on them, typically by flagellation (beating or whipping).

Sexual masochists may derive pleasure from various types of punishing experiences, including being restrained (a practice known as **bondage**), blindfolded (sensory bondage), spanked, whipped, or made to perform humiliating acts, such as walking around on all fours and licking the boots or shoes of the sex partner, or being subjected to vulgar insults. Some masochists have their partners humiliate them by urinating or defecating on them. Some masochists prefer a particular source of pain. Others seek an assortment. But we should not think that sexual masochists enjoy other types of pain that are not connected with their sexual practices. Sexual masochists are no more likely than anyone else to derive pleasure from the pain they experience when they accidentally stub their toes or touch a hot appliance. Pain has erotic value only within a sexual context. It must be part of an elaborate sexual ritual.

Sexual masochists and **sexual sadists** often form sexual relationships to meet each other's needs. Some sexual masochists enlist the services of prostitutes or obtain the cooperation of their regular sexual partners to enact their masochistic fantasies.

It might seem contradictory for pain to become connected with sexual pleasure. The association of sexual arousal with mildly painful stimuli is actually quite common, however. Kinsey and his colleagues (1953) reported that perhaps as many as one person in four has experienced erotic sensations from being bitten during lovemaking. The eroticization of mild forms of pain (love bites, hair pulls, minor scratches) might fall within the normal range of sexual variation. Pain from these sources increases overall bodily arousal, which might enhance sexual excitement. Some of us become sexually excited when our partners "talk dirty" to us or call us vulgar names. When the urge for pain for purposes of sexual arousal becomes so persistent or strong that it overshadows other sources of sexual stimulation, or when the masochistic experience causes physical or psychological harm, we might say that the boundary between normality and abnormality has been breached.

It is in fact considered normal to enjoy some mild forms of pain during sexual activity. Love bites, hair pulls, and minor scratches are examples of sources of pain that are considered to fall within normal limits. ■

Bondage Ritual restraint, as by shackles, as practiced by many sexual masochists.

Sexual sadists People who become sexually aroused by inflicting pain or humiliation on others.

Hypoxyphilia A practice in which a person seeks to enhance sexual arousal, usually during masturbation, by becoming deprived of oxygen. (From the Greek root meaning "under" [*hypo*-].)

Baumeister (1988a) proposes that independent and responsible selfhood become burdensome or stressful at times. Sexual masochism provides a temporary reprieve from the responsibilities of independent selfhood. It is a blunting of one's ordinary level of self-awareness that is achieved by "focusing on immediate sensations (both painful and pleasant) and on being a sexual object" (Baumeister, 1988a, p. 54).

Sexual masochism can range from relatively benign to potentially lethal practices, such as **hypoxyphilia.** Hypoxyphiliacs put plastic bags over their heads, nooses around their necks, or pressure on their chests to temporarily deprive themselves of oxygen and enhance their sexual arousal. They usually fantasize that they are being strangled by a lover. They try to discontinue oxygen deprivation before they lose consciousness, but some miscalculations result in death by suffocation or strangulation (Blanchard & Hucker, 1991; Cosgray et al., 1991).

Sexual Sadism

Sexual sadism is named after the infamous Marquis de Sade (1774–1814), a Frenchman who wrote tales of becoming sexually aroused by inflicting pain or humiliation on others. The virtuous Justine, the heroine of his best-known novel of the same name, endures terrible suffering at the hands of fiendish men. She is at one time bound and spread-eagled so that bloodhounds can savage her. She then seeks refuge with a surgeon who tries to dismember her. Later, she falls into the clutches of a saber-wielding mass murderer, but Nature saves her with a timely thunderbolt.

Sexual sadism is characterized by persistent, powerful urges and sexual fantasies involving the inflicting of pain and suffering on others to achieve sexual excitement or gratification. The urges are acted on or are disturbing enough to cause personal distress. Some sexual sadists cannot become sexually aroused unless they make their sex partners suffer. Others can become sexually excited without such acts.

S&M Paraphernalia. People who participate in S&M often incorporate handcuffs and other paraphernalia into their sadomasochistic encounters.

Some sadists hurt or humiliate willing partners, such as prostitutes or sexual masochists. Others—a small minority—stalk and attack nonconsenting victims.

SADOMASOCHISM Sadomasochism (S&M) involves *mutually gratifying sexual interactions* between *consenting partners*. Occasional S&M is quite common among the general population. Couples might incorporate mild or light forms of S&M in their lovemaking now and then, such as mild dominance and submission games or gentle physical restraint. It is also not uncommon for lovers to scratch or bite their partners to heighten their mutual arousal during coitus. They generally do not inflict severe pain or damage, however.

Twenty-two percent of the men and 12% of the women surveyed by Kinsey and his colleagues (1953) reported at least some sexual response to sadomasochistic stories. Although some milder forms of sadomasochism might fall within the boundaries of normal sexual variation, sadomasochism becomes pathological when such fantasies are acted upon in ways that become destructive, dangerous, or distressing to oneself or others, as we find in the following case example:

> A 25-year-old female graduate student described a range of masochistic experiences. She reported feelings of sexual excitement during arguments with her husband when he would scream at her or hit her in a rage. She would sometimes taunt him to make love to her in a brutal fashion, as though she were being raped. She found the brutality and sense of being punished to be sexually stimulating. She had also begun having sex with strange men and enjoyed being physically punished by them during sex more than any other type of sexual stimulus. Being beaten or whipped produced the most intense sexual experiences she had ever had. Although she recognized the dangers posed by her sexual behavior, and felt somewhat ashamed about it, she was not sure that she wanted treatment for "it" because of the pleasure that it provided her. (adapted from Spitzer et al., 1989, pp 87–88)

In one subculture, sadomasochism is the preferred or even the exclusive form of sexual gratification. People in this subculture seek one another out through mutual contacts, S&M social organizations, or personal ads in S&M magazines. The S&M subculture has spawned magazines and clubs catering to people who describe themselves as "into S&M," as well as sex shops that sell sadomasochistic paraphernalia. These include leather restraints and leather face masks that resemble the ancient masks of executioners.

Sexual sadism A paraphilia characterized by the desire or need to inflict pain or humiliation on others to enhance sexual arousal so that gratification is attained. (From the name of the Marquis de Sade.)

Sadomasochism A mutually gratifying sexual interaction between consenting sex partners in which sexual arousal is associated with the infliction and receipt of pain or humiliation. Commonly known as *S&M*.

It is true that there is a subculture in the United States in which sexual sadists and sexual masochists form liaisons to inflict and receive pain and humiliation during sexual activity. It is called the S&M subculture and is catered to by sex shops and magazines. ■

Participants in sadomasochism often engage in highly elaborate rituals involving dominance and submission. Rituals are staged, as if they were scenes in a play (Weinberg et al., 1984). In the "master and slave" game, the sadist leads the masochist around by a leash. The masochist performs degrading or menial acts. In bondage and discipline (B&D), the dominant partner restrains the submissive partner and flagellates (spanks or whips) or sexually stimulates the submissive partner. The erotic appeal of bondage seems to be connected with controlling or being controlled.

Various types of stimulation may be used to administer pain during S&M encounters, but pain is not always employed. When it is, it is usually mild or moderate. Psychological pain, or humiliation, is perhaps be as common as physical pain. Pain might also be used symbolically, as in the case of a sadist who uses a harmless, soft rubber paddle to spank the masochist. So the erotic appeal of pain for some S&M participants might derive from the ritual of control rather than from the pain itself (Weinberg, 1987).

Extreme forms of pain, such as torture or severe beatings, are rarely reported by sadomasochists (Breslow et al., 1985). Masochists might seek pain, but they usually avoid serious injury and dangerous partners (Baumeister, 1988b).

S&M participants may be heterosexual, gay, or bisexual (Breslow et al., 1986). They may assume either the masochistic or the sadistic role or may alternate roles depending on the sexual script. People who seek sexual excitement by enacting both sadistic and masochistic roles are known as *sadomasochists*. In heterosexual relationships, the partners might reverse traditional gender roles. The man might assume the submissive or masochistic role, and the woman might take the dominant or sadistic role (Reinisch, 1990).

A survey of S&M participants drawn from ads in S&M magazines found that about three out of four were male and about one in four were female (Breslow et al., 1985). Most were married. Women respondents engaged in S&M more frequently and had a greater number of different partners than men. (Apparently, a greater number of men than women seek partners for S&M.)

The causes of sexual masochism and sadism, as of other paraphilias, are unclear. Ford and Beach (1951) speculated that humans might possess a physiological capacity to experience heightened sexual arousal from the receipt or infliction of pain (which may explain the prevalence of love bites). Mild pain might heighten physiological arousal both in the aggressor and victim, adding to the effects of sexual stimulation. Yet intense pain is likely to decrease rather than increase sexual arousal.

Pain might also have more direct biological links to pleasure. Natural chemicals called *endorphins*, similar to opiates, are released in the brain in response to pain and produce feelings of euphoria and general well-being. Perhaps, then, pleasure is derived from pain because of the release or augmentation of endorphins (Weinberg, 1987). This theory fails to explain the erotic appeal of sadomasochistic encounters that involve minimal or symbolic pain, however. Nor does it explain the erotic appeal to the sadist of inflicting pain.

Whatever their causes, the roots of sexual masochism and sadism apparently date to childhood. Sadomasochistic behavior commonly begins in early adulthood, but sadomasochistic fantasies are likely to have been present during childhood (American Psychiatric Association, 1994; Breslow et al., 1986).

Frotteurism

Frotteurism (also known as "mashing") is rubbing against or touching a nonconsenting person. As with other paraphilias, a diagnosis of frotteurism requires either acting upon these urges or being distressed by them. Mashing has been reported exclusively among males (Spitzer et al., 1989).

Most mashing takes place in crowded places, such as buses, subway cars, or elevators. The man finds the rubbing or the touching, not the coercive nature of the act, to be sexually stimulating. While rubbing against a woman, he might fantasize a consensual, af-

Frotteurism A paraphilia characterized by recurrent, powerful sexual urges and related fantasies involving rubbing against or touching a nonconsenting person. (From the French *frotter,* meaning "to rub.")

fectionate sexual relationship with her. Typically, the man incorporates images of his mashing within his masturbation fantasies. Mashing also incorporates a related practice, **toucherism:** fondling nonconsenting strangers.

Mashing may be so fleeting and furtive that the woman might not realize what has happened (Spitzer et al., 1989). Mashers therefore stand little chance of being caught. Consider the case of a man who victimized a thousand or so women within a decade but was arrested only twice:

> Charles, 45, was seen by a psychiatrist following his second arrest for rubbing against a woman in the subway. He would select as his target a woman in her 20s as she entered the subway station. He would then position himself behind her on the platform and wait for the train to arrive. He would then follow her into the subway car and when the doors closed would begin bumping his penis against her buttocks, while fantasizing that they were enjoying having intercourse in a loving and consensual manner. About half of the time he would ejaculate into a plastic bag that he had wrapped around his penis to prevent staining his pants. He would then continue on his way to work. Sometimes when he hadn't ejaculated he would change trains and seek another victim. While he felt guilty for a time after each episode, he would soon become preoccupied with thoughts about his next encounter. He never gave any thought to the feelings his victims might have about what he had done to them. While he was married to the same woman for 25 years, he appears to be rather socially inept and unassertive, especially with women. (adapted from Spitzer et al., 1989, pp. 106–107)

Although this masher was married, many mashers have difficulties forming relationships with women and are handicapped by fears of rejection. Mashing provides sexual contact in a relatively nonthreatening context.

Other Paraphilias

Let us consider some other less common paraphilias.

ZOOPHILIA   A person with **zoophilia** experiences repeated, intense urges and related fantasies involving sexual contact with animals. As with other paraphilias, the urges may be acted upon or cause personal distress. A child or adolescent who shows some sexual response to an occasional episode of rough-and-tumble play with the family pet is not displaying zoophilia.

The term *bestiality* applies to actual sexual contact with an animal. Human sexual contact with animals, mythical and real, has a long history. Michelangelo's painting *Leda and the Swan* depicts the Greek god Zeus taking the form of a swan to mate with a woman, Leda. Zeus was also portrayed as taking the form of a bull or serpent to mate with humans. In the Old Testament, God is said to have put to death people who had sexual relations with animals. The Greek historian Herodotus notes that goats at the Egyptian temple at Mendes were trained to copulate with people.

Although the prevalence of zoophilia in the general population is unknown, Kinsey and his colleagues (1948, 1953) found that about 8% of the men and 3% to 4% of the women interviewed admitted to sexual contacts with animals. Men more often had sexual contact with farm animals, such as calves and sheep. Women more often reported sexual contacts with household pets. Men were more likely to masturbate or copulate with the animals. Women more often reported general body contact. People of both genders reported encouraging the animals to lick their genitals. A few women reported that they had trained a dog to engage in coitus with them. Urban-rural differences also emerged. Rates of bestiality were higher among boys who were reared on farms. Compared with only a few city boys, 17% of farm boys had reached orgasm at some time through sexual contact with dogs, cows, and goats. These contacts were generally restricted to adolescence, when human outlets were not available. Still, adults sometimes engage in sexual contacts with animals, generally because of curiosity or novelty or for a sexual release when human partners are unavailable. Whether or not such contacts constitute zoophilia depends upon their frequency and intensity or whether they cause the person distress. In most cases, true zoophilia is associated with deep-seated psychological problems and difficulties in developing intimate relationships with people.

Toucherism A practice related to frotteurism and characterized by the persistent urge to fondle nonconsenting strangers.

Zoophilia A paraphilia involving persistent or repeated sexual urges and related fantasies involving sexual contact with animals.

a CLOSER look

Paraphilias as Sexual Addictions

In his book *Don't Call It Love* (1991), Patrick Carnes suggests that some people with paraphilias suffer from a sexual addiction, a nonchemical form of addiction. Sexual addicts ("sexaholics") might feel unable to resist their sexual urges and might act upon them indiscriminately, remaining oblivious to resultant harm or damage they cause. Carnes argues that sexual addicts use sex in much the same way that drug addicts and alcoholics use drugs or alcohol: to alter their moods and temporarily relieve psychological states of discomfort, such as depression or anxiety. In the end, however, the destructive nature of the paraphilia reinforces feelings of shame and worthlessness.

Carnes identifies a four-step cycle through which sexual addictions progress and gather strength. Let us apply this model to exhibitionism:

1. *Preoccupation.* The person enters a trancelike state characterized by a preoccupation with thoughts about exposing himself, leading to a strong cravings to commit the act.
2. *Ritualization.* The person begins to act upon the exhibitionistic urge. He engages in rituals that precede the act to increase his level of sexual arousal, such as driving a route through a park frequented by women walking alone.
3. *Compulsive sexual behavior.* The person exposes himself, while feeling that he cannot control or prevent the act.
4. *Despair.* Whereas most people feel pleasure and a release from sexual tension following sex, the exhibitionist sinks into feelings of hopelessness and despair over his inability to control his exhibitionistic urges. Such feelings may be temporarily offset by recurrent preoccupation with the paraphilia, leading to the completion of a new cycle. But the completion of each cycle provides further confirmation of personal unworthiness.

The concept of sexual addiction might not apply to all paraphilias or to all people with paraphilias. Fetishists and transvestites, for example, might feel in control of their sexual urges, not controlled by them. They might not become preoccupied with paraphilic thoughts and fantasies or experience irresistible cravings to perform paraphilic acts.

The model of sexual addiction might hold some promise in the development of treatment approaches for paraphilias. Treatment might be modeled after approaches for the chemical addictions and alcoholism, such as Alcoholics Anonymous (AA), in which people with chemical dependencies are encouraged to confront their addictions and learn to cope with their urges. Self-help groups in this mold, such as Sexaholics Anonymous and Sex Addicts Anonymous, have been formed.

Necrophilia A paraphilia characterized by desire for sexual activity with corpses. (From the Greek *nekros,* meaning "dead body.")

Klismaphilia A paraphilia in which sexual arousal is derived from use of enemas.

Coprophilia A paraphilia in which sexual arousal is attained in connection with feces. (From the Greek *copros,* meaning "dung.")

Urophilia A paraphilia in which sexual arousal is associated with urine.

Nymphomania An excessive, insatiable sexual appetite or drive in women. (From the Greek roots *nymphe,* meaning "a bride," and *mania,* which means "madness.")

Satyriasis An excessive, insatiable sexual appetite or drive in men. (After *satyr,* a sexually insatiable, goat-legged creature with pointed ears and short horns in Greek mythology. Satyrs were part man, part beast.)

NECROPHILIA In **necrophilia,** a rare paraphilia, a person desires sex with corpses. Three types of necrophilia have been identified (Rosman & Resnick, 1989). In *regular necrophilia,* the person has sex with a deceased person. In *necrophilic homicide,* the person commits murder to obtain a corpse for sexual purposes. In *necrophilic fantasy,* the person fantasizes about sex with a corpse but does not actually carry out necrophilic acts. Necrophiles often obtain jobs that provide them with access to corpses, such as working in cemeteries, morgues, or funeral homes. The primary motivation for necrophilia appears to be the desire to sexually possess a completely nonresistent and nonrejecting partner (Rosman & Resnick, 1989). Many necrophiles are clearly mentally disturbed.

LESS COMMON PARAPHILIAS In **klismaphilia,** sexual arousal is derived from use of enemas. Klismaphiles generally prefer the receiving role to the giving role. Klismaphiles may have derived sexual pleasure in infancy or childhood from the anal stimulation provided by parents giving them enemas.

In **coprophilia,** sexual arousal is connected with feces. The person might desire to be defecated on or to defecate on a sex partner. The association of feces with sexual arousal might also be a throwback to childhood. Many children appear to obtain anal sexual pleasure by holding in and then purposefully expelling feces. It might also be that the incidental connection between erections or sexual arousal and soiled diapers during infancy eroticizes feces.

In **urophilia,** sexual arousal is associated with urine. As with coprophilia, the person might desire to be urinated upon or to urinate upon a sexual partner. Also like coprophilia, urophilia might have childhood origins. Stimulation of the urethral canal during urination might become associated with sexual pleasure. Or urine might have become eroticized by experiences in which erections occurred while the infant was clothed in a wet diaper.

NYMPHOMANIA, SATYRIASIS, AND THE SEXUAL DOUBLE STANDARD

Sarah R., a never-married, 39-year-old artist, became sexually active in her junior year in high school and has rarely been without at least one or two lovers ever since. Whenever she has not had an opportunity for sexual intercourse for several weeks or longer, for one reason or another, she has felt quite uncomfortable, or as she put it, "horny and hard-up." She has had two unwanted pregnancies, both of which resulted in abortions, and has contracted gonorrhea on three separate occasions and has suffered several times from infestations of pubic lice. She continues to be troubled with recurrent episodes of genital herpes. She generally limits her sexual relationships to one or two partners, but has on occasion maintained sexual relationships at the same time with three or four men. She engages in sexual intercourse two or three times a week, on the average, and engages in masturbation to relieve her sexual urges when intercourse is not possible.

Both her family practitioner and gynecologist, who have treated her for years, consider her to be a nymphomaniac. Her gynecologist says of her, "Of course she has herpes. What can you expect with the kind of sexual excesses she indulges in? She's a real nympho." (Goldberg, 1987, p. 204)

Would you have reached the same conclusion as Sarah's physicians did? Why or why not? What criteria would you use to define **nymphomania**? Perhaps most readers have heard of nymphomania, but only a few are likely to be acquainted with the term describing the same condition in men, **satyriasis. Don Juanism** is another term for the condition.

What Is Hypersexuality? Can one really be "oversexed"? Where are the boundaries between a "healthy sexual appetite" and hypersexuality? Why are people usually more familiar with the term *nymphomania* than its male counterpart, *satyriasis*? How do cultural stereotypes affect our perceptions of these behavior patterns?

The fact that nymphomania is more commonly used in our society than the male counterpart underscores the traditional double standard in Western society (Groneman, 1994). Greater sexual liberties are allowed to men than women. A man who has a number of flings is likely to be labeled a "playboy," a "Casanova," or even a "stud." A woman who does so is likely to be branded with labels that carry negative connotations, such as "nympho," "slut," or "whore."

Clinicians prefer to use the term **hypersexuality** to refer to nymphomania in women and satyriasis in men, thereby avoiding disparaging connotations. No absolute criteria exist for determining hypersexuality or establishing the boundary between normal sexuality and hypersexuality, however. Some people might consider a person who requires a sexual release through masturbation or coitus more than once daily to be hypersexual. Others draw the line at two, three, or perhaps six or ten or more times daily. Among some couples, the partner who desires less frequent sexual activity might label the other "oversexed." But what defines "oversexed" in one relationship may be considered normal, or even "undersexed," in another.

Clinicians might weigh the compulsive or self-defeating nature of the behavior in determining the boundaries of hypersexuality, not the sheer frequency of sexual activity. Hypersexual people might use sex as a means of buttressing a flagging sense of self-esteem. They might feel driven to a series of sexual conquests or brief encounters to reassure themselves that they are desirable or masculine or feminine enough. Because they lack true intimacy, however, the encounters leave them feeling empty and sexually unfulfilled. Such relationships provide only a temporary salve for feelings of self-doubt or unworthiness. The person quickly loses sexual interest in the new partner once the conquest or brief encounter has occurred and begins searching for another. Partners are treated like objects to be used and discarded.

Return to Sarah. Do the facts of her case suggest hypersexuality? Did Sarah feel a lack of control over her sexual urges? Did she feel compelled to engage in sexual behaviors that put herself at risk of incurring unwanted pregnancies or sexually transmitted diseases?

Goldberg (1987) argues that Sarah's physicians labeled her a nymphomaniac because her behavior did not meet social expectations of female sexuality. Goldberg (1987) comments, "In all likelihood, a 39-year-old man living the sort of life that Sarah is living would not be regarded as suffering from satyriasis or, indeed, as being sexually abnormal in any way" (p. 204). Does the label of nymphomania represent a sexist tendency to judge women and men by different sets of social standards?

Reflections

- Are the women on your campus who enjoy dressing in men's-style clothing to be considered transvestites? Why or why not?
- Are lovers who are excited when their partners see their bodies to be considered exhibitionists? Why or why not?
- Are lovers who become excited by seeing their partners undressing or in the nude to be considered voyeurs? Why or why not?

Don Juanism An excessive, insatiable sexual appetite or drive in men. (After the fictional Spanish nobleman who was unable to obtain true sexual gratification despite numerous affairs.)

THEORETICAL PERSPECTIVES

The paraphilias are among the most fascinating and perplexing variations in sexual behavior. We might find it difficult to understand how people can become sexually excited by fondling an article of clothing or by cross-dressing. It might also be difficult to identify with people who feel compelled to exhibit their genitals or to rub their genitals against unsuspecting victims in crowded places. Perhaps we can recognize some voyeuristic tendencies in ourselves, but we cannot imagine peeping through binoculars while perched in a nearby tree or, for that matter, risking the social and legal consequences of being discovered in the act. Nor might we understand how people can become sexually turned on by inflicting or receiving pain.

Let us consider explanations that have been advanced from the major theoretical perspectives.

Biological Perspectives

Little is known about whether there are biological factors in paraphilic behavior. Efforts to date to find concrete evidence of brain damage or abnormalities among people with paraphilias have failed (e.g., Langevin et al., 1989). Because testosterone is linked to sex drive, researchers have also focused on differences in testosterone levels between people with paraphilias and people without them. A recent study found evidence of some hormonal differences between a group of 16 male exhibitionists and controls (Lang et al., 1989). Although no differences in overall levels of testosterone were found, researchers reported that the exhibitionists evidenced significantly elevated levels of the measure of testosterone that is believed to be most closely linked to sex drive. This difference suggests that exhibitionists might have biologically elevated sex drives. The significance of the finding is limited by the fact that hormone levels among many of the people with paraphilias who were studied fell within the normal range.

Psychoanalytic Perspectives

Classical psychoanalytic theory suggests that paraphilias are psychological defenses, usually against unresolved castration anxiety dating back to the Oedipus complex (Fenichel, 1945). To the transvestic man, the sight of a woman's vagina threatens to arouse castration anxiety. It reminds him that women do not have penises and that he might suffer the same fate. Sequestering his penis beneath women's clothing symbolically asserts that women do have penises, which provides unconscious reassurance against his own fears of castration.

By exposing his genitals, the exhibitionist unconsciously seeks reassurance that his penis is secure. It is as if he were asserting, "Look! I have a penis!" Shock or surprise on the victim's face acknowledges that his penis still exists, temporarily relieving unconscious castration anxiety.

Masturbation with a fetishistic object (a shoe, for example) allows the fetishist to gratify his sexual desires while keeping a safe distance from the fantasized dangers that he unconsciously associates with sexual contact with women. Or the fetishistic object itself—the shoe—might unconsciously symbolize the penis. Stroking a woman's shoe during sexual relations or fantasizing about one might unconsciously provide reassurance that the man's own penis, symbolically represented by the fetishistic object, is secure.

In one psychoanalytic view of voyeurism, the man is unconsciously denying castration by searching for a penis among women victims. Other psychoanalytic views suggest that the voyeur is identifying with the man in the observed couple as he had identified with his own father during childhood observations of the parental

Hypersexuality An excessive or apparently insatiable sex drive that disrupts the person's ability to concentrate on other needs or leads to self-defeating behavior, such as indiscriminate sexual contacts.

coitus—the so-called *primal scene*. Perhaps he is trying to master the primal scene by compulsively reliving it.

Psychoanalytic explanations of sadism suggest that sadists are attempting to defend themselves against unconscious feelings of impotence and powerlessness by inflicting pain on others. The recipients' shouts of pain or confessions of unworthiness make sadists feel masculine and powerful.

Psychoanalytic theory suggests that masochism in the male might be the turning inward of aggressive impulses originally aimed toward the powerful, threatening father. The flagellation or bondage might also be unconsciously preferred to castration as a form of punishment for having unacceptable sexual feelings. Like the child who experiences relief when punishment is over, the sexual masochist willingly accepts immediate punishment in the form of flagellation or bondage in place of the future punishment of castration. Or a woman who witnessed her parents having coitus at an early age might have misperceived the father to be assaulting the mother. Her masochism then represents her unconscious reliving of her mother's (imagined) role with her father. Sexual masochists of either gender might also have such high levels of sex guilt that they can permit themselves to experience sexual pleasure only if they are adequately punished for it during sex.

The paraphilias have provided a fertile ground for psychoanalytic theories. However, there is a lack of evidence to support the role of such unconscious processes as unresolved castration anxiety. The basic shortcoming of psychoanalytic theory is that many of its key concepts involve unconscious mechanisms that cannot be directly observed or measured. So psychoanalytic theories remain interesting but speculative hypotheses about the origins of these unusual sexual behavior patterns.

Learning Perspectives

Learning theorists believe that fetishes and other paraphilias are learned behaviors that are acquired through experience. An object might acquire sexually arousing properties through association with sexual arousal or orgasm. Early proponents of the learning theory viewpoint were Alfred Kinsey and his colleagues, who wrote in *Sexual Behavior in the Human Female* (1953):

> Even some of the most extremely variant types of human sexual behavior may need no more explanation than is provided by our understanding of the processes of learning and conditioning. Behavior which may appear bizarre, perverse, or unthinkably unacceptable to some persons, and even to most persons, may have significance for other individuals because of the way in which they have been conditioned. (pp. 645–646)

Like Pavlov's dogs, who learned to salivate to the ringing of a bell that had been repeatedly paired with food,

> an animal may become conditioned to respond not only to particular stimuli, but to objects and other phenomena which were associated with the original experience. . . . In the laboratory, male animals may respond to particular dishes, to particular boards, or to particular pieces of furniture with which some female has had contact. (Kinsey et al., 1953, p. 647)

According to the conditioning model, a boy who catches a glimpse of his mother's stockings hanging on the towel rack while he is masturbating might go on to develop a fetish for stockings (Breslow, 1989). Orgasm in the presence of the object would reinforce the erotic connection, especially if the experience occurs repeatedly.

In an early experimental test of the conditioning model, Rachman (1966) showed normal (nonfetishistic) males slides of nude women interspersed with slides of women's boots. After numerous repetitions, the men showed a sexual response to the boots alone.

This "fetish" was weak and short-lived, however. It could still be argued that more persistent fetishes might be learned if pairings of such stimuli were to occur repeatedly during childhood. If fetishes were mechanically acquired by association, however, we might expect fetishists to be more attracted to objects that are inadvertently (and often repeatedly) associated with sexual activity, such as pillows, bedsheets, and even ceilings (Breslow, 1989). Yet we do not find this to be the case. The *meaning* of the object also seems to play a role.

Along these lines, Breslow (1989) proposed a learning theory explanation that describes the development of paraphilias in terms of the gradual acquisition of sexual arousal to an unusual object or activity through its incorporation in masturbatory fantasies. A transvestite, for example, might have achieved an erection while trying on his mother's panties in childhood. The paraphilic object or activity is then incorporated within masturbatory fantasies and is reinforced by orgasm. The paraphilic object or activity is then repeatedly used as a masturbatory aid, further strengthening the erotic bond.

We can also consider a role for parental approval as a reinforcing agent in the early development of transvestism. Parents who really wanted to have a girl have been known to occasionally dress their little boys in girls' clothing. The reinforcement of parental approval for cross-dressing might lead the boy to experiment with cross-dressing himself, which might then become eroticized if it is combined with masturbation or sexual fantasies and reinforced by sexual arousal or orgasm.

Fetishistic interests can often be traced to early childhood. Some rubber fetishists, for example, recall erotic interests in rubber objects since early childhood. Reinisch (1990) speculates that for some rubber fetishists, the earliest awareness of sexual arousal or response (such as erection) might have been associated with the presence of rubber pants, diapers, and so forth, such that a connection was formed between the two. Or perhaps the sexual attraction to objects that are associated with infancy derives from their association with feelings of being completely loved and cared for. The fetishistic act might represent an attempt to recapture sexual or loving feelings from early childhood.

McGuire and his colleagues (1965) report a case that provides some support for the role of learning in the development of exhibitionism. Two young males were surprised by an attractive woman while urinating. Although embarrassed at the time, their memories of the incident were sexually stimulating, and they masturbated repeatedly while fantasizing about it. The fantasies persisted, possibly reinforced by frequent orgasms. After a while, the young men purposely began to expose themselves to rekindle the high level of sexual excitement. Still, we should caution that only a very small percentage of men who have accidentally been discovered exposed have become exhibitionists.

Friedrich & Gerber (1994) studied five adolescent boys who practiced hypoxyphilia and found extensive early histories of choking in combination with physical or sexual abuse. The combination seems to have encouraged each of the boys to associate choking with sexual arousal.

Blair and Lanyon (1981) suggest that modeling plays a role in some cases. Parents might inadvertently model exhibitionistic behavior to young sons, which can lead the sons to eroticize the act of exposing themselves.

Learning explanations of sexual masochism focus on the pairing of sexual excitement with punishment. For example, a child might be punished when discovered masturbating. Or a boy might reflexively experience an erection if his penis accidentally rubs against the parent's body as he is being spanked. With repeated encounters like these, pain and pleasure might become linked in the person's sexual arousal system. Another learning explanation focuses on the association of pain with parental affection (Breslow, 1989; Sue et al., 1981). A child with cold and indifferent parents might be hugged only after a spanking. The pain or humiliation that is associated with the spanking becomes associated with the affection of the hug, which leads in later life to pain becoming a prerequisite for sexual pleasure. Yet these learning approaches fail to account for how sexual masochism develops within a larger and more complex sadomasochistic lifestyle (Breslow, 1989).

Learning theories of the origins of paraphilias also fail to consider the predisposing factors that might explain why some people who are exposed to early conditioning experiences develop paraphilic interests and others do not. Such predisposing factors might include poor self-esteem and difficulties forming intimate relationships. Many exhibitionists, voyeurs, frotteurs, and other people with paraphilias have few interpersonal skills in relating to women. They might avoid customary social interactions with women for fear of rejection. Their furtive, paraphilic behaviors might provide a sexual release with minimal risks of rejection or apprehension and be maintained because they represent the only available source of sexual gratification or reinforcement. Some paraphilias, such as voyeurism, exhibitionism, and frotteurism, can also be conceptualized as *courtship disorders*, involving an exaggeration or distortion of the steps that are normally taken during courtship in identifying, approaching, and becoming more intimate with new sexual partners (Freund & Blanchard, 1986).

Sociological Perspectives

Most people indulge paraphilias privately. Sexual masochists and sadists require a partner, however, save for the few masochists who practice only autoerotic forms of masochism and the few sadists who stalk nonconsenting partners. Most sadomasochists also relate in one way or another to the sadomasochistic subculture. It is within the S&M subculture—the loosely connected network of S&M clubs, specialty shops, organizations, magazines, and so on—that S&M rituals are learned, sexual contacts are made, sadomasochistic identities are confirmed, and sexual paraphernalia is acquired. But the S&M subculture exists in the context of the larger society, and the rituals that it invents mirror the social and gender roles that exist in the larger society.

Martin Weinberg (1987) proposes a sociological model that focuses on the social context of sadomasochism. Weinberg notes that S&M rituals generally involve some form of dominance and submission and attributes their erotic appeal to the opportunity to reverse the customary power relationships that exist between the genders and social classes in society at large. Within the confines of the carefully scripted S&M encounter, the meek can be powerful and the powerful can be meek (Geer et al., 1984). People from lower social classes or in menial jobs might be drawn to S&M by the opportunities it affords to enact a dominant role. They might have the opportunity to bark orders and commands that are followed unquestioningly. Those who customarily hold high-status positions that require them to be in control and responsible might be attracted by the opportunity to surrender control to another person. Dominance and submission games also allow opportunities to accentuate or reverse the gender stereotypes that identify masculinity with dominance and femininity with submissiveness.

Individual sadomasochistic interests might become institutionalized as an S&M subculture in societies (like ours) that have certain social characteristics: (1) Dominance-submission relationships are embedded within the culture, and aggression is socially valued; (2) there is an unequal distribution of power between people from different gender or social class categories; (3) there are enough affluent people to enable them to participate in such leisure-time activities; and (4) imagination and creativity, important elements in the development of S&M scripts and fantasies, are socially valued and encouraged (Weinberg, 1987).

An Integrated Perspective: The "Lovemap"

Like other sexual patterns, the paraphilias may have multiple biological, psychological, and sociocultural origins (Money, 1994). Our understanding of them may therefore be best approached from a theoretical framework that incorporates multiple perspectives, as found in the work of John Money and his colleagues.

Money and Lamacz (1989) trace the origins of paraphilias to childhood. They believe that childhood experiences etch a pattern in the brain, called a **lovemap,** that determines the types of stimuli and activities that become sexually arousing to the individual. In the case of paraphilias, these lovemaps become distorted or "vandalized" by early traumatic experiences, such as incest, overbearing antisexual upbringings, and physical abuse or neglect.

Research suggests that voyeurs and exhibitionists often were the victims of childhood sexual abuse (Dwyer, 1988). Not all children who are exposed to such influences develop paraphilic compulsions, however. For reasons that remain unknown, some children who are exposed to such influences appear to be more vulnerable to developing distorted lovemaps than are others. A genetic predisposition, hormonal factors, brain abnormalities, or a combination of these and other factors might play a role in determining one's vulnerability to vandalized lovemaps (Brody, 1990a).

Reflections

■ Psychoanalytic theories of paraphilias have been quite popular over the years. How would you account for their popularity?

■ Agree or disagree with the following statement and support your answer: Paraphilias are caused by early learning experiences.

■ Agree or disagree with the following statement, and support your answer: Despite the amount of theorizing and research that has gone into the paraphilias, we know very little about their origins.

TREATMENT OF THE PARAPHILIAS

The treatment of these atypical patterns of sexual behavior raises a number of issues. First, people with paraphilias usually do not want or seek treatment, at least not voluntarily. They often deny that they are offenders, even after they are apprehended and convicted. They are generally seen by mental health workers only when they come into conflict with the law or at the urging of their family members or sexual partners who have discovered them performing the paraphilic behavior or found evidence of their paraphilic interests.

Paraphilic behavior is a source of pleasure, so many people are not motivated to give it up. The individual typically perceives his problems as stemming from society's intolerance, not from feelings of guilt or shame.

Second, helping professionals might encounter ethical problems when they are asked to contribute to a judicial process by trying to persuade a sex offender that he (virtually all are male) *ought* to change his behavior. Helping professionals traditionally help clients to clarify or meet their own goals; it is not their role to impose societal goals on the individual. Many helping professionals believe that the criminal justice system, not they, ought to enforce social standards.

The third issue is a treatment problem. Therapists realize that they are generally less successful with resistant or recalcitrant clients. Unless the motivation to change is present, therapeutic efforts is often wasted.

The fourth problem is the issue of perceived responsibility. Sex offenders almost invariably claim that they are unable to control their urges and impulses. Such claims of uncontrollability are often self-serving and might lead others to treat offenders with greater sympathy and understanding. Most therapies, however, are based on the belief that whatever causes may have led to the problem behavior and however difficult it

Lovemap A mentally ingrained representation of the idealized lover and the idealized erotic activity with the lover.

might be to resist these unusual sexual urges, accepting personal responsibility for one's actions is a prelude to change. Therefore, if therapy is to be constructive, it is necessary to break through the client's personal mythology that he or she is powerless to control his or her behavior.

Despite these issues, many offenders are referred for treatment by the courts. A few seek therapy themselves because they have come to see how their behavior harms themselves or others. Let us consider some of the ways in which therapists treat people with these atypical sexual behavior patterns.

Psychotherapy

Psychoanalysis focuses on resolving the unconscious conflicts that are believed to originate in childhood and to give rise in adulthood to pathological problems such as paraphilias. The aim of therapy is to help bring unconscious conflicts, principally Oedipal conflicts, into conscious awareness so that they might be worked through in the light of the individual's adult personality.

Although some favorable case results have been reported (e.g., Rosen, 1967), psychoanalytic therapy of the paraphilias has not been subjected to experimental analysis. We therefore do not know whether successes are due to the psychoanalytic treatment itself or to other factors, such as spontaneous improvement or a client's willingness to change.

Behavior Therapy

Whereas traditional psychoanalysis tends to entail a lengthy process of exploration of the childhood origins of problem behaviors, **behavior therapy** is relatively briefer and focuses directly on changing behavior. Behavior therapy has spawned a number of techniques to help eliminate paraphilic behaviors and strengthen appropriate sexual behaviors. These techniques include systematic desensitization, aversion therapy, social skills training, covert sensitization, and orgasmic reconditioning, to name a few.

Systematic desensitization attempts to break the link between the sexual stimulus (such as a fetishistic stimulus) and the inappropriate response (sexual arousal). The client is first taught to relax selected muscle groups in the body. Muscle relaxation is then paired repeatedly with each of a series of progressively more arousing paraphilic images or fantasies. Relaxation comes to replace sexual arousal in response to each of these stimuli, even the most provocative. In one case study, a fetishistic transvestite who had become attracted to his mother's lingerie at age 13 was taught to relax when presented with audiotaped scenes representing transvestite or fetishistic themes (Fensterheim & Kantor, 1980). He played such tapes daily while remaining relaxed. He later reported a complete absence of transvestite thoughts or activities.

In **aversion therapy,** the undesirable sexual behavior (for example, masturbation to fetishistic fantasies) is paired repeatedly with an aversive stimulus (such as a harmless but painful electric shock or a nausea-inducing chemical) in the hope that the client will develop a conditioned aversion toward the paraphilic behavior.

Covert sensitization is a variation of aversion therapy in which paraphilic fantasies are paired with an aversive stimulus in imagination. In a broad-scale application, 38 **pedophiles** and 62 exhibitionists, more than half of whom were court referred, were treated by pairing imagined aversive odors with fantasies of the problem behavior (Maletzky, 1980). Clients were instructed to fantasize pedophiliac or exhibitionistic scenes. Then,

> at a point . . . when sexual pleasure is aroused, aversive images are presented. . . . Examples might include a pedophiliac fellating a child, but discovering a festering sore on the boy's penis, an exhibitionist exposing to a woman but suddenly being discovered by his wife or the police, or a pedophiliac laying a young boy down in a field, only to lie next to him in a pile of dog feces. (Maletzky, 1980, p. 308)

Behavior therapy The systematic application of the principles of learning to help people modify problem behavior.

Systematic desensitization A method for terminating the connection between a stimulus (such as a fetishistic object) and an inappropriate response (such as sexual arousal to the paraphilic stimulus). Muscle relaxation is practiced in connection with each stimulus in a series of increasingly arousing stimuli so that the person learns to remain relaxed (and not sexually aroused) in their presence.

Aversion therapy A method for terminating undesirable sexual behavior in which the behavior is repeatedly paired with an aversive stimulus such as electric shock so that a conditioned aversion develops.

Covert sensitization A form of aversion therapy in which thoughts of engaging in undesirable behavior are paired repeatedly with imagined aversive stimuli.

Pedophile A person with pedophilia, a paraphilia involving sexual interest in children.

Appropriate or Not? The debate rages over how parents introduce their children to human sexuality. Therapy for atypical sexual behaviors often examines the childhood and learning environment of the person and explores deep-seated attitudes about sex.

Maletzky used this treatment weekly for six months, then followed it with booster sessions every three months over a three-year period. The procedure resulted in at least a 75% reduction of the deviant activities and fantasies for over 80% of the study participants at follow-up periods of up to 36 months.

Social skills training focuses on helping the individual improve his ability to relate to the other gender. The therapist might first model a desired behavior, such as how to ask a woman out on a date or how to handle a rejection. The client might then role play the behavior, with the therapist playing the part of the woman. Following the role-play enactment, the therapist would provide feedback and additional guidance and modeling to help the client improve his skills. This process would be repeated until the client mastered the skill.

Orgasmic reconditioning aims to increase sexual arousal to socially appropriate sexual stimuli by pairing culturally appropriate imagery with orgasmic pleasure. The person is instructed to become sexually aroused by masturbating to paraphilic images or fantasies. But as he approaches the point of orgasm, he switches to appropriate imagery and focuses on it during orgasm. In a case example, Davison (1977) reports reduction of sadistic fantasies in a 21-year-old college man. The client was instructed to attain an erection in any way he could, even through the use of the sadistic fantasies that he wished to eliminate. But once erection was achieved, he was to masturbate while looking at photos of *Playboy* models. Orgasm was thus paired with nonsadistic images. These images and fantasies eventually acquire the capacity to elicit sexual arousal. Orgasmic reconditioning is often combined with other techniques, such as social skills training, so that more desirable social behaviors can be strengthened as well (Adams et al., 1981).

Although behavior therapy techniques tend to have higher reported success rates than most other methods, they too are limited by reliance on uncontrolled case studies. Without appropriate controls, we cannot isolate the effective elements of therapy or determine that the results were not due merely to the passage of time or other factors unrelated to the treatment. It is possible that clients who are highly motivated to change might succeed in doing so with any systematic approach.

Social skills training Behavior therapy methods for building social skills that rely on a therapist's coaching and practice.

Orgasmic reconditioning A method for strengthening the connection between sexual arousal and appropriate sexual stimuli (such as fantasies about an adult of the other gender) by repeatedly pairing the desired stimuli with orgasm.

Biochemical Approaches

There is no biological "cure" for the paraphilias. No drug or surgical technique eliminates paraphilic urges and behavior. Yet some progress has recently been reported in using a popular antidepressant, Prozac (fluoxetine hydrochloride), in treating exhibitionism, voyeurism, and fetishism (Lorefice, 1991; Miller, 1995). Why Prozac? In addition to treating depression, Prozac has been helpful in treating obsessive-compulsive disorder, a type of emotional disorder involving recurrent obsessions (intrusive ideas) and/or compulsions (urges to repeat a certain behavior or thought). Researchers speculate that paraphilias may be linked to obsessive-compulsive disorder (Kruesi et al., 1992). People with paraphilias often experience intrusive, repetitive thoughts or images of the paraphilic object or stimulus, such as mental images of young children. Many also report feeling compelled to repeatedly carry out the paraphilic acts. Paraphilias might belong to what researchers have dubbed an obsessive-compulsive spectrum of behaviors (Kruesi et al., 1992).

People who experience such intense urges that they are at risk of committing sexual offenses might be helped by **antiandrogen drugs,** which reduce the level of testosterone in the bloodstream (Marshall et al., 1991). Testosterone is closely linked to sex drive and interest. *Medroxyprogesterone acetate* (MPA) (trade name: Depo-Provera), which is administered in weekly injections, is the antiandrogen that has been used most extensively in the treatment of sex offenders. In men, antiandrogens reduce testosterone to a level that is typical of a prepubertal boy (Bradford, 1998). They consequently reduce sexual desire and the frequencies of erections and ejaculations (Bradford, 1998).

Depo-Provera suppresses the sexual appetite in men. It can lower the intensity of sex drive and erotic fantasies and urges so that the man might feel less compelled to act upon them (Berlin, 1989). Antiandrogens do not, however, eliminate paraphilic urges or behavior. As an analogy, consider the relationship between the accelerator pedal and the steering wheel of a car. The accelerator pedal controls the car's speed but not its direction. In much the same way that releasing pressure on the accelerator pedal slows the car, the use of antiandrogens reduces the intensity of sex drives and desires. The types of stimuli that have erotic value are not affected by antiandrogens, however, any more than easing up on the accelerator alters the direction of a car.

The use of antiandrogens is sometimes incorrectly referred to as *chemical castration.* Surgical castration, the surgical removal of the testes, has sometimes been performed on convicted rapists and violent sex offenders ("Sex offender," 1998). Surgical castration eliminates testicular sources of testosterone. Antiandrogens suppress, but do not eliminate, testicular production of testosterone. Also, unlike surgical castration, the effects of antiandrogens can be reversed when the treatment is terminated.

Evidence suggests that antiandrogens help some people when they are used in conjunction with psychological treatment (Marshall et al., 1991; Murray, 1988). The value of antiandrogens has been limited by high refusal and dropout rates, however (Marshall et al., 1991). Questions also remain concerning side effects.

Although we have amassed a great deal of research on atypical variations in sexual behavior, our understanding of them and our treatment approaches to them remain largely in their infancy.

Reflections

- What problems do therapists come across when they seek to treat people with paraphilias?
- What are the limitations in using antiandrogen drugs to treat people with paraphilias?
- Do you have any thoughts on why nearly all people with paraphilias are males?

Antiandrogen drug A chemical substance that reduces the sex drive by lowering the level of testosterone in the bloodstream.

s u m m i n g   u p

NORMAL VERSUS DEVIANT SEXUAL BEHAVIOR

What is considered normal in one culture or at a particular time might be considered abnormal in other cultures and at other times. Atypical patterns of sexual arousal or behavior that become problematic in the eyes of the individual or society are labeled *paraphilias.*

THE PARAPHILIAS

Paraphilias involve sexual arousal in response to unusual stimuli such as children or other nonconsenting persons, certain objects, or pain or humiliation. The psychiatric diagnosis of paraphilia requires that the person has acted on these persistent urges or is distinctly distressed by them. Except in the case of sexual masochism, paraphilias are believed to occur almost exclusively among men.

Fetishism

In fetishism, an inanimate object comes to elicit sexual arousal. In partialism, people are inordinately aroused by a particular body part, such as the feet.

Transvestism

Whereas other fetishists become sexually aroused by handling the fetishistic object while they masturbate, transvestites become excited by wearing articles of clothing—the fetishistic objects—of the other gender.

Exhibitionism

An exhibitionist experiences the compulsion to expose himself to strangers. The typical exhibitionist does not attempt further sexual contact with the victim and so does not usually pose a physical threat.

Obscene Telephone Calling

The obscene phone caller is motivated to become sexually aroused by shocking his victim. Such callers typically masturbate during the phone call or shortly afterward.

Voyeurism

Voyeurs become sexually aroused by watching and do not seek sexual relations with the target. The voyeur might masturbate while peeping or afterward while engaging in voyeuristic fantasies. Like exhibitionists, voyeurs tend to harbor feelings of inadequacy and poor self-esteem and to lack social and sexual skills.

Sexual Masochism

Sexual masochists associate the receipt of pain or humiliation with sexual arousal. Sexual masochists and sexual sadists sometimes form liaisons to meet each other's needs.

Sexual Sadism

Sexual sadism is characterized by persistent, powerful urges and sexual fantasies involving the inflicting of pain and suffering on others to achieve sexual excitement or gratification. Sadomasochists enjoy playing both sadistic and masochistic roles.

Frotteurism

Most frotteuristic acts—rubbing against nonconsenting persons, also known as mashing—take place in crowded places, such as buses, subway cars, or elevators.

Other Paraphilias

Zoophiles desire to have sexual contact with animals. Necrophiles desire to have sexual contact with dead bodies.

THEORETICAL PERSPECTIVES

Biological Perspectives

The links between paraphilias and biological factors have yet to be fully explored in research.

Psychoanalytic Perspectives

Classical psychoanalytic theory suggests that paraphilias in males are psychological defenses against castration anxiety.

Learning Perspectives

Some learning theorists have argued that unusual stimuli acquire sexually arousing properties through association with sexual arousal or orgasm. Another possibility is that unusual stimuli gradually acquire sexually arousing properties through incorporation in masturbatory fantasies.

Sociological Perspectives

According to Weinberg's sociological model, the erotic appeal of S&M rituals might result from the opportunity to reverse the customary power relationships that exist between different gender and social class categories in society at large.

An Integrated Perspective: The "Lovemap"

Money and Lamacz suggest that childhood experiences etch a pattern in the brain—a lovemap—that determines the types of stimuli and activities that become sexually arousing. In the case of paraphilias, these lovemaps become distorted by early traumatic experiences.

TREATMENT OF THE PARAPHILIAS

People with paraphilias might be motivated to seek help because of fears of exposure, criminal prosecution, or humiliation, but they seldom desire to surrender their sexual preferences.

Psychotherapy

Psychoanalysis aims to bring unconscious Oedipal conflicts into awareness so that they can be worked through in adulthood.

Behavior Therapy

Behavior therapy attempts to eliminate paraphilic behaviors through techniques such as systematic desensitization, aversion therapy, social skills training, covert sensitization, and orgasmic reconditioning.

Biochemical Approaches

The antidepressant Prozac has shown some promise in treating paraphilias. By reducing sex drives, antiandrogen drugs can help people who have difficulty combating paraphilic urges. They might be most helpful when used in conjunction with psychological treatment.

Jackson Pollock. *Naked Man with Knife*. 1938-1941. Oil on canvas, 127 x 91.4 cm. Tate Gallery, London/Art Resource, New York

18

Sexual Coercion

o u t l i n e

TRUTH OR FICTION?

RAPE

A WORLD OF DIVERSITY:
Not All Sex Offenders Are Men

Incidence of Rape

Types of Rapes

A CLOSER LOOK:
Anatomy of a Date Rape: Ann and Jim

Social Attitudes and Myths
That Encourage Rape

Sociocultural Factors in Rape

Psychological Characteristics of Rapists

A WORLD OF DIVERSITY:
*Rape-Prone and Rape-Free Societies:
Whither the United States?*

Adjustment of Rape Survivors

Treatment of Rape Survivors

Rape Prevention

A CLOSER LOOK:
Rape Prevention

VERBAL SEXUAL COERCION

WHAT DO YOU SAY NOW?
Handling Sexual Pressure Lines

SEXUAL ABUSE OF CHILDREN

What Is Sexual Abuse of Children?

Patterns of Abuse

Pedophilia

Incest

Effects of Sexual Abuse of Children

IN THE NEW MILLENNIUM:
*New Methods for Getting to the Truth
in Cases of Child Abuse*

Prevention of Sexual Abuse of Children

Treatment of Survivors of Sexual Abuse

**TREATMENT OF RAPISTS AND
CHILD MOLESTERS**

SEXUAL HARASSMENT

Sexual Harassment in the Workplace

Sexual Harassment on Campus

Sexual Harassment in the Schools

How to Resist Sexual Harassment

SUMMING UP

Truth or Fiction?

_____ A woman is raped every five minutes in the United States.

_____ The prevalence of rape is 20 times greater in the United States than in Japan.

_____ The majority of rapes are committed by strangers in deserted neighborhoods or darkened alleyways.

_____ Men who rape other men are gay.

_____ Many women say no when they mean yes.

_____ Most rapists are mentally ill.

_____ Women who encounter a rapist should attempt to fight him off.

_____ Father-daughter incest is the most common type of incest.

n recent years, the airwaves have been flooded with allegations of sexual assault and sexual harassment involving celebrities, highly placed politicians, and members of the armed services. In late 1991 and early 1992, media sharks went on a feeding frenzy in covering the rape trials of William Kennedy Smith and Mike Tyson and the Senate confirmation hearings of Supreme Court nominee Clarence Thomas, who faced charges of sexual harassment leveled by a former assistant, law professor Anita Hill. In 1998, the media turned its attention to an affair between President Bill Clinton and a young White House intern named Monica Lewinsky. Many argued that their relationship constituted sexual harassment because of the disparity in their power, even though Lewinsky was a willing partner.

Other high-profile cases include sexual abuse at an army training center in Maryland, the Tailhook incident, and sexual harassment by former U.S. Senator Robert Packwood of Oregon ("Sex complaints," 1996). The Senate Ethics Committee voted unanimously to expel Packwood from the Senate in September 1995. Packwood resigned.

A team of professional writers could not have tickled the public's fancy more, but the plots and the characters in these media series were very real. Many observers winced as they saw aspects of themselves—as either aggressors or victims—being laid bare before the nation.

This chapter is about sexual coercion. Our topic includes rape and other forms of sexual pressure, including lying to seduce one's partner and sexual harassment. Sexual coercion also includes *any* sexual activity between an adult and a child. Even when children cooperate, sexual relations with children are considered coercive in our culture because children are below the legal age of consent. Although sexual coercion is most often perpetrated by men, some offenders are in fact women.

RAPE

> I wanted to knock the woman off her pedestal, and I felt rape was the worst thing I could do to her.

> She wanted it, she was asking for it. She just said "no" so I wouldn't think she was easy. The only reason she yelled rape was she got home late and her husband knew she hadn't been out with her girlfriend.

> I found myself having sexual fantasies that would put women in precarious positions. I was thinking about this more and more, like devising a rack, perhaps, that would spread her legs as wide open as they could possibly be spread—something of this nature. I acted tough with them. The first one and the last pleaded for their virginity. I told them to do what they were told and they wouldn't get hurt. I said that if they didn't do what they were told, they would be sorry. I don't know if I actually threatened to kill them or not, but I very strongly feel that I never would have. The only thing is, perhaps if I continued on and hadn't been caught this time, seeing what happened from the first three times to the second three times—I just wonder—maybe in the next set of three somebody would have gotten hurt, you know, somebody would have really gotten hurt. (Groth & Birnbaum, 1979)

Rape Sexual intercourse that takes place as a result of force or threats of force rather than consent. (The legal definition of rape varies from state to state.) See also *forcible rape* and *statutory rape.*

These statements by rapists show that **rape** is the subjugation of women by men by force or threat of force. Many social scientists view rape as an act of violence that is more connected with domination, anger, power, and sadism than with passion or sexual desire (Tedeschi & Felson, 1994). Sexual motivation does play a role in rape. However, the use of sex to express domination, anger, and so on is more central to our understanding of rape.

NOT ALL SEX OFFENDERS ARE MEN

She wore red coveralls—the uniform of the female prisoner. She looked exhausted and disheveled as she stood for sentencing. She is Mary Kay LeTourneau, a 35-year-old former grade school teacher in suburban Seattle. She is the woman who had sexual relations, and a baby, with a former student—a 13-year-old boy. LeTourneau wept as her lawyer pleaded for mercy and made no comment when the judge offered her a chance to speak. She was sentenced to seven years and five months in prison and was denounced by the judge who had been lenient some months earlier, in a case that has raised questions as to whether female sex offenders can be held to different standards than men. In November 1997, she had pleaded guilty to raping the boy and promised King County Superior Court Judge Linda Lau that she would have no further contact with him.

"I give you my word," LeTourneau had said. "It will not happen again." LeTourneau is the mother of four children by her ex-husband. She had no previous criminal record and was given a suspended prison sentence and ordered to undergo treatment. But in February 1998, after hearing testimony that LeTourneau had again seen the boy and possibly planned to flee with him, Judge Lau revoked the suspension and sent LeTourneau to prison. Prosecutors, state legislators, and professionals who treat sex offenders note that LeTourneau had escaped an earlier prison sentence largely because she was attractive and presented herself as being in love with an emotionally mature boy.

When LeTourneau escaped the prison sentence the previous November, critics pointed to a similar case with a male teacher, Mark Blilie, who was 42 years old. He also had no previous criminal history but was convicted of having sex with a 15-year-old former student. Blilie was imprisoned for at least four years. But women make up only a small fraction—less than 2%—of convicted sex offenders, a fact that might have played a part in the judge's earlier sentence.

The victim? The boy repeatedly protested to the media that he was *not* a victim, that he was in love with his former teacher and deeply saddened by her conviction. LeTourneau had claimed that the boy was emotionally mature beyond his years But people who treat sex offenders say that they often justify sex with underage people by saying that the victim is emotionally mature. "Exploiting a young teenager's desire to be older, to be liked, to be accepted is the currency of sex offenders who prey on children of that age," said Lucy Berliner, research director of the Seattle's Harborview Center for Sexual Assault.

Mary Kay LeTourneau. Not all sex offenders are male. LeTourneau, a former grade school teacher, had sexual relations and a baby with a 13-year-old former student. A judge sentenced her to prison after she violated a pledge to have no further contact with the boy. LeTourneau has since had a second child with the boy after their brief encounter during the parole violation.

For the first few thousand years of recorded history, the only rapes that were punished were those that defiled virgins. These rapes were considered crimes against property (virgins being the property of their fathers)—not crimes against persons. In ancient Babylonia, rape laws applied to married women as well. Babylonian law required the assailant *and his victim* to be bound and thrown into a river. As the injured party (after all, *his* property had been damaged), the husband could choose to let his wife drown or save her. The unfair stigmatization of rape survivors is therefore an age-old tradition. The ancient Hebrews stoned to death a married woman who was raped and her assailant. In both the ancient Babylonian and Hebrew cultures, the wife was seen as guilty of adultery. Virgins who were raped within the protection of the city gates would also be stoned by the Hebrews. It was thought that they could have maintained their purity by crying out.

The current definition of rape varies from state to state. **Forcible rape** is usually defined as sexual intercourse with a nonconsenting person by the use of force or the threat of force. **Statutory rape** refers to sexual intercourse with a person who is below the age of consent, even if the person cooperates.

> **Forcible rape** Sexual intercourse with a nonconsenting person that is obtained by the use of force or the threat of force.
>
> **Statutory rape** Sexual intercourse with a person who is below the age of consent. Sexual intercourse under such conditions is considered statutory rape even if the person who is attacked cooperates.

Forcible Rape. Forcible rape is the use of force or threats of force to compel a person into sexual intercourse. A rapist's motives typically have more to do with the desire to control, abuse, or punish the victim than to attain sexual gratification.

Traditionally, a man could not be convicted for raping his wife, though he might have forced her to submit to sexual activity by physical power or threats. This marital exclusion was derived from the English common law that held that a woman "gives herself over" to her husband when she becomes his wife and cannot then retract her consent. Today, however, most states have rape statutes that permit the prosecution of husbands who rape their wives. Many states have also broadened the scope of rape laws to include forced sexual acts other than coitus, such as anal intercourse and oral-genital relations. Rape laws are now also applied to men who rape men and to women who coerce men into sexual activity or assist men in raping other women. Forcible rape is a form of **sexual assault.** Even when a sexual attack does not meet the legal definition of rape, as in the case of forced penetration of the anus by an object such as a bottle or a broom handle, it can be prosecuted as sexual assault (Powell, 1996).

Incidence of Rape

The government's National Crime Victimization Survey (1995) estimates that 500,000 women are sexually assaulted each year. This figure includes 170,000 rapes and 140,000 attempted rapes. This means that a rape was reported to have occurred about every three minutes on the average. The number of rapes has been outpacing population growth (Federal Bureau of Investigation, 1991; U.S. Senate Committee on the Judiciary, 1991).

Historical studies have seriously underreported the incidence of rape (Schafran, 1995). They have largely relied on crime statistics. However, the majority of rapes are not reported to the police or prosecuted (Gibbs, 1991). Many women choose not to report assaults because of concern that they will be humiliated by the criminal justice system. Others fear reprisal from their families or the rapist. Some simply assume that the offender will not be apprehended or prosecuted.

Truth or Fiction?
REVISITED

It is true that in the United States a woman is raped at least every five minutes. Every three minutes is actually closer to the truth. ■

Sexual assault Any sexual activity that involves the use of force or the threat of force.

According to Schafran (1995), there are two reasons that even the National Crime Victimization Survey underestimates the incidence of rape in the United States. First, many women mistakenly believe that coercive sex is rape only when the rapist is a stranger. Second, many women mistakenly assume that only forced vaginal penetration is defined as rape. But many states define rape more broadly.

Other surveys report the following prevalence of rape or sexual assaults:

- 21% of a sample of more than 5,000 female members of a health maintenance plan reported having been sexually assaulted (Koss, 1988).

- 18.5% of a sample of women clients of 257 psychotherapists in North Carolina reported having been sexually assaulted (Dye & Roth, 1990).

- 15% of the 3,187 women sampled in a national survey of college students reported that they had been raped. An additional 12% reported that they had been victims of an attempted rape (Koss et al., 1987).

- Nearly 22% of the women in the NHSLS study reported having been forced to do something sexual by a man (Laumann et al., 1994).

The weight of the evidence suggests that between 14% and 25% of women in the United States are raped at some point during their lifetimes (Calhoun & Atkeson, 1991; Koss, 1993). The prevalence of reported rapes in the United States is 13 times greater than that in Great Britain and more than 20 times greater than that in Japan. Later, we consider some of the cultural influences that make our society a breeding ground for rape.

It is true that the prevalence of rape is 20 times greater in the United States than in Japan. (That is, the prevalence of *reported* rape is more than 20 times greater in the United States.) ■

Truth or Fiction?
REVISITED

Women of all ages, races, and social classes are raped. Young women, however, are at greater risk than older women. Women of ages 16 to 24 are two to three times more likely to be raped than are other women (National Crime Victimization Survey, 1995).

Types of Rapes

One of the central myths about rape in our culture is that most rapes are perpetrated by strangers lurking in dark alleyways or by intruders who climb through open windows in the middle of the night. However, most women are raped by men they know—often by men they have come to trust. Figure 18.1 shows that only 4% of the women in the NHSLS study were "forced to do something sexual that they did not want to do" by a stranger. According to the National Crime Victimization Survey, 80% of rapes were committed by acquaintances of the victim (Schafran, 1995). The types of rape include stranger rape, acquaintance rape, male rape, marital rape, and rape by females.

It is not true that the majority of rapes are committed by strangers in deserted neighborhoods or darkened alleyways. Actually, most women are raped by men they know, not by strangers. ■

Truth or Fiction?
REVISITED

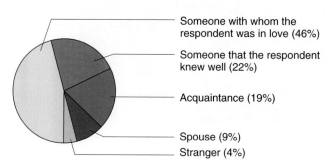

Someone with whom the respondent was in love (46%)

Someone that the respondent knew well (22%)

Acquaintance (19%)

Spouse (9%)

Stranger (4%)

figure 18.1

Women's Relationships with Men Who Forced Them to Do Something Sexual That They Did Not Want to Do. Only 4% of the sexual assaults reported in the NHSLS study were perpetrated by strangers.

(Source: Adapted from Laumann, E. O., Gagnon, J. H., Michael, R. T., & Michaels, S. [1994]. *The social organization of sexuality: Sexual practices in the United States*. Chicago: University of Chicago Press, figure 9.3, p. 338.)

STRANGER RAPE   **Stranger rape** refers to a rape that is committed by an assailant (or assailants) who was not previously known to the person attacked. The stranger rapist often selects targets who seem vulnerable—women who live alone, who are older or retarded, who are walking down deserted streets, or who are asleep or intoxicated. After choosing a target, the rapist might search for a safe time and place to commit the crime—a deserted, run-down part of town; a darkened street; a second-floor apartment without window bars or locks.

ACQUAINTANCE RAPE   Women are more likely to be raped by men they know, such as classmates, fellow office workers, and even their brothers' friends, than by strangers (Schafran, 1995). **Acquaintance rapes** are much less likely than stranger rapes to be reported to the police (Schafran, 1995). One reason is that rape survivors might not perceive sexual assaults by acquaintances as rapes. Only 27% of the women in the national college survey who had been sexually assaulted saw themselves as rape victims (Koss et al., 1987). Despite the increased public awareness of acquaintance rape, the belief is still common that rapists are strangers lurking in shadows and that a woman should be able to resist a sexual advance unless the man uses a weapon (Calhoun & Atkeson, 1991). Acquaintance rapists tend to believe in myths that serve to legitimize their behavior to themselves, such as the traditional view that men are expected to assume a sexually aggressive role in dating relationships and the belief that rapists are strangers. Even when acquaintance rapes are reported to police, they are often treated as "misunderstandings" or lovers' quarrels rather than as violent crimes.

DATE RAPE   Date rape is a form of acquaintance rape. Studies of college women show a consistent trend: 10% to 20% of women report being forced into sexual intercourse by dates (Tang et al., 1995). These figures hold at the Chinese University of Hong Kong as well as in the United States (Tang et al., 1995). In one U.S. study, most reported date rapes were committed by men whom the women had known for nearly a year on the average (Muehlenhard & Linton, 1987). Rapes were more likely to occur when the couple had too much to drink and then parked in the man's car or went back to his residence. The man tended to perceive his partner's willingness to return home with him as a signal of sexual interest, even if she resisted his advances. Most of the men ignored the women's protests and overcame their resistance by force. None of the men used a weapon. Only a few used threats of violence.

Combating Rape on Campus. Many colleges and universities have instituted rape awareness programs to combat the problem of rape on campus. What is the prevalence of rape on your campus? What are you going to do about it?

Stranger rape Rape that is committed by an assailant who was previously unknown to the person who is assaulted.

Acquaintance rape Rape by an acquaintance of the person who is assaulted.

a CLOSER look

Anatomy of a Date Rape: Ann and Jim

Date rape is a pressing concern on college campuses, where thousands of women have been raped by men they knew or had dated and where there is much controversy as to what exactly constitutes date rape (Gibbs, 1991). Consider the case of Ann.

I first met him at a party. He was really good looking and he had a great smile. I wanted to meet him but I wasn't sure how. I didn't want to appear too forward. Then he came over and introduced himself. We talked and found we had a lot in common. I really liked him. When he asked me over to his place for a drink, I thought it would be OK. He was such a good listener, and I wanted him to ask me out again.

When we got to his room, the only place to sit was on the bed. I didn't want him to get the wrong idea, but what else could I do? We talked for awhile and then he made his move. I was so startled. He started by kissing. I really liked him so the kissing was nice. But then he pushed me down on the bed. I tried to get up and I told him to stop. He was so much bigger and stronger. I got scared and I started to cry. I froze and he raped me.

It took only a couple of minutes and it was terrible, he was so rough. When it was over he kept asking me what was wrong, like he didn't know. He had just forced himself on me and he thought that was OK. He drove me home and said he wanted to see me again. I'm so afraid to see him. I never thought it would happen to me.

College men on dates frequently perceive their dates' protests as part of an adversarial sex game. One male under-graduate said "Hell, no" when asked whether a date had consented to sex. He added, "but she didn't say no, so she must have wanted it, too. . . . It's the way it works" (Celis, 1991). Consider the comments of Jim, the man who raped Ann.

I first met her at a party. She looked really hot, wearing a sexy dress that showed off her great body. We started talking right away. I knew that she liked me by the way she kept smiling and touching my arm while she was speaking. She seemed pretty relaxed so I asked her back to my place for a drink. . . . When she said yes, I knew that I was going to be lucky!

When we got to my place, we sat on the bed kissing. At first, everything was great. Then, when I started to lay her down on the bed, she started twisting and saying she didn't want to. Most women don't like to appear too easy, so I knew that she was just going through the motions. When she stopped struggling, I knew that she would have to throw in some tears before we did it.

She was still very upset afterwards, and I just don't understand it! If she didn't want to have sex, why did she come back to the room with me? You could tell by the way she dressed and acted that she was no virgin, so why she had to put up such a big struggle I don't know.

Accepting a date is not the equivalent of consenting to coitus. Accompanying a man to his room or apartment is not the equivalent of consenting to coitus. Nor are kissing and petting the equivalent of consenting to coitus. Let us reiterate a point worth restating: When the woman says no, the man is obligated to take no for an answer.

Men who commit date rape might believe that acceptance of a date indicates willingness to engage in coitus. They might think that women should reciprocate with coitus if they are taken to dinner. Some men assume that women who frequent settings such as singles bars are expressing tacit agreement to engage in coitus with men who show interest in them. Some date rapists believe that a woman who resists advances is merely "protesting too much" so that she will not seem "easy." They interpret resistance as coyness, a ploy in the cat-and-mouse game that typifies the "battle of the sexes" to them. They might believe that when a woman says no, she means maybe. When she says maybe, she means yes. They might therefore not see themselves as committing rape. But they are.

The issue of consent lies at heart of determining whether a sexual act is rape. Unlike cases of stranger rape, date rape occurs within a context in which sexual relations could occur voluntarily. Thus, the issue of consent can become murky. Juries and judges are often faced with a woman plaintiff who alleges that the male defendant, who might appear neatly dressed and looking like the boy next door, forced her into sexual relations against her will. As in the William Kennedy Smith and Mike Tyson trials, the defendant might concede that sexual intercourse took place but claim that it was consensual. Judges and juries face the task of discerning subtle shadings in meaning regarding the issue of consent. Attorneys on both sides vie to persuade them to see things their way.

Charges of date rape often come down to a case of his word against hers. Her word often becomes less persuasive in the eyes of the jury if it was clear that she had consented to a series of consensual acts beforehand, such as sharing dinner, attending the movies together, accompanying him to his home, sharing a drink alone, and perhaps kissing or petting. Let us state in no uncertain terms, however, that it does not matter whether the woman wore a "sexy" outfit, was "on the pill," or shared a passionate kiss or embrace with the man. If the encounter ended with the woman's being forcibly violated, then it is rape. When a woman says no, a man must take no for an answer.

The problem of date rape has been brought within closer public scrutiny in recent years. "Take Back the Night" marches have become a common form of student protest on college campuses against the sexual misconduct of men (Gross, 1993). Many colleges have mandated date rape seminars and workshops.

THE GANG RAPE   Groth and Birnbaum (1979) relate the story of Kurt, a 23-year-old White, married father of three who was involved in a number of rapes with a friend, Pete:

> I always looked up to Pete and felt second-class to him. I felt I owed him and couldn't chicken out on the rapes. I worshiped him. He was the best fighter, lover, water-skier, motorcyclist I knew. Taking part in the sexual assaults made me feel equal to him. . . . I didn't have any friends and felt like a nobody. . . . He brought me into his bike club. He made me a somebody.
>
> I'd go to a shopping center and find a victim. I'd approach her with a knife or a gun and then bring her to him. He'd rape her first and then I would. . . . We raped about eight girls together over a four-month period. (p. 113)

By participating in a gang rape, the follower, like Kurt, is attempting to conform to the stereotype of the tough, competent, "masculine" he-man. Followers, however, appear to fortify the courage of the instigator of the act. One of Groth and Birnbaum's planners of such an assault remarked: "Having a partner is like having something to drink. I felt braver. I felt stronger. This gave me the courage to do something I might not have done on my own" (1979, p. 112).

Exercise of power appears to be the major motive behind gang rapes, although some attackers might also be expressing anger against women. Gang members often believe that once women engage in coitus, they are "whores." Therefore, each offending gang member might become more aggressive as he takes his turn.

The Koss college survey (Koss et al., 1987) showed that sexual assaults involving a group of assailants tend to be more vicious than individual assaults (Gidycz & Koss, 1990). Relatively few survivors of gang rape reported the attack to police or sought support from a crisis center.

MALE RAPE   The prevalence of male rape is unknown because most assaults are not reported. Some estimates suggest that perhaps 1 in 10 rape survivors is a man (Gibbs, 1991). Most men who rape other men are heterosexual. Their motives tend to include domination and control, revenge and retaliation, sadism and degradation, and (when the rape is carried out by a gang member) status and affiliation (Groth & Birnbaum, 1979). Sexual motives are generally absent.

Truth or Fiction?
REVISITED

It is not true that men who rape other men are gay. Most men who rape other men are heterosexual. ∎

Most male rapes occur in prison settings, but some occur outside prison walls. Male rape survivors tend to suffer greater physical injury than female survivors (Kaufman et al., 1980). Males are more often attacked by multiple assailants, are held captive longer, and are more often reluctant to report the assault (Gerrol & Resick, 1988; Groth & Burgess, 1980; Myers, 1989). After all, victimization does not fit the male stereotype of capacity for self-defense. Men are expected to be not only strong but silent. Male rape survivors may suffer traumatic effects similar to those suffered by female rape survivors, however (Calhoun & Atkeson, 1991).

MARITAL RAPE

> The typical marital rapist is a man who still believes that husbands are supposed to "rule" their wives. This extends, he feels, to sexual matters. When he wants her, she should be glad, or at least willing. If she isn't, he has the right to force her. But in forcing her he gains far more than a few minutes of sexual pleasure; he humbles her and reasserts, in the most powerfully emotional way possible, that he is the ruler and she is the subject. (Hunt, 1979, p. 38)

When Hunt wrote these words, most states would not prosecute husbands for even the most violent of rapes. A number of recent legal changes have made it possible for sexually assaultive husbands to be convicted on rape charges, however. Nearly half the states have completely removed preferential treatment for assaultive husbands. In many other states, husbands still receive the benefit of the doubt unless there is evidence of gross brutality (Gibbs, 1991).

Marital rapes are probably more common than date rapes because a sexual relationship has already been established. A husband might believe that he is entitled to sexual access to his wife any time he desires it. He might be less willing to accept a rebuff. He might believe that it is his wife's duty to satisfy his sexual needs even when she is uninterested. Although there are no precise statistics on marital rape, a committee of the U.S. Congress estimated that one wife in seven is likely to be raped by her husband (Gibbs, 1991).

Marital rape goes largely unreported and unrecognized by survivors as rape (Russell, 1982). Women might fail to report marital rape because of fear that no one will believe them.

Motives for marital rape vary. Some men use sex to dominate their wives. Others degrade their wives through sex, especially after arguments. Sexual coercion often occurs within a context of a pattern of marital violence, battering, and physical intimidation (Finkelhor & Yllo, 1982; Russell, 1982). In some cases, though, violence is limited to the sexual relationship (Finkelhor & Yllo, 1982). Some men see sex as the solution to all marital disputes. They think that if they can force their wives into coitus, "everything will be OK."

Survivors of marital rape might be as fearful as survivors of stranger rape of serious injury or death (Kilpatrick et al., 1987). The long-term effects of marital rape on survivors are also similar to those experienced by survivors of stranger rape (Calhoun & Atkeson, 1991), including fear, depression, and sexual dysfunctions (Kilpatrick et al., 1987). Moreover, the woman who is raped by her husband usually continues to live with her assailant and might fear repeated attacks.

RAPE BY FEMALES   Rape by women is rare. When it does occur, it often involves aiding or abetting men who are attacking another woman. Rape by women might occur in gang rape in which women follow male leaders to gain their approval. In such cases, a woman might be used to lure another woman to a reasonably safe place for the rape. Or the woman might hold the other woman down while she is assaulted.

But men have actually been raped by women (Sarrel & Masters, 1982; Struckman-Johnson, 1988). Sarrel and Masters reported 11 cases of men who were sexually assaulted by women, including one case of a 37-year-old man who was coerced into sexual intercourse by two women who accosted him at gunpoint. In another case, a 27-year-old man fell asleep in his hotel room with a woman he had just met in a bar and then awakened to find that he was bound to his bed, gagged, and blindfolded. He was then forced into sexual intercourse with four different women, who threatened him with castration if he did not perform satisfactorily. Rape of a man might not be recognized as rape in states that adhere to a legal definition that requires forced vaginal penetration of a woman by a man. In such cases, the assailant or assailants might be charged under other statutes governing physical or sexual assaults.

Social Attitudes and Myths That Encourage Rape

Many people believe a number of myths about rape, such as "women say no when they mean yes," "all women like a man who is aggressive and forceful," "the way women dress, they are just asking to be raped," and "rapists are crazed by sexual desire" (Powell, 1996, p. 139). Yet another myth is that deep down inside, women want to be raped. Many women report rape fantasies, but they are in control of their fantasies. Rape is a complete lack of control, which no one wants (Powell, 1996). The belief that women desire to be overpowered and forced by men into sexual relations is a rationalization for violence (Powell, 1996).

Truth or Fiction?
REVISITED

It is not true that many women say no when they mean yes. This myth has the effect of encouraging rape. ■

Rape myths create a social climate that legitimizes rape. Though both men and women are susceptible to rape myths, researchers find that college men show greater acceptance of rape myths than do college women (Brady et al., 1991; Margolin et al., 1989). Men also cling more stubbornly to myths about date rape than do women, even after date rape education classes that are designed to challenges these views (Lenihan et al., 1992). College men who endorse rape myths are more likely to see themselves as likely to commit rape (Malamuth, 1981). Such myths do not occur in a social vacuum. They are related to other social attitudes, including gender-role stereotyping, the perception of sex as adversarial, and the acceptance of violence in interpersonal relationships.

Sociocultural Factors in Rape

Many observers contend that our society breeds rapists by socializing males into socially and sexually dominant roles (Lisak, 1991; Powell, 1996). Men are often reinforced from early childhood to behave in stereotypical aggressive and competitive ways (Lisak, 1991). Gender typing may also lead men to reject or repress traits that might restrain sexual aggression but are associated with the feminine gender role, such as tenderness and empathy (Lisak, 1991).

Research with college students supports the connection between stereotypical masculine identification and tendencies to rape or condone rape. One study compared college men who believed strictly in traditional gender roles with men holding less rigid attitudes. The "traditionalists" expressed a greater likelihood of committing rape, were more accepting of violence against women, were more likely to blame rape survivors, and were more aroused by depictions of rape (Check & Malamuth, 1983). Other researchers found that college men who more closely identified with the traditional masculine gender role more often reported having engaged in verbal sexual coercion and forcible rape (Muehlenhard & Falcon, 1990).

Women may be socialized into assuming the helpless role. The stereotypical feminine gender role includes characteristics such as submissiveness, passivity, cooperativeness, even obedience to male authority. Such qualities might make it difficult for a woman to resist when faced with the possibility of rape. A woman might lack skills in aggressiveness and believe that physical resistance is inappropriate or that she is incapable of resisting. Women are also taught that is important to be sexually attractive to men. Women might thus unfairly blame themselves for the assault, believing that they somehow enticed the assailant.

Social influences might reinforce cultural themes that underlie rape, such as the belief that a truly masculine man is expected to be sexually aggressive and overcome a woman's resistance until she "melts" in his arms (Stock, 1991). The popular belief that women fantasize about being overpowered sanctions coercive tactics to "awaken" a woman's sexual desires. Images from popular books and movies reinforce these themes, such as that of Rhett Butler in *Gone with the Wind*, carrying a protesting Scarlett O'Hara up the stairs to her bedroom. Violent pornography, which fuses violence and erotic arousal, might also serve to legitimize rape (Stock, 1991).

Young men might come to view dates not as chances to get to know their partners but as opportunities for sexual conquest, in which the object is to overcome their partners' resistance. In one study, male college students expressed support for a man's right to kiss his female partner even if she resists (Margolin et al., 1989). Malamuth (1981) found that 35% of the college men in his sample said that they would force a woman into sexual relations if they knew they could get away with it.

The social philosopher Myriam Miedzian suggests that lessons learned in competitive sports might also predispose young Americans to sexual violence (Levy, 1991). Boys are often exposed to coaches who emphasize winning at all costs. They are taught to be dominant and to vanquish their opponents, even if winning means injuring or "taking out" the opposition. This philosophy, Miedzian argues, could be carried from the playing field into relationships with women. Some athletes distinguish between sports and dating relationships. Others do not. Evidence shows that student athletes commit a disproportionate number of sexual assaults (Eskenazi, 1990). Many of these are gang rapes committed by groups of student athletes who live together and bond so strongly that they even share sexual experiences.

Sexual behavior and sports in our culture are linked through common idioms. A young man might be taunted by his friends after a date with a woman with such questions as "Did you score?" or, more bluntly, "Did you get in?" Consider, for example, the aggressive competitiveness with which this male college student views dating relationships between men and women:

> A man is supposed to view a date with a woman as a premeditated scheme for getting the most sex out of her. Everything he does, he judges in terms of one criterion—"getting laid." He's supposed to constantly pressure her to see how far he can get. She is his adversary, his opponent in a battle, and he begins to view her as a prize, an object, not a person. While she's dreaming about love, he's thinking about how to conquer her. (Powell, 1991, p. 55)

Psychological Characteristics of Rapists

Although sexual aggressiveness might be embedded within our social fabric, not all men are equally vulnerable to such cultural influences (Burkhart & Fromuth, 1991). Personal factors are thus also involved. What are they? Are rapists mentally disturbed? Are they retarded? Are they driven by insatiable sexual urges?

Much of our knowledge of the psychological characteristics of rapists derives from studies of samples of incarcerated rapists (Harney & Muehlenhard, 1991). One conclusion that emerges is that there is no single type of rapist. Rapists vary in their psychological characteristics, family backgrounds, mental health, and criminal histories (Prentky & Knight, 1991). Generally speaking, rapists are no less intelligent or more mentally ill than other people (Renzetti & Curran, 1989). Many rapists show no evidence of psychological disturbance (Dean & de Bruyn-Kops, 1982). This does not mean that their behavior is "normal." It means that most rapists are in control of their behavior and know that it is illegal.

It is not true that most rapists are mentally ill, even though their crimes might strike observers as being "sick." ▪

Truth or Fiction?
REVISITED

Some rapists feel socially inadequate and report that they cannot find willing partners. Some lack social skills and avoid social interactions with women (Overholser & Beck, 1986). Others are no less skillful socially than nonrapists in the same socioeconomic group, however (Segal & Marshall, 1985). Some rapists are basically antisocial and have long histories of violent behavior (Knight et al., 1991). They tend to act on their impulses regardless of the cost to the person they attack. Some were sexually victimized or physically assaulted as children (Groth, 1978; Sack & Mason, 1980). As adults, they might be identifying with the aggressor role in interpersonal relationships. The use of alcohol can also dampen self-restraint and spur sexual aggressiveness.

For some rapists, violence and sexual arousal become enmeshed. Therefore, they seek to combine sex and violence to enhance their sexual arousal (Quinsey et al., 1984). Some rapists are more sexually aroused (as measured by the size of erections) by verbal descriptions, films, or audiotapes that portray themes of rape than are other people (Barbaree & Marshall, 1991). Other researchers, however, have failed to find deviant patterns of arousal in rapists (e.g., Baxter et al., 1986; Hall, 1989). These researchers find that, as a group, rapists, like most other people, are more aroused by stimuli depicting mutually consenting sexual activity than by rape stimuli.

Studies of incarcerated rapists can be criticized on grounds that the samples might not represent the total population of rapists. It is estimated that fewer than 4% of rapists are caught and eventually imprisoned (Gibbs, 1991). Most rapes are committed by acquaintances. Acquaintance rapists are even less likely than stranger rapists to be arrested, convicted, and incarcerated.

To offset this methodological concern, researchers have turned to the survey method to study men who anonymously report that they have engaged in sexually coercive behaviors, including rape, but have not been identified by the criminal justice system.

Koss and her colleagues (1987) found that about 1 man in 13 (7.7%) in their national college sample of nearly 3,000 college men admitted to committing or attempting rape. Harney and Muehlenhard (1991) summarized research findings on self-identified sexually aggressive men. They are more likely than other men to:

- Condone rape and violence against women
- Hold traditional gender-role attitudes
- Be sexually experienced
- Be hostile toward women
- Engage in sexual activity to express social dominance
- Be sexually aroused by depictions of rape
- Be irresponsible and lack a social conscience
- Have peer groups, such as fraternities, that pressure them into sexual activity

THE MOTIVES OF RAPISTS: THE SEARCH FOR TYPES   Although sexual arousal is an obvious and important element in rape (Barbaree & Marshall, 1991), some researchers argue that sexual desire is not the basic motivation for rape (Gebhard et al., 1965; Groth & Birnbaum, 1979). Other researchers believe that sexual motivation plays a key role in at least some rapes (Hall & Hirschman, 1991). On the basis of their clinical work with more than 1,000 rapists, Groth and Birnbaum believe that there are three basic kinds of rape—anger rape, power rape, and sadistic rape:

- *Anger rape.* The **anger rape** is a vicious, unplanned attack that is triggered by anger and resentment toward women. The anger rapist usually employs more force than is needed to obtain compliance. The person he rapes is often coerced into performing degrading and humiliating acts, fellatio, or anal intercourse. Typically, the anger rapist reports that he had suffered humiliations at the hands of women and used the rape as a means of revenge.
- *Power rape.* The man who commits a **power rape** is motivated by the desire to control and dominate the woman he rapes. Sexual gratification is secondary. The power rapist uses rape as an attempt "to resolve disturbing doubts about [his] masculine identity and worth, [or] to combat deep-seated feelings of insecurity and vulnerability" (Groth & Hobson, 1983, p. 165). Only enough force to subdue the woman is used.

Anger rape A vicious, unplanned rape that is triggered by feelings of intense anger and resentment toward women.

Power rape Rape that is motivated by the desire to control and dominate the person who is assaulted.

RAPE-PRONE AND RAPE-FREE SOCIETIES: Whither the United States?

Cross-cultural studies suggest that sexual violence is not unique to our culture. It may in fact be culturally sanctioned in some societies. Rape is more common in violent cultures, especially in the minority of cultures in which violence toward women is legitimized (Ember & Ember, 1990; Powell, 1996). Among the Yanomamö people of the Amazon jungle, a tribe that is among the fiercest and most aggressive people in the world, men often raid neighboring villages and literally carry away the women to keep as their wives (Ember & Ember,

1990). Wives are often savagely beaten, stabbed with sticks, or burned with glowing firewood by husbands as punishment for misbehavior. Wives come to accept punishment as part of their marital role. They may also come to regard the scars as signs that their husbands must care deeply for them to have beaten them.

Sanday (1981) characterized 18% of the 156 cultures she studied as *rape-prone*. These rape-prone societies or "cultures of violence" tended to treat women as property. By contrast, Sanday found 45 "rape-free" cultures in which rape was absent or rare. Rape-free societies were characterized by sexual equality in which both genders shared power and were deemed to make

important contributions, albeit in different ways, to the welfare of the society. In such societies, women did not economically depend on men and were able to control their own resources. Such societies also reared their children to be nurturant and to shun interpersonal violence. It therefore appears that sexual violence occurs within the cultural context of interpersonal violence and male dominance (Stock, 1991).

Such cultural factors might help to explain the high rate of rape in the United States (Renzetti & Curran, 1989). The United States has both a high level of violent behavior, including the highest homicide rate among industrialized nations, and unequal gender relations.

■ *Sadistic rape.* The **sadistic rape** is a ritualized, savage attack. Sadistic rapists often carefully plan their assaults and use a con or pretext to approach their targets, such as asking for directions or offering or requesting assistance (Dietz et al., 1990). Some sadists bind their victims and subject them to humiliating and degrading experiences and threats. Some torture or murder their victims (Dietz et al., 1990). Mutilation of the victim is unfortunately common. Groth and Birnbaum (1979) suggest that sadistic rapists are often preoccupied with violent pornography but have little or no interest in nonviolent (consensual) pornography. Groth and Birnbaum (1979) estimated that about 40% of rapes are anger rapes, 55% are power rapes, and 5% are sadistic rapes.

What Motivates Rapists? Rapists may be after sex, but many social scientists find that rapists are typically more motivated to express anger toward women, or assert power over women, than to find sexual release.

Sadistic rape A highly ritualized, savage rape in which the person who is attacked is subjected to painful and humiliating experiences and threats.

565

Adjustment of Rape Survivors

Many women who are raped fear for their lives during the attack (Calhoun & Atkeson, 1991). Whether or not weapons or threats are used, the experience of being dominated by an unpredictable and threatening assailant is terrifying. The woman does not know whether she will survive and might feel helpless to do anything about it. Afterward, many survivors enter a state of **crisis.**

Many survivors are extremely distraught in the days and weeks after the rape (Koss, 1993; Valentiner et al., 1996). They have trouble sleeping and cry frequently. They tend to report eating problems, cystitis, headaches, irritability, mood changes, anxiety and depression, and menstrual irregularity. They might become withdrawn, sullen, and mistrustful (McArthur, 1990). People in the United States tend to believe that women who are raped are at least partly to blame for the assault (Bell et al., 1994). Therefore, some survivors experience feelings of guilt and shame (McArthur, 1990). Emotional distress tends to peak in severity by about three weeks after the assault and generally remains high for about a month before beginning to abate about a month or two later (Koss, 1993; Valentiner et al., 1996). About one survivor in four encounters emotional problems that linger beyond a year (Calhoun & Atkeson, 1991; Hanson, 1990).

According to a community survey of sexual assault survivors (both women and men) from Los Angeles, the most frequent emotional reactions to sexual assault were anger (59%), sadness (43%), and anxiety (40%) (see Table 18.1). A total of 447 people from the sample of more than 3,000 adults reported that they had suffered a sexual assault, which included a range of coercive acts from fondling of the breasts or sex organs to sexual intercourse (Siegel et al., 1990). As shown in Table 18.1, women were significantly more likely to report 12 of 14 listed reactions. Survivors who were physically threatened by

table 18.1

Prevalence of emotional and behavioral reactions to sexual assault in Los Angeles community sample (in percents)			
Reaction	**Women (%)**	**Men (%)**	**Total (%)**
Fearful	45.5	15.9[*]	35.1
Stopped doing things	31.8	15.2[*]	25.9
Fearful of sex	21.6	7.9[*]	16.8
Less sexual interest	32.5	6.9[*]	23.5
Less sexual pleasure	27.1	8.0[*]	20.4
Felt dishonored or spoiled	33.9	20.0[*]	29.1
Guilt	35.0	25.9[*]	31.8
Sad, blue, or depressed	50.6	28.8[*]	43.0
Anger	72.0	34.8[*]	59.0
Tense, nervous, or anxious	49.9	22.9[*]	40.4
Insomnia	25.2	11.6[*]	20.4
Loss/increase in appetite	15.8	8.4	13.2
Alcohol/drug use	5.1	5.9	5.4
Fearful of being alone	23.0	2.2[*]	15.7

[*]Indicates that the differences between men and women were statistically significant at the .05 level of significance; that is, there is less than a 5% chance that the differences between men and women were due to chance fluctuations.

Source: Siegel, J. M. et al. (1990). Reactions to sexual assault: A community study. *Journal of Interpersonal Violence, 5,* 229–246. Reprinted by permission of Sage Publications, Inc.

Crisis A highly stressful situation that can involve shock, loss of self-esteem, and lessened capacity for making decisions.

their assailants reported greater fear and anxiety, depression, and sexual distress (reduced interest and pleasure, fear of sex). Attacks that resulted in forced intercourse were more distressing than those that did not.

Rape survivors might also suffer physical injuries and sexually transmitted diseases, even AIDS, as a result of a sexual assault. In one study, concerns about contracting AIDS were reported by about one in four survivors (Baker et al., 1990).

Rape survivors might also be at risk for long-term health complications. In one study, survivors reported more current physical complaints, including gynecological problems, when they were assessed *two or more years* following the attack than did a reference group matched on demographic variables such as race and age (Waigandt et al., 1990).

Survivors might also encounter problems at work, such as problems relating to coworkers or bosses or difficulties in concentrating. Work adjustment, however, usually returns to normal levels within a year (Calhoun & Atkeson, 1991). Relationships with spouses or partners might also be impaired. Disturbances in sexual functioning are common and might last for years or a lifetime. Survivors often report a lack of sexual desire, fears of sex, and difficulty becoming sexually aroused (Becker et al., 1986). Some women simply do not experience the level of sexual enjoyment they found before the assault (Calhoun & Atkeson, 1991).

SURVIVORS' REACTIONS TO THE ASSAULT: WHOM TO TELL? About two thirds (65%) of the 447 sexual assault survivors in the Los Angeles survey reported they had told someone about the assault (Golding et al., 1989). The person was usually a friend or a relative. Only 1 in 10 reported the assault to the police. Only 1 in 6 consulted a mental health professional. Survivors were more likely to inform police or physicians of attacks by strangers than by acquaintances.

Most women fail to report sexual assaults to police. Why? Reasons include fears of retaliation, the social stigma attached to the survivors of rape, doubts that others will believe them, feelings that it would be hopeless to try to bring charges against the perpetrator, concerns about negative publicity, and fears about the emotional distress to which they would be subjected if the case were to go to trial.

RAPE AND PSYCHOLOGICAL DISORDERS Rape survivors are at higher-than-average risk of developing anxiety disorders and depression and of abusing alcohol and other substances (Koss, 1993). One anxiety disorder is **posttraumatic stress disorder** (PTSD) (Valentiner et al., 1996). PTSD is brought on by exposure to a traumatic event and is also often seen in soldiers who were in combat (American Psychiatric Association, 1994). People with PTSD might have flashbacks to the traumatic experience, disturbing dreams, emotional numbing, and nervousness. PTSD can persist for years. The person might also develop fears of situations connected with the traumatic event. For example, a woman who was raped on an elevator might develop a fear of riding elevators by herself. Researchers also report that women who blame themselves for the rape tend to suffer more severe depression and adjustment problems, including sexual problems (Frazier, 1990; Wyatt et al., 1990).

RAPE TRAUMA SYNDROME Ann Burgess and Lynda Holmstrom (1974) identified some common response patterns in survivors of rape, which they labeled the **rape trauma syndrome.** Through emergency room interviews with 92 women at Boston City Hospital and telephone or in-person follow-up interviews, Burgess and Holmstrom found two phases in rape trauma syndrome:

The acute phase: disorganization. The acute phase typically lasts for several weeks after the attack. Many survivors are disorganized during this time and often can benefit from rape trauma counseling. The woman might cry uncontrollably and experience feelings of anger, shame, fear, and nervousness.

Some women present a calm, composed face to the world but inwardly have not yet come to terms with the traumatic experience. Calmness often gives way to venting of feelings later on.

The long-term process: reorganization. The long-term reorganization phase might last for years. The woman gradually comes to deal with her feelings and to reorganize her life.

Posttraumatic stress disorder A type of stress reaction that is brought on by a traumatic event and characterized by flashbacks of the experience in the form of disturbing dreams or intrusive recollections, a sense of emotional numbing or restricted range of feelings, and heightened body arousal. Abbreviated *PTSD.*

Rape trauma syndrome A two-phase reaction to rape that is characterized by disruption of the survivor's lifestyle (the acute phase) and reorganization of the survivor's life (the long-term phase).

Lingering fears might lead rape survivors to move to safer surroundings. Women who informed the police might fear retaliation by the rapist. They might change their phone numbers, often to unlisted numbers. Some take out-of-state trips, often visiting parents, although they do not necessarily tell them of the rape. Many survivors continue to be bothered by frightening dreams.

Burgess and Holmstrom noted that many survivors of rape who do not disclose their attacks have a silent rape reaction. Unfortunately, concealing the rape might prevent them from receiving social support. If survivors are children or adolescents when assaulted, their feelings might go unresolved for years.

IF YOU ARE RAPED . . .   Elizabeth Powell (1996) offers the following suggestions if you should be raped:

1. Don't change anything about your body—don't wash, don't even comb your hair. Leave your clothes as they are. Otherwise, you could destroy evidence.
2. Strongly consider reporting the incident to police. You might prevent another woman from being assaulted, and you will be taking charge, starting on the path from victim to survivor.
3. Ask a relative or friend to take you to a hospital if you can't get an ambulance or a police car. If you call the hospital tell them why you're requesting an ambulance in case they are able to send someone who is trained to deal with rape cases.
4. Seek help in an assertive way. Seek medical help. Injuries that you are unaware of might be detected. Insist that a written or photographic record be made to document your condition. If you decide to file charges, the prosecutor might need this evidence to obtain a conviction.
5. Question health professionals. Ask about your biological risks. Ask what treatments are available. Ask for whatever will help make you comfortable. Call the shots. Demand confidentiality if that's what you want. Refuse what you don't want.

You might also wish to call a rape hotline or rape crisis center for advice if one is available in your area. A rape crisis volunteer might be available to accompany you to the hospital and help see you through the medical evaluation and police investigation if you report the attack. It is not unusual for rape survivors to try to erase the details of the rape from their minds. However, trying to remember details clearly will permit you to provide an accurate description of the rapist to the police, including his clothing, type of car, and so on. This information might help police to apprehend the rapist and assist in the prosecution.

Treatment of Rape Survivors

Treatment of rape survivors typically involves a two-stage process of helping the woman (the vast majority of rape survivors are female) through the crisis following the attack and then helping to foster long-term adjustment. Crisis intervention typically provides the survivor with support and information to help her express her feelings and develop strategies for coping with the trauma (Resick & Schnicke, 1990). Psychotherapy, involving group or individual approaches, can help the survivor to cope with the emotional consequences of rape, avoid self-blame, improve self-esteem, validate the welter of feelings surrounding the experience, and help the survivor to establish or maintain loving relationships. Therapists also recognize the importance of helping the rape survivor to mobilize social support (Ledray, 1990; Valentiner et al., 1996). Family, friends, religious leaders, and health care specialists are all potential sources of help. In major cities and many towns, concerned men and women have formed rape crisis centers and hotlines, peer counseling groups, and referral agencies geared to assessing and treating survivors' needs after the assault. Some counselors are specially trained to mediate between survivors of rape and their loved ones—husbands, lovers, and so forth. These counselors help people to discuss and work through the often complex emotional legacy of rape. Phone numbers for these services can be obtained from feminist groups (for example, your local office of the National Organization for Women [NOW]), the police department, or the telephone directory.

a CLOSER look

Rape Prevention

The New Our Bodies, Ourselves (Boston Women's Health Book Collective, 1992) lists several suggestions that might help to prevent rape:

- Establish a set of signals with other women in your building or neighborhood.
- List yourself in the phone directory and on the mailbox by your first initials only.
- Use deadbolt locks.
- Lock windows, and install iron grids on first-floor windows.
- Keep doorways and entries well lit.
- Keep your keys handy when approaching the car or the front door.
- Do not walk by yourself after dark.
- Avoid deserted areas.
- Do not allow strange men into your house or apartment without first checking their credentials.
- Keep your car doors locked and the windows up.
- Check out the back seat before you get in your car.
- Don't live in a risky building. (We realize that this suggestion might be of little use to poor women who have relatively little choice about where they live.)
- Don't give rides to hitchhikers (including women hitchhikers).
- Don't converse with strange men on the street.
- Shout "Fire!," not "Rape!" People are likely to flock to fires but to avoid scenes of violence.

Powell (1996) adds the following suggestions for avoiding date rape:

- Communicate your sexual limits to your date. Tell your partner how far you would like to go so that he will know what the limits are. For example, if your partner starts fondling you in ways that make you uncomfortable, you might say, "I'd prefer if you didn't touch me there. I really like you, but I prefer not getting so intimate at this point in our relationship."
- Meet new dates in public places and avoid driving with a stranger or a group of people you've met. When meeting a new date, drive in your own car and meet your date at a public place. Don't ride with strangers or offer rides to strangers or groups of people. In some cases of date rape, the group disappears just before the assault.
- State your refusal definitively. Be firm in refusing a sexual overture. Look your partner straight in the eye. The more definite you are, the less likely it is that your partner will misinterpret your wishes.
- Become aware of your fears. Take notice of any fears of displeasing your partner that might stifle your assertiveness. If your partner is truly respectful of you, you need not fear an angry or demeaning response. But if your partner is not respectful, it is best to become aware of it and end the relationship right there.
- Pay attention to "vibes." Trust your gut-level feelings. Many victims of acquaintance rape said afterward that they had had a strange feeling about the man but failed to pay attention to it.
- Be especially cautious if you are in a new environment, such as a college or a foreign country. You might be especially vulnerable to exploitation when you are becoming acquainted with a new environment, different people, and different customs.
- If you have broken off a relationship with someone you don't really like or feel good about, don't let him into your place. Many so-called date rapes are committed by ex-lovers and ex-boyfriends.

Rape Prevention

The elimination of rape would probably require massive changes in cultural attitudes and socialization processes. Educational intervention on a smaller scale might reduce its incidence, however. A study of 276 undergraduates at Pitzer College in California showed that college men who were more knowledgeable about the trauma caused by rape were less likely to report that they might commit a rape (Hamilton & Yee, 1990). Many colleges and universities offer educational programs about date rape. The University of Washington, for example, offers students lectures and seminars on date rape (and provides women with escorts to their homes or dorms after dark). Brown University requires all first-year students to attend orientation sessions on rape (Celis, 1991). The point of such programs is for men to learn that no means no, despite the widespread belief that some women like to be "talked into" sex.

Until the basic cultural attitudes that support rape change, however, rape prevention means that women take a number of precautions. Why should women be advised to take

Taking Back the Night. Many women—and men who care about them—have marched to demonstrate their anger toward the men who might victimize them if they were out walking alone, and toward the society that too often seems to condone rape. They frequently complain that society often blames the victim of rape and other sexual crimes, such as sexual harassment.

measures to avoid rape? Is not the very listing of such measures a subtle way of blaming the woman if she should fall prey to an attacker? No, providing information does not place responsibility on the person who is attacked. The rapist is *always* responsible for the assault. Women can take precautions, as discussed in the nearby A Closer Look feature, that might lower their risk of being assaulted.

CONFRONTING A RAPIST: SHOULD YOU FIGHT, FLEE, OR PLEAD?   What if you are accosted by a rapist? Should you try to fight him off, flee, or try to plead with him to stop? Some women have thwarted attacks by pleading or crying. Yet research has shown that less forceful forms of resistance, such as pleading, begging, or reasoning, can be dangerous strategies. They might not fend off the attack and could heighten the probability of injury (Bart & O'Brien, 1985). Screaming may be particularly effective in warding off some attacks (Byers & Lewis, 1988). Running away is sometimes an effective strategy for avoiding a rape (Bart & O'Brien, 1985), for example, but running might not be effective if the woman is outnumbered by a group of assailants (Gidycz & Koss, 1990). No single suggestion is likely to be helpful in all rape cases.

Self-defense training might help women to become better prepared to fend off an assailant. But physical resistance might spur some rapists to become more aggressive (Powell, 1996). Federal statistics show that women who resist increase their chances of preventing the completion of a rape by 80%. However, resistance increases the odds of being physically injured by as much as threefold (Brody, 1992a). A study of 116 rapes showed that women were more likely to physically resist if the attacker was a friend or relative, if the attacker made verbal threats, and if the attacker physically restrained or injured the woman (Atkeson et al., 1989).

It is difficult, if not impossible, for people to think through their options clearly and calmly when they are suddenly attacked. Rape experts recommend that women rehearse alternative responses to a rape attack. The Boston Police Department recommends that whatever form of self-defense a woman intends to use, she should carefully think through how it is used and practice using it (Brody, 1992a). Thompson (1991) suggests that effective self-defense is built upon the use of multiple strategies, ranging from attempts to avoid potential rape situations (such as by installing home security systems or by walking

Self-Defense Against Rape. Many women take self-defense classes to help them become better prepared to fend off an assailant. Yet no one strategy is likely to be effective in all situations.

only in well-lit areas) to acquiescence when active resistance would seem too risky to the use of more active verbal or physical forms of resistance in some low-risk situations.

It is questionable whether women who encounter a rapist should attempt to fight off the assailant. Women must make their own decisions about whether to physically resist a rapist, based on their assessment of the rapist, the situation, and their own ability to resist. ▨

Truth or Fiction?
REVISITED

Reflections

▨ Agree or disagree with the following statement and support your answer: A woman who walks in a dangerous neighborhood or talks to a stranger deserves what she gets.

▨ Agree or disagree with the following statement and support your answer: Our society breeds rapists by socializing males into socially and sexually dominant roles.

▨ What can you do to decrease the incidence of rape in our society? Will you do it?

VERBAL SEXUAL COERCION

Verbal sexual coercion is persistent verbal pressure or the use of seduction "lines" to manipulate a person into sexual activity. A study of 194 male undergraduates in a southeastern university showed that 42% admitted to verbally coercing a woman into sex (Craig et al., 1989). In a survey of 325 college undergraduates from a northwestern state university, about one in five of the men reported having said things to women they didn't mean to engage in sexual intercourse (Lane & Gwartney-Gibbs, 1985). Women were more likely than men to have been pressured into sexual relations. One in four of the women respondents reported that they had engaged in sexual intercourse with someone they would otherwise have rejected because they had "felt pressured by his continual arguments" (p. 56). About 1 in 15 of the *men* reported engaging in sexual intercourse unwillingly as a result of sexual pressure.

The use of verbal pressure and seduction "lines" is so common in dating relationships that they are seldom recognized as coercion. Consider the man who deceives his partner into believing that he really loves her to persuade her to engage in sexual activity with him. His use of lies or deception can be considered a form of sexual coercion because it employs devious means to exploit his partner's emotional needs in order to curry sexual favors.

what do you say now?

Handling Sexual Pressure Lines

Rape is an extreme form of sexual pressure that involves the use of threats or force to coerce an unwilling person into a sexual act. But sexual pressure can take a more subtle form, such as persistent verbal pressure or the use of seduction "lines" that aim to manipulate, by deception or trickery, another person into having sexual relations.

Following are sexual pressure lines noted by Powell (1996, pp. 71–73) that men usually use with women. What would you say in response to each of them? Responses suggested by Powell are shown in parentheses.

Kind of Pressure Line	The Line	Your Response
Lines that reassure you about the negative consequences	"Don't worry, I'm sterile."	_____ _____ _____ ("I know you want to make me feel safer, but . . . well, I'm just not comfortable about sex without a condom. I've known a few people who were more fertile than they thought.")
	"You can't get pregnant the first time."	_____ _____ _____ ("Hey, where did you get your sex education? People can get pregnant any time they have intercourse, even if it's just for one second.")
	"Don't worry— I'll pull out."	_____ _____ _____ ("I know you want to reassure me, but people can get pregnant that way, even without ejaculation.")
Lines that threaten you with rejection	"If you don't have sex, I'll find someone who will."	_____ _____ _____ ("I can't believe you are making a threat like this. I'm furious that you would treat lovemaking like some kind of job, as if anyone will do.")
Lines that attempt to put down the refuser	"You're such a bitch."	_____ _____ _____ ("It's hard to believe you want to make love to me and think calling names will put me in the mood. I need to leave now.")
	"Are you frigid?"	_____ _____ _____ ("I resent being called names just because I tell you what I want to do with my body.")

Kind of Pressure Line	The Line	Your Response
Lines that stress the beautiful experience being missed	"Our relationship will grow stronger."	_____ _____
		("I know you really would like to get more involved right now. But I need to wait. And lots of people have had their relationship grow stronger without intercourse.")
Lines that might settle for less	"I don't want to do anything. I just want to lie next to you."	_____ _____
		("The way we're attracted to each other, I don't think that would be a good idea. As much as I care about you, I'd better not spend the night.")
Lines to make you prove yourself	"If you loved me, you would."	_____ _____
		("You know I care a lot about you. But I feel very pressured when you try to get me to do something I'm not ready for. It's not fair to me. Please consider my feelings.")
Lines that attempt to be logical, but aren't	"You're my girlfriend— it's your obligation."	_____ _____
		("If you think sex is an obligation, we need to think about this relationship right now.") [Watch out for any such talk—it is very common in abusers and rapists. At best, it's an irrational comment by an immature person.]
Lines that are totally transparent	"I'll say I love you after we do it."	_____ _____
		("Bye, now.") [There is no way to deal with a person who would say such a thing.]

Although these sample responses can help you to resist specific pressure lines, do not think that saying no to sexual pressure is a privilege that you earn by winning an argument. As Powell recognizes, "You don't *have* to explain." Your body is not debatable. You don't have to say anything except "I don't want to."

Reflections

▨ To what forms of sexual verbal coercion have you been exposed? What forms of verbal coercion have you used?

▨ Have you ever lied to convince someone to engage in sexual activity? Have you lied to avoid sexual activity? Are you happy with the way you handled the situation? Why or why not?

SEXUAL ABUSE OF CHILDREN

Many people view sexual abuse of children as among the most heinous of crimes. Children who are sexually assaulted often suffer social and emotional problems that impair their development and persist into adulthood, affecting their self-esteem and their ability to form intimate relationships.

No one knows how many children are sexually abused. Although most sexually abused children are girls (Knudsen, 1991), one quarter to one third are boys (Finkelhor, 1990). A randomized national telephone survey of more than 2,600 adults showed that 9.5% of the men and 14.6% of the women reported having been sexually abused (a completed or attempted act of sexual intercourse) before age 19 (Finkelhor et al., 1990). These estimates might underrepresent the actual prevalence, as people might fail to report such incidents because of faulty memories or because of shame or embarrassment. In addition, about one in four people refused to participate in the survey, a number that casts doubt on the sample's representativeness. Other researchers estimate that the prevalence of sexual abuse among boys ranges from 4% to 16% (Genuis et al., 1991; Janus & Janus, 1993; Kohn, 1987) and that among girls exceeds 20% (Janus & Janus, 1993; Kohn, 1987). Whatever the actual prevalence, sexual abuse of children cuts across all racial, ethnic, and economic boundaries (Alter-Reid et al., 1986).

What Is Sexual Abuse of Children?

Sexual abuse of children ranges from exhibitionism, kissing, fondling, and sexual touching to oral sex and anal intercourse and, with girls, vaginal intercourse. In our culture, any form of sexual contact between an adult and a child is abusive, even if the child is willing, since children are legally incapable of consenting to sexual activity. Although the age of consent varies among the states, sexual relations between adults and children under the age of consent is a criminal offense in every state.

Voluntary sexual activity *between children* of similar ages is not sexual abuse. Children often engage in consensual sex play with peers or siblings, as in "playing doctor" or in mutual masturbation. Although such experiences may be recalled in adulthood with feelings of shame or guilt, they are not typically as harmful as experiences with adults. When the experience involves coercion or when the other child is significantly older or in a position of power over the younger child, the sexual contact can be considered sexual abuse.

Patterns of Abuse

Children from stable, middle-class families appear to be generally at lower risk of encountering sexual abuse than are children from poorer, less cohesive families (Finkelhor, 1984). In most cases, children who are sexually abused are not accosted by the proverbial stranger lurking in the schoolyard. In perhaps 75% to 80% of cases, the molesters are people who are close to them: relatives, steprelatives, family friends, and neighbors (Waterman & Lusk, 1986). Estimates of the percentage of sexually molested children who are abused by family members have ranged from 10% to 50% of cases (Waterman & Lusk,

1986). In a random survey of 521 Boston parents, 55% of the respondents who said that they had been sexually abused as children reported that the perpetrator was a family member or acquaintance (Finkelhor, 1984).

Parents who discover that their child has been abused by a family member are often reluctant to notify authorities. Some might believe that such problems are family matters that are best kept private. Others might be reluctant to notify authorities for fear that it may shame the family or that they may be held accountable for failing to protect the child. The decision to report the abuse to the police depends largely on the relationship between the abuser and the person who discovers the abuse (Finkelhor, 1984). In the Boston community survey, none of the parents whose children were sexually abused by family members notified the authorities. By contrast, 23% of the parents whose children had been abused by acquaintances notified the authorities, and 73% of the parents whose children were abused by strangers did so (Finkelhor, 1984).

Typically, the child initially trusts the abuser. Physical force is seldom needed to gain compliance, largely because of the child's helplessness, gullibility, and submission to adult authority. Although most sexually abused children are abused only once, those who are abused by family members are more likely to suffer repeated acts of abuse (Briere & Runtz, 1987; Dube & Hebert, 1988).

Genital fondling is the most common type of abuse (Knudsen, 1991). In one sample of women who had been molested in childhood, most of the contacts involved genital fondling (38% of cases) or exhibitionism (20% of cases). Intercourse occurred in only 4% of cases (Knudsen, 1991). Repeated abuse by a family member, however, commonly follows a pattern that begins with affectionate fondling during the preschool years, progressing to oral sex or mutual masturbation during the early school years and then to sexual penetration (vaginal or anal intercourse) during preadolescence or adolescence (Waterman & Lusk, 1986).

Abused children rarely report the abuse, often because of fear of retaliation from the abuser or because they believe that they will be blamed for it. Adults might suspect abuse if a child shows sudden personality changes or develops fears, problems in school, or eating or sleeping problems. A pediatrician might discover physical signs of abuse during a medical exam.

The average age at which most children are first sexually abused ranges from 6 to 12 years for girls and from 7 to 10 years for boys (Knudsen, 1991). Boys are relatively more likely than girls to be abused in public places and by strangers and non-family members (Faller, 1989a; Knudsen, 1991). Boys are also more likely to be threatened and physically injured.

TYPES OF ABUSERS   Researchers find that the overwhelming majority of people who sexually abuse children (both boys and girls) are males (Thomlison et al., 1991). Although most child abusers are adults, some are adolescents. Male adolescent sex offenders are more likely than other adolescents to have been molested themselves as boys (Becker et al., 1989; Muster, 1992). Some adolescent sex offenders might be imitating their own victimization. Adolescent child molesters also tend to feel socially inadequate and to be fearful of social interactions with age-mates of the other gender (Katz, 1990).

Although the great majority of sexual abusers are male, the number of female sexual abusers might be greater than has been generally believed (Banning, 1989). Many female sexual abusers may go undetected because society accords women a much freer range of physical contact with children than it does men. A woman who fondles a child might be seen as affectionate, or at worst seductive, whereas a man would be more likely to be perceived as a child molester (Banning, 1989).

So there really was a monster in her bedroom.

For many kids, there's a real reason to be afraid of the dark.

Last year in Indiana, there were 6,912 substantiated cases of sexual abuse. The trauma can be devastating for the child and for the family. So listen closely to the children around you.

If you hear something you don't want to believe, perhaps you should. For helpful information on child abuse prevention, contact the LaPorte County Child Abuse Prevention Council, 7451 Johnson Road, Michigan City, IN 46360. (219) 874-0007

LaPorte County Child Abuse Prevention Council

The Monster in the Bedroom. Not all monsters are make-believe. Some, like perpetrators of incest, are members of the family.

What motivates a woman to sexually abuse children, even her own children? Some female abusers have histories of becoming dependent on, or rejected by, abusive males (Matthews et al., 1990). Some appear to have been manipulated into engaging in sexual abuse by their husbands. Others appear to have unmet emotional needs and low self-esteem and might have been seeking acceptance, closeness, and attention though sexual acts with children. Some, motivated by unresolved feelings of anger, revenge, powerlessness, or jealousy, might view their own and others' children as safe targets for venting these feelings. Some view their crimes as expressions of love.

The great majority of child molesters are male. Why? Banning (1989), arguing from a sociocultural framework, suggests that males in our culture are socialized into seeking partners who are younger and weaker, whom they can easily dominate. This pattern of socialization might take the extreme form of development of sexual interest in children and adolescent girls, who because of their age are more easily dominated than adult women. Yet sexual interest in children might also be motivated by unusual patterns of sexual arousal in which children become the objects of sexual desire, sometimes to the exclusion of more appropriate (adult) stimuli. This brings us to pedophilia.

Pedophilia

The prevalence of **pedophilia** in the general population is unknown (Ames & Houston, 1990). Some pedophiles are so distressed by their urges that they never act on them. Many, however, molest young children and adolescents, often repeatedly. Some pedophiles are responsible for large numbers of sexual assaults on children. One study of 232 convicted pedophiles showed that they had molested an average of 76 children each (Abel et al., 1989). Incarcerated pedophiles have usually committed many more offenses than those for which they were convicted (Ames & Houston, 1990).

Although pedophiles are sometimes called child molesters, not all child molesters are pedophiles. Pedophilia involves persistent or recurrent sexual attraction to children. Some molesters, however, might seek sexual contacts with children only when they are under unusual stress or lack other sexual outlets. Thus, they do not meet the clinical definition of pedophilia.

Pedophiles are almost exclusively male, although some isolated cases of female pedophiles have been reported (Cooper et al., 1990). Some pedophiles are sexually attracted only to children. Others are sexually attracted to adults as well. Some pedophiles limit their sexual interest in children to incestuous relationships with family members. Others abuse children to whom they are unrelated. Some pedophiles limit their sexual interest in children to looking at them or undressing them. Others fondle them or masturbate in their presence. Some manipulate or coerce children into oral, anal, or vaginal intercourse.

Children tend not to be worldly-wise. They can often be taken in by pedophiles who tell them that they would like to "show them something," "teach them something," or do something with them that they would "like." Some pedophiles seek to gain the child's affection and discourage the child from disclosing the sexual activity by showering the child with attention and gifts. Others threaten the child or the child's family to prevent disclosure.

There is no consistent personality profile of the pedophile (Okami & Goldberg, 1992). Most pedophiles do not fit the common stereotype of the "dirty old man" in the trench coat who hangs around schoolyards. Most are otherwise law-abiding, well-respected citizens, generally in their 30s and 40s. Many are married or divorced, with children of their own.

Research suggests that sexual attraction to children might be more common than is generally believed. Researchers in one study administered an anonymous survey to a sample of 193 college men (Briere & Runtz, 1989). A high percentage of the students—21%—admitted to having been sexually attracted to small children. Nine percent reported sexual fantasies involving young children. Five percent reported masturbating to

Pedophilia A type of paraphilia that is defined by sexual attraction to unusual stimuli: children. (From the Greek *paidos,* meaning "child," not the Latin *pedis,* meaning "foot.")

such fantasies. Seven percent reported that there was some likelihood that they would have sex with a young child if they knew that they could avoid detection and punishment. Fortunately, most people with such erotic interests never act upon them.

Pedophilia may have complex and varied origins. Some pedophiles who are lacking in social skills might turn to children after failing to establish gratifying relationships with adult women (Overholser & Beck, 1986; Tollison & Adams, 1979). Research generally supports the stereotype of the pedophile as weak, passive, and shy—a socially inept, isolated man who feels threatened by mature relationships (Ames & Houston, 1990; Wilson & Cox, 1983).

Pedophiles who engage in incestuous relationships with their own children tend to present a somewhat different picture. They tend to fall at one or the other end of the dominance spectrum. Some are very dominant; others are very passive. Few are found between these extremes (Ames & Houston, 1990).

Some pedophiles were sexually abused as children and might be attempting to establish feelings of mastery by reversing the situation (De Young, 1982). Cycles of abuse may be perpetuated from generation to generation if children who are sexually abused become victimizers or partners of victimizers as adults.

Fired. Former Phillips Academy prep school teacher David Cobb was convicted in 1996 of trying to pay a 12-year-old boy to perform sexual acts on him. He was also convicted for possessing and exhibiting child pornography.

Incest

Incest involves people who are related by blood, or *consanguineous*. The law may also proscribe coitus between, say, a stepfather and stepdaughter. Although a few societies have permitted incestuous pairings among royalty, all known cultures have some form of an incest taboo.

PERSPECTIVES ON THE INCEST TABOO   Speculations about the origin of incest taboos abound. One explanation holds that the incest taboo developed because it was adaptive for ancient humans to prevent the harmful effects of inbreeding that can result when genetic defects or diseases are carried within family bloodlines (Leavitt, 1990). Our ancient ancestors lacked knowledge of the mechanisms of genetics, but they might have observed that certain diseases or defects tended to run in families. Evidence does show that marriage between close relations is associated with an increased rate of genetic diseases, mental retardation, and other physical abnormalities (Ames & Houston, 1990). Inbreeding might also be counterproductive to survival because it reduces the amount of genetic variation in the gene pool. Therefore, it can reduce the population's ability to adapt to changes in the environment.

Other theorists explain the incest taboo in terms of the role that it might play in maintaining stability in the family and establishing kinship ties within the larger social grouping (Ember & Ember, 1990). The anthropologist Bronislaw Malinowski (1927), for example, argued that the incest taboo serves to reduce sexual competition within the family. If left uncontrolled, competition would create rivalry and hostility such that the family might be unable to function as a social unit. Since the family unit fosters survival of a society, the incest taboo might have developed as a means of keeping the family intact.

Cooperation theory emphasizes the importance to the survival of the society of cooperative ties between family groups (Ember & Ember, 1990). Society is complex. Its survival requires the cooperation of large numbers of people. Marriage establishes kinship ties that lessen suspiciousness and hostility between family groups and foster cooperation. According to cooperation theory, the incest taboo was established to help ensure that people would marry outside their own families and thus create cohesive communities. Such theories are fascinating but remain speculative.

TYPES OF INCEST   Most of our knowledge of incestuous relationships concerns father-daughter incest. Why? Because, most identified cases involve fathers who were eventually incarcerated.

Incest Marriage or sexual relations between people who are so closely related (by "blood") that sexual relations are prohibited and punishable by law. (From the Latin *in-*, meaning "not," and *castus*, meaning "chaste.")

About 1% of a sample of women in five American cities reported a sexual encounter with a father or stepfather (Cameron et al., 1986). Brother-sister incest, not parent-child incest, is the most common type of incest, however (Waterman & Lusk, 1986). Brother-sister incest is also believed to be greatly underreported, possibly because it tends to be transient and is apparently less harmful than parent-child incest. Finkelhor (1990) found that 21% of the college men in his sample and 39% of the college women reported incestuous relationships with a sibling of the other gender. Only 4% reported an incestuous relationship with their fathers. Incest between siblings of the same gender is rare (Waterman & Lusk, 1986). Mother-daughter incest is the rarest form of incest (Waterman & Lusk, 1986).

It is not true that father-daughter incest is the most common type of incest. Father-daughter incest might be the most highly publicized variety of incest, but brother-sister incest is actually more common. ▪

Let us further consider the two most common incest patterns: father-daughter incest and brother-sister incest.

Father-Daughter Incest   Father-daughter incest often begins with affectionate cuddling or embraces and then progresses to teasing sexual play, lengthy caresses, hugs, kisses, and genital contact, even penetration. In some cases, genital contact occurs more abruptly, usually when the father has been drinking or arguing with his wife. Force is not typically used to gain compliance, but daughters are sometimes physically overcome and injured by their fathers.

Brother-Sister Incest   In sibling incest, the brother usually initiates sexual activity and assumes the dominant role (Meiselman, 1978). Some brothers and sisters might view their sexual activity as natural and not know that it is taboo (Knox, 1988).

Evidence on the effects of incest between brothers and sisters is mixed. In a study of college undergraduates, those who reported childhood incest with siblings did not reveal greater evidence of sexual adjustment problems than other undergraduates (Greenwald & Leitenberg, 1989). Sibling incest might be harmful for some children, however (Sorrenti-Little et al., 1984). Sibling incest is most likely to be harmful when it is recurrent or forced or parental response is harsh (Knox, 1988; Laviola, 1989).

Family Factors in Incest   Incest frequently occurs within the context of general family disruption, as in families in which there is spouse abuse, a dysfunctional marriage, or alcoholic or physically abusive parents (Alter-Reid et al., 1986; Sirles & Franke, 1989; Waterman, 1986). Stressful events in the father's life, such as the loss of a job or problems at work, often precede the initiation of incest (Waterman, 1986).

Fathers who abuse older daughters tend to be domineering and authoritarian with their families (Waterman, 1986). Fathers who abuse younger, preschool daughters are more likely to be passive, dependent, and low in self-esteem. As Waterman (1986a) notes:

> [The fathers] may need soothing and comforting, and may feel especially safe with preschool children: "I felt safe with her. . . . I didn't have to perform. She was so little that I knew she wouldn't and couldn't hurt me." (p. 215)

Marriages in incestuous families tend to be characterized by an uneven power relationship between the spouses. The abusive father is usually dominant. Another thread that frequently runs through incestuous families is a troubled sexual relationship between the spouses. The wife often rejects the husband sexually (Waterman, 1986).

Gebhard and his colleagues (1965) found that many fathers who committed incest with their daughters were religiously devout, fundamentalist, and moralistic. Perhaps such men, when sexually frustrated, are less likely to seek extramarital and extrafamilial sexual outlets or to turn to masturbation as a sexual release. In many cases, the father is under stress but does not find adequate emotional and sexual support from his wife (Gagnon, 1977). He turns to a daughter as a wife surrogate, often when he has been drinking alcohol (Gebhard et al., 1965). The daughter might become, in her father's fantasies, the "woman of the house." This fantasy might become his justification for continuing the incestuous relationship. In some incestuous families, a role reversal occurs. The abused daughter assumes many of the mother's responsibilities for managing the household and caring for the younger children (Waterman, 1986).

Incestuous abuse is often repeated from generation to generation. One study found that in 154 cases of children who were sexually abused within the family, more than one third of the male offenders and about half of the mothers either had been abused themselves or were exposed to abuse as children (Faller, 1989b).

Sociocultural factors, such as poverty, overcrowded living conditions, and social or geographical isolation, might contribute to incest in some families (Waterman, 1986). Sibling incest might be encouraged by the crowded living conditions and open sexuality that occur among some economically disadvantaged families (Waterman, 1986).

Effects of Sexual Abuse of Children

Sexual abuse often inflicts great psychological harm on the child, whether perpetrated by a family member, an acquaintance, or a stranger. Children who are sexually abused often suffer from a litany of short- and long-term psychological complaints, including anger, depression, anxiety, eating disorders, inappropriate sexual behavior, aggressive behavior, self-destructive behavior, sexual promiscuity, drug abuse, suicide attempts, posttraumatic stress disorder, low self-esteem, sexual dysfunction, mistrust of others, and feelings of detachment (Beitchman et al., 1992; Finkelhor, 1990; Goodwin et al., 1990; McLaren & Brown, 1989). Sexual abuse can also have physical effects such as genital injuries and can cause psychosomatic problems such as stomachaches and headaches.

Abused children commonly "act out." Younger children have tantrums or display aggressive or antisocial behavior. Older children turn to substance abuse (Finkelhor, 1990; Waterman & Lusk, 1986). Some abused children become withdrawn and retreat into fantasy or refuse to leave the house. Regressive behaviors, such as thumb sucking, fear of the dark, and fear of strangers, are also common among sexually abused children. On the heels of the assault and in the ensuing years, many survivors of childhood sexual abuse—like many rape survivors—show signs of posttraumatic stress disorder. They have flashbacks, nightmares, numbing of emotions, and feelings of estrangement from others (Finkelhor, 1990).

The sexual development of abused children can also become shaped in dysfunctional ways. For example, the survivor might become prematurely sexually active or promiscuous in adolescence and adulthood (Finkelhor, 1990; Waterman & Lusk, 1986; Tharinger, 1990). Researchers find that adolescent girls who are sexually abused tend to engage in consensual coitus at earlier ages than nonabused peers (Wyatt, 1988).

Researchers generally find more similarities than differences between the genders with respect to the effects of sexual abuse in childhood (Finkelhor, 1990). For example, both boys and girls tend to suffer fears and sleep disturbance. There are some gender differences, however. The most consistent gender difference appears to be that boys more often externalize their problems, perhaps by becoming more physically aggressive. Girls more often internalize their difficulties, as by becoming depressed (Finkelhor, 1990; Gomez-Schwartz et al., 1990).

There has been comparatively little research comparing survivors of childhood sexual abuse from different ethnic groups. In one of the few reported studies, researchers compared Asian American children who had been sexually abused with random samples of African, White, and Hispanic American sexually abused children drawn from the same child sex abuse clinic (Rao et al., 1992). Compared to the other groups, Asian American children were more likely to become suicidal. Asian Americans were also less likely to exhibit anger and sexual acting out.

New Methods for Getting to the Truth in Cases of Child Abuse

As we edge over into the new millennium, what are the brightest prospects for determining the truth in cases of child abuse? The American Academy of Child and Adolescent Psychiatry (1998) points out that no particular pattern of behavior in children shows that they have been abused—or who has abused them. As many as one-third of victims of sexual abuse show *no* symptoms. Roles for microbiology and DNA testing would apply only in cases in which there is physical evidence, such as semen. There was a time when hopes were pinned on anatomically detailed dolls as vehicles for allowing children to describe incidences of sexual abuse. However, children's natural interest in the dolls' anatomy can be misinterpreted as a sign of abuse. Therefore, the American Professional Society on the Abuse of Children (1998) has taken the position that "Anatomical dolls should not be used as a diagnostic test for sexual abuse."

Asking children what has happened to them has led to many *false positives*—that is, instances in which innocent adults have been fingered as being guilty of abuse. The problem, according to Cornell University psychologist Stephen Ceci (1998), is that children are highly suggestible. They pick up on interviewers' suggestions—made in the form of leading questions ("Did Mark touch your penis?")—and then often respond inaccurately. Suggestibility is also highlighted in the use of anatomically correct dolls. McGill University researcher Maggie Bruck (1998) notes that reports of inappropriate touching increase each time children are shown the dolls.

It would appear that the best hope for unearthing childhood sexual abuse might simply be more careful interviewing. Guidelines for interviews that avoid suggesting abuse include the following (Goldberg, 1998):

■ Interview the children in an open-ended way rather than describing specific events and asking whether they occurred. *Don't* say, "Did he touch your vagina?" (a leading question).

Rather, say, "Tell me everything that happened in John's apartment."

■ Use interviewers who are unbiased—who have no preconceived ideas as to whether abuse occurred or about who might have been guilty of it.

■ Keep numbers of questions and interviews to a minimum. Not only are interviews taxing to children, but exposure to many questions or interviews begins to plant suggestions in children's minds.

■ Children should not be asked to imagine sexual acts, because they might then become confused as to what is real and what is fantasy.

■ Children should not be pressured to respond, especially by bribing them or threatening them. Aside from the obvious inappropriateness of such courses of action, they might pressure children to invent abuses that did not occur.

Thus, it could be that obtaining accurate information about childhood sexual abuse will not involve fancy electronic circuitry or microbiology. It might rely on careful questioning and common sense.

How Can We Get at the Truth in Cases of Child Abuse? Serious doubts have been raised about the use of "anatomically correct" dolls and questioning child victims. However, asking children open-ended rather than leading questions may lead to more accurate reports.

The long-term consequences of sexual abuse in childhood tend to be greater for children who were abused by their fathers or stepfathers, who experienced penetration, who were forced, and who suffered more prolonged and severe abuse (Beitchman et al., 1992; Cheasty, 1998; Wyatt & Newcomb, 1990). Children who suffer incest often feel a deep sense of betrayal by the offender and, perhaps, by other family members—especially their mothers, whom they perceive as failing to protect them (Finkelhor, 1990). Incest survivors might feel powerless to control their bodies or their lives.

Late adolescence and early adulthood seem to be especially difficult periods for survivors of childhood sexual abuse. Studies of women in these age groups reveal more psychological and social problems in abused women (Jackson et al., 1990; Roland et al., 1989).

Effects of childhood sexual abuse are often long-lasting. In one study, researchers found evidence of greater psychological distress in a group of 54 adult women, ranging from 23 to 61 years of age, who had been sexually abused as children than in a matched group of nonabused women (Greenwald & Leitenberg, 1989). A Dublin study found that female survivors of sexual abuse were more likely to feel depressed and to get divorces than the general population (Cheasty, 1998). Women who blame themselves for the abuse apparently have relatively lower self-esteem and more depression than those who do not (Hoagwood, 1990).

Prevention of Sexual Abuse of Children

Many of us were taught by our parents never to accept a ride or an offer of candy from a stranger. However, many instances of sexual abuse are perpetrated by familiar adults, often a family member or friend. Prevention programs help children to understand what sexual abuse is and how they can avoid it. A national survey showed that two of three children in the United States have participated in school-based sex abuse prevention programs (Goleman, 1993). In addition to learning to avoid strangers, children need to recognize the differences between acceptable touching, such as an affectionate embrace or pat on the head, and unacceptable or "bad" touching. Even elementary-school-age children can learn the distinction between "good touching and bad touching" (Tutty, 1992). Good school-based programs are generally helpful in preparing children to handle an actual encounter with a potential molester (Goleman, 1993). Children who receive comprehensive training are more likely to use strategies such as running away, yelling, or saying no when they are threatened by an abuser. They are also more likely to report incidents to adults.

Researchers recognize that children can easily be intimidated or overpowered by adults or older children. Children might be unable to say no in a sexually abusive situation, even though they want to and know that it is the right thing to do (Waterman et al., 1986). Although children might not always be able to prevent abuse, they can be encouraged to tell someone about it. Most prevention programs emphasize teaching children messages such as "It's not your fault," "Never keep a bad or scary secret," and "Always tell your parents about this, especially if someone says you shouldn't tell them" (Waterman et al., 1986).

Children also need to be alerted to the types of threats they might receive for disclosing the abuse. They are more likely to resist threats if they are reassured that they will be believed if they disclose the abuse, that their parents will continue to love them, and that they and their families will be protected from the molester.

School-based prevention programs focus on protecting the child. In most states, teachers and helping professionals are required to report suspected abuse to authorities. Tighter controls and better screening are needed to monitor the hiring of day care employees. Administrators and teachers in preschool and day care facilities also need to be educated to recognize the signs of sexual abuse and to report suspected cases (Waterman et al., 1986). Treatment programs to help people who are sexually attracted to children *before* they commit abusive acts would also be of use.

Treatment of Survivors of Sexual Abuse

At least 75% of cases of sexual abuse of children go unreported. Psychotherapy in adulthood often becomes the first opportunity for survivors to confront leftover feelings of pain, anger, and misplaced guilt (Alter-Reid et al., 1986; Ratican, 1992). Group or individual therapy can help improve survivors' self-esteem and ability to develop intimate relationships. Confronting the trauma within a supportive therapeutic relationship might also help to prevent the cycle of abuse from perpetuating itself from one generation to another (Alter-Reid et al., 1986).

Special programs have begun to appear that provide therapeutic services to abused children and adolescents. Most therapists recommend a multicomponent treatment approach, which might involve individual therapy for the child, mother, and father; group therapy for the adolescent or even preadolescent survivor; art therapy or play therapy for the younger child (e.g., using drawings or puppets to express feelings); marital counseling for the parents; and family therapy for the entire family (de Luca et al., 1992; Waterman, 1986).

Reflections

- Agree or disagree with the following statement and support your answer: Any form of sexual contact between an adult and a child is abusive.
- Do you know of anyone who was exposed to childhood sexual abuse? What was the experience like at the time? What were its lingering effects? Was the perpetrator reported to authorities? Why or why not?
- Why do you think the great majority of child molesters are male?

TREATMENT OF RAPISTS AND CHILD MOLESTERS

What does *treatment* mean? When a helping professional treats someone, the goal is usually to help that individual. When we speak of treating a sex offender, the goal is as likely, or more likely, to be to help society by eliminating the problem behavior.

Rapists and child molesters are criminals, not patients. Most convicted rapists and child molesters are incarcerated as a form of punishment, not treatment. They might receive psychological treatment or rehabilitation in prison to help prepare them for release and reentry into society, however. The most common form of treatment is group therapy, which is based on the belief that though offenders might fool counselors, they do not easily fool one another. Yet the great majority of incarcerated sex offenders receive little or no treatment in prison (Goleman, 1992). In California, for example, which has 15,000 incarcerated sex offenders, treatment has been provided in but one experimental program for only 46 rapists and child molesters (Goleman, 1992).

The results of prison-based treatment programs are mixed at best. Consider a Canadian study of 54 rapists who participated in a treatment program. After release from prison, 28% were later convicted of a sexual offense, and 43% were convicted of a violent offense (Rice et al., 1990). Treatment also failed to curb recidivism among a sample of 136 child molesters (Rice et al., 1991).

More promising findings resulted from innovative programs in prison facilities in California and Vermont (Goleman, 1992). In the Vermont program, the average rate of conviction for additional sex crimes after release was reduced by at least half in a group of sex offenders who received the treatment program, compared to a control group who did not. These innovative programs used a variety of techniques. Empathy training was used to increase the offender's sensitivity to his victims. One empathy exercise had offenders write about their crimes from the perspective of the victim. The technique of covert sensitization was used to help offenders resist deviant sex fantasies, which often lead to deviant behavior. The offender would pair, in his imagination, scenes involving rape and molestation with aversive consequences. An exhibitionist, for example, might be asked to practice imagining that he is about to expose himself and is discovered in the act by his parents. A child molester might fantasize about sexually approaching a child, only to find himself confronted by police officers.

Another approach uses medical interventions such as castration to reduce testosterone levels and, consequently, offenders' sex drives. Experts do not agree on whether castration helps sex offenders to control their sexual urges ("Sex offender," 1998). Many castrated rapists report lowered sex drives, as might be expected from the reductions in testosterone production that result from the removal of the testes. They might retain sexual interest and remain capable of erection, however. And some do repeat their crimes. Other researchers report lower recidivism rates among castrated offenders than among other offenders.

Surgical castration is an extreme measure. It raises ethical concerns because of its invasive character and irreversibility. Antiandrogen drugs such as Depo-Provera chemically reduce testosterone levels (Ayres, 1996). Unlike surgical castration, "chemical castration"—via antiandrogen drugs—is reversible (Ayres, 1996). In 1996, California passed a bill that requires repeat child molesters to undergo chemical castration upon release unless they have undergone voluntary surgical castration ("Injections approved," 1996). An Illinois child sex offender recently underwent surgical castration in an effort to win a lighter sentence ("Sex offender," 1998).

Reflections

- Agree or disagree with the following statement and support your answer: We should punish sex offenders and not worry about treating them.
- Agree or disagree with the following statement and support your answer: It is futile to attempt to provide treatment for a sex offender.

SEXUAL HARASSMENT

Many Americans were spellbound by the 1994 Michael Douglas–Demi Moore film *Disclosure*. In the film, Demi Moore plays Michael Douglas's supervisor. She uses her power over him to attempt to harass him into sexual activity.

What *is* **sexual harassment**?

Sexual harassment can be difficult to define (Lewin, 1998b). For example, President Bill Clinton was accused of sexually touching or "groping" a resistant White House volunteer, Kathleen Willey, and of placing her hand on his penis (Lewin, 1998b). Such behavior would clearly constitute sexual harassment. Clinton also engaged in fellatio with a young White House intern, Monica Lewinsky. Although Lewinsky participated voluntarily, some critics note that the White House is a workplace and that Clinton's power over the intern caused their interaction to constitute sexual harassment.

For legal purposes, sexual harassment in the workplace is usually defined as the "deliberate or repeated unsolicited verbal comments, gestures, or *physical contact*[1] of a sexual nature that is considered to be unwelcome by the recipient" (U.S. Merit Systems Protection Board, 1981, p. 2). Examples of sexual harassment can range from unwelcome sexual jokes, overtures, suggestive comments, and sexual innuendos to outright sexual assault and might include behaviors such as the following (Powell 1996):

- Verbal harassment or abuse
- Subtle pressure for sexual activity
- Remarks about a person's clothing, body, or sexual activities
- Leering at or ogling a person's body
- Unwelcome touching, patting, or pinching
- Brushing against a person's body
- Demands for sexual favors accompanied by implied or overt threats concerning one's job or student status
- Physical assault. The idea here is that sexual assault, of the kind of which President Clinton was accused, would be sexual harassment but could also be much more.

Men or women can both commit, and be subjected to, sexual harassment, however, about 99% of harassers are men (see Table 18.2 on page 584; American Psychological Association, 1998a).

Charges of sexual harassment are often ignored or trivialized by coworkers and employers. The victim might hear comments such as, "Why make a big deal out of it? It's

---

[1]Our italics.

> **Sexual harassment** Deliberate or repeated unsolicited verbal comments, gestures, or physical contact of a sexual nature that is considered to be unwelcome by the recipient.

t a b l e   1 8 . 2

Sexual harassment: Myths and realities

Myths	Realities
Sexual harassment is rare.	Sexual harassment is extremely widespread. It touches the lives of 40% to 60% of working women, and similar proportions of female students in colleges and universities.
The seriousness of sexual harassment has been exaggerated; most so-called harassment is really trivial and harmless flirtation.	Sexual harassment can be devastating. Studies indicate that most harassment has nothing to do with "flirtation" or sincere sexual or social iterest. Rather, it is offensive, often frightening, and insulting to women. Research shows that women are often forced to leave school or jobs to avoid harassment and may experience serious psychological and health-related problems.
Many women make up and report stories of sexual harassment to get back at their employers or others who have angered them.	Research shows that less than 1% of complaints are false. Women rarely file false complaints or file complaints even when they are justified in doing so.
Women who are sexually harassed generally provoke harassment by the way they look, dress and behave.	Harassment does not occur because women dress provocatively or initiate sexual activity in the hope of getting promoted and advancing their careers. Studies have found that victims of sexual harassment vary in physical appearance, type of dress, age, and behavior. The only thing they have in common is that over 99% of them are female.
If you ignore harassment, it will go away.	It will not. Research has shown that simply ignoring the behavior is ineffective; harassers generally will not stop on their own. Ignoring such behavior may even be seen as agreement or encouragement.

Source: American Psychological Association (1998, March 16). Sexual harassment: Myths and realities. APA Public Information Home Page; www.apa.org.

not like you were attacked in the street." Evidence shows, however, that people who are subjected to sexual harassment do suffer from it. In one study, 75% of people who were sexually harassed reported reactions such as anxiety, irritability, lowered self-esteem, and anger (Gruber & Bjorn, 1986; Loy & Stewart, 1984). Some find harassment on the job so unbearable that they resign. College women have dropped courses, switched majors, or changed graduate programs or even colleges because they were unable to stop professors from sexually harassing them (Dziech & Weiner, 1984; Fitzgerald, 1993a, 1993b).

One reason that sexual harassment is so stressful is that, as with so many other forms of sexual exploitation or coercion, the blame tends to fall on the victim (Powell, 1996). Some harassers seem to believe that charges of harassment were exaggerated or that the victim "overreacted" or "took me too seriously." In our society, women are expected to be "nice"—to be passive and not "make a scene." The woman who assertively protects her rights might be seen as "strange" and disturbing or a "troublemaker." "Women are damned if they assert themselves and victimized if they don't" (Powell, 1991, p. 114).

Sexual harassment might have more to do with the abuse of power than with sexual desire (Goleman, 1991; Tedeschi & Felson, 1994). Relatively few cases of sexual harassment involve outright requests for sexual favors. Most involve the expression of power as a tactic to control or frighten someone, usually a woman. The harasser is usually in a dominant position and abuses that position by exploiting the victim's vulnerability. Sexual harassment might be used as a tactic of social control. It might be a means of keeping women "in their place." This is especially so in work settings that are traditional male preserves, such as the firehouse, the construction site, or the military academy. Sexual harassment expresses resentment and hostility toward women who venture beyond the boundaries of the traditional feminine role (Fitzgerald, 1993b).

Sexual Harassment. Where do we draw the line between a sexual invitation and sexual harassment? According to the U.S. government, sexual harassment in the workplace is the "deliberate or repeated unsolicited verbal comments, gestures, or physical contact of a sexual nature that is considered to be unwelcome by the recipient." Sexual harassment can range from unwelcome sexual jokes, overtures, suggestive comments, and sexual innuendos to outright sexual assault.

Sexual harassment is not confined to the workplace or the university. It can also occur between patients and doctors and between therapists and clients. Therapists might use their power and influence to pressure clients into sexual relations. The harassment might be disguised, expressed in terms of the "therapeutic benefits" of sexual activity.

Two of the most common settings in which sexual harassment occurs are the workplace and the university.

Sexual Harassment in the Workplace

Harassers in the workplace can be employers, supervisors, coworkers, or clients of a company. In some cases clients make unwelcome sexual advances to employees that are ignored or approved of by the boss. If a worker asks a coworker for a date and is refused, it is not sexual harassment. If the coworker persists with unwelcome advances and does not take no for an answer, however, the behavior crosses the line and becomes harassment.

Perhaps the most severe form of sexual harassment, short of an outright assault, involves an employer or supervisor who demands sexual favors as a condition of employment or advancement. In 1980, the Equal Employment Opportunity Commission drafted a set of guidelines that expanded the definition of sexual harassment in the workplace to include any behavior of a sexual nature that interferes with an individual's work performance or creates a hostile, intimidating, or offensive work environment.

In 1986, the U.S. Supreme Court recognized sexual harassment as a form of sex discrimination under Title VII of the Civil Rights Act of 1964. It held that employers could be held accountable if such behavior was deemed to create a hostile or abusive work environment or to interfere with an employee's work performance. A 1993 Supreme Court ruling held that a person need not suffer psychological damage to sue an employer on grounds of sexual harassment ("Court, 9–0," 1993). Moreover, employers can be held responsible not only for their own actions, but also for sexual harassment by their employees when they either knew *or should have known* that harassment was taking place and failed to eliminate it promptly (McKinney & Maroules, 1991). To protect themselves, many companies and universities have developed programs to educate workers about sexual harassment, established mechanisms for dealing with complaints, and imposed sanctions against harassers.

Under the law, individuals who are subjected to sexual harassment can obtain a court order to have the harassment stopped, have their jobs reinstated (when they have lost them by resisting sexual advances), receive back pay and lost benefits, and obtain monetary awards for the emotional strain imposed by the harassment. However, proving charges of sexual harassment is generally difficult because there are usually no corroborating witnesses or evidence. As a result, relatively few people who encounter sexual harassment in the workplace file formal complaints or seek legal remedies.

One survey found that most people who were sexually harassed handled the situation by ignoring the harasser (32%) or by saying something directly to the harasser (39%) (Loy & Stewart, 1984). Seventeen percent sought job transfers or quit their jobs. Relatively few, 2%, sought legal help. Only about 3% of women who have been sexually harassed file a formal complaint (Goleman, 1991). Like people who are subjected to other forms of sexual coercion, people who experience sexual harassment often do not report the offense for fear that they will not be believed or will be subjected to retaliation. Some fear that they will be branded as troublemakers or that they will lose their jobs (Goleman, 1991).

How common is sexual harassment in the workplace? Two thirds of the men interviewed by the *Harvard Business Review* said that reports of sexual harassment in the workplace were exaggerated (Castro, 1992). However, a survey by *Working Woman* magazine showed that more than 90% of the Fortune 500 companies had received complaints of sexual harassment from their employees. More than one third of the companies had been sued on charges of sexual harassment (Sandross, 1988). A survey of federal employees by the U.S. Merit System Protection Board found that 42% of females and 14% of males reported instances of sexual harassment (DeWitt, 1991). A 1991 *The New York Times/ CBS News* poll found that 38% of the women who were sampled reported that they had been the object of sexual advances or remarks from supervisors or other men in positions of power (Kolbert, 1991). Overall, it might be that as many as one in two women encounters some form of sexual harassment on the job or in college. Sexual harassment would thus be the most common form of sexual victimization (Fitzgerald, 1993b). Research overseas finds that about 70% of the women who work in Japan and 50% of those who work in Europe have encountered sexual harassment (Castro, 1992). Sexual harassment of women is more common in workplaces in which women have traditionally been underrepresented (Fitzgerald, 1993b), such as construction sites and shipyards.

Sexual Harassment on Campus

Estimates of the frequency of sexual harassment of undergraduate and graduate students vary widely across studies, from 7% to 27% of men and from 12% to 65% of women (McKinney & Maroules, 1991). Overall, 25% to 30% of students report at least one incident of sexual harassment in college. The federal law prohibiting sex discrimination in academic institutions permits students to sue their schools for monetary damages for sexual harassment (Greenhouse, 1992).

Sexual harassment on campus usually involves the less severe forms of harassment, such as sexist comments and sexual remarks, as well as come-ons, suggestive looks, propositions, and light touching (McKinney & Maroules, 1991). Relatively few acts involve the use of direct pressure for sexual intercourse. Harassers are typically (but not always) male. Most students who encounter sexual harassment do not report the incident. If they do, it is usually to a confidant, not to a person in authority.

Most forms of harassment involve unequal power relationships between the harasser and the person harassed. *Peer harassment* involves cases between people who are equal in power, as in the cases of repeated sexual taunts from fellow employees, students, or colleagues. In some cases, the harasser might even have less formal power than the person who is harassed. For example, women professors have been sexually harassed by students (Grauerholz, 1989). Here, of course, the traditional social dominance of the male overrides the academic position of the woman—at least in the mind of the offender.

The most common form of harassment by students, reported by nearly one third of the female professors polled in a recent survey, involved sexist remarks. Other common forms of harassment include obscene phone calls, undue attention, and sexual remarks. Outright sexual advances were reported by a few professors (Grauerholz, 1989).

Male faculty and staff members might also be subject to harassment. Six percent of 235 male faculty members polled at one university reported being sexually harassed by a student. However, nearly double that percentage (11%) reported that they had attempted to stroke, caress, or touch a student (Fitzgerald et al., 1988).

Sexual Harassment in the Schools

Playful sexual antics are common during adolescence. However, unwelcome sexual advances and lewd comments go beyond playfulness and have become a concern to many of America's teens. A nationwide survey of high school and junior high school students found that many boys and girls had encountered harassment in the form of others grabbing or groping them or subjecting them to sexually explicit put-downs when walking through school hallways (Henneberger, 1993).

The picture that emerges from a 1993 Louis Harris nationwide poll of teenagers in grades 8 through 11 indicates that sexual taunts and advances have become part of an unwelcome ritual for many students, especially girls, in trying to make their way through the hallways and stairwells of high schools (Barringer, 1993c; Henneberger, 1993). More than two out of three of the girls, and more than four out of ten of the boys, reported being touched, grabbed, or pinched at school. Two of three boys and about one in two girls reported harassing other students. Many of the harassers (41% of the boys and 31% of the girls) viewed their actions as "just part of school life" and "no big deal." Unwelcome sexual comments and advances had negative impact on both boys and girls, but especially on girls. One in three girls who experienced sexual harassment at school reported that it made them feel that they didn't want to go to school. Twenty-eight percent said that it made it more difficult to pay attention in class, and 20% said that it lowered their grades.

One problem is that teachers tend to tolerate sexually harassing behavior by male students against female classmates (Chira, 1992). Most of the harassment (about 80%) reported in the Harris survey was committed by other students, but some students reported being harassed by teachers, coaches, custodians, and other adults.

How to Resist Sexual Harassment

What would you do if you were sexually harassed by an employer or a professor? How would you handle it? Would you try to ignore it and hope that it would stop? What actions might you take? We offer some suggestions, adapted from Powell (1996), that might be helpful. Recognize, however, that responsibility for sexual harassment always lies with the perpetrator and the organization that permits sexual harassment to take place, not with the person who is subjected to the harassment.

1. *Convey a professional attitude.* Harassment might be stopped cold by responding to the harasser with a businesslike, professional attitude.
2. *Discourage harassing behavior, and encourage appropriate behavior.* Harassment might also be stopped cold by shaping the harasser's behavior. Your reactions to the harasser might encourage businesslike behavior and discourage flirtatious or suggestive behavior. If a harassing professor suggests that you come back after school to review your term paper so that the two of you will be undisturbed, set limits assertively. Tell the professor that you would feel more comfortable discussing the paper during regular office hours. Remain task-oriented. Stick to business. The harasser should quickly get the message that you wish to maintain a strictly professional relationship. If the harasser persists, do not blame yourself. You are responsible only for your own actions. When the harasser persists, a more direct response may be appropriate: "Professor Jones, I'd like to keep our relationship on a purely professional basis."

Preventing Sexual Harassment. Growing awareness of sexual harassment issues have led people to be much more careful about encounters with others, particularly when levels of rank or authority differ. Many organizations have taken steps to educate and train their staff in preventing potential situations from arising. Organizations that do not act promptly and aggressively to stem sexual harassment are liable for damages.

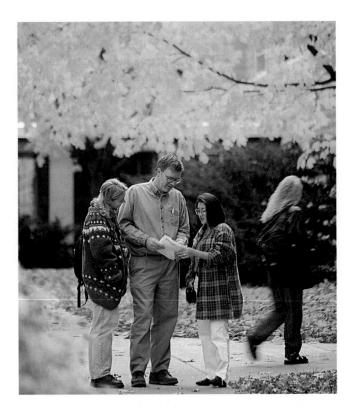

3. *Avoid being alone with the harasser.* If you are being harassed by your professor but need some advice about preparing your term paper, approach him or her after class when other students are milling about, not privately during office hours. Or bring a friend to wait outside the office while you consult the professor.

4. *Maintain a record.* Keep a record of all incidents of harassment as documentation in the event you decide to lodge an official complaint. The record should include the following: (1) where the incident took place; (2) the date and time; (3) what happened, including the exact words that were used, if you can recall them; (4) how you felt; and (5) the names of witnesses. Some people who have been subjected to sexual harassment have carried a hidden tape recorder during contacts with the harasser. Such recordings might not be admissible in a court of law, but they are persuasive in organizational grievance procedures. A hidden tape recorder might be illegal in your state, however. It is therefore advisable to check the law.

5. *Talk with the harasser.* It might be uncomfortable to address the issue directly with a harasser, but doing so puts the offender on notice that you are aware of the harassment and want it to stop. It might be helpful to frame your approach in terms of a description of the specific offending actions (e.g., "When we were alone in the office, you repeatedly attempted to touch me or brush up against me"), your feelings about the offending behavior ("It made me feel like my privacy was being violated. I'm very upset about this and haven't been sleeping well"), and what you would like the offender to do ("So I'd like you to agree never to attempt to touch me again"). Having a talk with the harasser might stop the harassment. If the harasser denies the accusations, it might be necessary to take further action.

6. *Write a letter to the harasser.* Set down on paper a record of the offending behavior, and put the harasser on notice that the harassment must stop. Your letter might (1) describe what happened ("Several times you have made sexist comments about my body"), (2) describe how you feel ("It made me feel like a sexual object when you

talked to me that way"), and (3) describe what you would like the harasser to do ("I want you to stop making sexist comments to me").

7. *Seek support.* Support from people you trust can help you through the often trying process of resisting sexual harassment. Talking with others allows you to express your feelings and receive emotional support, encouragement, and advice. In addition, it might strengthen your case if you have the opportunity to identify and talk with other people who have been harassed by the offender.

8. *File a complaint.* Companies and organizations are required by law to respond reasonably to complaints of sexual harassment. In large organizations, a designated official (sometimes an ombudsman, affirmative action officer, or sexual harassment advisor) is usually charged to handle such complaints. Set up an appointment with this official to discuss your experiences. Ask about the grievance procedures in the organization and your right to confidentiality. Have available a record of the dates of the incidents, what happened, how you felt about it, and so on.

    The two major government agencies that handle charges of sexual harassment are the Equal Employment Opportunity Commission (look in the government section of your phone book for the telephone number of the nearest office) and your state's Human Rights Commission (listed in your phone book under state or municipal government). These agencies can offer advice on how you can protect your legal rights and proceed with a formal complaint.

9. *Seek legal remedies.* Sexual harassment is illegal and actionable. If you are considering legal action, consult an attorney who is familiar with this area of law. You might be entitled to back pay (if you were fired for reasons arising from the sexual harassment), job reinstatement, and punitive damages.

In closing, we ask not what people who suffer rape, incest, and sexual harassment will do to redress the harm that has been done to them. We ask what all of us will do to reshape our society so that sex is no longer used as an instrument of power, coercion, and violence.

Reflections

- Agree or disagree with the following statement and support your answer: Because of all the publicity, people who are intolerant of normal sexual advances or who want to punish their supervisors are now crying sexual harassment.
- Have you or a friend been exposed to sexual harassment? How did you or the friend handle the situation? Are you happy with the way the situation was handled? Why or why not?
- Imagine that you are sexually harassed and want to report it, but a friend advises, "Why make such a fuss? Is it really worth it? After all, complaining could backfire." How would you respond?

summing up

RAPE

Although sexual motivation plays a role in many rapes, the use of sex to express aggression, anger, and power is more central to our understanding of rape. The definition of rape varies from state to state but usually refers to obtaining sexual intercourse with a nonconsenting person by the use of force or the threat of force.

Incidence of Rape
Surveys suggest that there are about 310,000 rapes and sexual assaults each year in the United States. Many rapes go unreported.

Types of Rapes
Types of rapes include stranger rape, acquaintance rape, marital rape, gang rape, male rape, and rape by females.

Women are more likely to be raped by men they know than by strangers. Most male rapes occur in prison settings. Husbands who rape their wives can now be prosecuted under the rape laws in many states.

Social Attitudes and Myths That Encourage Rape

Social attitudes such as gender-role stereotyping, seeing sex as adversarial, and acceptance of violence in interpersonal relationships all help to create a climate that encourages rape.

Sociocultural Factors in Rape

Many observers contend that our society breeds rapists by socializing males to be socially and sexually dominant.

Psychological Characteristics of Rapists

Incarcerated rapists vary in their psychological characteristics. Self-identified sexually aggressive men are more likely than other men to condone rape and violence against women, have traditional gender-role attitudes, be hostile toward women, engage in sexual activity to express social dominance, be sexually aroused by rape, lack a social conscience, and have peer groups such as fraternities that pressure them into sexual activity. Groth and Birnbaum identified three basic kinds of rape: anger rape, power rape, and sadistic rape.

Adjustment of Rape Survivors

Rape survivors often experience posttraumatic stress disorder (PTSD). Burgess and Holmstrom identified some common response patterns in rape survivors that they labeled the rape trauma syndrome.

Treatment of Rape Survivors

Treatment of rape survivors typically involves helping them through the crisis period after the attack and then helping to foster long-term adjustment.

Rape Prevention

Rape prevention involves education of society at large and the taking of a number of precautions that are available to women. Whether or not women take precautions to prevent rape, however, the rapist is always the one responsible for the assault.

VERBAL SEXUAL COERCION

Verbal sexual coercion involves the use of verbal pressure or seduction lines to manipulate a person into having sexual relations.

SEXUAL ABUSE OF CHILDREN

Like rape, sexual abuse of children is greatly underreported.

What Is Sexual Abuse of Children?

Any form of sexual contact between an adult and a child is abusive, even if force or physical threat is not used, since children are legally incapable of consenting to sexual activity with adults.

Patterns of Abuse

Sexual abuse of children, like rape and other forms of sexual coercion, cuts across all socioeconomic classes. In most cases, the molesters are close to the children they abuse—relatives, steprelatives, family friends, and neighbors. Genital fondling is the most common type of abuse.

Pedophilia

Pedophilia is a type of paraphilia in which adults are sexually attracted to children. Pedophiles are almost exclusively male.

Incest

Incest is marriage or sexual relations between people who are so closely related that sex is prohibited and punished by virtue of the kinship tie. Several theories have been expounded to explain the development of the incest taboo, including theories based on the dangers of inbreeding, the role played by the taboo in maintaining stability in the family, and cooperation theory. Father-daughter incest is most likely to be reported and prosecuted, but brother-sister incest is the most common type of incest. Incest frequently occurs within the context of general family disruption.

Effects of Sexual Abuse of Children

Children who are sexually abused often suffer social and emotional problems that impair their development and persist into adulthood, affecting their self-esteem and their formation of intimate relationships.

Prevention of Sexual Abuse of Children

In addition to learning to avoid strangers, children need to learn the difference between acceptable touching, such as an affectionate embrace or pat on the head, and unacceptable or "bad" touching. Children who might not be able to prevent abuse can nevertheless be encouraged to tell someone about the experience.

Treatment of Survivors of Sexual Abuse

Psychotherapy might help adult survivors of sexual abuse to improve their self-esteem and ability to develop intimate relationships. Special programs provide therapeutic services to abused children and adolescents.

TREATMENT OF RAPISTS AND CHILD MOLESTERS

The effectiveness of prison-based rehabilitation programs and antiandrogen drugs in curbing repeat offenses requires further empirical support.

SEXUAL HARASSMENT

Sexual Harassment in the Workplace

Sexual harassment in the workplace involves "deliberate or repeated unsolicited verbal comments, gestures, or physical contact of a sexual nature that [are] unwelcome [to] the recipient." Sexual harassment may be used as a tactic to keep women "in their place," especially in work settings that have traditionally been male preserves.

Sexual Harassment on Campus

About 25% to 30% of students report at least one incident of sexual harassment in college. Professors are also sometimes harassed by students.

Sexual Harassment in the Schools

Sexual harassment at school has become an unwelcome ritual that many junior and senior high school students are forced to endure.

How To Resist Sexual Harassment

There is no guaranteed way to put an end to sexual harassment, but some suggestions that have helped many individuals include conveying a professional attitude, avoiding being alone with the harasser, keeping a record of incidents, and seeking legal remedies.

Bohill Wong. *Beauty Contest*. Watercolor, ink on rag paper, 15 x 22 in. *Courtesy of Gateway Crafts Gallery, Brookline, Massachusetts*

chapter

19

Commercial Sex

outline

TRUTH OR FICTION?

**THE WORLD OF COMMERCIAL SEX:
A DISNEYLAND FOR ADULTS**

PROSTITUTION

Incidence of Prostitution in the United
States Today

A WORLD OF DIVERSITY:
From Russia, with . . . Sex?

Types of Female Prostitutes

Characteristics of Female Prostitutes

Customers of Female Prostitutes

A WORLD OF DIVERSITY:
Schoolgirls as Sex Toys

Male Prostitution

HIV, AIDS, and Prostitution

PORNOGRAPHY AND OBSCENITY

What Is Pornographic?

Pornography and the Law

Prevalence and Use of Erotica
and Pornography

IN THE NEW MILLENNIUM:
Surfing for Sex

Pornography and Sexual Coercion

SEX IN ADVERTISING

Advertising and Gender-Role
Stereotypes

SUMMING UP

Truth or Fiction?

_____ Prostitution is illegal throughout the United States.

_____ The massage and escort services advertised in the
Yellow Pages are fronts for prostitution.

_____ Most female prostitutes were sexually abused
as children.

_____ Typical customers of prostitutes have difficulty
forming sexual relationships with other women.

_____ Most prostitutes take precautions to avoid becoming
infected by or transmitting the AIDS virus.

_____ Only males are sexually aroused by pornography.

_____ If advertisements are too sexy, consumers might
forget what the product was.

a few years ago, England's floppy-haired actor Hugh Grant was caught with a prostitute in a BMW on Hollywood's Sunset Boulevard. Why? His girlfriend was supermodel Elizabeth Hurley, who at the time was promoting the perfume called "Pleasures." Grant exemplified good looks, charm, innocence, and success. Still, he sought the sexual services of a woman for hire.

Why, indeed. Why have millions of men (and some women) paid for sex throughout the ages? In the caverns of Wall Street, brokers and traders sell stocks and other financial instruments that drive the nation's commercial enterprises. On the floor of Chicago's Board of Trade, brokers trade commodities—soybeans, corn, wheat, and other goods. Prices go up, prices go down, responding to the law of supply and demand. On street corners a few short blocks from these financial institutions, another sort of commerce takes place. In New York City and Chicago, as in Hollywood and the nation's smaller towns and villages, prostitutes exchange sex for money or for goods such as drugs.

Sex is also used to sell more legitimate goods and services. "Sex sells" is a common catchphrase that has driven the imaginations of countless copywriters to create advertising campaigns projecting a "sexy" image for products ranging from automobiles to blue jeans, from beer to bread sticks.

THE WORLD OF COMMERCIAL SEX: A DISNEYLAND FOR ADULTS

Sex as commerce runs the gamut from adult movie theaters and bookshops to strip shows, sex toy shops, erotic hotels and motels, escort/outcall services, "massage parlors," "900" telephone services, cybersex (e.g., sex over the Internet), and the use of sex appeal in advertisements for legitimate products. The "world of commercial sex is a kind of X-rated amusement park—Disneyland for Adults" (Edgley, 1989, p. 372).

In this chapter, we discuss three commercial aspects of sexuality: prostitution, pornography, and the use of sex in advertising. Though the streetwalker, the purveyor of "adult" movies, and the Madison Avenue copywriter might otherwise have little else in common, they all have learned to use sex to make a profit.

PROSTITUTION

Hugh Grant ran afoul of the law because prostitution is illegal in California. **Prostitution** is illegal everywhere in the United States except for some rural counties in Nevada, where it is restricted to state-licensed brothels.

It is not true that prostitution is illegal throughout the United States. It is legal in some counties in the state of Nevada, although it is restricted to regulated, state-licensed brothels. ■

Prostitution The sale of sexual activity for money or goods of value, such as drugs. (From the Latin *prostituere,* meaning "to cause to stand in front of." The implication is that one is offering one's body for sale.)

Soliciting the services of a prostitute is also illegal in many states. Police rarely crack down on customers, or "johns," however. Hugh Grant came to their attention because he was engaging in a "lewd act" in a car parked on a public street (Beller, 1995). The few customers who are arrested are usually penalized with a small fine. On occasion, the names of convicted johns are published in local newspapers, which might deter men who fear publicity. On the other hand, some people believe that Hugh Grant's indiscretion *boosted* receipts for his film *Nine Months,* which opened a few days later. Although prostitutes and their clients can be male or female, most prostitutes are female, and virtually all customers are male.

Prostitution is often called "the world's oldest profession"—for good reason. It can be traced at least to ancient Mesopotamia, where temple prostitution flourished. The Greek historian Herodotus noted that all women in the city were expected to put in some time at the temple. They would offer their bodies to passing strangers, who would make a "religious" donation.

Prostitution flourished in medieval Europe and during the sexually repressive Victorian period in the nineteenth century. Then, as now, the major motive for prostitution was economic. Many poor women were drawn to prostitution as a means of survival. In Victorian England, prostitution was widely regarded as a necessary outlet for men to satisfy their sexual appetites. It was widely held that women lacked the potential to enjoy sex. Therefore, it was commonly believed that it was better for a man to visit a prostitute than to "soil" his wife with his carnal passions.

In the nineteenth-century United States, married and unmarried men frequented prostitutes regularly. Use of prostitution cut across all economic and social boundaries. Prostitution most often occurred within two contexts: sexual initiation for young males and regular brothel visitation.

Incidence of Prostitution in the United States Today

No one knows how many prostitutes there are in the United States. The little we know of prostitution derives from sex surveys.

Almost two-thirds of the White males in Kinsey's sample (Kinsey et al., 1948) reported visiting a prostitute at least once. About 15% to 20% visited them regularly. The use of prostitutes varied with educational level, however. By the age of 20, about 50% of Kinsey's non-college-educated single males, but only 20% of his college-educated males, had visited a prostitute. By the age of 25, the figures swelled to about two-thirds for non-college-educated males but only slightly above 25% for college men.

Kinsey's data foreshadowed a falling off of experience with prostitutes that seems linked to the decay of the sexual double standard. Kinsey found that 20% of his college-educated men had been sexually initiated by prostitutes. This figure was more than cut in half among generations who came of age in the 1960s and 1970s (Hunt, 1974). Less than 10% of both college-educated *and* non-college-educated males in the Playboy survey (Hunt, 1974) of the 1970s reported being sexually initiated by a prostitute.

A " Streetwalker." No one knows how many prostitutes there are in the United States, although it is estimated that there are hundreds of thousands. Some prostitutes walk the streets; others are called after customers' fingers do the walking through the Yellow Pages. Still others advertise online.

FROM RUSSIA, WITH . . . SEX?

Tamara, 19, has classic Slavic features, long blond hair, and deep green eyes. "I answered an ad to be a waitress," she told a reporter in a massage parlor near Tel Aviv's old Central Bus Station (cited in Specter, 1998). "I'm not sure I would go back now if I could. What would I do there, stand on a bread line or work in a factory for no wages?"

"I didn't plan to do this," she added, surrounded by the red walls and leopard prints that decorate the brothel. "They took my passport, so I don't have much choice. But they do give me money. And believe me, it's better than anything I could ever get at home."

From Russia, with Love is the title of a James Bond novel by Ian Fleming, of course. But a new chapter is being written in the annals of prostitution, and it could very easily be titled *From Russia, with Sex.* Russia and its Slavic neighbors Ukraine and Belarus have largely replaced Thailand and the Philippines as the center of the worldwide business in trafficking women. Economic problems in the former Soviet Union have opened a profitable market to the criminal gangs that have risen since the fall of Communism. The routes that traffic women run eastward to Thailand and Japan, where thousands of young Eastern European women now work against their will as prostitutes, and westward to the Adriatic Coast. Russian crime gangs based in Moscow arrange for security, connections with brothel owners in various countries, and false documents.

"It's no secret that the highest prices now go for the white women," says Marco Buffo (Specter, 1998), executive director of "On the Road," an organization that fights the trafficking of women in Italy. "They are the novelty item now. It used to be Nigerians and Asians at the top of the market. Now it's [Eastern Europeans]."

Irina's is another case in point. Irina is from Ukraine, 21, and self-confident. Like many other Ukranian women, she wound up in Israel. She had answered a newspaper ad, crossed the Mediterranean on a tour boat for Haifa, intending to make her fortune dancing in the nude on tabletops. For her, Israel was a new world, filled with hope, until she was driven to a brothel and her boss burned her passport while she watched.

"I own you," he said (Specter, 1998). "You are my property, and you will work until you earn your way out. Don't try to leave. You have no papers and you don't speak Hebrew. You will be arrested and deported. Then we will get you and bring you back."

European women are in demand, and Ukraine has an apparently endless supply. Why? Because the economy of Ukraine is in turmoil, and more than two-thirds of the unemployed are women. Irina and others like her begin their hellish journeys seeking a better life. The average salary in Ukraine at the turn of the millennium was $30 a month, and young women are lured by local ads for lucrative jobs in foreign countries. Israel is a typical destination. Prostitution is legal there, although brothels are not. Brothel owners are sometimes fined, but they usually remain in business.

The women who are seeking their fortune usually do not understand what is happening to them until it is too late. Once they reach their destination, their passports are confiscated, their cash is taken, and they become sexual slaves.

Why are young men less likely to visit prostitutes than they were in Kinsey's day? For one thing, young men in recent generations were more likely to become sexually initiated with their girlfriends. As Edgley (1989) put it, "An old and hallowed economic principle was at work; those who charge for a service cannot compete with those who give it away" (p. 392). Increased concern about sexually transmitted infections, especially AIDS, has also limited the use of prostitution. Nevertheless, prostitution continues to flourish.

Types of Female Prostitutes

Female prostitutes—commonly called *hookers, whores, working girls,* or *escorts*—are usually classified according to the settings in which they work. The major types of prostitutes today are streetwalkers; brothel or "house" prostitutes, many of whom work in massage parlors; and "escorts" or call girls (many prostitutes today have their customers "let their fingers do the walking through the Yellow Pages"). Traditional brothel prostitution is much less common today than before World War II.

STREETWALKERS Part of the mystery about Hugh Grant was why he would seek the services of any prostitute. Another part of it was why he would seek out a **streetwalker.**

Although most prostitutes are streetwalkers, streetwalkers occupy the bottom rung in the hierarchy of prostitutes. They earn the lowest incomes and are usually the least desirable. They also incur the greatest risk of abuse by customers and **pimps.** Streetwalkers tend to come from poverty and to have had unhappy childhoods (Edgley, 1989). Perhaps

Streetwalkers Prostitutes who solicit customers on the streets.

Pimps Men who serve as agents for prostitutes and live off their earnings. (From the Middle French *pimper,* meaning "to dress smartly.")

as many as 80% are survivors of rape, sexual abuse, or incest (Gordon & Snyder, 1989). Many were teenage runaways who turned to prostitution to survive.

Streetwalkers operate in the open. They are thus more likely than other prostitutes to draw attention to themselves and risk arrest. To avoid arrest, streetwalkers are often indirect about their services. They might ask passersby if they are interested in a "good time" or some "fun" rather than sex per se. In many cities, streetwalkers dress in revealing or provocative fashions.

There is a stereotype of the prostitute as a sexually unresponsive woman who feigns sexual arousal with johns while she keeps one eye glued to the clock. Most street prostitutes in a Philadelphia sample, however, reported that some forms of sex with customers were "very satisfying" (Savitz & Rosen, 1988). More than 60% of the prostitutes reported achieving orgasm with customers at least occasionally. Most prostitutes also reported that they had enjoyable sexual relationships in their private lives and were regularly orgasmic. Not surprisingly, they garnered more sexual enjoyment from their personal relationships than from their customers.

In most locales, penalties for prostitution involve small fines or short jail terms. Many police departments, besieged by crimes such as drug peddling and violent crimes, consider prostitution a "minor" or "nuisance" crime (Carvajal, 1995). Many prostitutes find the criminal justice system a revolving door. They pay the fine. They spend a night or two in jail. They return to the streets.

A bar prostitute is a variation of the streetwalker. She approaches men in a bar she frequents, rather than on the streets. Payoffs to bar owners or managers secure their cooperation, although the women are sometimes tolerated because they draw customers. Some streetwalkers work X-rated, or "adult," movie houses and may service their patrons in their seats with manual or oral sex. Payoffs may secure the cooperation of the management.

Many streetwalkers support a pimp. A pimp acts as lover-father-companion-master. He provides the streetwalker with protection, bail, and sometimes room and board in exchange for a high percentage of her earnings, often more than 90%. As Chris, a streetwalker explains, a prostitute cannot expect to survive long on the streets without a pimp:

> CHRIS: You can't really work the streets for yourself unless you got a man—not for a long length of time. . . . 'cause the other pimps are not going to like it because you don't have anybody to represent you. They'll rob you, they'll hit you in the head if you don't have nobody to take up for you. Yea, it happens. They give you a hassle. . . . [The men] will say, "Hey baby, what's your name? Where your man at? You got a man?"
>
> INTERVIEWER: So you can't hustle on your own?
>
> CHRIS: Not really, no. You can, you know, but not for long.
> (Romenesko & Miller, 1989, pp. 116–117)

Prostitutes are often physically abused by their pimps, who might use threats and beatings as means of control. In a study of young streetwalkers in Boston, Virginia Ann Price (1989) observed that as the relationship progressed, the beatings became more vicious. Kim Romenesko and Eleanor Miller (1989), who studied streetwalkers in Milwaukee, commented, "Clearly, 'men' are the rulers of the underworld" (p. 117).

Streetwalkers do not stay in the business (sometimes referred to as "the life") very long (Edgley, 1989). Some make the transition to a more traditional life or get married. Others die young from drug abuse, disease, suicide, or physical abuse from pimps or customers. Those who survive become less marketable with age.

Streetwalkers who work hotels and conventions generally hold a higher status than those that work the streets or bars. Clients are typically conventioneers or businessmen traveling away from home. The hotel prostitute must be skilled in conveying subtle messages to potential clients without drawing the attention of hotel management or security. They usually provide sexual services in the client's hotel room. Some hotel managers will tolerate known prostitutes (usually for a payoff under the table) as long as the women conduct themselves discreetly.

BROTHEL PROSTITUTION Many brothel prostitutes occupy a middle status in the hierarchy of prostitutes, between streetwalkers on one end and call girls on the other (Edgley, 1989). They work in a brothel or, more commonly today, in a massage parlor.

The life of the brothel (or "house") prostitute is usually neither as lucrative as that of the call girl nor as degrading as that of the streetwalker. Some prostitutes in massage parlors or working for escort services might not consider themselves to be "real prostitutes" because they do not walk the streets and because they work for businesses that present a legitimate front (Edgley, 1989). *Cathouse, bordello, cat wagon, parlor house, whorehouse, joy house, sport house, house of ill repute*—these are but a handful of the names given to the establishments in which prostitutes work. The heyday of the brothel is all but over in the United States. Formal brothels today are rare, except in some parts of Nevada, where they are legal but regulated.

Brothel prostitutes may attempt to maintain a traditional life apart from their prostitution activities. Ricker (1980) tells the story of one dual-world prostitute:

> Jan has been married 15 years and is the mother of three children—her earnings help keep them in a snooty Northern California boarding school. A relative newcomer [at the Chicken Ranch, a licensed Nevada brothel], she tried massage parlors, escort services, and other forms of "the business" [earlier]. Jan got into this line of work because she needed extra money. . . . Jan feels her home relationship has been improved by her job. "Before I went to work, my husband and I were always entertaining, trying to keep up that affluent suburban image. Now, when we're together we just enjoy each other and the children." She also feels her work has made her more interesting to her husband. "I've had to learn to relate to all kinds of different people. And I've learned how to play a variety of roles—I can be nurse, sophisticated companion, psychologist, temptress. . . ." No, Jan doesn't tell her children what she does (p. 282).

Jan, like other brothel prostitutes, splits her fees with the management. In addition to her split, she receives free room and board. They are on duty three weeks a month and on call 24 hours a day during that time. When a customer arrives, they step into the living room lineup. After one has been chosen, they wait again, resting, reading, or watching television.

Jan doesn't see herself as having a bad life. Yet some brothel prostitutes lead lives of complete degradation. Many poor Asian women have recently been lured to the United States by promises of the good life. Upon arrival, they have found themselves enslaved in brothels—working for tips and not allowed to leave. Such a brothel was recently closed by police at 208 Bowery in New York City. It housed more than 30 women who had been smuggled from Thailand. It came to the attention of police when one woman jumped from a window (Goldberg, 1995).

THE MASSAGE PARLOR Nature abhors a vacuum. "Massage parlors" have sprung up from coast to coast to fill the vacuum left by the departure of the brothels. Many massage parlors are legitimate establishments that provide massage, and only massage, to customers. Masseuses and masseurs are licensed in many states, and laws prohibit them from offering sexual services. Many localities require that the masseuse or masseur keep certain parts of her or his body clothed (some masseuses in suburban Detroit wear a scarf or a garter to comply) and not touch the client's genitals.

Many massage parlors serve as fronts for prostitution, however. They are often found in malls in middle-class suburbs, where there is ample parking (Carvajal, 1995). In these establishments, clients typically pay fees for a standard massage and then tip the workers for sexual extras.

Massage parlor prostitutes generally offer to perform manual stimulation of the penis ("a local"), oral sex, or, less frequently, coitus ("full service"). Some massage parlor prostitutes are better educated than streetwalkers and brothel workers and would not work in those other venues.

ESCORT SERVICES If Hugh Grant had hired an "escort," we probably would never have learned of it. Conventioneers and businessmen are more likely to turn to the listings for "massage" and "escort services" in the telephone directory or under the personal ads in local newspapers than to seek hotel prostitutes. Services that provide "outcall" send masseuses (or masseurs) or escorts to the hotel room.

Escort services are typically (but not always) fronts for prostitution. Escort services are found in every major American city and present themselves as legitimate businesses providing escorts for men. Indeed, one will find female companionship for corporate functions and for unattached men traveling away from home under "escort services." Many escort services provide only prostitution, however, and clients of other escort services sometimes negotiate sexual services after formal escort duties are completed—or in their stead.

Not all of the massage and escort services advertised in the Yellow Pages are fronts for prostitution. Legitimate masseuses and masseurs often advertise that they are licensed by their states. ■

Truth or Fiction?
REVISITED

Prostitutes who work for escort services often come from middle-class backgrounds and are well educated—so much the better to help prepare them to hold their own in social conversation. Escort services might establish arrangements with legitimate companies to provide "escorts" for visiting customers or potential clients. Escort services also provide female escorts to "entertain" at conventions. Because of her high-society background, Sidney Biddle Barrow, the so-called Mayflower Madam, attracted a great deal of publicity when it was discovered that she ran an exclusive escort service in New York City in the 1980s.

CALL GIRLS   **Call girls** occupy the highest status on the social ladder of female prostitution. Many of them overlap with escorts. Call girls tend to be the most attractive and well-educated prostitutes and tend to charge more for their services. Many come from middle-class backgrounds (Edgley, 1989). Unlike other types of prostitutes, call girls usually work on their own. Thus, they need not split their income with a pimp, escort service, or massage parlor. Consequently, they can afford to lead a luxurious lifestyle when business is good, living in expensive neighborhoods and wearing stylish clothes, and to be more selective about the customers they will accept. Yet they incur expenses for answering services and laundry services and for payoffs to landlords, doormen, and sometimes police to maintain their livelihood and avoid arrest.

Call girls often escort their clients to dinner and social functions and are expected to provide not only sex but also charming and gracious company and conversation (Edgley,

Heidi Fleiss—"The Hollywood Madam." Heidi Fleiss, the "madam" who arranged trysts for many of Hollywood's most rich and famous, is shown leaving federal court after being arraigned on charges of money laundering in an alleged effort to conceal income from her prostitution ring.

Call girls Prostitutes who arrange for their sexual contacts by telephone. *Call* refers both to telephone calls and to being "on call."

1989). Call girls often give clients the feeling that they are important and attractive. They might effectively simulate pleasure and orgasm and can create the illusion that time does not matter. It does, of course. To the call girl, as to other entrepreneurs, time is money.

Call girls might receive clients in their apartments (incalls) or make outcalls to clients' homes and hotels. Some call girls trade or sell "black books" that list clients and their sexual preferences. To protect themselves from police and abusive clients, call girls might insist on reviewing a client's business card or learning his home telephone number before personal contact is made. They might investigate whether the customer is in fact the person he purports to be.

Characteristics of Female Prostitutes

No single factor explains entry into female prostitution. Yet poverty and sexual and/or physical abuse figure prominently in the backgrounds of many prostitutes. They often come from conflict-ridden or single-parent homes in poor urban areas or rural farming communities.

For young women of impoverished backgrounds and marginal skills, the life of the prostitute might seem alluring. It is an alternative to the menial and dismal work that is otherwise available. On the basis of their studies of streetwalkers in Milwaukee, Romensko and Miller (1989) concluded that

> poverty, and the many concomitants of poverty manifest in American society, were the factors pushing these women into the world of illicit work. Conversely, the bright lights, money, and independence that the street seemingly offered—things that were largely absent from these women's lives prior to their entrance into street life—were enticements that drew women to street life. (p. 112)

Researchers also find a high level of psychological disturbance among prostitutes. Melissa Farley and her colleagues (1998) interviewed nearly 500 prostitutes from the United States, Europe, Africa, and Asia and found that nearly two-thirds of them could be diagnosed with **posttraumatic stress disorder** (PTSD). Only 5% of the general population have PTSD, and only 20% to 30% of combat veterans. The incidence of PTSD was the same for streetwalkers and brothel workers, although brothel prostitutes encountered less violence (Zuger, 1998). The prostitutes also developed high numbers of medical problems (other than sexually transmitted infections). Ninety percent said that they wanted to get out of "the life."

Cross-cultural evidence from a study of 41 prostitutes in Belgium showed similar patterns of psychopathology (de Schampheleire, 1990). Compared to other women (female flight attendants), streetwalkers in the Belgian study were more fearful, anxious, resentful, and depressed. They also had poorer relationships with their families and were in poorer health. In a study in the United States, teenage female prostitutes were more likely than normal female adolescents or delinquents who did not engage in prostitution to show signs of psychological disturbance and to have been placed in special-education classes in school (Gibson et al., 1988).

Poverty accounts for the entry of young women into prostitution in many countries. In some Third World nations, such as Thailand, many rural, impoverished parents in effect sell daughters to recruiters, who place them in brothels in cities (Erlanger, 1991; Goldberg, 1995). Many of the women send home whatever money they can and also work hard to try to pay off the procurers and break free of their financial bonds.

In the United States and Canada, many initiates into prostitution are teenage runaways. The family backgrounds of teenage runaways vary in socioeconomic status (some come from middle-class or affluent homes, whereas others are reared in poverty). However, family discord and dysfunction frequently set the stage for their entry into street life and prostitution (Price, 1989). Many teenage runaways perceive life on the street to be the only possible escape from family strife and conflict or from the physical, emotional, or sexual abuse they suffer at home. Despite its dangers, life on the streets appears more attractive than remaining in the troubled family environment. A study of teenage prostitutes in Boston found that a majority had come from broken homes and were reared by

Posttraumatic stress disorder A type of stress reaction brought on by a traumatic event and characterized by flashbacks of the experience in the form of disturbing dreams or intrusive recollections, a sense of emotional numbing or restricted range of feelings, and heightened body arousal. Abbreviated *PTSD*.

single parents or in reconstituted families consisting of half-siblings and stepsiblings (Price, 1989). Those who came from intact families reported high levels of family conflict.

Teenage runaways are at particularly high risk of unsafe sexual practices, such as unprotected sex with multiple partners. The average male teenage runaway in a New York City study reported having had 11 female sexual partners in his lifetime (Rotheram-Borus et al., 1992). Only 8% of the teenage boys reported using condoms consistently.

Teenage runaways with marginal skills and limited means of support might find few alternatives to prostitution. Adolescent prostitution results from the "necessities of street life—it is survival behavior more than it is sexual behavior" (Seng, 1989, p. 674). It is not long before the teenage runaway is approached by a pimp or a john. A study of 149 teenage runaways in Toronto found that 67% of the boys and 82% of the girls who had been away from home for more than a year had been offered money to engage in sexual activity with an adult (Hartman et al., 1987).

Studies of teenage prostitutes in the United States show that perhaps as many as one-half to two-thirds of female prostitutes had been sexually abused as children (Seng, 1989). One sample of 45 former prostitutes in Canada showed that 73% had been sexually abused in childhood (Bagley & Young, 1987).

It appears that the majority of female prostitutes were in fact sexually abused as children. ■

Truth or Fiction?
REVISITED

Some teenagers who have endured sexual abuse or incest learn how to detach themselves emotionally from sex to survive unwanted sexual experiences. The transition to prostitution might represent an extension of this unfortunate learning experience. Though teenage prostitutes might turn to prostitution primarily for money, Price (1989) recognized that survivors of sexual abuse or incest might also be attracted to prostitution because they have learned that it is through their sexuality that they can obtain attention or love from adults:

> For a lonely adolescent, attention from tricks or a sugar daddy is not all that different from the attention he or she received at home. In fact, it may be preferable, as there may not be any physical abuse involved. (p. 84)

Not all sexually abused children become prostitutes, of course. Only 12% of one sample of predominantly female 16- to 18-year-olds who had been sexually abused became involved in prostitution (Seng, 1989). Abused children who run away from home are much more likely to become involved in prostitution than those who do not (Seng, 1989). Runaways are also more likely to become drug and alcohol abusers.

Nor do all teenage runaways become prostitutes. Though information on prevalence of prostitution among runaways is scarce, a Boston study of homeless street youths in the mid-1980s found that fewer than 20% had engaged in prostitution (Price, 1989). Though most had been approached for prostitution within a few days of living on the streets, the overwhelming majority refused.

In sum, evidence suggests that most female prostitutes are survivors of sexual abuse or incest. Running away from home appears to funnel many survivors of childhood sexual abuse into prostitution, yet not all survivors of sexual abuse, nor all teenage runaways, become prostitutes.

Customers of Female Prostitutes

Hugh Grant was a *john* or a *trick*. That is how many prostitutes refer to their customers. Terms such as *patron, meatball, sucker*, and *beefbuyer* are also heard. Men who use female prostitutes come from all walks of life and represent all socioeconomic and racial groups. Many, perhaps most, are married men of middle-class background. A study of the address listings of customers (seized by the local police) of an escort service in a southern city showed that most of the clients lived in relatively affluent neighborhoods consisting of a high percentage of well-educated, largely White, married residents (Adams, 1987).

Most patrons are *occasional johns*. Examples include traveling salesmen or military personnel who are stopping over in town and away from their regular sex partners. One study of 30 occasional johns showed that all had regular sex partners. They used prostitutes because they desired novelty or sexual variety, not because they lacked other sexual outlets (Holzman & Pines, 1982).

Habitual johns use prostitutes as their major or exclusive sexual outlet. Some habitual johns have never established an intimate sexual relationship. Some wealthy men who wish to avoid intimate relationships habitually patronize call girls.

Compulsive johns feel driven to prostitutes to meet some psychological or sexual need. They might repeatedly resolve to stop using prostitutes but feel unable to control their compulsions. Some compulsive johns engage in acts of fetishism or transvestism with prostitutes but would not inform their wives or girlfriends of their variant interests. Some men who are compulsive users of prostitutes suffer from a **whore-madonna complex.** They see women as either sinners or saints. They can permit themselves to enjoy sex only with prostitutes or would ask only prostitutes to engage in acts such as fellatio. They see marital coitus as a duty or obligation.

MOTIVES FOR USING PROSTITUTES　Though the reasons for using prostitutes vary, researchers have identified six of the most common motives (Edgley, 1989; Gagnon, 1977):

1. *Sex without negotiation.* Prostitution might be attractive to men who do not want to spend the time, effort, and money involved in dating and getting to know someone simply to obtain sex. As Edgley (1989) comments, the customer "gives [the prostitute] money for sex, she gives sex in return. The entire matter is simple, direct, and sure" (p. 393). Hugh Grant might have wanted to have sex, and his girlfriend was a continent and an ocean away. The streetwalker was willing to supply sex in the absence of a relationship.
2. *Sex without commitment.* Prostitutes require no commitment from the man other than payment for services rendered. The prostitute will not call him at home or expect to be called in return.
3. *Sex for eroticism and variety.* Many prostitutes offer something extra in the way of novel or kinky sex—for example, oral sex, use of costumes (e.g., leather attire), and S&M rituals (such as bondage and discipline or spanking). Men might desire such activity but not obtain it with their regular partners. They might even be afraid to mention the idea. Prostitutes might also be attractive to men who seek variety or novelty in sex partners.
4. *Prostitution as sociability.* In the nineteenth and early twentieth centuries, the brothel served not only as a place to obtain sex, but also as a kind of stopping off place between home and work—referred to by some writers as a "third place" (Oldenberg & Brissett, 1980). The local tavern or pool hall are nonsexual "third places." At times, sex was secondary to the companionship and amiable conversation that men would find in brothels, especially in the days of the "bawdy houses" of the pioneer West.
5. *Sex away from home.* The greatest contemporary use of prostitution occurs among men who are away from home, such as businessmen at conventions and sports fans at out-of-town sporting events. In these typical all-male preserves, there is often intense peer pressure to engage in sexual adventures.

Truth or Fiction?
REVISITED

It is not true that typical customers of prostitutes have difficulty forming sexual relationships with other women. Many men often turn to prostitutes for sexual variety or because they seek sexual activity when they are away from home. ■

6. *Problematical sex.* People who have physical disabilities or disfiguring conditions sometimes seek the services of prostitutes because of difficulty in attracting other partners or because of fears of rejection. (One prostitute at a Nevada brothel said that she was a favorite of the management because she accepted johns with cerebral palsy.) Though some prostitutes are selective about the clients they will accept, others will accept any client who is willing to pay. Men with sexual dysfunctions might also turn to prostitutes to help them overcome their problems. Some lonely men who lack sex partners might seek prostitutes as substitutes.

Whore-madonna complex A rigid stereotyping of women as either sinners or saints.

SCHOOLGIRLS AS SEX TOYS

A disturbing new national pastime has taken root in Japan: a male obsession with schoolgirls dressed in uniforms.

In Tokyo there are now several hundred "image clubs," where Japanese men pay $150 an hour to act out their fantasies with make-believe schoolgirls in make-believe classrooms, locker rooms or commuter trains. A customer may, for example, act the part of a teacher who walks into a classroom and tears the clothes off a schoolgirl. Or he may choose to fondle a schoolgirl on a crowded commuter train.

The clubs are but one part of a growing national obsession—and a growing national market—that the Japanese call "Loli-con," after Lolita. Hiroyuki Fukuda edits one Japanese magazine called Anatomical Illustrations of Junior High School Girls and another called V-Club, featuring pictures of naked elementary school girls. And a number of schoolgirls earn extra money as prostitutes.

Why? First because it's legal for men in Tokyo to have sex with children who are older than 12. And second, says Masao Miyamoto, a male psychiatrist, because many Japanese men feel threatened by the growing sophistication of older women. So they turn to schoolgirls.

Source: Schoolgirls as sex toys. (1997, April 6). *The New York Times*, p. E2.

Male Prostitution

Male prostitution includes both male-male and male-female activities. Males prostitutes who service female clients—*gigolos*—are rare. Gigolos' clients are typically older, wealthy, unattached women. Gigolos might serve as escorts or as surrogate sons for the women and might or might not offer sexual services. Many gigolos are struggling actors or models.

The overwhelming majority of male prostitutes service gay men. Men who engage in male prostitution are called **hustlers.** Their patrons are typically called **scores.** Hustlers average 17 to 18 years of age and become initiated into prostitution at an average age of 14 or so (Coleman, 1989). They typically have less than eleventh-grade educations and few, if any, marketable skills. The majority come from working-class and lower-class backgrounds. Many male prostitutes, like many female prostitutes, come from families troubled by conflict, alcoholism, or abuse (Coleman, 1989). More than 4 out of 5 (83%) of a sample of 47 male prostitutes in Seattle, Washington, had been survivors of sexual abuse (Boyer, 1989). Two of three are survivors of rape or attempted rape. In another study, the factor that most clearly distinguished juvenile male prostitutes and male delinquent street youths was the absence of sexual victimization in the histories of the delinquents (Janus et al., 1984).

Hustlers can be gay, bisexual, or heterosexual in orientation. At least half of the male prostitutes surveyed are gay. Seventy percent of the male prostitutes in the Seattle study identified themselves as gay or bisexual. Only 30% identified themselves as heterosexual (Boyer, 1989).

The major motive for male prostitution, like that for female prostitution, is money. In one study, 69% of male prostitutes cited money as their principal motive (Fisher et al., 1982). Running away from home typically serves as an entry point for male as well as female prostitution. In one study, three of four male prostitutes had run away by an average age of 15 (Weisberg, 1985). Some had run away because of family problems, others because of a desire for adventure or independence (Coleman, 1989). Some gay male prostitutes are literally thrown out because their families cannot accept their sexual orientation (Coleman, 1989; Kruks, 1991). Researcher Debra Boyer (1989) comments:

The responses of families to the [sexual orientation] of their sons ranged from strong condemnation to total rejection, for example "it's disgusting"; "we refuse to accept it"; "we don't want to talk about it"; "that's it, you are leaving." These young men suffered outright rejection from their families and were often literally thrown away as sullied human beings. (pp. 168–169)

Hustlers Men who engage in prostitution with male customers.

Scores Customers of hustlers.

603

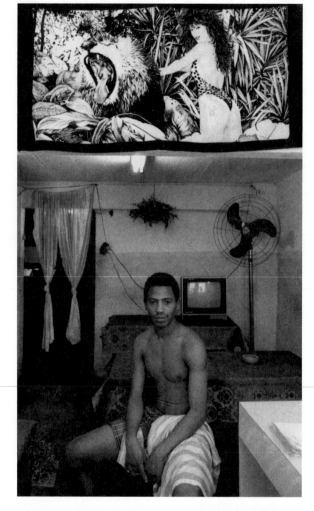

Male Prostitutes. They average between 17 and 18 years of age. Many come from troubled families of working-class and lower-class backgrounds. Their principal motive for prostitution is money.

For many of these gay "throwaways," prostitution might represent a way of obtaining adult acceptance, albeit within the context of exchanging sex for money. Another distinguishing characteristic of the gay prostitutes in the Seattle study was the lack of a network of gay friends. These young gay males became initiated into the gay subculture in the life of the street. Their only contacts with other gay men were through turning tricks or hanging out with other young hustlers. The ability to attract clients and the money they received inflated their self-esteem. As Boyer (1989) put its, they were "no longer outcasts, but stars" (p. 177). Many hoped to find companionship or a meaningful relationship through prostitution. Some would fall in love with tricks, only to be disappointed when the encounter or relationship fizzled.

Heterosexual hustlers might try to psychologically detach themselves from male clients by refusing to kiss or hug them or to perform fellatio. Gagnon (1977) writes, "As long as the [client's] head is below the [hustler's] belly button and contact is on the penis, it is the other person who is [gay]" (p. 264). To become aroused, heterosexual hustlers might fantasize about women while the "score" is fellating them. Many heterosexual male prostitutes maintain heterosexual relationships in their private lives while "turning tricks" with men to earn money.

Most hustlers are part-timers who continue some form of educational or vocational activity as they support themselves through prostitution. Drug dealing and drug use are also common among hustlers (Coleman, 1989). In one study, about three in four male prostitutes used drugs while they were hustling (Fisher et al., 1982).

Unlike female prostitutes, hustlers typically are not attached to a pimp (Luckenbill, 1985). They generally make contacts with clients in gay bars and social clubs or by working the streets in areas that are frequented by gay men. They typically learn to hustle through their interactions with other hustlers and by watching other hustlers ply their trade (Luckenbill, 1985).

Coleman (1989) identifies several types of male prostitutes:

- *Kept boys* have relationships with older, economically secure men who keep them in an affluent lifestyle. The older male, or "sugar daddy," often assumes a parental role.
- *Call boys*, like call girls, might work on their own or through an agency or escort service.
- *Punks* are prison inmates who are used sexually by other inmates and rewarded with protection or goods such as cigarettes or drugs.
- *Drag prostitutes* are transvestites or presurgical male-to-female transsexuals who impersonate female prostitutes and have sex with men who are frequently unaware of their gender. Some drag prostitutes limits themselves to fellatio on their customers to conceal their genders. Others take the passive role in anal sex (Boles & Elifson, 1994).
- *Brothel prostitutes* are rarer than their female counterparts. Fewer houses of male prostitution exist.
- *Bar hustlers* and *street hustlers*, like their female counterparts, occupy the lowest status and ply their trade in gay bars or on streets frequented by gay passersby. Street hustlers are the most common and typically the youngest subtype. They are

also the most visible and consequently the ones most likely to draw the attention of the police.

Male prostitutes typically have shorter careers than their female counterparts (Price, 1989). By and large, male prostitution is an adolescent enterprise. The younger the hustler, the higher the fee he can command and the more tricks he can turn. By the time he reaches his mid-20s, he might be forced to engage in sexual activities that he might have rejected when younger or to seek clients in sleazier places.

HIV, AIDS, and Prostitution

Concerns about the spread of sexually transmitted infections by prostitution is nothing new. In the 1960s, two of three prostitutes surveyed by Gebhard (1969) had contracted gonorrhea or syphilis. Though prostitutes are still exposed to a heightened risk of contracting or spreading these and other sexually transmitted infections, such as chlamydia, today the risk of AIDS poses a more deadly threat. The risk of HIV transmission has been linked to both male and female prostitution (Campbell, 1991; Van den Hoek et al., 1990; Yates et al., 1991).

Sex with prostitutes is the most important factor in the male-female transmission of HIV in Africa, where the infection is spread predominantly via male-female sexual intercourse (see Chapter 16). A Florida study showed that regular contact with female street prostitutes was a risk factor in the transmission of HIV in U.S. men (Castro et al., 1988). Prostitutes incur a greater risk of HIV transmission because they have sexual relations with many partners, often without protection (Quadagno et al., 1991). Moreover, many prostitutes and their clients and other sex partners inject drugs and share contaminated needles (Bloor et al., 1990; Freund et al., 1989). HIV may be spread by unprotected sex from prostitutes to customers, then to the customers' wives or lovers. Nationwide, about 12% of the prostitutes who were tested in the late 1980s were seropositive for HIV (Lambert, 1988).

Men who frequent male prostitutes may represent a vector, or conduit, for male-female sexual transmission of HIV. The rate of HIV infection is high among male prostitutes, and many if not most of their male customers describe themselves as either bisexual or heterosexual (Morse et al., 1992). One study found that the rate of HIV infection was 50% for gay male prostitutes, 36.5% for bisexual male prostitutes, and 18.5% for heterosexual male prostitutes (Boles & Elifson, 1994). Customers of such men might thus be exposing their wives and girlfriends to HIV.

Despite the obvious dangers of HIV transmission, many U.S. prostitutes have not altered either their sexual behavior or their patterns of drug use to any large extent. Only 30% of a sample of 20 street prostitutes in Camden, New Jersey, reported always using condoms (Freund et al., 1989). A study of 72 heroin-addicted female street prostitutes in southern California showed a high level of knowledge and fear about AIDS but a failure to change patterns of sexual behavior or drug use (Bellis, 1990). The prostitutes who were sampled did nothing to protect themselves or their clients from HIV. Their need for money led them to deny the risks to which they were exposing themselves. Surveys of adolescent prostitutes show a similar pattern of denial, as Price (1989) observes:

> Some [adolescent prostitutes] simply believe it will not happen to them, while others say they are willing to take the risk. Still others do not care whether they live or die, and expect their lives to end shortly anyway. (p. 86)

Some changes in prostitution practices have taken place. Brothel owners in Nevada, for example, now require customers to wear condoms. But prostitutes who are bent on denial or are so filled with despair that they care nothing about their own or clients' lives might be most resistant to change.

Truth or Fiction?

It is not true that most prostitutes take precautions to avoid becoming infected by or transmitting the AIDS virus. Most street prostitutes in the United States and many brothel workers in foreign nations do not take precautions against becoming infected by or transmitting HIV. ■

Reflections

■ Agree or disagree with the following statement and support your answer: Prostitution should be legalized throughout the United States.

■ What are the connections between prostitution, child sexual abuse, and drug abuse?

■ Why do you think an attractive, popular actor such as Hugh Grant would turn to a prostitute?

PORNOGRAPHY AND OBSCENITY

The production and distribution of sexually explicit materials are a boom industry. In the United States, 20 million "adult" magazines are sold each month. X-rated or adult movies (also called *porn* movies) have moved from sleazy adult theaters to the living rooms of middle America in the form of videocassette rentals and sales. According to a Gallup poll, X-rated films account for about one in five video sales (Linsley, 1989). Nobody knows how many people bring X-rated photos, videos, or even live sex from foreign nations onto their computer monitors or Web TV sets via the Internet every day.

Pornography is indeed popular, but it is also highly controversial. Many people are opposed to pornography on moral grounds. Many feminists oppose pornography on the grounds that it portrays women in degrading and dehumanizing roles, as sex objects who are subservient to men's wishes, as sexually insatiable nymphomaniacs, or as sexual masochists who enjoy being raped and violated. Moreover, some feminists hold that depictions of women in sexually subordinate roles may encourage men to treat them as sex objects and increase the potential for rape (Scott & Schwalm, 1988).

Yet feminists are split on the issue of legal suppression of pornography. For example, the feminist writer Kate Millett argues that "We're better off hanging tight to the First Amendment so that we have freedom of speech" (Press et al., 1985).

What is pornography? How is it defined? Who uses it? Why? How does it affect users?

What Is Pornographic?

Webster's Deluxe Unabridged Dictionary defines **pornography** as "writing, pictures, etc., intended to arouse sexual desire." The inclusion of the word *intended* places the determination of what is pornographic in the mind of the person who composes the work. Applying this definition makes it all but impossible to determine what is pornographic. If a filmmaker admits that he or she wanted to arouse the audience sexually, we might judge the work to be pornographic even if no naked bodies or explicit sex scenes are shown. On the other hand, explicit representations of people engaged in sexual activity would not be pornographic if the work were intended as an artistic expression, rather than created for its **prurient** value. Many works that were once prohibited in this country because of explicit sexual content, such as the novels *Tropic of Cancer* by Henry Miller, *Lady Chatterley's Lover* by D. H. Lawrence, and *Ulysses* by James Joyce, are now generally considered literary works rather than excursions into pornography. Even Mark Twain's *Huckleberry Finn*, John Steinbeck's *The Grapes of Wrath*, and Ernest Hemingway's *For Whom the Bell Tolls* have been banned in some places because local citizens found them to be offensive, obscene, or morally objectionable (Linsley, 1989).

Pornography Written, visual, or audiotaped material that is sexually explicit and produced for purposes of eliciting or enhancing sexual arousal. (From Greek roots meaning "to write about prostitutes.")

Prurient Tending to excite lust; lewd. (From the Latin *prurire*, meaning "to itch" in the sense of "to long for.")

figure 19.1

Art or Obscenity? The left-hand photo shows Madonna in concert. Madonna and other performers engage in pelvic thrusting on stage. Is their behavior obscene according to contemporary community standards? Should companies employ such performers to advertise their wares? Should the government ban them, or would you rather cast your vote by buying—or not buying—tickets, recordings, and the products that they promote? The right-hand photo, *Patrice*, is from the *X Portfolio* of Robert Mapplethorpe. Photographs from Mapplethorpe's *X Portfolio* stimulated authorities in Cincinnati, Ohio, to indict a gallery director for "pandering to obscenity." The gallery director was subsequently acquitted, however.

There is thus a subjective element in the definition of pornography. An erotic statue that sexually arouses viewers might not be considered pornographic if the sculptor's intent was artistic. A grainy photograph of a naked body that was intended to excite sexually might be pornographic. One alternative definition finds material pornographic when it is judged to be offensive by others. This definition, too, relies on the subjective judgment of the person who is exposed to the material. In other words, one person's pornography is another person's work of art. Are the photos shown in Figure 19.1 pornographic? Why or why not?

Legislative bodies usually write laws about **obscenity** rather than pornography. Even the Supreme Court, however, has had a difficult time defining obscenity and determining where, if anywhere, laws against obscenity do not run afoul of the Bill of Rights' guarantee of free speech. In the case of *Miller* v. *California* (1973), Supreme Court Justice William Brennan wrote that obscenity is "incapable of definition with sufficient clarity to withstand attack on vagueness grounds." Such vagueness did not deter Supreme Court Justice Potter Stewart from quipping that although he could not define obscenity in objective terms, he knew it when he saw it. Recall that *Huckleberry Finn* was once considered obscene, however.

Let us follow Mosher (1988) and define pornography as written, visual, or audiotaped material that is sexually explicit or graphic and produced for purposes of eliciting or enhancing sexual arousal. **Erotica** may be as sexually explicit as pornography is, but many writers use the term to refer to sexual materials that are artistically produced or motivated. Although some people find any erotic material to be offensive or obscene, it makes little sense to lump together artistic expressions of erotic themes and hard-core pornography.

Pornography is often classified as either *hard-core* (X-rated) or *soft-core* (R-rated). Hard-core pornography includes graphic and sexually explicit depictions of sex organs and sexual acts. Soft-core porn, as represented by R-rated films and *Playboy* photo spreads,

Obscenity That which offends people's feelings or goes beyond prevailing standards of decency or modesty. (From the Latin *caenum*, meaning "filth.")

Erotica Books, pictures, and so on that have to do with sexual love (from the Greek *eros*, meaning "love"). Many contemporary writers use the term *erotica* to refer to sexual material that is artistically produced or motivated by artistic intent.

features more stylized nude photos and suggested (or simulated) rather than explicit sexual acts. *Penthouse* has made the transition from soft-core to hard-core in many of its photo spreads.

Pornography and the Law

Laws against obscenity provide the legal framework for outlawing the dissemination of pornography. Since the definition of obscenity relies on offending people or running afoul of community standards, that which is deemed obscene can vary from person to person and from culture to culture. Women going topless on a public beach might be deemed obscene in some locales but not on beaches along the French Riviera or in Rio de Janeiro, where this style of (un)dress is customary. The word *obscene* extends beyond sexual matters. One could judge TV violence or beer commercials to be obscene because they are personally offensive or are offensive to women, even if such depictions do not meet legal standards of obscenity.

In the United States, legal prohibition of pornography as a form of obscenity dates to the nineteenth century. In 1873, Congress passed an antiobscenity bill, the Comstock Act. One effect of the bill was to outlaw the dissemination of information about birth control. The Comstock Act and similar laws made it a felony to mail obscene books, pamphlets, photographs, drawings, or letters. But what is obscene?

A landmark case in 1957 helped to establish the legal basis of obscenity in the United States. In *Roth* v. *United States*, the U.S. Supreme Court ruled that portrayal of sexual activity was protected under the First Amendment to the Constitution unless its dominant theme dealt with "sex in a manner appealing to prurient interest" (*Roth* v. *United States*, 1957, p. 487). In a 1973 case, *Miller* v. *California*, the U.S. Supreme Court held that obscenity is based upon a determination of

> (a) Whether the average person, applying contemporary community standards, would find that the work, taken as a whole, appeals to the prurient interest. . . ; (b) whether the work depicts or describes, in a patently offensive way, sexual conduct specifically defined by the applicable state law; and (c) whether the work, taken as a whole, lacks serious literary, artistic, political, or scientific value. (*Miller* v. *California*, 1973, p. 24).

Courts have since had to grapple with the *Miller* standard in judging whether material is obscene. *Miller* recognizes that judgments of obscenity may vary with "community standards." As a result, the same material might be considered obscene in one community but not in another. The *Miller* standard raises some obvious and unresolved questions. For example, who is the "average person" who can speak for a community? Many of us live in ethnically, racially, and religiously diverse communities. Can one viewpoint in *any* community truly represent the community? Even in relatively homogeneous communities, a diversity of opinion might exist on particular issues. Moreover, what is a *community*? Is it one's neighborhood, police precinct, municipality, county, or a larger political unit? What does "patently" offensive mean? Who judges "serious" literary, artistic, political, or scientific value? An attempt to clarify this last question was made in a 1987 case, *Pope* v. *Illinois*, in which the Supreme Court held that

> the proper inquiry is not whether an ordinary member of any given community would find serious literary, artistic, political, or scientific value in allegedly obscene material, but whether a reasonable person would find such value in the material, taken as a whole. (p. 445)

In this ruling, the court held that sexually explicit material could not be declared obscene if many or most people in a particular community held it to lack serious literary, artistic, political, or scientific value, unless a "reasonable person" were to reach the same judgment. Whether the concept of a "reasonable person" will provide the courts with a clearer standard than that of an "average" or "ordinary" person for adjudicating obscenity cases remains to be seen.

Child pornography and violent, degrading, or dehumanizing pornography complicate matters further. People who do not find depictions, however explicit, of consensual sexual activity between adults to be obscene might regard child pornography or violent pornography to be obscene. Child pornography is clearly psychologically harmful to the juvenile actors or models (Silbert, 1989). Many people also object to sexually explicit material that portrays women as sex objects or in a position subordinate to men—gratifying men's sexual appetites.

Some footnotes: The U.S. Supreme Court ruled (in *Stanley v. Georgia*, 1969) that the possession of obscene material in one's home is not a criminal act (Sears, 1989). However, states may make it illegal to possess child pornography (Sears, 1989). Some communities (such as Indianapolis) have sought to ban pornography on the grounds that it discriminates against women. Pornography, that is, damages women's opportunities for equal rights by perpetuating stereotypes of women as subservient to men. The Indianapolis ordinance was overturned by a federal court on the grounds that it represented an unconstitutional infringement of free speech (Lewin, 1992). However, in a 1992 ruling, the Supreme Court of Canada redefined obscenity as involving sexually explicit material containing violence toward women or material that degrades or dehumanizes women (Lewin, 1992).

Prevalence and Use of Erotica and Pornography

Most of us have been exposed to sexually explicit materials, whether in the form of a novel, an article in *Playboy* or *Playgirl* (purchased, no doubt, for its literary value), or an X-rated film. The NHSLS study found that about one man in four (23%) and one woman in ten (11%) had bought an X-rated movie or video within the past year (Michael et al., 1994). Sixteen percent of the men and 4% of the women had bought sexually explicit magazines or books.

People in the United States are typically introduced to pornography by their high school years, often by peers (Bryant & Brown, 1989). Females are more likely to have been exposed to pornography by their boyfriends than the reverse (Bryant & Brown, 1989).

Pornography is typically used to elicit or enhance sexual arousal, often as a masturbation aid (Michael et al., 1994). Pornographic materials may also be used by couples to enhance sexual arousal during lovemaking. Couples might find that running a soft- or hard-core video on the VCR or reading an erotic story aloud enlivens their sexual appetite or suggests novel sexual techniques.

Researchers have found that both men and women are physiologically sexually aroused by pornographic pictures, movies, or audiotaped passages (Goleman, 1995). That is, both men and women respond to pornographic stimuli with vasocongestion of the genitals and myotonia (muscle tension). However, there is a significant difference between physiological response and subjective feelings of arousal in women. Despite what is happening within their bodies, women tend to rate romantic scenes as more sexually arousing than sexually explicit scenes (Laan & Heiman, 1994).

Women are less accepting of sex without emotional involvement (Townsend, 1995). "Women like sex to come from an emotional connection," says marital and sex therapist Lonnie Barbach (1995). "For women there's a predisposition to allowing themselves to become turned on that romance allows. This wouldn't necessarily be measured by genital arousal."

Repeated exposure to the same pornographic materials progressively lessens the sexual response to them. People might become aroused by the familiar materials again if some time is allowed to go by. Novel materials are also likely to reactivate a sexual response (Meuwissen & Over, 1990; Zillmann, 1989).

It is not true that only males are sexually aroused by pornography. Most men *and* women are sexually aroused by erotica, physiologically speaking. As we see in the following section, however, their interest in, and subjective responses to, pornography can differ quite a bit. ∎

Surfing for Sex

It's everywhere. Singles do it, marrieds do it, even kids do it. State laws, electrical blackouts, even parental controls can barely control it. What is it? Surfing for sex, of course. Sex is now available on the Internet. What was once found outside the arenas in ancient Rome ("fornicating"), in the brothels of Victorian England, in the bars that followed men out West, and in some adult bookstores and theaters now travels the world at the speed of light and enters homes (and offices!) through phone and cable lines. And millions of people around the world are clicking in to it.

Some are businessmen looking for companionship on their next trip. So they might click into night life in San Francisco to find massage parlors, lap dancing, or particular "escorts" (Figure 19.2). Escorts' photos and some of their sales pitch have been uploaded, and it takes little skill to save the data on one's hard drive. In fact, many men never leave home without it; check out the hard drive (no pun intended) in the laptop (no pun intended) of the businessman in the next seat in the airplane.

Some are adolescents looking for XXX-rated pictures. If their parents have placed parental controls on their Internet browsers, perhaps their friends' parents have not. They simply type key phrases such as "sex pictures" or "Asian erotica" in a search engine, click "Find," and wait while the search engine comes up with a list of likely hits. None of these hits quite does it? The user is prompted to modify the key phrase and try it again or to simply click "More" to obtain more hits. More and more and more.

What do they find? It varies. Sometimes, they find something posted on the Web by an individual. Sometimes they find a particular vendor of hard-core photos and "live sex" (only necrophiliacs would prefer "dead sex," we imagine) that asks for credit card information to sign them up ("Only $9.95 per month" or whatever). The vendors often, but not always, ask to run "Adult checks" to verify that the user is over 18 and a resident of a state that allows access to pornographic materials by users of that age. Sometimes, users find electronic switchboards that invite them to click here or here or here for live sex, raw sex, amateur sex, she-male sex, the 1,000 top adult Web sites, the 5,000 top adult Web sites, college women, Japanese women, Japanese animated sex, live sex from Amsterdam, or live sex from your neighbor's basement (your neighbor might have created a Web site and be offering . . . whatever).

Some find other sites, other things. Consider Vancouver's multipurpose Consensual Sex Information Service (www.walnet.org/csis). This is about as traditional and honorable a Web site as one is likely to click across. Its home page is a bit raunchy, but compared to XXX-rated home pages, it looks like Mom and apple pie. CSIS does offer information about local and some not-so-local massage parlors and escort services. It also provides the electronic pathways that allow you to click your way to their electronic portals. But it also offers legal and medical information that is intended to be of help to prostitutes and other sex workers (e.g., updates on efforts to have prostitution redefined as sex work). For example, sex workers would like prostitution to be legalized so that prostitutes are protected by police (rather than harassed by police) and can obtain medical and retirement benefits.

As we enter the new millennium, it seems that we become less and less likely to find "dirty old men" leafing through adult magazines in the back of news shops. Rather, they—and younger men and women, many of whom are very freshly scrubbed—appear to be more and more likely to be spending their time surfing the Internet for sex.

figure 19.2

Eros Guide San Francisco. Businessmen looking for sex on a trip to San Francisco can click into Web sites such as this one to find escorts, masseuses, nightlife, and the like.

GENDER DIFFERENCES IN RESPONSE TO PORNOGRAPHY   Both genders can become physiologically aroused by erotic materials. Yet men and women do not necessarily share the same subjective response to them or level of interest in them. Visual pornography (sexually explicit pictures or films) is actually largely a male preserve (Symons, 1995; Winick, 1985). The majority of erotic visual materials are produced by men for men. Attempts to market visual materials to females have been largely unsuccessful (Symons, 1995). Women might read erotic romance novels, but they show little interest in acquiring erotic pictures, films, or videotapes (Lawrence & Herold, 1988). Women respondents to the Bryant (1985) survey were twice as likely to be disgusted by their initial exposure to X-rated material as to enjoy it. Men, by contrast, were twice as likely to report a positive response.

The reasons for these gender differences remain unclear (Bryant & Brown, 1989). Women might find erotica a turnoff when it portrays women in unflattering roles, as whorish, as subservient to the sexual demands of men, and as sexually aroused by male domination and coercion. Symons (1979), a sociobiologist, believes that a basic evolutionary process is at work. He argues that ancestral men who were more sexually aroused by the sight of a passing female might have had reproductive advantages over their less arousable peers:

> The male's desire to look at female genitals, especially genitals he has not seen before, and to seek out opportunities to do so, is part of the motivational process that maximizes male reproductive opportunities. (p. 181)

Women, however, have fewer mating opportunities than men and must make the most of any reproductive opportunity by selecting the best possible mate and provider. To be sexually aroused by the sight of male genitalia might encourage random matings, which would undermine their reproductive success.

Pornography and Sexual Coercion

Is pornography a harmless diversion or an impetus to sexual violence or other antisocial acts? Let us consider several sources of evidence in examining these highly charged questions, beginning with the findings of a 1970 government commission that was impaneled to review the evidence that was available at the time.

THE COMMISSION ON OBSCENITY AND PORNOGRAPHY   In the 1960s, Congress created the Commission on Obscenity and Pornography to study the effects of pornography. Upon reviewing the existing research, the commission (Abelson et al., 1970) concluded that there was no evidence that pornography led to crimes of violence or sexual offenses such as exhibitionism, voyeurism, or child molestation. Some people were sexually aroused by pornography and increased the frequency of their usual sexual activity, such as masturbation or coitus with regular partners, after exposure. They did not engage in antisocial behavior, however. These results have been replicated many times.

The commission found no causal link between pornography and delinquent behavior or sexual violence against women. The commission noted, for example, that when pornographic material became widely available in Denmark following its legalization in late 1960s, there was no corresponding increase in the incidence of sex crimes. Finding pornography basically harmless (Edgley, 1989), the commission recommended that "federal, state, and local legislation should not seek to interfere with the right of adults who wish to read, obtain, or view explicit sexual materials" (Abelson et al., 1970, p. 58). Congress and then-president Richard Nixon rejected the commission's findings and recommendation, however, on moral and political—not scientific—grounds.

PORNOGRAPHY AND SEX OFFENDERS   Another approach to examining the role of pornography in crimes of sexual violence involves comparing the experiences of sex offenders and nonoffenders with pornographic materials. A review of the research literature found little or no difference in the level of exposure to pornography between incarcerated sex offenders and comparison groups of felons who were incarcerated for nonsexual crimes (Marshall, 1989).

Yet evidence also shows that as many as one in three rapists and child molesters use pornography to become sexually aroused immediately before and during the commission of their crimes (Marshall, 1989). These findings suggest that pornography might stimulate sexually deviant urges in certain subgroups of men who are predisposed to commit crimes of sexual violence (Marshall, 1989).

THE MEESE COMMISSION REPORT   In 1985, President Ronald Reagan appointed a committee headed by Attorney General Edwin Meese to reexamine the effects of pornography. In 1986, the U.S. Attorney General's Commission on Pornography, known as the Meese Commission, issued a report that reached very different conclusions than the 1970 commission. The Meese Commission said that it found a causal link between sexual violence and exposure to violent pornography (U.S. Department of Justice, 1986). The commission asserted that a substantial increase in the proliferation of violent pornography had occurred since the earlier commission had been convened. Moreover, the report concluded that exposure to pornography that portrayed women in degrading or subservient roles increased acceptability of rape in the minds of viewers. The commission found no evidence linking exposure to nonviolent, nondegrading pornography (consensual sexual activity between partners in equal roles) and sexual violence but noted that only a small fraction of the pornographic materials on the market was of this type.

The commission issued 92 recommendations for tighter enforcement of obscenity laws and greater restrictions on the dissemination of pornography. Some recommendations focused on the enforcement and prosecution of existing child pornography laws. Others encouraged states that had not already done so to make the knowledgeable possession of child pornography a felony.

The commission's findings are controversial. Critics claim that although the Meese Commission did not blatantly falsify the data, its conclusions reflected an overgeneralization of laboratory-based findings (Wilcox, 1987). Two researchers in the area, Edward Donnerstein and Daniel Linz (1987), contended that the Meese Commission failed to distinguish between the effects of sexually explicit materials per se and the effects of violent materials. Evidence of links between exposure to sexually explicit materials (without violent content) and sexual aggression is lacking. Donnerstein and Linz concluded that violence, not sex, is the obscenity. Nor do researchers confirm the Meese Commission's belief in the rising incidence of violent pornography. Evidence does not show depictions of violence in media such as in the magazines *Playboy* and *Hustler*, or in X-rated movies and videos, to have increased in recent years (Scott & Cuvelier, 1993). In fact, X-rated movies and videos contain less violence than do general-release movies.

If nothing else, the Meese Commission raised awareness about different types of pornography and their potential effects on viewers' behaviors and attitudes. Let us take a look at the scientific evidence on the effects of violent and nonviolent pornography.

VIOLENT PORNOGRAPHY   Laboratory-based studies have shown that men who are exposed to violent pornography are more likely to become aggressive against females and to show less sensitivity toward women who have been sexually assaulted. In one study (Donnerstein, 1980), 120 college men interacted with a male or female confederate (accomplice) of the experimenter, who treated them in either a neutral or a hostile manner. The study participants were then shown neutral, nonviolent pornographic films or violent pornographic films. In the latter, a man forced himself into a woman's home and raped her. Participants were then given the opportunity to deliver an electric shock to the male or female confederate, presumably to assist the confederate in learning a task. The measure of aggression was the intensity of the shock chosen. No shock was actually delivered, but participants did not know that the shock apparatus was fake. Unprovoked men who viewed violent pornographic films showed greater aggression toward the women than did unprovoked men who viewed nonviolent films, however. Provoked men who were shown violent pornography selected the highest shock levels of all. The film might have served as a model for retaliation.

In another study, aggression by males against female confederates following exposure to violent pornography (a rape scene) was increased by depictions of the woman being raped as either enjoying the experience or becoming sexually aroused during the rape (Donnerstein & Berkowitz, 1981). These findings suggest that depictions of women enjoying or becoming aroused by their victimization might legitimize violence against women in the viewer's mind, reinforcing the cultural myth that some women need to be dominated and are sexually aroused by an overpowering male.

Other research has shown that exposure to violent pornography leads men to become more accepting of rape, less sensitive to women survivors of rape, and more accepting of the use of violence in interpersonal relationships (Donnerstein & Linz, 1987; Malamuth, 1984).

Yet research suggests that it is the violence in violent pornography, not sexual explicitness, that hardens men's attitudes toward rape survivors. In one study (Donnerstein & Linz, 1987), college men were exposed to films consisting of either violent pornography, nonviolent pornography (a couple having consensual intercourse), or violence that was not sexually explicit. The violent pornographic and nonpornographic films both showed a woman being tied up and slapped at gunpoint, but the nonpornographic version contained no nudity or explicit sexual activity. The men had first been either angered or treated in a neutral manner by a female confederate of the experimenter. The results showed that, in comparison with nonviolent pornography, both violent pornographic films and violent *non*pornographic films produced greater acceptance of rape myths, increased reported willingness to force a woman into sexual activity, and greater reported likelihood of engaging in rape (if the man also knew that he could get away with it). These effects occurred regardless of whether the man was angered by the woman or not.

In another study, Linz and his colleagues (1988) assigned college men, at random, to watch five feature-length films over a two-week period. One group saw X-rated nonviolent films. A second group watched R-rated "slasher-type" violent films such as *Friday the 13th, Part 2.* ("Slasher films" show graphic violence, primarily directed at women, intermingled with mild erotic scenes.) A third group saw R-rated, nonviolent "teenage sex films" such as *Porky's.* Afterward, the men viewed a videotaped reenactment of a trial in which a woman accused a man of raping her. Men who had watched the R-rated slasher films showed less sensitivity toward the woman complainant than did men who had been exposed to the R- or the X-rated nonviolent films. Exposure to sexually explicit material *without violence,* whether soft-core (R-rated) or hard-core (X-rated), did not reduce sympathy toward the woman complainant.

On the basis of a review of the research literature, Linz (1989) concluded that short-term and prolonged exposure to sexual violence, whether sexually explicit or not, lessens sensitivity toward survivors of rape and increases acceptance of the use of force in sexual encounters. "Slasher" films are connected with the strongest antisocial effects.

Research on the effects of pornography should be interpreted with caution, however. Most of it has employed college students, whose behavior might or might not be typical of people in general or of people with propensities toward sexual violence. On the other hand, research discussed in Chapter 18 shows that a large percentage of college men have engaged in rape, attempted rape, or some other form of sexual coercion. Another issue is that most studies in this area are laboratory-based experiments that involve simulated aggression or judgments of sympathy toward hypothetical women who have been portrayed as rape victims. None measured *actual* violence against women outside the lab. We are still bereft of evidence that normal men have been, or would be, spurred to rape or to sexually violate women because of exposure to violent pornography or other forms of violent media.

NONVIOLENT PORNOGRAPHY Nonviolent pornography might not contain scenes of sexual violence, but it typically portrays women in degrading or dehumanizing roles—as sexually promiscuous, insatiable, and subservient. Might such portrayals of women reinforce traditional stereotypes of women as sex objects? Might they lead viewers to condone acts of rape by suggesting that women are essentially promiscuous? Might the depiction of women as readily sexually accessible inspire men to refuse to take no for an answer on dates?

Zillmann and Bryant (1984) exposed male and female study participants to six sessions of pornography over six consecutive weeks. Participants were exposed to either a massive dose of pornography, consisting of six nonviolent pornographic films ("Swedish Erotica") during each weekly session; to an intermediate dose consisting of three pornographic and three neutral films during each session; or to a no-dose control, consisting of six nonsexual films during each session. When later tested in a purportedly independent study, both males and females who received extended exposure to pornography, especially those who received the massive dose, gave more lenient punishments to a rapist who was depicted in a newspaper article. Moreover, males became more callous in their attitudes toward women.

Zillmann and Weaver (1989) argue that making women appear sexually permissive and promiscuous increases men's callousness toward women who have been sexually assaulted. Once men brand women as promiscuous, they lose respect for them. They see women as "public property" who have forfeited their right to exercise choice in sex partners.

Not all researchers, however, find exposure to nonviolent pornography to increase callousness toward women. Some report finding that nonviolent pornography did not reduce the sensitivity of men (Linz et al., 1988) and women (Krafka, 1985) to female victims of sexual assault. Others report that nonviolent pornography did not increase men's aggression toward women in laboratory studies (Malamuth & Ceniti, 1986). Still others did not find repeated exposure to nonviolent pornography to make men adopt more callous attitudes toward women or increase their acceptance of rape myths (Padgett et al., 1989).

Given the inconsistencies in the research findings and the limited amount of research on nonviolent pornography, Linz (1989) concludes that

> the data, *overall*, do not support the contention that exposure to nonviolent pornography has significant adverse effects on attitudes toward rape as a crime or more general evaluations of rape victims. (p. 74)

Moreover, if nonviolent pornography can be connected with negative attitudes toward women, Linz (1989) suggests that such attitudes might result from the demeaning portrayals of women as sexual playthings who are valued only for their physical attributes and sexual availability, rather than from sexual explicitness per se.

Yet another concern is the possible effect of nonviolent pornography on the viewer's sexual and family values. Nonviolent pornography typically features impromptu sexual encounters between new acquaintances. Might repeated exposure to such material alter viewers' attitudes toward traditional sexual and family values? Zillmann (1989) reports intriguing evidence that repeated exposure to this type of nonviolent pornography loosens traditional sexual and family values. When compared to people who viewed nonsexual films, men and women who were exposed to weekly, hour-long sessions involving scenes of explicit sexual encounters between new acquaintances over a six-week period showed attitudinal changes including greater acceptance, in comparison to controls who viewed nonsexual films, of premarital and extramarital sex and of simultaneous sexual relationships with multiple partners. Men and women who viewed such pornography also reported desiring fewer children than people in the control groups and were relatively less committed to marriage as an "essential institution."

Zillmann (1989) argues that nonviolent pornography loosens traditional family values by projecting an image of sexual enjoyment without responsibility or obligations. Prolonged exposure to such pornography might also foster dissatisfaction with the physical appearance and sexual performance of one's intimate partners (Zillmann, 1989).

In sum, research on the effects of nonviolent pornography does not permit definite conclusions. The effects of nonviolent pornography might be more connected with whether or not women are presented in a dehumanizing manner than with sexual explicitness per se. No research has yet linked sexual explicitness itself with undesirable effects. It is of interest to note that only a minority of people in the United States support legislation making sexually explicit materials illegal, yet three out of four favor the criminalization of *violent* pornography (Harris, 1988).

Reflections

- Agree or disagree with the following statement and support your answer: One person's pornography is another person's art.
- Why do you think men are more interested in pornography than women are?
- In *Miller* v. *California*, the U.S. Supreme Court held that obscenity is based on "whether the average person, applying contemporary community standards, would find that the work, taken as a whole, appeals to the prurient interest." What is your "community"? What are its standards? What types of films, photographs, or written stories would an average person in your community consider to be obscene? Why?
- Which do you consider to be the greater danger: the danger of having pornography available or the danger of censorship? Why?

SEX IN ADVERTISING

In the 1980s, a coquettish Brooke Shields was featured in a TV commercial that showed her spreading her denim-clad legs, smiling coyly at the camera, and murmuring that nothing came between her and her Calvins (Calvin Klein jeans, that is). The advertising campaign evoked a storm of complaints from viewers who thought that it was vulgar and obscene. Meanwhile, the sales of Calvin Klein jeans went through the roof. In short, sex sells.

The use of sexual imagery in advertising ranges from more subtle uses of innuendo and double entendre, such as slogans like "Take it off, take it all off" (for Noxema shaving cream) and *"It's* better in the Bahamas," to the use of an attractive woman who says her men wear "English Leather or they wear nothing at all."

Sex in advertising operates according to the principle of association. Advertisers hope that people will link the product with the sexual imagery that is incorporated within the advertisement. Perhaps the use of a sexy ad will make consumers think that the product will make them more sexually alluring or enhance their sexual arousal, ideas that, in turn, will prompt them to purchase the product rather than that of a competitor.

Researchers caution, however, that sexy ads can backfire. Viewers might pay such careful attention to the sexy imagery that they tune out the advertising message or product claims or even forget what the product is (Edgley, 1989; Severn et al., 1990). Sexy advertising might not only be distracting. It might also turn people off to the advertisement and, by extension, to the product, especially if the sexual image is unrelated to the nature of the product.

It is true that advertisements that are too sexy might cause consumers to focus on the sexual content of the advertisements and forget the products. ■

Truth or Fiction?
REVISITED

Advertisers also need to consider the gender of the target audience. Researchers find that men tend to react more positively and women more negatively toward various forms of sexual content in advertising, whether it be sexual innuendo uttered by female models in TV commercials (Bello et al., 1983) or female nudity in print advertising (LaTour, 1990).

Advertising and Gender-Role Stereotypes

The frequent use of sexy female models in advertisements raises broader concerns about the depiction of women in advertising. As Edgley (1989) notes, "Despite years of feminist consciousness-raising about the issue, commercials still tend to depict women in stereotypical ways." What Komisar said of advertising in 1971 may be as true today as it was then:

> If television commercials are to be believed, most American women go into uncontrollable ecstasies at the sight and smell of tables and cabinets that have been lovingly caressed with long-lasting, satin-finish, lemon-scented, spray-on furniture polish. Or they glow with rapture at the blinding whiteness of their wash—to the green-eyed envy of their neighbors. . . . it is an amazing feat of hocus-pocus worthy of Tom Sawyer and P. T. Barnum to lovingly declare that domestic labor is the true vocation of women wearing wedding bands. (p. 209)

"Pushing the Envelope." Calvin Klein's ad campaigns have been accused of using child pornography to sell jeans. What do you think? How far is too far?

Studies of TV commercials in the United States, Canada, the United Kingdom, and Italy show a consistent pattern: Females are more likely to be portrayed visually on screen, whereas males are more likely to do voice-overs as the "voice of authority" (Ferrante et al., 1988; Furnham & Voli, 1989; Lovdal, 1989). A study of 320 U.S. TV commercials employing voice-overs showed that 91% used male voices. Only 9% used female voices (Lovdal, 1989).

TV commercials also tend to portray men in a wider variety of occupational roles than women (Bretl & Cantor, 1988; Lovdal, 1989). Despite increased awareness of gender-role stereotypes, the image of women in TV commercials has not changed much in recent years (Lovdal, 1989). Women's roles are still generally stereotyped in traditional roles as wives, mothers, brides, waitresses, actresses, and so on. Rarely are they photographers, athletes, or businesswomen. Still, we can report some signs of change, at least with respect to the portrayal of men's roles. Men today are increasingly represented in commercials as spouses and parents (Bretl & Cantor, 1988). Women, however, are still more likely to be seen in domestic settings, advertising products that they can use in the home (Bretl & Cantor, 1988).

Why should we be concerned about how women are portrayed in advertising? For one thing, stereotypical advertising might serve to perpetuate traditional gender-role expectations by portraying women primarily in domestic roles or as sex objects. TV commercials (and programs), for example, might influence viewers' perceptions of acceptable gender-role behaviors (Lovdal, 1989). Girls and young women who are continually exposed to images of women in domestic roles might perceive themselves as having fewer career options than their male counterparts.

Reflections

- Agree or disagree with the following statement and support your answer: Advertising practices today are contributing to the moral decay of the United States.
- What advertisements in magazines and on television today seem to rely heavily on sex appeal? Have they affected your attitudes toward the products involved? Have they affected your purchasing practices? (Be honest!)
- Agree or disagree with the following statement and support your answer: Sex in advertising perpetuates traditional gender-role stereotypes.

THE WORLD OF COMMERCIAL SEX: A DISNEYLAND FOR ADULTS

Commercial sex runs the gamut from "adult" movie theaters and bookshops to strip shows, sex toy shops, brothels, escort services, massage parlors, "900" telephone services, and the use of sex in advertising.

PROSTITUTION

In the United States, prostitution is illegal everywhere except some rural counties in Nevada.

Incidence of Prostitution in the United States Today

Fewer young men in the United States use prostitutes than in Kinsey's day, apparently because of the liberalizing trends of the sexual revolution.

Types of Female Prostitutes

The major types of female prostitutes are streetwalkers, brothel prostitutes (many of whom work in massage parlors and for "escort services"), and call girls. Streetwalkers often support, and are abused by, pimps.

Characteristics of Female Prostitutes

No single factor explains entry into female prostitution, but poverty and sexual and/or physical abuse figure prominently in the backgrounds of many prostitutes. Teenage runaways with marginal skills and limited means of support might find few alternatives to prostitution.

Customers of Female Prostitutes

The consumers of prostitutes are often referred to as "johns" or "tricks." Most patrons are "occasional johns" with regular sex partners. Some people use prostitutes habitually or compulsively, however.

Male Prostitution

Most male prostitutes are "hustlers" who service male clients. Hustlers typically begin selling sex in their teens and may be gay or heterosexual in orientation.

HIV, AIDS, and Prostitution

Prostitutes are at greater risk of transmission of HIV because they have sexual relations with many partners, often without protection. Many prostitutes and their clients and other sex partners also inject drugs and share contaminated needles. HIV can be spread by unprotected sex from prostitutes to customers, then to the customers' wives or lovers. Despite the dangers of HIV transmission, many U.S. prostitutes have not altered either their sexual behavior or their patterns of drug use.

PORNOGRAPHY AND OBSCENITY

What Is Pornographic?

Pornography is "writing, pictures, etc., intended to arouse sexual desire." Erotica, by contrast, refers to sexual materials that are artistically produced or motivated. The judgment as to what is pornographic or obscene varies from person to person and from culture to culture.

Pornography and the Law

In *Miller* v. *California*, the U.S. Supreme Court held that obscenity is based upon a determination of "whether the average person, applying contemporary community standards, would find that the work . . . appeals to the prurient interest . . . ; whether the work depicts [sexual behavior] in a patently offensive way, [and] whether the work, taken as a whole, lacks serious literary, artistic, political, or scientific value." *Miller* recognizes that judgments of obscenity may vary with "community standards."

Prevalence and Use of Erotica and Pornography

People in the United States are typically introduced to pornography by their high school years. Although both genders can become physiologically aroused by erotic materials, men are relatively more interested in sexually explicit pictures and films than women are.

Pornography and Sexual Coercion

A 1970 U.S. government commission found no harmful effects of pornographic material on normal people. A later government commission, the Meese Commission, issued a report in 1986 linking exposure to violent pornography with sexual aggression, and exposure to degrading but nonviolent pornography with increased acceptability of rape in the minds of viewers. Research evidence suggests that exposure to pornography might stimulate sexually deviant urges in some men who are predisposed to commit crimes of sexual violence. Research evidence in laboratory settings also suggests that violent pornography might stimulate college men to act more aggressively toward women. Some researchers argue that it is the violence in violent pornography, not sexual explicitness, that promotes violence against women. The effects of nonviolent pornography on normal populations remain unclear.

SEX IN ADVERTISING

Sex in advertising operates according to the principle of association. Advertisers hope that people will link the product with the sexual imagery that is incorporated within the advertisement. Sexy ads can backfire, however, by diverting attention from the product or turning people off to the product.

Advertising and Gender-Role Stereotypes

Women in TV commercials are still generally stereotyped as wives, mothers, brides, waitresses, actresses, and so on.

Bharati Chaudhuri. *Invisible Tension*. 1992. Oil on canvas, 36 x 40 in. SuperStock

chapter

20

Making Responsible Sexual Decisions—An Epilogue

outline

CHOICES, INFORMATION, AND DECISION MAKING

Conflict

Decisions, Decisions, Decisions . . .

VALUE SYSTEMS

Legalism

Situation Ethics

Ethical Relativism

Hedonism

Asceticism

Utilitarianism

Rationalism

THE BALANCE SHEET FOR DECISION MAKING

making choices is deeply intertwined with our sexual experience. Although sex is a natural function, the ways in which we express our sexuality are matters of personal choice. We choose how, where, and with whom to become sexually involved. We might face a wide array of sexual decisions: Whom should I date? When should my partner and I become sexually intimate? Should I initiate sexual relations or wait for my partner to approach me? Should my partner and I practice contraception? If so, which method? Should I use a condom to protect against sexually transmitted diseases (or insist that my partner does)? Should I be tested for HIV? Should I insist that my partner be tested for HIV before we engage in sexual relations?

CHOICES, INFORMATION, AND DECISION MAKING

We have presented you with information that can help you to make responsible sexual decisions. Information alone cannot determine whether the options you consider are morally acceptable to you, however. Many issues raise moral concerns, such as premarital and extramarital sex, contraception, and abortion. Gathering information and weighing the scientific evidence will alert you to what is possible in the contemporary world, but only you can determine which of your options are compatible with your own moral values. We all have unique sets of moral values—as Americans, as members of one of America's hundreds of subcultures, as individuals. No single value system defines us all. Indeed, the world of diversity in which we live is a mosaic of different moral codes and cultural traditions and beliefs.

Conflict

The most difficult decisions involve choices between alternatives that each have positive and negative aspects or that each have compelling negative features.

Consider the issue of deciding whether to obtain screening for cancer. The pluses include freedom from anxiety (when results are negative) and early detection (when cancer is found). The negatives include the costs of screening, inconvenience, discomfort (in some techniques), and hearing results one would rather not hear (if cancer is found) (White et al., 1994).

Consider contraceptive techniques. The pill is effective and does not interfere with sexual spontaneity, but it is costly and has side effects. The condom has no side effects (for the great majority of users), but some people find that it disrupts lovemaking and reduces sexual sensations. It is also not as effective as the pill.

Or consider the plight of Kim, a college student who becomes pregnant as a result of date rape: Should she have an abortion, which might be morally offensive to her, or bear an unwanted child? Then, too, should she report the crime and hope the criminal justice system will successfully prosecute her assailant, or should she try to swallow her bitter feelings and protect her anonymity? Or consider the college student who feels morally committed to remaining a virgin until marriage but fears earning the disapproval of dating partners or having no dates at all.

When we are pulled in different directions at the same time, we experience psychological conflict. Conflict can be extremely stressful, especially if it is prolonged. People in conflict often feel "damned if they do and damned if they don't." They might also vacillate—take tentative steps in one direction and then in the other. Kim, a survivor of date rape, takes a bus to an abortion clinic across town and gets off at the next stop. She checks the telephone number of the police but then hesitates to pick up the telephone. She is obsessed with the question as to what is the right thing to do.

Part of Kim's conflict is over a moral issue. She would very much like to terminate her unwanted pregnancy by having an abortion, but she holds back because she firmly believes that the embryo within is a precious human life. Her conflict over whether or not to report her assailant is in part moral, in part practical. It is morally proper to report him, but what if she is not believed? What if the incident becomes widely known on campus and to her family? Moreover, she realizes that the longer she waits, the more it might appear that she is making up the story.

Decisions, Decisions, Decisions . . .

The way out of conflict is to make decisions. Making decisions involves choosing among various courses of action. The act of not making a formal decision may itself represent a tacit decision. For example, we might vacillate about whether to use a particular form of birth control but continue to engage in unprotected sex. Is this because we have not made a decision or because we have decided to let happen what will happen?

Gathering information helps us to predict the outcomes of the decisions we make. This textbook provides you with a broad data base concerning scientific developments and ways of relating to other people—including people who come from other cultures. By talking to people who have had similar questions or been in similar conflicts, you can also learn which decisions worked for them, which did not, and, perhaps, why. Or you might be able to learn what happens when people do not make decisions but simply hope for the best. You can also talk to your parents, friends, religious counselors, course instructors, psychologists, and other helping professionals. Regarding which contraceptive method to use, you might wish to discuss the information in this book with a physician, nurse, or other health counselor.

VALUE SYSTEMS

Our value systems provide another framework for judging the moral acceptability of sexual options. We often approach sexual decisions by determining whether the choices we face are compatible with our moral values. Our value systems do not necessarily determine the outcomes of all of our sexual decisions, however—any more than laws strictly determine people's behavior. Some of us adhere to stricter moral values. Some people make choices that bend or violate their values but try not to focus on the discrepancies too closely. Many of us also act on impulse, especially sexual impulses, without thinking through the consequences of our actions. Afterward, we may regret our decisions or feel guilty if our behavior was inconsistent with our values.

Our value systems—our sexual standards—have many sources: parents, peers, religious training, ethnic subcultures, the larger culture, and our appraisal of all these influences. Value systems that provide a guiding framework to determine the moral acceptability of sexual choices include legalism, situation ethics, hedonism, asceticism, utilitarianism, and rationalism.

Legalism

The legalistic approach formulates ethical behavior on the basis of a code of moral laws derived from an external source, such as the creed of a particular religion (Knox, 1988). The Bible contains many examples of the moral code of the Jewish and Christian religions. In the Book of Leviticus (20:10–17) in the Old Testament, we find many of the biblical prohibitions against adultery, incest, sexual activity with people of one's own gender, and bestiality:

> And the man that committeth adultery with another man's wife, even he that committeth adultery with his neighbor's wife, both the adulterer and the adulteress shall surely be put to death. And the man that lieth with his father's wife . . . both of them shall surely be put to death; their blood shall be upon them. . . . And if a man lie with mankind, as with womankind, both of them have committed abomination: they shall surely be put to death; . . . And if a man lie with a beast, he shall surely be put to death; and ye shall slay the beast. . . . And if a man shall take his sister, . . . and see her nakedness, and she sees his nakedness: it is a shameful thing; and they shall be cut off in the sight of the children of their people. . . .

Leviticus also proscribes intercourse during menstruation and the forcing of daughters into prostitution.

Throughout the centuries, many Christians and Jews have adhered to religious laws that are intended to promote the solidarity of the family and the community by minimizing interpersonal jealousies and frictions. Adultery, for example, could set neighbor against neighbor. Religious laws have also directed followers to be "fruitful and multiply" so as to ensure that an ample number of progeny would be available to meet the needs for labor and defense of the family and the community of religious followers.

Many religious followers today accept the moral codes of their religions as a matter of faith and commitment, not necessarily because they can logically or rationally derive them from contemporary societal needs. Some people find it reassuring to be informed by religious authorities or scripture that a certain course of action is right or wrong. Others, however, have questioned how closely one must adhere to religious teachings if one is to be ethical. A number of fundamentalist Protestants, conservative Catholics, and orthodox Jews would argue that the Bible is to be followed to the letter, not just "in spirit." They see the Bible, in all its literal details, as the revealed word of God.

Other Christians and Jews take a more liberal view. They say that the Bible was inspired by God but that it was written or transcribed by fallible humans and is subject to various interpretations. They might also assert that the Bible reflects the social setting of the time in which it was written, not just divine inspiration. At a time of burgeoning population growth in many parts of the world, biblical injunctions to be fruitful and multiply might no longer be socially and environmentally sound. Prohibitions, such as that against coitus during menstruation, might have been based on prescientific perceptions of danger. Thus, religious teachings might be viewed as a general framework for decision making rather than as a set of absolute rules.

Situation Ethics

Episcopal theologian Joseph Fletcher (1966, 1967) argued that ethical decision making should be guided by genuine love for others rather than by rigid moral rules. Fletcher advocated that sexual decision making should be based on the context of the particular situation that the person faces. For this reason, his view is termed *situation ethics*. According to Fletcher, a Roman Catholic woman will have been taught that abortion is the taking of a human life. Her situation, however—her love for her existing family and her recognition of her limited resources for providing for another child—might influence her to decide in favor of an abortion.

Fletcher argues that one's rules for conduct should not be inflexible. Rather, they should be general guidelines. "The situationist is prepared in any concrete case to suspend, ignore, or violate any principle if by doing so he can effect more good than by following it" (1966, p. 34).

Note that situation ethics is not an excuse for selfishness. The moral situation ethicist acts in a manner that he or she believes will lead to the greater good. Now and then, such an act may be frustrating, painful, or difficult. Situation ethicists also may find it difficult, as psychologist David Knox (1988) points out, to make sexual decisions on a case-by-case basis:

> "I don't know what's right anymore" reflects the uncertainty of a situation ethics view. Once a person decides that mutual love is the context justifying intercourse, how often and how soon should the person fall in love? Can love develop after two hours of conversation? How does one know that her or his own love feelings and those of a partner are genuine? The freedom that situation ethics brings to sexual decision making requires responsibility, maturity, and judgment. In some cases, individuals may deceive themselves by believing they are in love so they will not feel guilty about having intercourse. (Knox, 1988, p. 97. Reprinted by permission.)

Ethical Relativism

Ethical relativism assumes that diverse values are fundamental to human existence. Ethical relativists reject the idea that there is a single correct moral view. One person might believe that premarital sex is unacceptable under any circumstances, whereas another might hold that "being in love" makes it acceptable. Still another person might believe that premarital sex is morally permissible without an emotional commitment between the partners.

The ethical relativist believes that there is no objective way of justifying one set of moral values over another. In this view, the essence of human morality is to derive one's own principles and apply them according to one's own conscience. From this perspective, whatever a person believes is right is right for him or her. Subscribing to ethical relativism does not free us of the need to develop moral beliefs, however. It challenges us, instead, to take responsibility for our decisions and to live up to them.

Opponents of ethical relativism believe that allowing people free rein to determine what is right or wrong can bring about social chaos and decay.

One form of ethical relativism is cultural relativism. From this perspective, what is right or wrong must be understood in terms of the cultural beliefs that affect sexual decision making. In some cultures, premarital sex is tolerated or even encouraged; in others, it is considered immoral. Cultural relativism, like ethical relativism, does not ascribe moral superiority to one cultural tradition over another.

Hedonism

The hedonist is guided by the pursuit of pleasure, not by whether a particular behavior is morally or situationally justified (Knox, 1988). "If it feels good, do it" expresses the hedonistic ethic. The hedonist believes that sexual desires, like hunger or thirst, do not invoke moral considerations.

Of course, one could make the case that there are two kinds of hedonism: short-sighted and long-term hedonism. Basing decisions upon what feels good at the moment might fail to account for the long-term consequences of one's actions. The short-sighted hedonist might risk becoming so driven by the pursuit of pleasure that sex becomes a form of "addiction" in which sexual pleasure overshadows other important aspects of life.

On the other hand, taking a long-term hedonistic view, one can attempt to make responsible sexual decisions that can lead to a lifetime of sexual pleasure. Choosing to do what is necessary to maintain our sexual health, for instance, can help us to lead long lives and to enjoy our bodies throughout our span of years.

Asceticism

Religious celibates, such as Roman Catholic priests and nuns, choose asceticism (self-denial of material and sexual desires) to devote themselves to spiritual pursuits. Many ascetics in Eastern and Western religions seek to transcend physical and worldly desires.

Utilitarianism

Some people believe that it is necessary to adhere to specific religious principles or teachings if one is to be a moral or ethical person, but others believe that ethical guidelines can be based on principles other than religious ones. The English philosopher John Stuart Mill (1806–1873), for example, proposed an ethical system based on utilitarianism.

The core ethic of utilitarianism is that moral conduct is based on that which will bring about "the greatest good for the greatest number" (Mill, 1939/1863). The utilitarian characterizes behavior as ethical when it does the greatest good and causes the least harm. This is not license. Utilitarians might come down hard in opposition to premarital sex and bearing children out of wedlock, for example, if they believe that these behavior patterns jeopardize a nation's health and social fabric. Mill's ethics generally require that we treat one another justly and honestly, because it serves the greater good for people to be true to their word and just in their dealings with others.

Rationalism

Rationalism involves the use of reason as the means of determining a course of action (Knox, 1988). The rationalist believes that decisions should be based on intellect and reasoning, rather than emotions or strict obedience to a particular faith. The rationalist attempts to assess the facts in a sexual situation and then logically weigh the consequences of each course of action before making a decision. The rationalist shares with the utilitarian the belief that reasoning can lead to a course of ethical behavior. The rationalist is not bound, however, to the utilitarian code that makes choices on the basis of the greatest good for the greatest number. The rationalist might contend that personal needs and desires outweigh the needs of the many.

The utilitarian might decide, for example, to prolong an unhappy marriage because of the belief that the greater good (of the family and the community) is better served by maintaining an unhappy marriage than by dissolving it. The rationalist might decide that the personal consequences of continuing an unhappy marriage outweigh the consequences to the family or the community at large. The religious follower, adopting a legalistic view, might decide that divorce is or is not acceptable, depending on the tenets of the person's religion. The situation ethicist might interpret religious principles in light of how the greater good would be served in a particular situation.

These ethical systems represent general frameworks of moral reasoning or pathways for judging the moral acceptability of sexual and nonsexual behavior. Whereas some of us might adopt one or another of these systems in their purest forms, others adopt a system of moral reasoning that involves some combination or variation of these ethical systems. Some also shift from one ethical system to another from time to time, sometimes reasoning legalistically and sometimes adopting a more flexible situationist approach. Despite these variations, these general guidelines of moral reasoning assist our understanding of how people approach questions of moral acceptability of sexual choices.

Reflections

- Do any of the value systems discussed in the chapter seem similar to your own? What role does your sociocultural background play in your value system? Explain.
- Agree or disagree with the following statement and support your answer: There is no objective way of justifying one set of moral values over another.
- Agree or disagree with the following statement and support your answer: Sexual decisions should be based on intellect and reasoning, rather than emotions or strict obedience to a particular faith.

THE BALANCE SHEET FOR DECISION MAKING

You might use a balance sheet to help weigh the pluses and minuses of alternatives when making decisions. Sheri Oz (1994, 1995) suggests that it is particularly important to weigh the costs of deciding in one direction or another. Oz notes that in making decisions about sex, marriage, and divorce, we frequently weigh costs in self-esteem against costs in terms of the approval of other people—often our intimate partners.

Rosa, a Mexican American student at a California state college, has been involved in a sexual relationship for several weeks and is contemplating going on the pill. Rosa uses the balance sheet to list the projected gains and losses for herself and her partner according to five criteria:

1. *Experiential:* How will it feel? What is its effect on sexual relations? How does it affect sexual sensations and spontaneity?
2. *Biological:* How do contraceptive methods work? What are the side effects of birth-control methods? What are the risks involved? What are the effects on preventing STIs?

3. *Financial:* Can I afford it—literally? For example, how much do pills cost? How much do babies cost?
4. *Ethical:* Is what I am considering consistent with my religious and parental teachings? Is that important to me? Will I experience guilt, anxiety, or shame? Is the course of behavior consistent with my ideas concerning sex roles and who takes the responsibility for the decision? (For example, should the responsibility for birth control be placed on the woman's shoulders only?)
5. *Legal:* Am I contemplating something that is against the law? What could happen to my partner and me?

As shown in Table 20.1, Rosa filled in some of the spaces on the sheet to indicate the following pieces of information:

- Sex can be spontaneous.
- For all practical purposes, the pill can be considered 100% effective (I'm assuming I'll take them as directed).
- I'm 20 years old (young enough and healthy enough not to be too worried about the pill's potential effect on my health).
- The pill is kind of expensive.
- I have some moral concerns about using the pill.
- The pill is legal.

The remaining blank spaces prompted Rosa to consider other issues. For example, she realized that she had forgotten to think about the side effects of the pill and the fact that it is useless against STIs. The information prompted by using the balance sheet is placed in parentheses.

table 20.1

Rosa's balance sheet for deciding whether or not to use birth-control pills			
Issues		**Positive Anticipations**	**Negative Anticipations**
Experiential gains and losses	For self	Sex would be spontaneous	(Possible side effects: nausea, bloating, etc.)
	For partner	Sex would be spontaneous	None
Biological gains and losses	For self	High effectiveness	Probably no negative impact on health; (useless against STIs)
	For partner	High effectiveness	None
Financial gains and losses	For self	(Needn't worry about the cost of a child)	Expensive!
	For partner	(Needn't worry about the cost of a child)	(None!)
Ethical gains and losses	For self	Would not risk bearing unwanted child or having to decide whether to have an abortion if became pregnant	Moderate concern about using artificial means of birth control; responsibility for birth control would be all mine
	For partner	Would not have to worry about causing pregnancy	None!
Legal factors	For self		None
	For partner		None

Rosa decided not to go on the pill for several reasons: (1) She was concerned about side effects; (2) she did not want to spend the money; and (3) she felt that by taking the pill, she was assuming all responsibility for birth control and that she would rather share it with her partner. Her periods were regular, and she decided (1) to use the rhythm method (to abstain from intercourse for a week in the middle of her cycle) and (2) to have her partner use condoms (and spermicide containing nonoxynol-9) every time they made love. The condoms and spermicide would also afford protection against STIs.

After completing a balance sheet, Rosa might fill out a similar one for the alternative of using the condom before making a decision. The balance sheet does not automatically lead to one "correct" choice. You might, for example, reach a different decision than Rosa if you were faced with the same situation. Rather, it is a means of organizing one's perceptions of the positive and negative features of each alternative for oneself and one's partner. Research has shown that balance sheet users hold fewer regrets about the road not taken and are more likely to stick with their decisions.

Reflections

- What decisions are you facing in your own sex life? What sexual decisions are you likely to face in the future? As we return to our worlds of diversity, what value systems will you draw upon in making these decisions?
- What kinds of conflicts may emerge if your partner comes from another cultural background and holds different values? How can the information in this book be of help to you?
- Will you use the information in this textbook to critically examine stereotypes and folklore, or will you think "Oh, it's just another textbook" and toss it aside at the end of the term?

We have come a long way together, and we wish you well. Perhaps we have helped you to phrase the most important questions and to find some answers. We also hope that we have encouraged you to try to understand other people's sexual beliefs and values in light of their cultural backgrounds. Understanding is an essential stopping point on the pathway to respect, and respect is vital to resolving conflicts and establishing healthy relationships.

Scoring Keys for Self-Scoring Questionaires

**SCORING KEY FOR THE LOVE ATTITUDES SCALE
(CHAPTER 7, pp. 200–201)**

First add your scores on the 30 items of the scale to yield a total score.

Write down your total score here: _____

Note that each of the items is keyed so that lower-numbered responses represent more romantic responses; higher-numbered responses represent more realistic responses. The lower your total score (30 is the lowest possible score), the more you identify with a romantic view of love. The higher your score (150 is the highest possible score), the more realistic you are in your love attitudes. A score of 90 places you at the midpoint on the romantic-realist dimension. You might wish to compare your score with your partner's score to see who is more the romantic or more the realist.

**SCORING KEY FOR STERNBERG'S TRIANGULAR LOVE SCALE
(CHAPTER 7, pp. 206–207)**

First add your scores for the items on each of the three components—Intimacy, Passion, and Decision/Commitment—and divide each total by 15. This will yield an average rating for each subscale. An average rating of 5 on a particular subscale indicates a moderate level of the component represented by the subscale. A higher rating indicates a greater level. A lower rating indicates a lower level. Examining your ratings on these components will give you an idea of the degree to which you perceive your love relationship to be characterized by these three components of love. For example, you might find that passion is stronger than decision/commitment, a pattern that is common in the early stages of an intense romantic relationship. You might find it interesting to complete the questionnaire a few months or perhaps a year or so from now to see how your feelings about your relationship change over time. You might also ask your partner to complete the scale so that the two of you can compare your respective scores. Comparing your ratings for each component with those of your partner will give you an idea of the degree to which you and your partner see your relationship in a similar way.

Sternberg (1988) reports the results of administering the scale to a sample of 50 men and 51 women (average age of 31 years) from the New Haven (Connecticut) area who were either married or currently involved in a close relationship. Average scores for the three components were 7.39 for intimacy, 6.51 for passion, and 7.20 for commitment. High scores (scores representing approximately the top 15 percent of scores) were 8.6 for intimacy, 8.2 for passion, and 8.7 for commitment. Low scores, representing the bottom 15 percent of scores, were 6.2, 4.9, and 5.7 for the three components, respectively. Since romantic ardor might be more difficult to maintain over time, the lower average scores for passion might reflect the length of the relationships in which the people in the sample were involved, which averaged 6.3 years in length. Although you might want to compare your scores with those from this sample, we caution that the Sternberg sample was small and most likely does not accurately represent the general population.

SCORING KEY FOR REASONING ABOUT ABORTION SCALE (CHAPTER 12, p. 373)

First tally your scores for the following items: 1, 3, 7, 8, 9, 11, 13, 14, 17, 20. This score represents your support for a *pro-choice* point of view: _____ .

Now tally your scores for the remaining items: 2, 4, 5, 6, 10, 12, 15, 16, 18, 19. This score represents your support for a *pro-life* point of view: _____ .

Now subtract your *pro-choice* score from your *pro-life* score. Write the difference, including the sign, here: _____. A positive score indicates agreement with a pro-life philosophy. A negative score indicates agreement with a pro-choice philosophy. The higher your score, the more strongly you agree with the philosophy that you endorsed. Scores may range from –40 to +40.

One sample of 230 undergraduate students (115 of each gender) obtained a mean score of –7.48 and a median score of –13.33 (Parsons et al., 1990). This indicates that the students tended to be pro-choice in their attitudes. Another sample of 38 graduate students (31 women and 7 men) obtained mean scores of –11 to –12 and median scores of –17 to –18 on two separate occasions. Scores for other samples may vary.

SCORING KEY FOR STI ATTITUDE SCALE (CHAPTER 16, pp. 487–488)

Scores on this scale are interpreted in terms of a predisposition to high-risk sexual behavior. The scale is composed of three subscales, which measure your predisposition to high-risk behavior on the basis of your *beliefs* about STIs (items 1–9), your *feelings* about STIs (items 10–18), and your *intentions to act* (items 19–27). Calculate a total for each subscale and for the total scale by using the point values below.

For items 1, 10–14, 16, 25:

Strongly Agree	=	5 points
Agree	=	4 points
Undecided	=	3 points
Disagree	=	2 points
Strongly Disagree	=	1 point

For items 2–9, 15, 17–24, 26, 27:

Strongly Agree	=	1 point
Agree	=	2 points
Undecided	=	3 points
Disagree	=	4 points
Strongly Disagree	=	5 points

Subtotal for *Beliefs* subscale (items 1–9): _____

Subtotal for *Feelings* subscale (items 10–18): _____

Subtotal for *Intentions to Act* subscale (items 19–27): _____

Total score (based on all items): _____

The higher your subscale and total scores, the greater the likelihood that your attitudes, feelings and intentions put you at risk of contracting an STI. The lower your scores, the less risk you are likely to incur. Although we have no norms at present, we suggest that subscale scores higher than 27 and total scores higher than 81 indicate that your responses are weighted more toward risky than safe behavior. We suggest that you weigh your particular risk by examining not only your scores but your responses to the individual scale items as well. Ask yourself, "How do my responses to these items increase or decrease my risk of contracting an STI?" Then ask yourself, "How might I change my attitudes to reduce my chances of contracting an STI?"

appendix B

Additional Readings: Books on Human Sexuality and Related Topics

Barbach, L. G. (1975). *For yourself: The fulfillment of female sexuality*. Garden City, NY: Doubleday & Co., Inc. A popular self-help book for women who have difficulty achieving orgasm.

Barbach, L. (1984). *For each other*. New York: Signet. Suggestions for enhancing communication and sexual satisfaction in relationships.

Barrett, M. B. (1990). *Invisible lives: The truth about millions of women-loving women*. New York: Morrow. Based upon interviews with 125 lesbians, this book reveals what it is like to be a lesbian in contemporary America and seeks to bridge an understanding between lesbians and parents, children, and friends.

Beck, A. (1988). *Love is never enough*. New York: Harper & Row. Aaron Beck, a leading psychiatrist and originator of cognitive therapy, examines the factors that underlie relationship problems and presents specific techniques that couples can use to resolve conflicts and improve their relationships.

Blumstein, P., & Schwartz, P. (1983) *American couples*. New York: Morrow. A major study of relationships in contemporary American, based on a sample of heterosexual and homosexual couples.

Bornoff, N. (1991). *Pink samurai: Love, marriage & sex in contemporary Japan*. New York: Pocket Books. An enlightening account of sexual customs and practices in modern Japan.

Boston Women's Health Book Collective (1984). *The New Our Bodies, Ourselves*. New York: Simon & Schuster. A highly popular repository of information concerning women's health care and sexuality.

Bridge, T. P., Mirsky, A. F., & Goodwin, F. K. (Eds.) (1988). *Psychological, neuropsychiatric, and substance abuse aspects of AIDS*. New York: Raven Press. A scholarly compendium of information about the medical, behavioral, and legal aspects of AIDS.

Butler, R., & Lewis, M. (1988). *Love and sex after 60* (rev. ed.). New York: Harper & Row. Practical information about adjusting to sexual changes in later life.

Calderone, M. S., & Johnson, E. W. (1989). *Family book about sexuality* (rev. ed.). New York: Harper & Row. A straightforward and balanced compendium of information and advice about sexual development through the life cycle.

Calderone, M., S. & Ramey, J. (1982). *Talking with your child about sex*. New York: Random House. A practical guide for parents about raising sexually healthy children. Provides parents with answers to questions that children frequently ask about sex.

Cass, V. (1988). *There's more to sex than AIDS: The A to Z guide to safe sex*. Richmond, Victoria, Australia: Greenhouse Publications. A comprehensive guide to safer sexual techniques.

Coles, R., & Stokes, G. (1985). *Sex and the American teenager*. New York: Harper & Row. Findings of a survey of the sexual attitudes and practices of a national sample of 1,067 teenagers in the United States.

Cook, E. P. (1985). *Psychological androgyny*. New York: Pergamon. An examination of psychological androgyny that compares and contrasts androgyny to traditional masculine and feminine gender roles.

Donnerstein, E., Linz, D., & Penrod, S. (1987). *The question of pornography*. New York: The Free Press. A comprehensive review of scientific knowledge of the effects of exposure to pornography and legal issues in the debate over pornography.

Eisenberg, A., Murkoff, H., & Hathaway, S. E. (1989). *What to expect the first year*. New York: Workman Publishing. A comprehensive guide to infant development during the first year of life.

Ford, C. S., & Beach, F. A. (1951). New York: Harper. *Patterns of sexual behavior*. A classic study of sexuality from a cross-cultural and cross-species perspective.

Gilligan, C. (1982). *In a different voice*. Cambridge, MA: Harvard University Press. An influential book that examines the differences between men and women with respect to issues of autonomy and intimacy.

Grauerholz, E., & Koralewski, M. A. (Eds.) (1991). *Sexual coercion: A sourcebook on its nature, causes, and prevention*. Lexington, MA: D.C. Heath and Company. A number of leading scholars address the nature, causes, and prevention of sexual coercion.

Greenburg, M. (1985). *The birth of a father.*. New York: Continuum. A first-hand account of the experience of fatherhood.

Griffin, C., Wirth, M., & Wirth, A. (1986). *Beyond acceptance*. Englewood Cliffs, NJ: Prentice-Hall. Written by parents of gay and lesbian children for parents of gay and lesbian children, this book sensitively discusses issues and conflicts that arise in the context of discovering that one's child is homosexual.

Hatcher, R. A., et al. (1998). *Contraceptive technology*. (17th rev. ed.). New York: Ardent Media. The authoritative guide to the most recent developments in contraception.

629

Hatfield, E., & Sprecher, S. (1986). *Mirror, mirror . . . The importance of looks in everyday life.* Albany, NY: SUNY Press. An examination of the role of physical appearance in interpersonal attraction and relationships.

Heiman, J., & LoPiccolo, J. (1988). *Becoming orgasmic: A sexual and personal growth program for women.* Englewood Cliffs, NJ: Prentice-Hall. A self-help guide to help women learn to become orgasmic and enhance their sexual pleasure in masturbation and lovemaking.

Holmes, K. K., et al. (1990). *Sexually transmitted diseases* (2nd ed.). New York: McGraw-Hill Information Services Company. A scholarly, technical resource book on sexually transmitted diseases.

Janus, S. S., & Janus, C. L. (1993). *The Janus Report on sexual behavior.* New York: Wiley. The findings of a new nationwide survey of sexual behavior in the U.S. Conducted from 1988 to 1992, the Janus Report was based on a survey of 2,765 adults who anonymously completed written questionnaires assessing a wide range of sexual behaviors and attitudes.

Kaplan, H. S. (1979). *Disorders of sexual desire.* New York; Brunner/Mazel. A leading sex therapist, Helen Singer Kaplan, examines the causes and treatments of sexual desire disorders.

Kaplan, H. (1987). *The illustrated manual of sex therapy.* New York: Brunner/Mazel. A well-illustrated manual which clearly describes the steps involved in sex therapy for various sexual dysfunctions in men and women.

Kinsey, A. C., Pomeroy, W., & Martin, C. (1948). *Sexual behavior in the human male.* Philadelphia, PA: W. B. Saunders Co.

Kinsey, A. C., Pomeroy, W., Martin, C., & Gebhard, P. (1953). *Sexual behavior in the human female.* Philadelphia, PA: W. B. Saunders Co. The classic "Kinsey reports" containing statistical tables and data describing the sexual behavior patterns of men and women in the U.S., based on interviews of nearly 12,000 people.

Langston, D. (1983). *Living with herpes.* Garden City, NY: Doubleday & Co. A sensitive, practical guide that will be useful to people coping with herpes and to their sexual partners.

Leach, P. (1989). *Your baby & child: From birth to age five* (rev. ed.). New York: Knopf. A comprehensive, clearly presented, and well-illustrated guide to child care.

MacFarlane, K., Waterman, J., and others (Eds.) (1986). *Sexual abuse of young children: Evaluation and treatment.* New York: Guildford. This edited volume features a compilation of clinical and research findings on the problem of child sexual abuse.

Madaras, L. (1983). *The what's happening to my body? Book for Girls: A growing up guide for parents and daughters.* New York: Newmarket Press

Madaras, L. (1984). *The what's happening to my body? Book for boys: A growing up guide for parents and sons.* New York: Newmarket Press. Down-to-earth guides about the changes of puberty and adolescence.

Margulis, L., & Sanga, D. (1991). *Mystery dance: On the evolution of human sexuality.* New York: Summit Books. An exploration of the ancestral origins of human sexuality.

Marshall, D., & Suggs, R. (Eds.) (1971). *Human sexual behavior: Variations in the ethnographic spectrum.* Englewood Cliffs, NJ: Prentice-Hall. A splendid compendium of ethnographic accounts of sexual behavior and customs in various cultures around the world.

Masters, W. H., & Johnson, V. (1970). *Human sexual inadequacy.* This classic book describes the treatment protocol and results of Masters and Johnson's sex therapy program.

Masters, W., & Johnson, V. (1966). *Human sexual response.* Boston: Little, Brown. An account of the classic scientific studies of sexual arousal and response in men and women by Masters and Johnson. "Must" reading for students seeking more detailed knowledge of sexual physiology and functioning.

McNaught, B. (1988). *On being gay.* New York: St. Martin's Press. The author discusses various aspects of the experience of being gay, including the coming-out process, dealing with conflicts with family members, developing gay relationships, and confronting the AIDS crisis.

McWhirter, D. P., Sanders, S. A., & Reinisch, J. M. (Eds.) (1990). *Homosexuality/heterosexuality: Concepts of sexual orientation. The Kinsey Institute Series, Volume II.* New York: Oxford University Press. A compendium of scholarly articles on the classification and understanding of sexual orientation.

Millet, K. (1976). *The prostitution papers.* New York: Ballantine Books. A leading feminist examines the role of prostitutes in our society and argues for decriminalization, but not legalization, of prostitution.

Money, J. (1988). *Gay, straight, and in-between: The sexology of erotic orientation.* New York: Oxford University Press. Written by a leading researcher, this is a scholarly treatise on the biological and psychosocial factors underlying sexual orientation.

Money, J., & Ehrhardt, A. (1972). *Man and woman, boy and girl.* Baltimore: Johns Hopkins Press. A comprehensive analysis of the biological and psychosocial factors that determine gender identity.

Nillson, L. (1977). *A child is born.* New York: Dell. Breathtaking pictures of fetal development with accompanying text.

Peters, B. (1988). *Terrific sex in fearful times.* New York: St. Martin's Press. A guide to safer sex in the age of AIDS.

Pomeroy, W., Flax, C., & Wheeler, C. (1982). *Taking a sex history: Interviewing and recording.* New York: Free Press. The authors review the interviewing methods used in the original Kinsey research and discuss contemporary issues in conducting sex surveys.

Reinisch, J. (1990). *The Kinsey Institute new report on sex: What you must know to be sexually literate.* New York: St. Martin's Press. The findings of a national survey of sexual knowledge, along with a comprehensive and well-researched compendium of information on contraception, sexually transmitted diseases, sexual development, sexual health, problems with sexual functioning, and sex with a partner.

Reinisch, J., & Rosenblum, L. (Eds.) (1987). *Masculinity-femininity: Basic perspectives.* New York: Oxford University Press. A compendium of scientific articles that address issues of gender differences from multiple perspectives, including the biological, psychosocial, and developmental perspectives.

Rubin, L. B. (1983). *Intimate strangers: Men and women together.* New York: Harper & Row. A sensitive and probing study of the struggle of men and women, both within themselves and with their partners, to establish intimate relationships.

Samuels, M., & Samuels, N. (1986). *The well pregnancy book.* A comprehensive and sensitive guide to pregnancy and childbirth. New York: Harper & Row.

Shilts, R. (1987). *And the band played on: Politics, people, and the AIDS epidemic.* New York: Viking Penguin. A national best-seller. Investigative reporter Randy Shilts provides a compelling account of the chronology of the AIDS epidemic and the lack of governmental response to the AIDS crisis.

Spark, R. F. (1991). *Male sexual health: A couple's guide.* Mount Vernon, NY: Consumer Reports Books. A concise up-to-date guide to male sexual problems ranging from infertility to erectile dysfunction.

Starr, B., & Weiner, M. (1981). *The Starr-Weiner report on sex and sexuality in the mature years.* New York: Stein & Day. Findings of a survey of the sexual interests and practices of a sample of more than 800 people from 60 to 91 years of age.

Stephenson, L. (1987). *Give us a child: Coping with the personal crisis of infertility.* New York: Harper & Row. A sensitive guide to couples coping with infertility.

Sternberg, R. J., & Barnes, M. L. (Eds.) (1988). *The psychology of love.* New Haven, CT: Yale University. Modern scholars examine the concept of love from a scientific standpoint.

Symons, D. (1979). *The evolution of human sexuality.* New York: Oxford University Press. A provocative exploration of the evolutionary roots of human sexuality.

Tannahill, R. (1980). *Sex in history.* New York: Stein & Day. A highly readable and entertaining account of the history of sexual practices and customs in Western and Eastern societies.

Tannen, D. (1990). *You just don't understand: Women and men in conversation.* New York: Morrow. Written by a linguistics professor, this down-to-earth, best-selling book discusses how gender-based differences in conversational styles lead to misunderstandings in relationships between men and women.

Tennov, D. (1979). *Love and limerence: The experience of being in love.* New York: Stein & Day. A clearly written book describing the experience of love.

Warshaw, R. (1988). *I never called it rape.* New York: Harper & Row. A probing review of problem of acquaintance rape and date rape.

Zilbergeld, B. (1992). *The new male sexuality: A guide to sexual fulfillment.* New York: Bantam. A thorough updating of this informative guide to male sexuality.

ABCDE model Levinger's view, which approaches romantic relationships in terms of five stages: attraction, building, continuation, deterioration, and ending.

Acquaintance rape Rape by an acquaintance of the person who is assaulted.

Acquired immunodeficiency syndrome (AIDS) A condition caused by the human immunodeficiency virus (HIV) and characterized by destruction of the immune system so that the body is stripped of its ability to fend off life-threatening diseases.

Activating effects Those effects of sex hormones that influence the level of the sex drive but not sexual orientation.

Agape (AH-gah-pay) Selfless love; a kind of loving that is similar to generosity and charity.

Age of viability The age at which a fetus can sustain independent life.

Amenorrhea The absence of menstruation.

Amniocentesis A procedure for drawing off and examining fetal cells in the amniotic fluid to determine the presence of various disorders in the fetus.

Amniotic fluid Fluid within the amniotic sac that suspends and protects the fetus.

Amniotic sac The sac containing the fetus.

Ampulla A sac or dilated part of a tube or canal; the wide segment of a fallopian tube near the ovary. (A Latin word meaning "bottle.")

Analogous Similar in function.

Analogue Something that is similar or comparable to something else.

Anaphrodisiacs Drugs or other agents whose effects are antagonistic to sexual arousal or sexual desire.

Androgen-insensitivity syndrome A form of pseudohermaphroditism in which a genetic male is prenatally insensitive to androgens. As a result, his genitals do not become normally masculinized.

Androgenital syndrome A form of pseudohermaphroditism in which a genetic female has internal female sexual structures but masculinized external genitals.

Androgens Male sex hormones. (From the Greek *andros*, meaning "man" or "males," and *-gene*, meaning "born.")

Anger rape A vicious, unplanned rape that is triggered by feelings of intense anger and resentment toward women.

Anilingus Oral stimulation of the anus.

Anorexia nervosa A potentially life-threatening eating disorder characterized by refusal to maintain a healthy body weight, intense fear of being overweight, a distorted body image, and, in females, lack of menstruation (amenorrhea.)

Anorgasmic Never having reached orgasm. (Literally, "without orgasm.")

Anovulatory Without ovulation.

Anoxia Oxygen deprivation.

Anthropomorphism The attributing of human characteristics to an animal.

Antiandrogen A substance that decreases the levels of androgens in the bloodstream.

Antiandrogen drug A chemical substance that reduces the sex drive by lowering the level of testosterone in the bloodstream.

Antibodies Specialized proteins produced by the white blood cells of the immune system in response to disease organisms and other toxic substances. Antibodies recognize and attack the invading organisms or substances.

Antigen A protein, toxin, or other substance to which the body reacts by producing antibodies. (Combined word formed from *anti*body *gen*erator.)

Aphrodisiac Any drug or other agent that is sexually arousing or increases sexual desire. (From *Aphrodite*, the Greek goddess of love and beauty.)

Areola The dark ring on the breast that encircles the nipple.

Arthritis A progressive disease that is characterized by inflammation or pain in the joints.

Artificial contraception A method of contraception that applies a human-made device.

Artificial insemination The introduction of sperm in the reproductive tract through means other than sexual intercourse.

Asexuals Bell and Weinberg's term for gay people who live alone and have few sexual contacts.

Asymptomatic Without symptoms.

Autoimmune response The production of antibodies that attack naturally occurring substances that are (incorrectly) recognized as being foreign or harmful.

Autonomic nervous system The division of the nervous system that regulates automatic bodily processes, such as

633

heartbeat, pupil dilation, respiration, and digestion. Abbreviated *ANS*.

Aversion therapy A method for terminating undesirable sexual behavior in which the behavior is repeatedly paired with an aversive stimulus such as electric shock so that a conditioned aversion develops.

Bacteria Plural of *bacterium*, a class of one-celled microorganisms that have no chlorophyll and can give rise to many illnesses. (From the Greek *baktron*, meaning "stick," referring to the fact that many bacteria are rod-shaped.)

Bacterial vaginosis A form of vaginitis usually caused by the *Gardnerella vaginalis* bacterium.

Bartholin's glands Glands that lie just inside the minor lips and secrete fluid just before orgasm.

Basal body temperature (BBT) method A fertility awareness method of contraception that relies on prediction of ovulation by tracking the woman's temperature during the course of the menstrual cycle.

Behavior therapy The systematic application of the principles of learning to help people modify problem behavior.

Behaviorists Learning theorists who argue that a scientific approach to understanding behavior must refer only to observable and measurable behaviors.

Benign Doing little or no harm.

Benign prostatic hyperplasia Enlargement of the prostate gland due to hormonal changes associated with aging and characterized by symptoms such as urinary frequency, urinary urgency, and difficulty starting the flow of urine.

Bestiality Sexual relations between a person and an animal.

Bisexual Sexually responsive to either gender. (From the Latin *bi-*, meaning "two.")

Bisexuality Erotic attraction to, and interest in developing romantic relationships with, males and females.

Blastocyst A stage within the germinal stage of prenatal development at which the embryo is a sphere of cells surrounding a cavity of fluid.

Bondage Ritual restraint, as by shackles, as practiced by many sexual masochists.

Braxton-Hicks contractions So-called false labor contractions that are relatively painless.

Breech presentation Emergence of the baby feetfirst from the womb.

Bulbourethral glands Another term for *Cowper's glands*.

Butch A lesbian who assumes a traditional masculine gender role.

Calendar method A fertility awareness (rhythm) method of contraception that relies on prediction of ovulation by tracking menstrual cycles, typically for a 10- to 12-month period, and assuming that ovulation occurs 14 days before menstruation.

Call girls Prostitutes who arrange for their sexual contacts by telephone. *Call* refers both to telephone calls and to being "on call."

Candidiasis A form of vaginitis caused by a yeastlike fungus, *Candida albicans*.

Case study A carefully drawn, in-depth biography of an individual or a small group of individuals that may be obtained through interviews, questionnaires, and historical records.

Castration anxiety In psychoanalytic theory, a man's fear that his genitals will be removed. Castration anxiety is an element of the Oedipus complex and is implicated in the directionality of erotic interests.

Celibacy Complete sexual abstinence. (Sometimes used to describe the state of being unmarried, especially in the case of people who take vows to remain single.)

Cephalic presentation Emergence of the baby headfirst from the womb.

Cephalocaudal From the head downward. (From Latin roots meaning "head" and "tail.")

Cerebellum A part of the hindbrain that governs muscle coordination and balance.

Cerebral cortex The wrinkled surface area (gray matter) of the cerebrum.

Cerebral palsy A muscular disorder that is caused by damage to the central nervous system (usually before or during birth) and characterized by spastic paralysis.

Cerebrum The large mass of the forebrain, which consists of two hemispheres.

Cervicitis Inflammation of the cervix.

Cervix The lower end of the uterus. (Latin for "neck.")

Cesarean section A method of childbirth in which the fetus is delivered through a surgical incision in the abdomen.

Chancre A sore or ulcer.

Chancroid An STI caused by the *Hemophilus ducreyi* bacterium. Also called *soft chancre*.

Chattel A movable piece of personal property, such as furniture or livestock. (From the Old French word meaning "cattle.")

Chromosomes The rodlike structures that reside in the nuclei of every living cell and carry the genetic code in the form of genes.

Cilia Hairlike projections from cells that beat rhythmically to produce locomotion or currents.

Circumcision Surgical removal of the foreskin of the penis. (From the Latin *circumcidere*, meaning "to cut around.")

Climacteric A long-term process, including menopause, that involves the gradual decline in the reproductive capacity of the ovaries.

Clitoridectomy Surgical removal of the clitoris.

Clitoris A female sex organ consisting of a shaft and glans located above the urethral opening. It is extremely sensitive to sexual sensations.

Cloaca The cavity in birds, reptiles, and many fish into which the genitourinary and intestinal tracts empty. (From the Latin *cluere*, meaning "to cleanse.")

Clomiphene A synthetic hormone that is chemically similar to LH and induces ovulation.

Close couples Bell and Weinberg's term for gay couples whose relationships resemble marriage in their depth of commitment and exclusiveness.

Cohabitation Living together as though married but without legal sanction.

Coitus (co-it-us or co-EET-us) Sexual intercourse.

Coitus interruptus A method of contraception in which the penis is withdrawn from the vagina before ejaculation. Also referred to as the *withdrawal method.*

Comarital sex Swinging; *mate-swapping.*

Combination pill A birth-control pill that contains synthetic estrogen and progesterone.

Complete hysterectomy Surgical removal of the ovaries, fallopian tubes, cervix, and uterus.

Concordance Agreement.

Concubine A secondary wife, usually of inferior legal and social status. (From Latin roots meaning "lying with.")

Condom A sheath made of animal membrane or latex that covers the penis during coitus and serves as a barrier to sperm following ejaculation.

Congenital syphilis A syphilis infection that is present at birth.

Consensual adultery Extramarital sex that is engaged in openly with the knowledge and consent of one's spouse.

Control group A group of study participants who do not receive the experimental treatment. However, other conditions are held comparable to those of individuals in the experimental group.

Conventional adultery Extramarital sex that is kept clandestine (hidden) from one's spouse.

Coprophilia A paraphilia in which sexual arousal is attained in connection with feces. (From the Greek *copros*, meaning "dung.")

Copulation Sexual intercourse. (From the Latin *copulare*, meaning "to unite" or "to couple.")

Corona The ridge that separates the glans from the body of the penis. (From the Latin for "crown.")

Corpora cavernosa Cylinders of spongy tissue in the penis that become congested with blood and stiffen during sexual arousal; masses of spongy tissue in the clitoral shaft that become engorged with blood and stiffen in response to sexual stimulation. (Latin for "cavernous bodies.")

Corpus luteum The follicle that has released an ovum and then produces copious amounts of progesterone and estrogen during the luteal phase of a woman's cycle. (From Latin roots meaning "yellow body.")

Corpus spongiosum The spongy body that runs along the bottom of the penis, contains the penile urethra, and enlarges at the tip of the penis to form the glans.

Correlation A statistical measure of the relationship between two variables.

Correlation coefficient A statistic that expresses the strength and direction (positive or negative) of the relationship between two variables.

Courtesan A prostitute, especially the mistress of a noble or wealthy man. (From Italian roots meaning "court lady.")

Covert sensitization A form of aversion therapy in which thoughts of engaging in undesirable behavior are paired repeatedly with imagined aversive stimuli.

Cowper's glands Structures that lie below the prostate and empty their secretions into the urethra during sexual arousal.

Cremaster muscle The muscle that raises and lowers the testicle in response to temperature changes and sexual stimulation.

Crisis A highly stressful situation that can involve shock, loss of self-esteem, and lessened capacity for making decisions.

Critical fat hypothesis The view that girls must reach a certain body weight to trigger pubertal changes such as menarche.

Critical period of vulnerability A period of time during which an embryo or fetus is vulnerable to the effects of a teratogen.

Cruising The name homosexuals give to searching for a sex partner.

Crura Anatomical structures resembling legs that attach the clitoris to the pubic bone. (Singular: crus. A Latin word meaning "leg" or "shank.")

Cryptorchidism A condition in which one or both testicles fail to descend from the abdomen into the scrotum. (From roots meaning "hidden testes.")

Culpotomy A kind of tubal sterilization in which the fallopian tubes are approached through an incision in the back wall of the vagina.

Cunnilingus Oral stimulation of the female genitals.

Cystitis An inflammation of the urinary bladder. (From the Greek *kystis*, meaning "sac.")

Cysts Saclike structures filled with fluid or diseased material.

D&C Abbreviation for *dilation and curettage*, an operation in which the cervix is dilated and uterine contents are then gently scraped away.

D&E Abbreviation for *dilation and evacuation*, an abortion method in which the cervix is dilated before vacuum aspiration.

Dartos muscle The muscle in the middle layer of the scrotum that contracts and relaxes in response to temperature changes.

Defense mechanisms In psychoanalytic theory, automatic processes that protect the ego from anxiety by disguising or ejecting unacceptable ideas and urges.

Defloration Destruction of the hymen (especially as a cultural ritual).

Demographic Concerning the vital statistics (density, race, age, etc.) of human populations.

Dependent variables The measured results of an experiment, which are believed to be a function of the independent variables.

DES Diethylstilbestrol: an estrogen that was once given to women at risk for miscarriage to help maintain pregnancy.

Diaphragm A shallow rubber cup or dome, fitted to the contour of a woman's vagina, that is coated with a spermicide and inserted before coitus to prevent conception.

Dilate To open or widen.

Dildo A penis-shaped object used in sexual activity.

Displacement In psychoanalytic theory, a defense mechanism that allows one to transfer unacceptable wishes or desires onto more appropriate or less threatening objects.

Dizygotic (DZ) twins Twins who develop from different fertilized ova. Fraternal twins.

DNA Deoxyribonucleic acid, the chemical substance whose molecules make up genes and chromosomes.

Dominican Republic syndrome A form of pseudohermaphroditism in which a genetic enzyme disorder prevents testosterone from masculinizing the external genitalia.

Don Juanism An excessive, insatiable sexual appetite or drive in men. (After the fictional Spanish nobleman who was unable to obtain true sexual gratification despite numerous affairs.)

Donor IVF A variation of in vitro fertilization in which the ovum is taken from one woman, fertilized, and then injected into the uterus or fallopian tube of another woman.

Douche Application of a jet of liquid to the vagina as a rinse. (From the Italian *doccia*, meaning "shower bath.")

Down syndrome A chromosomal abnormality that leads to mental retardation, caused by an extra chromosome on the twenty-first pair.

Dysfunctionals Bell and Weinberg's term for gay people who live alone and have sexual, social, or psychological problems.

Dysmenorrhea Pain or discomfort during menstruation.

Dyspareunia A sexual dysfunction characterized by persistent or recurrent pain during sexual intercourse. (From roots meaning "badly paired.")

Ectoderm The outermost cell layer of the newly formed embryo, from which the skin and nervous system develop.

Ectoparasites Parasites that live on the outside of the host's body—in contrast to *endo*parasites, which live within the body. (From the Greek *ektos*, meaning "outside.")

Ectopic pregnancy A pregancy in which the fertilized ovum implants outside the uterus, usually in the fallopian tube. (*Ectopic* derives from Greek roots meaning "out of place.")

Efface To become thin.

Ego In Freud's theory, the second mental structure to develop, which is characterized by self-awareness, planning, and delay of gratification.

Ejaculatory duct A duct formed by the convergence of a vas deferens with a seminal vesicle through which sperm pass through the prostate gland and into the urethra.

Embryo The stage of prenatal development that begins with implantation of a fertilized ovum in the uterus and concludes with development of the major organ systems at about two months after conception.

Embryonic disk The platelike inner part of the blastocyst, which differentiates into the ectoderm, mesoderm, and endoderm of the embryo.

Embryonic stage The stage of prenatal development that lasts from implantation through the eighth week and is characterized by the differentiation of the major organ systems.

Embryonic transfer A method of conception in which a woman volunteer is artificially inseminated by the male partner of the intended mother, after which the embryo is removed from the volunteer and inserted within the uterus of the intended mother.

Emission phase The first phase of ejaculation, which involves contractions of the prostate gland, seminal vesicles, and the upper part of the vasa deferentia.

Empirical Derived from or based on observation and experimentation.

Endocrine gland A ductless gland that releases its secretions directly into the bloodstream.

Endoderm The inner layer of the newly formed embryo, from which the lungs and digestive system develop.

Endometriosis An abnormal condition in which endometrial tissue is sloughed off into the abdominal cavity rather than out of the body during menstruation. The condition is characterized by abdominal pain and may cause infertility.

Endometrium The innermost layer of the uterus. (From Latin and Greek roots meaning "within the uterus.")

Epididymis A tube that lies against the back wall of each testicle and serves as a storage facility for sperm. (From Greek roots meaning "upon testicles.")

Epididymitis Inflammation of the epididymis.

Episiotomy A surgical incision in the perineum that may be made during childbirth to protect the vagina from tearing. (From the Greek roots *epision*, meaning "pubic region," and *tome*, meaning "cutting.")

Erection The enlargement and stiffening of the penis as a consequence of engorgement with blood.

Erogenous zones Parts of the body that are especially sensitive to tactile sexual stimulation. (*Erogenous* is derived from roots meaning "giving birth to erotic sensations.")

Eros The kind of love that is closest in meaning to the modern-day concept of passion.

Erotic Arousing sexual feelings or desires. (From the Greek word for love, *eros*.)

Erotica Books, pictures, and so on that have to do with sexual love (from the Greek *eros*, meaning "love"). Many contemporary writers use the term *erotica* to refer to sexual material that is artistically produced or motivated by artistic intent.

Estrogen A generic term for female sex hormones (including estradiol, estriol, estrone, and others) or synthetic compounds that promote the development of female sex characteristics and regulate the menstrual cycle. (From the roots meaning "generating" [-*gen*] and "estrus.")

Estrous cycle The female reproductive cycle of most mammals (other than primates), which is under hormonal control and includes a period of heat, followed by ovulation.

Estrus The periodic sexual excitement when female mammals (other than primates) are most receptive to the sexual advances of males.

Ethnocentric Adjectival form of the noun *ethnocentrism*, meaning the tendency to view other groups or cultures according to the standards of one's own. (From the Greek *ethnos*, meaning "race," "culture," or "people," and *kentric*, meaning "center.")

Ethnography The branch of anthropology that deals descriptively with specific cultures, especially preliterate societies.

Evolution The development of a species to its present state, which is believed to involve adaptations to its environment.

Excitement phase The first phase of the sexual response cycle, which is characterized by erection in the male, vaginal lubrication in the female, and muscle tension and increases in heart rate in both males and females.

Exhibitionism A paraphilia characterized by persistent, powerful urges and sexual fantasies involving exposing one's genitals to unsuspecting strangers for the purpose of achieving sexual arousal or gratification.

Experiment A scientific method that seeks to confirm cause-and-effect relationships by manipulating independent variables and observing their effects on dependent variables.

Experimental group A group of study participants who receive a treatment.

Expulsion stage The second stage of ejaculation, during which muscles at the base of the penis and elsewhere contract rhythmically, forcefully expelling semen and providing pleasurable sensations.

Extramarital sex Sexual relations between a married person and someone other than his or her spouse.

Fallopian tubes Tubes that extend from the upper uterus toward the ovaries and conduct ova to the uterus. (After the Italian anatomist Gabriello Fallopio, who is credited with their discovery.)

Fellatio Oral stimulation of the male genitals.

Female-superior position A coital position in which the woman is on top.

Femme A lesbian who assumes a traditional feminine gender role.

Fetal alcohol syndrome A cluster of symptoms caused by maternal drinking, in which the child shows developmental lags and characteristic facial features such as an underdeveloped upper jaw, a flattened nose, and widely spaced eyes.

Fetishism A paraphilia in which an inanimate object such as an article of clothing or items made of rubber, leather, or silk elicit sexual arousal.

Fibroadenoma A benign, fibrous tumor.

Fimbriae Projections from a fallopian tube that extend toward an ovary. (Singular: fimbria. Latin for "fiber" or "fringe.")

Fixation In psychoanalytic theory, arrested development, which includes attachment to objects of an earlier stage of psychosexual development.

Follicle A capsule within an ovary that contains an ovum. (From a Latin word meaning "small bag.")

Follicle-stimulating hormone (FSH) A gonadotropin that stimulates development of follicles in the ovaries.

Forcible rape Sexual intercourse with a nonconsenting person that is obtained by the use of force or the threat of force.

Foreplay Mutual sexual stimulation that precedes sexual intercourse.

Foreskin The loose skin that covers the penile glans. Also referred to as the *prepuce*.

Fornication Sexual intercourse between people who are not married to one another. (If one of the partners is married, the act may be labeled *adultery*.)

Frenulum The sensitive strip of tissue that connects the underside of the penile glans to the shaft. (From the Latin *frenum*, meaning "bridle.")

Frequency The number of times an action is repeated within a given period.

Frotteurism A paraphilia characterized by recurrent, powerful sexual urges and related fantasies involving rubbing against or touching a nonconsenting person. (From the French *frotter*, meaning "to rub.")

Functionals Bell and Weinberg's term for gay people who live alone, have adapted well to a swinging lifestyle, and are sociable and well adjusted.

Fundus The uppermost part of the uterus. (*Fundus* is a Latin word meaning "base.")

Gamete intrafallopian transfer (GIFT) A method of conception in which sperm and ova are inserted into a fallopian tube to encourage conception.

Gay bashing Violence against homosexuals.

Gay males Males who are erotically attracted to and desire to form romantic relationships with other males.

Gender One's personal, social, and legal status as male or female.

Gender assignment The labeling of a newborn as a male or female.

Gender constancy The concept that people's genders do not change, even if they alter their dress or behavior.

Gender dysphoria The subjective experience of incongruity between genital anatomy and gender identity or role.

Gender identity The psychological sense of being male or female.

Gender roles Complex clusters of ways in which males and females are expected to behave within a given culture.

Gender schema A cluster of mental representations about male and female physical qualities, behaviors, and personality traits.

Gender stability The concept that people retain their genders for a lifetime.

Gender typing The process by which children acquire behavior that is deemed appropriate to their gender.

General anesthesia The use of drugs to put people to sleep and eliminate pain, as during childbirth.

General paresis A progressive form of mental illness caused by neurosyphilis and characterized by gross confusion.

Generalize To go from the particular to the general.

Genes The basic units of heredity, which consist of chromosomal segments of DNA.

Genital herpes An STI caused by the herpes simplex virus type 2 and characterized by painful shallow sores and blisters on the genitals.

Genital warts An STI that is caused by the human papilloma virus and takes the form of warts that appear around the genitals and anus.

Germ cell A cell from which a new organism develops. (From the Latin *germen*, meaning "bud" or "sprout.")

Germinal stage The period of prenatal development before implantation in the uterus.

Gonadotropin-releasing hormone (Gn-RH) A hormone secreted by the hypothalamus that stimulates the pituitary to release gonadotropins.

Gonadotropins Pituitary hormones that stimulate the gonads. (Literally, "that which feeds the gonads").

Gonorrhea An STI that is caused by the *Neisseria gonorrhoeae* bacterium and characterized by a discharge and burning urination. Left untreated, gonorrhea can give rise to pelvic inflammatory disease (PID) and infertility. (From the Greek *gonos*, meaning "seed," and *rheein*, meaning "to flow," referring to the fact that in ancient times, the penile discharge characteristic of the illness as erroneously interpreted as a loss of seminal fluid.)

Grafenberg spot A part of the anterior wall of the vagina, whose prolonged stimulation is theorized to cause particularly intense orgasms and a female ejaculation. Abbreviated *G-spot*.

Granuloma inguinale A tropical STI caused by the *Calymmatobacterium granulomatis* bacterium.

Group marriage A social arrangement in which three or more people share an intimate relationship. Group marriages are illegal in the United States.

Gynecologist A physician who treats women's diseases, especially of the reproductive tract. (From the Greek *gyne*, meaning "woman.")

Gynecomastia Overdevelopment of a male's breasts. (From Greek roots meaning "woman" [*gyne*] and "breast" [*mastos*].)

Hegar's sign Softness of a section of the uterus between the uterine body and the cervix, which indicates that a woman is pregnant.

Hepatitis An inflammation of the liver. (From the Greek *hepar*, meaning "liver.")

Hermaphrodites People who possess both ovarian and testicular tissue. (From the names of the male and female Greek gods *Hermes* and *Aphrodite*.)

Herpes simplex virus type 1 The virus that causes oral herpes, which is characterized by cold sores or fever blisters on the lips or mouth. Abbreviated *HSV-1*.

Herpes simplex virus type 2 The virus that causes genital herpes. Abbreviated *HSV-2*.

Heteroerotic Of an erotic nature and involving members of the other gender.

Heterosexual orientation Erotic attraction to, and preference for developing romantic relationships with, members of the other gender.

Homoerotic Of an erotic nature and involving members of one's own gender.

Homogamy The practice of marrying people who are similar in social background and standing. (From Greek roots meaning "same" [*homos*] and "marriage" [*gamos*].)

Homologous Similar in structure; developing from the same embryonic tissue.

Homophobia A cluster of negative attitudes and feelings toward gay people, including intolerance, hatred, and fear. (From Greek roots meaning "fear" [of members of the] "same" [gender]).

Homosexual orientation Erotic attraction to, and preference for developing romantic relationships with, members of one's own gender. (From the Greek *homos*, meaning "same," not the Latin *homo*, which means "man").

Hormone-replacement therapy (HRT) Replacement of naturally occurring estrogen or estrogen and progesterone with synthetic equivalents, following menopause.

Hormone A substance secreted by an endocrine gland that regulates various body functions. (From the Greek *horman*, meaning "to stimulate" or "to goad.")

Human chorionic gonadotropin A hormone produced by women shortly after conception that stimulates the corpus luteum to continue to produce progesterone. The presence of HCG in a woman's urine indicates that she is pregnant.

Human immunodeficiency virus (HIV) A sexually transmitted virus that destroys white blood cells in the immune system, leaving the body vulnerable to life-threatening diseases.

Human sexuality The ways in which we experience and express ourselves as sexual beings.

Hustlers Men who engage in prostitution with male customers.

Hyaluronidase An enzyme that briefly thins the zona pellucida, enabling one sperm to penetrate. (From roots meaning "substance that breaks down a glasslike fluid.")

Hymen A fold of tissue across the vaginal opening that is usually present at birth and remains at least partly intact until a woman engages in coitus. (Greek for "membrane.")

Hypersexuality An excessive or apparently insatiable sex drive that disrupts the person's ability to concentrate on other needs or leads to self-defeating behavior, such as indiscriminate sexual contacts.

Hypogonadism An endocrine disorder that reduces the output of testosterone.

Hypothalamus A brain structure below the thalamus that regulates body temperature, motivation, and emotion.

Hypothesis A precise prediction about behavior that is tested through research.

Hypoxyphilia A practice in which a person seeks to enhance sexual arousal, usually during masturbation, by becoming deprived of oxygen. (From the Greek root meaning "under" [*hypo-*].)

Hysterectomy Surgical removal of the uterus. (*Not* appropriate as a method of sterilization.)

Hysterosalpingogram A test in which a dye is injected into the reproductive tract and its progress is tracked by X-rays to determine whether or not the fallopian tubes are blocked. (From roots meaning "uterus," "fallopian tubes," and "record of.")

Hysterotomy An abortion method in which the fetus is removed by cesarean section.

Id In Freud's theory, the mental structure that is present at birth, embodies physiological drives, and is fully unconscious.

Identification In psychoanalytic theory, the process of incorporating within ourselves our perceptions of the behaviors, thoughts, and feelings of others.

Immune system A term for the body's complex of mechanisms for protecting itself from disease-causing agents such as pathogens.

Impotence Recurrent difficulty in achieving or sustaining an erection sufficient to successfully engage in sexual intercourse. (The term has been replaced by the terms *male erectile disorder* or *erectile dysfunction*, as discussed in Chapter 15.)

In vitro fertilization (IVF) A method of conception in which mature ova are surgically removed from an ovary and placed in a laboratory dish along with sperm.

Incest Marriage or sexual relations between people who are so closely related (by "blood") that sexual relations are prohibited and punishable by law. (From the Latin *in-*, meaning "not," and *castus*, meaning "chaste.")

Incest taboo The prohibition against intercourse and reproduction among close blood relatives.

Incidence A measure of the occurrence or the degree of occurrence of an event.

Independent variable A condition in a scientific study that is manipulated so that its effects may be observed.

Induced abortion The purposeful termination of a pregnancy before the embryo or fetus is capable of sustaining independent life. (From the Latin *abortio*, meaning "that which is miscarried.")

Infatuation A state of intense absorption in or focus on another person, which is usually accompanied by sexual desire, elation, and general physiological arousal or excitement; passion.

Inference Conclusion or opinion.

Infertility Inability to conceive a child.

Inflammation Redness and warmth that develop at the site of an injury, reflecting dilation of blood vessels that permits the expanded flow of leukocytes to the region.

Informed consent The term used by researchers to indicate that people have agreed to participate in research after receiving information about the purposes and nature of the study, and its potential risks and benefits.

Infundibulum The outer, funnel-shaped part of a fallopian tube. (A Latin word meaning "funnel.")

Inguinal canal A fetal canal that connects the scrotum and the testes, allowing their descent. (From the Latin *inguinus*, meaning "near the groin.")

Interstitial cells Cells that lie between the seminiferous tubules and secrete testosterone. (*Interstitial* means "set between.")

Intimacy Feelings of closeness and connectedness that are marked by sharing of inmost thoughts and feelings.

Intra-amniotic infusion An abortion method in which a substance is injected into the amniotic sac to induce premature labor. Also called *instillation*.

Intracytoplasmic sperm injection A method of conception in which a single sperm is injected directly into an ovum.

Intrauterine device A small object that is inserted into the uterus and left in place to prevent conception. Abbreviated *IUD*.

Introitus The vaginal opening. (From the Latin for "entrance.")

Isthmus The segment of a fallopian tube closest to the uterus. (A Latin word meaning "narrow passage.")

Jaundice A yellowish discoloration of the skin and the whites of the eyes. (From the Old French *jaune*, meaning "yellow.")

Klinefelter's syndrome A sex-chromosomal disorder caused by an extra X sex chromosome.

Klismaphilia A paraphilia in which sexual arousal is derived from use of enemas.

Labia majora Large folds of skin that run downward from the mons along the sides of the vulva. (Latin for "large lips" or "major lips.")

Labia minora hairless, light-colored membranes, located between the labia majora. (Latin for "small lips" or "minor lips.")

Lactation Production of milk by the mammary glands.

Lamaze method A childbirth method in which women learn about childbirth, learn to relax and to breathe in patterns that conserve energy and lessen pain, and have a coach (usually the father) present at childbirth. Also termed *prepared childbirth*.

Laparoscopy A medical procedure in which a long, narrow tube (laparoscope) is inserted through an incision in the navel, permitting the visual inspection of organs in the pelvic cavity, tubal sterilization by means of a laparoscope, used to cauterize, cut, or clamp the fallopian tubes. Sometimes referred to as "belly button surgery." (From the Greek *lapara*, meaning "flank.")

Larynx A structure of muscle and cartilage at the upper end of the trachea that contains the vocal cords; the voice box.

Lesbians Females who are erotically attracted to, and desire to form romantic relationships with, other females. (After *Lesbos*, the Greek island on which, legend has it, female-female sexual activity was idealized).

Leukocytes White blood cells that are essential to the body's defenses against infection. (From the Greek *leukos*, meaning "white," and *kytos*, meaning "a hollow," and used in combination with other word forms to mean *cell*.)

Leydig's cells Another term for *interstitial cells*.

Limbic system A group of structures active in memory, motivation, and emotion; the structures that are part of this system form a fringe along the inner edge of the cerebrum.

Local anesthesia Anesthesia that eliminates pain in a specific area of the body, as during childbirth.

Lochia A reddish vaginal discharge that may persist for a month after delivery. (From the Greek *lochios*, meaning "of childbirth.")

Lovemap A mentally ingrained representation of the idealized lover and the idealized erotic activity with the lover.

Lumpectomy Surgical removal of a lump from the breast.

Luteinizing hormone (LH) A gonadotropin that helps regulate the menstrual cycle by triggering ovulation.

Lymphogranuloma venereum A tropical STI caused by the *Chlamydia trachomatis* bacterium.

Male erectile disorder Persistent difficulty in achieving or maintaining an erection sufficient to allow the man to engage in or complete sexual intercourse. Also termed *erectile dysfunction*.

Male-superior position. A coital position in which the man is on top.

Malignant Lethal; causing or likely to cause death.

Mammary glands Milk-secreting glands. (From the Latin *mamma*, which means both "breast" and "mother.")

Mammography A special type of X-ray test that detects cancerous lumps in the breast.

Mastalgia A swelling of the breasts that sometimes causes premenstrual discomfort.

Mastectomy Surgical removal of the entire breast.

Masturbation Sexual self-stimulation.

Matching hypothesis The concept that people tend to develop romantic relationships with people who are similar to themselves in attractiveness.

Mating gradient The tendency for women to "marry up" (in social or economic status) and for men to "marry down."

Medulla An oblong area of the hindbrain that is involved in regulation of heartbeat and respiration.

Menarche The onset of menstruation; first menstruation. (From Greek roots meaning "month" [*men*] and "beginning" [*arche*].)

Menopause The cessation of menstruation.

Menstrual phase The fourth phase of the menstrual cycle, during which the endometrium is sloughed off in the menstrual flow.

Menstruation The cyclical bleeding that stems from the shedding of the uterine lining (endometrium).

Mesoderm The central layer of the embryo, from which the bones and muscles develop.

Minilaparotomy A kind of tubal sterilization in which a small incision is made in the abdomen to provide access to the fallopian tubes.

Minipill A birth-control pill that contains synthetic progesterone but no estrogen.

Miscarriage A spontaneous abortion.

Missionary position The coital position in which the man is on top. Also termed the *male-superior position*.

Mittelschmerz Pain that occurs during ovulation. (German for "middle pain," reflecting the fact that the pain occurs midway between menstrual periods).

Modeling Acquiring knowledge and skills by observing and imitating others.

Molluscum contagiosum An STI caused by a pox virus that causes painless raised lesions to appear on the genitals, buttocks, thighs, or lower abdomen.

Monogamy Marriage to one person. (From the Greek *mono-*, meaning "single" or "alone.")

Monozygotic (MZ) twins Twins who develop from the same fertilized ovum. Identical twins.

Mons veneris A mound of fatty tissue that covers the joint of the pubic bones in front of the body, below the abdomen and above the clitoris. (The name is a Latin phrase meaning hill or "mount of Venus," the Roman goddess of love. Also known as the *mons pubis*, or simply *mons*.)

Morning sickness Symptoms of pregnancy, including nausea, aversions to specific foods, and vomiting.

Motility Self-propulsion. A measure of the viability of sperm cells.

Multiple orgasms One or more additional orgasms following the first, which occur within a short period of time and before the body has returned to a preplateau level of arousal.

Mutations Random changes in the molecular structure of DNA.

Mutuality A phase in building a relationship in which members of a couple come to regard themselves as "we," no longer two "I's" who happen to be in the same place at the same time.

Myometrium The middle, well-muscled layer of the uterus. (*Myo-* stems from the Greek *mys*, meaning "muscle.")

Myotonia Muscle tension.

Natural childbirth A method of childbirth in which women use no anesthesia but are given other strategies for coping with discomfort and are educated about childbirth.

Natural selection The evolutionary process by which adaptive traits enable members of a species to survive to reproductive age and transmit these traits to future generations.

Naturalistic observation A method in which organisms are observed in their natural environments.

Necrophilia A paraphilia characterized by desire for sexual activity with corpses. (From the Greek *nekros*, meaning "dead body.")

Neural tube A hollow area in the blastocyst from which the nervous system will develop.

Neurosyphilis Syphilitic infection of the central nervous system, which can cause brain damage and death.

Neurotransmitter A chemical that transmits messages from one brain cell to another.

Nocturnal emission Involuntary ejaculation of seminal fluid while asleep. Also referred to as a "wet dream," although the individual need not be dreaming about sex, or dreaming at all, at the time.

Nymphomania An excessive, insatiable sexual appetite or drive in women. (From the Greek roots *nymphe*, meaning "a bride," and *mania*, which means "madness.")

Obscenity That which offends people's feelings or goes beyond prevailing standards of decency or modesty. (From the Latin *caenum*, meaning "filth.")

Observer effect A distortion of individuals' behavior caused by the act of observation.

Ocular herpes A herpes infection of the eye, usually caused by touching an infected area of the body and then touching the eye.

Oedipus complex In psychoanalytic theory, a conflict of the phallic stage in which the boy wishes to possess his mother sexually and perceives his father as a rival in love. (The analogous conflict for girls is the *Electra complex*.)

Open couples Bell and Weinberg's term for gay couples who live together but engage in secret affairs.

Open marriage A marriage that is characterized by the personal privacy of the spouses and the agreed-upon liberty of each spouse to form intimate relationships, which may include sexually intimate relationships, with people other than the spouse.

Operational definition A definition of a construct or variable in terms of the methods used to measure it.

Ophthalmia neonatorum A gonorrheal infection of the eyes of newborn children, who contract the disease by passing through an infected birth canal. (From the Greek *ophthalmos*, meaning "eye.")

Opportunistic diseases Diseases that take hold only when the immune system is weakened and unable to fend them off.

Kaposi's sarcoma and *Pneumocystis carinii* pneumonia (PCP) are examples of opportunistic diseases found in people with AIDS.

Oral contraceptive A contraceptive, consisting of sex hormones, that is taken by mouth.

Orgasm The climax of sexual excitement.

Orgasmic disorders Sexual dysfunctions in which people persistently or recurrently have difficulty reaching orgasm or reach orgasm more rapidly than they would like, despite attaining a level of sexual stimulation of sufficient intensity to normally result in orgasm.

Orgasmic platform The thickening of the walls of the outer third of the vagina, due to vasocongestion, that occurs during the plateau phase of the sexual response cycle.

Orgasmic reconditioning A method for strengthening the connection between sexual arousal and appropriate sexual stimuli (such as fantasies about an adult of the other gender) by repeatedly pairing the desired stimuli with orgasm.

Os The opening in middle of the cervix. (Latin for "mouth.")

Osteoporosis A condition caused by estrogen deficiency and characterized by a decline in bone density, such that bones become porous and brittle. (From the Greek *osteon*, meaning "bone," and the Latin *porus*, meaning "pore.")

Outercourse Forms of sexual expression, such as massage, hugging, caressing, mutual masturbation, and rubbing bodies together that do not involve the exchange of body fluids. (Contrast with *intercourse*.)

Outing The revelation of the identities of gay people by other gay people. The method is intended to combat discrimination against gay people by forcing individuals out of the closet and into the fray.

Ova Egg cells. (Singular: ovum.)

Ovariectomy Surgical removal of the ovaries.

Ovaries Almond-shaped organs that produce ova and the hormones estrogen and progesterone.

Ovulation The release of an ovum from an ovary.

Ovulation method A fertility awareness method of contraception that relies on prediction of ovulation by tracking the viscosity of the cervical mucus.

Ovulatory phase The second stage of the menstrual cycle, during which a follicle ruptures and releases a mature ovum.

Oxytocin A pituitary hormone that stimulates uterine contractions in labor and the ejection of milk during nursing.

Pap test A test of a sample of cervical cells that screens for cervical cancer and other abnormalities. (Named after the originator of the technique, Dr. Papanicolaou.)

Paraphilia A diagnostic category used by the American Psychiatric Association to describe atypical patterns of sexual arousal or behavior that become problematic in the eyes of the individual or society, such as fetishism or exhibitionism. The urges are recurrent and either are acted on or are distressing to the individual. (From Greek roots meaning "to the side of" [*para-*] and "loving" [*philos*].)

Paraplegic A person with sensory and motor paralysis of the lower half of the body.

Parasympathetic The branch of the ANS that is most active during processes that restore the body's reserves of energy, such as digestion. The parasympathetic ANS largely controls erection.

Partialism A paraphilia related to fetishism in which sexual arousal is exaggeratedly associated with a particular body part, such as feet, breasts, or buttocks.

Participant observation A method in which observers interact with the people they study as they collect data.

Pathogen An agent, especially a microorganism, that can cause a disease. (From the Greek *pathos*, meaning "suffering" or "disease," and *genic*, meaning "forming" or "coming into being.")

Patriarchy A form of social organization in which the father or eldest male runs the group or family; government, rule, or domination by men. (From the Greek *pater*, meaning "father," and *archein*, meaning "to rule.")

Peak days The days during the menstrual cycle during which a woman is most likely to be fertile.

Pederasty Sexual love of boys. (From the Greek *paidos*, meaning "boy.")

Pediculosis A parasitic infestation by pubic lice (*Phthirus pubis*) that causes itching.

Pedophile A person with pedophilia, a paraphilia involving sexual interest in children.

Pedophilia A type of paraphilia that is defined by sexual attraction to unusual stimuli: children. (From the Greek *paidos*, meaning "child," not the Latin *pedis*, meaning "foot.")

Pelvic inflammatory disease Inflammation of the pelvic region—possibly including the cervix, uterus, fallopian tubes, abdominal cavity, and ovaries—that can be caused by organisms such as *Neisseria gonorrhoeae*. Its symptoms are abdominal pain, tenderness, nausea, fever, and irregular menstrual cycles. The condition may lead to infertility. Abbreviated *PID*.

Penile strain gauge A device for measuring sexual arousal in men in terms of changes in the circumference of the penis.

Penis The male organ of sexual intercourse. (From the Latin for "tail.")

Penis envy In psychoanalytic theory, the girl's wish to have a penis.

Performance anxiety Feelings of dread and foreboding experienced in connection with sexual activity (or any other activity that might be judged by another person).

Perimetrium The outer layer of the uterus. (From roots meaning "around the uterus.")

Perineum The skin and underlying tissue that lie between the vaginal opening and the anus. (From Greek roots meaning "around" and "to empty out.")

Period of the ovum The germinal stage.

Peyronie's disease An abnormal condition characterized by an excessive curvature of the penis that can make erections painful.

Phallic symbols Images of the penis that are usually suggestive of generative power.

Phallic worship Worship of the penis as a symbol of generative power.

Pharyngeal gonorrhea A gonorrheal infection of the pharynx (the cavity leading from the mouth and nasal passages to the larynx and esophagus) that is characterized by a sore throat.

Pheromones Chemical substances, secreted externally by certain animals, which convey information to, or produce specific responses in, other members of the same species. (From the Greek *pherien*, meaning "to bear [a message]" and *hormone*.)

Philia (FEEL-yuh) Friendship love, which is based on liking and respect rather than sexual desire.

Phimosis An abnormal condition in which the foreskin is so tight that it cannot be withdrawn from the glans. (From the Greek *phimos*, meaning "muzzle.")

Pimps Men who serve as agents for prostitutes and live off their earnings. (From the Middle French *pimper*, meaning "to dress smartly.")

Pituitary gland The gland that secretes growth hormone, prolactin, oxytocin, and others.

Placenta An organ connected to the fetus by the umbilical cord. The placenta serves as a relay station between mother and fetus, allowing the exchange of nutrients and wastes.

Plateau phase The second phase of the sexual response cycle, which is characterized by increases in vasocongestion, muscle tension, heart rate, and blood pressure in preparation for orgasm.

Polyandry A form of marriage in which a woman has two or more husbands. (From the Greek *andros*, meaning "man" or "male.")

Polygamy The practice of having two or more spouses at the same time. (From the Greek roots meaning "many" [*poly-*] and "marriage" [*gamos*].)

Polygyny A form of marriage in which a man has two or more wives. (From the Greek *gyne*, meaning "woman.")

Polymorphous perverse In psychoanalytic theory, being receptive to all forms of sexual stimulation.

Pons A structure of the hindbrain that regulates respiration, attention, sleep, and dreaming.

Population A complete group of organisms or events.

Pornography Written, visual, or audiotaped material that is sexually explicit and produced for purposes of eliciting or enhancing sexual arousal. (From Greek roots meaning "to write about prostitutes.")

Postpartum Following birth.

Postpartum depression Persistent and severe mood changes during the postpartum period, involving feelings of despair and apathy and characterized by changes in appetite and sleep, low self-esteem, and difficulty concentrating.

Posttraumatic stress disorder A type of stress reaction brought on by a traumatic event and characterized by flashbacks of the experience in the form of disturbing dreams or intrusive recollections, a sense of emotional numbing or restricted range of feelings, and heightened body arousal. Abbreviated *PTSD*.

Power rape Rape that is motivated by the desire to control and dominate the person who is assaulted.

Premature ejaculation A sexual dysfunction in which the male persistently ejaculates too early to afford the couple adequate sexual gratification.

Premenstrual syndrome (PMS) A combination of physical and psychological symptoms (e.g., anxiety, depression, irritability, weight gain from fluid retention, and abdominal discomfort) that regularly afflicts many women during the four- to six-day interval that precedes their menses each month.

Prepuce The fold of skin covering the glans of the clitoris (or penis). (From Latin roots meaning "before a swelling.")

Preterm Born prior to 37 weeks of gestation.

Primary amenorrhea Lack of menstruation in a woman who has never menstruated.

Primary dysmenorrhea Menstrual pain or discomfort that occurs in the absence of known organic problems.

Primary erogenous zones Erogenous zones that are particularly sensitive because they are richly endowed with nerve endings.

Primary sex characteristics Physical characteristics that differentiate males and females and are directly involved in reproduction, such as the sex organs.

Probability sample A sample in which the probability of inclusion in the sample of any particular member is known.

Prodromal symptoms Warning symptoms that signal the onset or flare-up of a disease. (From the Greek *prodromos,* meaning "forerunner.")

Progesterone A steroid hormone secreted by the corpus luteum or prepared synthetically that stimulates proliferation of the endometrium and is involved in regulation of the menstrual cycle.

Prolactin A pituitary hormone that stimulates production of milk. (From roots meaning "for milk.")

Proliferative phase The first phase of the menstrual cycle, which begins with the end of menstruation and lasts about nine or ten days. During this phase, the endometrium proliferates.

Prophylactic An agent that protects against disease.

Prostaglandins Hormones that cause muscle fibers in the uterine wall to contract, as during labor.

Prostate gland The gland that lies beneath the bladder and secretes prostatic fluid, which gives semen its characteristic odor and texture.

Prostatitis Inflammation of the prostate gland.

Prostitution The sale of sexual activity for money or goods of value, such as drugs. (From the Latin *prostituere,* meaning "to cause to stand in front of." The implication is that one is offering one's body for sale.)

Proximodistal From the central axis of the body outward. (From Latin roots meaning "near" and "far.")

Prurient Tending to excite lust; lewd. (From the Latin *prurire,* meaning "to itch" in the sense of "to long for.")

Pseudohermaphrodites People who possess the gonads of one gender but external genitalia that are ambiguous or typical of the other gender.

Psychoanalysis The theory of personality originated by Sigmund Freud, which proposes that human behavior represents the outcome of clashing inner forces.

Psychological androgyny Possession of stereotypical masculine traits, such as assertiveness and instrumental skills, along with stereotypical feminine traits, such as expressiveness, nurturance, and cooperation.

Psychosexual development In psychoanalytic theory, the process by which sexual feelings shift from one erogenous zone to another.

Puberty The stage of development during which reproduction first becomes possible. Puberty begins with the appearance of secondary sex characteristics and ends when the long bones make no further gains in length. (From the Latin *puber,* meaning "of ripe age.")

Pubococcygeus muscle The muscle that encircles the entrance to the vagina.

Pudendum The external female genitals.

Radiotherapy Treatment of a disease by X-rays or by emissions from a radioactive substance.

Random sample A sample in which every member of a population has an equal chance of participating.

Rape Sexual intercourse that takes place as a result of force or threats of force rather than consent. (The legal definition of rape varies from state to state.) See also *forcible rape* and *statutory rape.*

Rape trauma syndrome A two-phase reaction to rape that is characterized by disruption of the survivor's lifestyle (the acute phase) and reorganization of the survivor's life (the long-term phase).

Recessive trait A trait that is not expressed when the gene or genes involved have been paired with dominant genes. Recessive traits are transmitted to future generations, however, and are expressed if they are paired with other recessive genes.

Reciprocity Mutual exchange.

Reflex A simple, unlearned response to a stimulus that is mediated by the spine rather than the brain.

Refractory period A period of time following a response (e.g., orgasm) during which an individual is no longer responsive to stimulation (e.g., sexual stimulation).

Reliability The consistency or accuracy of a measure.

Repression In psychoanalytic theory, the most basic defense mechanism through which threatening ideas and impulses are ejected from conscious awareness.

Resolution phase The fourth phase of the sexual response cycle, during which the body gradually returns to its prearoused state.

Respiratory distress syndrome A cluster of breathing problems, including weak and irregular breathing, to which preterm babies are especially vulnerable.

Reticular activating system A part of the brain that is active during attention, sleep, and arousal.

Retrograde ejaculation Ejaculation in which the ejaculate empties into the bladder. (From the Latin *retrogradi*, meaning "to go backward.")

Rh incompatibility A condition in which antibodies produced by a pregnant woman are transmitted to the fetus and may cause brain damage or death.

Romantic love A kind of love characterized by feelings of passion and intimacy.

Root The base of the penis, which extends into the pelvis.

Rubella A viral infection that can cause mental retardation and heart disease in an embryo. Also called *German measles*.

Rubin test A test in which carbon dioxide gas is blown through the cervix and its progress through the reproductive tract is tracked to determine whether or not the fallopian tubes are blocked.

Sacrum The thick, triangular bone located near the bottom of the spinal column.

Sadism The practice of achieving sexual gratification through hurting or humiliating others.

Sadistic rape A highly ritualized, savage rape in which the person who is attacked is subjected to painful and humiliating experiences and threats.

Sadomasochism A mutually gratifying sexual interaction between consenting sex partners in which sexual arousal is associated with the infliction and receipt of pain or humiliation. Commonly known as *S&M*.

Sample Part of a population.

Satyriasis An excessive, insatiable sexual appetite or drive in men. (After *satyr*, a sexually insatiable, goat-legged creature with pointed ears and short horns in Greek mythology. Satyrs were part man, part beast.)

Scabies A parasitic infestation caused by a tiny mite (*Sarcoptes scabiei*) that causes itching.

Schema Concept; way of interpreting experience or processing information.

Scores Customers of hustlers.

Scrotum The pouch of loose skin that contains the testes. (From the same linguistic root as the word *shred*, meaning "a long, narrow strip," and probably referring to the long furrows on the scrotal sac.)

Secondary amenorrhea Lack of menstruation in a woman who has previously menstruated.

Secondary dysmenorrhea Menstrual pain or discomfort that is caused by identified organic problems.

Secondary erogenous zones Parts of the body that become erotically sensitized through experience.

Secondary sex characteristics Physical characteristics that differentiate males and females and that usually appear at puberty but are not directly involved in reproduction, such as the bodily distribution of hair and fat, development of the muscle mass, and deepening of the voice.

Secretory phase The third phase of the menstrual cycle, which follows ovulation. Also referred to as the *luteal phase*, after the *corpus luteum*, which begins to secrete large amounts of progesterone and estrogen following ovulation.

Selection factor A bias that may operate in research when people are allowed to determine whether or not they will receive a treatment.

Self-disclosure The revelation of personal, perhaps intimate, information.

Semen The whitish fluid that constitutes the ejaculate, consisting of sperm and secretions from the seminal vesicles, prostate, and Cowper's glands.

Seminal vesicles Small glands that lie behind the bladder and secrete fluids that combine with sperm in the ejaculatory ducts.

Seminiferous tubules Tiny, winding, sperm-producing tubes that are located within the lobes of the testes. (From Latin roots meaning "seed bearing.")

Sensate focus exercises Exercises in which sex partners take turns giving and receiving pleasurable stimulation in nongenital areas of the body.

Serial monogamy A pattern of involvement in one exclusive relationship after another, as opposed to engaging in multiple sexual relationships at the same time.

Seronegative Lacking a pathogen or antibodies to that pathogen in the bloodstream.

Seropositive Having a pathogen or antibodies to that pathogen in the bloodstream.

Sex flush A reddish rash that appears on the chest or breasts late in the excitement phase of the sexual response cycle.

Sex skin Reddening of the labia minora that occurs during the plateau phase.

Sex therapy A collective term for short-term behavioral models for treatment of sexual dysfunctions.

Sexism The prejudgment that because of gender, a person will possess negative traits.

Sexologist A person who engages in the scientific study of sexual behavior.

Sexual arousal disorders Sexual dysfunctions in which people persistently or recurrently fail to become adequately sexually aroused to engage in or sustain sexual intercourse.

Sexual assault Any sexual activity that involves the use of force or the threat of force.

Sexual desire disorders Sexual dysfunctions in which people have persistent or recurrent lack of sexual desire or aversion to sexual contact.

Sexual differentiation The process by which males and females develop distinct reproductive anatomy.

Sexual dysfunctions Persistent or recurrent difficulties in becoming sexually aroused or reaching orgasm.

Sexual harassment Deliberate or repeated unsolicited verbal comments, gestures, or physical contact of a sexual nature that is considered to be unwelcome by the recipient.

Sexual masochism A paraphilia characterized by the desire or need for pain or humiliation to enhance sexual arousal so that gratification may be attained. (From the name of Leopold von Sacher-Masoch.)

Sexual orientation The directionality of one's sexual interests—toward members of the same gender, the other gender, or both genders.

Sexual pain disorders Sexual dysfunctions in which people persistently or recurrently experience pain during coitus.

Sexual response cycle Masters and Johnson's model of sexual response, which consists of four phases.

Sexual sadism A paraphilia characterized by the desire or need to inflict pain or humiliation on others to enhance sexual arousal so that gratification is attained. (From the name of Marquis de Sade.)

Sexual sadists People who become sexually aroused by inflicting pain or humiliation on others.

Sexually transmitted infections (STIs) Infections that are communicated through sexual contact. Some, such as HIV/AIDS, can also be transmitted in other ways.)

Shaft The body of the penis, which expands as a result of vasocongestion.

Shigellosis An STI caused by the *Shigella* bacterium.

Small talk A superficial kind of conversation that allows exchange of information but stresses breadth of topic coverage rather than in-depth discussion.

Social desirability A response bias to a questionnaire or interview in which the person provides a socially acceptable response.

Social-exchange theory The view that the development of a relationship reflects the unfolding of social exchanges—that is, the rewards and costs of maintaining the relationship as opposed to ending it.

Social-learning theory A cognitively oriented learning theory in which observational learning, values, and expectations play key roles in determining behavior.

Social skills training Behavior therapy methods for building social skills that rely on a therapist's coaching and practice.

Socialization The process of guiding people into socially acceptable behavior patterns by means of information, rewards, and punishments.

Sociobiology The theory that dispositions toward behavior patterns that enhance reproductive success may be genetically transmitted.

Spectator role A role, usually taken on because of performance anxiety, in which people observe rather than fully participate in their sexual encounters.

Sperm The male germ cell. (From a Greek root meaning "seed.")

Spermatic cord The cord that suspends a testicle within the scrotum and contains a vas deferens, blood vessels, nerves, and the cremaster muscle.

Spermatids Cells formed by the division of spermatocytes. Each spermatid has 23 chromosomes.

Spermatocyte An early stage in the development of sperm cells, in which each parent cell has 46 chromosomes, including one X and one Y sex chromosome.

Spermatogenesis The process by which sperm cells are produced and developed.

Spermatozoa Mature sperm cells.

Sphincters Ring-shaped muscles that surround body openings and open or close them by expanding or contracting. (From the Greek for "that which draws close.")

Spontaneous abortion The sudden, involuntary expulsion of the embryo or fetus from the uterus before it is capable of independent life.

Squeeze technique A method for treating premature ejaculation whereby the tip of the penis is squeezed temporarily to prevent ejaculation.

Statutory rape Sexual intercourse with a person who is below the age of consent. Sexual intercourse under such conditions is considered statutory rape even if the person who is attacked may cooperate.

Stereotype A fixed, conventional idea about a group of people.

Sterilization Surgical procedures that render people incapable of reproduction without affecting sexual activity.

Stillbirth The birth of a dead fetus.

Storge (STORE-gay) Loving attachment and nonsexual affection; the type of emotion that binds parents to children.

Stranger rape Rape that is committed by an assailant who was previously unknown to the person who is assaulted.

Stratified random sample A random sample in which known subgroups in a population are represented in proportion to their numbers in the population.

Streetwalkers Prostitutes who solicit customers on the streets.

Superego In Freud's theory, the third mental structure, which functions as a moral guardian and sets forth high standards for behavior.

Surface contact A probing phase of building a relationship in which people seek common ground and check out feelings of attraction.

Surfactant Substance that prevent the walls of the airways from sticking together.

Surrogate mother A woman who is impregnated through artificial insemination with the sperm of a prospective father, carries the embryo and fetus to term, and then gives the child to the prospective parents.

Survey A detailed study of a sample obtained by means such as interviews and questionnaires.

Swinging A form of consensual adultery in which both spouses share extramarital sexual experiences. Also referred to as *mate-swapping*.

Sympathetic The branch of the ANS most active during emotional responses that spend the body's reserves of energy, such as fear and anxiety. The sympathetic ANS largely controls ejaculation.

Sympathetic pregnancy The experiencing of a number of signs of pregnancy by the father.

Syphilis An STI that is caused by the *Treponema pallidum* bacterium, which may progress through several stages of development—often from a chancre to a skin rash to damage to the cardiovascular or central nervous systems. (From the Greek *siphlos*, meaning "maimed" or "crippled.")

Systematic desensitization A method for terminating the connection between a stimulus (such as a fetishistic object) and an inappropriate response (such as sexual arousal to the paraphilic stimulus). Muscle relaxation is practiced in connection with each stimulus in a series of increasingly arousing stimuli so that the person learns to remain relaxed (and not sexually aroused) in their presence.

Tampon A cylindrical plug of cotton that is inserted into the vagina and left in place to absorb menstrual fluid. (A French word, meaning a gun barrel "plug.")

Telephone scatologia A paraphilia characterized by the making of obscene telephone calls. (From the Greek *skatos*, meaning "excrement.")

Teratogens Environmental influences or agents that can damage an embryo or fetus. (From the Greek *teras*, meaning "monster.")

Testes The male sex glands, suspended in the scrotum, that produce sperm cells and male sex hormones. Singular: *testis*.

Testicles Testes.

Testosterone The male sex hormone that fosters the development of male sex characteristics and is connected with the sex drive.

Thalamus An area near the center of the brain that is involved in the relay of sensory information to the cortex and in the functions of sleep and attention.

Toucherism A practice related to frotteurism and characterized by the persistent urge to fondle nonconsenting strangers.

Toxemia A life-threatening condition that is characterized by high blood pressure.

Transition The process during which the cervix becomes nearly fully dilated and the head of the fetus begins to move into the birth canal.

Transsexual A person with a gender-identity disorder who feels that he or she is really a member of the other gender and is trapped in a body of the wrong gender.

Transverse position A crosswise birth position.

Transvestism A paraphilia in which a person repeatedly cross-dresses to achieve sexual arousal or gratification, or is troubled by persistent, recurring urges to cross-dress. (From the Latin roots *trans-*, meaning "cross," and *vestis*, meaning "garment.") Also known as *transvestic fetishism*.

Treatment In experiments, an intervention that is administered to participants (e.g., a test, a drug, or sex-education program) so that its effects may be observed.

Trichomoniasis A form of vaginitis caused by the protozoan *Trichomonas vaginalis*.

Trophoblast The outer part of the blastocyst, from which the amniotic sac, placenta, and umbilical cord develop.

Tubal sterilization The most common method of female sterilization, in which the fallopian tubes are surgically blocked to prevent the meeting of sperm and ova. Also called *tubal ligation*.

Tumescence Swelling; erection. (From the Latin *tumere*, meaning "to swell." *Tumor* has the same root.)

Turner syndrome A sex-chromosomal disorder caused by loss of some X chromosome material.

Umbilical cord A tube that connects the fetus to the placenta.

Unconscious mind Those parts or contents of the mind that lie outside of conscious awareness.

Urethral bulb The small tube that makes up the prostatic part of the urethral tract and that balloons out as muscles close at either end, trapping semen prior to ejaculation.

Urethral opening The opening through which urine passes from the female's body.

Urethritis An inflammation of the bladder or urethra.

Urologist A physician who specializes in the diagnosis and treatment of diseases of the urogenital system.

Urophilia A paraphilia in which sexual arousal is associated with urine.

Uterus The hollow, muscular, pear-shaped organ in which a fertilized ovum implants and develops until birth.

Vacuum aspiration Removal of the uterine contents by suction. An abortion method that is used early in pregnancy. (From the Latin *aspirare*, meaning "to breathe upon.")

Vagina The tubular female sex organ that contains the penis during sexual intercourse and through which a baby is born. (Latin for "sheath.")

Vaginal plethysmograph A tampon-shaped probe that is inserted in the vagina and suggests the level of vasocongestion by measuring the light reflected from the vaginal walls.

Vaginismus A sexual dysfunction characterized by involuntary contraction of the muscles surrounding the vaginal barrel, preventing penile penetration or rendering penetration painful.

Vaginitis Any type of vaginal infection or inflammation.

Validity With respect to tests, the degree to which a particular test measures the constructs or traits it purports to measure.

Values The qualities in life that are deemed important or unimportant, right or wrong, desirable or undesirable.

Variables Quantities or qualities that vary or may vary.

Vas deferens A tube that conducts sperm from the testicle to the ejaculatory duct of the penis. Plural: vasa deferentia.

Vasectomy The surgical method of male sterilization in which sperm are prevented from reaching the urethra by cutting each vas deferens and tying it back or cauterizing it.

Vasocongestion The swelling of the genital tissues with blood, which causes erection of the penis and engorgement of the area surrounding the vaginal opening. (From the Latin *vas*, meaning "vessel.")

Vasovasostomy The surgical method of reversing vasectomy in which the cut or cauterized ends of each vas deferens are sewn together.

VDRL The test named after the Venereal Disease Research Laboratory of the U.S. Public Health Service that tests for the presence of antibodies to *Treponema pallidum* in the blood.

Vestibular bulbs Cavernous structures that extend downward along the sides of the introitus and swell during sexual arousal.

Viscosity Stickiness, consistency.

Volunteer bias A slanting of research data that is caused by the characteristics of individuals who volunteer to participate, such as willingness to discuss intimate behavior.

Voyeurism A paraphilia characterized by strong, repetitive urges and related sexual fantasies of observing unsuspecting strangers who are naked, disrobing, or engaged in sexual relations. (From the French verb *voir*, meaning "to see.")

Vulva The external sexual structures of the female.

Whore-madonna complex A rigid stereotyping of women as either sinners or saints.

Zona pellucida A gelatinous layer that surrounds an ovum. (From roots meaning "zone through which light can shine.")

Zoophilia A paraphilia involving persistent or repeated sexual urges and related fantasies involving sexual contact with animals.

Zygote A fertilized ovum (egg cell).

Zygote intrafallopian transfer (ZIFT) A method of conception in which an ovum is fertilized in a laboratory dish and then placed in a fallopian tube.

A

ABC News *Nightline* Poll. (1995, February 17). *Most favor sex ed in schools, believing it changes behavior.*

Abel, G. G., et al. (1984). Complications, consent, and cognitions in sex between children and adults. *International Journal of Law and Psychiatry, 7,* 89–103.

Abel, G. G., et al. (1989). The measurement of the cognitive distortions of child molesters. *Annals of Sex Research, 2,* 135–152.

Abelson, H., et al. (1970). Public attitudes toward and experience with erotic materials. In *Technical Reports of the Commission on Obscenity and Pornography, Vol. 6.* Washington, DC: U.S. Government Printing Office.

Abramowitz, S. (1986). Psychosocial outcomes of sex reassignment surgery. *Journal of Consulting and Clinical Psychology, 54,* 183–189.

Acker, M., & Davis, M. H. (1992). Intimacy, passion and commitment in adult romantic relationships: A test of the triangular theory of love. *Journal of Social and Personal Relationships, 9,* 21–50.

Ackerman, D. (1990). *A natural history of the senses.* New York: Random House.

Ackerman, D. (1991). *The moon by whale light.* New York: Random House.

Adams, H. E., et al. (1981). Behavior therapy with sexual deviations. In S. M. Turner, K. S. Calhoun, & H. E. Adams (Eds.), *Handbook of clinical behavior therapy* (pp. 318–346). New York: Wiley.

Adams, H. E., Wright, L. W., Jr., & Lohr, B. A. (1996). Is homophobia associated with homosexual arousal? *Journal of Abnormal Psychology, 105,* 440–445.

Adams, R. (1987). The role of prostitution in AIDS and other STDs. *Medical Aspects of Human Sexuality, 21,* 27–33.

Adams, R. A., et al. (1992). Components of a model adolescent AIDS/drug abuse prevention program: A delphi study. *Family Relations, 41,* 312–317.

Adams, V. (1980, August). Sex therapists in perspective. *Psychology Today,* pp. 35–36.

Ade-Ridder, L. (1985). Quality of marriage: A comparison between golden-wedding couples and couples married less than fifty years. *Lifestyles, 7,* 224–237.

Adelson, A. (1990, November 19). Study attacks women's roles in TV. *The New York Times,* p. C18.

Adler, J. (1993, April 26). Sex in the snoring '90s. *Newsweek,* pp. 55, 57.

A flock with changing views. (1993, August 1). *The New York Times,* p. A26.

Ahmed, R. A. (1991). Women in Egypt and the Sudan. In L. L. Adler (Ed.), *Women in cross-cultural perspective* (pp. 107–134). New York: Praeger.

AIDS without needles or sex. (1993, December 20). *Newsweek,* pp. 106–107.

Aiken, L. S., West, S. G., Woodward, C. K., & Reno, R. R. (1994). Health beliefs and compliance with mammography-screening recommendations in asymptomatic women. *Health Psychology, 13,* 122–129.

Akhtar, S. (1988). Four culture-bound psychiatric syndromes in India. *The International Journal of Social Psychiatry, 34,* 70–74.

Alan Guttmacher Institute. (1991). *Facts in brief.* New York: Author.

Alan Guttmacher Institute. (1994). *Sex and America's teenagers.* New York: Author.

Alan Guttmacher Institute. (1998). Cited in Brody, J. E. (1998, September 15), Teen-agers and sex: Younger and more at risk. *The New York Times;* America Online.

Alexander, C. J., Sipski, M. L., & Findley, T. W. (1993). Sexual activities, desire, and satisfaction in males pre- and post-spinal cord injury. *Archives of Sexual Behavior, 22,* 217–228.

Allen, J. R., & Setlow, V. P. (1991). Heterosexual transmission of HIV: A view of the future. *Journal of the American Medical Association, 266,* 1695–1696.

Allen, M., & Burrell, N. (1996). Comparing the impact of homosexual and heterosexual parents on children: Meta-analysis of existing research. *Journal of Homosexuality, 32*(2), 19–35.

Alterman, E. (1997, November). Sex in the '90s. *Elle,* pp. 128–134.

Alter-Reid, K., et al. (1986). Sexual abuse of children: A review of the empirical findings. *Clinical Psychology Review, 6,* 249–266.

Althof, S. E. (1994). Paper presented to the annual meeting of the American Urological Association. San Francisco.

Altman, L. K. (1991, April 15). Study challenges federal research on risks of IUD's. *The New York Times,* p. A1.

Altman, L. K. (1992a, July 21). Women worldwide nearing higher rate for AIDS than men. *The New York Times,* p. C3.

Altman, L. K. (1992b, February 17). 2 new studies link vasectomy to higher prostate cancer risk. *The New York Times*, p. C12.

Altman, L. K. (1993, February 21). New caution, and some reassurance, on vasectomy. *The New York Times*, Section 4, p. 2.

Altman, L. K. (1995a, February 2). Combination of drugs appears to slow AIDS virus, studies say. *The New York Times*, p. A20.

Altman, L. K. (1995b, February 7). Protein in saliva found to block AIDS virus in test tube study. *The New York Times*, p. C3.

Altman, L. K. (1995c, July 7). Drug for treating impotence is ready for sale, F. D. A. says. *The New York Times*, p. A13.

Altman, L. K. (1997, January 19). With AIDS advance, more disappointment. *The New York Times*, pp. A1, A14.

Altman, L. K. (1998a, February 3). Big drop in AIDS deaths attributed to drug therapies. *The New York Times*; America Online.

Altman, L. K. (1998b, February 5). Doctors discuss unwanted side effects of new AIDS drugs. *The New York Times*; America Online.

Altman, L. K. (1998c, April 7). Researchers find the first drug known to prevent breast cancer. *The New York Times*, pp. A1, A21.

Altman, L. K. (1998d, April 21). Studies show second drug can prevent breast cancer. *The New York Times*; America Online.

Altman, L. K. (1998e, May 26). Good news from the front in the war against cancer. *The New York Times*, p. F3.

Alzate, H. (1985). Vaginal eroticism: A replication study. *Archives of Sexual Behavior, 14*, 529–537.

Alzate, H., & Londono, M. L. (1984). Vaginal erotic sensitivity. *Journal of Sex and Marital Therapy, 10*, 49–56.

Amaro, H. (1995). Love, sex, and power: Considering women's realities in HIV prevention. *American Psychologist, 50*, 437–447.

Amato, P. R., & Keith, B. (1991). Parental divorce and the well-being of children: A meta-analysis. *Psychological Bulletin, 110*, 26–46.

American Academy of Child and Adolescent Psychiatry. (1998). Cited in Goldberg, C. (1998, September 8). Getting to the truth in child abuse cases: New methods. *The New York Times*, pp. F1, F5.

American Cancer Society. (1990). *For men only: Testicular cancer and how to do TSE* (rev. ed.). Atlanta: Author.

American Cancer Society. (1991). *Cancer facts and figures*. New York: Author.

American Cancer Society. (1995a). America Online. Document ID: ACS049.

American Cancer Society. (1995b). America Online. Document ID: ACS050.

American Cancer Society. (1995c). America Online. Document ID: ACS052.

American Cancer Society. (1995d). America Online. Document ID: ACS053.

American Cancer Society. (1995e). America Online. Document ID: ACS058.

American Professional Society on the Abuse of Children. (1998). Cited in Goldberg, C. (1998, September 8). Getting to the truth in child abuse cases: New methods. *The New York Times*, pp. F1, F5.

American Psychiatric Association. (1994). *Diagnostic and statistical manual of mental disorders* (4th ed.). Washington, DC: Author.

American Psychological Association, Committee on Gay and Lesbian Concerns. (1991). Avoiding heterosexual bias in language. *American Psychologist, 46*, 973–974.

American Psychological Association (1998a, March 16). Sexual harassment: Myths and realities. APA Public Information Home Page; www.apa.org.

American Psychological Association (1998b, October 4). Answers to your questions about sexual orientation and homosexuality. APA Public Information Home Page; www.apa.org.

Americans generally well-informed about AIDS, but many lack knowledge about preventive aspects. (1993). *Family Planning Perspectives, 25*, 139–140.

Ames, M. A., & Houston, D. A. (1990). Legal, social, and biological definitions of pedophilia. *Archives of Sexual Behavior, 19*, 333–342.

Anderson, J. L., et al. (1992). Was the Duchess of Windsor right? A cross-cultural review of the socioecology of ideals of female body shape. *Ethology and Sociobiology, 13*, 197–227.

Anderson, P. B., & Aymami, R. (1993). Reports of female initiating of sexual contact: Male and female differences. *Archives of Sexual Behavior, 22*, 335–343.

Anderson, V. N. (1992). For whom is this world just? Sexual orientation and AIDS. *Journal of Applied Social Psychology, 22*, 248–259.

Angier, N. (1990, July 19). Scientists say gene on Y chromosome makes a man a man. *The New York Times*, pp. A1, A19.

Angier, N. (1991, August 30). Zone of brain linked to men's sexual orientation. *The New York Times*, pp. A1, D18.

Angier, N. (1992, January 30). Odor receptors discovered in sperm cells. *The New York Times*, p. A19.

Angier, N. (1993a). Future of the pill may lie just over the counter. *The New York Times*, Section 4, p. 5.

Angier, N. (1993b). Reports suggest homosexuality is linked to genes. *The New York Times*, pp. A12, D21.

Angier, N. (1995, November 2). Study links brain to transexuality. *The New York Times*; America Online.

Angier, N. (1997). Chemical tied to fat control could help trigger puberty. *The New York Times*, pp. C1, C3.

Ansen, D., with others. (1993, January 18). A lost generation. *Newsweek*, pp. 16–23.

Antill, J. K. (1983). Sex role complementarity versus similarity in married couples. *Journal of Personality and Social Psychology, 52*, 260–267.

Antonarakas, S. E., et al. (1991). Prenatal origin of the extra chromosome in trisomy 21 as indicated by analysis of DNA polymorphisms. *New England Journal of Medicine, 324,* 872–876.

Antoni, M. H., et al. (1990). Psychoneuroimmunology and HIV-1. *Journal of Consulting and Clinical Psychology, 58,* 38–49.

Antoni, M. H., et al. (1991). Cognitive-behavioral stress management intervention buffers distress responses and immunologic changes following notification of HIV-1 seropositivity. *Journal of Consulting and Clinical Psychology, 59,* 906–915.

Armsworth, M. W. (1991). Psychological response to abortion. *Journal of Counseling and Development, 69,* 377–379.

Asbell, B. (1995). *The pill: A biography of the drug that changed the world.* New York: Random House.

Assalian, P. (1994). Premature ejaculation: Is it really psychogenic? *Journal of Sex Education and Therapy, 20*(1), 1–4.

Astley, S. J., et al. (1992). Analysis of facial shape in children gestationally exposed to marijuana, alcohol, and/or cocaine. *Pediatrics, 89,* 67–77.

Atkeson, B. M., Calhoun, K. S., & Morris, K. T. (1989). Victim resistance to rape: The relationship of previous victimization, demographics, and situational factors. *Archives of Sexual Behavior, 18,* 497–507.

Ayres, B. D. (1996, August 27). California bill would require "chemical castration" for repeat sex offenders. *The New York Times;* America Online.

Axinn, W. G. (1991). The influence of interviewer sex on responses to sensitive questions in Nepal. *Social Science Research, 20,* 303–318.

Azar, B. (1998). Communicating through pheromones. *APA Monitor, 29*(1), 1, 12.

B

Bach, G. R., & Deutsch, R. M. (1970). *Pairing.* New York: Peter H. Wyden.

Bachu, A. (1991, December 4). Cited in Pear, R. Larger number of new mothers are unmarried. *The New York Times,* p. A20.

Bagatell, C. J., & Bremner, W. J. (1996). Drug therapy: Androgens in men—Uses and abuses. *New England Journal of Medicine, 334,* 707–714.

Bagley, C., & Young, L. (1987). Juvenile prostitution and child sexual abuse: A controlled study. *Canadian Journal of Community Mental Health, 6,* 5–26.

Bailey, J. M., & Pillard, R. C. (1991). A genetic study of male sexual orientation. *Archives of General Psychiatry, 48,* 1089–1096.

Bailey, J. M., Pillard, R. C., Neale, M. C., & Agyei, Y. (1993). Heritable factors influence sexual orientation in women. *Archives of General Psychiatry, 50,* 217–223.

Bailey, J. M., & Zucker, K. J. (1995). Childhood sex-typed behavior and sexual orientation: A conceptual analysis and quantitative review. *Developmental Psychology, 31,* 43–55.

Baker, J. N. (1990, Summer/Fall). Coming out. (Special Issue). *Newsweek,* pp. 60–61.

Baker, S., Thalberg, S., & Morrison, D. (1988). Parents' behavioral norms as predictors of adolescent sexual activity and contraceptive use. *Adolescence, 23,* 278–281.

Baker, T. C., et al. (1990). Rape victims' concerns about possible exposure to HIV infection. *Journal of Interpersonal Violence, 5,* 49–60.

Baldwin, J. D., & Baldwin, J. I. (1989). The socialization of homosexuality and heterosexuality in a non-Western society. *Archives of Sexual Behavior, 18,* 13–29.

Baldwin, J. D., Whiteley, S., & Baldwin, J. I. (1992). The effect of ethnic group on sexual activities related to contraception and STDs. *Journal of Sex Research, 29,* 189–205.

Bancroft, J. (1984). Hormones and human sexual behavior. *Journal of Sex and Marital Therapy, 10,* 3–21.

Bancroft, J. (1990). Commentary: Biological contributions to sexual orientation. In D. P. McWhirter, S. A. Sanders, & J. M. Reinisch (Eds.), *Homosexuality/heterosexuality: Concepts of sexual orientation* (pp. 101–111). New York: Oxford University Press.

Bancroft, J., et al. (1983). Mood, sexuality, hormones, and the menstrual cycle. III: Sexuality and the role of androgens. *Psychosomatic Medicine, 45,* 509–516.

Banmen, J., & Vogel, N. (1985). The relationship between marital quality and interpersonal sexual communication. *Family Therapy, 12,* 45–58.

Banning, A. (1989). Mother-son incest: Confronting a prejudice. *Child Abuse and Neglect, 13,* 563–570.

Bar-Tal, D., & Saxe, L. (1976). Perceptions of similarly and dissimilarly physically attractive couples and individuals. *Journal of Personality and Social Psychology, 33,* 772–781.

Barbach, L. G. (1975). *For yourself: The fulfillment of female sexuality.* New York: Doubleday.

Barbach, L. G. (1995). Cited in Goleman, D. (1995, June 14). Sex fantasy research said to neglect women. *The New York Times,* p. C14.

Barbaree, H. E., & Marshall, W. L. (1991). The role of male sexual arousal in rape: Six models. *Journal of Consulting and Clinical Psychology, 59,* 621–630.

Barboza, D. (1998, January 19). Video world is smitten by a gun-toting, tomb-raiding sex symbol. *The New York Times,* p. D3.

Barisic, S. (1998, February 18). Study: Breast milk is still best. The Associated Press; America Online.

Barlow, D. H. (1986). Causes of sexual dysfunction: The role of anxiety and cognitive interference. *Journal of Consulting and Clinical Psychology, 54,* 140–148.

Barlow, D. H., & Durand, V. M. (1995). *Abnormal psychology.* Pacific Grove, CA: Brooks/Cole.

Barr, H. M., Streissguth, A. P., Darby, B. L., & Sampson, P. D. (1990). Prenatal exposure to alcohol, caffeine, tobacco, and aspirin. *Developmental Psychology, 26,* 339–348.

Barrett, M. B. (1990). *Invisible lives: The truth about millions of women-loving women.* New York: Harper & Row (Perennial Library).

Barringer, F. (1990, August 17). After long decline, teen births are up. *The New York Times*, p. A14.

Barringer, F. (1991, June 7). Changes in family patterns: Solitude and single parents. *The New York Times*, pp. A1, A18.

Barringer, F. (1992a, July 17). Rate of marriage continues decline. *The New York Times*, p. A20.

Barringer, F. (1992b, July 19). More Americans are saying, "I don't." *The New York Times*, p. E2.

Barringer, F. (1993a, April 1). Viral sexual diseases are found in 1 of 5 in U.S. *The New York Times*, pp. A1, B9.

Barringer, F. (1993b, April 15). Sex survey of American men finds 1% are gay. *The New York Times*, p. A1.

Barringer, F. (1993c, June 2). School hallways as gauntlets of sexual taunts. *The New York Times*, p. B7.

Bart, P. B., & O'Brien, P. B. (1985). *Stopping rape: Successful survival strategies*. Elsmford, NY: Pergamon Press.

Bartel, G. D. (1970). Group sex among mid-Americans. *Journal of Sex Research*, 6, 113–131.

Bartlett, J. G. (1993). Zidovudine now or later? *New England Journal of Medicine*, 329, pp. 351–352.

Bartoshuk, L. M., & Beauchamp, G. K. (1994). Chemical senses. *Annual Review of Psychology*, 45, 419–449.

Baumeister, R. F. (1988a). Gender differences in masochistic scripts. *Journal of Sex Research*, 25, 478–499.

Baumeister, R. F. (1988b). Masochism as escape from self. *Journal of Sex Research*, 25, 28–59.

Baxter, D. J., Barbaree, H. E., & Marshall, W. L. (1986). Sexual responses to consenting and forced sex in a large sample of rapists and nonrapists. *Behaviour Research and Therapy*, 17, 215–222.

Beck, A. (1988). *Love is never enough*. New York: Harper & Row.

Beck, J. G. (1993). Vaginismus. In W. O'Donohue & J. H. Geer (Eds.), *Handbook of sexual dysfunctions: Assessment and treatment* (pp. 381–397). Boston: Allyn & Bacon.

Beck, J. G., & Davies, D. K. (1987). Teen contraception: A review of perspectives on compliance. *Archives of Sexual Behavior*, 16, 337–368.

Becker, J. V., et al. (1986). Level of postassault sexual functioning in rape and incest victims. *Archives of Sexual Behavior*, 15, 37–49.

Becker, J. V., et al. (1989). Factors associated with erection in adolescent sex offenders. *Journal of Psychopathology and Behavioral Assessment*, 11, 353–362.

Beitchman, J. H., et al. (1992). A review of the long-term effects of child sexual abuse. *Child Abuse and Neglect*, 16, 101–118.

Belcastro, P. A. (1985). Sexual behavior differences between black and white students. *Journal of Sex Research*, 21, 56–67.

Bell, A. P., & Weinberg, M. S. (1978). *Homosexualities: A study of diversity among men and women*. New York: Simon & Schuster.

Bell, A. P., Weinberg, M. S., & Hammersmith, S. K. (1981). *Sexual preference: Its development in men and women*. Bloomington, IN: University of Indiana Press.

Bell, S., Kuriloff, P. J., & Lottes, I. (1994) Understanding attributions of blame in stranger rape and date rape situations: An examination of gender, race, identification, and students' social perceptions of rape victims. *Journal of Applied Social Psychology*, 24(19), 1719–1734.

Beller, T. (1995, July 13). Why? Don't ask. *The New York Times*, p. A23.

Bellis, D. J. (1990). Fear of AIDS and risk reduction among heroin-addicted female street prostitutes: Personal interviews with 72 Southern California subjects. *Journal of Alcohol and Drug Education*, 35, 26–37.

Bello, D. C., Pitts, R. E., & Etzel, M. J. (1983). The communications effects of controversial sexual content in television programs and commercials. *Journal of Advertising*, 12(3), 32–42.

Bem, S. L. (1974). The measurement of psychological androgyny. *Journal of Consulting and Clinical Psychology*, 42, 151–162.

Bem, S. L. (1975). Sex role adaptability: One consequence of psychological androgyny. *Journal of Personality and Social Psychology*, 31, 634–643.

Bem, S. L. (1981). Gender schema theory: A cognitive account of sex typing. *Psychological Review*, 88, 354–364.

Bem, S. L. (1983). Gender schema theory and its implications for child development: Raising gender-aschematic children in a gender-schematic society. *Signs*, 8, 598–616.

Bem, S. L. (1985). Androgyny and gender schema theory: A conceptual and empirical integration. In T. B. Sonderegger (Ed.), *Nebraska symposium on motivation, 1984: Psychology and gender*. Lincoln: University of Nebraska Press.

Bem, S. L. (1993). *The lenses of gender*. New Haven: Yale University Press.

Bem, S. L., Martyna, W., & Watson, C. (1976). Sex typing and androgyny: Further explorations of the expressive domain. *Journal of Personality and Social Psychology*, 34, 1016–1023.

Bennett, N. G. (1998, September 16). Who should decide the sex of a baby? *The New York Times*, p. A28.

Bennett, N. G., Blanc, A. K., & Bloom, D. E. (1988). Commitment and the modern union: Assessing the link between premarital cohabitation and subsequent marital stability. *American Sociological Review*, 53, 127–138.

Bentler, P. M. (1976). A typology of transsexualism: Gender identity theory and data. *Archives of Sexual Behavior*, 5, 567–584.

Berke, R. L. (1997, June 15). Suddenly, the new politics of morality. *The New York Times*, p. E3.

Berke, R. L. (1998, August 2). Chasing the polls on gay rights. *The New York Times*, p. WK3.

Berlin, F. S. (1989). The paraphilias and Depo-Provera: Some medical, ethical and legal considerations. *Bulletin of the American Academy of Psychiatry and the Law*, 17, 233–239.

Berliner, D. (1993). Cited in Blakeslee, S. (1993, September 7). Human nose may hold an additional organ for a real sixth sense. *The New York Times*, p. C3.

Bernstein, S. J., et al. (1993). The appropriateness of hysterectomy: A comparison of care in seven health plans. *Journal of the American Medical Association*, 269, 2398–2402.

Bernstein, W. M., et al. (1983). Causal ambiguity and heterosexual affiliation. *Journal of Experimental Social Psychology, 19,* 78–92.

Berscheid, E. (1988). Some comments on love's anatomy: Or, whatever happened to old-fashioned lust? In R. J. Sternberg & M. L. Barnes (Eds.), *The psychology of love* (pp. 359–374). New Haven: Yale University Press.

Berscheid, E., & Walster, E. (1978). *Interpersonal attraction.* Reading, MA: Addison-Wesley.

Bianchi, S. M., & Spain, D. (1997). *Women, work and family in America.* Population Reference Bureau.

Bieber, I. (1976). A discussion of "Homosexuality: The ethical challenge." *Journal of Consulting and Clinical Psychology, 44,* 163–166.

Bieber, I., et al. (1962). *Homosexuality.* New York: Basic Books.

Biggar, R. J., & Melbye, M. (1992). Responses to anonymous questionnaires concerning sexual beahvior: A method to examine potential biases. *American Journal of Public Health, 82,* 1506–1512.

Billingham, R. E., & Sack, A. Z. (1986). Gender differences in college students' willingness to participate in alternative marriage and family relationships. *Family Perspectives, 20,* 37–44.

Billy, J. O. G., et al. (1993). The sexual behavior of men in the United States. *Family Planning Perspectives, 25,* 52–60.

Binion, V. J. (1990). Psychological androgyny: A Black female perspective. *Sex Roles, 22,* 487–507.

Bixler, R. H. (1981). The incest controversy. *Psychological Reports, 49,* 267–283.

Bjorklund, D. F., & Kipp, K. (1996). Parental investment theory and gender differences in the evolution of inhibition mechanisms. *Psychological Bulletin, 120,* 163–188.

Blair, C. D., & Lanyon, R. I. (1981). Exhibitionism: A critical review of the etiology and treatment. *Psychological Bulletin, 89,* 439–463.

Blakeslee, S. (1992, January 22). An epidemic of genital warts raises concern but not alarm. *The New York Times,* p. C12.

Blanchard, R., & Hucker, S. J. (1991). Age, transvestism, bondage, and concurrent paraphilic activities in 117 fatal cases of autoerotic asphyxia. *British Journal of Psychiatry, 159,* 371–377.

Blanchard, R., Steiner, B. W., & Clemmensen, L. H. (1985). Gender dysphoria, gender reorientation, and the clinical management of transsexualism. *Journal of Consulting and Clinical Psychology, 53,* 295–304.

Bloom, B. J., Asher, S. J., & White, S. W. (1978). Marital disruption as a stressor: A review and analysis. *Psychological Bulletin, 85,* 867–894.

Bloor, M., McKeganey, N., & Barnard, M. (1990). An ethnographic study of HIV-related risk practices among Glasgow rent boys and their clients: Report of a pilot study. *AIDS Care, 2,* 17–24.

Blumstein, P., & Schwartz, P. (1983). *American couples: Money, work, sex.* New York: William Morrow.

Blumstein, P., & Schwartz, P. (1990). Intimate relationships and the creation of sexuality. In D. P. McWhirter, S. A. Sanders, & J. M. Reinisch (Eds.), *Homosexuality/heterosexuality: Concepts of sexual orientation* (pp. 307–320). New York: Oxford University Press.

Blustein, J. (1995). Medicare coverage, supplemental insurance, and the use of mammography by older women. *New England Journal of Medicine, 332,* 1138–1143.

Bogert, C., Chubbuck, K., & Hammer, J. (1995, September 25). "Making men listen." Africa: Women bear the brunt of the AIDS crisis. *Newsweek,* p. 52.

Bohlen, C. (1995, April 4). Almost anything goes in birth science in Italy. *The New York Times,* p. A14.

Boles, J., & Elifson, K. W. (1994). Sexual identity and HIV: The male prostitute. *Journal of Sex Research, 31,* 39–46.

Boskind-White, M., & White, W. C. (1986). Bulmariexia: A historical-sociocultural perspective. In K. D. Brownell & J. P. Foreyt (Eds.), *Handbook of eating disorders: Physiology, psychology, and treatment of obesity, anorexia, and bulimia* (pp. 353–378). New York: Basic Books.

Bostick, R. M., et al. (1994). Predictors of cancer prevention attitudes and participation in cancer screening examinations. *Preventive Medicine: An International Journal Devoted to Practice and Theory, 23*(6), 816–826.

Boston Women's Health Book Collective. (1992). *The New Our Bodies, Ourselves.* New York: Simon & Schuster.

Boswell, J. (1990). Sexual and ethical categories in premodern Europe. In D. P. McWhirter, S. A. Sanders, & J. M. Reinisch (Eds.), *Homosexuality/Heterosexuality: Concepts of sexual orientation* (pp. 15–31). New York: Oxford University Press.

Boulton, M., Hart, G., & Fitzpatrick, R. (1992). The sexual behaviour of bisexual men in relation to HIV transmission. *AIDS Care, 4,* 165–175.

Bowie, W. R. (1990). Approach to men with urethritis and urologic complications of sexually-transmitted diseases. *Medical Clinics of North America, 74,* 1543–1557.

Bowlby, J. (1969). *Attachment and loss, Vol. 1.* New York: Basic Books.

Boyer, D. (1989). Male prostitution and homosexual identity. [Special Issue: Gay and lesbian youth: I]. *Journal of Homosexuality, 17,* 151–184.

Bozzette, S. A., et al. (1995). A randomized trial of three anti-pneumocystis agents in patients with advanced human immunodeficiency virus infection. *New England Journal of Medicine, 332,* 693–699.

Bradbard, M. R., & Endsley, R. C. (1983). The effects of sex typed labeling on preschool children's information-seeking and retention. *Sex Roles, 9,* 247–261.

Bradford, J. M. W. (1998). Treatment of men with paraphilia. *New England Journal of Medicine, 338,* 464–465.

Brady, E. C., et al. (1991). Date rape: Expectations, avoidance strategies, and attitudes toward victims. *Journal of Social Psychology, 131,* 427–429.

Breast fears fade. (1993, November). *Prevention,* pp. 19–20.

Brecher, E. M, and the Editors of Consumer Reports Books. (1984). *Love, sex, and aging*. Boston: Little, Brown.

Breslow, N. (1989). Sources of confusion in the study and treatment of sadomasochism. *Journal of Social Behavior and Personality, 4*, 263–274.

Breslow, N., Evans, L., & Langley, J. (1985). On the prevalence and roles of females in the sadomasochistic subculture: Report on an empirical study. *Archives of Sexual Behavior, 14*, 303–317.

Breslow, N., Evans, L., & Langley, J. (1986). Comparisons among heterosexual, bisexual and homosexual male sadomasochists. *Journal of Homosexuality, 13*, 83–107.

Bretl, D. J., & Cantor, J. (1988). The portrayal of men and women in U.S. television commercials: A recent content analysis and trends over 15 years. *Sex Roles, 18*, 595–609.

Bretschneider, J., & McCoy, N. (1988). Sexual interest and behavior in healthy 80- to 102-year olds. *Archives of Sexual Behavior, 17*, 109.

Brewer, J. J. (1982). A history of erotic art as illustrated in the collectors of the Institute for Sex Research (The "Kinsey Institute"). In A. Hoch & H. I. Lief (Eds.), *Sexology: Sexual biology, behavior and therapy* (pp. 318–321). Amsterdam, The Netherlands: Excerpta Medica.

Briere, J., & Runtz, M. (1987). Post sexual abuse trauma: Data and implications for clinical practice. *Journal of Interpersonal Violence, 2*, 367–379.

Briere, J., & Runtz, M. (1989). University males' sexual interest in children: Predicting potential indices of "pedophilia" in a nonforensic sample. *Child Abuse and Neglect, 13*, 65–75.

Bright, S. (1995). *Susie Bright's sexwise*. Cleis.

Brody, J. E. (1989, July 27). Research casts doubt on need for many Caesarean births as their rate soars. *The New York Times*, p. B5.

Brody, J. E. (1990a, January 23). Scientists trace aberrant sexuality. *The New York Times*, pp. C11, C12.

Brody, J. E. (1990b, August 2). In fight against breast cancer, mammograms are a crucial tool, but not foolproof. *The New York Times*, p. B5.

Brody, J. E. (1992a, April 29). How to outwit a rapist: Rehearse. *The New York Times*, p. C13.

Brody, J. E. (1992b, November 11). PMS is a worldwide phenomenon. *The New York Times*, p. C14.

Brody, J. E. (1993, August 4). A new look at an old quest for sexual stimulants. *The New York Times*, p. C12.

Brody, J. E. (1995a, May 3). Breast scans may indeed help women under 50. *The New York Times*, p. C11.

Brody, J. E. (1995b, July 19). Revolution in treating infertile men turns hopelessness to parenthood. *The New York Times*, p. C8.

Brody, J. E. (1995c, August 30). Hormone replacement therapy for men: When does it help? *The New York Times*, p. C8.

Brody, J. E. (1996, August 28). PMS need not be the worry it was just decades ago. *The New York Times*, p. C9.

Brody, J. E. (1997a, February 12). Abortion doesn't affect well-being, study says. *The New York Times*; America Online.

Brody, J. E. (1997b, March 4). Drug researchers working to design customized estrogen. *The New York Times*, pp. C1, C10.

Brody, J. E. (1997c, August 20). Estrogen after menopause? A tough dilemma. *The New York Times*, p. C8.

Brody, J. E. (1998a, February 10). Genetic ties may be factor in violence in stepfamilies. *The New York Times*, pp. F1, F4.

Brody, J. E. (1998b, February 18). Studies confirm alcohol's link to breast cancer. *The New York Times*; America Online.

Brody, J. E. (1998c). Sour note in the Viagra symphony. *The New York Times*, p. F7.

Brody, J. E. (1998d, August 4). Personal health: Giving men directions to the road to better health. *The New York Times*; America Online.

Brody, J. E. (1998e, September 15). Teen-agers and sex: Younger and more at risk. *The New York Times*; America Online.

Brody, J. E. (1998f, September 8). Weighing the pros and cons of hormone therapy. *The New York Times*, p. F7.

Bronner, E. (1998, February 1). Just say maybe. No sexology, please. We're Americans. *The New York Times*, p. WK6.

Brookoff, D., et al. (1997). Characteristics of participants in domestic violence: Assessment at the scene of domestic assault. *Journal of the American Medical Association, 277*, 1369–1373.

Brooks, V. R. (1982). Sex differences in student dominance behavior in female and male professors' classrooms. *Sex Roles, 8*, 683–690.

Brooks-Gunn, J., & Furstenberg, F. F. (1989). Adolescent sexual behavior. *American Psychologist, 44*, 249–257.

Brooks-Gunn, J., & Matthews, W. S. (1979). *He and she: How children develop their sex-role identity*. Englewood Cliffs, NJ: Spectrum.

Brooks-Gunn, J., et al. (1986). Physical similarity of and disclosure of menarchal status to friends: Effects of grade and pubertal status. *Journal of Early Adolescence, 6*, 3–14.

Broude, G. J., & Greene, S. J. (1976). Cross-cultural codes on twenty sexual attitudes and practices. *Ethnology, 15*, 409–429.

Brown, R. A. (1994). Romantic love and the spouse selection criteria of male and female Korean college students. *The Journal of Social Psychology, 134*(2), 183–189.

Bruck, M. (1998). Cited in Goldberg, C. (1998, September 8). Getting to the truth in child abuse cases: New methods. *The New York Times*, pp. F1, F5.

Bryant, H., & Brasher, P. (1995). Breast implants and breast cancer—Reanalysis of a linkage study. *New England Journal of Medicine, 332*, 1535–1539.

Bryant, J. (1985, September). *The effects of massive exposure to pornography on everyday moral behavior*. Testimony given to the U.S. Attorney General's Commission on Pornography, Houston, TX.

Bryant, J., & Brown, D. (1989). Uses of pornography. In D. Zillmann & J. Bryant (Eds.), *Pornography: Research advances and policy considerations* (pp. 25–55). Hillsdale, NJ: Lawrence Erlbaum Associates.

Buchanan, M., & Robbins, C. (1990). Early adult psychological consequences for males of adolescent pregnancy and its resolution. *Journal of Youth and Adolescence, 19*, 413–424.

Buhaug, H., et al. (1990). Should asymptomatic patients be tested for *Chlamydia trachomatis* in general practice? *British Journal of General Practice, 40*, 142–145.

Buhrich, N., et al. (1979). Plasma testosterone, serum FSH, and serum LH levels in transvestism. *Archives of Sexual Behavior, 8*, 49–54.

Bullough, V. (1990). The Kinsey Scale in historical perspective. In D. P. McWhirter, S. A. Sanders, & J. M. Reinisch (Eds.) *Homosexuality/heterosexuality: Concepts of sexual orientation* (pp. 3–14). New York: Oxford University Press.

Bullough, V. L. (1991). Transvestism: A reexamination. *Journal of Psychology and Human Sexuality, 4*, 53–67.

Bullough, V. L., & Weinberg, T. S. (1989). Women married to transvestites: Problems and adjustments. *Journal of Psychology & Human Sexuality, 1*, 83–104.

Bumiller, E. (1990, October 25). Japan's abortion agony: In a country that prohibits the pill, reality collides with religion. *Washington Post.*

Bumpass, L. (1991). Cited in Pear, R. (1991, December 4), Larger number of new mothers are unmarried. *The New York Times*, p. A20.

Bumpass, L. (1995). Cited in Steinhauer, J. (1995, July 6), No marriage, no apologies. *The New York Times*, pp. C1, C7.

Bumpass, L., Sweet, J., & Castro, T. (1988, August). Changing patterns of remarriage. Paper presented at the meeting of the American Sociological Association, Atlanta, Georgia.

Burgess, A. W., & Hartman, C. R. (1986). *Sexual exploitation of patients by health professionals.* New York: Praeger.

Burgess, A. W., & Holmstrom, L. L. (1974). Rape trauma syndrome. *American Journal of Psychiatry, 131*, 981–986.

Burkhart, B., & Fromuth, M. E. (1991). Individual psychological and social psychological understandings of sexual coercion. In E. Grauerholz & M. A. Koralewski (Eds.), *Sexual coercion: A sourcebook on its nature, causes, and prevention* (pp. 7–89). Lexington, MA: Lexington Books.

Burns, C. (1997, November 26). More AIDS cases than thought. The Associated Press; America Online.

Burstein, G. R., et al. (1998). Incident *Chlamydia trachomatis* infections among inner-city adolescent females. *Journal of the American Medical Association, 280*, 521–526.

Burt, M. R. (1980). Cultural myths and supports for rape. *Journal of Personality and Social Psychology, 38*, 217–230.

Buss, D. M. (1994). *The evolution of desire: Strategies of human mating.* New York: Basic Books.

Buxton, A. P. (1994). *The other side of the closet.* New York: John Wiley & Sons.

Byers, E. S., & Lewis, K. (1988). Dating couples' disagreements over the desired level of sexual intimacy. *Journal of Sex Research, 24*, 15–29.

Bynum, R. (1998, June 26). U.S. syphilis rate hits record low. Associated Press; America Online.

Byrnes, J., & Takahira, S. (1993). Explaining gender differences on SAT-math items. *Developmental Psychology, 29*, 805–810.

C

Caceres, C. F., & van Griensven, G. J. P. (1994). Male homosexual transmission of HIV-1. *AIDS, 8*(8), 1051–1061.

Cado, S., & Leitenberg, H. (1990). Guilt reactions to sexual fantasies during intercourse. *Archives of Sexual Behavior, 19*, 49–64.

Calderone, M. S., & Johnson, E. W. (1989). *Family book about sexuality* (rev. ed.). New York: Harper & Row.

Calhoun, K. S., & Atkeson, B. M. (1991). *Treatment of rape victims: Facilitating social adjustment.* New York: Pergamon Press.

Call, V., Sprecher, S., & Schwartz, P. (1995). The incidence and frequency of marital sex in a national sample. *Journal of Marriage and the Family, 57*, 639–652.

Cameron, P., et al. (1986). Child molestation and homosexuality. *Psychological Reports, 58*, 327–337.

Campbell, C. A. (1991). Prostitution, AIDS, and preventive health behavior. *Social Science and Medicine, 32*, 1367–1378.

Campbell, S. B., & Cohn, J. F. (1991). Prevalence and correlates of postpartum depression in first-time mothers. *Journal of Abnormal Psychology, 100*, 594–599.

Cancer survivor Bob Dole calls Viagra "great drug." (1998, May 7). Reuters; America Online.

Cannistra, S. A., & Niloff, J. M. (1996). Cancer of the uterine cervix. *New England Journal of Medicine, 334*, 1030–1038.

Cantalona, W. J. (1998). Cited in Story, P. (1998, June 2), Study: Prostate cancer deaths down. The Associated Press; America Online.

Cantalona, W. J., et al. (1993). Detection of organ-confined prostate cancer is increased through prostate-specific antigen-based screening. *Journal of the American Medical Association, 270*, 948–954.

Cappella, J. N., & Palmer, M. T. (1990). Attitude similarity, relational history, and attraction: The mediating effects of kinesic and vocal behaviors. *Communication Monographs, 5*, 161–183.

Carani, C., et al. (1990). Effects of androgen treatment in impotent men with normal and low levels of free testosterone. *Archives of Sexual Behavior, 19*, 223–234.

Carey, N., et al. (1992). Effectiveness of latex condoms as a barrier to human immunodeficiency virus-sized particles under conditions of simulated use. *Sexually Transmitted Diseases, 19*, 230–234.

Carlson, M. (1990, July 9). Abortion's hardest cases. *Time*, pp. 22–26.

Carnes, P. (1983). *The sexual addiction.* Minneapolis: CompCare Publications.

Carnes, P. (1991). *Don't call it love.* New York: Bantam Books.

Carreran, M. (1981). *Sex: The facts, the acts and your feelings.* New York: Crown.

Carrier, J. M. (1986). Childhood cross-gender behavior and adult homosexuality. *Archives of Sexual Behavior, 15*, 89–93.

Cartwright, R. D., et al. (1983). The traditional-liberated woman dimension: Social stereotype and self-concept. *Journal of Personality and Social Psychology, 44,* 581–588.

Carvajal, D. (1995). Oldest profession's newest home. *The New York Times,* pp. L29, L32.

Cash, T. F., & Duncan, N. C. (1984). Physical attractiveness stereotyping among black American college students. *Journal of Social Psychology, 122,* 71–77.

Castro, J. (1992, January 20). Sexual harassment: A guide. *Time,* p. 37.

Castro, K. G., et al. (1988). Transmission of HIV in Belle Glade, Florida: Lessons for other communities in the United States. *Science, 239,* 193–197.

Catalan, J., Hawton, K., & Day, A. (1990). Couples referred to a sexual dysfunction clinic: Psychological and physical morbidity. *British Journal of Psychiatry, 156,* 61–67.

Catania, J. A., et al. (1991). Changes in condom use among homosexual men in San Francisco. *Health Psychology, 10,* 190–199.

Catania, J. A., et al. (1992). Prevalence of AIDS-related risk factors and condom use in the United States. *Science, 258,* 1101–1106.

Cates, W., Jr. (1998). Reproductive tract infections. In Hatcher, R. A., et al. (1998), *Contraceptive technology* (17th rev. ed., pp. 179–210). New York: Ardent Media, Inc.

Cates, W., Jr., & Raymond, E. G. (1998) Vaginal spermicides. In Hatcher, R. A., et al. (1998). *Contraceptive technology* (17th rev. ed., pp. 357–370). New York: Ardent Media, Inc.

Cates, W., Jr., & Wasserheit, J. N. (1991). Genital chlamydial infections: Epidemiology and reproductive sequelae. *American Journal of Obstetrics and Gynecology, 164,* 1171–1181.

CBS News. (1991, May 22). *48 hours: For better or worse.*

CDC tackles surge in sexual diseases (1998, March 24). The Associated Press; America Online.

Ceci, S. (1998). Cited in Goldberg, C. (1998, September 8). Getting to the truth in child abuse cases: New methods. *The New York Times,* pp. F1, F5.

Celis, W. (1991, January 2). Students trying to draw line between sex and an assault. *The New York Times,* pp. B1, B8.

Centers for Disease Control. (1985). *Chlamydia trachomatis* infections. *Morbidity and Mortality Weekly Report, 34,* 53.

Centers for Disease Control. (1988). Leads from the MMWR/Morbidity and Mortality Weekly Report (Vol. 37/No. 7, 9, 1988): Condoms for prevention of sexually transmitted diseases. *Journal of the American Medical Association, 259,* 1925–1927.

Centers for Disease Control. (1989a). Summaries of identifiable diseases in the United States. *Morbidity and Mortality Weekly Report, 38,* No. S-8.

Centers for Disease Control. (1989b). Treatment guidelines for sexually transmitted diseases. *Morbidity and Mortality Weekly Report, 38,* No. S-8.

Centers for Disease Control. (1992, January). *HIV infection and AIDS: Are you at risk?* Atlanta: Centers for Diseases Control.

Centers for Disease Control. (1993). Evaluation of surveillance for *Chlamydia trachomatis* infections in the United States, 1987 to 1991. *Mortality and Morbidity Weekly Report, 42* (SS-3), 21–27.

Centers for Disease Control and Prevention. (1996). *HIV/AIDS surveillance report: U.S. HIV and AIDS cases reported through June 1996, 8*(1).

Centers for Disease Control and Prevention. (1998). *HIV/AIDS surveillance report: U.S. HIV and AIDS cases reported through June 1998, 10*(1).

The cervical cancer virus. (1995, September). *Discover,* pp. 24–26.

Chadda, R. K., & Ahuja, N. (1990). Dhat syndrome: A sex neurosis of the Indian subcontinent. *British Journal of Psychiatry, 156,* 577–579.

Chan, C. (1992). Cultural considerations in counseling Asian American lesbians and gay men. In S. Dworkin & F. Gutierrez (Eds.), *Counseling gay men and lesbians: Journey to the end of the rainbow.* Alexandria, VA: American Association for Counseling and Development.

Chan, D. W. (1990). Sex knowledge, attitudes, and experiences of Chinese medical students in Hong Kong. *Archives of Sexual Behavior, 19,* 73–93.

Charny, I. W., & Parnass, S. (1995). The impact of extramarital relationships on the continuation of marriages. *Journal of Sex and Marital Therapy, 21,* 100–115.

Cheasty, M. (1998). Cited in "Sexually abused women prone to divorce as adults." (1998, January 15). Reuters; America Online.

Cheating going out of style but sex is popular as ever. (1993, October 19). *Newsday,* p. 2.

Check, J. V. P., & Malamuth, N. M. (1983). Sex-role stereotyping and reactions to depictions of stranger versus acquaintance rape. *Journal of Personality and Social Psychology, 45,* 344–356.

Chesney, M. A. (1996). Cited in Freiberg, P. (1996). New drugs give hope to AIDS patients. *APA Monitor, 27*(6), 28.

Chideya, F., et al. (1993, August 30). Endangered family. *Newsweek,* pp. 17–27.

China develops electronic contraceptive for men. (1998, March 15). Reuters; CNN.

Chira, S. (1992, February 12). Bias against girls is found rife in schools, with lasting damage. *The New York Times,* pp. A1, A23.

Choi, P. Y. (1992). The psychological benefits of physical exercise: Implications for women and the menstrual cycle. Special issue: The menstrual cycle. *Journal of Reproductive and Infant Psychology, 10,* 111–115.

Christensen, C. (1995). Prescribed masturbation in sex therapy: A critique. *Journal of Sex and Marital Therapy, 21*(2), 87–99.

Clapper, R. L., & Lipsitt, L. P. (1991). A retrospective study of risk-taking and alcohol-mediated unprotected intercourse. *Journal of Substance Abuse, 3,* 91–96.

Clark, M. S., Mills, J. R., & Corcoran, D. M. (1989). Keeping track of needs and inputs of friends and strangers. *Personality and Social Psychology Bulletin, 15,* 533–542.

Clay, R. A. (1996a). Beating the "biological clock" with zest. *APA Monitor, 27*(2), 37.

Clay, R. A. (1996b). Older men are more involved fathers, studies show. *APA Monitor, 27*(2), 37.

Clumeck, N. (1995). Primary prophylaxis against opportunistic infections in patients with AIDS. *New England Journal of Medicine, 332,* 739–740.

Cnattingius, S., Bergstrom, R., Lipworth, L., & Kramer, M. S. (1998). Prepregnancy weight and the risk of adverse pregnancy outcomes. *New England Journal of Medicine, 338,* 147–152.

Cobb, J. (1996, January). The genes of 1995. *Discover,* p. 36.

Cochran, W. G., Mosteller, F., & Tukey, J. W. (1953). Statistical problems of the Kinsey Report. *Journal of the American Statistical Association, 48,* 673–716.

Cohen, E. (1998, March 26). Study: "Male pill" proves 95% effective. CNN.

Cohen, J. (1993). AIDS research: The mood is uncertain. *Science, 260,* 1254–1255.

Cohen, J. B. (1990, December 13). *A crosscutting perspective on the epidemiology of HIV infection in women.* Paper presented at the Women and AIDS Conference, Washington, DC (abstract).

Cohen, R. (1996). Cited in Clay, R. A. (1996). Beating the "biological clock" with zest. *APA Monitor, 27*(2), 37.

Cohn, L. D., Macfarlane, S., Yanez, C., & Imai, W. K. (1995). Risk-perception: Differences between adolescents and adults. *Health Psychology, 14,* 217–222.

Colditz, G. A., et al. (1993). Family history, age, and risk of breast cancer: Prospective data from the nurses' health study. *Journal of the American Medical Association, 270,* 338–343.

Cole, C. J. (1995, August). Cited in "Sex, the single lizard, and the missing parent." *National Geographic.*

Cole, H. M. (Ed.). (1989). Intrauterine devices. *Journal of the American Medical Association, 261,* 2127–2130.

Cole, S. S. (1988). Women's sexuality, and disabilities. *Women and Therapy, 7,* 277–294.

Coleman, E. (1986, July). Sexual compulsion vs. sexual addiction: The debate continues. *SIECUS Report,* 7–10.

Coleman, E. (1989). The development of male prostitution activity among gay and bisexual adolescents [Special Issue: Gay and lesbian youth]. *Journal of Homosexuality, 17,* 131–149.

Coleman, M., & Ganong, L. H. (1985). Love and sex role stereotypes: Do macho men and feminine women make better lovers? *Journal of Personality and Social Psychology, 49,* 170–176.

Coles, C. (1994) Critical periods for prenatal alcohol exposure: Evidence from animal and human studies. *Alcohol Health and Research World, 18*(1), 22–29.

Coles, R., & Stokes, G. (1985). *Sex and the American teenager.* New York: Harper & Row.

Collaer, M. L., & Hines, M. (1995). Human behavioral sex differences: A role for gonadal hormones during early development? *Psychological Bulletin, 118,* 55–107.

Collins, N. L., & Miller, L. C. (1994). Self-disclosure and liking: A meta-analytic review. *Psychological Bulletin, 116,* 457–475.

Condon, J. W., & Crano, W. D. (1988). Inferred evaluation and the relation between attitude similarity and interpersonal attraction. *Journal of Personality and Social Psychology, 54,* 789–797.

Connor, E. M., et al. (1994). Reduction of maternal-infant transmission of human immunodeficiency virus type 1 with zidovudine treatment. *New England Journal of Medicine, 331,* 1173–1180.

Constantine, L., & Constantine, J. (1973). *Group marriage.* New York: Macmillan.

Consumer's Union. (1995, May). Consumer reports: How reliable are condoms? America Online.

Cooper, A. J., et al. (1990). A female sex offender with multiple paraphilias: A psychologic, physiologic (laboratory sexual arousal) and endocrine case study. *Canadian Journal of Psychiatry, 35,* 334–337.

Corey, L., & Holmes, K. K. (1996). Therapy for HIV infection—What have we learned? *New England Journal of Medicine, 335,* 1142–1144.

Cosgray, R. E., et al. (1991). Death from auto-erotic asphyxiation in a long-term psychiatric setting. *Perspectives in Psychiatric Care, 27,* 21–24.

Court, 9–0, makes sex harassment easier to prove. (1993, November 10). *The New York Times,* pp. A1, A22.

Cowley, G., & Rogers, A. (1997, November 17). Rebuilding the male machine. *Newsweek,* pp. 66–67.

Cox, D. J. (1988). Incidence and nature of male genital exposure behavior as reported by college women. *Journal of Sex Research, 24,* 227–234.

Craig, M. E., Kalichman, S. C., & Follingstad, D. R. (1989). Verbal coercive sexual behavior among college students. *Archives of Sexual Behavior, 18,* 421–434.

Cramer, D., et al. (1998, January). *The Lancet.* Cited in Associated Press (1998, January 9). Painkiller may lower cancer risk. America Online.

Crews, D. (1994). Animal sexuality. *Scientific American, 270*(1), 108–114.

Cronin, A. (1993, June 27). Two viewfinders, two views of Gay America. *The New York Times,* Section 4, p. 10.

Crossette, B. (1998, March 23). Mutilation seen as risk for the girls of immigrants. *The New York Times,* p. A3.

Crowe, L. C., & George, W. H. (1989). Alcohol and human sexuality: Review and integration. *Psychological Bulletin, 105,* 374–386.

Crum, C., & Ellner, P. (1985). Chlamydia infections: Making the diagnosis. *Contemporary Obstetrics and Gynecology, 25,* 153–159, 163, 165, 168.

Cunningham, G., Cordero, E., & Thornby, J. (1989). Testosterone replacement with transdermal therapeutic systems. *Journal of the American Medical Association, 261,* 2525–2531.

Cunningham, M. R., et al. (1995). "Their ideas of beauty are, on the whole, the same as ours": Consistency and variability in the cross-cultural perception of female physical attractiveness. *Journal of Personality and Social Psychology, 68*(2), 261–279.

Curtis, R. C., & Miller, K. (1986). Believing another likes or dislikes you: Behavior making the beliefs come true. *Journal of Personality and Social Psychology, 51,* 284–290.

Cutler, W. B., & Preti, G. (1986). Human axillary secretions influence women's menstrual cycles: The role of donor extract from men. *Hormones and Behavior, 20,* 463–473.

Cutrona, C. E. (1983). Causal attributions and perinatal depression. *Journal of Abnormal Psychology, 92,* 161–172.

D

Dabbs, J. M., Jr., & Morris, R. (1990). Testosterone, social class, and antisocial behavior in a sample of 4,462 men. *Psychological Science, 1,* 1–3.

Daly, M., & Wilson, M. (1998). Cited in Brody, J. E. (1998, February 10). Genetic ties may be factor in violence in stepfamilies. *The New York Times,* pp. F1, F4.

Danner, S. A., et al. (1995). A short-term study of the safety, pharmacokinetics, and efficacy of ritonavir, an inhibitor of HIV-1 protease. *New England Journal of Medicine, 333,* 1528–1533.

Darabi, K. F., Dryfoos, J., & Schwartz, D. (1986). Hispanic adolescent fertility. *Hispanic Journal of Behavioral Sciences, 8,* 157–171.

Darling, C. A., & Davidson, J. K., Sr. (1986). Coitally active university students: Sexual behaviors, concerns, and challenges. *Adolescence, 21,* 403–419.12.

Darling, C. A., Davidson, J. K., & Jennings, D. A. (1991). The female sexual response revisited: Understanding the multiorgasmic experience in women. *Archives of Sexual Behavior, 20,* 527–540.

Darling, C. A., Davidson, J. K., & Passarello, L. C. (1992). The mystique of first intercourse among college youth: The role of partners, contraceptive practices, and psychological reactions. *Journal of Youth and Adolescence, 21,* 97–117.

D'Augelli, A. R. (1992a). Lesbian and gay male undergraduates' experiences of harassment and fear on campus. *Journal of Interpersonal Violence, 7,* 383–395.

D'Augelli, A. R. (1992b). Sexual behavior patterns of gay university men: Implications for preventing HIV infection. *Journal of American College Health, 41,* 25–29.

Davenport, W. (1965). Sexual patterns and their regulation in a society of the Southwest Pacific. In F. A. Beach (Ed.), *Sex and behavior.* New York: Wiley.

Davenport, W. (1977). Sex in cross-cultural perspective. In F. Beach (Ed.), *Human sexuality in four perspectives* (pp. 115–163). Baltimore: Johns Hopkins University Press.

Davidson, J. K., & Hoffman, L. E. (1986). Sexual fantasies and sexual satisfaction: An empirical analysis of erotic thought. *Journal of Sex Research, 22,* 184–205.

Davidson, K. J., Darling, C., & Conway-Welch, C. (1989). The role of the Grafenberg spot and female ejaculation in the female orgasmic response: An empirical analysis. *Journal of Sex and Marital Therapy, 15,* 102–119.

Davidson, N. E. (1995). Hormone-replacement therapy—Breast versus heart versus bone. *New England Journal of Medicine, 332,* 1638–1639.

Davies, P. T., & Cummings, E. M. (1994). Marital conflict and child adjustment. *Psychological Bulletin, 116,* 387–411.

Davison, G. C. (1977). Elimination of a sadistic fantasy by a client-controlled counterconditioning technique. In J. Fischer & H. Gochios (Eds.), *Handbook of behavior therapy with sexual problems.* New York: Pergamon Press.

Dawes, R. M. (1989). Statistical criteria for establishing a truly false consensus effect. *Journal of Experimental Social Psychology, 25,* 1–17.

Day, N. L., & Richardson, G. A. (1994). Comparative teratogenicity of alcohol and other drugs. *Alcohol Health and Research World, 18*(1), 42–48.

de Luca, R. V., et al. (1992). Group treatment for child sexual abuse. Special Issue: Violence and its aftermath. *Canadian Psychology, 33,* 168–179.

de Raad, B., & Doddema-Winsemius, M. (1992). Factors in the assortment of human mates: Differential preferences in Germany and the Netherlands. *Personality and Individual Differences, 13,* 103–114.

de Schampheleire, D. (1990). MMPI characteristics of professional prostitutes: A cross-cultural replication. *Journal of Personality Assessment, 54,* 343–350.

de Young, M. (1982). *The sexual victimization of children.* Jefferson, NC: McFarland & Company.

Dean, C. W., & de Bruyn-Kops, E. (1982). *The crime and consequences of rape.* Springfield, IL: Charles C. Thomas.

DeAngelis, T. (1994). Educators reveal keys to success in classroom. *APA Monitor, 25*(1), 39–40.

Deaux, K. (1985). Sex and gender. *Annual Review of Psychology, 36,* 49–81.

Deaux, K., & Lewis, L. L. (1983). Assessment of gender stereotypes: Methodology and components. *Psychological Documents, 13,* 25 (Ms. No. 2583).

Deepening shame: A *Newsweek* investigation into the scandal that is rocking the navy. (1992, August 10). *Newsweek,* pp. 30–36.

Defense dept. suspends its policy on homosexuals. (1993, October 8). *The New York Times,* p. A25.

Dekker, J. (1993). Inhibited male orgasm. In W. O'Donohue & J. H. Geer (Eds.), *Handbook of sexual dysfunctions: Assessment and treatment* (pp. 279–301). Boston: Allyn & Bacon.

Del Priore, G., et al. (1995). Risk of ovarian cancer after treatment for infertility. *New England Journal of Medicine, 332,* 1300.

Delgado, J. (1969). *Physical control of the mind.* New York: Harper & Row.

Delmas, P. D., et al. (1997). Effects of raloxifene on bone mineral density, serum cholesterol concentrations, and uterine endometrium in postmenopausal women. *New England Journal of Medicine, 337,* 1641–1648.

Denny, N., Field, J., & Quadagno, D. (1984). Sex differences in sexual needs and desires. *Archives of Sexual Behavior, 13,* 233–245.

DeParle, J. (1993, July 14). Big rise in birth outside wedlock. *The New York Times,* pp. A1, A14.

Desmond, A. M. (1994). Adolescent pregnancy in the United States: Not a minority issue. *Health Care for Women International, 15*(4), 325–331.

Deutsch, F. M., LeBaron, D., & Fryer, M. M. (1987). What is in a smile? *Psychology of Women Quarterly, 11,* 341–352.

DeWitt, K. (1991, October). The evolving concept of sexual harassment. *The New York Times.*

Diamond, M. (1993). Homosexuality and bisexuality in different populations. *Archives of Sexual Behavior, 22,* 291–310.

Diaz-Mitoma, F., et al. (1998, September 9). Oral famciclovir for the suppression of recurrent genital herpes: A randomized controlled trial. *Journal of the American Medical Association;* America Online.

Dick-Read, G. (1944). *Childbirth without fear: The principles and practices of natural childbirth.* New York: Harper & Bros.

DiClemente, R. J. (1992). Epidemiology of AIDS, HIV prevalence, and HIV incidence among adolescents. *Journal of School Health, 62,* 325–330.

Dietz, P. E., Hazelwood, R. R., & Warren, J. (1990). The sexually sadistic criminal and his offenses. *Bulletin of the American Academy of Psychiatry and the Law, 18,* 163–178.

DiMatteo, M. R., et al. (1996). Cesarean childbirth and psychosocial outcomes: A meta-analysis. *Health Psychology, 15,* 303–314.

Dindia, K., & Allen, M. (1992). Sex differences in self-disclosure: A meta-analysis. *Psychological Bulletin, 112,* 106–124.

Disease discovered Europe first? (1992, November 24). *New York Newsday,* p. 49.

Dixon, J. (1991). Feminist reforms of sexual coercion. In E. Grauerholz & M. A. Koralewski (Eds.), *Sexual coercion: A sourcebook on its nature, causes, and prevention* (pp. 161–171). Lexington, MA: Lexington Books.

"Doctors tie male mentality to shorter life span." (1995, June 14). *The New York Times,* p. C14.

Donnerstein, E. (1980). Aggressive erotica and violence against women. *Journal of Personality and Social Psychology, 39,* 269–277.

Donnerstein, E., & Berkowitz, L. (1981). Victim reactions in aggressive erotic films as a factor in violence against women. *Journal of Personality and Social Psychology, 41,* 710–724.

Donnerstein, E. I., & Linz, D. G. (1987). *The question of pornography.* New York: The Free Press.

Donoghue, D. (1995, August 20). The politics of homosexuality. *The New York Times Book Review,* pp. 3, 20.

Doorn, C. D., Poortinga, J., & Verschoor, A. M. (1994). Cross-gender identity in transvestites and male transsexuals. *Archives of Sexual Behavior, 23*(2), 185–201.

Douglas, J. M., Jr. (1990). Molluscum contagiosum. In K. K. Holmes, P. Mardh, P. F. Sparling, & P. J. Wiesner (Eds.), *Sex-ually transmitted diseases* (2nd ed., pp. 443–448). New York: McGraw-Hill.

Drapers, P. (1975). !Kung women: Contrasts in sexual egalitarianism in foraging and sedentary contexts. In R. R. Reiter (Ed.), *Toward an anthropology of women* (pp. 77–109). New York: Monthly Review Press.

Drews, C. D., et al. (1996, April). *Pediatrics.* Cited in "Smokers more likely to bear retarded babies, study says." (1996, April 10). *The New York Times,* p. B7.

Dreyfuss, I. A. (1998, February 8). Exercise may cut breast cancer risk. Associated Press; America Online.

Dube, R., & Hebert, M. (1988). Sexual abuse of children 12 years of age: A review of 511 cases. *Child Abuse and Neglect, 12,* 321–330.

Duffy, S. M., & Rusbult, C. E. (1985/1986). Satisfaction and commitment in homosexual and heterosexual relationships. *Journal of Homosexuality, 12,* 1–24.

Dugger, C. W. (1996a, September 11). A refugee's body is intact but her family is torn. *The New York Times,* pp. A1, B6.

Dugger, C. W. (1996b, October 12). New law bans genital cutting in United States. *The New York Times,* pp. A1, A28.

Dunlap, D. W. (1995, May 1). Support for gay adoptions seems to wane. *The New York Times,* p. A13.

Dunn, M. E. (1998). Cited in Leary, W. E. (1998, September 29), Older people enjoy sex, survey says. *The New York Times,* p. F8.

Dunn, M. E., & Trost, J. E. (1989). Male multiple orgasms: A descriptive study. *Archives of Sexual Behavior, 18,* 377–387.

DuRant, R. H., & Sanders, J. M. (1989). Sexual behavior and contraceptive risk taking among sexually active adolescent females. *Journal of Adolescent Health Care, 10,* 1–19.

DuRant, R. H., Seymore, C., Pendergrast, R., & Beckman, R. (1990). Contraceptive behavior among sexually active Hispanic adolescents. *Journal of Adolescent Health Care, 11,* 490–496.

Durfee, M. (1989). Prevention of child sexual abuse. *Psychiatric Clinics of North America, 12,* 445–453.

Dutch surgeons "restore virginity" to reduce shame. (1998, February 6). Reuters; America Online.

Dwyer, M. (1988). Exhibitionism/voyeurism. *Journal of Social Work and Human Sexuality, 7,* 101–112.

Dye, E., & Roth, S. (1990). Psychotherapists' knowledge about and attitudes toward sexual assault victim clients. *Psychology of Women Quarterly, 14,* 191–212.

Dziech, B. W., & Weiner, L. (1984). *The lecherous professor: Sexual harassment on campus.* Boston: Beacon Press.

E

Early prostate surgery is found very effective. (1996, August 28). *The New York Times,* p. C9.

Eastell, R. (1998). Treatment of postmenopausal osteoporosis. *New England Journal of Medicine, 338,* 736–746.

Eckert, E. D., et al. (1986). Homosexuality in monozygotic twins reared apart. *British Journal of Psychiatry, 148,* 421–425.

Edgley, C. (1989). Commercial sex: Pornography, prostitution, and advertising. In K. McKinney & S. Sprecher (Eds.), *Human sexuality: The societal and interpersonal context* (pp. 370–424). Norwood, NJ: Ablex Publishing Corporation.

Edlin, B. R., et al. (1994). Intersecting epidemics: Crack cocaine use and HIV infection among inner-city young adults. *New England Journal of Medicine, 331*, 1422–1427.

Edmonson, B. (1988). Disability and sexual adjustment. In V. B. Van Hasselt, P. S. Strain, & M. Hersen (Eds.), *Handbook of developmental and physical disabilities* (pp. 91–106). New York: Pergamon Press.

Ehrhardt, A. A. (1998). Cited in Bronner, E. (1998, February 1), "Just say maybe. No sexology, please. We're Americans." *The New York Times*, p. WK6.

Eisen, M., & Zellman, G. (1987). Changes in incidence of sexual intercourse of unmarried teenagers following a community-based sex education program. *The Journal of Sex Research, 23*, 527–544.

Ellis, A. (1962). *Reason and emotion in psychotherapy.* New York: Lyle Stuart.

Ellis, A. (1977). The basic clinical theory of rational-emotive therapy. In A. Ellis & R. Grieger (Eds.), *Handbook of rational-emotive therapy.* New York: Springer.

Ellis, L., & Ames, M. A. (1987). Neurohormonal functioning and sexual orientation: A theory of homosexuality-heterosexuality. *Psychological Bulletin, 101*, 233–258.

Ellis, L., Burke, D., & Ames, M. A. (1987). Sexual orientation as a continuous variable: A comparison between the sexes. *Archives of Sexual Behavior, 16*, 523–529.

Ember, C. R., & Ember, M. (1990). *Anthropology* (6th ed., Instructor's Edition). Englewood Cliffs, NJ: Prentice-Hall.

English, P. B., & Eskenazi, B. (1992). Reinterpreting the effects of maternal smoking on infant birthweight and perinatal mortality: A multivariate approach to birthweight standardization. *International Journal of Epidemiology, 21*, 1097–1105.

Erel, O., & Burman, B. (1995). Interrelatedness of marital relations and parent-child relations: A meta-analytic review. *Psychological Bulletin, 118*, 108–132.

Erlanger, S. (1991, July 14). A plague awaits. *The New York Times Magazine*, pp. 24, 26, 49, 53.

Eron, J. J., et al. (1995). Treatment with lamivudine, zidovudine, or both in HIV-positive patients with 200 to 500 CD4+ cells per cubic millimeter. *New England Journal of Medicine, 333*, 1662–1669.

Eskenazi, G. (1990, June 3). The male athlete and sexual assault. *The New York Times*, pp. L1, L4.

"Estrogen may aid fertility in men." (1997, December 16). *The New York Times*, p. F9.

Etaugh, C., & Rathus, S. A. (1995). *The world of children.* Fort Worth: Harcourt Brace College Publishers.

Everaerd, W. (1993). Male erectile disorder. In W. O'Donohue & J. H. Geer (Eds.), *Handbook of sexual dysfunctions: Assessment and treatment* (pp. 201–224). Boston: Allyn & Bacon.

Everitt, B. J. (1990). Sexual motivation: A neural and behavioural analysis of the mechanisms underlying appetitive and copulatory responses of male rats. *Neuroscience and Biobehavioral Reviews, 14*, 217–232.

Exner, J. E., et al. (1977). Some psychological characteristics of prostitutes. *Journal of Personality Assessment, 41*, 474–485.

F

Faller, K. C. (1989a). The role relationship between victim and perpetrator as a predictor of characteristics of intrafamilial sexual abuse. *Child and Adolescent Social Work Journal, 6*, 217–229.

Faller, K. C. (1989b). Why sexual abuse? An exploration of the intergenerational hypothesis. *Child Abuse and Neglect, 13*, 543–548.

Fallon, A. E., & Rozin, P. (1985). Sex differences in perceptions of desirable body shape. *Journal of Abnormal Psychology, 94*, 102–105.

Farley, A. U., Hadler, J. L., & Gunn, R. A. (1990). The syphilis epidemic in Connecticut: Relationship to drug use and prostitution. *Sexually Transmitted Diseases, 17*, 163–168.

Fay, R. E., et al. (1989). Prevalence and patterns of same-gender sexual contact among men. *Science, 243*, 338–348.

FDA allows large-scale AIDS vaccine trial. (1998, June 3). The Associated Press; CNN.

FDA approves an AIDS drug that is taken just once a day. (1998, September 19). *The New York Times*; America Online.

Federal Bureau of Investigation. (1991). *Uniform crime reports.* Washington, DC: U.S. Department of Justice.

Federman, D. D. (1994). Life without estrogen. *The New England Journal of Medicine, 331*, 1088–1089.

Feingold, A. (1991). Sex differences in the effects of similarity and physical attractiveness on opposite-sex attraction. *Basic and Applied Social Psychology, 12*, 357–367.

Feingold, A. (1994). Gender differences in personality: A meta-analysis. *Psychological Bulletin, 116*, 429–456.

Felsman, D., Brannigan, G., & Yellin, P. (1987). Control theory in dealing with adolescent sexuality and pregnancy. *Journal of Sex Education and Therapy, 13*, 15–16.

Feng, T. (1993). Substance abuse in pregnancy. *Current Opinions in Obstetrics and Gynecology, 5*, 16–23.

Fenichel, O. (1945). *The psychoanalytic theory of neurosis.* New York: W. W. Norton & Co.

Fensterheim, H., & Kantor, J. S. (1980). Behavioral approach to sexual disorders. In B. Wolman & J. Money (Eds.), *Handbook of human sexuality.* Englewood Cliffs, NJ: Prentice-Hall.

Ferrante, C. L., Haynes, A. M., & Kingsley, S. M. (1988). Image of women in television advertising. *Journal of Broadcasting and Electronic Media, 32*, 231–237.

Fichner-Rathus, L. (1998). *Understanding art* (5th ed.). Upper Saddle River, NJ: Prentice Hall.

Finkelhor, D. (1984). *Child sexual abuse: Theory and research.* New York: Free Press.

Finkelhor, D. (1990). Early and long-term effects of child sexual abuse: An update. *Professional Psychology: Research and Practice, 21*, 325–330.

Finkelhor, D., & Hotaling, G. T. (1984). Sexual abuse in the National Incidence Study of Child Abuse and Neglect: An appraisal. *Child Abuse and Neglect, 8,* 22–33.

Finkelhor, D., & Russell, D. (1984). Women as perpetrators: Review of the evidence. In D. Finkelhor (Ed.), *Child sexual abuse: Theory and research.* New York: The Free Press.

Finkelhor, D., & Yllo, K. (1982). Rape in marriage: A sociological view. In D. Finkelhor, R. J. Gelles, G. T. Hotaling, & M. A. Straus (Eds.), *The dark side of families: Current family violence research* (pp. 119–130). Beverly Hills, CA: Sage.

Finkelhor, D., et al. (1990). Sexual abuse in a national survey of adult men and women: Prevalence, characteristics, and risk factors. *Child Abuse and Neglect, 14,* 19–28.

Fish, L. S., Busby, D., & Killian, K. (1994). Structural couple therapy in the treatment of inhibited sexual drive. *American Journal of Family Therapy, 22*(2), 113–125.

Fisher, B., Weisberg, D. K., & Marotta, T. (1982). *Report on adolescent male prostitution.* San Francisco: Urban and Rural Systems Associates.

Fisher, J. (1992, January 11). Cited in "Associated Press, Boy beaver foils experts." *The New York Times,* p. 6.

Fisher, J. D., & Misovich, S. J. (1991). *1990 technical report on undergraduate students' AIDS-preventive behavior, AIDS-knowledge, and fear of AIDS.* Storrs, CT: University of Connecticut, Department of Psychology.

Fisher, T. D., & Hall, R. H. (1988). A scale for the comparison of the sexual attitudes of adolescents and their parents. *The Journal of Sex Research, 24,* 90–100.

Fisher, W. A., Fisher, J. D., & Rye, B. J. (1995). Understanding and promoting AIDS-preventive behavior: Insights from the theory of reasoned action. *Health Psychology, 14,* 255–264.

Fisher-Thompson, D. (1990). Adult sex typing of children's toys. *Sex Roles, 23,* 291–303.

Fitzgerald, L. F. (1993a). *Sexual harassment in higher education: Concepts and issues.* Washington, DC: National Education Association.

Fitzgerald, L. F. (1993b). Sexual harassment: Violence against women in the workplace. *American Psychologist, 48,* 1070–1076.

Fitzgerald, L. F., et al. (1988). Academic harassment: Sex and denial in scholarly garb. *Psychology of Women Quarterly, 12,* 329–340.

Fletcher, J. (1966). *Situation ethics.* Philadelphia: Westminster Press.

Fletcher, J. (1967). *Moral responsibility: Situation ethics at work.* Philadelphia: Westminster Press.

Fletcher, J. M., et al. (1991). Neurobehavioral outcomes in diseases of childhood: Individual change models for pediatric human immunodeficiency viruses. *American Psychologist, 46,* 1267–1277.

Flexner, C. (1998). Drug therapy: HIV-protease inhibitors. *New England Journal of Medicine, 338,* 1281–1292.

Floyd, R. L., Rimer, B. K., Giovino, G. A., Mullen, P. D., & Sullivan, S. E. (1993). A review of smoking in pregnancy: Effects on pregnancy outcomes and cessation efforts. *Annual Review of Public Health, 14,* 379–411.

For high school girls, Norplant debate hits home. (1993, March 7). *The New York Times,* p. 28.

Ford, C. S., & Beach, F. A. (1951). *Patterns of sexual behavior.* New York: Harper & Row.

Forrest, J. D., & Fordyce, R. R. (1993). Women's contraceptive attitudes and use in 1992. *Family Planning Perspectives, 25,* 175–179.

Forster, P., & King, J. (1994). Fluoxetine for premature ejaculation. *American Journal of Psychiatry, 151*(10), 1523.

Frank, E., & Wenger, N. K. (1997, December 15). Women doctors in menopause are twice as likely as other women to use hormone-replacement therapy. *Emory University's Annals of Internal Medicine.*

Franzoi, S. L., & Herzog, M. E. (1987). Judging physical attractiveness: What body aspects do we use. *Personality and Social Psychology Bulletin, 13,* 19–33.

Fraser, A. M., Brockert, J. E., & Ward, R. H. (1995). Association of young maternal age with adverse reproductive outcomes. *New England Journal of Medicine, 332,* 1113–1117.

Frayser, S. (1985). *Varieties of sexual experience: An anthropological perspective on human sexuality.* New Haven, CT: Human Relations Area Files Press.

Frazier, P. A. (1990). Victim attributions and post-rape trauma. *Journal of Personality and Social Psychology, 59,* 298–304.

Freiberg, P. (1995). Psychologists examine attacks on homosexuals. *APA Monitor, 26*(6), 30–31.

Freiberg, P. (1996). New drugs give hope to AIDS patients. *APA Monitor, 27*(6), 28.

Freud, S. (1922/1959). Analysis of a phobia in a 5-year-old boy. In A. J. Strachey (Ed. & Trans.), *Collected papers, Vol. 3.* New York: Basic Books. (Original work published 1909.)

Freund, K., & Blanchard, R. (1986). The concept of courtship disorder. *Journal of Sex and Marital Therapy, 12,* 79–92.

Freund, K., Watson, R., & Rienzo, D. (1988). The value of self-reports in the study of voyeurism and exhibitionism. *Annals of Sex Research, 1,* 243–262.

Freund, M., Leonard, T. L., & Lee, N. (1989). Sexual behavior of resident street prostitutes with their clients in Camden, New Jersey. *Journal of Sex Research, 26,* 460–478.

Frey, K. S., & Ruble, D. N. (1992). Gender constancy and the "cost" of sex-typed behavior: A test of the conflict hypothesis. *Developmental Psychology, 28,* 714–721.

Friday, N. (1973). *My secret garden.* New York: Trident.

Fried, P. A. (1986). Marijuana use in pregnancy. In I. J. Chasnott (Ed.), *Drug use in pregnancy: Mother and child.* Boston: MTP Press.

Friedman, L. C., et al. (1994). Dispositional optimism, self-efficacy, and health beliefs as predictors of breast self-examination. *American Journal of Preventive Medicine, 10*(3), 130–135.

Friedman, R. C., & Downey, J. I. (1994). Homosexuality. *New England Journal of Medicine, 331,* 923–930.

Friedrich, W. N. (1998). Cited in Gilbert, S. (1998). "New light shed on normal sexual behavior in a child." *The New York Times,* p. F7.

Friedrich, W. N., & Gerber, P. N. (1994). Autoerotic asphyxia: The development of a paraphilia. *Journal of the American Academy of Child and Adolescent Psychiatry, 33*(7), 970–974.

Frisch, R. (1997). Cited in Angier, N. (1997a). Chemical tied to fat control could help trigger puberty. *The New York Times*, pp. C1, C3.

Frodi, A. M., Macauley, J., & Thome, P. R. (1977). Are women always less aggressive than men? A review of the experimental literature. *Psychological Bulletin, 84*, 634–660.

Fuchs, C. S., et al. (1995). Alcohol consumption and mortality among women. *New England Journal of Medicine, 332*, 1245–1250.

Fuentes, A. (1993, June 30). AIDS rising among Latinos. *New York Daily News*, p. 21.

Fugger, E. F., et al. (1998). *Human Reproduction*. Cited in Kolata, G. (1998, September 9). Researchers report success in method to pick baby's sex. *The New York Times*; America Online.

Fuleihan, G. E. (1997). Tissue specific estrogens—The promise for the future. *New England Journal of Medicine, 337*, 1686–1687.

Furnham, A., & Voli, V. (1989). Gender stereotypes in Italian television advertisements. *Journal of Broadcasting and Electronic Media, 33*, 175–185.

Furstenberg, F. F., Jr., Brooks-Gunn, J., Chase-Lansdale, L. (1989). Teenaged pregnancy and childbearing. *American Psychologist, 44*, 313–320.

G

Gabelnick, H. L., (1998). Future methods. In Hatcher, R. A., et al. (Eds.), (1998). *Contraceptive technology* (17th rev. ed., pp. 615–622). New York: Ardent Media, Inc.

Gabriel, T. (1995a, April 23). When one spouse is gay and a marriage unravels. *The New York Times*, pp. A1, A22.

Gabriel, T. (1995b, June 12). A new generation seems ready to give bisexuality a place in the spectrum. *The New York Times*, p. A12.

Gaddis, A., & Brooks-Gunn, J. (1985). The male experience of pubertal change. *Journal of Youth and Adolescence, 14*, 61.

Gagnon, J. H. (1977). *Human sexualities*. Glenview, IL: Scott, Foresman.

Gagnon, J. H. (1990). Gender preferences in erotic relations: The Kinsey scale and sexual scripts. In D. P. McWhirter, S. A. Sanders, & J. M. Reinisch (Eds.), *Homosexuality/heterosexuality: Concepts of sexual orientation* (pp. 177–207). New York: Oxford University Press.

Gagnon, J. H., & Simon, W. (1973). *Sexual conduct: The social origins of human sexuality*. Chicago: Aldine.

Gagnon, J. H., & Simon, W. (1987). The sexual scripting of oral genital contacts. *Archives of Sexual Behavior, 16*, 1–25.

Ganitsch, C. (1998). Personal communication.

Garber, M. (1995). *Vice versa*. New York: Simon & Schuster.

Gardiner, H. W., & Gardiner, O. S. (1991). Women in Thailand. In L. L. Adler (Ed.), *Women in cross-cultural perspective* (pp. 175–187). New York: Praeger.

Garland, S. M., Lees, M. I., & Skurrie, I. J. (1990). *Chlamydia trachomatis*: Role in tubal infertility. *Australian and New Zealand Journal of Obstetrics and Gynaecology, 30*, 83–86.

Garnets, L., & Kimmel, D. (1991). In J. D. Goodchilds (Ed.). *Psychological perspectives on human diversity in America*. Washington, DC: American Psychological Association.

Garwood, S. G., et al. (1980). Beauty is only "name deep": The effect of first name in ratings of physical attraction. *Journal of Applied Social Psychology, 10*, 431–435.

Gay, P. (1984). *The bourgeois experience: Victoria to Freud*. New York: Oxford University Press.

Gayle, J., Selik, R., & Ccu, S. (1990). Surveillance for AIDS and HIV infection among Black and Hispanic children and women of childbearing age, 1981–1989. *Morbidity and Mortality Weekly Report: Progress in Chronic Disease Prevention, 39*, 23–29. Washington, DC: U.S. Department of Health and Human Services.

Gebhard, P. H. (1969). Misconceptions about female prostitutes. *Medical Aspects of Human Sexuality, 3*, 24–26.

Gebhard, P. H. (1976). The institute. In M. S. Weinberg (Ed.), *Sex research: Studies from the Kinsey Institute*. New York: Oxford University Press.

Gebhard, P. H. (1977). *Memorandum on the incidence of homosexuals in the United States*. Bloomington, IN: Indiana University Institute for Sex Research.

Gebhard, P. H., et al. (1965). *Sex offenders: An analysis of types*. New York: Harper & Row.

Geer, J., Heiman, J., & Leitenberg, H. (1984). *Human sexuality*. Englewood Cliffs, NJ: Prentice-Hall.

Geiger, R. (1981). Neurophysiology of sexual response in spinal cord injury. In D. Bullard & S. Knight (Eds.), *Sexuality and physical disability: Personal perspectives*. St. Louis: C. V. Mosby.

Gelles, R. J., & Cornell, C. P. (1985). *Intimate violence in families*. Beverly Hills, CA: Sage.

Gelman, D., with P. Kandell. (1993, January 18). Isn't it romantic? *Newsweek*, pp. 60–61.

Genuis, M., Thomlison, B., & Bagley, C. (1991, Fall). Male victims of child sexual abuse: A brief overview of pertinent findings. Special issue: Child sexual abuse. *Journal of Child and Youth-Care*, 1–6.

Geringer, W. M., et al. (1993). Knowledge, attitudes, and behavior related to condom use and STDs in a high risk population. *Journal of Sex Research, 30*, 75–83.

Gerrard, M. (1987). Sex, sex guilt, and contraceptive use revisited: The 1980s. *Journal of Personality and Social Psychology, 52*, 975–980.

Gerrol, R., & Resick, P. A. (1988, November). Sex differences in social support and recovery from victimization. Paper presented at the meeting of the Association for Advancement of Behavior Therapy, New York, NY.

Gibbs, N. (1991, June 3). When is it rape? *Time*, pp. 48–54.

Gibson, A. I., et al. (1988). Adolescent female prostitutes. *Archives of Sexual Behavior, 17,* 431–438.

Gidycz, C. A., & Koss, M. P. (1990). A comparison of group and individual sexual assault victims. *Psychology of Women Quarterly, 14,* 325–342.

Gijs, L., & Gooren, L. (1996). Hormonal and psychopharmacological interventions in the treatment of paraphilias: An update. *Journal of Sex Research, 33,* 273–290.

Gilbert, S. (1996, September 25). No long-term link is found between pill and breast cancer. *The New York Times,* p. C9.

Gilbert, S. (1998, September 22). Doctors report rise in elective Caesareans. *The New York Times,* p. F7.

Gillis, J. S., & Avis, W. E. (1980). The male-taller norm in mate selection. *Personality and Social Psychology Bulletin, 6,* 396–401.

Gilmartin, B. G. (September 1975). That swinging couple down the block. *Psychology Today, 54.*

Giovannucci, E., et al. (1993a). A prospective cohort study of vasectomy and prostate cancer in U.S. men. *Journal of the American Medical Association, 269,* 873–877.

Giovannucci, E., et al. (1993b). A retrospective cohort study of vasectomy and prostate cancer in U.S. men. *Journal of the American Medical Association, 269,* 878–882.

Gitlin, M. J., & Pasnau, R. O. (1989). Psychiatric syndromes linked to reproductive function in women: A review of current knowledge. *American Journal of Psychiatry, 146,* 1413–1422.

Glass, S. P., & Wright, T. L. (1992). Justifications of extramarital relationships: The association between attitudes, behaviors, and gender. *Journal of Sex Research, 29,* 361–387.

Gold, R. S., & Skinner, M. J. (1992). Situational factor and thought processes associated with unprotected intercourse in young gay men. *AIDS, 6,* 1021–1030.

Gold, S. R., & Gold, R. G. (1993). Sexual aversions: A hidden disorder. In W. O'Donohue & J. H. Geer (Eds.), *Handbook of sexual dysfunctions: Assessment and treatment* (pp. 83–102). Boston: Allyn & Bacon.

Goldberg, C. (1995, September 11). Sex slavery, Thailand to New York. *The New York Times,* pp. B1, B6.

Goldberg, C. (1998, September 8). Getting to the truth in child abuse cases: New methods. *The New York Times,* pp. F1, F5.

Goldberg, C., & Elder, J. (1998, January 16). Public still backs abortion, but wants limits, poll says. *The New York Times,* pp. A1, A16.

Goldberg, L. H., et al. (1993). Longterm suppression of recurrent genital herpes with acyclovir. *Archives of Dermatology, 129,* 582–587.

Goldberg, M. (1987). Understanding hypersexuality in men and women. In G. R. Weeks and Larry Hof (Eds.), *Integrating sex and marital therapy: A clinical guide* (pp. 202–220). New York: Brunner/Mazel.

Goldenberg, R. L., & Klerman, L. V. (1995). Adolescent pregnancy—Another look. *New England Journal of Medicine, 332,* 1161–1162.

Golding, J. M., et al. (1989, January). Social support sources following sexual assault. *Journal of Community Psychology, 17*(1), 92–107.

Goldman, J. A., & Harlow, L. L. (1993). Self-perception variables that mediate AIDS-preventive behavior in college students. *Health Psychology, 12,* 489–498.

Goldstein, A. M., & Clark, J. H. (1990). Treatment of uncomplicated gonococcal urethritis with single-dose ceftriaxone. *Sexually Transmitted Diseases, 17,* 181–183.

Goldstein, I. (1998). Cited in Kolata, G. (1998, April 4). Impotence pill: Would it also help women? *The New York Times,* pp. A1, A6.

Goldstein, I., et al. (1998). Oral sildenafil in the treatment of erectile dysfunction. *New England Journal of Medicine, 338,* 1397–1404.

Goleman, D. (1988, October 18). Chemistry of sexual desire yields its elusive secrets. *The New York Times,* pp. C1, C15.

Goleman, D. (1991, October 22). Sexual harassment: It's about power, not lust. *The New York Times,* pp. C1, C12.

Goleman, D. (1992). Therapies offer hope for sex offenders. *The New York Times,* pp. C1, C11.

Goleman, D. (1993, October 6). Abuse-prevention efforts aid children. *The New York Times,* p. C13.

Goleman, D. (1995, June 14). Sex fantasy research said to neglect women. *The New York Times,* p. C14.

Gomez, J., & Smith, B. (1990). Taking the home out of homophobia: Black lesbian health. In E. C. White (Ed.), *The Black women's health book: Speaking for ourselves.* Seattle: Seal Press.

Gomez-Schwartz, B., Horowitz, J., & Cardarelli, A. (1990). *Child sexual abuse: The initial effects.* Newbury Park, CA: Sage.

Gonsiorck, J. (1988). Mental health issues of gay and lesbian adolescents. *Journal of Adolescent Health Care, 9,* 114–122.

Goodwin, J. M., Cheeves, K., & Connell, V. (1990). Borderline and other severe symptoms in adult survivors of incestuous abuse. *Psychiatric Annals, 20,* 22–32.

Gordon, S., & Snyder, C. W. (1989). *Personal issues in human sexuality: A guidebook for better sexual health* (2nd ed.). Boston: Allyn & Bacon.

Gottlieb, M. S. (1991, June 5). AIDS—the second decade: Leadership is lacking. *The New York Times,* p. A29.

Goulart, M., & Madover, S. (1991). An AIDS prevention program for homeless youth. *Journal of Adolescent Health, 12,* 573–575.

Graber, B. (1993). Medical aspects of sexual arousal disorders. In W. O'Donohue & J. H. Geer (Eds.), *Handbook of sexual dysfunctions: Assessment and treatment* (pp. 103–156). Boston: Allyn & Bacon.

Graca, L. M., Cardoso, C. G., Clode, N., & Calhaz-Jorge, C. (1991). Acute effects of maternal cigarette smoking on fetal heart rate and fetal body movements felt by the mother. *Journal of Perinatal Medicine, 19,* 385–390.

Graham, J. M., & Blanco, J. D. (1990). Chlamydial infections. *Primary Care: Clinics in Office Practice, 17,* 85–93.

Graham, S., et al. (1982). Sex patterns and herpes simplex virus type 2 in the epidemiology of cancer of the cervix. *American Journal of Epidemiology, 115,* 729–735.

Grauerholz, E. (1989). Sexual harassment of women professors by students: Exploring the dynamics of power, authority, and gender in a university setting. *Sex Roles, 21,* 789–301.

Green, R. (1978). Sexual identity of 37 children raised by homosexual or transsexual parents. *American Journal of Psychiatry, 135,* 692–697.

Green, R. (1987). *The "sissy boy syndrome" and the development of homosexuality.* New Haven, CT: Yale University Press.

Greenberg, E. R., et al. (1984). Breast cancer in mothers given diethylstilbestrol in pregnancy. *New England Journal of Medicine, 311,* 1393–1398.

Greene, B. (1994). Ethnic-minority lesbians and gay men: Mental health and treatment issues. *Journal of Consulting and Clinical Psychology, 62,* 243–251.

Greenhouse, L. (1992, February 27). Court opens path for student suits in sex-bias cases. *The New York Times,* pp. A1, A16.

Greenwald, E., & Leitenberg, H. (1989). Long-term effects of sexual experiences with siblings and non-siblings during childhood. *Archives of Sexual Behavior, 18,* 389–399.

Griffin, E., & Sparks, G. G. (1990). Friends forever: A longitudinal exploration of intimacy in same-sex friends and platonic pairs. *Journal of Social and Personal Relationships, 7,* 29–46.

Grodstein, F., Goldman, M. G., & Cramer, D. W. (1993). Relation of tubal infertility to history of sexually transmitted diseases. *American Journal of Epidemiology, 137,* 577–584.

Grodstein, F., et al. (1996). Postmenopausal estrogen and progestin use and the risk of cardiovascular disease. *New England Journal of Medicine, 335,* 453–461.

Grodstein, F., et al. (1997). Postmenopausal hormonal therapy and mortality. *New England Journal of Medicine, 336,* 1769–1775.

Grogger, J., & Bronars, S. (1993). The socioeconomic consequences of teenage childbearing: Findings from a natural experiment. *Family Planning Perspectives, 25,* 156–161.

Groneman, C. (1994). Nymphomania: The historical construction of female sexuality. *Signs, 19*(2), 337–367.

Gross, J. (1991, February 11). New challenge of youth: Growing up in a gay home. *The New York Times,* pp. A1, B7.

Gross, J. (1992, July 13). Suffering in silence no more: Fighting sexual harassment. *The New York Times,* pp. A10, D10.

Gross, J. (1993, September 25). Combating rape on campus in a class on sexual consent. *The New York Times,* pp. 1, 9.

Grossman, S. (1991, December 22). Cited in "Undergraduates drink heavily, survey discloses." *The New York Times,* p. 46.

Groth, A. N. (1978). Patterns of sexual assault against children and adolescents. In A. W. Burgess, A. N. Groth, L. L. Holmstrom, & S. M. Sgroi (Eds.), *Sexual assault of children and adolescents.* Toronto: Lexington Books.

Groth, A. N., & Birnbaum, H. J. (1979). *Men who rape: The psychology of the offender.* New York: Plenum Press.

Groth, A. N., & Burgess, A. W. (1980). Male rape: Offenders and victims. *American Journal of Psychiatry, 137,* 806–810.

Groth, A., & Hobson, W. (1983). The dynamics of sexual assault. In L. Schlesinger & E. Revitch (Eds.), *Sexual dynamics of antisocial behavior.* Springfield, IL: Thomas.

Gruber, J. E., & Bjorn, L. (1986). Women's responses to sexual harassment: An analysis of sociocultural, organizational, and personal resource models. *Social Science Quarterly, 67,* 814–826.

Grunfeld, C. (1995). What causes wasting in AIDS? *New England Journal of Medicine, 333,* 123–124.

Grych, J. H., & Fincham, F. D. (1993). Children's appraisals of marital conflict. *Child Development, 64,* 215–230.

Guinan, M. E. (1992). Cited in Leary, W. E. (1992, February 1). U.S. panel backs approval of first condom for women. *The New York Times,* p. 7.

Gupta, M. (1994). Sexuality in the Indian subcontinent. *Sexual and Marital Therapy, 9*(1), 57–69.

H

Haas-Hawkings, G., et al. (1985). A study of relatively immediate adjustment to widowhood in late life. *International Journal of Women's Studies, 8,* 158–165.

Haddow, J. E., et al. (1998). Screening of maternal serum for fetal Down's syndrome in the first trimester. *New England Journal of Medicine, 338,* 955–961.

Haffner, D. (1993, August). Sex education: Trends and issues. Paper presented at the meeting of the American Psychological Association, Toronto, Canada.

Haglund, B., & Cnattingius, S. (1990). Cigarette smoking as a risk factor for sudden infant death syndrome: A population based study. *American Journal of Public Health, 80,* 29–32.

Hall, C. S. (1984). "A ubiquitous sex difference in dreams" revisited. *Journal of Personality and Social Psychology, 46,* 1109–1117.

Hall, G. C. N. (1989). Sexual arousal and arousability in a sexual offender population. *Journal of Abnormal Psychology, 98,* 145–149.

Hall, G. C. N., & Hirschman, R. (1991). Toward a theory of sexual aggression: A quadripartite model. *Journal of Consulting and Clinical Psychology, 59,* 662–669.

Hamer, D. H., et al. (1993, July 16). A linkage between DNA markers on the X chromosome and male sexual orientation. *Science, 261,* 321–327.

Hamilton, M., & Yee, J. (1990). Rape knowledge and propensity to rape. *Journal of Research in Personality, 24,* 111–122.

Handler, A. (1990). The correlates of the initiation of sexual intercourse among young urban Black females. *Journal of Youth and Adolescence, 19,* 159–170.

Handsfield, H. (1984). Gonorrhea and uncomplicated gonococcal infection. In K. K. Holmes et al. (Eds.), *Sexually transmitted diseases* (pp. 205–220). New York: McGraw-Hill.

Haney, D. Q. (1997, September 30). AIDS virus resisting new drugs. *Daily Record,* pp. A1, A10.

Hanrahan, J. P., et al. (1992). The effect of maternal smoking during pregnancy on early infant lung function. *American Review of Respiratory Disease, 145,* 1129–1135.

Hanson, R. K. (1990). The psychological impact of sexual assault on women and children: A review. *Annals of Sex Research, 3,* 187–232.

Hanson, S. L., Morrison, D. R., & Ginsburg, A. L. (1989). The antecedents of teenage fatherhood. *Demography, 26,* 579–596.

Harding, J. J. (1989). Postpartum psychiatric disorders: A review. *Comprehensive Psychiatry, 30,* 109–112.

Hariton, E. B., & Singer, J. L. (1974). Women's fantasies during sexual intercourse: Normative and theoretical implications. *Journal of Consulting and Clinical Psychology, 42,* 313–322.

Harney, P. A., & Muehlenhard, C. L. (1991). Rape. In E. Grauerholz & M. A. Koralewski (Eds.), *Sexual coercion: A sourcebook on its nature, causes, and prevention* (pp. 3–16). Lexington, MA: Lexington Books.

Harold, G. T., Fincham, F. D., Osborne, L. N., & Conger, R. D. (1997). Mom and Dad are at it again: Adolescent perceptions of marital conflict and adolescent psychological distress. *Developmental Psychology, 33,* 333–350.

Harris, L. (1988). *Inside America.* New York: Vintage.

Harris, L., & Associates (1995). Cited in "Mom the Provider." (1995, May 14). *The New York Times,* p. A14.

Hart, J., et al. (1991). Sexual behavior in pregnancy: A study of 219 women. *Journal of Sex Education and Therapy, 17,* 86–90.

Hartge, P. (1997). Abortion, breast cancer, and epidemiology. *New England Journal of Medicine, 336,* 127–128.

Hartman, C. R., Burgess, A. W., & McCormack, A. (1987). Pathways and cycles of runaways: A model for understanding repetitive runaway behavior. *Hospital and Community Psychiatry, 38,* 292–299.

Harvey, S. (1987). Female sexual behavior: Fluctuations during the menstrual cycle. *Journal of Psychosomatic Research, 31,* 101–110.

Hass, A. (1979). *Teenage sexuality.* New York: Macmillan.

Hatcher, R. A. (1998). Depo-Provera, Norplant, and progestin-only pills (minipills). In R. A. Hatcher et al. (1998), *Contraceptive technology* (17th rev. ed., pp. 467–510). New York: Ardent Media, Inc.

Hatcher, R. A., & Guillebaud, J. (1998). The pill: Combined oral contraceptives. In R. A. Hatcher et al. (1998), *Contraceptive technology* (17th rev. ed., pp. 405–466). New York: Ardent Media, Inc.

Hatcher, R. A., et al. (1998). *Contraceptive technology* (17th rev. ed.). New York: Ardent Media, Inc.

Hatfield, E. (1988). Passionate and companionate love. In R. J. Sternberg & M. L. Barnes (Eds.), *The psychology of love* (pp. 191–217). New Haven, CT: Yale University Press.

Hatfield, E., & Sprecher, S. (1986). Measuring passionate love in intimate relationships. *Journal of Adolescence, 9,* 383–410.

Hausknecht, R. U. (1995). Methotrexate and misoprostol to terminate early pregnancy. *New England Journal of Medicine, 333,* 537–540.

Hausknecht, R. U. (1998). Cited in Hitt, J. (1998, January 18). Who will do abortions here? *The New York Times Magazine,* p. 42.

Havemann, E., & Lehtinen, M. (1990). *Marriages and families: New problems, new opportunities* (2nd ed.). Englewood Cliffs, NJ: Prentice-Hall, Inc.

Hayes, C. D. (Ed.). (1987). *Risking the future, Vol. 1.* Washington, DC: National Academy Press.

Hawton, K. (1991). Sex therapy. Special Issue: The changing face in behavioral psychotherapy. *Behavioral Psychotherapy, 19,* 131–136.

Hawton, K., & Catalan, J. (1990). Sex therapy for vaginismus: Characteristics of couples and treatment outcomes. *Sexual and Marital Therapy, 5,* 39–48.

Hazan, C., & Shaver, P. (1987). Love conceptualized as an attachment process. *Journal of Personality and Social Psychology, 52,* 511–524.

Heath, R. (1972). Pleasure and brain activity in man. *Journal of Nervous and Mental Disease, 154,* 3–18.

Hechtman, L. (1989). Teenage mothers and their children: Risks and problems: A review. *Canadian Journal of Psychiatry, 34,* 569–575.

Hegeler, S., & Mortensen, M. (1977). Sexual behavior in elderly Danish males. In R. Gemme & C. Wheeler (Eds.), *Progress in sexology* (pp. 285–292). New York: Plenum Press.

Heiman, J. R., & LoPiccolo, J. (1987). *Becoming orgasmic* (2nd ed.). Englewood Cliffs, NJ: Prentice-Hall Books.

Hendrick, C., & Hendrick, S. (1986). A theory and method of love. *Journal of Personality and Social Psychology, 50,* 392–402.

Henneberger, M. (with M. Marriott). (1993). For some, rituals of abuse replace youthful courtship. *The New York Times,* pp. A1, A33.

Henry, J. (1963). *Culture against man.* New York: Random House.

Hensley, W. E. (1992). Why does the best-looking person in the room always seem to be surrounded by admirers? *Psychological Reports, 70,* 457–458.

Hensley, W. E. (1994). Height as a basis for interpersonal attraction. *Adolescence 29,* 469–474.

Herdt, G. H. (1981). *Guardians of the flutes: Idioms of masculinity.* New York: McGraw-Hill.

Herdt, G. H. (1987). *The Sambia: Ritual and gender in New Guinea.* New York: Holt, Rinehart & Winston.

Hernandez, J. T., & Smith, F. J. (1990). Inconsistencies and misperceptions putting college students at risk of HIV infection. *Journal of Adolescent Health Care, 11,* 295–297.

Herzog, L. (1989). Urinary tract infections and circumcision. *American Journal of Diseases of Children, 143,* 348–350.

Hess, B. B., Markson, E. W., & Stein, P. J. (1993). *Sociology* (4th ed.). New York: Macmillan.

Hillier, S., & Holmes, K. K. (1990). Bacterial vaginosis. In K. K. Holmes, P. Mardh, P. F. Sparling, & P. J. Wiesner (Eds.), *Sexually transmitted diseases* (2nd ed., pp. 547–560). New York: McGraw-Hill.

Hilton, E., et al. (1992). Ingestion of yogurt containing *Lactobacillus acidophilus* as prophylaxis for candidal vaginitis. *Annals of Internal Medicine, 116,* 353–357.

Hingson, R. W., et al. (1990). Beliefs about AIDS, use of alcohol and drugs, and unprotected sex among Massachusetts adolescents. *American Journal of Public Health, 80,* 295–298.

Hirsch, M. S., et al. (1998). Antiretroviral drug resistance testing in adults with HIV infection. *Journal of the American Medical Association, 279,* 1984–1991.

Hite, S. (1976). *The Hite report.* New York: Macmillan.

Hite, S. (1977). *The Hite report: A nationwide study of female sexuality.* New York: Dell.

Hite, S. (1981). *The Hite report on male sexuality.* New York: Knopf.

Hitt, J. (1998, January 18). Who will do abortions here? *The New York Times Magazine,* pp. 20–27, 42, 45–46, 54–55.

HIV clue supports early use of condom. (1992, December 18). *The New York Times,* p. C9.

HIV infection rate in U.S. holds steady. (1998, April 24). The Associated Press; America Online.

Ho, D. D. (1995). Time to hit HIV, early and hard. *New England Journal of Medicine, 333,* 450–451.

Ho, G. Y. F., et al. (1998, February 12). *New England Journal of Medicine, 338.* Cited in "Sexually active coeds at higher risk for HPV" (1998, February 11). Reuters; America Online.

Hoagwood, K. (1990). Blame and adjustment among women sexually abused as children. *Women and Therapy, 9,* 89–110.

Hobfoll, S. E., Jackson, A. P., Lavin, J., Britton, P. J., & Shepherd, J. B. (1993). Safer sex knowledge, behavior, and attitudes of inner-city women. *Health Psychology, 12,* 481–488.

Hock, Z. (1983). The G spot. *Journal of Sex and Marital Therapy, 9,* 166–167.

Hodges, B. C., et al. (1992). Gender-differences in adolescents' attitudes toward condom use. *Journal of School Health, 62,* 103–106.

Hodgson, R., et al. (1990). *Chlamydia trachomatis:* The prevalence, trend and importance in initial infertility management. *Australian and New Zealand Journal of Obstetrics and Gynaecology, 30,* 251–254.

Hodson, D. S., & Skeen, P. (1994). Sexuality and aging: The hammerlock of myths. *Journal of Applied Gerontology, 13*(3), 219–235.

Hofferth, S. L., & Hayes, C. D. (Eds.). (1987). *Risking the future: Adolescent sexuality, pregnancy, and childbearing: Vol. 2. Working papers and statistical reports.* Washington, DC: National Academy Press.

Hoffman, C., & Hurst, N. (1990). Gender stereotypes: Perception or rationalization? *Journal of Personality and Social Psychology, 58,* 197–208.

Hogan, D. P., & Kitigawa, E. M. (1985). The impact of social status, family structure and neighborhood on the fertility of black adolescents. *Family Planning Perspectives, 17,* 165–169.

Holden, G. W., & Ritchie, K. L. (1991). Linking extreme marital discord, child rearing, and child behavior problems. *Child Development, 62,* 311–327.

Holmes-Farley, S. R. (1998, September 16). Who should decide the sex of a baby? *The New York Times,* p. A28.

Holtzman, D., et al. (1992). HIV education and health education in the United States: A national survey of local school district policies and practices. *Journal of School Health, 62,* 421–427.

Holzman, H. R., & Pines, S. (1982). Buying sex: The phenomenology of being a john. *Deviant Behavior, 4,* 89–116.

Horowitz, R. (1983). *Honor and the American dream: Culture and identity in a Chicano community.* New Brunswick, NJ: Rutgers University Press.

Howard, J. A., Blumstein, P., & Schwartz, P. (1987). Social or evolutionary theories: Some observations on preferences in mate selection. *Journal of Personality and Social Psychology, 53,* 194–200.

Howard, M., & McCabe, J. B. (1990). Helping teenagers postpone sexual involvement. *Family Planning Perspectives, 22,* 21–26.

Howard, M. C. (1989). *Contemporary cultural anthropology* (3rd ed.). Glenview, IL: Scott, Foresman and Company.

Howards, S. S. (1995). Current concepts: Treatment of male infertility. *New England Journal of Medicine, 332,* 312–317.

Hsu, B., et al. (1994). Gender differences in sexual fantasy and behavior in a college population: A ten-year replication. *Journal of Sex and Marital Therapy, 20*(2), 103–118.

Hu, S. (1992, January 24). Cited in "Immune deficiency vaccine for monkeys succeeds." *The New York Times,* p. A17.

Huang, K., & Uba, L. (1992). Premarital sexual behavior among Chinese college students in the United States. *Archives of Sexual Behavior, 21,* 227–240.

Hubbard, R., & Wald, E. (1993). *Exploding the gene myth.* Boston: Beacon Press.

Huffman, T., Chang, K., Rausch, P., & Schaffer, N. (1994). Gender differences and factors related to the disposition toward cohabitation. *Family Therapy, 21*(3), 171–184.

Huge gains, huge worries, on AIDS. (1998, October 9). *The New York Times,* p. A26.

Hunt, M. (1974). *Sexual behavior in the 1970's.* New York: Dell Books.

Hunt, M. (1979). Legal rape. *Family Circle,* January 9.

Hunter, D. J., et al. (1996). Cohort studies of fat intake and the risk of breast cancer—A pooled analysis. *New England Journal of Medicine, 334,* 356–361.

Hyde, J. S., & Linn, M. C. (1988). Gender differences in verbal ability: A meta-analysis. *Psychological Bulletin, 104,* 53–69.

Hyde, J. S., Fennema, E., & Lamon, S. J. (1990). Gender differences in mathematics performance: A meta-analysis. *Psychological Bulletin, 107,* 139–155.

Hyde, J. S., & Plant, E. A. (1995). Magnitude of psychological gender differences: Another side to the story. *American Psychologist, 50,* 159–161.

I

Imperato-McGinley, J., et al. (1974). Steroid 5 reductase deficiency in man: An inherited form of male pseudohermaphroditism. *Science, 186,* 1213–1215.

Ingrassia, M. (1993, October 25). Abused and confused. *Newsweek,* pp. 57–58.

Injections approved for child molesters. (1996, August 31). *The New York Times,* p. L7.

Irvine, M. (1998, January 10). California AIDS deaths drop sixty percent. Associated Press; America Online.

Isay, R. A. (1990). Psychoanalytic theory and the therapy of gay men. In D. P. McWhirter, S. A. Sanders, & J. M. Reinisch (Eds.), *Homosexuality/heterosexuality: Concepts of sexual orientation* (pp. 283–303). New York: Oxford University Press.

Isay, R. A. (1993, April 23). Sex survey may say most about society's attitudes to gays. *The New York Times,* Section 4, p. 16 (Letter).

Ison, C. A. (1990). Laboratory methods in genitourinary medicine: Methods of diagnosing gonorrhoea. *Genitourinary Medicine, 66,* 453–459.

J

Jacklin, C. N., DiPietro, J. A., & Maccoby, E. E. (1984). Sex-typing behavior and sex-typing pressure in child-parent interaction. *Archives of Sexual Behavior, 13,* 413–425.

Jackson, B. B., Taylor, J., & Pyngolil, M. (1991). How age conditions the relationship between climacteric status and health symptoms in African American women. *Research in Nursing and Health, 14,* 1–9.

Jackson, J., et al. (1990). Young adult women who report childhood intrafamilial sexual abuse: Subsequent adjustment. *Archives of Sexual Behavior, 19,* 211–221.

Jackson, L. A., & Ervin, K. S. (1992). Height stereotypes of women and men: The liabilities of shortness for both sexes. *Journal of Social Psychology, 132,* 433–445.

Jacobsen, C. (1991). Redefining censorship: A feminist view. *Art Journal, 50*(4), 42–55.

Jacobson, J. L., & Jacobson, S. W. (1994). Prenatal alcohol exposure and neurobehavioral development: Where is the threshold? *Alcohol Health and Research World, 18*(1), 30–36.

Jamison, P. L., & Gebhard, P. H. (1988). Penis size increase between flaccid and erect states. An analysis of the Kinsey data. *Journal of Sex Research, 24,* 177–183.

Jankowiak, W. R., & Fischer, E. F. (1992). A cross-cultural perspective on romantic love. *Ethnology, 31,* 149–155.

Janus, M. D., Scanlon, B., & Prince, V. (1984). Youth prostitution. In A. W. Burgess (Ed.), *Sex rings and child pornography.* Lexington, MA: Heath.

Janus, S. S., & Janus, C. L. (1993). *The Janus report on sexual behavior.* New York: Wiley.

Jencks, C., & Mayer, S. E. (1990). Residential segregation, job proximity, and Black job opportunities. In L. E. Lynn and M. McGeary (Eds.), *Inner-city poverty in the United States.* Washington, DC: National Academy Press.

Jenks, R. (1985). Swinging: A replication and test of a theory. *The Journal of Sex Research, 21,* 199–210.

Jennings, V. H., Lamprecht, V. M., & Kowal, D. (1998). Fertility awareness methods. In R. A. Hatcher et al. (1998), *Contraceptive technology* (17th rev. ed., pp. 309–324). New York: Ardent Media, Inc.

Johannes, L. (1998, July 14). Drug firms focus on female sex dysfunction. *The Wall Street Journal Europe,* p. 5.

Johnson, D. (1990, March 8). AIDS clamor at colleges muffling older dangers. *The New York Times,* p. A18.

Johnson, K. A., & Williams, L. (1993). Risk of breast cancer in the nurses' health study: Applying the Gail model. *Journal of the American Medical Association, 270,* 2925–2926.

Jones, A., et al. (1994). Erectile disorder and the elderly: An analysis of the case for funding. *Sexual and Marital Therapy, 9*(1), 9–15.

Jones, E. F., et al. (1985). Teenage pregnancy in developed countries: Determinants and policy implications. *Family Planning Perspectives, 17,* 53–62.

Jones, H. W., & Toner, J. P. (1993). The infertile couple. *New England Journal of Medicine, 329,* 1710–1715.

Jones, J. (1994). Embodied meaning: Menopause and the change of life. Special Issue: Women's health and social work: Feminist perspectives. *Social Work in Health Care, 19*(3–4), 43–65.

Jorgensen, S. R., et al. (1980). Dyadic and social network influences on adolescent exposure to pregnancy risk. *Journal of Marriage and the Family, 42,* 141–155.

Journal of the American Medical Association. (1993). Preventing HIV/AIDS among adolescents; Schools as agents of behavior change. *Journal of the American Medical Association, 269,* 760–762 (Editorial).

Judson, F. N. (1990). Gonorrhea. *Medical Clinics of North America, 74,* 1353–1366.

K

Kagay, M. R. (1991, June 19). Poll finds AIDS causes single people to alter behavior. *The New York Times,* p. C3.

Kalick, S. M. (1988). Physical attractiveness as a status cue. *Journal of Experimental Social Psychology, 24,* 469–489.

Kallmann, F. J. (1952). Comparative twin study on the genetic aspects of male homosexuality. *Journal of Nervous and Mental Disease, 115,* 283–298.

Kamb, M. L., et al. (1998). Efficacy of risk-reduction counseling to prevent human immunodeficiency virus and sexually transmitted diseases: A randomized controlled trial. *Journal of the American Medical Association, 280,* 1161–1167.

Kammeyer, K. C. W. (1990). *Marriage and family: A foundation for personal decisions* (2nd ed.). Boston: Allyn & Bacon.

Kammeyer, K. C. W., Ritzer, G., & Yetman, N. R. (1990). *Sociology: Experiencing changing societies.* Boston: Allyn & Bacon.

Kang, S. H., Bloom, J. R., & Romano, P. S. (1994). Cancer screening among African-American women: Their use of tests and social support. *American Journal of Public Health, 84*(1), 101–103.

Kanin, E. J. (1985). Date rapists: Differential sexual socialization and relative deprivation. *Archives of Sexual Behavior, 14,* 219–231.

Kantner, J. F., & Zelnik, M. (1972). Sexual experience of young unmarried women in the United States. *Family Planning Perspectives, 4,* 9–18.

Kantrowitz, B. (1990a, Summer/Fall Special Issue). High school homeroom. *Newsweek,* pp. 50–54.

Kantrowitz, B. (1990b, Summer/Fall Special Issue). The push for sex education. *Newsweek,* p. 52.

Kantrowitz, B. (1992, December 14). "A silver bullet" against teen pregnancies? Baltimore offers Norplant at school. *Newsweek,* p. 43.

Kaplan, H. S. (1974). *The new sex therapy: Active treatment of sexual dysfunctions.* New York: Brunner/Mazel.

Kaplan, H. S. (1979). *Disorders of sexual desire.* New York: Simon and Schuster.

Kaplan, H. S. (1987). *Sexual aversion, sexual phobias, and panic disorder.* New York: Brunner/Mazel.

Kaplan, H. S. (1990). Sex, intimacy, and the aging process. *Journal of the American Academy of Psychoanalysis, 18,* 185–205.

Karney, B. R., & Bradbury, T. N. (1995). The longitudinal course of marital quality and stability: A review of theory, method, and research. *Psychological Bulletin, 118,* 3–34.

Kash, K. (1998). Cited in Zuger, A. (1998, January 6). Do breast self-exams save lives? Science still doesn't have answer. *The New York Times;* America Online.

Katz, J. N. (1995). *The invention of heterosexuality.* New York: Dutton.

Katz, M. H., & Gerberding, J. L. (1997). Postexposure treatment of people exposed to the human immunodeficiency virus through sexual contact or injection-drug use. *New England Journal of Medicine, 336,* 1097–1100.

Katz, R. C. (1990). Psychosocial adjustment in adolescent child molesters. *Child Abuse and Neglect, 14,* 567–575.

Kaufman, A., et al. (1980). Male rape victims: Noninstitutionalized assault. *American Journal of Psychiatry, 137,* 221–223.

Kay, D. S. (1992). Masturbation and mental health: Uses and abuses. *Sexual and Marital Therapy, 7,* 97–107.

Kedia, K. (1983). Ejaculation and emission: Normal physiology, dysfunction, and therapy. In R. J. Krane, M. B. Siroky, & I. Goldstein (Eds.), *Male sexual dysfunction* (pp. 37–54). Boston: Little, Brown.

Keen, S., & Zur, O. (1989). Who is the new ideal man? *Psychology Today, 23*(11), pp. 54–60.

Kegel, A. H. (1952). Sexual functions of the pubococcygeus muscle. *Western Journal of Surgery, 60,* 521–524.

Keith, J. B., et al. (1991). Sexual activity and contraceptive use among low-income urban Black adolescent females. *Adolescence, 26,* 769–785.

Kellerman, J., Lewis, J., & Laird, J. D. (1989). Looking and loving: The effects of mutual gaze on feelings of romantic love. *Journal of Research in Personality, 23,* 145–161.

Kelly, M. P., Strassberg, D. S., & Kircher, J. R. (1990). Attitudinal and experiential correlates of anorgasmia. *Archives of Sexual Behavior, 19,* 165–177.

Kenney, A. M., Guardad, S., & Brown, L. (1989). Sex education and AIDS education in the schools. *Family Planning Perspectives, 21,* 56–64.

Kerns, J. G., & Fine, M. A. (1994). The relation between gender and negative attitudes toward gay men and lesbians: Do gender role attitudes mediate this relation? *Sex Roles, 31*(5–6), 297–307.

Kettl, P., et al. (1991). Female sexuality after spinal cord injury. *Sexuality and Disability, 9,* 287–295.

Killmann, P. R., & Auerbach, R. (1979). Treatment of premature ejaculation and psychogenic impotence. *Archives of Sexual Behavior, 8,* 81–100.

Killmann, P. R., et al. (1987). The treatment of secondary orgasmic dysfunction II. *Journal of Sex and Marital Therapy, 13,* 93–105.

Kilpatrick, D. G., et al. (1987, January). *Rape in marriage and dating relationships: How bad are they for mental health?* Paper presented at the meeting of the New York Academy of Science, New York, NY.

Kimble, D. P. (1992). *Biological psychology* (2nd ed.). Fort Worth, TX: Harcourt Brace Jovanovich.

Kimlicka, T., Cross, H., & Tarnai, J. (1983). A comparison of androgynous, feminine, masculine, and undifferentiated women on self-esteem, body satisfaction, and sexual satisfaction. *Psychology of Women Quarterly, 1,* 291–294.

Kinard, E., & Reinherz, H. (1987). School aptitude and achievement in children of adolescent mothers. *Journal of Youth and Adolescence, 16,* 69–78.

Kinder, B. N., & Curtiss, G. (1988). Specific components in the etiology, assessment, and treatment of male sexual dysfunctions: Controlled outcome studies. *Journal of Sex and Marital Therapy, 14,* 40–48.

Kinsey, A. C., Pomeroy, W. B., & Martin, C. E. (1948). *Sexual behavior in the human male.* Philadelphia: W. B. Saunders Co.

Kinsey, A. C., Pomeroy, W. B., Martin, C. E., & Gebhard, P. H. (1953). *Sexual behavior in the human female.* Philadelphia: W. B. Saunders Co.

Kintsch, W. (1994). Text comprehension, memory, and learning. *American Psychologist, 49,* 294–303.

Kirby, D., Waszak, C., & Ziegler, J. (1992). School-based clinics: Their reproductive health services and impact on sexual behavior. *Family Planning Perspectives, 23,* 6–16.

Kirby, D., et al. (1993). The effects of school-based health clinics in St. Paul on school-wide birthrates. *Family Planning Perspectives, 25,* 12–16.

Kirn, W. (1997, August 18). The ties that bind. *Time,* pp. 48–50.

Kite, M. E. (1992). Individual differences in males' reactions to gay males and lesbians. *Journal of Applied Social Psychology, 22,* 1222–1239.

Klepinger, D. H., et al. (1993). Perceptions of AIDS risk and severity and their association with risk-related behavior among U.S. men. *Family Planning Perspectives, 25,* 74–82.

Klüver, H., & Bucy, P. C. (1939). Preliminary analysis of functions of the temporal lobes in monkeys. *Archives of Neurology and Psychiatry, 42*, 979.

Knapp, M. L. (1978). *Social intercourse: A behavioral approach to counseling.* Champaign, IL: Research Press.

Knight, R. A., et al. (1991). *Antisocial personality disorder and Hare assessments of psychopathy among sexual offenders.* Manuscript in preparation.

Knight, S. E. (1989). Sexual concerns of the physically disabled. In B. W. Heller, L. M. Flohr, & L. S. Zegans (Eds.), *Psychosocial interventions with physically disabled persons* (pp. 183–199). New Brunswick, NJ: Rutgers University Press.

Knox, D. (1983). *The love attitudes inventory* (rev. ed.). Saluda, NC: Family Life Publications.

Knox, D. (1988). *Choices in relationships.* St. Paul: West.

Knudsen, D. D. (1991). Child sexual coercion. In E. Grauerholz & M. A. Koralewski (Eds.), *Sexual coercion: A sourcebook on its nature, causes, and prevention* (pp. 17–28). Lexington, MA: Lexington Books.

Knussman, R., Christiansen, K., & Couwenbergs, C. (1986). Relations between sex hormone levels and sexual behavior in men. *Archives of Sexual Behavior, 15*, 429–445.

Kockott, G., & Fahrner, E. (1987). Transsexuals who have not undergone surgery: A follow-up study. *Archives of Sexual Behavior, 16*, 511–522.

Kohlberg, L. (1966). A cognitive-developmental analysis of children's sex-role concepts and attitudes. In E. E. Maccoby (Ed.), *The development of sex differences.* Stanford, CA: Stanford University Press.

Kohn, A. (1987, February). Shattered innocence. *Psychology Today*, pp. 54–58.

Kolata, G. (1993a, February 26). Studies say mammograms fail to help many women. *The New York Times*, pp. A1, A15.

Kolata, G. (1993b, March 7). Targeting urged in attack on AIDS. *The New York Times*, pp. A1, A26.

Kolata, G. (1993c, December 14). Breast cancer screening under 50: Experts disagree if benefit exists: Statisticians find no proof that screening saves lives. *The New York Times*, pp. C1, C17.

Kolata, G. (1995, May 28). Will the lawyers kill off Norplant? *The New York Times*, pp. F1, F5.

Kolata, G. (1996a, February 28). Study reports small risk, if any, from breast implants. *The New York Times*, p. A12.

Kolata, G. (1996b, September 15). AIDS patients slipping through safety net. *The New York Times*, p. A24.

Kolata, G. (1998a, April 4). Impotence pill: Would it also help women? *The New York Times*, pp. A1, A6.

Kolata, G. (1998b, April 25). Doctors debate use of drug to help women's sex lives. *The New York Times*; America Online.

Kolata, G. (1998c, September 9). Researchers report success in method to pick baby's sex. *The New York Times*; America Online.

Kolbe, L. (1998). Cited in Poll shows decline in sex by high school students (1998, September 18). *The New York Times*, p. A26.

Kolbert, E. (1991, October 11). Sexual harassment at work is pervasive, survey suggests. *The New York Times*, pp. A1, A17.

Kolodny, R. C. (1981). Evaluating sex therapy: Process and outcome at the Masters & Johnson Institute. *Journal of Sex Research, 17*, 301–318.

Komisar, L. (1971). The image of women in advertising. In V. Gornick & B. Moran (Eds.), *Women in sexist society.* New York: Basic Books.

Kon, I. S. (1995). *The sexual revolution in Russia.* New York: The Free Press.

Kontula, O., Rimpela, M., & Ojanlatva, A. (1992). Sexual knowledge, attitudes, fears and behaviors of adolescents in Finland (the KISS study). *Health Education Research, 7*, 69–77.

Koop, C. E. (1988). *Understanding AIDS.* HHS Publication No. HHS-88–8404. Washington, DC: U.S. Government Printing Office.

Koren, G., Pastuszak, A., & Ito, S. (1998). Drug therapy: Drugs in pregnancy. *New England Journal of Medicine, 338*, 1128–1137.

Kornblum, W. J. (1994). *Sociology in a changing world* (3rd ed.). Ft. Worth, TX: Harcourt Brace.

Koss, M. P. (1988). Stranger and acquaintance rape: Are there differences in the victim's experience? *Psychology of Women Quarterly, 12*, 1–24.

Koss, L. (1989). The Papanicolaou test for cervical cancer detection. *The Journal of Sex Research, 261*, 737.

Koss, M. P. (1993). Rape: Scope, impact, interventions, and public policy responses. *American Psychologist, 48*, 1062–1069.

Koss, M. P., Gidycz, C. A., & Wisniewski, N. (1987). The scope of rape: Incidence and prevalence of sexual aggression and victimization in a national sample of higher education students. *Journal of Consulting and Clinical Psychology, 55*, 162–170.

Koutsky, L. A., et al. (1992). A cohort study of the risk of cervical intraepithelial neoplasia Grade 2 or 3 in relation to papilloma virus infection. *New England Journal of Medicine, 327*, 1272.

Kouzi, A. C., et al. (1992). Contraceptive behavior among intravenous drug users at risk for AIDS. *Psychology of Addictive Behaviors.*

Kowal, D. (1998). Coitus interruptus (withdrawal). In R. A. Hatcher et al. (1998), *Contraceptive technology* (17th rev. ed., pp. 303–308). New York: Ardent Media, Inc.

Krafka, C. L. (1985). *Sexually explicit, sexually violent, and violent media: Effects of multiple naturalistic exposures and debriefing on female viewers.* Unpublished doctoral dissertation, University of Wisconsin-Madison.

Kresin, D. (1993). Medical aspects of inhibited sexual desire disorder. In W. O'Donohue & J. H. Geer (Eds.), *Handbook of sexual dysfunctions: Assessment and treatment* (pp. 15–52). Boston: Allyn & Bacon.

Kruesi, M. J. P., et al. (1992). Paraphilias: A double-blind crossover comparison of clomipramine versus desipramine. *Archives of Sexual Behavior, 21*, 587–594.

Kruks, G. (1991). Gay and lesbian homeless/street youth: Special issues and concerns. Special issue: Homeless youth. *Journal of Adolescent Health, 12*, 515–518.

Ku, L. C., Sonenstein, F. L., & Pleck, J. H. (1992). The association of AIDS education and sex education with sexual behavior and condom use among teenage men. *Family Planning Perspectives, 24,* 100–106.

Kuiper, B., & Cohen-Kettenis, P. (1988). Sex reassignment surgery: A study of 141 Dutch transsexuals. *Archives of Sexual Behavior, 17,* 439–457.

Kulin, H., et al. (1989). The onset of sperm production in pubertal boys. *American Journal of Diseases of Children, 143,* 190–193.

Kumar, U. (1991). Life stages in the development of the Hindu woman in India. In L. L. Adler (Ed.), *Women in cross-cultural perspective* (pp. 143–158). New York: Praeger.

Kunkel, L. E., & Temple, L. L. (1992). Attitudes towards AIDS and homosexuals: Gender, marital status, and religion. *Journal of Applied Social Psychology, 22,* 1030–1040.

Kurdek, L. A., & Schmitt, J. P. (1986a). Relationship quality of gay men in closed or open relationships. *Journal of Homosexuality, 12*(2), 85–99.

Kurdek, L. A., & Schmitt, J. P. (1986b). Relationship quality of partners in heterosexual married, heterosexual cohabiting, gay, and lesbian relationships. *Journal of Personality and Social Psychology, 51,* 711–720.

L

Laan, E., & Heiman, J. (1994). *Archives of Sexual Behavior.*

Lackritz, E. M., et al. (1995). Estimated risk of transmission of the human immunodeficiency virus by screened blood in the United States. *New England Journal of Medicine, 333,* 1721–1725.

Ladas, A. K., Whipple, B., & Perry, J. D. (1982). *The G spot and other recent discoveries about human sexuality.* New York: Holt, Rinehart & Winston.

Laird, J. (1994). A male pill? Gender discrepancies in contraceptive commitment. *Feminism and Psychology, 4*(3), 458–468.

Lamanna, M. A., & Riedmann, A. (1997). *Marriages and families,* 6th ed. Belmont, CA: Wadsworth.

Lamaze, F. (1981). *Painless childbirth.* New York: Simon & Schuster.

Lambert, B. (1988, September 20). AIDS among prostitutes not as prevalent as believed, studies show. *The New York Times,* p. B1.

Lamberti, D. (1997). Cited in Alterman, E. (1997, November), Sex in the '90s. *Elle,* pp. 128–134.

Lamke, L. K. (1982a). Adjustment and sex-role orientation. *Journal of Youth and Adolescence, 11,* 247–259.

Lamke, L. K. (1982b). The impact of sex-role orientation on self-esteem in early adolescence. *Child Development, 53,* 1530–1535.

Lane, K. E., & Gwartney-Gibbs, P. A. (1985). Violence in the context of dating and sex. *Journal of Family Issues, 6,* 45–59.

Lang, A. R. (1985). The social psychology of drinking and human sexuality. *Journal of Drug Issues, 15,* 273–289.

Lang, A. R., et al. (1980). Expectancy, alcohol, and sex guilt as determinants of interest in and reaction to sexual stimuli. *Journal of Abnormal Psychology, 89,* 644–653.

Lang, R. A., et al. (1989). An examination of sex hormones in genital exhibitionists. *Annals of Sex Research, 2,* 67–75.

Langevin, R., et al. (1979). Experimental studies of the etiology of genital exhibitionism. *Archives of Sexual Behavior, 8,* 307–332.

Langevin, R., et al. (1985). Sexual aggression: Constructing a predictive equation. In R. Langevin, (Ed.), *Erotic preference, gender identity, and aggression in men: New research studies* (pp. 39–76). Hillsdale, NJ: Erlbaum.

Langevin, R., Wright, P., & Handy, L. (1989). Characteristics of sex offenders who were sexually victimized as children. *Annals of Sex Research, 2,* 227–253.

Lansky, D., & Wilson, G. T. (1981). Alcohol, expectations, and sexual arousal in males: An information-processing analysis. *Journal of Abnormal Psychology, 90,* 35–45.

LaTour, M. S. (1990). Female nudity in print advertising: An analysis of gender differences in arousal and ad response. *Psychology and Marketing, 7,* 65–81.

Laumann, E. O. (1997). Cited in Gilbert, S. (1997, April 2), Study adds to doubts about benefits of circumcision. *The New York Times*; America Online.

Laumann, E. O., Gagnon, J. H., Michael, R. T., & Michaels, S. (1994). *The social organization of sexuality: Sexual practices in the United States.* Chicago: University of Chicago Press.

Laumann, E. O., et al. (1997, April 2). Circumcision in the United States: Prevalence, prophylactic effects, and sexual practice. *The Journal of the American Medical Association, 277,* 1052–1057.

Laviola, M. (1989). Effects of older brother-younger sister incest: A review of four cases. *Journal of Family Violence, 4,* 259–274.

Lavoisier, P., et al. (1995). Clitoral blood flow increases following vaginal pressure stimulation. *Archives of Sexual Behavior, 24,* 37–45.

Lawrence, K., & Herold, E. S. (1988). Women's attitudes toward and experience with sexually explicit materials. *Journal of Sex Research, 24,* 161–169.

Lawson, C. (1993, August 5). Single but mothers by choice: "Who is my daddy?" can be answered in different ways. *The New York Times,* pp. C1, C9.

Leary, W. E. (1990, September 13). New focus on sperm brings fertility successes. *The New York Times,* p. B11.

Leary, W. E. (1992, December 10). Medical panel says most sexual impotence in men can be treated without surgery. *The New York Times,* p. D20.

Leary, W. E. (1993, April 28). Screening of all newborns urged for sickle cell disease. *The New York Times,* p. C11.

Leary, W. E. (1995, May 11). When it comes to giant sperm, this tiny fruit fly is a whale. *The New York Times,* p. A26.

Leary, W. E. (1998, September 29). Older people enjoy sex, survey says. *The New York Times,* p. F8.

Leavitt, G. C. (1990). Sociobiological explanations of incest avoidance: A critical review of evidential claims. *American Anthropologist, 92,* 971–993.

Ledray, L. E. (1990). Counseling rape victims: The nursing challenge. *Perspectives in Psychiatric Care, 26,* 21–27.

Lee, J. A. (1988). Love-styles. In R. J. Sternberg & M. L. Barnes (Eds.), *The psychology of love* (pp. 38–67). New Haven: Yale University Press.

Leiblum, S. R., & Rosen, R. C. (1991). Couples therapy for erectile disorders: Conceptual and clinical considerations. Special issue: The treatment of male erectile disorders. *Journal of Sex and Marital Therapy, 17,* 147–159.

Leigh, B. C., Morrison, D. M., Trocki, K., & Temple, M. T. (1994). Sexual behavior of American adolescents: Results from a U.S. national survey. *Journal of Adolescent Health, 15*(2), 117–125.

Leitenberg, H., Detzer, M. J., & Srebnik, D. (1993). Gender differences in masturbation and the relation of masturbation experience in preadolescence and/or early adolescence to sexual behavior and sexual adjustment in young adulthood. *Archives of Sexual Behavior, 22,* 87–98.

Leitenberg, H., Greenwald, E., & Tarran, M. J. (1989). The relation between sexual activity among children during preadolescence and/or early adolescence and sexual behavior and sexual adjustment in young adulthood. *Archives of Sexual Behavior, 18,* 299–313.

Leitenberg, H., & Henning, K. (1995). Sexual fantasy. *Psychological Bulletin, 117,* 469–496.

Leland, J. (1997, November 17). A pill for impotence? *Newsweek,* pp. 62–68.

Leland, N. L., & Barth, R. P. (1992). Gender differences in knowledge, intentions, and behaviors concerning pregnancy and sexually transmitted disease prevention among adolescents. *Journal of Adolescent Health, 13,* 589–599.

Lemon, S. J., & Newbold, J. E. (1990). Viral hepatitis. In K. K. Holmes, P. Mardh, P. F. Sparling, & P. J. Wiesner (Eds.), *Sexually transmitted diseases* (2nd ed., pp. 449–466). New York: McGraw-Hill.

Lenihan, G., Rawlins, M. E., Eberly, C. G., Buckley, B., & Masters, B. (1992). Gender differences in rape supportive attitudes before and after a date rape education intervention. *Journal of College Student Development, 33,* 331–338.

Lesnik-Oberstein, M., & Cohen, L. (1984). Cognitive style, sensation seeking, and assortive mating. *Journal of Personality and Social Psychology, 46,* 57–66.

Letourneau, E., & O'Donohue, W. (1993). Sexual desire disorders. In W. O'Donohue & J. H. Geer (Eds.), *Handbook of sexual dysfunctions: Assessment and treatment* (pp. 53–81). Boston: Allyn & Bacon.

LeVay, S. (1991). A difference in hypothalamic structure between heterosexual and homosexual men. *Science, 253,* 1034–1037.

Lever, J., et al. (1992). Behavior patterns and sexual identity of bisexual males. *Journal of Sex Research, 29,* 141–167.

Levine, G. I. (1991). Sexually transmitted parasitic diseases. *Primary Care: Clinics in Office Practice, 18,* 101–128.

Levinger, G. (1980). Toward the analysis of close relationships. *Journal of Experimental Social Psychology, 16,* 510–544.

Levitt, E. E. (1988). Alternative life style and marital satisfaction: A brief report. *Annals of Sex Research, 1,* 455–461.

Levitt, E. E., & Mulcahy, J. J. (1995). The effect of intracavernosal injection of papaverine hydrochloride on orgasm latency. *Journal of Sex and Marital Therapy, 21,* 39–41.

Levy, D. S. (1991, September 16). Why Johnny might grow up violent and sexist. *Time,* pp. 16–19.

Levy, G. D., & Carter, D. B. (1989). Gender schema, gender constancy, and gender-role knowledge: The roles of cognitive factors in preschoolers' gender-role stereotype attributions. *Developmental Psychology, 25,* 444–449.

Levy, R. I. (1973). *The Tahitians.* Chicago: University of Chicago Press.

Lewan, T. (1998, May 2). Not all women thrilled with Viagra. The Associated Press; America Online.

Lewin, T. (1991, February 8). Studies on teen-age sex cloud condom debate. *The New York Times,* p. A14.

Lewin, T. (1992, February 28). Canada court says pornography harms women. *The New York Times,* p. B7.

Lewin, T. (1995). Women are becoming equal providers. *The New York Times,* p. A27.

Lewin, T. (1998a, January 17). Debate distant for many having abortions. *The New York Times,* pp. A1, A9.

Lewin, T. (1998b, March 23). Debate centers on definition of harassment. *The New York Times,* pp. A1, A28.

Lewis, D. K., & Watters, J. K. (1991). Sexual risk behavior among heterosexual intravenous drug users: Ethnic and gender variations. *AIDS, 5,* 77–83.

Lewis, P. H. (1995, August 21). Planet Out: "Gay global village" of cyberspace. *The New York Times,* p. D3.

Lewis, P. H. (1998, July 16). Videoconferencing's killer app may be sex. *The New York Times;* America Online.

Libman, E. (1989). Sociocultural and cognitive factors in aging and sexual expression: Conceptual and research issues. *Canadian Psychology, 30,* 560–567.

Libman, E., Fichten, C. S., & Brender, W. (1985). The role of therapeutic format in the treatment of sexual dysfunction: A review. *Clinical Psychology Review, 5,* 103–117.

Lief, H. I., & Hubschman, L. (1993). Orgasm in the postoperative transsexual. *Archives of Sexual Behavior, 22* 145–155.

Lindermalm, G., Korlin, D., & Uddenberg, N. (1986). Long-term follow-up of "sex change" in 134 male to female transsexuals. *Archives of Sexual Behavior, 15,* 187–210.

Linet, O. I., & Ogrinc, F. G. (1996). Efficacy and safety of intracavernosal alprostadil in men with erectile dysfunction. *New England Journal of Medicine, 334,* 873–877.

Linsley, W. A. (1989). The case against censorship of pornography. In D. Zillmann & J. Bryant (Eds.), *Pornography: Research advances and policy considerations* (pp. 343–359). Hillsdale, NJ: Lawrence Erlbaum Associates.

Linz, D. (1989). Exposure to sexually explicit materials and attitudes toward rape: A comparison of study results. *Journal of Sex Research, 26,* 50–84.

Linz, D., Donnerstein, E., & Penrod, S. (1988). The effects of long-term exposure to violent and sexually degrading depictions of women. *Journal of Personality and Social Psychology, 55,* 758–767.

Lipshultz, L. I. (1996). Injection therapy for erectile dysfunction. *New England Journal of Medicine, 334,* 913–914.

Lisak, D. (1991). Sexual aggression, masculinity, and fathers. *Signs, 16,* 238–262.

Lisak, D., & Roth, S. (1990). Motives and psychodynamics of self-reported, unincarcerated rapists. *American Journal of Orthopsychiatry, 60,* 268–280.

Liskin, L., Wharton, C., & Blackburn, R. (1990). Condoms—now more than ever. *Population Reports, No. 8,* 1–36.

Logsman, A., et al. (1998). *The British Medical Journal.* Cited in "Dutch surgeons 'restore virginity' to reduce shame." (1998, February 6). Reuters; America Online.

LoPiccolo, J. (1994) The evolution of sex therapy. *Sexual and Marital Therapy, 9*(1), 5–7.

LoPiccolo, J., & Friedman, J. (1988). Broad-spectrum treatment of low sexual desire: Integration of cognitive, behavioral, and systemic therapy. In S. Leiblum & R. Rosen (Eds.), *Sexual desire disorders.* New York: Guilford Press.

LoPiccolo, J., & Stock, W. E. (1986). Treatment of sexual dysfunction. *Journal of Consulting and Clinical Psychology, 54,* 158–167.

Lorch, D. (1993a, February 23). Uganda, scared by AIDS, turns to its youth. *The New York Times,* pp. A1, A10.

Lorch, D. T. (1993b, December 18). After years of ignoring AIDS epidemic, Kenya has begun facing up to it. *The New York Times,* p. A5.

Lorefice, L. S. (1991) Fluoxetine treatment of a fetish. *Journal of Clinical Psychiatry, 52.*

Lott, B. (1985). The potential enhancement of social/personality psychology through feminist research and vice versa. *American Psychologist, 40,* 155–164.

Lottes, I. L., & Kuriloff, P. J. (1992). The effects of gender, race, religion, and political orientation on the sex role attitudes of college freshmen. *Adolescence, 27,* 675–688.

Lovdal, L. T. (1989). Sex role messages in television commercials: An update. *Sex Roles, 21,* 715–724.

Lown, J., & Dolan, E. (1988). Financial challenges in remarriage. *Lifestyles: Family and Economic Issues, 9,* 73–88.

Lowry, R., et al. (1994). Substance use and HIV-related sexual behaviors among US high school students: Are they related? *American Journal of Public Health, 84*(7), 1116–1120.

Loy, P. H., & Stewart, L. P. (1984). The extent and effects of the sexual harassment of working women. *Sociological Focus, 17,* 31–43.

Lublin, J. (1995, September 28). Survey finds more Fortune 500 firms have at least two female directors. *Wall Street Journal,* p. B16.

Luckenbill, D. F. (1985). Entering male prostitution. *Urban Life, 14,* 131–153.

Lundstrom, B., Pauly, I., & Walinder, J. (1984). Outcome of sex reassignment surgery. *Acta Psychiatrica Scandinavica, 70,* 289–294.

Lynxwiler, J., & Gay, D. (1994). Reconsidering race differences in abortion attitudes. *Social Science Quarterly, 75*(1), 67–84.

Lyons, J. (1991). Artistic freedom and the university. *Art Journal, 50*(4), 77–83.

M

Macallan, D. C., et al. (1995). Energy expenditure and wasting in human immunodeficiency virus infection. *New England Journal of Medicine, 333,* 83–88.

Maccoby, E. E. (1990). Gender and relationships: A developmental account. *American Psychologist, 45,* 513–520.

Maccoby, E. E., & Jacklin, C. N. (1974). *The psychology of sex differences.* Stanford, CA: Stanford University Press.

MacDonald, N. E., et al. (1990). High-risk STD/HIV behavior among college students. *Journal of the American Medical Association, 263,* 3155–3159.

MacFarquhar, N. (1996, August 8). Mutilation of Egyptian girls: Despite ban, it goes on. *The New York Times,* p. A3.

Macrae, C. N., & Shepherd, J. W. (1989). Sex differences in the perception of rape victims. *Journal of Interpersonal Violence, 4,* 278–288.

Magdol, L., et al. (1997). Gender differences in partner violence in a birth cohort of 21-year olds: Bridging the gap between clinical and epidemiological approaches. *Journal of Consulting and Clinical Psychology, 65,* 68–78.

Mahoney, E. R., et al. (1986). Sexual coercion and assault: Male socialization and female risk. *Sexual Coercion and Assault, 1,* 2–8.

Major, B., & Cozzarelli, C. (1992). Psychosocial predictors of adjustment to abortion. *Journal of Social Issues, 48,* 121–142.

Malamuth, N. M. (1981). Rape proclivity among males. *Journal of Social Issues, 37,* 138–157.

Malamuth, N. M. (1984). Aggression against women: Cultural and individual causes. In N. M. Malamuth & E. Donnerstein (Eds.), *Pornography and sexual aggression* (pp. 19–52). Orlando, FL: Academic Press.

Malamuth, N. M., & Ceniti, J. (1986). Repeated exposure to violent and nonviolent pornography: Likelihood of raping ratings and laboratory aggression against women. *Aggressive Behavior, 12,* 129–137.

Male birth control. (1995, August 1). *Newsday,* p. B31.

Maletzky, B. M. (1980). Self-referred vs. court-referred sexually deviant patients: Success with assisted covert sensitization. *Behavior Therapy, 11,* 306–314.

Malinowski, B. (1927). *Sex and repression in savage society.* London: Kegan Paul, Trench, Trubner & Co.

Malinowski, B. (1929). *The sexual life of savages in north-western Melanesia.* New York: Eugenics.

Malloy, M. H., Hoffman, H. J., Peterson, D. R. (1992). Sudden infant death syndrome and maternal smoking. *American Journal of Public Health, 82,* 1380–1382.

Mammograms on rise, federal study finds. (1992, April 29). *The New York Times,* p. C13.

Marchbanks, P., et al. (1988). Risk factors for ectopic pregnancy. *Journal of the American Medical Association, 259,* 1823–1827.

Marcus, A. J. (1995). Aspirin as a prophylaxis against colorectal cancer. *New England Journal of Medicine, 333,* 656–658.

Margolin, L., Miller, M., & Moran, P. B. (1989). When a kiss is not just a kiss: Relating violations on consent in kissing to rape myth acceptance. *Sex Roles, 20,* 231–243.

Markowitz, M., et al. (1995). A preliminary study of ritonavir, an inhibitor of HIV-1 protease, to treat HIV-1 infection. *New England Journal of Medicine, 333,* 1534–1539.

Marks, G., Miller, N., & Maruyama, G. (1981). Effect of targets' physical attractiveness on assumption of similarity. *Journal of Personality and Social Psychology, 41,* 198–206.

Marshall, D. (1971). Sexual behavior on Mangaia. In D. Marshall & R. Suggs (Eds.), *Human sexual behavior: Variations in the ethnographic spectrum* (pp. 103–162). New York: Basic Books.

Marshall, W. L. (1989). Pornography and sex offenders. In D. Zillmann & J. Bryant (Eds.), *Pornography: Research advances and policy considerations* (pp. 185–214). Hillsdale, NJ: Lawrence Erlbaum Associates.

Marshall, W. L., et al. (1991). Treatment outcome with sex offenders. *Clinical Psychology Review, 11,* 465–485.

Marsiglio, W. (1993a). Adolescent male's orientation toward paternity and contraception. *Family Planning Perspectives, 25,* 22–31.

Marsiglio, W. (1993b). Attitudes toward homosexual activity and gays as friends: A national survey of heterosexual 15- to 19-year-old males. *Journal of Sex Research, 30,* 12–17.

Martin, C. L., & Halverson, C. F., Jr. (1981). A schematic processing model of sex typing and stereotyping in children. *Child Development, 54,* 1119–1134.

Martin, C. L., & Halverson, C. F., Jr. (1983). The effects of sex-typing schemas on young children's memory. *Child Development, 54,* 563–574.

Martin, D. H. (1990). Chlamydial infections. *Medical Clinics of North America, 74,* 1367–1387.

Martin, J. N., et al. (1998). Sexual transmission and the natural history of human herpesvirus 8 infection. *New England Journal of Medicine, 338,* 948–954.

Martinez, F. D., Cline, M., & Burrows, B. (1992). Increased incidence of asthma in children of smoking mothers. *Pediatrics, 89,* 21–26.

Martinson, F. M. (1976). Eroticism in infancy and childhood. *The Journal of Sex Research, 2,* 251–262.

Masters, W. H., & Johnson, V. E. (1966). *Human sexual response.* Boston: Little, Brown.

Masters, W. H., & Johnson, V. E. (1970). *Human sexual inadequacy.* Boston: Little, Brown.

Masters, W. H., & Johnson, V. E. (1979). *Homosexuality in perspective.* Boston: Little, Brown.

Masters, W. H., et al. (1989). *Human sexuality* (4th ed.). New York: HarperCollins.

Matek, O. (1988). Obscene phone callers. *Journal of Social Work and Human Sexuality, 7,* 113–130.

Matlin, M. W. (1996). *The psychology of women* (3rd ed.). Fort Worth: Harcourt Brace College Publishers.

Matthews, K. A., et al. (1990). Influences of natural menopause on psychological characteristics and symptoms of middle-aged healthy women. *Journal of Consulting and Clinical Psychology, 58,* 345–351.

Matus, I. (1996.) Cited in Clay, R. A. (1996). Beating the "biological clock" with zest. *APA Monitor, 27*(2), 37.

Maybach, K. L., & Gold, S. R. (1994). Hyperfemininity and attraction to macho and non-macho men. *Journal of Sex Research, 31*(2), 91–98.

Mayer, J. P., Hawkins, B., & Todd, R. (1990). A randomized evaluation of smoking cessation interventions for pregnant women at a WIC clinic (Women, Infants and Children). *American Journal of Public Health, 80,* 76–79.

McArthur, M. J. (1990). Reality therapy with rape victims. *Archives of Psychiatric Nursing, 4,* 360–365.

McCabe, M. P., & Delaney, S. M. (1992). An evaluation of therapeutic programs for the treatment of secondary inorgasmia in women. *Archives of Sexual Behavior, 21,* 69–89.

McCloskey, L. A. (1996). Socioeconomic and coercive power within the family. *Gender and Society, 10,* 449–463.

McConaghy, M. J. (1979). Gender performance and the genital basis of gender: Stages in the development of constancy of gender. *Child Development, 50,* 1223–1226.

McConaghy, N. (1987). Heterosexuality/homosexuality: Dichotomy or continuum. *Archives of Sexual Behavior, 16,* 411–424.

McConaghy, N., & Blaszczynski, A. (1980). A pair of monozygotic twins discordant for homosexuality: Sex-dimorphic behavior and penile volume responses. *Archives of Sexual Behavior, 9,* 123–124.

McCormack, W. M. (1990). Overview. *Sexually Transmitted Diseases, 57,* 187–191.

McCusker, J., et al. (1992). Maintenance of behavioral change in a cohort of homosexually active men. *AIDS, 6,* 861–868.

McDonough, Y. Z. (1998, January 24). What Barbie really taught me. *The New York Times Magazine,* p. 70.

McGuire, R. J., Carlisle, J. M., & Young, B. G. (1965). Sexual deviation as conditioned behavior: A hypothesis. *Behaviour Research and Therapy, 2,* 185–190.

McKeachie, W. (1994) Cited in DeAngelis, T. (1994), Educators reveal keys to success in classroom. *APA Monitor, 25*(1), 39–40.

McKinney, K. (1989). Social factors in contraceptive and abortion attitudes and behaviors. In K. McKinney & S. Sprecher (Eds.), *Human sexuality: The societal and interpersonal context.* Norwood, NJ: Ablex Publishing Corporation.

McKinney, K., & Maroules, N. (1991). Sexual harassment. In E. Grauerholz & M. A. Koralewski (Eds.), *Sexual coercion: A sourcebook on its nature, causes, and prevention* (pp. 29–44). Lexington, MA: Lexington Books.

McKirnan, D. J., Stokes, J. P., Doll, L., & Burzette, R. G. (1995). Bisexually active men: Social characteristics and sexual behavior. *Journal of Sex Research, 32,* 65–76.

McLaren, J., & Brown, R. E. (1989). Childhood problems associated with abuse and neglect. *Canada's Mental Health, 37*(3), 1–6.

McLaughlin, F. J., et al. (1992). Randomized trial of comprehensive prenatal care for low-income women: Effect on infant birth weight. *Pediatrics, 89,* 128–132.

McLean, P. M. (1976). Brain mechanisms of elemental sexual functions. In B. J. Sadock et al. (Eds.), *The sexual experience.* Baltimore: Williams & Wilkins.

McMahon, M. J., et al. (1996). Comparison of a trial of labor with an elective second cesarean section. *The New England Journal of Medicine, 335,* 689–695.

Mead, M. (1935). *Sex and temperament in three primitive societies.* New York: Dell.

Mead, M. (1967). *Male and female: A study of the sexes in a changing world.* New York: William Morrow.

Meana, M., & Binik, Y. M. (1994). Painful coitus: A review of female dyspareunia. *Journal of Nervous and Mental Disease, 182*(5), 264–272.

Meckler, L. (1998, June 26). Teen abortion, pregnancy rates fall. Associated Press; America Online.

Meier, B. (1997, June 8). In war against AIDS, battle over baby formula reignites. *The New York Times,* pp. A1, A16.

Meiselman, K. C. (1978). *Incest: A psychological study of causes and effects with treatment recommendations.* San Francisco: Jossey-Bass.

Meisler, A. W., & Carey, M. P. (1990). A critical reevaluation of nocturnal penile tumescence monitoring in the diagnosis of erectile dysfunction. *Journal of Nervous and Mental Disease, 178,* 78–89.

Melbye, M., et al. (1997). Induced abortion and the risk of breast cancer. *New England Journal of Medicine, 336,* 81–85.

Mertz, G. J., et al. (1992). Risk factors for the sexual transmission of genital herpes. *Annals of Internal Medicine, 116,* 197–202.

Messenger, J. C. (1971). Sex and repression in an Irish folk community. In D. S. Marshall and R. C. Suggs (Eds.), *Human sexual behavior: Variations in the ethnographic spectrum* (pp. 3–37). New York: Basic Books.

Meston, C. M., & Gorzalka, B. B. (1992). Psychoactive drugs and human sexual behavior: The role of serotonergic activity. *Journal of Psychoactive Drugs, 24,* 1–40.

Meuwissen, I., & Over, R. (1990). Habituation and dishabituation of female sexual arousal. *Behaviour Research and Therapy, 28,* 217–226.

Meyer, J. K., & Reter, D. J. (1979). Sex reassignment: Follow-up. *Archives of General Psychiatry, 36,* 1010–1015.

Meyer, T. (1998, February 18). AZT short treatment works. The Associated Press; America Online.

Meyer-Bahlburg, H. F. L., et al. (1995). Prenatal estrogens and the development of homosexual orientation. *Developmental Psychology, 31*(1), 12–21.

Michael, R. T., Gagnon, J. H., Laumann, E. O., & Kolata, G. (1994). *Sex in America: A definitive survey.* Boston: Little, Brown.

Mill, J. S. (1939). Utilitarianism. In E. A. Burtt (ed.), *The English philosophers.* New York: The Modern Library. (Original work published 1863.)

Miller, B. C., & Bingham, C. R. (1989). Family configuration in relation to the sexual behavior of female adolescents. *Journal of Marriage and the Family, 51,* 499–506.

Miller, B. C., McCoy, J. K., & Olson, T. D. (1986). Dating age and stage as correlates of adolescent sexual attitudes and behavior. *Journal of Adolescent Research, 1,* 361–371.

Miller, D. (1995). Personal communication.

Miller, H. G., Turner, C. F., & Moses, L. E. (Eds.) (1990). *AIDS: The second decade.* Washington, DC: National Academy.

Miller, M. (1998). Cited in Bronner, E. (1998, February 1). Just say maybe. No sexology, please. We're Americans. *The New York Times,* p. WK6.

Miller, S. M., Shoda, Y., & Hurley, K. (1996). Applying cognitive-social theory to health-protective behavior: Breast self-examination in cancer screening. *Psychological Bulletin, 199,* 70–94.

Minai, N. (1981). *Women in Islam: Tradition and transition in the Middle East.* London: John Murray.

Minkoff, H. L., et al. (1990). The relationship of cocaine use to syphilis and human immunodeficiency virus infections among inner city parturient women. *American Journal of Obstetrics and Gynecology, 163,* 521–526.

Mirotznik, J. (1991). Genital herpes: A survey of the attitudes, knowledge, and reported behaviors of college students at-risk for infection. *Journal of Psychology and Human Sexuality, 4,* 73–99.

Mirotznik, J., et al. (1987). Genital herpes: An investigation of its attitudinal and behavioral correlates. *Journal of Sex Research, 23,* 266–272.

Mishell, D. R., Jr. (1989). Medical progress: Contraception. *New England Journal of Medicine, 320,* 777–787.

MMWR (1995). Update: AIDS among women—United States, 1994. *Morbidity and Mortality Weekly Report, 44,* 81–84.

Mohr, D. C., & Beutler, L. E. (1990). Erectile dysfunction: A review of diagnostic and treatment procedures. *Clinical Psychology Review, 10,* 123–150.

Money, J. (1988). *Gay, straight, and in-between.* New York: Oxford University Press.

Money, J. (1990). Agenda and credenda of the Kinsey Scale. In D. P. McWhirter, S. A. Sanders, & J. M. Reinisch (Eds.), *Homosexuality/heterosexuality: Concepts of sexual orientation* (pp. 41–60). New York: Oxford University Press.

Money, J. (1994). The concept of gender identity disorder in childhood and adolescence after 39 years. *Journal of Sex and Marital Therapy, 20*(3), 163–177.

Money, J., & Ehrhardt, A. (1972). *Man and woman, boy and girl.* Baltimore: The Johns Hopkins University Press.

Money, J., & Lamacz, M. (1989). *Vandalized lovemaps.* Buffalo, NY: Prometheus Books.

Money, J., Lehne, G., & Pierre-Jerome, F. (1984). Micropenis: Adult follow-up and comparison of size against new norms. *Journal of Sex and Marital Therapy, 10,* 105–116.

Money, J., & Wiedeking, C. (1980). Gender identity/role: Normal differentiation and its transpositions. In B. Wolman & J. Money (Eds.), *Handbook of human sexuality* (pp. 269–284). Englewood Cliffs, NJ: Prentice-Hall.

Montagnier, L. (1996). Cited in Altman, L. K. (1996, August 7). Urine test for H.I.V. is approved. *The New York Times,* p. A14.

Moore, K. A., & Stief, T. M. (1992). Changes in marriage and fertility behavior: Behavior versus attitudes of young adults. *Youth and Society, 22,* 362–386.

Morales, A. (1993). Nonsurgical management options in impotence. *Hospital Practice, 28*(15–6), 19–20, 23–24.

Morales, E. (1992). Latino gays and Latina lesbians. In S. Dworkin & F. Gutierrez (Eds.), *Counseling gay men and lesbians: Journey to the end of the rainbow.* Alexandria, VA: American Association for Counseling and Development.

Moran, J. S., & Zenilman, J. M. (1990). Therapy for gonococcal infections: Options in 1989. *Reviews of Infectious Diseases,* (Suppl. 6), S633-S644.

More single mothers. (1993, July 26). *Time,* p. 16.

Morgan, T. O., et al. (1996). Age-specific reference ranges for serum prostate-specific antigen in black men. *New England Journal of Medicine, 335,* 304–310.

Morokoff, P. J. (1993). Female sexual arousal disorder. In W. Donohue and J. H. Greer (Eds.) *Handbook of sexual dysfunctions: Assessment and treatment* (pp. 157–199). Boston: Allyn & Bacon.

Morris, N., et al. (1987). Marital sex frequency and midcycle female testosterone. *Archives of Sexual Behavior, 7,* 157–173.

Morrison, E. S., et al. (1980). *Growing up sexual.* New York: Van Nostrand Reinhold Co.

Morse, E., et al. (1992). Sexual behavior patterns of customers of male street prostitutes. *Archives of Sexual Behavior, 21,* 347.

Mortola, J. F. (1998). Premenstrual syndrome—Pathophysiologic considerations. *New England Journal of Medicine, 338,* 256–257.

Mosher, D. L. (1988). Pornography defined: Sexual involvement theory, narrative context, and goodness-of-fit. *Journal of Psychology and Human Sexuality, 1,* 67–85.

Mosher, W. D., & Bachrach, C. A. (1987). First premarital contraceptive use. *Studies in Family Planning, 18,* 83.

Mrs. Dole calls Viagra "great drug." (1998, May 9). Associated Press; America Online.

Ms. (1995, July/August), p. 17.

Muehlenhard, C. L., & Falcon, P. L. (1990). Men's heterosocial skill and attitudes toward women as predictors of verbal sexual coercion and forceful rape. *Sex Roles, 23,* 241–259.

Muehlenhard, C. L., & Linton, M. A. (1987). Date rape and sexual aggression in dating situations: Incidence and risk factors. *Journal of Counseling Psychology, 34,* 186–196.

Mueser, K. T., et al. (1984). You're only as pretty as you feel: Facial expression as a determinant of physical attractiveness. *Journal of Personality and Social Psychology, 46,* 469–478.

Mulry, G., Kalichman, S. C., Kelly, J. A. (1994). Substance use and unsafe sex among gay men: Global versus situational use of substances. *Journal of Sex Education and Therapy, 20*(3), 175–184.

Murray, J. B. (1988). Psychopharmacological therapy of deviant sexual behavior. *Journal of General Psychology, 115,* 101–110.

Murstein, B. I. (1988). A taxonomy of love. In R. J. Sternberg & M. L. Barnes (Eds.), *The psychology of love* (pp. 13–37). New Haven: Yale University Press.

Murstein, B., Merighi, J. R., & Vyse, S. A. (1991). Love styles in the United States and France: A cross-cultural comparison. *Journal of Social and Clinical Psychology, 10,* 37–46.

Muster, N. J. (1992). Treating the adolescent victim-turned-offender. *Adolescence, 27,* 441–450.

Myers, A. M., & Gonda, G. (1982). Utility of the masculinity-femininity construct: Comparison of traditional and androgyny approaches. *Journal of Personality and Social Psychology, 43,* 514–523.

Myers, M. F. (1989). Men sexually assaulted as adults and sexually abused as boys. *Archives of Sexual Behavior, 18,* 203–215.

N

Nadeau, R., et al. (1993) Knowledge and beliefs regarding STDs and condoms among students. *Canadian Journal of Public Health, 84,* 181–185.

Nadler, R. D. (1990). Homosexual behavior in nonhuman primates. In D. P. McWhirter, S. A. Sanders, & J. M. Reinisch (Eds.), *Homosexuality/heterosexuality: Concepts of sexual orientation* (pp. 138–170). New York: Oxford University Press.

Nakanishi, M. (1986). Perceptions of self-disclosure in initial interaction: A Japanese sample. *Human Communication Research, 13,* 167–190.

Narod, S. A., et al. (1998). Oral contraceptives and the risk of hereditary ovarian cancer. *New England Journal of Medicine, 339,* 424–428.

National Academy of Sciences, Institute of Medicine. (1982). *Marijuana and health.* Washington, DC: National Academic Press.

National Academy of Sciences. (1995). Cited in "A strong endorsement for clean needles." (1995, September 25). *The New York Times,* p. A14.

National Crime Victimization Survey (1995). U.S. Bureau of Justice Statistics. Washington, DC: U.S. Department of Justice.

National Research Council (1993). *Losing generations: Adolescents in high risk settings.* Washington, DC: National Academy Press.

Navarro, M. (1993, February 18). New York needle exchanges called surprisingly effective. *The New York Times*, pp. A1, B4.

Navarro, M. (1996, August 31). Lesbian loses court appeal for custody of daughter. *The New York Times*, p. L7.

Nelson, R. (1988). Nonoperative management of impotence. *Journal of Urology, 139*, 2–5.

Nevid, J. S. (1984). Sex differences in factors of romantic attraction. *Sex Roles, 11*, 401–411.

Nevid, J. S., Rathus, S. A., & Greene, B. A. (2000). *Abnormal psychology in a changing world* (4th ed.). Upper Saddle River, NJ: Prentice Hall.

"New fertility treatment may increase birth defects." (1997, November 13). Reuters; America Online.

A new use for Prozac. (1995, June 19). *Newsweek*, p. 85.

Newcomb, P. A., & Storer, B. E. (1995). Postmenopausal hormone use and risk of large-bowel cancer. *Journal of the National Cancer Institute, 87*(14), 1067–1071.

Newcomer, S. F., & Udry, J. R. (1985). Oral sex in an adolescent population. *Archives of Sexual Behavior, 14*, 41–46.

Nichols, M. (1990). Lesbian relationships: Implications for the study of sexuality and gender. In D. P. McWhirter, S. A. Sanders, & J. M. Reinisch (Eds.), *Homosexuality/heterosexuality: Concepts of sexual orientation* (pp. 350–364). New York: Oxford University Press.

Niebuhr, G. (1998, April 17). More clergy willing to perform same-sex marriages. *The New York Times*; America Online.

Nock, S. L. (1995). A comparison of marriages and cohabiting relationships. *Journal of Family Issues, 16*(1), 53–76.

Norman, J., & Harris, M. (1981). *The private life of the American teenager*. New York: Rawson Wade.

Nosek, M. A., et al. (1994). Wellness models and sexuality among women with physical disabilities. *Journal of Applied Rehabilitation Counseling, 25*(1), 50–58.

Novello, A. C. (1991). Women and HIV infection. *Journal of the American Medical Association, 265*, 1805.

Nuland, S. B. (1998, May 10). Medicine isn't just for the sick anymore. *The New York Times*, Section 4, pp. 1, 5.

O

O'Connell, M. (1991). Cited in Pear, R. (1991, December 4), Larger number of new mothers are unmarried. *The New York Times*, p. A20.

O'Donohue, W., Letourneau, E., & Geer, J. H. (1993). Premature ejaculation. In W. O'Donohue & J. H. Geer (Eds.), *Handbook of sexual dysfunctions: Assessment and treatment.* (pp. 303–333). Boston: Allyn & Bacon.

O'Hara, M. W., Neunaber, D. J., & Zekoski, E. M. (1984). Prospective study of postpartum depression: Prevalence, course, and predictive factors. *Journal of Abnormal Psychology, 93*, 158–171.

O'Hara, M. W., et al. (1991). Prospective study of postpartum blues: Biological and psychosocial factors. *Archives of General Psychiatry, 48*, 801–806.

O'Neill, N., & O'Neill, G. (1972). *Open marriage*. New York: Evans.

Ochs, R. (1993a, December 7). Breast cancer risk: What the numbers mean. *New York Newsday*, pp. 72–75.

Ochs, R. (1993b, December 7). Prostate cancer jolt: 16% increase attributed to wider screening. *New York Newsday*, p. 7.

Ochs, R. (1994, January 11). Cervical cancer comeback. *New York Newsday*, pp. 55, 57.

Okami, P., & Goldberg, A. (1992). Personality correlates of pedophilia: Are they reliable indicators? *Journal of Sex Research, 29*, 297–328.

Oldenburg, R., & Brissett, D. (1980, April). The essential hangout. *Psychology Today*, pp. 81–84.

Olds, J. (1956). Pleasure centers in the brain. *Scientific American, 193*, 105–116.

Olds, J., & Milner, P. (1954). Positive reinforcement produced by electrical stimulation of the septal area and other regions of the rat brain. *Journal of Comparative and Physiological Psychology, 47*, 419–427.

Osborne, N. G., & Adelson, M. D. (1990). Herpes simplex and human papillomavirus genital infections: Controversy over obstetric management. *Clinical Obstetrics and Gynecology, 33*, 801–811.

Osterhout, M. B., Formichella, A., & McIntyre, S. (1991). *Tell it like it is: Straight talk about sex*. New York: Avon Books.

Oswalt, R., & Matsen, K. (1993). Sex, AIDS, and the use of condoms: A survey of compliance in college students. *Psychological Reports, 72*, 764–766.

Overholser, J. C., & Beck, S. (1986). Multimethod assessment of rapists, child molesters, and three control groups on behavioral and psychological measures. *Journal of Consulting and Clinical Psychology, 54*, 682–687.

Oz, S. (1994). Decision making in divorce therapy: Cost-cost comparisons. *Journal of Marital and Family Therapy, 20*, 77–81.

Oz, S. (1995). A modified balance-sheet procedure for decision-making in therapy: Cost-cost comparisons. *Professional Psychology: Research and Practice, 26*, 78–81.

P

Padesky, C. (1988). Attaining and maintaining positive lesbian self-identity: A cognitive therapy approach. *Women and Therapy, 8*, 145–156.

Padgett, V. R., Brislin-Slütz, J. A., & Neal, J. A. (1989). Pornography, erotica, and attitudes toward women: The effects of repeated exposure. *Journal of Sex Research, 26*, 479–491.

Padilla, E. R., & O'Grady, K. E. (1987). Sexuality among Mexican Americans: A case of sexual stereotyping. *Journal of Personality and Social Psychology, 52*, 5–10.

Padma-Nathan, H., et al. (1997). Treatment of men with erectile dysfunction with transurethral alprostadil. *New England Journal of Medicine, 336*, 1–7.

Palace, E. M. (1995). Modification of dysfunctional patterns of sexual arousal through autonomic arousal and false physiological feedback. *Journal of Consulting and Clinical Psychology, 63*, 604–615.

Palella, F. J., et al. (1998). Declining morbidity and mortality among patients with advanced human immunodeficiency virus infection. *New England Journal of Medicine, 338*, 853–860.

Palmore, E. (1981). *Social patterns in normal aging: Findings from the Duke Longitudinal Study.* Durham, NC: Duke University Press.

Palson, C., & Palson, R. (1972). Swinging in wedlock. *Society, 9*(4), 28–37.

"Panel says Pap tests could almost end cervical cancer deaths." (April 4, 1996). *The New York Times,* p. A18.

Parsons, N. K., Richards, H. C., & Kanter, G. D. (1990). Validation of a scale to measure reasoning about abortion. *Journal of Counseling Psychology, 37*, 107–112.

Patterson, C. J. (1995). Special issue: Sexual orientation and human development. *Developmental Psychology, 31*, 3–140.

Paul, R. H. (1996). Toward fewer cesarean sections—The role of a trial of labor. *The New England Journal of Medicine, 335*, 735–736.

Pauly, B., & Edgerton, M. (1986). The gender-identity movement. *Archives of Sexual Behavior, 15*, 315–329.

Pauly, I. B. (1974). Female transsexualism: Part 1. *Archives of Sexual Behavior, 3*, 487–508.

Pear, R. (1991, December 4). Larger number of new mothers are unmarried. *The New York Times,* p. A20.

Pearson, C. A. (1992). Cited in Leary, W. E. (1992, February 1), U.S. panel backs approval of first condom for women. *The New York Times,* p. 7.

Peckham, C., & Gibb, D. (1995). Mother-to-child transmission of the human immunodeficiency virus. *New England Journal of Medicine, 333*, 298–302.

Penn, F. (1993, October 21). Cancer confusion: The risks and realities of human papilloma virus. *Manhattan Spirit,* pp. 14–15.

Peplau, L. A., & Cochran, S. D. (1980, September). *Sex differences in values concerning love relationships.* Paper presented at the annual meeting of the American Psychological Association, Montreal, Canada.

Peplau, L. A., & Cochran, S. D. (1990). A relationship perspective on homosexuality. In D. P. McWhirter, S. A. Sanders, & J. M. Reinisch (Eds.), *Homosexuality/heterosexuality: Concepts of sexual orientation* (pp. 321–349). New York: Oxford University Press.

Peplau, L. A., Garnets, L. D., Spalding, L. R., Conley, T. D., & Veniegas, R. C. (1998). A critique of Bem's "Exotic Becomes Erotic" theory of sexual orientation. *Psychological Review, 105*(2), 387–394.

Peplau, L. A., & Gordon, S. L. (1985). Women and men in love: Sex differences in close heterosexual relationships. In V. O'Leary et al. (Eds.), *Women, gender, and social psychology.* Hillsdale, NJ: Erlbaum.

Perduta-Fulginiti, P. S. (1992). Sexual functioning of women with complete spinal cord injury: Nursing implications. Special Issue: Nursing roles and perspectives. *Sexuality and Disability, 10*, 103–118.

Perrett, D. I. (1994). *Nature.* Cited in Brody, J. E. (1994, March 21), Notions of beauty transcend culture, new study suggests. *The New York Times,* p. A14.

Perry, D. G., & Bussey, K. (1979). The social learning theory of sex differences: Imitation is alive and well. *Journal of Personality and Social Psychology, 37*, 1699–1712.

Perry, J. D., & Whipple, B. (1981). Pelvic muscle strength of female ejaculation: Evidence in support of a new theory of orgasm. *Journal of Sex Research, 17*, 22–39.

Perry, M. J., et al. (1994). High risk sexual behavior and alcohol consumption among bar-going gay men. *AIDS, 8*(9), 1321–1324.

Persky, H., et al. (1982). The relation of plasma androgen levels to sexual behaviors and attitudes of women. *Psychosomatic Medicine, 44*, 305–309.

Person, E. S., et al. (1989). Gender differences in sexual behaviors and fantasies in a college population. *Journal of Sex and Marital Therapy, 15*, 187–198.

Pillard, R. C. (1990). The Kinsey Scale: Is it familial? In D. P. McWhirter, S. A. Sanders, & J. M. Reinisch (Eds.), *Homosexuality/heterosexuality: Concepts of sexual orientation* (pp. 88–100). New York: Oxford University Press.

Pillard, R. C., & Weinrich, J. D. (1986). Evidence of familial nature of male homosexuality. *Archives of Sexual Behavior, 43*, 808–812.

Pines, A., & Aronson, E. (1983). Antecedents, correlates, and consequences of sexual jealousy. *Journal of Personality, 51*, 108–109.

Pinkerton, S. D., & Abramson, P. R. (1992). Is risky sex rational? *Journal of Sex Research, 29*, 561–568.

Pitnick, S. (1995, May 11). *Nature.*

Plan for wider use of Norplant by girls dividing Baltimore. (1993, February 11). *The New York Times,* p. B16.

Platt, R., Rice, P., & McCormack, W. (1983). Risk of acquiring gonorrhea and prevalence of abnormal adrenal findings among women recently exposed to gonorrhea. *Journal of the American Medical Association, 250*, 3205–3209.

Pliner, A. J., & Yates, S. (1992). Psychological and legal issues in minors' rights to abortion. *Journal of Social Issues, 48*, 203–216.

Podolsky, D. (1991, April 15). Charting premenstrual woes. *U.S. News & World Report,* pp. 68–69.

Polit-O'Hara, D., & Kahn, J. (1985). Communication and adolescent contraceptive practices in adolescent couples. *Adolescence, 20*, 33–43.

Pollak, M., et al. (1998). *Science.* Cited in Weinraub, M. (1998, January 22), Study finds possible predictor of prostate cancer. Reuters.

Pollack, W. S. (1996). Cited in Clay, R. A. (1996). Older men are more involved fathers, studies show. *APA Monitor, 27*(2), 37.

Pomeroy, W. B. (1966). Normal vs. abnormal sex. *Sexology, 32*, 436–439.

Population Council (1995). Cited in Brody, J. E. (1995, August 31), Abortion method using two drugs gains in a study. *The New York Times*, pp. A1, B12.

Porter, N., Geis, F. L., Cooper, E., & Newman, E. (1985). Androgyny and leadership in mixed-sex groups. *Journal of Personality and Social Psychology, 49*, 808–823.

Poussaint, A. (1990, September). An honest look at Black gays and lesbians. *Ebony*, pp. 124, 126, 130–131.

Powderly, W. G., et al. (1995). A randomized trial comparing fluconazole with clotrimazole troches for the prevention of fungal infections in patients with advanced human immunodeficiency virus infection. *New England Journal of Medicine, 332*, 700–705.

Powell, E. (1991). *Talking back to sexual pressure*. Minneapolis: CompCare Publishers.

Powell, E. (1996). *Sex on your terms*. Boston: Allyn & Bacon.

Pratt, C., & Schmall, V. (1989). College students' attitudes toward elderly sexual behavior: Implications for family life education. *Family Relations, 38*, 137–141.

Prentky, R. A., & Knight, R. A. (1991). Identifying critical dimensions for discriminating among rapists. *Journal of Consulting and Clinical Psychology, 59*, 643–661.

Press, A., et al. (1985, March 18). The war against pornography. *Newsweek*, pp. 58–66.

Preti, G., Cutler, W. B., et al. (1986). Human axillary secretions influence women's menstrual cycles: The role of donor extract of females. *Hormones and Behavior, 20*, 474–482.

Price, V. A. (1989). Characteristics and needs of Boston street youth: One agency's response [Special Issue: Runaway, homeless, and shut-out children and youth in Canada, Europe, and the United States]. *Children and Youth Services Review, 11*, 75–90.

Proctor, F., Wagner, N., & Butler, J. (1974). The differentiation of male and female orgasm: An experimental study. In N. Wagner (Ed.), *Perspectives on human sexuality*. New York: Behavioral Publications.

Pryde, N. A. (1989). Sex therapy in context. *Sexual and Marital Therapy, 4*, 215–227.

Purdy, M. (1995, November 6). A kind of sexual revolution: At some nursing homes, intimacy is a matter of policy. *The New York Times*, pp. B1, B6.

Purifoy, F. E., Grodsky, A., & Giambra, L. M. (1992). The relationship of sexual daydreaming to sexual activity, sexual drive, and sexual attitudes for women across the life-span. *Archives of Sexual Behavior, 21*, 369–375.

Q

Quadagno, D., et al. (1991). Women at risk for human immunodeficiency virus. *Journal of Psychology and Human Sexuality, 4*, 97–110.

Quam, J. K., & Whitford, G. S. (1992). Adaptation and age-related expectations of older gay and lesbian adults. *Gerontologist, 32*, 367–374.

Quevillon, R. P. (1993). Dyspareunia. In W. O'Donohue & J. H. Geer (Eds.), *Handbook of sexual dysfunctions: Assessment and treatment* (pp. 367–380). Boston: Allyn & Bacon.

Quinsey, V. L., Chaplin, T. C., & Upfold, D. (1984). Sexual arousal to nonsexual violence and sadomasochistic themes among rapists and non-sex-offenders. *Journal of Consulting and Clinical Psychology, 52*, 651–657.

R

Rachman, S. (1966). Sexual fetishism: An experimental analogue. *Psychological Record, 16*, 293–296.

Radlove, S. (1983). Sexual response and gender roles. In E. R. Allgeier & N. B. McCormick (Eds.), *Changing boundaries: Gender roles and sexual behavior*. Palo Alto, CA: Mayfield.

Rajfer, J., et al. (1992). Nitric oxide as a mediator of relaxation of the corpus cavernosum in response to nonadrenergic, noncholinergic neurotransmission. *New England Journal of Medicine, 326*, 90–94.

Ramirez, A. (1990, August 12). The success of sweet smell. *The New York Times*, p. 10F.

Rao, K., DiClemente, R. J., & Ponton, L. E. (1992). Child sexual abuse of Asians compared with other populations. *Journal of the American Academy of Child and Adolescent Psychiatry, 31*, 880–886.

Rate of births for teen-agers drops again. (1995, September 22). *The New York Times*, p. A18.

Rathus, S. A. (1978). Treatment of recalcitrant ejaculatory incompetence. *Behavior Therapy, 9*, 962.

Rathus, S. A., & Fichner-Rathus, L. (1997). *The Right Start*. New York: Addison Wesley Longman.

Ratican, K. L. (1992). Sexual abuse survivors: Identifying symptoms and special treatment considerations. *Journal of Counseling and Development, 71*, 33–38.

Rawlins, R. (1998). Cited in Kolata, G. (1998, September 9), Researchers report success in method to pick baby's sex. *The New York Times*; America Online.

Raychaba, B. (1989). Canadian youth in care: Leaving care to be on our own with no direction from home [Special Issue: Runaway, homeless, and shut-out children and youth in Canada, Europe, and the United States]. *Children and Youth Services Review, 11*, 61–73.

Reaney, P. (1998, January 15). Discovery may lead to cervical cancer vaccine. Reuters; America Online.

Reichart, C. A., et al. (1990). Evaluation of Abbott Testpack Chlamydia for detection of *Chlamydia trachomatis* in patients attending sexually transmitted diseases clinics. *Sexually Transmitted Diseases, 17*, 147–151.

Reid, T. R. (1990, December 24). Snug in their beds for Christmas Eve: In Japan, December 24th has become the hottest night of the year. *Washington Post*.

Rein, M. F., & Muller, M. (1990). *Trichomonas vaginalis* and trichomoniasis. In K. K. Holmes, P. Mardh, P. F. Sparling, & P. J. Wiesner (Eds.), *Sexually transmitted diseases* (2nd ed., pp. 481–492). New York: McGraw-Hill.

Reinisch, J. M. (1990). *The Kinsey Institute new report on sex: What you must know to be sexually literate.* New York: St. Martin's Press.

Reiss, B. F. (1988, Spring/Summer). The long-lived person and sexuality. *Dynamic Psychotherapy, 6,* 79–86.

Reiss, I. L. (1980). *Family systems in America.* New York: Holt, Rinehart & Winston.

Remafedi, G. (1990). Study group report on the impact of television portrayals of gender roles on youth. *Journal of Adolescent Health Care, 11*(1), 59–61.

Renzetti, C. M., & Curran, D. J. (1989). *Women, men, and society: The sociology of gender.* Boston: Allyn and Bacon.

Research panel concludes AIDS has small impact on most of U.S. (February 5, 1993). *The New York Times,* p. A11.

Resick, P. A., & Schnicke, M. K. (1990). Treating symptoms in adult victims of sexual assault. *Journal of Interpersonal Violence, 5,* 488–506.

Reuters. (1996, September 18). The RU 486 abortion pill got a tentative seal of approval. America Online.

Rice, M. E., Harris, G. T., & Quinsey, V. L. (1990). A follow-up of rapists assessed in a maximum-security psychiatric facility. *Journal of Interpersonal Violence, 5,* 435–448.

Rice, M. E., Quinsey, V. L., & Harris, G. T. (1991). Sexual recidivism among child molesters released from a maximum security psychiatric institution. *Journal of Consulting and Clinical Psychology, 59,* 381–386.

Richardson, L. (1997, September 30). Condoms in school said not to affect teenage sex rate. *The New York Times,* pp. A1, B6.

Riche, M. (1988, November 23–26). Postmarital society. *American Demographics, 60.*

Ricker, A. L. (1980, November). Sex for sale in Las Vegas. *Cosmopolitan,* pp. 280–315.

Riggio, R. E., & Woll, S. B. (1984). The role of nonverbal cues and physical attractiveness in the selection of dating partners. *Journal of Social and Personal Relationships, 1,* 347–357.

Rindfuss, R. R. (1991). Cited in Pear, R. (1991, December 4), Larger number of new mothers are unmarried. *The New York Times,* p. A20.

Roberto, L. G. (1983). Issues in diagnosis and treatment of transsexualism. *Archives of Sexual Behavior, 12,* 445–473.

Roberts, R. (1998). Cited in Story, P. (1998, June 2), Study: Prostate cancer deaths down. Associated Press; America Online.

Roddy, R. E., et al. (1998). A controlled trial of Nonoxynol 9 film to reduce male-to-female transmission of sexually transmitted diseases. *New England Journal of Medicine, 339,* 504–510.

Roehrich, L., & Kinder, B. N. (1991). Alcohol expectancies and male sexuality: Review and implications for sex therapy. *Journal of Sex & Marital Therapy, 17,* 45–54.

Rogan, H. (1984, October 30). Executive women find it difficult to balance demands of job, home. *The Wall Street Journal,* pp. 35, 55.

Roland, B., Zelkart, P., & Dubes, R. (1989). MMPI correlates of college women who reported experiencing child/adult sexual contact with father, stepfather, or with other persons. *Psychological Reports, 64,* 1159–1162.

Rolfs, R. T., Goldberg, M., & Sharrar, R. G. (1990) Risk factors for syphilis: Cocaine use and prostitution. *American Journal of Public Health, 80,* 853–857.

Rolfs, R. T., & Nakashima, A. K. (1990). Epidemiology of primary and secondary syphilis in the United States: 1981 through 1989. *Journal of the American Medical Association, 264,* 1432–1437.

Romenesko, K., & Miller, E. M. (1989). The second step in double jeopardy: Appropriating the labor of female street hustlers. *Crime and Delinquency, 35,* 109–135.

Ronald, A. R., & Albritton, W. (1990). Chancroid and *Haemophilus ducreyi.* In K. K. Holmes, P. Mardh, P. F. Sparling, & P. J. Wiesner (Eds.), *Sexually transmitted diseases* (2nd ed., pp. 263–272). New York: McGraw-Hill.

Roper Organization. (1985). *The Virginia Slims American Women's Poll.* New York: Roper Organization.

Rose, P. G. (1996). Endometrial carcinoma. *New England Journal of Medicine, 335,* 640–649.

Rose, R. J. (1995). Genes and human behavior. *Annual Review of Psychology, 46,* 625–654.

Rosen, I. (1967). *Pathology and treatment of sexual deviations.* London: Oxford University Press.

Rosen, R. C., & Beck, J. G. (1988). *Patterns of sexual arousal.* New York: Guilford.

Rosen, R. C., Leiblum, S. R., & Spector, I. P. (1994). Psychologically based treatment for male erectile disorder: A cognitive-interpersonal model. *Journal of Sex and Marital Therapy, 20*(2), 67–85.

Rosenberg, P. S., & Biggar, R. J. (1998). Trends in HIV incidence among young adults in the United States. *Journal of the American Medical Association, 279,* 1894–1899.

Rosenthal, A. M. (1995, June 13). The possible dream. *The New York Times,* p. A25.

Rosenthal, D. A., Hall, C., & Moore, S. M. (1992). AIDS, adolescents, and sexual risk taking: A test of the Health Belief Model. *Australian Psychologist, 27,* 166–171.

Rosenthal, E. (1992, July 22). Her image of his ideal, in a faulty mirror. *The New York Times,* p. C12.

Rösler, A., & Witztum, E. (1998). Treatment of men with paraphilia with a long-acting analogue of gonadotropin releasing hormone. *New England Journal of Medicine, 338,* 416–422.

Rosman, J. P., & Resnick, P. J. (1989). Sexual attraction to corpses: A psychiatric review of necrophilia. *Bulletin of the American Academy of Psychiatry and the Law, 17,* 153–163.

Ross, M., & Need, J. (1989). Effects of adequacy of gender reassignment surgery on psychological adjustment: A follow-up of fourteen male-to-female patients. *Archives of Sexual Behavior, 18,* 145–153.

Roth v. *United States,* 354 U.S. 4/6 (1957).

Rotheram-Borus, M. J., & Koopman, C. (1991a). HIV and adolescents. Special Issue: Preventing the spread of the human immunodeficiency virus. *Journal of Primary Prevention, 12,* 65–82.

Rotheram-Borus, M. J., & Koopman, C. (1991b). Sexual risk behaviors, AIDS knowledge, and beliefs about AIDS among runaways. *American Journal of Public Health, 81,* 209–211.

Rotheram-Borus, M., et al. (1992). Lifetime sexual behaviors among predominantly minority male runaways and gay/bisexual adolescents in New York City. *AIDS Education and Prevention, Fall Suppl.,* 34–42.

Rovet, J., & Ireland, L. (1994). Behavioral phenotype in children with Turner syndrome. *Journal of Pediatric Psychology, 19,* 779–790.

Roving mates called factor in cancer. (1996, August 7). *The New York Times,* p. A10.

Royce, R. A., Seña, A., Cates, W., Jr., & Cohen, M. S. (1997). Sexual transmission of HIV. *New England Journal of Medicine, 336,* 1072–1078.

Rozin, P., & Fallon, A. (1988). Body image, attitudes to weight, and misperceptions of figure preferences of the opposite sex: A comparison of men and women in two generations. *Journal of Abnormal Psychology, 97,* 342–345.

Rubin, A., & Adams, J. (1986). Outcomes of sexually open marriages. *Journal of Sex Research, 22,* 311–319.

Rubinow, D. R., & Schmidt, P. J. (1995). The treatment of premenstrual syndrome—Forward into the past. *New England Journal of Medicine, 332,* 1574–1575.

Ruefli, T., Yu, O., & Barton, J. (1992). Sexual risk taking in smaller cities: The case of Buffalo, New York. *Journal of Sex Research, 29,* 95–108.

Russell, D. (1982). *Rape in marriage.* New York: Macmillan.

Russo, N. F., Horn, J. D., & Schwartz, R. (1992). U.S. abortion in context: Selected characteristics and motivations of women seeking abortions. *Journal of Social Issues, 48,* 183–202.

Russo, N. F., & Marin, A. D. (1997, February). *Professional Psychology: Research and Practice.* Cited in Brody, J. E. (1997, February 12), Abortion doesn't affect well-being, study says. The New York Times; America Online.

S

Sack, W. H., & Mason, R. (1980). Child abuse and conviction of sexual crimes: A preliminary finding. *Law and Human Behavior, 4,* 211–215.

Sadalla, E. K., Kenrick, D. T., & Vershure, B. (1987). Dominance and heterosexual attraction. *Journal of Personality and Social Psychology, 52,* 730–738.

Sadava, S. W., & Matejcic, C. (1987). Generalized and specific loneliness in early marriage. *Canadian Journal of Behavioural Science, 19,* 56–66.

Sadker, M., & Sadker, D. (1994). *How America's schools cheat girls.* New York: Scribners.

Saenger, P. (1996). Turner's syndrome. *New England Journal of Medicine, 335,* 1749–1754.

Safer, J. (1996, January 17). Childless by choice. *The New York Times,* p. A19.

Sagan, C., & Dryan, A. (1990, April 22). The question of abortion: A search for answers. *Parade Magazine,* pp. 4–8.

Sagarin, E. (1973). Power to the peephole. *Sexual Behavior, 3,* 2–7.

Saluter, A. F. (1992). Marital status and living arrangements: *Current Population Reports,* March, Series P20–468.

Samuels, M., & Samuels, N. (1986). *The well pregnancy book.* New York: Simon & Schuster.

Sanchez-Guerrero, J., et al. (1995). Silicone breast implants and the risk of connective tissue diseases and symptoms, *New England Journal of Medicine, 332,* 1666–1670.

Sanday, P. R. (1981). The socio-cultural context of rape: A cross-cultural study. *Journal of Social Issues, 37,* 5–27.

Sanders, S. A., Reinisch, J. M., & McWhirter, D. P. (1990). Homosexuality/heterosexuality: An overview. In D. P. McWhirter, S. A. Sanders, & J. M. Reinisch (Eds.), *Homosexuality/heterosexuality: Concepts of sexual orientation* (pp. xix–xxvii). New York: Oxford University Press.

Sandross, R. (1988, December). Sexual harassment in the Fortune 500. *Working Woman,* p. 69.

Sanger, M. (1938). *Margaret Sanger: An autobiography.* New York: Norton.

Sargent, T. O. (1988). Fetishism. *Journal of Social Work and Human Sexuality, 7,* 27–42.

Sarrel, P., & Masters, W. (1982). Sexual molestation of men by women. *Archives of Sexual Behavior, 11,* 117–131.

Sauer, M. V., Paulson, R. J., & Lobo, R. A. (1990). A preliminary report on oocyte donation extending reproductive potential to women over 40. *New England Journal of Medicine, 323,* 1157–1160.

Savitz, L., & Rosen, L. (1988). The sexuality of prostitutes: Sexual enjoyment reported by "streetwalkers." *Journal of Sex Research, 24,* 200–208.

Schachter, J. (1989). Why we need a program for the control of *Chlamydia trachomatis. New England Journal of Medicine, 320,* 802–804.

Schafer, R. B., & Keith, P. M. (1990). Matching by weight in married couples: A life cycle perspective. *Journal of Social Psychology, 130,* 657–664.

Schafran, L. H. (1995, August 26). Rape is still underreported. *The New York Times,* p. A19.

Schiavi, R. C., et al. (1990). Healthy aging and male sexual function. *American Journal of Psychiatry, 147,* 766–771.

Schillinger, L. (1995, June 10). More sex please, we're Russian. *The New York Times Book Review,* p. 49.

Schmidt, G. (1994). Sex therapy 1970–1994. *Nordisk-Sexologi, 12*(3), 178–183.

Schmidt, K. W., et al. (1992). Sexual behaviour related to psycho-social factors in a population of Danish homosexual and bisexual men. *Social Science and Medicine, 34,* 1119–1127.

Schmidt, P. J., et al. (1998). Differential behavioral effects of gonadal steroids in women with and in those without premenstrual syndrome. *New England Journal of Medicine, 338,* 209–216.

Schmitt, E. (1996, September 11). Senators reject both job-bias ban and gay marriage. *The New York Times*, pp. A1, A16.

Schneemann, C. (1991). The obscene body/politic. *Art Journal, 50*(4), 28–35.

Schnell, D. J., O'Reilly, K. R. (1991). Patterns of sexual behavior change among homosexual/bisexual men—selected U.S. sites, 1987–1990. *Mortality and Morbidity Weekly Report, 40, 46,* 792–794.

Schoendorf, K. C., & Kiely, J. L. (1992). Relationship of sudden infant death syndrome to maternal during and after pregnancy. *Pediatrics, 90,* 905–908.

Schoolgirls as sex toys. (1997, April 6). *The New York Times*, p. E2.

Schork, K. (1990, August 19). The despair of Pakistan's women: Not even Benazir Bhutto could stop the repression. *Washington Post.*

Schott, R. L. (1995). The childhood and family dynamics of transvestites. *Archives of Sexual Behavior, 24,* 309–327.

Schreiber, G. B., et al. (1996). The risk of transfusion-transmitted viral infections. *New England Journal of Medicine, 334,* 1685–1690.

Schreiner-Engle, P., & Schiavi, R. (1986). Lifetime psychopathology in individuals with low sexual desire. *Journal of Nervous and Mental Disease, 174,* 646–651.

Schultz, N. R., Jr., & Moore, D. W. (1984). Loneliness: Correlates, attributions, and coping among older adults. *Personality and Social Psychology Bulletin, 10,* 67–77.

Schuster, M. A., et al. (1998, March–April). *Family Planning Perspectives.* Cited in Study: Condom availability increases use, not sex (1998, April 17). Associated Press; America Online.

Schwartz, I. M. (1993). Affective reactions of American and Swedish women to their first premarital coitus: A cross-cultural comparison. *Journal of Sex Research, 30,* 18–26.

Schwartz, M. F., & Masters, W. H. (1984). The Masters and Johnson treatment program for dissatisfied homosexual men. *American Journal of Psychiatry, 141,* 173–181.

Scott, J. E., & Cuvelier, S. J. (1993). Violence and sexual violence in pornography: Is it really increasing. *Archives of Sexual Behavior, 22,* 357–371.

Scott, J. E., & Schwalm, L. A. (1988). Rape rates and the circulation rates of adult magazines. *Journal of Sex Research, 24,* 241–250.

Seachrist, L. (1995, September 23). Amount of virus sets cancer risk. *Science News*, p. 197.

Sears, A. E. (1989). The legal case for restricting pornography. In D. Zillmann & J. Bryant (Eds.), *Pornography: Research advances and policy considerations.* Hillsdale, NJ: Lawrence Erlbaum Associates.

Seattle–King County Department of Public Health (1991). The AIDS Prevention Project. The Seattle Star: A report to the communiity on what we're learning from the "Be A Star Study." Seattle: Author.

Seftel, A. D., Oates, R. D., & Krane, R. J. (1991). Disturbed sexual function in patients with spinal cord disease. *Neurologic Clinics, 9,* 757–778.

Segal, Z. V., & Marshall, W. L. (1985). Heterosexual social skills in a population of rapists and child molesters. *Journal of Consulting and Clinical Psychology, 53,* 55–63.

Segraves, R. T. (1988a). Drugs and desire. In S. Leiblum & R. Rosen (Eds.), *Sexual desire disorders.* New York: Guilford Press.

Segraves, R. T. (1988b). Sexual side-effects of psychiatric drugs. *International Journal of Psychiatry in Medicine, 18,* 243–252.

Segraves, R. T., & Segraves, K. B. (1993). Medical aspects of orgasm disorders. In W. O'Donohue & J. H. Geer (Eds.), *Handbook of sexual dysfunctions: Assessment and treatment* (pp. 225–252). Boston: Allyn & Bacon.

Self magazine (1995, June), p. 75.

Seligmann, J. (1993, July 26). Husbands no, babies yes. *Newsweek*, p. 53.

Sell, R. L., Wells, J. A., & Wypij, D. (1995). The prevalence of homosexual behavior and attraction in the United States, the United Kingdom, and France: Results of national, population-based samples. *Archives of Sexual Behavior, 24,* 235–248.

Seltzer, R. (1992). The social location of those holding antihomosexual attitudes. *Sex Roles, 26,* 391–398.

Selvin, B. W. (1993, June 1). Transsexuals are coming to terms with themselves and society. *New York Newsday*, pp. 55, 58, 59.

Semans, J. (1956). Premature ejaculation: A new approach. *Southern Medical Journal, 49,* 353–358.

Seng, M. J. (1989). Child sexual abuse and adolescent prostitution: A comparative analysis. *Adolescence, 24,* 665–675.

Severn, J., Belch, G. E., & Belch, M. A. (1990). The effects of sexual and non-sexual advertising appeals and information level on cognitive processing and communication effectiveness. *Journal of Advertising, 19,* 14–22.

Sex complaints flood phones set up by Army. (1996, November 12). *The New York Times*, p. A13.

Sex offender agrees to be castrated. (1998, January 18). *The New York Times*, p. A19.

Shafer, M. A., et al. (1993). Evaluation of urine-based screening strategies to detect *Chlamydia trachomatis* among sexually active asymptomatic young men. *Journal of the American Medical Association, 270,* 2065–2070.

Shalala, D. (1998). Cited in Meckler, L. (1998, June 26), Teen abortion, pregnancy rates fall. Associated Press; America Online.

Shapiro, J. P. (1992, July 13). The teen pregnancy boom. *U.S. News & World Report*, p. 38.

Shaver, P., Hazan, C., & Bradshaw, D. (1988). Love as attachment. In R. J. Sternberg & M. L. Barnes (Eds.), *The psychology of love* (pp. 68–99). New Haven: Yale University Press.

Sheehy, G. (1995). *New passages: Mapping your life across time.* New York: Random House.

Sheehy, G. (1997, November 17). Beyond virility, a new vision. *Newsweek*, p. 69.

Sheehy, G. (1998). *Understanding men's passages.* New York: Random House.

Shenon, P. (1995, July 15). New Zealand seeks causes of suicides by young. *The New York Times*, p. A3.

Sheppard, J. A., & Strathman, A. J. (1989). Attractiveness and height: The role of stature in dating preference, frequency of dating, and perceptions of attractiveness. *Personality and Social Psychology Bulletin, 15*, 617–627.

Sherman, K. J., et al. (1990). Sexually transmitted diseases and tubal pregnancy. *Sexually Transmitted Diseases, 17*, 115–121.

Sherwin, B. B., Gelfand, M. M., & Brender, W. (1985). Androgen enhances sexual motivation in females: A prospective, crossover study of sex steroid administration in the surgical menopause. *Psychosomatic Medicine, 47*, 339–351.

Shettles, L. (1982, June). Predetermining children's sex. *Medical Aspects of Human Sexuality*, 172.

Shilts, R. (1987). *And the band played on: Politics, people, and the AIDS epidemic*. New York: Penguin Books.

Siegel, J. M., et al. (1990). Reactions to sexual assault: A community study. *Journal of Interpersonal Violence, 5*, 229–246.

Siegel, K., et al. (1988). Patterns of change in sexual behavior among gay men in New York City. *Archives of Sexual Behavior, 17*, 481–497.

Siegler, I. C., Feaganes, J. R., & Rimer, B. K. (1995). Predictors of adoption of mammography in women under age 50. *Health Psychology, 14*, 274–278.

Signorielli, N. (1990). Children, television, and gender roles: Messages and impact. *Journal of Adolescent Health Care, 11*(1), 50–58.

Silber, S. J. (1991). *How to get pregnant with the new technology*. New York: Time-Warner.

Silbert, M. H. (1989). The effects on juveniles of being used for pornography and prostitution. In D. Zillmann & J. Bryant (Eds.), *Pornography: Research advances and policy considerations* (pp. 215–234). Hillsdale, NJ: Lawrence Erlbaum Associates.

Simpson, J. A., Campbell, B., & Berscheid, E. (1986). The association between romantic love and marriage: Kephart (1967) twice revisited. *Personality and Social Psychology Bulletin*, 363–372.

Singer, J., & Singer, I. (1972). Types of female orgasm. *Journal of Sex Research, 8*, 255–267.

Singh, D. (1994a). Body fat distribution and perception of desirable female body shape by young Black men and women. *International Journal of Eating Disorders, 16*(3), 289–294.

Singh, D. (1994b). Is thin really beautiful and good? Relationship between waist-to-hip ratio (WHR) and female attractiveness. *Personality and Individual Differences, 16*(1), 123–132.

Singh, G. K., & Yu, S. M. (1995). Cited in Pear, R. (1995, July 10), Infant mortality rate drops but racial disparity grows. *The New York Times*, p. B9.

Sirles, E. A., & Franke, P. J. (1989). Factors influencing mothers' reactions to intrafamily sexual abuse. *Child Abuse & Neglect, 13*, 131–139.

Skate, S. (1998). Cited in Story, P. (1998, June 2), Study: Prostate cancer deaths down. Associated Press; America Online.

Slattery, M. L., & Kerber, R. A. (1993). A comprehensive evaluation of family history and breast cancer risk: The Utah population database. *Journal of the American Medical Association, 270*, 1563–1568.

Sleek, S. (1997). Resolution raises concerns about conversion therapy. *APA Monitor, 27*(10), 15.

Slonim-Nevo, V. (1992). First premarital intercourse among Mexican-American and Anglo-American adolescent women: Interpreting ethnic differences. *Journal of Adolescent Research, 7*, 332–351.

Smart, C. R., et al. (1995, April). *Cancer*. Cited in Brody, J. E. (1995, May 3), Breast scans may indeed help women under 50. *The New York Times*, p. C11.

Smith, E. A., & Udry, J. R. (1985). Coital and non-coital sexual behaviors of white and black adolescents. *American Journal of Public Health, 75*, 1200–1203.

Smith, E. P., et al. (1994). Estrogen resistance caused by a mutation in the estrogen-receptor gene in a man. *The New England Journal of Medicine, 331*, 1056–1061.

Smolowe, J. (1993, June 14). New, improved and ready for battle. *Time*, pp. 48–51.

Sobel, J. D. (1997). Current concepts: Vaginitis. *New England Journal of Medicine, 337*, 1896–1903.

Sodroski, J., et al. (1998). *Nature*. Cited in "Scientists uncover 'key' to AIDS virus." (1998, June 18). Associated Press; CNN.

Solano, C. H., Batten, P. G., & Parish, E. A. (1982). Loneliness and patterns of self-disclosure. *Journal of Personality and Social Psychology, 43*, 524–531.

Sonenstein, F. L., Pleck, J. H., & Ku, L. C. (1989). Sexual activity, condom use and AIDS awareness among adolescent males. *Family Planning Perspectives, 21*, 152–157.

Sorensen, R. C. (1973). *Adolescent sexuality in contemporary America*. New York: World.

Sorrenti-Little, I., Bagley, C., and Robertson, S. (1984). An operational definition of the long-term harmfulness of sexual relations with peers and adults by young children. *Canadian Child, 9*, 46–57.

Sourander, L. B. (1994). Geriatric aspects on estrogen effects and sexuality. *Gerontology, 40*(Suppl. 3), 14–17.

Southerland, D. (1990, May 27). Limited "sexual revolution" seen in China: Nationwide survey shows more liberal attitudes developing in conservative society. *Washington Post*.

Spark, R. F. (1991). *Male sexual health: A couple's guide*. Mount Vernon, NY: Consumer Reports Books.

Speckens, A. E. M., et al. (1995). Psychosexual functioning of partners of men with presumed non-organic erectile dysfunction: Cause or consequence of the disorder? *Archives of Sexual Behavior, 24*, 157–172.

Specter, M. (1998, January 11). Traffickers' new cargo: Naive Slavic women. *The New York Times*; America Online.

Spiro, M. E. (1965). *Children of the kibbutz*. New York: Schocken Books.

Spitz, I. M., et al. (1998). Early pregnancy termination with mifepristone and misoprostol in the United States. *New England Journal of Medicine, 338*, 1241–1247.

Spitzer, R. L., et al. (1989). *DSM-III-R casebook.* Washington, DC: American Psychiatric Press.

Sprecher, S. (1989). Premarital sexual standards for different categories of individuals. *Journal of Sex Research, 26,* 232–248.

Sprecher, S., Barbee, A., & Schwartz, P. (1995). "Was it good for you, too?": Gender differences in first sexual intercourse experiences. *The Journal of Sex Research, 32,* 3–15.

Sprecher, S., Sullivan, Q., & Hatfield, E. (1994). Mate selection preferences: Gender differences examined in a national sample. *Journal of Personality and Social Psychology, 66*(6), 1074–1080.

Spring, J. A. (1997). Cited in Alterman, E. (1997, November). Sex in the '90s. *Elle,* p. 130.

St. Lawrence, J. S., Brasfield, T. L., Jefferson, K. W., Alleyne, E., O'Bannon, R. E., & Shirley, A. (1995). Cognitive-behavioral intervention to reduce African American adolescents' risk for HIV infection. *Journal of Consulting and Clinical Psychology, 63,* 221–237.

Stamm, W. E., & Holmes, K. K. (1990). *Chlamydia trachomatis* infections of the adult. In K. K. Holmes, P. Mardh, P. F. Sparling, & P. J. Wiesner (Eds.), *Sexually transmitted diseases* (2nd ed., pp. 181–194). New York: McGraw-Hill.

Stampfer, M. J., et al. (1988). A prospective study of past use of oral contraceptive agents and risk of cardiovascular diseases. *New England Journal of Medicine, 319,* 1313–1317.

Stampfer, M. J., et al. (1991). Ten-year follow-up study of estrogen replacement therapy in relation to cardiovascular disease and mortality. Paper presented at the 24th annual meeting of the Society for Epidemiologic Research, Buffalo, New York, June 11–14, 1991.

Stangor, C., & Ruble, D. N. (1989). Differential influences of gender schemata and gender constancy on children's information processing and behavior. *Social Cognition, 7,* 353–372.

Starr, B. D., & Weiner, M. B. (1981). *The Starr-Weiner report on sex and sexuality in the mature years.* New York: Stein & Day.

Steele, C. M., & Josephs, R. A. (1990). Alcohol myopia: Its prized and dangerous effects. *American Psychologist, 45,* 921–933.

Steiner, M., et al. (1995). Fluoxetine in the treatment of premenstrual dysphoria. *New England Journal of Medicine, 332,* 1529–1534.

Steinhauer, J. (1995, July 6). No marriage, no apologies. *The New York Times,* pp. C1, C7.

Stericker, A., & LeVesconte, S. (1982). Effect of brief training on sex-related differences in visual-spatial skill. *Journal of Personality and Social Psychology, 43,* 1018–1029.

Stephens, W. N. (1982). *The family in cross-cultural perspective.* Washington, DC: University Press of America.

Sternberg, R. J. (1986). A triangular theory of love. *Psychological Review, 93,* 119–135.

Sternberg, R. J. (1987). Liking versus loving: A comparative evaluation of theories. *Psychological Bulletin, 102,* 331–345.

Sternberg, R. J. (1988). *The triangle of love: Intimacy, passion, commitment.* New York: Basic Books.

Sternberg, R. J., & Grajek, S. (1984). The nature of love. *Journal of Personality and Social Psychology, 47,* 312–329.

Stewart, F. H. (1992). Cited in Leary, W. E. (1992, February 1), U.S. panel backs approval of first condom for women. *The New York Times,* p. 7.

Stewart, G. K. (1998). Intrauterine devices (IUDs). In R. A. Hatcher et al. (1998), *Contraceptive technology* (17th rev. ed., pp. 511–544). New York: Ardent Media, Inc.

Still no pill for Japan. (1992, March 22). *The New York Times,* Section 4, p. 7.

Stock, W. E. (1991). Feminist explanations: Male power, hostility, and sexual coercion. In E. Grauerholz & M. A. Koralewski (Eds.), *Sexual coercion: A sourcebook on its nature, causes, and prevention* (pp. 61–73). Lexington, MA: Lexington Books.

Stock, W. E. (1993). Inhibited female orgasm. In W. O'Donohue & J. H. Geer (Eds.), *Handbook of sexual dysfunctions: Assessment and treatment* (pp. 253–301). Boston: Allyn & Bacon.

Stolberg, S. G. (1998a, January 18). Quandary on donor eggs: What to tell the children. *The New York Times,* pp. 1, 20.

Stolberg, S. G. (1998b, March 9). U.S. awakes to epidemic of sexual diseases. *The New York Times,* pp. A1, A14.

Stoller, R. J. (1969). Parental influences in male transsexualism. In R. Green & J. Money (Eds.), *Transsexualism and sex reassignment.* Baltimore: Johns Hopkins University Press.

Stoller, R. J. (1977). Sexual deviations. In R. Beach (Ed.), *Human Sexuality in Four Perspectives* (pp. 190–214). Baltimore: Johns Hopkins University Press.

Stoller, R. J., & Herdt, G. H. (1985). Theories of origins of male homosexuality. *Archives of General Psychiatry, 42,* 399–404.

Stone, S. (1989). Assessing oral contraceptive risks. *Medical Aspects of Human Sexuality,* 112–122.

Storms, M. D. (1980). Theories of sexual orientation. *Journal of Personality and Social Psychology, 38,* 783–792.

Story, P. (1998, June 2). Study: Prostate cancer deaths down. Associated Press; America Online.

Strassberg, D. S., et al. (1990). The role of anxiety in premature ejaculation: A psychophysiological model. *Archives of Sexual Behavior, 19,* 251–257.

Strickland, B. R. (1995). Research on sexual orientation and human development: A commentary. *Developmental Psychology, 31,* 137–140.

Strom, S. (1993, April 18). Human pheromones. *The New York Times,* p. V12.

Struckman-Johnson, C. (1988). Forced sex on dates: It happens to men, too. *The Journal of Sex Research, 24,* 234–241.

Study finds some promise in alternative to estrogen. (1998, May 13). *The New York Times,* p. A21.

Sue, D. (1979). Erotic fantasies of college students during coitus. *Journal of Sex Research, 15,* 299–305.

Sue, D., Sue, D. W., & Sue, S. (1981). *Understanding abnormal behavior.* Boston: Houghton Mifflin Co.

Sullivan, A. (1995). *Virtually normal.* New York: Knopf.

Suppe, F. (1994). Explaining homosexuality: Philosophical issues, and who cares anyhow? *Journal of Homosexuality, 27*(3–4), 223–268.

Swann, W. B., Jr., et al. (1987). Cognitive-affective crossfire: When self-consistency meets self-enhancement. *Journal of Personality and Social Psychology, 52,* 881–889.

Symons, D. (1979). *The evolution of human sexuality.* New York: Oxford University Press.

Symons, D. (1995). Cited in Goleman, D. (1995, June 14), Sex fantasy research said to neglect women. *The New York Times,* p. C14.

Szasz, G., & Carpenter, C. (1989). Clinical observations in vibratory stimulation of the penis of men with spinal cord injury. *Archives of Sexual Behavior, 18,* 461–474.

T

Tanfer, K., Grady, W. R., Klepinger, D. H., & Billy, J. O. G. (1993). Condom use among U.S. men, 1991. *Family Planning Perspectives, 25,* 61–66.

Tang, C. S., Critelli, J. W., & Porter, J. F. (1995). Sexual aggression and victimization in dating relationships among Chinese college students. *Archives of Sexual Behavior, 24,* 47–53.

Tannahill, R. (1980). *Sex in history.* Briarcliff Manor, NY: Stein & Day.

Tannen, D. (1990). *You just don't understand.* New York: Ballantine Books.

Tannenbaum, J. (1991). Robert Mapplethorpe: The Philadelphia story. *Art Journal, 50*(4), 71–76.

Tavris, C., & Sadd, S. (1977). *The Redbook report on female sexuality.* New York: Delacorte.

Tedeschi, J. T., & Felson, R. B. (1994). *Violence, aggression, & coercive actions.* Washington, DC: American Psychological Association.

Telushkin, J. (1991). *Jewish literacy.* New York: Morrow.

Teen-agers and aids: The risk worsens. (1992, April 14). *The New York Times,* p. C3.

Tharinger, D. (1990). Impact of child sexual abuse on developing sexuality. *Professional Psychology: Research and Practice, 21,* 331–337.

Thomason, J. L., & Gelbart, S. M. (1989). *Trichomonas vaginalis. Obstetrics and Gynecology, 74,* 536–541.

Thomlison, B., et al. (1991). Characteristics of Canadian male and female child sexual abuse victims. Special Issue: Child sexual abuse. *Journal of Child and Youth Care,* Fall, 65–76.

Thompson, D. S. (Ed.). (1993). *Every woman's health: The complete guide to body and mind.* New York: Simon & Schuster.

Thompson, J. K., & Tantleff, S. (1992). Female and male ratings of upper torso: Actual, ideal, and stereotypical conceptions. *Journal of Social Behavior and Personality, 7,* 345–354.

Thompson, M. E. (1991). Self-defense against sexual coercion: Theory, research, and practice. In E. Grauerholz & M. A. Koralewski (Eds.), *Sexual coercion: A sourcebook on its nature, causes, and prevention* (pp. 111–121). Lexington, MA: Lexington Books.

Thompson, S. (1995). *Going all the way.* New York: Hill & Wang.

Thornton, A., & Camburn, D. (1987). The influence of the family on premarital sexual attitudes and behavior. *Demography, 24,* 323–340.

Tierney, J. (1994, January 9). Porn, the low-flung engine of progress. *The New York Times,* Section 2, pp. 1, 18.

Ting, D., & Carter, J. H. (1990). Behavioral change through empowerment: Prevention of AIDS. *Journal of the National Medical Association, 84,* 225–228.

Tobias, S. (1982). Sexist equations. *Psychology Today, 16*(1), pp. 14–17.

Tollison, C. D., & Adams, H. E. (1979). *Sexual disorders: Treatment, theory, and research.* New York: Gardner Press.

Tomlinson, J. A. (1991). Burn it, hide it, flaunt it. *Art Journal, 50*(4), 59–64.

Toner, J. P., et al. (1991). Basal follicle-stimulating hormone level is a better predictor of in vitro fertilization performance than age. *Fertility and Sterility, 55,* 784–791.

Toomey, K. E., & Barnes, R. C. (1990). Treatment of *Chlamydia trachomatis* genital infection. *Reviews of Infectious Diseases* (Suppl. 6).

Townsend, J. M. (1995). Sex without emotional involvement: An evolutionary interpretation of sex differences. *Archives of Sexual Behavior, 24,* 173–206.

Trenton State College. (1991, Spring). Sexual Assault Victim Education and Support Unit (SAVES-U) Newsletter.

Trieschmann, R. (1989). Psychosocial adjustment to spinal cord injury. In B. W. Heller, L. M. Flohr, & L. S. Zegans (Eds.), *Psychosocial interventions with physically disabled persons* (pp. 117–136). New Brunswick, NJ: Rutgers University Press.

Trovato, F. (1986). The relationship between marital dissolution and suicide: The Canadian case. *Journal of Marriage and the Family, 48,* 341–348.

Trujillo, C. (Ed.). (1991). *Chicana lesbians: The girls our mothers warned us about.* Berkeley, CA: Third Woman Press.

Trussell, J., Strickler, J., & Vaughan, B.(1993). Contraceptive efficacy of the diaphragm, the sponge, and the cervical cap. *Family Planning Perspectives, 25,* 100–105.

Tseng, W., et al. (1992). Koro epidemics in Guangdong, China: A questionnaire survey. *Journal of Nervous & Mental Disease, 180,* 117–123.

Tutty, L. M. (1992). The ability of elementary school children to learn child sexual abuse prevention concepts. *Child Abuse and Neglect, 16,* 369–384.

Two viewfinders, two views of Gay America. (1993, June 27). *The New York Times,* Section 4, p. 10.

U

U.S. Bureau of the Census. (1990). Marital status and living arrangements: March 1990. *Current Population Reports,* Series P-20, No. 450. Washington, DC: U.S. Government Printing Office.

U.S. Bureau of the Census. (1996). *Statistical abstract of the United States* (116th ed.). Washington, DC: U.S. Government Printing Office.

U.S. Bureau of the Census. (1998). *Statistical abstract of the United States* (118th ed.). Washington, DC: U.S. Government Printing Office.

U.S. Department of Health and Human Services (USDHHS). (1990). *The health benefits of smoking cessation: A report of the Surgeon General* (DHHS Publication No. CDC 90–8416). Rockville, MD: Public Health Service, Centers for Disease Control, Center for Chronic Disease Prevention and Health Promotion, Office on Smoking and Health.

U.S. Department of Health and Human Services (USDHHS). (1991). *Strategies to control tobacco use in the United States: A blueprint for public health action in the 1990's* (NIH Publication No. 92–3316). Washington, DC: National Cancer Institute, Public Health Service, National Institutes of Health, National Cancer Institute.

U.S. Department of Health and Human Services (USDHHS). (1992). *Smoking and health in the Americas* (DHHS Publication No. (CDC) 92–8419). Atlanta: Public Health Service, Centers for Disease Control, National Center for Chronic Disease Prevention and Health Promotion. Office on Smoking and Health.

U.S. Department of Justice. (1986). *Attorney general's commission on pornography: Final report.* Washington, DC: U.S. Government Printing Office.

U.S. Merit Systems Protection Board. (1981). *Sexual harassment in the federal workplace: Is it a problem?* Washington, DC: Office of Merit Systems Review and Studies.

U.S. scientists admit cocktail might not cure AIDS. (1997, November 13). Reuters; America Online.

U.S. Senate Committee on the Judiciary. (1991). Violence against women: The increase of rape in America 1990. *Response to the Victimization of Women and Children, 14* (79, No. 2), 20–23.

Udry, J. R., & Billy, J. O. G. (1987). Initiation of coitus in early adolescence. *American Sociological Review, 52,* 841–855.

Udry, J., et al. (1985). Serum androgenic hormones motivate sexual behavior in adolescent boys. *Fertility and Sterility, 43,* 90–94.

Udry, J. R., Talbert, L., & Morris, N. M. (1986). Biosocial foundations for adolescent female sexuality. *Demography, 23*(2), 217–230.

V

Vaginal yeast infection can be an HIV warning. (1992, November 24). *New York Newsday,* p. 51.

Valentiner, D. P., Foa, E. B., Riggs, D. S., & Gershuny, B. S. (1996). Coping strategies and posttraumatic stress disorder in female victims of sexual and nonsexual assault. *Journal of Abnormal Psychology, 105,* 455–458.

Valian, V. (1998). *Why so slow? The advancement of women.* Cambridge, MA: MIT Press.

Van den Hoek, A., Van Haastrecht, H. J., & Coutinho, R. A. (1990). Heterosexual behaviour of intravenous drug users in Amsterdam: Implications for the AIDS epidemic. *AIDS, 4,* 449–453.

Van der Velde, F. W., van der Pligt, J., & Hooykaas, C. (1994). Perceiving AIDS-related risk: Accuracy as a function of differences in actual risk. *Health Psychology, 13,* 25–33.

Van Steirteghem, A. C., et al. (1993). High fertilization and implantation rates after intracytoplasmic sperm injection. *Human Reproduction, 8,* 1061–1066.

Vazi, R., Best, D., Davis, S., & Kaiser, M. (1989). Evaluation of a testicular cancer curriculum for adolescents. *Journal of Pediatrics, 114,* 150–162.

Vinacke, W., et al. (1988). Similarity and complementarity in intimate couples. *Genetic, Social, and General Psychology Monographs, 114,* 51–76.

Voeller, B. (1991). AIDS and heterosexual anal intercourse. *Archives of Sexual Behavior, 20,* 233–276.

Von Krafft-Ebbing, R. (1978). *Psychopathia sexualis.* Philadelphia: F. A. Davis. (Original work published 1886.)

Voyer, D., Voyer, S., & Bryden, M. P. (1995). Magnitude of sex differences in spatial abilities: A meta-analysis and consideration of critical variables. *Psychological Bulletin, 117,* 250–270.

Vyas, G. N., Rawal, D. B., & Busch, M. P. (1996). The risk of HIV transmission by screened blood. *New England Journal of Medicine, 334,* 992.

W

Waigandt, A., et al. (1990). The impact of sexual assault on physical health status. *Journal of Traumatic Stress, 3,* 93–102.

Wald, A., et al. (1995). Virologic characteristics of subclinical and symptomatic genital herpes infections. *New England Journal of Medicine, 333,* 770–775.

Waldinger, M. D., Hengeveld, M. W., & Zwinderman, A. H. (1994). Paroxetine treatment of premature ejaculation: A double-blind, randomized, placebo-controlled study. *American Journal of Psychiatry, 151*(9), 1377–1379.

Walfish, S., & Myerson, M. (1980). Sex role identity and attitudes toward sexuality. *Archives of Sexual Behavior, 9,* 199–204.

Wallace, H. M., & Vienonen, M. (1989). Teenage pregnancy in Sweden and Finland. *Journal of Adolescent Health Care, 10,* 231–236.

Wallerstein, J. S., & Blakeslee, S. (1989). *Second chances: Women and children a decade after divorce.* New York: Ticknor & Fields.

Wallerstein, J. S., & Kelly, J. B. (1980). *Surviving the breakup: How children and parents cope with divorce.* New York: Basic Books.

Walsh, P. C. (1996). Treatment of benign prostatic hyperplasia. *New England Journal of Medicine, 335,* 586–587.

Walster, E., & Walster, G. W. (1978). *A new look at love.* Reading, MA: Addison-Wesley.

Walt, V. (1993, July 26). Some 2nd thoughts on depo. *New York Newsday,* p. 13.

Walter, H. J., & Vaughan, R. D. (1993). AIDS risk reduction among a multiethnic sample of urban high school students. *Journal of the American Medical Association, 270,* 725–730.

Wardlaw, G. M., & Insel, P. M. (1990). *Perspectives in nutrition.* St. Louis: Times Mirror/Mosby College Publishing.

Warner, D. L., & Hatcher, R. A. (1998). Male condoms. In Hatcher, R. A., et al. (1998). *Contraceptive technology* (17th rev. ed., pp. 325–356). New York: Ardent Media, Inc.

Warren, C. W., et al. (1990). Assessing the reproductive behavior of on- and off-reservation American Indian females: Characteristics of two groups in Montana. *Social Biology, 37,* 69–83.

Washington, A. C., Rosser, P. L., & Cox, E. P. (1983). Contraceptive practices of teenage mothers. *Journal of the National Medical Association, 75,* 1059–1063.

Wasson, J. H. (1998). Finasteride to prevent morbidity from benign prostate hyperplasia. *New England Journal of Medicine, 338,* 612–613.

Waterman, J. (1986). Overview of treatment issues. In K. MacFarlane et al. (Eds.), *Sexual abuse of young children: Evaluation and treatment.* (pp. 197–203). New York: Guilford.

Waterman, J., & Lusk, R. (1986). Scope of the problem. In K. MacFarlane et al. (Eds.), *Sexual abuse of young children: Evaluation and treatment* (pp. 3–14). New York: Guilford Press.

Waterman, J., et al. (1986). Challenges for the future. In K. MacFarlane et al. (Eds.), *Sexual abuse of young children: Evaluation and treatment* (pp. 315–332). New York: Guilford.

Waterman, J., & Lusk, R. (1986). Scope of the problem. In K. MacFarlane, et al. (Eds.), *Sexual abuse of young children: Evaluation and treatment* (pp. 3–14). New York: Guilford Press.

Weinberg, M. S., Williams, C. J., & Moser, C. (1984). The social constituents of sadomasochism. *Social Problems, 31,* 379–389.

Weinberg, M. S., et al. (1994). *Dual attraction.* New York: Oxford University Press.

Weinberg, T. S. (1987). Sadomasochism in the United States: A review of recent sociological literature. *Journal of Sex Research, 23,* 50–69.

Weinberg, T. S., & Bullough, V. L. (1986). *Women married to transvestites: Problems and adjustments.* Paper presented at the annual meeting of the Society for the Study of Social Problems, New York.

Weinberg, T. S., & Bullough, V. L. (1988). Alienation, self-image, and the importance of support groups for the wives of transvestites. *Journal of Sex Research, 24,* 262–268.

Weingarten, H. (1985). Marital status and well-being: A national study comparing first-married, currently divorced, and remarried adults. *Journal of Marriage and the Family, 47,* 653–662.

Weinraub, M. (1998, January 22). Study finds possible predictor of prostate cancer. Reuters.

Weinstock, H. S., et al. (1993). Factors associated with condom use in a high-risk heterosexual pouplation. *Sexually Transmitted Diseases, 20,* 14–20.

Weisberg, D. K. (1985). *Children of the night: A study of adolescent prostitution.* Lexington, MA: D.C. Heath.

Weiss, D. L. (1983). Affective reactions of women to their initial experince of coitus. *Journal of Sex Research, 19,* 209–237.

Weiss, R. D., & Mirin, S. M. (1987). *Cocaine.* Washington, DC: American Psychiatric Press.

Wells, C. (1991). *Women, sport, & performance: A physiological perspective* (2nd ed.). Champaign, IL: Human Kinetics Publishers, Inc., 1991.

Werner, D., & Cohen, A. (1990). Instructor's edition. In C. R. Ember & M. Ember, *Anthropology.* (6th ed., pp. I-1–I-146). Englewood Cliffs, NJ: Prentice-Hall.

Westrom, L. V. (1990). Chlamydia trachomatis—Clinical significance and strategies of intervention. *Seminars in Dermatology, 9,* 117–125.

Whalen, R. E., Geary, D. C., & Johnson, F. (1990). Models of sexuality. In D. P. McWhirter, S. A. Sanders, & J. M. Reinisch (Eds.), *Homosexuality/heterosexuality: Concepts of sexual orientation* (pp. 61–70). New York: Oxford University Press.

Wheeler, J., & Kilmann, P. R. (1983). Comarital sexual behavior: Individual and relationship variables. *Archives of Sexual Behavior, 12,* 295–306.

Whiffen, V. E. (1992). Is postpartum depression a distinct diagnosis? *Clinical Psychology Review, 12,* 485–508.

Whipple, B., & Komisaruk, B. R. (1988). Analgesia produced in women by genital self-stimulation. *Journal of Sex Research, 24,* 130–140.

Whitam, F. L. (1977). Childhood indicators of male homosexuality. *Archives of Sexual Behavior, 6,* 89–96.

Whitam, F. L., Diamond, M., & Martin, J. (1993). Homosexual orientation in twins: A report on 61 pairs and three triplet sets. *Archives of Sexual Behavior, 22,* 187–206.

White, G. L. (1981). Some correlates of romantic jealousy. *Journal of Personality, 49,* 129–146.

White, J. W. (1983). Sex and gender issues in aggression research. R. G. Green & E. I. Donnerstein (Eds.), *Aggression: Theoretical and empirical reviews, Vol. 2.* New York: Academic Press.

White, S. D., & DeBlassie, R. R. (1992). Adolescent sexual behavior. *Adolescence, 27,* 183–191.

White, V. M., Wearing, A. J., & Hill, D. J. (1994). Is the conflict model of decision making applicable to the decision to be screened for cervical cancer? A field study. *Journal of Behavioral Decision Making, 7*(1), 57–72.

Whitley, B. E., Jr. (1983). Sex role orientation and self-esteem: A critical meta-analysis. *Journal of Personality and Social Psychology, 44,* 765–788.

Whitley, B. E., Jr., & Kite, M. E. (1995). Sex differences in attitudes toward homosexuality. *Psychological Bulletin, 117,* 146–154.

Whitley, R., et al. (1991). Predictors of morbidity and mortality in infants with herpes simplex virus infections. *New England Journal of Medicine, 324,* 450–454.

Whittemore, A. S. (1994). The risk of ovarian cancer after treatment for infertility. *New England Journal of Medicine, 331,* 805–806.

Whittemore, A. S., et al. (1992). Characteristics relating to ovarian cancer risk: Collaborative analysis of 12 U.S. case-control studies: II. Invasive ovarian cancers in white women. *American Journal of Epidemiology, 136,* 1184–1203.

WHO. (1995). Cited in "Rise in STDs concerns group." (1995, September 12). *Newsday*, p. B27.

Wilcox, A. J. (1995). Fertility in men exposed prenatally to diethylstilbestrol. *New England Journal of Medicine, 332,* 1411–1416.

Wilcox, A. J., et al. (1995). Timing of sexual intercourse in relation to ovulation: Effects on the probability of conception, survival of the pregnancy, and sex of the baby. *New England Journal of Medicine, 333,* 1517–1521.

Wilcox, B. L. (1987). Pornography, social science and politics: When research and ideology collide. *American Psychologist, 42,* 941–943.

Wildman, B. G., & White, P. A. (1986). Assessment of dysmenorrhea using the Menstrual Symptom Questionnaire: Factor structure and validity. *Behaviour Research & Therapy, 24,* 547–551.

Wilford, J. N. (1992, November 17). Clues etched in bone debunk theory of a plague's spread. *The New York Times,* p. C1, C8.

Williams, D. E., & D'Alessandro, J. D. (1994) A comparison of three measures of androgyny and their relationship to psychological adjustment. *Journal of Social Behavior and Personality, 9*(3), 469–480.

Williams, J. E., & Best, D. L. (1994). Cross-cultural views of women and men. In W. J. Lonner & R. Malpass (Eds.), *Psychology and culture.* Boston: Allyn & Bacon.

Williams, S. S., et al. (1992). College students use implicit personality theory instead of safer sex. *Journal of Applied Social Psychology, 22,* 921–933.

Willis, R. J., & Michael, R. T. (1994). Innovation in family formation: Evidence on cohabitation in the United States. In J. Eruisch & K. Ogawa (Eds.), *The family, the market and the state in aging societies.* London: Oxford University Press.

Willoughby, T., Wood, E., & Khan, M. (1994). Isolating variables that impact on or detract from the effectiveness of elaboration strategies. *Journal of Educational Research, 86,* 279–289.

Wilmore, J. (1991). Importance of differences between men and women for exercise testing and exercise prescription. In J. Skinner, (Ed.) *Exercise testing and exercise prescription* (pp. 41–56). Malverne, PA: Lea & Febbiger.

Wilson, G., & Cox, D. (1983). Personality of pedophile club members. *Personality and Individual Differences, 4,* 323–329.

Wilson, J. D. (1995). The promiscuous receptor: Prostate cancer comes of age. *New England Journal of Medicine, 332,* 1440–1441.

Wilson, J. D., George, F., & Griffin, J. (1981). The hormonal control of sexual development. *Science, 211,* 1278–1284.

Wilson, M. I., & Daly, M. (1996). Male sexual proprietariness and violence against wives. *Current Directions in Psychological Science, 5,* 2–7.

Wilson, M. R., & Filsinger, E. E. (1986). Religiosity and marital adjustment: Multidimensional interrelationships. *Journal of Marriage and the Family, 48,* 147–151.

Wilson, S. N., & Sanderson, C. A. (1988). The sex report curriculum: Is "just say no" effective? *SIECUS Report, 17,* 10–11.

Winick, C. (1985). A content analysis of sexually explicit magazines sold in an adult bookstore. *Journal of Sex Research, 21,* 206–210.

Wise, T. N. (1994). Sertraline as a treatment for premature ejaculation. *Journal of Clinical Psychiatry, 55*(9), 417.

Wisell, T. E., et al. (1987). Declining frequency of circumcision: Implications for changes in the absolute incidence and male to female sex ratio of urinary tract infections in early infancy. *Pediatrics, 79,* 338–342.

Wolman, T. (1985). Drug addiction. In M. Farber (Ed.), *Human sexuality* (pp. 277–285). New York: Macmillan.

Woloshyn, V. E., Paivio, A., & Pressley, M. (1994). Use of elaborative interrogation to help students acquire information consistent with prior knowledge and information inconsistent with prior knowledge. *Journal of Educational Psychology, 86,* 79–89.

Women might mark millennium with "orgasm pill." (1998, June 6). Reuters; America Online.

Wooldridge, W. E. (1991). Syphilis: A new visit from an old enemy. *Postgraduate Medicine, 89,* 199–202.

Wortman, C. B., et al. (1976). Self-disclosure: An attributional perspective. *Journal of Personality and Social Psychology, 33,* 184–191.

WuDunn, S. (1995, July 9). Many Japanese women are resisting servility. *The New York Times,* p. 10.

WuDunn, S. (1996, January 25). In Japan, a ritual of mourning for abortions. *The New York Times,* A1, A8.

Wulfert, E., & Wan, C. K. (1993). Condom use: A self-efficacy model. *Health Psychology, 12,* 346–353.

Wyatt, G. E. (1985). The sexual abuse of Afro-American and white American women in childhood. *Child Abuse and Neglect, 9,* 507–519.

Wyatt, G. E. (1988). The relationship between child sexual abuse and adolescent sexual functioning in Afro-American and white American women. *The Annals of the New York Academy of Sciences, 528,* 111–122.

Wyatt, G. E. (1989). Reexamining factors predicting Afro-American and white American women's age at first coitus. *Archives of Sexual Behavior, 18,* 271–298.

Wyatt, G. E., & Newcomb, M. (1990). Internal and external mediators of women's sexual abuse in childhood. *Journal of Consulting and Clinical Psychology, 58,* 758–767.

Wyatt, G. E., Notgrass, C. M., & Newcomb, M. (1990). Internal and external mediators of women's rape experiences. *Psychology of Women Quarterly, 14,* 153–176.

Wyatt, G. E., Peters, S. D., & Guthrie, D. (1988a). Kinsey revisited, Part I: Comparisons of the sexual socialization and sexual behavior of white women over 33 years. *Archives of Sexual Behavior, 17*(3), 201–209.

Wyatt, G. E., Peters, S. D., & Guthrie, D. (1988b). Kinsey revisited, Part II: Comparisons of the sexual socialization and sexual behavior of black women over 33 years. *Archives of Sexual Behavior, 17*(4), 289–332.

Y

Yarber, W. L., & Parillo, A. V. (1992). Adolescents and sexually transmitted diseases. *Journal of School Health, 62,* 331–338.

Yarber, W. L., Torabi, M. R., & Veenker, C. H. (1989). Development of a three-component sexually transmitted diseases attitude scale. *Journal of Sex Education & Therapy, 15,* 36–49.

Yates, G. L., et al. (1991). A risk profile comparison of homeless youth involved in prostitution and homeless youth not involved. Special Issue: Homeless youth. *Journal of Adolescent Health, 12,* 545–548.

Yorburg, B. (1995, July 9). Why couples choose to live together. *The New York Times,* p. 14.

Z

Zaviacic, M., & Whipple, B. (1993). Update on the female prostate and the phenomenon of female ejaculation. *Journal of Sex Research, 30,* 148–151.

Zaviacic, M., et al. (1988a). Concentrations of fructose in female ejaculate and urine: A comparative biochemical study. *Journal of Sex Research, 24,* 319–325.

Zaviacic, M., et al. (1988b). Female urethral expulsions evoked by local digitial stimulation of the G-spot: Differences in the response patterns. *Journal of Sex Research, 24,* 311–318.

Zeman, N. (1990, Summer/Fall). The new rules of courtship (Special Edition). *Newsweek,* 24–27.

Zenker, P. N., & Rolfs, R. T. (1990). Treatment of syphilis, 1989. *Reviews of Infectious Diseases* (Suppl. 6), S590–S609.

Zhang, J., & Fried, D. B. (1992). Relationship of maternal smoking during pregnancy to placenta previa. *American Journal of Preventative Medicine, 8,* 278–282.

Zilbergeld, B. (1978). *Male sexuality.* Boston: Little, Brown.

Zilbergeld, B., & Evans, M. (1980). The inadequacy of Masters & Johnson. *Psychology Today, 14,* pp. 29–34, 47–53.

Zillmann, D. (1989). Effects of prolonged consumption of pornography. In D. Zillmann & J. Bryant (Eds.), *Pornography: Research advances and policy considerations* (pp. 127–157). Hillsdale, NJ: Lawrence Erlbaum Associates.

Zillmann, D., & Bryant, J. (1984). Effects of massive exposure to pornography. In N. M. Malamuth & E. Donnerstein (Eds.), *Pornography and sexual aggression* (pp. 115–138). New York: Academic Press.

Zillmann, D., & Weaver, J. B. (1989). Pornography and men's sexual callousness toward women. In D. Zillmann & J. Bryant (Eds.), *Pornography: Research advances and policy considerations* (pp. 95–125). Hillsdale, NJ: Lawrence Erlbaum Associates.

Zimmer, D., Borchardt, E., & Fischle, C. (1983). Sexual fantasies of sexually distressed and nondistressed men and women: An empirical investigation. *Journal of Sex and Marital Therapy, 9,* 38–50.

Zuger, A. (1998, January 6). Do breast self-exams save lives? Science still doesn't have answer. *The New York Times;* America Online.

Abel, G. G., 532, 576
Abelson, H., 611
Abramowitz, S., 163
Abramson, P. R., 518–519
Achilles, 13
Acker, M., 208
Ackerman, D., 126, 160
Acton, W., 18
Adams, H. E., 162, 280, 548, 577
Adams, J., 438
Adams, R., 601
Adams, V., 478
Ade-Ridder, L., 442
Adelson, A., 177
Adelson, M. D., 512
Adler, J., 47
Agyei, Y., 282
Ahmed, R. A., 15
Ahuja, N., 461
Aiken, L. S., 83
Akhtar, S., 461
Albritton, W., 497
Alexander, C. J., 444
Allen, J. R., 504
Allen, M., 171, 217, 266, 278
Allen, W., 212, 425f
Alleyne, E., 509, 518
Alter-Reid, K., 574, 578, 581
Alterman, E., 430, 432–433
Althof, S. E., 477
Altman, L. K., 75, 78–81, 113, 353, 366–367, 370, 470, 507–508
Alzate, H., 149
Amaro, H., 508
Amato, P. R., 436
Ames, M. A., 137, 283, 576–577
Anderson, J. L., 190
Anderson, P. B., 181
Anderson, V. N., 280
Angier, N., 108, 154–155, 162, 284, 301, 347–348, 355, 360, 397
Antill, J. K., 182
Aristophanes, 12–13
Armsworth, M. W., 380
Aronson, E., 219
Asbell, B., 20
Ashe, A., 504
Asher, S. J., 436
Assalian, P., 477

Astley, S. J., 323
Atkeson, B. M., 557–558, 560–561, 566–567, 570
Auerbach, R., 479
Augustine, Saint, 14
Avis, W. E., 190
Axinn, W. G., 47
Aymami, R., 181
Ayres, B. D., 583
Azar, B., 127

Bach, G. R., 188
Bachrach, C. A., 410
Bagatell, C. J., 470
Bagley, C., 574, 601
Bailey, J. M., 282, 287
Baker, C., 508
Baker, J. N., 408
Baker, S., 410
Baker, T. C., 567
Baldwin, J. D., 275–276, 404
Baldwin, J. I., 275–276, 404
Bancroft, J., 138–139, 282
Banks, S., 215
Banmen, J., 430
Banning, A., 575–576
Bar-Tal, D., 197
Barbach, L. G., 70, 144, 246, 474, 609
Barbaree, H. E., 564
Barbee, A., 406–407
Barboza, D., 193
Barisic, S., 336
Barlow, D. H., 283, 479
Barnard, M., 605
Barr, H. M., 323–324, 335
Barrett, M. B., 292
Barringer, F., 271, 416, 418, 435, 485, 587
Bart, P. B., 570
Bartell, G. D., 51
Barth, R. P., 410
Bartoshuk, L. M., 127
Batten, P. G., 221
Baulieu, E-E., 379
Baumeister, R. F., 536, 538
Baxter, D. J., 564
Beach, F., 24–25
Beach, F. A., 171, 190, 196, 248, 255, 275, 388, 424, 432, 538
Beauchamp, G. K., 127
Beaupre, D., 214

Beck, A., 462
Beck, J. G., 52, 410, 412, 457, 479
Beck, S., 563, 577
Becker, J. V., 567, 575
Beckman, R., 404
Beitchman, J. H., 579–580
Belcastro, P. A., 253
Belch, G. E., 615
Belch, M. A., 615
Bell, A. P., 43, 47, 269, 286–288, 290–292, 294–296
Bell, S., 566
Beller, T., 594
Bellis, D. J., 605
Bello, D. C., 615
Bem, S. L., 179, 181–182, 267, 272
Bennett, N. G., 304, 420
Bentler, P. M., 163
Bentley, A., 214
Berke, R. L., 278, 432
Berkowitz, L., 613
Berlin, F. S., 549
Berliner, L., 555
Bernstein, S. J., 74
Bernstein, W. M., 197
Berscheid, E., 199–200, 202, 208
Best, D., 112
Best, D. L., 167
Beutler, L. E., 459–460, 466
Bianchi, S. M., 436
Bieber, I., 285–286, 290
Biggar, R. J., 41, 508
Billy, J.O.G., 47, 138, 253, 262
Bingham, C. R., 406
Binik, Y. M., 456
Birnbaum, H. J., 554, 560, 564–565
Bjorklund, D. F., 23, 174, 195
Bjorn, L., 584
Blair, C. D., 532, 544
Blakeslee, S., 437, 515
Blanc, A. K., 420
Blanchard, R., 163, 532, 536, 545
Blanco, J. D., 496
Blaszczynski, A., 282
Blilie, M., 555
Bloom, B. J., 436
Bloom, D. E., 420
Bloom, J. R., 81

Bloor, M., 605
Blumstein, P., 49, 53, 195, 295–296, 427–428, 432
Blustein, J., 83
Bogert, C., 508
Bohlen, C., 91
Boles, J., 604–605
Borchardt, E., 260
Bostick, R. M., 76
Boswell, J., 274, 343
Bousacos, J., 215
Bowie, W. R., 496
Bowlby, J., 387
Boyer, D., 603–604
Bozzette, S. A., 508
Bradbard, M. R., 179
Bradbury, T. N., 212, 220
Bradford, J.M.W., 138, 549
Bradshaw, D., 208
Brady, E. C., 562
Brannigan, G., 409
Brasfield, T. L., 509, 518
Brasher, P., 80
Brecher, E. M., 442
Bremner, W. J., 470
Brender, W., 139, 466
Brennan, W., 607
Breslow, N., 538, 543–545
Bretl, D. J., 616
Bretschneider, J., 442
Briere, J., 575–576
Brislin-Slütz, J. A., 614
Brissett, D., 602
Britton, P. J., 519
Brockert, J. E., 409
Brody, J. E., 79–81, 92, 94, 107, 129–131, 171, 308, 331, 380, 402, 452, 459, 511, 527–528, 546, 570
Bronars, S., 408
Bronner, E., 45, 393
Brookoff, D., 434
Brooks, V. R., 171
Brooks-Gunn, J., 159, 400, 403–404, 406–407, 409–411
Broude, G. J., 24, 247, 275, 388
Brown, D., 609, 611
Brown, L., 309, 393
Brown, R. A., 195
Brown, R. E., 579
Bruck, M., 580
Bryant, H., 80

Bryant, J., 609, 611, 614
Bryden, M. P., 170
Buchanan, M., 404–405
Buckley, B., 562
Bucy, P., 135
Buffo, M., 596
Buhaug, H., 521
Buhrich, N., 529
Bullough, V., 271, 274
Bullough, V. L., 530–531
Bumiller, E., 7
Bumpass, L., 418–421
Burgess, A., 567
Burgess, A. W., 560, 601
Burkhart, B., 563
Burman, B., 437
Burns, C., 501
Burrell, N., 266, 278
Burrows, B., 324
Burstein, G. R., 496
Busby, D., 462
Busch, M. P., 504
Buss, D. M., 23, 196, 424–425
Bussey, K., 176, 178
Butler, J., 143
Buxton, A. P., 292
Byers, E. S., 570
Bynum, R., 494
Byrnes, J., 170

Caceres, C. F., 504
Cado, S., 260
Caesar, J., 13–14
Calderone, M. S., 350, 390, 394–395
Calhaz-Jorge, C., 324
Calhoun, K. S., 557–558, 560–561, 566–567, 570
Caligula, 14
Call, V., 428
Calvin, J., 17
Camburn, D., 405
Cameron, P., 578
Campbell, B., 200
Campbell, C. A., 605
Campbell, S. B., 336
Cannistra, S. A., 73, 484–485, 515
Cantalona, W. J., 114
Cantor, E., 227
Cantor, J., 616
Capella, J. N., 197
Carani, C., 138, 452, 470
Cardarelli, A., 579
Cardoso, C. G., 324
Carey, M. P., 459–460
Carlisle, J. M., 544
Carlson, M., 374
Carnes, P., 540
Carpenter, C., 444
Carrera, M., 281
Carrier, J. M., 288
Carroll, L., 212
Carter, D. B., 179
Carvajal, D., 597–598

Casanova, G., 343
Castro, J., 586
Castro, K. G., 605
Catalan, J., 462, 479
Catania, J. A., 293
Cates, W., Jr., 103, 355, 357–358, 492–493, 495–498, 500–501, 505, 513–515
Ccu, S., 484
Ceci, S., 580
Celis, W., 559, 569
Ceniti, J., 614
Chadda, R. K., 461
Chan, C., 276
Chan, D. W., 404
Chang, K., 419
Chaplin, T. C., 564
Charny, I. W., 433
Chase-Lansdale, L., 409, 411
Cheasty, M., 580–581
Check, J.V.P., 562
Cheeves, K., 579
Chesney, M. A., 506–507
Chira, S., 177, 587
Choi, P. Y., 96
Christensen, C., 479
Christiansen, K., 138
Chubbuck, K., 508
Church, C., 192–193
Churchill, W., 438
Clark, M. S., 198
Clay, R. A., 303
Clemmensen, L. H., 163
Cline, M., 324
Clinton, W., 20, 50, 294, 430–431, 431f, 554, 583
Clode, N., 324
Clumeck, N., 508
Cnattingius, S., 320, 324
Cobb, D., 577f
Cochran, S. D., 289, 295
Cochran, W. G., 44
Cohen, A., 175, 438
Cohen, E., 369
Cohen, L., 424
Cohen, M. S., 103, 505
Cohen, R., 303
Cohen-Kettenis, P., 163
Cohn, J. F., 336
Cohn, L. D., 518
Colditz, G. A., 79
Cole, C. J., 306
Cole, H. M., 355
Cole, S. S., 443, 445
Coleman, E., 603–604
Coleman, M., 183
Coleman, S., 381
Coles, C., 323–324
Coles, R., 43, 394, 400–401, 404–408, 410
Collaer, M. L., 160, 174, 283
Collins, N. L., 216
Columbus, C., 493–494
Comstock, A., 343–344
Condon, J. W., 198

Conger, R. D., 437
Connell, V., 579
Connolly, M., 129
Connor, E. M., 507
Constantine, J., 438
Constantine, L., 438
Conway-Welch, C., 149
Cook, E., 375
Cooper, A., 214
Cooper, A. J., 576
Cooper, E., 182
Corcoran, D. M., 198
Cordero, E., 138
Cordero, W., 434f
Cornell, C. P., 278
Cosby, B., 430
Cosgray, R. E., 536
Coutinho, R. A., 605
Couwenbergs, C., 138
Cowley, G., 469
Cox, D., 577
Cox, D. J., 531
Cox, E. P., 411
Cozzarelli, C., 380
Craig, M. E., 571
Cramer, D., 75
Cramer, D. W., 500
Crano, W. D., 198
Crews, D., 283
Critelli, J. W., 558
Croft, L., 192–193
Cronin, A., 271, 288
Cross, H., 183
Crossette, B., 66–67
Crowe, L. C., 132
Cummings, E. M., 436–437
Cunningham, G., 138
Cunningham, M. R., 194
Curran, D. J., 563, 565
Curtis, R. C., 198
Curtiss, G., 464, 479
Cutler, W. B., 127
Cutrona, C. E., 336
Cuvelier, S. J., 612

Dabbs, J. M., Jr., 138
D'Alessandro, J. D., 182
Daly, M., 23, 434
Dante Alighieri, 199
Darabi, K. F., 404
Darby, B. L., 323–324, 335
Darling, C., 149
Darling, C. A., 145, 353, 406–407
Darwin, C., 22, 194
D'Augelli, A. R., 280
Davenport, W., 6, 25, 275
Davidson, J. K., 145, 246, 260, 353, 406–407
Davidson, J. K., Sr., 406
Davidson, K. J., 149
Davidson, N. E., 92
Davies, D. K., 410, 412
Davies, P. T., 436–437
Davis, M. H., 208

Davis, S., 112
Davison, G. C., 548
Dawes, R. M., 198
Day, A., 462
Day, N. L., 324
de Bruyn-Kops, E., 563
de Luca, R. V., 581
de Raad, B., 195
de Schampheleire, D., 600
de Young, M., 577
Dean, C. W., 563
DeAngelis, T., 8, 192
Deaux, K., 167, 171
DeBlassie, R. R., 406
Dekker, J., 455, 479
Del Priore, G., 75
Delaney, S. M., 479
Delgado, J., 136
Delmas, P. D., 91–92
Denny, N., 248
Desmond, A. M., 408
Detzer, M. J., 240, 242, 400
Deutsch, F. M., 191
Deutsch, R. M., 188
DeWitt, K., 586
Diamond, M., 271, 282
Diaz-Mitoma, F., 513
Dick-Read, G., 331
DiClemente, R. J., 579
Dietz, P. E., 565
DiMatteo, M. R., 332
Dindia, K., 171, 217
DiPietro, J. A., 176
Doddema-Winsemius, M., 195
Dolan, E., 437
Dole, E., 471
Dole, R., 459, 471
Donne, J., 212
Donnerstein, E., 612–614
Donoghue, D., 275
Doorn, C. D., 529
Douglas, J. M., Jr., 516
Douglas, M., 583
Downey, J. I., 283, 287
Drapers, P., 175
Drews, C. D., 324
Dreyfuss, I. A., 79, 81
Dryan, A., 372, 374
Dryden, J., 218
Dryfoos, J., 404
Dube, R., 575
Dubes, R., 580
Duffy, S. M., 289
Dugger, C. W., 66–67
Dumas, A., 295f
Dunlap, D. W., 266
Dunn, M. E., 146, 442
Durand, V. M., 283
DuRant, R. H., 404, 410
Dwyer, M., 532, 535, 546
Dye, E., 557
Dylan, B., 20
Dziech, B. W., 584

Eastell, R., 92
Eberly, C. G., 562
Eckert, E. D., 282
Edgerton, M., 163
Edgley, C., 594, 596–600, 602, 611, 615
Edmonson, B., 444, 446
Ehrhardt, A., 159–160, 393–394
Eisen, M., 393
Elder, J., 351, 371, 374–375, 378–379
Elias, M., 215
Elifson, K. W., 604–605
Ellis, A., 464
Ellis, H., 19, 240
Ellis, L., 137, 283
Ember, C. R., 12, 25, 421, 424, 426, 432, 565, 577
Ember, M., 12, 25, 421, 424, 426, 432, 565, 577
Endsley, R. C., 179
English, P. B., 324
Erel, O., 437
Erlanger, S., 600
Ervin, K. S., 190
Eskenazi, B., 324
Eskenazi, G., 563
Etaugh, C., 148, 175, 325t, 396–397
Etzel, M. J., 615
Evans, L., 538
Evans, M., 478
Everaerd, W., 479
Everitt, B. J., 135

Fahrner, E., 163–164
Falcon, P. L., 562
Faller, K. C., 575, 579
Fallon, A., 190
Fallon, A. E., 190
Fallopius, 343
Farley, A. U., 494
Farrow, M., 425f
Fay, R. E., 270
Feaganes, J. R., 81
Federman, D. D., 155
Feingold, A., 171, 198
Felsman, D., 409
Felson, R. B., 554, 584
Feng, T., 324
Fenichel. O., 542
Fennema, E., 170
Fensterheim, H., 547
Ferrante, C. L., 616
Fichner-Rathus, L., 11, 222
Fichten, C. S., 466
Field, J., 248
Filsinger, E. E., 53
Fincham, F. D., 437
Findley, T. W., 444
Fine, M. A., 279–280
Finkelhor, D., 561, 574–575, 578–580
Fischer, E. F., 198
Fischle, C., 260

Fish, L. S., 462
Fisher, B., 518, 603–604
Fisher, J. D., 518
Fisher, N., 353
Fisher, T. D., 389
Fisher-Thompson, D., 177
Fitzgerald, L. F., 584, 586–587
Fleiss, H., 599f
Fleming, I., 596
Fletcher, J., 622
Flexner, C., 507–508
Flinn, K., 430, 431f
Flowers, G., 430–431
Floyd, R. L., 324–325
Foa, E. B., 566–568
Follingstead, D. R., 571
Ford, C., 24–25
Ford, C. S., 171, 190, 196, 248, 255, 275, 388, 424, 432, 538
Fordyce, R. R., 360
Formichella, A., 403, 405
Forrest, J. D., 360
Forster, P., 477
Fracastero, G., 493
Frank, E., 92
Frank, P. J., 578
Franz, W., 380
Franzoi, S. L., 190
Fraser, A. M., 409
Frayser, S., 24–25, 190, 248, 424, 432
Frazier, P. A., 567
Freud, S., 19, 26, 42, 146, 176, 284–285, 386, 392, 464
Freund, K., 531–532, 545
Freund, M., 605
Frey, K. S., 179
Friday, N., 246
Fried, D. B., 324
Fried, P. A., 323
Friedman, J., 467
Friedman, L. C., 82
Friedman, R. C., 283, 287
Friedrich, W. N., 389–390, 391t, 544
Frisch, R., 308, 397
Frodi, A. M., 177
Fromuth, M. E., 563
Fryer, M. M., 191
Fuchs, C. S., 79
Fuentes, A., 510
Fugger, E., 305
Fukuda, H., 603
Fuleihan, G. E., 92
Furnham, A., 616
Furstenberg, F. F., 403–404, 406–407, 410
Furstenberg, F. F., Jr., 409, 411

Gabelnick, H. L., 368–369
Gabriel, T., 273, 292
Gaddis, A., 400
Gagnon, J. H., 19, 28, 29t, 43, 45–46, 48, 197, 213, 239t, 240–241, 241t, 246, 251–253,

255, 262, 271, 273, 276, 287, 294, 401, 403–405, 419–420, 424–425, 427–428, 428t, 428–429, 429t, 435, 442, 579, 602, 604, 609
Galen, 488
Ganitsch, C., 331
Ganong, L. H., 183
Garber, M., 273–274
Gardiner, H. W., 400
Gardiner, O. S., 400
Garland, S. M., 496
Garnets, L., 276
Garwood, S. G., 192
Gauguin, P., 494
Gay, D., 375
Gay, P., 18
Gayle, J., 484
Geary, D. C., 283
Gebhard, P., 43–45, 145, 240, 242, 244–245, 251, 269–270, 270t, 294, 387, 392, 403, 426–427
Gebhard, P. H., 19, 104, 271, 533, 535, 564, 578–579, 605
Geer, J., 248, 530, 532, 545
Geer, J. H., 464, 479
Geiger, R., 444
Geis, F. L., 182
Gelfand, M. M., 139
Gelles, R. J., 278
Gelman, D., 198
Genuis, M., 574
George, W. H., 132
Gerber, P. N., 544
Geringer, W. M., 518
Gerrol, R., 560
Gershuny, B. S., 566–568
Giambra, L. M., 246, 439
Gibb, D., 321, 504
Gibbs, N., 556, 559–561, 564
Gibson, A. I., 600
Gidycz, C. A., 557–558, 560, 564, 570
Gifford, F., 430
Gijs, L., 138
Gilbert, S., 79, 103, 192, 331–332, 348, 350, 391t
Gillis, J. S., 190
Ginsburg, A. L., 410
Giovannucci, E., 366
Giovino, G. A., 324–325
Gitlin, M. J., 336
Glass, S. P., 431
Gold, R. G., 467
Gold, S. R., 192, 467
Goldberg, A., 576
Goldberg, C., 351, 371, 374–375, 378–379, 580, 598, 600
Goldberg, M., 494, 541
Goldenberg, R. L., 409
Golding, J. M., 567
Goldman, J. A., 519
Goldman, M. G., 500

Goldstein, I., 451, 453, 459, 471, 476
Goleman, D., 138, 581–582, 584, 586, 609
Gomez, J., 276
Gomez-Schwartz, B., 579
Gonsiorck, J., 279
Goodwin, J. M., 579
Goodyear, C., 343
Gooren, L., 138
Gordon, S., 202, 224, 278, 375, 441, 597
Gordon, S. L., 425
Gorzalka, B. B., 131
Gottlieb, M. S., 501
Graber, B., 454
Graca, L. M., 324
Grady, W. R., 47
Grafenberg, E., 149
Graham, J. M., 496
Graham, S., 18, 239
Grajek, S., 202
Grant, H., 594, 596, 598, 601
Grauerholz, E., 586–587
Gray, T., 192
Green, R., 278, 287
Greenberg, E. R., 323
Greene, B., 276–277
Greene, B. A., 434, 436
Greene, S., 24
Greene, S. J., 247, 275, 388
Greenhouse, L., 586
Greenwald, E., 392–393, 578, 580
Greer, G., 77
Gregory III, Pope, 274
Griffin, E., 197
Grodsky, A., 246, 439
Grodstein, F., 73, 92, 500
Grogger, J., 408
Groneman, C., 541
Gross, J., 266, 560
Grossman, S., 132
Groth, A. N., 554, 560, 564–565
Gruber, J. E., 584
Grunfeld, C., 504
Grych, J. H., 437
Guardad, S., 393
Guillebaud, J., 350
Guinan, M. E., 368
Gunn, R. A., 494
Gupta, M., 16
Guthrie, D., 48–49
Gwartney-Gibbs, P. A., 571

Haddow, J. E., 327
Hadler, J. L., 494
Haffner, D., 393
Haglund, B., 324
Hall, C., 519
Hall, C. S., 171
Hall, G.C.N., 564
Hall, R. H., 389
Halverson, C. F., Jr., 179
Hamer, D. H., 271, 282

Hamilton, M., 569
Hamilton, S., 112*f*
Hammer, J., 508
Hammersmith, S. K., 43, 47, 286–287
Handler, A., 410
Handy, L., 542
Hanrahan, J. P., 324
Hanson, R. K., 566
Hanson, S. L., 410
Harding, J. J., 335–336
Hariton, E. B., 261
Harlow, L. L., 519
Harney, P. A., 563–564
Harold, G. T., 437
Harris, G. T., 582
Harris, L., 614
Harris, M., 393
Hart, J., 314
Hartge, P., 79
Hartman, C. R., 601
Harvey, S., 89
Hass, A., 400
Hatcher, R. A., 306, 347*t*, 350–352, 357, 359, 361–362, 367–368, 370–371, 520
Hatfield, E., 189, 195, 202
Hausknecht, R. U., 322, 378
Havemann, E., 50, 175, 226, 433, 438
Hawkins, B., 324
Hawton, K., 462, 479
Hayashi, H., 417
Hayes, C. D., 406
Haynes, A. M., 616
Hazan, C., 199, 208
Hazelwood, R. R., 565
Heath, R., 136
Hebert, M., 575
Hechtman, L., 409
Hegeler, S., 442
Heiman, J., 248, 530, 532, 545, 609
Heiman, J. R., 247, 474, 479
Helms, J., 45
Hemingway, E., 100, 606
Hendrick, C., 203
Hendrick, S., 203
Hengeveld, M. W., 477
Henneberger, M., 587
Henning, K., 245–247
Henry III, King of France, 530
Hensley, W. E., 189–190
Hercules, 13
Herdt, G. H., 175, 275
Herodotus, 539
Herold, E. S., 611
Herzog, L., 103
Herzog, M. E., 190
Hess, B. B., 409
Hihara, H., 381
Hill, A., 554
Hill, D. J., 620
Hillier, S., 499

Hillingdon, Lady Alice, 18
Hilton, E., 500
Hines, M., 160, 174, 283
Hippocrates, 488
Hirsch, M. S., 507–508
Hirschman, R., 564
Hite, S., 46, 243–245, 253
Hitt, J., 374, 376, 379
Ho, D. D., 506–507
Ho, G.Y.F., 484–485, 515
Hoagwood, K., 581
Hobfoll, S. E., 519
Hobson, W., 564
Hock, Z., 149
Hodges, B. C., 518
Hodgson, R., 496
Hodson, D. S., 441
Hofferth, S. L., 406
Hoffman, H. J., 324
Hoffman, L. E., 246, 260
Hogan, D. P., 407
Holden, G. W., 437
Holmes, K. K., 497, 499
Holmes-Farley, S. R., 305
Holmstrom, L., 567
Holzman, H. R., 602
Hooykaas, C., 519
Horn, J. D., 372
Horowitz, J., 579
Horowitz, R., 404
Houston, D. A., 576–577
Howard, J. A., 195
Howard, M., 411
Howard, M. C., 24
Howards, S. S., 306–307, 310
Hsu, B., 246
Huang, K., 404
Hubbard, R., 326
Hubschman, L., 163
Hucker, S. J., 536
Huffman, T., 419
Hunt, M., 41, 43, 45–49, 246, 251, 403, 426–428, 433, 561, 595
Hunter, D. J., 79
Hurley, E., 594
Hurley, K., 78, 81
Hyde, J. S., 170

Imai, W. K., 518
Imperato-McGinley, J., 159
Ireland, L., 157
Irvine, M., 508
Isay, R. A., 271, 286–287, 292
Ito, S., 320, 322–323

Jacklin, C. N., 170, 176–177
Jackson, A. P., 519
Jackson, B. B., 90
Jackson, J., 580
Jackson, L. A., 190
Jacobson, J. L., 323–324
Jacobson, S. W., 323–324
Jamison, P. L., 104
Jankowiak, W. R., 198

Janus, C. L., 42, 46, 199–200, 271, 403, 574
Janus, M. D., 603
Janus, S. S., 42, 46, 199–200, 271, 403, 574
Javier, R. A., 168
Jefferson, K. W., 509, 518
Jenks, R., 433
Jennings, D. A., 145
Jennings, V. H., 365
Jesus, 14
Johannes, L., 139, 467
Johnson, D., 519
Johnson, E., 390
Johnson, E. W., 350, 394–395
Johnson, F., 283
Johnson, K. A., 79
Johnson, V. E., 51–53, 93, 104, 121, 128, 140, 144–148, 243, 250–251, 269, 290, 293–294, 314, 427, 455, 457, 459, 466, 468, 473, 476–479
Jones, A., 442
Jones, F. P., 232
Jones, H. W., 306
Jones, J., 90
Jorgensen, C., 161
Jorgensen, S. R., 410–411
Josephs, R. A., 132
Joyce, J., 606

Kahn, J., 410
Kaiser, M., 112
Kajiwara, H., 417
Kalichman, S. C., 571
Kalick, S. M., 197
Kallmann, F. J., 282
Kamb, M. L., 485, 518
Kammeyer, K.C.W., 6, 224, 421, 442
Kang, S. H., 81
Kanter, G. D., 373
Kantner, J. F., 403
Kantor, J. S., 547
Kantrowitz, B., 408, 411–412
Kaplan, H. S., 144–145, 442, 453, 455–456, 464, 466–467, 476
Karney, B. R., 212, 220
Kash, K., 82
Kassindja, F., 66
Kassindja, H. Z., 66
Katz, J. N., 272, 274, 276, 278–280
Katz, R. C., 575
Kaufman, A., 560
Kay, D. S., 240
Keaston, D., 212
Kedia, K., 455, 459
Kegel, A., 70
Keith, B., 436
Keith, J. B., 406
Keith, P. M., 197, 424
Kellerman, J., 226
Kellogg, J. H., 238, 240

Kelly, J. B., 437
Kelly, M. P., 242, 461
Kenney, A. M., 393
Kenrick, D. T., 192
Kerber, R. A., 78
Kerns, J. G., 279–280
Kettl, P., 445
Khan, M., 8
Kiely, J. L., 324–325
Killian, K., 462
Killmann, P. R., 466, 476, 479
Kilpatrick, D. G., 561
Kimble, D. P., 135, 137
Kimlicka, T., 183
Kimmel, D., 276
Kinard, E., 409
Kinder, B. N., 132, 464, 479
King, J., 477
Kingsley, S. M., 616
Kinsey, A. C., 19, 43–45, 47, 49, 128, 145, 240, 242–245, 251, 269–270, 270*t*, 272, 294, 387, 392, 403, 426–427, 429, 465, 536–537, 539, 543, 595
Kintsch, W., 8
Kipp, K., 23, 174, 195
Kirby, D., 412
Kircher, J. R., 242, 461
Kirn, W., 435, 436*t*
Kite, M. E., 280
Kitigawa, E. M., 407
Klepinger, D. H., 47, 518
Klerman, L. V., 409
Klett, S., 193
Klorfein, E., 472
Klüver, H., 135
Knapp, M. L., 216
Knight, R. A., 563
Knight, S. E., 443–446
Knox, D., 200–201, 380, 423*t*, 438, 442, 578, 621–624
Knudsen, D. D., 574–575
Knussman, R., 138
Kockott, G., 163–164
Kohlberg, L., 178–179
Kohn, A., 574
Kolata, G., 45, 80, 197, 213, 240, 304–305, 310, 352, 403–405, 425, 428–429, 429*t*, 472, 476, 509, 609
Kolbe, L., 393, 402
Kolbert, E., 586
Kolodny, R. C., 478, 478*t*
Komisar, L., 615
Komisaruk, B. R., 149
Kon, I. S., 7
Koopman, C., 518
Koren, G., 320, 322–323
Korlin, D., 163
Kornblum, W. J., 418
Koss, M. P., 557–558, 560, 564, 566–567, 570
Koutsky, L. A., 515
Kowal, D., 363, 365

Kowalski, G., 275
Krafka, C. L., 614
Krane, R. J., 444–445
Kresin, D., 89, 452
Kruesi, M.J.P., 549
Kruks, G., 603
Ku, L. C., 293
Kuiper, B., 163
Kulin, H., 399
Kumar, U., 400
Kunkel, L. E., 279
Kurdek, L. A., 289
Kuriansky, J., 214
Kuriloff, P. J., 279, 566

Laan, E., 609
Lackritz, E. M., 504
Ladas, A. K., 149
Laemmel, T., 535
Laird, J., 369
Laird, J. D., 226
Lamacz, M., 546
Lamanna, M. A., 430–431
Lamaze, F., 331
Lambert, B., 605
Lamberti, D., 433
Lamke, L. K., 183
Lamon, S. J., 170
Lamprecht, V. M., 365
Landon, A., 41
Lane, K. E., 571
Lang, A. R., 132, 542
Langevin, R., 532, 535, 542
Langley, J., 538
Lansky, D., 132
Lanyon, R. I., 532, 544
LaTour, M. S., 615
Lau, L., 555
Laumann, E. O., 28, 29t, 43,
    45–46, 48, 103–104, 197,
    213, 239t, 240–241, 241t,
    246, 251–253, 262, 271, 273,
    276, 403–405, 419–420,
    424–425, 427–428, 428t,
    428–429, 429t, 432, 435, 442,
    450, 450t, 452, 457, 457t,
    557, 609
Lavin, J., 519
Laviola, M., 578
Lavoisier, P., 147
Lawrence, D. H., 427, 606
Lawrence, K., 611
Leary, W. E., 108–109, 307, 326,
    442, 460
Leavitt, G. C., 577
LeBaron, D., 191
Ledray, L. E., 568
Lee, J. A., 199
Lee, N., 605
Lees, M. I., 496
Lehne, G., 104
Lehtinen, M., 50, 175, 226, 433,
    438
Leiblum, S. R., 452, 462–463,
    465, 467

Leitenberg, H., 240, 242,
    245–248, 260, 392–393, 400,
    530, 532, 545, 578, 580
Leland, J., 459, 471
Leland, N. L., 410
Lemon, S. J., 514
Lenihan, G., 562
Leonard, T. L., 605
Lesnik-Oberstein, M., 424
Letourneau, E., 452, 464, 479
LeTourneau, M. K., 555
LeVay, S., 283–284
Lever, J., 268
LeVesconte, S., 171
Levinger, G., 213, 217
Levy, D. S., 563
Levy, G. D., 179
Lewin, T., 130, 169, 260,
    371–372, 376–377, 380,
    411–412, 583, 609
Lewinsky, M., 20, 430, 431f,
    554, 583
Lewis, J., 226
Lewis, K., 570
Lewis, L. L., 167
Lewis, P. H., 293, 535
Lewis, R., 518
Lewis, S., 198
Libman, E., 442, 466
Lief, H. I., 163
Lindermalm, G., 163
Linet, O. I., 470
Linn, M. C., 170
Linsley, W. A., 606
Linton, M. A., 558
Linz, D., 612–614
Linz, D. G., 613
Lipshultz, L. I., 470–471
Lisak, D., 562
Liu, D., 48–49
Lobo, R. A., 91
Lohr, B. A., 280
Londono, M. L., 149
LoPiccolo, J., 247, 457, 465,
    467, 474, 476, 478–479
Lorch, D., 508
Lorefice, L. S., 549
Lott, B., 182
Lottes, I., 566
Lottes, I. L., 279
Lovdal, L. T., 616
Lown, J., 437
Lowry, R., 485
Loy, P. H., 584, 586
Luckenbill, D. F., 604
Lundstrom, B., 163
Lusk, R., 574–575, 578–579
Luther, M., 17
Lynxwiler, J., 375

Macallan, D. C., 504
Macauley, J., 177
Maccoby, E. E., 170, 176–177
Macfarlane, S., 518
MacFarquhar, N., 66

Madonna, 16, 607f
Magdol, L., 434
Maheu, M., 214
Maier, F., 214
Major, B., 380
Malamuth, N. M., 562–563,
    613–614
Maletzky, B. M., 547–548
Malinowski, B., 23–24, 51, 577
Malloy, M. H., 324
Mapplethorpe, R., 607f
Marchbanks, P., 74
Marcus, A. J., 354
Margolin, L., 562–563
Marin, A. D., 380
Marks, G., 198
Markson, E. W., 409
Marotta, T., 603–604
Maroules, N., 585–586
Marshall, D., 458
Marshall, W. L., 549, 563–564,
    612
Marsiglio, W., 278–279, 410
Martin, C. E., 43–45, 145, 240,
    242–245, 251, 269–270, 270t,
    294, 387, 392, 403, 426–427,
    539, 595
Martin, C. L., 179
Martin, J., 282
Martin, J. N., 511
Martinez, F. D., 324
Martinson, F. M., 386
Martyna, W., 182
Maruyama, G., 198
Masi, C. M., 103, 432
Mason, R., 564
Masters, B., 562
Masters, W., 561
Masters, W. H., 51–53, 93, 104,
    121, 128, 140, 144–149, 243,
    250–251, 269, 290, 293–294,
    314, 427, 455, 457, 459, 466,
    468, 473, 476–479
Matejcic, C., 221
Matek, O., 533
Matlin, M. W., 400
Matsen, K., 518
Matthews, K. A., 90, 576
Matthews, W. S., 159
Matus, I., 302
Maybach, K. L., 192
Mayer, J. P., 324
McAndrew, N., 193
McArthur, M. J., 566
McCabe, J. B., 411
McCabe, M. P., 479
McCloskey, L. A., 434
McConaghy, N., 282, 287–288
McCormack, A., 601
McCormack, K. D., 345
McCoy, J. K., 400, 407
McCoy, N., 442
McDonough, Y. Z., 391
McGuire, R. J., 544
McIntyre, S., 403, 405

McKeachie, W., 8
McKeganey, N., 605
McKinney, K., 585–586
McLaren, J., 579
McLaughlin, F. J., 334–335
McLean, P. M., 135
McMahon, M. J., 332
McWhirter, D. P., 271–273
Mead, M., 23–24, 51, 171, 174,
    196
Meana, M., 456
Meckler, L., 402, 408
Meese, E., 612
Meier, B., 321, 336
Meiselman, K. C., 578
Meisler, A. W., 459–460
Melbye, M., 41, 79
Mendel, G., 22
Mertz, G. J., 511
Messenger, J., 458
Meston, C. M., 131
Meuwissen, I., 609
Meyer, J. K., 163
Meyer, T., 507
Meyer-Bahlburg, H. F. L., 283
Michael, R. T., 28, 29t, 43,
    45–46, 48, 197, 213, 239t,
    240–241, 241t, 246, 251–253,
    262, 271, 273, 276, 403–405,
    419–420, 424–425, 427–428,
    428t, 428–429, 429t, 435, 442,
    609
Michaels, S., 28, 29t, 43, 45–46,
    48, 197, 239t, 241, 241t, 246,
    251–253, 262, 271, 273, 276,
    419–420, 424, 427–428, 428t,
    429, 429t, 435, 442
Michelangelo, 539
Miedzian, M., 563
Mill, J. S., 623
Miller, B. C., 400, 406–407
Miller, D., 549
Miller, E. M., 597, 600
Miller, H., 427, 606
Miller, K., 198
Miller, L. C., 216
Miller, M., 393, 562–563
Miller, N., 198
Miller, S. M., 78, 81
Millett, K., 606
Mills, J. R., 198
Milner, P., 135
Minai, N., 15
Minkoff, H. L., 494
Mirin, S. M., 133, 460
Mirotznik, J., 513
Mishell, D. R., Jr., 349–352, 355,
    359
Mitterand, F., 430
Miyamoto, M., 603
Mohr, D. C., 459–460, 466
Money, J., 104, 137, 159–160,
    162, 166, 174, 275, 283, 288,
    527–528, 545–546
Montagnier, L., 506

Moore, D., 583
Moore, D. W., 221
Moore, K. A., 408, 424
Moore, S. M., 519
Morales, A., 130
Morales, E., 276
Moran, P. B., 562–563
Morgan, T. O., 113–114
Morris, K. T., 570
Morris, N., 139
Morris, N. M., 138
Morris, R., 138
Morrison, D., 410
Morrison, D. R., 410
Morrison, E. S., 67, 77,
    389–392, 400, 406
Morse, E., 605
Mortensen, M., 442
Mortola, J. F., 94–96
Moser, C., 538
Mosher, C. D., 18
Mosher, D. L., 607
Mosher, W. D., 410
Mosteller, F., 44
Muehlenhard, C. L., 558,
    562–564
Mueser, K. T., 191
Muhammad, 15
Mullen, P. D., 324–325
Muller, M., 500
Murphy, E., 430
Murray, J. B., 549
Murstein, B. I., 208
Muster, N. J., 575
Myers, M. F., 560
Myerson, M., 183

Nadeau, R., 518
Nadler, R. D., 277
Nakamura, R., 284
Nakanishi, M., 218
Nakashima, A. K., 494
Narod, S. A., 350
Navarro, M., 266
Nazir, C., 473
Neal, J. A., 614
Neale, M. C., 282
Need, J., 163
Neisser, A. L. S., 488
Nelson, R., 460
Neunaber, D. J., 336
Nevid, J. S., 193, 195, 336, 434,
    436
Newbold, J. E., 514
Newcomb, M., 567, 580
Newcomb, P. A., 92
Newcomer, S. F., 401, 405
Newman, E., 182
Nichols, M., 461
Niebuhr, G., 266, 275
Niloff, J. M., 73, 484–485, 515
Nixon, R., 611
Nock, S. L., 419
Nordheimer, J., 473

Norman, J., 393
Nosek, M. A., 443
Notgrass, C. M., 567
Novello, A. C., 504
Nuland, S. B., 79, 81

Oates, R. D., 444–445
O'Bannon, R. E., 509, 518
O'Brien, P. B., 570
Ochs, R., 78, 113, 515
O'Donohue, W., 452, 464, 479
O'Grady, K. E., 404
Ogrine, F. G., 470
O'Hara, M. W., 336
Okami, P., 576
Oldenberg, R., 602
Olds, J., 135
Olson, T. D., 400, 407
O'Neill, G., 438
O'Neill, N., 438
Osborne, L. N., 437
Osborne, N. G., 512
Osgood, C., 418
Osterhout, M. B., 403, 405
Oswalt, R., 518
Over, R., 609
Overholser, J. C., 563, 577
Oz, S., 624

Packwood, R., 554
Padesky, C., 292
Padgett, V. R., 614
Padilla, E. R., 404
Padma-Nathan, H., 469, 471
Paivio, A., 8
Palace, E. M., 133
Palella, F. J., 507
Palmer, M. T., 197
Palmore, E., 442
Palson, C., 51
Palson, R., 51
Parillo, A. V., 486, 496
Parish, E. A., 221
Parnass, S., 433
Parsons, N. K., 373
Pasnau, R. O., 336
Passarello, L. C., 353, 406–407
Pastuszak, A., 320, 322–323
Patterson, C. J., 266, 278
Paul, R. H., 332
Paul, Saint, 14
Paulson, R. J., 91
Pauly, B., 163
Pauly, I., 163
Pauly, I. B., 161–162, 164
Pear, R., 408
Pearson, C., 368
Peckham, C., 321, 504
Pendergrast, R., 404
Penn, F., 485
Penrod, S., 613–614
Peplau, L. A., 289, 295, 425
Perduta-Fulginiti, P. S., 445
Perrett, D. I., 194
Perry, D. G., 176, 178

Perry, J. D., 148–149
Person, E. S., 240, 246
Peters, S. D., 48–49
Peterson, D. R., 324
Pierre-Jerome, F., 104
Pillard, R. C., 157, 282, 286
Pines, A., 219
Pines, S., 602
Pinkerton, S. D., 518–519
Pitisci, J. H., 473
Pitnick, S., 109
Pitts, R. E., 615
Pius IX, Pope, 374
Plant, E. A., 170
Pleck, J. H., 293
Pliny, 89
Polit-O'Hara, D., 410
Pollack, W. S., 303
Pollak, M., 114
Pomeroy, W. B., 43–45, 145,
    240, 242–245, 251, 269–270,
    270t, 294, 387, 392, 403,
    426–427, 539, 595
Ponton, L. E., 579
Poortinga, J., 529
Porter, J. F., 558
Porter, N., 182
Poussaint, A., 276
Powderly, W. G., 508
Powell, E., 556, 562–563, 565,
    568–570, 572–573, 583–584,
    587
Prentky, R. A., 563
Press, A., 606
Pressley, M., 8
Preti, G., 127
Price, V. A., 597, 600–601, 605
Prince, V., 603
Proctor, F., 143
Pryde, N. A., 480
Purifoy, F. E., 246, 439
Pyngolil, M., 90

Quadagno, D., 248, 605
Quam, J. K., 289
Quevillon, R. P., 456
Quinsey, V. L., 564, 582

Rachman, S., 543
Radlove, S., 183
Rajfer, J., 459
Ramirez, A., 126
Rao, K., 579
Raskin, R., 161
Rathus, S. A., 27t, 148, 175, 222,
    325t, 396–397, 434, 436, 455
Ratican, K. L., 581
Rausch, P., 419
Rawal, D. B., 504
Rawlins, M. E., 562
Rawlins, R., 304
Raymond, E. G., 357–358
Reagan, R., 612
Reaney, P., 515
Reed, H. M., 473

Reid, T. R., 7, 417
Rein, M. F., 500
Reinherz, H., 409
Reinisch, J. M., 104, 112,
    246–247, 251–252, 271–273,
    308, 347t, 349–351, 354–355,
    357–359, 363–367, 371, 387,
    390–391, 394–395, 398–399,
    441, 444, 446, 479, 494, 496,
    499–501, 512, 515–517,
    520–521, 533, 538, 544
Reiss, B. F., 439
Reiss, I. L., 288
Remafedi, G., 177
Reno, R. R., 83
Renzetti, C. M., 563, 565
Resick, P. A., 560, 568
Resnick, P. J., 540
Reter, D. J., 163
Rice, M. E., 582
Richards, H. C., 373
Richards, R., 161
Richardson, G. A., 324
Richardson, L., 393, 411–412
Riche, M., 420
Ricker, A. L., 598
Riedmann, A., 430–431
Rienzo, D., 531–532
Riggio, R. E., 192
Riggs, D. S., 566–568
Rimer, B. K., 81, 324–325
Ritchie, K. L., 437
Ritzer, G., 6, 224
Robbins, C., 404–405
Roberto, L. G., 162
Roberts, R., 114
Roddy, R. E., 357
Roehrich, L., 132
Rogan, H., 30
Rogers, A., 469
Rogers, R., 214
Roland, B., 580
Rolfs, R. T., 494
Romano, P. S., 81
Romenesko, K., 597, 600
Ronald, A. R., 497
Roosevelt, F. D., 41
Rose, R. J., 73, 282
Rosen, I., 547
Rosen, L., 597
Rosen, R. C., 52, 452, 462–463,
    465, 467
Rosenberg, P. S., 508
Rosenthal, A. M., 67
Rosenthal, D. A., 519
Rosenthal, E., 190
Rösler, A., 138
Rosman, J. P., 540
Ross, M., 163
Rosser, P. L., 411
Roth, S., 557
Rotheram-Borus, M. J., 518, 601
Rovet, J., 157
Royce, R. A., 103, 505
Rozin, P., 190

Rubin, A., 438
Rubinow, D. R., 95
Ruble, D. N., 179
Rudner, R., 435
Runtz, M., 575–576
Rusbult, C. E., 289
Rush, B., 239
Russell, D., 561
Russo, N. F., 372, 380
Rye, B. J., 518

Sacher-Masoch, L. von, 536
Sack, W. H., 564
Sadalla, E. K., 192
Sadava, S. W., 221
Sadd, S., 430
Sade, Marquis de, 537
Sadker, D., 171, 177
Sadker, M., 171, 177
Saenger, P., 157
Safer, J., 302
Sagan, C., 372, 374
Sagan, F., 154
Sagarin, E., 526
St. Lawrence, J. S., 509, 518
Saluter, A. F., 419, 421, 435
Sampson, P. D., 323–324, 335
Samuels, M., 326t, 336
Samuels, N., 326t, 336
Sanchez-Guerrero, J., 80
Sanday, P. R., 565
Sanders, J. M., 410
Sanders, S. A., 271–273
Sanderson, C. A., 411
Sandross, R., 586
Sanger, M., 342, 343f, 344–345
Sargent, T. O., 529
Sarrel, P., 561
Sato, S., 417
Sauer, M. V., 91
Savitz, L., 597
Saxe, L., 197
Scanlon, B., 603
Schafer, R. B., 197, 424
Schaffer, N., 419
Schafran, L. H., 556–558
Schaudinn, F., 493
Scherer, C., 214
Schiavi, R., 452, 462
Schiavi, R. C., 441
Schillinger, L., 7
Schmidt, G., 452
Schmidt, P. J., 95
Schmitt, E., 266
Schmitt, J. P., 289
Schnicke, M. K., 568
Schoendorf, K. C., 324–325
Schork, K., 6
Schott, R. L., 529
Schreiber, G. B., 504, 509
Schreiner-Engle, P., 452, 462
Schroeder, P., 67
Schultz, N. R., Jr., 221
Schuster, M. A., 412
Schwalm, L. A., 606

Schwartz, D., 404
Schwartz, I. M., 406
Schwartz, M. F., 290
Schwartz, P., 49, 53, 195,
    295–296, 406–407, 427–428,
    432
Schwartz, R., 372
Scott, J. E., 606, 612
Sears, A. E., 609
Seftel, A. D., 444–445
Segal, Z. V., 563
Segraves, K. B., 452, 454, 459
Segraves, R. T., 452, 454,
    459–460
Selik, R., 484
Sell, R. L., 271
Seltzer, R., 280
Selvin, B. W., 161, 164
Semans, J., 477
Seña, A., 103, 505
Seng, M. J., 601
Setlow, V. P., 504
Severn, J., 615
Seymore, C., 404
Shafer, M. A., 496
Shakespeare, W., 104, 131, 218
Shalala, D., 402
Sharlip, I., 472
Sharrar, R. G., 494
Shaver, P., 199, 208
Sheehy, G., 107, 306
Shenon, P., 291
Shepard, M., 279f
Shepherd, J. B., 519
Sheppard, J. A., 190
Sherman, K. J., 496
Sherwin, B. B., 139
Shettles, L., 304
Shields, B., 615
Shirley, A., 509, 518
Shoda, Y., 78, 81
Siegel, J. M., 566
Siegel, K., 296
Siegler, I. C., 81
Signorielli, N., 177
Silber, S. J., 307
Silbert, M. H., 609
Simon, W., 255, 287, 401
Simpson, J. A., 200
Simpson, O. J., 434
Singer, I., 147–148
Singer, J., 147–148
Singer, J. L., 261
Singh, D., 190
Singh, G. K., 334
Sipski, M. L., 444
Sirles, E. A., 578
Skates, S., 114
Skeen, P., 441
Skinner, B. F., 27
Skurrie, I. J., 496
Slattery, M. L., 78
Sleek, S., 291
Slonim-Nevo, V., 404
Smart, C. R., 80

Smith, B., 64, 276
Smith, E. A., 404
Smith, E. P., 399
Smith, W. K., 554, 559
Smolowe, J., 372, 378
Snyder, C. W., 202, 224, 278,
    375, 441, 597
Sobel, J. D., 498–501
Sodroski, J., 502
Solano, C. H., 221
Sonenstein, F. L., 293
Sorensen, R. C., 403, 408
Sourander, L. B., 75, 92
Southerland, D., 49
Spain, D., 436
Spark, R. F., 118, 120,
    444–445, 453, 459–460,
    467, 470–471
Sparks, G. G., 197
Speckens, A.E.M., 457
Specter, M., 504, 508, 596
Spector, I. P., 465
Spiro, M. E., 388
Spitz, I. M., 378
Spitzer, R. L., 463, 537–539
Sprecher, S., 189, 195, 406–408,
    428
Spring, J. A., 430–431
Srebnik, D., 240, 242, 400
Stamm, W. E., 497
Stampfer, M. J., 92, 350
Stanfield, B., 214
Stangor, C., 179
Starr, B. D., 439, 442
Steele, C. M., 132
Stein, G., 147
Stein, P. J., 409
Steinbeck, J., 606
Steinem, G., 154
Steiner, B. W., 163
Steiner, M., 95
Steinhauer, J., 419–420
Stephens, W. N., 25, 37
Stericker, A., 171
Sternberg, R. J., 202–208, 223,
    627
Stewart, F. H., 368
Stewart, G. K., 353–355
Stewart, L. P., 584, 586
Stewart, P., 607
Stief, T. M., 408, 424
Stock, W. E., 456–457, 476,
    478–479, 562–563, 565
Stokes, G., 43, 394, 400–401,
    404–408, 410
Stolberg, S. G., 309, 484–485,
    494, 505
Stoller, R. J., 162, 275, 532
Storer, B. E., 92
Storms, M., 272
Storms, M. D., 176, 181
Story, P., 114
Strassberg, D. S., 242, 461, 464
Strathman, A. J., 190
Streissguth, A. P., 323–324, 335

Strickland, B. R., 288
Strickler, J., 357, 359
Struckman-Johnson, C., 561
Sue, D., 261, 544
Sue, D. W., 544
Sue, S., 544
Sugimoto, Y., 381
Sullivan, A., 275
Sullivan, Q., 195
Sullivan, S. E., 324–325
Suppe, F., 267
Swann, W. B., Jr., 198
Symons, D., 196, 246, 611
Syphilus, 493
Szasz, G., 444

Takahira, S., 170
Talbert, L., 138
Tanfer, K., 47
Tang, C. S., 558
Tannahill, R., 11–13, 16–17
Tannen, D., 217, 224–225
Tantleff, S., 190
Tarnai, J., 183
Tarran, M. J., 392–393
Tavris, C., 430
Taylor, J., 90
Tedeschi, J. T., 554, 584
Telushkin, J., 12
Temple, L. L., 279
Thabit, S. M., 66
Thalberg, S., 410
Tharinger, D., 579
Thomas, C., 554
Thomas, J., 164–165
Thomas Aquinas, Saint, 372,
    374
Thome, P. R., 177
Thomlinson, B., 574–575
Thompson, D. S., 108–109, 313,
    320, 378
Thompson, J. K., 190
Thompson, M. E., 570
Thompson, S., 403
Thornby, J., 138
Thornton, A., 405
Tissot, S. A. D., 239
Tobias, S., 171
Todd, R., 324
Tollison, C. D., 162, 577
Toner, J. P., 306, 310
Torabi, M. R., 487–488
Townsend, J. M., 23, 431,
    609
Trieschmann, R., 444
Trost, J. E., 146
Trovato, F., 436
Trujillo, C., 276
Trussell, J., 357, 359
Tseng, W., 461
Tukey, J. W., 44
Turkle, S., 215
Tutty, L. M., 581
Twain, M., 100, 606
Tyson, M., 554, 559

Uba, L., 404
Uddenberg, N., 163
Udry, J., 138
Udry, J. R., 138, 401, 404
Upfold, D., 564

Valentiner, D. P., 566–568
Van den Hoek, A., 605
van der Pligt, J., 519
van der Velde, F. W., 519
van Griensven, G.J.P., 504
Van Haastrecht, H. J., 605
Van Steirteghem, A. C., 310
Vatsyayana, 16
Vaughan, B., 357, 359
Vazi, R., 112
Veenker, C. H., 487–488
Verschoor, A. M., 529
Vershure, B., 192
Victoria, Queen of England, 18, 327, 330
Vinacke, W., 198
Vinci, L. da, 42
Voeller, B., 263
Vogel, N., 430
Voli, V., 616
Volker, M., 472
Von Krafft-Ebing, R., 19, 240
Voyer, D., 170
Voyer, S., 170
Vyas, G. N., 504

Wagner, N., 143
Waigandt, A., 567
Wald, A., 511
Wald, E., 326
Waldinger, M. D., 477
Walfish, S., 183
Walinder, J., 163
Walker, A., 67
Walker, D., 472
Wallerstein, J. S., 437

Walsh, P. C., 112
Walster, E., 202, 208
Walster, G. W., 202
Walt, V., 368
Wan, C. K., 518
Ward, R. H., 409
Warner, D. L., 361–362
Warren, C. W., 48
Warren, J., 565
Washington, A. C., 411
Wasson, J. H., 113
Waszak, C., 412
Waterman, J., 574–575, 578–579, 581
Watson, C., 182
Watson, J. B., 27
Watson, R., 531–532
Wearing, A. J., 620
Weaver, J. B., 614
Weideking, C., 528
Weinberg, M., 47, 545
Weinberg, M. S., 43, 47, 269, 273–274, 286–288, 290–292, 294–296, 538
Weinberg, T. S., 531, 538
Weiner, L., 584
Weiner, M. B., 439, 442
Weingarten, H., 437
Weinraub, M., 113
Weinrich, J. D., 157, 282, 286
Weisberg, D. K., 603–604
Weiss, D. L., 407
Weiss, R. D., 133, 460
Wells, C., 172
Wells, J. A., 271
Wenger, N. K., 92
Werner, D., 175, 438
West, M., 100
West, S. G., 83
Whalen, R. E., 283
Whiffen, V. E., 336
Whipple, B., 148–149

Whitam, F. L., 282, 287
White, G. L., 219
White, J. W., 171
White, P. A., 93
White, S. D., 406
White, S. W., 436
White, V. M., 620
Whiteley, S., 404
Whitford, G. S., 289
Whitley, B. E., Jr., 182, 280
Whitley, R., 512
Whittemore, A. S., 75, 350
Whitton, C., 154
Wilcox, A. J., 304, 323
Wilcox, B. L., 612
Wildman, B. G., 93
Williams, C. J., 538
Williams, D. E., 182
Williams, J. E., 167
Williams, L., 79
Williams, S. S., 192
Willis, R. J., 419–420
Willoughby, T., 8
Wilmore, J., 172
Wilson, G., 577
Wilson, G. T., 132
Wilson, J. D., 113
Wilson, M., 23
Wilson, M. I., 434
Wilson, M. R., 53
Wilson, S. N., 411
Winick, C., 611
Wise, T. N., 477
Wisniewski, N., 557–558, 560, 564
Witztum, E., 138
Woll, S. B., 192
Wolman, T., 132
Woloshyn, V. E., 8
Wood, E., 8
Woodward, C. K., 83
Wooldridge, W. E., 495

Wordsworth, W., 386
Wortman, C. B., 218
Wright, L. W., Jr., 280
Wright, P., 542
Wright, T. L., 431
WuDunn, S., 381
Wulfert, E., 518
Wyatt, G., 48–49, 260
Wyatt, G. E., 48–49, 567, 579–580
Wypij, D., 271

Yanez, C., 518
Yarber, W. L., 486–488, 496
Yates, G. L., 605
Yee, J., 569
Yellin, P., 409
Yetman, N. R., 6, 224
Yllo, K., 561
Yorburg, B., 419–420
You, S., 425f
Young, B. G., 544
Young, K., 215
Young, L., 601
Youngman, H., 435
Yu, S. M., 334

Zaviacic, M., 149
Zekoski, E. M., 336
Zelkart, P., 580
Zellman, G., 393
Zelnick, M., 403
Zeman, N., 403
Zhang, J., 324
Ziegler, J., 412
Zilbergeld, B., 105, 478
Zillman, D., 609, 614
Zimmer, D., 260
Zucker, K. J., 287
Zuckerman, E. W., 103, 432
Zuger, A., 82, 600
Zwinderman, A. H., 477

Page numbers followed by *t* and *f* indicate tables and figures, respectively.

AASECT, 480
Abbott Testpak, 497
ABC(DE) model of romance, 212–221
Abkhazians, sexual beliefs and behaviors of, 6
Abortion
   in adolescence, ethnic differences in, 404–405
   attitudes toward, 7, 371–373
   and breast cancer risk, 79
   critical thinking about, 10, 373
   definition of, 342
   drug-induced, 378–379
   ethical considerations with, 372–373
   historical perspective on, 374–377
   induced, 371
   legal perspective on, 345, 374–377
   methods of, 377–379
   for minors, 374–375, 402
   partial-birth, 379
   psychological consequences of, 380
   spontaneous, 300, 313–314
Abstinence
   for adolescents, 411
   to prevent STIs, 518
Abuse, sexual. *See* Sexual abuse of children
Acculturation
   definition of, 168
   machismo/marianismo stereotypes and, 168
Accutane, fetal effects of, 322
Acquaintance rape, 558
Acquired erectile dysfunction, 453
Acquired immunodeficiency syndrome (AIDS), 484–485, 491*t*, 501–510
   in adolescents, 402
      prevention of, 411–412, 517–521
   deaths from, in sub-Saharan Africa, 508
   diagnosis of, 506
   drug therapy for, 507–508
   ethnicity and, 502
   gay activism and, 281
   and gay bashing, 280
   and gay lifestyles, 295–296
   hotline, 510, 522
   immune system and, 502
   incidence of, 508
   information about, sources for, 522
   maternal, effects on prenatal development, 321
   prevalence of, 501

prevention of, 509, 518–519
   condoms and, 360, 363
   targeting special populations for, 509–510
   progression of, 503–504
   prostitution and, 605–606
   rape and, 567
   risk factors for, 501, 505
   sexual practices and, research on, 47
   testing for, before initiating sexual relations, 521
   treatment of, 506–509
      future of, 31, 509
   vaccines against, 506–507, 509
Act-Up, 281
Activating effects, of testosterone, 283
Acyclovir, 513
Adolescence
   abortion in, ethnic differences in, 404–405
   abstinence in, 411
   AIDS in, 402
      prevention of, 411–412, 517–521
   coitus in, 400–403
      motives for, 403–405
   condom use in, 410–411, 518–519
   contraceptive use in, 402, 410–411
      ethnic differences in, 404–405
   cunnilingus in, 401
   fellatio in, 401
   first coitus in, adolescents' attitudes toward, 406–407
   gay identity in, 408
   kissing in, 401
   masturbation in, 241*t*, 242–243, 400
   oral sex in, 401
   petting in, 401
   pregnancy in. *See* Pregnancy, adolescent
   premarital sex in, 401–407
   sexual behavior in
      ethnic differences in, 404–405
      factors affecting, 406–407
      male-female, 400–408
      male-male or female-female, 408
   sexual pressure on, 402, 404–405
   sexuality in, 20, 395–408
      cultural attitudes toward, 6
   STIs in, 402
      prevention of, 411–412
Adoption, 311
Adrenogenital syndrome, 158–159, 159*f*
Adultery. *See also* Extramarital sex
   consensual, 431–433

   conventional, 431
   definition of, 14
   historical perspective on, 12, 17
Advertising
   and gender-role stereotypes, 615–616
   sex in, 615–616
Advocate, 281
Affair(s). *See* Extramarital sex
Africa
   female genital mutilation in, 66–67
   sub-Saharan, AIDS in, 508
African Americans
   adolescent, sexual behavior of, 404–405
   AIDS and, 502, 508–509
   cohabitation rate of, 419
   incidence of sexual dysfunctions in, 457*t*
   infant mortality rate for, 334–335
   male, prostate cancer screening for, 114
   number of sex partners, 29*t*, 30
   and oral sex, 252–253
   sexual behavior of, surveys on, 48–49
   and sexual orientation, 276–277
   and sexual permissiveness, 260
After the Affair, 431
Afterbirth, 319
Agape, 199
Age
   at marriage, 421
   and masturbation, 241, 241*t*
   at menarche, 396–397, 398*f*
   and number of sex partners, 29*t*, 30
   and prostate cancer, 113
Age homogamy, 425
Age of viability, 319
Ageism, in media, 177
Aggression, social-learning theory of, 177
Aggressiveness, gender differences in, 171
Aging
   of gay men and lesbians, 289
   and sexuality, 439–443
AIDS. *See* Acquired immunodeficiency syndrome (AIDS)
AIDS Hotline for Hearing Impaired, 522
AIDS Hotline for Teens, 522
AIDS-related complex, 503
Alcohol
   and breast cancer, 79
   maternal use of, effects on prenatal development, 323–324
   and sexual behavior, 131–132, 132*f*, 519
   sexual dysfunctions caused by, 460
Aleuts, attitude toward extramarital sex, 432

Alofilox, 515

Alprostadil, 469–471

Amenorrhea, 94

American Association of Sex Educators, Counselors, and Therapists, 480

Amitriptyline (Elavil), anaphrodisiac effects, 131

Amniocentesis, 300, 327

Amniotic fluid, 318

Amniotic sac, 318
  rupture of, 328

Amphetamines, and sexual behavior, 133

Amphett Islanders, sexuality among, 24

Ampulla
  definition of, 121
  of fallopian tubes, 74
  of vas deferens, 120–121

Amputee(s), coital positions for, 445

Amyl nitrate, 130

Anal intercourse, 262–263
  in gay couples, 281–282, 293

Analogous, definition of, 65

Analogues
  definition of, 21
  of human sexual behavior, 21

Anaphrodisiacs, 130–131

Androgen(s), 106
  production of, 136
    pubertal, 398
  and sexual behavior, 138
    in females, 139
  in sexual differentiation, 155–156

Androgen-insensitivity syndrome, 159

Androgyny, psychological, 181–183, 182f

Anesthesia, for childbirth, 330–331

Anger rape, 564

Anilingus, 262–263, 520

Animals, experimental research using, 55–56

Anorexia nervosa, 94, 190

Anorgasmia
  definition of, 456
  treatment of, 473–474, 474f

Anovulatory, definition of, 398

Anoxia, prenatal or perinatal, 333–334

Anthropomorphism, 37

Antiandrogen(s)
  anaphrodisiac effects, 131
  for paraphilias, 549
  and sexual behavior, 138

Antibiotic(s)
  for bacterial vaginosis, 499
  for chancroid, 497
  for chlamydial infection, 497
  fetal effects of, 322
  for gonorrhea, 493
  for granuloma inguinale, 498
  for shigellosis, 498
  for syphilis, 495

Antibody(ies)
  definition of, 495
  to *Treponema pallidum*, 495

Antidepressant(s)
  anaphrodisiac effects, 131
  for premature ejaculation, 477

and sex drive, 130
  sexual dysfunctions caused by, 460

Antigens, 502

Antihistamine(s), fetal effects of, 322

Antihypertensive agent(s)
  as anaphrodisiacs, 130
  sexual dysfunctions caused by, 460

Antipsychotic agent(s), sexual dysfunctions caused by, 460

Anxiety. *See also* Performance anxiety
  and hypoactive sexual desire, 452
  sexual dysfunctions caused by, 462, 464–465

Aphrodisiacs, 13, 129–130, 137–138
  definition of, 126, 129
  foods as, 129–130

Apinaye people, attitudes toward childhood sexuality, 388

Apomorphine, 471

Arapesh tribe, gender roles in, 175

ARC, 503

Areola, 77–78

Arousal. *See* Sexual arousal

Arthritis, and sexual functioning, 445

Artificial contraception, 345

Artificial insemination, 307–308
  and AIDS, 504–505

Asceticism, and sexual decision making, 623

Asexuals, 296
  definition of, 272f

Asian Americans
  adolescent, sexual behavior of, 404–405
  and sexual orientation, 276

Assisted reproductive technology, 21, 309–311

Athletic achievement, gender differences in, 172–173

Attraction, 189–198
  in romance, 213

Attractiveness
  attitude similarity and, 197–198
  facial, 194
  gender differences in perception of, 193–195, 195t, 196–197
  personal qualities and, 193–195
  physical, 189–197
  reciprocity in, 198

Autoimmune response
  definition of, 307
  against sperm, 307

Autonomic nervous system
  definition of, 119
  in sexual arousal and response, 119

Aversion therapy, 547

AZT, 507

B&D, 538

Baby blues, 335–336

Bacteria
  definition of, 488
  sexually transmitted infections caused by, 488–498, 489t

Bacterial vaginosis, 489t, 498–499

Bar prostitutes, 597

Barbiturates, as anaphrodisiacs, 130

Bartholin's glands, 69f, 69–70

Basal body temperature
  in fertility awareness, 364–365
  in menstrual cycle, 86f, 87
  in predicting ovulation, 303f, 303–304, 364–365

Beavers, birth control for, 353

Behavior therapy
  definition of, 547
  for paraphilias, 547–548

Behaviorists
  definition of, 27
  learning theory of, 27

Benign, definition of, 79

Benign prostatic hyperplasia, 112–113

Benign tumors, in breasts, 79

Bestiality, 14, 19, 539

Between Two Absolutes, 375–376

Bias, in sampling, 41

Bible, and sexual decision making, 621–622

Bichloroacetic acid, 515

Billings Indian Health Service Survey, 48

Biological clock, older parents and, 302–303

Birth centers, 333

Birth control
  artificial. *See* Contraception
  natural. *See* Fertility awareness

Birth-control pill. *See* Oral contraceptives

Bisexuality, 272–274
  in ancient Greece, 13
  definition of, 13, 267

Bladder, inflammation, prevention of, 66–67

Blastocyst, 316, 317f

Blended orgasm, 147–148

Blindness, sex and, 445

Bondage, 536
  and discipline, 538

Bottle-feeding, 336–337

Brain
  geography of, 133–134, 134f
  pleasure centers in, 135–136
  prenatal organization of, and gender-typed behavior, 174
  in sexual arousal and response, 118–119, 133–136
  sexual differentiation of, 137, 162, 174
    prenatal, 157, 174
  structure of, and gay male sexual orientation, 283–284
  toxoplasmosis of, in HIV-infected (AIDS) patients, 503–504

Braxton-Hicks contractions, 328

Breakthrough bleeding, 351

Breast(s)
  anatomy of, 77f, 77–78, 78f
  benign tumors in, 79
  clinical examination of, guidelines for, 80
  cysts in, 79
  kissing, 248
  malignant tumors in, 79
  in pregnancy, 313
  pubertal changes in, 398
  self-examination of
    guidelines for, 80
    technique for, 82, 82f

during sexual response cycle, 142, 143*f*
size of, and attractiveness, 190
stimulation of, 251
Breast cancer, 78–83
deaths from, 78, 81
detection of, 79–81, 83
oral contraceptives and, 351
risk factors for, 78–79, 81
survival rates for, 78, 81
treatment of, 79–83
Breast-feeding, 336–337
Breast implants, 80
Breech presentation, 319
Brothel prostitution, 598
Buddhism, and abortion, 381
Bulbourethral glands, 110
Bupropion (Wellbutrin), and sex
drive, 130
Butch, 282

Calendar method, of fertility awareness, 346*t*,
364
Call girls, 599–600
Caller ID, 533–534
Calymmatobacterium granulomatis, 498
Canadian Toll-Free Hotline, 522
Candida albicans, 490*t*
Candidiasis, 490*t*, 498, 499*f*, 499–500
Cantharidin, 129
Cardiorespiratory endurance, gender
differences in, 172
Case study, 42–43
limitations of, 43
Castration
chemical, 549
of sex offenders, 582–583
and sexual behavior, 138
surgical, 549
Castration anxiety, 284–285
Catholicism
and contraception, 345, 363
and homosexuality, 274–275
and number of sex partners, 29*t*, 30
and opposition to abortion, 374
and sexuality, 16
CD4 cells, 503
Celibacy, 418
historical perspective on, 14–15
Cephalic presentation, 319
Cephalocaudal development, 317, 318*f*
Cerebellum, 134, 134*f*
Cerebral cortex, 134, 135*f*
in sexual functioning, 134–135
Cerebral palsy, sexuality and, 444
Cerebrum, 134
Cervical cancer, 73
oral contraceptives and, 351
Cervical cap, 346*t*, 359
Cervical mucus
ovulatory, 365
in predicting ovulation, 305, 346*t*, 365
viscosity of, 365
Cervicitis
chlamydial, 495–496
in gonorrhea, 492

Cervix
anatomy of, 71*f*, 72–73
dilation of, 328
effacement of, 328
os of, 72–73
Cesarean section, 331–332, 332*f*
Chancre
soft. *See* Chancroid
syphilitic, 494, 495*f*
Chancroid, 497
Chattel, 13, 422
Cheating. *See* Extramarital sex
Chemical castration, 549
Chewu people, attitudes toward childhood
sexuality, 388
Child abuse. *See also* Sexual abuse of children
sociobiological theory of, 23
Child pornography, 609
Childbirth, 327–333
anesthesia for, 330–331
anoxia in, 333–334
at birth centers, 333
at home, 333
methods of, 330–332
natural, 331
prepared (Lamaze method), 331
problems in, 333–335
stages of, 328–330, 329*f*
Childfree by choice, 302, 303*f*
Children
cohabitation and, 419
consensual sex play by, 574
of divorce, 436–437
female (schoolgirls), as sex toys in
Japan, 603
psychosexual development of, Freud's
theory of, 26
sex education and sex information for,
393–395
sexual abuse of. *See* Sexual abuse of
children
sexual attraction to. *See* Pedophilia
sexual coercion of, 528
sexuality of, cultural attitudes toward, 6
China
ancient, sexuality in, 15
koro in, 461
Chinese Americans
adolescent, sexual behavior of, 404–405
infant mortality rate for, 334
Chinese people, sexual behavior of, survey
on, 49
Chlamydia, 495–497
incidence of, 496
Chlamydia trachomatis, 484, 489*t*, 495–498
Chorionic villus sampling, 327
Christians, early, sexuality and, 14
Christmas Eve, as erotic day in Japan, 7, 417
Chromosomal abnormalities, 325*t*, 325–327
averting, 327
Chromosomes, 22, 108, 108*f*, 154
number of, 108, 108*f*
Chukchee people
attitude toward extramarital sex, 432
sexual attitudes of, 24

Cigarette smoking, effects on prenatal
development, 324–325
Cilia
in fallopian tubes, 74
of vas deferens, 110
Circumcision, 102–104, 103*f*
rates, by ethnic group, 103, 103*f*
risks and benefits of, 103–104
sexual effects of, 103–104
Climacteric, 90–91
Clitoral orgasm, 146–148
Clitoridectomy, 65–67
Clitoris, 62, 63*f*, 64–65
corpora cavernosa of, 64
crura of, 69, 69*f*
glans of, 64
prepuce of, 64
shaft of, 64
stimulation of, 250
Cloaca, 102
Clomiphene (Clomid), 87, 308
Clomipramine, 477
Close couples, 296
Cocaine
and sexual behavior, 133
sexual dysfunctions caused by, 460
Cognitive abilities, gender differences in,
170*f*, 170–171
Cohabitation, 418–421
critical thinking about, 10
demographics of, 419
and later marriage, 420–421, 421*f*
modern practice of, 18
reasons for, 419–420
Coitus
in adolescence, 400–403
motives for, 403–405
definition of, 5
fantasy during, 260–261
first, adolescents' attitudes toward,
406–407
frequency of
age-related changes in, 442
cross-cultural perspective on, 24
and sexual satisfaction, 53–54, 54*f*
marital
duration of, 428–429
frequency of, 427*t*, 427–428, 428*t*
sexual satisfaction in, 428*t*, 429–430
techniques, 428–429
during menstruation, 89–90
painful, 456–457
position for, 255–260
amputation and, 445
arthritis and, 445
disability and, 445
female-superior (woman-on-top), 180,
256–258, 257*f*, 428, 473, 475*f*
lateral-entry (side-entry), 258, 258*f*
male-superior (man-on-top), 180,
255–256, 256*f*, 305, 428
rear-entry, 259*f*, 259–260, 305
postpartum resumption of, 337
during pregnancy, 314
Coitus interruptus, 239, 343, 346*t*, 363

Colpotomy, for tubal sterilization, 370
Comarital sex, 433. *See also* Mate-swapping
Combination pills, 348–349
Coming out, 291–293
Commercial sex, 594. *See also* Prostitution
Commission on Obscenity and
        Pornography, 611
Commitment
    and cohabitation, 419
    and intimacy, 224
    in triangular model of love, 203–208
Communication
    about contraception, 344
    delivering criticism in, 231–232
    difficulties in, 227
    and disagreement, 234
    impasses in, 233–234
    of information, 229–230
    and intimacy, 224–225
    listening and, 228–229
    of needs, 229
    nonverbal, 225–226, 230
    questions in, 228–229
    receiving criticism in, 232–233
    for relationship enhancement, 226–234
    requests in, 230–231
    sexual, 226–234
    and sexual satisfaction, 430
    styles of, gender differences in, 171
Companionate love, 205, 205t, 208
Compatibility, in triangular model of love,
        204, 205f
Comstock Law, 344, 608
Conception, 300–306
    optimizing chances of, 301–306
Concordance
    definition of, 282
    for sexual orientation, in twins, 282
Concubine, definition of, 13
Condom(s), 347t, 359–363
    adolescents' use of, 410–411, 518–519
    application of, 361f, 361–362
    composition and shape of, 360, 360f
    definition of, 343
    distribution in schools, 412
    female, 368
    historical perspective on, 343
    latex, to prevent STIs, 520
    nonlatex, 368
    to prevent STIs, 360, 363, 515, 518–520
Congenital syphilis, 494
Consanguineous, definition of, 577
Consensual adultery, 431–433
Constructs, 38
Consummate love, 205t, 207, 207f, 208
Contraception, 342–348
    adolescents' use of, 402, 410–411
        ethnic differences in, 404–405
    artificial, 345
    barrier methods
        chemical, 368
        mechanical, 368
    definition of, 342
    discussion of, with partner, 344
    future trends in, 31, 368–369

historical perspective on, 342–343
hormonal methods
    future trends in, 368–369
    for men, 369
ideal method for, 369
immunologic methods, 369
male, future trends in, 369
methods, 348–371
    effectiveness of, 346t-347t, 347
    failure rates, 346t-347t
    selection of, 345–348
    school-based programs for, 353,
        411–413
    in United States, legal battles over,
        343–345
Control group, 55
Conventional adultery, 431
Cooperation theory, 577
Copper T 380A (IUD), 347t, 353, 354f
Coprophilia, 540
Copulation
    definition of, 21
    positions for, 21
Corona, of penis, 101f, 102
Corpora cavernosa, 115
    of clitoris, 64
    of penis, 101f, 102
Corpus luteum, 83, 88
Corpus spongiosum, 115
    of penis, 101f, 102
Correlation
    definition of, 53–54
    positive versus negative, 53–54
Correlation coefficient, definition of,
        53–54
Correlational research, 53–54
    limitations of, 54
Courtesan, definition of, 13
Courtship disorders, 545
Covert sensitization, 547
Cowper's glands, 110
Crabs. *See* Pediculosis
Cranberry juice, 111
Cremaster muscle, 104
Crisis
    definition of, 566
    sexual assault and, 566
Critical fat hypothesis, 397
Critical periods of vulnerability, in prenatal
        development, 320, 321f
Critical thinking
    characteristics of, 9–10
    about sexuality, 9–10
Crocodile, sex determination in, 160
Cross-dressing. *See* Transvestism
Crowning, 328
Cruising, 295
Crura, clitoral, 69, 69f
Cryotherapy
    for genital warts, 515
    for molluscum contagiosum, 516
Cryptorchidism, 157
    definition of, 112
    and testicular cancer, 112
Cultural relativism, 623

Culture
    and gender differences in mate
        preferences, 196
    and ideal beauty, 194
    and sexual beliefs and behaviors, 6–7
Cunnilingus
    in adolescence, 401
    definition of, 14, 251
    and prevention of STIs, 520
    techniques of, 253–254
Cyberbabes and cyberhunks, 192–193
Cybersex, 249
Cyberspace. *See also* Internet
    gay global village of, 293
    matchmaking in, 214–215
Cystic fibrosis, 325t
    prenatal diagnosis of, 327
Cystitis, 66
Cysts, in breasts, 79

D&C, 377–378
D&E, 378
Daddy's Roommate, 266
Dahomey people
    sexual attitudes of, 25
    sexual practices of, 37
Dartos muscle, 105
Date rape, 558–560
Date-seeking skills, improving, 216–217
Daughters of Bilitis, 281
Deaf people, sex and, 445
Decision making, sexual
    balance sheet for, 624–626
    conflict and, 620
    information gathering for, 620–621
    value systems and, 621–624
Deep Throat, 20
Defense mechanisms, 26
    definition of, 27
Defloration, 68
Delayed ejaculation, 455
Delivery date, calculation of, 315
Delta hepatitis. *See* Hepatitis
Demographics, 38
Denial, and bias in sex survey research, 50
Dependent variables, 55
Depo-Provera, 346t, 368–369
    for paraphilias, 549
Depressants, as anaphrodisiacs, 130
Depression
    maternal, postpartum, 335–336
    paternal, postpartum, 336
    sexual dysfunctions caused by, 462
Descent of Man, 194
Desire, in three-stage model of sexual
        response cycle, 144–145
Dhat, 461
Diabetes mellitus
    erectile disorder in, 459
    sexual arousal disorder in, 454–455
Diaphragm (contraceptive), 346t, 355–357,
        356f
    silicone, 368
Didanosine (ddI), 507
Diet, and prostate cancer, 113

Diethylstilbestrol (DES)
    and cryptorchidism, 112
    prenatal exposure to, effects of, 323
Dihydrotestosterone, in sexual
        differentiation, 155
Dilate, definition of, 328
Dilation and curettage, 377–378
Dilation and evacuation, 378
Dildo(s), 521
    definition of, 238
Disability
    physical, sex and, 443–445
    psychological, sex and, 445–446
    sensory, sex and, 445
    sex and, 443–446
Disease, maternal, effects on prenatal
        development, 320
Displacement, as defense mechanism, 284
Divorce, 435–437
    children of, 436–437
    cost of, 436–437
    historical perspective on, 12–14, 422
    no-fault, 435
    premarital cohabitation and, 420–421,
        421f
    rates, in U.S., 435, 435f
    reasons for, 436, 436t
    remarriage and, 437
Dizygotic (DZ) twins, 97
    concordance for sexual
        orientation, 282
    definition of, 282
DNA, 22
Doggy style, 260
Domestic violence, 434–435
Dominican Republic syndrome, 159–160
Don Juanism, 541
Donor IVF, 309
Don't Call It Love, 540
L-Dopa, and sex drive, 130
Double standard, adolescents' attitudes
        toward, 407–408
Douche, 72, 521
    contraceptive effects of, 363
    definition of, 363
Down syndrome, 300, 325t, 326
    maternal age and, 326, 326t
    prenatal diagnosis of, 327
Dreams, symbols in, 26, 27t
Droit de seigneur, 68
Drosophila bifurca, sperm of, 109
Drug(s)
    maternal or paternal use of, fetal effects
        of, 322–323
    and risky sexual behavior, 519
    sexual dysfunctions caused by, 460
Dry orgasm, 120, 122, 146
Ductus deferens. *See* Vas deferens
Dysfunctionals, 296
Dysmenorrhea, 92–94
    biological aspects of, 93–94
    primary, 92–93
    secondary, 93
Dyspareunia, 451, 456–457
    treatment of, 477

East Bay islanders, sexual attitudes of, 24–25
Eclampsia, 322
Ectoderm, 317
Ectoparasite(s)
    definition of, 516
    infestations of, sexually transmitted, 491t,
        516–517
Ectopic pregnancy, 74, 322
Education
    and attitudes toward abortion, 375, 376f
    and masturbation, 241t, 242
    and number of sex partners, 29t, 30
    and oral sex, 252
Eebu, in Japan, 7, 417
Efface, definition of, 328
Egg cells. *See* Ova
Egg donation, 310
Ego, definition of, 26
Egypt
    ancient
        brother-sister marriages in, 12
        father-daughter marriages in, 12
    female genital mutilation in, 66–67
Ejaculation, 120–122, 141f, 143
    brain structures regulating, 135
    delayed, 455
    emission stage of, 120–121
    expulsion stage of, 121
    female, 148–149
    first, in puberty, 399
    by paraplegics, 120
    premature. *See* Premature ejaculation
    reflexes governing, 116–117
    retarded, 455
    retrograde. *See* Retrograde ejaculation
Ejaculatory ducts, 109–110, 110f
Ejaculatory incompetence, 455
Elderly, sexuality of, 439–443
Electra complex, 176, 284–285, 464
Elephantiasis, 498
ELISA, 506
Elmer Gantry, 198
Embryo, 154–155
Embryonic disk, 316
Embryonic stage, of prenatal development,
        315, 317–319, 318f
Embryonic transfer, 310
Emission stage, of ejaculation, 120–121
Empirical approach, 36
Empty love, in triangular model of
        love, 205t, 207
Endocrine gland(s)
    corpus luteum as, 83
    definition of, 83
    in regulation of testes, 106, 106f
Endocrine system, 84, 84f
    feedback loop in, 106
Endoderm, 317
Endometrial cancer, 73–74
    oral contraceptives and, 350
Endometriosis, 73
    definition of, 308
    and infertility, 308
Endometritis, chlamydial, 495
Endometrium, 73

Endorphins, 538
Ensoulment, 372, 374
Enzyme-linked immunosorbent assay, 506
Epididymis, 109
Epididymitis
    chlamydial, 495, 497
    in gonorrhea, 492
Epidural block, for childbirth, 331
Episiotomy, 69, 328–329
ErecAid, 471
Erectile dysfunction, 119, 453–454. *See also*
        Impotence
    acquired, 453
    alprostadil for, 469–471
    generalized, 453
    lifelong, 453
    organic causes of, 459
    phentolamine for, 470–471
    situational, 453
    treatment of, 468f, 468–473
        biological approaches to, 469–471, 470t
        medications for, 469–471
        penile implants for, 469, 469f
        vacuum pumps for, 471
        vascular surgery for, 469
    Viagra for, 130, 471–473
Erection
    abnormalities, 120
    age-related changes in, 440
    brain structures regulating, 135
    infant's capacity for, 386
    physiology of, 115–116
    psychogenic, 444
    in puberty, 399
    reflexes governing, 116–118
    reflexive, 117–118
        after spinal cord injury, 444
Erogenous zones, 26, 127–128
    definition of, 27
    primary, 128
    secondary, 128
Eros, 199
Erotic, definition of, 5
Erotica, 607
    prevalence of, 609
    use of, 609
Erythroblastosis, fetal, 322
Escort services, 598–599
Estratest, 467
Estrogen, 75
    and breast cancer, 79
    deficit, in menopause, 91–92
    in menstrual cycle, 86f, 87–89
    placental secretion of, 319
    production of, 85, 136
    pubertal production of, 398–399
    replacement therapy
        plus androgens, and sexual behavior, 139
        and sexual behavior, 139
    and sexual behavior, in females, 138–139
Estrous cycle, 84
Estrus, 84, 139
Ethical relativism, and sexual decision
        making, 622–623
Ethics, in sex research, 56–58

Ethnicity. *See* Race/ethnicity
Ethnocentrism
    and cultural attitudes, 25
    definition of, 25
Ethnography, 51
Evolution
    definition of, 22
    and sexual behavior, 22–23
Exaggeration, and bias in sex survey
        research, 50
Excitement phase
    of sexual response cycle, 140*f*, 140–141,
        141*f*-142*f*
    in three-stage model of sexual response
        cycle, 144–145
Exercise, and sex drive, 130, 131*f*
Exhibitionism, 528, 531–532
    biological perspective on, 542
    learning perspective on, 544–545
    psychoanalytic perspective on, 542
    responding to, 533
Experiment, definition of, 54
Experimental group, 55
Experimental research, 54–56
    with animals, 55–56
    experimental and control groups for, 55
    independent and dependent variables in, 55
    limitations of, 56
Expulsion stage, of ejaculation, 121
External sex organs
    development of, 154–155, 156*f*
    female, 62–71, 63*f*
        structures underlying, 69*f*, 69–70
    male, 100–105, 101*f*
Extramarital sex, 430–433. *See also* Adultery
    attitudes toward, 432
    cross-cultural perspective on, 24, 432
    effects of, 433
    historical perspective on, 17–18
    incidence of, 432
    motivations for, 430–431
Eye contact, in communication, 226

Facial expression, and attractiveness, 191, 191*f*
Fallopian tubes, 71*f*, 74
    blockage, tests for, 308–309
    fertilization in, 301
    ligation, for sterilization, 370, 370*f*
Famciclovir, 513
Family Book about Sexuality, 394
Family planning. *See also* Contraception
    natural, 363
Fantasy, 245–247
    coital, 260–262, 261*t*
    homoerotic, 269
    and masturbation, 246–247
    necrophilic, 540
    in paraphilias, 527–528
    sexual orientation and, 272–273
Fatuous love, 205*t*, 207
Fellatio
    in adolescence, 401
    definition of, 14, 251
    and prevention of STIs, 520
    techniques of, 252–253

Female(s). *See also* Women
    as child molesters, 575–576
    fertility problems of, 308–309
    number of sex partners, 29*t*, 30
    pubertal changes in, 396*t*, 398
    rape by, 561
    sexual anatomy and physiology of, 60–96
    sexuality of, age-related changes in, 439*t*,
        439–440
Female impersonators, 530
Female orgasmic disorder, 456
Female sexual arousal disorder, 454–455
Female-superior position, 180, 256–258,
        257*f*, 428, 473, 475*f*
Femme, 282
Fertility awareness, 346*t*, 363–366
    basal body temperature method of,
        364–365
    calendar method of, 346*t*, 364
    ovulation method of, 346*t*, 365
Fertility problems. *See* Infertility
Fertility symbols, 11, 13*f*
Fertilization, 154
Fetal alcohol syndrome (FAS), 323–324
Fetal erythroblastosis, 322
Fetal movements, 319–320
Fetal stage, of prenatal development, 315,
        318*f*, 319–320
Fetishism, 528–529
    learning perspective on, 544
    psychoanalytic perspective on, 542
    transvestic. *See* Transvestism
Fibroadenomas, in breasts, 79
Field study, 50–51
Fijians, attitude toward extramarital sex, 432
Fimbriae, of fallopian tubes, 74
Fisting, 293, 520
Fitness, gender differences in, 172–173
Fixations
    definition of, 27
    Freud's theory of, 26
Flagyl, 501
Flashing. *See* Exhibitionism
Fluoxetine hydrochloride. *See* Prozac
Follicle, ovarian, 75
    maturation of, 87, 87*f*
Follicle-stimulating hormone (FSH), 85
    in menstrual cycle, 87–88
    pubertal production of, 398
    in regulation of testes, 106, 106*f*
Food(s), as aphrodisiacs, 129–130
For Whom the Bell Tolls, 606
Forcible rape, definition of, 555
Forebrain, 133–134, 134*f*
Foreplay, 247–248
    definition of, 5
    marital, 427
Foreskin, 101*f*, 102
Fornication, definition of, 14
Fraternal twins. *See* Dizygotic (DZ) twins
Frenulum, of penis, 101*f*, 102
Frequency
    definition of, 44
    of sexual behaviors, faulty estimation of, 47
    of sexual intercourse

cross-cultural perspective on, 24
        and sexual satisfaction, 53–54, 54*f*
Frigidity, 453
Frotteurism, 538–539
    learning perspective on, 545
Fruit fly, sperm of, 109
Functionals, 296
Fundus, uterine, 71*f*, 73

G-spot. *See* Grafenberg spot
Gamete intrafallopian transfer (GIFT), 309
Gang rape, 560
Gardnerella vaginalis, 489*t*
Gay activism, 281
Gay bashing, 279–280
Gay community, 295
Gay identity, 292
    in adolescence, 408
Gay lifestyles, 294–295
    differences between gay males and
        lesbians, 295–296
    variations in, 296
Gay males. *See also* Gay people
    definition of, 267
    as prostitutes, 603–604
Gay people. *See also* Homosexuality;
        Lesbians; Sexual orientation
    adjustment of, 288–291
    and AIDS, 280, 508
    brain structure of, 283–284
    discrimination against, 294
    ethnicity and, 276–277
    as female impersonators, 530
    and gender identity, 268
    Kinsey Institute Reports on, 47
    lifestyles of, 288–289, 295–296
    in military, 294–295
    number of, in population, 271
    as parents, 266, 278
    sexual behavior of, 281–282, 293–294
    sexual dysfunctions in, 462
    stereotypes of, 281–282
    treatment of, 289–291
Gay rights, 295
Gender
    definition of, 5
    and mate selection preferences, 193–195,
        195*t*, 196–197
    and number of sex partners, 29*t*, 30
Gender assignment, definition of, 157–158
Gender constancy, 178–179
Gender differences, 169–171
    in aggressiveness, 171
    in cognitive abilities, 170*f*, 170–171
    in communication styles, 171
    in fitness, 172–173
    in personality, 171
    in self-disclosure, 217
    in styles of love, 203
    in willingness to seek health care, 171
Gender dysphoria, 161
Gender identity, 157–164
    definition of, 5, 157
    gender schema theory of, 179–180
    nature and nurture in, 158

pseudohermaphroditism and, 159–160
psychosocial factors affecting, 159–160
sexual orientation and, 268
Gender identity disorder, 164–165
Gender nonconformity, sexual orientation
and, 287–288
Gender polarization, future trends in, 31
Gender reassignment, 161–163
outcomes of, 163–164
Gender roles, 154, 165
acquisition of, social-learning theory
of, 28, 28f
cross-cultural perspective on, 24
as cultural adaptation, 175
definition of, 5
historical perspective on, 11–13, 15–16
psychosocial factors affecting, 160
and sexual behavior, 180–181
sociocultural perspectives on, 30
stereotypes, 166–167, 167t
advertising and, 615–616
and attractiveness, 192
Gender schema
definition of, 179
theory of, 179–180
Gender selection, for child, 304–305
Gender stability, 178–179
Gender typing, 173–180, 178f
biological perspective on, 173
cognitive-developmental theory
of, 178–179
cross-cultural perspectives on, 174–175
parental roles in, 176–177
psychodynamic theory of, 176
psychological perspectives on, 175–180
social-learning theory of, 176–178
sociobiological perspective on, 173–174
General anesthesia, for childbirth, 330–331
General paresis, 495
Generalize, definition of, 40
Genes
definition of, 22
and sexual behavior, 22–23
Genetic abnormalities, 325t, 325–327
averting, 327
sex-linked, 326–327
Genetics, 22–23
and sexual orientation, 282–283
Genital mutilation, ritual, of females, 65–67
Genital play
in infancy, 388
in sex therapy, 473, 474f
Genital stimulation
in gay couples, 293–294
manual, 250–251
oral, 251–255, 520
Genital warts. *See* Warts
Genitals. *See also* External sex organs
age-related changes in, 439t, 439–441
washing, before and after sex, 520
Germ cells, 106
German measles. *See* Rubella
Germinal stage, of prenatal development,
315–316, 317f
Girls Inc., 402

Glans
of clitoris, 64
of penis, 101f, 102, 115
Gonadotropin-releasing hormone, 85
in menstrual cycle, 87–88
Gonadotropins, 85
Gonads, 106
hormone production by, 84–85
Gonorrhea, 488–493, 489t
incidence of, 485
pharyngeal, 492
Gossypol, as male contraceptive, 369
Graafian follicle, 87
Grafenberg spot, 148f, 149–150
Graham crackers, 18
Granuloma inguinale, 498
The Grapes of Wrath, 606
Greece, ancient
patriarchy in, 422
sexuality in, 12–13, 100
Griswold v. *Connecticut*, 345
Group marriage, 438
Growing Together, 402
Growth, pubertal, 399
Gymnophthalmus underwoodi, 306
Gynecologist, 66
Gynecomastia, 399

H-Y antigen, 155
Haemophilus ducreyi, 497
Hallucinogens
effects on prenatal development, 323
and sexual behavior, 132–133
Hardwick v. *Bowers*, 281
Harris v. *McRae*, 374
Hawaii, royal family of, brother-sister
marriages among, 12
Headache, with menstrual discomfort, 93–94
Health care, willingness to seek, gender
differences in, 171
Hearing, in sexual arousal, 128–129
Heather Has Two Mommies, 266
Hebrews, ancient, sexuality of, 12
Hedonism, and sexual decision making, 623
Hegar's sign, 313
Height, and attractiveness, 190
The Helper, 522
Hemophilia, 325t, 326–327
Hepatitis
definition of, 514
transmission of, 514
viral, 490t, 514
Herceptin, 80–81
Hermaphroditism, 158f, 158–160
Heroin
effects on prenatal development, 323
sexual dysfunctions caused by, 460
Herpes, 510–514
diagnosis of, 513
genital, 490t, 511, 511f
coping with, 513–514
in HIV-infected (AIDS) patients, 504
hotline, 522
incidence of, 510
information about, sources for, 522

ocular, 512
oral, 490t, 512
prodromal symptoms in, 512
recurrences of, 512
symptoms of, 512
transmission of, 511–512
treatment of, 513
Herpes Resource Center, 522
Herpes simplex virus (HSV)
type 1, 490t, 511
type 2, 490t, 511
Heteroeroticism, 272
definition of, 269
Heterosexual orientation, 266
Hindbrain, 133–134, 134f
Hindus
attitudes toward menarche, 400
marriage among, 421
and sexuality, 16
Hispanic Americans
adolescent, sexual behavior of, 404–405
AIDS and, 502, 508–510
and sexual orientation, 276
Hispanic culture, *machismo/marianismo*
stereotypes and, 168
The Hite Report, 46
The Hite Report on Male Sexuality, 46
HIV (human immunodeficiency virus),
484–485, 491t, 501, 501f
infection, 501–510. *See also* Acquired
immunodeficiency syndrome (AIDS)
diagnosis of, 506
drug therapy for, 507–508
immune system and, 502–503
immunity to, 505
incidence of, 508
maternal, effects on prenatal
development, 321
prevalence of, 501
prevention of, 509–510, 518–519
progression of, 503–504
risk factors for, 501, 505
testing for, before initiating sexual
relations, 521
transmission, 504–505, 508
in breast milk, 336
to fetus, 321
misinformation about, 505–506
perinatal, 321
prostitution and, 605–606
vaccines against, 506–507, 509
HIV-infected (AIDS) patients, treatment
of, 506–509
future of, 31, 509
Home births, 333
Homicide, necrophilic, 540
Homoeroticism, 272
definition of, 269
Homogamy, 424–425
Homologous, definition of, 65
Homophile, 267
Homophobia, 279f, 279–280
internalized, 279
Homosexual Citizen, 281
Homosexual identity, 292

Homosexual orientation, 267. *See also* Gay people; Lesbians; Sexual orientation
versus transsexualism, 161
Homosexualities, 47
Homosexualities: A Study of Diversity among Men and Women, 294
Homosexuality in Perspective, 52
Honesty, and intimacy, 224
Honeymoon cystitis, 66
Hopi, sexual attitudes of, 24
Hormone(s), 84. *See also* Sex hormones
definition of, 136
designer, for contraception, 369
and sexual orientation, 283
Hormone replacement therapy
future of, 31
for hypoactive sexual desire disorder, 467
for men, 107
risks and benefits of, 92
Hotline(s)
AIDS, 510, 522
for adolescents, 522
Canadian toll-free, 522
for hearing impaired, 522
Spanish, 522
herpes, 522
STI, 522
Huckleberry Finn, 606–607
Hudood Ordinance, 6
Human chorionic gonadotropin
beta subunit radioimmunoassay, 313
placental secretion of, 319
in pregnancy testing, 313
Human immunodeficiency virus. *See* HIV
(human immunodeficiency virus)
Human papilloma virus (HPV), 484–485, 491*t*, 515
vaccine against, 515
Human Sexual Response, 51
Huntington's chorea, 325*t*
prenatal diagnosis of, 327
Hustlers, 603–605
Hyaluronidase, 301
Hyde Amendment, 374
Hymen, 67–68, 68*f*
imperforate, 68
surgical restoration of, 69
and virginity, 68–69
Hypersexuality, 541
Hypoactive sexual desire disorder, 452
treatment of, 467
Hypogonadism, 452
definition of, 138
and sexual behavior, 138
Hypothalamus, 84–85, 134, 134*f*
in regulation of testes, 106, 106*f*
and sex hormone secretion, 136
sexual differentiation of, 157, 162
in sexual functioning, 135
Hypothesis
definition of, 36
testing, 36–37
Hypoxyphilia, 536
learning perspective on, 544

Hysterectomy, 74
complete, 74
partial, 74
for sterilization, 370
Hysterosalpingography, 308–309
Hysterotomy, 378

I-talk, 231
Id, definition of, 26
Identical twins. *See* Monozygotic (MZ) twins
Identification
and gender typing, 176
psychoanalytic definition of, 162
in social-learning theory, 176
and transsexualism, 162
Imipramine (Tofranil), anaphrodisiac
effects, 131
Imiquimod, 515
Immune system, and HIV infection
(AIDS), 502–503
Immunocontraceptives, 369
Implanon, 368
Implantation, 316, 317*f*
Impotence, 453. *See also* Erectile dysfunction
definition of, 240
masturbation and, 240
In vitro fertilization (IVF), 309
donor, 309
Incas, brother-sister marriages
among, 12
Incest
brother-sister, 578
cross-cultural perspective on, 25, 37
definition of, 577
family factors in, 578–579
father-daughter, 578–579
mother-daughter, 578
prevalence of, 578
types of, 577–579
victims of, and prostitution, 601
Incest taboo, 12
perspectives on, 577
prevalence of, 25
Incidence, definition of, 44
Independent variables, 55
India
ancient, sexuality in, 16
attitudes toward menarche in, 400
attitudes toward menstruation in, 89
dhat syndrome in, 461
marriage in, 421
sexual attitudes in, 24
Individuality, and intimacy, 224
Induced abortion, 371
Infancy, sexuality in, 386–389
Infant mortality, ethnicity and, 334–335
Infanticide, sociobiological theory of, 23
Infatuation, 204–205
versus love, 202
Inference
anthropomorphic, 37
definition of, 37
versus description, 37
Infertility
definition of, 306

female, 308–309
STIs and, 485
incidence of, 306
male, 306–308
treatments for, 21
Infibulation, 66
Infidelity. *See* Extramarital sex
Inflammation, 502
Informed consent
definition of, 57
for sex research, 57
Infundibulum, of fallopian tubes, 74
Inguinal canal, 157
Inis Beag, sexual attitudes and practices
in, 458
Injecting drug users, and HIV infection
(AIDS), 502, 508, 510
Intercourse. *See* Coitus
Internal sex organs
development of, 154–156, 155*f*
female, 65*f*, 71*f*, 71–76
male, 105–111
Internet. *See also* Cyberspace
pornography on, future trends in, 31
sex available on, 610
Interstitial-cell-stimulating hormone, 106
Interstitial cells, 106, 106*f*
Intimacy
definition of, 223
elements of, 223–226
sexual versus emotional, 223
in triangular model of love, 203–208, 223
Intra-amniotic infusion, 378
Intracytoplasmic sperm injection, 310
Intrauterine device (IUD), 347*t*, 353–355, 354*f*, 369
Introitus, 67–68, 68*f*
Invisible Lives, 292
Islamic society
attitudes toward menstruation in, 89
clitoridectomy in, 66–67
sexual beliefs and behaviors in, 6, 15, 15*f*
Isthmus, of fallopian tubes, 74

The Janus Report on Sexual Behavior, 46
Japan
Christmas Eve dating in, 7, 417
schoolgirls as sex toys in, 603
Japanese
attitude toward abortion, 7, 381
contraceptive options for, 381
self-disclosure by, 218
Japanese Americans, infant mortality
rate for, 334
Jaundice, 514
Jealousy, 218–219
John(s)
compulsive, 602
definition of, 601
habitual, 602
occasional, 601–602

Kama Sutra, 16, 16*f*
Kaposi's sarcoma (KS), 503, 511
Karma, 16

Kegel exercises, 70
Kinsey Institute Reports, on gay people, 47
Kinsey reports, 19, 44–46, 48
Kissing
    in adolescence, 401
    cross-cultural perspective on, 24
    cultural attitudes toward, 6–7, 20
    deep, 248
    in foreplay, 248
    and HIV, 504, 504*f*
    simple, 248
Kissing gourami, 37
Klinefelter syndrome, 157
Klismaphilia, 540
Koro, 461
!Kung people, gender roles in, 175
Kurtatchi people, attitudes toward
        menarche, 400
Kwell, 517
Kwoma people, attitudes toward childhood
        sexuality, 388

Labia majora, 62, 63*f*, 63–64
Labia minora, 62, 63*f*, 64
Labor. *See also* Childbirth
    induction of, by intra-amniotic
        infusion, 378
    onset of, maternal-fetal signals for, 328
    stages of, 328–330
Laboratory observation, in sex
        research, 51–53
Lactation, 336–337
Ladder, 281
Lady Chatterley's Lover, 20, 427, 606
Lamaze method, for prepared childbirth, 331
Laminaria, 377–378
Laparoscopy, 308
    for tubal sterilization, 370, 370*f*
Larynx, pubertal changes in, 399
Latency period, 392
Learning theory, 27–28
    of paraphilias, 543–545
    of sexual orientation, 286–287
Lecha people, attitudes toward childhood
        sexuality, 388
Leda and the Swan, 539
Legalism, 621–622
Leptin, 397
Lesbians. *See also* Gay people;
        Homosexuality; Sexual orientation
    adjustment of, 288–291
    definition of, 267
    ethnicity and, 276–277
    lifestyles of, 288–289, 295–296
    as parents, 266, 278
    sexual behavior of, 282, 293–294
    treatment of, 289–291
Lesu people, attitudes toward childhood
        sexuality, 388
Leukocytes, 502
Leydig's cells, 106, 106*f*
Librium, effects on prenatal
        development, 323
Lice, pubic. *See* Pediculosis
Life on the Screen, 215

Liking, 205, 205*t*
Limbic system, 134, 135*f*
    pleasure centers in, 135–136
    in sexual functioning, 134–135
Lindane, 517
Listening, and communication, 228–229
Liu Report, 49
Lizard, all-female species of, 306
Local anesthetics, for childbirth, 331
Lochia, 337
Loneliness, 221–222
    causes of, 221
    coping with, 221–222
Looking for Love Online, 214
Love, 198–208. *See also* Romantic love
    ancient Greek concepts of, 199
    arousal and, 202–203
    companionate, 205, 205*t*, 208
    consummate, 205*t*, 207, 207*f*, 208
    courtly, 17
    empty, in triangular model of love, 205*t*,
        207
    fatuous, 205*t*, 207
    gender differences in, 203
    versus infatuation, 202
    Sternberg's triangular theory of, 203–208,
        204*f*-205*f*, 205*t*, 207*f*, 627
    styles of, 203
Love Attitudes Scale, 200–201, 627
Love Online, 215
Lovemap, 546
Low-birthweight infants, 334–335
LSD
    effects on prenatal development, 323
    and sexual behavior, 133
Lumpectomy, 79
Luteinizing hormone, 85
    analysis of urine or saliva for, in predicting
        ovulation, 304–305
    in menstrual cycle, 87–88
    pubertal production of, 398
    in regulation of testes, 106, 106*f*
Luteinizing hormone-releasing hormone, in
        regulation of testes, 106, 106*f*
Lymphogranuloma venereum, 498
Lysergic acid diethylamide. *See* LSD

Machismo, 168
Madonna/whore concept, 16–17, 17*f*
Magazines, surveys on sexuality, 46–47
Male(s). *See also* Men
    as child molesters, 575–576
    fertility problems of, 306–308
    number of sex partners, 29*t*, 30
    proactive approach to sexual health, future
        of, 31
    pubertal changes in, 397*t*, 398–399
    sexual functions of, 115–122
    sexuality of, age-related changes in, 439*t*,
        440–441
Male erectile disorder. *See* Erectile
        dysfunction
Male menopause, 107
Male orgasmic disorder, 455
    treatment of, 476

Male rape, 560
Male Sexuality, 105
Male-superior position, 180, 255–256, 256*f*,
        305, 428
Malignant, definition of, 79
Malnutrition, maternal, effects on prenatal
        development, 320, 322
Mammary glands, 77, 77*f*
Mammography, 78
    in breast cancer detection, 79–81, 83
    guidelines for, 80
Mangaia, sexual attitudes and practices
        in, 458
Manopause, 107
Marianismo, 168
Marijuana
    effects on prenatal development, 323
    and sexual behavior, 132–133
    sexual dysfunctions caused by, 460
Marital fidelity. *See also* Extramarital sex
    cultural attitudes toward, 6
Marital rape, 556, 561
Marital sexuality, 426–430
    historical perspective on, 422–423
    sexual revolution and, 426–429
Marital status
    and masturbation, 241*t*, 242
    and number of sex partners, 29*t*, 30
Marriage, 421–426
    age and, 421
    ages of mates in, 425
    alternative forms of, 437–438
    characteristics of mates in, 424–425
    cohabitation and, 420–421, 421*f*
    effects of extramarital sex on, 433
    emotional satisfaction in, 430
    gay, 266, 275
    group, 438
    historical perspective on, 12, 14–15, 17,
        421–423
    motivations for, 423–424
    open, 20, 438
    and romantic love, 423
    sexual satisfaction in, 428*t*, 429–430
    social purposes of, 423
    traditional versus modern, 423
    trends in, in U.S., 416, 418
    types of, 424
Marshall Islanders, attitude toward
        extramarital sex, 432
Mashing. *See* Frotteurism
Masochism. *See also* Sexual masochism
    definition of, 536
Massage parlors, 598
Mastalgia, 93
Mastectomy, 79
Master gland, pituitary gland as, 85
Masturbation, 5, 144, 238–245. *See also*
        Fetishism
    in adolescence, 241*t*, 242–243, 400
    attitudes toward, modern, 240–243
    childhood, 389–390
        cross-cultural perspective on, 388
        parental reaction to, 390
    cross-cultural perspective on, 24–25

Masturbation (*continued*)
definition of, 238
devices for prevention of, 240, 240*f*
fantasy and, 246–247
historical perspective on, 15, 239–240
incidence of, 240–242, 241*t*
in infancy, 387
Judeo-Christian attitudes toward, 238–239
in old age, 442
orgasm in, physiologic intensity and psychological experience of, 147
and orgasmic potential, 242*f*, 242–243
in preadolescence, 392
in sex therapy, 474–476
techniques
female, 244*f*, 244–245
male, 243*f*, 243–244
Matching hypothesis, 197
Matchmaking, 213, 213*f*, 214–215
Mate(s)
matching hypothesis and, 197
selection
for marriage, 424–425
preferences in, 193–195, 195*t*, 196–197
Mate-swapping, 20, 432–433
investigator participation in, for research, 51
Maternity blues, 335–336
Mathematical abilities, gender differences in, 170–171
Mating gradient, 425
Mattachine Society, 281
Meatus, urethral, 101, 101*f*, 102
Media, gender stereotypes in, 177
Medroxyprogesterone acetate. *See* Depo-Provera
Medulla, 134, 134*f*
Meese Commission, 612
Men. *See also* Male(s)
divorce and, 436
and domestic violence, 434–435
older, as fathers, 303
as romantics, 425–426
as sexually aggressive, stereotype of, 180–181, 426–427
as sexually overaroused, stereotype of, 181, 426–427
spinal-cord-injured, sexuality of, 444–445
Menarche, 83, 396–398, 398*f*
cross-cultural perspective on, 400
Menopause, 90–92
male, 107
myths about, 90–91
and sexuality, 90–91
Menstrual cycle, 83–92
anovulatory, 83, 398
changes occurring in, 86*f*
luteal (secretory) phase of, 83, 85*f*–86*f*, 87–88
menstrual phase of, 83, 85*f*
ovulatory phase of, 83, 85*f*–86*f*, 87
peak days of, 365
phases of, 83, 85*f*, 85–89, 86*f*
proliferative phase of, 83, 85*f*–86*f*, 87

regulation of, 84*f*, 84–85
and sexual behavior, 139
Menstrual discomfort, 93–94. *See also* Dysmenorrhea
management of, 95*f*, 95–96
Menstrual problems, 92–96, 93*t*
management of, 95*f*, 95–96
Menstrual synchrony, 127
Menstruation, 83, 85–86, 88–89
coitus during, 89–90
cross-cultural perspective on, 89, 400
versus estrus, 84
historical perspective on, 89
postpartum resumption of, 337
Mentally retarded people, sexuality of, 445–446
Mescaline, and sexual behavior, 133
Mesoderm, 317
Methadone, effects on prenatal development, 323
Methotrexate, for induced abortion, 379
Metronidazole, 501
Mexican Americans, adolescent, sexual behavior of, 404–405
Midbrain, 133–134, 134*f*
Middle Ages, sexuality in, 16–17
Middle East, female genital mutilation in, 66–67
Mifepristone, 378–379
Migraine, as menstrual discomfort, 94
Miller v. *California*, 607–608
Minilaparotomy, for tubal sterilization, 370
Minipill, 348–349, 351
Mirena (IUD), 369
Miscarriage, 313–314. *See also* Spontaneous abortion
maternal syphilis and, 321
Misoprostol, for induced abortion, 379
Mittelschmerz, 87
Modeling
definition of, 28
of sexual behavior, 28
Molluscum contagiosum, 516
Mongolism. *See* Down syndrome
Moniliasis. *See* Candidiasis
Monogamy, 424
cross-cultural perspective on, 25
definition of, 12
to prevent STIs, 518
Monozygotic (MZ) twins, 87
concordance for sexual orientation, 282
definition of, 282
Mons veneris, 62–63, 63*f*
Mormon church, and polygyny, 25
Morning-after pill, 351
Morning sickness, 313
with oral contraceptives, 350
Morphine, sexual dysfunctions caused by, 460
Müllerian (female) ducts, 155, 155*f*, 156
Müllerian-inhibiting substance, 155
Multiple orgasms, 145–146
Multiple sclerosis, erectile disorder in, 459
Mundugumor tribe, gender roles in, 175
Muria Gond people, attitudes toward childhood sexuality, 388

Muscular dystrophy, prenatal diagnosis of, 327
Mutations, 22
Mutuality, 217
My Fair Lady, 166
Myometrium, 74
Myotonia, in sexual response cycle, 140, 144

Nagele's rule, 315
Nama tribe, attractiveness in, 190
Name(s), and attractiveness, 192–193
Narcotics
effects on prenatal development, 323
sexual dysfunctions caused by, 460
National AIDS Hotline, 510, 522
National Health and Social Life Survey, 45–46, 48
National Herpes Hotline, 522
National STI Hotline, 522
National Survey of Family Growth, 48
Native Americans
attitude toward extramarital sex, 432
sexual behavior of, survey on, 48
and sexual orientation, 277
Natural childbirth, 331
Natural selection, definition of, 22
Naturalistic observation, 50–51
Navajo culture, attitudes toward menstruation in, 89
Necrophilia, 19, 540
Neisseria gonorrhoeae, 488, 489*t*
penicillin-resistant, 493
Neural tube, 317
Neural tube defects, 325*t*
Neurosyphilis, 495
Neurotransmitters, 477
The New Our Bodies, Ourselves, 569
Newborn, testing and treatment of, 330
NGU. *See* Nongonococcal urethritis
Nicotine, anaphrodisiac effects, 131
Nipples, 77–78
Nitric oxide (NO), and erectile disorder, 459–460
Nocturnal emission, 399
Nocturnal penile tumescence, 460
Nongonococcal urethritis, 489*t*
chlamydial, 495–497
trichomonal, 500
Nonoxynol-9, protection against STIs, 357
Nonverbal communication, 225–226, 230
Norplant, 347*t*, 352*f*, 352–353
for adolescents, 412–413
Nymphomania, 541

Obesity, and pregnancy outcome, 320
Obscene telephone calling, 533–534
Obscenity, definition of, 607–608
Observational learning, and gender typing, 176
Observational research
case study method of, 42–43
ethnographic method of, 51
laboratory method of, 51–53
limitations of, 52–53
methods of, 42–53

naturalistic method of, 50–51
participant method of, 51
Observer effect, 52
Ocular herpes, 512
Oedipus complex, 26, 176, 284–285, 464, 542
definition of, 27
Old age, sexuality in, 439–443
Old Testament, attitudes toward
menstruation in, 89
Onanism, 239
Open couples, 296
Open marriage, 438
Opening lines, 214–216
Operational definitions, 38–40
definition of, 38–39
Ophthalmia neonatorum, 492
Opportunistic diseases, in HIV-infected
(AIDS) patients, 504, 508
Oral-anal sex, 262–263, 520
Oral contraceptives, 347t, 348–351
definition of, 348
healthful side effects of, 350
for men, 369
postcoital ("morning-after pill"), 351
safety of, 79
and sexual revolution, 20
Oral-genital stimulation, 251–255
abstaining from, 254–255
and prevention of STIs, 520
sociocultural factors and, 252–253
Oral sex
in adolescence, 401
and prevention of STIs, 520
Orgasm(s)
coital, physiologic intensity and
psychological experience of, 147
controversies about, 145–149
dry, 120, 122, 146
female, 142f, 143
blended, 147–148
clitoral, 146–148
types of, 146–148
uterine, 147–148
vaginal, 146–148
vulval, 147–148
in infancy, 387
male, 120, 141f, 142–143
in marital sex, 428t, 429–430
in masturbation, physiologic intensity and
psychological experience of, 147–148
and menstrual discomfort, 93
multiple, 146–147
in old age, 440
rapid, 456
in spinal-cord-injured people, 444–445
subjective experience of, 143
in three-stage model of sexual response
cycle, 144–145
through masturbation, 243
Orgasmic disorder(s), 451, 455–456
female, 456
treatment of, 473–476
male, 455
treatment of, 476
treatment of, 473–477

Orgasmic phase, of sexual response cycle,
140f–142f, 142–143
Orgasmic platform, 141, 142f
Orgasmic reconditioning, 548
Orthodox Jews, attitudes toward
menstruation, 89
Os, cervical, 72–73
Osteoporosis, 91–92
Outercourse, 521
Outing, 281
Ova, 62, 75, 75f
passage through fallopian tubes, 74
Ovarian cancer, 75
oral contraceptives and, 350
Ovariectomy
definition of, 139
and sexual behavior, 139
Ovaries
anatomy of, 71f, 74–75
hormone production by, 84–85
in menopause, 91
prenatal development of, 156–157
Ovulation, 83, 86f, 87
failure of, 308
induction of, 308
postpartum resumption of, 337
prediction of, 301–305. See also Fertility
awareness
kits for, 365
Ovulation method, of fertility awareness,
346t, 365
Ovulatory mucus, 365
Oxytocin, 85
and labor, 328

Pain, and pleasure, 538
Pair bonding, 56
Pap test, 73, 76, 76f
ParaGard, 347t, 353, 354f
Paraphilia(s)
behavior therapy for, 547–548
biochemical therapy for, 549
biological perspective on, 542
definition of, 527
features of, 528–541
harmless versus harmful, 528
integrated perspective on, 545–546
learning perspective on, 543–545
psychoanalytic perspective on, 542–543
psychotherapy for, 547
as sexual addictions, 540
sociological perspective on, 545
theoretical perspective on, 542–546
treatment of, 546–549
types of, 527–541
Paraplegia, 444
Paraplegics
definition of, 121
ejaculation by, 120
Parasite(s). See Ectoparasite(s)
Parasympathetic nervous system, 119
Parenthood, pros and cons of, analyzing,
312–313
Parenting, contemporary attitudes toward,
302–303

Parents, middle-aged, 302–303
Partial-birth abortion, 379
Partialism, 529
Participant observation, 51
Passion, in triangular model of love, 203–208
Paternity blues, 336
Pathogens, 502
Patriarchy, 421–422
Peak days, of menstrual cycle, 365
Pederasty
in ancient Greece, 13
definition of, 13
Pediculosis, 491t, 516–517, 517f
Pedophile(s), characteristics of, 577
Pedophilia, 528, 576–577
behavior therapy for, 547–548
definition of, 576
prevalence of, 576–577
Peeping Toms, 534
Peer harassment, 586
Pelvic examination, 75–76, 76f
Pelvic inflammatory disease
chlamydial, 495–496
in gonorrhea, 492
and infertility, 308
IUD and, 355
risk factors for, 355
Pelvic thrusting, in infancy, 387
Penicillin
for gonorrhea, 493
for syphilis, 495
Penile implants, 469, 469f
Penile strain gauge, 38–39
Penis
anatomy of, 100–105, 101f
corona of, 101f, 102
corpora cavernosa of, 101f, 102
corpus spongiosum of, 101f, 102
frenulum of, 101f, 102
functions of, 101
glans of, 101f, 102
pubertal changes in, 398
root of, 101f, 102
shaft of, 101f, 102
size of, 104–105
stimulation of, 250
Penis envy, 285
Performance anxiety, 116, 453
sexual dysfunctions caused by, 464–465
treatment of, 468–469
Pergonal, 308
Perimetrium, 74
Perineum, 69
in childbirth, 329
definition of, 329
Period of the ovum. See Germinal stage
Personality
Freud's theory of, 26
gender differences in, 171
Petting, in adolescence, 401
Peyronie's disease, 120
Phallic symbols, 12, 100
Phallic worship, 11
Pharaonic circumcision, 66
Pharyngeal gonorrhea, 492

Phenobarbital, effects on prenatal
    development, 323
Phentolamine, 470
Phenylketonuria, 325*t*
Pheromones, 127
Philia, 199, 267
Phimosis, 104
Physical attractiveness, 189–197
Physique, and attractiveness, 190–193
Phthirus pubis, 491*t*, 516, 517*f*
Pill, the. *See* Oral contraceptives
Pimp(s), 596–597
Piperonyl butoxide, 517
Pituitary gland, 84–85, 134*f*
    as master gland, 85
    in regulation of testes, 106, 106*f*
    and sex hormone secretion, 136
Placenta, 319
    expulsion of, 330
Planet Out, 293
Plateau phase, of sexual response cycle, 140*f*-
    141*f*, 141–142
Play It Again, Sam, 212
Playboy Foundation survey, 45–46
Pneumocystis carinii pneumonia (PCP), 503
Podophyllin, 515–516
Polyandry, 424
    cross-cultural perspective on, 25
    definition of, 25
Polygamy, 424
    cross-cultural perspective on, 25
    definition of, 12
    in Islamic society, 15
Polygyny, 424
    cross-cultural perspective on, 25
    definition of, 25
Polymerase chain reaction, 506
Polymorphous perversity, 284
Pons, 134, 134*f*
Pope v. *Illinois*, 608
Population
    definition of, 40
    of interest, 40
    target, 40
Pornography, 606–615
    child, 609
    definition of, 606–607, 607*f*
    hard-core (X-rated), 607–608
    on Internet, future trends in, 31
    legal perspective on, 608–609
    nonviolent, social effects of, 613–614
    popularity of, 606
    prevalence of, 609
    and sex offenders, 611–612
    and sexual coercion, 611–615
    sexual response to, 609
        gender differences in, 609, 611
    soft-core (R-rated), 607–608
    use of, 609
    violent, 609
        social effects of, 612–613
Possessing the Secret of Joy, 67
POSSLQ, 418
Postpartum depression, 335–336
Postpartum period, 335–337

Posttraumatic stress disorder
    definition of, 567
    in prostitutes, 600
    in rape survivor, 567
Posture, in communication, 225
Potassium nitrate, as anaphrodisiac, 130
Power rape, 564
Preeclampsia, 321–322
Pregnancy, 311–315
    adolescent, 400–402, 408–410
        ethnic differences in, 404–405
        future trends in, 31
        school-based preventive programs
            for, 411–413
    coitus during, 314
    dating, Nagele's rule for, 315
    early effects of, 313
    early signs of, 311
    ectopic, 74, 322
    psychological changes during, 314–315
    sympathetic, 315
    weight gain in, 320
Pregnancy tests, 312
Prejudice, against gays and lesbians, future
    trends in, 31
Premarital sex
    in adolescence, 401–403
        ethnic differences in, 404–405
        factors affecting, 406–407
        motives for, 403–405
    cross-cultural perspective on, 388
    historical perspective on, 14, 17, 19
    incidence of, 20
Premature ejaculation, 119, 121, 456, 464
    antidepressants for, 477
    clomipramine for, 477
    treatment of, 468*f*, 476–477
        biological approaches to, 477
Premenstrual syndrome (PMS), 94*t*,
    94–95
Prenatal development, 315–327
    critical periods of vulnerability in, 320,
        321*f*
    environmental factors affecting, 320–325
    stages of, 315, 316*f*
Preorgasmic, definition of, 456
Prepared childbirth, 331
Prepuce
    of clitoris, 64
    of penis, 101*f*, 102
Preterm infants, 334–335
Priapism, 120, 470
Primal scene, 543
Primary amenorrhea, 94
Primary dysmenorrhea, 92–93
Primary erogenous zones, 128
Primary sex characteristics, 396
Procreation, sex and, historical perspective
    on, 11–12, 14, 18, 20–21
Prodromal symptoms, in herpes, 512
Progestasert T, 347*t*, 353–354, 354*f*
Progesterone, 75
    deficit, in menopause, 91
    in menstrual cycle, 86*f*, 87–89
    placental secretion of, 319

production of, 85, 136
    and sexual behavior, in females, 138–139
Progestin, effects on prenatal
    development, 323
Prolactin, 85, 336
Prophylactic. *See also* Condom(s)
    definition of, 359
Prostaglandins
    actions of, 93
    definition of, 93
    and labor, 328
    and menstrual cramps, 93
Prostate gland, 110
    cancer of, 113–115
        future developments in detection and
            treatment of, 114
    disorders of, 112–115
Prostate-specific antigen, and prostate cancer
    detection, 114
Prostatectomy, erectile disorder after, 459
Prostatic fluid, 110
Prostatitis, 115
Prostitute(s)
    female
        in bars and hotels, 597
        in brothels, 598
        call girls as, 599–600
        characteristics of, 600–601
        customers of, 601–602
        in escort services, 598–599
        from former Soviet Union, 596
        in massage parlors, 598
        teenage runaways as, 600–601
        types of, 596–600
    male
        motivations of, 603
        types of, 604–605
Prostitution
    in ancient Greece, 13
    brothel, 598
    definition of, 594
    historical perspective on, 595
    incidence of, in United States, 595–596
    legality of, 594
    male, 603–605
    in Victorian era, 18–19
Protease inhibitors, 507
Protestant Reformation, and sexuality, 17
Proximodistal development, 317–318,
    318*f*
Prozac
    anaphrodisiac effects, 131
    for paraphilias, 549
Prurient, definition of, 606
Pseudohermaphroditism, 158–159, 159*f*
    and gender identity, 159–160
Psychoactive drugs, and sex drive, 131–133
Psychoanalysis, definition of, 26
Psychoanalytic theory
    of paraphilias, 542–543
    of sexual dysfunctions, 464
    of sexual orientation, 284–286
    of transsexualism, 162
Psychodynamic theory, of gender
    typing, 176

Psychological androgyny, 181–183, 182*f*
  and personal development, 182–183
  and psychological well-being, 182–183
  and self-esteem, 182–183
  and sexual behavior, 183
Psychopathia Sexualis, 19, 240
Psychosexual development
  definition of, 27
  Freud's theory of, 26
Psychosexual therapy, 466–467
Psychosexual trauma, sexual dysfunctions
      caused by, 462
Psychotherapy, for paraphilias, 547
Puberty, 395–400
  definition of, 395
  in females, 396*t*, 398
  growth during, gender differences
      in, 172
  in males, 397*t*, 398–399
Pubic hair, 63, 395–396
Pubic lice. *See* Pediculosis
Pubococcygeus (P-C) muscles, 70
Pudendal block, for childbirth, 331
Pudendum, 62
Pyrethrins, 517

Quadriplegia, 444
Questions, in communication, 228–229
Quickening, 374. *See also* Fetal movements

Race/ethnicity
  and HIV infection (AIDS), 502
  and infant mortality, 334–335
  and number of sex partners, 29*t*, 30
  and oral sex, 252–253
  and sexual orientation, 276–277
Radiotherapy
  for cervical cancer, 73
  definition of, 73
Raloxifene, 79–81
Rape, 554–571
  acquaintance, 558
  anger, 564
  attitudes toward, violent pornography
      and, 612–613
  cross-cultural perspective on, 565
  date, 558–560
  definition of, 554
  by females, 561
  forcible, definition of, 555
  gang, 560
  historical perspective on, 555–556
  incidence of, 556–557
  male, 560
  marital, 556, 561
  myths about, 562
  in nonhuman species, 21–22
  power, 564
  prevention of, 569–571
  psychological disorders caused by, 567
  sadistic, 565
  social attitudes and, 562
  sociocultural factors in, 562–563
  statutory, definition of, 555
  stranger, 558

survivors
  adjustment of, 566–568
  treatment of, 568
  types of, 557–561
victims
  cultural attitudes toward, 6
  demographics of, 557
Rape-prone culture, 565
Rape trauma syndrome, 567–568
Rapid female orgasm, 456
Rapist(s)
  attack by, response to, 570–571
  motives of, 564–565
  psychological characteristics of, 563–565
  treatment of, 582–583
Rationalism, and sexual decision making, 624
Reality (female condom), 368
Reasoning About Abortion Questionnaire,
      373, 628
Recessive traits, 327
Reciprocity, in attractiveness, 198
Recreational sex, 427
Rectal examination, and prostate cancer
      detection, 114
Reflection, definition of, 8
Reflex
  definition of, 116, 117*f*
  spinal. *See* Spinal reflexes
Reflex arc, 117, 117*f*
Refractory period, of sexual response
      cycle, 144, 146
  age-related changes in, 441
  definition of, 144
Regional anesthesia, for childbirth, 331
Relationship problems, sexual dysfunctions
      caused by, 462–463
Reliability, of research measures, 44
Religion
  Eastern, and sexuality, 15–16
  and number of sex partners, 29*t*, 30
  and sexual decision making, 621–622
  and sexuality, 11, 14, 16–18
Repression
  as defense mechanism, 26, 285
  definition of, 27
Reproductive success, sexual behavior
      and, 22–23
Reproductive system
  female, 65*f*, 71*f*, 71–76
  male, 98–122, 101*f*
Research
  and confidentiality, 57
  correlational method for, 53–54
  ethics in, 56–58
  experimental method for, 54–56
  informed consent for, 57
  observational methods for, 42–53
  and pain and stress, 57
  sampling methods for, 41–42, 55
  on sexuality, Kinsey's, 19
  and use of deception, 57–58
Research questions, formulation of, 36
Resolution phase, of sexual response cycle,
      140*f*-142*f*, 144
Respiratory distress syndrome, 335

Retarded ejaculation, 455
Reticular activating system (RAS), 134
Retinoblastoma, 325*t*
Retrograde ejaculation, 121–122
Reverse transcriptase, 503
Rh incompatibility, 322
  diagnosis of, 327
RhoGAM, 322
Rhythm methods (of birth control). *See*
      Fertility awareness
RID, 517
Roe v. *Wade*, 345, 374, 376
Romantic love
  ABC(DE) model of, 212–221
  arousal and, 202–203
  in contemporary Western culture, 198–202
  and marriage, 423
  sexual arousal and, 202–203
  in triangular model of love, 205*t*, 207–208
Rome, ancient
  attitudes toward menstruation in, 89
  patriarchy in, 422
  sexuality in, 12–14, 100
Root, of penis, 101*f*, 102
Roth v. *United States*, 608
RU-486, 378–379
Rubbers. *See* Condom(s)
Rubella, maternal, effects on prenatal
      development, 320–321
Rubin test, 308–309
Russia, sexual attitudes in, 7

Sacrum, 118
Sadism, 14. *See also* Sexual sadism
Sadistic rape, 565
Sadomasochism, 19, 537*f*, 537–538
  sociological perspective on, 545
Safes. *See* Condom(s)
Saltpeter, as anaphrodisiac, 130
Sambian people
  gender roles in, 175
  sexual practices of, 275–276
Sample
  of convenience, 42
  definition of, 40
  methods of choosing, 41–42
  probability, 41
  random, 41
  representative, 40
  stratified random, 41
Sarcoptes scabiei, 491*t*, 517
Satyriasis, 541
Scabies, 491*t*, 517
The Scarlet Letter, 17
Schema. *See also* Gender schema
  definition of, 178
School(s)
  and contraception, 353, 411–413
  in prevention of teenage
      pregnancy, 411–413
  sex education in, 393–394
  sexism in, 177
  sexual harassment in, 587
Science, and sexuality, 11
Scientific method, 36–37

Scrotum, 104–105
Secondary amenorrhea, 94
Secondary dysmenorrhea, 93
Secondary erogenous zones, 128
Secondary sex characteristics, 395–396
    definition of, 77, 137
    female, 77, 396t
    male, 106, 397t, 398–399
    sex hormones and, 137
Secondhand smoke, effects on prenatal
    development, 325
Sedatives, effects on prenatal
    development, 323
Selection factor, 55
Self-disclosure
    in building relationships, 216–217
    cross-cultural differences in, 218
    in intimacy, 229
Self-esteem, psychological androgyny
    and, 182–183
Semen, 110f, 111
    in manhood initiation rites, 275
    swallowing, in oral sex, 255
Seminal fluid, 111
Seminal vesicles, 109–111
Seminiferous tubules, 101f, 107, 110f
Seniang people, attitudes toward childhood
    sexuality, 388
Sensate focus exercises, 466
Sensory disability, sex and, 445
Serial monogamy, 418
Seronegative, 506
Seropositive, 506
Serotonin, 477
Sex
    biology of, 21
    definition of, 4–5
*Sex and Temperament in Three Primitive
    Societies*, 24
Sex chromosomes, 108, 154, 300
    abnormalities of, 157
    of sperm, and gender selection,
    305
Sex education, 393–395, 411–412
    for disabled people, 444
    for hearing impaired people, 445
    for visually impaired people, 445
Sex flush, 141
Sex hormones
    actions of, 136–137
    deficit, in menopause, 91
    male, 106
    prenatal, and sexual orientation, 283
    production of, 84–85
    secretion of, 136
    and sexual behavior, 137–138
        in female, 138–139
        in male, 138
    in sexual differentiation, 155–156
Sex in America: A Definitive Survey, 45
Sex-linked disorders, 326–327
Sex manuals, historical perspective on, 15–16,
    16f
Sex offenders. *See also* Rapist(s)
    pornography and, 611–612

treatment of, 582–583
    women as, 555
Sex organs. *See also* External sex organs;
    Internal sex organs
    female, 62–96
    male, 98–122
Sex partners, number of, 28–30, 29t
Sex research. *See* Research
Sex (sexual) organs, definition of, 5
Sex skin, 142
Sex talk, 227
Sex therapist, qualified, finding, 480
Sex therapy, 465–480
    definition of, 465
    effectiveness of, 478–480
    ethics of, 480
    goals of, 465
    Helen Singer Kaplan approach
        to, 466–467
    Masters and Johnson approach to, 466
Sexism, 168–169
    in American schools, 177
    definition of, 168
    and stereotypes, 169
Sexologists
    definition of, 19
    historical perspective on, 19
Sexual abuse of children, 574–582. *See also*
    Incest; Pedophilia
    effects of, 579–581
    and female sexual arousal disorder, 455
    interviewing children about, 580
    patterns of, 574–576
    perpetrators
        adolescent, 575
        demographics of, 574–575
        female, 575–576
        male, 575–576
        treatment of, 582–583
        types of, 575–576
    prevention of, 581
        future trends in, 31
    survivors of
        long-term problems of, 579–581
        and prostitution, 601
        treatment of, 581
    types of, 574
    victims, age of, 575
Sexual activity. *See also* Coitus; Sexual
    behavior
    of older people, 441–443
    postpartum resumption of, 337
    of spinal-cord-injured people, 444–445
Sexual addictions, 540
Sexual anesthesia, 18
Sexual arousal
    age-related changes in, 439t, 439–441
    brain in, 118–119, 133–136
    measurement of, 38–39, 51–52
    operational definition of, 38–39
    and romantic love, 202–203
    senses in, 126–129
Sexual arousal disorders, 451, 453–455
    female, 454–455
    treatment of, 468–473

Sexual assault. *See also* Rape
    definition of, 556
    perpetrators of, demographics
        of, 557, 557f
    prevalence of, 557
    reporting of, 567
    survivors' reactions to, 566t, 566–568
Sexual aversion disorder, 453
    treatment of, 467
Sexual behavior
    in adolescence
        ethnic differences in, 404–405
        factors affecting, 406–407
    atypical variations in, 527
    definition of, 5
    of gay people, 281–282
    male-female
        in adolescence, 400–408
        in early childhood, 390–391
        in preadolescence, 392
    male-male or female-female. *See also* Gay
        people; Homosexuality; Lesbians
        in adolescence, 408
        biological perspectives on, 282–284
        contemporary attitudes toward, 278–282
        cross-cultural perspective on, 275–276
        cross-species perspective on, 276–277
        in early childhood, 391
        historical perspective on, 274–275
        in preadolescence, 392–393
        psychological perspectives on, 284–287
    noncoital, 521
    normal versus deviant, 526–527
    of older people, 441–443
    with partners, 247–263
    and reproductive success, 22–23
    risky, and STIs, 518–519
    solitary, 238–247. *See also* Fantasy;
        Masturbation
    sports and, 563
*Sexual Behavior in the Human
    Female*, 19, 543
Sexual Behavior in the Human Male, 19
Sexual Behavior in the 1970's, 45
Sexual coercion. *See also* Rape
    pornography and, 611–615
    verbal, 571–574
Sexual competition, 196
Sexual desire disorder(s), 451–453
    hypoactive, 452, 467
    treatment of, 467
Sexual deviations, 19
    cross-cultural perspective on, 37–38
    in nonhuman species, 21–22
Sexual differentiation
    definition of, 154
    prenatal, 154–157
    sex hormones in, 155–156
Sexual dysfunction(s)
    acquired, 451
    childhood origins of, 27
    cultural factors in, 460–461
    definition of, 450–451
    features of, 450
    generalized, 451

incidence of, 450*t*, 450–451
  by race and sex, 457*t*
  lifelong, 451
  organic causes of, 459–460
  origins of, 459–465
  psychosocial causes of, 460–465
  situational, 451
  treatment of, 465–480
    future trends in, 31
  types of, 451–459
Sexual harassment, 583–589
  on campus, 586–587
  definition of, 583
  how to resist, 587–589
  myths about, 584*t*
  perpetrators of, 584
  responding to, 587–589
  in schools, 587
  victims of, 583–584
  in workplace, 585–586
    definition of, 583
    prevalence of, 586
Sexual intercourse. *See* Coitus
Sexual masochism, 535–536
  learning perspective on, 544–545
  psychoanalytic perspective on, 543
  sociological perspective on, 545
Sexual orientation. *See also* Gay people;
    Homosexuality; Lesbians
  biological perspectives on, 282–284
  classification of, 268–273
  contemporary attitudes toward, 278–282
  critical thinking about, 10
  declaration of ("coming out"), 291–293
  definition of, 266
  development of, family characteristics
    and, 286
  ethnicity and, 276–277
  and fantasy, 272–273
  and gender identity, 268
  and gender nonconformity, 287–288
  genetics and, 282–283
  hormonal influences and, 283
  Kinsey continuum of, 269*f*, 269–272, 270*t*
  learning theory of, 286–287
  legal considerations regarding, 280–281
  origin of, 278–279, 284, 288
  psychoanalytic theory of, 284–286
  psychological perspectives on, 284–287
  sexologists' views on, 19
  and sexual dysfunctions, 462
  terminology for, 267
  treatment for, 289–291
  twin studies of, 282–283
Sexual pain disorders, 451, 456–457
  treatment of, 477–478
Sexual panic state, 453
Sexual phobia, 453
Sexual repression, 18
  sexual dysfunctions caused by, 461
Sexual response
  brain in, 118–119, 133–136
  cognitive and experiential factors
    affecting, 138–139
  infant's capacity for, 386–387

measurement of, 51–52
  spinal reflexes and, 116–120
  stages of, 52
Sexual response cycle, 140*f*, 140–145
  age-related changes in, 439*t*, 439–441
  breasts during, 142, 143*f*
  definition of, 140
  excitement phase of, 140*f*, 140–141, 141*f*
  orgasmic phase of, 140*f*-142*f*,
    142–143
  phases of, 140*f*, 140–145
    three-stage model of, 144–145
  plateau phase of, 140*f*-141*f*, 141–142
  refractory period of, 144, 146, 441
  resolution phase of, 140*f*-142*f*, 144
Sexual revolution, 20–21
  effects on marital sexuality, 426–429
Sexual sadism, 527, 537–538
  psychoanalytic perspective on, 543
  sociological perspective on, 545
Sexual sadists, 536
Sexual satisfaction
  coital frequency and, 53–54, 54*f*
  in marriage, 428*t*, 429–430
  of older people, 442
Sexuality
  in adolescence, 395–408
  biological perspective on, 21
  childhood, cross-cultural perspective
    on, 388
  communicating with children
    about, 394–395
  critical thinking about, 9–10
  cross-cultural perspective on, 23–25
  cross-species perspective on, 21–23
  definition of, 4–9
  in early childhood, 389–392
  future trends in, 31
  historical perspective on, 11–21
  in infancy, 386–389
  marital. *See* Marital sexuality
  multiple perspectives on, 31–32
  for older people, 439–443
  of people with disabilities, 443–446
  perspectives on, 10–32
  in preadolescence, 392–395
  prehistoric, 11–12
  premarital. *See* Premarital sex
  psychological perspectives on, 25–28
  scientific approach to, 36–40
    foundations for, 19
    goals of, 37–38
    methods of, 37–38
  sociocultural perspectives on, 28–30
  study of, 5–6
  and values, 5–7
Sexually transmitted infections, 484–485. *See
  also* Pelvic inflammatory disease
  in adolescents, 402
    prevention of, 411–412
  attitudes toward, 487–488
  bacterial, 488–498, 489*t*
  communication about, 486
  exposure to
    management of, 521

prevention of, 521–522
  and HIV transmission, 505
  hotlines, 522
  incidence of, 485
  information about, sources for, 522
  prevention of, 517–521
    contraception and, 357, 360, 363
    contraceptives and, 346, 346*t*-347*t*
  prostitution and, 605–606
  rape and, 567
  risk factors for, 485, 518–519
  symptomless, 485, 496, 500
  testing for, before initiating sexual
    relations, 521
  viral, 490*t*-491*t*, 501–516
  visible signs of, inspecting partners
    for, 519–520
Shaft, of penis, 101*f*, 102
Shigellosis, 497–498
Shinto, and abortion, 381
Sickle cell anemia, 325*t*, 326
  prenatal diagnosis of, 327
Sildenafil, 471
Silver nitrate, for molluscum
    contagiosum, 516
Singlehood, 416–418
Situation ethics, and sexual decision
    making, 622
Sixty-nine, 254, 254*f*
Skene's glands, 149
Skins. *See* Condom(s)
Slasher films, antisocial effects
    of, 613
S&M. *See* Sadomasochism
Small talk, 213–214
Smegma, 102
Smell, in sexual arousal, 126–127
Smiling, and attractiveness, 191
Smoking
  maternal, effects on prenatal
    development, 324
  secondhand, effects on prenatal
    development, 325
Social desirability
  and bias in sex survey research, 50
  definition of, 50
Social-exchange theory, 212
Social-learning theory
  of aggression, 177
  definition of, 28
  of gender typing, 176–178
  of sexual behavior, 28
*The Social Organization of Sexuality: Sexual
  Practices in the United States*, 45
Social skills training, 548
Socialization, 176
  and gender typing, 176
Sociobiology, 22–23
  perspective on gender
    typing, 173–174
Sodomy laws, 280–281
Soixante-neuf, 254, 254*f*
Spanish AIDS/SIDA Hotline, 522
Spanish fly, 129
Spectator role, 456

Sperm, 107–109
  abnormalities, and male fertility
      problems, 307
  in fertilization, 300–301, 301*f*
  intracytoplasmic injection of, 310
  motility, 109, 307
  odor receptors of, 301
  production, 106–108, 110*f*
      factors affecting, 307
  separation procedures, for gender
      selection, 304–305
  sex chromosomes of, and gender
      selection, 305
Sperm banks, 310
Sperm count, low, 307
Sperm donation, 310
Spermatic cord, 104
Spermatids, 108
Spermatocyte, 108
Spermatogenesis, 106–108, 110*f*
Spermatozoa. *See* Sperm
Spermicide(s), 346*t*, 357–359, 358*f*, 368
  with diaphragm, 356–357
  protection against STIs, 357
Sphincters, 69
Spina bifida, prenatal diagnosis
      of, 327
Spinal block, for childbirth, 331
Spinal cord
  injuries, sexuality and, 444–445
  in sexual arousal and response, 118
Spinal reflexes
  reflex arc, 117, 117*f*
  and sexual response, 116–120
Spirochete, 493
Spontane, 471
Spontaneous abortion, 300, 313–314
Sports
  achievement in, gender differences
      in, 172
  and sexual behavior, 563
Spousal abuse. *See* Domestic violence
Squeeze technique, 476–477
Stanley v. *Georgia*, 609
Staphylococcus aureus, and toxic shock
      syndrome, 88
Statutory rape, definition of, 555
Stepfamilies, 437
Stereotype(s)
  definition of, 166
  of feminine role in sexual
      behavior, 180–181
      and rape, 562–563
  of gay people, 281–282
  gender-role, 166–167, 167*t*
  of masculine role in sexual
      behavior, 180–181
      and rape, 562–563
  in media, 177
  of mentally retarded people, 445–446
  sexism and, 169
Sterilization, 109
  advantages and disadvantages
      of, 371
  definition of, 366

female, 347*t*, 370–371
  male, 347*t*, 366–367, 367*f. See also*
      Vasectomy
Sternberg's triangular love model, 203–208,
      204*f*-205*f*, 205*t*, 207*f*, 627
STI Attitude Scale, 487–488, 628
Stillbirth, maternal syphilis and, 321
Stimulants, and sexual behavior, 133
STIs. *See* Sexually transmitted
      infections
Stop-start technique, 477
Storge, 199
Straight(s), 266
Stranger rape, 558
Streetwalkers, 595*f*, 596–597
Studies in the Psychology of Sex, 19, 240
The Sun Also Rises, 100
Superego, definition of, 26
Surface contact, 213
Surfactant, 334
Surrogate mother, 310–311
Surveys
  definition of, 43
  interviews for, 43
  limitations of, 47–50
  questionnaires for, 43
  on sexuality, techniques of, 44–50
  of specific populations, 46–47
Swan people, sexual practices of, 275
Swinging, 20, 432–433
  investigator participation in,
      for research, 51
Sympathetic nervous system, 119
Sympathetic pregnancy, 315
Syphilis, 489*t*, 493–495
  congenital, 321, 494
  erectile disorder with, 459
  incidence of, 494
  maternal, effects on prenatal
      development, 321
Systematic desensitization, 547

Tamoxifen
  in breast cancer treatment, 79, 81
  side effects of, 79, 80*f*
Tampons, 88
Taoism, and sexuality, 15–16
Target population, 40
Taste, in sexual arousal, 128
Taxol, 80–81
Tay-Sachs disease, 325*t*, 326
  prenatal diagnosis of, 327
Tchambuli tribe, gender roles in, 175
Teenage pregnancy. *See* Pregnancy,
      adolescent
Telephone scatologia, 533–534
Teratogens, 320
Terminology, and bias in sex survey
      research, 50
Test-tube baby, 309
Testes, 100, 106–109, 110*f*
  age-related changes in, 441
  anatomy of, 107
  cancer of, 111–112, 112*f*
  descent of, 156–157

hormonal control of, 106, 106*f*
  hormone production by, 84–85, 106
  prenatal development of, 156–157
  pubertal changes in, 398
  self-examination of, 112–113
  sperm production by, 107–109
  temperature of, regulation of, 104–105
Testicles. *See* Testes
  undescended. *See* Cryptorchidism
Testosterone, 85, 106–107
  activating effects of, 283
  aphrodisiac effects of, 137–138
  definition of, 155
  levels, age-related changes in, 107
  production
      age-related changes in, 441
      pubertal, 172, 398
  secretion of, 136
  and sex drive, 130
  and sexual behavior, 137–138
      in females, 139
  in sexual differentiation, 155–156
  therapy, for erectile dysfunction,
      469–470
Thalamus, 134, 134*f*
  in sexual functioning, 135
Thalidomide, 322
Third place(s), 602
Thonga people, sexual attitudes of, 24
Thrush. *See* Candidiasis
Tobrianders
  attitudes toward childhood
      sexuality, 388
  sexuality among, 24
Toda people, sexual attitudes of, 24
Tomboys, 287
Touch, in sexual arousal, 127–128
Toucherism, 539
Touching
  in communication, 225–226
  in foreplay, 248–251
Toxemia, effects on prenatal
      development, 321–322
Toxic shock syndrome, 88–89
Toxoplasmosis, of brain, in HIV-infected
      (AIDS) patients, 503–504
Traits, genetic, 22–23
Tranquilizers
  as anaphrodisiacs, 130
  effects on prenatal development, 323
Transition, in childbirth, 328
Transsexualism, 161–164
  definition of, 137, 161
  gender reassignment for, 162–163
      outcomes of, 163–164
  versus homosexuality, 161
  theoretical perspective on, 162
  transvestism and, comparison of, 529
Transverse position, of fetus, 332
Transvestic fetishism. *See* Transvestism
Transvestism, 528, 529*f*, 529–531
  learning perspective on, 544
  psychoanalytic perspective on, 542
  versus transsexualism, 529
Treatment, definition of, 54

Treponema pallidum, 489t, 493, 493f
Trichloroacetic acid, 515–516
Trichomonas vaginalis, 490t, 500, 516
Trichomoniasis, 490t, 498, 500–501
Triple X, 517
Trophoblast, 316
Tropic of Cancer, 427, 606
Trukese people, attitudes toward childhood
    sexuality, 388
Tuamotuan people, 64
Tubal pregnancy. *See* Ectopic pregnancy
Tubal sterilization, 370, 370f
Tunica albuginea, 115
Turner syndrome, 157
Twins
    dizygotic (DZ) (fraternal), 87
        concordance for sexual orientation, 282
        definition of, 282
    monozygotic (MZ) (identical), 87
        concordance for sexual orientation, 282
        definition of, 282

Uganda, AIDS in, 508
Ultrasonography (US)
    in male sterilization, 369
    prenatal, 327, 327f
Ulysses, 606
Umbilical cord, 319
    cutting of, 330
Unconscious mind, 26
Undescended testicles. *See*
    Cryptorchidism
Ureaplasma urealyticum, 489t
Urethra, penile, 101f, 102
Urethral bulb, 121
Urethral meatus, 101, 101f, 102
Urethral opening, 65f, 65–67
Urethritis, 111
    chlamydial, 495–496
    nongonococcal. *See* Nongonococcal
        urethritis
    prevention of, 111
Urinary frequency
    with cystitis, 66
    with prostate cancer, 113
    with urethritis, 111
Urinary tract infection, 66
Urinary urgency
    with cystitis, 66
    with urethritis, 111
Urination, difficulty with, with prostate
    cancer, 113
Urogenital system, diseases of, 111–115
Urologist, 111
Urophilia, 540
Uterine orgasm, 147–148
Uterine tubes. *See* Fallopian tubes
Uterus
    anatomy of, 71f, 73–74
    antroverted, 73
    fundus of, 71f, 73
    layers of, 73–74
    retroverted, 73
Utilitarianism, and sexual decision
    making, 623

Vaccination, 502
Vaccine(s)
    AIDS, 506–507, 509
    human papilloma virus (HPV), 515
Vacuum aspiration, 377, 377f
Vacuum pumps, 471
Vagina
    anatomy of, 71f, 71–72
    lubrication of, 70
    physiology of, 71–72
    stimulation of, 250–251
Vaginal infections, 498–501
Vaginal mucus, in predicting ovulation. *See*
    Cervical mucus
Vaginal opening, 67–68
Vaginal orgasm, 146–148
Vaginal photoplethysmograph, 39
Vaginal ring, 368
Vaginal secretions, 71–72
Vaginismus, 451, 457
    treatment of, 477–478
Vaginitis, 489t-490t
    causes of, 498
    definition of, 72, 498
    nonspecific. *See* Bacterial vaginosis
    prevention of, 72
Valacyclovir, 513
Validity, of research measures, 45
Valium
    effects on prenatal development, 323
    sexual dysfunctions caused by, 460
Value systems, and sexual decision
    making, 621–624
Values
    definition of, 5
    and sexuality, 5–7
Variables
    definition of, 38
    demographic, 38
    dependent, 55
    independent, 55
Vas deferens, 104, 109, 110f
    ampulla of, 120–121
Vasectomy, 109–111, 366–367, 367f
Vasocongestion, 453
    definition of, 38
    measurement of, 38–39
    in sexual response cycle, 140, 144
Vasomax, 471
Vasovasostomy, 367
VDRL, 495
Venereal disease. *See* Sexually transmitted
    infections
Venereal warts. *See* Warts
Venus of Willendorf, 13f
Verbal abilities, gender differences
    in, 170–171
Vestibular bulbs, 69, 69f
Vestibule, 65
Viagra, 130, 471–473
    adverse effects and side effects
        of, 471
    for women, 476
Vibrators, 244–245, 245f, 521
Victorian era, sexuality in, 18

Violence, and rape, 565
Virgin Mary, cult of, 16
Virginity
    hymen and, 68–69
    technical, 401
Virtual sex, 249
Virus(es), sexually transmitted infections
    caused by, 490t-491t, 501–516
Viscosity, of cervical mucus, 365
Vision, in sexual arousal, 126
Visual-spatial abilities, gender differences
    in, 170–171
Vitamins, effects on prenatal
    development, 323
Volunteer bias, 41, 47
Vomeronasal organ, 127
Voyeurism, 534–535
    learning perspective on, 545
    psychoanalytic perspective on, 542–543
Vulva, 62, 63f
Vulval orgasm, 147–148

Warrior Marks, 67
Warts
    genital, 491t, 515, 515f
    venereal, 491t
Wasting syndrome, in HIV-infected (AIDS)
    patients, 504
Weight
    and attractiveness, 190
    gain
        with oral contraceptives, 350
        in pregnancy, 320
    and pregnancy outcome, 320
Wellbutrin. *See* Bupropion
Western blot, 506
Wet dreams, 399
Wheat Ridge, Colorado, 353
White Americans
    adolescent, sexual behavior
        of, 404–405
    cohabitation rate of, 419
    incidence of sexual dysfunctions
        in, 457t
    number of sex partners, 29t, 30
    and oral sex, 252–253
    sexual behavior of, survey on, 48–49
Wife beating. *See* Domestic violence
Will Power/Won't Power, 402
Withdrawal method of birth control, 110. *See*
    also Coitus interruptus
Wolffian (male) ducts, 155, 155f
The Woman Rebel, 344
Womb. *See* Uterus
Women. *See also* Female(s); Working women
    AIDS and, 508–509
    as chattel, 422
    childfree by choice, 302, 303f
    divorce and, 436
    and domestic violence, 434–435
    earning power of, 169
    Madonna/whore concept and, 16–17,
        17f
    middle-aged, as mothers, 303
    as pragmatists, 425–426

Women (*continued*)
   as sex offenders, 555
   as sexually passive, stereotype of, 180–181,
      426–427
   as sexually underaroused, stereotype of,
      181, 426–427
   social status of, historical perspective on,
      11–13, 15–18
   spinal-cord-injured, sexuality
      of, 445
Women, Work and Family in America, 436
Woodstock generation, 20

Working women
   media's portrayal of, 177
   as providers, 169
Wyatt Survey on African American
     and White Women in Los
     Angeles, 48–49

X chromosome, 108, 154, 300
   and gay male sexual orientation,
     282–283
X-rays, fetal effects of, 325
Xanax, sexual dysfunctions caused by, 460

Y chromosome, 108, 154–155, 300
Yeast infection. *See* Candidiasis
Yohimbine, 130

Zalcitabine (ddC), 507
Zidovudine, 507
Zona pellucida, 301
Zoophilia, 539
Zovirax, 513
Zygote(s), 87, 154, 300
   division of, 316, 317*f*
Zygote intrafallopian transfer (ZIFT), 309